T0268900

HIPPOCRENE PRACTICAL DICTIONARY
SPANISH-ENGLISH
ENGLISH-SPANISH

Arthur Swift Butterfield

HIPPOCRENE BOOKS
New York

Revised Hippocrene Edition with larger type, 1993.
Nineteenth printing, 2024.

First Hippocrene Edition, 1983.
Copyright © Laurence Urdang Associates, 1982.

Glossary of Menu Terms and special American Usage entries:
  Copyright © Hippocrene Books, 1983.

All rights reserved.

For information, address:
HIPPOCRENE BOOKS, INC.
171 Madison Avenue
New York, NY 10016

ISBN-13: 978-0-7818-0179-9
ISBN-10: 0-7818-0179-6

Printed in the United States of America.

Abbreviations/Abreviaciones

adj adjective, adjetivo
adv adverb, adverbio
aero aeronautics, aeronáutica
agr agriculture, agricultura
anat anatomy, anatomía
arch architecture
arq arquitectura
art article, artículo
astrol astrology, astrología
astron astronomy, astronomía
auto automobile, automóvil
bot botany, botánica
chem chemistry
coll colloquial
com comercio
comm commerce
conj conjunction, conjunción
culin culinario
derog derogatory
econ economics, economía
elec electricity, electricidad
f feminine, femenino
fam familiar, colloquial
ferr ferrocarril
fig figurative, figurativo
foto fotografía
geog geography, geografía
geol geology, geología
gram gramática
gramm grammar
impol impolite

interj interjection, interjección
interrog interrogative,
    interrogativo
invar invariable
jur jurisprudencia
m masculine, masculino
mar marítimo
mat matemáticas
math mathematics
mec mecánica
mech mechanics
med medicine, medicina
mil military, militar
mot motoring
n noun
naut nautical
phone telephone
phot photography
pl plural
pol politics, política
prep preposition, preposición
pron pronoun, pronombre
psych psychology
quím química
rail railways
rel religion, religión
s sustantivo
sing singular
tech technology, technical
tecn tecnología
v verb, verbo
V vide (see, vea)
zool zoology, zoología

Spanish pronunciation

a cada ['kaða]
e entre ['entre]
i libro ['liβro]
o loco ['loko]
u lunes ['lunes]
j nieve ['njeβe]
b bueno ['bweno]
d desde ['desðe]
f fácil ['faθil]
g grande ['grande]
k poco ['poko]
l salud [sa'luð]

m hombre ['ombre]
n noche ['notʃe]
p lápiz ['lapiθ]
r cerca ['θerka]
rr perro ['perro]
s servir [ser'βir]
t todo ['toðo]
w luego ['lwego]
θ cerveza [θer'βeθa]
β hábil ['aβil]
tʃ muchacho [mu'tʃatʃo]
ð ciudad [θju'ðað]
ʎ calle ['kaʎe]
ɲ señor [se'ɲor]
x ojo, ágil ['oxo], ['axil]

The symbol ' indicates that the following syllable should be stressed.

Pronunciación del inglés

a hat [hat]
e bell [bel]
i big [big]
o dot [dot]
ʌ bun [bʌn]
u book [buk]
ə alone [ə'loun]
aː card [kaːd]
əː word [wəːd]
iː team [tiːm]
oː torn [toːn]
uː spoon [spuːn]
ai die [dai]
ei ray [rei]
oi toy [toi]
au how [hau]
ou road [roud]
eə lair [leə]
iə fear [fiə]
uə poor [puə]
b back [bak]
d dull [dʌl]
f find [faind]

g gaze [geiz]
h hop [hop]
j yell [jel]
k cat [kat]
l life [laif]
m mouse [maus]
n night [nait]
p pick [pik]
r rose [rouz]
s sit [sit]
t toe [tou]
v vest [vest]
w week [wiːk]
z zoo [zuː]
θ think [θiŋk]
ð those [ðouz]
ʃ shoe [ʃuː]
ʒ treasure ['treʒə]
tʃ chalk [tʃoːk]
dʒ jump [dʒʌmp]
ŋ sing [siŋ]

El signo de acentuación ' se coloca directamente delante de la sílaba aguda.
El signo , se coloca delante de la sílaba aguda secundaria.

Guide to the dictionary

The infinitives of all irregular verbs appearing in the headword list are marked with an asterisk. These and examples of Spanish stem-changing verbs, and the tenses in which such changes occur, can be found in the following verb tables. Composite verbs, such as *deshacer* from *hacer*, are also included under the parent verb.

The Spanish alphabet includes three symbols or combinations of letters that are not found in the English alphabet. These are **ch, ll,** and **ñ,** which are treated as individual letters and follow **c, l,** and **n** respectively in the alphabetical order.

The plurals of almost all Spanish nouns are formed regularly by the addition of *s* or *es* to the singular form. Occasional irregular plural forms are shown immediately after the part of speech referring to the headword. Some nouns do not change in the plural and these are marked *invar* (invariable).

Adverbs are regularly formed by adding *-mente* to the feminine (or occasionally masculine) form of the adjective, and are not normally shown unless a different translation is called for.

Guía al diccionario

Los plurales irregulares de los sustantivos se hallen junto al
encabezamiento. Las categorías siguientes de los plurales se
consideran regulares en inglés:

cat	cats
glass	glasses
fly	flies
half	halves
wife	wives

Los verbos irregulares en la lista de encabezamientos se señalan por
medio de un asterisco y se hallen en las tablas de los verbos.

Los adverbios regulares no se indican. Los adverbios ingleses que se
forman añadiendo -(al)ly al adjetivo, se consideran regulares. Los
adverbios españoles que se forman añadiendo -mente al adjetivo
femenino (de vez en cuando masculino), se consideran regulares y no
se indican sino exigiendo una traducción diferente.

Spanish verb tables

1. The final consonants preceding the infinitive endings (-ar, -er, and -(u)ir) change, for reasons of euphony, when they occur before certain vowels.

Infinitives	Change	Before
-car	the c to qu	e
-cer	the c to z	a or o
-cir	the c to z	a or o
-gir	the g to j	a or o
-guir	the gu to g	a or o
-quir	the qu to c	a or o
-gar	the ga to gu	e
-zar	the z to c	e

2. Verbs adding z. There are numerous verbs ending in -ecer (e.g. parecer) and other verbs ending in a vowel + -cer (e.g. conocer). When the ending of these verbs is a or o (specifically, present indicative 1 *sing*, and present subjunctive, all persons), a z is added before the c (e.g. parezco, conozco).

3. Verbs in the following tables change the vowels in their stems in certain persons and tenses. The sections below are arranged according to the vowel change involved and are followed by a selection of verbs exemplifying the change. Note that composite verbs (e.g. desplegar) are conjugated in the same way as their base forms (e.g. plegar).

   (i) Stem changes e to ie in present indicative and present subjunctive 1, 2, 3 *sing* and 3 *pl*, and in imperative *sing*.

acertar	aterrar	comenzar	dentar	entender
acrecentar	aventar	concertar	desalentar	entesar
aferrar	calentar	confesar	descender	fregar
apretar	cegar	contender	desempedrar	gobernar
arrendar	cerner	decentar	despernar	hacendar
ascender	cerrar	defender	despertar	heder

helar	merendar	recentar	sembrar	tentar
hender	negar	recomendar	sentar	trascender
herrar	nevar	regar	serrar	trasegar
incensar	pensar	remendar	sosegar	trasverter
invernar	perder	restregar	soterrar	tropezar
manifestar	plegar	reventar	temblar	verter
mentar	quebrar	segar	tender	

(ii) Stem changes **o** to **ue** in present indicative and present subjunctive 1, 2, 3 *sing* and 3 *pl*, and in imperative *sing*.

acordar	colar	jugar	resollar	soñar
acostar	colgar	moler	rodar	torcer
aforar	contar	mostrar	rogar	tostar
almorzar	costar	mover	solar	trocar
apostar	doler	poblar	soldar	tronar
aprobar	encontrar	probar	soler	voler
avergonzar	forzar	recordar	soltar	volcar
azolar	holgar	renovar	sonar	volver

(iii) Stem changes from **e** to **i** in present indicative 1, 2, 3 *sing* and 3 *pl*; preterite 3 *sing* and *pl*; present, imperfect, and future subjunctives, all persons; imperative *sing* and present participle.

colegir	derretir	henchir	regir	seguir
concebir	elegir	medir	rendir	servir
corregir	gemir	pedir	repetir	vestir

(iv) Stem changes **e** to **ie** in present indicative and present subjunctive 1, 2, 3 *sing* and 3 *pl*; imperative *sing*.
Stem changes **e** to **i** in preterite 3 *sing* and *pl*; present subjunctive 1, 2 *pl*; imperfect and future subjunctives, all persons; present participle.

advertir	digerir	hervir	preferir
cernir	divertir	inferir	requerir
convertir	hendir	ingerir	sentir
diferir	herir	mentir	sugerir

4. The verbs shown below change in various ways. In the table,
1 and 3 *sing* are shown under the present indicative and 1 *sing*
under the preterite and future.

Infinitive	Present Indicative	Preterite	Future	Past Participle
andar	ando, anda	anduve	andaré	andado
caber	quepo, cabe	cupe	cabré	cabido
caer	caigo, cae	caí	caeré	caido
dar	doy, da	di	daré	dado
decir	digo, dice	dije	diré	dicho
dormir	duermo, duerme	dormí	dormiré	dormido
erguir	yergo, yergue	erguí	erguiré	erguido
errar	yerro, yerra	erré	erraré	errado
estar	estoy, está	estuve	estaré	estado
haber	he, ha	hube	habré	habido
hacer	hago, hace	hice	haré	hecho
huir	huyo, huye	huí	huiré	huido
ir	voy, va	fui	iré	ido
oír	oigo, oye	oí	oiré	oido
oler	huelo, huele	olí	oleré	olido
poder	puedo, puede	pude	podré	podido
poner	pongo, pone	puse	pondré	puesto
querer	quiero, quiere	quise	querré	querido
reducir	reduzco, reduce	reduje	reduciré	reducido
reír	río, ríe	reí	reiré	reido
saber	sé, sabe	supe	sabré	sabido
ser	soy, es	fui	seré	sido
tener	tengo, tiene	tuve	tendré	tenido
traer	traigo, trae	traje	traeré	traído
valer	valgo, vale	valí	valdré	valido
venir	vengo, viene	vine	vendré	venido
ver	veo, ve	vi	veré	visto

Verbos irregulares ingleses

Infinitivo	Pretérito	Participo Pasado	Infinitive	Pretérito	Participo Pasado
abide	abode	abode	deal	dealt	dealt
arise	arose	arisen	dig	dug	dug
awake	awoke	awoken	do	did	done
be	was	been	draw	drew	drawn
bear	bore	borne	dream	dreamed	dreamed
		or born		or dreamt	or dreamt
beat	beat	beaten	drink	drank	drunk
become	became	become	drive	drove	driven
begin	began	begun	dwell	dwelt	dwelt
behold	beheld	beheld	eat	ate	eaten
bend	bent	bent	fall	fell	fallen
bet	bet	bet	feed	fed	fed
beware			feel	felt	felt
bid	bid	bidden	fight	fought	fought
		or bid	find	found	found
bind	bound	bound	flee	fled	fled
bite	bit	bitten	fling	flung	flung
bleed	bled	bled	fly	flew	flown
blow	blew	blown	forbid	forbade	forbidden
break	broke	broken	forget	forgot	forgotten
breed	bred	bred	forgive	forgave	forgiven
bring	brought	brought	forsake	forsook	forsaken
build	built	built	freeze	froze	frozen
burn	burnt	burnt	get	got	got
	or burned	or burned	give	gave	given
burst	burst	burst	go	went	gone
buy	bought	bought	grind	ground	ground
can	could		grow	grew	grown
cast	cast	cast	hang	hung	hung
catch	caught	caught		or hanged	or hanged
choose	chose	chosen	have	had	had
cling	clung	clung	hear	heard	heard
come	came	come	hide	hid	hidden
cost	cost	cost	hit	hit	hit
creep	crept	crept	hold	held	held
cut	cut	cut	hurt	hurt	hurt

Infinitivo	Pretérito	Participo Pasado	Infinitivo	Pretérito	Participo Pasado
keep	kept	kept	say	said	said
kneel	knelt	knelt	see	saw	seen
knit	knitted	knitted	seek	sought	sought
	or knit	or knit	sell	sold	sold
know	knew	known	send	sent	sent
lay	laid	laid	set	set	set
lead	led	led	sew	sewed	sewn
lean	leant	leant			or sewed
	or leaned	or leaned	shake	shook	shaken
leap	leapt	leapt	shear	sheared	sheared
	or leaped	or leaped			or shorn
learn	learnt	learnt	shed	shed	shed
	or learned	or learned	shine	shone	shone
leave	left	left	shoe	shod	shod
lend	lent	lent	shoot	shot	shot
let	let	let	show	showed	shown
lie	lay	lain	shrink	shrank	shrunk
light	lit	lit	shut	shut	shut
	or lighted	or lighted	sing	sang	sung
lose	lost	lost	sink	sank	sunk
make	made	made	sit	sat	sat
may	might		sleep	slept	slept
mean	meant	meant	slide	slid	slid
meet	met	met	sling	slung	slung
mow	mowed	mown	slink	slunk	slunk
must			slit	slit	slit
ought			smell	smelt	smelt
pay	paid	paid		or smelled	or smelled
put	put	put	sow	sowed	sown
quit	quitted	quitted			or sowed
	or quit	or quit	speak	spoke	spoken
read	read	read	speed	sped	sped
rid	rid	rid		or speeded	or speeded
ride	rode	ridden	spell	spelt	spelt
ring	rang	rung		or spelled	or spelled
rise	rose	risen	spend	spent	spent
run	ran	run	spill	spilt	spilt
saw	sawed	sawn		or spilled	or spilled
		or sawed	spin	spun	spun

Infinitivo	Pretérito	Participo Pasado	Infinitivo	Pretérito	Participo Pasado
spit	spat	spat	swim	swam	swum
split	split	split	swing	swung	swung
spread	spread	spread	take	took	taken
spring	sprang	sprung	teach	taught	taught
stand	stood	stood	tear	tore	torn
steal	stole	stolen	tell	told	told
stick	stuck	stuck	think	thought	thought
sting	stung	stung	throw	threw	thrown
stink	stank	stunk	thrust	thrust	thrust
	or stunk		tread	trod	trodden
stride	strode	stridden	wake	woke	woken
strike	struck	struck	wear	wore	worn
string	strung	strung	weave	wove	woven
strive	strove	striven	weep	wept	wept
swear	swore	sworn	win	won	won
sweep	swept	swept	wind	wound	wound
swell	swelled	swollen	wring	wrung	wrung
	or swelled		write	wrote	written

Glossary of menu terms

Americans dining in Spain, Mexico, and the Spanish Caribbean are in for a pleasant surprise, for Spanish cooking is far more diverse than the few dishes that have become part of the American diet would indicate. Neither is it as hot and spicy (**picante**) as the food often served in the Southwest. Food in Spain is tasty but relatively bland; even in Mexico, the "hot" comes mainly from the red and green sauces found on the table.

The Spanish menu lacks the gourmet tradition of France. Dishes tend to be less delicate, heartier and more filling. Menu items not imported are those that are grown locally, hence many ingredients are those that have always been readily available: rice and olive oil, for instance, are used over and over. Caribbean cooking makes frequent use of such fruits as pineapples, bananas and the smaller plaintain, and other, less familiar, tropical fruits. Mexican cooking combines corn, beans, tomatoes (both red and green), and countless varieties of peppers and **chiles** in intriguing combinations.

A first-time visitor to Spanish-speaking countries may find the times for eating more exotic than the food itself. Full breakfasts are seldom found in Spain outside of large hotels catering to tourists. In the Americas, however, a large breakfast is easy to get — often to be eaten about the middle of the morning rather than first thing (coffee or hot chocolate help tide you over). The midday meal, the **comida,** is taken between 1:00 and 3:00 p.m. in Mexico, 2:00 and 4:00 in Spain. Most "business dinners" take place at **comida.** Traditionally, most offices closed for the delightful custom, the **siesta,** although long commuting times have made the break for a nap less common in large cities. The last meal of the day, the **cena,** is much lighter than **comida** and is eaten late in the evening, sometimes very late (any time between 8:00 and midnight with the emphasis on the later hours).

You would have to work hard, however, to go hungry. It often seems that Spanish-speaking societies never stop eating. Snacking is not only common, but the occasion for sampling some of the most representative local foods. Spain has even institutionalized the between-meal snack, the **merienda,** which consists of a variety of hors d'oeuvre eaten with a few **copas** of wine around 6:00 p.m. No visitor should leave Spain without visiting a few taverns for **merienda** and sampling the local specialties, **tapas.** Indeed, it is considered customary to have a light snack whenever one stops for morning coffee or after-work cocktails.

In general, restaurants of comparable quality are less expensive than their U.S. counterparts, especially in Mexico and the Caribbean. Service appears more formal, although it is often acceptable to attract a waiter's attention by hissing, making a kissing sound, or slapping hands, depending on local custom. Better not try it until you see someone else do it first! The economy-minded visitor should be warned that such ordinary extras as soft drinks, coffee, even bread, are sometimes priced out of proportion to the rest of the menu; second cups of coffee are seldom free. On the other hand, one is never rushed to pay the bill and leave; you may linger forever over one drink or coffee. Indeed, getting a waiter to bring the check (**cuenta**) can be a major challenge. You have to ask for it and probably remind the waiter a few times before he produces it. Finally, as a general rule, the more American-looking a restaurant, the higher its prices.

A typical Spanish menu is completely à la carte. The standard headings include **entremeses** and/or **tapas** (appetizers); **sopas** (soups); sometimes **sopas secas** (literally dry soups, usually a pasta or rice course); **carnes** (red meats); **aves** (poultry); **pescados** (fish); **mariscos** (shellfish); **ensaladas** (salads); **legumbres** (vegetables); **postres** (desserts); and **bebidas** (beverages). The people who live in the country you are visiting will probably eat an astonishing number of courses, but you can order from as many or as few categories as you like to make up a meal that suits your tastes and appetite.

An exception to the à la carte menu is the multicourse combination usually available at the midday meal, the **comida**. Called the **menu turístico, comida corrida**, or simply **comida**, it offers few choices and (sometimes) smaller portions, but it is a good bargain. Be sure to inform the waiter that you are having the set meal and restrict yourself to the choices offered.

Finally, it is important to remind yourself that although the menu may be in English, the waiter does not always speak English. Spanish and English entrées are usually listed in the same order for this reason.

Basic Terms

a la mexicana Mexican-style: mixed with peppers, tomatoes, onions, and **chiles**

caldo thick stew-like soup with solid ingredients

cilantro fresh coriander; if you don't like the taste, ask for your food **sin** (without) **cilantro**

mole a spicy sauce with many variations, some quite **picante,** others bland; the famous dish is **mole poblano de guajolote,** turkey in dark chocolate-flavored sauce in the style of Puebla

rellenos stuffed, often vegetables with stuffing

salsa sauce; some common ones are **salsa mexicana** (see above), **salsa verde** (made with green tomatoes called **tomatillos**), and **salsa ranchera** (quite hot, used for **huevos rancheros**)

sofrito common base of tomatoes, vegetables, onions, garlic lightly fried in olive oil

tortillas The Mexican tortilla is, with beans and peppers, the basic ingredient in Mexican cooking. A tortilla is a flat pancake made from **masa harina,** a flour made of corn from which the husks and germ have been removed, and water. Tortillas are baked on an ungreased griddle and are used as bread with many meals and combined with other ingredients to make a number of common Mexican menu items:

chalupas small tortillas filled with meat or other toppings, served as hors d'oeuvre

chilaquiles strips of stale tortillas fried, then combined with meat or chicken, sauces, and meats and baked; green chilaquiles feature chicken and green **tomatillo** sauce while red chilaquiles usually have beef and red tomato (**jitomate**) sauce; both topped with cheese

enchiladas tortillas dipped in **chile** sauce, then fried to receive various fillings, e.g. chicken, cheese, and sour cream to make **enchiladas suizas** (Swiss enchiladas)

nachos similar to chalupas

quesadillas small raw tortillas, filled with cheese or other savory fillings, sealed, and baked or fried on a grill

taco ubiquitous Mexican counterpart of the American sandwich; a tortilla is rolled around filling and either eaten as is or fried on a grill; **taco al carbón:** a taco made with meat only

tamales not tortillas, but soft dumplings made by wrapping tortilla dough around various fillings, securing the whole in corn husks, and steaming

tostado taco for which the tortilla is first fried until crisp in deep fat

Entremeses or Tapas (Appetizers)

ceviche a seafood cocktail made of raw fish or shellfish "cooked" by marinating in lime juice and mixed with spices; many different versions exist

chalupas see **tortillas**

cóctel de camarones shrimp cocktail

cóctel de ostiones oyster-like cocktail; shellfish is served out of the shell in cocktail sauce

nachos see **tortillas**

pescado Santo Domingo cold sea bass served as hors d'oeuvre

quesadillas see **tortillas**

Sopas (Soups)

albóndigas very thick soup made with ground beef and rice

caldo de pescado fish soup

caldo Tlalpeño rich clear chicken soup with vegetables and dried **chiles**; very good

gazpacho classic cold soup made of raw tomatoes and other vegetables and oil and vinegar

menudo tripe soup; very hearty and filling

pozole soup made of pork, hominy, and **chiles**; often very hot, always very filling

sopa de ajo popular garlic soup prepared by browning garlic cloves and bread in oil

sopa de cebolla onion soup, often with cheese

sopa de frijol negro black bean soup

sopa de judías coloradas black bean soup with ham and hard-cooked egg

sopa de tortilla delicious soup made with chicken broth, tortilla strips, and many flavorings

Entrées or Platillo Fuerte or Platos Principales (Main Dishes)

Carnes (Red Meats)

albóndigas meat balls, often very **picante**, sometimes served as an appetizer as well

carne asada literally grilled meat, this is almost always filet of beef sliced fair-

ly thin **with** the grain, broiled medium-well, and served with any combination of a number of side dishes; a safe dish to order almost anywhere

cocido popular stew with many variations but usually including meat, chicken, bacon, chick peas, and vegetables

cocido de riñones kidney stew in a sofrito base

cochinillo asado roast suckling pig; no one should go through life without it

cochinillo pibil Yucatecan-style barbecued pork

chiles rellenos stuffed **chile poblanos** (stuffing is usually ground pork but can be cheese)

chorizo popular red-colored sausage

empanada Galacian hot turnover usually filled with a meat mixture

fabada stew of pork, beans, and spices

guisado stew, usually of meat and other vegetables

higado liver

jamón en dulce ham preserved in sugar, i.e. sugar-cured ham, served cold

lechón asada another name for roast suckling pig

lengua de res ox tongue

lomo de cerdo loin of pork

olla podrida same as **cocido**

piononos deep-fried plaintain rings with tasty ground-beef filling

pote same as **cocido**

puchero same as **cocido**

puerco en mole verde pork in green mole sauce; also called **pipián verde** sauce (**pipián** means a sauce made with ground nuts or seeds, in this case with green pumpkin seeds, **pepitas**)

riñones kidneys

Aves (Poultry)

arroz con pollo common rice with chicken dish including saffron, peas, and other vegetables and seasonings in endless variations; always a good and safe bet

guisado de pollo chicken stew with potatoes, peas, and wine sauce

mole poblano one of the national dishes of Mexico, traditionally made with turkey, though chicken is often used

pato duck

pechuga de pollo breast of chicken

pollo a la chilindrón chicken sautéed with peppers, tomatoes, and olives

pollo en pipián rojo chicken in a red sauce flavored with sesame seeds; may be referred to as **en pipián colorado** (red **pipián**)

Huevos (Eggs)

huevos a la flamenca fried eggs on a sofrito base

huevos motuleños as they are made in the town of Motul in Yucatán, incorporating chopped ham and peas

huevos rancheros soft fried eggs on tortillas covered with hot sauce (**salsa ranchera**) served with refried beans; guaranteed to wake you up

huevos revueltos a la mexicana eggs scrambled with chopped tomatoes, onions, and **chiles**

pisto manchego mixed vegetables, bits of ham, and eggs, a sort of omelette, easy on the eggs; there are many variations from region to region

tortilla in Spain only, a sturdy omelette containing many combinations of ingredients other than eggs

Pescados y Mariscos (Fish and Shellfish)

adobo de pescado fish casserole with tomatoes

aguacates rellenos literally stuffed avocados; often the stuffing is a seafood salad or a vegetable mixture; sometimes served as an appetizer or first course

asopao Puerto Rican rice stew with seafood

bacalao a la Vizcaina salt cod and tomatoes, of Basque origin

blanco de Pátzcuaro white fish from Lake Pátzcauro in Mexico

calamares en su tinta squid in a sauce made with their ink; much tastier than it sounds

camarones shrimp

huachinango a la Veracruzana red snapper in the style of Veracruz: baked with tomatoes, onions, and chiles

paella famous rice-based casserole usually containing shellfish, chicken, peas, and sometimes sausages; spices include saffron; every chef has his own version, but be prepared to wait because it is always cooked to order

pescado guisado fish stew

zarzuela mixed seafood stew in a sauce of wine and brandy; many variations, almost all delicious

Snacks, Side Dishes, etc.

bocadillo literally sandwich, it is also the standard hard roll, very soft inside; a real staple

bolillo the Mexican standard roll

bombas de camarones deep-fried potato cakes with shrimp in the dough

burritos wheat-flour tortillas rolled around a variety of fillings similar to those used for the corn tortillas; if then fried, usually called **chimachangas**

churros long deep-fried pastry made from a doughnut-like dough and dipped in granulated sugar; served for breakfast in Spain and also for late-night **merienda** with coffee or chocolate in Mexico

frijoles refritos "refried" beans; actually the beans are cooked tender, then fried only once, being mashed in the process; served with practically everything in Mexico

guacamole avocado purée with onions, peppers, often fresh coriander (**cilantro**), and possibly chopped tomatoes; usually bland, it is sometimes made with hot **chiles**, so taste cautiously

migas bread bits fried in olive oil and flavored with garlic; a distinctively Spanish crouton

pan dulce literally sweet bread, this term covers a huge variety of pastries and sweet breads made in bakeries that seem to be on every corner; don't miss these delicious sweets, but buy only what you will eat in one day since they lose their bloom if kept longer

torta Mexico City only: a carved out bolillo filled with meat, avocado, tomato, etc.; a great takeout

Postres (Desserts)

Spanish desserts are relatively simple and not difficult to understand. Fruits are popular, sometimes in cream (**con crema**) or with whipped cream (**nata,** thicker than the American version). One can order a variety of pastries (**pastales** or, in Spain, **tortas**) or ice cream (**helado**).

arroz con leche rice pudding

chongos a kind of cross between custard and cheese made by letting gently heated milk separate into curds and whey, these are served with a sweet syrup; don't miss them

natillas universally available soft custard served cold

flan sometimes called **crème caramel,** this custard baked with caramel syrup on the bottom is probably the best known distinctly Spanish dessert; usually on every menu

Bebidas (Beverages)

atole a hot drink made with **masa harina,** rather like a thin cornmeal mush sweetened and flavored in various ways; not everybody's cup, but interesting to try — perhaps the chocolate version, called **champurrado**

café coffee; be careful how you order:

café americano American-style coffee

café con crema American-style coffee with cream (in small or very rural places, the cream may be evaporated milk, so be advised)

café con leche coffee with warm milk (**café au lait**)

café de olla coffee made in a clay pot served black flavored with stick cinnamon and sweetened with raw brown sugar

café solo espresso-style black coffee

chocolate spelled the same way but pronounced choco-LAHT-tay, this popular beverage in Mexico comes in many styles among which are mexicana (made with water) and francesca (made with milk and, possibly, an egg)

cerveza beer; light is **clara,** dark is **negra;** dark Mexican beer is labeled **oscura** and the very dark, once-a-year treat around Christmas is **nochebuena**

coñac brandy (no particular brand)

jerez sherry, our corruption of the name of the city that gave rise to the wine, Jerez, Spain, pronounced (both city and drink) *hereth*

jugo de naranja orange juice

Kalaúa the coffee-flavored, chocolatey liqueur of Mexico

refresco any soft drink, usually ordered by brand

tequila Mexican liquor distilled from the agave plant; other forms of agave products, including **mescal** and **pulque;** ask local advice

vino wine; red (**tinto**), rose (**rosado**), or white (**blanco**); local table wine is **vino corriente, vino de mesa,** or **vino del país**

English–Español

A

a, an [ə, ən] *art* un, -a.
aback [ə'bak] *adv* be taken aback quedar desconcertado.
abandon [ə'bandən] *v* abandonar. *n* abandono *m.*
abashed [ə'baʃt] *adj* avergonzado, confundido.
abate [ə'beit] *v* disminuir. **abatement** *n* disminución *f.*
abattoir ['abətwaɪ] *n* matadero *m.*
abbey ['abi] *n* abadía *f.* **abbess** *n* abadesa *f.* **abbot** *n* abad *m.*
abbreviate [ə'briːvieit] *v* abreviar. **abbreviation** *n* abreviación *f.*
abdicate ['abdikeit] *v* abdicar. **abdication** *n* abdicación *f.*
abdomen ['abdəmən] *n* abdomen *m.* **abdominal** *adj* abdominal.
abduct [əb'dʌkt] *v* raptar. **abduction** *n* rapto *m.*
aberration [abə'reiʃən] *n* extravío *m,* engaño *m.* **abberant** *adj* extraviado.
abet [ə'bet] *v* instigar, inducir.
abeyance [ə'beiəns] *n* in abeyance en suspenso.
abhor [əb'hoɪ] *v* aborrecer, odiar. **abhorrence** *n* aborrecimiento *m,* odio *m.* **abhorrent** *adj* aborrecible.
***abide** [ə'baid] *v* residir, habitar; (*tolerate*) aguantar, sufrir. **abide by** atenerse a, cumplir con.
ability [ə'biləti] *n* habilidad *f,* capacidad *f.* **to the best of one's ability** lo mejor que pueda.
abject [,abdʒekt] *adj* abyecto.
ablaze [ə'bleiz] *adj* en llamas.
able ['eibl] *adj* capaz; (*talented*) hábil.

able-bodied *adj* entero. **able-bodied seaman** marinero de primera *m.* **be able** poder. **ably** *adv* hábilmente.
abnormal [ab'noɪml] *adj* anormal. **abnormality** *n* anormalidad *f.*
aboard [ə'boɪd] *adv, prep* a bordo (de). **all aboard!** ¡viajeros a bordo! **go aboard** embarcarse.
abode [ə'boud] *n* domicilio *m.*
abolish [ə'boliʃ] *v* abolir. **abolition** *n* abolición *f.*
abominable [ə'bominəbl] *adj* abominable. **abominate** *v* abominar (de). **abomination** *n* abominación *f.*
Aborigine [abə'ridʒini] *n* aborigen *m.*
abortion [ə'boɪʃən] *n* aborto *m.* **abort** *v* abortar.
abound [ə'baund] *v* abundar.
about [ə'baut] *adv* (*approximately*) casi, alrededor de, más o menos. **all about** por todas partes. *prep* (*place*) alrededor de; (*near*) cerca de; (*concerning*) de, acerca de.
above [ə'bʌv] *adv* encima, arriba. *prep* (*place*) encima de, sobre; (*number*) más de; (*rank*) superior a. **above-mentioned** *adj* susodicho, citado.
abrasion [ə'breiʒən] *n* raspadura *f.* **abrasive** *adj* raspante.
abreast [ə'brest] *adv* de frente. **keep abreast of** *or* **with** ir al paso de.
abridge [ə'bridʒ] *v* abreviar, resumir. **abridgement** *n* abreviación *f,* resumen *m.*
abroad [ə'broɪd] *adv* en el extranjero.
abrupt [ə'brʌpt] *adj* abrupto, brusco.
abscess ['abses] *n* absceso *m.*
abscond [əb'skond] *v* fugarse.
absent ['absənt] *adj* ausente. **absent-minded** *adj* distraído. **absent onself** ausentarse. **absence** *n* ausencia *f.* **absentee** *n* ausente *m, f.* **absenteeism** *n* absentismo *m.*

absolute ['absəluɪt] *adj* absoluto. **absolutely** *adv* absolutamente; (*interj*) categóricamente. **absolutism** *n* absolutismo *m*.
absolve [əb'zolv] *v* absolver. **absolution** *n* absolución *f*.
absorb [əb'zoɪb] *v* absorber. **be absorbed in** enfrascarse en. **absorbent** *adj* absorbente. **absorbing** *adj* (*coll*) sumamente interesante.
abstain [əb'stein] *v* abstenerse (de). **abstention** *n* abstención *f*. **abstinence** *n* abstinencia *f*.
abstemious [əb'stiɪmiəs] *adj* abstemio.
abstract ['abstrakt; *v* ab'strakt] *adj* abstracto. *n* resumen *m*. *v* extractar. **abstractedly** *adv* distraídamente. **abstraction** *n* abstracción *f*.
absurd [əb'səɪd] *adj* absurdo. **absurdity** *n* absurdidad *f*.
abundance [ə'bʌndəns] *n* abundancia *f*. **abundant** *adj* abundante.
abuse [ə'bjuɪz; *n* ə'bjuɪs] *v* abusar (de). *n* abuso *m*; injuria *f*. **abusive** *adj* abusivo; injurioso.
abyss [ə'bis] *n* abismo *m*. **abysmal** *adj* abismal; profundo.
academy [ə'kadəmi] *n* academia *f*. **academic** *adj* académico.
accede [ak'siɪd] *v* acceder.
accelerate [ək'seləreit] *v* acelerar. **acceleration** *n* aceleración *f*. **accelerator** *n* acelerador *m*.
accent ['aksənt] *n* acento *m*. *v* acentuar.
accept [ək'sept] *v* aceptar. **acceptable** *adj* aceptable. **acceptance** *n* aceptación *f*.
access ['akses] *n* acceso *m*. **accessible** *adj* asequible.
accessory [ak'sesəri] *nm, adj* accessorio. *n* (*law*) cómplice *m, f*. **accessories** *pl n* (*mot, etc.*) complementos *m pl*.
accident ['aksidənt] *n* accidente *m*. **by accident** sin querer, por casualidad. **accidental** *adj* accidental.
acclaim [ə'kleim] *v* aclamar, aplaudir. *n* also **acclamation** aclamación *f*, aplauso *m*.
acclimatize [ə'klaimətaiz] *v* aclimatar.
accolade ['akəleid] *n* acolada *f*.
accommodate [ə'komədeit] *v* acomodar; (*lodge*) alojar, hospedar; adaptar; (*provide*) proveer (de). **accommodating** *adj* complaciente. **accommodation** *n* alojamiento *m*.

accompany [ə'kʌmpəni] *v* acompañar. **accompaniment** *n* acompañamiento *m*. **accompanist** *n* acompañante, -a *m, f*.
accomplice [ə'kʌmplis] *n* cómplice *m, f*.
accomplish [ə'kʌmpliʃ] *v* cumplir. **accomplished** *adj* (*talented*) talentoso. **accomplishment** *n* efectuación *f*; talentos *m pl*.
accord [ə'koɪd] *v* conceder; concordar. *n* acuerdo *m*. **of one's own accord** espontáneamente. **in accordance with** conforme a. **accordingly** *adv* en consecuencia. **according to** según.
accordion [ə'koɪdiən] *n* acordeón *m*.
accost [ə'kost] *v* abordar.
account [ə'kaunt] *n* (*bank, etc.*) cuenta *f*; (*narrative*) relato *m*; (*status*) importancia *f*. **on account of** a causa de. **on no account** de ninguna manera. **take into account** tener en cuenta. **account for** dar una explicación de. **accountant** *n* contador *m*; (*chartered*) contador colegiado.
accrue [ə'kruɪ] *v* crecer.
accumulate [ə'kjuɪmjuleit] *v* acumular. **accumulation** *n* acumulación *f*.
accurate ['akjurət] *adj* exacto. **accuracy** *n* precisión *f*.
accuse [ə'kjuɪz] *v* acusar. **accusation** *n* acusación *f*. **the accused** acusado, -a *m, f*.
accustom [ə'kʌstəm] *v* acostumbrar.
ace [eis] *n* as *m*. **within an ace of** de dos dedos de.
ache [eik] *n* dolor *m*. *v* doler.
achieve [ə'tʃiɪv] *v* ejecutar. **achievement** *n* ejecución *f*; (*feat*) hazaña *f*.
acid ['asid] *nm, adj* ácido. **acidity** *n* acidez *f*.
acknowledge [ək'nolidʒ] *v* reconocer, aceptar. **acknowledge receipt of** acusar recibo de. **acknowledgement** *n* reconocimiento *m*; acuse de recibo *m*.
acne ['akni] *n* acné *m*.
acorn ['eikoɪn] *n* bellota *f*.
acoustic [ə'kuɪstik] *adj* acústico. **acoustics** *pl n* acústica *f sing*.
acquaint [ə'kweint] *v* informar, avisar. **acquaintance** *n* (*knowledge*) conocimiento *m*; (*person*) conocido, -a *m, f*. **be acquainted with** conocer(a).
acquiesce [akwi'es] *v* consentir, conformarse. **acquiescence** *n* conformidad *f*. **acquiescent** *adj* sumiso.
acquire [ə'kwaiə] *v* adquirir. **acquisition** *n* adquisición *f*. **acquisitive** *adj* adquisitivo; (*derog*) ahorrativo.

acquit [ə'kwit] v absolver. **acquit oneself** portarse. **acquittal** (*law*) absolución *f*.
acrid ['akrid] *adj* acre.
acrimony ['akriməni] *n* acrimonia *f*. **acrimonious** *adj* áspero.
acrobat ['akrəbat] *n* acróbata *m*, *f*. **acrobatic** *adj* acrobático. **acrobatics** *pl n* acrobacia *f sing*.
across [ə'kros] *adv* a través, al través. *prep* a través de, al través de, de través de; al otro lado de, del otro lado de.
acrylic [ə'krilik] *adj* acrílico.
act [akt] v (*theatre*) representar; (*function*) funcionar, marchar; (*behave*) comportarse; (*take action*) obrar, tomar medidas; (*affect*) afectar. *n* acto *m*, acción *f*; obra *f*; (*law*) decreto; (theatre) acto *m*. **actor** *n* actor *m*. **actress** *n* actriz *f*.
action ['akʃən] *n* acción *f*, hecho *m*; (*mil*) acción *f*, batalla *f*; (*mech*) mecanismo *m*. **bring an action against** entablar demanda contra. **put out of action** inutilizar.
active ['aktiv] *adj* activo. **activate** v activar. **activist** *n* activista *m*, *f*. **activity** *n* actividad *f*; movimiento *m*.
actual ['aktʃuəl] *adj* verdadero, efectivo. **actually** *adv* en realidad.
actuate ['aktjueit] v mover; accionar.
acupuncture ['akjupʌŋktʃə] *n* acupuntura *f*.
acute [ə'kjuit] *adj* agudo.
adamant ['adəmənt] *adj* firme, seguro.
Adam's apple [adəm'zapl] *n* nuez de la garganta *f*.
adapt [ə'dapt] v adaptar; ajustar; (*play, book*) refundir; (*music*) arreglar. **adaptable** *adj* adaptable. **adaptation** *n* adaptación *f*; refundición *f*; arreglo *m*. **adapter** *n* (theatre) refundidor *m*; (*elec*) enchufe de reducción *m*.
add [ad] v añadir; (*increase*) aumentar. **add up** sumar. **add up to** subir a. **addition** *n* el añadir *m*; (*math*) suma *f*, adición *f*.
additional *adj* adicional.
addendum [ə'dendəm] *n invar* adenda *f*.
adder ['adə] *n* víbora *f*.
addict ['adikt] *n* partidario, -a *m*, *f*; (*drugs*) toxicómano, -a *m*, *f*. **addiction** *n* adicción *f*; propensión *f*. **be addicted to** ser adicto a.
additive ['aditiv] *n* aditivo *m*.
address [ə'dres] v (*letter*) dirigir; (*meeting, etc.*) pronunciar un discurso ante. **address oneself to** dirigirse. *n* (*postal*) dirección *f*; (*speech*) discurso *m*; (*envelope*) sobrescrito *m*. **addressee** *n* destinatario, -a *m*, *f*.
adenoids ['adənoidz] *pl n* amígdalas vegetaciones *f pl*.
adept [ə'dept] *nm, adj* experto.
adequate ['adikwət] *adj* adecuado, suficiente.
adhere [əd'hiə] v pegarse; (*to a policy*) adherirse a. **adhesion** *n* adhesión *f*. **adhesive** *adj* adhesivo. **adhesive tape** esparadrapo *m*.
adherent [əd'hiərənt] *n* partidario, -a *m*, *f*.
adjacent [ə'dʒeisənt] *adj* próximo, contiguo.
adjective ['adʒiktiv] *n* adjetivo *m*.
adjoin [ə'dʒoin] v lindar (con). **adjoining** *adj* contiguo.
adjourn [ə'dʒəin] v aplazar; (*session*) levantar la sesión. **adjournment** *n* aplazamiento *m*; (*of a session*) suspensión *f*.
adjudicate [ə'dʒuidikeit] v adjudicar; (*law*) juzgar. **adjudication** *n* adjudicación *f*; (*law*) fallo *m*. **adjudicator** *n* árbitro *m*.
adjust [ə'dʒʌst] v arreglar; (*tech*) ajustar. **adjustment** *n* arreglo *m*; ajuste *m*.
ad-lib ['ad'lib] *adv* a voluntad, a discreción. v improvisar.
administer [əd'ministə] v administrar; (*law*) aplicar; (*med*) suministrar. **administration** *n* administración *f*; (*ministry*) gobierno *m*. **administrative** *adj* administrativo. **administrator** *n* administrador *m*.
admiral ['admərəl] *n* almirante *m*.
admire [əd'maiə] v admirar. **admirable** *adj* admirable. **admiration** *n* admiración *f*.
admit [əd'mit] v dar entrada a; (*concede*) conceder; (*acknowledge*) reconocer. **admission** *n* entrada *f*; (*acknowledgement*) confesión *f*.
adolescence [adə'lesns] *n* adolescencia *f*. **adolescent** *n(m+f), adj* adolescente.
adopt [ə'dopt] v adoptar; (*report*) aprobar. **adopted** *adj* (*child*) adoptivo. **adoption** *n* adopción *f*.
adore [ə'doi] v adorar. **adoration** *n* adoración *f*.
adorn [ə'doin] v adornar, embellecer. **adornment** *n* adorno *m*.
adrenaline [ə'drenəlin] *n* adrenalina *f*.

adrift [ə'drift] *adv* a la deriva.
adroit [ə'droit] *adj* diestro, hábil.
adulation [adju'leiʃən] *n* adulación *f*.
adult ['adʌlt] *n, adj* adulto, -a.
adulterate [ə'dʌltəreit] *v* adulterar.
adultery [ə'dʌltəri] *n* adulterio *m*. **adulterer** *n* adúltero, -a *m, f*.
advance [əd'vains] *v* adelantar; avanzar. *n* progreso *m*, avance *m*, adelanto *m*; (*cash*) anticipo *m*.
advantage [əd'vaintidʒ] *n* ventaja *f*. **take advantage of** aprovecharse de. **advantageous** *adj* ventajoso.
advent ['advənt] *n* advenimiento *m*. **Advent** *n* Adviento *m*.
adventure [əd'ventʃə] *n* aventura *f*; (*comm*) especulación *f*. **adventurer** *n* aventurero *m*. **adventurous** *adj* aventurero.
adverb ['advəib] *n* adverbio *m*.
adversary ['advəsəri] *n* adversario, -a *m, f*.
adverse ['advəis] *adj* adverso. **adversity** *n* adversidad *f*.
advertise ['advətaiz] *v* anunciar; publicar. **advertisement** *n* anuncio *m*. **advertising** *n* publicidad *f*.
advise [əd'vaiz] *v* aconsejar; avisar. **advisable** *adj* conveniente. **advisedly** *adv* con intención. **adviser** *n* consejero *m*. **advice** *n* consejo *m*.
advocate ['advəkeit] *v* recomendar.
aerial ['eəriəl] *adj* aéreo. *n* antena *f*.
aerodynamics [eərədai'namiks] *n* aerodinámica *f sing*.
aeronautics [eərə'noitiks] *n* aeronáutica *f sing*.
aeroplane ['eərəplein] *n* avión *m*.
aerosol ['eərəsol] *n* aerosol *m*.
aesthetic [iis'θetik] *adj* estético. **aesthetics** *n* estética *f sing*.
affair [ə'feə] *n* asunto *m*; episodio *m*; (*love*) aventura amorosa *f*. **affairs** (*business*) negocios *m pl*.
affect[1] [ə'fekt] *v* (*influence*) influir en; (*move*) conmover.
affect[2] [ə'fekt] *v* (*pretend*) afectar.
affection [ə'fekʃən] *n* cariño *m*.
affiliate [ə'filieit] *v* afiliarse (a). **affiliation** *n* afiliación *f*.
affinity [ə'finəti] *n* afinidad *f*.
affirm [ə'fəim] *v* afirmar. **affirmation** *n* afirmación *f*. **affirmative** *adj* afirmativo.
affix [ə'fiks] *v* fijar; añadir; pegar; poner.

afflict [ə'flikt] *v* afligir, aquejar. **affliction** *n* aflicción *f*, dolor *m*.
affluent ['afluənt] *adj* afluente, opulento. **affluence** *n* afluencia *f*, opulencia *f*.
afford [ə'foid] *v* tener medios; (*produce*) dar; ofrecer.
affront [ə'frʌnt], *v* afrentar. *n* afrenta *f*, ofensa *f*.
afloat [ə'flout] *adv* a flote.
afoot [ə'fut] *adv* a pie; (*fig*) en proyecto.
aforesaid [ə'foised] *adj* susodicho, mencionado.
afraid [ə'freid] *adj* temeroso, espantado. **be afraid** tener miedo (a *or* de).
afresh [ə'freʃ] *adv* de nuevo.
Africa ['afrikə] *n* África *f*. **African** *n, adj* africano, -a.
aft [aift] *adv* a popa.
after ['aiftə] *prep* (*time*) después de; (*place*) detrás de; tras. *adv* (*time*) después; (*place*) detrás. *conj* después (de) que. **after all** con todo. **afterwards** *adv* después. **after-effect** *n* consecuencia *f*. **aftershave** *n* loción de afeitar *f*.
afternoon [aiftə'nuin] *n* tarde *f*. **good afternoon!** ¡buenas tardes!
again [ə'gen] *adv* de nuevo, otra vez; además. **again and again** aún una y otra vez. **now and again** de vez en cuando.
against [ə'genst] *prep* contra; (*touching*) tocante.
age [eidʒ] *n* edad *f*; (*era*) época *f*. **of age** mayor de edad. **under age** menor de edad. *v* envejecer. **aged** *adj* de la edad de; (*old*) viejo.
agency ['eidʒənsi] *n* agencia *f*; mediación *f*.
agenda [ə'dʒendə] *n* agenda *f*.
agent ['eidʒənt] *n* agente *m, f*; (*comm*) representante *m, f*.
aggravate ['agrəveit] *v* agravar; (*coll*) exasperar. **aggravation** *n* agravamiento *m*; (*coll*) irritación *f*.
aggregate ['agrigət] *m, adj* agregado. *v* agregar, juntar.
aggression [ə'greʃən] *n* agresión *f*. **aggressive** *adj* agresivo. **aggressiveness** *n* belicosidad *f*. **agressor** *n* agresor, -a *m, f*.
aghast [ə'gaist] *adj* horrorizado.
agile ['adʒail] *adj* ágil, ligero. **agility** *n* agilidad *f*.
agitate ['adʒiteit] *v* agitar, excitar. **agitate for** luchar por. **agitation** *n* agitación *f*; perturbación *f*.

agnostic [ag'nostik] *n, adj* agnóstico, -a.
agnosticism *n* agnosticismo *m.*
ago [ə'gou] *adv* hace, ha. **long ago** hace mucho tiempo. **a short time ago** hace poco.
agog [ə'gog] *adj* ansioso.
agony ['agəni] *n* agonía *f,* angustia *f.* **agonize** *v* atormentar.
agree [ə'griː] *v* estar de acuerdo, convenir (en); (*consent*) consentir (en); (*gram*) concordar; (*correspond*) estar conforme (con). **agreeable** *adj* agradable. **agreement** *n* (*pact*) pacto *m;* (*comm*) contrato *m.*
agriculture ['agrikʌltʃə] *n* agricultura *f.* **agricultural** *adj* agrícola.
aground [ə'graund] *adv* encallado. **run aground** encallar, varar.
ahead [ə'hed] *adv* delante, al frente. **be ahead** estar adelante. **go ahead!** ¡adelante!
aid [eid] *v* ayudar, socorrer. *n* ayuda *f.* **in aid of** en beneficio de. **first aid** primera cura. **go to the aid of** acudir en defensa de.
aim [eim] *v* (*weapon*) apuntar (a); (*remark*) dirigir (a). *n* (*weapon*) puntería *f;* (*fig*) propósito *m,* meta *f,* blanco *m.* **aimless** *adj* sin objeto. **aimlessly** *adv* a la ventura.
air [eə] *n* aire *m;* (*music*) aire *m,* tonada *f;* (*aspect*) aspecto *m. v* airear, ventilar.
airbed ['eəbed] *n* colchón de viento *m.*
airborne ['eəbɔin] *adj* en el aire.
aircraft ['eəkraift] *n* avión *m.* **aircraft-carrier** *n* portaaviones *m invar.*
airfield ['eəfiild] *n* campo de aviación *m.*
air force *n* fuerza *or* flota aérea *f.*
air-hostess *n* azafata *f.*
air lift *n* puente aéreo *m.*
airline ['eəlain] *n* línea aérea *f.*
airmail ['eəmeil] *n* correo aéreo *m.*
airport ['eəpɔit] *n* aeropuerto *m.*
air-raid *n* bombardeo aéreo *m.*
airtight ['eətait] *adj* hermético, herméticamente cerrado.
airy ['eəri] *adj* aéreo; (*flippant*) frívolo.
aisle [ail] *n* nave lateral *f.*
ajar [ə'dʒɑi] *adv* entreabierto, entornado.
alabaster ['aləbaistə] *n* alabastro *m. adj* alabastrino.
alarm [ə'laim] *n* alarma *f. v* alarmar. **alarm clock** *n* despertador *m.*
alas [ə'las] *interj* ¡ay!

Albania [al'beinjə] *n* Albania *f.* **Albanian** *n, adj* albanés, -esa.
albatross ['albɔtros] *n* albatros *m.*
albino [al'biinou] *n, adj* albino, -a.
album ['albəm] *n* álbum *m.*
alchemy ['alkəmi] *n* alquimia *f.* **alchemist** *n* alquimista *m.*
alcohol ['alkəhol] *n* alcohol *m.* **alcoholic** *n, adj* alcohólico, -a. **alcoholism** *n* alcoholismo *m.*
alcove ['alkouv] *n* nicho *m,* hueco *m.*
alderman ['ɔildəmən] *n* teniente de alcalde *m,* concejal *m.*
ale [eil] *n* cerveza *f.*
alert [ə'lɔit] *adj* alerto, vivo, despierto. *v* poner sobre aviso, alertar.
algebra ['aldʒibrə] *n* álgebra *f.*
Algeria [al'dʒiəriə] *n* Argelia *f.* **Algerian** *n, adj* argelino, -a.
alias ['eiliəs] *nm, adv* alias.
alibi ['alibai] *n* coartada *f.*
alien ['eiliən] *n, adj* extranjero, -a. **alienate** *v* enajenar, alejar. **alienation** *n* alienación *f.*
alight¹ [ə'lait] *v* desmontar, bajar, apearse.
alight² [ə'lait] *adj* encendido, iluminado, en llamas.
align [ə'lain] *v* alinear. **alignment** *n* alineación *f.*
alike [ə'laik] *adj* igual, parecido, semejante. *adv* igualmente, del mismo modo.
alimentary canal [ali'mentəri] *n* tubo digestivo *m.*
alimony ['aliməni] *n* alimentos *m pl.*
alive [ə'laiv] *adj* vivo, activo. **alive to** sensible de. **alive with** rebosante de.
alkali ['alkəlai] *n* álcali *m.*
all [ɔil] *adj* todo. *pron* todo el mundo. *n* todo *m,* totalidad *f. adv* todo, enteramente. **all but** casi. **all right** está bien. **all the more** cuanto más. **all the same** sin embargo.
allay [ə'lei] *v* aliviar, calmar.
allege [ə'ledʒ] *v* alegar, afirmar.
allegiance [ə'liidʒəns] *n* fidelidad *f,* lealtad *f.*
allegory ['aligəri] *n* alegoría *f.*
allergy ['alədʒi] *n* alergia *f.* **allergic** *adj* alérgico.
alleviate [ə'liivieit] *v* aliviar. **alleviation** *n* alivio *m.*
alley ['ali] *n* callejuela *f,* paseo *m.* **blind alley** callejón sin salida *m.*
alliance [ə'laiəns] *n* alianza *f.*

allied ['alaid] *adj* aliado.
alligator ['aligeitə] *n* caimán *m*.
alliteration [əlitə'reiʃən] *n* aliteración *f*.
allocate ['aləkeit] *v* asignar, distribuir.
allocation *n* asignación *f*, repartimiento *m*.
allot [ə'lot] *v* asignar. **allotment** *n* lote *m*.
allow [ə'lau] *v* permitir, admitir. **allow for** tener en cuenta. **allowable** *adj* permisible, legítimo. **allowance** *n* ración *f*; pensión *f*. **monthly allowance** mesada *f*.
alloy ['aloi; *v* ə'loi] *n* aleación *f*; (*fig*) mezcla *f*. *v* alear, ligar.
allude [ə'luːd] *v* aludir. **allusion** *n* alusión *f*. **allusive** *adj* alusivo.
allure [ə'ljuə] *v* seducir, fascinar. **allurement** *n* incentivo *m*, anzuelo *m*. **alluring** *adj* halagüeño, tentador.
ally ['alai; *v* ə'lai] *n* aliado, -a *m*, *f*, asociado, -a *m*, *f*. *v* unir.
almanac ['oɪlmənak] *n* almanaque *m*.
almighty [oɪl'maiti] *adj* omnipotente, todopoderoso.
almond ['aɪmənd] *n* (*nut*) almendra *f*; (*tree*) almendro *m*.
almost ['oɪlmoust] *adv* casi.
alms [aɪmz] *n* limosna *f*. **almsgiving** *n* caridad *f*. **almshouse** *n* hospicio *m*.
aloft [ə'loft] *adv* en alto, arriba.
alone [ə'loun] *adj* solo, único. *adv* solamente, a solas. **leave alone** dejar en paz.
along [ə'loŋ] *prep* a lo largo de. **along with** en compañía de, junto con. **come along!** ¡ven! **alongside** *adv* al lado; (*naut*) al costado de.
aloof [ə'luːf] *adv* a distancia. *adj* altanero, reservado. **keep aloof** mantenerse alejado. **aloofness** *n* alejamiento *m*.
aloud [ə'laud] *adv* en voz alta, recio, alto.
alphabet ['alfəbit] *n* alfabeto *m*.
Alps [alps] *n* Alpes *m pl*.
already [oɪl'redi] *adv* ya.
also ['oɪlsou] *adv* también, además.
altar ['oɪltə] *n* altar *m*. **high altar** altar mayor. **altar boy** monaguillo *m*. **altarpiece** retablo *m*.
alter ['oɪltə] *v* cambiar, modificar, corregir, transformar; (*clothes*) arreglar. **alteration** *n* cambio *m*, modificación *f*; (*building*) reforma *f*.
alternate [oɪl'təɪnət; *v* 'oɪltəneit] *adj* alterno. *v* alternar. **alternating current** corriente alterna.
alternative [oɪl'təɪnətiv] *n* alternativa *f*.

adj alternativo. **have no alternative but** ... no poder menos de ....
although [oɪl'ðou] *conj* aunque.
altitude ['altitjuɪd] *n* altura *f*, altitud *f*.
altogether [oɪltə'geðə] *adv* en total, en conjunto, del todo.
altruistic [altru'istik] *adj* altruista. **altruism** *n* altruismo. **altruist** *n* altruista *m*, *f*.
aluminium [alju'miniəm] *n* aluminio *m*.
always ['oɪlweiz] *adv* siempre.
am [am] *V* be.
amalgamate [ə'malgəmeit] *v* amalgamar, combinar, unir; combinarse, unirse. **amalgamation** *n* amalgamación *f*; mezcla *f*.
amass [ə'mas] *v* acumular, amontonar.
amateur ['amətə] *n*, *adj* aficionado, -a. **amateurish** *adj* de aficionado, superficial.
amaze [ə'meiz] *v* asombrar, sorprender, confundir. **amazement** *n* asombro *m*. **amazing** *adj* asombroso.
ambassador [am'basədə] *n* embajador *m*.
amber ['ambə] *n* ámbar *m*. *adj* ambarino.
ambidextrous [ambi'dekstrəs] *adj* ambidextro.
ambiguous [am'bigjuəs] *adj* ambiguo. **ambiguity** *n* ambigüedad *f*.
ambition [am'biʃən] *n* ambición *f*. **ambitious** *adj* ambicioso.
ambivalent [am'bivələnt] *adj* ambivalente.
amble ['ambl] *v* amblar, andar lentamente. *n* paso de andadura *m*.
ambulance ['ambjuləns] *n* ambulancia *f*.
ambush ['ambuʃ] *n* emboscada *f*, asechanza *f*. *v* emboscar, asechar.
ameliorate [ə'miːliəreit] *v* mejorar. **amelioration** *n* mejora *f*.
amenable [ə'miːnəbl] *adj* tratable, dócil, sujeto.
amend [ə'mend] *v* enmendar, modificar, rectificar. **amendment** *n* enmienda *f*. **make amends** dar satisfacción, indemnizar.
amenity [ə'miːnəti] *n* amendidad *f*, comodidad *f*.
America [ə'merikə] *n* América *f*. **American** *n*, *adj* americano, -a *m*, *f*.
amethyst ['aməθist] *n* amatista *f*.
amiable ['eimiəbl] *adj* amistoso, afable.
amicable ['amikəbl] *adj* amigable.
amid [ə'mid] *prep* entre, rodeado por, en medio de.
amiss [ə'mis] *adv* mal, de más, impropiamente. **take amiss** llevar a mal.

ammonia [ə'mouniə] n amoníaco m.
ammunition [amju'niʃən] n municiones f pl.
amnesia [am'niːziə] n amnesia f.
amnesty ['amnəsti] n amnistía f.
amoeba [ə'miːbə] n ameba f.
among [ə'mʌŋ] prep entre, en medio de.
amoral [ei'morəl] adj amoral.
amorous ['amərəs] adj amoroso.
amorphous [ə'mɔːfəs] adj amorfo.
amount [ə'maunt] n cantidad f, importe m, suma f. v llegar a, subir a, valer. **gross amount** importe bruto m. **net amount** importe neto m. **it amounts to this** se reduce a esto.
ampere ['ampeə] n amperio m.
amphetamine [am'fetəmiːn] n anfetamina f.
amphibian [am'fibiən] nm, adj anfibio.
amphitheatre ['amfiθiətə] n anfiteatro m.
ample ['ampl] adj amplio, abundante; (enough) bastante, suficiente.
amplify ['amplifai] v ampliar, amplificar, aumentar. **amplifier** n amplificador m.
amputate ['ampjuteit] v amputar. **amputation** n amputación f.
amuse [ə'mjuːz] v divertir, distraer, entretener. **amuse oneself** divertirse. **amusement** n diversión f, entretenimiento m, recreo m; (hobby) pasatiempo m. **amusement park** parque de atracciones m. **amusing** adj divertido, gracioso.
anachronism [ə'nakrənizəm] n anacronismo m. **anachronistic** adj anacrónico.
anaemia [ə'niːmiə] n anemia f. **anaemic** adj anémico.
anaesthetic [anəs'θetik] nm, adj anestésico.
anagram ['anəgram] n anagrama m.
analogy [ə'nalədʒi] n analogía f. **analogous** adj análogo.
analysis [ən'aləsis] n, pl -ses análisis m. **analyst** n analista m, f. **analytic(al)** adj analítico.
anarchy ['anəki] n anarquía f. **anarchic** adj anárquico. **anarchist** n anarquista m, f.
anathema [ə'naθəmə] n anatema m, f.
anatomy [ə'natəmi] n anatomía f. **anatomical** adj anatómico.
ancestor ['ansestə] n antepasado m. **ancestral** adj ancestral, hereditario. **ancestry** n linaje m.

anchor ['aŋkə] n ancla f; (fig) áncora f. v anclar, fijar, fondear.
anchovy ['antʃəvi] n anchoa f.
ancient ['einʃənt] adj anciano, antiguo. **ancients** pl n los antiguos m pl. **from ancient times** de antiguo.
ancillary [an'siləri] adj auxiliar.
and [and] conj y, e.
anecdote ['anikdout] n anécdota f.
anemone [ə'neməni] n anémona f.
anew [ə'njuː] adv de nuevo, otra vez.
angel ['eindʒəl] n ángel m. **angelic** adj angélico.
anger ['aŋgə] n cólera f, ira f, enojo m. v enojar, enfadar, encolerizar. **angry** adj enojado, enfadado.
angina [an'dʒainə] n angina f. **angina pectoris** angina de pecho.
angle ['aŋgl] n ángulo m, rincón m; (viewpoint) punto de vista m.
angling ['aŋgliŋ] n pesca con caña f. **angler** n pescador, -a m, f.
anguish ['aŋgwiʃ] n angustia f, agonía f, dolor m.
animal ['animəl] n animal m, bestia f. adj animal. **animal kingdom** reino animal m. **animal spirits** brío m, energía f, exuberancia vital f.
animate ['animeit; adj 'animət] v animar, alentar, vivificar. adj viviente, animado. **animated** adj animado, vivo. **animated cartoon** dibujo animado.
animosity [ani'mosəti] n animosidad f, hostilidad f.
aniseed ['anisiːd] n grano de anís m.
ankle ['aŋkl] n tobillo m.
annals ['anlz] pl n anales m pl.
annex ['aneks; v ə'neks] n anexo m. v anexar, anexionar; unir, juntar. **annexation** n anexión f.
annihilate [ə'naiəleit] v aniquilar. **annihilation** n aniquilación f.
anniversary [ˌani'vəːsəri] n aniversario m.
annotate ['anəteit] v anotar, acotar, glosar. **annotation** n anotación f, nota f.
announce [ə'nauns] v anunciar, publicar, proclamar. **announcement** n anuncio m, aviso m, publicación f; (of engagement) participación f. **announcer** n annuncidor, -a m, f; (radio) locutor, -a m, f.
annoy [ə'noi] v molestar, irritar, fastidiar. **annoyance** n molestia f, disgusto m. **annoyed** adj enojado. **annoying** adj fastidioso, enojoso, molesto.

annual ['anjuəl] *adj* anual. *n* (*book*) anuario *m*; (*plant*) planta anual *f*.
annul [ə'nʌl] *v* anular; (*law*) abrogar.
annulment *n* anulación *f*.
Annunciation [ə,nʌnsi'eiʃən] *n* (*rel*) Anunciación *f*.
anode ['anoud] *n* ánodo *m*.
anomaly [ə'noməli] *n* anomalía *f*. **anomalous** *adj* anómalo.
anonymous [ə'noniməs] *adj* anónimo.
anorak ['anərak] *n* anorak *m*.
another [ə'nʌðə] *adj* otro. *pron* otro, -a *m*, *f*. **one after another** uno después de otro.
answer ['ainsə] *n* contestación *f*, respuesta *f*; (*solution*) solución *f*; (*math*) resultado *m*. *v* contestar, responder; (*a bell*) acudir; (*door*) abrir. **answer back** replicar. **answer by return** contestar a vuelta de correo. **answerable** *adj* responsable.
ant [ant] *n* hormiga *f*.
antagonize [an'tagənaiz] *v* antagonizar, contender. **antagonism** *n* antagonismo *m*, oposición *f*. **antagonist** *n* antagonista *m*, *f*. **antagonistic** *adj* antagónico.
antecedent [anti'siidənt] *nm*, *adj* antecedente.
antelope ['antəloup] *n* antilope *m*.
antenatal [anti'neitl] *adj* antenatal.
antenna [an'tenə] *n* antena *f*.
anthem ['anθəm] *n* motete *m*. **national anthem** himno nacional *m*.
anthology [an'θolədʒi] *n* antología *f*.
anthropology [anθrə'polədʒi] *n* antropología *f*.
anti-aircraft [anti'eəkraift] *adj* anti-aéreo.
antibiotic [antibai'otik] *nm*, *adj* antibiótico.
antibody ['anti,bodi] *n* anticuerpo *m*.
anticipate [an'tisipeit] *v* prever, esperar; anticiparse a. **anticipation** *n* anticipación *f*, esperanza *f*, adelantamiento *m*. **in anticipation of** en espera de.
anticlimax [anti'klaimaks] *n* anticlimax *m*.
anticlockwise [anti'klokwaiz] *adj* en dirección contraria a las agujas del reloj.
antics ['antiks] *pl n* cabriola *f sing*, travesura *f sing*, payasadas *f pl*.
anticyclone [anti'saikloun] *n* anticiclón *m*.
antidote ['antidout] *n* antídoto *m*, contraveneno *m*.
antifreeze ['antifriiz] *n* anticongelante *m*.
antipathy [an'tipəθi] *n* antipatía *f*, aversión *f*.

antique [an'tiik] *n* antigualla *f*, antigüedad *f*. *adj* antiguo. **antique dealer** antiquario *m*. **antique shop** tienda de antigüedades. **antiquity** *n* antigüedad *f*.
anti-Semitic [antisə'mitik] *adj* antisemítico. **anti-Semitism** *n* antisemitismo *m*.
antiseptic [anti'septik] *nm*, *adj* antiséptico.
antisocial [anti'souʃəl] *adj* antisocial.
anti-tank [anti'taŋk] *adj* antitanque.
antithesis [an'tiθəsis] *n*, *pl* -ses antítesis *f*.
antler ['antlə] *n* asta *f*, cuerno *m*.
antonym ['antənim] *n* antónimo *m*.
anus ['einəs] *n* ano *m*. **anal** *adj* anal.
anvil ['anvil] *n* yunque *m*.
anxious ['aŋkʃəs] *adj* ancioso, preocupado, inquieto. **anxiety** *n* inquietud *f*, ansiedad *f*, intranquilidad *f*.
any ['eni] *adv* cualquier; (*some*) algún, ningún; (*every*) todo. *pron* alguno, -a *m*, *f*; cualquiera *m*, *f*; ninguno, -a *m*, *f*. *adv* algo. **anybody** *or* **anyone** *pron* cualquiera, alguien, nadie. **anyhow** *adv* de cualquier modo. **anything** *n* algo *m*; (*negative*) nada *f*. **anywhere** *adv* dondequiera.
apart [ə'pait] *adv* aparte.
apartment [ə'paitmənt] *n* apartamento *m*, cuarto *m*, habitación *f*; (*flat*) piso *m*.
apathy ['apəθi] *n* apatía *f*, indiferencia *f*. **apathetic** *adj* apático.
ape [eip] *n* simio *m*, mono, -a *m*, *f*. *v* imitar.
aperitive [ə'peritiv] *nm*, *adj* aperitivo.
aperture ['apətjuə] *n* abertura *f*, orificio *m*, agujero *m*.
apex ['eipeks] *n* ápice *m*.
aphrodisiac [afrə'diziak] *n* afrodisiaco *m*.
apiece [ə'piis] *adv* por persona, por cabeza, cada uno.
apology [ə'polədʒi] *n* disculpa *f*, apología *f*, excusa *f*. **apologize** *v* disculparse, pedir perdón; (*regret*) sentir.
apoplexy ['apəpleksi] *n* apoplejía *f*. **apoplectic** *adj* apoplético.
apostle [ə'posl] *n* apóstol *m*.
apostrophe [ə'postrəfi] *n* (*punctuation*) apóstrofo *m*; (*speech*) apóstrofe *m*, *f*.
appal [ə'poil] *v* espantar, aterrar. **appalling** *adj* espantoso, horrible.
apparatus [apə'reitəs] *n* aparato *m*, máquina *f*.
apparent [ə'parənt] *adj* aparente; notable, obvio, evidente, claro. **apparently** *adv* al parecer.

apparition [apə'riʃən] *n* aparición *f*, fantasma *m*.
appeal [ə'piːl] *v* (*law*) apelar; (*attract*) atraer. *n* (*law*) apelación *f*; atractivo *m*.
appeal against suplicar de.
appear [ə'piə] *v* aparecer; (*seem*) parecer; (*in court*) comparecer. **appearance** *n* aparición *f*; (*aspect*) apariencia *f*, aspecto *m*; (*arrival*) llegada *f*.
appease [ə'piːz] *v* aplacar, apaciguar. **appeasement** *n* aplacamiento *m*, apaciguamiento *m*.
appendix [ə'pendiks] *n* apéndice *m*. **appendicitis** *n* apendicitis *f*.
appetite ['apitait] *n* apetito *m*. **have an appetite** tener ganas. **appetizing** *adj* apetitoso.
applaud [ə'plɔid] *v* aplaudir. **applause** *n* aplauso *m*.
apple ['apl] *n* (*fruit*) manzana *f*; (*tree*) manzano *m*. **apple sauce** compota de manzanes *f*.
apply [ə'plai] *v* dirigirse a, recurrir; aplicar; (*use*) emplear; (*for a job*) proponerse a. **apply oneself to** dedicarse a. **appliance** *n* aparato *m*. **applicable** *adj* aplicable. **applicant** *n* aspirante *m*, *f*. **application** *n* aplicación *f*.
appoint [ə'point] *v* nombrar, designar. **be appointed to** colocarse a. **be appointed as** ser nombrado. **appointment** *n* puesto *m*, empleo *m*; (*assignation*) cita *f*. **make an appointment with** citar.
apportion [ə'pɔːʃən] *v* distribuir, repartir.
appraisal [ə'preizl] *n* valoración *f*, estimación *f*. **appraise** *v* valorizar, tasar.
appreciate [ə'priːʃieit] *v* apreciar, darse cuenta de; (*affection*) encarecer; (*in value*) tener en alza. **appreciation** *n* apreciación *f*, aprecio *m*; (*understanding*) percepción *f*; (*of shares, etc.*) aumento de valor *m*.
apprehend [apri'hend] *v* (*arrest*) prender, capturar; (*understand*) aprehender, percibir; (*fear*) temer. **apprehension** *n* (*arrest*) aprehensión *f*; (*understanding*) comprensión *f*; (*fear*) aprensión *f*. **apprehensive** *adj* aprensivo.
apprentice [ə'prentis] *n* aprendiz *m*. **apprenticeship** *n* aprendizaje *m*.
approach [ə'proutʃ] *v* acercarse a, aproximar; (*speak to*) hablar con. *n* acercamiento *m*, aproximación *f*; (*arrival*) llegada *f*; (*entrance*) entrada *f*.

appropriate [ə'prouprieit; *adj* ə'proupriət] *v* tomar posesión de, apropiar; (*assign*) asignar, destinar. *adj* propio, pertinente, correspondiente. **appropriateness** *n* conveniencia *f*.
approve [ə'pruːv] *v* aprobar. **approval** *n* aprobación *f*. **on approval** a prueba. **approved** *adj* bien visto.
approximate [ə'proksimeit; *adj* ə'proksimət] *v* aproximar, aproximarse. *adj* aproximado. **approximately** *adv* poco más o menos.
apricot ['eiprikot] *n* (*fruit*) albaricoque *m*; (*tree*) albaricoquero *m*.
April ['eiprəl] *n* abril *m*.
apron ['eiprən] *n* delantal *m*; (*stage*) proscenio *m*.
apt [apt] *adj* apto; propenso; (*suitable*) apropiado.
aptitude ['aptitjuːd] *n* aptitud *f*.
aqualung ['akwəlʌŋ] *n* aparato de aire comprimido *m*.
aquarium [ə'kweəriəm] *n* acuario *m*.
Aquarius [ə'kweəriəs] *n* Acuario *m*.
aquatic [ə'kwatik] *adj* acuático.
aqueduct ['akwidʌkt] *n* acueducto *m*.
Arab ['arəb] *n*(*m*+*f*), *adj* árabe. **Arabia** *n* Arabia *f*. **Arabic** *adj* arábigo.
arable ['arəbl] *adj* arable.
arbitrary ['aibitrəri] *adj* arbitrario.
arbitrate ['aibitreit] *v* arbitrar. **arbitration** *n* arbitraje *m*. **arbiter** *or* **arbitrator** *n* árbitro *m*.
arc [aik] *n* arco *m*. **arc lamp** lámpara de arco *f*.
arcade [ai'keid] *n* arcada *f*, galería *f*.
arch¹ [aitʃ] *n* arco *m*. *v* arquear.
arch² [aitʃ] *adj* (*chief*) principal; archi-.
archaeology [aiki'olədʒi] *n* arqueología *f*. **archaeologist** *n* arqueólogo *m*.
archaic [ai'keiik] *adj* arcaico, arcaizante.
archbishop [aitʃ'biʃəp] *n* arzobispo *m*.
archduke [aitʃ'djuik] *n* archiduque *m*.
archery ['aitʃəri] *n* tiro con arco *m*. **archer** *n* arquero, -a *m*, *f*.
archetype ['aikitaip] *n* arquetipo *m*.
archipelago [aiki'peləgou] *n* archipiélago *m*.
architect ['aikitekt] *n* arquitecto *m*. **architecture** *n* arquitectura *f*.
archives ['aikaivz] *n pl* archivo *m sing*.
arctic ['aiktik] *adj* ártico. **the Arctic** el Ártico.
ardent ['aidənt] *adj* ardiente, apasionado.

ardour ['aɪdə] *n* ardor *m*.
arduous ['aɪdjuəs] *adj* arduo.
are [aɪ] *V* be.
area ['eəriə] *n* área *f*, superficie *f*; extensión *f*.
arena [ə'riːnə] *n* arena *f*, liza *f*.
Argentina [aɪdʒən'tiːnə] *n* Argentina *f*.
Argentinian *n*, *adj* argentino, -a.
argue ['aɪgjuː] *v* debatir, disputar, discutir. **argue against** oponer. **arguable** *adj* discutible. *argument n* argumento *m*.
argumentative *adj* contencioso.
arid ['arid] *adj* árido, seco.
Aries ['eəriɪz] *n* (*astrol*) Aries *m*.
***arise** [ə'raiz] *v* elevarse, subir; (*revolt*) sublevarse; (*from bed*) levantarse.
aristocracy [ari'stokrəsi] *n* aristocracia *f*. **aristocrat** *n* aristócrata *m*, *f*. **aristocratic** *adj* aristocrático.
arithmetic [ə'riθmətik] *n* aritmética *f*.
ark [aɪk] *n* arca *f*. **Noah's Ark** arca de Noé *f*.
arm[1] [aɪm] *n* (*limb*) brazo *m*. **armchair** *n* sillón *m*. **arm in arm** de bracete, de bracero. **armpit** *n* sobaco *m*. **within arm's reach** al alcance del brazo.
arm[2] [aɪm] *n* arma *f*. *v* armar. **to arms!** ¡a las armas! **take up arms** alzarse en armas. **under arms** sobre las armas.
armistice ['aɪmistis] *n* armisticio *m*.
armour ['aɪmə] *n* armadura *f*, arnés *m*; (*ships, vehicles*) blindaje *m*. *v* blindar, acorazar. **armour-plate** *n* coraza *f*.
armoury *n* armería *f*.
army ['aɪmi] *n* ejército *m*.
aroma [ə'roumə] *n* aroma *m*, fragancia *f*.
aromatic *adj* aromático.
around [ə'raund] *prep* alrededor de, cerca de; a la vuelta de. *adv* alrededor, en torno, por todas partes.
arouse [ə'rauz] *v* despertar, excitar.
arrange [ə'reindʒ] *v* arreglar, disponer; organizar; (*music*) adaptar; concertarse. **arrangement** *n* arreglo *m*; (*agreement*) acuerdo *m*; (*music*) adaptación *f*. **arrangements** *pl n* preparativos *m pl*.
array [ə'rei] *v* ataviar, poner en orden de batalla. *n* (*dress*) atavio *m*; (*troops*) formación *f*.
arrears [ə'riəz] *pl n* atrasos *m pl*. **in arrears** atrasado en pagos.
arrest [ə'rest] *v* arrestar, detener. *n* (*stop*) parada *f*; (*detention*) detención *f*. **under arrest** bajo arresto.

arrive [ə'raiv] *v* llegar. **arrival** *n* llegada *f*, venida *f*. **on arrival** al llegar.
arrogant ['arəgənt] *adj* arrogante, altanero. **arrogance** *n* arrogancia *f*.
arrow ['arou] *n* flecha *f*, saeta *f*.
arse [aɪs] *n* (*vulgar*) culo *m*, ojete *m*.
arsenal ['aɪsənl] *n* arsenal *m*.
arsenic ['aɪsnik] *n* arsénico *m*.
arson ['aɪsn] *n* incendiarismo *m*, incendio premeditado *m*.
art [aɪt] *n* arte *m*; (*cunning*) artificio *m*. **art gallery** museo de pinturas *m*. **artful** *adj* artero, mañoso.
artery ['aɪtəri] *n* arteria *f*.
arthritis [aɪ'θraitis] *n* artritis *f*.
artichoke ['aɪtitʃouk] *n* alcachofa *f*.
article ['aɪtikl] *n* artículo *m*; (*object*) objeto *m*.
articulate [aɪ'tikjuleit; *adj* aɪ'tikjulət] *v* articular. *adj* claro, distinto.
artifice ['aɪtifis] *n* artificio *m*.
artificial [aɪti'fiʃəl] *adj* artificial, falso. **artificiality** *n* lo artificial. **artificial respiration** respiracíon artificial *f*.
artillery [aɪ'tiləri] *n* artillería *f*.
artisan [aɪti'zan] *n* artesano, -a *m*, *f*.
artist ['aɪtist] *n* artista *m*, *f*. **artistic** *adj* artístico.
as [az] *adv* tan. *prep*, *conj* como, ya que, según, a medida que; (*when*) cuando; (*since*) puesto que; (*because*) porque; (*although*) aunque. **as a rule** por regla general. **as far as** en cuanto a. **as from** desde. **as good as** tan bueno como. **as if** como si. **as it were** en cierto modo. **as soon as** en cuanto. **as soon as possible** cuanto antes. **as usual** como de costumbre. **as well** también. **as well as** además de.
asbestos [az'bestos] *n* asbesto *m*.
ascend [ə'send] *v* subir. **ascendancy** *n* ascendiente *m*. **be in the ascendant** ir en aumento. **ascension** *n* subida *f*. **ascent** *n* subida *f*; (*slope*) cuesta *f*.
ascetic [ə'setik] *adj* ascético. *n* asceta *m*, *f*.
ash[1] [aʃ] *n* (*cinder*) ceniza *f*, cenizas *f pl*. **ashtray** *n* cenicero *m*.
ash[2] [aʃ] *n* (*tree*) fresno *m*.
ashamed [ə'ʃeimd] *adj* avergonzado.
ashore [ə'ʃoɪ] *adv* a tierra. **go ashore** desembarcar.
Ash Wednesday *n* miércoles de ceniza *m*.

Asia ['eɪʃə] n Asia f. Asian n, adj asiático, -a.
aside [ə'said] adv aparte, a un lado. n (theatre) aparte m.
ask [aɪsk] v preguntar, pedir, invitar. ask for trouble buscársela. for the asking sin más que pedirlo.
askew [ə'skjuɪ] adj oblicuamente, a un lado.
asleep [ə'sliːp] adj, adv dormido. fall asleep dormirse.
asparagus [ə'sparəgəs] n espárrago m.
aspect ['aspekt] n aspecto m, vista f.
asphalt ['asfalt] n asfalto m.
asphyxiate [əs'fiksieit] v asfixiar.
aspire [ə'spaɪə] v aspirar. aspiration n aspiración f.
aspirin ['aspərin] n aspirina f.
ass [as] n asno m. asinine adj asnal.
assail [ə'seil] v atacar. assailant n asaltador, -a m, f.
assassinate [ə'sasineit] v asesinar. assassin n asesino m, f. assassination n asesinato m.
assault [ə'soɪlt] n asalto m. v asaltar.
assemble [ə'sembl] v (people) convocar; (things) juntar; (machines) armar. assemblage n reunión f. assembly n asamblea f. assembly line línea de montaje f.
assent [ə'sent] v asentir. n asentimiento m.
assert [ə'soɪt] v afirmar, declarar. assertion n afirmación f, aserción f.
assess [ə'ses] v evaluar, asesorar. assessment n valoración f.
asset ['aset] n ventaja f. assets pl n activo m sing, haber m sing, bienes m pl.
assiduous [ə'sidjuəs] adj asiduo, aplicado.
assign [ə'sain] v asignar, señalar; (law) consignar; (goods) traspasar. assignment n asignación f.
assimilate [ə'simileit] v asimilar, incorporarse. assimilation n asimilación f.
assist [ə'sist] v asistir, ayudar. assistance n ayuda f. assistant n ayudante m, colaborador m.
associate [ə'sousiət; v ə'sousieit] n socio, -a m, f, compañero, -a m, f, cómplice m, f. v asociar, juntar. associate with ir con. association n asociación f, sociedad f.
assorted [ə'soɪtid] adj surtido, mezclado. assortment n clasificación f, mezcla f.
assume [ə'sjuɪm] v asumir, tomar; (suppose) suponer. assumed adj fingido.

assuming that dado que. assumption n asunción f.
assure [ə'ʃuə] v asegurar, garantizar. assurance n seguridad f, certeza f; (comm) seguro m. assuredly adv seguramente.
asterisk ['astərisk] n asterisco m.
asthma ['asmə] n asma f.
astonish [ə'stoniʃ] v asombrar. astonishment n asombro m.
astound [ə'staund] v aturdir. be astounded quedarse muerto.
astray [ə'strei] adv desviado. go astray perderse.
astride [ə'straid] adv a horcajadas. prep a horcajadas sobre.
astringent [ə'strindʒənt] adj astringente.
astrology [ə'strolədʒi] n astrología f. astrologer n astrólogo, -a m, f.
astronaut ['astrənoɪt] n astronauta m, f.
astronomy [ə'stronəmi] n astronomía f. astronomer n astrónomo m. astronomical adj astronómico.
astute [ə'stjuɪt] adj astuto, agudo. astuteness n astucia f, sagacidad f.
asunder [ə'sʌndə] adv separadamente, en dos.
asylum [ə'sailəm] n (refuge) asilo m; (for the insane) manicomio m.
at [at] prep a, en.
ate [et] V eat.
atheism ['eiθiizəm] n ateísmo m. atheist n ateo, -a m, f.
Athens ['aθinz] n Atenas f. Athenian n(m+f), adj ateniense.
athlete ['aθliːt] n atleta m, f. athletic adj atlético. athletics n atletismo m.
Atlantic [ət'lantik] n Atlántico m. adj atlántico.
atlas ['atləs] n atlas m.
atmosphere ['atməsfiə] n atmósfera f, aire m; (feeling) ambiente m. atmospheric adj atmosférico. atmospherics pl n perturbaciones atmosféricas f pl.
atom ['atəm] n átomo m. atomic adj atómico.
atone [ə'toun] v expiar. atonement n expiación f.
atrocious [ə'trouʃəs] adj atroz. atrocity n atrocidad f.
attach [ə'tatʃ] v atar, adherir, pegar. attach oneself to asociarse con. attachment n unión f; (hook) enganche m; (friendship) amistad f.

attaché [ə'taʃei] *n* agregado *m*. **attaché case** maletín *m*.

attack [ə'tak] *v* atacar. *n* ataque *m*; (*mil*) ofensiva *f*. **attacker** *n* atacador, -a *m, f*.

attain [ə'tein] *v* lograr, alcanzar. **attainable** *adj* asequible, realizable. **attainment** *n* logro *m*. **attainments** *pl n* prendas *f pl*.

attempt [ə'tempt] *n* tentativa *f*. *v* procurar, tratar de.

attend [ə'tend] *v* atender, servir; concurrir; (*the sick*) asistir; (*listen*) escuchar. **attendance** *n* servicio *m*, asistencia *f*; (*audience*) auditorio *m*. **attendant** *n* criado, -a *m, f*, servidor, -a *m, f*.

attention [ə'tenʃən] *n* atención *f*. **call attention to** destacar, hacer presente. **pay attention** prestar atención. **attentive** *adj* atento, cortés. **attentiveness** *n* cuidado *m*.

attic ['atik] *n* desván *m*, sotabanco *m*.

attire [ə'taiə] *n* atavió *m*, ropaje *m*, traje *m*, adorno *m*. *v* ataviar, vestir.

attitude ['atitjuid] *n* actitud *f*, postura *f*, ademán *m*.

attorney [ə'təmi] *n* (*agent*) apoderado, -a *m, f*; (*solicitor*) abogado, -a *m, f*. **power of attorney** poderes *m pl*.

attract [ə'trakt] *v* atraer, llamar. **attraction** *n* atracción *f*, imán *m*. **attractive** *adj* atractivo, atrayente.

attribute ['atribjuit; *v* ə'tribjuit] *n* atributo *m*. *v* atribuir. **attributable** *adj* atribuible. **attribution** *n* atributo *m*.

attrition [ə'triʃən] *n* atrición *f*.

atypical [ei'tipikl] *adj* atípico.

aubergine ['oubəʒiin] *n* berenjena *f*.

auburn ['oibən] *adj* castaño rojizo.

auction ['oikʃən] *n* remate *m*, almoneda *f*, subasta *f*. *v* rematar, subastar. **auctioneer** *n* subastador *m*.

audacious [oi'deiʃəs] *adj* audaz, arrojado. **audacity** *n* audacia *f*, arrojo *m*, atrevimiento *m*.

audible ['oidəbl] *adj* audible. **audibility** *n* audibilidad *f*.

audience ['oidjəns] *n* audiencia *f*; oyentes *m pl*.

audiovisual [oidiou'viʒuəl] *adj* audiovisual.

audit ['oidit] *v* intervenir. *n* intervención *f*, ajuste (de cuentas) *m*. **auditor** *n* inteventor *m*, contador *m*.

audition [oi'diʃən] *n* audición *f*. *v* dar audición.

auditorium [oidi'toiriəm] *n* auditorio *m*, sala de espectáculos *f*.

augment [oig'ment] *v* aumentar, engrosar; acrecentarse.

august [oi'gʌst] *adj* augusto.

August ['oigəst] *n* agosto *m*.

aunt [aint] *n* tía *f*. **great-aunt** *n* tía abuela *f*.

aura ['oirə] *n* aura *f*; exhalación *f*.

auspicious [oi'spiʃəs] *adj* propicio.

austere [oi'stiə] *adj* austero, severo. **austerity** *n* austeridad *f*, severidad *f*.

Australia [o'streiljə] *n* Australia *f*. **Australian** *n, adj* australiano, -a.

Austria ['ostriə] *n* Austria *f*. **Austrian** *n, adj* austríaco, -a.

authentic [oi'θentik] *adj* auténtico.

author ['oiθə] *n* autor, -a *m, f*.

authority [oi'θorəti] *n* autoridad *f*. **on good authority** de buena fuente. **authoritarian** *adj* autoritario.

authorize ['oiθəraiz] *v* autorizar. **authorization** *n* autorización *f*.

autobiography [oitoubai'ogrəfi] *n* autobiografía *f*. **autobiographical** *adj* autobiográfico.

autocratic [oitou'kratik] *adj* autocrático. **autocrat** *n* autócrata *m, f*.

autograph ['oitəgraif] *n* autógrafo *m*. *v* firmar, dedicar.

automatic [oitə'matik] *adj* automático. **automation** *n* automatización *f*.

automobile ['oitəməbiil] *n* automóvil *m*.

autonomous [oi'tonəməs] *adj* autónomo.

autopsy ['oitopsi] *n* autopsia *f*.

autumn ['oitəm] *n* otoño *m*. **autumnal** *adj* otoñal.

auxiliary [oig'ziljəri] *adj* auxiliar. *n* auxiliador *m*.

avail [ə'veil] *v* servir, valer, importar; aprovechar. **avail oneself of** aprovecharse de. **to no avail** en balde.

available [ə'veiləbl] *adj* útil, disponible. **availability** *n* utilidad *f*, disponibilidad *f*.

avalanche ['avəlainʃ] *n* avalancha *f*, alud *m*.

avarice ['avəris] *n* avaricia *f*, codicia *f*. **avaricious** *adj* avariento.

avenge [ə'vendʒ] *v* vengar, vindicar. **avenge oneself** vengarse de. **avenger** *n* vengador, -a *m, f*.

avenue ['avinjui] *n* avenida *f*.

average ['avəridʒ] *n* promedio *m*, término medio *m*. *adj* de promedio, corriente. *v* hallar el término medio. **on average** por regla general.

aversion [ə'vəːʃən] n aversión f. **averse** adj opuesto. **be averse to** ser enemigo de.
avert [ə'vəːt] v apartar; (avoid) evitar.
aviary ['eiviəri] n avería f.
aviation [eivi'eiʃən] n aviación f. **aviator** n aviador, -a m. f.
avid ['avid] adj ávido, codicioso, voraz.
avidity n avidez f. codicia f.
avocado [avə'kaːdou] n aguacate m.
avoid [ə'void] v evitar, eludir, evadir. **avoidance** n evitación f.
await [ə'weit] v esperar, aguardar.
***awake** [ə'weik] v despertar; despertarse. adj despierto, atento (a). **awakening** n despertamiento m.
award [ə'woːd] n fallo m. premio m. recompensa f. v otorgar, conceder, conferir.
aware [ə'weə] adj enterado, vigilante, consciente. **become aware of** darse cuenta de. **make aware of** hacer saber. **awareness** n conocimiento m.
away [ə'wei] adv a lo lejos, ausente, fuera, en otro lugar.
awe [oː] n temor m. pasmo m; reverencia f. v intimidar, atemorizar. **awesome** adj pavoroso, imponente.
awful ['oːful] adj tremendo, atroz, terrible, espantoso. **how awful!** ¡i qué barbaridad! **awfully** adv (coll) muy.
awkward ['oːkwəd] adj difícil; (clumsy) desmañado; (ungraceful) sin gracia.
awl [oːl] n punzón m. lezna f.
awning ['oːniŋ] n toldo m.
axe [aks] n hacha f.
axiom ['aksiəm] n axioma m.
axis ['aksis] n eje m.
axle ['aksl] n eje m. peón m. árbol m.

B

babble ['babl] v balbucear; garlar. n murmullo m. cháchara f.
baboon [bə'buːn] n babuino m.
baby ['beibi] n bebé m. criatura f. nene m; (animals) crio m. **babyhood** n niñez f. **babyish** adj infantil.
bachelor ['batʃələ] n soltero m; (of Arts or Science) licenciado m. bachiller m.
back [bak] n (anat) espalda f; dorso m;

(sport) defensa f. adj trasero, posterior, de atrás; (of pay, etc.) atrasado. adv atrás; detrás; otra vez, de nuevo. v retroceder; (support) apoyar; (bet on) apostar a. **back down** abandonar. **back out** echarse atrás; (retract) desdecirse.
backache ['bakeik] n dolor de espaldas m.
backbone ['bakboun] n espinazo m.
backdate [ˌbak'deit] v poner fecha atrasada.
backfire [ˌbak'faiə] n petardeo m. v petardear.
backgammon ['bakˌgamən] n chaquete m.
backhand ['bakhand] n (sport) revés m. **back-handed** adj de revés; (fig) ambiguo.
backing ['bakiŋ] n forro m; (support) apoyo m; (lining) refuerzo m; (betting) el apostar (a) m.
backlash ['baklaʃ] n reacción f.
backlog ['baklog] n atrasos m pl.
backside ['baksaid] n trasero m, parte trasera f.
backward ['bakwəd] adj atrasado, vuelto hacia atrás. **backwardness** n atraso m, torpeza f. **backward and forward** de acá para allá.
backwards ['bakwədz] adv hacia atrás, al revés.
backwater ['bakwoːtə] n (pool) remanso m.
bacon ['beikən] n tocino m.
bacteria [bak'tiəriə] n pl bacteria f pl.
bad [bad] adj malo; (ill) enfermo; (rotten) podrido; (debt) incobrable; (dangerous) peligroso; (coin) falso; (pain) fuerte; (unlucky) desgraciado. **bad-tempered** adj de mal genio. **from bad to worse** de mal en peor. **badly** adv mal; (seriously) gravemente.
badge [badʒ] n insignia f, marca f, divisa f.
badger ['badʒə] n tejón m. v molestar.
badminton ['badmintən] n volante m, badminton m.
baffle ['bafl] v frustrar, desconcertar, confundir. **baffling** adj desconcertante, difícil; (person) enigmático.
bag [bag] n bolsa f, saco m, valija f; (sewing) costurera f; (suitcase) maleta f. v ensacar; (coll, esp. game) matar, tomar. **pack one's bags** liar el petate. **baggage** m equipaje m.
baggy ['bagi] adj holgado.

bagpipes ['bagpaips] *n pl* gaita *f*.
bail¹ [beil] *n (law)* fianza *f*, caución *f*. *v* poner bajo fianza.
bail² *or* **bale** [beil] *v* **bail out** (*flooded boat*) achicar, baldear; (*from aircraft*) lanzarse en paracaídas.
bailiff ['beilif] *n (law)* alguacil *m*; (*of estate*) capataz *m*.
bait [beit] *n (fishing)* cebo *m*, anzuelo *m*; (*lure*) añagaza *f*. *v* cebar, azuzar; (*annoy*) molestar.
bake [beik] *v* cocer al horno. **baker's dozen** la docena del fraile *f*. **baker** *m* panadero *m*. **bakery** *n* panadería *f*. **baking powder** levadura en polvo *f*.
balance ['baləns] *n* equilibrio *m*; (*scales*) balanza *f*; (*comm*) balance *m*. *v* equilibrar; (*comm*) saldar.
balcony ['balkəni] *n* balcón *m*, galería *f*; (*theatre*) anfiteatro *m*.
bald [boıld] *adj* calvo, pelado; (*tyre*) desgastado. **baldness** *n* calvicie *f*.
bale¹ [beil] *n* fardo *m*, bala *f*. *v* embalar.
bale² *V* **bail²**.
ball¹ [boıl] *n* pelota *f*; globo *m*, bola *f*; (*shot*) bala *f*; (*of wool*) ovillo *m*; (*of the foot*) planta del pie *f*. **ball-and-socket joint** articulación esférica *f*. **ball bearings** cojinete de bolas *m sing*. **ball-point pen** bolígrafo *m*.
ball² [boıl] *n (dance)* baile *m*. **fancy-dress ball** baile de disfraces. **ballroom** *n* salón de baile *m*.
ballad ['baləd] *n* balada *f*, romance *m*, trova *f*; (*music*) canción *f*.
ballast ['baləst] *n* lastre. *v* lastrar.
ballet ['balei] *n* ballet *m*, danza *f*. **ballet dancer** bailarín, bailarina *m*, *f*.
ballistic [bə'listik] *adj* balístico. **ballistic missile** proyectil balístico *m*.
balloon [bə'luın] *n* globo *m*. **balloonist** *n* aeronauta *m*, *f*.
ballot ['balət] *n* votación *f*, sufragio *m*. *v* votar, balotar. **ballot-box** *n* urna electoral *f*.
bamboo [bam'buı] *n* bambú *m*.
ban [ban] *n* prohibición *f*, interdicción *f*. *v* prohibir, proscribir.
banal [bə'naıl] *adj* trivial, trillado.
banana [bə'naınə] *n (fruit and tree)* plátano *m*; (*S. Am.*) (*fruit*) banana, (*tree*) banano *m*.
band¹ [band] *n (troop)* grupo *m*, banda *f*; (*music*) orquesta *f*, banda *f*. *v* congregar, unir, asociar.

band² [band] *n (strip)* lista *f*, tira *f*, banda *f*.
bandage ['bandidʒ] *n* venda *f*. *v* vendar.
bandit ['bandit] *n* bandido *m*.
bandy ['bandi] *adj also* **bandy-legged** estevado. *v* trocar.
bang [baŋ] *n* golpazo *m*, detonación *f*, golpe *m*. *v* golpear, estallar.
bangle ['baŋgl] *n* ajorca *f*, pulseta *f*, brazalete *m*.
banish ['baniʃ] *v* desterrar, despedir, exilar, deportar. **banishment** *n* destierro *m*.
banister ['banistə] *n* baranda *f*, pasamano *m*.
banjo ['bandʒou] *n* banjo *m*.
bank¹ [baŋk] *n (of river, etc.)* ribera *f*, orilla *f*, margen *m*.
bank² [baŋk] *n* banco *m*. **bank account** cuenta bancaria *f*. **bank holiday** día festivo *m*. *v* depositar en el banco. **banker** *n* banquero *m*.
bankrupt ['baŋkrʌpt] *n* quebrado, -a *m*, *f*. *adj* insolvente, quebrado. **go bankrupt** hacer bancarrota, declararse en quiebra. **bankruptcy** *n* bancarrota *f*, quiebra *f*.
banner ['banə] *n* bandera *f*, estandarte *m*.
banns [banz] *n pl* amonestaciones *f pl*. **publish the banns** decir las amonestaciones.
banquet ['baŋkwit] *m* banquete *m*. *v* banquetear.
bantam ['bantəm] *n* gallina enana *f*. **bantamweight** *n* peso gallo *m*.
banter ['bantə] *n* burla *f*, chanza *f*. *v* burlarse, tomar el pelo a.
baptize [bap'taiz] *v* bautizar. **baptism** *n* bautismo *m*. **baptist** *n* bautista *m*. **baptistry** *n* baptisterio *m*, bautisterio *m*.
bar [baı] *n* barra *f*; (*soap, chocolate, etc.*) pastilla *f*; (*music*) barra *f*, compás *m*; (*barrier*) barrera *f*; (*refreshments*) bar *m*; (*law*) foro *m*, curia *f*; *v* atrancar, obstruir, impedir. **barman** *n* mozo de bar *m*. **barmaid** *n* camarera *f*.
barb [baıb] *n* púa *f*; (*fish-hook*) lengüeta *f*.
barbarian [baı'beəriən] *n*, *adj* bárbaro, -a *m*, *f*. **barbaric** *adj* barbárico. **barbarity** *n* barbaridad *f*.
barbecue ['baıbikjuı] *n* barbacoa *f*.
barber ['baıbə] *n* barbero *m*, peluquero *m*. **barber's shop** barbería *f*, peluquería *f*.
barbiturate [baı'bitjurət] *n* barbitúrico *m*.
bare [beə] *adj* desnudo, descubierto. *v* desnudar, descubrir. **barefaced** *adj*

descarado. **barefoot** *adj* descalzo. **bare-
headed** *adj* sin sombrero. **barely** *adv*
apenas.
bargain ['ba:gin] *n* (*cheap*) ganga *f*;
(*agreement*) pacto *m*, ajuste *m*, convenio
m. *v* negociar, regatear. **bargain sale**
saldo *m*. **into the bargain** por más señas.
barge [ba:dʒ] *n* barca *f*, bote *m*, barcaza
f. **barge in** irrumpir. **barge into** entrometerse.
baritone ['baritoun] *n* barítono *m*.
bark¹ [ba:k] *n* (*dog*) ladrido *m*. *v* ladrar.
bark² [ba:k] *n* (*tree*) corteza *f*.
barley ['ba:li] *n* cebada *f*. **barley water** *n*
hordiate *m*.
barn [ba:n] *n* granero *m*, pajar *m*.
barometer [bə'romitə] *n* barómetro *m*.
baron ['barən] *n* barón *m*. **baroness** *n*
baronesa *f*. **baronet** *n* baronet *m*.
baroque [bə'rok] *adj* barroco.
barracks ['barəks] *pl n* cuartel *m*, barraca
f.
barrage ['bara:ʒ] *n* presa *f*; (*mil*)
bombardeo *m*, cortina de fuego *f*.
barrel ['barəl] *n* (*cask*) barril *m*; (*gun,
etc.*) cañón *m*. **barrel organ** organillo *m*.
barren ['barən] *adj* (*land*) yermo, árido;
estéril. **barrenness** *n* aridez *f*; esterilidad
f.
barricade [bari'keid] *n* barrera *f*, barricada *f*, empalizada *f*. *v* barrear, obstruir.
barrier ['bariə] *n* barrera *f*; impedimento
m; valla *f*.
barrister ['baristə] *n* abogado, -a *m, f*.
barrow ['barou] *n* carretilla *f*.
barter ['ba:tə] *v* cambiar, trocar. *n*
trueque *m*, cambio *m*, tráfico *m*.
base¹ [beis] *n* base *f*, fundamento *m*, pie
m. *v* fundar, apoyarse, basar. **baseless**
adj sin base.
base² [beis] *adj* bajo, vil, impuro. **base-
ness** *n* bajeza *f*, vileza *f*.
baseball ['beisbo:l] *n* béisbol *m*.
basement ['beismənt] *n* sótano *m*.
bash [baʃ] *n* golpe *m*. *v* golpear.
bashful ['baʃful] *adj* vergonzoso, tímido,
encogido. **bashfulness** *n* vergüenza *f*,
encogimiento *m*.
basic ['beisik] *adj* fundamental; (*chem*)
básico.
basil ['bazl] *n* albahaca *f*.
basilica [bə'zilikə] *n* basílica *f*.
basin ['beisin] *n* bacia *f*, jofaina *f*; (*wash-
basin*) palangana *f*; (*dock*) dársena *f*;
(*river*) cuenca *f*.

basis ['beisis] *n* base *f*, fundamento *m*.
bask [bask] *v* calentarse.
basket ['ba:skit] *n* cesta *f*, canasta *f*. **basketball** *n* baloncesto *m*.
Basque [bask] *n*, *adj* vasco, -a *m, f*; (*language*) vascuence *m*.
bas-relief ['basri.li:f] *n* bajorrelieve *m*.
bass¹ [beis] *n* (*voice*) bajo *m*. **bass clef** *n*
clave de fa *f*.
bass² [bas] *n* (*freshwater*) róbalo *m*; (*sea*)
lobina *f*.
bassoon [bə'su:n] *n* bajón *m*.
bastard ['ba:stəd] *n* bastardo, -a *m, f*.
baste [beist] *v* (*cookery*) enlardar, pringar; (*sewing*) bastear, hilvanar.
bastion ['bastjən] *n* bastión *m*, baluarte
m.
bat¹ [bat] *n* maza *f*, palo *m*; (*cricket*)
paleta *f*; (*table tennis*) pala *f*. *v* golpear
con le paleta.
bat² [bat] *n* (*zool*) murciélago *m*.
batch [batʃ] *n* grupo *m*; (*loaves*) hornada
f.
bath [ba:θ] *n* baño *m*. *v* bañar, lavar,
tomar un baño. **bath-chair** *n* cochecillo
de inválido *m*. **bathrobe** *n* albornoz *m*.
bathroom *n* cuarto de baño *m*. **bathtowel**
n toalla de baño *f*. **swimming baths** *n pl*
piscina *f sing*.
bathe [beið] *v* bañar, bañarse. **bathing cap**
gorra de baño *f*. **bathing costume** traje de
baño *m*. **bathing pool** piscina *f*. **bathing
trunks** pantalones de baño *m pl*.
baton ['batn] *n* (*mil*) bastón de mando *m*;
(*police*) porra *f*; (*music*) batuta *f*.
battalion [bə'taljən] *n* batallón *m*.
batter¹ ['batə] *v* apalear, golpear, derribar.
batter² ['batə] *n* (*cookery*) batido *m*, pasta
f.
battery ['batəri] *n* (*elec*) pila *f*, batería *f*;
(*mil*) batería; (*law*) agresión *f*. **storage
battery** acumulador *m*. **battery cell** pila
de batería eléctrica *f*.
battle ['batl] *n* batalla *f*, combate *m*. *v*
batallar, luchar. **battlefield** *n* campo de
batalla *m*. **battlement** *n* almenaje *m*. **bat-
tleship** *n* buque de guerra *m*.
bawdy ['bo:di] *adj* obsceno, escabroso.
bawl [bo:l] *v* vocear.
bay¹ [bei] *n* (*geog*) bahía *f*.
bay² [bei] *v* (*cry*) aullar. **at bay** acor-
ralado.
bay³ [bei] *n* (*tree*) laurel *m*.

bayonet ['beiənit] *n* bayoneta *f. v* dar un bayonetazo.

bay window *n* mirador *m.*

bazaar [bə'zɑɪ] *n* bazar *m.*

*be [biɪ] *v* ser, existir; estar; (*place*) encontrarse, quedar.

beach [biɪtʃ] *n* playa *f*; costa *f. v* varar, encallar en la costa.

beacon ['biɪkən] *n* fanal *m*, faro *m*; (*naut*) boya *f.*

bead [biɪd] *n* cuenta *f*, perla *f*, gota *f.* **beads** *n pl* rosario *m sing.*

beagle ['biɪgl] *n* sabueso *m.*

beak [biɪk] *n* pico *m*; punta *f.* **beaked** *adj* picudo.

beaker ['biɪkə] *n* vaso *m*, copa *f.*

beam [biɪm] *n* (*light*) rayo *m*, destello *m*; (*arch*) madero *m*; (*width of a ship*) manga *f*; (*smile*) sonrisa brillante *f. v* irradiar; (*smile*) sonreir radiantemente.

bean [biɪn] *n* (*broad*) haba *f*; (*black*) fréjol *m*; (*kidney*) habichuela *f*, alubia *f*, judía *f.*

*bear¹ [beə] *v* soportar, aguantar, sufrir; (*carry*) llevar; (*have*) tener, (*fruit*) dar; (*give birth to*) parir; (*a strain*) resistir. **bear in mind** tener presente. **bearing** *n* porte *m*, aspecto *m*; relación *f.*

bear² [beə] *n* oso *m.*

beard [biəd] *n* barba *f. v* enfrentarse con, mesar la barba a. **bearded** *adj* barbudo. **beardless** *adj* imberbe.

bearings ['beəriŋz] *n pl* situación *f sing*, relación *f sing*, camino *m sing.* **lose one's bearings** desorientarse, desatinar. **take one's bearings** orientarse.

beast [biɪst] *n* bestia *f*; res *f*; (*wild*) fiera *f.* **beastly** *adj* bestial; desagradable.

*beat [biɪt] *v* batir; (*games*) derrotar, vencer; (*with weapon*) golpear; (*carpet*) sacudir. **beat down** atropellar. *n* (*med*) latido *m*, pulsación *f*; golpe *m*; (*music*) compás *m.*

beauty ['bjuɪti] *n* hermosura *f*, belleza *f*; (*coll*) lo mejor. **beauty spot** lunar *m.* **beautiful** *adj* bello, hermoso; guapo. **beautify** *v* embellecer.

beaver ['biɪvə] *n* castor *m.*

because [bi'koz] *conj* porque. **because of** a causa de.

beckon ['bekən] *v* llamar con señas, atraer, invitar.

*become [bi'kʌm] *v* convenir; llegar a ser, ponerse, hacerse. **becoming** *adj* que

sienta bien, propio, decoroso. **becomingly** *adv* con gracia.

bed [bed] *n* cama *f*, lecho *m*; (*coal, etc.*) yacimiento *m*; (*flowers*) macizo *m.* **bedding** *n* ropa de cama *f.* **bedroom** *n* dormitorio *m.* **bedsitter** *n* salón con cama *m.* **bedspread** *n* colcha *f.*

bedbug ['bedbʌg] *n* chinche *f.*

bedraggled [bi'dragld] *adj* mojado y sucio, enlodado.

bee [biɪ] *n* abeja *f.* **bee line** línea recta *f.* **beehive** *n* colmena *f.* **bumble-bee** *n* abejorro *m.*

beech [biɪtʃ] *n* (*tree*) haya *f*; (*nut*) hayuco *m.*

beef [biɪf] *n* carne de vaca *f.* **roast beef** rosbif *m.*

been [biɪn] *V* be.

beer [biə] *n* cerveza *f.*

beetle ['biɪtl] *n* (*zool*) escarabajo *m*; (*tech*) pisón *m.* **death-watch beetle** carcoma *f.* **beetle-browed** *adj* cejijunto.

beetroot ['biɪtruɪt] *n* remolacha *f.*

before [bi'foɪ] *adv* delante; al frente; (*time*) antes; (*already*) ya. *prep* delante de; frente de; (*time*) ante; (*rather than*) antes de. *conj* antes (que). **beforehand** *adv* de antemano.

befriend [bi'frend] *v* favorecer, amistar, proteger, ayudar.

beg [beg] *v* pedir, suplicar; mendigar. **I beg your pardon?** ¿cómo dice? **I beg your pardon!** ¡Vd dispense! **beg the question** dejar a un lado. **beggar** *n* mendigo *m.*

*begin [bi'gin] *v* comenzar, empezar, iniciar. **to begin with** en primer lugar. **beginner** *n* principiante, -a *m, f.* **beginning** *n* principio *m.*

begrudge [bi'grʌdʒ] *v* envidiar; conceder de mala gana.

beguile [bi'gail] *v* engañar; (*charm*) encantar.

behalf [bi'haɪf] *n* provecho *m.* **on behalf of** en nombre de, a favor de.

behave [bi'heiv] *v* comportarse, manejarse, portarse; funcionar, obrar. **behaviour** *n* comportamiento *m*, conducta *f*; funcionamiento *m.*

behead [bi'hed] *v* decapitar.

behind [bi'haind] *adv* atrás, detrás, hacia atrás; (*time*) después; (*late*) con retraso. *prep* detrás de, por detrás de. *n* (*coll*) trasero *m.* **fall behind** retrasarse. **behind the times** pasado de moda.

*behold [bi'hould] *v* mirar, contemplar.
interj ¡aqui está!, ¡he aquí!
beige [beiʒ] *adj* beige.
being ['biiiŋ] *n* ser *m*, existencia *f*, estado *m*. **human being** ser humano *m*. **wellbeing** *n* bienestar *m*.
belated [bi'leitid] *adj* tardío.
belch [beltʃ] *n* eructo *m*. *v* eructar, arrojar.
belfry ['belfri] *n* campanario *m*.
Belgium ['beldʒəm] *m* Bélgica *f*. **Belgian** *n(m+f)*, *adj* belga.
believe [bi'liiv] *v* creer, pensar; opinar. **believer** *n* creyente *m*, *f*, fiel *m*. **belief** *n*, *pl* -s creencia *f*; opinión *f*.
bell [bel] *n* campana *f*, campanilla *f*; (*electric*) timbre *m*; (*hand*) esquila *f*.
belligerent [bi'lidʒərənt] *n*, *adj* beligerante, -a *m*, *f*.
bellow ['belou] *v* bramar, rugir. *n* bramido *m*.
bellows ['belouz] *n pl* fuelle *m sing*.
belly ['beli] *n* barriga *f*, panza *f*, vientre *m*. **bellyful** *n* hartón *m*.
belong [bi'loŋ] *v* pertenecer, tocar a. **belong to** ser de. **belongings** *n pl* bienes *m pl*.
beloved [bi'lʌvid] *n* amado, -a *m*, *f*, querido, -a *m*, *f*. **favorito, -a** *m*, *f*.
below [bi'lou] *adv* abajo, debajo. *prep* (por) debajo de.
belt [belt] *n* cinturón *m*, cinto *m*, faja *f*; (*tech*) correa *f*; (*geog*) zona *f*. *v* ceñir, rodear, fajar.
bench [bentʃ] *n* banco *m*, banca *f*, escaño *m*, (*law*) tribunal *m*.
*bend [bend] *v* torcer, doblar; inclinar, encorvar. *n* recodo *m*, curva *f*.
beneath [bi'niiθ] *adv* abajo, debajo. (*prep*) bajo, debajo de. **beneath regard** indigno de consideración.
benefactor ['benəfaktə] *n* bienhechor *m*, patrono *m*.
benefit ['benəfit] *n* beneficio *m*, provecho *m*. *v* beneficiar. **beneficial** *adj* ventajoso. **beneficiary** *n* beneficiaro *m*.
benevolent [bi'nevələnt] *adj* benévolo; caritativo. **benevolence** *n* benevolencia *f*, caridad *f*.
benign [bi'nain] *adj* benigno.
bent [bent] *adj* torcido, encorvado; (*on a course of action*) resuelto (a); (*fam*) invertido. *n* talento *m*, inclinación *f*.
bequeath [bi'kwiið] *v* legar; transmitir. **bequest** *n* legado *m*.

bereaved [bi'riivd] *adj* afligido. **bereave** *v* quitar; afligir. **bereavement** *n* pérdida *f*, aflicción *f*.
beret ['berei] *n* boina *f*.
berry ['beri] *n* baya *f*, grano *m*.
berserk [bə'səik] *adj* demente.
berth [bəiθ] *n* camarote *m*; (*dock*) fondeadero *m*. *v* fondear. **give a wide berth to** apartarse de.
beside [bi'said] *prep* junto a, cerca de. **beside oneself** fuera de sí. **beside the point** no venir al caso. **besides** *adv* (*as well*) también; (*moreover*) además.
besiege [bi'siidʒ] *v* asediar, sitiar.
bespoke [bi'spouk] *adj* hecho a medida. **bespeak** *v* reservar.
best [best] *adj*, *adv* mejor. **at best** a lo mejor. **do one's best** hacer todo lo posible. **make the best of** sacar el mayor provecho de. **best man** padrino de boda *m*. **best-seller** *n* éxito de librería *m*.
bestow [bi'stou] *v* conferir, otorgar.
*bet [bet] *v* apostar; jugar. *n* apuesta *f*, postura *f*. **better, bettor** *n* apostador, -a *m*, *f*. **betting shop** establecimiento de apuesta *m*.
betray [bi'trei] *v* traicionar; engañar; revelar. **betrayal** *n* traición *f*.
better ['betə] *adj*, *adv* mejor. **get better** mejorarse. **better half** (*coll*) media naranja *f*. **better off** mejor situado. **so much the better** tanto mejor. *v* mejorarse.
between [bi'twiin] *prep* entre. *adv* entre los dos. **far between** a grandes intervalos. **between ourselves** entre nosotros.
beverage ['bevəridʒ] *n* bebida *f*, brebaje *m*.
*beware [bi'weə] *v* tener cuidado de. *interj* ¡atención!
bewilder [bi'wildə] *v* desconcertar, aturrullar, aturdir. **bewilderment** *n* aturdimiento *m*, anonadamiento *m*.
beyond [bi'jond] *adv* más alla, más lejos. *prep* superior a, fuera de. **beyond doubt** fuera de duda. **beyond measure** sobremanera. **beyond question** indiscutible.
bias ['baiəs] *n* sesgo *m*, través *m*; propensión *f*, prejuicio *m*. *v* sesgar; influir, predisponer. **biased** *adj* predispuesto. **cut on the bias** contar al sesgo.
bib [bib] *n* babero *m*, pechera *f*.

Bible ['baibl] n Biblia f. **biblical** adj bíblico.
bibliography [bibli'ografi] n bibliografía f.
bibliographer n bibliógrafo m. **bibliographical** adj bibliográfico.
biceps ['baiseps] n bíceps m.
bicker ['bikə] v disputar, reñir, altercar.
bickering n altercado m.
bicycle ['baisikl] n bicicleta f.
***bid** [bid] v ofrecer, pujar; (command) mandar; rogar. n oferta f; (attempt) tentativa f. **make a bid for** procurar. **no bid** (cards) paso. **bidder** n postor m.
bidet ['biːdei] n bidé m.
biennial [bai'eniəl] adj bienal, bianual.
bifocals [bai'foukəlz] pl n lentes bifocales m pl.
big [big] adj grande; grueso; abultado; importante.
bigamy ['bigəmi] n bigamia f. **bigamist** n bígamo, -a m, f. **bigamous** adj bígamo.
bigot ['bigət] n beatón, -ona m, f, fanático, -a m, f. **bigoted** adj fanático, intolerante. **bigotry** n fanatismo m, intolerancia f.
bikini [bi'kiːni] n bikini m.
bilingual [bai'lingwəl] adj bilingüe.
bilious ['biljəs] adj bilioso. **bile** n bilis f.
bill¹ [bil] n (comm) cuenta f, factura f; (poster) cartel m; (pol) proyecto de ley m; anuncio m. **billboard** n cartelera f. **bill of lading** conocimiento de embarque m. **bill of sale** escritura de venta f. v enviar una cuenta; anunciar. **bill and coo** arrullar; (coll) besuquearse.
bill² [bil] n (beak) pico m.
billiards ['biljədz] n billar m.
billion ['biljən] n (10¹²) billón m; (10⁹) mil millones m pl.
bin [bin] n arcón m, hucha f; papelera f; (wine) estante m.
binary ['bainəri] adj binario.
***bind** [baind] v atar; ligar, unir; (bandage) vendar; (sheaves) agavillar, (books) encuadernar; (captive) aprisionar; (sewing) ribetear; (oblige) comprometer.
binding ['baindiŋ] n (books) encuadernación f; atadura f. adj válido; obligatorio.
binge [bindʒ] n (coll) parranda f. **go on the binge** ir de parranda.
binoculars [bi'nokjuləz] n pl binóculos m pl, prismáticos m pl, gemelos m pl.
biography [bai'ografi] n biografía f. **biographer** n biógrafo, -a m, f. **biographical** adj biográfico.

biology [bai'olədʒi] n biología f. **biological** adj biológico. **biologist** n biólogo m.
birch [bəːtʃ] n abedul m. v varear.
bird [bəːd] n pájaro m, ave f; (slang) chica f. **bird's eye view** vista de pájaro f. **birdcage** n jaula f. **birdseed** n alpiste m.
birth [bəːθ] n nacimiento m, parto m; linaje m; comienzo m. **give birth to** dar a luz; parir. **birth certificate** partida de nacimiento f. **birth control** anticoncepcionismo m. **birthday** n cumpleaños m. **birthplace** n lugar de nacimiento m. **birthrate** n natalidad f. **birthright** n herencia f.
biscuit ['biskit] n bizcocho m, galleta f.
bishop ['biʃəp] n obispo m; (chess) alfil m.
bison ['baisən] n bisonte m.
bit¹ [bit] n (drill) barrena f, taladro m; (horse) bocado m. **take the bit between one's teeth** desbocarse.
bit² [bit] n pedazo m, poco m, trocito m; (time) ratito m; (jot) jota f. **bit by bit** poco a poco. **not a bit** nada de eso.
bitch [bitʃ] n (dog) perra f; (slang) zorra f.
***bite** [bait] v morder; (insect, etc.) picar. n mordedura f; picadura f. **biting** adj (remark, etc.) mordaz.
bitter ['bitə] adj amargo, áspero. **to the bitter end** hasta la muerte. **bitterness** n amargura f.
bizarre [bi'zaɪ] adj extravagante, grotesco.
black ['blak] n, adj negro, -a m, f. **blacken** v ennegrecer; (character) denigrar.
blackberry ['blakbəri] n (bush) zarza f; (fruit) zarzamora f.
blackbird ['blakbəːd] n mirlo m.
blackboard ['blakboːd] n pizarra f.
blackcurrant [,blak'kʌrənt] n grosella negra f.
black eye n ojo a la funerala m.
blackhead ['blakhed] n espinilla f.
blackleg ['blakleg] n esquirol m.
blackmail ['blakmeil] n chantaje m. v hacer chantaje. **blackmailer** n chantajista m, f.
black market n mercado negro m.
blackout ['blakaut] n apagón m, apagamiento m; (fainting) desmayo m.
black pudding n morcilla f.
blacksmith ['blaksmiθ] n herrero m.
bladder ['bladə] n vejiga f.
blade [bleid] n (grass) brizna f; (razor) hoja f; (propeller) paleta f; (oar) pala f.

blame [bleim] *n* culpa *f. v* culpar. **blameless** *adj* inculpable. **blameworthy** *adj* culpable.

bland [bland] *adj* afable; dulce.

blank [blaŋk] *adj* en blanco; (*empty*) vacío; confuso. *n* blanco *m*, hueco *m*; vacío *m*. **blank cartridge** cartucho para salvas *m*. **blank verse** verso libre *m*, verso suelto *m*.

blanket ['blaŋkit] *n* manta *f*, frazada *f*; (*of dust*) capa *f. v* cubrir con manta. *adj* comprensivo.

blare [bleə] *v* vociferar, rugir. *n* trompetazo *m*, fragor *m*; estrépito *m*.

blaspheme [blas'fiɪm] *v* blasfema. **blasphemer** *n* blasfemador, -a *m, f*. **blasphemous** *adj* blasfemo. **blasphemy** *n* blasfemia *f*.

blast [blaɪst] *n* explosión *f*; (*trumpet*) trompetazo *m*; (*wind*) ráfaga *f. v* (*rocks*) barrenar; (*wither*) marchitar; (*curse*) maldecir. **full blast** en plena marcha. **blast furnace** alto horno *m*.

blatant ['bleitənt] *adj* discarado, vocinglero, llamativo.

blaze [bleiz] *n* incendio *m*, llamarada *f*, conflagración *f. v* llamear, flamear; arder. **blaze a trail** abrir un camino. **blaze of colour** masa de color *f*. **blazer** *n* chaqueta deportiva *f*.

bleach [bliɪtʃ] *v* blanquear, descolorar. *n* lejía *f*

bleak [bliɪk] *adj* desabrido, desierto, crudo; (*prospect*) sombrío.

bleat [bliɪt] *v* balar. *n* balido *m*.

*bleed [bliɪd] *v* sangrar. **bleed to death** morir desangrado. **bleeding** *n* hemorragia *f*.

blemish ['blemiʃ] *n* mácula *f*, defecto *m*, mancha *f. v* empañar, manchar.

blend [blend] *v* mezclar, combinar, fundir; (*colour*) matizar. *n* mezcla *f*, combinación *f*.

bless [bles] *v* bendecir; consagrar; favorecer. **blessedness** *n* felicidad *f*. **blessing** *n* bendición *f*; merced *f*; favor *m*.

blew [bluɪ] *V* **blow²**.

blight [blait] *n* (*plants*) tizne *m*; (*fig*) influencia maligna *f. v* atizonar; (*fig*) malograr.

blind [blaind] *adj* ciego. *n* pretexto *m*; (*window*) persiana *f. v* cegar. **blindness** *n* ceguera *f*. **turn a blind eye** hacer la vista gorda.

blindfold ['blaindfould] *n* venda *f. v* vendar los ojos de.

blink [bliŋk] *v* parpadear, pestañear, guiñar. *n* parpadeo *m*, guiño *m*; (*of light*) destello *m*. **blinkers** *pl n* anteojeras *f pl*.

bliss [blis] *n* bienaventuranza *f*, felicidad *f*. **blissful** *adj* bienaventurado, feliz.

blister ['blistə] *n* vesícula *f*, ampolla *f. v* ampollar.

blizzard ['blizəd] *n* ventisca *f*.

bloated ['bloutid] *adj* abotagado.

blob [blob] *n* gota *f*, goterón *m*; borrón *m*.

bloc [blok] *n* (*pol*) bloque *m*.

block [blok] *n* bloque *m*; (*butcher's*) tajo *m*; (*houses*) manzana *f*; (*obstruction*) atasco *m. v* bloquear, obstruir, cerrar el paso. **block and tackle** polea con aparejo *f*.

blockade [blo'keid] *n* bloqueo *m. v* bloquear.

bloke [blouk] *n* (*coll*) tío *m*, fulano *m*.

blond [blond] *adj* rubio. **blonde** *n* rubia *f*.

blood [blʌd] *n* sangre *f*; (*lineage*) parentesco *m*. **bloodless** *adj* exangüe. **blood donor** donante de sangre *m, f*. **blood group** grupo sanguíneo *m*. **blood poisoning** envenenamiento de la sangre *m*. **blood pressure** *n* presión arterial *f*. **bloodshed** *n* matanza *f*. **bloodshot** *adj* inyectado de sangre. **bloodstream** *n* corriente sanguínea *f*. **bloodthirsty** *adj* sanguinario. **bloody** *adj* sangriento; (*slang*) maldito.

bloom [bluɪm] *n* flor *f*; florecimiento *m*; (*prime*) lozanía *f. v* florecer. **in bloom** en flor. **blooming** *adj* floreciente.

blossom ['blosəm] *n* flor *f. v* florecer.

blot [blot] *n* borrón *m*; mancha *f. v* manchar, tachar; (*dry*) secar. **blot out** borrar. **blotter** *n* libro borrador *m*. **blotting paper** papel secante *m*.

blotch [blotʃ] *n* mancha *f*; (*med*) erupción *f. v* manchar, ennegrecer.

blouse [blauz] *n* blusa *f*.

blow¹ [blou] *n* (*hit*) golpe *m*, bofetada *f*; (*shock*) choque *m*; (*misfortune*) revés *m*. **come to blows** venir a las manos.

*blow² [blou] *n* soplido *m. v* soplar, hacer viento; (*pant*) jadear; (*fuse*) fundirse; (*music*) tocar. **blow away** disipar. **blow one's nose** sonarse las narices. **blow out** (*a light*) apagar soplando. **blow up** (*explode*) volar; (*inflate*) inflar.

blubber ['blʌbə] *n* grasa de ballena *f. v* gimotear.

blue [bluɪ] *adj* azul; (*mournful*) deprimido; (*obscene*) verde. **bluebell** *n* campanilla *f*. **bluebottle** *n* moscón *m*.

blueprint *n* fotocopia *f*, plan *m*.

bluff [blʌf] *v* fanfarronear. *n* fanfarronada *f*; (*cliff*) morro *m*, tisco *m*, peñasco. *adj* campechano, brusco.

blunder [blʌndə] *n* desatino *m*, yerro *m. v* desatinar; tropezar (con); (*coll*) meter la pata. **blunderer** *n* desatinado *m*.

blunt [blʌnt] *adj* desafilado, embotado; (*abrupt*) franco, descortés; (*plain*) claro. *v* despuntar, desafilar, embotar; (*pain*) mitigar. **bluntness** *n* embotamiento *m*.

blur [bləɪ] *v* empañar; emborronar. *n* borrón *m*. **blurred** *adj* borroso.

blush [blʌʃ] *v* ruborizarse, enrojecerse. *n* rubor *m*, sonrojo *m*; (*of shame*) bochorno *m*.

boar [boɪ] *n* jabalí *m*.

board [boɪd] *n* tabla *f*; (*chess, draughts*) tablero *m*; (*for notices*) tablón *m*; (*table*) mesa *f*; (*food*) comida *f*; (*committee*) junta *f*, tribunal *m*; (*naut*) bordo *m. v* (*carpentry*) enmaderar, entablar; (*embark*) embarcarse en.

boast [boust] *n* jactancia *f*, alarde *m*, baladronada *f. v* jactarse, presumir. **boastful** *adj* jactancioso.

boat [bout] *n* bote *m*, lancha *f*, barca *f*; buque *m*, barco *m. v* navegar, ir en bote. **boatman** *n* barquero *m*. **boatswain** *n* contramaestre *m*. **lifeboat** *n* lancha de socorro *f*.

boater ['boutə] *n* (*hat*) canotié *m*, canotier *m*.

bob [bob] *v* bambolean, menear. *n* balanceo *m*; borla *f*.

bobbin ['bobin] *n* (*sewing-machine, loom*) bobina *f*.

bobsleigh ['bobslei] *n* trineo doble *m. v* ir en trineo.

bodice ['bodis] *n* corpiño *m*.

body ['bodi] *n* cuerpo *m*, masa *f*, entidad *f*; (*corpse*) cadáver *m*; (*mot*) carrocería *f*. **bodyguard** *n* guardia de corps *f*.

bog [bog] *n* pantano *m*.

bogus ['bougəs] *adj* espurio, fingido, falso.

bohemian [bə'hiːmiən] *adj* bohemio.

boil¹ [boil] *v* hervir. *n* hervor *m*. **boil over** irse. **boiler** *n* caldera *f*. **boiling point** punto de ebullición *m*.

boil² [boil] *n* divieso *m*, grano *m*, furúnculo *m*.

boisterous ['boistərəs] *adj* borrascoso, bullicioso. **boisterousness** *n* bullicio *m*.

bold [bould] *adj* osado, arrojado, atrevido; resuelto; (*showy*) llamativo. **bold-faced** *adj* descarado. **bold-faced type** letra negra *f*. **boldness** *n* temeridad *f*, intrepidez *f*.

Bolivia [bə'liviə] *n* Bolivia *f*. **Bolivian** *adj*, *n* boliviano, -a *m*, *f*.

bolster ['boulstə] *n* travesaño *m*; almohada *f. v* estribar, levantar, apoyar.

bolt [boult] *n* (*door*) cerraja *f*, cerrojo *m*; (*for nut*) perno *m*; rayo *m. v* (*run*) huir; (*secure*) empernar; (*food*) zampar. **bolt upright** enhiesto. **thunderbolt** *n* rayo *m*.

bomb [bom] *n* bomba *f. v* bombardear.

bombard [bəm'baɪd] *v* bombardear. **bombardment** *n* bombardeo *m*.

bonafide [bounə'faidi] *adj* fidedigno.

bond [bond] *n* lazo *m*, unión *f*, vínculo *m*; (*comm*) obligación *f*; (*security*) fianza *f*; (*customs*) depósito *m. v* unir, ligar; dar fianza. **bonds** *n pl* cadenas *f pl*. **bondage** *n* esclavitud *f*.

bone [boun] *n* hueso *m*; (*fish*) espina *f. v* desosar. **bony** *adj* huesudo. **all skin and bones** estar en los huesos. **pick a bone with** arreglar las cuentas con.

bonfire ['bonfaiə] *n* hoguera *f*.

bonnet ['bonit] *n* capota *f*, gorra *f*; (*mot*) capó *m*.

bonus ['bounəs] *n* extra *m*, prima *f*.

booby trap ['buɪbi] *n* trampa *f*; (*mil*) mina *f*.

book [buk] *n* libro *m*; tomo *m. v* (*a seat*) tomar; (*reserve*) reservar; (*engage*) contratar.

bookcase ['bukkeis] *n* librería *f*.

book-ends ['bukendz] *n pl* sujetalibros *m pl*.

booking ['bukin] *n* taquilla *f*.

book-keeper ['buk,kiɪpə] *n* tenedor de libros *m*.

booklet ['buklit] *n* folleto *m*.

bookmark ['bukmaɪk] *n* marcador *m*.

bookseller ['buksələ] *n* librero *m*.

bookshop ['bukʃop] *n* librería *f*.

boom [buɪm] *n* (*noise*) ruido *m*; (*econ*) auge repentino *m. v* (*comm*) prosperar, estar en bonanza; sonar, bramar.

boost [buɪst] *v* (*advertise*) dar bombo (a); (*coll*) empujar. *n* (*coll*) empujón *m*.

boot [buːt] n (*shoe*) bota f; (*mot*) maleta f. **get the boot** ser despedido.
booth [buːð] n cabina f, quiosco m.
booze [buːz] n (*coll*) bebida alcohólica f. v (*coll*) emborracharse, coger una turca.
border ['bɔːdə] n confín m; frontera f; margen m; (*sewing*) ribete m; (*garden*) arriate m. v lindar con. **borderline** n límite m.
bore¹ [bɔː] v (*hole, etc.*) perforar, horadar, taladrar. n taladro m, barreno m; (*gun*) calibre m.
bore² [bɔː] v aburrir, fastidiar. n aburrimiento m; (*person*) pelmazo m. **boredom** n tedio m, hastío m. **boring** adj aburrido, tedioso.
bore³ [bɔː] V **bear¹**.
born [bɔːn] adj nacido, nato. **be born** nacer.
borne [bɔːn] V **bear¹**.
borough ['bʌrə] n municipio m.
borrow ['borou] v tomar prestado, pedir prestado. **borrower** n prestatario m.
bosom ['buzəm] n seno m; pecho m.
boss [bos] n amo m, jefe m, patrón m; (*political*) cacique m. v dominar, dirigir.
botany ['botəni] n botánica f. **botanical** adj botánico. **botanist** n botánico, -a m, f.
both [bouθ] adj, pron ambos, los dos.
bother ['boðə] v molestar; (*worry*) preocuparse. n molestia f; preocupación f.
bottle ['botl] n botella f, frasco m; (*water*) cantimplora f; (*wine*) porrón m. v embotellar.
bottom ['botəm] n fondo m; casco m; (*anat*) trasero m, (*vulgar*) culo m; (*river*) lecho m; (*page*) pie m; (*chair*) asiento m. adj más bajo. **bottomless** adj sin fondo.
boudoir ['buːdwaː] n tocador m, gabinete m.
bough [bau] n rama f.
bought [bɔːt] V **buy**.
boulder ['bouldə] n peñasco m, pedrusco m.
bounce [bauns] v rebotar, botar, saltar; (*cheque*) ser rechazado. n rebote m, respingo m.
bound¹ [baund] v (*leap*) saltar, brincar. n salto m, brinco m.
bound² [baund] n límite m. **within bounds** dentro del límite.
bound³ [baund] V **bind**.
bound⁴ [baund] adj **bound for** destinado a, con rumbo a.

boundary ['baundəri] n lindero m, término m.
bouquet [buːkei] n ramo m, ramillete m; perfume m; (*wine*) nariz f.
bourgeois ['buəʒwaː] adj burgués.
bout [baut] n turno m; (*illness*) ataque m.
bow¹ [bau] v (*bend*) inclinarse, saludar; (*submit*) someterse (a). n inclinación f; reverencia f.
bow² [bou] n (*music, weapon*) arco m; (*ribbon*) lazo m. **bow-legged** adj patiestevado. **bow window** ventana arqueada f.
bow³ [bau] n (*naut*) proa f.
bowels ['bauəlz] n pl intestinos m pl, entrañas f pl.
bowl¹ [boul] n receptáculo m; (*soup*) escudilla f; (*washing*) jofaina f.
bowl² [boul] v tirar; (*cricket*) sacar. **bowl over** (*fig*) desconcertar. **bowls** pl n juego de bolos m sing.
bowler hat n hongo m.
box¹ [boks] n caja f, cajón m; (*luggage*) baúl m; (*theatre*) palco m; (*sentry*) garita f, casilla f. v encajonar. **box office** taquilla f. **post-office box** apartado de correos m.
box² [boks] v (*sport*) boxear. **boxer** n boxeador m, puglista m. **boxing** n boxeo m, pugilato m.
Boxing Day n Día de San Esteban m.
boy [boi] n muchacho m, niño m, chico m. **boyfriend** n novio m. **boy scout** muchacho explorador m. **boyhood** niñez f.
boycott ['boikot] n boicot m. v boicotear.
bra [braː] n (*coll*) sostén m.
brace [breis] n refuerzo m; (*tech*) abrazadera f; (*pair*) par m. v reforzar; refrescar. **braces** n pl tirantes m pl. **bracing** adj tónico.
bracelet ['breislit] n pulsera f; brazalete m.
bracken ['brakən] n helecho m.
bracket ['brakit] n soporte m; (*writing*) paréntesis m, corchete m.
brag [brag] v jactarse. n jactancia f.
Braille [breil] n Braille m, alfabeto para los ciegos m.
brain [brein] n cerebro m, sesos m pl. v romper la crisma. **brains** n pl talento m sing. **brainwash** v lavar el cerebro. **brainwave** n idea luminosa f. **brainy** adj sesudo. **rack one's brains** devanarse los sesos.

braise [breiz] v estofar.

brake [breik] n freno m. v frenar.

bramble ['brambl] n zarza f. maleza f. **bramble patch** breña f. matorral m.

bran [bran] n salvado m.

branch [braintʃ] n rama f; (of learning) ramo m; (river) tributario m; (road, rail) ramal m; (company) dependencia f. v echar ramas, dividirse.

brand [brand] n (manufacture) marca f; (animals) hierro m; (fire) tizón m; (stigma) estigma m. v marcar; tildar. **brand-new** adj enteramente nuevo.

brandish ['brandiʃ] v blandir.

brandy ['brandi] n coñac m.

brass [brais] n latón m; (music) cobre m, metal m; (coll) pasta f. **brassy** adj de latón; (coll) presuntuoso.

brassière ['brasiə] V **bra**.

brave [breiv] adj valiente, intrépido. v desafiar. **bravery** n valentía f.

brawl [broil] n alboroto m, riña f. v alborotar.

brawn [broin] n carnosidad f, músculo m; (food) carne de cerdo adobada f. **brawny** adj musculoso.

brazen ['breizn] adj (metal) de latón; (fig) desahogado.

Brazil [brə'zil] n (el) Brasil m. **Brazilian** n, adj brasileño, -a m, f. **Brazil nut** nuez del Brasil f.

breach [briitʃ] n brecha f. v abrir brecha; romper. **breach of promise** infracción f. **breach of the peace** alteración de orden público f.

bread [bred] n pan m. **breadcrumb** n migaja f. **breadcrumbs** n pl pan rallado m sing. **slice of bread** rebanada f.

breadth [bredθ] n anchura f.

***break** [breik] v romper; quebrar; quebrantar; (burst) reventar; (violate) infringir. **break away** desprenderse. **break down** (mech) averiarse; (cry) deshacerse en lágrimas. **break in** forzar la entrada. **break out** estallar. **break up** desmenuzar. n ruptura f, rotura f; (opening) abertura f; (interruption) interrupción f. **breakdown** n colapso m. **breakthrough** n avance m.

breakfast ['brekfəst] n desayuno m. v desayunar.

breast [brest] n pecho m; (female) mama f, teta f. **breastbone** n esternón m. **breast pocket** bolsillo de pecho m. **breaststroke** n brazada de pecho f.

breath [breθ] n respiración f, aliento m; (breeze) soplo m. **breathless** adj sin aliento. **under one's breath** en voz baja.

breathalyser ['breθəlaizə] n alcohómetro m.

breathe [briið] v respirar, exhalar, inspirar. **breathing** n respiración f.

***breed** [briid] v criar, engendrar. n raza f, casta f. **breeding** n cría f, reproducción f; (upbringing) crianza f, educación f.

breeze [briiz] n brisa f. **breezy** adj fresco; (of manner) animado.

brew [brui] v (infuse) infusionar; (beer) fabricar. n poción f. **brewery** n fábrica de cerveza f.

bribe [braib] n soborno m. v sobornar. **bribery** n soborno m.

brick [brik] n ladrillo m. v enladrillar. **bricklayer** n albañil m. **brickyard** n ladrillar m.

bride [braid] n novia f, desposada f. **bridal** adj nupcial. **bridegroom** m novio m, desposado m. **bridesmaid** n dama de honor f, madrina de boda f.

bridge¹ [bridʒ] n puente m. **drawbridge** n puente levadizo m. **suspension bridge** puente colgante m. v pontear.

bridge² [bridʒ] n (cards) bridge m.

bridle ['braidl] n brida f, freno m. v enfrenar; picarse.

brief [briif] adj breve. n resumen m; (law) escrito m, relacion f. v (law) instruir. **briefcase** n cartera f. **briefly** adv brevemente.

brigade [bri'geid] n brigada f.

bright [brait] adj brillante; (intelligent) inteligente. **brighten** v hacer brillar; (make happy) alegrar; (polish) pulir; (weather) aclarar. **brightness** n brillantez f; (intelligence) talento m.

brilliant ['briljənt] adj brillante. **brilliance** n brillo m, fulgor m.

brim [brim] n (of a container) borde m; (hat) ala f.

brine [brain] n salmuera f.

***bring** [briŋ] v traer, llevar, conducir. **bring about** causar, ocasionar. **bring down** rebajar. **bring in** introducir. **bring off** lograr, conseguir. **bring out** sacar; publicar. **bring together** reunir. **bring to light** descubrir. **bring up** criar, educar.

brink [briŋk] n borde m. **on the brink of a** dos dedos de.

brisk [brisk] adj animado, vivo.
bristle ['brisl] n cerda f. v erizarse. **bristly**
adj erizado.
Britain ['britn] n Gran Bretaña f. **British**
adj británico. **Briton** n britano, -a m, f,
británico, -a m, f.
brittle ['britl] adj quebradizo.
broad [broid] adj ancho; (fig) lato,
amplio; (accent) fuerte. **broad-minded** adj
tolerante. **broaden** v ensanchar. **broadly**
adv en general. **broadness** n anchura f.
broadcast ['broidkaist] n emisión f, radiodifusión f; v emitir, radiar. **broadcasting**
station n emisora f.
broccoli ['brokəli] n bróculi m, brécol m.
brochure ['broufuə] n folleto m.
broke [brouk] V **break**. adj (coll) pelado,
sin blanca.
broken ['broukn] V **break**.
broker ['broukə] n corredor de bolsa m.
bronchitis [broŋ'kaitis] m bronquitis f.
bronze [bronz] n bronce m.
brooch [broutʃ] n broche m.
brood [bruid] n (chickens) pollada f;
(birds) nidada f; (other animals) cría f. v
empollar. **brood over** ruminar.
brook [bruk] n arroyo m.
broom [bruim] n escoba f; (bot) retama f.
broth [broθ] n caldo m.
brothel ['broθl] n burdel m, lupanar m.
brother ['brʌðə] n hermano m. **brother-in-
law** n cuñado m. **brotherhood** n
fraternidad f. **brotherly** adv fraternal.
brow [brau] n frente f; (hill) cumbre f.
browbeat v intimidar verbalmente.
brown [braun] adj castaño, moreno. v
(cookery) dorar; (tan) tostar. **brown
paper** papel de estraza m. **brownish** adj
pardusco.
browse [brauz] v pacer.
bruise [bruiz] n contusión f, magulladura
f. v magullar.
brunette [brui'net] n morena f.
brush [brʌʃ] n cepillo m; (broom) escoba
f; (for painting) pincel m; (undergrowth)
matorral m. v cepillar; (sweep) barrer;
(touch) rozar. **brush aside** echar a un
lado. **brush off** sacudir(se).
brusque [brusk] adj brusco, rudo.
Brussels ['brʌsəlz] n Bruselas. **Brussels
sprouts** coles de Bruselas f pl.
brute [bruit] n bruto m, bestia m, f. **brutal**
adj brutal, bestial. **brutality** n brutalidad
f.

bubble ['bʌbl] n burbuja f; borbollón m.
v burbujear, borbollar.
buck [bʌk] n gamo m. v encorvarse. **buck
up** animarse.
bucket ['bʌkit] n cubo m, balde m.
buckle ['bʌkl] n hebilla f. v enhebillar;
doblarse.
buck-tooth n diente saliente m.
bud [bʌd] n brote m. v brotar, germinar.
budge [bʌdʒ] v mover, moverse,
menearse.
budgerigar ['bʌdʒərigai] n periquito m.
budget ['bʌdʒit] n presupuesto m. v
presupuestar.
buffalo ['bʌfəlou] n búfalo m.
buffer ['bʌfə] n parochoque m.
buffet[1] ['bʌfit] n (blow) bofetón m,
bofetada f. v abofetear, golpear.
buffet[2] ['bufei] n fonda f, bar m.
bug [bʌg] n chinche m. v (coll) ocultar un
micrófono en.
bugger ['bʌgə] n sodomita m. v cometer
sodomía. interj ¡joder! **bugger off!** ¡vete a
la mierda! **buggery** m sodomía f.
bugle ['bjuigl] n corneta f. **bugler** n
trompetero m.
***build** [bild] v construir; edificar; fundar.
building n edificio m. **building site** n solar
m. **built-up area** n zona urbana f.
bulb [bʌlb] n (elec) bombilla f; (bot)
bulbo m.
Bulgaria [bʌl'geəriə] n Bulgaria f. **Bulgarian** n, adj búlgaro, -a m, f.
bulge [bʌldʒ] n hinchazón f, bulto m. v
hincharse. **bulging** adj hinchado (de).
bulk [bʌlk] n bulto m; masa f; (larger
part) grueso m. **in bulk** (comm) en bruto.
bulky adj voluminoso.
bull [bul] n toro m. **bullfight** n corrida de
toros f. **bullfighter** n torero m. **bull in a
china shop** un caballo loco en una
cacharrería. **bullring** n plaza de toros f.
bull's-eye n centro del blanco m.
bulldozer ['buldouzə] n bulldozer m,
excavadora f.
bullet ['bulit] n bala f. **bullet-proof** adj a
prueba de balas.
bulletin ['bulətin] n boletín m.
bullion ['buliən] n (gold) oro en barras m;
(silver) plata en barras f.
bully ['buli] n valentón m, rufián m. v
intimidar.
bum [bʌm] n (coll) posaderas f pl. v holgazanear.

bump [bʌmp] *n* (*swelling*) hinchazón *f*; (*blow*) golpe *m*. *v* chocar, golpear.

bumper ['bʌmpə] *n* (*mot*) parachoques *m invar. adj* abundante.

bun [bʌn] *n* buñuelo *m*; (*hair*) moño *m*.

bunch [bʌntʃ] *n* (*flowers*) ramo *m*; (*fruit*) racimo *m*; (*coll: gang*) pandilla *f. v* agruparse.

bundle ['bʌndl] *n* fardo *m*, bulto *m. v* enfardar, liar.

bungalow ['bʌngəlou] *n* chalet *m*, casa de un solo piso *f*.

bungle ['bʌngl] *v* estropear, chapucear. *n* chapucería *f*. **bungler** *n* chapucero, -a *m*, *f*. **bungling** *adj* chapucero.

bunion ['bʌnjən] *n* juanete *m*.

bunk [bʌŋk] *n* litera *f*; (*coll: nonsense*) palabrería *f*. **do a bunk** pirarse.

bunker ['bʌŋkə] *n* (*refuge*) refugio *m*; (*coal*) carbonera *f*; (*golf*) bunker *m*, hoya de arena *f*. .

buoy [boi] *n* boya *f*. **buoyancy** *n* fluctuación *f*. **buoyant** *adj* boyante.

burden ['bɔɪdn] *n* carga *f. v* cargar.

bureau ['bjuərou] *n* (*desk*) escritorio *m*; (*office*) oficina *f*; departmento *m*.

bureaucracy [bju'rokrəsi] *n* burocracia *f*. **bureaucrat** *n* burócrata *m, f*. **bureaucratic** *adj* burocrático.

burglar ['bɔɪglə] *n* ladrón *m*. **burglar alarm** alarma contra ladrones *f*. **burglary** *n* robo *m*. **burgle** *v* robar.

***burn** [bɔɪn] *v* quemar, incendiar. *n* quemadura *f*. **burner** *n* quemador *m*. **burning** *adj* ardiente.

burrow ['bʌrou] *n* madriguera *f. v* amadrigar, minar.

***burst** [bɔɪst] *n* estallido *m*, explosión *f. v* reventar, estallar. **burst into tears** romper a llorar. **burst open** forzar.

bury ['beri] *v* enterrar, sepultar. **burial** *n* entierro *m*.

bus [bʌs] *n* autobús *m*, ómnibus *m*. **double-decker bus** ómnibus de dos pisos *m*. **bus station** término *m*. **bus-stop** *n* parada de autobús *or* ómnibus.

bush [buʃ] *n* arbusto *m*; (*undergrowth*) maleza *f*. **bushy** *adj* denso, espeso, matoso.

business ['biznis] *n* negocio *m*, comercio *m*; ocupación *f*. **business hours** horas de trabajo *f pl*. **businesslike** *adj* práctico,

sistemático. **businessman** *n* hombre de negocios *m*. **mean business** estar resuelto. **mind one's own business** no meterse donde no le llaman.

bust¹ [bʌst] *n* (*anat*) pecho *m*; (*art*) busto *m*.

bust² [bʌst] *adj* (*fam*) quebrado, reventado. **go bust** quebrar.

bustle ['bʌsl] *n* animación *f. v* menearse, dar prisa (a).

busy ['bizi] *adj* ocupado; activo, diligente. **busybody** *n* entrometido *m*.

but [bʌt] *conj* pero, sino. *prep* excepto. *adv* solamente. **but for** a no ser por. **nothing but** nada más que.

butane ['bjuɪtein] *n* butano *m*.

butcher [butʃə] *n* carnicero *m*. **butcher's shop** carnicería *f. v* matar, destrozar.

butler ['bʌtlə] *n* mayordomo *m*.

butt¹ [bʌt] *n* (*gun*) culata *f*; (*cigarette*, *etc.*) colilla *f*.

butt² [bʌt] *n* (*of jokes, etc.*) objeto *m*.

butt³ [bʌt] *v* topar, acornear. **butt in** entrometerse.

butter ['bʌtə] *n* mantequilla *f*; *v* untar con mantequilla.

buttercup ['bʌtəkʌp] *n* ranúnculo *m*.

butterfly ['bʌtəflai] *n* mariposa *f*.

butterscotch ['bʌtəskotʃ] *n* dulce de azúcar y mantequilla *m*.

buttocks ['bʌtəks] *n pl* nalgas *f pl*.

button ['bʌtn] *n* botón *m. v* abotonear. **buttonhole** *n* ojal *m. v* (*coll*) importunar.

buttress ['bʌtris] *n* estribo *m*, contrafuerte *m*; (*fig*) apoyo *m. v* estribar.

***buy** [bai] *v* comprar. *n* compra *f*. **buy up** acaparar. **buyer** *n* comprador, -a *m, f*.

buzz [bʌz] *v* zumbar. *n* zumbido *m*. **buzzer** *n* zumbador *m*; (*bell*) timbre *m*.

by [bai] *prep* por, de, a; (*near*) cerca de. *adv* al lado, cerca; aparte. **by all means** naturalmente. **by and large** en general. **by the way** de paso.

bye-law ['bailɔɪ] *n* reglamento *m*.

by-election ['baii,lekʃən] *n* elección parcial *f*.

bypass ['bai,paɪs] *n* desviación *f. v* desviar.

by-product ['baiprodəkt] *n* subproducto *m*.

bystander ['bai,standə] *n* espectador, -a *m, f*.

C

cab [kab] n taxi m; (lorry) cabina f.
cabaret ['kabərei] n cabaret m; (show) attracciones f pl.
cabbage ['kabidʒ] n col f, repollo m.
cabin ['kabin] n cabaña f; (naut) camarote m; (aircraft, etc.) cabina f. cabin cruiser n motonave f.
cabinet ['kabinit] n (cupboard) armario m; (display) vitrina f; (pol) gabinete m, consejo de ministros m. medicine cabinet botiquín m. cabinet-maker n ebanista m.
cable ['keibl] n (rope, wire) cable m; (message) cablegrama m. cable address dirección telegráfica f. cable car funicular m. v cablegrafiar.
cackle ['kakl] v carcarear. n carcareo m.
cactus ['kaktəs] n pl -i or -uses cacto m.
caddie ['kadi] n caddy m; (trolley) carrito m.
cadence ['keidəns] n cadencia f.
cadet [kə'det] n cadete m.
café ['kafei] n café m, restaurante m.
cafeteria [kafə'tiəriə] n cafetería f, restaurante de autoservicio m.
caffeine ['kafiɪn] n cafeina f.
cage [keidʒ] n jaula f. v enjaular.
cake [keik] n pastel m; (soap) pastilla f. Christmas cake tarta de Navidad f. a piece of cake (coll) ser pan comido. sell like hot cakes (coll) venderse como rosquillas. take the cake (coll) llevarse la palma. v endurecerse.
calamine ['kaləmain] n calamina f.
calamity [kə'laməti] n calamidad f.
calcium ['kalsiəm] n calcio m.
calculate ['kalkjuleit] v calcular; (guess, suppose) confiar en. calculated adj intencional, deliberado. calculating adj calculador. calculation n cálculo m. calculator n calculador m.
calendar ['kaləndə] n calendario m. calendar month mes civil m.
calf¹ [kaɪf] n (zool) becerro m, ternero m.
calf² [kaɪf] n (anat) pantorrilla f.
calibre ['kalibə] n (measurement) calibre m; (talent) capacidad f, talento m.
call [koɪl] n llamada f, llamamiento m; (cry) grito m; (visit) visita f. on call de guardia. trunk call conferencia f. v llamar. call for pedir. call off cancelar. call on visitar. call up evocar; convocar.

callous ['kaləs] adj insensible, duro.
calm [kaɪm] adj calmoso, sosegado, tranquilo. n calma f, tranquilidad f. v calmar, sosegar.
calorie ['kaləri] n caloría f.
came [keim] V come.
camel ['kaməl] n camello m.
camera ['kamərə] n máquina fotográfica f. in camera a puerta cerrada. cameraman n cameraman m.
camouflage ['kaməflaɪʒ] n camuflaje m. v camuflar.
camp¹ [kamp] n (site) campamento m. camp-bed n cama plegable f. holiday camp campamento de vacaciones m. v acampar.
camp² [kamp] adj (coll) afeminado; afectado; homosexual.
campaign [kam'pein] n campaña f. advertising campaign campaña publicitaria f. election campaign campaña electoral f. v hacer (una) campaña.
campus ['kampəs] n recinto universitario m, campus m, ciudad universitaria f.
*can¹ [kan] v (be able) poder; (know how to) saber.
can² [kan] n (container) lata f. can-opener n abrelatas m invar. v enlatar, conservar en lata. canned adj enlatado.
Canada ['kanədə] n Canadá m. Canadian n(m+f), adj canadiense.
canal [kə'nal] n canal m.
canary [kə'neəri] n canario m.
Canary Islands n pl (islas) Canarias f pl.
cancel ['kansəl] v (contract, decree, etc.) cancelar; (cheque, order, invitation) anular; (delete) tachar; (maths) eliminar. cancel out anularse. cancellation n cancelación f; anulación f.
cancer ['kansə] n cáncer m. cancerous adj canceroso.
Cancer ['kansə] n Cáncer m.
candid ['kandid] adj franco, sincero.
candidate ['kandidət] n candidato m. candidacy n candidatura f.
candle ['kandl] n vela f; (in a church) cirio m. burn the candle at both ends hacer de la noche día. candlestick n candelero m.
candour ['kandə] n franqueza f, sinceridad f.
candy ['kandi] n caramelo m. v escarchar, cristalizar.

cane [kein] *n* caña *f*; (*walking stick*) bastón *m*; (*school*) palmeta *f*, vara *f*. **sugar cane** caña de azúcar *f*. **cane furniture** muebles de mimbre *m pl*. *v* castigar con la palmeta *or* vara.
canine ['keinain] *adj* canino. **canine tooth** diente canino *m*.
cannabis ['kanəbis] *n* marijuana *f*.
cannibal ['kanibəl] *n(m+f)*, *adj* caníbal. **cannibalism** *n* canibalismó *m*.
cannon ['kanən] *n* cañón *m*. **cannonball** *n* bala de cañón *f*.
canoe [kə'nuː] *n* canoa *f*. *v* ir en canoa.
canon ['kanən] *n* canónigo *m*. **canonical** *adj* canónico. **canonize** *v* canonizar. **canonization** *n* canonización *f*.
canopy ['kanəpi] *n* (*awning*) toldo *m*; (*over a bed*) dosel *m*, baldaquín *m*.
canteen [kan'tiːn] *n* (*restaurant*) cantina *f*; (*flask*) cantimplora *f*; (*cutlery*) juego de cubiertos *m*.
canter ['kantə] *n* medio galope *m*. *v* ir a medio galope.
canton ['kantən] *n* cantón *m*.
canvas ['kanvəs] *n* (*fabric*) lona *f*; (*art*) lienzo.
canvass ['kanvəs] *v* solicitar votos de; (*comm*) buscar clientes; (*public opinion*) sondear.
canyon ['kanjən] *n* cañón *m*.
cap [kap] *n* gorra *f*; (*military or bathing*) gorro *m*; (*cover*) tapa *f*; (*bottle*) chapa *f*; (*pen*) capuchón *m*. *v* (*fig: crown*) coronar; (*do better than*) superar.
capable ['keipəbl] *adj* capaz, hábil. **capability** *n* capacidad *f*, habilidad *f*.
capacity [kə'pasəti] *n* capacidad *f*; (*mot*) cilindrada *f*.
cape¹ [keip] *n* (*cloak*) capa *f*; (*cycling*) impermeable de hule *m*.
cape² [keip] *n* (*geog*) cabo *m*.
caper ['keipə] *n* (*jump*) cabriola *f*; (*prank*) travesura *f*; (*cookery*) alcaparra *f*.
capillary [kə'piləri] *n* capilar *m*.
capital ['kapitl] *adj* capital. **capital punishment** pena capital *f*. *n* (*letter*) mayúscula *f*; (*city*) capital *f*; (*money*) fondo de operaciones *m*. **capitalism** *n* capitalismo *m*. **capitalist** *n* capitalista *m*, *f*. **capitalistic** *adj* capitalista. **capitalize** *v* capitalizar. **capitalization** *n* capitalización *f*.
capitulate [kə'pitjuleit] *v* capitular. **capitulation** *n* capitulación *f*.
capricious [kə'priʃəs] *adj* caprichoso.
caprice, capriciousness *n* capricho *m*.

Capricorn ['kaprikoːn] *n* Capricornio *m*.
capsicum ['kapsikəm] *n* pimiento *m*, chile *m*.
capsize [kap'saiz] *v* volcar, zozobrar.
capsule ['kapsjuːl] *n* cápsula *f*.
captain ['kaptin] *n* capitán *m*. *v* capitanear. **captaincy** *n* capitanía *f*.
caption ['kapʃən] *n* encabezamiento *m*, pie *m*. *v* poner pie a.
captive ['kaptiv] *n*, *adj* cautivo, -a. **captivate** *v* cautivar. **captivity** *n* cautividad *f*.
capture ['kaptʃə] *v* capturar; (*place*) tomar; (*market*) acaparar; (*fig*) atraer. *n* captura *f*, apresamiento *m*; (*place*) toma *f*.
car [kaː] *n* coche *m*, automóvil *m*; (*rail*) vagón *m*; (*cable*) cabina *f*. **car park** aparcamiento *m*. **car wash** lavado de coches *m*. **dining car** coche comedor *m*. **racing car** coche de carreras *m*. **sleeping car** coche cama *m*.
caramel ['karəmel] *n* caramelo *m*, azúcar quemado *m*.
carat ['karət] *n* quilate *m*.
caravan ['karəvan] *n* (*mot*) remolque *m*; (*travellers*) caravana *f*; (*gipsy*) carromato *m*.
caraway ['karəwei] *n* (*seed*) carvi *m*; (*plant*) alcaravea *f*.
carbohydrate [kaːbə'haidreit] *n* carbohidrato *m*.
carbon ['kaːbən] *n* (*chem*) carbono *m*; carbón *m*. **carbon dioxide** bióxido de carbono *m*. **carbon paper** papel carbón *m*.
carbuncle ['kaːbʌŋkl] *n* (*med*) carbunco *m*, carbunclo *m*.
carburettor ['kaːbjuretə] *n* carburador *m*.
carcass ['kaːkəs] *n* (*animal*) res muerta *f*.
card [kaːd] *n* tarjeta *f*; (*visiting*) tarjeta de visita *f*; (*postcard*) tarjeta postal *f*; (*playing card*) carta *f*, naipe *m*; (*membership*) carnet *m*; (*thin cardboard*) cartulina *f*; (*coll*) gracioso, -a *m*, *f*. **cardboard** *n* cartón *m*. **card index** fichero *m*.
cardiac ['kaːdiak] *adj* cardiaco.
cardigan ['kaːdigən] *n* rebeca *f*.
cardinal ['kaːdənl] *n* (*church, bird*) cardenal *m*. *adj* cardinal, esencial. **cardinal number** número cardinal *m*.
care [keə] *n* cuidado *m*, atención *f*; (*worry*) inquietud *f*; (*responsibility*) cargo *m*. **medical care** asistencia médica *f*. **care of** para entregar a. **handle with care** frágil. **take care!** ¡ojo! *v* importar, preocuparse

por. **take care of** guardar, tener cuidado de. **careful** *adj* cuidadoso. **carefulness** *n* cuidado *m*, esmero *m*. **careless** *adj* descuidado, desatento.

career [kə'rɪə] *n* carrera *f*, curso *m*. *v* correr a toda velocidad.

caress [kə'res] *n* caricia *f*. *v* acariciar.

cargo ['kaɪgou] *n* carga *f*, cargamento *m*.

caricature ['karɪkətjuə] *n* caricatura *f*. *v* caricaturizar.

carnage ['kaɪnɪdʒ] *n* carnicería *f*.

carnal ['kaɪnl] *adj* carnal. **carnality** *n* carnalidad *f*.

carnation [kaɪ'neɪʃən] *n* clavel *m*.

carnival ['kaɪnɪvəl] *n* carnaval *m*.

carnivorous [kaɪ'nɪvərəs] *adj* carnívoro. **carnivore** *n* carnívoro, -a *m, f*.

carol ['karəl] *n* villancico *m*.

carpenter ['kaɪpəntə] *n* carpintero *m*. **carpentry** *n* carpintería *f*.

carpet ['kaɪpɪt] *n* alfombra *f*; (*fitted*) moqueta *f*. **carpet-sweeper** escoba mecánica *f*. *v* alfombrar.

carriage ['karɪdʒ] *n* carruaje *m*, carro *m*; vagón *m*; (*posture*) manera de andar *f*; (*comm*) porte *m*. **carriageway** *n* calzada *f*. **dual carriageway** carretera de doble calzada *f*.

carrier ['karɪə] *n* portador *m*; (*comm*) empresa de transportes *f*; (*med*) portador, -a *m, f*.

carrot ['karət] *n* zanahoria *f*.

carry ['kari] *v* llevar; (*bring*) traer; (*a load*) transportar; (*by pipes*) conducir; (*sustain*) sostener. **carry forward** (*comm*) pasar. **carry out** realizar. **carrycot** *n* cuna portátil *f*.

cart [kaɪt] *n* carro *m*; (*handcart*) carro de mano *m*; (*trolley*) carrito *m*. *v* carretear. **cart horse** caballo de tiro *m*.

cartilage ['kaɪtəlidʒ] *n* cartílago *m*.

cartography [kaɪ'togrəfi] *n* cartografía *f*.

carton ['kaɪtən] *n* cartón *m*, caja de cartón *f*.

cartoon [kaɪ'tuɪn] *n* caricatura *f*, chiste *m*; (*art*) cartón *m*; (*film*) dibujos animados *m pl*. **cartoonist** *n* caricaturista *m, f*, humorista *m, f*.

cartridge ['kaɪtridʒ] *n* cartucho *m*; (*blank*) cartucho sin bala *m*.

carve [kaɪv] *v* (*meat*) trinchar; (*cut*) cortar; (*sculpture*) tallar. **carve up** (*divide*) dividir; (*stab*) acuchillar. **carving knife** cuchillo de trinchar *m*.

cascade [kas'keid] *n* cascada *f*, salto de agua *m*. *v* caer en cascada.

case¹ [keis] *n* caso *m*; (*affair*) asunto *m*. **in any case** en todo caso. **in case** en caso. **in no case** de ningún modo. **in the case of** en cuanto a. **it's not a case of ...** no se trata de .... **just in case** por si acaso. **state the case** exponer los hechos.

case² [keis] *n* (*box*) caja *f*; (*rigid*) estuche *m*; (*soft*) funda. **suitcase** *n* maleta *f*. *v* encajonar, embalar.

cash [kaʃ] *n* dinero al constante *m*; (*comm*) pago al contado *m*. **cash account** cuenta de caja *f*. **cash book** libro de caja *m*. **cash discount** descuento por pago al contado *m*. **cash on delivery** envío contra reembolso *m*. **cash register** caja registradora *f*. **petty cash** dinero para gastos menores *m*.

cashier¹ [ka'ʃɪə] *n* (*bank*) cajero, -a *m, f*.

cashier² [ka'ʃɪə] *v* (*mil*) dar de baja.

cashmere [kaʃ'mɪə] *n* cachemira *f*.

casing ['keisiŋ] *n* cubierta *f*; (*wrapping*) envoltura *f*; (*cylinder*) camisa *f*.

casino [kə'siɪnou] *n* casino *m*.

cask [kaɪsk] *n* barril *m*.

casket ['kaɪskit] *n* joyero *m*, cofre *m*.

casserole ['kasəroul] *n* (*dish*) cacerola *f*; (*food*) cazuela *f*.

cassette [kə'set] *n* (*tape*) cassette *m*; (*phot*) cartucho *m*.

cassock ['kasək] *n* sotana *f*.

*cast ['kaɪst] *n* (*acting*) reparto *m*; (*throw*) lanzamiento *m*; (*appearance*) aspecto *m*; (*tech*) molde *m*; (*squint*) estrabismo *m*; (*plaster*) escayola *f*. *v* echar, arrojar; (*tech*) moldear, fundir. **castaway** *n* náufrago *m*. **cast aside** desechar. **cast down** bajar. **cast iron** hierro colado *m*. **cast off** abandonar; (*naut*) desamarrar.

castanets [kastə'nets] *pl n* castañuelas *f pl*.

caste [kaɪst] *n* casta *f*.

castle ['kaɪsl] *n* castillo *m*.

castor ['kaɪstə] *n* (*wheel*) ruedecilla *f*.

castor oil *n* aceite de ricino *m*.

castrate [kə'streit] *v* castrar. **castration** *n* castración *f*.

casual ['kaʒuəl] *adj* casual, informal; (*carefree*) despreocupado. **casual clothes** ropa de sport *f sing*. **casually** *adv* de paso.

casualty ['kaʒuəlti] *n* accidente *m*; víctima *f*; (*mil*) baja *f*.

cat [kat] *n* gato, -a *m, f.* **let the cat out of the bag** descubrir el pastel.
catalogue ['katəlog] *n* catálogo *m.* *v* catalogar.
catalyst ['katəlist] *n* catalizador *m.*
catapult ['katəpʌlt] *n* catapulta *f*, honda *f.* *v* catapultar.
cataract ['katərakt] *n* catarata *f.*
catarrh [kə'tɑː] *n* catarro *m.*
catastrophe [kə'tastrəfi] *n* catástrofe *f.* **catastrophic** *adj* catastrófico.
*catch [katʃ] *v* (*seize*) agarrar, cojer; (*capture*) prender, atrapar; (*disease*) contraer; (*hook*) engancharse. **catch on** (*coll*) comprender. **catch out** sorprender. **catch up** alcanzar. *n* (*act of catching*) cogida *f*; (*prey*) presa *f*; (*bolt*) pestillo *m*; (*buckle*) hebijón *m*; (*drawback*) trampa *f*; (*trick*) truco *m.* **safety catch** fiador *m.* **catching** *adj* contagioso. **catchy** *adj* pegadizo.
category ['katəgəri] *n* categoría *f.* **categorical** *adj* categórico, rotundo. **categorize** *v* clasificar.
cater ['keitə] *v* proveer de comida. **cater for** atender a. **caterer** *n* proveedor, -a *m, f.* **catering** *n* abastecimiento *m.*
caterpillar ['katəpilə] *n* oruga *f.*
cathedral [kə'θiːdrəl] *n* catedral *f.*
cathode ['kaθoud] *n* cátodo *m.* **cathode-ray tube** tubo de rayos catódicos *m.*
catholic ['kaθəlik] *n, adj* católico, -a. *adj* universal; ortodoxo. **catholicism** *n* catolicismo *m.* **catholicity** *n* catolicidad *f.*
catkin ['katkin] *n* candelilla *f.*
cattle ['katl] *n* ganado *m.*
catty ['kati] *adj* malicioso.
caught [kɔːt] *V* catch.
cauliflower ['koliflauə] *n* coliflor *f.*
cause [kɔːz] *n* causa *f*, motivo *m.* *v* causar, provocar. **in the cause of** por.
causeway ['kɔːzwei] *n* terraplén *m.*
caustic ['kɔːstik] *adj* cáustico, mordaz.
caution ['kɔːʃən] *n* cautela *f*, cuidado *m*; (*warning*) advertencia *f.* *v* (*reprimand*) amonestar; (*warn*) advertir. **cautionary** *adj* amonestador. **cautious** *adj* cauteloso, precavido.
cavalry ['kavəlri] *n* caballería *f.*
cave [keiv] *n* cueva *f*, caverna *f.* **cave in** derrumbarse. **cavernous** *adj* cavernoso.
caviar ['kaviɑː] *n* caviar *m.*
cavity ['kavəti] *n* cavidad *f*; (*dental*) cavies *f invar.*
cayenne [kei'en] *n* pimentón *m.*

cease [siːs] *v* cesar. **cease-fire** *n* alto el fuego. **ceaseless** *adj* incesante.
cedar ['siːdə] *n* cedro *m.*
cedilla [si'dilə] *n* cedilla *f.*
ceiling ['siːliŋ] *n* techo *m*; (*aero*) altura *f*; (*fig*) tope *m*, limite *m.* **hit the ceiling** subirse por las paredes.
celebrate ['seləbreit] *v* celebrar, festejar. **celebrated** *adj* célebre. **celebration** *n* celebración *f.* **celebrant** *n* celebrante *m.*
celery ['seləri] *n* apio *m.*
celestial [sə'lestiəl] *adj* celestial; (*astron*) celeste.
celibate ['selibət] *n(m+f), adj* célibe. **celibacy** *n* celibato *m.*
cell [sel] *n* celda *f*; (*biol*) célula *f*; (*elec*) pila *f.*
cellar ['selə] *n* sótano *m*; (*wine*) bodega *f.*
cello ['tʃelou] *n* violoncelo *m.* **cellist** *n* violoncelista *m, f.*
cellular ['seljulə] *adj* celular.
cement [sə'ment] *n* cemento. *v* (*tech*) cementar; (*fig*) cimentar.
cemetery ['semətri] *n* cementerio *m.*
cenotaph ['senətaːf] *n* cenotafio *m.*
censor ['sensə] *n* censor *m.* *v* censurar; (*delete*) tachar. **censorious** *adj* censorador. **censorship** *n* censura *f.*
censure ['senʃə] *n* censura *f.* *v* censurar. **censurable** *adv* censurable.
census ['sensəs] *n* censo *m.* **take a census of** empadronar.
cent [sent] *n* centavo *m.*
centenary [sen'tiːnəri] *nm, adj* centenario. **centenarian** *n, adj* centenario, -a. **centennial** *adj* centenario.
centigrade ['sentigreid] *adj* centígrado.
centimetre ['sentimiːtə] *n* centimetro *m.*
centipede ['sentipiːd] *n* ciempiés *m invar.*
centre ['sentə] *n* centro *m.* **community centre** centro social *m.* *v* centrar. **central** *adj* central, céntrico. **central heating** calefacción central *f.* **centralize** *v* centralizar. **centralization** *n* centralización *f.*
centrifugal [sen'trifjugəl] *adj* centrifugo.
century ['sentʃuri] *n* siglo *m.*
ceramic [sə'ramik] *adj* cerámico. **ceramics** *n* cerámica *f sing.*
cereal ['siəriəl] *nm, adj* cereal.
ceremony ['serəməni] *n* ceremonia *f.* **stand on ceremony** andarse con ceremonias. **ceremonial** *nm, adj* ceremonial. **ceremonious** *adj* ceremonioso.
certain ['səːtn] *adj* cierto, seguro. **make certain** asegurarse. **certainly** *adv* desde

luego, naturalmente. **certainly not** de ninguna manera. **certainty** n certeza f. certidumbre f; seguridad f.
certificate [sə'tifikət] n certificado m; (*academic*) título m, diploma f. **birth certificate** partida de nascimiento f. **death certificate** partida de defunción f. **marriage certificate** partida de matrimonio f. **certify** v certificar; garantizar.
cesspool ['sespuːl] n pozo negro m.
chafe [tʃeif] v (*rub*) rozar; (*irritate*) irritar; (*for warmth*) frotar; (*fig*) enfadar. n rozadura f; irritación f.
chaffinch ['tʃafintʃ] n pinzón m.
chain [tʃein] n cadena f. **chain store** sucursal m. v encadenar.
chair [tʃeə] n silla f; (*university*) cátedra f; (*meeting*) presidencia f. **folding chair** silla plegable f. **take the chair** tomar la presidencia. **chairman** n presidente m. v presidir.
chalet ['ʃalei] n chalet m.
chalk [tʃoːk] n (*geol*) creta f; (*for writing*) tiza f. **not by a long chalk** ni mucho menos. v marcar con tiza. **chalk up** apuntarse. **chalky** adj cretáceo, yesoso.
challenge ['tʃalindʒ] n reto m, desafío m; (*sentry*) alto m; (*incentive*) estímulo m; (*law*) recusación f. v desafiar, retar. **challenger** n desafiador m, retador m.
chamber ['tʃeimbə] n (*room, legislative body*) cámara f; (*tech*) recámara f. **chambermaid** n doncella f, camarera f. **chamber music** música de cámara f. **chamber pot** orinal m.
chameleon [kəmiːliən] n camaleón m.
chamois ['ʃamwaɪ] n gamuza f.
champagne [ʃam'pein] n champaña f.
champion ['tʃampiən] n, adj campeón, -ona. v defender, hacerse el campeón de. **championship** n campeonato m.
chance [tʃains] n casualidad f, suerte f, azar m; oportunidad f, ocasión f; posibilidad f; riesgo m. adj casual, fortuito. v arriesgar; probar; (*happen*) acaecer. **chance upon** tropezarse con.
chancellor [tʃainsələ] n canciller m. **chancellery** n cancillería f.
chandelier [ʃandə'liə] n araña f.
change [tʃeindʒ] n cambio m; (*money*) suelto m; (*clothes*) muda f. **for a change** para variar. v cambiar; mudar. **changeable** adj (*character, weather*) variable; (*inconsistent*) cambiadizo; (*able to be*

changed) cambiable. **changing room** vestuario m.
channel ['tʃanl] n canal m; (*of a river*) cauce m; (*fig*) vía f; (*groove*) ranura f. **English Channel** Canal de la Mancha m.
chant [tʃaint] n canción f, canto m. v cantar; entonar.
chaos ['keios] n caos m. **chaotic** adj caótico.
chap¹ [tʃap] v (*skin*) agrietar. n grieta f.
chap² [tʃap] n (*coll*) tipo m, sujeto m.
chapel ['tʃapəl] n capilla f.
chaperon ['ʃapəroun] n carabina f. v acompañar.
chaplain ['tʃaplin] n capellán m.
chapter ['tʃaptə] n capítulo m; (*rel*) cabildo m. **quote chapter and verse** citar literalmente.
char¹ [tʃaɪ] v (*burn*) carbonizar.
char² [tʃaɪ] n (*charwoman*) asistenta f.
character ['karəktə] n carácter m; (*person*) personaje m; (*role*) papel m; (*coll*) tipo m. **character reference** informe m. **characterize** v caracterizar. **characterization** n caracterización f.
characteristic [ˌkarəktə'ristik] adj característico. n característica f.
charcoal ['tʃaɪkoul] n carbón de leña m.
charge [tʃaɪdʒ] n (*responsibility*) cargo m; (*task*) tarea f; (*battery, explosive, attack*) carga f. **charge account** cuenta a cargo f. **in charge of** encargado de. **take charge of** hacerse cargo de. v (*accuse*) acusar; (*bill*) cobrar; (*mil*) atacar.
chariot ['tʃariət] n carro m.
charity ['tʃarəti] n caridad f; (*alms*) limosna f; (*society*) sociedad benéfica f. **charitable** adj caritativo.
charm [tʃaɪm] n encanto m; (*spell*) hechizo m. v encantar; hechizar. **charming** adj encantador, simpático.
chart [tʃaɪt] n (*naut*) carta marina f; (*map*) mapa m; (*table*) tabla f; (*graph*) gráfico m. v tabular; trazar.
charter ['tʃaɪtə] n (*law*) carta; (*comm*) flete m, fletamento m, fletamiento m; (*transport*) alquiler m. v fletar; alquilar; (*grant a charter*) conceder carta a. **charter flight** vuelo charter' m. **charter member** socio fundador m.
chase [tʃeis] v perseguir; (*hunt*) cazar. **chase after** ir detrás de. **chase away/off** ahuyentar. n persecución f; caza f.
chasm ['kazəm] n sima f, abismo m.

chassis ['ʃasi] n (mech) chasis m.
chaste [tʃeist] adj casto; (style) sobrio.
chastity n castidad f.
chastise [tʃas'taiz] v castigar.
chat [tʃat] n charla f. v charlar. **chatty** adj charlador.
chatter ['tʃatə] v chacharear, parlotear; (teeth) castañetear. n cháchara f, parloteo m; castañeteo m. **chatterbox** n charlatán, -ana m, f.
chauffeur ['ʃoufə] n chófer m, conductor, -a m, f.
chauvinism ['ʃouvinizəm] n chauvinismo m. **chauvinist** n(m+f), adj chauvinista.
cheap [tʃiːp] adj barato. **dirt cheap** baratísimo adj, adv. **cheapen** v abaratar.
cheat [tʃiːt] v (swindle) timar, estafar; (deceive) engañar; (at games) hacer trampas; (in exams) copiar. n timador, -a m, f, estafador, -a m, f; tramposo, -a m, f; (trick) trampa f.
check [tʃek] v parar, detener; (restrain) reprimir, refrenar; (inspect) inspeccionar; (facts) comprobar; (mark) poner contraseña a; (chess) dar jaque a. **check in** registrarse. **check on** averiguar. **check with** cotejar con. n parada f, detención f; (restraint) restricción f; (control) inspección f; (pattern) cuadro m; (chess) jaque m. **checkmate** v dar el mate; n jaque mate m. **checkpoint** n control m. **checkup** n (med) reconocimiento general m.
cheek [tʃiːk] n carillo m, mejilla f; (coll) caradura f. **turn the other cheek** poner la otra mejilla. **cheekbone** n pómulo m. **cheeky** adj descarado.
cheer [tʃiə] v (shout) vitorear, aclamar; (gladden) alegrar. **cheer on** animar. **cheer up** alentar. n (shout) viva m; (comfort) consuelo m; (joy) ánimo m. **cheers!** interj ¡a su salud! **cheerful** adj alegre, animado. **cheerfulness** n alegría f. **cheerio!** interj ¡hasta luego! **cheerless** adj triste.
cheese [tʃiːz] n queso m. **cheesecake** n pastel de queso m. **cheesecloth** n estopilla f.
cheetah ['tʃiːtə] n leopardo cazador m.
chef [ʃef] n jefe de cocina m.
chemistry ['kemistri] n química f. **chemical** adj químico. **chemist** n químico m; farmacéutico m. **chemist's shop** farmacia f.
check [tʃek] n cheque m. **checkbook** n talonario de cheques m. **check card**

tarjeta de credito f. **traveler's check** cheque de viaje m.
cherish ['tʃeriʃ] v (love) querer; (nourish) abrigar; (take care of) cuidar.
cherry ['tʃeri] n (fruit) cereza f; (tree) cerezo m.
chess [tʃes] n ajedrez m. **chessboard** n tablero de ajedrez m. **chessman** n pieza de ajedrez f.
chest [tʃest] n (anat) pecho m; (box) caja f. **chest of drawers** n cómoda f. **chesty** adj (cough) delicado de los broncios.
chestnut ['tʃesnʌt] n (fruit) castaña f; (tree) castaño m. adj (hair) castaño.
chew [tʃuː] v masticar. **chewing gum** chicle m. **chew the cud** rumiar. **chew up** estropear.
chick pea ['tʃik,piː] n garbanzo m.
chicken ['tʃikin] n pollo m. **chickenpox** n varicela f. **chicken out** (slang) ser una gallina.
chicory ['tʃikəri] n (coffee) achicoria f; (salad) escarola f.
chief [tʃiːf] n pl -s jefe m, f. adj principal. **chiefly** adv principalmente; sobre todo.
chilblain ['tʃilblein] n sabañón m.
child [tʃaild] n pl -ren niño, -a m, f. **childbirth** n parto m. **childhood** n niñez f. **childish** adj infantil, pueril. **childless** adj sin hijos.
Chile ['tʃili] n Chile m. **Chilean** n, adj chileno, -a.
chill [tʃil] n frío m; (med) tiritona f; (shiver) escalofrío m; (fig) frialdad f. v enfriar. **chilled to the bone** enfriado hasta los huesos. **chilly** adj fresco.
chilli ['tʃili] n chile m.
chime [tʃaim] v sonar, repicar. **chime in** intervenir. n carillón m.
chimney ['tʃimni] n chimenea f. **chimney pot** cañón de chimenea m. **chimney sweep** deshollinador m.
chimpanzee [tʃimpən'ziː] n chimpancé m.
chin [tʃin] n barbilla f, mentón m.
china ['tʃainə] n porcelana f.
China ['tʃainə] n China f. **Chinese** n, adj chino, -a. **the Chinese** los chinos.
chink[1] [tʃiŋk] n (fissure) raja f, grieta m.
chink[2] [tʃiŋk] n (sound) sonido metálico m. v hacer tintinear.
chip [tʃip] n (fragment) pedacito m; (in cup, etc.) desportilladura f; (gambling) ficha f. **chipboard** n madera aglomerada f. **chips** pl n (cookery) patata frita f. v

astillar. **chip in** (*interrupt*) interrumpir; (*contribute money*) poner.
chiropodist [ki'rɔpədist] *n* pedicuro, -a *m*, *f*. **chiropody** *n* quiropodia *f*.
chirp [tʃɔɪp] *v* (*birds*) gorjear; (*crickets*) chirriar. *n* gorjeo *m*; chirrido *m*. **chirpy** *adj* animado.
chisel ['tʃɪzl] *n* cincel *m*. *v* cincelar.
chivalry ['ʃɪvəlri] *n* caballerosidad *f*. **chivalrous** *adj* caballeroso.
chive [tʃaiv] *n* cebolleta *f*.
chlorine ['klɔɪriɪn] *n* cloro *m*. **chlorinate** *v* tratar con cloro.
chloroform ['klorəfoim] *n* cloroformo *m*. *v* cloroformizar.
chlorophyll ['klorəfil] *n* clorofila *f*.
chocolate ['tʃokələt] *n* chocolate *m*. **drinking chocolate** chocolate a la taza *m*.
choice [tʃois] *n* elección *f*, selección *f*; preferencia *f*. *adj* (*best*) flor y nata.
choir ['kwaiə] *n* coro *m*, coral *f*. **choirboy** *n* niño de coro *m*. **choirmaster** *n* director de coro *m*.
choke [tʃouk] *v* (*strangle*) estrangular; (*block*) obstruir. *n* (*mot*) estrangulador *m*.
cholera ['kolərə] *n* cólera *m*.
***choose** [tʃuɪz] *v* escoger, elegir.
chop¹ [tʃop] *n* (*meat*) chuleta *f*; (*blow*) golpe *m*. *v* (*cut*) cortar; (*mince*) picar; (*lop*) tronchar. **chop down** talar. **chopper** *n* hacha *f*; (*slang*) helicóptero *m*.
chop² [tʃop] *v* **chop and change** cambiar de opinión. **choppy** *adj* (*sea*) picado.
chops [tʃops] *pl n* (*jaws*) morros *m pl*. **lick one's chops** relamerse.
chopstick ['tʃopstik] *n* palillo *m*.
chord [koɪd] *n* (*music*) acorde *m*; (*anat*) cuerda *f*.
chore [tʃoɪ] *n* (*unpleasant*) tarea penosa *f*. **chores** *pl n* (*household*) faenas de la casa *f pl*.
choreography [kori'ogrəfi] *n* coreografía *f*. **choreographer** *n* coreógrafo *m*.
chorus ['koɪrəs] *n* (*refrain*) estribillo *m*; (*singers*) coro *m*. **chorus girl** corista *f*. **choral** *adj* coral. **choral society** orfeón *m*.
chose [tʃouz] *V* **choose**.
christen ['krisn] *v* bautizar; (*nickname*) llamar. **christening** *n* bautismo *m*.
Christian ['kristʃən] *n*, *adj* cristiano, -a *m*, *f*. **Christian name** nombre de pila *m*. **Christianity** *n* cristianismo *m*.

Christmas ['krisməs] *n* Navidad *f*. **Christmas Day** día de Navidad *m*. **Christmas Eve** Nochebuena *f*.
chromatic [krə'matik] *adj* cromático.
chrome [kroum] *n* cromo *m*.
chromium ['kroumiəm] *n* cromo *m*. **chromium-plated** *adj* cromado.
chronic ['kronik] *adj* crónico; (*coll: dreadful*) terrible.
chronicle ['kronikl] *n* crónica *f*.
chronological [kronə'lodʒikəl] *adj* cronológico.
chrysalis ['krisəlis] *n* crisálida *f*.
chrysanthemum [kri'sanθəməm] *n* crisantemo *m*.
chubby ['tʃʌbi] *adj* gordinflón.
chuck [tʃʌk] *v* (*coll: throw*) tirar; (*give up*) abandonar.
chuckle ['tʃʌkl] *v* reir entre de dientes. *n* risa *f*.
chunk [tʃʌŋk] *n* pedazo *m*; (*large amount*) cantidad grande *f*.
church [tʃɔɪtʃ] *n* iglesia *f*. **church service** oficio religioso *m*. **churchyard** *n* cementerio *m*.
churn [tʃɔɪn] *n* mantequera *f*. *v* batir. **churn out** producir en profusión.
chute [ʃuɪt] *n* tolva *f*.
cider ['saidə] *n* sidra *f*.
cigar [si'gaɪ] *n* cigarro puro *m*.
cigarette [sigə'ret] *n* cigarillo *m*. **cigarette case** pitillera *f*. **cigarette holder** boquilla *f*. **cigarette lighter** encendedor *m*, mechero *m*. **cigarette paper** papel de fumar *m*.
cinder ['sində] *n* carbonilla *f*, ceniza *f*.
cinema ['sinəmə] *n* cine *m*. **cinematography** *n* cinematografía *f*.
cinnamon ['sinəmən] *n* canela *f*.
circle ['sɔɪkl] *n* círculo *m*; (*theatre*) piso principal *m*. **go round in circles** dar vueltas. *v* rodear; (*surround*) circundar. **circular** *adj*, *n* circular *f*.
circuit ['sɔɪkit] *n* (*route*) circuito *m*; (*perimeter*) perímetro *m*; (*law*) distrito *m*; (*cinemas, theatres*) cadena *f*. **short circuit** cortocircuito *m*. **circuitous** *adj* indirecto.
circulate ['sɔɪkjuleit] *v* circular. **circulation** *n* circulación *f*.
circumcise ['sɔɪkəmsaiz] *v* circuncidar. **circumcision** *n* circuncisión *f*.
circumference [sɔɪ'kʌmfərəns] *n* circunferencia *f*.
circumflex ['sɔɪkəmfleks] *n* circunflejo *m*.

circumscribe ['sɔːkəmskraib] v circunscribir. circumscription n circunscripción f.

circumstance ['sɔːkəmstəns] n circunstancia f. extenuating circumstances circunstancias atenuantes f pl. under no circumstances de ninguna manera. under the circumstances en estas circunstancias. circumstantial adj (incidental) circunstancial; (detailed) circunstanciado. circumstancial evidence testimonio indirecto m.

circus ['sɔːkəs] n circo m.

cistern ['sistən] n cisterna f, aljibe m.

cite [sait] v citar. citation n citación f; (mil) mención f.

citizen ['sitizn] n ciudadano, -a m, f. citizenship n ciudadanía f.

citrus ['sitrəs] n cidro m. citrus fruit n agrios m pl. citric acid ácido cítrico m.

city ['siti] n ciudad f.

civic ['sivik] adj cívico.

civil ['sivl] adj civil; (polite) cortés. civil engineering ingeniería civil f. civil rights derechos civiles m pl. civil servant funcionario, -a m, f. civil service administración pública f. civil war guerra civil f.

civilian [sə'viljən] adj civil, de paisano. n paisano, -a m, f.

civilization [,sivilai'zeiʃən] n civilización f. civilize v civilizar.

clad [klad] adj vestido (de).

claim [kleim] v (damages) exigir; (a right) reclamar; (assert) declarar; (need) requerir. n (right) derecho m; (demand) demanda f, reclamación f; (statement) declaración f; (land) propiedad f. claimant (law) n demandante m, f; (pretender) pretendiente m, f.

clairvoyant [kleə'voiənt] n(m+f), adj clarividente. clairvoyance n clarividencia. f.

clam [klam] n almeja f.

clamber ['klambə] v trepar.

clammy ['klami] adj pegajoso.

clamour ['klamə] n clamor m. v clamar, vociferar.

clamp [klamp] n abrazadera f. v sujetar con abrazadera. clamp down on suprimir.

clan [klan] n clan m. clannish adj exclusivista.

clandestine [klan'destin] adj clandestino.

clang [klaŋ] v sonar estripitosamente. n sonido metálico m.

clap [klap] v aplaudir, dar palmadas. n (with hands) palmada f; (noise) ruido seco m. clap of thunder trueno m.

claret ['klarət] n clarete m.

clarify ['klarəfai] v aclarar; (liquid) clarificar. clarification n aclaración f; clarificación f.

clarinet [klarə'net] n clarinete m.

clarity ['klarəti] n claridad f.

clash [klaʃ] v (collide) chocar; (cymbals) golpear; (interests) estar en desacuerdo; (dates) coincidir; (colours) matarse. n ruido metálico m; (encounter) choque m; (interests) conflicto m; coincidencia f; disparidad f.

clasp [klɑːsp] v (grasp) agarrar; (fasten) abrochar. n (hands) apretón m; (fastening) cierre m; (belt) broche m.

class [klɑːs] n clase f.

classic ['klasik] adj clásico. classical adj clásico. classics n pl clásicas f pl.

classify ['klasifai] v clasificar. classification n clasificación f. classified advertisement anuncio por palabras m.

clatter ['klatə] n estruendo m; (hooves) chacoloteo m. v sonar con estrépito; chacolotear.

clause [klɔːz] n (law) cláusula f; (gramm) oración f.

claustrophobia [klɔːstrə'foubiə] n claustrofobia f.

claw [klɔː] n (talon) garra f; (cat) uña f; (crab) pinza f; (tech) garfio m. v agarrar; arañar; (tear) desgarrar.

clay [klei] n arcilla f, barro m.

clean [kliːn] adj limpio; (irreproachable) sin tocha. v limpiar. clean out (empty) vaciar. clean up (tidy) ordenar; (win) ganarse. clean-cut adj bien hecho, perfilado. cleaner (person) n asistenta f. cleanliness n limpieza f. clean-shaven adj bien afeitado.

cleanse [klenz] v limpiar, purificar.

clear [kliə] adj claro, transparente; (conscience) tranquilo; evidente; (free) libre; (unobstructed) despejado; (profit) neto. adv claramente. v aclarar; despejar; (law) absolver. clearance n espacio m, altura libre f, margen m; despeje m; acreditación f. clearance sale liquidación f.

clef [klef] n clave f.

clench [klentʃ] v apretar, sujetar.

clergy ['klɔːdʒi] n clero m. clergyman n clérigo m.

clerical ['klerikəl] *adj* (*clerk*) de oficina; (*rel*) clerical. **clerical error** error de copia *m*.

clerk [klaik] *n* oficinista *m, f*; (*law*) escribano *m*.

clever ['klevə] *adj* listo; inteligente; (*skilful*) hábil; (*cunning*) astuto. **cleverness** *n* habilidad *f*; ingenio *m*.

cliché ['kliːʃei] *n* cliché *m*, clisé *m*.

click [klik] *n* chasquido *m*; taconeo *m*. *v* chascar, chasquear; taconear.

client ['klaiənt] *n* cliente *m, f*.

cliff [klif] *n* (*coast*) acantilado *m*; (*crag*) risco *m*.

climate ['klaimət] *n* clima *m*; (*atmosphere*) ambiente *m*. **climatic** *adj* climático.

climax ['klaimaks] *n* punto culminante *m*; climax *m*. *v* llevar al punto culminante.

climb [klaim] *v* subir, escalar; (*plants*) trepar. *n* subida *f*, escalada *f*. **climber** *n* escalador, -a *m, f*; (*mountaineer*) alpinista *m, f*; (*plant*) planta trepadora *f*.

***cling** [kliŋ] *v* agarrarse; (*stick to*) adherirse a, pegarse a. **clinging** *adj* ceñido; pegajoso.

clinic ['klinik] *n* dispensario *m*; clínica *f*. **clinical** *adj* clínico.

clip¹ [klip] *v* (*trim*) recortar; (*animals*) esquilar; (*ticket*) picar; (*coll: cuff*) abofetear. *n* (*film*) fragmento; (*cuff*) bofetada *f*.

clip² [klip] *v* (*fasten*) sujetar. *n* grapa *f*; sujetapapeles *m invar*; (*hair*) horquilla *f*; (*pen, pencil*) prendedor *m*.

cloak [klouk] *n* capa *f*; (*fig*) manto *m*; (*mil*) capote. **cloak-and-dagger** *adj* de capa y espada. **cloakroom** *n* guardarropa *m*; (*toilet*) servicios *m pl*. *v* encubrir, cubrir, encapotar.

clock [klok] *n* reloj *m*. **against the clock** contra reloj. **alarm clock** despertador *m*. **around the clock** durante 24 horas. **clockwise** *adj* en el sentido de las agujas del reloj. **clockwork** *n* aparato de relojería *m*. *v* registrar.

clog [klog] *n* zueco *m*. *v* atascar, obstruir.

cloister ['kloistə] *n* claustro *m*. *v* enclaustrar.

close [klouz; *adj, adv* klous] *v* cerrar; (*block*) tapar; (*end*) acabar; (*account*) saldar; (*distance*) acortar. **close in** acercarse. *n* conclusión *f*; final *m*. *adj* cercano; íntimo; (*air*) cargado; (*game*) reñido. *adv* cerca. **close-up** *n* primer plano *m*.

closet ['klozit] *n* (*WC*) retrete *m*. **water** *m*; armario *m*.

clot [klot] *n* (*blood*) coágulo *m*; (*liquid*) grumo *m*. *v* coagular, cuajar.

cloth [kloθ] *n* (*rag*) trapo *m*; (*fabric*) paño *m*; (*tablecloth*) mantel *m*.

clothe [klouð] *v* vestir; (*cover*) cubrir.

clothes [klouðz] *pl n also* **clothing** ropa *f sing*; vestidos *m pl*. **clothes basket** cesta de la ropa sucia *f*. **clothes brush** cepillo de la ropa *m*. **clothes line** tendedero *m*. **clothes peg** pinza *f*.

cloud [klaud] *n* nube *f*; (*gas*) capa *f*. *v* nublar; (*darken*) ensombrecer, oscurecer. **cloudburst** *n* chaparrón *m*. **cloudiness** *n* nubosidad *f*. **cloudless** *adj* despejado. **cloudy** *adj* nuboso; nublado.

clove¹ [klouv] *n* (*spice*) clavo *m*.

clove² [klouv] *n* (*of garlic, etc.*) diente *m*.

clover ['klouvə] *n* trébol *m*.

clown [klaun] *n* payaso *m*. *v* hacer el payaso.

club [klʌb] *n* (*association*) club *m*; (*stick*) porra *f*, garrote *m*; (*golf*) palo *m*. *v* (*beat*) aporrear. **clubfoot** *n* pie zopo *m*.

clue [kluː] *n* (*police lead*) pista *f*; (*piece of evidence*) indicio *m*.

clump [klʌmp] *n* (*trees*) grupo *m*; (*flowers*) matar *f*; (*earth*) terrón *m*; (*noise*) pisada fuerte *f*. *v* agrupar; andar con pisadas fuertes.

clumsy ['klʌmzi] *adj* (*awkward*) torpe; (*unskilful*) desmañado; (*tactless*) sin tacto. **clumsiness** *n* torpeza *f*; desmaña *f*.

cluster ['klʌstə] *n* grupo *m*; (*fruits*) racimo *m*. *v* agruparse, arracimarse.

clutch [klʌtʃ] *v* agarrar, apretar. *n* (*grip*) agarrón *m*; (*mot*) embrague *m*. **engage the clutch** embragar.

clutter ['klʌtə] *n* desorden *m*, confusión *f*. *v* desordenar, atentar.

coach [koutʃ] *n* (*carriage*) coche *m*; (*ceremonial carriage*) carroza *f*; (*mot*) autocar *m*; (*tutor*) profesor particular *m*; (*trainer*) entrenador *m*. *v* dar clases particulares; entrenar.

coagulate [kou'agjuleit] *v* coagular. **coagulation** *n* coagulación *f*.

coal [koul] *n* carbón *m*, hulla *f*. **coal cellar** carbonera *f*. **coalman** *n* carbonero *m*. **coalmine** *n* mina de carbón *f*. **coalminer** *n* minero de carbón *m*. **coal scuttle** cubo para el carbón *m*.

coalesce [kouə'les] *v* (*unite*) unirse; (*merge*) fundirse.
coalition [kouə'liʃən] *n* coalición *f*.
coarse [kɔɪs] *adj* (*gross*) grosero; (*ill-made*) basto. **coarse-grained** *adj* de grano grueso. **coarseness** *n* grosería *f*; basteza *f*.
coast [koust] *n* costa *f*. **the coast is clear** no hay moros en la costa. *v* (*freewheel*) deslizarse cuesta abajo. **coastguard** *n* guardacostas *m invar*. **coastline** *n* litoral *m*.
coat [kout] *n* chaqueta *f*; (*overcoat*) abrigo *m*; (*animal*) pelo *m*. **coat-hanger** percha *f*. **coat of arms** escudo de armas *m*. **coat of paint** mano de pintura *f*. *v* cubrir; dar una mano de pintura; (*cookery*) rebozar. **coating** *n* capa *f*; mano *f*; rebozo *m*.
coax [kouks] *v* engatusar.
cobbler ['koblə] *n* zapatero *m*.
cobra ['koubrə] *n* cobra *f*.
cobweb ['kobweb] *n* telaraña *f*.
cocaine [kə'kein] *n* cocaína *f*.
cock¹ [kok] *n* (*male fowl*) gallo *m*; (*male bird*) macho *m*; (*impol: penis*) polla *f*. **cocky** *adj* engreído.
cock² [kok] *v* (*gun*) amartillar; (*ears*) aguzar el oído.
cockle ['kokl] *n* berberecho *m*.
cockpit ['kokpit] *n* (*aero*) cabina del piloto *f*; (*cockfighting*) reñidero *m*.
cockroach ['kokroutʃ] *n* cucaracha *f*.
cocktail ['kokteil] *n* cóctel *m*. **cocktail shaker** coctelera *f*.
cocoa ['koukou] *n* cacao *m*.
coconut ['koukənʌt] *n* coco *m*. **coconut palm** cocotero *m*.
cocoon [kə'kuɪn] *n* capullo *m*.
cod [kod] *n* bacalao *m*.
code [koud] *n* código *m*; (*signals*) cifra *f*, clave *f*; (*area code*) prefijo *m*. **highway code** codigo de la circulación *m*. **Morse code** alfabeto Morse *m*. *v* cifrar.
codeine ['koudiɪn] *n* codeína *f*.
coeducation [kouedju'keiʃən] *n* coeducación *f*.
coerce [kou'əɪs] *v* forzar, obligar.
coexist [kouig'zist] *v* coexistir. **coexistence** *n* coexistencia *f*.
coffee ['kofi] *n* café *m*. **black/white coffee** café solo/con leche *m*. **coffee bean** grano de café *m*. **coffee pot** cafetera *f*. **coffee table** mesita de café *f*.
coffin ['kofin] *n* ataúd *m*.

cog [kog] *n* diente *m*; (*wheel*) rueda dentada *f*.
cognac ['konjak] *n* coñac *m*.
cohabit [kou'habit] *v* cohabitar, vivir juntos. **cohabitation** *n* cohabitación *f*.
cohere [kə'hiə] *v* adherirse, pegarse. **coherence** *n* coherencia *f*. **coherent** *adj* coherente.
coil [koil] *n* (*rope*) rollo *m*; (*smoke*) espiral *m*; (*elec*) carrete *m*. **coil spring** muelle en espiral *m*. *v* enrollar, arrollar.
coin [koin] *n* moneda *f*. **toss a coin** echar a cara o cruz. *v* acuñar; inventar. **coinage** *n* moneda *f*.
coincide [kouin'said] *v* coincidir. **coincidence** *n* coincidencia *f*. **coincidental** *adj* coincidente.
colander ['koləndə] *n* escurridor *m*.
cold [kould] *adj* frío. **be cold** (*person*) tener frío; (*weather*) hacer frío. **cold front** frente frío *m*. **cold storage** conservación *f*. **cold war** guerra fría *f*. **catch a cold** resfriarse. **cold-blooded** *adj* (*biol*) de sangre fría; (*fig*) insensible.
colic ['kolik] *n* cólico *m*.
collaborate [kə'labəreit] *v* colaborar. **collaboration** *n* colaboración *f*. **collaborator** *n* (*colleague*) colaborador, -a *m, f*; (*pol*) colaboracionista *m, f*.
collapse [ke'laps] *v* derrumbar; (*med*) sufrir un colapso. *n* derrumbamiento *m*; colapso; (*failure*) fracaso *m*. **collapsible** *adj* plegable.
collar ['kolə] *n* cuello *m*; (*dog, etc.*) collar *m*. **collarbone** *n* clavícula *f*. *v* (*seize*) agarrar por el cuello; (*put a collar on*) acollarar.
collate [ko'leit] *v* cotejar. **collation** *n* (*food*) colación *f*; (*texts*) cotejo *m*.
colleague ['koliɪg] *n* colega *m, f*.
collect [kə'lekt] *v* (*bring together*) juntar, reunir; (*hobby*) coleccionar; (*funds*) allegar; (*taxes*) recaudar; (*bills*) cobrar; (*gather*) recoger. **collected works** obras completas *f pl*. **collection** (*hobby*) colección *f*; (*charity*) colecta *f*; (*people*) grupo *m*; (*things*) reunión *f*; (*rent, bills*) cobro *m*; (*taxes*) recaudación *f*; (*postal*) recogida *f*. **collective** *adj* colectivo. **collector** *n* (*tax*) recaudador, -a *m, f*; (*bills, rent*) cobrador *m*; (*hobbies*) coleccionista *m, f*.
college ['kolidʒ] *n* colegio *m*. **collegiate** *adj* colegiado.

collide [kə'laid] v chocar. collision n choque m.
colloquial [kə'loukwiəl] adj familiar, popular. colloquialism n expresión familiar f.
Colombia [kə'lombiə] n Colombia f. Colombian n, adj colombiano, -a.
colon ['koulon] n dos puntos m pl; (anat) colon m.
colonel ['kɜːnl] n coronel m.
colony ['koləni] n colonia f. colonial adj colonial. colonialist n(m+f), adj colonialista. colonist n colono m. colonization n colonización f. colonize v colonizar.
colossal [kə'losəl] adj colosal.
colour ['kʌlə] n color m. colour bar barrera racial f. colour-blind adj daltoniano. colourful adj animado. fast colour color sólido m. in colour en colores. v colorear; (dye) teñir.
colt [koult] n potro m.
column ['koləm] n columna f. columnist n columnista m, f.
coma ['koumə] n coma m.
comb [koum] n peine m; (honey) panal m. v peinar.
combat ['kombat] n combate m. v combatir, luchar contra. combatant n(m+f), adj combatiente.
combine [kəm'bain; n 'kombain] v combinar, reunir. n (comm) cártel m. combination n combinación f, asociación f.
combustion [kəm'bʌstʃən] n combustión f. combustible adj combustible.
*come [kʌm] v venir, llegar; proceder; salir. come about ocurrir. come across dar con. come along! ¡vamos! come back volver. comeback n restablecimiento m. come off desprender; (succeed) tener éxito. come out salir. come to (from faint) volver ensí; (total) ascender a.
comedy ['komədi] n comedia f. comedian n cómico m.
comet ['komit] n cometa m.
comfort ['kʌmfət] n (relief) alivio m; (consolation) consuelo m; (well-being) bienestar m; (convenience) comodidad f. v aliviar; consolar; animar. comfortable adj cómodo; agradable. comfortably adv cómodamente; confortablemente.
comic ['komik] adj cómico, divertido. n (magazine) tebeo m. comical adj cómico.
comma ['komə] n coma f. inverted commas comillas f pl.
command [kə'maind] n (order) orden f; (authority) mando m; (mastery) dominio

m. v mandar, ordenar; dominar. commandant n comandante m. commander n comandante m; (leader) jefe m. commander-in-chief n comandante-en-jefe m. commandment n mandamiento m.
commandeer [komən'diə] v expropiar.
commando [kə'maindou] n comando m.
commemorate [kə'meməreit] v conmemorar. commemoration n conmemoración f. commemorative adj conmemorativo.
commence [kə'mens] v empezar, comenzar. commencement n comienzo m.
commend [kə'mend] v (recommend) recomendar; (entrust) encomendar; (praise) alabar. commendable adj recomendable. commendation n alabanza f, elogio m, encomio m.
comment ['koment] n observación f; (explanation) comentario. no comment sin comentarios. v comentar, hacer observaciones. commentary n comentario m, observación f. running commentary reportaje en directo m.
commerce ['komɜːs] n comercio m. commercial adj comercial. commercial traveller agente comercial m. commercialism n mercantilismo m. commercialize v comercializar.
commiserate [kə'mizəreit] v compadecerse. commiseration n conmiseración f.
commission [kə'miʃən] n (profit) comisión f; (to a post, etc.) nombramiento m; (assignment) cometido m; (charge) encargo; (crime) ejecución f; (mil) grado de oficial m. v comisionar; encargar; (mil) nombrar. commissionaire n portero m. commissioner n comisionado m. High Commissioner alto comisario m.
commit [kə'mit] v (crime) cometer; (entrust) confiar; (imprison) encarcelar. commit oneself comprometerse. commitment n (assignment) cometido m; (pledge) compromiso m.
committee [kə'miti] n comité m, comisión f.
commodity [kə'modəti] n mercancia f, producto m, artículo m.
common ['komən] adj común; público; ordinario; frecuente. commoner n plebeyo, -a m, f. Common Market Mercado Común m. commonness n frecuencia f; vulgaridad f. commonplace

adj común, trivial. **commonsense** *adj* lógico. **commonwealth** *n* república *f*.
commotion [kə'mouʃən] *n* disturbio *m*; tumulto *m*.
commune¹ [kə'mjuːn] *v* (*communicate*) comunicarse; (*meditate*) meditar. **communion** *n* comunión *f*.
commune² ['komjuːn] *n* comuna *f*. **communal** *adj* comunal.
communicate [kə'mjuːnikeit] *v* comunicar. **communication** *n* comunicación *f*. **communicative** *adj* comunicativo.
communism ['komjunizəm] *n* comunismo *m*. **communist** *n*(*m+f*), *adj* comunista.
community [kə'mjuːnəti] *n* comunidad *f*. **community centre** centro social *m*.
commute [kə'mjuːt] *v* (*travel*) viajar; (*law*) conmutar. **commuter** *n*, *adj* viajero, -a.
compact¹ [kəm'pakt] *adj* compacto; recogido; conciso; denso. *v* condensar; comprimir.
compact² ['kompakt] *n* pacto *m*; (*powder*) polvera *f*.
companion [kəm'panjən] *n* compañero, -a *m*, *f*; (*professional*) acompañante *m*, *f*. **companionship** *n* compañerismo *m*.
company ['kʌmpəni] *n* (*comm*) compañiá *f*, empresa *f*; (*companionship*) compañerismo *m*, sociedad *f*.
compare [kəm'peə] *v* comparar. **comparable** *adj* comparable. **comparative** *adj* relativo; (*gram*) comparativo. **comparison** *n* comparación *f*.
compartment [kəm'paːtmənt] *n* compartimiento *m*, departamento *m*.
compass ['kʌmpəs] *n* (*naut*) brújula *f*; (*extent*) extensión *f*. **compasses** *n* *pl* (*maths*) compás *m*.
compassion [kəm'paʃən] *n* compasión *f*. **compassionate** *adj* compasivo.
compatible [kəm'patəbl] *adj* compatible. **compatibility** *n* compatibilidad *f*.
compel [kəm'pel] *v* compeler, obligar. **compelling** *adj* convincente.
compensate ['kompənseit] *v* (*make up for*) compensar; (*repay*) indemnizar. **compensation** *n* compensación *f*; indemnización *f*; (*reward*) recompensa *f*.
compete [kəm'piːt] *v* competir. **competition** *n* competición *f*; (*contest*) concurso *m*; (*comm*) competencia *f*. **competitive** *adj* competitivo; (*spirit*) de competencia. **competitor** *n* competidor, -a *m*, *f*. (*contestant*) concursante *m*, *f*.

competent ['kompətənt] *adj* competente; (*suitable*) adecuado. **competence** *n* competencia *f*, aptitud *f*.
compile [kəm'pail] *v* compilar. **compilation** *n* compilación *f*. **compiler** *n* compilador, -a *m*, *f*.
complacent [kəm'pleisnt] *adj* complaciente. **complacence, complacency** *n* satisfacción de si mismo *f*.
complain [kəm'plein] *v* quejarse. **complaint** *n* queja *f*; (*med*) enfermedad *f*; (*law*) demanda *f*.
complement ['kompləmənt] *n* complemento *m*. *v* complementar. **complementary** *adj* complementario.
complete [kəm'pliːt] *adj* completo; (*finished*) acabado, concluido, terminado; (*entire*) entero. *v* completar; terminar; (*fill in*) llenar. **completion** *n* cumplimiento *m*; terminación *f*.
complex ['kompleks] *adj* complejo, complicado. *n* complejo *m*. **complexity** *n* complejidad *f*.
complexion [kəm'plekʃən] *n* tez *f*, cutis *m*; aspecto *m*.
complicate ['komplikeit] *v* complicar. **complicated** *adj* complicado. **complication** *n* complicación *f*.
complicity [kəm'plisəti] *n* complicidad *f*.
compliment ['kompləmənt] *n* cumplido *m*. **compliments** *n* *pl* saludos *m* *pl*. **complimentary** *adj* elogioso; (*gratis*) de favor.
comply [kəm'plai] *v* conformarse; (*obey*) obeceder.
component [kəm'pounənt] *nm*, *adj* componente.
compose [kəm'pouz] *v* componer; calmar. **composed** *adj* sereno. **be composed of** constar de. **composer** *n* compositor, -a *m*, *f*. **composite** *adj* compuesto. **composition** *n* composición *f*.
compost ['kompost] *n* abono *m*.
composure [kəm'pouʒə] *n* calma *f*, serenidad *f*.
compound¹ [kəm'paund; *n*, *adj* 'kompaund] *v* componer; mezclar. *nm*, *adj* compuesto. **compound fracture** fractura complicada *f*.
compound² ['kompaund] *n* (*enclosure*) recinto cercado *m*.
comprehend [kompri'hend] *v* comprender. **comprehensible** *adj* comprensible. **comprehension** *n* comprensión *f*.

comprehensive *adj* extenso, amplio. **comprehensive insurance** seguro a todo riesgo *m*. **comprehensive school** colegio integrado *m*.

compress ['kɔmpres; *v* kəm'pres] *n* (*med*) compresa *f*. *v* comprimir; (*condense*) condensar. **compression** *n* compresión *f*.

comprise [kəm'praiz] *v* comprender.

compromise ['kɔmprəmaiz] *n* compromiso *m*, arreglo *m*. *v* (*agree*) llegar a un arreglo; (*yield*) transigir; (*endanger*) comprometer. **compromising** *adj* comprometedor.

compulsion [kəm'pʌlʃən] *n* obligación *f*; (*coercion*) coacción *f*; (*impulse*) impulso *m*. **compulsive** *adj* compulsivo. **compulsory** *adj*

computer [kəm'pjuːtə] *n* computador *m*, computadora *f*, ordenador *m*. **compute** *v* computar, calcular. **computerize** *v* tratar.

comrade ['kɔmrid] *n* camarada *m*, *f* compañero, -a *m*, *f*. **comradeship** *n* camaradería *f*.

concave [kɔn'keiv] *adj* cóncavo. **concavity** *n* concavidad *f*.

conceal [kən'siːl] *v* ocultar. **concealed** *adj* oculto. **concealment** *n* encubrimiento *m*.

concede [kən'siːd] *v* conceder; (*admit*) reconocer. **concede victory** darse por vencido.

conceit [kən'siːt] *n* presunción *f*, vanidad *f*. **conceited** *adj* engreído, vanidoso.

conceive [kən'siːv] *v* concebir. **conceive of** imaginarse. **conceivable** *adj* concebible.

concentrate ['kɔnsəntreit] *v* concentrar. *n* concentrado. **concentration** *n* concentración *f*. **concentration camp** campo de concentración *m*.

concentric [kən'sentrik] *adj* concéntrico.

concept ['kɔnsept] *n* concepto *m*. **conception** *n* concepción *f*; idea *f*.

concern [kən'səːn] *n* asunto *m*; (*interest*) interés *m*; (*business*) empresa *f* (*worry*) preocupación *f*. *v* (*have as a subject*) tratar de; (*affect*) afectar; (*be related to*) referirse a. **concerned** *adj* preocupado. **concerning** *prep* con respecto a.

concert ['kɔnsət; *v* kən'səːt] *n* concierto *m*. *v* concertar.

concertina [kɔnsə'tiːnə] *n* concertina *f*.

concerto [kən'tʃəːtou] *n* concierto *m*.

concession [kən'seʃən] *n* concesión *f*.

conciliate [kən'silieit] *v* conciliar. **conciliation** *n* conciliación *f*. **conciliator** *n* conciliador, -a *m*, *f*. **conciliatory** *adj* conciliatorio.

concise [kən'sais] *adj* conciso.

conclude [kən'kluːd] *v* acabar, terminar; (*treaty*) concertar; (*deduce*) concluir. **conclusion** *n* conclusión *f*. **conclusive** *adj* conclusivo; concluyente.

concoct [kən'kɔkt] *v* (*mix*) confeccionar; (*plot*) urdir; inventar. **concoction** *n* (*mixture*) mezcla *f*; (*lies*) fabricación *f*.

concrete ['kɔnkriːt] *n* hormigón *m*. **concrete mixer** hormigonera *f*. **reinforced concrete** hormigón armado *m*. *adj* concreto; (*tech*) de hormigón.

concussion [kən'kʌʃən] *n* conmoción cerebral *f*. **concuss** *v* conmocionar.

condemn [kən'dem] *v* condenar; (*building*) declarar en ruina. **condemnation** *n* condenación *f*. **condemnatory** *adj* condenatorio. **condemned** *adj* condenado.

condense [kən'dens] *v* (*cut*) abreviar, resumir; (*physics*) condensar. **condensation** *n* condensación *f*; (*vapour*) vaho *m*; (*abbreviation*) resumen *m*. **condenser** *n* condensador *m*.

condescend [kɔndi'send] *v* condescender, dignarse. **condescending** *adj* condescendiente, superior. **condescension** *n* condescendencia *f*.

condition [kən'diʃən] *n* condición *f*, estado *m*. *v* condicionar, determinar. **conditional** *adj* condicional. **conditionally** *adv* con reservas. **conditioning** *n* condicionamiento *m*.

condolence [kən'douləns] *n* condolencia *f*, pésame *m*. **condole** *v* condolerse, dar el pésame.

condom ['kɔndom] *n* condón *m*.

condone [kən'doun] *v* condonar, perdonar.

conducive [kən'djuːsiv] *adj* conducivo; (*helpful*) propicio.

conduct ['kɔndʌkt; *v* kən'dʌkt] *n* conducta *f*, comportamiento *m*. *v* (*lead*) conducir; (*music, business*) dirigir; (*behave*) comportarse. **conductance** *n* conductancia *f*. **conduction** *n* conducción *f*. **conductivity** *n* conductividad *f*.

conductor [kən'dʌktə] *n* (*music*) director, -a *m*, *f*; (*guide*) guía *m*; (*bus*) cobrador *m*; (*physics*) conductor *m*. **lightning conductor** pararrayos *m sing*.

cone [koun] *n* cono *m*; (*bot*) piña *f*; (*ice*

cream) cucurucho de helado *m*. **cone-shaped** *adj* cónico.
confectioner [kən'fekʃənə] *n* confitero, -a *m, f*. **confection** *n* dulce *m*. **confectionery** *n* (*sweets*) dulces *m pl*; (*shop*) confitería *f*; (*cake shop*) repostería *f*.
confederate [kən'fedərət] *nm, adj* confederado, *v* confederar. **confederation** *n* confederación *f*.
confer [kən'fəɪ] *v* consultar, conferir; (*hold a conference*) conferenciar. **conference** *n* consulta *f*; (*meeting*) conferencia *f*; (*talks*) entrevista *f*.
confess [kən'fes] *v* confesar. **confession** *n* confesión *f*. **confessional** *n* (*rel*) confesionario *m*. **confessor** *n* confesor *m*; (*priest*) director espiritual *m*.
confetti [kən'feti] *n* confeti *m*.
confide [kən'faid] *v* confiar. **confidence** *n* (*trust*) confianza *f*; (*secret*) confidencia *f*; (*self-reliance*) seguridad en si mismo *f*. **confidence trick** estafa *f*. **confident** *adj* lleno de confianza. **confidential** *adj* confidencial. **confidentially** *adv* en confianza.
confine [kən'fain] *n* confín *m*; limite *m*. *v* confinar; limitar; (*med*) estar de parto. **confined** *adj* reducido. **confinement** *n* encierro *m*; (*med*) parto *m*.
confirm [kən'fəɪm] *v* confirmar; (*treaty*) ratificar. **confirmation** *n* confirmación *f*; ratificación *f*. **confirmed** *adj* confirmado; (*inveterate*) empedernido.
confiscate ['konfiskeit] *v* confiscar. **confiscation** *n* confiscación *f*.
conflict ['konflikt] *v* kən'flikt] *n* conflicto *m*. *v* luchar; (*clash*) chocar. **conflicting** *adj* contrapuesto.
conform [kən'foɪm] *v* conformarse. **conformist** *n*(*m+f*), *adj* conformista. **conformity** *n* conformidad *f*.
confound [kən'faund] *v* confundir; (*foil*) frustrar; (*disconcert*) desconcertar.
confront [kən'frʌnt] *v* hacer frente a; (*present with*) presentarse; (*bring face to face*) enfrentar, confrontar. **confrontation** *n* confrontación *f*.
confuse [kən'fjuːz] *v* confundir; desconcertar; complicar. **confused** *adj* confuso; perplejo. **confusing** *adj* confuso; desconcertante. **confusion** *n* confusión *f*, desorden *m*.
congeal [kən'dʒiːl] *v* congelar; coagular.
congenial [kən'dʒiːniəl] *adj* (*pleasant*) agradable; (*suitable*) conveniente; (*similar*) compatible.

congenital [kən'dʒenitl] *adj* congénito.
congested [kən'dʒestid] *adj* congestionado; (*crowded*) superpoblado. **congestion** *n* congestión *f*; superpoblación *f*.
conglomeration [kənˌglomə'reiʃən] *n* conglomeración *f*. **conglomerate** *v* conglomerar.
congratulate [kən'gratjuleit] *v* felicitar, dar la enhorabuena. **congratulations** *pl n* felicitaciones *f pl*; *interj* ¡felicidades!
congregate ['kongrigeit] *v* congregarse. **congregation** *n* congregación *f*, asamblea *f*; (*rel*) feligreses *m pl*.
congress ['kongres] *n* congreso *m*.
conical ['konikəl] *adj* cónico.
conifer ['konifə] *n* conífera *f*. **coniferous** *adj* conífero.
conjecture [kən'dʒektʃə] *n* conjetura *f*. *v* conjeturar. **conjectural** *adj* conjetural.
conjugal ['kondʒugəl] *adj* conyugal.
conjugate ['kondʒugeit] *v* conjugar. **conjugation** *n* conjugación *f*.
conjunction [kən'dʒʌŋkʃən] *n* (*gramm*) conjunción *f*. **conjunctive** *adj* conjuntivo.
conjunctivitis [kənˌdʒʌŋkti'vaitis] *n* conjuntivitis *f*.
conjure ['kʌndʒə; (*appeal to*) kən'dʒuə] *v* (*magic*) hacer juegos de manos; (*appeal to*) conjurar. **conjurer** *n* ilusionista *m*, prestidigitador *m*. **conjuring trick** juego de manos *m*.
connect [kə'nekt] *v* (*join*) unir, juntar; (*relate*) relacionar; (*elec*) conectar. **connected** *adj* (*joined*) conectado, unido; (*related*) emparentado; (*associated*) relacionado; coherente. **connection** *n* relación *f*; (*transport*) empalme *m*; (*elec*) conexión *f*; (*joint*) unión *f*; (*relative*) pariente *m*. **in connection with** con respecto a.
connoisseur [konə'səɪ] *n* experto, -a *m, f*, conocedor, -a *m, f*.
connotation [konə'teiʃən] *n* connotación *f*.
conquer ['koŋkə] *v* vencer, triunfar. **conquering** *adj* victorioso. **conqueror** *n* conquistador *m*, vencedor, -a *m, f*. **conquest** *n* conquista *f*.
conscience ['konʃəns] *n* conciencia *f*.
conscientious [konʃi'enʃəs] *adj* concienzudo. **conscientious objector** objetor de conciencia *m*. **conscientiousness** *n* escrupulosidad *f*.

conscious ['konʃəs] *adj* (*aware*) consciente; (*deliberate*) intencional. **be conscious** tener conocimiento. **be conscious of** tener conciencia de. **become conscious** volver en si. **become conscious of** darse cuenta de. **consciousness** *n* conocimiento *m*.

conscript ['konskript] *n* recluta *m*.

consecrate ['konsikreit] *v* consagrar. **consecration** *n* consagración *f*.

consecutive [kən'sekjutiv] *adj* consecutivo.

consensus [kən'sensəs] *n* consenso *m*.

consent [kən'sent] *n* consentimiento *m*. **by common consent** de acuerdo mutuo. *v* consentir (en).

consequence ['konsikwəns] *n* consecuencia *f*, resultado *m*. **consequent** *adj* consiguiente. **consequently** *adv* consecuentemente, por lo tanto.

conserve [kən'səːv] *v* conservar. *n* conserva *f*. **conservation** *n* conservación *f*. **conservative** *adj* conservador, moderado. **conservatory** *n* (*plants*) invernadero *m*; (*music*) conservatorio *m*.

consider [kən'sidə] *v* considerar; (*think*) pensar (en); (*study*) examinar; (*realize*) darse cuenta de; (*take into account*) tener en cuenta. **considerable** *adj* considerable. **considerably** *adv* considerablemente. **consideration** *n* consideración *f*; (*payment*) retribución *f*. **considerate** *adj* considerado.

consign [kən'sain] *v* consignar; (*send*) enviar; (*entrust*) confiar. **consignee** *n* consignatario *m*. **consignment** *n* consignación *f*; envío *m*.

consist [kən'sist] *v* consistir; (*made up of*) constar, componerse. **consistency** *n* (*density*) consistencia *f*; (*agreement*) conformidad *f*. **consistent** *adj* de acuerdo; firme. **consistently** *adv* constantemente; consecuentemente.

console¹ ['konsoul] *n* (*table, organ*) consola *f*; (*support*) ménsula *f*; mesa de control *f*; pupitre *m*.

console² [kən'soul] *v* consolar. **consolation** *n* consuelo *m*. **consolation prize** premio de consolación *m*.

consolidate [kən'solideit] *v* consolidar. **consolidation** *n* consolidación *f*.

consommé [kən'somei] *n* consomé *m*, caldo *m*.

consonant ['konsənənt] *n* consonante *f*. *adj* conforme.

consortium [kən'soːtiəm] *n* consorcio *m*.

conspicuous [kən'spikjuəs] *adj* visible; (*remarkable*) notable; (*attracting attention*) llamativo.

conspire [kən'spaiə] *v* conspirar. **conspiracy** *n* conspiración *f*. **conspirator** *n* conspirador, -a *m*, *f*.

constable ['kʌnstəbl] *n* policía *m*, guardia *m*. **constabulary** *n* policía *f*.

constant ['konstənt] *adj* (*continuous*) constante; (*faithful*) fiel, leal. **constancy** *n* constancia *f*; fidelidad *f*, lealtad *f*.

constellation [konstə'leifən] *n* constelación *f*.

constipation [konsti'peifən] *n* estreñimiento *m*. **constipated** *adj* estreñido.

constitute ['konstitjuːt] *v* constituir. **constituency** *n* distrito electoral *m*. **constituent** *n* (*component*) componente *m*; (*pol*) votante *m*. *adj* (*component*) constitutivo, constituyente; electoral. **constitution** *n* constitución *f*. **constitutional** *adj* constitucional. *n* (*coll*) paseo *m*.

constraint [kən'streint] *n* (*restriction*) encierro *m*; (*compulsion*) coacción *f*; (*inhibition*) turbación *f*. **constrain** *v* encerrar; (*compel*) constreñir; (*inhibit*) incomodar.

constrict [kən'strikt] *v* (*narrow*) estrechar; (*compress*) oprimir. **constricted** *adj* estrecho. **constriction** *n* constricción *f*.

construct [kən'strʌkt] *v* construir. **construction** *n* construcción *f*; (*structure*) estructura *f*; (*meaning*) interpretación *f*. **constructive** *adj* constructivo. **constructor** *n* constructor *m*.

consul ['konsəl] *n* cónsul *m*. **consular** *adj* consular. **consulate** *n* consulado *m*.

consult [kən'sʌlt] *v* consultar. **consultant** *n* (*adviser*) asesor *m*; (*med*) especialista *m*; (*tech*) consejero técnico *m*. **consultation** *n* consulta *f*. **consulting room** consultorio *m*.

consume [kən'sjuːm] *v* consumir; (*time*) tomar; (*food*) comerse; (*drink*) beberse. **consumer** *n* consumidor, -a *m*, *f*. **consumer goods** bienes de consumo *m pl*. **consumption** *n* consumo *m*; (*med: tuberculosis*) tisis *f*. **consumptive** *n*, *adj* (*med*) tísico, -a.

contact ['kontakt] *n* contacto *m*. **contact lens** lente de contacto *f*. *v* ponerse en contacto con.

contagious

contagious [kən'teidʒəs] *adj* contagioso.
contagion *n* contagio *m*.
contain [kən'tein] *v* contener. **container** *n* (*package*) envase *m*; (*receptacle*) recipiente *m*. (*transport*) contenedor *m*. **containment** *n* contención *f*.
contaminate [kən'tæməneit] *v* contaminar. **contamination** *n* contaminación *f*.
contemplate ['kontəmpleit] *v* contemplar; (*expect*) contar con; (*consider*) considerar. **contemplation** *n* contemplación *f*, meditación *f*; consideración *f*. **contemplative** *adj* contemplativo.
contemporary [kən'tempərəri] *nm, adj* contemporáneo.
contempt [kən'tempt] *n* desprecio *m*, desdén *m*. **contempt of court** desacato a los tribunales *m*. **hold in contempt** despreciar. **contemptible** *adj* despreciable, desdeñable. **contemptuous** *adj* despreciativo, desdeñoso.
contend [kən'tend] *v* (*struggle*) contender; (*compete*) competir; (*dispute*) disputir; (*affirm*) afirmar. **contender** *n* competidor, -a *m, f*. **contention** *n* contienda *f*; (*argument*) discusión *f*; (*opinion*) opinión *f*. **contentious** *adj* (*person*) pendenciero; (*issue*) discutible. **contentiousness** *n* carácter pendenciero *m*.
content¹ ['kontent] *n* contenido *m*.
content² [kən'tent] *adj* also **contented** contento, satisfecho. **be contented with** contentarse con. **contentment** *n* contento *m*.
contest [kən'test; *n* 'kontest] *v* (*dispute*) disputar; (*question*) impugnar. *n* (*struggle*) contienda *f*; (*competition*) competición *f*; (*controversy*) controversia *f*. **contestant** *n* contrincante *m*; (*election*) candidato, -a *m, f*.
context ['kontekst] *n* contexto *m*.
continent ['kontinənt] *n* continente *m*. **the Continent** el continente europeo *m*. **continental** *adj* continental.
contingency [kən'tindʒənsi] *n* (*possibility*) contingencia *f*, eventualidad *f*; (*event*) acontecimiento fortuito *m*. **contingent** *adj* (*accidental*) fortuito; (*probable*) contingente; (*incidental*) derivado; (*dependent*) subordinado; (*dependent on chance*) aleatorio.
continue [kən'tinjuː] *v* continuar, seguir; (*extend*) prolongar. **continual** *adj* continuo. **continually** *adv* constantemente.

continuation *n* continuación *f*. **continuity** *n* continuidad *f*; (*cinema, radio*) guión *m*. **continuous** *adj* continuo.
contort [kən'toːt] *v* retorcer, torcer. **contortion** *n* contorsión *f*; deformación *f*. **contortionist** *n* contorsionista *m, f*.
contour ['kontuə] *n* (*map*) curva de nivel *f*; (*outline*) contorno *m*.
contraband ['kontrəbænd] *n* contrabando *m*. *adj* de contrabando.
contraception [kontrə'sepʃən] *n* contracepción *f*. **contraceptive** *nm, adj* contraceptivo. **contraceptive pill** píldora contraceptiva *f*.
contract ['kontrakt; *v* kən'trakt] *n* contrato *m*. *v* (*shrink*) contraer; (*make a contract*) contratar; (*ailment*) coger. **contraction** *n* contracción *f*. **contractor** *n* contratista *m*. **contractual** *adj* contractual.
contradict [kontrə'dikt] *v* contradecir. **contradiction** *n* contradicción *f*. **contradictory** *adj* contradictorio.
contralto [kən'traltou] *n* contralto *m, f*.
contraption [kən'trapʃən] *n* (*coll*) chisme *m*.
contrary ['kontrəri] *adj* contrario. **on the contrary** al contrario.
contrast {kən'traːst; *n* 'kontraːst] *v* contrastar. *n* contraste *m*. **in contrast** por contraste. **in contrast to** a diferencia de. **contrasting** *adj* contrastante.
contravene [kontrə'viːn] *v* contravenir. **contravention** *n* contravención *f*.
contribute [kən'tribjut] *v* contribuir (con); (*write*) escribir; (*give information*) aportar. **contribution** *n* contribución *f*; artículo *m*; aportación *f*; (*to conversation*) intervención *f*. **contributive** *adj* contributivo. **contributor** *n* contribuyente *m*, *f*; (*writer*) colaborador, -a *m, f*. **contributory** *adj* contribuyente.
contrive [kən'traiv] *v* idear, inventar; (*manage*) conseguir. **contrived** *adj* artificial. **contrivable** *adj* realizable; imaginable. **contrivance** *n* aparato *m*; invención *f*; (*resourcefulness*) ingenio *m*.
control [kən'troul] *n* control *m*; autoridad *f*; dominación *f*; (*standard of comparison*) testigo *m*. **remote control** mando a distancia *m*. **controls** *pl n* mandos *m pl*. *v* controlar; tener autoridad sobre; (*direct*) dirigir; (*regulate*) regular; (*vehicle*)

manejar. **controller** *n* director *m*. **air traffic controller** controlador del tráfico aéreo *m*. **controlling** *adj* predominante; (*decisive*) determinante.

controversy [kən'trovəsi] *n* controversia *f*. **controversial** *adj* discutible.

convalesce [konvə'les] *v* convalecer. **convalescence** *n* convalecencia *f*.

convector [kən'vektə] *n* estufa de convección *f*. **convection** *n* convección *f*.

convenience [kən'viɪnjəns] *n* conveniencia *f*; (*comfort*) comodidad *f*; (*advantage*) ventaja *f*; (*useful object*) dispositivo útil *m*. **at your convenience** cuando le sea posible. **public convenience** servicios *m pl*. **convenient** *adj* (*handy*) cómodo; (*suitable*) conveniente; (*place*) bien situado; (*time*) oportuno.

convent ['konvənt] *n* convento *m*.

convention [kən'venʃən] *n* (*usage*) convención *f*; (*assembly*) asamblea *f*; (*international agreement*) convenio *m*. **conventions** *n pl* conveniencias *f pl*. **conventional** *adj* (*not original*) convencional; (*traditional*) clásico.

converge [kən'vəɪdʒ] *v* convergir, converger. **convergence** *n* convergencia *f*. **converging** *adj* convergente.

converse[1] [kən'vəɪs] *v* conversar, hablar. **conversant** *adj* versado, familiarizado. **conversation** *n* conversación *f*.

converse[2] ['konvəɪs] *n* lo opuesto *m*. *adj* opuesto, contrario.

convert ['konvəɪt; *v* kən'vəɪt] *n* converso, -a *m*, *f*. *v* convertir. **conversion** *n* conversión *f*; transformación *f*.

convertible [kən'vəɪtəbl] *adj* convertible; transformable. *n* (*mot*) descapotable *m*.

convex ['konveks] *adj* convexo.

convey [kən'vei] *v* (*carry*) llevar, transportar; (*suggest*) sugerir, dar a entender; (*transmit*) transmitir; (*meaning*) expresar. **conveyance** *n* transporte *m*; transmisión *f*; (*deed*) escritura de traspaso *f*. **conveyancer** *n* notario que hace escritura de traspaso *m*. **conveyancing** *n* redacción de una escritura de traspaso *f*.

convict ['konvikt; *v* kən'vikt] *n* presidiario, -a *m*, *f*. *v* (*prove guilty*) condenar; (*betray*) traicionar.

conviction [kən'vikʃən] *n* condena *f*; (*belief*) convicción *f*.

convince [kən'vins] *v* convencer. **convincing** *adj* convincente.

convivial [kən'viviəl] *adj* alegre, sociable, festivo.

convoy ['konvoi] *n* convoy *m*. *v* convoyar.

convulsion [kən'vʌlʃən] *n* (*med*) convulsión *f*; (*laughter*) carcajadas *f pl*. **convulse** *v* convulsionar.

cook [kuk] *v* cocinar; (*coll*: *the books*) falsificar. *n* cocinero, -a *m*, *f*. **cooker** *n* cocina *f*; olla *f*. **pressure cooker** olla de presión *f*. **cookery** *n* arte de cocina *m*; cocción *f*; cocina *f*. **cookery book** libro de cocina *m*. **do the cooking** guisar.

cool [kuɪl] *adj* fresco; (*calm*) tranquilo; (*unenthusiastic*) frío. *v* enfriar; calmar. **cooler** *n* enfriador *m*. **cooling** *adj* refrescante. **cooling system** *n* sistema de refrigeración *m*. **coolish** *adj* fresquito. **coolly** *adv* fríamente; tranquilamente. **coolness** *n* frescor *m*; frialdad *f*; serenidad *f*; sangre fría *f*.

coop [kuɪp] *n* (*poultry*) gallinero *m*. **coop up** encerrar.

cooperate [kou'opəreit] *v* cooperar. **cooperation** *n* cooperación *f*. **cooperative** *adj* cooperativo.

coordinate [kou'oɪdineit] *n* coordenada *f*. *adj* igual. *v* coordinar. **coordination** *n* coordinación *f*.

cope[1] [koup] *v* arreglárselas; dar abasto; poder con.

cope[2] [koup] *n* (*rel*) capa pluvial *f*.

Copenhagen [koupən'heigən] *n* Copenhague.

copious ['koupiəs] *adj* copioso, abundante.

copper[1] ['kopə] *n* (*metal*) cobre *m*. *adj* de cobre; (*colour*) cobrizo. **copper plate** plancha de cobre *f*.

copper[2] ['kopə] *n* *also* cop (*slang*) poli *m*.

copulate ['kopjuɪleit] *v* copular. **copulation** *n* cópula *f*.

copy ['kopi] *n* copia *f*; (*book*) ejemplar *m*; (*pattern*) modelo *m*; (*reportage*) asunto *m*. **carbon copy** papel carbón *m*. **fair copy** copia en limpio *f*. **rough copy** borrador *m*. *v* copiar; imitar. **copyright** *n* propiedad literaria.

coral ['korəl] *n* coral *m*. *adj* coralino.

cord [koɪd] *n* (*string, rope*) cuerda *f*; (*insulated wire*) cordón *m*. **spinal cord** médula espinal *f*. **umbilical cord** cordón umbilical *m*. **vocal cords** cuerdas vocales *f pl*.

cordial ['koɪdiəl] *adj*, *nm* cordial. **cordiality** *n* cordialidad *f*.

cordon ['kɔɪdn] *n* cordón *m*. **cordon off** acordonar.

corduroy ['kɔɪdəroɪ] *n* pana *f*.

core [kɔɪ] *n* (*fruit*) corazón *m*; (*geol*) núcleo; (*fig*) centro *m*, esencia *f*. *v* quitar el corazón de.

cork [kɔɪk] *n* (*bot*) corcho *m*; (*stopper*) tapón *m*. **cork tree** alcornoque *m*. **corktipped** *adj* con boquilla de corcho. *v* taponar. **uncork** *v* (*bottle*) descorchar. **corked** *adj* (*bottle*) taponado; (*wine*) que sabe a corcho. **corkscrew** *n* sacacorchos *m invar*.

corn¹ [kɔɪn] *n* (*wheat*) trigo *m*; (*maize*) maíz *m*; (*cereals*) granos cereales *m pl*. **corn on the cob** maíz en la mazorca *m*.

corn² [kɔɪn] *n* (*med*) callo *m*.

corner ['kɔɪnə] *n* (*inside angle*) rincón *m*; (*outside angle*) esquina *f*; (*of an object*) pico *m*. **cut corners** tomar atajos. *v* poner en un aprieto; (*accost*) abordar; (*mot*) tomar una curva; (*comm*) monopolizar.

cornet ['kɔɪnit] *n* corneta *f*; (*ice cream*) cucurucho *m*.

coronary ['kɔrənəri] *adj* coronario. **coronary thrombosis** trombosis coronaria *f*.

coronation [kɔrə'neiʃən] *n* coronación *f*.

corporal¹ ['kɔɪpərəl] *adj* corporal. **corporal punishment** castigo corporal *m*.

corporal² ['kɔɪpərəl] *n* (*mil*) cabo *m*.

corporation [ˌkɔɪpə'reiʃən] *n* corporación *f*; sociedad anónima *f*. **municipal corporation** ayuntamiento *m*. **corporate** *adj* colectivo, corporativo.

corps [kɔɪ] *n* cuerpo *m*. **corps de ballet** cuerpo de ballet. **diplomatic corps** cuerpo diplomático.

corpse [kɔɪps] *n* cadáver *m*.

correct [kə'rekt] *adj* (*accurate*) exacto; (*behaviour*) correcto; (*right*) justo. *v* corregir. **correction** *n* corrección *f*. **corrective** *adj* correctivo. **correctness** *n* corrección *f*; exactitud *f*; (*judgment*) rectitud *f*.

correlate ['kɔrəleit] *v* correlacionar. **correlation** *n* correlación *f*.

correspond [kɔrə'spond] *v* corresponder; (*write*) escribirse. **correspondence** *n* correspondencia *f*. **correspondent** *n* corresponsal *m*; (*newspaper*) corresponsal *m, f*.

corridor ['kɔridɔɪ] *n* pasillo *m*, corredor *m*.

corroborate [kə'robəreit] *v* corroborar. **corroboration** *n* corroboración *f*.

corrode [kə'roud] *v* corroer. **corrosion** *n* corrosión *f*. **corrosive** *adj* corrosivo.

corrugated ['kɔrəgeitid] *adj* ondulado.

corrupt [kə'rʌpt] *adj* corrupto; corrompido; (*rotten*) estragado; (*perverted*) pervertido; (*bribable*) venal. *v* corromper; (*bribe*) sobornar. **corruptible** *adj* corruptible. **corruption** *n* corrupción *f*.

corset ['kɔɪset] *n* faja *f*.

Corsica ['kɔɪsikə] *n* Córcega *f*. **Corsican** *n, adj* corso, -a *m, f*.

cosmetic [koz'metik] *nm, adj* cosmético.

cosmic ['kozmik] *adj* cósmico.

cosmopolitan [kozmə'politən] *n(m+f), adj* cosmopolita.

*cost [kost] *n* costo *m*, coste *m*; (*price*) precio *m*; (*expenses*) gastos *m pl*. **costs** *pl n* (*law*) costas *f pl*. **at all costs** cueste lo que cueste. **cost of living** coste de vida *m*. **to one's cost** a expensas de uno. *v* costar; valer. **costly** *adj* caro.

Costa Rica [ˌkostə'riːkə] *n* Costa Rica. **Costa Rican** *n(m+f), adj* costarriquense; *n, adj* costarriqueño, -a *m, f*.

costume ['kostjuːm] *n* traje *m*. **bathing costume** traje de baño. **costume jewellery** bisutería *f*.

cosy ['kouzi] *adj* confortable; (*place*) acogedor.

cot [kot] *n* cuna *f*.

cottage ['kotidʒ] *n* casa de campo *f*; chalet *m*. **cottage cheese** requesón *m*.

cotton ['kotn] *n* algodón *m*. *adj* de algodón. **cotton-wool** *n* algodón hidrófilo *m*.

couch [kautʃ] *n* sofá *m*; (*bed*) lecho *m*. *v* (*express*) expresar.

cough [kof] *n* tos *f*. *v* toser. **cough up** (*coll*) cascar.

could [kud] *V* can¹.

council ['kaunsəl] *n* consejo *m*; (*assembly*) ayuntamiento *m*. **council house** vivienda protegida *f*. **town council** concejo municipal *m*. **councillor** *n* concejal *m*.

counsel ['kaunsəl] *n* consejo *m*; (*lawyer*) abogado *m*; (*legal adviser*) asesor jurídico *m*. *v* aconsejar; pedir consejo.

count¹ [kaunt] *v* contar, calcular; (*consider*) considerar. **count against** ir en contra de. **count for** valer por. **countable** *adj* contable. **countdown** *n* cuenta atrás *f*. **countless** *adj* incontable. *n* cuenta *f*, cálculo *m*; (*sum*) total *m*; (*votes*) escrutinio *m*.

43

craft

count² [kaunt] n (noble) conde m. countess n condesa f.
countenance ['kauntinəns] n semblante m. cara f. v (approve) aprobar; (support) apoyar.
counter¹ ['kauntə] n (disc) ficha f; (table top) mostrador m. contador m. Geiger counter contador Geiger m. under the counter bajo mano.
counter² ['kauntə] adj (opposed) contrario, opuesto. v contraatacar; oponerse. go counter to ir en contra de.
counterattack ['kauntərə,tak] n contraataque m. v contraatacar.
counterfeit ['kauntəfit] adj falso, falsificado. v falsificar. n falsificación f.
counterfoil ['kauntə,foil] n talón m.
counterpart ['kauntə,pait] n contraparte f.
country ['kʌntri] n (state) país m; (out of town) campo. country estate finca f. country house casa de campo f. countryman n campesino m; compatriota m.
countryside n campo m; (landscape) paisaje m.
county ['kaunti] n condado m. county council diputación provincial f.
coup [kuɪ] n golpe m. coup d'état golpe de estado m.
couple ['kʌpl] n par m; (married, engaged, etc.) pareja f. v emparejar; (associate) asociar; (vehicles) enganchar; (elec) conectar; (copulate) copular.
coupon ['kuɪpon] n cupón m; (pools) boleto m.
courage ['kʌridʒ] n valor m, valentía f. pluck up courage armarse de valor. take courage cobrar ánimo. courageous adj valiente.
courgette [kuə'ʒet] n calabacín m.
courier ['kuriə] n guía m, f; agente de turismo m, f; mensajero, -a m, f.
course [kois] n (direction) dirección f, rumbo m; (progress) curso m; (way, means) camino m; (action, conduct) línea f; (meal) plato m; (track) pista f; (golf) campo m. in due course a su debido tiempo. main course plato fuerte m. of course claro, por supuesto. set course for hacer rumbo a. v (hunt) cazar; (run: liquid) correr.
court [koit] n (royalty) corte f; (alley) callejón sin salida m; (law) audiencia f, tribunal m; (sport) cancha f. court order orden judicial f. go to court acudir a los tribunales. courtyard n patio m. v (woo)

cortejar, hacer la corte a; buscar; pedir, solicitar. courtier n cortesano m. courtly adj cortés. court-martial n consejo de guerra m. courtship n noviazgo m.
courteous ['kɔitiəs] adj cortés. courtesy n cortesía f.
cousin ['kʌzn] n primo, -a m, f. first cousin primo, -a carnal m, f.
cove [kouv] n cala f; (slang) tío m.
cover ['kʌvə] n cubierta f; (lid) tapa f; (bed) colcha f; (table) tapete m; (refuge) refugio m; (parcel) envoltura f; (envelope) sobre m; (pretence) excusa f; (protection) amparo m. cover charge precio del cubierto m. take cover ponerse a cubierto. v cubrir, tapar. coverage n alcance m.
cow [kau] n vaca f; (female animal) hembra f. v intimidar. cowboy n vaquero m, (Amer) gaucho m. cowshed n establo m.
cowslip n prímula f.
coward ['kauəd] n cobarde m, f. cowardice n cobardía f. cowardly adj cobarde.
cower ['kauə] v encojerse; agacharse.
coy [koi] adj (shy) tímido; (demure) remilgado.
crab [krab] n cangrejo m. crab apple manzana silvestre f. crabbed adj (badtempered) malhumorado; (writing) indescifrable.
crack [krak] n (noise) restallido m, chasquido m; (opening) abertura f; (split) raja f; (in walls, etc.) hendidura f; (slit) rendija f; (blow) golpe m; (coll: joke) chiste m. crack of dawn al amanecer. have a crack at intentar. v restallar, chasquear; golpear; (break) romper; (a nut) cascar; hender; rajar; (burst) reventar; (give in) ceder; (break down) hundirse; (coll: joke) bromear; (coll: safe) forzar. get cracking darse prisa. crackpot n, adj (coll) chiflado, -a m, f.
cracker ['krakə] n (Christmas) sorpresa f; (firework) buscapiés m invar; (biscuit) galleta f.
crackle ['krakl] n crepitación f, crujido m. v crepitar, crujir. crackling n (cookery) chicharrón m.
cradle ['kreidl] n cuna f; sorporte m. v acunar; (in one's arms) mecer; sopartar.
craft [kraift] n (trade) trabajo manual m; (skill) arte m; (guild) gremio m; (cunning) astucia f, maña f; (ship) embarcación f; (aircraft) avión m. craftily adv astutamente. craftsman n artesano m.

cram 44

craftsmanship n artesanía f. **crafty** adj astuto, socarrón.

cram [kram] v (fill up) aborratar; (force in) meter a la fuerza; (for exam) empollar.

cramp [kramp] n (med) calambre m. v dar calambre a. **cramped** adj (crowded) apiñado; (writing) apretado.

cranberry ['kranbəri] n arándano m.

crane [krein] n (hoist) grúa f; (bird) grulla f. v (neck) estirar.

crank [kraŋk] n (tech) manivela f; (fool) chiflado, -a m, f. v arrancar con la manivela. **crankcase** n cárter m. **crankiness** n irritabilidad f; excentricidad f; chifladura f. **crankshaft** n cigüeñal m.

crap [krap] n (slang: nonsense) disparate; (impol) mierda f. v (impol) cagar.

crash [kraʃ] n accidente m, choque m; (noise) estrépito m; (aircraft) caída f; (business) quiebra f. **crash course** curso intensivo m. **crash helmet** casco protector m. v chocar; caer; quebrar; (make a loud noise) retumbar. **crash-land** hacer un aterrizaje de emergencia.

crate [kreit] n cajón de embalaje m. v embalar.

crater ['kreitə] n cráter m.

crave [kreiv] v (desire) ansiar; (beg) suplicar; (attention) reclamar. **craving** n ansia f.

crawl [krɔːl] v arrastrarse, andar a gatas; (move slowly) andar lentamente. n arrastramiento m; marcha lenta f.

crayfish ['kreifiʃ] n ástaco m, cangrejo de río m.

crayon ['kreiən] n lápiz de tiza m. v dibujar al pastel.

craze [kreiz] n (wild enthusiasm) locura f; (fad) manía f; (fashion) moda f. v enloquecer. **craziness** n locura f. **crazy** adj loco.

creak [kriːk] n crujido m. v crujir. **creaky** adj que cruje.

cream [kriːm] n nata f, crema f. **whipped cream** nata batida. adj color crema. v (beat) batir; (skim) desnatar. **cream cheese** queso de nata m.

crease [kriːs] n (fold) pliegue m; (wrinkle) arruga f; (trousers) raya f. **crease-resistant** adj inarrugable. v plegar; arrugar; hacer la raya de.

create [kri'eit] v crear. **creation** n creación f. **creator** n creador, -a m, f.

credentials [kri'denʃəlz] pl n credenciales f pl.

credible ['kredəbl] adj creíble. **credibility** n credibilidad f.

credit[1] ['kredit] n crédito m; (comm) haber m; (prestige) honor m. **credits** pl n (film) ficha técnica f sing. **credit balance** saldo acreedor m. **credit card** tarjeta de crédito f. **credit rating** solvabilidad f. **on credit** a plazos. **we do not give credit** no se fía.

credit[2] ['kredit] v (believe) creer; (fig) atribuir; (an account) abonar en cuenta.

creditable adj (believable) digno de crédito; (praiseworthy) encomiable; (well spoken of) de buena reputación. **creditably** adv honrosamente. **creditor** n acreedor, -a m, f.

credulous ['kredjuləs] adj crédulo.

creed [kriːd] n credo m.

***creep** [kriːp] v deslizarse, arrastrarse; (flesh) ponerse a uno la carne de gallina. n (coll) pelotillero, -a m, f. **creepy** adj horripilante.

cremate [kri'meit] v incinerar. **cremation** n incineración f. **crematorium** n horno crematorio m.

crescent ['kresnt] n medialuna f, luna creciente f. adj creciente.

cress [kres] n berro m.

crest [krest] n (on animal's head, wave) cresta f; (hill) cima f, cumbre f; (heraldry) timbre m. **crested** adj crestado. **crestfallen** adj alicaído.

crevice ['krevis] n grieta f; hendedura f.

crew [kruː] n (body of workers) equipo m; (ship, aircraft) tripulación f; (mob) banda f. **ground crew** personal de tierra m.

crib [krib] n (rack) pesebre m; (small cot) cuna f; (coll: exam) chuleta f. v plagiar.

cricket[1] ['krikit] n (insect) grillo m.

cricket[2] ['krikit] n (sport) criquet m.

crime [kraim] n crimen m; criminalidad f. **criminal** nm, adj criminal.

crimson ['krimzn] nm, adj carmesí.

cringe [krindʒ] v agacharse, encogerse. **cringing** adj servil.

crinkle ['kriŋkl] n arruga f. v arrugarse.

cripple ['kripl] n, adj tullido, -a m, f. v (person) tullir; (object) estropear; (fig) paralizar.

crisis ['kraisis] n pl -ses crisis f invar.

crisp [krisp] adj fresco; (bread) curruscante; (style) crespo; (snow) crujiente; (talk) animado. v encrespar, rizar. **potato**

crisp patata frita a la inglesa *f*. **crispness** *n* encrespado *m*.

criterion [krai'tiəriən] *n pl* **-a** criterio *m*.

criticize ['kriti̦saiz] *v* criticar. **critic** (*faultfinder*) criticón, -ona *m*, *f*; (*reviewer*) crítico *m*. **critical** *adj* crítico. **criticism** *n* crítica *f*.

crochet ['krəʊʃei] *n* croché *m*, ganchillo *m*. *v* hacer a ganchillo.

crockery ['krokəri] *n* loza *f*, vajilla *f*.

crocodile ['krokə̦dail] *n* cocodrilo *m*.

crocus ['krəʊkəs] *n* azafrán *m*.

crook [kruk] *n* (*shepherd's*) cayado *m*; (*bishop's*) báculo *m*; (*coll*) ladrón *m*, timador *m*.

crooked ['krukid] *adj* (*bent*) curvado; (*twisted*) torcido; (*path*) sinuoso; (*nose*) ganchudo; (*coll*) poco limpio. **crookedness** *n* sinuosidad *f*; (*coll*) falta de honradez *f*.

crop [krop] *n* (*harvest*) cosecha *f*; (*cultivated produce*) cultiva *f*; (*whip*) fusta *f*; (*bird*) buche *m*; (*haircut*) corte de pelo *m*. **crop rotation** rotación de cultivos *f*. *v* (*graze*) pacer; (*ears*) desorejar; (*tail*) cortar la cola de; (*hair*) cortar muy corto. **come a cropper** darse un batacazo.

croquet ['krəʊkei] *n* croquet *m*.

cross [kros] *n* cruz *f*; (*breeding*) cruce *f*. **make the sign of the cross** santiguarse. *adj* cruzado; (*angry*) enfadado. *v* (*move*) atravesar; (*limbs*) cruzar; (*oppose*) contrariar; (*mark*) marcar con una cruz. **cross out** tachar. **cross one's mind** ocurrírsele a.

cross-country *adj* a campo traviesa.

cross-current *n* contracorriente *f*.

cross-examination *n* repregunta *f*.

cross-eyed *adj* bizco.

crossfire ['kroșfaiə] *n* fuego cruzado *m*.

crossing ['krosiŋ] *n* (*intersection*) cruce *f*; (*voyage*) travesía *f*; (*pedestrian*) paso de peatones *m*.

cross-purposes *pl n* fines opuestos *m pl*.

cross-reference *n* remisión *f*.

crossroads ['kroșroudz] *pl n* cruce *f sing*; (*fig*) encrucijada *f sing*.

cross section *n* sección transversal *f*.

crossword ['kroșwəd] *n* crucigrama *m*.

crotchet ['krotʃit] *n* (*music*) negra *f*. **crotchety** *adj* de mal genio.

crouch [krautʃ] *v* agacharse, encogerse.

crow¹ [krou] *n* (*bird*) cuervo *m*. **as the crow flies** en línea recta. **crowbar** *n* palanca *f*.

crow² [krou] *v* cantar; cacarear. *n* cacareo *m*.

crowd [kraud] *n* muchedumbre *f*, multitud *f*. *v* amontonar; congregarse. **crowded** *adj* lleno.

crown [kraun] *n* corona *f*; (*hat*) copa *f*; (*hill*) cumbre *f*; (*head*) coronilla *f*. **crown jewels** joyas reales *f pl*. **crown prince** príncipe heredero *m*. *v* coronar. **to crown it all** para rematarlo todo. **crowning** *adj* supremo.

crucial ['kruʃəl] *adj* crucial, decisivo.

crucify ['krusi̦fai] *v* crucificar. **crucifix** *n* crucifijo *m*. **crucifixion** *n* crucifixión *f*.

crude [kruid] *adj* (*raw*) crudo; (*steel*) bruto; (*oil*) sin refinar; (*vulgar*) basto; (*ill-made*) tosco. **crudeness**, **crudity** *n* crudeza *f*; tosquedad *f*.

cruel ['kruəl] *adj* cruel. **cruelty** *n* crueldad *f*.

cruise [kruiz] *n* crucero *m*. *v* hacer un crucero; (*patrol*) patrullar; (*at cruising speed*) ir a una velocidad de crucero. **cruiser** *n* (*naut*) crucero *m*.

crumb [krʌm] *n* migaja *f*, miga *f*.

crumble ['krʌmbl] *v* desmenuzar; desmigar. **crumbly** *adj* desmenuzable.

crumple ['krʌmpl] *v* arrugar, ajar. **crumple up** desplomarse.

crunch [krʌntʃ] *n* crujido *m*; (*coll*) punto decisivo *m*. *v* crujir; mascar. **crunchy** *adj* crujiente.

crusade [kru'seid] *n* cruzada *f*; (*fig*) campaña *f*. *v* hacer una cruzada. **crusader** *n* cruzado *m*.

crush [krʌʃ] *n* aplastamiento *m*; (*crowd*) aglomeración *f*; (*squeeze*) apretón *m*. **have a crush on** (*coll*) estar loco perdido por. *v* aplastar; apretar; (*pulverize*) machacar; (*overwhelm*) abrumar. **crushing** *adj* aplastante.

crust [krʌst] *n* (*of a loaf*) corteza *f*. **upper crust** la flor y nata *f*. **crusty** *adj* de corteza dura; (*coll*) brusco.

crutch [krʌtʃ] *n* (*support*) muleta *f*; (*fig*) apoyo *m*.

crux [krʌks] *n* quid *m*.

cry [krai] *n* grito *m*. *v* (*call*) gritar; (*weep*) llorar. **cry out** clamar.

crypt [kript] *n* cripta *f*. **cryptic** *adj* secreto; enigmático.

crystal ['kristl] *n* cristal *m*. *adj* de cristal. **crystal clear** cristalino. **crystallize** *v* cristalizar.

cub [kʌb] *n* (*bear, lion, tiger, wolf*) cachorro *m*; (*other animals*) cría *f.* **cub scout** niño explorador *m.*
Cuba ['kjuːbə] *n* Cuba *f.* **Cuban** *n, adj* cubano, -a.
cube [kjuːb] *n* (*math*) cubo *m*; (*sugar, etc.*) terrón *m.* *v* (*math*) cubicar. **cube root** raíz cúbica *f.* **cubic** *adj* cúbico.
cubicle ['kjuːbikl] *n* cubículo *m*; (*for sleeping*) cubilla *f*; (*for changing*) caseta *f.*
cuckoo ['kukuː] *n* cuco *m*, cuclillo *m.*
cucumber [kjuˈkʌmbə] *n* pepino *m.*
cuddle ['kʌdl] *n* abrazo *m.* *v* abrazar. **cuddly** *adj* mimoso.
cue¹ [kjuː] *n* (*theatre*) señal *f*; entrada *f.* *v* indicar.
cue² [kjuː] *n* (*billiards*) taco *m.*
cuff¹ [kʌf] *n* (*shirt*) puño *m.* **cufflinks** *pl n* gemelos *m pl.* **off the cuff** de improviso.
cuff² [kʌf] *n* (*hit*) bofetada *f.* *v* abofetear.
culinary ['kʌlinəri] *adj* culinario.
culminate ['kʌlmiˌneit] *v* culminar. **culmination** *n* culminación *f.*
culprit ['kʌlprit] *n* culpado, -a *m, f*; culpable *m, f.*
cult [kʌlt] *n* culto *m.*
cultivate ['kʌltiˌveit] *v* cultivar. **cultivated** *adj* (*land*) cultivado; (*person*) culto. **cultivation** *n* cultivo *m.*
culture ['kʌltʃə] *n* cultura *f*; cultivo *m.* **cultured** *adj* culto.
cumbersome ['kʌmbəsəm] *adj* molesto; (*annoying*) incómodo.
cunning ['kʌniŋ] *adj* (*sly*) taimado; (*clever*) astuto; (*skilful*) mañoso. *n* astucia *f*; maña *f.*
cup [kʌp] *n* taza *f*; (*prize*) copa *f.*
cupboard ['kʌbəd] *n* armario *m.*
curate ['kjuərət] *n* cura *m.*
curator [kjuəˈreitə] *n* conservador, -a *m, f.*
curb [kəːb] *v* contener, refrenar. *n* (*obstacle*) estorbo *m*; (*fig*) freno *m.*
curdle ['kəːdl] *v* cuajar, cuajarse. **curd** cuajada *f.*
cure [kjuə] *n* (*course of treatment; smoking food*) cura *f*; (*remedy*) remedio *m*; (*of leather*) curtido *m*; (*salting*) salazón *m.* *v* curar; remediar; salar; curtir. **cure-all** *n* curalotodo *m.*
curfew ['kəːfjuː] *n* toque de queda *m.*
curious ['kjuəriəs] *adj* curioso. **curiosity** *n* curiosidad *f.*
curl [kəːl] *n* (*hair*) bucle *m*; (*smoke*) voluta *f*; (*twist*) torcedura *f*; serpenteo *m.*
v (*hair*) rizar. **curl oneself up** hacerse un ovillo. **curler** *n* rulo *m.* **curly** *adj* rizado; sinuoso; en espiral.
currant ['kʌrənt] *n* (*dried grape*) pasa *f*; (*berry*) grosella *f*; (*bush*) grosellero *m.*
currency ['kʌrənsi] *n* moneda *f*; (*general use*) uso corriente *m.*
current ['kʌrənt] *n* corriente *f*; curso *m.* **alternating/direct current** corriente alterna/continua *f.* *adj* (*general*) corriente, prevalente; (*now*) actual; (*accepted*) admitido. **current account** cuenta corriente *f.* **current affairs** actualidades *f pl.* **current rate of exchange** cambio del día *m.* **current year** año en curso. **currently** *adv* corrientemente; actualmente.
curry ['kʌri] *n* cari *m*, curry *m.* *v* preparar con cari. **curry powder** especias en polvo *f pl.*
curse [kəːs] *n* maldición *f.* *v* maldecir; (*swear*) decir palabrotas; (*blaspheme*) blasfemar.
curt [kəːt] *adj* brusco. **curtness** *n* brusquedad *f.*
curtail [kəːˈteil] *v* (*cut short*) abreviar; (*expenses*) reducir. **curtailment** *n* abreviación *f*; reducción *f.*
curtain ['kəːtn] *n* cortina *f*; (*theatre*) telón *m.* **curtain call** llamada a escena *f.* **draw the curtain** correr la cortina. *v* poner cortinas en; encubrir.
curtsy ['kəːtsi] *n* reverencia *f.* *v* hacer una reverencia.
curve [kəːv] *n* curva *f*; vuelta *f.* *v* doblar; encorvar. **curvature** *n* curvatura *f*; (*earth*) esfericidad *f*; (*spine*) encorvamiento *m.* **curved** *adj* curvo; doblado.
cushion ['kuʃən] *n* cojín *m*, almohadón *m.* *v* amortiguar, acolchar.
custard ['kʌstəd] *n* natillas *f pl.*
custody ['kʌstədi] *n* custodia *f*, guardia *f*; prisión *f.* **in custody** bajo custodia. **take into custody** detener. **custodian** *n* custodio *m*; guardián, -ana *m, f.*
custom ['kʌstəm] *n* (*habit*) costumbre *f*; (*customers*) clientela *f sing.* **customs** *n* derechos de aduana *m pl.* **customary** *adj* de costumbre. **custom-built** *adj* hecho de encargo. **customer** *n* cliente *m, f.*
*cut [kʌt] *n* corte *m*; (*wound*) herida *f*; (*notch*) muesca *f*; (*reduction*) reducción *f*; (*med*) incisión *f.* **short cut** atajo *m.* **cut-and-dried** previsto. **cut and thrust** la lucha *f.* *v* cortar; reducir; (*reap*) segar; (*shorten*) acortar. **cut short** cortar en

seco. *adj* cortado; reducido. **cut-price** *adj* a precio reducido.
cute [kjuːt] *adj* (*attractive*) mono, lindo; (*clever*) astuto. **cuteness** *n* monería *f*; astucia *f*.
cuticle ['kjuːtikl] *n* cutícula *f*.
cutlery ['kʌtləri] *n* cubiertos *m pl*.
cutlet ['kʌtlit] *n* chuleta *f*.
cycle ['saikl] *n* ciclo *m*; bicicleta *f*. *v* pasar por un ciclo; ir en bicicleta. **cyclical** *adj* cíclico. **cycling** *n* ciclismo *m*. **cyclist** *n* ciclista *m*, *f*.
cyclone ['saikloun] *n* ciclón *m*.
cylinder ['silində] *n* cilindro *m*. **cylinder block** bloque de cilindros *m*. **cylindrical** *adj* cilíndrico.
cymbal ['simbəl] *n* címbalo *m*, platillo *m*.
cynic ['sinik] *n*, *adj* cínico, -a *m*, *f*. **cynical** *adj* cínico. **cynicism** *n* cinicismo *m*.
cypress ['saiprəs] *n* ciprés *m*.
Cyprus ['saiprəs] *n* Chipre. **Cypriot** *n*(*m*+*f*), *adj* chipriota.
cyst [sist] *n* quiste *m*. **cystitis** *n* cistitis *f*.
Czechoslovakia [ˌtʃekəsləˈvakiə] *n* Checoslovaquia *f*. **Czechoslovakian, Czechoslovak, Czech** *n*, *adj* checoslovaco, -a.

D

dab [dab] *n* (*light blow*) golpe ligero *m*; (*touch*) toque *m*; (*bit*) pizca *f*. *v* golpear ligeramente; dar unos toques de. *adj* **be a dab hand at** ser un hacha en.
dabble ['dabl] *v* (*splash*) salpicar; (*wet*) mojar. **dabble in** (*water*) chapotear; (*participation*) meterse en.
dad [dad] *n* (*coll*) papá *m*.
daffodil ['dafədil] *n* narciso *m*.
daft [daːft] *adj* (*coll*) tonto.
dagger ['dagə] *n* daga *f*; puñal *m*.
daily ['deili] *adj* diario, cotidiano. *adv* diariamente, cada día. *n* (*coll: newspaper*) diario *m*.
dainty ['deinti] *adj* (*taste*) delicado, fino; (*fussy*) difícil. **daintiness** *n* delicadeza *f*; elegancia *f*.
dairy ['deəri] *n* lechería *f*. **dairy cattle** vacas lecheras *f pl*. **dairy farm** granja de vacas *f*. **dairy products** productos lácteos *m pl*.

daisy ['deizi] *n* margarita *f*.
dam [dam] *n* (*barrier*) dique *m*; (*reservoir*) embalse *m*; (*zool*) madre *f*. *v* construir un dique; embalsar.
damage ['damidʒ] *n* daño *m*; (*fig*) perjuicio *m*. **damages** *pl n* (*law*) daños y perjuicios *m pl*. *v* dañar; perjudicar; (*spoil*) estropear.
damn [dam] *v* (*condemn*) condenar; (*curse*) maldecir. *damn!* (*interj*) ¡mechacis! **damnable** *adj* condenable; detestable. **damnation** *n* condenación *f*; (*interj*) ¡maldición! **damned** *adj* condenado; (*coll*) maldito; tremendo. *adv* sumamente.
damp [damp] *adj* húmedo. *n* humedad *f*. **damp course** aislante hidráfugo *m*. *v* (*also* **dampen**) humedecer; (*extinguish*) apagar, sofocar; (*discourage*) desanimar; (*sound*) amortiguar. **damper** *n* humedecedor *m*; (*chimney*) regulador *m*. **put a damper on** caer como un jarro de agua fría en.
damson ['damzən] *n* (*fruit*) ciruela damascena *f*; (*tree*) ciruelo damasceno *m*.
dance [daːns] *n* baile *m*; (*ritual*) danza *f*. **dance band** orquesta de baile *f*. **dance floor** pista de baile *f*. **dance hall** sala de baile *f*. *v* bailar. **dancer** *n* bailarín, -ina *m*, *f*.
dandelion ['dandiˌlaiən] *n* diente de león *m*.
dandruff ['dandrəf] *n* caspa *f*.
Dane [dein] *n* danés, -esa *m*, *f*. **Danish** *nm*, *adj* danés. **Great Dane** perro danés *m*.
danger ['deindʒə] *n* peligro *m*. **danger zone** área de peligro. **dangerous** *adj* peligroso.
dangle ['daŋgl] *v* (*hang*) colgar, dejar colgado; (*swing*) balancear en el aire.
dare [deə] *v* (*challenge*) desafiar; (*have the impudence to*) atreverse a. **I dare say** quizás. *n* desafío *m*, reto *m*. **daredevil** *n* temerario, -a *m*, *f*. **daring** *adj* atrevido; osado. *n* osadía *f*.
dark [daːk] *adj* oscuro; (*hair, complexion*) moreno; (*sombre*) triste; (*menacing*) amenazador; (*mysterious*) misterioso. **Dark Ages** edad de las tinieblas *f*. **dark room** cámara oscura *f*. **grow dark** anochecer. *n* oscuridad *f*. **after dark** después del anochecer. **be in the dark** estar a oscuras. **darken** *v* oscurecer; entristecer. **darkness** *n* oscuridad *f*.

darling ['daːlɪŋ] *n, adj* querido, -a *m, f.*
darn [daːn] *v* zurcir. *n* zurcido *m.* **darning needle** aguja de zurcir *f.*
dart [daːt] *n* (*missile*) dardo *m*; (*movement*) movimiento rápido *m. v* lanzar. **dartboard** *n* blanco *m.* **darts** *pl n* (*sport*) dardos *m pl.*
dash [daʃ] *n* (*rush*) carrera *f*; (*printing*) guión *m*; (*cookery*) poco *m*, gotas *f pl*; (*verve*) brio *m. v* (*rush*) precipitarse, ir de prisa; (*hopes*) defraudar. **dash off** (*letter, etc.*) escribir deprisa. **dashboard** *n* salpicadero *m.* **dashing** *adj* gallardo.
data ['deɪtə] *pl n* datos *m pl.* **data processing** proceso de datos *m.*
date¹ [deɪt] *n* (*calendar*) fecha *f*; época *f.* **be up to date** estar al día. **out of date** anticuado. **to date** hasta la fecha. **date line** meridiano de cambio de fecha *m. v* fechar.
date² [deɪt] *n* (*fruit*) dátil *m.* **date palm** palmera datilera *f.*
dative ['deɪtɪv] *nm, adj* dativo.
daughter ['dɔːtə] *n* hija *f.* **daughter-in-law** *n* nuera *f*, hija política *f.*
daunt [dɔːnt] *v* (*dishearten*) desanimar; (*intimidate*) intimidar. **dauntless** *adj* intrépido.
dawdle ['dɔːdl] *v* (*loiter*) holgazanear; (*waste time*) malgastar; (*walk slowly*) andar despacio.
dawn [dɔːn] *n* alba *m*, amanecer *m*; (*fig*) alborear *m.* **from dawn to dusk** de sol a sol. *v* alborear, amanecer.
day [deɪ] *n* día *m*; (*of work*) jornada *f.* **all day** todo el día. **every day** todos los días. **the day after tomorrow** pasado mañana. **the day before yesterday** anteayer. **from day to day** de día en día. **daybreak** *n* amanecer *m.* **daydream** *n* ensueño *m*; *v* soñar despierto. **daylight** *n* luz del día *f.* **in broad daylight** en pleno día. **good day!** ¡buenos días!
daze [deɪz] *n* aturdimiento *m. v* aturdir. **be in a daze** estar aturdido.
dazzle ['dazl] *n* brillo *m. v* deslumbrar. **dazzling** *adj* deslumbrante, deslumbrador.
dead [ded] *adj* muerto; (*absolute*) absoluto; (*insensible*) insensible; (*battery*) descargado; (*extinguished*) apagado. **deadline** *n* fecha *f.* **deadly** *adj* mortal; (*unerring*) absoluto; (*habit*) pernicioso.
deaden ['dedn] *v* (*sound, etc.*) amortiguar;

(*pain*) calmar; (*feeling*) embotar. **deadening** *adj* (*tech*) aislante.
deaf [def] *adj* sordo. **turn a deaf ear** hacerse el sordo. **deaf-and-dumb** *adj* sordomudo. **deafen** *v* ensordecer. **deafening** *adj* ensordecedor. **deafness** *n* sordera *f.*
***deal** [diːl] *v* repartir, distribuir. **deal in** comercir en. *n* transacción *f*, negocio *m*; (*treatment*) trato *m*; (*agreement*) convenio *m*; (*amount*) cantidad *f*; (*cards*) reparto *m*; (*wood*) abeto *m.* **it's a deal!** ¡trato hecho! **your deal** te toca. **dealer** *m* comerciante *m, f*; (*cards*) mano *f.* **dealing** *n* trato *m*; (*behaviour*) conducta *f.* **dealings** *pl n* relaciones *f pl.*
dean [diːn] *n* (*rel*) deán *m*; (*academic*) decano *m.*
dear [dɪə] *adj* querido; (*costly*) caro, costoso. **dear me!** ¡Dios mío! **dear sir** estimado señor. **dearly** *adv* (*affectionately*) cariñosamente; (*costly*) caro.
death [deθ] *n* muerte *f*; (*formal*) fallecimiento *m.* **death certificate** certificado de defunción *m.* **death duty** derechos de sucesión *m pl.* **deathless** *adj* inmortal. **deathly** *adj* (*appearance*) cadavérico; (*silence*) sepulcral. **death penalty** pena de muerte *f.* **death rate** mortalidad *f.*
debase [dɪ'beɪs] *v* degradar; (*coins*) alterar. **debasement** *n* degradación *f*; alteración *f.*
debate [dɪ'beɪt] *n* debate *m*, discusión *f*; controversia *f. v* discutir; controvertir; considerar. **debatable** *adj* discutible. **debating society** asociación que organiza debates *f.*
debit ['debɪt] *n* (*entry of debt*) débito *m*; (*left-hand side of account*) debe *m. v* cargar en cuenta.
debris ['deɪbriː] *n* escombros *m pl.*
debt [det] *n* deuda *f.* **run into debt** contraer deudas. **debtor** *n* deudor, -a *m, f.*
decade ['dekeɪd] *n* decenio *m.*
decadent ['dekədənt] *n*(*m*+*f*), *adj* decadente. **decadence** decadencia *f.*
decant [dɪ'kant] *v* decantar. **decanter** *n* garrafa *f*, jarra *f.*
decapitate [dɪ'kapɪteɪt] *v* decapitar. **decapitation** *n* decapitación *f.*
decay [dɪ'keɪ] *n* decomposición *f*; (*teeth*) caries *f invar*; decadencia *f*; (*physics*) desintegración progresiva *f. v* descomponerse; cariarse; decaer.

decease [di'siis] n fallecimiento m. v fallecer. **deceased** n, adj difunto, -a.
deceit [di'siit] n (cheating) engaño m; fraude m; decepción; (lying) mentira f.
deceitful adj engañoso; fraudulento; mentiroso. **deceitfulness** n lo engañoso m; falsedad f.
deceive [di'siiv] v engañar; defraudar. **deceiver** n embustero, -a m, f.
December [di'sembə] n diciembre m.
decent ['diisənt] adj decente; (satisfactory) razonable; (coll) bueno, simpático.
decency n decencia f, decoro m.
deceptive [di'septiv] adj engañoso. **deceptiveness** n apariencia engañosa f.
decibel ['desi,bel] n decibel m, decibelio m.
decide [di'said] v decidir; (line of action) determinar; (conflict) resolver; (choose) optar por. **decided** adj decidido; determinado; resuelto; (difference) marcado.
deciduous [di'sidjuəs] adj de hoja caduca.
decimal ['desiməl] nf, adj decimal. **decimal point** coma de decimales f.
decipher [di'saifə] v descifrar.
decision [di'siʒən] n decisión f. **decisive** adj decisivo; concluyente; (manner) decidido; (tone) tajante. **decisively** adv con decisión.
deck [dek] n (ship) cubierta f; (bus) piso m. **deck chair** tumbona f.
declare [di'kleə] v declarar; proclamar. **declaration** n declaración f; proclamación f. **declaratory** adj declaratorio.
decline [di'klain] n (decrease) disminución f; (life) ocaso m; (decay) decaimiento; (number) baja f. v (to act) negarse (a); (an offer) rehusar; (gramm) declinar; bajar; (med) debilitarse. **declining** adj declinante.
decompose [,diikəm'pouz] v (break up) descomponer; (rot) pudrir. **decomposition** n descomposición f; putrefacción f.
decorate ['dekə,reit] v decorar, adornar; (medal) condecorar; (paint) pintar. **decoration** n (medal) condecoración f; (ornament) adorno m; (décor) decoración f. **decorative** adj decorativo. **decorator** n decorador, -a m, f.
decoy ['diikoi] n señuelo m.
decrease [di'kriis] v disminuir, reducir. n disminución f, reducción f. **decreasing** adj decresciente.

decree [di'krii] n decreto m. v decretar; pronunciar.
decrepit [di'krepit] adj decrépito.
dedicate ['dedi,keit] v (book, life, etc.) dedicar; (church) consagrar. **dedication** n (devotion) dedicación f; (inscription) dedicatoria f. **dedicatory** adj dedicatorio.
deduce [di'djuis] v deducir.
deduct [di'dʌkt] v descontar. **deductible** adj deducible. **deduction** n (discount) deducción f, rebaja f, descuento m; (conclusion) conclusión f, deducción f.
deed [diid] n acto m, acción f; (something done) hecho m; (feat) hazaña f; (law) escritura f.
deep [diip] adj profundo, hondo. **a hole a metre deep** un pozo de un metro de hondo. **deep in debt** cargado de deudas. **go off the deep end** perder los estribos. n (sea) piélago m. **deepfreeze** n congelador m.
deer [diə] n ciervo m.
deface [di'feis] v desfigurar; multilar. **defacement** n desfiguración f; mutilación f.
default [di'foilt] n (debt) falta de pago; (absence) falta f; (law) contumacia f, rebeldía f. **judgment by default** sentencia en rebeldía f. **win by default** ganar por incomparecencia del adversario. v dejar de pagar; condenar en rebeldía; (a contest) perder por incomparecencia.
defeat [di'fiit] n derrota f. v derrotar, vencer. **defeatism** n derrotismo m. **defeatist** n(m+f), adj derrotista.
defect ['diifekt; v di'fekt] n defecto m. v desertar. **defection** n deserción f. **defective** adj defectuoso; incompleto; (gramm) defectivo. **defectiveness** n imperfección f.
defend [di'fend] v defender. **defence** n defensa f. **self-defence** n autodefensa f. **defenceless** adj indefenso. **defendant** n (civil) demandado, -a m, f; (criminal) acusado, -a m, f. **defender** n defensor, -a m, f. **defensible** adj defensible; justificable. **defensive** adj defensivo. **on the defensive** a la defensiva.
defer [di'fəi] v (postpone) diferir; (submit) someter; (delay) tardar. **deference** n deferencia f. **in deference to** por respeto a. **deferential** adj deferente, respetuoso. **deferment** n aplazamiento m; (mil) prórroga f. **deferrable** adj diferible. **deferred** adj diferido; aplazado.

defiant [di'faiənt] *adj* provocativo; (*challenging*) desafiante. **defiance** *n* desafío *m*. **in defiance of** con desprecio de.
deficient [di'fiʃənt] *adj* deficiente; (*med*) atrasado.
deficit ['defisit] *n* déficit. *adj* deficitario.
define [di'fain] *v* definir; caracterizar; formular; determinar. **definition** *n* definición *f*; (*phot*) claridad *f*.
definite ['definit] *adj* definido; determinado; claro; definitivo; seguro. **definitely** *adv* claramente; categóricamente; (*without doubt*) seguramente.
deflate [di'fleit] *v* desinflar; (*comm*) provocar la deflación de; (*hopes*) reducir. **deflation** *n* desinflado *m*; (*comm*) deflación *f*.
deform [di'fɔːm] *v* deformar, desfigurar. **deformation** *n* deformación *f*.
defraud [di'frɔːd] *v* defraudar, estafar.
defrost [diːˈfrɒst] *v* deshelar.
deft [deft] *adj* hábil, diestro. **deftness** *n* habilidad *f*, destreza *f*.
defunct [di'fʌŋkt] *adj* difunto.
defy [di'fai] *v* (*challenge*) desafiar, retar; (*resist*) resistir a.
degenerate [di'dʒenəˌreit; *n, adj* di'dʒenərit] *v* degenerar. *n, adj* degenerado, -a. **degeneration** *n* degeneración *f*. **degenerative** *adj* degenerativo.
degrade [di'greid] *v* (*humiliate, reduce in rank*) degradar; (*quality*) rebajar; (*morals*) envilecer. **degradation** *n* degradación *f*. **degrading** *adj* degradante.
degree [di'griː] *v* (*stop*) grado *m*; categoría *f*; (*university*) título *m*. **bachelor's degree** licenciatura *f*. **by degrees** poco a poco. **doctor's degree** doctorado *m*. **to some degree** hasta cierto punto.
dehydrate [diːˈhaidreit] *v* deshidratar. **dehydration** *n* deshidratación *f*.
de-icer [diːˈaisə] *n* descongelador *m*.
deity ['diːiti] *n* deidad *f*.
dejected [di'dʒektid] *adj* descorazonado, desanimado. **dejection** *n* desaliento *m*, abatimiento *m*.
delay [di'lei] *n* dilación *f*, retraso *m*; (*wait*) demora *f*. *v* retrasar; (*postpone*) aplazar. **delaying** *adj* dilatorio.
delegate ['deləgit; *v* 'deləgeit] *n* delegado, -a *m, f*. *v* delegar. **delegation** *n* delegación *f*.
delete [di'liːt] *v* tachar, borrar. **deletion** *n* supresión *f*.
deliberate [di'libərət; *v* di'libəreit] *adj*

(*intentional*) deliberado; (*unhurried*) lento; (*premeditated*) premeditado; (*cautious*) prudente. *v* deliberar; (*ponder*) reflexionar. **deliberately** *adv* (*on purpose*) a propósito; prudentemente; lentamente. **deliberation** *n* deliberación *f*; lentitud *f*; reflexión *f*.
delicate ['delikət] *adj* delicado; (*food*) exquisito; refinado; escrupuloso; (*touch*) ligero; (*health*) frágile. **delicacy** *n* delicadeza *f*, fragilidad *f*.
delicious [di'liʃəs] *adj* delicioso.
delight [di'lait] *n* deleite *m*; encanto *m*. *v* deleitar; encantar. **delightful** *adj* delicioso; encantador.
delinquency [di'liŋkwənsi] *n* delincuencia *f*. **delinquent** *n*(*m*+*f*), *adj* delincuente.
delirious [di'liriəs] *adj* delirante. **be delirious** delirar. **delirium** *n* delirio *m*.
deliver [di'livə] *v* (*hand over*) entregar; (*goods, post*) repartir; (*message*) dar; (*opinion*) expresar; (*speech*) pronunciar; (*baby*) asistir para dar a luz; (*free*) liberar. **deliverance** *n* liberación *f*. **delivery** *n* entrega *f*; reparto *m*; pronunciación *f*; lanzamiento *m*; (*med*) parto *m*; manera de expresarse *f*. **delivery service** servicio a domicilio *m*. **delivery van** furgoneta de reparto *f*. **take delivery of** recibir.
delta ['deltə] *n* delta *m*.
delude [di'luːd] *v* engañar. **delusion** *n* engaño, *m*, error *m*, ilusión *f*.
deluge ['deljuːdʒ] *n* diluvio *m*. *v* inundar; (*fig*) abrumar.
delve [delv] *v* cavar. **delve into** ahondar.
demand [di'maːnd] *n* (*comm*) demanda *f*; (*request*) petición *f*; (*for payment*) reclamación *f*. *v* (*require*) requerir; (*ask urgently*) exigir; reclamar. **demanding** *adj* (*tiring*) agotador; (*absorbing*) aborbente; (*person*) exigente.
demented [di'mentid] *adj* demente, loco. **dementia** *n* demencia *f*.
democracy [di'mokrəsi] *n* democracia *f*. **democrat** *n* demócrata *m, f*. **democratic** *adj* democrático.
demolish [di'moliʃ] *v* (*building*) demoler, derribar; (*fig*) destruir. **demolition** *n* demolición *f*, derribo *m*; destrucción *f*.
demon ['diːmən] *n* demonio *m*, diablo *m*.
demonstrate ['demənˌstreit] *v* demostrar, probar; (*show how something operates*) mostrar; (*pol*) hacer la manifestación. **demonstration** *n* demostración *f*, prueba *f*; manifestación *f*. **demonstrative** *adj*

demostrativo. **demonstrator** *n* ayudante *m, f; (protester)* manifestante *m, f.*
demoralize [di'morǝ,laiz] *v* desmoralizar.
demoralization *n* desmoralización *f.*
demoralizing *adj* desmoralizador, desmoralizante.
demure [di'mjuǝ] *adj* recatado.
den [den] *n (of animals, etc.)* guardia *f; (study)* estudio *m.*
denial [di'naiǝl] *n (refusal)* negativa *f; (disavowal)* negación *f; (rejection)* rechazamiento *m.* **self-denial** abnegación *f.*
denim ['denim] *n* mahón *m.*
Denmark ['denmaːk] *n* Dinamarca *f.*
denomination [di,nomi'neiʃǝn] *n (measure)* denominación *f; (rel)* secta *f,* confesión *f; (coins)* valor *m; (type)* clase *f,* tipo *m.* **denominational** *adj* sectario. **denominator** *n (math)* denominador *m.*
denote [di'nout] *v* denotar.
denounce [di'nauns] *v* denunciar.
dense [dens] *adj (thick)* denso; *(coll: person)* torpe. **densely** *adv* densamente. **density** *n* densidad *f;* torpeza *f.*
dent [dent] *n* abolladura *f. v* abollar.
dental ['dentl] *adj* dental.
dentist ['dentist] *n* dentista *m, f.* **dentistry** *n* odolontogia *f.*
denture ['dentʃǝ] *n* dentadura *f,* postiza *f.*
denude [di'njuːd] *v* desnudar.
denunciation [dinʌnsi'eiʃǝn] *n* denuncia *f; (condemnation)* condena *f; (criticism)* censura *f.*
deny [di'nai] *v (refuse, dispute)* negar; *(request)* denegar; *(give the lie to)* desmentir; *(repudiate)* repudiar.
deodorant [diː'oudǝrǝnt] *n* desodorante *m.*
depart [di'paːt] *v (go away)* marcharse; *(set off)* salir; *(deviate)* apartarse. **departed** *adj* pasado; *(dead)* difunto. **departure** *n* marcha *f;* salida *f;* desviación *f.*
department [di'paːtmǝnt] *n (in a shop)* departamento *m; (in a business)* servicio *m; (college, university)* sección *f; (ministry)* negociado *m; (branch)* ramo *m; (fig: sphere)* esfera *f.* **department store** gran almacén *m.* **departmental** *adj* departamental.
depend [di'pend] *v* depender. **dependence** *n* dependencia *f.* **dependent** *adj* dependiente; subordinado.
depict [di'pikt] *v (art)* pintar; *(fig)*

describir. **depiction** *n* pintura *f;* descripción *f.*
deplete [di'pliːt] *v* vaciar, agotar. **depletion** *n* agotamiento *m.*
deplore [di'plɔː] *v* deplorar, lamentar. **deplorable** *adj* deplorable, lamentable.
deport [di'pɔːt] *v* expulsar. **deport oneself** comportarse. **deportation** *n* expulsión *f.* **deportment** *n* porte *m;* conducta *f.*
depose [di'pouz] *v* deponer.
deposit [di'pozit] *n (bank)* depósito *m; (substance)* sedimento *m,* poso *m; (pledge)* señal *f; (on accommodation)* entrada *f. v* depositar; *(money in account)* ingresar; dar de señal. **deposit account** cuenta de depósitos a plazo *f.*
depot ['depou] *n (store)* almacén *m; (buses)* cochera *f; (mil)* depósito *m.*
deprave [di'preiv] *v* depravar. **depravity** *n* depravación *f.*
depreciate [di'priːʃi,ǝit] *v (belittle, money)* despreciar; *(goods)* abaratar; *(price)* bajar. **depreciation** *n* depreciación *f;* abaratamiento *m; (fig)* desprecio *m.*
depress [di'pres] *v (dishearten)* deprimir; *(weaken)* debilitar; *(lessen)* disminuir; *(lower)* bajar; *(push down)* presionar; *(pedal)* pisar. **depressed** *adj* deprimido; *(indigent)* necesitado; *(comm)* de depresión. **depressing** *adj* deprimente. **depression** *n (dejection)* abatimiento *m; (geog, med, comm)* depresión *f.*
deprive [di'praiv] *v* privar, desposeer. **deprivation** *n* privación *f; (loss)* pérdida *f.*
depth [depθ] *n* profundidad *f; (colour)* intensidad *f; (sound)* gravedad *f.* **out of one's depth** perder pie; *(fig)* no entender nada.
deputy ['depjuti] *n* delegado *m; (substitute)* suplente *m; (politician)* diputado *m.* **deputation** *n* delegación *f.* **deputize** *v* diputar; delegar; sustituir.
derail [di'reil] *v* hacer descarrilar. **derailment** *n* descarrilamiento *m.*
derelict ['derilikt] *adj* abandonado. *n (neut)* derrelicto *m; (person)* deshecho *m.* **dereliction** *n* abandono *m; (negligence)* negligencia *f.*
deride [di'raid] *v* ridicular. **derision** *n* mofas *f pl.* **derisive** *or* **derisory** *adj (mocking)* mofador; *(petty)* irrisorio.
derive [di'raiv] *v* derivar; *(profit)* sacar. **derivation** *n* derivación *f.* **derivative** *nm, adj* derivado.

derogatory [di'rogətəri] *adj* despectivo, rebajante.
descend [di'send] *v* descender, bajar.
descendant *n(m+f)*, *adj* descendiente.
descent *n* descenso *m*, bajada *f*; (*slope*) declive *m*; (*lineage*) descendencia *f*.
describe [di'skraib] *v* describir; (*draw*) trazar. **describe oneself as** presentarse como. **description** *n* descripción *f*; (*sort*) clase *f*. **descriptive** *adj* descriptivo.
desert¹ ['dezət] *n* (*land*) desierto *m*.
desert² [di'zəɪt] *v* abandonar; (*mil*) desertar de. **deserter** *n* desertor *m*. **desertion** *n* (*mil*) deserción *f*; abandono *m*.
deserts [di'zəɪts] *pl n* **get one's deserts** llevarse su merecido.
deserve [di'zəɪv] *v* merecer; ser digno de. **deserving** *adj* digno; (*deed*) meritorio.
design [di'zain] *n* (*intention*) propósito *m*; (*plan*) proyecto *m*; (*drawing*) dibujo *m*; (*style*) estilo *m*. **have designs on** haber puesto sus miras en. *v* (*prepare plans for*) diseñar; dibujar; proyectar; inventar; (*create*) crear; imaginar. **designer** *n* diseñador, -a *m,f*. (*draughtsman*) delineante *m*. **dress designer** modista *m*. **designing** *adj* intrigante.
designate ['dezig,neit] *v* (*name for a duty*) designar; (*name*) denominar; (*appoint*) nombrar; (*point out*) señalar. *adj* designado; nombrado. **designation** *n* designación *f*; denominación *f*; nombramiento *m*.
desire [di'zaiə] *n* deseo *m*; (*request*) petición *f*. *v* desear; pedir; (*want*) querer. **desirable** *adj* deseable; atractivo. **desirability** *n* lo atractivo; conveniencia *f*. **desirous** *adj* deseoso.
desk [desk] *n* (*office*) escritorio *m*; (*school*) pupitre *m*.
desolate ['desələt] *adj* (*waste*) desolado; solitario; desierto; disconsolado. *v* (*lay waste*) asolar; abandonar; desconsolar. **desolating** *adj* desolador. **desolation** *n* desolación *f*; soledad *f*.
despair [di'speə] *n* desesperación *f*, desesperanza *f*. *v* desesperar.
desperate ['despərət] *adj* desesperado; (*resistance*) enérgico; (*urgent*) apremiante. **desperation** *n* desesperación *f*.
despise [di'spaiz] *v* despreciar. **despicable** *adj* despreciable. **despicableness** *n* bajeza *f*.
despite [di'spait] *prep* a pesar de.

despondent [di'spondənt] *adj* desanimado, desalentado. **despondency** *n* desánimo *m*, desaliento *m*.
despot ['despot] *n* déspota *m*. **despotic** *adj* despótico. **despotism** *n* despotismo *m*.
dessert [di'zəɪt] *n* postre *m*. **dessertspoon** *n* cuchara de postre *f*.
destine ['destin] *v* destinar. **destination** *n* destinación *f*. **destiny** *n* destino *m*.
destitute ['destitjuɪt] *adj* indigente, menesteroso. **be destitute** estar en la miseria. **destitution** *n* indigencia *f*, miseria *f*.
destroy [di'stroi] *v* destruir, destrozar. **destroyer** *n* (*naut*) destructor *m*. **destruction** *n* destrucción *f*; ruina *f*. **destructive** *adj* destructivo.
detach [di'tatʃ] *v* despegar; separar. **detachable** *adj* separable; (*collar*) postizo. **detached** *adj* independiente; (*untroubled*) indiferente. **detachment** *n* separación *f*; indiferencia *f*; (*mil*) destacamento *m*.
detail ['diɪteil] *n* detalle *m*. *v* detallar; (*itemize*) enumerar; (*mil*) destacar.
detain [di'tein] *v* retener; (*law*) detener. **detention** *n* detención *f*, arresto, *m*.
detect [di'tekt] *v* (*discover*) descubrir; (*perceive*) percibir; (*note*) advertir; (*tech*) detectar. **detection** *n* descubrimiento *m*; detección *f*. **detective** *n* detective *m*. **detective story** novela policíaca *f*. **detector** *n* detector *m*. **lie detector** detector de mentiras *m*.
deter [di'təɪ] *v* desuadir. **deterrent** *adj* disuasivo. *n* fuerza de disuasión *f*.
detergent [di'təɪdʒənt] *nm*, *adj* detergente.
deteriorate [di'tiəriə,reit] *v* (*wear out*) deteriorar; (*become worse*) empeorar; (*in value*) depreciar. **deterioration** *n* deterioro *m*; empeoramiento *m*; (*decline*) decadencia *f*.
determine [di'təɪmin] *v* (*fix*) determinar; (*cause*) provocar; (*limits*) definir; (*decide*) decidir; resolver. **determination** *n* determinación *f*; resolución *f*; decisión *f*. **determined** *adj* resuelto; decidido; determinado.
detest [di'test] *v* detestar, odiar. **detestable** *adj* detestable, odioso. **detestation** *n* odio *m*.
detonate ['detə,neit] *v* detonar. **detonating** *adj* detonante. **detonation** *n* detonación *f*.
detour ['diɪtuə] *n* desvío *m*, desviación *f*; vuelta *f*. **make a detour** dar un rodeo.

detract [di'trakt] v (take away) quitar,
reducir; (denigrate) denigrar. **detraction**
n denigración f.
detriment ['detrimənt] n detrimento m,
perjuicio m. **detrimental** adj perjudicial.
devalue [diː'valjuː] v devaluar,
desvalorizar. **devaluation** n devaluación f.
devastate ['devəˌsteit] v devastar. **devastating** adj devastador. **devastation** n
devastación f.
develop [di'veləp] v (expand) desarrollar;
(business) explotar; (land) urbanizar;
(resources) aprovechar; (promote)
fomentar; (taste) adquirir; (ailment) contraer; (tendency) manifestar; (talent)
mostrar; (phot) revelar. **developer** n
(phot) revelador m. **development** n desarrollo m; evolución f; progreso m.
deviate ['diːviˌəit] v desviarse. **deviation** n
desviación f; (from truth) alejamiento m;
(sexual) inversión f. **deviationism** n
desviacionismo m. **deviationist** n desvia-
cionista m, f.
device [di'vais] n (tech) mecanismo;
ingenio; (scheme) ardid m; estratagema
f.
devil ['devl] n diablo. **devilish** adj
diabólico. **devil's advocate** abogado del
diablo m.
devise [di'vaiz] v inventar; (plan) concebir; (plot) tramar.
devoid [di'void] adj desprovisto.
devolution [ˌdiːvə'luːʃən] n (powers) delegación f. **devolve** v delegar; transmitir.
devote [di'vout] v dedicar. **devoted** adj
dedicado; (loyal) leal; (devout) devoto.
devotion n dedicación f; lealtad f; devoción f. **devotional** adj piadoso.
devour [di'vauə] v devorar. **devouring** adj
devorador.
devout [di'vaut] adj devoto; sincero.
devoutness n devoción f.
dew [djuː] n rocío m.
dexterous ['dekstrəs] adj diestro, hábil.
dexterity n destreza f, habilidad f.
diabetes [ˌdaiə'biːtiːz] n diabetes f. **diabet-
ic** n, adj diabético, -a.
diagnose [ˌdaiəg'nouz] v diagnosticar.
diagnosis n diagnóstico m.
diagonal [dai'agənəl] nf, adj diagonal.
diagonally adv diagonalmente.
diagram ['daiəˌgram] n (math) figura;
(chart) gráfico m; (sketch) esquema;
(explanatory) diagrama m. **diagrammatic**
adj esquemático.

dial ['daiəl] n (clock) esfera f; (selector)
botón m; (telephone) disco m. v marcar.
dialling tone señal para marcar f.
dialect ['daiəlekt] n dialecto m.
dialogue ['daiəlog] n diálogo m.
diameter [dai'amitə] n diámetro m. **dia-
metrically** adv diametralmente.
diamond ['daiəmənd] n diamante m. **dia-
mond-shaped** adj romboidal.
diaper ['daiəpə] n (US) pañal m.
diaphragm ['daiəˌfram] n diafragma m.
diarrhoea [ˌdaiə'riə] n diarrea f.
diary ['daiəri] n diario m; (for appoint-
ments) agenda f.
dice [dais] n pl dados m pl. ∵ jugar a los
dados. **dice with death** jugar con la
muerte.
dictate [dik'teit] v dictar; (order) mandar;
(impose) imponer. n mandato m. **dictation** n dictado m. **dictator** n dictador m.
dictatorial adj dictatorial. **dictatorship** n
dictadura f.
dictionary ['dikʃənəri] n diccionario m.
did [did] V **do**.
die [dai] v morrir, fallecer. **die away**
(sound) desvanecer. **die down** (fire) apagarse; (wind) amainar; (conversation)
decaer. **die out** desaparecer.
diesel ['diːzəl] nm, adj diesel. **diesel
engine** motor diesel m. **diesel oil** gasoil
m.
diet ['daiət] n dieta f, régimen m. v poner
a dieta or régimen. **dietary** adj dietético.
dietetics n dietética f. **dietician** n dietético m.
differ ['difə] v ser diferente, ser distinto.
difference n diferencia f; (disagreement)
desacuerdo m. **different** adj diferente,
distinto. **differential** nf, adj diferencial.
differentiate v diferenciar, distinguir.
difficult ['difikəlt] adj difícil. **difficulty** n
dificultad f.
*dig [dig] v cavar; excavar; (coal, etc.)
extraer. **dig in** enterrar. **dig into** clavar.
dig up desenterrar. n (in the ribs) golpe
m; excavación arquelógica f; (fig)
pinchazo m.
digest [dai'dʒest] n resumen m. v digerir;
(summarize) resumir; (fig) asimilar.
digestible adj digerible. **digestion** n digestión f. **digestive** adj digestivo. **digestive
system** aparato digestivo m.
digit ['didʒit] n (finger, toe) dedo m;
(math) dígito m. **digital** adj digital.

dignified ['digni,faid] *adj* digno; solemne.
dignify *v* dignificar.
dignity ['dignəti] *n* dignidad *f*. **dignitary** *n* dignatorio *m*.
digress [dai'gres] *v* desviarse, apartarse.
digression *n* digresión *f*.
digs [digz] *n pl* (*coll*) pensión *f sing*.
dilapidated [di'lapi,deitid] *adj* (*building*) ruinoso; (*clothes*) muy estropeado. **dilapidate** *v* deteriorar; estropear. **dilapidation** *n* estado ruinoso *m*.
dilate [dai'leit] *v* dilatar.
dilemma [di'lemə] *n* dilema *m*.
diligent ['dilidʒent] *adj* diligente. **diligence** *n* diligencia *f*.
dilute [dai'luit] *v* diluir, aguar; (*fig*) atenuar. *adj* diluido; atenuado. **dilution** *n* dilución *f*.
dim [dim] *adj* oscuro; (*memory*) lejano; (*sound*) sordo; (*sight*) turbio; (*light*) débil; (*vague*) borroso; (*colour*) apagado; (*slang*) tonto. **take a dim view of** ver con malos ojos. *v* (*light*) bajar; (*sight*) nublar.
dimly *adv* vagamente; poco iluminado.
dimension [di'menʃən] *n* dimensión *f*.
diminish [di'miniʃ] *v* disminuir.
diminutive [di'minjutiv] *adj* diminuto. *nm*, *adj* (*gramm*) diminutivo.
dimple ['dimpl] *n* hoyuelo *m*. *v* formar hoyuelos en.
din [din] *n* estrépito *m*, alboroto *m*.
dine [dain] *v* cenar. **dining car** coche restaurante *m*. **diningroom** *n* comedor *m*.
dinghy ['diŋgi] *n* bote *m*.
dingy ['dindʒi] *adj* sucio, sórdido.
dinner ['dinə] *n* (*evening*) cena *f*; (*midday*) comida *f*. **dinner jacket** esmoquin *m*. **dinner party** cena *f*. **dinner table** mesa de comedor *f*.
dinosaur ['dainə,soː] *n* dinosaurio *m*.
diocese ['daiəsis] *n* diócesis *f*. **diocesan** *n*, *adj* diocesano, -a.
dip [dip] *v* (*wet*) mojar; (*immerse*) sumergir; (*someone*) zambullir; (*scoop*) sacar; (*put a hand in*) meter; (*flag*) inclinar; (*headlights*) poner luz de cruce; (*road*) bajar; *n* baño *m*; (*slope*) declive *m*.
diphthong ['difθoŋ] *n* diptongo *m*.
diploma [di'ploumə] *n* diploma *m*.
diplomacy [di'ploumɔsi] *n* diplomacia *f*.
diplomat *n* diplomático *m*. **diplomatic** *adj* diplomático. **diplomatic corps** cuerpo diplomático *m*. **diplomatic immunity** inmunidad diplomática *f*.

dipstick ['dipstik] *n* varilla graduada *f*.
dire [daiə] *adj* extremo; terrible.
direct [di'rekt] *adj* (*straight*) directo; (*blunt*) tajante; (*frank*) franco. **direct current** corriente continua *f*. *v* dirigir; (*order*) mandar; (*show the way*) indicar; (*gaze, attention*) señalar. **direction** *n* dirección *f*. **directions** *n pl* instrucciones *f pl*. **directive** *n* instrucción *f*. **directly** *adv* directamente; (*at once*) en seguida. **directness** *n* franqueza *f*. **director** *m* director *m*. **board of directors** consejo de administración *n*. **managing director** director gerente *m*.
dirt [dəːt] *n* suciedad *f*; (*filth*) mugre *f*; (*rubbish*) basura *f*. **dirt-cheap** *adj* baratísimo. **dirty** *adj* sucio; (*obscene: person*) verde; (*language*) grosero. **dirty trick** mala pasada *f*.
disability [disə'biləti] *n* incapacidad *f*. **disable** *v* incapacitar; (*cripple*) lisiar. **disabled** *adj* inválido. **disablement** *n* incapacidad *f*.
disadvantage [,disəd'vaːntidʒ] *n* desventaja *f*. **be at a disadvantage** estar en situación desventajosa.
disagree [,disə'griː] *v* discrepar; no estar de acuerdo. **disagreeable** *adj* desagradable. **disagreement** *n* desacuerdo *m*.
disappear [,disə'piə] *v* desaparecer. **disappearance** *n* desaparición *f*.
disappoint [,disə'point] *v* decepcionar; defraudar. **disappointing** *adj* decepcionante. **disappointment** *n* decepción *f*; disgusto *m*.
disapprove [,disə'pruːv] *v* desaprobar; estar en contra. **disapproval** *n* desaprobación *f*. **disapproving** *adj* desaprobador. **disapprovingly** *adv* con desaprobación.
disarm [dis'aːm] *v* desarmar. **disarmament** *n* desarme *m*.
disaster [di'zaːstə] *n* desastre *m*. **disastrous** *adj* desastroso.
disband [dis'band] *v* disolver; (*mil*) licenciar.
disc or *US* **disk** [disk] *n* disco *m*. **disc jockey** presentador de discos *m*.
discard [dis'kaːd; *n* 'diskaːd] *v* (*cast away*) desechar; (*cards*) descartar; (*fig*) renunciar. *n* descarte *m*.
discern [di'səːn] *v* discernir. **discernible** *adj* perceptible. **discerning** *adj* perspicaz.
discharge [dis'tʃaːdʒ] *v* descargar; (*debt*) saldar; (*gun*) disparar; (*sack*) despedir;

(*law*) absolver; (*duty*) desempeñar; (*prisoner*) liberar; (*patient*) dar de alta; (*bankrupt*) rehabilitar. *n* descarga *f*; (*debt*) descargo; (*gas*) escape *m*; liberación *f*; rehabilitación *f*; absolución *f*; desempeño *m*; alta *f*; disparo *m*.

disciple [di'saipl] *n* discipulo, -a *m, f*.

discipline ['disiplin] *n* disciplina *f*. *v* castigar. **disciplinarian** *n* disciplinario, -a *m, f*. **disciplinary** *adj* disciplinario.

disclaim [dis'kleim] *v* rechazar; (*law*) renunciar. **disclaimer** *n* (*denial*) denegación *f*; (*law*) renuncia *f*.

disclose [dis'klouz] *v* revelar. **disclosure** *n* revelación *f*; descubrimiento *m*.

discolour [dis'kʌlə] *v* descolorar; (*stain*) manchar. **discolouration** *n* descoloración *f*.

discomfort [dis'kʌmfət] *n* molestia *f*; incomodidad *f*; malestar. *v* molestar.

disconcert [diskən'sɔɪt] *v* desconcertar, perturbar. **disconcerting** *adj* desconcertante.

disconnect [diskə'nekt] *v* (*elec*) desconectar; (*separate*) separar. **disconnection** *n* desconexión *f*; separación *f*.

disconsolate [dis'konsələt] *adj* desconsolado. **disconsolateness** *n* desconsuelo *m*.

discontinue [diskən'tinjuː] *v* discontinuar, interrumpir; suspender. **discontinuance** *or* **discontinuation** *n* cesación *f*; suspensión *f*. **discontinuity** *n* discontinuidad *f*; interrupción *f*. **discontinuous** *adj* discontinuo.

discord ['diskɔɪd] *n* discordia *f*; (*music*) disonancia *f*. **discordant** *adj* discordante; (*music*) discorde.

discotheque ['diskətek] *n* discoteca *f*.

discount ['diskaunt] *n* descuento *m*; (*reduction*) rebaja *f*. *v* descontar; rabajar; (*disregard*) no hacer caso de.

discourage [dis'kʌridʒ] *v* desanimar. **discourage from** recomendar que no. **discouragement** *n* desánimo *m*. **discouraging** *adj* desalentador.

discover [dis'kʌvə] *v* descubrir; (*realize*) darse cuenta de. **discoverer** *n* descubridor, -a *m, f*. **discovery** *n* descubrimiento *m*.

discredit [dis'kredit] *v* desacreditar; (*disbelieve*) dudar de; (*dishonour*) deshonrar. *n* descrédito *m*; duda *f*. **discreditable** *adj* indigno; vergonzoso.

discreet [dis'kriːt] *adj* discreto; prudente.

discretion *n* discreción; circunspección *f*. **at your discretion** a su gusto. **discretionary** *adj* discrecional.

discrepancy [di'skrepənsi] *n* discrepancia *f*; diferencia *f*. **discrepant** *adj* discrepante; diferente.

discrete [di'skriːt] *adj* discreto.

discriminate [di'skrimi,neit] *v* distinguir. **discriminate against** discriminar contra. **discriminating** *adj* (*law*) discriminatorio; (*taste*) muy bueno. **discrimination** *n* discriminación *f*; discernimiento *m*; buen gusto *m*. **discriminatory** *adj* discriminatorio.

discus ['diskəs] *n* disco *m*.

discuss [di'skʌs] *v* discutir; hablar de. **discussion** *n* discusión *f*.

disease [di'ziːz] *n* enfermedad *f*. **diseased** *adj* enfermo.

disembark [disim'baɪk] *v* desembarcar. **disembarkation** *n* (*people*) desembarco *m*; (*cargo*) desembarque *m*.

disengage [disin'geidʒ] *v* (*detach*) soltar; (*unhook*) desenganchar; (*free*) liberar; (*mil*) retirar; (*gears*) desengranar; (*clutch*) desembragar. **disengagement** *n* liberación *f*; retirada *f*; desembrague *m*.

disfigure [dis'figə] *v* desfigurar; (*spoil*) afear. **disfigurement** *n* desfiguración *f*; afeamiento *m*.

disgrace [dis'greis] *n* (*disfavour*) desgracia *f*; (*cause of shame*) vergüenza *f*; deshonra *f*; ignominia *f*. *v* deshonrar. **disgraceful** *adj* deshonroso; vergonzoso.

disgruntled [dis'grʌntld] *adj* malhumorado.

disguise [dis'gaiz] *v* disfrazar. *n* disfraz *m*.

disgust [dis'gʌust] *n* repugnancia *f*. *v* repugnar.

dish [diʃ] *n* plato *m*; (*serving vessel*) fuente *f*. *v* servir. **dish out** dar. **dishwasher** *n* lavaplatos *m*.

dishearten [dis'haɪtn] *v* descorazonar, desanimar. **disheartening** *adj* descorazonador.

dishevelled [di'ʃevəld] *adj* despeinado; desarreglado.

dishonest [dis'onist] *adj* fraudulento.

dishonour [dis'onə] *n* deshonra *f*; deshonor *m*. *v* deshonrar.

disillusion [disi'luːʒən] *v* desilusionar. *n* desilusión *f*.

disinfect [disin'fekt] *v* desinfectar. **disinfectant** *nm, adj* desinfectante.

disinherit [disin'herit] *v* desheredar. **disinheritance** *n* desheramiento *m*.
disintegrate [dis'inti,greit] *v* desintegrar.
disintegration *n* desintegración *f*.
disinterested [dis'intristid] *adj* desinteresado; imparcial. **disinterest** *n* desinterés *m*.
disjointed [dis'dʒointid] *adj* desarticulado; (*incoherent*) inconexo.
disk *V* **disc**.
dislike [dis'laik] *v* aborrecer, tener aversión a. *n* aversión *f*, antipatía *f*.
dislocate ['dislə,keit] *v* (*joint*) dislocar; (*plans*) desarreglar. **dislocation** *n* dislocación *f*; desarreglo *m*.
dislodge [dis'lodʒ] *v* desalojar. **dislodgement** *n* desalojamiento.
disloyal [dis'loiəl] *adj* desleal. **disloyalty** *n* deslealtad *f*.
dismal ['dizməl] *adj* triste; (*face*) sombrío; (*voice*) lúgubre.
dismantle [dis'mantl] *v* desmantelar; desmontar.
dismay [dis'mei] *n* consternación *f*; (*fright*) espanto *m*. *v* consternar; espantar; (*discourage*) desalentar.
dismiss [dis'mis] *v* despedir; (*discharge*) licenciar; (*assembly*) disolver; (*mil*) romper filas; (*idea*) descartar. **dismissal** *n* (*employee*) despido *m*; abandono *m*.
dismount [dis'maunt] *v* desmontar.
disobey [disə'bei] *v* desobedecer. **disobedience** *n* desobediencia *f*. **disobedient** *adj* desobediente.
disorder [dis'ɔɪdə] *n* desorden *m*; (*riot*) disturbio *m*; (*illness*) trastorno *m*. *v* desordenar. **disorderliness** *n* desorden *m*.
disorderly *adj* (*person*) desordenado; (*place*) desarreglado; (*meeting*) alborotado.
disorganize [dis'ɔɪgənaiz] *v* desorganizar. **disorganization** *n* desorganización *f*.
disown [dis'oun] *v* repudiar; (*deny*) negar; no reconocer.
disparage [di'sparidʒ] *v* desacreditar; (*belittle*) menospreciar; (*denigrate*) denigrar. **disparagement** *n* descrédito *m*; menosprecio *m*; denigración *f*. *adj* despectivo; menospreciativo; denigrante. **disparagingly** *adv* con desprecio.
disparity [dis'pariti] *n* disparidad *f*. **disparate** *adj* dispar.
dispassionate [dis'paʃənit] *adj* desapasionado; imparcial.
dispatch [di'spatʃ] *n* (*message*) despacho

m, expedición *f*; (*messenger*, *parcels*) envío *m*; (*promptness*) diligencia *f*. *v* despachar; enviar; matar.
dispel [di'spel] *v* disipar.
dispense [di'spens] *v* (*drugs*) preparar; (*justice*) administrar; (*distribute*) distribuir; (*laws*) aplicar. **dispense with** prescindir de. **dispensable** *adj* prescindible. **dispensary** *n* dispensario *m*; farmacia *f*. **dispensation** *n* distribución *f*; administración *f*; (*exemption*) dispensa *f*.
disperse [di'spɔɪs] *v* dispersar. **dispersal** *n* dispersión *f*.
displace [dis'pleis] *v* desplazar; (*oust*) quitar el puesto; (*remove from office*) destituir. **displacement** *n* desplazamiento *m*; destitución *f*; reemplazo *m*.
display [di'splei] *v* exhibir; demostrar. *n* exhibición *f*; demostración *f*; despliegue *m*; (*emotion*) alarde *m*; (*show*) exposición *f*; (*parade*) desfile *m*; (*tech*) representación visual *f*.
displease [dis'plitz] *v* desagradar, disgustar. **displeasing** *adj* desagradable. **displeasure** *n* desagrado *m*, disgusto *m*.
dispose [di'spouz] *v* (*arrange*) disponer; determinar; inclinar; mover. **dispose of** tirar; (*transfer*) traspasar; (*argument*) echar por tierra; (*kill*) liquidar; (*sell*) vender; (*consume*) consumir. **disposable** *adj* disponible; (*to be thrown away*) para tirar. **disposal** (*arrangement*) desposición *f*; eliminación *f*; resolución *f*; traspaso *m*; venta *f*. **disposition** *n* disposición *f*; traspaso *m*; predisposición *f*.
disprove [dis'pruɪv] *v* refutar.
dispute [di'spjutt] *n* disputa *f*; discusión *f*; controversia *f*; (*law*) litigio *m*. *v* disputar; discutir; (*question*) poner en duda. **disputation** *n* discusión *f*; controversia *f*.
disqualify [dis'kwoli,fai] *v* (*render unfit*) incapacitar; (*competitor*) descalificar. **disqualification** *n* incapacidad *f*; descalificación *f*.
disregard [disrə'gaɪd] *v* (*neglect*) descuidar; desatender. *n* descuido *m*; indiferencia *f*.
disreputable [dis'repjutəbl] *adj* (*shabby*) lamentable; (*not respectable*) de mala fama. **disrepute** *n* descrédito *m*.
disrespect [disrə'spekt] *n* falta de respeto *f*. **disrespectful** *adj* irrespetuoso.
disrupt [dis'rʌpt] *v* (*upset*) trastornar; (*interrupt*) interrumpir; (*break up*) romper; desorganizar. **disruption** *n* trastorno

m; ruptura *f*; interrupción *f*; desorganización *f*. **disruptive** *adj* perjudicial.
dissatisfy [di'satisfai] *v* no satisfacer. **dissatisfaction** *n* descontento *m*.
dissect [di'sekt] *v* disecar. **dissection** *n* disección *f*.
dissent [di'sent] *n* disensión *f*; (*disagreement*) disentimiento *m*. *v* (*disagree*) disentir. **dissension** *n* disensión *f*.
dissident ['disidənt] *n*(*m*+*f*). *adj* disidente. **dissidence** *n* disidencia *f*.
dissimilar [di'similə] *adj* desigual; distinto. **dissimilarity** *n* desigualdad *f*.
dissociate [di'sousieit] *v* disociar. **dissociation** *n* disociación *f*.
dissolute ['disəluːt] *adj* disoluto. **dissolution** *n* (*society, marriage, melting*) disolución *f*.
dissolve [di'zolv] *v* disolver; (*disintegrate*) descomponer; disipar; (*law*; *contract*) rescindir.
dissuade [di'sweid] *v* disuadir. **dissuasion** *n* disuasión *f*. **dissuasive** *adj* disuasivo.
distance ['distəns] *n* distancia *f*. *v* distanciar. **distant** *adj* distante, lejano.
distaste [dis'teist] *n* disgusto *m*, aversión *f*. **distasteful** *adj* desagradable.
distemper [di'stempə] *n* (*dogs*) moquillo *m*; (*paint*) temple *m*.
distend [di'stend] *v* distender. **distension** *n* distensión *f*.
distil [di'stil] *v* destilar. **distillation** *n* destilación *f*. **distillery** *n* destilería *f*.
distinct [di'stiŋkt] *adj* (*clear*) claro; (*different*) distinto; (*definite*) bien determinado. **distinction** *n* distinción *f*. **distinctive** *adj* distintivo. **distinctness** *n* claridad *f*; diferencia *f*.
distinguish [di'stiŋgwiʃ] *v* distinguir. **distinguishable** *adj* distinguible. **distinguished** *adj* (*elegant*) distinguido; (*eminent*) eminente.
distort [di'stoːt] *v* torcer; (*fig*) desvirtuar. **distortion** *n* torcimiento *m*; desvirtuación *f*.
distract [di'strakt] *v* (*divert attention*) distraer; (*confuse*) aturdir; (*madden*) enloquecer. **distraction** *n* distracción *f*; aturdimiento *m*; locura *f*.
distraught [di'stroːt] *adj* distraído; enloquecido.
distress [di'stres] *n* aflicción *f*; (*poverty*) miseria *f*; (*danger*) peligro *m*. *v* afligir; angustiar. **distressed** *adj* afligido; en la

miseria; en peligro. **distressing** *adj* angustioso.
distribute [di'stribjut] *v* distribuir, repartir. **distribution** *n* distribución *f*; reparto *m*. **distributor** *n* distribuidor, -a *m, f*; (*mot*) distribuidor *m*.
district ['distrikt] *n* (*pol*) distrito *m*; (*town*) barrio *m*; (*region*) región *f*. **district manager** representante regional *m*.
distrust [dis'trʌst] *n* desconfianza *f*. *v* desconfiar. **distrustful** *adj* desconfiado.
disturb [di'stəːb] *v* molestar; perturbar; agitar; preocupar. **disturbance** *n* molestia *f*; perturbación *f*; agitación *f*; preocupación *f*; (*row*) alboroto *m*; (*public disorder*) disturbio *m*. **disturbing** *adv* molesto; perturbador; preocupante.
disuse [dis'juːs] *n* desuso *m*; abandono *m*.
ditch [ditʃ] *n* (*trench*) zanja *f*; (*roadside*) cuneta *f*; (*irrigation*) acequia *f*; (*drainage*) canal *m*. *v* (*coll*; *get rid of*) tirar; (*coll*; *abandon*) abandonar.
ditto ['ditou] *n* idem *m*.
divan [di'van] *n* diván *m*.
dive [daiv] *v* zambullida *f*. *v* zambullirse; saltar; bajar en picado; sumergirse. **diver** *n* buzo *m*; saltador, -a *m, f*.
diverge [dai'vəːdʒ] *v* divergir; desviar. **divergence** *n* divergencia *f*. **divergent** *adj* divergente.
diverse [dai'vəːs] *adj* diverso; distinto; diferente; variado. **diversity** *n* diversidad *f*.
divert [dai'vəːt] *v* (*reroute*) desviar; (*distract*) distraer; (*amuse*) divertir. **diversion** *n* desviación *f*; diversión *f*.
divide [di'vaid] *v* dividir. **division** *n* división *f*; separación *f*; distribución *f*; sección *f*; (*fig*; *opinions*) discrepancia *f*; (*fig*; *discord*) desunión *f*.
dividend ['dividend] *n* dividendo *m*.
divine [di'vain] *adj* divino. *v* adivinar. **divinity** *n* divinidad *f*; teología *f*.
divorce [di'voːs] *n* divorcio *m*. **sue for a divorce** pedir el divorcio. *v* divorciar; divorciarse de. **divorcee** *n* divorciado, -a *m, f*.
divulge [dai'vʌldʒ] *v* divulgar.
dizzy ['dizi] *adj* mareado; (*height, speed*) vertiginoso. **dizziness** *n* mareo *m*, vértigo *m*.
*do [duː] *v* (*act*) hacer; (*deal with*) ocuparse de; (*fulfil*) cumplir con; (*serve*) venir bien; (*feel*) estar, sentirse; (*be suitable*) valer; (*work*) trabajar; **do away with**

docile   58

suprimir. **do for** llevar la casa a; **do up**
(buttons, belt, etc.) abrocharse; *(laces)*
atarse; *(renovate)* renovar. **do well** ir
bien, salir bien; recuperarse. **do without**
prescindir de. **doesn't do to** no conviene.
how do you do? *(after being introduced)*
encantado; *(how are you?)* ¿cómo está
usted? **make do with** arreglárselas con.
please do por supuesto, por favor.
docile ['dousail] *adj* dócil. **docility** *n*
docilidad *f*.
dock¹ [dok] *n (wharf)* dársena *f*; *v (ship)*
atracar al muelle; *(arrive)* llegar.
dock² [dok] *n (law)* banquillo de los
acusados *m*.
dock³ [dok] *v (cut, shorten)* cortar;
reducir; *(coll: deduct)* descontar; *(coll:
fine)* multar.
doctor ['doktə] *n* médico, -a *m, f*; *(university title)* doctor, -a *m, f. v* atender;
adulterar; falsificar. **doctorate** *n*
doctorado *m*.
doctrine ['doktrin] *n* doctrina *f*. **doctri-
naire** doctrinario. **doctrinal** *adj* doctrinal.
document ['dokjumənt] *n* documento *m.
v* documentar. **documentary** *nm, adj* doc-
umental.
dodge [dodʒ] *v* esquivarse; eludir; *(bide)*
echarse; *(avoid)* evitar. *n (manoeuvre)*
regate *m*; *(trick)* truco *m*. **dodgy** *(coll) adj*
astuto; *(unreliable)* incierto.
dog [dog] *n* perro *m*. **beware of the dog**
cuidado con el perro. *v* seguir; perseguir.
dog biscuit *n* galleta de perro *f*.
dog days *n pl* canícula *f sing.*
dog-eared *adj* sobado.
dogged ['dogid] *adj* tenaz. **doggedness** *n*
tenacidad *f*.
doggerel ['dogərəl] *n* aleluyas *f pl.*
dogma ['dogmə] *n* dogma *m*. **dogmatic** *adj*
dogmático.
do-it-yourself [,duːitjoːˈself] *adj* hágalo
usted mismo.
dole [doul] *n (alms)* limosna *f*; *(unemployment pay)* subsidio de paro *m*. **be on the
dole** estar parado. **dole out** repartir.
doleful ['doulful] *adj* triste. **dolefulness** *n*
tristeza *f*.
doll [dol] *n* muñeca *f*.
dollar ['dolə] *n* dólar *m*.
dolphin ['dolfin] *n* delfín *m*.
domain [dəˈmein] *n* dominio *m*; *(fig)*
campo *m*.
dome [doum] *n (arch)* cúpula *f*, domo *m*.

domestic [dəˈmestik] *adj* doméstico;
(home-loving) hogareño; *(market)*
nacional. **domestic animal** animal doméstico *m*. **domestic help** doméstico, -a *m, f*.
domesticate domesticar. **domestication** *n*
domesticación *f*. **domesticity** *n* domesticidad *f*.
dominate ['domi,neit] *v* dominar. **dominant** *adj* dominante. **domineering** *adj*
dominante.
dominion [dəˈminjən] *n* dominio *m*.
domino ['dominou] *n* dominó *m*. **play
dominoes** jugar al dominó.
don [don] *v* ponerse. *n* catedrático *m*.
donate [dəˈneit] *v* donar. **donation** *n*
donativo *m*.
done [dʌn] *V* do.
donkey ['doŋki] *n* burro *m*.
donor ['dounə] *n* donante *m, f*.
doom [duːm] *n* perdición *f. v* condenar.
doomsday *n* día del juicio final *m*.
door [doː] *n* puerta *f*. **next door** en la casa
de al lado.
doorbell ['doːbel] *n* timbre *m*.
door-keeper *n* portero *m*; conserje *m*.
door-handle *n* mano de la puerta *f*.
doorknob ['doːnob] *n* tirador de puerta
m.
door-knocker *n* llamador *m*.
doormat ['doːmat] *n* felpudo *m*.
doorstep ['doːstep] *n* peldaño *m*; *(threshold)* umbral *m*.
doorway ['doːwei] *n* portal *m*.
dope [doup] *n (coll: drug)* droga *f*; *(coll:
varnish)* barniz *m*; *(coll: information)*
informes *m pl. v* drogar.
dormant ['doːmənt] *adj* letárgico; inactivo; latente.
dormitory ['doːmitəri] *n* dormitorio *m*.
dormouse ['doː,maus] *n* lirón *m*.
dose [dous] *n* dosis *f invar. v* dar la dosis.
dosage *n* dosis *f invar*.
dot [dot] *n* punto *m*. **on the dot** puntual-
mente. *v* poner el punto a; *(scatter)*
salpicar.
dote [dout] *v* chochear. **dote on** estar
chocho por. **dotage** *n* chochez *f*. **doting**
adj chocho.
double ['dʌbl] *nm, adj, adv* doble. *v*
doblar.
double bass *n* contrabajo *m*.
double bed *n* cama de matrimonio *f*.
double-breasted [,dʌblˈbrestid] *adj* cruzado.

double-cross [ˌdʌbl'kros] *n* traición *f*. *v* traicionar.

double-edged [ˌdʌbl'edʒd] *adj* de dos filos.

double-entendre [duɪblä'tädr] *n* expresión con doble sentido *f*.

double entry *n* (*comm*) partida doble *f*.

doubt [daut] *n* duda *f*. **no doubt** sin duda. *v* dudar. **doubtful** *adj* dudozo; sospechoso. **doubtless** *adv* indudablemente.

dough [dou] *n* masa *f*. **doughnut** *n* buñuelo *m*.

dove [dʌv] *n* paloma *f*.

dowdy ['daudi] *adj* desaliñado. **dowdiness** *n* desaliño *m*.

down¹ [daun] *adv* hacia abajo. *prep* abajo. *adj* descendente, bajo. **down payment** al contado. *v* derribar; tirar al suelo; (*food*) tragar; (*drink*) vaciar de un trago.

down² [daun] *n* plumón *m*; (*fine hair*) vello *m*; (*upland*) loma *f*.

downcast ['daunˌkaɪst] *adj* (*sad*) abatido; (*in a downward direction*) bajo.

downfall ['daunˌfoɪl] *n* ruina *f*; perdición *f*; caida *f*; (*rain*) chaparrón *m*.

downhearted [ˌdaun'haɪtid] *adj* descorazonado.

downhill [ˌdaun'hil] *adj* en pendiente. *adv* cuesta abajo.

downpour ['daunˌpoɪ] *n* aguacero *m*, chaparrón *m*.

downright ['daunˌrait] *adj* categórico; sincero; evidente; verdadero. *adv* categóricamente; verdaderamente; completamente.

downstairs. ['daunˌsteəz; *adv* ˌdaun'steəz] *adj* de abajo. *adv* abajo.

downstream [ˌdaun'striɪm] *adj*, *adv* río abajo.

downtrodden ['daunˌtrodn] *adj* (*fig*) oprimido.

downward ['daunwəd] *adj* descendente. *adv* hacia abajo.

downwards ['daunwədz] *adv* hacia abajo.

dowry ['dauəri] *n* dote *f*.

doze [douz] *v* dormitar. *n* cabezada *f*.

dozen ['dʌzn] *n* docena *f*. **baker's dozen** docena del fraile *f*.

drab [drab] *adj* pardo; monótono.

draft [draift] *n* (*version*) redacción *f*; (*drawing*) esbozo *m*; (*plan*) bosquejo *m*; (*payment*) libramiento *m*; (*bill*) letra de cambio *f*; (*naut*) calado *m*; (*conscription*) quinta *f*. *v* hacer un proyecto; (*draw up*) redactar; esbozar; (*conscript*) reclutar.

drag [drag] *v* arrastrar; (*river, etc.*) dragar. **drag down** hundir. *n* (*tow*) arrastre *m*; (*that which hinders*) estorbo *m*; (*device for dragging rivers, etc.*) rastra *f*; (*theatre*) disfraz de mujer *m*; (*aero*) resistencia aerodinámica; (*tech: brake*) galga *f*. **what a drag!** ¡qué lata!

dragon ['dragən] *n* drágon *m*. **dragonfly** *n* libélula *f*.

drain [dreiɴ] *n* desaguadero *m*; (*sewer inlet*) sumidero *m*; (*strength*) pérdida *f*. *v* desaguar; (*drink empty*) vaciar; (*marshes*) desecar; (*strength*) agotar. **drainage** *n* desagüe *m*; desecación *f*. **drawing board** escurridero *m*. **drainpipe** *n* tubo de desagüe *m*.

drama ['draɪmə] *n* drama *m*. **dramatic** *adj* dramático. **dramatics** *n pl* teatro *m*. **dramatist** *n* dramaturgo, -a *m*, *f*. **dramatize** *v* adaptar al teatro.

drape [dreip] *v* cubrir con ropa, adornar con colgaduras. *n* colgadura *f*. **draper** *n* pañero, -a *m*, *f*. **drapery** *n* telas *f pl*.

drastic ['drastik] *adj* drástico.

draught [draift] *n* (*air*) corriente de aire *f*; (*plan*) bosquejo *m*; (*drink*) trago *m*. *adj* (*animals*) de tiro. **draughtboard** *n* tablero de damas *m*. **draughtsman** *n* delineante *m*. **draughtsmanship** *n* dibujo lineal *m*.

*draw [droɪ] *n* (*sport*) empate *m*; (*lots*) sorteo *m*; (*lottery*) lotería *f*. *v* (*pull*) tirar de; (*extract*) extraer; (*attract*) atraer; (*art*) dibujar; (*a line*) trazar; (*nail, water, confession, profits, etc.*) sacar; (*comparisons*) hacer; (*breath*) tomar; (*earn*) cobrar; (*cheque*) librar; (*prize*) ganar; sortear; (*close curtains*) descorrer; (*blinds*) bajar; (*cards*) robar. **draw attention** llamar la atención. **draw up** (*document*) redactar a.

drawback ['droɪbak] *n* (*disadvantage*) desventaja *f*; (*shortcoming*) inconveniente *m*.

drawer ['droɪə] *n* (*container*) cajón *m*; (*art*) dibujante *m*, *f*.

drawing ['droɪiɴ] *n* (*art*) dibujo *m*; (*extraction*) extracción *f*. **drawing board** tablero de dibujo *m*. **drawing pin** chincheta *f*. **drawing room** salón *m*.

drawl [droɪl] *n* voz lenta *f*. *v* arrastrar las palabras.

drawn [droɪn] *adj* (*weary*) cansado. **drawn to** atraído por.

dread [dred] n miedo; terror. v temer.
dreadful adj terrible; espantoso.
*dream [driːm] v soñar; imaginarse. n sueño m. **bad dream** pesadilla f. **daydream** n ensueño m. **dream up** inventar.
dreary ['driəri] adj triote; monótono; (boring) aburrido. **dreariness** n tristeza f; monotonía f.
dredge [dredʒ] v dragar. n draga f.
dregs [dregz] n pl heces f pl.
drench [drentʃ] v empapar, mojar. **drenched to the skin** estar mojada hasta los huesos.
dress [dres] n (frock) vestido m; (clothing) ropa; (evening dress: men) traje de etiqueta m, (women) traje de noche m; (wedding) traje de novia m. v vestir. **dress up** poner de tiros largos. **dress up as** disfrazarse de.
dress circle n piso principal m.
dress coat n frac m.
dress designer n modelista m, f.
dresser ['dresə] n aparador m.
dressing ['dresiŋ] n (act) vestir m; (clothes) ropa f; (med) vendaje m; (cookery) aliño m; (agriculture) abono m. **dressing gown** bata f.
dressmaker ['dresmeikə] n modista m, f. **dressmaking** n costura f.
dress rehearsal n ensayo general m.
dress shirt n camisa de frac f.
dressy ['dresi] adj elegante.
dribble ['dribl] n goteo m. v gotear.
drier ['draiə] n secador m; (for clothes) secadora f.
drift [drift] n arrastramiento m; (snow) ventisquero m; (sand) montón m; (naut, aero) deriva f. v ser arrastrado; amontonarse; derivar; (fig) vivir sin rumbo. **drift along** vagar. **drifter** n (vagrant) vagabundo m; (boat) trainera f.
drill [dril] n (tech) taladro m; (dental) fresa f; (mil) instrucción f. v (mil) ejercitar; (bore) taladrar, perforar. **drilling** n instruccion f; perforación f.
*drink [driŋk] v beber; tomar; (toast) brindar por. **drink down** beber de um trago. **drink in** beberse. **drink up** bebérselo todo. n bebida f; (alcoholic) copa; (water, milk) vaso m; algo de beber. **soft drink** bebida no alcohólica f. **have a drink** tomar algo.
drinkable ['driŋkəbl] adj potable.
drinker ['driŋkə] n bebedor, -a m, f.

drinking ['driŋkiŋ] n beber m; bebida f. **drinking fountain** fuente de agua potable f. **drinking water** agua potable f.
drip [drip] n goteo m; (drop) gota f. v gotear. **drip-dry** adj de lava y pon.
*drive [draiv] v (push onwards) empujar; (control a vehicle) conducir; (carry in a vehicle) llevar; (some distance) recorrer; (force someone out) echar; (compel) obligar. **drive at** (physically) dirigirse hacia; (fig) insinuar. **drive away** irse; alejar. **drive by** passar (por). **drive in** entrar; clavar. **drive into** chocar contra. **drive on** seguir su camino. **drive up** llegar. n paseo m; excursión f; (journey) viaje m; (fig) vigor m; (mil) ofensiva f; (tennis, golf) drive m; (mot) tracción f; transmisión f; propulsión f; (instinct) instinto m. **driver** n conductor, -a m, f; chófer m; (taxi) taxista m, f; (train) maquinista m. **driveway** n camino de entrada m.
drivel ['drivl] n tonterías f pl. v decir tonterías.
driving ['draiviŋ] n conducción f. **driving licence** carnet de conducir m. **driving school** autoescuela f. **driving test** examen para sacar el carnet de conducir m.
drizzle ['drizl] n llovizna f. v lloviznar.
drone [droun] n (noise) zumbido m; (voices) murmullo m; (bee) zángano m; (aero) teledirigido m. v zumbar; murmurar.
droop [druːp] n (shoulders) encorvamiento m; (head) inclinación f. v estar encorvado; inclinarse; (flowers) marchitarse; (eyelids) caerse; (fig) desanimarse; debilitarse.
drop [drop] n gota f; (sweet) pastilla f; (bit) pizca f; (fall) caída f; (in value) disminución f; (in prices) baja f; (in temperature) descenso m. v (release) soltar; (let fall) dejar caer; (tears) derramar; (a friend) dejar; (prices, eyes, voice) bajar; (give up a habit) dejar de; (leave behind) despegarse de. **drop behind** quedarse atrás. **drop dead** caerse muerto. **drop in on** pasar por casa de. **drop off** dormirse.
dropout ['dropaut] n abandono m; marginado, -a m, f.
dropsy ['dropsi] n hidropesía f.
drought [draut] n sequía f.
drown [draun] v ahogar.
drowsy ['drauzi] adj soñoliento. **be drowsy** tener sueño. **drowse** v dormitar.

61   **dwindle**

drudge [drʌdʒ] *n* esclavo *m*. *v* currelar.
drudgery *n* trabajo penoso *m*.
drug [drʌg] *n* droga *f*; medicamento *m*. *v* drogar. **drug addict** drogadicto, -a *m*, *f*.
drug addiction toxicomania *f*.
drum [drʌm] *n* (*music*) tambor *m*; (*container*) bidón *m*; (*ear*) tímpano *m*. *v* tocar el tambor; (*fingers*) tamborilear.
drummer *n* tambor *m*; batería *f*. **drumstick** *n* palillo de tambor *m*.
drunk [drʌŋk] *adj* borracho; (*fig*) ebrio.
get drunk emborracharse. **drunkard** *n* borracho, -a *m*, *f*. **drunkenness** *n* embriaguez *f*.
dry [drai] *adj* seco; (*measure*) para áridos; (*boring*) aburrido; (*thirsty*) sediento; (*wit*) agudo; (*subject*) árido. *v* secar. **dry-clean** *v* limpiar en seco. **dry cleaner** tintorero, -a *m*, *f*.
dual ['djuəl] *adj* doble. **dual carriageway** pista doble *f*. **dual-purpose** *adj* de dos usos.
dubbed ['dʌbd] *adj* (*named*) apodado; (*knighted*) armado; (*film*) doblado. *v* apodar; armar; doblar.
dubious ['djuːbiəs] *adj* dudoso; ambiguo; indeciso; discutible; sospechoso.
duchess ['dʌtʃis] *n* duquesa *f*.
duck¹ [dʌk] *n* (*bird*) pata *f*; (*drake*) pato *m*; (*dodging*) esquiva *f*; (*in water*) zambullida *f*.
duck² [dʌk] *v* (*crouch*) agachar; zambullir.
duckling ['dʌkliŋ] *n* patito *m*.
duct [dʌkt] *n* (*anat*) canal *m*; (*gas*) conducto *m*; (*elec*) tubo *m*.
dud [dʌd] *n* (*coll*) desastre *m*; (*mil*) projectil fallido *m*. *adj* falso; inútil; defectuoso; (*cheque*) sin fondos.
due [djuː] *adj* (*care, time*) debido; (*payable*) pagadero. **due date** vencimiento *m*. **be due to** deberse a. *n* merecido *m*. *adv* derecho hacia. **dues** *pl n* derechos *m pl*.
duly *adv* debidamente; a su debido tiempo.
duel ['djuəl] *n* duelo *m*. *v* batirse en duelo. **duellist.** *n* duelista *m*.
duet [djuˈet] *n* dúo *m*.
duke [djuːk] *n* duque *m*.
dull [dʌl] *adj* monótono; (*obtuse*) torpe; (*slow*) tardo; (*tedious*) pesado; (*colour*) apagado; (*surface*) mate; (*weather*) gris; (*sullen*) sombrío; (*blunt*) embotado. *v* (*emotions*) enfriarse; (*pain*) aliviar; (*sound*) apagar. **dullness** *n* monotonía *f*;

torpeza *f*; pesadez *f*. **dully** *adv* torpemente; lentamente.
dumb [dʌm] *adj* mudo; (*coll*) estúpido.
dumbbell *n* pesa *f*. **dumbfound** *v* dejar sin habla. **dumbfounded** *adj* confuso, atónito. **dumbwaiter** *n* carrito *m*.
dummy ['dʌmi] *n* (*teat*) chupete *m*; (*tailor's*) maniquí *m*; (*puppet*) muñeco *m*; (*cards*) muerto *m*; (*coll*) lobo, -a *m*, *f*. *adj* ficticio, falso. *v* (*sport*) fintar.
dump [dʌmp] *n* (*rubbish dump*) depósito de basura *m*; (*heap*) montón *m*; (*scrapheap*) vertedero *m*; (*coll: wretched place*) tugurio *m*. *v* (*throw away*) tirar; (*get rid of*) deshacerse de; (*unload*) descargar. **dumping** *n* descarga *f*. **dumpy** *adj* regordete.
dumpling ['dʌmpliŋ] *n* masa hervida *f*.
dunce [dʌns] *n* tonto *m*, burro *m*.
dune [djuːn] *n* duna *f*.
dung [dʌŋ] *n* excrementos *m pl*; (*manure*) estiércol *m*.
dungarees [ˌdʌŋgəˈriːz] *n pl* mono *m sing*.
dungeon ['dʌndʒən] *n* calabozo *m*, mazmorra *f*.
duplicate ['djuːplikət; *v* 'djuːplikeit] *n* copia *f*, doble *m*, duplicado *m*. *adj* duplicado. *v* duplicar; multicopiar. **duplicating machine** multicopista *f*. **duplication** *n* duplicación *f*; copia *f*.
durable ['djuərəbl] *adj* duradero. **durability** *n* durabilidad *f*.
duration [djuˈreiʃən] *n* duración *f*.
during ['djuəriŋ] *prep* durante.
dusk [dʌsk] *n* crepúsculo *m*. **dusky** *adj* oscuro; (*complexion*) moreno.
dust [dʌst] *n* polvo *m*. *v* (clean) limpiar el polvo; (*powder*) espolvorear. **dustbin** *n* cajón de basura *m*. **duster** (*cloth*) trapo *m*; (*feather*) plumero *m*. **dustman** *n* basurero *m*. **dustpan** *n* recogedor *m*. **dusty** *adj* polvoriento; cubierto de polvo.
duty ['djuːti] *n* deber *m*, obligación *f*; (*tax*) impuesto *m*. (*at customs*) derechos de aduana *m pl*. **off duty** estar libre. **on duty** de servicio. **dutiful** *adj* obediente; deferente. **duty-free** *adj* libre de derechos de aduana.
duvet ['duːvei] *n* colcha de plumón *f*.
dwarf [dwɔːf] *n*, *adj* enano, -a. *v* achicar.
***dwell** [dwel] *v* vivir. **dwell on** (*emphasize*) insistir en; (*a subject*) extender en.
dwelling *n* vivienda *f*.
dwindle ['dwindl] *v* disminuir, menguar.

dye [dai] *n* (*colouring substance*) tinte *m*; (*colour*) fast dye color sólido *m*. *v* teñir.
dyke [daik] *n* (*ditch*) zanja *f*; (*bank*) dique *m*.
dynamic [dai'namik] *adj* dinámico.
dynamite ['dainə‚mait] *n* dinamita *f*. *v* dinamitar.
dynamo ['dainə‚mou] *n* dínamo *f*.
dynasty ['dinəsti] *n* dinastía *f*. **dynastic** *adj* dinástico.
dysentery ['disəntri] *n* disentería *f*.
dyslexia [dis'leksiə] *n* dislexia *f*.
dyspepsia [dis'pepsiə] *n* dispepsia *f*. **dyspeptic** *adj* dispéptico.

E

each [iɪtʃ] *adj* cada. *pron* cada uno, cada una. **each other** el uno al otro.
eager ['iɪgə] *adj* ávido; ansioso; impaciente. **eagerness** *n* ansia *f*; impaciencia *f*.
eagle ['iɪgl] *n* águila *f*. **eagle-eyed** *adj* tener ojos de lince.
ear¹ [iə] *n* oreja *f*; (*fig*) oído *m*. **earache** dolor de oído *m*. **eardrum** *n* tímpano *m*.
earmark *v* reservar; destinar. **earring** *n* pendiente *m*; **earshot** *n* alcance del oído *m*.
ear² [iə] *n* (*grain*) espiga *f*.
earl [əɪl] *n* conde *m*.
early ['əɪli] *adv* temprano; pronto; al principio. *adj* temprano; próximo; pronto.
earn [əɪn] *v* ganar; merecer. **earnings** *pl n* (*income*) ingresos *m pl*; (*salary*) sueldo *m sing*.
earnest ['əɪnist] *adj* sincero; aplicado; serio. **in earnest** en serio.
earth [əɪθ] *n* tierra *f*. **earthenware** *n* alfarería *f*.
earwig ['iəwig] *n* tijereta *f*.
ease [iɪz] *n* facilidad *f*; naturalidad *f*; (*comfort*) comodidad *f*; (*from pain*) alivio *m*. *v* facilitar; aliviar; tranquilizar; (*tension*) relajar.
easel ['iɪzl] *n* caballete *m*.
east [iɪst] *n* este *m*. *adj also* **easterly, eastern** oriental; del este; *adv* al este, hacia el este. **eastward** *adj, adv* hacia el este.

Easter ['iɪstə] *n* Pascua de Resurrección *f*. **Easter egg** huevo de Pascua *m*.
easy ['iɪzi] *adj* fácil. **easy chair** sillón *m*. **easy-going** *adj* acomodadizo; indolente. **take it easy!** ¡tómatelo con calma! **easiness** *n* facilidad *f*.
*eat [iɪt] *v* comer. **eat up** comerse. **eatable** *adj also* **edible** comestible.
eavesdrop ['iɪvzdrop] *v* fisgonear. **eavesdropper** *n* fisgón, -era *m*, *f*.
ebb [eb] *n* reflujo *m*, menguante *m*. *v* menguar; decaer. **ebb tide** marea menguante *f*.
ebony ['ebəni] *n* ébano *m*.
eccentric [ik'sentrik] *n*, *adj* excéntrico, -a. **eccentricity** *n* excentricidad *f*.
ecclesiastical [iklıɪziɪ'astikl] *adj also* **ecclesiastic** eclesiástico.
echo ['ekou] *n* eco *m*; resonancia *f*; repetición *f*. *v* resonar; repetir; imitar.
eclair [ei'kleə] *n* relámpago *m*.
eclipse [i'klips] *n* eclipse *m*. *v* eclipsar.
ecology [i'kolədʒi] *n* ecología *f*. **ecological** *adj* ecológico. **ecologist** *n* ecólogo *m*.
economy [i'konəmi] *n* economía *f*. **economic** *adj also* **economical** económico. **economics** *n* economía *f*. **economist** *n* economista *m*, *f*. **economize** *v* economizar.
ecstasy ['ekstəsi] *n* éxtasis *m*. **ecstatic** *adj* extático. **go into ecstasies over** extasiarse ante.
Ecuador ['ekwədoɪ] *n* Ecuador *m*. **Ecuadoran, Ecuadorean,** *or* **Ecuadorian** *n*, *adj* ecuatoriano, -a.
eczema ['eksimə] *n* eczema *m*.
edge [edʒ] *n* borde *m*; (*blade*) filo *m*, corte *m*. **have the edge on** llevar ventaja. **be on edge** tener los nervios de punta. *v* bordear; mover poco a poco. **edging** (*sewing*) orla *f*; (*path*) borde *m*. **edgy** *adj* nervioso.
edible ['edəbl] *adj* comestible.
Edinburgh ['edinbərə] *n* Edimburgo *m*.
edit ['edit] *v* (*text*) redactar; (*film*) montar; (*direct a paper, magazine*) dirigir. **editor** *n* radactor *m*; director *m*. **editorial** *n* editorial *m*; artículo de fondo *m*. **editorial staff** redacción *f*.
edition [i'diʃən] *n* edición *f*; tirada *f*.
educate ['edjuˌkeit] *v* educar. **educated** *adj* culto. **education** *n* educación *f*; (*teaching*) enseñanza *f*; (*specific*) instrucción *f*. **educational** *adj* educativo; (*teaching*) docente.

63

eel [iːl] *n* anguila *f*.
eerie ['iəri] *adj* misterioso; espantoso.
effect [i'fekt] *n* efecto *m*; resultado *m*; impresión *f*; (*meaning*) significado *m*. **side effect** efecto secundario. **take effect** (*drugs, etc.*) surtir efecto; (*law, etc.*) tener efecto. *v* efectuar. **effective** *adj* (*efficient*) eficaz; (*real*) efectivo; (*in force*) vigente. **effectiveness** *n* eficacia *f*; efecto *m*; vigencia *f*.
effeminate [i'feminət] *adj* afeminado.
effervescent [,efə'vesənt] *adj* efervescente. **effervesce** *v* estar en efervescencia.
efficient [i'fiʃənt] *adj* eficaz, eficiente. **efficiency** *n* eficacia *f*, eficiencia *f*.
effigy ['efidʒi] *n* efigie *f*.
effort ['efət] *n* esfuerzo *m*. **effortless** *adj* sin esfuerzo.
egg [eg] *n* huevo *m*. **bad egg** huevo podrido. **boiled egg** huevo pasado por agua. **hard-boiled egg** huevo duro. **new-laid egg** huevo fresco. **poached egg** huevo escalfado. **scrambled eggs** huevos revueltos *m pl*. **eggcup** *n* huevera *f*. **egg-shaped** *adj* oviforme. **eggshell** *n* cascarón de huevo *m*. **egg on** incitar.
egotism ['egətizm] *n* egotismo *m*. **egotist** *n* (*self-important person*) egotista *m, f*; (*selfish person*) egoísta *m, f*.
Egypt ['iːdʒipt] *n* Egipto *m*. **Egyptian** *n, adj* egipcio, -a.
eiderdown ['aidədaun] *n* edredón *m*.
eight [eit] *nm, adj* ocho. **eighth** *n, adj* octavo, -a.
eighteen [ei'tiːn] *nm, adj* dieciocho. **eighteenth** *n, adj* decimoctavo, -a.
eighty ['eiti] *nm, adj* ochenta. **eightieth** *n, adj* octogésimo, -a.
either ['aiðə] *adj* cada, ambos. *pron* uno u otro; cualquiera de los dos. *adv* tampoco. *conj* o. **either ... or ...** o ... o....
ejaculate [i'dʒakjuleit] *v* exclamar; (*med*) eyacular. **ejaculation** *n* exclamación *f*; eyaculación *f*.
eject [i'dʒekt] *v* expulsar; echar; (*tenant*) desahuciar. **ejection** *n* expulsión *f*; desahucio *m*. **ejector seat** asiento eyectable *m*.
eke [iːk] *v* **eke out** (*add to*) complementar; (*make last*) escatimar.
elaborate [i'labərət; *v* i'labəreit] *adj* complicado; detallado. *v* elaborar. **elaborate**

elm

on ampliar. **elaborately** *adv* cuidadosamente; complicadamente; detalladamente. **elaboration** *n* elaboración *f*; explicación *f*; complicación *f*.
elapse [i'laps] *v* transcurrir.
elastic [i'lastik] *nm, adj* elástico. **elastic band** goma elástica *f*. **elasticity** *n* elasticidad *f*.
elated [i'leitid] *adj* jubiloso; exaltado. **elation** *n* júbilo *m*; exaltación *f*.
elbow ['elbou] *n* codo *m*. **elbow grease** fuerza de puños *f*. **elbow room** espacio suficiente *m*.
elder[1] ['eldə] *nm, adj* mayor. **elderly** *adj* mayor de edad. **eldest** *adj* mayor.
elder[2] ['eldə] *n* (*bot*) saúco *m*. **elderberry** *n* baya del saúco.
elect [i'lekt] *v* elegir. *adj* elegido. **election** *n* elección *f*. **electoral** *adj* electoral. **electorate** *n* electorado *m*.
electric [ə'lektrik] *adj also* **electrical** eléctrico. **electric blanket** manta eléctrica *f*. **electric fire** estufa eléctrica *f*. **electric shock** electrochoque *m*. **electrician** *n* electricista *m, f*. **electricity** *n* electricidad *f*. **electrify** *v* (*rail, industry*) electrificar; (*produce electricity*) electrizar; (*fig*) entusiasmar.
electrocute [i'lektrəkjuːt] *v* electrocutar. **electrocution** *n* electrocución *f*.
electrode [i'lektroud] *n* electrodo *m*.
electronic [elək'tronik] *adj* electrónico. **electronics** *n* electrónica *f*.
elegant ['eligənt] *adj* elegante; bello. **elegance** *n* elegancia *f*.
elegy ['elidʒi] *n* elegía *f*.
element ['eləmənt] *n* elemento *m*; factor *m*. **elementary** *adj* elemental; fundamental.
elephant ['elifənt] *n* elefante *m*.
elevate ['eliveit] *v* elevar; (*voice, eyes*) levantar; (*honour*) enaltecer. **elevation** *n* elevación *f*; (*hill*) altura *f*; (*thought*) nobleza *f*.
elevator ['eliveitor] *n* ascensor *m*.
eleven [i'levn] *nm, adj* once. **eleventh** *n* undécimo, -a *m, f*; *adj* onceavo.
elf [elf] *n* duende *m*.
eligible ['elidʒəbl] *adj* elegible; atractivo.
eliminate [i'limineit] *v* eliminar. **elimination** *n* eliminación *f*.
elite [ei'liːt] *n* élite *f*.
ellipse [i'lips] *n* elipse *f*. **elliptical** *adj* elíptico.
elm [elm] *n* olmo *m*.

elocution [elə'kjuːʃən] n elocución f; declamación f.

elope [i'loup] v fugarse. **elopement** n fuga f.

eloquent ['eləkwənt] adj elocuente. **eloquence** n elocuencia f.

else [els] adv más, de otra manera. **or else** si no. **elsewhere** adv otro sitio.

elude [i'luːd] v eludir, escapar; (a blow) evitar. **elusive** adj escurridizo.

emaciated [i'meisieitid] adj demacrado. **emaciation** n demacración f.

emanate ['eməneit] v emanar. **emanation** n emanación f.

emancipate [i'mansipeit] v emancipar. **emancipation** n emancipación f.

embalm [im'baːm] v embalsamar.

embankment [im'baŋkmənt] n (road, rail) terraplén m; (river) dique m.

embargo [im'baːgou] n prohibición f.

embark [im'baːk] v embarcar. **embark on** emprender. **embarkation** n (people) embarco m; (cargo) embarque m.

embarrass [im'barəs] v desconcertar; molestar. **embarrassment** n desconcierto m; molestia f. **financial embarrassment** apuros de dinero m pl.

embassy ['embəsi] n embajada f.

embellish [im'beliʃ] v embellecer; adornar. **embellishment** n embellicimiento m; adorno m.

ember ['embə] n ascua f.

embezzle [im'bezl] v malversar. **embezzlement** n malversación f. **embezzler** n malversador, -a m, f.

embitter [im'bitə] v (person) amargar. **embittered** adj amargado; rencoroso.

emblem ['embləm] n emblema m. **emblematic** adj emblemático.

embody [im'bodi] v personificar; materializar; incluir. **embodiment** n personificación f; incorporación f.

emboss [im'bos] v grabar en relieve; (paper) gofrar; (leather, silver) repujar. **embossed** adj (letterhead) gofrado.

embrace [im'breis] v abrazar; (encompass) abarcar; (opportunity) aprovecharse de. n abrazo m.

embroider [im'broidə] v bordar; (fig) adornar. **embroidery** n bordado m; adorno m.

embryo ['embriou] n embrión m. **in embryo** en embrión. **embryonic** adj embrionario.

emerald ['emərəld] n esmeralda f.

emerge [i'məːdʒ] v salir; sacarse. **emergence** n salida f.

emergency [i'məːdʒənsi] n emergencia f; (med) urgencia f. **emergency exit** salida de emergencia f. **emergency landing** aterrizaje forzoso m. **in case of emergency** en caso de emergencia.

emigrate ['emigreit] v emigrar. **emigrant** (m+f), adj emigrante. **emigration** n emigración f.

eminent ['eminənt] adj eminente. **eminence** n eminencia f.

emit [i'mit] v (light, sound) emitir; (cry) dar; (heat) desprender; (smoke) echar; (smell) despedir. **emission** n emisión f.

emotion [i'mouʃən] n emoción f. **emotional** adj (concerning the emotions) emocional; (occasion, person) emotivo. **emotionally** adv con emoción.

empathy ['empəθi] n empatía f.

emperor ['empərə] n emperador m. **empress** n emperatriz f.

emphasis ['emfəsis] n, pl -ses (fig) énfasis m; importancia f; (stress) acento m. **emphasize** v subrayar; (stress) acentuar. **emphatic** adj enfático; enérgico; categórico.

empire ['empaiə] n imperio m.

empirical [im'pirikəl] adj empírico. **empiricism** n empirismo m.

employ [im'ploi] v emplear. n also **employment** empleo m. **employee** n empleado, -a m, f. **employer** n empresario, -a m, f; empleador, -a m, f. **employment agency** agencia de colocaciones f.

empower [im'pauə] v autorizar, habilitar.

empty ['empti] adj vacío; vacante; desocupado; desierto. **empty-handed** adj con las manos vacías. **empty-headed** adj casquivano. v vaciar; (river) desaguar. **emptiness** n vacío m; vacuidad f.

emu ['iːmjuː] n emú m.

emulate ['emjuːleit] v emular. **emulation** n emulación f.

emulsion [i'mʌlʃən] n emulsión f. **emulsify** v emulsionar.

enable [i'neibl] v permitir; capacitar.

enact [i'nakt] v (represent) representar; (a law) promulgar; (decree) decretar; (do) hacer. **enactment** n promulgación f; decreto m.

enamel [i'naməl] n esmalte m. v esmaltar.

enamour [i'namə] *v* enamorar. **be enamoured of** estar enamorado de.
encase [in'keis] *v* (*enclose*) encerrar; (*box*) encajonar.
enchant [in'tʃaɪnt] *v* encantar. **enchanter** *n* (*magician*) hechicero *m*; encanto *m*.
enchanting *adj* encantador. **enchantment** *n* (*charm*) encanto *m*; (*magic*) hechizo *m*.
enchantress *n* hechicera *f*; encanto *m*.
encircle [in'sɜikl] *v* cercar, rodear.
enclose [in'klouz] *v* (*shut in*) encerrar; (*surround*) rodear; (*in a letter*) adjuntar.
enclosed *adj* adjunto. **enclosure** *n* encierro *m*; carta adjunta *f*.
encore ['oŋkɔɪ] *interj* ¡bis! ¡otra vez! *n* repetición *f*. *v* pedir la repetición; repetir.
encounter [in'kauntə] *v* encontrarse con; enfrentarse a. *n* encuentro *m*.
encourage [in'kʌridʒ] *v* animar, alentar; estimular; incitar. **encouragement** *n* ánimo *m*, aliento *m*; estimulación *f*; incitación *f*. **encouraging** *adj* alentador; prometedor.
encroach [in'kroutʃ] *v* invadir; usurpar. **encroachment** *n* invasión *f*; usurpación *f*.
encumber [in'kʌmbə] *v* (*humper*) estorbar; (*load*) cargar; (*block*) obstruir. **encumbrance** *n* estorbo *m*; obstáculo *m*.
encyclopaedia [insaiklə'piːdiə] *n* enciclopedia *f*.
end [end] *n* (*tip*) punta *f*; (*tail end*) cabo *m*; (*finish*) fin *m*, final *m*. **end product** (*comm*) producto final *m*; (*result*) resultado *m*. **make ends meet** pasar con lo que se tiene. *v* acabar, terminar. **ending** *n* fin *m*, final *m*. **endless** *adj* interminable.
endanger [in'deindʒə] *v* arriesgar, poner en peligro.
endeavour [in'devə] *n* esfuerzo *m*, empeño *m*. *v* esforzarse, procurar.
endemic [en'demik] *adj* endémico.
endive ['endiv] *n* escarola *f*, endibia *f*.
endorse [in'dɔis] *v* (*cheque, etc.*) endosar; (*approve*) aprobar. **endorsement** *n* endoso *m*; aprobación *f*; (*mot*) nota de inhabilitación *f*.
endow [in'dau] *v* dotar; (*prize, etc.*) fundar. **endowment** *n* dotación *f*; fundación *f*.
endure [in'djuə] *v* (*support*) aguantar; (*last*) durar. **endurable** *adj* soportable. **endurance** *n* aguante *m*; resistencia *f*. **enduring** *adj* resistente; duradero.

enemy ['enəmi] *n* enemigo, -a *m, f*.
energy ['enədʒi] *n* energía *f*. **energetic** *adj* enérgico.
enfold [in'fould] *v* envolver; abrazar.
enforce [in'fɔis] *v* (*discipline*) imponer; (*law*) hacer cumplir.
engage [in'geidʒ] *v* (*employ*) ajustar; (*pledge*) comprometer; (*attention*) llamar; (*keep busy*) ocupar; (*clutch*) embragar. **engaged** *adj* prometido; ocupado. **get engaged** comprometerse. **engagement** *n* compromiso *m*; (*appointment*) cita *f*; (*encounter*) encuentro *m*. **engagement ring** sortija de pedida *f*.
engine ['endʒin] *n* motor *m*; máquina *f*. **engine driver** maquinista *m*. **engine room** sala de máquinas *f*.
engineer [endʒi'niə] *n* ingeniero *m*; (*workman*) mecánico *m*. **engineering** *n* ingeniería *f*.
England ['iŋglənd] *n* Inglaterra *f*. **English** *nm, adj* inglés. **the English** los ingleses.
English Channel *n* Canal de la Mancha *m*.
engrave [in'greiv] *v* grabar. **engraver** *n* grabador, -a *m, f*. **engraving** *n* grabado *m*.
engross [in'grous] *v* absorber. **engrossing** *adj* absorbente.
engulf [in'gʌlf] *v* tragarse; (*sink*) hundir.
enhance [in'hains] *v* (*prices, etc.*) aumentar; (*beauty*) realzar. **enhancement** *n* aumento *m*; realce *m*.
enigma [i'nigmə] *n* enigma *m*. **enigmatic** *adj* enigmático.
enjoy [in'dʒoi] *v* (*like*) gustar; (*delight in, have the use of*) gozar de, disfrutar de; (*party*) divertirse en. **enjoyable** *adj* agradable; divertido. **enjoyment** *n* placer *m*; diversión *f*.
enlarge [in'laidʒ] *v* ampliar, agrandar; (*expand*) extender. **enlargement** *n* aumento *m*; extensión *f*; (*phot*) ampliación *f*. **enlarger** *n* (*phot*) ampliadora *f*.
enlighten [in'laitn] *v* iluminar; (*inform*) informar; aclarar. **enlightenment** *n* aclaración *f*.
enlist [in'list] *v* alistar; alistarse; (*obtain support*) conseguir. **enlistment** *n* alistamiento *m*.
enmity ['enməti] *n* enemistad *f*.
enormous [i'nɔiməs] *adj* enorme. **enormity** *n* enormidad *f*. **enormously** *adv* enormemente.

enough 66

enough [i'nʌf] adj, adv bastante. n lo bastante. **enough is enough** basta y sobra.
curiously enough por extraño que parez-
ca. **sure enough** más que seguro. **that's
enough** con eso basta.
enquire [in'kwaiə] V **inquire.**
enrage [in'reidʒ] v enfurecer.
enrich [in'ritʃ] v enriquecer; (soil) fertilizar. **enrichment** n enriquecimiento m;
fertilización f.
enrol [in'roul] v inscribir; registrar;
matricular; (mil) alistar. **enrolment** n
inscripción f; registro m; matriculación
f; alistamiento m.
ensign ['ensain] n (flag) enseña f; (badge)
insignia f; (naut) bandera de popa f.
enslave [in'sleiv] v esclavizar. **enslavement**
n esclavitud f.
ensue [in'sjuː] v seguir; resultar. **ensuing**
adj siguiente; resultante.
ensure [in'ʃuə] v asegurar.
entail [in'teil] v (involve) suponer; (follow
as a result of) acarrear; (law) vincular.
entailment n vinculación f.
entangle [in'taŋgl] v enredar; complicar.
entanglement n enredo m; (fig) lío m.
enter ['entə] v entrar en; penetrar;
meterse en; registrar; matricular;
presentar. **enter for** tomar parte en. **enter
into** empezar; establecer; comprender.
enterprise ['entəpraiz] n empresa f;
iniciativa f. **enterprising** adj
emprendedor.
entertain [ˌentə'tein] v (host) recibir;
(amuse) divertir; (ideas) abrigar. **entertainer** n artista m, f. **entertaining** adj
divertido, entretenido. **entertainment** n
entretenimiento m.
enthral [in'θrɔil] v encantar. **enthralling**
adj cautivador.
enthusiasm [in'θuːziˌazəm] n entusiasmo
m. **enthusiast** n entusiasta m, f. **enthusiastic** adj (person) entusiasta; (praise, etc.)
entusiástico.
entice [in'tais] v tentar, seducir. **enticing**
adj tentador; atractivo. **enticement** n
atracción f; seducción f.
entire [in'taiə] adj entero, completo.
entirety n totalidad f.
entitle [in'taitl] v (authorize) dar derecho
a; (written work) titular. **be entitled** tener
derecho.
entity ['entəti] n entidad f, ente m.
entrails ['entreilz] pl n entrañas f pl.

entrance¹ ['entrəns] n entrada f; ingreso
m. **entrance examination** examen de
ingreso m. **entrance hall** vestíbulo m.
tradesmen's entrance entrada de servicio
f.
entrance² [in'trains] v arrebatar. **entranc-
ing** adj encantador.
entrant ['entrənt] n participante m, f.
entreat [in'triit] v suplicar, implorar.
entreaty n súplica f, imploración f.
entrée ['ontrei] n entrada f.
entrench [in'trentʃ] v atrincherar.
entrenchment n atrincheramiento m;
(encroachment) invasión f.
entrepreneur [ˌontrəprə'nəi] n empresario
m; intermediario m.
entrust [in'trʌst] v (commit) confiar;
(someone) encargar.
entry ['entri] n (entrance) entrada f; (into
profession) ingreso m; (in a book) anotación f; (book-keeping) asiento m. **no
entry** dirección prohibida f.
entwine [in'twain] v entrelazar.
enunciate [i'nʌnsiˌeit] v enunciar. **enunciation** n enunciación f.
envelop [in'veləp] v envolver. **enveloping**
adj envolvente.
envelope ['envəˌloup] n sobre m.
environment [in'vaiərənmənt] n ambiente
m. **environmental** adj ambiental.
envisage [in'vizidʒ] v (imagine)
imaginarse; (foresee) prever.
envoy ['envoi] n enviado m.
envy ['envi] n envidia f. v envidiar. **envia-
ble** adj envidiable. **envious** adj envidioso.
enviously adv con envidia.
enzyme ['enzaim] n enzima f.
epaulet ['epəlet] n charretera f.
ephemeral [i'femərəl] adj efímero.
epic ['epik] n poema épica f. adj épico.
epidemic [epi'demik] n epidemia f. adj
epidémico.
epilepsy ['epilepsi] n epilepsia f. **epileptic**
n, adj epiléptico, -a. **epileptic fit** ataque
epiléptico m.
Epiphany [i'pifəni] n Epifanía f.
episcopal [i'piskəpəl] adj episcopal.
episode ['episoud] n episodio m. **episodic**
adj episódico.
epitaph ['epiˌtaif] n epitafio m.
epitome [i'pitəmi] n epítome m; (fig) personificación f. **epitomize** v compendiar;
ser la personificación de.
epoch ['iipok] n época f.

equable ['ekwəbl] *adj* uniforme; *(calm)* tranquilo.

equal ['iːkwəl] *n* (*m*+*f*), *adj* igual. *v* igualar. **equality** *n* igualdad *f*. **equalize** *v* igualar; *(draw)* empatar.

equanimity [ekwə'niməti] *n* ecuanimidad *f*.

equate [i'kweit] *v* igualar; comparar; poner en ecuación. **equation** *n* ecuación *f*.

equator [i'kweitə] *n* ecuador *m*. **equatorial** *adj* ecuatorial.

equestrian [i'kwestriən] *adj* ecuestre. *n* caballista *m*.

equilateral [iːkwi'latərəl] *n* figura equilátera *f*. *adj* equilátero.

equilibrium [iːkwi'libriəm] *n* equilibrio *m*.

equinox ['ekwinoks] *n* equinoccio *m*. **equinoctial** *adj* equinoccial.

equip [i'kwip] *v* equipar. **equipment** *n* equipo *m*; *(tools)* herramientas *f pl*.

equity ['ekwəti] *n* equidad *f*, justicia *f*.

equivalent [i'kwivələnt] *nm*, *adj* equivalente.

era ['iərə] *n* era *f*.

eradicate [i'radi,keit] *v* erradicar. **eradication** *n* erradicación *f*.

erase [i'reiz] *v* borrar. **eraser** *n* goma de borrar. **erasure** *n* borradura *f*.

erect [i'rekt] *adj* erguido. *v* erigir; *(assemble)* montar. **erection** *n* erección *f*; *(building)* construcción *f*; montaje *m*.

ermine ['əːmin] *n* ermiño *m*.

erode [i'roud] *v* corroer; *(wear away)* erosionar. **erosion** *n* corrosión *f*; erosión *f*. **erosive** *adj* erosivo.

erotic [i'rotik] *adj* erótico. **eroticism** *n* erotismo *m*.

err [əː] *v* errar, desviarse; *(sin)* pecar. **erring** *adj* extraviado; pecaminoso.

errand ['erənd] *n* recado *m*. **run an errand** hacer un recado. **errand boy** recadero *m*.

erratic [i'ratik] *adj* desigual; errático.

error ['erə] *n* (*mistake*) error *m*; *(wrongdoing)* extravío *m*.

erudite ['erudait] *adj* erudito. **erudition** *n* erudición *f*.

erupt [i'rupt] *v* estar en erupción, salir con fuerza. **eruption** *n* erupción *f*. **eruptive** *adj* eruptivo.

escalate ['eskə,leit] *v* intensificar, agravar. **escalation** *n* intensificación *f*. **escalator** *n* escalera mecánica *f*.

escalope ['eskə,lop] *n* escalope *m*.

escape [is'keip] *n* *(flight)* fuga *f*; *(liquid)* salida *f*; *(gas)* escape *m*; *(responsibilities, etc.)* evasión *f*. **escape hatch** escotilla de salvamento *f*. **fire escape** escalera de incendios *f*. *v* escapar de; evadir; eludir. **escape notice** pasar inadvertido. **escapism** *n* evasión *f*.

escort ['eskoːt; *v* i'skoːt] *n* acompañante *m*; *(mil)* escolta *f*. *v* acompañar; *(mil)* escoltar.

esoteric [esə'terik] *adj* esotérico.

especial [i'speʃəl] *adj* especial, particular; excepcional. **especially** *adv* especialmente, sobre todo.

espionage ['espiə,naːʒ] *n* espionaje *m*.

esplanade [,esplə'neid] *n* explanada *f*, bulevar *m*, pasco *m*.

essay ['esei] *n* ensayo *m*; composición *f*; *(attempt)* intento *m*. *v* probar; intentar. **essayist** *n* ensayista *m*, *f*.

essence ['esns] *n* esencia *f*. **essential** *adj* esencial, imprescindible; fundamental. *n* lo esencial. **essentials** *pl n* elementos esenciales *m pl*.

establish [i'stabliʃ] *v* establecer. **establishment** *n* establecimiento *m*. **The Establishment** clase dirigente *f*.

estate [i'steit] *n* *(property)* propiedad *f*; *(land)* finca *f*, *(S. Am.)* hacienda *f*, estancia *f*; *(inheritance)* herencia *f*; *(fortune)* fortuna *f*; *(social class)* estado *m*; *(of the deceased)* testamentaría *f*. **estate agency** agencia inmobiliaria *f*. **estate agent** agente inmobiliario *m*. **estate car** furgoneta *f*.

esteem [i'stiːm] *v* estimar, apreciar. *n* estima *f*, aprecio *m*.

estimate ['estimət; *v* 'esti,meit] *n* *(valuation)* estimación *f*; *(statement of cost)* presupuesto *m*. *v* estimar; hacer un presupuesto de. **estimation** *n* juicio *m*; *(esteem)* aprecio *m*.

estuary ['estjuəri] *n* estuario *m*.

eternal [i'təːnl] *adj* eterno. **eternity** *n* eternidad *f*.

ether ['iːθə] *n* éter *m*. **ethereal** *adj* etéreo.

ethical ['eθikl] *adj* ético. **ethics** *pl n* ética *f sing*.

ethnic ['eθnik] *adj* étnico.

etiquette ['eti,ket] *n* etiqueta *f*.

etymology [,eti'molədʒi] *n* etimología *f*. **etymologist** *n* etimólogo, -a *m*, *f*.

Eucharist ['juːkərist] *n* Eucaristía *f*.

eunuch ['juːnək] *n* eunuco *m*.

euphemism ['juːfəˌmizəm] n eufemismo m. euphemistic adj eufemístico.
euphoria [juˈfɔɪrɪə] n euforia f. euphoric adj eufórico.
Europe ['juərəp] n Europa f. European n, adj europeo, -a.
European Economic Community (EEC) n Comunidad Económica Europea (CEE) f.
euthanasia [juːθəˈneɪzɪə] n eutanasia f.
evacuate [iˈvakjuˌeit] v evacuar. evacuation n evacuación f. evacuee n evacuado, -a m, f.
evade [iˈveid] v evadir, eludir. evasion n evasión f. evasive evasivo.
evaluate [iˈvaljuˌeit] v evaluar. evaluation n evaluación f.
evangelical [ˌiːvanˈdʒelikəl] adj evangélico. evangelist n evangelizador, -a m, f.
evaporate [iˈvapəˌreit] v evaporar; deshidratar. evaporated milk leche evaporada f. evaporation n evaporación f; deshidratación f.
eve [iːv] n víspera f. Christmas Eve Nochebuena f. New Year's Eve Noche Vieja f. on the eve of en vísperas de.
even ['iːvən] adj (surface) uniforme; (smooth) suave; (calm) ecuánime; (fair) justo; (same level) a nivel; (equal) igual; (number) par. break even quedar igual. get even desquitarse. adv siquiera; incluso. even if incluso si. even so aun así. even though aunque. even-tempered adj sereno. v nivelar; igualar. evenly adv uniformemente; imparcialmente.
evening ['iːvnɪŋ] n tarde f; anochecer m. evening class clase nocturna f. evening dress (man) traje de etiqueta m; (woman) traje de noche m. good evening! (early) ¡buenas tardes! (late) ¡buenas noches!
event [iˈvent] n (occurrence) acontecimiento m; (case) caso m; (outcome) consecuencia f; (in a programme) número m; (sport) prueba f. in the event of en caso de. eventful adj agitado; memorable. eventual adj final; consiguiente. eventuality n eventualidad f. eventually adv finalmente; con el tiempo.
ever ['evə] adv (always) siempre; nunca, jamás. we hardly ever go out casi nunca salimos. not ever nunca jamás. ever after desde (que).
evergreen ['evəgriːn] adj de hoja perenne.

everlasting [ˌevəˈlaːstɪŋ] adj eterno; perpetuo.
every ['evri] adj (all) todo; (each) cada. everybody also everyone pron todo el mundo. everyday adj diario. every other day cada dos días. everything pron todo. everywhere adv por also en todas partes.
evict [iˈvikt] v desahuciar. eviction n desahucio m.
evidence ['evidəns] n evidencia f; (sign) indicio m; (law: proof) prueba f; (law: testimony) testimonio m. v evidenciar. give evidence declarar como testigo. evident adj evidente, patente.
evil ['iːvl] adj malo; perverso; maligno. n mal m; desgracia f. evildoer n malhechor, -a m, f. evil-minded adj malpensado.
evoke [iˈvouk] v evocar. evocation n evocación f. evocative adj evocador.
evolve [iˈvolv] v evolucinar; (develop) desarrollarse. evolution n evolución f; desarrollo m. evolutionary adj evolutivo.
ewe [juː] n oveja f.
exacerbate [igˈzasəˌbeit] v exacerbar. exacerbation n exacerbación f.
exact [igˈzakt] adj exacto. v exigir. exacting adj (person) exigente; (condition) severo; (work) duro. exactly adv exactamente; precisamente.
exaggerate [igˈzadʒəˌreit] v exagerar; acentuar. exaggerated adj exagerado. exaggeration n exageración f.
exalt [igˈzolt] v exaltar, elevar; (praise) glorificar. exaltation n exaltación f; (ecstasy) arrobamiento. exalted adj exaltado, eminente.
examine [igˈzamin] v examinar; (search) reconocer; (by touch) analizar; (law) interrogar. examination examen m; (law) interrogatorio m. sit an exam examinarse. written exam prueba escrita f. examiner n examinador, -a m, f; inspector, -a m, f.
example [igˈzaɪmpl] n ejemplo m. follow someone's example tomar ejemplo de uno. for example por ejemplo. set an example dar ejemplo.
exasperate [igˈzaɪspəˌreit] v exasperar. exasperation n exasperación f.
excavate ['ekskəˌveit] v excavar. excavation n excavación f. excavator (person) excavador m; (tech) excavadora f.
exceed [ikˈsiːd] v exceder. exceedingly adv sumamente.

excel [ik'sel] v superar, sobresalir. **excellence** n excelencia f. **His Excellency** su Excelencia m. **excellent** adj excelente.
except [ik'sept] prep excepto, salvo, con excepción de. **except for** excepto. v excluir, exceptuar. **exception** n exclusión f; excepción f. **take exception to** ofenderse por. **exceptional** adj excepcional.
excerpt ['eksəıpt] n extracto m. v extractar.
excess [ik'ses] n exceso m. adj excedente. **excess fare** suplemento m. **excess luggage** exceso de equipaje also peso m. **excessive** adj excesivo. **excessively** adv excesivamente.
exchange [iks'tʃeindʒ] v (change) cambiar; (interchange) intercambiar; (courtesies) hacerse; (prisoners) canjear; (blows) darse. n cambio m; intercambio m. **exchange control** control de divisas. **exchange rate** tipo de cambio m. **Stock Exchange** bolsa de valores f. **telephone exchange** central telefónica f.
exchequer [iks'tʃekə] n (finances) hacienda f; tesoro público m. **Chancellor of the Exchequer** Ministro de Hacienda m.
excise ['eksaiz] n impuestos sobre el consumo m pl.
excite [ik'sait] v (stimulate) excitar; emocionar; entusiasmar; (irritate) poner nervioso; (urge) incitar; (imagination) despertar; (admiration, etc.) provocar. **get excited** emocionarse; entusiasmarse. **excitement** n excitación f; emoción f; entusiasmo m; agitación f. **exciting** adj excitante; emocionante; apasionante.
exclaim [ik'skleim] v exclamar. **exclamation** n exclamación f. **exclamation mark** punto de admiración m.
exclude [ik'skluːd] v excluir. **exclusion** n exclusión f. **exclusive** adj (policy) exclusivista; (sole) exclusivo; (select) selecto.
excommunicate [ekskə'mjuːniˌkeit] v excomulgar. **excommunication** n excomunión f.
excrete [ik'skriːt] v excretar. **excrement** n excremento m. **excretion** n excreción f.
excruciating [ik'skruːʃieitiŋ] adj (noise) intolerable; (pain) atroz.
excursion [ik'skəːʃən] n excursión f.
excuse [ik'skjuːz] n excusa f, disculpa f. v

excusar, disculpar, perdonar; (duty) dispensar de. **excuse me!** ¡perdón! ¡discúlpeme! **excusable** adj excusable, disculpable, perdonable.
execute ['eksiˌkjuːt] v (order, will, criminal) ejecutar; (carry out) llevar a cabo. **execution** n ejecución f; (of order) cumplimiento m. **executioner** n verdugo m.
executive [ig'zekjutiv] adj (power) ejecutivo; (function) dirigente; (ability) de ejecución. n (government branch) poder ejecutivo m; (person) ejecutivo m.
exemplify [ig'zempliˌfai] v ilustrar con ejemplos. **exemplification** n ejemplificación f.
exempt [ig'zempt] adj exento. v exentar, dispensar. **exemption** n exención f.
exercise ['eksəˌsaiz] n ejercicio m; gimnasia f. **exercise book** n cuaderno m. **take exercise** hacer ejercicio. v (rights, etc.) ejercer; (physically) ejercitarse; (patience) usar de.
exert [ig'zəːt] v ejercer. **exert oneself** esforzarse. **exertion** n esfuerzo m; (of strength) empleo m.
exhale [eks'heil] v exhalar; (breathe out) espirar. **exhalation** n exhalación f; espiración f.
exhaust [ig'zɔːst] v agotar. n (system) escape m. **exhaust pipe** tubo de escape m. **exhausting** adj agotador. **exhaustion** n agotamiento m. **exhaustive** adj exhaustivo. **exhaustively** adv exhaustivamente.
exhibit [ig'zibit] v (display) mostrar; (paintings, etc.) exponer; (documents) presentar. n objeto expuesto m. **exhibition** n exposición f. **make an exhibition of oneself** ponerse en ridículo. **exhibitor** n expositor m.
exhilarate [ig'ziləˌreit] v alegrar, animar. **exhilarating** adj estimulante. **exhilaration** n alegría f, regocijo m.
exile ['eksail] n exilio m, destierro m; (person) exiliado, -a m, f; desterrado, -a m, f. **go into exile** exiliarse, exilarse. v exiliar, exilar, desterrar.
exist [ig'zist] v existir; (live) vivir. **existence** n existencia f. **existent** also **existing** adj existente; (present) actual. **existentialism** n existencialismo m. **existentialist** n (m+f). adj existencialista.
exit ['egzit] n salida f; (theatre) mutis m. v (theatre) hacer mutio.
exonerate [ig'zonəˌreit] v (from blame)

disculpar; (*from obligation*) dispensar de.
exoneration *n* disculpa *f*; dispensa *f*.
exorbitant [ig'zo:bitənt] *adj* exorbitante.
exorcize ['ekso:saiz] *v* exorcizar. **exorcism**
n exorcismo *m*. **exorcist** *n* exorcista *m*, *f*.
exotic [ig'zotik] *adj* exótico. **exoticism** *n*
exotismo *m*.
expand [ik'spand] *v* (*cause to increase*)
desarrollar; (*make larger*) dilatar; (*add to*) ampliar. **expansion** *n* expansión *f*;
desarollo *m*; dilatación *f*; ampliación *f*.
expansive *adj* (*person*) expansivo; (*wide*)
extenso. **expansiveness** *n* expansibilidad
f.
expanse [ik'spans] *n* extensión *f*; (*wings*)
envergadura *f*.
expatriate [eks'peitriət; *v* eks'peitrieit] *n*,
adj expatriado, -a. *v* desterrar. **expatriation** *n* expatriación *f*.
expect [ik'spekt] *v* (*anticipate, hope for, require*) esperar; (*suppose*) suponer.
expectant *adj* expectante. **expectant mother** futura madre *f*. **expectation** *n*
expectación *f*; (*hope*) esperanza *f*; (*anticipation*) previsión *f*.
expedient [ik'spi:diənt] *adj* expeditivo,
oportuno. *n* expediente. **expedience** *also*
expediency *n* conveniencia *f*.
expedition [ˌekspi'diʃən] *n* expedición *f*.
expel [ik'spel] *v* expulsar.
expenditure [ik'spenditʃə] *n* gasto *m*.
expend *v* gastar; (*effort*) dedicar. **expendable** *adj* (*objects*) gastable; (*people*)
prescindible.
expense [ik'spens] *n* gasto *m*. **at the expense of** a costa de. **expense account**
cuenta de gastos de representación *f*.
expensive *adj* caro, costoso.
experience [ik'spiəriəns] *n* experiencia *f*.
v experimentar; (*difficulty*) tener. **experienced** *adj* experimentado; experto.
experiment [ik'sperimənt] *n* experimento
m. *v* hacer experimentos, experimentar.
experimental *adj* experimental.
expert ['ekspə:t] *n*, *adj* experto, -a.
expertise [ˌekspə'ti:z] *n* pericia *f*.
expire [ik'spaiə] *v* (*finish, die*) expirar;
(*become void*) caducar; (*expel air*)
espirar. **expiration** *also* **expiry** *n* expiración *f*; (*comm*) vencimiento *m*.
explain [ik'splein] *v* explicar. **explanation**
n explicación *f*. **explanatory** *adj* explicativo.
expletive [ek'spli:tiv] *n* (*gramm*) expletiva
f; (*oath*) taco *m*.

explicit [ik'splisit] *adj* explícito.
explode [ik'sploud] *v* estallar, hacer
explotar; (*myth*) refutar; (*rumour*)
desmentir. **explosion** *n* explosión *f*.
explosive *nm*, *adj* explosivo.
exploit[1] ['eksploit] *n* hazaña *f*.
exploit[2] [ik'sploit] *v* explotar. **exploitation**
n explotación *f*.
explore [ik'splo:] *v* explorar. **exploration** *n*
exploración *f*. **exploratory** *adj*
exploratorio. **explorer** *n* explorador, -a
m, *f*.
exponent [ik'spounənt] *n* exponente *m*, *f*.
export ['ekspo:t; *v* ik'spo:t] *n* exportación
f. *v* exportar. **exporter** *n* exportador, -a
m, *f*.
expose [ik'spouz] *v* (*leave uncovered*)
exponer; (*reveal*) revelar; (*plot, etc.*)
descubrir; (*phot*) exponer. **exposure** *n*
exposición *f*; revelación *f*;
descubrimiento *m*; (*denunciation*)
denuncia *f*; (*phot*) fotografía *f*. **exposure
meter** exposímetro *m*. **indecent exposure**
exhibicionismo *m*.
expound [ik'spaund] *v* exponer;
comentar.
express [ik'spres] *v* expresar; (*press*)
exprimir. *n* (*train*) rápido *m*; (*mail*) correo urgente *m*. *adj*, *adv* expreso; rápido.
expression *n* expressión *f*. **expressive** *adj*
expresivo; (*mot*) **expressway** autopista
expulsion [ik'spʌlʃən] *n* expulsión *f*.
exquisite ['ekswizit] *adj* exquisito;
intenso.
extend [ik'stend] *v* extender, aumentar;
(*widen*) ampliar; (*lengthen*) prolongar;
(*stretch*) estirar; (*invitation*) enviar; (*aid*)
ofrecer; (*hand*) tender; (*time-limit*)
proragar. **extension** extensión *f*; prolongación *f*; aumento *m*; prórroga *f*. **telephone extension** extensión *f*. **extensive**
adj extenso.
extent [ik'stent] *n* (*length*) extensión *f*;
(*degree*) punto *m*; (*scope*) alcance *m*.
exterior [ik'stiəriə] *nm*, *adj* exterior.
exterminate [ik'stə:mi,neit] *v* exterminar.
extermination *n* exterminio *m*.
external [ik'stə:nl] *adj* externo. **for external use only** sólo para uso externo.
extinct [ik'stiŋkt] *adj* extinto; (*fire, volcano*) extinguido. **extinction** *n* extinción *f*.
extinguish [ik'stiŋgwiʃ] *v* extinguir; apagar; (*hope*) destruir. **extinguisher** *n* (*fire*)
extintor.

extort [ik'stɔtt] *v* arrancar, sacar por fuerza. **extortion** *n* extorsión *f*. **extortionate** *adj* exorbitante.

extra ['ekstrə] *adj* extra; de más; adicional; extraordinario; no incluido. *n (extra charge)* recargo *m*; *(actor)* extra *m, f. adv* extraordinariamente.

extract [ik'strakt; *n* 'ekstrakt] *v* extraer; *(obtain, parts of books, etc.)* sacar. *n* extracto *m*. **extraction** *n* extracción *f*; *(descent)* origen *m*.

extradite ['ekstrə,dait] *v* conceder la extradición de; obtener la extradición de. **extradition** *n* extradición *f*.

extramural [,ekstrə'mjuərəl] *adj* para estudiantes libres.

extraordinary [ik'strɔɪdənəri] *adj* extraordinario; raro.

extravagant [ik'stravəgənt] *adj (lavish)* pródigo; *(wasteful)* despilfarrador; *(taste)* dispendioso; *(language, ideas)* extravagante. **extravagance** *n* prodigalidad *f*; despilfarro *m*; extravagancia *f*.

extreme [ik'striɪm] *nm, adj* extremo. **go to extremes** llegar a extremos. **extremist** *n* *(m + f)*, *adj* extremista. **extremity** *n (end)* extremidad *f*; *(necessity)* apuro *m*.

extrovert ['ekstrəvəɪt] *n, adj* extrovertido, -a.

exuberant [ig'zjuɪbərənt] *adj* exuberante; enfórico. **exuberance** *n* exuberancia *f*; enforia *f*.

exude [ig'zjuɪd] *v* exudar.

exult [ig'zʌlt] *v* exultar. **exult over** triunfar sobre. **exultant** *adj* exultante. **exultation** *n* exultación *f*.

eye [ai] *n* ojo *m*. **an eye for an eye** ojo por ojo. **private eye** detective *m*. **make eyes at** echar miradas a. **see eye to eye with** ver con los mismos ojos que. **turn a blind eye** cerrar los ojos. **up to one's eyes in work** estar hasta aquí en trabajo. **with an eye to** con miras a. **with the naked eye** a simple vista. *v* mirar.

eyeball ['aibɔɪl] *n* globo del ojo *m*.

eyebrow ['aibrau] *n* ceja *f*.

eye-catching ['aikatʃiŋ] *adj* llamativo.

eyelash ['ailaʃ] *n* pestaña *f*.

eyelid ['ailid] *n* párpado *m*.

eye shadow *n* sombreador de ojos *m*.

eyesight ['aisait] *n* vista *f*.

eyesore ['aisɔɪ] *n* algo que ofende la vista.

eyewitness ['ai,witnis] *n* testigo ocular *m*.

F

fable ['feibl] *n* fábula *f*.

fabric ['fabrik] *n (cloth)* tejido *m*; estructura *f*, construcción *f*. **fabricate** *v (invent)* fingir. **fabrication** *n* fabricación *f*; invención *f*.

fabulous ['fabjuləs] *adj* fabuloso; *(coll)* macanudo.

façade [fə'saɪd] *n* fachada *f*.

face [feis] *n* cara *f*, rostro *m*; *(side)* lado *m*; *(aspect)* aspecto *m*; *(grimace)* mueca *f*; *(surface)* superficie *f*; *(clock)* esfera *f*. **face down** boca abajo. **face up** boca arriba. **face to face** cara a cara. **on the face of it** a primera vista. **fly in the face of** burlarse de. **in the face of** frente a. **keep a straight face** mantenerse impávido. **lose face** quedar mal. **pull faces** hacer muecas. **save face** salvar las apariencias. *v* mirar hacia, dar a; estar en frente de; enfrentarse con; presentarse ante; *(consequences)* arrostrar; *(stand)* aguantar; *(resurface)* revestir.

face cloth *n* paño *m*.

facelift ['feislift] *n (coll)* lavado *m*.

face pack *n* mascarilla de belleza *f*.

face powder *n* polvos para la cara *m pl*.

facet ['fasit] *n* faceta *f*.

facetious [fə'siɪʃəs] *adj* chistoso; gracioso.

face value *n (bill)* valor nominal *m*; *(stamps)* valor facial. **take something at face value** creer algo a pie juntillas.

facing ['feisiŋ] *n (sewing)* guarnición *f*; *(building)* revestimiento *m*. *adj* de enfrente.

facsimile [fak'siməli] *nm, adj* facsímil.

fact [fakt] *n* hecho *m*; realidad *f*. **as a matter of fact** en realidad. **in fact** en verdad. **factual** *adj* objetivo.

faction ['fakʃən] *n* facción *f*. **factious** *adj* faccioso.

factor ['faktə] *n* factor *m*, elemento *m*; *(comm)* agente *m*.

factory ['faktəri] *n* fábrica *f*.

faculty ['fakəlti] *n (university)* facultad *f*; *(gift)* facilidad *f*.

fad [fad] *n* manía *f*; novedad *f*. **faddish** *adj* maniático.

fade [feid] *v (colour)* descolorarse; *(light)* apagarse; *(sound)* desvanecerse; *(interest)* decaer. **faded** *adj* descolorido; marchito.

fag [fag] *n* (*coll: cigarette*) pitillo *m*. **fag end** sobras *f pl*; (*cigarette*) colilla *f*. **fagged out** rendido.

fail [feil] *v* fallar; (*not succeed*) fracasar, no lograr; (*hopes*) frustrarse; (*run out*) acabarse; (*weaken*) decaer; (*exams*) ser suspendido; (*neglect*) dejar (de). **without fail** sin falta. **failing** *n* defecto *m*. **failure** *n* fracaso *m*; fallo *m*; suspenso *m*; (*breakdown*) avería *f*.

faint [feint] *adj* (*near collapse*) mareado; (*weak*) débil; (*colour*) pálido; (*timid*) timorato; (*slight*) ligero; vago; indistinto. *v* desmayarse. *n* desmayo *m*.

fair[1] [feə] *adj* bello; hermoso; (*skin*) blanco; (*hair*) rubio; (*just*) justo; (*reputation, weather*) bueno; (*prospects*) favorable; (*play*) limpio; (*price*) razonable; (*comment*) acertado; (*average*) mediano. **by fair means or foul** por las buenas o por las malas. **fairly** *adv* con justicia; (*reasonably*) bastante. **fairness** *n* belleza *f*; justicia *f*.

fair[2] [feə] *n* (*amusements*) verbena *f*; (*market*) feria *f*. **fun fair** parque de atracciones *m*. **fairground** *n* real *m*.

fairy ['feəri] *n* hada *f*. *adj* de hada. **fairy lights** bombillas de colores *f pl*.

faith [feiθ] *n* confianza *f*. **have faith in** fiarse de. **religious faith** fe religiosa *f*. **faithful** *adj* fiel; exacto. **faithfulness** *n* fidelidad *f*; exactitud *f*. **faithless** *adj* desleal; infiel.

fake [feik] *n* falsificación *f*; impostor *m*. *adj* falso; falsificado; (*feigned*) fingido. *v* falsificar; fingir.

falcon ['fɔːlkən] *n* halcón *m*.

*fall [fɔːl] *v* caer; (*prices, temperature, water*) bajar; (*wind*) amainar; (*decay*) decaer; (*task, duty, privilege*) tocar; (*accent*) recaer. **fall apart** caerse a pedazos. **fall back on** echar mano a. **fall behind** retrasarse. **fall in love** enamorarse. **fall out** (*quarrel*) reñir. **fall through** venirse abajo. *n* (*body, earth, leaves*) caida *f*; (*prices*) baja *f*; (*slope*) declive *m*; (*US: season*) otoño *m*.

fallacy ['faləsi] *n* falacia *f*; (*deception*) engaño *m*. **fallacious** *adj* erróneo.

fallible ['faləbl] *adj* falible. **fallibility** *n* falibilidad *f*.

fallow ['falou] *adj* (*land*) en barbecho; inculto.

false [fɔːls] *adj* falso; erróneo. **false alarm** falsa alarma *f*. **false pretences** estafa *f*. **false teeth** dientes postizas *m pl*. **falsehood** *n* falsedad *f*; mentira *f*. **falseness** *n* falsedad *f*; inexactitud *f*; perfidia *f*. **falsify** *v* falsificar; desvirtuar. **falsification** *n* falsificación *f*.

falsetto [fɔːl'setou] *n* falsete *m*. *adj* de falsete.

falter ['fɔːltə] *v* (*action*) vacilar; (*voice*) titubear. **faltering** *adj* vacilante; titubeante. **falteringly** *adv* con paso vacilante; con voz titubeante.

fame [feim] *n* fama *f*.

familiar [fə'miljə] *adj* familiar, conocido. **be familiar with** estar familiarizado con. **familiarity** *n* familiaridad *f*. **familiarize** *v* familiarizar.

family ['faməli] *n* familia *f*. **family allowance** subsidio familiar *m*. **family doctor** médico de cabecera *m*. **family planning** planificación familiar *f*. **family tree** árbol genealógico *m*.

famine ['famin] *n* (*general scarcity*) escasez *f*; (*food*) hambre *f*.

famished ['famiʃt] *adj* famélico. **be famished** estar muerto de hambre.

famous ['feiməs] *adj* famoso, célebre.

fan[1] [fan] *n* (*hand*) abanico *m*; (*tech*) ventilador *m*. **fan belt** correa del ventilador *f*. *v* abanicar; agitar.

fan[2] [fan] *n* aficionado, -a *m*, *f*; admirador, -a *m*, *f*. **fan club** club de admiradores *m*. **fan mail** correspondencia de los admiradores *f*.

fanatic [fə'natik] *n, adj* fanático, -a. **fanaticism** *n* fanatismo *m*.

fancy ['fansi] *adj* de adorno; de fantasía. *n* fantasía *f*; (*whim*) capricho *m*; (*desire*) afición *f*; (*delusion*) ilusión *f*; (*taste*) gusto *m*. *v* imaginarse; suponer; gustar; (*suspect*) parecerle(a); (*desire*) apetecer. **fancy oneself** ser un creído. **fancy that!** ¡imagínate! **fancy dress** disfraz *m*. **fancied** *adj* favorito; imaginario. **fanciful** *adj* imaginario; caprichoso.

fanfare ['fanfeə] *n* fanfarria *f*.

fang [faŋ] *n* colmillo *m*; (*snake*) diente *m*.

fantastic [fan'tastik] *adj* fantástico.

fantasy ['fantəsi] *n* fantasía *f*; capricho *m*.

far [fɑː] *adv* lejos; (*much*) mucho; muy. *adj* lejano; distante. **as far as** hasta; por lo que. **far and wide** por todas partes. **far away** lejos. **far-away** *adj* remoto. **Far East** Extremo Oriente *m*. **far-fetched** *adj* inverosímil. **far-reaching** *adj* de mucho

alcance. **so far so good** hasta ahora todo va bien.
farce [fɑːs] *n* farsa *f.* **farcical** *adj* ridículo, absurdo.
fare [feə] *n* precio del billete *m,* tarifa *f;* (*boat*) pasaje *m;* (*passenger*) pasajero, -a; (*in a taxi*) cliente *m, f;* (*in a bus*) viajero, -a *m, f;* (*food*) comida *f. v* (*get on*) irle bien (a uno).
farewell [feəˈwel] (*interj*) ¡adiós! **say farewell** decir adiós, despedirse de. *adj* de despedida.
farm [fɑːm] *n also* **farmhouse** granja *f,* finca *f;* (*S. Am.*) estancia *f,* hacienda *f.* **farmhand** *n* peón *m.* **farmland** *n* tierras de labrantío *f pl.* **farmyard** *n* corral *m. v* cultivar. **farm out** mandar hacer fuera. **farmer** *n* agricultor *m;* granjero *m.* **farming** *n* labranza *f;* agricultura *f.*
fart [fɑːt] (*impol*) n pedo *m. v* peerse.
farther [ˈfɑːðə] *adv* (*space*) más lejos; (*time*) más adelante. *adj* (*space, time*) más lejano.
farthest [ˈfɑːðist] *adv* más lejos. *adj* (*most distant*) más lejano; (*longest*) más largo.
fascinate [ˈfasiˌneit] *v* fascinar. **fascinating** *adj* fascinador. **fascination** *n* fascinación *f.*
fascism [ˈfaʃizəm] *n* fascismo *m.* **fascist** *n*(*m*+*f*), *adj* fascista.
fashion [ˈfaʃən] *n* manera *f,* modo *m;* moda *f.* **after a fashion** en cierto modo. **fashion show** desfile de modas *m.* **in fashion** de modo. **out of fashion** pasado de moda. *v* hacer; formar; (*mould*) moldear.
fast[1] [fɑːst] *adj* rápido, veloz; (*colour*) sólido; (*clock, etc.*) adelantado; (*secure*) seguro; firme. **fast asleep** profundamente dormido. **make fast** sujetar, atar. **pull a fast one** jugar una mala jugada. **stuck fast** (*in mud*) completamente atascado.
fast[2] [fɑːst] *n* ayuno *m. v* ayunar.
fasten [ˈfɑːsn] *v* (*fix*) fijar; (*attach*) sujetar; (*dress*) abrochar; (*close*) cerrar. **fastener** *or* **fastening** *n* corchete *m;* fijación *f.*
fastidious [faˈstidiəs] *adj* quisquilloso; (*demanding*) exigente. **fastidiousness** *n* melindre *m.*
fat [fat] *n* grasa *f;* (*on meat*) gordo *m. adj* grueso; gordo. **fatten** *v* (*person*) engordar; (*animal*) cebar. **fattening** *adj* que engorda.
fatal [ˈfeitl] *adj* fatal, mortal. **fatality** *n* fatalidad *f.*
fate [feit] *n* destino *m;* suerte *f.* **fated** *adj*

predestinado; condenado. **fateful** *adj* profético; fatal.
father [ˈfɑːðə] *n* padre *m.* **Father Christmas** Papa Noel *m.* **father-in-law** *n* suegro *m.* **fatherland** *n* patria *f.* **fatherless** *adj* huérfano de padre *m.* **fatherly** *adj* paternal.
fathom [ˈfaðəm] *n* braza *f. v* (*water depth*) sondar, sondear; (*unravel*) desentrañar. **fathomless** *adj* insondable.
fatigue [fəˈtiːg] *n* fatiga *f. v* fatigar.
fatuous [ˈfatjuəs] *adj* fatuo; necio. **fatuity** *or* **fatuousness** *n* fatuidad *f;* necedad *f.*
fault [fɔːlt] *n* culpa *f;* defecto *m;* error *m;* falta *f;* (*geol*) falla *f.* **be at fault** tener la culpa. **faultiness** *n* imperfección *f.* **faultless** *adj* perfecto. **faulty** *adj* malo; erróneo; defectuoso.
fauna [ˈfɔːnə] *n* fauna *f.*
favour [ˈfeivə] *n* favor *m;* favoritismo *m;* (*gift*) obsequio *m;* (*comm*) carta *f.* atenta *f.* **be in favour of** estar a favor de. *v* favorecer. **favourable** *adj* favorable. **favourite** *n, adj* favorito, -a.
fawn [fɔːn] *n* cervato *m. adj* color de gamuza *m.* **fawn on** *or* **upon** adular.
fear [fiə] *n* miedo *m;* temor *m. v* temer; tener miedo de *or* a. **fearful** *adj* (*frightening*) espantoso; (*frightened*) temeroso. **fearless** *adj* intrépido, audaz.
feasible [ˈfiːzəbl] *adj* factible. **feasibility** *n* viabilidad *f.*
feast [fiːst] *n* fiesta *f;* banquete *m.* **feast day** día festivo *m.*
feat [fiːt] *n* hazaña *f.*
feather [ˈfeðə] *n* pluma *f.* **feather bed** colchón de plumas *m.*
feature [ˈfiːtʃə] *n* característica *f;* (*shape*) figura *f;* (*face*) rasgo *m;* (*written article*) artículo principal *m.* **feature film** película principal *f. v* presentar; representar; (*emphasize*) destacar.
February [ˈfebruəri] *n* febrero *m.*
fed [fed] *V* **feed**.
federal [ˈfedərəl] *adj* federal.
federate [ˈfedəˌreit] *v* federar. **federation** *n* federación *f.*
fee [fiː] *n* (*professional*) honorarios *m pl;* (*club*) cuota *f.* **entrance fee** entrada *f.*
feeble [ˈfiːbl] *adj* débil; (*unconvincing*) de poco peso. **feebleness** *n* debilidad *f.*
*****feed** [fiːd] *v* alimentar; dar de comer; (*eat*) comer. **be fed up with** (*coll*) estar harto de. **feed on** alimentarse con. *n* (*for babies*) comida *f;* (*fodder*) foraje *m;*

(*tech*) alimentación *f*. **feedback** *n* reaprovechamiento *m*; (*tech*) realimentación *f*.
*feel [fiːl] *v* tocar; mirar; sentir; (*realize*) darse cuenta de; (*caress*) sobar; (*think*) pensar. *n* tacto *m*; sensación *f*; atmósfera *f*; sentido *m*. **feeler** *n* antena *f*; tentáculo *m*. **feeling** *n* sentimiento *m*; sentido *m*; sensación *f*; opinión *f*; impresión *f*.
feet [fiːt] *V* **foot**.
feign [fein] *v* fingir; inventar.
feline ['fiːlain] *nm, adj* felino.
fell¹ [fel] *V* **fall**.
fell² [fel] *v* derribar; (*trees*) talar.
fellow ['felou] *n* hombre *m*; compañero; (*coll*) tipo *m*; (*of a society*) miembro *m*. **fellowship** *n* comunidad *f*; asociación *f*.
felony ['feləni] *n* delito grave *m*. **felon** *n* criminal *m*.
felt¹ [felt] *V* **feel**.
felt² [felt] *n* fieltro *m*. **felt-tip pen** rotulador *m*.
female ['fiːmeil] *adj* hembra; femenino. *n* (*animal*) hembra *f*; (*person*) mujer *f*.
feminine ['feminin] *nm, adj* femenino. **femininity** *n* feminidad *f*. **feminism** *n* feminismo *m*. **feminist** *n*(*m*+*f*), *adj* feminista.
fence [fens] *n* cerca f, valla *f*. *v* cercar, vallar; (*sport*) practicar la esgrima. **fencing** *n* (*sport*) esgrima *f*.
fend [fend] *v* **fend for oneself** arreglárselas. **fend off** desviar.
fender ['fendə] *n* guardafuegos *m invar*; (*US: car*) guardabarros *m invar*.
fennel ['fenl] *n* hinojo *m*.
ferment [fə'ment; *n* 'fəːment] *v* fermentar. *n* fermento *m*; agitación *f*. **fermentation** *n* fermentación *f*.
fern [fəːn] *n* helecho *m*.
ferocious [fə'rouʃəs] *adj* feroz. **ferocity** *n* ferocidad *f*.
ferret ['ferit] *n* hurón *m*. **ferret out** conseguir, descubrir.
ferry ['feri] *n* transbordador *m*. *v* transportar.
fertile ['fəːtail] *adj* fértil; (*person*) fecundo. **fertility** *n* fertilidad *f*; fecundidad *f*. **fertilization** *n* fertilización *f*; fecundación *f*. **fertilize** *v* abonar; fecundar. **fertilizer** *n* abono *m*.
fervent ['fəːvənt] *adj* ferviente. **fervour** *n* fervor *m*.
fester ['festə] *v* supurar; (*fig*) enconarse.
festival ['festəvəl] *n* fiesta *f*.

festoon [fə'stuːn] *v* festonear. *n* guirnalda *f*.
fetch [fetʃ] *v* (*bring*) traer; (*procure*) buscar; (*reach*) alcanzar. **fetching** *adj* atractivo.
fête [feit] *n* fiesta *f*. *v* festejar.
fetid ['fiːtid] *adj* fétido.
fetish ['fetiʃ] *n* fetiche *m*.
fetter ['fetə] *v* encadenar. **fetters** *pl n* grilletes *m pl*; (*fig*) trabas *f pl*.
feud [fjuːd] *n* enemistad hereditaria *f*. *v* pelear, reñir.
feudal ['fjuːdl] *adj* feudal. **feudalism** *n* feudalismo *m*.
fever ['fiːvə] *n* fiebre *f*. **feverish** *adj* febril.
few [fjuː] *adj* poco. *n* pocos, -as *pl*. **a few** algunos, unos, unos pocos. **quite a few** bastante. **fewer** *adj* menos. **the fewer the better** cuantos menos mejor. **fewest** *adj* menos.
fiancé [fi'onsei] *n* novio *m*. **fiancée** *n* novia *f*.
fiasco [fi'askou] *n* fiasco *m*.
fib [fib] *n* mentirijilla *f*. *v* decir una mentirijilla.
fibre ['faibə] *n* fibra *f*. **fibreglass** *n* fibra de vidrio *f*.
fickle ['fikl] *adj* inconstante, veleidoso.
fiction ['fikʃən] *n* (*stories*) novela *f*; (*invention*) ficción *f*. **fictional** *or* **fictitious** *adj* novelesco; ficticio.
fiddle ['fidl] *n* violín *m*; (*coll: trick*) trampa *f*. *v* tocar el violín; (*coll: cheat*) camelar; (*coll: falsify*) amañar. **fiddle with** juguetear con. **fiddling** *adj* trivial; fútil.
fidelity [fi'deləti] *n* fidelidad *f*.
fidget ['fidʒit] *v* agitar nerviosamente. **fidgety** *adj* nervioso, agitado.
field [fiːld] *n* campo *m*; (*fig*) esfera *f*. **field glasses** gemelos *m pl*. **field marshal** mariscal de campo *m*. **fieldwork** *n* trabajo en el terreno *m*.
fiend [fiːnd] *n* demonio *m*, diablo *m*; (*coll*) fanático, -a *m*, *f*. **fiendish** *adj* diabólico.
fierce [fiəs] *adj* feroz, fiero; (*person*) violento; (*heat*) intenso; (*battle*) encarnizado. **fierceness** *or* **ferocity** *n* ferocidad *f*; violencia *f*; furia *f*; intensidad *f*.
fiery ['faiəri] *adj* (*burning*) ardiente; (*flaming*) llameante; (*passionate*) apasionado; (*temper*) fogoso.

fifteen [fif'tiin] *nm, adj* quince. **fifteenth** *n,*
adj decimoquinto, -a.
fifth [fifθ] *n, adj* quinto, -a.
fifty ['fifti] *nm, adj* cincuenta. **go fifty-fifty**
ir a medias. **fiftieth** *n, adj* quincuagésimo,
-a. **fiftyish** *adj* cincuentón.
fig [fig] *n (fruit)* higo *m*; *(tree)* higuera *f.*
***fight** [fait] *v* luchar contra, combatir. *n*
lucha *f,* pelea *f.*
figment ['figmənt] *n* invención *f.*
figure ['figə] *n (number)* número *m*, cifra
f; *(price)* precio *m*; *(statue, design, per-*
sonage) figura *f*; *(human)* línea *f.*
figurehead *n* mascarón de proa *m*; *(fig)*
testaferro *m.* **figure skating** patinaje
artístico *m. v (math)* poner en cifras;
(calculate) calcular. **figure out** comprender; resolver.
filament ['filəmənt] *n* filamento *m.*
file[1] [fail] *n (folder)* carpeta *f*; *(card index)*
fichero *m*; *(document holder)* archivador
m; *(dossier)* expediente *m. v* archivar; *(a*
claim) presentar. **file in/out** entrar/salir
en fila. **file past** desfilar ante. **in single**
file en fila de a uno. **filing** *n* clasificación
f. **filing cabinet** archivo *m.* **filing clerk**
archivero, -a *m, f,* archivista *m, f.*
file[2] [fail] *n (tool)* lima *f. v* limar. **filings** *pl*
n limaduras *f pl.*
filial ['filiəl] *adj* filial.
fill [fil] *v* llenar; *(space, time)* ocupar;
(vacancy) cubrir; *(tooth)* empastar; *(hole)*
tapar; *(cookery)* rellenar; *(requirements)*
satisfacer. **fill in** *(form)* rellenar. **fill up**
llenar. **filling** *n* relleno *m*; empaste *m.*
filling station estación de servicio *f.*
fillet ['filit] *n* filete *m. v* cortar en filetes.
film [film] *n (phot, cinema)* película *f*;
(layer) capa *f*; *(eye)* nube *f*; *(mist, etc.)*
velo *m.* **roll of film** rollo de película *m.*
filmgoer *n* aficionado al cine *m.* **film star**
astro de cine *m,* estrella de cine *f.*
filter ['filtə] *n* filtro *m. v* filtrar. **filtering** *n*
filtración *f.* **filter-tipped** *adj* con filtro,
emboquillado.
filth [filθ] *n* inmundicia *f,* suciedad *f*; *(fig)*
obscenidades *f pl.* **filthy** *adj* asqueroso,
inmundo; obsceno.
fin [fin] *n* aleta *f.*
final ['fainl] *adj (last)* último; decisivo;
definitivo. *n* final *f.* **finalist** *n* finalista *m,*
f. **finalize** *v* finalizar. **finally** *adv* finalmente.
finance [fai'nans] *n* finanzas *f pl. v*

finanzar. **financial** *adj* financiero.
financial year año económico *m.*
financier *n* financiero *m.*
finch [fintʃ] *n* pinzón *m.*
***find** [faind] *v* encontrar, hallar. **find out**
averiguar; descubrir. *n* hallazgo *m.*
findings *pl n* hallazgos *m pl*; resultados *m*
pl.
fine[1] [fain] *adj* excelente; elegante; *(pleas-*
ant) agradable; bueno; fino; delicado.
that's fine! ¡muy bien! *adv* en trozos
pequeños; fino; muy bien. **fine arts** be-
llas artes *f pl.* **finely** *adv (small)*
finamente; *(well)* primorosamente. **finery**
n galas *f pl.*
fine[2] [fain] *n* multa *f. v* multar.
finesse [fi'nes] *n* fineza *f,* delicadeza *f*;
tácto *m*; *(bridge)* impás *m.*
finger ['fiŋgə] *n* dedo *m.* **little finger**
mañique *m. v* tocar. **fingernail** *n* uña *f.*
fingerprint *n* huella dactilar *f.* **fingertip** *n*
punta del dedo *f.* **have at one's fingertips**
saberse al dedillo.
finish ['finiʃ] *v* terminar, acabar; *(sport)*
llegar. **finish off** rematar. *n* fin *m,* conclusión *f*; *(surface)* acabado *m*; *(sport)* llegada. **finishing line** meta *f.* **finishing**
touch última mano *f.*
finite ['fainait] *adj* finito.
Finland ['finlənd] *n* Finlandia *f.* **Finn** *n*
finlandés, -esa *m, f.* **Finnish** *nm, adj*
finlandés.
fir [fəɪ] *n* abeto *m.* **fir cone** piña *f.*
fire ['faiə] *n* fuego *m*; *(uncontrolled)*
incendio *m*; *(electric or gas)* estufa *f.* **be**
on fire estar ardiendo. **catch fire**
encenderse. **set on fire, set fire to** pegar
fuego, incendiar. *v (with enthusiasm, etc.)*
infundir (a); *(gun)* disparar; *(salute)*
tirar; *(missile)* lanzar; *(sack)* echar. **fire**
on hacer fuego sobre.
fire alarm *n* alarma de incendios *f.*
firearm ['faiə,aɪm] *n* arma de fuego *f.*
fire brigade *n* cuerpo de bomberos *m.*
fire door *n* puerta incombustible *f.*
fire drill *n* ejercicios para casos de
incendio *m pl.*
fire engine *n* bomba de incendios *f.*
fire-escape *n* escalera de incendios *f.*
fire-extinguisher *n* extintor *m.*
firefly ['faiəflai] *n* luciérnaga *f.*
fire-guard *n* guardafuego *m.*
firelight ['faiə,lait] *n* lumbre *m.*
fireman ['faiəmən] *n* bombero *m.*

fireplace ['faiə,pleis] *n* chimenea *f.*
fireproof ['faiə,pruːf] *adj* ininflamable, incombustible.
fireside ['faiə,said] *n* hogar *m.*
fire station *n* parque de bomberos *m.*
firewood ['faiə,wud] *n* leña *f.*
firework ['faiə,wɜːk] *n* fuego de artificio *m.*
firing squad *n* pelotón de ejecución *m.*
firm¹ [fɜːm] *adj* firme, sólido; estable.
firmness *n* firmeza *f.*
firm² [fɜːm] *n* empresa *f*, firma *f.*
first¹ [fɜːst] *adj* primero; básico; elemental. **first aid** primeros auxilios *m pl.* **first-class** *adj* de primera clase. **first cousin** primo hermano *m.* **first edition** edición príncipe *m.* **first floor** primer piso *m.* **first name** nombre de pila *m.* **first-rate** *adj* de primera calidad. **in the first place** en primer lugar.
first² [fɜːst] *adv* antes, primero. **first and foremost** antes que nada. **first and last** en todos los aspectos. **travel first** viajar en primera. **you go first** usted primero.
first³ [fɜːst] *n* primero, -a *m, f;* sobresaliente *m.* **at first** al principio. **be the first to** ser el primero en. **get a first** sacar sobresaliente.
fiscal ['fiskəl] *adj* fiscal.
fish [fiʃ] *n* (*food*) pescado *m*; (*in water*) pez *m.* **fish and chips** pescado frito con patatas fritas. *v* pescar. **fishy** *adj* (*coll*) sospechoso.
fishbone ['fiʃ,boun] *n* espina *f.*
fish-bowl *n* pecera *f.*
fisherman ['fiʃəmən] *n* pescador *m.*
fish fingers *n* filete de pescado empanado *m.*
fish hook *n* anzuelo *m.*
fishing ['fiʃiŋ] *n* pesca *f.* **fishing line** sedal *m.* **fishing net** red de pesca *f.* **fishing rod** caña de pescar *f.* **fishing tackle** aparejo de pescar *m.* **go fishing** ir de pesca.
fish market *n* mercado de pescado.
fishmonger ['fiʃ,mʌŋgə] *n* pescadero *m.* **fishmonger's** *n* pescadería *f.*
fission ['fiʃən] *n* fisión *f*, escisión *f.*
fissure ['fiʃə] *n* grieta *f.*
fist [fist] *n* puño *m.* **fistful** *n* puñado *m.*
fit¹ [fit] *adj* conveniente; apto; adecuado; (*qualified*) capacitado; (*competent*) capaz; (*worthy*) digno; (*healthy*) sano. **not fit to eat** no se puede comer. **see fit** juzgar conveniente. *v* (*try on*) probar; (*qualify*) capacitar; (*tally with*) cuadrar

con; adaptar; preparar; unir; (*supply with*) equipar con; (*clothes*) sentar bien a; (*tailor*) entallar. **fitness** *n* conveniencia *f*; salud *f*; aptitud *f.* **fitter** *n* (*tailor*) probador, -a *m, f*; (*tech*) ajustador *m.* **fitting** *adj* oportuno; digno; apropiado; propio. **fitting room** cuarto de pruebas *m.* **fittings** *pl n* muebles *m pl*; accesorios *m pl.*
fit² [fit] *n* (*med*) ataque *m.*
five [faiv] *nm, adj* cinco.
fix [fiks] *v* fijar; sujetar; (*decide*) establecer; (*date*) señalar; (*hopes*) poner; (*coll: put right*) arreglar. *n* aprieto *m*; (*coll*) una dosis de froga *f.* **fixation** *n* obsesión *f.* **fixed** *adj* fijo; (*coll: rigged*) amañado. **fixture** *n* instalación *f*; (*sport*) partido *m*; (*coll*) permanencia *f.*
fizz [fiz] *n* burbujeo *m*; (*coll*) gaseosa *f. v* burbujear.
flabbergasted ['flabe,gaistid] *adj* pasmado.
flabby ['flabi] *adj* fláccido; (*spineless*) blandengue. **flabbiness** *n* flaccidez *f*; blandura *f.*
flag¹ [flag] *n* bandera *f*; (*stone*) baldosa *f.* **flag down** detener haciendo señales. **flagpole** *n* asta de bandera *f.* **flagship** *n* buque insignia *m.*
flag² [flag] *v* (*weaken*) flaquear; (*interest*) decaer. **flagging** *adj* flojo; desmadejado.
flagon ['flagən] *n* ⟨*jug*⟩ jarra *f*; (*bottle*) botella (de dos litros) *f.*
flagrant ['fleigrənt] *adj* flagrante; escandaloso.
flair [fleə] *n* don *m*; instinto *m*; talento *m.*
flake [fleik] *n* (*snow*) copo *m*; (*soap*) escama *f*; (*paint*) desconchón *m. v* caer en copos; desconchar. **flaky** *adj* escamoso. **flaky pastry** hojaldre *m.*
flamboyant [flam,boiənt] *adj* llamativo. **flamboyance** *n* extravagancia *f.*
flame [fleim] *n* llama *f.* **burst into flames** incendiarse. *v* llamear. **flammable** *adj* inflamable.
flamingo [flə'miŋgou] *n* flamenco *m.*
flan [flan] *n* flan *m.*
flank [flaŋk] *n* (*animal*) ijada *f*; (*person*) costado *m*; (*mil*) flanco *m. v* bordear.
flannel ['flanl] *n* (*fabric*) franela *f*; (*face cloth*) pañito para lavarse la cara *m.* **flannels** *pl n* pantalones de franela *m pl.*
flap [flap] *v* (*shake*) sacudir; (*arms*) agitar; (*wings*) batir. *n* (*pocket*) carterita *f*; (*envelope, etc.*) solapa *f*; (*table*) ala

abatible *f*; (*coat*) faldón *m*; (*aero*) alerón *m*; (*coll*) crisis *f*.

flare [fleə] *n* (*blaze*) llamarada *f*; (*signal*) cohete de señales *m*; (*widening*) ensanchamiento *m*. *v* llamear; ensanchar; (*clothes*) acampanar. **flare up** (*anger*) ponerse furioso.

flash [flaʃ] *n* destello *m*; (*sparkle*) centelleo *m*; (*phot*) flash *m*; (*moment*) instante *m*; (*inspiration*) ráfaga *f*; (*genius*) rasgo *m*; (*hope*) resquicio *m*. **flashback** *n* escena retrospectiva *f*. **flash bulb** bombilla de magnesio *f*. **flashlight** *n* linterna *f*. *v* despedir; lanzar; encender; destellar; centellear. **flashing** *adj* intermitente.

flask [flɑːsk] *n* frasco *m*; (*vacuum*) termo *m*.

flat¹ [flat] *adj* plano, llano, chato; horizontal; (*fig*) categórico; monótono; (*boring*) pesado; (*rate*) fijo; (*below pitch*) desafinado; (*tyre*) desinflado; (*battery*) descargado; (*horse racing*) sin obstáculos. **flat beer** cerveza muerta *f*. **flat-footed** *adj* de pies planos. **be flat broke** estar sin blanca. **go flat out** ir a todo gas. **flatly** *adv* categóricamente; completamente. *n* (*music*) bemol *m*; (*land*) llano *m*; (*tyre*) pinchazo *m*. **flatten** *v* (*make flat*) aplanar; (*crush*) aplastar; (*smooth*) alisar.

flat² [flat] *n* apartamento *m*. **flatlet** *n* piso pequeño *m*.

flatter ['flatə] *v* adular, halagar; favorecer. **flatterer** *n* adulador, -a *m, f*. **flattering** *adj* (*words*) halagüeño; (*person*) halagador; (*clothes*) favorecedor. **flattery** *n* halago *m*, adulación *f*.

flatulence ['flatjuləns] *n* flatulencia *f*.

flaunt [flɔːnt] *v* ostentar. **flaunt oneself** pavonearse.

flautist ['flɔːtist] *n* flautista *m, f*.

flavour ['fleivə] *n* sabor *m*, gusto *m*; (*cookery*) sazón *m*, sainete *m*. *v* saborear; condimentar. **flavouring** *n* condimento *m*, sainete *m*.

flaw [flɔː] *n* defecto *m*; (*error*) fallo *m*. *v* (*crack*) agrietar; (*spoil*) estropear. **flawed** *adj* falto; imperfecto. **flawless** *adj* sin tacha; perfecto.

flax [flaks] *n* lino *m*. **flaxen** *adj* de lino; (*hair*) rubio.

flea [fliː] *n* pulga *f*. **fleabite** *n* picadura de pulga *f*.

fleck [flek] *n* (*speck*) mota *f*; (*colour*)

mancha *f*; (*dust*) partícula *f*. *v* motear; (*paint*) salpicar.

fled [fled] *V* **flee**.

***flee** [fliː] *v* evitar; escapar de.

fleece [fliːs] *n* (*wool*) lana *f*; (*sheared wool*) velón *m*. *v* (*coll*) pelar. **fleecy** *adj* (*woolly*) lanoso.

fleet [fliːt] *n* flota *f*; (*navy*) armada *f*. *adj* veloz. **fleeting** *adj* fugaz, breve.

Flemish ['flemiʃ] *nm, adj* flamenco. **Fleming** *n* flamenco, -a *m, f*.

flesh [fleʃ] *n* carne *f*. **flesh-coloured** *adj* de color carne. **flesh-eating** *adj* carnívoro. **flesh wound** herida superficial *f*. **in the flesh** en carne y hueso. **fleshy** *adj* gordo.

flew [fluː] *V* **fly**.

flex [fleks] *n* flexible *m*. *v* doblar. **flexibility** *n* flexibilidad *f*. **flexible** *adj* (*pliable*) flexible; (*fig*) elástico.

flick [flik] *v* dar un golpecito a. **flick through** (*book*) hojear. *n* (*whip*) latigazo suave *m*; (*light stroke*) golpecito *m*; (*duster*) pasada *f*; (*wrist*) movimiento rápido *m*. **the flicks** (*coll*) el cine *m*.

flicker ['flikə] *v* (*light*) parpadear; (*flames*) vacilar. *n* parpadeo *m*; (*flame*) llama vacilante *f*; (*hope, etc.*) requicio *m*.

flight¹ [flait] *n* (*birds*) bandada *f*; (*aircraft*) escuadrilla *f*; (*act of flying*) vuelo *m*; (*distance flown*) recorrido *m*. **flight crew** tripulación *f*. **flight deck** cubierta de aterrizaje *f*. **flight of stairs** tramo de escalera *m*. **flight path** trayectoria de vuelo *f*. **in flight** en vuelo. **flightiness** *n* ligereza *f*. **flightless** *adj* incapacitado para volar. **flighty** *adj* volátil; caprichoso.

flight² [flait] *n* (*escape*) huida *f*, fuga *f*.

flimsy ['flimzi] *adj* (*lacking substance*) poco sólido; (*fragile*) frágil; (*weak*) débil; (*paper*) fino; (*cloth*) ligero; (*excuse*) flojo. **flimsiness** *n* fragilidad *f*; debilidad *f*; finura *f*; ligereza *f*.

flinch [flintʃ] *v* (*draw back*) retroceder; (*hesitate*) vacilar; (*muscular movement*) encogerse.

***fling** [fliŋ] *v* arrojar, tirar; (*dash*) precipitarse. **fling aside** dejar de lado. *n* (*throw*) lanzamiento; (*wild tune*) juerga *f*.

flint [flint] *n* pedernal *m*; (*of lighter*) piedra de mechero *f*.

flip [flip] *v* (*flick*) dar un capirotazo; (*coin*) echar a cara o cruz. *n* capirotazo *m*. **flipper** *n* aleta *f*.

flippant ['flipənt] *adj* frívolo. **flippancy** *n* ligereza *f*.

flirt [flɜːt] n (female) coqueta f; (male) mariposón m. v flirtear, coquetear. **flirtation** n coqueteo m.
flit [flit] v revolotear.
float [flout] v flotar; (support) hacer flotar. n flotador m; (angling) corcho m; (carnival) carroza f.
flock[1] [flok] n (sheep, goats) rebaño m; (birds) bandada f; (people) muchedumbre f. v congregarse.
flock[2] [flok] n (filling) borra f.
flog [flog] v (beat) azotar; (coll: sell) vender. **flogging** n paliza f; flagelación f.
flood [flʌd] v inundar; irrigar; (overflow) desbordar. n inundación f; flujo m; diluvio m. **in flood** crecido.
***floodlight** ['flʌdlait] n foco m. v iluminar con focos. **floodlighting** n iluminación con focos f.
floor [flɔː] n suelo m, piso m; (ocean) fondo m; (dance) pista f. **first floor** primer piso m. **ground floor** planta baja f. **take the floor** (speak) tomar la palabra. v (knock down) echar al suelo. **floorboard** n tabla del suelo f. **floorcloth** n trapo m. **flooring** n solado m. **floor polish** cera para el suelo f. floor show espectáculo de cabaret m. **floorwalker** n supervisor de división m.
flop [flop] v desplomarse; (fail) fracasar. n (coll) fracaso m. **floppy** adj flojo; colgante.
flora ['flɔːrə] n flora f.
florist ['florist] n florista m, f. **florist's shop** florería f.
flounce[1] [flauns] v **flounce in/out** entrar/salir enfadado. n movimiento brusco m.
flounce[2] [flauns] n (of dress) volante m.
flounder ['flaundə] v forcejar; confundirse.
flour ['flauə] n harina f. v enharinar. **flour mill** molino harinero m. **floury** adj (covered with flour) enharinado; (like flour) harinoso.
flourish ['flʌriʃ] v (prosper) florecer; (wave) agitar; (brandish) esgrimir. n ostentación f; (gesture) ademán m; (writing) rasgo m. **flourishing** adj floreciente.
flout [flaut] v burlarse de.
flow [flou] v (liquid) fluir; (tears) correr; (blood in the body) circular; (blood from the body) derramarse; (tide) subir. **flow away** irse. **flow from** salir de. **flow in/out** entrar/salir a raudales. **flow into**

desembocar. n circulación f; movimiento m. **flow chart** organigrama m. **flowing** adj (river) fluente; (style) fluido; (hair) suelto; (beard) largo.
flower ['flauə] n flor f. **flower arrangement** ramillete m. **flower bed** arriate m. **flowerpot** n maceta f. **flower shop** florería f. **flower show** exposición de flores f. v florecer. **flowering** adj floreciente; n florecimiento m. **flowery** adj florido.
flown [floun] V **fly.**
flu [fluː] n gripe f.
fluctuate ['flʌktjuˌeit] v fluctuar; vacilar. **fluctuation** n fluctuación f.
flue [fluː] n chimenea f; conducto de humo m.
fluent ['fluənt] adj (language) bueno; (writing) fluido. **fluency** n facilidad f; dominio m. **fluently** adv (speech) con soltura; (writing) con fluidez.
fluff [flʌf] n pelusa f; mota f; masa esponjosa f. **fluffy** adj (pillow, cushion) mullido; (downy) velloso; (cloth) que tiene pelusa.
fluid ['fluid] nm, adj fluido.
fluke [fluːk] n chiripa f. **fluky** adj de suerte.
flung [flʌŋ] V **fling.**
fluorescent [fluə'resnt] adj fluorescente. **fluorescence** n fluorescencia f.
fluoride ['fluəraid] n fluoruro m. **fluoridation** n fluoración f.
flurry ['flʌri] n (excitement) agitación f; (snow) borrasca f; (rain) chaparrón m; (wind) ráfaga f.
flush[1] [flʌʃ] n (blush) rubor m; (fever) sofoco m; (lavatory) cisterna f. v ruborizarse; tener sofocos; (light) resplandecer. **flush the toilet** tirar de la cadena. **flushed** adj rebosante.
flush[2] [flʌʃ] adj (abundant) copioso; (lavish) liberal; (coll: well off) adinerado. **flush with** (level) a nivel con.
fluster ['flʌstə] v poner nervioso. n agitación f.
flute [fluːt] n flauta f.
flutter ['flʌtə] v (leaves, etc.) revolotear; (wings) batir; (curtains, flags) ondular; (heart) palpitar; (flap) agitar. n ondulación f; (wings) aleteo m; agitación f; (eyelids) parpadeo m; palpitación f.
flux [flʌks] n (flow) flujo m; (changes) cambios frecuentes m pl. **be in a state of flux** estar siempre cambiando.

*fly¹ [flai] *v* volar; (*escape*) huir; (*time*) pasar volando; (*kite*) echar a volar; (*aircraft*) pilotar; (*flag*) izar, enarbolar; (*go across*) atravesar; (*mileage*) recorrer. **fly away** emprender el vuelo. **fly over** sobrevolar. **fly past** desfilar. **flies** *pl n* (*trousers*) bragueta *f*.

fly² [flai] *n* mosca *f*.

fly-blown *adj* cochambroso.

fly-fishing *n* pesca con moscas *f*.

flying ['flaiiŋ] *adj* volador; volante. *n* aviación *f*.

flying colours *pl n* éxito rotundo *m*.

flying field *n* campo de aviación *m*.

flying fish *n* pez volador *m*.

flying saucer *n* platillo volante *m*.

flying squirrel *n* ardilla volante *f*.

flying start *n* salida lanzada *f*; (*fig*) principio feliz *m*.

flyleaf ['flailiɪf] *n* guarda *f*.

flyover ['flai‚ouvə] *n* paso elevado *m*.

fly-paper *n* papel matamoscas *m*.

fly swatter *n* matamoscas *m invar*.

flyweight ['flaiweit] *n* peso mosca *m*.

flywheel ['flaiwiɪl] *n* volante *m*.

foal [foul] *n* potro, -a *m, f. v* parir.

foam [foum] *n* espuma *f. v* espumar; (*animal*) espumajear. **foam rubber** gomespuma *f*. **foaming** *adj* espumoso.

focal ['foukəl] *adj* focal. **focal point** punto focal.

focus ['foukəs] *n* foco *m*. **in focus** enfocado. **out of focus** fuera de foco. *v* enfocar; concentrar.

fodder ['fodə] *n* forraje *m*.

foe [fou] *n* enemigo, -a *m, f*.

foetus ['fiɪtəs] *n* feto *m*. **foetal** *adj* fetal.

fog [fog] *n* niebla *f*, bruma *f*. **fogbound** *adj* (*foggy*) cubierto de niebla; (*immobilized*) detenido por la niebla. **foghorn** *n* sirena de niebla *f*. **foglamp** *or* **foglight** (*mot*) faro antiniebla *m*. **fogginess** *n* nebulosidad *f*. **foggy** *adj* nebuloso, brumoso.

foible ['foibl] *n* extravagancia *f*; (*fad*) manía *f*.

foil¹ [foil] *v* frustrar.

foil² [foil] *n* hoja fina de metal *f*; (*fig*) contraste *m*.

foil³ [foil] *n* (*fencing*) florete *m*.

foist [foist] *v* colar; meter.

fold¹ [fould] *n* (*crease*) pliegue *m*; (*wrinkle*) arruga *f*. *v* doblar, plegar; (*surround*) envolver; (*coll: close down*) liquidarse. **fold one's arms** cruzar los brazos. **folder**

n carpeta *f*. **folding** *adj* plegable. **folding door** puerta de fuelle *f*.

fold² [fould] *n* (*sheep*) redil *m*; (*religion*) grey *f*.

foliage ['fouliidʒ] *n* follaje *m*.

folk [fouk] *pl n* gente *f sing*; pueblo *m*. **folks** *pl n* (*coll*) familia *f sing*. **folk art** arte popular. **folk dance** baile foklórico *m*. **folklore** *n* folklore *m*. **folk music** música popular *f*. **folk singer** cantante de canciones populares. **folk song** canción popular *f*.

follicle ['folikl] *n* folículo *m*.

follow ['folou] *v* seguir; (*pursue*) perseguir; (*practise*) ejercer; (*ensue*) resultar. **follow up** investigar sobre; reforzar. **follower** *n* seguidor, -a *m, f*; discípulo *m*; aficionado, -a *m, f*. **following** *adj* siguiente. *n* partidarios *m pl*.

folly ['foli] *n* locura *f*.

fond [fond] *adj* cariñoso; indulgente. **be fond of** tenerle cariño a. **fondly** *adj* cariñosamente. **fondness** *n* cariño *m*.

fondle ['fondl] *v* acariciar; mimar.

font [font] *n* (*baptismal*) pila *f*; (*printing*) fundición *f*.

food [fuɪd] *n* comida *f*, alimento *m*; comestibles *m pl*. **food and drink** comida y bebida *f*. **food poisoning** intoxicación alimentica *f*. **food shop** tienda de comestibles *f*. **foodstuff** *n* producto alimenticio *m*.

fool [fuɪl] *n* tonto, -a *m, f*; bobo, -a *m, f*; idiota *m, f*; (*jester*) bufón *m*. **foolproof** *adj* infalible. *v* (*deceive*) engañar; (*joke*) bromear. **fool about** *or* **around** juguetear. **foolhardy** *adj* temerario. **foolhardiness** *n* temeridad *f*. **foolish** *adj* insensato; tonto. **foolishly** *adv* neciamente. **foolishness** *n* insensatez *f*; tontería *f*.

foolscap ['fuɪlskap] *n* papel de barba *m*.

foot [fut] *n, pl* **feet** pie *m*; (*animal*) pata *f*. **from head to foot** de pies a cabeza. **on foot** a pie. **get cold feet** tener miedo.

football ['fut‚boɪl] *n* fútbol *m*; (*ball*) pelota *f*. **football pools** *pl n* quinielas *f pl*.

foot brake *n* freno de pedal *m*.

footbridge ['fut‚bridʒ] *n* pasarela *f*.

foothills ['futhilz] *pl n* estribaciones *f pl*.

foothold ['fut‚hould] *n* punto de apoyo para el pie *m*; (*fig*) posición *f*.

footing ['futiŋ] *n* pie *m*, equilibrio *m*; condición *f*; posición *f*. **on an equal footing** en un pie de igual.

footlights 80

footlights ['fut,laits] pl n candilejas f pl.
footloose ['futluːs] adj libre.
footnote ['fut,nout] n nota f.
footpath ['fut,paːθ] n senda f; (pavement) acera f.
footprint ['fut,print] n pisada f.
footstep ['fut,step] n paso m.
for [foɪ] prep para; por; de; (time) desde; durante; (in favour of) en favor de; (in honour of) en honor de; (in place of) en lugar de; (as regards) en cuanto a; (against) contra; (in order that) para que. conj pues, puesto que, ya que.
forage ['forɪdʒ] v forrajear; (fig: seek) buscar. n forraje m.
*forbear [fəˈbeə] v contenerse; abstenerse. forbearance n abstención f; indulgencia f; paciencia f.
*forbid [fəˈbid] v prohibir; (prevent) impedir. forbidding adj impresionante; inhóspito; severo; (threatening) amenazador.
force [foːs] n fuerza f; (mil) cuerpo m. in force en vigor. sales force vendedores m pl. join forces unirse. v forzar; obligar; (tech) inyectar. be forced to verse obligado a. forceful adj fuerte; contundente.
forceps ['foːseps] pl n fórceps m sing.
ford [foːd] n vado m. v vadear.
fore [foɪ] adj delantero; anterior. adv delante. n (naut) proa f. come to the fore empezar a destacar. interj (golf) ¡cuidado!
forearm ['foːraɪm] n antebrazo m. v prevenir.
forebears ['foːbeəz] pl n antepasados m pl.
foreboding [foːˈboudiŋ] n presentimiento m.
*forecast ['foːkaɪst] n previsión f; pronóstico m; plan m. v pronosticar. weather forecast pronóstico meteorológico m.
forecourt ['foːkoɪt] n antepatio m.
forefather ['foːfaːðə] n antepasado m.
forefinger ['foːfiŋgə] n dedo índice m.
forefront ['foːfrʌnt] n delantera f; sitio de mayor importancia m.
foregone ['foːgon] adj conocido de antemano. foregone conclusion conclusión inevitable f.
foreground ['foːgraund] n primer plano m; primer término m.
forehand ['foːhand] n (tennis) golpe derecho m.

forehead ['forid] n frente f.
foreign ['forən] adj extranjero; ajeno. foreign affairs asuntos exteriores m pl. foreign trade comercio exterior m. foreign exchange cambio exterior m. foreign legion legión extranjera f. foreigner n extranjero, -a m, f.
foreleg ['foːleg] n pata delantera f.
foreman ['foːmən] n capataz m.
foremost ['foːmoust] adj delantero; principal. first and foremost ante todo.
forename ['foːneim] n nombre de pila m.
forensic [fəˈrensik] adj forense. forensic medicine medicina legal f.
forerunner ['foːrʌnə] n precursor, -a m, f; (herald) anunciador, -a m, f.
*foresee [foːˈsiː] v prever. foreseeable adj previsible.
foreshadow [foːˈʃadou] v presagiar; prefigurar.
foresight ['foːsait] n previsión f.
foreskin ['foːskin] n prepucio m.
forest ['forist] n selva f; bosque m. forester n guardabosque m. forestry n silvicultura f. Forestry Commission administración de montes f.
forestall [foːˈstoːl] v prevenir; impedir; anticiparse a.
foretaste ['foːteist] n anticipación f.
*foretell [foːˈtel] v predecir; presagiar.
forethought ['foːθoːt] n premeditación f.
forever [fəˈrevə] adv siempre, para siempre. forever more por siempre jamás.
forewarn [foːˈwoːn] v avisar, advertir. forewarning n aviso m, advertencia f.
foreword ['foːwoːd] n prefacio m; prólogo m.
forfeit ['foːfit] v (right) perder; (property) comisar.
forge¹ [foːdʒ] v (counterfeit) falsificar; (metal) fraguar. n fragua f. forger n falsificador m; (metal) herrero m. forgery n falsificación f; (things forged) documento falsificado m; moneda falsificada f.
forge² [foːdʒ] v forge ahead hacer grandes progresos.
*forget [fəˈget] v olvidar, olvidarse de. forget-me-not n nomeolvides f. forgetful adj olvidadizo; descuidado. forgetfulness n olvido m; descuido m.
*forgive [fəˈgiv] v perdonar; dispensar. forgiveness n perdón m; remisión f. forgiving adj indulgente, clemente.
*forgo [foːˈgou] v abstenerse; renunciar.

fork [fɔɪk] *n* (*cutlery*) tenedor *m*; (*gardening*) horca *f*; (*tree*) horcadura *f*; (*road*) bifurcación *f*; (*river*) horcajo *m*. **tuning fork** diapasón *m*. *v* bifurcarse. **forked** *adj* bifurcado.

forlorn [fə'lɔɪn] *adj* desamparado; triste.

form [fɔɪm] *n* (*shape*) forma *f*; (*figure*) figura *f*; (*type*) tipo *m*; (*document*) formulario *m*; (*school year*) curso *m*. *v* (*make*) hacer; (*model*) modelar; (*habit*) crear; (*constitute*) constituir; (*put together*) formar. **form a queue** ponerse en cola. **formation** *n* formación *f*. **formative** *adj* de formación, formativo.

formal ['fɔɪməl] *adj* formal; solemne; (*person*) formalista; ceremonioso; de cortesía; en debida forma. **formality** *n* (*requirement*) formalidad *f*; ceremonia *f*; rigidez *f*.

format ['fɔɪmat] *n* formato *m*.

former ['fɔɪmə] *adj* (*previous*) anterior; (*ex-*) antiguo, pasado. *pron* ése, ésa, aquél, equélla, el primero, la primera. **formerly** *adv* anteriormente; antiguamente.

formidable ['fɔɪmidəbl] *adj* formidable.

formula ['fɔɪmjulə] *n, pl* -ae fórmula *f*.

formulate ['fɔɪmjuleit] *v* formular. **formulation** *n* formulación *f*.

*forsake [fə'seik] *v* abandonar.

fort [fɔɪt] *n* fuerte *m*, fortaleza *f*.

forte ['fɔɪtei] *n* fuerte *m*.

forth [fɔɪθ] *adv* en adelante. **and so forth** y así sucesivamente. **forthcoming** *adj* próximo; (*approaching*) venidero; (*person*) abierto. **forthright** *adj* franco. **forthwith** *adv* en seguida; en el acto.

fortify ['fɔɪtifai] *v* (*health, moral strength*) fortalecer; (*town*) fortificar; (*wine*) encabezar; (*argument*) reforzar. **fortification** *n* fortalecimiento *m*; fortificación *f*; reforzamiento *m*.

fortitude ['fɔɪtitjuɪd] *n* fortaleza *f*; firmeza *f*.

fortnight ['fɔɪtnait] *n* quincena *f*. **fortnightly** *adj* quincenal. *adv* quincenalmente.

fortress ['fɔɪtris] *n* fortaleza *f*.

fortuitous [fə'tjuɪitəs] *adj, adv* casual.

fortunate ['fɔɪtʃənət] *adj* afortunado; oportuno. **fortunately** *adv* afortunadamente.

fortune ['fɔɪtʃən] *n* (*fate*) fortuna *f*; (*luck*) suerte *f*. **cost a fortune** costar un

dineral. **stroke of fortune** golpe de suerte *m*. **fortune-teller** *n* adivino, -a *m*, *f*.

forty ['fɔɪti] *nm, adj* cuarenta. **fortieth** *nm, adj* cuarentavo.

forum ['fɔɪrəm] *n* foro *m*; (*meeting*) tribuna *f*.

forward ['fɔɪwəd] *adj* (*front*) delantero; (*movement*) hacia adelante; (*progressive*) avanzado; (*impertinent*) impertinente. *v* (*send*) expedir; (*promote*) promover. **please forward** remítase al destinario. *n* (*football*) delantero *m*. **forwards** *adv* adelante.

fossil ['fosl] *nm, adj* fósil. **fossilized** *adj* fosilizado.

foster ['fostə] *v* (*child*) criar; (*idea*) abrigar; (*project*) patrocinar; (*favour*) favorecer. *adj* adoptivo.

fought [fɔɪt] *V* fight.

foul [faul] *adj* asqueroso; (*dirty*) sucio; (*air*) viciado; (*language*) grosero; (*smell*) fétido. **foul play** jugada sucia *f*. *n* falta *f*. *v* ensuciar; (*reputation*) manchar; (*sport*) cometer una falta.

found¹ [faund] *V* find.

found² [faund] *v* fundar; construir; (*opinion*) fundamentar. **foundation** *n* (*establishment*) fundación *f*; (*building*) cimientos *m pl*; (*fig*) fundamento *m*. **founder** *n* fundador, -a *m*, *f*.

founder ['faundə] *v* (*ship*) hundirse; (*fall*) derrumbarse.

foundry ['faundri] *n* fundición *f*.

fountain ['fauntin] *n* fuente *f*. **fountainhead** *n* manantial *m*. **fountain pen** pluma estilográfica *f*.

four [fɔɪ] *nm, adj* cuatro. **fourth** *m, adj* cuarto, -a *m*, *f*.

fourteen [fɔɪ'tiɪn] *nm, adj* catorce. **fourteenth** *n, adj* decimocuarto, -a *m*, *f*.

fowl [faul] *n* aves de corral *f pl*; (*cock*) gallo *m*; (*hen*) gallina *f*; (*chicken*) pollo *m*.

fox [foks] *n* zorro, -a *m*, *f*. *v* (*baffle*) desconcertar; (*trick*) engañar. **foxglove** *n* digital *f*. **foxhound** *n* perro raposero *m*. **foxhunting** *n* caza de zorros *f*.

foyer ['foiei] *n* foyer *m*.

fraction ['frakʃən] *n* fracción *f*; pequeña parte *f*. **fractional** *adj* fraccionario.

fracture ['fraktʃə] *n* fractura *f*. *v* fracturarse.

fragile ['fradʒail] *adj* frágil. **fragility** *n* fragilidad *f*.

fragment ['fragmənt] *n* fragmento *m*. *v* fragmentar.
fragrant ['freigrənt] *adj* fragante. **fragrance** *n* fragancia *f*.
frail [freil] *adj* frágil; débil; delicado. **frailty** *n* fragilidad *f*; debilidad *f*; delicadez *f*.
frame [freim] *n* (*building*) armazón *f*; (*picture*) marco *m*; (*bicycle*) cuadro *m*; (*spectacles*) montura *f*; (*film*) imagen *f*. **frame of mind** estado de ánimo *m*. *v* (*enclose*) enmarcar; (*devise*) elaborar; (*shape*) formar; hacer la armazón de.
France [frains] *n* Francia *f*.
franchise ['frantʃaiz] *n* derecho de voto *m*.
frank [fraŋk] *adj* franco; abierto. **frankness** *n* franqueza *f*.
frankfurter ['fraŋkfəitə] *n* salchicha alemana *f*.
frantic ['frantik] *adj* frenético; loco.
fraternal [frə'təinl] *adj* fraternal. **fraternity** *n* (*brotherhood*) fraternidad *f*; (*association*) asociación *f*; (*religious*) hermandad *f*. **fraternize** *v* fraternizar.
fraud [froid] *n* (*law*) fraude *m*; (*deception*) engaño *m*; (*person*) impostor *m*. **fraudulent** *adj* fraudulento.
fraught [froit] *adj* **fraught with** cargado de.
fray¹ [frei] *v* raer, desgastar.
fray² [frei] *n* (*brawl*) riña *f*; (*fight*) combate *m*.
freak [friik] *n* capricho *m*; fantasís *f*; monstruosidad *f*. *adj* imprevisto; extraño.
freckle ['frekl] *n* peca *f*. **freckled** *adj* pecoso.
free [frii] *adj* libre; gratis; (*loose*) suelto; generoso; sincero; (*manner*) desenvuelto.
free and easy *adj* poco ceremonioso.
freedom ['friidəm] *n* libertad *f*; soltura *f*.
free-for-all *n* refriega *f*.
freehand ['friihand] *adj* a pulso.
freehold ['friihould] *n* propiedad absoluta *f*.
freelance ['friilains] *n* persona que trabaja independientemente *f*.
freely ['friili] *adj* libremente; voluntariamente; gratuitamente.
freemason ['friimeisn] *n* francmasón. **freemasonry** *n* francmasonería *f*.
freesia ['friiziə] *n* fresia *f*.
freestyle ['friistail] *n* estilo libre *m*.
free trade *n* librecambio *m*.

free will *n* libre albedrío *m*.
*freeze [friiz] *v* (*preserve*) congelar; (*chill*) refrigerar; (*from cold*) helarse; (*prices, etc.*) bloquear; (*turn to ice*) helar; (*stand still*) quedarse inmóvil. *n* helada *f*; bloqueo *m*. **freezer** *n* congelador *m*. **freezing** *adj* glacial. **freezing point** punto de congelación.
freight [freit] *n* (*load*) carga *f*; (*transportation*) transporte *m*; (*by ship, plane*) flete *m*; (*other*) mercancías *f pl*. **freight train** tren de mercancías *m*. **freighter** *n* (*ship*) buque de carga *m*; (*aircraft*) avión de carga *m*.
French [frentʃ] *nm, adj* francés. **the French** los franceses. **French bean** judía verde *f*. **French horn** trompa de llaves *f*. **French polish** barniz de muebles *m*. **french fries** patata frita *f*. *v*
frenzy ['frenzi] *n* frenesí *m*, delirio *m*. **frenzied** *adj* frenético.
frequent ['friikwənt; *v* fri'kwent] *adj* frecuente; (*usual*) común. *v* frecuentar. **frequency** *n* frecuencia *f*. **frequently** *adv* frecuentemente.
fresco ['freskou] *n* fresco *m*.
fresh [freʃ] *adj* fresco; (*bread*) tierno; (*water*) dulce; (*air*) puro; (*complexion*) de buen color; (*new*) nuevo. *adv* recientemente. **freshwater** *adj* (*fish*) de aqua dulce. **freshen up** refrescarse. **freshness** *n* frescura *f*; novedad *f*.
fret¹ [fret] *v* irritar; (*complain*) quejarse. **fretful** *adj* mal humorado; (*upset*) apenado.
fret² [fret] *n* (*music*) traste *m*. *v* adornar con calados. **fretsaw** *n* sierra de calar *f*. **fretwork** *n* calado *m*.
friar ['fraiə] *n* fraile *m*, monje *m*. **friary** *n* monasterio *m*.
friction ['frikʃən] *n* fricción *f*.
Friday ['fraidei] *n* viernes *m*. **Good Friday** Viernes Santo *m*.
fridge [fridʒ] *n* (*coll*) nevera *f*.
fried [fraid] *adj* frito.
friend [frend] *n* amigo, -a *m, f*. **make friends with** hacerse amigo de. **the best of friends** muy amigos. **friendliness** *n* simpatía *f*. **friendly** *adj* simpático; amistoso. **friendship** *n* amistad *f*.
frieze [friiz] *n* friso *m*.
frigate ['frigit] *n* fragata *f*.
fright [frait] *n* susto *m*; miedo *m*; terror *m*. **frighten** *v* asustar. **be frightened** tener

miedo. **frightening** *adj* espantoso. **frightful** *adj* horrible; *(fig)* tremendo.
frigid ['frɪdʒɪd] *adj* glacial; *(manner)* frío; *(med)* frígido. **frigidity** *n* frialdad *f*; *(med)* frigidez *f.*
frill [fril] *n* (*shirt*) pechera *f*; *(fluting)* encañonado *m*; *(flared edge)* volante *m*; *(ruff)* gorguera *f.* **frilly** *adj* con volantes.
fringe [frɪndʒ] *n* franja *f*; *(edge)* borde *m.* **fringe benefits** beneficios complementarios *m pl.* *v* franjar.
frisk [frisk] *v* brincar; *(coll: search)* cachear. **friskiness** *n* viveza *f.* **frisky** *adj* juguetón.
fritter¹ ['fritə] *v* **fritter away** malgastar.
fritter² ['fritə] *n* *(cookery)* buñuelo *m.*
frivolity [fri'voliti] *n* frivolidad *f.* **frivolous** *adj* frívolo; trivial.
frizz [friz] *v* *(hair)* rizar. **frizzy** *adj* crespo.
fro [frou] *adv* **to and fro** de un lado a otro. **go to and fro** ir y venir.
frock [frok] *n* vestido *m.*
frog [frog] *n* rana *f.* **frogman** *n* hombre rana *m.* **frogs' legs** ancas de rana *f pl.* **have a frog in one's throat** tener carraspera.
frolic ['frolik] *n* juego *m*; diversión *f.* *v* juguetar; divertirse. **frolicsome** *adj* juguetón.
from [from] *prep* de; desde; *(made from)* con; *(steal, buy, take, etc.)* a; *(drink, learn)* en; *(speak, act)* por; *(according to)* según.
front [frʌnt] *n* *(building)* fachada *f*; *(shop)* escaparate *m*; parte delantera *f*; principio *m*; *(face)* cara *f*; *(weather)* frente *m.* **in front of** delante de. *adj* delantero; principal; primero.
frontier ['frʌntiə] *n* frontera *f.* *adj* fronterizo.
frost [frost] *n* escarcha *f*; helada *f.* **frostbite** *n* congelación *f.* **frostbitten** *adj* congelado. *v* cubrir de escarcha. **frosted glass** vidrio deslustrado *m.* **frosty** *adj* escarchado; helado.
froth [froθ] *n* espuma *f*; *(fig)* frivolidad *f.* *v* espumar. **frothy** *adj* espumoso; frívolo.
frown [fraun] *n* ceño *m.* *v* fruncir el entrecejo. **frown on** *or* **upon** desaprobar. **frowning** *adj* severo; amenazador.
froze [frouz] *V* **freeze**.
frozen ['frouzn] *adj* congelado, helado. **frozen food** comestibles congelados *m pl.*
frugal ['fruɪɡəl] *adj* frugal; sobrio. **frugality** *n* frugalidad *f*; sobriedad *f.*

fruit [fruɪt] *n* *(on tree)* fruto *m*, *(as food)* fruta *f.* **fruit cake** pastel de fruta *m.* **fruit machine** máquina tragaperras *f.* **fruit salad** ensalada de frutas *f.* *v* dar fruto. **fruitful** *adj* fructífero; *(fig)* fructuoso. **fruition** *n* fruición *f*; realización *f*; *(bot)* fructificación *f.*
frustrate [frʌ'streit] *v* *(plans, etc.)* frustrar; impedir.
*****fry** [frai] *v* freír. **frying pan** sartén *f.*
fuchsia ['fjuɪʃə] *n* fucsia *f.*
fuck [fʌk] *v* *(impol)* joder.
fudge [fʌdʒ] *v* fallar; inventar.
fuel ['fjuəl] *n* combustible *m*; gasolina *f*; *(mot)* carburante *f.* **fuel gauge** indicador del nivel de gasolina *m.* **fuel pump** gasolinera *f.* *v* *(mot)* echar gasolina a; *(furnace)* alimentar; *(ship)* abastecer de combustible.
fugitive ['fjuɪdʒitiv] *n*, *adj* fugativo, -a.
fulcrum ['fulkrəm] *n* fulcro *m.*
fulfil [ful'fil] *v* *(promise, obligation)* cumplir; *(ambition)* realizar; *(purpose)* servir; *(wishes)* satisfacer; *(function)* desempeñar; *(plan)* llevar a cabo. **fulfilment** *n* cumplimiento *m*; realización *f*; satisfacción *f*; *(instructions)* ejecución *f.*
full [ful] *adj* lleno; completo; *(text)* íntegro; *(whole)* entero; *(price)* sin descuento; *(extensive)* extenso; *(daylight, development)* pleno; *(speed)* todo; *(capacity)* máximo; *(measure, weight)* exacto; *(flavour)* mucho. **full employment** pleno empleo *m.* **full up** completamente lleno. **I'm full** no puedo más. **in full colour** a todo color.
full-blooded *adj* *(thoroughbred)* de pura sangre; *(robust)* vigoroso; *(true blue)* verdadero.
full-bodied *adj* *(wine)* de mucho cuerpo.
full-dress *adj* de etiqueta; de gala.
full-grown *adj* crecido; adulto.
full-hearted *adj* completo.
full house *n* *(theatre or cinema notice)* no hay localidades.
full-length *adj* de cuerpo entero.
full-scale *adj* de tamaño natural.
full stop *n* punto *m.*
full-time *adj* de jornada completa.
fumble ['fʌmbl] *v* tojetear; *(drop)* dejar caer; *(feel)* hurgar; *(search)* buscar.
fume [fjuɪm] *v* *(fig)* bufar de cólera. **fumes** *pl n* numo *m.*

fun [fʌn] *n* alegría *f*; gracia *f*; diversión *f*. **for fun** en broma. **funfair** *n* parque de atracciones *m*. **have fun** divertirse. **make fun of** reírse de. **what fun!** ¡qué divertido!

function ['fʌŋkʃən] *n* función *f*; acto *m*; recepción *f*. *v* funcionar. **functional** *adj* funcional.

fund [fʌnd] *n* fondo *m*; (*source*) fuente *f*.

fundamental [fʌndə'mentl] *adj* fundamental.

funeral ['fjuːnərəl] *n* funeral *m*; (*state*) exequias nacionales *f pl*. **funeral parlour** funeraria *f*. **funeral procession** cortejo fúnebre *m*. **funeral service** misa de cuerpo presente *f*.

fungus ['fʌŋgəs] *n*, *pl* **-i** (*bot*) hongo *m*; (*med*) fungo *m*.

funnel ['fʌnl] *n* (*pourer*) embudo; (*smoke-stack*) chimenea *f*. *v* verter por un embudo; (*direct*) encauzar.

funny ['fʌni] *adj* divertido; gracioso; (*curious*) extraño. **taste funny** tener un sabor extraño. **funny business** cosas varas *f pl*. **funny-bone** hueso de la alegría *m*. **funnily** *adv* graciosamente.

fur [fəː] *n* pelo *m*; (*pelt*) piel *f*; (*kettle*) sarro *m*; (*tongue*) saburra *f*. **fur coat** abrigo de pieles *m*. *v* forrar con pieles; incrustar; cubrir de sarro. **furrier** *n* peletero *m*; (*shop*) peletería *f*. **furry** *adj* peludo; sarroso.

furious ['fjuəriəs] *adj* furioso; violento.

furnace ['fəːnis] *n* horno *m*; (*domestic*) estufa *f*; (*boiler*) hogar *m*.

furnish ['fəːniʃ] *v* (*house*) amueblar; (*supply*) suministrar; (*give*) facilitar; (*opportunity*) dar; (*proof*) aducir. **furnishings** *pl n* muebles *m pl*; mobiliario *m*.

furniture ['fəːnitʃə] *n* muebles *m pl*. **furniture van** camión de mudanzas *m*.

furrow ['fʌrou] *n* (*ploughing*) surco *m*; (*forehead*) arruga *f*; (*groove*) ranura *f*. *v* surcar; arrugar.

further ['fəːðə] *adj* (*distant, additional*) otro; (*another*) nuevo; (*later*) posterior; (*education*) superior. *adv* más; más lejos, más allá; (*moreover*) además. *v* favorecer. **furtherance** *n* adelantamiento *m*; formento *m*. **furthermore** *adv* además. **furthermost** *adj* más lejano. **furthest** *adj* más lejano; extremo.

furtive ['fəːtiv] *adj* furtivo.

fury ['fjuəri] *n* furia *f*, furor *m*.

fuse¹ [fjuːz] *n* (*elec*) fusible *m*. **fuse box** caja de fusibles *f*. *v* (*join*) fusionar; (*melt*) fundir.

fuse² [fjuːz] *n* (*explosives*) mecha *f*; (*detonator*) espoleta *f*.

fuselage ['fjuːzəˌlaːʒ] *n* fuselaje *m*.

fusion ['fjuːʒən] *n* fusión *f*.

fuss [fʌs] *n* (*trouble*) lío *m*; (*commotion*) alboroto *m*; (*complaints*) quejas *f pl*. **a lot of fuss about nothing** mucho ruido y pocas nueces. *v* agitarse; quejarse; preocuparse; molestar. **fussiness** *n* agitación *f*. **fussy** *adj* escrupuloso; exigente; melindroso.

futile ['fjuːtail] *adj* vano; frívolo.

future ['fjuːtʃə] *n* futuro *m*; porvenir *m*. *adj* futuro; venidero.

fuzz [fʌz] *n* (*on face*) vello *m*; (*fluff*) pelusa *f*. **fuzzy** *adj* velloso; (*blurred*) borroso.

G

gabble ['gabl] *v* chacharear. *n* cháchara *f*. **gabbler** *n* chacharero, -a *m*, *f*.

gable ['geibl] *n* gablete *m*.

gadget ['gadʒit] *n* aparato *m*; accesorio *m*.

gag¹ [gag] *v* amordazar. *n* mordaza *f*.

gag² [gag] *n* (*joke*) broma *f*; chiste *m*.

gaiety ['geiəti] *n* alegría *f*; jovialidad *f*.

gain [gein] *n* ganancia *f*; provecho *m*; aumento *m*. *v* ganar; avanzar.

gait [geit] *n* modo de andar *m*.

gala ['gaːlə] *n* fiesta *f*, gala *f*.

galaxy ['galəksi] *n* galaxia *f*.

gale [geil] *n* vendaval *m*.

gallant ['galənt] *adj* (*to women*) galante; (*brave*) valiente; (*stately*) elegante. **gallantry** *n* galantería *f*; valor *m*; (*courtesy*) cortesía *f*.

gall-bladder ['gɔːlˌbladə] *n* vesícula biliar *f*.

galleon ['galiən] *n* galeón *m*.

gallery ['galəri] *n* galería *f*; (*spectators*) tribuna *f*; (*theatre*) gallinero *m*.

galley ['gali] *n* (*ship*) galera *f*; (*kitchen*) cocina *f*.

gallon ['galən] *n* galón *m*.

gallop ['galəp] *n* galope *m*. *v* galopar.

gallows ['galouz] *pl n* cadalso *m sing*.

gallstone ['goːlstoun] *n* cálculo biliar *m*.
galore [gə'loː] *adj, adv* en cantidad.
galvanize ['galvənaiz] *v* galvanizar.
gamble ['gambl] *v* (*bet*) apostar; (*risk*) arriesgar. **gamble on** contar con. *n* (*risky enterprise*) empresa arriesgada *f*; (*game*) jugada *f*. **gambler** *n* jugador, -a *m, f*. **gambling** *n* juego *m*. **gambling den** garito *m*.
game [geim] *n* juego *m*; (*sport*) deporte *m*; (*of football, tennis, etc.*) partido *m*; (*cards, chess, etc.*) partida *f*; (*hunting*) caza *f*. **game bird** ave de caza *f*. **gamekeeper** *n* guardabosque *m*. **play the game** jugar limpio. *adj* (*coll*) valiente.
gammon ['gamən] *n* jamón ahumado *m*.
gang [gaŋ] *n* (*band*) cuadrilla *f*; (*of gangsters*) banda *f*. *v* **gang up on** conspirar contra. **gangster** *n* gángster *m*.
gangrene ['gaŋgriːn] *n* gangrena *f*. **gangrenous** *adj* gangrenoso.
gangway ['gaŋwei] *n* (*passage*) pasillo *m*; (*naut*) pasarela *f*.
gaol *V* **jail.**
gap [gap] *n* (*empty space*) vacío *m*; (*breach*) brecha *f*; (*cavity*) hueco *m*; (*in a wall*) portillo *m*; (*between hills*) quebrada *f*; (*in education*) laguna *f*; (*crack*) resquicio *m*; (*in a wood*) claro *m*.
gape [geip] *v* (*stare*) quedarse boquiabierto; (*open wide*) abrirse mucho.
garage ['garaidʒ] *n* garaje *m*.
garbage ['gaːbidʒ] *n* basura *f*. **garbage can** cubo de la basura *m*. **garbage disposal** vertedero de basuras *m*. **garbage man** basurero *m*.
garble ['gaːbl] *v* amañar; mutilar. **garbled** *adj* amañado; mutilado.
garden ['gaːdn] *n* jardín *m*; huerto *m*. *v* cultivar un huerto. **garden city** ciudad jardín *f*. **garden party** recepción al aire libre *f*. **garden produce** hortalizas *f pl*. **gardener** *n* jardinero, -a *m, f*. **gardening** *n* jardinería *f*.
gargle ['gaːgl] *v* hacer gárgaras. *n* gárgaras *f pl*.
garland ['gaːlənd] *n* guirnalda *f*. *v* enguirnaldar.
garlic ['gaːlik] *n* ajo *m*.
garment ['gaːmənt] *n* prenda *f*, traje *m*, vestido *m*.
garnish ['gaːniʃ] *v* adornar, embellecer; (*cookery*) aderezar. *n* adorno *m*; aderezo *m*.

garrison ['garisn] *n* guarnición *f*. *v* guarnecer.
garter ['gaːtə] *n* liga *f*. **Order of the Garter** orden de la jarretera *f*.
gas [gas] *n* gas *m*; (*petrol*) gasolina *f*, bencina *f*. **step on the gas** (*coll*) acelerar. *v* asfixiar con gas. **gaseous** *adj* gaseoso. **gas burner** *n* mechero de gas *m*. **gas fire** *n* estufa de gas *f*. **gas main** *n* cañería maestra de gas *f*. **gasmask** *n* máscara para gases *f*. **gas meter** *n* contador de gas *m*. **gaspipe** *n* cañería de gas *f*. **gas-ring** *n* fogón de gas *m*. **gas stove** *n* cocina de gas *f*. **gasworks** *n* fábrica de gas *f*.
gash [gaʃ] *n* herida *f*; cuchillada *f*. *v* acuchillar.
gasket ['gaskit] *n* junta de culata *f*.
gasoline ['gasəliːn] *n* gasolina *f*.
gasp [gaːsp] *n* (*breathing difficulty*) jadeo *m*; (*surprise*) boqueada *f*. *v* jadear; boquear.
gastric ['gastrik] *adj* gástrico. **gastric fever** fiebre gástrica *f*. **gastric juice** jugo gástrico. **gastric ulcer** ulcera gástrica *f*. **gastritis** *n* gastritis *f*. **gastroenteritis** *n* gastroenteritis *f*.
gastronomic [gastrə'nomik] *adj* gastronómico. **gastronomy** *n* gastronomía *f*.
gate [geit] *n* puerta *f*, entrada *f*; (*metal*) verja *f*; (*level-crossing*) barrera *f*. **gatecrash** *v* asistir sin invitación. **gatekeeper** *n* portero, -a *m, f*. **gatepost** *n* soporte de la puerta *m*. **gateway** *n* entrada *f*, paso *m*.
gateau ['gatou] *n* tarta *f*.
gather ['gaðə] *v* coger, amontonar; (*strength*) cobrar; (*harvest*) cosechar; (*understand*) colegir; (*money*) recaudar; (*sewing*) fruncir. **gather together** reunirse, congregarse. **gathering** *n* reunión *f*, afluencia *f*.
gaudy ['goːdi] *adj* chillón, cursi.
gauge [geidʒ] *n* (*rail*) entrevía *f*; (*gun*) calibre *m*; (*measure*) indicador *m*; (*fig*) medida *f*. *v* medir, juzgar; calibrar. **broad/narrow gauge railway** ferrocarril de vía ancha/estrecha *m*. **pressure gauge** manómetro *m*.
gaunt [goːnt] *adj* demacrado; (*grim*) feroz; (*fig*) lúgubre.
gauze [goːz] *n* gasa *f*.
gave [geiv] *V* **give**.
gay [gei] *adj* alegre; gozoso; (*dress*) guapo; (*event*) festivo; (*coll*) homosexual. *n* (*coll: homosexual*) maricón *m*.

gaze [geiz] *v* mirar fijamente. *n* mirada fija *f*.

gazelle [gə'zel] *n* gacela *f*.

gazetteer [gazə'tiə] *n* gacetero *m*.

gear [giə] *n* (*mech*) engranaje *m*, juego *m*, marcha *f*; (*dress*) traje *m*; (*tackle*) utensilios *m pl*; (*naut*) aparejo *m*. **gearbox** caja de velocidades *f*. **gear lever** palanca de cambio de velocidad. **in gear** engranado. *v* aparejar; engranar; adaptar.

geese [giɪs] *V* **goose**.

gelatine ['dʒeləˌtiɪn] *n* gelatina *f*.

gelignite ['dʒeligˌnait] *n* gelignita *f*.

gem [dʒem] *n* joya *f*, gema *f*; (*delight*) preciosidad *f*.

Gemini ['dʒemini] *pl n* Géminis *m*.

gender ['dʒendə] *n* género *m*; sexo *m*.

gene [dʒiɪn] *n* gene *m*.

genealogy [dʒiɪniˌalədʒi] *n* genealogía *f*. **genealogical** *adj* genealógico.

general ['dʒenərəl] *nm, adj* general. **general election** elección general *f*. **general opinion** voz común *f*. **general practitioner** médico, -a general *m, f*. **in general** generalmente. **generalization** *n* generalización *f*. **generalize** *v* generalizar.

generate ['dʒenəreit] *v* producir; (*elec*) generar. **generation** *n* generación *f*. **generator** *n* generador *m*; dínamo *m*.

generic [dʒi'nerik] *adj* genérico.

generous ['dʒenərəs] *adj* generoso; magnánimo. **generosity** *n* generosidad *f*; liberalidad *f*.

genetic [dʒi'netik] *adj* genético. **genetics** *n* genética *f*.

Geneva [dʒi'niɪvə] *n* Ginebra. **Lake Geneva** Lago de Ginebra.

genial ['dʒiɪniəl] *adj* genial, cordial.

genital ['dʒenitl] *adj* genital. **genitals** *pl n* genitales *m pl*.

genitive ['dʒenitiv] *nm, adj* genitivo.

genius ['dʒiɪnjəs] *n* genio *m*.

genteel [dʒen'tiɪl] *adj* fino; melindroso.

gentle ['dʒentl] *adj* (*light*) lijero; (*mild*) suave; (*slow*) lento; (*tame*) manso; (*moderate*) moderado; (*friendly*) amable; (*kind*) bondadoso. **gentleman** *n* caballero *m*, señor *m*. **gentlemen** *pl n* (*in correspondence*) muy señores míos, muy señores nuestros *m pl*. **gentleness** *n* amabilidad *f*; bondad *f*; suavidad *f*.

gentry ['dʒentri] *n* pequeña nobleza *f*.

gents [dʒents] *n* (*sign*) caballeros *m pl*.

genuine ['dʒenjuin] *adj* puro; genuino; verdadero; auténtico.

genus ['dʒiɪnəs] *n* género *m*.

geography [dʒi'ogrəfi] *n* geografía *f*. **geographer** *n* geógrafo *m*. **geographic** *adj also* **geographical** geográfico.

geology [dʒi'olədʒi] *n* geología *f*. **geological** *adj* geológico. **geologist** *n* geólogo *m*.

geometry [dʒi'omətri] *n* geometría *f*. **geometrical** *adj* geométrico.

geranium [dʒə'reiniəm] *n* geranio *m*.

geriatric [dʒeri'atrik] *adj* geriátrico. **geriatrics** *n* geriatría *f*.

germ [dʒəɪm] *n* (*med*) bacilo *m*; microbio *m*; (*fig*) germen *m*.

Germany ['dʒəɪməni] *n* Alemania *f*. **German** *n, adj* alemán, -ana *m, f*. **German measles** rubéola *f*. **Germanic** *adj* germánico.

germinate ['dʒəɪmineit] *v* germinar, brotar. **germination** *n* germinación *f*.

gerund ['dʒerənd] *n* gerundio *m*.

gesticulate [dʒe'stikjuˌleit] *v* gesticular. **gesticulation** *n* gesticulación *f*.

gesture ['dʒestʃə] *v* gesticular. *n* gesto *m*.

*get [get] *v* obtener; tener; recibir; (*fetch*) buscar; (*buy*) comprar; (*call*) llamar; (*find*) encontrar; (*catch, reproduce*) coger; (*bring*) llevar; (*extract*) sacar; (*succeed*) conseguir; (*coll: understand*) llegar a comprender; (*coll: kill*) matar. **get about** desplazarse. **get across** (*cross*) atravesar; hacer comprender. **getaway** *n* huida *f*. **get at** (*reach*) alcanzar; (*tease*) meterse con. **get back** (*return*) volver; (*recover*) récobrar. **get by** (*manage*) arreglárselas. **get down** (*descend*) bajar; (*write*) poner por escrito. **get down to** ponerse a. **get off** bajarse de; escapar. **get on** (*mount*) subir a; (*progress*) progresar; (*agree*) llevarse bien; (*grow old*) envejecer. **get out** salir; (*fig*) sacar. **get up** (*arise*) levantarse; (*climb*) subirse.

geyser ['giɪzə] *n* (*hot spring*) géiser *m*; (*water-heater*) calentador de agua *m*.

ghastly ['gaɪstli] *adj* horroroso; (*pale*) de una palidez mortal.

gherkin ['gəɪkin] *n* cohombrillo *m*.

ghetto ['getou] *n* judería *f*.

ghost [goust] *n* fantasma *m*; espectro; (*spirit*) alma *f*. **ghost writer** escritor fantasma *m*. **Holy Ghost** Espíritu Santo *m*. **give up the ghost** entregar el alma.

ghostly *adj* espectral. **ghostliness** *n* espiritualidad *f*.

giant ['dʒaiənt] *nm, adj* gigante.
gibberish ['dʒibəriʃ] *n* galimatías *m invar.*
gibe [dʒaib] *n* mofa *f. v* **jibe at** mofarse de.
giblets ['dʒiblits] *pl n* menudillos *m pl.*
giddy ['gidi] *adj (dizzy)* mareado; *(height)* vertiginoso; *(scatter-brained)* frívolo. **giddiness** *n* mareo *m*, vértigo *m.*
gift [gift] *n* regalo *m*; *(talent)* don *m*; *(offering)* ofrenda *f.* **gift-token** vale para comprar un regalo *m.* **gifted** *adj* dotado; talentoso.
gigantic [dʒai'gantik] *adj* gigantesco.
giggle ['gigl] *v* reírse tontamente. *n* risita *f.* **the giggles** la risa tonta *f sing.*
gill [gil] *n (fish)* branquia *f*; *(plant)* laminilla *f*; *(measure)* medida de líquidos *f.*
gilt [gilt] *nm, adj* dorado. **gilt-edged** *(book)* con cantos dorados. **gilt-edged securities** valores de máxima garantía *m pl.*
gimmick ['gimik] *n (coll: gadget)* artefact *m*; *(coll: trick)* truco *m.*
gin [dʒin] *n* ginebra *f.*
ginger ['dʒindʒə] *n* jengibre *m.* **ginger beer** gaseosa *f.* **gingerbread** *n* pan de jengibre *m. adj (hair)* rojizo. *v (coll)* animar.
gingerly ['dʒindʒəli] *adv* delicadamente.
gipsy ['dʒipsi] *n* gitano, -a *m, f.*
giraffe [dʒi'raif] *n* jirafa *f.*
girder ['gəidə] *n* viga *f.*
girdle ['gəidl] *n (belt)* cinturón *m*; *(corset)* faja *f. v* ceñir; *(fig)* rodear.
girl [gəil] *n* niña *f*, chica *f*; muchacha *f*; señorita. **girlfriend** *n* amiguita *f*, novia *f.* **girlhood** *n* niñez *f*; juventud *f.* **girlish** *adj* de niña; *(of boys)* afeminado.
girth [gəiθ] *n* circumferencia *f*; *(waist, etc.)* gordura *f*; *(saddle)* cincha *f.*
gist [dʒist] *n* esencia *f*, importe *m.*
*****give** [giv] *v* dar; *(offer as a present)* regalar; *(deliver)* entregar; *(hand over)* pasar; *(provide with)* proveer de; *(grant)* conceder; *(infect)* contagiar; *(communicate)* comunicar; *(a speech)* pronunciar; *(med: administer)* poner; *(telephone: connect with)* poner con. **give-and-take** *n* toma y daca *m.* **give away** distribuir; regalar; revelar. **giveaway** *n* revelación *f.* **give back** devolver. **give in** darse por vencido; ceder; *(hand in)* entregar. **give off** despedir. **give out** distribuir; emitir; anunciar; divulgar; *(run out)* agotarse.
give up abandonar; renunciar a; rendirse; entregar; ceder. **give way to** retirarse ante; abandonarse a.
glacier ['glasiə] *n* glaciar *m.* **glaciation** *n* glaciación *f.*
glad [glad] *adj* feliz, alegre. **be glad** alegrarse. **gladden** *v* regocijar. **gladly** *adv* alegremente.
glamour [glamə] *n* encanto *m.* **glamorous** *adj* encantador.
glance [glains] *n (look)* vistazo *m*, ojeada *f*; *(light)* vislumbre *f*; *(projectile)* desviación *f. v* echar un vistazo, ojear; relumbrar; desviarse.
gland [gland] *n* glándula *f.* **glandular** *adj* glandular. **glandular fever** fiebre glandular *f.*
glare [gleə] *n (look)* mirada feroz *f*; *(dazzle)* deslumbramiento *m. v* mirar con ferocidad; deslumbrar. **glaring** *adj* feroz; deslumbrante; *(conspicuous)* manifiesto.
glass [glais] *n* vidrio *m*; cristal *m*; *(for drinking)* vaso *m*; *(mirror)* espejo *m*; *(lens)* lente *f.* **glasses** *pl n* gafas *f pl.* **glassware** *n* cristalería *f.* **glassworks** *n* fábrica de cristal y vidrio *f.* **glassy** *adj* vitreo; *(eyes)* vidrioso; *(smooth)* liso.
glaze [gleiz] *v (pottery)* vidriar; *(window)* poner cristales a; *(cookery)* glasear. *n* vidriado *m*; brillo *m.* **glazier** *n* vidriero *m.*
gleam [gliim] *n* rayo *m. v* relucir. **gleaming** reluciente.
glean [gliin] *v* espigar.
glee [glii] *n* alegría *f.* **gleeful** *adj* alegre.
glib [glib] *adj* locuaz; fácil. **glibly** *adv* con labia.
glide [glaid] *v (aero)* planear; *(slide)* resbalar. **glide away** escurrirse. *n* planeo *m*; *(slide)* deslizamiento *m.* **glider** *n* planeador *m.*
glimmer ['glimə] *n* luz trémula *f*; *(fig)* vislumbre *m. v* brillar con luz trémula.
glimpse [glimps] *v* entrever. *n* vistazo *m.* **catch a glimpse of** vislumbrar.
glint [glint] *n* destello *m. v* destellar.
glisten ['glisn] *v* relucir. **glistening** *adj* reluciente.
glitter ['glitə] *v* brillar. *n* brillo *m.* **glittering** *adj* brillante.
gloat [glout] *v* recrearse con.
globe [gloub] *n* globo *m.* **globe artichoke** alcachofa *f.* **globe-trotter** *n* trotamundos *m invar.* **global** *adj* global; mundial.

gloom [gluːm] *n* obscuridad *f*; (*fig*) melancolía *f*. **gloomy** *adj* obscuro; melancólico.

glory ['gloːri] *n* gloria *f*; esplendor. **glorify** *v* glorificar. **glorious** *adj* glorioso; espléndido.

gloss [glos] *n* brillo *m*; lustre *m*; (*fig*) apariencia *f*. *v* **gloss over** disculpar.

glossary ['glosəri] *n* glosario *m*.

glove [glʌv] *n* guante *m*. **boxing gloves** *pl n* guantes de boxeo *m pl*. **glovecompartment** guantera *f*. **fit like a glove** sentar como anillo al dedo. **hand in glove with** juntar diestra con diestra. *v* enguantar.

glow [glou] *v* (*shine*) brillar.

glucose ['gluːkous] *n* glucosa *f*.

glue [gluː] *n* cola *f*. *v* pegar.

glum [glʌm] *adj* deprimido, sombrío.

glut [glʌt] *n* exceso *m*. *v* hartar.

glutton ['glʌtən] *n* glotón, -ona *m, f*. **gluttonous** *adj* glotón. **gluttony** *n* glotonería *f*.

gnarled [naːld] *adj* nudoso; (*persons*) curtido.

gnash [naʃ] *v* **gnash one's teeth** crujir los dientes.

gnat [nat] *n* mosquito *m*.

gnaw [noː] *v* roer. **gnawing** *adj* roedor.

gnome [noum] *n* gnomo *m*.

*****go** [gou] *v* ir; (*depart*) irse; (*lead to*) conducir a; (*go towards*) dirigirse a; (*leave*) dejar; (*vanish*) desaparecer; (*be removed*) quitarse; (*turn, become*) ponerse; (*function*) funcionar. **go off** (*leave*) marcharse; (*rot*) estropearse; (*gun*) dispararse. **go out** salir; (*lights, fire, etc.*) apagarse. **go round** dar la vuelta. **go with** acompañar; (*harmonize*) hacer juego con. **go without** (*manage*) arreglárselas. *n* (*coll*) energía *f*. **it's your go** te toca a ti. **on the go** ocupado. **go-between** *n* intermediario, -a *m, f*.

goad [goud] *v* aguijar; (*fig*) incitar; *n* garrocha *f*; (*fig*) estímulo *m*.

goal [goul] *n* (*structure*) meta *f*; (*score*) gol *m*; (*destination*) destinación *f*; (*purpose*) objeto *m*. **goalkeeper** *n* portero *m*; **goalpost** *n* poste *m*.

goat [gout] *n* (*nanny*) cabra *f*; (*billy*) cabrón *m*.

gobble ['gobl] *v* engullir.

goblin ['goblin] *n* trasgo *m*, duende *m*.

god [god] *n* dios *m*. **by God!** ¡vive Dios! **for God's sake** por el amor de dios. **goddaughter** *n* ahijada *f*. **godfather** padrino

m. **godmother** *n* madrina *f*. **godsend** *n* don del cielo *m*. **godson** *n* ahijado *m*. **goddess** *n* diosa *f*.

goggles ['goglz] *pl n* anteojos *m pl*.

goings-on [ˌgouiŋz'on] *pl n* (*coll*) tejemanejes *m pl*.

gold [gould] *n* oro *m*. **golden** *adj* dorado; de oro.

goldfinch ['gouldfintʃ] *n* jilguero *m*.

goldfish ['gouldfiʃ] *n* pez de colores *m*. **goldfish bowl** pecera *f*.

goldsmith ['gouldsmiθ] *n* orfebre *m*.

golf [golf] *n* golf *m*. **golf course** campo de golf *m*. **golfer** *n* golfista *m, f*.

gondola ['gondələ] *n* góndola *f*. **gondolier** *n* gondolero *m*.

gone [gon] *V* go.

gong [goŋ] *n* gong *m*.

gonorrhoea [ˌgonə'riə] *n* gonorrea *f*.

good [gud] *adj* bueno; (*before m sing nouns*) buen; (*wholesome*) sano; (*pleasant*) amable; (*genuine*) legítmo; (*virtuous*) virtuoso. *n* bien *m*. **no good** inútil. **for good** para siempre. **goodness** *n* bondad *f*. **good-looking** *adj* guapo.

good afternoon *interj* buenas tardes *f pl*.

goodbye [gud'bai] *interj* ¡adios!

good evening *interj* buenas tardes *f pl*.

good-for-nothing *n*(*m+f*), *adj* inútil.

Good Friday *n* Viernes Santo *m*.

good morning *interj* buenos días *m pl*.

good night *interj* buenas noches *f pl*.

goods [gudz] *pl n* (*comm*) artículos *m pl*; (*possessions*) bienes *m pl*. **goods and chattels** muebles y enseres *m pl*. **goods train** tren de mercancías *m*.

goose [guːs] *n, pl* **geese** ganso *m*, oca *f*.

gooseberry ['guzbəri] *n* (*fruit*) grosella espinosa *f*; (*bush*) grosellero espinoso *m*.

gore[1] [goː] *v* cornear.

gore[2] [goː] *n* sangre *f*.

gorge [goːdʒ] *n* cañón *m*. *v* hartarse.

gorgeous ['goːdʒəs] *adj* magnífico.

gorilla [gə'rilə] *n* gorila *m*.

gorse [goːs] *n* tojo *m*.

gory [goːri] *adj* ensangrentado.

gospel ['gospəl] *n* evangelio *m*.

gossip ['gosip] *n* (*chat*) charla *f*; (*unkind*) chisme; (*person*) murmurador, -a *m, f*; chismoso, -a *m, f*. **gossip column** ecos de sociedad *m pl*. *v* (*talk scandal*) cotillear; (*chatter*) charlar.

got [got] V **get.**
Gothic ['goθik] *adj* gótico.
goulash ['guːlaʃ] *n* estofado húngaro *m*.
gourd [guəd] *n* calabaza *f*.
gourmet ['guəmei] *n* gastrónomo *m*.
gout [gaut] *n* gota *f*.
govern ['gʌvən] *v* (*rule*) gobernar; (*administer*) dirigir; (*determine*) guiar; (*restrain*) dominar; (*prevail*) prevalecer. **governess** *n* aya *f*. **government** *n* gobierno *m*. **governor** *n* gobernador *m*; administrador *m*; (*coll: boss*) jefe *m*.
gown [gaun] *n* traje largo *m*; (*law, university*) toga *f*. **dressing gown** bata *f*.
grab [grab] *v* agarrar, arrebatar. *n* asimiento *m*, presa *f*; (*mech*) gancho *m*.
grace [greis] *n* gracia *f*, elegancia; (*courtesy*) cortesía *f*; (*kindness*) bondad *f*; (*forgiveness*) perdón *m*; (*before meals*) bendición mesa *f*; (*favour*) favor; (*delay*) plazo *m*. **graceful** *adj* elegante; gracioso; cortés. **gracious** *adj* gracioso; grato.
grade [greid] *n* grado *m*; (*persons, things*) clase *f*; (*mark*) nota *f*; (*gradient*) pendiente *f*. *v* graduar; (*goods*) clasificar.
gradient ['greidiənt] *n* (*declivity*) decline *m*; (*slope*) cuesta *f*.
gradual ['gradjuəl] *adj* gradual.
graduate ['gradjuət; *v* 'gradjueit] *n*, *adj* graduado, -a. *v* graduarse; diplomarse.
graft [graift] *n* injerto *m*. *v* injertarse.
grain [grein] *n* grano *m*; (*wood*) fibra *f*.
gram [gram] *n* gramo *m*.
grammar ['gramə] *n* gramática *f*. **grammar school** instituto de segunda enseñanza *m*. **grammatical** *adj* gramático.
gramophone ['graməfoun] *n* gramófono *m*; tocadiscos *m invar*.
granary ['granəri] *n* granero *m*.
grand [grand] *adj* magnífico; grande; importante; espléndido. **grandiose** *adj* grandioso.
grand-dad *n also* **grandpa** (*coll*) abuelito *m*.
grandchild ['grantʃaild] *n* nieto, -a *m*, *f*.
grandfather ['gran,faiðə] *n* abuelo *m*.
grandma ['granmai] *n also* **granny** (*coll*) abuelita *f*.
grandmother ['gran,mʌðə] *n* abuela *f*.
grandparent ['gran,peərənt] *n* abuelo, -a *m*, *f*.
grand piano *n* piano de cola *m*.
grandstand ['granstand] *n* tribuna *f*.
granite ['granit] *n* granito *m*. *adj* granítico.

grant [graint] *v* conceder; (*agree to*) acceder; (*bestow*) otorgar; (*assume*) suponer. *n* concesión *f*; otorgamiento *m*; (*student*) beca *f*.
granule ['granjuil] *n* gránulo *m*. **granulated sugar** azúcar en polvo *m*.
grape [greip] *n* uva *f*. **grapevine** *n* vid *f*; (*coll*) rumores *m pl*.
grapefruit ['greipfruit] *n* pomelo *m*.
graph [graf] *n* gráfica *f*. **graph paper** papel cuadriculado *m*. **graphic** *adj* gráfico.
grapple ['grapl] *v* **grapple with** (*fight*) luchar cuerpo a cuerpo; (*fig*) intentar a resolver.
grasp [graisp] *v* agarrar; (*fig*) comprender. *n* agarro *m*; (*reach*) alcance *m*. **grasping** *adj* avaro.
grass [grais] *n* hierba *f*; (*pasture*) pasto *m*; (*lawn*) césped *m*. **grasshopper** *n* saltamontes *m*. **grass snake** culebra *f*. **grassy** *adj* cubierto de hierba; (*like grass*) herbáceo.
grate[1] [greit] *n* parrilla *f*. **grating** *n* rejilla *f*.
grate[2] [greit] *v* rallar; (*teeth*) hacer rechinar. **grater** *n* rallador *m*.
grateful ['greitful] *adj* agradecido.
gratify ['grati,fai] *v* satisfacer; (*please*) agradar. **gratifying** *adj* satisfactorio; agradable.
gratitude ['gratitjuid] *n* agradecimiento *m*.
gratuity [grə'tjuəti] *n* propina *f*.
grave[1] [greiv] *n* sepultura *f*; (*monument*) tumba *f*. **gravedigger** *n* sepulturero *m*. **gravestone** *n* lápida sepulcral. **graveyard** *n* cementerio *m*.
grave[2] [greiv] *adj* grave, serio.
gravel ['gravəl] *n* grava *f*.
gravity ['gravəti] *n* (*force*) gravedad *f*; (*seriousness*) solemnidad *f*.
gravy ['greivi] *n* salsa *f*.
graze[1] [greiz] *v* (*scrape*) raspar; (*rub*) rozar. *n* rozadura *f*.
graze[2] [greiz] *v* pastar.
grease [griis] *n* grasa *f*. **greasepaint** *n* maquillaje *m*. **greaseproof paper** papel vegetal *m*. *v* engrasar. **greasy** *adj* grasiento; (*slippery*) resbaladizo.
great [greit] *adj* gran, grande; famoso; poderoso; magnífico. **greatly** *adv* grandemente, enormemente. **greatness** *n* grandeza *f*.
great-aunt *n* tía abuela *f*.

Great Britain *n* Gran Bretaña *f.*
Great Dane *n* perro danés *m.*
great-grandchild *n* biznieto, -a *m, f.*
great-grandfather *n* bisabuelo *m.*
great-grandmother *n* bisabuela *f.*
great-uncle *n* tío abuelo *m.*
Greece [griːs] *n* Grecia *f.* **Greek** *n, adj*
griego, -a *m, f.*
greed [griːd] *n* avaricia *f;* *(for food)*
glotonería *f.* **adj** avaro; glotón.
green [griːn] *adj* verde; *(inexperienced)*
novato; *(fresh)* fresco; *(recent)* nuevo. *n*
(colour) verde *m;* *(meadow)* prado *m;*
(lawn) césped *m.* **greens** *pl n* verduras *f*
pl. **greenery** *n* verdor *m.*
greenfly ['griːnflaɪ] *n* pulgón *m.*
greengage ['griːngeɪdʒ] *n* ciruela claudia
f.
greengrocer ['griːngrousə] *n* verdulero *m.*
greengrocery *n* verdulería *f.*
greenhouse ['griːnhaus] *n* invernadero *m.*
Greenland ['griːnlənd] *n* Groenlandia *f.*
Greenlander *n* groenlandés, -esa *m, f.*
greet [griːt] *v* saludar. **greeting** *n* salutación *f.* **greetings** *pl n* recuerdos *m pl.*
gregarious [gri'geəˌriəs] *adj* gregario.
grew [gruː] *V* **grow.**
grey [greɪ] *nm, adj* gris; *(hair)* cano. **grey-
haired** *adj* canoso. **greyhound** *n* galgo *m.*
go grey *(hair)* encanecer.
grid [grid] *n* rejilla *f;* *(elec)* red *f.*
grief [griːf] *n* pena *f,* dolor *m.* **grief-strick-
en** *adj* desconsolado.
grieve [griːv] *v* afligir; lamentar. **grieve
for** echar de menos. **grievous** *adj* doloroso; grave; apenado; lamentable. **grievous
bodily harm** daños corporales *m pl.*
grill [gril] *v* *(cook)* asar a la parrilla;
(interrogate) interrogar. *n* arrilla *f;* *(meal)*
asado a la parrilla *m.* **grillroom** *n* parrilla
f.
grille [gril] *n* reja *f;* rejilla *f.*
grim [grim] *adj* feroz; severo; horrible;
(coll) desagradable. **grimly** *adv* severamente; horriblemente.
grimace [gri'meis] *n* mueca *f.* *v* hacer
muecas.
grime [graim] *n* mugre *f.* **grimy** *adj*
mugriento.
*****grind** [graind] *v* *(coffee, etc.)* moler;
(sharpen) afilar; *(teeth)* crujir. *n* *(coll)*
trabajo pesado *m.* **grinder** *n* afilador *m.*
grindstone *n* muela *f.* **keep one's nose to
the grindstone** batir al yunque.

grip [grip] *n* *(of hand)* mano *f;* *(hold)*
agarro *m;* *(bag)* maleta *f;* *(understanding)*
comprensión *f.* *v* **asir;** *(wheels)* agarrarse;
(press) apretar; *(the attention)* atraer.
gripping *adj* impresionante.
gripe [graip] *v* retortijón *m.* *v* *(coll)*
quejarse.
grisly ['grizli] *adj* espantoso; horroroso;
repugnante.
gristle ['grisl] *n* cartílago *m.*
grit [grit] *n* cascajo *m;* polvo *m;* *(coll:
courage)* valor *m.* *v* *(teeth)* rechinar.
groan [groun] *n* gemido *m;* *(dismay)*
gruñido *m.* *v* gemir; gruñir.
grocer ['grousə] *n* tendero, -a *m, f.* **groceries** *pl n* comestibles *m pl.* **grocery** *n*
tienda de comestibles *f.*
groin [groin] *n* ingle *f.*
groom [gruːm] *n* *(horse)* mozo de caballos
m; *(of bride)* novio *m.* *v* *(horse)*
almohazar; *(smarten)* arreglar.
groove [gruːv] *n* ranura *f,* muesca *f;* *(record)* surco *m;* *(fig)* rutina *f.* *v* hacer
ranuras en; estriar. **grooved** *adj*
acanalado; estriado. **groovy** *adj* *(coll)*
fenómeno.
grope [group] *v* andar a tientas. **grope for**
buscar a tientas. **gropingly** *adv* a tientas.
gross [grous] *adj* *(not net)* bruto; *(coarse)*
grosero; grueso, denso. *n* gruesa *f.*
grotesque [grə'tesk] *nm, adj* grotesco.
grotto ['grotou] *n* gruta *f.*
ground[1] [graund] *V* **grind.**
ground[2] [graund] *n* suelo *m;* *(earth)* tierra
f; *(sport)* campo *m;* *(basis)* base *f;* *(background)* fondo *m;* *(fig)* terreno *m.* *v*
poner en tierra; *(teach)* enseñar los rudi-
mentos de. **grounds** *pl n* jardines *m pl;*
(sediment) sedimento *m sing;* *(reason)*
causa *f sing.*
ground control *n* control desde tierra *m.*
ground floor *n* planta baja *f.*
grounding ['graundiŋ] *n* **have a good
grounding in** tener una buena base en.
groundless ['graundlis] *adj* sin fundamento.
ground level *n* nivel del suelo *m.*
ground rent *n* alquiler del terreno *m.*
groundsheet ['graundʃiːt] *n* tela impermeable *f.*
groundwork ['graundwərk] *n* base *f.*
group [gruːp] *n* grupo *m.* *v* agrupar.
grouse[1] [graus] *n* ortega *f.*
grouse[2] [graus] *v* *(coll)* quejarse.

grove [grouv] n boscaje m.
grovel ['grovl] v arrastrarse; (fig) humillarse.
*grow [grou] v crecer; (increase) aumentar; (become) hacerse; (turn) ponerse; (develop) desarrollarse; (cultivate) cultivar. grown-up n adulto, -a m, f. growth n crecimiento m; aumento m; desarrollo m; (med) bulto m; vegetación f.
growl [graul] v gruñir. n gruñido m.
grub [grʌb] n larva f; (coll: food) comida f. v cavar. grubby adj sucio.
grudge [grʌdʒ] v envidiar. n rencor m. bear a grudge tener ojeriza. grudging adj mezquino. grudgingly adv de mala gana.
gruelling ['gruəliŋ] adj penoso; agotador.
gruesome ['gruɪsəm] adj pavoroso, macabro.
gruff [grʌf] adj (manner) brusco; (voice) bronco. gruffness n brusquedad f; bronquedad f.
grumble ['grʌmbl] v quejarse. n queja f.
grumpy ['grʌmpi] adj malhumorado. grumpiness n malhumor m.
grunt [grʌnt] v gruñir. n gruñido m.
guarantee [garən'tiː] n garantía f. v garantizar. guarantor n garante m, f.
guard [gaɪd] n (soldier) guardia m; (sentry) centinela m; (escort) escolta f; (keeper) guardián m; (train) jefe de tren m; (protection) defensa f; (watchfulness) vigilancia f. be on guard estar de guardia. guard dog perro de guardia m. guard's van furgón de equipajes m. v guardar; proteger. guard against protegerse contra. guarded adj (cautious) cauteloso.
guardian n (custodian) guardián; (of an orphan) tutor, -a m, f. guardian angel ángel de la Guardia m.
guerrilla [gə'rilə] n guerrillero m. guerrilla warfare guerrilla f.
guess [ges] n cálculo m; conjetura f; suposición f. at a guess a primera vista. guesswork n conjetura f. v adivinar; suponer; acertar.
guest [gest] n invitado, -a m, f; (hotel) huésped, -a m, f. be my guest yo invito. guest of honour invitado de honor m. guest-house n casa de huéspedes f. guestroom cuarto de huéspedes m.
guide [gaid] n guía m, f; (counsellor) consejero, -a m, f. girl guide exploradora f. guidebook n guía turística f. v guiar; conducir; dirigir. guidance n consejo m.

guided missile projectil teledirigido m. guided tour visita acompañada f.
guild [gild] v (association) gremio m; (craftsmen, etc.) guilda f.
guillotine ['gilətiːn] n guillotina f. v guillotinar.
guilt [gilt] n culpabilidad f. guilty adj culpable. plead guilty confesarse culpable.
guinea pig ['ginipig] n conejillo de Indias m.
guitar [gi'taɪ] n guitarra f. guitarist n guitarrista m, f.
gulf [gʌlf] n golfo m; (abyss) abismo m.
gull [gʌl] n gaviota f.
gullet ['gʌlit] n esófago m; (throat) garganta f.
gullible ['gʌləbl] adj crédulo. gullibility n credulidad f.
gully ['gʌli] n hondonada f.
gulp [gʌlp] v tragar. n (drink) trago m; (food) bocado m.
gum[1] [gʌm] n goma f. v engomar.
gum[2] [gʌm] n (mouth) encía f.
gun [gʌn] n (weapon) arma f; revólver m; pistola f; (hunting) escopeta f; rifle m; cañón m. gunfire n cañonazos m pl. gunman n pistolero m. gunpowder pólvora f. gun-running n contrabanda de armas f. gunshot n disparo m.
gurgle ['gəɪgl] n (water) borboteo m; (child) gorjeo m. v borbotear; gorjear.
gush [gʌʃ] v derramar. n chorro m; (fig) efusión f. gushing adj (person) efusivo.
gust [gʌst] n (wind) ráfaga f; (smoke) bocanada f; (rain) aguacero m; (laughter, anger) accesión f. gusty adj borrascoso.
gusto ['gʌstou] n placer m; brío m; entusiasmo m.
gut [gʌt] n (anat) intestino m, tripa f. guts pl n (coll) agallas f pl. v destripar; vaciar.
gutter ['gʌtə] n (roof) canal m; (street) arroyo m.
guy[1] [gai] n (coll) tipo m.
guy[2] [gai] n (rope) tirante m.
gymnasium [dʒim'neiziəm] n gimnasio m. gymnast n gimnasta m, f. gymnastic adj gimnástico. gymnastics n gimnasia f.
gynaecology [gainə'kolədʒi] n ginecología f. gynaecological adj ginecológico. gynaecologist n ginecólogo, -a m, f.
gypsum ['dʒipsəm] n yeso m.
gyrate [,dʒai'reit] v girar. gyration n giro m.

H

gyroscope ['dʒairə‚skoup] giroscopio *m*.

haberdasher ['habədaʃə] *n* mercero, -a *m*, *f*. **haberdashery** *n* mercería *f*.
habit ['habit] *n* costumbre *f*; (*clothes*) traje *m*. **habitual** *adj* acostumbrado.
habitable ['habitəbl] *adj* habitable.
habitat ['habitat] *n* medio *m*, habitación *f*.
hack¹ [hak] *v* acuchillar, cortar; (*kick*) dar un puntapié. *n* corte *m*; puntapié *m*. **hacking** *adj* (*cough*) seco.
hack² [hak] *n* (*horse*) rocín *m*; (*writer*) escritorzuelo *m*.
hackneyed ['haknid] *adj* usado, trillado.
had [had] *V* have.
haddock ['hadək] *n* eglefino *m*.
haemorrhage ['heməridʒ] *n* hemorragia *f*.
haemorrhoids ['heməroidz] *pl n* hemorriodes *f pl*.
hag [hag] *n* (*coll*) bruja *f*.
haggard ['hagəd] *adj* ojeroso; extraviado.
haggle ['hagl] *v* regatear. *n* regateo *m*.
Hague, The [heig] *n* La Haya.
hail¹ [heil] *n* granizo *m*. **hailstone** *n* granizo *m*, piedra *f*. **hailstorm** *n* granizada *f*.
hail² [heil] *v* (*salute*) saludar; (*coll*) llamar. **hail from** proceder de.
hair [heə] *n* pelo *m*; (*human head*) cabello *m*. **comb one's hair** peinarse. **have one's hair done** ir a la peluquería. **let one's hair down** (*coll*) soltarse el pelo. **split hairs** hilar muy fino. **tear one's hair out** tirarse de los pelos. **hairy** *adj* peludo.
hairbrush ['heəbrʌʃ] *n* cepillo (para el pelo) *m*.
haircut ['heəkʌt] *n* corte de pelo *m*. **have a haircut** cortarse el pelo.
hairdresser ['heə‚dresə] *n* peluquero, -a *m*, *f*. **hairdresser's** *n* peluquería *f*. **hairdressing** *n* peluquería *f*.
hair dryer *n* secador (para el pelo) *m*.
hairnet ['heənet] *n* redecilla *f*.
hairpiece ['heəpiːs] *n* postizo *m*.
hairpin ['heəpin] *n* horquilla *f*.
hair-remover *n* depilatorio *m*.
hairspray ['heəsprei] *n* fijador (para el pelo) *m*.
hairstyle ['heəstail] *n* peinado *m*.

Haiti ['heiti] *n* Haití *m*. **Haitian** *n*, *adj* haitiano, -a.
half [haɪf] *n* mitad *f*; medio *m*; (*division of a match*) tiempo *m*. **by half** con mucho. **half-and-half** mitad y mitad. **in half** por la mitad. **go halves with** ir a medias con. *adj* medio. **half an hour** media hora. **half a dozen** media docena. *adv* a medias; media. **half as many** *or* **much** la mitad. **half as much again** la mitad más. **not half!** (*coll*) ¡no poco!
half-baked [‚haɪf'beikt] *adj* (*coll: idea*) mal concebido; (*coll: person*) disparatado.
half-breed ['haɪfbriːd] *n* mestizo, -a *m*, *f*.
half-brother ['haɪf‚brʌðə] *n* hermanastro *m*.
half-hearted [‚haɪf'haɪtid] *adj* poco entusiasta.
half-mast [‚haɪf'maɪst] *n* **at half-mast** a media asta.
half-price [‚haɪf'prais] *adj*, *adv* a mitad de precio.
half-sister ['haɪf‚sistə] *n* hermanastra *f*.
half-time [‚haɪf'taim] *n* (*sport*) descanso *m*. *adj* (*work*) de media jornada.
halfway [‚haɪf'wei] *adv* a medio camino. **meet halfway** (*compromise*) partir la diferencia (con). *adj* medio.
half-wit ['haɪfwit] *n* tonto, -a *m*, *f*.
halibut ['halibət] *n* halibut *m*.
hall [hoɪl] *n* (*entrance*) vestíbulo *m*; (*room*) sala *f*. **hall porter** conserje *m*. **hallstand** *n* perchero *m*.
hallmark ['hoɪlmaɪk] *n* contraste *m*; (*fig*) sello *m*. *v* contrastar.
hallowed ['haloud] *adj* santo. **hallow** santificar.
Hallowe'en [halou'iɪn] *n* víspera del Día de todos los Santos *f*.
hallucination [hə‚luːsi'neiʃən] *n* alucinación *f*.
halo ['heilou] *n* halo *m*; (*rel*) aureola *f*.
halt [hoɪlt] *n* alto *m*, parada *f*. *v* parar; interrumpir.
halter ['hoɪltə] *n* cabestro *m*.
halve [haɪv] *v* compartir; partir en dos; reducir a la mitad.
ham [ham] *n* jamón *m*.
hamburger ['hambɔɪgə] *n* hamburguesa *f*.
hammer ['hamə] *n* martillo *m*; (*firearm*) percursor *m*. **come under the hammer** salir a subasta. *v* martillar, martillear; (*nail*) clavar; (*iron*) batir. **hammer out** (*disputes*, *etc.*) elaborar.

hammock ['hamək] *n* hamaca *f.*
hamper[1] ['hampə] *v* impedir; embarazar.
hamper[2] ['hampə] *n* canasta *f.*
hamster ['hamstə] *n* hámster *m.*
hamstring ['hamstriŋ] *v* (*coll*) paralizar.
hand [hand] *n* mano *f*; (*watch, etc.*) aguja *f*; (*worker*) trabajador *m*; (*writing*) escritura *f*; (*applause*) ovación *f*; (*measure*) palmo *m*; (*naut*) marinero *m*. **at first hand** de primera mano. **at hand** a mano. **by hand** en mano. **hand and foot** de pies y manos. **hand in hand** de la mano. **hands up!** ¡arriba las manos! **hand to hand** cuerpo a cuerpo. **keep one's hand in** no perder la práctica. **on the other hand** por otra parte. *v* dar. **hand down** transmitir. **hand in** entregar. **hand over** ceder. **handful** *n* puñado *m.*
handbag ['handbag] *n* bolso *m.*
handbook ['handbuk] *n* manual *m*; guía *f.*
handbrake ['handbreik] *n* freno de mano *m.*
handcuff ['handkʌf] *v* poner las esposas a. **handcuffs** *pl n* esposas *f pl.*
handicap ['handikap] *n* desventaja *f*; (*sport*) handicap *m*. *v* perjudicar.
handicraft ['handikraıft] *n* mano de obra *f.*
handiwork ['handiwəık] *n* obra *f.*
handkerchief ['haŋkətʃif] *n* pañuelo *m.*
handle ['handl] *n* (*cup, bag, etc.*) asa *f*; (*grip of a tool*) mango *m*; (*stick, door knob*) pomo *m*; (*door lever*) tirador *m*; (*lever*) brazo *m*. *v* tocar; (*naut*) dirigir; (*mot*) conducir; (*tool*) manejar; (*lift, shift*) manipular; (*cope*) poder con; (*deal with*) ocuparse de. **handle with care** frágil. **handlebars** *pl n* manillar *m sing.*
handmade [,hand'meid] *adj* hecho a mano.
hand-out ['handaut] *n* (*leaflet*) prospecto *m*; (*charity*) limosna *f*. **hand out** dar; distribuir.
hand-pick [hand'pik] *v* (*people*) escoger a dedo; (*objects*) escoger con sumo cuidado.
handrail ['handreil] *n* pasamano *m.*
handshake ['handʃeik] *n* apretón de manos *m.*
handsome ['hansəm] *adj* hermoso, bello; guapo.
handstand ['hand,stand] *n* pino *m.*
handwriting ['hand,raitiŋ] *n* escritura *f.*
handwritten *adj* escrito a mano.

handy ['handi] *adj* (*near*) a mano; (*skilful*) mañoso; diestro; (*convenient*) cómodo; (*manageable*) manejable; (*useful*) útil. **come in handy** venir bien.
*hang [haŋ] *v* colgar, suspender; (*execute*) ahorcar; (*head*) bajar; (*wallpaper*) empapelar; (*of clothes*) caer. **hang about** *or* **around** vagar. **hang fire** estar en suspenso. **hang-gliding** *n* vuelo libre *m.*
hangman *n* verdugo *m.* **hang on** mantenerse firme; (*remain*) quedarse; (*hold on*) agarrarse; (*depend upon*) depender de. **hangover** *n* (*slang*) resaca *f.* **hang-up** *n* (*coll*) complejo *m.*
hangar ['haŋə] *n* hangar *m.*
hanker ['haŋkə] *v* **hanker for** *or* **after** anhelar. **hankering** *n* anhelo *m.*
haphazard [,hap'hazəd] *adj* fortuito.
happen ['hapən] *v* acontecer, suceder; (*take place*) tener lugar; (*arise*) sobrevenir. **happening** *n* suceso *m*, ocurrencia *f.*
happy ['hapi:] *adj* feliz, alegre. **happy birthday!** ¡feliz cumpleaños! **happy Christmas!** ¡felices Pascuas! **happy-go-lucky** *adj* descuidado. **happiness** *n* alegria *f.* **happily** *adv* felizmente.
harass ['harəs] *v* hostigar. **harassment** *n* hostigamiento *m.*
harbour ['haıbə] *n* puerto *m*; (*haven*) asilo *m*. *v* dar refugio a; (*cherish*) abrigar.
hard [haıd] *adj* duro; firme; violento; inflexible; cruel; (*unjust*) opresivo; (*weather*) severo; (*stiff*) tieso. *adv* duro; de firme, vigorosamente; (*raining*) a cántaros; (*closely*) de cerca; (*badly*) mal; (*heavily*) pesadamente. **hard-and-fast** *adj* (*rule*) inalterable. **hard-bitten** *adj* also **hard-boiled** (*fig*) duro, tenaz. **hard-hearted** *adj* insensible. **hard labour** trabajos forzados *m pl.* **hard up** (*coll*) apurado. **hardware** *n* ferretería *n.* **harden** *v* endurecer; (*make callous*) hacer insensible. **hardness** *n* dureza *f*; inhumanidad *f*; tiesura *f*; dificultad *f.* **hardship** *n* penas *f pl*; sufrimiento *m*; privación *f.*
hardy ['haıdi] *adj* audaz; fuerte; (*bot*) resistente.
hare [heə] *n* liebre *f.* **hare-brained** *adj* casquivano. **hare-lip** *n* labio leporino *m.*
haricot ['harikou] *n* judía *f.*
harm [haım] *n* mal *m*; daño *m.* **harmful** *adj* malo; dañino. **harmless** *adj* inofensivo; inocuo.

harmonic [haɪˈmonik] nm, adj armónico.
harmonica [haɪˈmonikə] n armónica f.
harmonize [ˈhaɪmənaiz] v armonizar.
harmony [ˈhaɪməni] n armonia f. harmonious adj armonioso.
harness [ˈhaɪnis] n guarniciones f pl. v enjaezar; (power, etc.) represar.
harp [haɪp] n arpa f. v harp on volver a repetir. harpist n arpista m, f.
harpoon [haɪˈpuɪn] n arpón m. v arponear.
harpsichord [ˈhaɪpsiˌkoɪd] n arpicordio m, clavicémbalo m.
harrowing [ˈharouiŋ] adj atormentador, patibulario.
harsh [haɪʃ] adj (features) duro; (voice) ronco; (sound) discordante; (texture) áspero.
harvest [ˈhaɪvist] n cosecha f. v cosechar.
has [haz] V have.
hash [haʃ] n (food) picadillo m; (coll) lío m. make a hash of estropear por completo. v (food) picar.
hashish [ˈhaʃiːʃ] n hachís m invar.
haste [heist] n prisa f. hasten v dar prisa a; apresurar. hastily adv de prisa; (rashly) a la ligera. hasty adj precipitado; (rash) apresurado.
hat [hat] n sombrero m. bowler hat sombrero hongo m. Panama hat jipijapa m. top hat sombrero de copa m. take one's hat off to descubrirse ante.
hatch[1] [hatʃ] v hacer salir del cascarón; (coll: plot) maquinar.
hatch[2] [hatʃ] n (serving) ventanilla f; (naut) escotilla f; (trapdoor) trampa f.
hatchet [ˈhatʃit] n hacha f.
hate [heit] v odiar, aborrecer. n also hatred odio m. pet hate pesadilla f. hateful adj odioso.
haughty [ˈhoɪti] adj altanero. haughtiness n altaneria f.
haul [hoɪl] v (drag) arrastrar; (transport) acarrear. n (pull) tirón m; (journey) recorrido m; (fish) redada f; (loot) botín m. haulage n acarreo m, transporte m.
haunt [hoɪnt] v (ghost) aparecer en; (follow) perseguir; (frequent) frecuentar; (memories) obsesionar. n lugar predilecto m. haunting adj obsesionante.
*have [hav] v tener; (receive) recibir; (drink, food) tomar; (get) conseguir; (coll: deceive) engañar. have on (wear) llevar; (coll: tease) tomar el pelo a. have to tener que.

haven [ˈheivn] n abrigo m; (fig) refugio m.
haversack [ˈhavəsak] n mochila f.
havoc [ˈhavək] n estragos m pl. play havoc with hacer estragos en.
hawk [hoɪk] n halcón m.
hawthorn [ˈhoɪθoɪn] n espino m.
hay [hei] n heno m. make hay while the sun shines hacer su agosto. hay fever fiebre del heno f. haystack n almiar m. go haywire (machine) estropearse; (plans) desorganizarse.
hazard [ˈhazəd] n peligro m; (chance) azar m. v arriesgar; (guess) aventurar. hazardous adj arriesgado, peligroso.
haze [heiz] n neblina f; (fig) confusión f. hazy adj nebuloso; (fig) confuso.
hazel [ˈheizl] n avellano m. hazel-nut n avellana f. adj de avellano.
he [hiɪ] pron él.
head (hed] n cabeza f; (chief) jefe m; (school) director, -a m, f; (bed, table, river) cabecera f; (coin) cara f; (spear, arrows) punta f; (steam) presión f; (hammer) cotillo m. v (demonstration, list, etc.) encabezar; (lead) estar a la cabeza de; dirigir; conducir; (goal) meter de cabeza. head off cortar el paso a. head for dirigirse hacia. headed adj (notepaper) con membrete. heading n título m. heady adj embriagador.
headache [ˈhedeik] n dolor de cabeza m.
headfirst [ˌhedˈfɜɪst] adv de cabeza.
headlamp [ˈhedlamp] or headlight n (mot) faro m.
headland [ˈhedlənd] n punta f, promontorio m.
headline [ˈhedlain] n (book) título m; (newspaper) titular m. make the headlines estar en primera plana.
headlong [ˈhedloŋ] adv (headfirst) de cabeza; (rush) precipitado.
headmaster [ˌhedˈmaɪstə] n director m. headmistress n directora f.
head-on [ˌhedˈon] adj, adv de frente.
headphones [ˈhedfounz] pl n auriculares m pl.
headquarters [ˌhedˈkwoɪtəz] n (mil) cuartel general m; (firm) domicilio social m; (organization) sede f.
headrest [ˈhedrest] n cabecero m, cabezal m.
headscarf [ˈhedskaɪf] n pañuelo m.
headstrong [ˈhedstroŋ] adj testarudo.

headway ['hedwei] n progreso m.
heal [hiːl] v (disease) curar, sanar; (wound) cicatrizar.
health [helθ] n salud f. **health certificate** certificado médico m. **health food** alimentos naturales m pl. **health officer** inspector de sanidad m. **health resort** balneario m. **Ministry of Health** Dirección General de Sanidad f. **public health** sanidad pública f. **your health!** ¡a su salud! **healthy** adj sano, saludable; salubre. **healthy appetite** buen apetito m.
heap [hiːp] n montón m, pila f; (people) muchedumbre f. v amontonar, apilar.
*hear [hiə] v oír; (listen) escuchar; (attend) asistir a; (give audience) dar audiencia; (news) enterarse de. **hear from** enterarse de. **hear hear!** ¡i muy bien! **hear about** or **of** oír hablar de. **hearing** n (sense) oído m; (act of hearing) audición f. **hearing aid** aparato para sordos m. **hearsay** n rumor m.
hearse [həːs] n coche fúnebre m.
heart [haːt] n (anat) corazón m; (feelings) entrañas f pl; (courage) ánimo m; (soul) alma f; (cards) copas f pl; (lettuce) repollo m. **by heart** de memoria. **set one's heart on** poner el corazón en. **to one's heart's content** hasta quedarse satisfecho. **a man after my own heart** un hombre de los que me gustan. **hearten** v animar. **heartless** adj cruel. **hearty** adj (welcome) cordial; (meal) abundante.
heart attack n ataque cardíaco m.
heartbeat ['haːtbiːt] n latido del corazón m.
heart-breaking ['haːtbreikiŋ] adj desgarrador. **heart-broken** adj acongojado.
heartburn ['haːtbəːn] n acedía f.
heart failure n colapso cardíaco m.
heartfelt ['haːtfelt] adj de todo corazón.
hearth [haːθ] n hogar m. **hearthrug** n alfombra f.
heart-throb ['haːtθrob] n ídolo m.
heart-to-heart adj franco, sincero. **have a heart-to-heart talk** tener una conversación íntima.
heartwarming ['haːtwoːmiŋ] adj caluroso.
heat [hiːt] n calor m; (animals) celo m; (fig) vehemencia f; (passion) ardor m; (of a race) carrera eliminatoria f. v calentar; excitar; (annoy) irritar. **heatstroke** n insolación f. **heatwave** n onda de calor f. **in the heat of the moment** en el calor del

momento. **heated** adj calentado; (argument) apasionado. **heater** n calentador m. **heating** n calefacción f. **central heating** calefacción central f.
heath [hiːθ] n (plant) brezo m; (land) brezal m.
heathen ['hiːðn] n, adj pagano, -a.
heather ['heðə] n brezo m.
heave [hiːv] n (lift) gran esfuerzo m; (pull) tirón m; (sea) movimiento m; (breast) palpitación f; (retching) náusea f. v (pull) tirar de; (lift) levantar; (sigh) exhalar; (waves) subir y. bajar; (retch) tener náusea; (breast) palpitar. **heave to** ponerse al pairo.
heaven ['hevn] n cielo m, paraíso m. **heavenly** adj celeste; (fig) delicioso.
heavy ['hevi] adj pesado, torpe; (slow) lento; (thick) grueso; (hard) duro; (strong) fuerte; (oppressive) opresivo; (cold) malo; (sky) anublado; (meal) abundante; (food) indigesto; (soil) recio. **heavyweight** nm, adj peso pesado. **heaviness** n peso m; torpor m; tristeza f; ponderosidad f.
Hebrew ['hiːbruː] n (people) hebreo, -a m, f; (language) hebreo m. adj hebreo.
heckle ['hekl] v interrumpir. **heckler** n perturbador, -a m, f. **heckling** n interrupción f.
hectare ['hektaː] n hectárea f.
hectic ['hektik] adj agitado.
hedge [hedʒ] n seto m. v cercar con un seto; (fig) vacilar; (a bet) compensar.
hedgehog ['hedʒhog] n erizo m.
heed [hiːd] v atender. n atención f, cuidado m. **heedless** adj desatento; negligente.
heel [hiːl] n (anat) talón m; (shoe) tacón m. v poner tacón a.
hefty ['hefti] adj (heavy) pesado; (robust) robusto.
heifer ['hefə] n novilla f.
height [hait] n altura f; (people) estatura f; (hill) colina f; (fig) colmo m; cumbre f. **heighten** v elevar; (fig) aumentar.
heir [eə] n heredero m; **heiress** n heredera f. **heirloom** n reliquia de familia f.
held [held] V **hold**.
helicopter ['helikoptə] n helicóptero m.
hell [hel] n infierno m. **go to hell!** (impol) ¡vete al infierno! **go hell for leather** ir como si se llevara el diablo. **to hell with it!** ¡qué diablos! **hellish** adj infernal; (fig) horrible.

hello [hə'lou] *interj* (*greeting*) ¡hola!; (*attract attention*) ¡oye!; (*phone*) ¡oiga!; (*answering the phone*) ¡diga!

helm [helm] *n* caña del timón *f*. **be at the helm** empuñar el timón.

helmet ['helmit] *n* casco *m*; (*of motorcyclist, labourer, etc.*) careta *f*.

help [help] *n* ayuda *f*; socorro *m*; auxilio *m*; remedio *m*; (*employee*) empleado *m*; (*servant*) criado, -a *m, f*. *interj* ¡socorro! *v* ayudar; auxiliar; socorrer; (*relieve*) aliviar; (*serve*) servir; (*avoid*) evitar; (*facilitate*) facilitar; (*prevent oneself from*) no poder menos que. **help yourself!** ¡sírvese! **it can't be helped!** ¡no hay más remedio! **helper** *n* ayudante *m*. **helpful** *adj* útil; provechoso; amable. **helping** *n* porción *f*. **helpless** *adj* desamparado.

hem [hem] *n* dobladillo *m*. *v* hacer un dobladillo en. **hem in** (*fig*) rodear. **hemline** *n* bajo *m*.

hemisphere ['hemi‚sfiə] *n* hemisferio *m*.

hemp [hemp] *n* cáñamo *m*.

hen [hen] *n* (*chicken*) gallina *f*; (*female of other birds*) hembra *f*. **henhouse** *n* gallinero *m*. **hen party** (*coll*) reunión de mujeres *f*. **henpecked** *adj* dominado por su mujer.

hence [hens] *adv* por eso, por lo consiguiente; (*time*) de ahora; (*place*) de aquí. **henceforth** *adv* desde aquí en adelante.

henna ['henə] *n* alheña *f*.

her [hɜː] *pron* ella; (*direct object*) la; (*indirect object*) le, a ella. *adj* su (*pl* sus).

herald ['herəld] *n* heraldo *m*. *v* proclamar. **heraldic** *adj* heráldico. **heraldry** *n* heráldica *f*.

herb [hɜːb] *n* hierba *f*. **herbal** *adj* herbario.

herd [hɜːd] *n* rebaño *m*, manada *f*. *v* (*round up*) reunir en manada; (*drive*) conducir; (*fig*) agrupar.

here [hiə] *adv* aquí. **hereafter** *adv* en lo futuro; en adelante. **here and now** ahora mismo. **here and there** aquí y allá. **here goes!** ¡vamos a ver! **here is/are** aquí está/están.

hereditary [hi'redətəri] *adj* hereditario.

heredity [hi'redəti] *n* herencia *f*.

heresy ['herəsi] *n* herejía *f*. **heretic** *n* hereje *m, f*. **heretical** *adj* herético.

heritage ['heritidʒ] *n* herencia *f*.

hermit ['hɜːmit] *n* ermitaño *m*.

hernia ['hɜːniə] *n* hernia *f*.

hero ['hiərou] *n* héroe *m*. **heroine** *n* heroína *f*. **hero-worship** *n* culto a los héroes *m*. **heroic** *adj* heroico. **heroism** *n* heroísmo *m*.

heroin ['herouin] *n* heroína *f*.

heron ['herən] *n* garza *f*.

herring ['heriŋ] *n* arenque *m*. **red herring** (*coll*) pista falsa *f*.

hers [hɜːz] *pron* suyo, suya.

herself [hɜː'self] *pron* (*reflexive*) se; (*emphatic*) ella misma. **by herself** a solas.

hesitate ['heziteit] *v* vacilar. **hesitant** *adj* vacilante. **hesitation** *n* vacilación *f*.

heterosexual [hetərə'sekʃuəl] *n(m+f)*, *adj* heterosexual.

hexagon ['heksəgən] *n* hexágono *m*. **hexagonal** *adj* hexagonal.

heyday ['heidei] *n* auge *m*, apogeo *m*.

hiatus [hai'eitəs] *n* laguna *f*.

hibernate ['haibəneit] *v* hibernar. **hibernation** *n* hibernación *f*.

hiccup ['hikʌp] *n* hipo *m*. **have the hiccups** tener hipo. *v* hipar.

hide[1] [haid] *v* esconder. **hide something from someone** ocultar algo a alguien. **hide-and-seek** *n* escondite *m*. **hide-out** *n* escondrijo *m*.

hide[2] [haid] *n* piel *f*; (*leather*) cuero *m*.

hideous ['hidiəs] *adj* horroroso.

hiding[1] ['haidiŋ] *n* **be in hiding** estar escondido. **go into hiding** esconderse. **hiding place** escondite *m*.

hiding[2] ['haidiŋ] *n* (*beating*) paliza *f*.

hierarchy ['haiəraːki] *n* jerarquía *f*. **hierarchical** *adj* jerárquico.

hi-fi ['hai‚fai] *n* alta fidelidad *f*.

high [hai] *adj* alto; de alto; (*speed, hopes, number*) grande; (*post*) importante; (*wind*) fuerte; (*altar, Mass*) mayor; (*voice*) agudo; (*quality*) superior; (*river*) crecido; (*noon*) pleno; (*game*) manido; (*shine, polish*) brillante; (*colour*) subido.

highbrow ['haibrau] *n(m+f)*, *adj* intelectual.

high chair *n* silla alta para niño *f*.

high frequency *adj* de alta frecuencia.

high-heeled *adj* de tacón alto.

high jump *n* salto de altura *m*.

highland ['hailənd] *n* tierras altas *f pl*. *adj* montañoso.

highlight ['hailait] *v* destacar. *n* (*art*) toque de luz *m*; (*fig*) atracción principal *f*.

Highness ['hainis] n Alteza f.
high-pitched adj de tono alto.
high-rise block n torre f.
high-speed adj de gran velocidad.
high-spirited adj brioso.
high street n calle principal f.
highway ['haiwei] n camino real m, carretera f. **highway code** código de la circulación m. **highwayman** n salteador de caminos m.
hijack ['haidʒak] v (aircraft) secuestrar; (people) asaltar; (goods) robar. n secuestro m; asalto m.
hike [haik] n excursión a pie f. v ir de excursión. **hiker** n excursionista m, f. **hiking** n excursionismo m.
hilarious [hi'leəriəs] adj (funny) hilarante; (merry) alegre. **hilarity** n hilaridad f.
hill [hil] n colina f, cerro m; (slope) cuesta f. **hillside** n ladera f. **hilly** adj montañoso.
him [him] pron él; (direct object) le, lo.
himself [him'self] pron (reflexive) se; sí, sí mismo; (emphatic) él mismo. **by himself** a solas.
hind [haind] adj trasero, posterior. **hindquarters** pl n cuarto trasero m sing. **hindsight** n percepción retrospectiva f.
hinder ['hində] v impedir; interrumpir. **hindrance** n impedimento m; obstáculo m.
Hindu [hin'duː] n(m+f), adj hindú. **Hinduism** n hinduismo m.
hinge [hindʒ] n bisagra f; (stamps) fijasellos m invar. v **hinge on** depender de.
hint [hint] n indirecta f; (tip) consejo m; (clue) pista f; indicación f; (trace) pizca f. **broad hint** una insinuación muy clara. **take the hint** (pejorative) darse por aludido; (follow advice) aprovechar el consejo. v insinuar; soltar indirectas.
hip [hip] n cadera f.
hippopotamus [hipə'potəməs] n hipopótamo m.
hire [haiə] v alquilar; (person) contratar. **hire out** alquilar. n (house, etc.) alquiler m; (engagement) contratación f; (wages) sueldo m. **for hire** de alquiler; (taxi) libre. **hire purchase** compra a plazos f.
his [hiz] adj su (pl sus); de él. pron suyo, suya.
hiss [his] n silbido m. v silbar.
history ['histəri] n historia f. **historian** n historiador, -a m, f. **historic** adj histórico.
*hit [hit] v golpear, pegar a; (target) dar

en; (wound) herir; (collide) chocar con. **hit home** dar en el blanco. **hit it off with** hacer buenas migas con. n golpe m; (mil) impacto m; (success) exito m. **hit-or-miss** adv a la buena de Dios.
hitch [hitʃ] n obstáculo m; problema m; (knot) vuelta de cabo m. v (travel) hacerse llevar en coche; (tie) atar; (link) enganchar. **hitch-hike** v hacer autostop. **hitch-hiker** n autostopista m, f. **hitch-hiking** n autostop m.
hitherto [ˌhiðə'tuː] adv hasta ahora.
hive [haiv] n colmena f.
hoard [hoːd] n acumulación f; tesoro m. v acumular, amasar.
hoarding ['hoːdiŋ] n (fence) valla f; (advertising) cartelera f.
hoarse [hoːs] adj ronco. **hoarsely** adv roncamente. **hoarseness** n ronquera f.
hoax [houks] n estafa f; engaño m; burla f. v estafar; engañar; burlar.
hobble ['hobl] v cojear. n (gait) cojera f.
hobby ['hobi] n pasatiempo m.
hock¹ [hok] n (pork, etc.) pernil m.
hock² [hok] n vino del Rín m.
hockey ['hoki] n hockey m. **hockey stick** bastón de hockey m.
hoe [hou] n azadón m. v azadonar.
hog [hog] n cerdo m, puerco m. v (coll) acaparar.
hoist [hoist] v (heavy objects) levantar; (sails, flag) izar. n (lifting) levantamiento m; (crane) grúa f; (lift) montacargas m invar; (lifting mechanism) cabria f.
*hold¹ [hould] v tener; mantener; agarrar; (believe) creer; (keep) guardar; (sustain) sostener; (opinion) defender. **hold back** reprimir. **hold forth** perorar. **hold on** sujetar; (wait) aguantar; (grip) agarrarse. **hold out** (hand) tender, ofrecer; (last) durar; (resist) resistir. **hold up** (raise) levantar; (support) sostener; (delay) retrasar. n (grip) asimiento m, agarro m; (handhold) asidero m; (control) autoridad f. dominio m. **get hold of** coger, agarrar. **hold-up** n interrupción f; (robbery) atraco a mano armada m; (traffic jam) embotellamiento m. **holder** n (person) poseedor, -a m, f; (object) receptáculo m.
hold² [hould] n (naut) bodega f.
hole [houl] n agujero m; (from digging) hoyo m; (in garments) boquete m; (mouse) ratonera f; (rabbit) madriguera f.

holiday ['holədi] *n* (*day*) fiesta *f*; (*several days*) vacaciones *f pl*. **holiday resort** centro de turismo *m*.

Holland ['holənd] *n* Holanda *f*.

hollow ['holou] *n* hueco *m*; (*in ground*) hondonada *f*. *adj*, *adv* hueco. *v* ahuecar.

holly ['holi] *n* acebo *m*.

hollyhock ['holihok] *n* malva loca *f*.

holster ['houlstə] *n* pistolera *f*.

holy ['houli] *adj* santo; sacro; sagrado; (*bread*, *water*) bendito. **holiness** *n* santidad *f*.

homage ['homidʒ] *n* homenaje *m*. **pay homage** rendir homenaje.

home [houm] *n* casa *f*; hogar *m*; domicilio *m*; (*fig*) morada *f*. **at home** en casa. **make yourself at home** está usted en su casa. *adv* a casa. **go home** volver a casa. **homeless** *adj* sin casa ni hogar. **home address** dirección privada *f*. **homesick** *adj* nostálgico.

homicide ['homisaid] *n* (*act*) homicidio *m*; (*person*) homicida *m*, *f*. **homicidal** *adj* homicida.

homogeneous [homə'dʒiɪniəs] *adj* homogéneo.

homosexual [homə'sekʃuəl] *n*(*m*+*f*), *adj* homosexual. **homosexuality** *n* homosexualidad *f*.

honest ['onist] *adj* honrado; sincero; franco. **honesty** *n* honradez *f*; sinceridad *f*; rectitud *f*.

honey ['hʌni] *n* miel *f*. **honeycomb** *n* panal *m*. **honeymoon** *n* luna de miel *f*. **honeysuckle** *n* madreselva *f*.

honour ['onə] *n* honor *m*; rectitud *f*. *v* honrar. **honorary** *adj* honorario. **honourable** *adj* honorable.

hood [hud] *n* capucha *f*; (*car*, *pram*) capota *f*.

hoof [huɪf] *n* casco *m*; (*cloven*) pezuña *f*.

hook [huk] *n* gancho *m*; (*fish*) anzuelo *m*; (*dress*) corchete *m*; (*hanger*) colgadero *m*. *v* enganchar; (*fish*) pescar; (*dress*) abrochar; colgar. **hooked** *adj* (*shaped*) ganchudo. **get hooked on** (*coll*) enviciarse en.

hooligan ['huɪligən] *n* rufián *m*. **hooliganism** *n* rufianería *f*.

hoop [huɪp] *n* (*toy*) aro *m*; (*barrel*) fleje *m*.

hoot [huɪt] *n* (*owl*) ululato *m*; (*person*) silbato *m*; (*shout*) grito *m*; (*boat*, *factory*) toque de sirena *m*. *v* ulular; silbar; dar un bocinazo; gritar; dar un toque de sirena; (*boo*) abuchear.

hop¹ [hop] *v* saltar; brincar; saltar con un pie. *n* salto *m*; brinco *m*; (*coll*: *dance*) baile *m*; (*coll*: *stage in a journey*) etapa *f*.

hop² [hop] *n* (*bot*) lúpulo *m*.

hope [houp] *n* esperanza *f*. *v* esperar. **hopeful** *adj* lleno de esperanzas; confiado. **hopeless** *adj* desesperado; (*coll*) inútil.

horde [hoɪd] *n* horda *f*.

horizon [hə'raizn] *n* horizonte *m*.

horizontal [hori'zontl] *adj* horizontal.

hormone ['hoɪmoun] *n* hormona *f*.

horn [hoɪn] *n* cuerno *m*; (*mot*) bocina *f*. **hornet** ['hoɪnit] *n* avispón *m*.

horoscope ['horəskoup] *n* horóscopo *m*.

horrible ['horibl] *adj* horrible, espantoso.

horrid ['horid] *adj* horroroso, odioso.

horrify ['horifai] *v* horrorizar. **horrific** *adj* horrífico, horrendo.

horror ['horə] *n* horror *m*. *adj* (*film*, *story*, *etc*.) de miedo.

hors d'œuvres [oɪ'dəɪvr] *pl n* entremeses *m pl*.

horse [hoɪs] *n* caballo *m*. **on horseback** a caballo. **horsepower** *n* caballo de vapor *m*. **horseradish** *n* rábano picante *m*. **horse show** concurso hípico *m*.

horticulture ['hoɪtikʌltʃə] *n* horticultura *f*. **horticultural** *adj* horticultural.

hose [houz] *n* manga *f*; manguera *f*; (*stockings*) medias *f pl*. *v* regar con una manga.

hosiery ['houziəri] *n* medias *f pl*; (*business*) calcetería *f*.

hospitable [ho'spitəbl] *adj* hospitalario.

hospital ['hospitl] *n* hospital *m*. **hospitalize** *v* hospitalizar.

hospitality [hospi'taliti] *n* hospitalidad *f*.

host¹ [houst] *n* huésped *m*. **hostess** *n* huéspeda *f*.

host² [houst] *n* (*crowd*) muchedumbre *f*.

hostage ['hostidʒ] *n* rehén *m*.

hostel ['hostəl] *n* hostería *f*; residencia *f*. **youth hostel** albergue juvenil *m*.

hostile ['hostail] *adj* hostil; enemigo. **hostility** *n* hostilidad *f*; enemistad *f*.

hot [hot] *adj* caliente; (*climate*) cálido; (*sun*) abrasador; (*day*) caluroso; (*spicy*) picante; (*temper*) vivo; (*issue*) controvertido; (*pursuit*) porfiado. **be hot** (*person*) tener calor; (*weather*) hacer calor. **hot dog** perro caliente *m*. **hot-house** invernadero *m*. **hotplate** *n* calientaplato

m invar. **hot-tempered** *adj* enfadadizo.
hot-water bottle bolsa de agua caliente *f.*
hotel [hou'tel] *n* hotel *m.*
hound [haund] *n* perro de caza *m. v (fig)*
perseguir.
hour ['auə] *n* hora *f.* **after hours** fuera de
horas. **by the hour** por horas. **hour by
hour** de hora en hora. **peak hours** horas
de mayor consumo. **rush hour** hora
punta. **small hours** altas horas. **zero hour**
hora H. **hourly** *adv* de cada hora.
house [haus; *v* hauz] *n* casa *f; (theatre)*
sala *f; (audience)* público *m. v (hold)*
alojar; *(put up)* albergar.
houseboat ['hausbout] *n* casa flotante *f.*
housecoat ['hauskout] *n* bata *f.*
household ['haushould] *n* casa *f,* familia *f.*
adj casero.
housekeeper ['hausˌkiːpə] *n (paid)* ama de
llaves *f; (housewife)* ama de casa *f.*
housekeeping *n (work)* quehaceres
domésticos *m pl; (money)* dinero para
gastos domésticos *m.*
housemaid ['hausmeid] *n* criada *f.*
house-to-house *adj, adv* de casa en casa.
house-trained ['haustreind] *adj* enseñado.
house-warming ['hausˌwɔːmiŋ] *n* **have a
house-warming party** inaugurar la casa.
housewife ['hauswaif] *n* ama de casa *f.*
housing ['hauziŋ] *n* alojamiento *m.* **housing estate** urbanización *f.*
hovel ['hovəl] *n* casucha *f.*
hover ['hovə] *v* cernerse; *(fig)* rondar.
hovercraft *n* aerodeslizador *m.*
how [hau] *adv (as)* como; *(in what way)*
cómo; *(in exclamation before adv or adj)*
qué. **how are you?** *or* **how do you do?**
¿cómo está usted? **how much?** ¿cuánto?
however [hau'evə] *conj* sin embargo. *adv*
de cualquier manera que.
howl [haul] *v (dog, wolf)* aullar; *(wind)*
bramar; *(pain)* dar alaridos; *(child)* berrear. *n* aullido *m;* bramido *m;* alarido *m;*
grito *m;* berrido *m.*
hub [hʌb] *n (wheel)* cubo *m; (fig)* centro
m. **hubcap** *n (mot)* tapacubos *m invar.*
huddle ['hʌdl] *v* amontonar. *n* grupo *m.*
hue [hjuː] *n* color *m.*
huff [hʌf] *n* **in a huff** enojado.
hug [hʌg] *v* abrazar. *n* abrazo *m.*
huge [hjuːdʒ] *adj* enorme.
hulk [hʌlk] *n (ship)* carraca *f; (derog: person)* armatoste *m.* **hulking** *adj* voluminoso.
hull [hʌl] *n (naut)* casco *m.*

hum [hʌm] *n (bees, engines)* zumbido *m;
(a tune)* canturreo *m. v* zumbar; cantur-
rear; *(fig: with activity)* hervir. **humming-
bird** *n* colibrí *m.*
human ['hjuːmən] *nm, adj* humano.
human being ser humano *m.* **human
nature** naturaleza humana *f.*
humane [hjuː'mein] *adj* humano.
humanity [hjuː'manəti] *n* humanidad *f.*
humanitarian *adj* humanitario.
humble ['hʌmbl] *adj* humilde. *v* humillar.
humdrum ['hʌmdrʌm] *adj* monótono.
humid ['hjuːmid] *adj* húmedo. **humidity** *n*
humedad *f.*
humiliate [hjuː'milieit] *v* humillar. **humiliation** *n* humillación *f.*
humility [hjuː'miləti] *n* humildad *f.*
humour ['hjuːmə] *n* humor *m; (temperament)* disposición *f. v* complacer. **humorist** *n* humorista *m, f.* **humorous** *adj*
humorístico.
hump [hʌmp] *n* horoba *f. v (coll: carry)*
cargar con.
hunch [hʌntʃ] *v* encorvarse. *n (coll)*
presentimiento *m.* **hunchback** *n*
jorobado, -a *m, f.*
hundred ['hʌndrəd] *n* ciento *m;* centenar
m; centena *f. adj* cien, ciento. **hundredth**
nm, adj centésimo.
hung [hʌŋ] *V* **hang.**
Hungary ['hʌŋgəri] *n* Hungría *f.* **Hungarian** *n, adj* húngaro, -a.
hunger ['hʌŋgə] *n* hambre *f. v* **also be
hungry** tener hambre, estar hambriento.
hunger for desear. **hungrily** *adv* ham-
brientamente.
hunt [hʌnt] *n* caza *f; (search)* busca *f. v*
cazar; buscar. **hunting** *n* caza *f.* **huntsman**
n cazador *m.*
hurdle ['həːdl] *n (sport)* valla *f; (fig)*
obstáculo *m. v* vallar.
hurl [həːl] *v* lanzar, arrojar; *(abuse)* soltar.
hurricane ['hʌrikən] *n* huracán *m.*
hurry ['hʌri] *n* prisa *f.* **be in a hurry** llevar
prisa. *v* dar prisa (a), apresurar. **hurried**
adj apresurdado. **hurriedly** *adj*
apresuradamente.
***hurt** [həːt] *v (cause pain)* doler; *(wound)*
herir; *(damage)* hacer daño (a); ofender;
(feelings) mortificar. *n* herida *f;* daño *m;*
mal *m. adj* lastimado; herido. **hurtful** *adj*
dañoso; perjudicial; *(words)* hiriente.
husband ['hʌzbənd] *n* marido *m,* esposo
m.

hush [hʌʃ] *n* silencio *m*. *interj* ¡calla! *v* silenciar. **hush up** echar tierra a. **hushed** *adj* callado.

husk [hʌsk] *n* (*cereals*) cáscara *f*; (*peas and beans*) vaina *f*; (*chestnut*) erizo *m*. *v* descascarar; desvainar; pelar.

husky ['hʌski] *n* (*dog*) perro esquimal *m*. *adj* (*hoarse*) ronco; (*strong*) fuerte. **huskily** *adv* con voz ronca. **huskiness** *n* ronquera *f*.

hussar [hə'zaɪ] *n* húsar *m*.

hustle ['hʌsl] *v* empujar; (*fig*) precipitar. *n* (*energy*) empuje *m*; (*hurry*) prisa *f*; (*push*) empujón *m*. **hustle and bustle** vaivén *m*.

hut [hʌt] *n* choza *f*, cabaña *f*.

hutch [hʌtʃ] *n* (*rabbit*) conejera *f*.

hyacinth ['haɪəsinθ] *n* jacinto *m*.

hybrid ['haibrid] *nm*, *adj* híbrido. **hybridization** *n* hibridación *f*.

hydraulic [hai'drɔilik] *adj* hidráulico.

hydrocarbon [ˌhaidrə'kaɪbən] *n* hidrocarburo *m*.

hydro-electric *adj* hidroeléctrico.

hydrofoil ['haidrəfoil] *n* aerodeslizador *m*.

hydrogen ['haidrədʒən] *n* hidrógeno *m*.

hyena [hai'iɪnə] *n* hiena *f*.

hygiene ['haidʒiɪn] *n* higiene *f*. **hygienic** *adj* higiénico.

hymn [him] *n* himno *m*. **hymn-book** *or* **hymnal** *n* himnario *m*.

hyphen ['haifən] *n* guión *m*.

hypnosis [hip'nousis] *n* hipnosis *f*. **hypnotic** *adj* hipnótico. **hynotism** *n* hipnotismo *m*. **hypnotist** *n* hipnotizador, -a *m*, *f*. **hypnotize** *v* hipnotizar.

hypochondria [haipə'kondriə] *n* hipocondría *f*. **hypochondriac** *n*, *adj* hipocondríaco, -a *m*, *f*.

hypocrisy [hi'pokrəsi] *n* hipocresía *f*. **hypocrite** *n* hipócrita *m*, *f*. **hypocritical** *adj* hipócrita.

hypodermic [haipə'dɔimik] *adj* hipodérmico. *n* jeringa hipodérmica *f*.

hypothesis [hai'poθəsis] *n*, *pl* -ses hipótesis *f*. **hypothetical** *adj* hipotético.

hysterectomy [ˌhistə'rektəmi] *n* histerectomía *f*.

hysteria [hi'stiəriə] *n* histeria *f*. **hysterical** *adj* histérico. **hysterics** *n* histerismo *m*; ataque histérico *m*.

I

I [ai] *pron* yo.

Iberian [ai'biəriən] *adj* ibérico. *n* ibero, -a *m*, *f*.

ice [ais] *n* hielo *m*. **iceberg** *n* iceberg *m*. **icebreaker** *n* rompehielos *m invar*. **ice-cold** *adj* helado. **ice cream** helado *m*. **ice-skate** *n* patín de cuchilla *m*. *v* (*turn into ice*) helar; (*chill*) enfriar. **icing** *n* escarchado *m*. **icing sugar** azúcar en polvo *m*, *f*. **icy** *adj* (*wind, place*) glacial; (*hand, foot*) helado.

Iceland ['aislənd] *n* Islandia *f*. **Icelander** *n* islandés, -esa *m*, *f*. **Icelandic** *adj* islandés.

icicle ['aisikl] *n* carámbano *m*.

icon ['aikon] *n* icono *m*.

idea [ai'diə] *n* idea *f*.

ideal [ai'diəl] *nm*, *adj* ideal. **idealist** *n* idealista *m*, *f*. **idealistic** *adj* idealista.

identical [ai'dentikəl] *adj* idéntico. **identical twins** gemelos homólogos *m pl*.

identify [ai'dentifai] *v* identificar. **identify with** identificarse con. **identification** *n* identificación *f*; (*papers*) documentos de identidad *m pl*.

identity [ai'dentiti] *n* identidad *f*. **identity card** carnet de identidad *m*.

ideology [aidi'olədʒi] *n* ideología *f*.

idiom ['idiəm] *n* (*expression*) idiotismo *m*; (*language*) idioma *m*. **idiomatic** *adj* idiomático.

idiosyncrasy [ˌidiə'siŋkrəsi] *n* idiosincrasia *f*.

idiot ['idiət] *n* imbécil *m*, *f*, idiota *m*, *f*. **idiotic** *adj* idiota.

idle ['aidl] *adj* (*lazy*) perezoso; (*at leisure*) ocioso; (*unemployed*) desocupado; (*machine*) parado; (*talk*) frívolo; (*fears*) infundado. *v* (*waste time*) perder el tiempo; (*be lazy*) holgazanear; (*mechanism*) girar loco. **idleness** *n* (*laziness*) holgazanería *f*; (*leisure*) ociosidad *f*; (*unemployment*) paro *m*.

idol ['aidl] *n* ídolo *m*. **idolatry** *n* idolatría *f*. **idolize** *v* idolatrar.

idyllic [i'dilik] *adj* idílico.

if [if] *conj* si. **as if** como si. **if not** si no. **if only** ¡ojalá que! **if so** si es así.

ignite [ig'nait] *v* encender, prender fuego a.

ignition [ig'niʃən] *n* ignición *f*; (*mot*)

encendido *m*. **ignition key** llave de contacto *f*. **ignition switch** interruptor del encendido *m*.

ignorant ['ignərənt] *adj* ignorante. **ignorance** *n* ignorancia *f*.

ignore [ig'nɔɪ] *v* (*warning*) no hacer caso de; (*person*) no hacer caso a; (*leave out*) pasar por alto.

ill [il] *adj* (*sick*) enfermo; (*bad*) malo. *nm*, *adv* mal. **ill-advised** *adj* malaconsejado. **ill-at-ease** *adj* molesto. **ill-mannered** *adj* mal educado. **ill health** mala salud *f*. **ill-treat** *v* maltratar. **ill will** mala voluntad *f*. **illness** *n* enfermedad *f*.

illegal [i'liɪgəl] *adj* ilegal.

illegible [i'ledʒəbl] *adj* ilegible.

illegitimate [ˌili'dʒitimit] *adj* ilegítimo. **illegitimacy** *n* ilegitimidad *f*.

illicit [i'lisit] *adj* ilícito.

illiterate [i'litərit] *n*, *adj* analfabeto, -a. **illiteracy** *n* analfabetismo *m*.

illogical [i'lodʒikəl] *adj* ilógico.

illuminate [i'luɪmiˌneit] *v* (*light up*) iluminar; (*clear*) aclarar. **illumination** *n* iluminación *f*; aclaración *f*.

illusion [i'luɪʒən] *n* ilusión *f*.

illustrate ['iləˌstreit] *v* ilustrar; (*demonstrate*) demostrar. **illustration** *n* ilustración *f*; ejemplo *m*. **illustrator** *n* ilustrador, -a *m*, *f*.

illustrious [i'lʌstriəs] *adj* ilustre.

image ['imidʒ] *n* imagen *f*; (*fig*) reputación *f*. **be the image of** ser el retrato de. **imagery** *n* imágenes *f pl*.

imagine [i'madʒin] *v* imaginar. **imaginary** *adj* imaginario. **imagination** *n* imaginación *f*. **imaginative** *adj* imaginativo.

imbalance [im'baləns] *n* desequilibrio *m*.

imbecile ['imbəsiɪl] *n* imbécil *m*, *f*.

imitate ['imiˌteit] *v* imitar. **imitation** *n* imitación *f*.

immaculate [i'makjulit] *adj* inmaculado.

immaterial [ˌimə'tiəriəl] *adj* indiferente; no importa.

immature [ˌimə'tjuə] *adj* inmaduro. **immaturity** *n* inmadurez *f*.

immediate [i'miɪdiət] *adj* inmediato; (*near*) cercano. **immediately** *adv* inmediatamente; directamente.

immense [i'mens] *adj* inmenso, enorme.

immerse [i'məɪs] *v* sumergir. **immersion** *n* sumersión *f*. **immersion heater** calentador de inmersión *m*.

immigrate ['imiˌgreit] *v* inmigrar. **immigrant** *n*(*m+f*), *adj* inmigrante. **immigration** *n* inmigración *f*.

imminent ['iminənt] *adj* inminente.

immobile [i'moubail] *adj* inmóvil. **immobilize** *v* inmovilizar.

immoral [i'morəl] *adj* inmoral. **immorality** *n* inmoralidad *f*.

immortal [i'moɪtl] *adj* inmortal. **immortality** *n* inmortalidad *f*. **immortalize** *v* inmortalizar.

immovable [i'muɪvəbl] *adj* inmóvil; (*steadfast*) inflexible.

immune [i'mjuɪn] *adj* inmune. **immunity** *n* inmunidad *f*. **immunization** *n* inmunización *f*. **immunize** *v* inmunizar.

imp [imp] *n* diablillo *m*.

impact ['impakt] *n* impacto *m*.

impair [im'peə] *v* dañar. **impairment** *n* daño *m*.

impale [im'peil] *v* atravesar.

impart [im'paɪt] *v* (*give*) impartir; (*grant*) conceder; (*make known*) comunicar.

impartial [im'paɪʃəl] *adj* imparcial. **impartiality** *n* imparcialidad *f*.

impasse [am'pais] *n* callejón *m*.

impassive [im'pasiv] *adj* impasible.

impatient [im'peiʃənt] *adj* impaciente. **become impatient** perder la paciencia. **impatience** *n* impaciencia *f*.

impeach [im'piɪtʃ] *v* acusar; (*prosecute*) encausar; (*a witness*) recusar. **impeachment** *n* acusación *f*; (*prosecution*) enjuiciamiento *m*; recusación *f*.

impeccable [im'pekəbl] *adj* impecable.

impede [im'piɪd] *v* estorbar; impedir. **impediment** [im'pedimənt] *n* estorbo *m*; obstáculo *m*; defecto *m*.

impel [im'pel] *v* impeler; mover; (*push*) empujar; obligar.

impending [im'pendiŋ] *adj* inminente; próximo.

imperative [im'perətiv] *adj* (*peremptory*) perentorio; (*urgent*) imperioso; (*necessary*) indispensable.

imperfect [im'pəɪfikt] *adj* imperfecto; incompleto. *n* (*gramm*) imperfecto *m*.

imperial [im'piəriəl] *adj* imperial; (*fig*) señorial. **imperialism** *n* imperialismo *m*.

impersonal [im'pəɪsənl] *adj* impersonal.

impersonate [im'pəɪsəˌneit] *v* hacerse pasar por; (*theatre*) imitar. **impersonation** *n* imitación *f*.

impertinent [im'pəɪtinənt] *adj* impertinente. **impertinence** *n* impertinencia *f*.

impervious [im'pɜːviəs] *adj* impenetrable; (*to criticism, pain, etc.*) insensible.

impetuous [im'petjuəs] *adj* impetuoso.

impetus ['impətəs] *n* (*force*) ímpetu *m*; (*fig*) impulso *m*; estímulo *m*.

impinge [im'pindʒ] *v* **impinge on** tropezar con; usurpar.

implement ['implimənt; *v* 'impliment] *n* (*tool*) herramienta *f*; (*utensil*) utensilio; **implements** *pl n* (*writing*) artículos *m pl*; (*agr*) aperos *m pl*. *v* llevar a cabo; (*law*) aplicar.

implication [impli'keiʃən] *n* implicación *f*; complicidad *f*; consecuencia *f*. **implicate** *v* implicar; comprometer.

implicit [im'plisit] *adj* implícito; absoluto.

implore [im'plɔː] *v* suplicar. **imploring** *adj* suplicante.

imply [im'plai] *v* implicar; presuponer; significar; dar a entender. **implied** *adj* implícito.

impolite [impə'lait] *adj* descortés.

import [im'pɔːt] *n* (*comm*) artículo importado *m*; (*meaning*) sentido *m*; importancia *f*. *v* (*comm*) importar; significar.

importance [im'pɔːtəns] *n* importancia *f*. **important** *adj* importante.

impose [im'pouz] *v* imponer; (*tax*) gravar con. **impose on** abusar de. **imposing** *adj* imponente. **imposition** *n* imposición *f*; abuso *m*; (*tax*) impuesto *m*.

impossible [im'posəbl] *adj* imposible.

impostor [im'postə] *n* impostor, -a *m, f*.

impotent ['impətənt] *adj* impotente. **impotence** *n* impotencia *f*.

impound [im'paund] *v* confiscar.

impoverish [im'povəriʃ] *v* (*people*) empobrecer; (*land*) agotar.

impregnate ['impreg,neit] *v* fecundar; (*saturate*) empapar. **impregnable** *adj* inexpugnable. **impregnation** *n* fecundación *f*; impregnación *f*.

impress [im'pres] *v* impresionar; (*print*) imprimir. **impression** *n* impresión *f*. **impressive** *adj* impresionante.

imprint ['imprint; *v* im'print] *n* impresión *f*. *v* imprimir.

imprison [im'prizn] *v* encarcelar. **imprisonment** *n* encarcelamiento *m*.

improbable [im'probəbl] *adj* improbable; (*story, etc.*) inverosímil.

impromptu [im'promptjuː] *adv* improvisadamente. *adj* improvisado.

improper [im'propə] *adj* indecente; indecoroso; incorrecto.

improve [im'pruːv] *v* mejorar; favorecer; perfeccionar. **improvement** *n* mejora *f*; progreso *m*; reforma *f*.

improvise ['imprə,vaiz] *v* improvisar. **improvisation** *n* improvisación *f*.

impudent ['impjudənt] *adj* impudente. **impudence** *n* impudencia *f*.

impulse ['impʌls] *n* impulso *m*. **impulsive** *adj* impulsivo.

impure [im'pjuə] *adj* impuro. **impurity** *n* impureza *f*.

in [in] *prep* en; de; durante; a. *adv* dentro. **be in** (*at home*) estar en casa. **be in on** estar enterado de.

inability [inə'biləti] *n* incapacidad *f*.

inaccessible [inak'sesəbl] *adj* inaccesible. **inaccessibility** *n* inaccesibilidad *f*.

inaccurate [in'akjurit] *adj* inexacto. **inaccuracy** *n* inexactitud *f*.

inactive [in'aktiv] *adj* inactivo. **inaction** *n* inacción *f*. **inactivity** *n* inactividad *f*.

inadequate [in'adikwit] *adj* insuficiente. **inadequacy** *n* insuficiencia *f*.

inadvertent [inəd'vɜːtənt] *adj* inadvertido; descuidado. **inadvertently** *adv* por inadvertencia.

inane [in'ein] *adj* (*futile*) inane; (*silly*) necio. **inanity** *n* inanidad *f*; necedad *f*.

inanimate [in'animit] *adj* inanimado.

inarticulate [inaɪ'tikjulit] *adj* (*sound*) inarticulado; (*person*) incapaz de expresarse.

inasmuch [inəz'mʌtʃ] *adv* **inasmuch as** puesto que, visto que.

inaudible [in'ɔːdəbl] *adj* inaudible.

inaugurate [i'nɔːgju,reit] *v* inaugurar. **inaugural** *adj* inaugural. **inauguration** *n* inauguración *f*.

inborn [in'bɔːn] *adj* innato; (*med*) congénito.

incapable [in'keipəbl] *adj* incapaz.

incendiary [in'sendiəri] *adj* incendiario. **incendiary bomb** bomba incendiaria *f*.

incense¹ ['insens] *n* incienso *m*.

incense² [in'sens] *v* encolerizar.

incentive [in'sentiv] *n* incentivo *m*, estímulo *m*.

incessant [in'sesənt] *adj* incesante, continuo.

incest ['insest] *n* incesto *m*. **incestuous** *adj* incestuoso.

inch [intʃ] *n* pulgada *f*. **inch by inch** poco a poco. **within an inch of** a dos pasos de. *v* **inch forward** avanzar poco a poco.

incident ['insidənt] *n* incidente *m*; (*in a story*) episodio *m*. **incidental** *adj* incidente; incidental; imprevisto; (*expense*) accesorio *m*; (*music*) de fondo; (*secondary*) secundario; (*casual*) fortuito. **incidentally** *adv* (*by the way*) a propósito. **incinerator** [in'sinə,reitə] *n* quemador de basuras *m*. **incinerate** *v* quemar. **incineration** *n* incineración *f*. **incite** [in'sait] *v* incitar; provocar. **incitement** *n* incitamiento *m*; estímulo *m*. **incline** [in'klain] *v* inclinar. **be inclined to** inclinarse a. *n* pendiente *f*. **inclination** *n* (*tilt*) inclinación *f*; (*slope*) pendiente *f*; (*leaning*) tendencia *f*. **include** [in'kluːd] *v* incluir; (*enclose in a letter*) adjuntar. **including** *adj* incluso. **inclusion** *n* inclusión *f*. **inclusive** *adj* inclusivo. **incognito** [,inkog'niːtou] *adv* de incógnito. **incoherent** [,inkə'hiərənt] *adj* incoherente. **incoherence** *n* incoherencia *f*. **incoherently** *adv* de modo incoherente. **income** ['inkʌm] *n* ingresos *m pl*. **income tax** impuesto de utilidades *m*. **incomparable** [in'kompərəbl] *adj* incomparable. **incomparably** *adv* incomparablemente. **incompatible** [inkəm'patəbl] *adj* incompatible. **incompatibility** *n* incompatibilidad *f*. **incompetent** [in'kompitənt] *adj* incompetente. **incompetence** *n* incompetencia *f*. **incomplete** [,inkəm'pliːt] *adj* incompleto; sin terminar. **incomprehensible** [in,kompri'hensəbl] *adj* incomprensible. **inconceivable** [inkən'siːvəbl] *adj* inconcebible. **incongruous** [in'koŋgruəs] *adj* incongruo; incompatible. **incongruity** *n* incongruidad *f*. **inconsiderate** [,inkən'sidərit] *adj* (*thoughtless*) inconsiderado; (*lacking consideration for others*) desconsiderado. **inconsistent** [,inkən'sistənt] *adj* (*substance*) inconsistente; (*actions, thoughts*) inconsecuente. **inconsistency** *n* inconsistencia *f*; inconsecuencia *f*. **incontinence** [in'kontinəns] *n* incontinencia *f*. **incontinent** *adj* incontinente. **inconvenient** [inkən'viːnjənt] *adj* (*place*) incómodo; (*time*) inoportuno. **inconvenience** *n* inconvenientes *m pl*, molestia *f*. *v* incomodar, molestar.

incorporate [in'kɔːpə,reit] *v* incorporar, incluir; (*contain*) contener; (*comm*) constituir en sociedad. **incorrect** [inkə'rekt] *adj* incorrecto; erróneo. **increase** [in'kriːs] *v* aumentar. *n* aumento *m*. **increasing** *adj* creciente. **increasingly** *adv* cada vez más. **incredible** [in'kredəbl] *adj* increíble. **incredulous** [in'kredjuləs] *adj* incrédulo. **incredulity** *n* incredulidad *f*. **increment** ['iŋkrəmənt] *n* aumento *m*. **incriminate** [in'krimineit] *v* incriminar. **incriminating** *adj* acriminador. **incubate** ['iŋkju,beit] *v* incubar. **incubation** *n* incubación *f*. **incubator** *n* incubadora *f*. **incur** [in'kəː] *v* incurrir; (*debt*) contraer; (*loss*) sufrir. **incurable** [in'kjuərəbl] *adj* incurable. **indebted** [in'detid] *adj* (*owing money*) endeudado (con); (*fig*) agradecido. **indebtedness** *n* deuda *f*; agradecimiento *m*. **indecent** [in'diːsnt] *adj* indecente. **indecency** *n* indecencia *f*. **indeed** [in'diːd] *adv* en efecto; realmente. **yes indeed!** ¡ya lo creo! **indefinite** [in'definit] *adj* indefinido; impreciso. **indelible** [in'deləbl] *adj* indeleble. **indemnity** [in'demnəti] *n* (*security*) indemnidad *f*; reparación *f*. **indent** [in'dent] *v* (*dent*) abollar; (*notch*) dentar; (*comm*) pedir; (*print*) sangrar. **indentation** *n* (*notch*) muesca *f*; (*print*) sangría *f*. **independent** [,indi'pendənt] *adj* independiente. **independence** *n* independencia *f*. **index** ['indeks] *n* índice *m*; (*math*) exponente *m*. **index finger** dedo índice *m*. **cost-of-living index** el índice del coste de la vida. *v* (*file*) clasificar; (*a book*) poner un índice a. **India** ['indjə] *n* India *f*. **Indian** *n* indio, -a *m, f*; (*language*) indio *m*. *adj* indio. **Indian ink** tinta china *f*. **Indian summer** veranillo de San Martín *m*. **india paper** papel de China *m*. **india rubber** goma de borrar *f*. **indicate** ['indikeit] *v* indicar, señalar. **indication** *n* indicación *f*; señal *f*. **indicative** *nm, adj* indicativo. **indicator** *n* indicador *m*.

indict [in'dait] v acusar. indictment n acusación f.

indifferent [in'difrant] adj indiferente; insignificante; (mediocre) regular. indifference n indiferencia f.

indigenous [in'didʒinəs] adj indígena.

indigestion [,indi'dʒestʃən] n indigestión f. indigestible adj indigesto.

indignant [in'dignənt] adj indignado. get indignant indignarse. indignantly adv con indignación. indignation n indignación f.

indignity [in'dignəti] n (lack of dignity) indignidad f; (outrage) afrenta f.

indirect [,indi'rekt] adj indirecto.

indiscreet [,indi'skriit] adj indiscreto. indiscretion n indiscreción f.

indiscriminate [,indi'skriminit] adj indistinto; universal; (person) sin criterio.

indispensable [,indi'spensəbl] adj indispensable.

indisposed [,indi'spouzd] adj (ill) indispuesto, enfermo; (reluctant) maldispuesto. indisposition n indisposición f; aversión f.

individual [,indi'vidjuəl] adj individual; personal. n individuo m. individuality n individualidad f.

indoctrinate [in'doktri,neit] v adoctrinar. indoctrination n adoctrinamiento m.

indolent ['indələnt] adj indolente. indolence n indolencia f.

indoor ['indoi] adj interior. indoor pool piscina cubierta f. indoors adv dentro; en casa.

induce [in'djuis] v (convince) inducir, persuadir; (cause) causar, provocar. inducement n incentivo m; (motive) móvil m.

indulge [in'dʌldʒ] v (pamper) mimar; (give way to) ceder a. indulge in entregarse a. indulgence n indulgencia f; satisfacción f; tolerancia f; (self-indulgence) desenfreno m. indulgent adj indulgente.

industry ['indəstri] n industria f; diligencia f. industrial adj industrial. industrial relations relaciones profesionales f pl. industrialist n industrial m. industrialize v industrializar. industrious adj trabajador.

inebriated [i'niibrieitid] adj ebrio.

inedible [in'edibl] adj incomible.

inefficient [,ini'fiʃnt] adj ineficaz; incompetente. inefficiency n ineficacia f; incompetencia f.

inept [i'nept] adj inepto.

inequality [,ini'kwoləti] n desigualdad f; injusticia f.

inert [i'nɔit] adj inerte. inertia n inercia f.

inevitable [in'evitəbl] adj inevitable. inevitability n inevitabilidad f.

inexpensive [,inik'spensiv] adj poco costoso, barato.

inexperienced [,inik'spiəriənst] adj inexperto.

infallible [in'faləbl] adj infalible.

infamous ['infəməs] adj de mala fama; odioso. infamy n infamia f.

infancy ['infənsi] n infancia f, niñez f.

infant ['infənt] n niño, -a m, f. adj naciente. infantile adj infantil.

infantry ['infəntri] n infantería f.

infatuate [in'fatjueit] v be infatuated with (person) estar chiflado por; (idea) estar encaprichado por. infatuation n enamoramiento m.

infect [in'fekt] v infectar; contaminar. infection n infección f; contaminación f. infectious adj infeccioso; contagioso.

infer [in'fəi] v deducir. inference n deducción f.

inferior [in'fiəriə] nm, adj inferior. inferiority n inferioridad f. inferiority complex complejo de inferioridad m.

infernal [in'fəinl] adj infernal; (coll) maldito.

infest [in'fest] v infestar. infestation n infestación f.

infidelity [,infi'deliti] n infidelidad f.

infiltrate [in'fil,treit] v infiltrarse. infiltration n infiltración f.

infinite ['infinit] nm, adj infinito. infinity n infinidad f; (math) infinito m.

infinitive [in'finitiv] nm, adj infinitivo.

infirm [in'fəim] adj débil. infirmity n debilidad f; (illness) enfermedad f.

infirmary [in'fəiməri] n enfermería f; hospital m.

inflame [in'fleim] v (set on fire) inflamar; (passion) avivar; (anger) encender. inflammable adj inflamable. inflammation n inflamación f. inflammatory adj incendiario.

inflate [in'fleit] v hinchar; (prices) provocar la inflación de. inflation n (air) inflado m; (comm) inflación f. inflationary adj inflacionista.

inflection [in'flekʃən] n inflexión f.

inflict [in'flikt] v infligir, imponer. infliction n (punishment) castigo m.

influence ['influəns] *n* influencia *f*. **under the influence of** bajo los efectos de. *v* (*person*) influenciar; (*decision*) influir en. **influential** *adj* influyente.
influenza [,influ'enzə] *n* gripe *f*.
influx ['inflʌks] *n* (*gas, etc.*) entrada *f*; (*people*) afluencia *f*.
inform [in'foːm] *v* informar. **informative** *adj* informativo. **informer** *n* denunciante *m, f*.
informal [in'foːml] *adj* sin ceremonia; (*person*) sencillo; (*tone*) familiar; (*unofficial*) no oficial. **informality** *n* ausencia de ceremonia *f*; sencillez *f*.
information [,infə'meiʃən] *n* información *f*. **information bureau** centro de informaciones *m*. **information desk** informaciones *f pl*.
infra-red [,infrə'red] *adj* infrarrojo.
infringe [in'frindʒ] *v* infringir, violar. **infringe on** usurpar. **infringement** *n* infracción *f*; usurpación *f*.
infuriate [in'fjuəri,eit] *v* enfurecer; exasperar. **infuriating** *adj* exasperante.
ingenious [in'dʒiːnjəs] *adj* ingenioso. **ingenuity** *n* ingeniosidad *f*.
ingot ['iŋgət] *n* lingote *m*.
ingredient [in'griːdjənt] *n* ingrediente *m*.
inhabit [in'habit] *v* (*occupy*) habitar; (*live in*) vivir en. **inhabitant** *n* habitante *m*.
inhale [in'heil] *v* inhalar; (*smoke*) tragar.
inherent [in'hiərənt] *adj* inherente.
inherit [in'herit] *v* heredar. **inheritance** *n* herencia *f*; sucesión *f*.
inhibit [in'hibit] *v* (*restrain*) inhibir; (*prevent*) impedir. **inhibition** *n* inhibición *f*.
inhuman [in'hjuːmən] *adj* inhumano; insensible. **inhumanity** *n* inhumanidad *f*.
iniquity [i'nikwəti] *n* iniquidad *f*. **iniquitous** *adj* inicuo.
initial [i'niʃl] *adj* inicial, primero. *n* inicial *f*; (*used as abbreviation*) siglas *f pl*. *v* poner iniciales a. **initially** *adv* al principio.
initiate [i'niʃi,eit] *v* iniciar; (*proceedings*) entablar; (*membership*) admitir. **initiation** *n* iniciación *f*.
initiative [i'niʃiətiv] *n* iniciativa *f*.
inject [in'dʒekt] *v* inyectar. **injection** *n* inyección *f*.
injure ['indʒə] *v* herir; lastimar; ofender. **injury** *n* herida *f*; daño *m*; ofensa *f*. **injurious** *adj* injurioso; ofensivo.
injustice [in'dʒʌstis] *n* injusticia *f*.

ink [iŋk] *n* tinta *f*. **ink-well** *n* tintero *m*. *v* entintar.
inkling ['iŋkliŋ] *n* idea *f*; algo *m*; sospecha *f*; indicio *m*.
inland ['inlənd; *adv* in'land] *adj* interior. **Inland Revenue** fisco *m*. *adv* hacia el interior.
in-laws ['in,loːs] *pl n* (*coll*) familia política *f sing*.
***inlay** [in'lei; *n* 'inlei] *v* incrustar; adornar con marquetería. *n* incrustación *f*; (*with coloured woods*) taracea *f*.
inlet ['inlet] *n* cala *f*; brazo de mar *m*; (*tech*) entrada *f*.
inmate ['inmeit] *n* (*prison*) preso *m*; (*asylum*) internado, -a *m, f*; (*hospital*) enfermo, -a *m, f*.
inn [in] *n* posada *f*; taberna *f*. **innkeeper** *n* posadero, -a *m, f*; tabernero, -a *m, f*.
innate [,i'neit] *adj* innato.
inner ['inə] *adj* interior; íntimo. **inner tube** cámara de neumático *f*.
innocent ['inəsnt] *adj* inocente. **innocence** *n* inocencia *f*.
innocuous [i'nokjuəs] *adj* inocuo; inofensivo.
innovation [inə'veiʃən] *n* innovación *f*.
innuendo [,inju'endou] *n* insinuación *f*.
innumerable [i'njuːmərəbl] *adj* innumerable.
inoculate [i'nokju,leit] *v* inocular. **inoculation** *n* inoculación *f*.
inorganic [,inoː'ganik] *adj* inorgánico.
input ['input] *n* entrada *f*; (*computer*) input *m*.
inquest ['inkwest] *n* encuesta *f*.
inquire [in'kwaiə] *v* informarse de; preguntar. **inquire into** investigar. **inquiring** *adj* (*mind*) curioso; (*look*) inquisidor.
inquiry *n* pregunta *f*; (*official*) investigación *f*; (*request for information*) petición de información *f*. **inquiry office** oficina de informaciones *f*. **inquiries** *pl n* (*sign*) información *f sing*.
inquisition [,inkwi'ziʃən] *n* investigación *f*. **the Inquisition** la Inquisición *f*.
inquisitive [in'kwizətiv] *adj* preguntón; curioso. **inquisitiveness** *n* curiosidad *f*.
insane [in'sein] *adj* loco. **insane asylum** manicomio *m*. **insanity** *n* locura *f*.
insatiable [in'seiʃəbl] *adj* insaciable.
inscribe [in'skraib] *v* inscribir; (*engrave*) grabar. **inscription** *n* inscripción *f*.
insect ['insekt] *n* insecto *m*; (*coll*) bicho *m*. **insecticide** *n* insecticida *f*.

insecure [ˌinsi'kjuə] *adj* inseguro; (*unstable*) inestable. **insecurity** *n* inseguridad *f.*
inseminate [in'semineit] *v* inseminar. **insemination** *n* inseminación *f.*
insensitive [in'sensətiv] *adj* insensible. **insensitivity** *n* insensibilidad *f.*
inseparable [in'sepərəbl] *adj* inseparable.
insert [in'səit; *n* 'insəit] *v* introducir; (*advert*) insertar; (*between pages*) intercalar. *n* (*in a book*) encarte *m.* **insertion** *n* inserción *f*; encarte *m*; (*advert*) anuncio *m.*
inshore [ˌin'ʃoi] *adj* cercano a la orilla.
inside [ˌin'said] *adv* dentro,· adentro. *prep* dentro de. *adj* interior; confidencial. *n* interior *m*; parte de adentro *f.* **inside out** al revés.
insidious [in'sidiəs] *adj* insidioso. **insidiousness** *n* insidia *f.*
insight ['insait] *n* perspicacia *f.*
insignificant [ˌinsig'nifikənt] *adj* insignificante. **insignificance** *n* insignificancia *f.*
insincere [ˌinsin'siə] *adj* insincero; hipócrita. **insincerity** *n* insinceridad *f*; hipocresía *f.*
insinuate [in'sinjueit] *v* insinuar. **insinuation** *n* insinuación *f.*
insipid [in'sipid] *adj* insípido, soso.
insist [in'sist] *v* insistir, empeñarse. **insistence** *n* insistencia *f*, empeño *m.* **insistent** *adj* insistente. **insistently** *adv* insistentemente.
insolent ['insələnt] *adj* insolente. **insolence** *n* insolencia *f.*
insoluble [in'soljubl] *adj* insoluble.
insomnia [in'somniə] *n* insomnio *m.* **insomniac** *n*(*m*+*f*), *adj* insomne.
inspect [in'spekt] *v* inspeccionar, examinar. **inspection** *n* inspección *f*, examen *m.* **inspector** *n* inspector *m*, *f.*
inspire [in'spaiə] *v* inspirar. **inspiration** *n* inspiración *f.* **inspirational** *adj* inspirador.
instability [ˌinstə'biləti] *n* inestabilidad *f*, instabilidad *f.*
install [in'stoil] *v* instalar. **installation** *n* instalación *f.*
instalment [in'stoilmənt] *n* (*payment*) plazo *m*; (*serial*) fascículo *m.* **monthly instalment** mensualidad *f.*
instance ['instəns] *n* ejemplo *m.* **for instance** por ejemplo.
instant ['instənt] *n* instante *m*, momento *m.* *adj* (*coffee, soup, etc.*) instantáneo; urgente; inmediato; inminente; (*this*

month) corriente. **instantaneous** *adj* instantáneo. **instantly** *adv* al instante.
instead [in'sted] *adv* en su lugar. **instead of** en vez de.
instep ['instep] *n* empeine *m.*
instigate ['instigeit] *v* instigar, incitar; fomentar. **instigation** *n* instigación *f.* **instigator** *n* instigador, -a *m*, *f.*
instil [in'stil] *v* instilar; inculcar.
instinct ['instiŋkt] *n* instinto *m.* **instinctive** *adj* instintivo.
institute ['institjuit] *n* instituto *m.* *v* instituir, establecer; (*start*) empezar. **institution** *n* institución *f*; establecimiento *m.*
instruct [in'strʌkt] *v* (*teach*) instruir; (*order*) mandar. **instruction** *n* instrucción *f.* **instructive** *adj* instructivo. **instructor** *n* instructor *m*; profesor *m*; maestro *m.*
instrument ['instrəmənt] *n* instrumento *m.* **instrumental** *adj* instrumental. **be instrumental in** contribuir a.
insubordinate [ˌinsə'boidənət] *adj* insubordinado. **insubordination** *n* insubordinación *f.*
insufficient [ˌinsə'fiʃənt] *adj* insuficiente. **insufficiency** *n* insuficiencia *f.*
insular ['insjulə] *adj* insular; (*outlook*) estrecho de miras.
insulate ['insjuleit] *v* aislar. **insulation** *n* aislamiento *m*; (*material*) aislador *m.*
insulin ['insjulin] *n* insulina *f.*
insult [in'sʌlt; *n* 'insʌlt] *v* insultar. *n* insulto *m.*
insure [in'ʃuə] *v* asegurar. **insurance** *n* seguro *m.* **insurance broker** corredor de seguros *m.* **insurance policy** póliza de seguro *f.* **fully comprehensive insurance** seguro a todo riesgo *m.* **third party insurance** seguro contra terceros *m.* **national insurance** seguros sociales *m pl.* **take out insurance** hacerse un seguro.
intact [in'takt] *adj* intacto.
intake ['inteik] *n* (*air, water*) toma *f*; (*mot*) entrada *f*; (*fuel, steam*) válvula de admisión *f*; (*food*) ración *f*; (*school*) número de personas admitidas *m*; (*thing taken in*) consumo *m.*
intangible [in'tandʒəbl] *adj* intangible. **intangibility** *n* intangibilidad *f.*
integral ['intigrəl] *adj* (*part*) integrante; (*complete*) integral. *n* integral *f.*
integrate ['intigreit] *v* integrar. **integration** *n* integración *f.*

integrity [in'tegrəti] *n* integridad *f.*
intellect ['intilekt] *n* intelecto *m,* inteligencia *f.* **intellectual** *n(m+f), adj* intelectual.
intelligent [in'telidʒənt] *adj* inteligente.
intelligence *n* inteligencia *f; (information)* noticia *f; (secret information)* información *f.*
intelligible [in'telidʒəbl] *adj* inteligible.
intend [in'tend] *v* proponerse.
intense [in'tens] *adj* intenso; fuerte; profundo; ardiente; enorme. **intensify** *v* intensificar; aumentar. **intensity** *n* intensidad *f.* **intensive** *adj* intensivo. **intensive care** asistencia intensiva *f.*
intent¹ [in'tent] *n* intención *f,* propósito *m.*
intent² [in'tent] *adj* atento; profundo; constante.
intention [in'tenʃən] *n* intención *f.* **intentional** *adj* intencional.
inter [in'tɜː] *v* enterrar. **interment** *n* entierro *m.*
interact [,intər'akt] *v* actuar recíprocamente. **interaction** *n* interacción *f.*
intercede [,intə'siːd] *v* interceder. **intercession** *n* intercesión *f.*
intercept [,intə'sept] *v* (*message*) interceptar; (*stop someone*) parar. **interception** *n* intercepción *f,* interceptación *f.*
interchange [,intə'tʃəindʒ] *n* intercambio *m;* cambio *m.* **interchangeable** *adj* intercambiable.
intercom ['intəkom] *n* interfono *m.*
intercourse ['intəkɔːs] *n* (*social*) trato *m;* (*pol, comm*) relaciones *f pl;* (*sexual*) contacto sexual *m.*
interest ['intrist] *n* interés *m;* (*advantage*) beneficio *m.* **business interests** negocios *m pl. v* interesar. **be interested** interesarse en.
interfere [,intə'fiə] *v* entrometerse. **interfere with** (*hinder*) estorbar; (*touch*) tocar; (*interests*) oponerse a. **interference** *n* intromisión *f;* obstrucción *f;* (*radio*) parásitos *m pl.* **interfering** *adj* (*person*) entrometido; interferente.
interim ['intərim] *n* ínterin *m. adj* provisional.
interior [in'tiəriə] *nm, adj* interior.
interjection [,intə'dʒekʃən] *n* interjección *f.*
interlude ['intəluːd] *n* intervalo *m;* (*theatre*) entremés *m;* (*music*) interludio *m.*

intermediate [,intə'miːdiət] *adj* intermedio. **intermediary** *n* intermediario, -a *m, f.*
interminable [in'tɜːminəbl] *adj* interminable.
intermission [,intə'miʃən] *n* (*interruption*) intermisión *f;* (*theatre*) entreacto *m;* (*cinema*) descanso *m.*
intermittent [,intə'mitənt] *adj* intermitente. **intermittently** *adv* a intervalos.
intern [in'tɜːn] *n* interno *m. v* internar. **internment** *n* internamiento *m.*
internal [in'tɜːnl] *adj* interno. **internal combustion engine** motor de combustión interna *m.*
international [,intə'naʃənl] *adj* internacional. **international date line** línea de cambio de fecha *f.*
interpose [,intə'pouz] *v* interponer; intervenir. **interposition** *n* interposición *f.*
interpret [in'tɜːprit] *v* interpretar. **interpretation** *n* interpretación *f.* **interpreter** *n* intérprete *m, f.*
interrogate [in'terəgeit] *v* interrogar. **interrogation** *n* interrogatorio *m.* **interrogator** *n* interrogador, -a *m, f.*
interrogative [,intə'rogətiv] *adj* (*sentence*) interrogativo; (*look*) interrogador. *n* palabra interrogativa *f.*
interrupt [,intə'rʌpt] *v* interrumpir. **interruption** *n* interrupción *f.*
intersect [,intə'sekt] *v* cruzar; (*math*) cortar. **intersection** *n* (*mot*) cruce *m;* (*math*) intersección *f.*
intersperse [,intə'spɜːs] *v* esparcir.
interval ['intəvəl] *n* (*time, space, music*) intervalo *m;* (*theatre*) entreacto *m;* (*cinema*) descanso *m.*
intervene [,intə'viːn] *v* intervenir; (*happen*) ocurrir; (*time*) transcurrir; (*distance*) mediar. **intervention** *n* intervención *f.*
interview ['intəvjuː] *n* entrevista *f,* interviú *f. v* entrevistar. **interviewer** *n* entrevistador, -a *m, f.*
intestine [in'testin] *n* intestino *m.* **intestinal** *adj* intestinal.
intimate¹ ['intimət] *adj* íntimo; (*individual*) personal; (*loving*) amoroso; (*detailed*) profundo. **intimacy** *n* relaciones íntimas *f pl.*
intimate² ['intimeit] *v* insinuar; anunciar. **intimation** *n* insinuación *f;* indicación *f;* indicio *m.*

intimidate [in'timideit] *v* intimidar. **intimidation** *n* intimidación *f.*
into ['intu] *prep* en; a; hacia; contra; dentro.
intolerable [in'tolərəbl] *adj* intolerable.
intolerant [in'tolərənt] *adj* intolerante. **intolerance** *n* intolerancia *f.*
intonation [‚intə'neiʃən] *n* entonación *f.* **intone** *v* entonar.
intoxicate [in'toksikeit] *v* embriagar, emborrachar. **intoxicated** *adj* borracho, ebrio. **intoxication** *n* embriaguez *f*, borrachera *f.*
intransitive [in'transitiv] *nm, adj* intransitivo.
intravenous [‚intrə'viinəs] *adj* intravenoso.
intrepid [in'trepid] *adj* intrépido.
intricate ['intriket] *adj* intrincado; complejo. **intricacy** *n* intrincamiento *m*; complejidad *f.*
intrigue ['intriig; *v* in'triig] *n* intriga *f. v* intrigar.
intrinsic [in'trinsik] *adj* intrínseco.
introduce [‚intrə'djuis] *v* presentar; introducir; (*acquaint*) iniciar. **introduction** *n* presentación *f*; introducción *f.* **introductory** *adj* introductorio.
introspective [‚intrə'spektiv] *adj* introspectivo. **introspection** *n* introspección *f.*
introvert ['intrə‚vəit] *n.* introvertido, -a *m, f.* **introverted** *adj* introvertido.
intrude [in'truid] *v* imponer; meter por fuerza. **intruder** *n* intruso, -a *m, f.* **intrusion** *n* entremetimiento *m.*
intuition [‚intjui'iʃən] *n* intuición *f.* **intuitive** *adj* intuitivo.
inundate ['inʌndeit] *v* inundar. **inundation** *n* inundación *f.*
invade [in'veid] *v* invadir. **invader** *n* invasor, -a *m, f.* **invasion** *n* invasión *f.*
invalid¹ ['invəlid] *nm, adj* (*disabled*) inválido; (*sick*) enfermo.
invalid² [in'valid] *adj* (*not valid*) nulo.
invaluable [in'valjuəbl] *adj* inestimable.
invariable [in'veəriəbl] *adj* invariable. **invariably** *adv* invariablemente; constantemente.
invective [in'vektiv] *n* invectiva *f.*
invent [in'vent] *v* inventar. **invention** *n* invención *f.* **inventive** *adj* inventivo. **inventor** *n* inventor, -a *m, f.*
inventory ['invəntri] *n* inventario *m.*
invert [in'vəit] *v* invertir. **inverted commas** comillas *f pl.* **inversion** *n* inversión *f.*

invertebrate [in'vəitibrət] *nm, adj* invertebrado.
invest [in'vest] *v* invertir; (*install*) investir. **invest in** (*fig*) comprarse. **invest with** (*fig*) envolver en. **investment** *n* inversión *f.* **investor** *n* inversionista *m, f.*
investigate [in'vestigeit] *v* investigar, examinar; estudiar. **investigation** *n* investigación *f*; estudio *m.*
invigorating [in'vigəreitiŋ] *adj* tónico, estimulante. **invigorate** *v* vigorizar, estimular.
invincible [in'vinsəbl] *adj* invencible.
invisible [in'vizəbl] *adj* invisible. **invisibility** *n* invisibilidad *f.*
invite [in'vait] *v* invitar, convidar; (*questions*) solicitar; (*ask for*) pedir; (*cause*) provocar. **invitation** *n* invitación *f.* **inviting** *adj* atractivo; seductor; tentador; apetitoso.
invoice ['invois] *n* factura *f. v* facturar.
invoke [in'vouk] *v* invocar; (*ask for*) pedir; (*fall back on*) recurrir. **invocation** *n* invocación *f.*
involuntary [in'voləntəri] *adj* involuntario. **involuntarily** *adv* sin querer.
involve [in'volv] *v* (*concern*) concernir; (*imply*) suponer; (*affect*) afectar; (*entail*) ocasionar; (*draw somebody in*) comprometer; mezclar; (*require*) exigir; (*complicate*) complicar. **involved** *adj* complicado. **involvement** *n* envolvimiento *m*; participación *f*; compromiso *m.*
inward ['inwəd] *adj* interior, interno; (*thoughts*) íntimo. **inwardly** *adv* interiormente. **inwards** *adv* hacia dentro.
iodine ['aiədiin] *n* yodo *m.*
ion ['aiən] *n* ion *m.*
irate [ai'reit] *adj* furioso.
Ireland ['aiələnd] *n* Irlanda *f.* **Irish** *nm, adj* irlandés. **the Irish** los irlandeses *m pl.*
iris ['aiəris] *n* lirio *m.*
irk [əik] *v* molestar. **irksome** *adj* molesto.
iron ['aiən] *n* (*metal*) hierro *m*; (*for pressing*) plancha *f*; (*golf*) palo de golf *m.* **cast iron** hierro colado *m.* **Iron Curtain** telón de acero *m.* **wrought iron** hierro forjado *m.* **ironmonger's** *n* quincallería *f. v* planchar. **iron out** (*fig*) allanar. **ironing** *n* planchado *m.* **ironing board** tabla de planchar.
irony ['aiərəni] *n* ironía *f.* **ironic** *adj* irónico.
irrational [i'raʃənl] *adj* irracional. *n* (*math*) número irracional *m.*

J

irregular [i'regjulə] *adj* irregular. **irregularity** *n* irregularidad *f*.

irrelevant [i'reləvənt] *adj* (*remark*) fuera de propósito; (*beside the point*) no pertinente.

irreparable [i'repərəbl] *adj* irreparable.

irresistible [,iri'zistəbl] *adj* irresistible.

irrespective [,iri'spektiv] *adj* **irrespective** of sin tener en cuenta.

irresponsible [,iri'sponsəbl] *adj* irresponsable; irreflexivo.

irrevocable [i'revəkəbl] *adj* irrevocable.

irrigate ['irigeit] *v* irrigar. **irrigation** *n* irrigación *f*.

irritate ['iriteit] *v* irritar. **irritable** *adj* irritable. **irritation** *n* irritación *f*.

is [iz] *V* be.

island ['ailənd] *n* isla; (*traffic*) refugio *m*.

isolate ['aisəleit] *v* aislar. **isolation** *n* aislamiento *m*.

issue ['iʃuɪ] *n* (*stamps, shares, etc.*) emisión *f*; (*publication*) publicación *f*; (*edition*) tirada *f*; (*copy*) número *m*; (*passport*) expedición *f*; (*distribution*) reparto *m*; (*outcome*) resultado *m*; (*question*) cuestión *f*; (*affair*) asunto *m̉*; (*offspring*) progenie *f*. **take issue with** estar en desacuerdo con. *v* salir; resultar; publicar; distribuir; (*give*) dar; emitir; (*decree*) promulgar; (*warrant, cheque*) extender; (*tickets*) expender; (*licence*) facilitar.

isthmus ['isməs] *n* istmo *m*.

it [it] *pron* él, ella ello; (*direct object*) lo, la; (*indirect object*) le.

italic [i'talik] *adj* itálico. **italics** *pl n* bastardilla *f sing*.

Italy ['itəli] *n* Italia *f*. **Italian** *n, adj* italiano, -a.

itch [itʃ] *n* picazón *f*; (*desire*) ganas *f pl. v* picar.

item ['aitəm] *n* artículo *m*; noticia *f*; detalle *m*; punto *m*. **itemize** *v* detallar.

itinerary [ai'tinərəri] *n* itinerario *m*.

its [its] *adj* su (*pl* sus).

itself [it'self] *pron* se; él/ello mismo, ella misma; (*after prep*) sí mismo, -a. **by itself** aislado; (*alone*) solo.

ivory ['aivəri] *n* marfil *m*.

ivy ['aivi] *n* hiedra *f*, yedra *f*.

jab [dʒab] *v* (*stab*) pinchar; (*elbow*) dar un codazo a. *n* pinchazo *m*; codazo *m*; (*blow*) golpe seco *m*; (*coll: injection*) injección *f*.

jack [dʒak] *n* (*mot*) gato *m*; (*cards*) valet *m*, jota *f*; (*Spanish cards*) sota *f*. *v* **jack up** levantar con el gato.

jackal ['dʒakoıl] *n* chacal *m*.

jackdaw ['dʒakdoı] *n* grajilla *f*.

jacket ['dʒakit] *n* chaqueta *f*; (*book*) sobrecubierta *f*; (*tech: cylinder, pipe, etc.*) camisa *f*.

jackpot ['dʒakpot] *n* premio gordo *m*.

jade [dʒeid] *nm, adj* jade *m*.

jaded ['dʒeidid] *adj* cansado.

jagged ['dʒagid] *adj* dentado.

jaguar ['dʒagjuə] *n* jaguar *m*.

jail [dʒeil] *n* cárcel *f*. *v* encarcelar. **jailer** *n* carcelero *m*.

jam¹ [dʒam] *v* (*force in*) meter a la fuerza; (*squash*) apretar; (*catch*) pillar; (*pack*) atestar; (*clog*) atorar; (*block*) bloquear; (*moving part*) atascar; (*radio*) interferir; (*become wedged*) atrancarse. *n* atasco *m*; (*people*) agolpamiento *m*; (*traffic*) embotellamiento *m*. **be in a jam** (*coll*) estar en un apuro.

jam² [dʒam] *n* mermelada *f*.

janitor ['dʒanitə] *n* portero *m*.

January ['dʒanjuəri] *n* enero *m*.

Japan [dʒə'pan] *n* Japón *m*. **Japanese** *nm, adj* japonés.

jar¹ [dʒaɪ] *n* (*vessel*) vasija *f*; (*jam pot*) tarro *m*; (*large pot*) tinaja *f*.

jar² [dʒaɪ] *v* (*sound*) chirriar; (*shake*) sacudir; (*colours*) chocar; (*music*) sonar mal; (*nerves*) irritar.

jargon ['dʒaɪgən] *n* jerga *f*.

jasmine ['dʒazmin] *n* jazmín *m*.

jaundice ['dʒoındis] *n* ictericia *f*; (*fig*) celos *m pl*.

jaunt [dʒoınt] *n* paseo *m*.

jaunty ['dʒoınti] *adj* vivaz; desenvuelto.

javelin ['dʒavəlin] *n* jabalina *f*.

jaw [dʒoı] *n* (*person*) mandíbula *f*; (*animal*) quijada *f*. **jawbone** *n* mandíbula *f*; quijada *f*.

jazz [dʒaz] *n* jazz *m*. **jazz band** orquesta de jazz *f*.

jealous ['dʒeləs] *adj* celoso; envidioso. **jealousy** *n* celos *m pl*; envidia *f*.

jeans [dʒiːns] *pl n* pantalones vaqueros *m pl.*

jeep [dʒiːp] *n* jeep *m.*

jeer [dʒiə] *v* (*boo*) abuchear; (*mock*) mofarse de. *n* abucheo *m*; mofa *f.*

jelly ['dʒeli] *n* jalea *f.* **jellyfish** *n* medusa *f.*

jeopardize ['dʒepədaiz] *v* arriesgar. **jeopardy** *n* riesgo *m*, peligro *m.*

jerk [dʒɜːk] *n* sacudida *f*; (*shove*) empujón *m*; (*pull*) tirón. *v* sacudir; mover a tirones. **jerkily** *adv* con sacudidas. **jerky** *adj* espasmódico.

jersey ['dʒɜːzi] *n* jersey *m.*

jest [dʒest] *v* bromear. *n* broma *f.* **jester** *n* bromista *m*, *f.*

jet [dʒet] *n* (*liquid*) chorro *m*; (*flame*) llama *f*; (*plane*) avión de reactor *m.* **jet-propelled** *adj* de reacción.

jetty ['dʒeti] *n* muelle *m.*

Jew [dʒuː] *n* judio, -a *m, f.* **Jewish** *adj* judio.

jewel ['dʒuːəl] *n* joya *f*, piedra preciosa *f*; (*in a watch*) rubí *m.* **jeweller** *n* joyero *m.* **jeweller's** *n* joyería *f.* **jewellery** *n* joyería *f.*

jig [dʒig] *n* giga *f.* *v* bailar la giga; dar saltitos.

jigsaw ['dʒigsɔː] *n* (*puzzle*) rompecabezas *m invar*; (*saw*) sierra de vaivén *f.*

jilt [dʒilt] *v* dejar plantado a.

jingle ['dʒiŋgl] *n* tintineo *m*; (*verse*) copla *f.* *v* tintinear.

jinx [dʒiŋks] *n* (*coll*) maleficio *m.* **put a jinx on** echar mal de ojo a.

job [dʒob] *n* trabajo *m*, empleo *m.* **job lot** colección miscelánea *f.* **make a good job of (something)** hacer (algo) bien. **odd-job man** factótum *m.*

jockey ['dʒoki] *n* jinete *m*; jockey *m.*

jocular ['dʒokjulə] *adj* jocoso; bromista.

jodhpurs ['dʒodpəz] *pl n* pantalones de montar *m pl.*

jog [dʒog] *n* sacudida *f*; (*with elbow*) codazo *m.* **jogtrot** *n* trote corto *m.* *v* sacudir; (*memory*) refrescar. **jog someone's elbow** darle en el codo a uno. **jogging** *n* jogging *m.*

join [dʒoin] *v* juntar, unir; (*roads*) ir a dar a; (*friends*) reunirse con; (*a company*) ingresar en; (*a club*) hacerse socio de; (*a political party*) afiliarse a; (*hands*) darse la mano; (*two pieces*) ensamblar; (*rivers*) confluir. **join in** participar en. **join up** (*mil*) alistarse. **joiner** carpintero *m.*

joint [dʒoint] *n* juntura *f*, unión *f*; (*anat*) articulación *f*; (*meat*) corte para asar; (*slang: place*) antro *m.* *adj* unido; colectivo; conjunto; mutuo. **jointly** *adv* en común.

joist [dʒoist] *n* vigueta *f.*

joke [dʒouk] *n* chiste *m*; (*prank*) broma *f.* *v* contar chistes; bromear. **joker** *n* chistoso, -a *m, f*; bromista *m, f*; (*fool*) payaso, -a *m, f*; (*cards*) comodín *m.*

jolly ['dʒoli] *adj* alegre, jovial; divertido. *adv* (*coll: emphatic*) muy. **jollity** *n* alegría *f*, jovialidad *f.*

jolt [dʒoult] *v* sacudir; (*vehicle*) traquetear. *n* sacudida *f*; choque *m*; (*fig: shock*) susto *m.*

jostle ['dʒosl] *v* (*push*) empujar; (*elbow*) codear. *n* empujones *m pl.*

jot [dʒot] *n* jota *f.* *v* **jot down** apuntar.

journal ['dʒɜːnl] *n* (*newspaper*) periódico *m*; (*magazine*) revista *f*; (*diary*) diario *m*; (*of a learned society*) boletín *m.* **journalism** *n* periodismo *m.* **journalist** *n* periodista *m, f.*

journey ['dʒɜːni] *n* viaje *m.* *v* viajar.

jovial ['dʒouviəl] *adj* jovial. **joviality** *n* jovialidad *f.*

joy [dʒoi] *n* alegría *f*; placer *m.* **joyful** *or* **joyous** *adj* alegre, gozoso.

jubilant ['dʒuːbilənt] *adj* jubiloso. **jubilation** *n* júbilo *m.*

jubilee ['dʒuːbiliː] *n* jubileo *m.*

Judaism ['dʒuːdei,izəm] *n* judaísmo·*m.*

judge [dʒʌdʒ] *n* juez *m*; árbitro *m.* *v* juzgar; arbitrar. **judging by** a juzgar por. **judgement** *n* (*trial*) juicio; (*legal sentence*) sentencia *f*; apreciación *f.*

judicial [dʒuː'diʃəl] *adj* judicial.

judicious [dʒuː'diʃəs] *adj* juicioso.

judo ['dʒuːdou] *n* judo *m.*

jug [dʒʌg] *n* jarra *f*; (*slang: prison*) chirona *f.*

juggernaut ['dʒʌgənɔːt] *n* camión grande *m.*

juggle ['dʒʌgl] *v* hacer juegos malabares. **juggler** *n* malabarista *m, f.* **juggling** *n* juegos malabares *m pl.*

jugular ['dʒʌgjulə] *nf, adj* yugular.

juice [dʒuːs] *n* jugo *m.* **juicy** *adj* jugoso.

jukebox ['dʒuːkboks] *n* máquina de discos *f.*

July [dʒu'lai] *n* julio *m.*

jumble ['dʒʌmbl] *v* embrollar; mezclar. *n* embrollo *m*; mezcolanza *f.* **jumble sale** venta de caridad *f.*

jump [dʒʌmp] *n* salto *m. v* saltar. jump at (*offer, etc.*) aprovechar. make someone jump sobresaltar a uno. jumpy *adj* (*coll*) nervioso.

jumper ['dʒʌmpə] *n* (*garment*) jersey *m*.

junction ['dʒʌŋktʃən] *n* (*join*) unión *f*; (*rail*) empalme *m*; (*road*) cruce *f*.

juncture ['dʒʌŋkʃə] *n* coyuntura *f*. at this juncture en esta coyuntura.

June [dʒuɪn] *n* junio *m*.

jungle ['dʒʌŋgl] *n* selva *f*.

junior ['dʒuɪnjə] *adj* (*younger*) hijo; (*lower rank*) subalterno. *n* menor *m, f*; subalterno, -a *m, f*; (*in school*) pequeño, -a *m, f*.

juniper ['dʒuɪnipə] *n* enebro *m*. juniper berry enebrina *f*.

junk¹ [dʒʌŋk] *n* trastos viejos *m pl*; (*coll: rubbish*) porquería *f*. junk-shop *n* baratillo *m*.

junk² [dʒʌŋk] *n* (*naut*) junco *m*.

jurisdiction [dʒuərisˈdikʃən] *n* jurisdicción *f*.

jury ['dʒuəri] *n* jurado *m*. juror *n* jurado, -a *m, f*.

just [dʒʌst] *adv* justo; justamente; precisamente. have just acabar de. *adj* justo; exacto.

justice ['dʒʌstis] *n* justicia *f*. Justice of the Peace juez de paz *m*.

justify ['dʒʌstifai] *v* justificar. justifiable *adj* justificable. justification *n* justificación *f*.

jut [dʒʌt] *v* jut out sobresalir.

jute [dʒuɪt] *n* yute *m*.

juvenile ['dʒuɪvənail] *n* joven *m, f*. adolescente *m, f*, menor *m, f*. *adj* juvenil; infantil. juvenile delinquent delincuente juvenil *m, f*.

juxtapose [,dʒʌkstəˈpouz] *v* yuxtaponer. juxtaposition *n* yuxtaposición *f*.

K

kaftan ['kaftan] *n* caftán *m*.

kaleidoscope [kəˈlaidəskoup] *n* calidoscopio *m*.

kangaroo [kaŋgəˈruɪ] *n* canguro *m*.

karate [kəˈraɪti] *n* karate *m*.

kebab [kiˈbab] *n* pincho *m*.

keel [kiɪl] *n* quilla *f*. keel over (*naut*) zozobrar; (*coll: faint*) desplomarse.

keen [kiɪn] *adj* entusiasta; fuerte, vivo; penetrante; (*prices*) competitivo; (*mind*) agudo; (*sharp*) afilado. keenly *adv* con entusiasmo; profundamente. keenness *n* entusiasmo *m*; deseo *m*; profundidad *f*; agudeza *f*; finura *f*.

*keep [kiɪp] *v* guardar; tener. (*promise*) cumplir; (*appointment*) acudir a; (*hang on to*) quedarse; (*support*) mantener; (*hold*) reservar; (*detain*) detener; (*look after*) cuidar; (*continue*) seguir. keep at seguir con. keep away mantener a distancia. keep down contener. keep fit mantenerse en forma. keep out! ¡prohibida la entrada! keep up with seguir. keeper *n* guarda *m*.

keg [keg] *n* barril *m*.

kennel ['kenl] *n* perrera *f*.

kerb [kəɪb] *n* bordillo *m*.

kernel ['kəɪnl] *n* (*nut*) pepita *f*; (*seed*) grano.

kerosene ['kerəsiɪn] *n* queroseno *m*.

ketchup ['ketʃəp] *n* salsa de tomate *f*.

kettle ['ketl] *n* hervidor *m*. kettledrum *n* timbal *m*.

key [kiɪ] *n* llave *f*; (*for a code*) clave *f*; (*music*) tono *m*; (*piano, typewriter*) tecla *f*. keyboard *n* teclado *m*. keyhold *n* ojo de la cerradura *m*. key-ring *n* llavero *m*. *adj* clave.

khaki ['kaɪki] *nm, adj* caqui.

kick [kik] *n* patada *f*, puntapié *m*; (*animal*) coz *f*; (*recoil*) culatazo *m*; (*fig: energy*) fuerza *f*. *v* dar una patada a; dar una coza. kick off (*football*) hacer el saque del centro; (*fig*) comenzar. kick-off *n* saque del centro *m*; (*coll*) comienzo *m*. kick out (*coll*) poner de patitas en la calle.

kid¹ [kid] *n* (*goat*) cabrito *m*; (*leather*) cabritilla *f*; (*coll: child*) niño, -a *m, f*.

kid² [kid] *v* (*coll*) tomar el pelo.

kidnap ['kidnap] *v* secuestrar, raptar. kidnapper *n* secuestrador, -a *m, f*, raptor, -ora *m, f*. kidnapping *n* secuestro *m*, rapto *m*.

kidney ['kidni] *n* riñón *m*.

kill [kil] *v* matar; (*fig: hopes*) arruinar. *n* muerte *f*; caza *f*. killjoy *n* aguafiestas *m, f invar*. killer *n* asesino, -a *m, f*. killing *n* (*murder*) asesinato *m*; (*slaughter*) matanza *f*.

kiln [kiln] *n* horno *m*.
kilo ['kiːlou] *n* kilo *m*.
kilogram ['kiləgram] *n* kilogramo *m*.
kilometre ['kiləmiːtə] *n* kilómetro *m*.
kin [kin] *n* parientes *m pl*. kinship *n* parentesco *m*.
kind¹ [kaind] *adj* amable; bueno. kind-hearted *adj* bondadoso. kindness *n* amabilidad *f*; bondad *f*.
kind² [kaind] *n* clase *f*, tipo *m*; género *m*; especie *f*. in kind en especie.
kindergarten ['kindəgaɪtn] *n* jardín de la infancia *m*.
kindle ['kindl] *v* encender; despertar.
kindred ['kindrid] *n* parientes *m pl*. *adj* (*related*) emparentado; (*similar*) semejante. kindred spirits almas gemelas *f pl*.
kinetic [kin'etik] *adj* cinético.
king [kiŋ] *n* rey *m*; (*draughts*) dama *f*. kingfisher *n* martín pescador *m*. kingdom *n* reino *m*. king-size *adj* enorme, gigante.
kink [kiŋk] *n* (*rope*) retorcimiento *m*; (*hair*) rizo *m*. *v* retorcer. kinky *adj* retorcido; (*coll*) extraño.
kiosk ['kiːosk] *n* quiosco *m*, kiosko *m*.
kipper ['kipə] *n* arenque ahumado *m*.
kiss [kis] *v* besar. *n* beso *m*. kiss of life respiración boca a boca *f*.
kit [kit] *n* (*tools*) herramientas *f pl*; (*sport*) equipo *m*; (*first aid*) botiquín *m*; (*model for assembling*) maqueta *f*. kit out equipar.
kitchen ['kitʃin] *n* cocina *f*. kitchen sink fregadero *m*.
kite [kait] *n* cometa *f*; (*bird*) milano *m*.
kitten ['kitn] *n* gatito *m*.
kitty ['kiti] *n* plato *m*, platillo *m*.
kleptomania [kleptə'meiniə] *n* cleptomanía *f*. kleptomaniac *n*(*m*+*f*), *adj* cleptómano.
knack [nak] *n* facilidad *f*; tino *m*; habilidad *f*. get the knack of coger el tino de.
knapsack ['napsak] *n* mochila *f*.
knead [niːd] *v* amasar.
knee [niː] *n* rodilla *f*. kneecap *n* rótula *f*.
*kneel [niːl] *v* arrodillarse.
knew [njuɪ] *V* know.
knickers ['nikəz] *pl n* bragas *f pl*.
knife [naif] *n* cuchillo *m*. *v* (*stab*) apuñalar.
knight [nait] *n* caballero *m*. *v* armar caballero. knighthood *n* título de caballero *m*.
knit [niːt] *v* tejer. knit together juntar;

(*bones*) soldarse. knitting *n* tejido de punto *m*. knitting machine máquina de hacer punto *f*. knitting needle aguja de hacer punto *f*.
knob [nob] *n* bulto *m*; (*door*) pomo *m*; (*radio*, *etç*.) botón *m*; (*drawer*) tirador *m*; (*butter*) pedazo *m*.
knobbly ['nobli] *adj* nudoso.
knock [nok] *n* golpe *m*, toque *m*. *v* golpear, pegar; (*fig*: *criticize*) meterse con. knock down (*price*) rebajar; (*person*) atropellar; (*object*) derribar. knock-kneed *adj* patizambo. knock out (*stun*) dejar K.O.; (*from contest*) eliminar. knockout *n* (*boxing*) knock out *m*, K.O. *m*. knock over tirar. knocker *n* aldaba *f*, aldabón *m*.
knot [not] *n* nudo *m*. *v* anudar. knotty (*problem*) espinoso.
*know [nou] *v* (*facts*) saber; (*people*, *places*) conocer; (*recognize*) reconocer; (*distinguish*) distinguir. know-all *n* (*coll*) sabelotodo *m*, *f*. know-how *n* (*coll*) habilidad *f*; conocimientos *m pl*. knowing *adj* astuto; (*look*) de entendimiento.
knowledge ['nolidʒ] *n* conocimiento *m*. knowledgeable *adj* informado; erudito.
knuckle ['nʌkl] *n* nudillo *m*. knuckle down to ponerse seriamente a. knuckle under someterse.

L

label ['leibl] *n* etiqueta *f*. *v* poner etiqueta a.
laboratory [lə'borətəri] *n* laboratorio *m*.
labour ['leibə] *n* (*work*) trabajo *m*; (*task*) tarea *f*; (*effort*) esfuerzo *m*; (*childbirth*) parto *m*; (*manpower*) trabajadores *m pl*. labour-saving *adj* que ahorra trabajo. *v* trabajar; esforzarse. laborious *adj* laborioso. labourer *n* obrero *m*; peón *m*.
labyrinth ['labərinθ] *n* laberinto *m*.
lace [leis] *n* (*fabric*) encaje *m*. (*shoe*) cordón *m*. *v* atar; (*drink*) rociar.
lacerate ['lasəreit] *v* lacerar. laceration *n* laceración *f*.
lack [lak] *n* falta *f*, carencia *f*. for lack of por falta de. *v* carecer de, faltar a; necesitar.

lackadaisical [ˌlakə'deizikəl] *adj* apático; descuidado; tardo.

lacquer ['lakə] *n* (*hair*) laca *f*; (*paint*) pintura al duco *f*. *v* echar laca a; pintar al duco.

lad [lad] *n* (*coll*) chico *m*, muchacho *m*.

ladder ['ladə] *n* escalera de mano *f*; (*stocking*) carrera *f*. **ladderproof** *adj* indesmallable.

laden ['leidn] *adj* cargado.

ladle ['leidl] *n* cucharón *m*.

lady ['leidi] *n* señora *f*. **ladies** (*sign*) servicios de señoras *m pl*. **ladies and gentlemen!** ¡señoras y señores! **ladybird** *n* mariquita *f*. **lady-in-waiting** *n* dama de honor *f*. **ladylike** *adj* distinguida.

lag¹ [lag] *v* (*be behind time*) retrasarse; (*trail*) quedarse atrás. *n* intervalo *m*; (*delay*) retraso *m*.

lag² [lag] *v* poner un revestimiento calorífugo a. **lagging** *n* revestimiento calorífugo *m*.

lager ['laɪgə] *n* cerveza dorada *f*.

lagoon [lə'guɪn] *n* laguna *f*.

laid [leid] *V* **lay¹**.

lain [lein] *V* **lie¹**.

lair [leə] *n* guarida *f*.

laity ['leiəti] *n* laicado *m*.

lake [leik] *n* lago *m*.

lamb [lam] *n* cordero *m*. **lamb chop** chuleta de cordero *f*.

lame [leim] *adj* cojo; (*excuse, etc.*) malo. **lame duck** incapaz *m, f*. *v* dejar cojo. **lamely** *adv* cojeando. **lameness** *n* cojera *f*; debilidad *f*.

lament [lə'ment] *n* lamento *m*. *v* lamentar, llorar. **lamentable** *adj* lamentable. **lamentation** *n* lamentación *f*.

laminate ['lamineit] *v* laminar. **laminated** *adj* laminado.

lamp [lamp] *n* lámpara *f*; (*street*) farol *m*; (*mot*) faro *m*. **lamppost** *n* poste de alumbrado *m*. **lampshade** *n* pantalla *f*.

lance [laɪns] *n* lanza *f*. *v* (*med*) abrir.

land [land] *n* tierra *f*; (*country*) país *m*. **landlady** *n* patrona *f*, dueña *f*. **landlord** *n* patrón *m*, dueño *m*. **landmark** *n* señal *f*. **landscape** *n* paisaje *m*. *v* desembarcar; (*aircraft*) aterrizar; (*fall*) caer; (*arrive*) llegar. **landing** *n* (*passengers*) desembarco *m*; (*cargo*) desembarque *m*; aterrizaje *m*. (*staircase*) rellano *m*. **landing stage** desembarcadero *m*.

lane [lein] *n* camino *m*; (*motorway*) banda *f*; (*running, swimming*) calle *f*.

language ['laŋgwidʒ] *n* (*means of expression*) lenguaje *m*; (*of a nation*) lengua *f*. **bad** *or* **foul language** palabrotas *f pl*.

languish ['laŋgwiʃ] *v* languidecer.

lanky ['laŋki] *adj* larguirucho.

lantern ['lantən] *n* farol *m*, linterna *f*.

lap¹ [lap] *n* (*sport*) vuelta *f*. *v* dar una vuelta; (*fold*) doblar; (*wrap*) envolver.

lap² [lap] *v* (*drink*) chapotear; beber a lengüetadas.

lap³ [lap] *n* rodillas *f pl*.

lapel [lə'pel] *n* solapa *f*.

lapse [laps] *n* (*time*) lapso *m*; (*failure*) fallo *m*; (*moral error*) desliz *m*; (*fall*) caída *f*. *v* (*time*) transcurrir; cometer un desliz; caer.

larceny ['laɪsəni] *n* ratería *f*.

larch [laɪtʃ] *n* alerce *m*.

lard [laɪd] *n* manteca de cerdo *f*.

larder ['laɪdə] *n* despensa *f*.

large [laɪdʒ] *adj* grande, amplio. **at large** libre. **large-scale** *adj* en gran escala. **largely** *adv* en gran parte.

lark¹ [laɪk] *n* (*zool*) alondra *f*.

lark² [laɪk] *n* (*coll*) juerga *f*; (*joke*) broma *f*. **lark about** hacer el tonto.

larva ['laɪvə] *n, pl* **larvae** larva *f*.

larynx ['lariŋks] *n* laringe *f*. **laryngitis** *n* laringitis *f*.

laser ['leizə] *n* laser *m*.

lash [laʃ] *n* (*whip*) azote *m*; (*tail*) coletazo *m*; (*waves*) embate *m*; (*eyelash*) pestaña *f*. *v* azotar; (*wind*) sacudir; (*bind*) atar. **lash out** repartir golpes a diestro y siniestro; (*coll: money*) gastar. **lashing** *n* flagelación *f*; **lashings** *pl n* (*coll*) montones *m pl*.

lass [las] *n* chica *f*, muchacha *f*.

lassitude ['lasitjuɪd] *n* lasitud *f*.

lasso [la'suɪ] *n* lazo *m*. *v* coger con el lazo.

last [laɪst] *adj* último. **last-minute** *adj* de última hora. **last night** anoche. *adv* el último, la última, lo último; por última vez; finalmente. *n* último, -a *m, f*; final *m*. **at least** por fin. **lastly** *adv* por último. *v* durar; permanecer; aguantar. **last out** resistir. **lasting** *adj* duradero.

latch [latʃ] *n* picaporte *m*. *v* cerrar.

late [leit] *adj* tardío; (*recent*) reciente; (*last*) último; (*delayed*) retrasado; (*former*) antiguo; (*dead*) fallecid. *adv* (*not on time*) tarde; (*after the appointed time*) con retraso; recientemente; anteriormente. **lately** *adv* hace poco. **lateness** *n* retraso *m*. **later** *adj* más tarde. **see you**

later! ¡hasta luego! **latest** adj (most recent) último. **at the latest** a más tardar.
latent ['leitənt] adj latente.
lateral ['latərəl] adj lateral.
lathe [leið] n torno m.
lather ['laːðə] n (soap) espuma f; (horse) sudor m. v enjabonar.
Latin ['latin] n, adj latino, -a. n (language) latín m.
Latin America n América Latina f. **Latin American** n, adj latinoamericano, -a m, f.
latitude ['latitjuːd] n latitud f.
latrine [lə'triːn] n letrina f; retrete m.
latter ['latə] adj último. **the latter** éste, ésta.
lattice ['latis] n celosía f; enrejado m.
laugh [laːf] v reír, reírse. **laugh at** reírse de. n risa f. **laughable** adj ridículo. **it's no laughing matter** no es cosa de risa. **laughing-stock** n hazmerreír m invar. **laughter** n risa f, risas f pl.
launch¹ [loːntʃ] v (ship) botar; (lifeboat) echar al mar; (missile) lanzar; (issue) emitir; (an attack) emprender; (a company) funder; (film, play) estrenar. **launching** n botadura f; lanzamiento m; fundación f; iniciación f.
launch² [loːntʃ] n lancha f. **motor launch** lancha motora f.
launder ['loːndə] v lavar. **launderette** n lavandería automática f. **laundry** n (place) lavandería f.
laurel ['lorəl] n laurel m.
lava ['laɪvə] n lava f.
lavatory ['lavətəri] n retrete m; servicios m pl.
lavender ['lavində] n espliego m.
lavish ['laviʃ] adj pródigo; generoso; abundante; lujoso. v prodigar.
law [loː] n ley f; (profession) derecho m, leyes f pl. **law-abiding** adj respetuoso de las leyes. **lawsuit** n proceso m. **lawful** adj legal; lícito. **lawyer** n jurista m, f; abogado m.
lawn [loːn] n césped m. **lawn-mower** n cortacéspedes m invar.
lax [laks] adj flojo; elástico; negligente. **laxity** n laxitud f; elasticidad f; negligencia f; flojedad f.
laxative ['laksətiv] nm, adj laxante.
*lay¹ [lei] v (place) poner; (table) cubrir. **layabout** n holgazán, -ana m, f. **lay-by** n área de aparcamiento f. **lay off** (workers)

despedir. **lay on** (provide) proveer de. **layout** n (arrangement) disposición f; (printing) composición f; (money) gasto m.
lay² [lei] adj laico. **layman** n seglar m.
lay³ [lei] V **lie**.
layer ['leiə] n capa f.
lazy ['leizi] adj perezoso. **laze around** holgazanear. **laziness** n pereza f.
*lead¹ [liːd] v llevar, conducir; remitir; (orchestra) dirigir; ir a la cabeza. **lead on** (encourage) animar; (seduce) seducir a. **lead up to** conducir a; preparar el terreno para. n (role) primer papel m; supremacía f; (clue) pista f; ejemplo; primer lugar; (advantage) ventaja f; (elec) cable m; (newspaper) noticia más importante f. **leader** n guía m, f; jefe m, f; caudillo m; editorial m. **leadership** n dirección f, mando m; jefatura f. **leading** adj primero principal; que encabeza.
lead² [led] n plomo m; (pencil) mina f.
leaf [liːf] n hoja f; página f; (table) hoja abatible f. v **leaf through** hojear. **leaflet** n (pamphlet) folleto m.
league [liːg] n liga f; **in league with** asociado con.
leak [liːk] n gotera f; (hole) agujero m; (gas, liquid) fuga f, salida f; (information) filtración f. v gotear; (boat) hacer agua; salirse; perder; filtrarse.
*lean¹ [liːn] v inclinarse. **lean back** reclinarse. **lean on** apoyarse. **lean over backwards to** (coll) no escatinar esfuerzos para. **leaning** (liking) predilección f; (tendency) tendencia f.
lean² [liːn] adj magro, sin grasa; (person) flaco. n carne magra f. **leanness** n magrez f; flaqueza f.
*leap [liːp] v saltar; lanzarse. n salto m, brinco m. **by leaps and bounds** a pasos agigantados. **leapfrog** n pídola f. **leap year** año bisiesto m.
*learn [ləːn] v aprender. **learn of** enterarse de. **learned** adj instruido; erudito. n carne magra f. **learner** n principiante m, f; (driver) aprendiz, -a m, f. **learning** n erudición f, saber m.
lease [liːs] n arrendamiento m. v arrendar. **leasehold** adj arrendado.
leash [liːʃ] n correa f.
least [liːst] adj menor. pron lo menos. adv menos. **at least** por lo menos.
leather ['leðə] n cuero m, piel f. **patent leather** charol m. **leathery** adj (meat) correoso; (skin) curtido.

*leave¹ [liːv] v irse, marcharse; (*abandon*) dejar; (*go out of*) salir de. **be left** quedar. **leave off** dejar de. **leave out** omitir. **left-luggage office** consigna f. **left-overs** pl n sobras f pl.

leave² [liːv] n permiso m. **be on leave** estar de permiso. **take leave of** despedirse de.

lecherous ['letʃərəs] adj lascivo. **lecher** n lascivo, -a m, f. **lechery** n lascivia f.

lectern ['lektən] n atril m.

lecture ['lektʃə] n conferencia f. **lecture hall** sala de conferencias f. v dar una conferencia; dar clase. **lecturer** n conferenciante m, f; (*university*) profesor, -a m, f.

led [led] V **lead¹**.

ledge [ledʒ] n saliente m; (*window*) antepecho m; (*shelf*) repisa f.

ledger ['ledʒə] n libro mayor m.

lee [liː] n (*shelter*) abrigo m; (*naut*) sotavento m. **leeward** adj, adv a sotavento.

leech [liːtʃ] n sanguijuela f; (*person*) lapa f.

leek [liːk] n puerro m.

leer [liə] v mirar de soslayo. n mirada de soslayo f. **leering** adj de soslayo.

leeway ['liːwei] n (*naut*) deriva f; (*fig*) campo m.

left¹ [left] V **leave¹**.

left² [left] adj izquierdo. n izquierda f. adv a or hacia la izquierda. **left-handed** adj zurdo. **left-wing** adj izquierdista.

leg [leg] n (*person*) pierna f; (*animal*) pata f; (*furniture*) pie; (*trousers*) pernera f; (*cookery: lamb*) pierna f; (*chicken*) muslo m; (*pork, venison*) pernil m; (*sport, journey*) etapa f.

legacy ['legəsi] n legado m, herencia f.

legal ['liːgəl] adj jurídico; legal; legítimo; lícito. **legality** n legalidad f. **legalize** v legalizar.

legend ['ledʒənd] n leyenda f. **legendary** adj legendario.

legible ['ledʒəbl] adj legible. **legibility** n legibilidad f.

legion ['liːdʒən] n legión f.

legislate ['ledʒisleit] v legislar; establecer por ley. **legislation** n legislación f. **legislature** n legislatura f.

legitimate [lə'dʒitimət] adj legítimo; válido; auténtico. **legitimacy** n legitimidad f.

leisure ['leʒə] n ocio n; tiempo libre m.

lemon ['lemən] n (*fruit*) limón m; (*tree*) limonero m; (*colour*) amarillo limón m. **lemonade** n limonada f. **lemon squeezer** exprimelimones m invar.

*lend [lend] v prestar. **lending library** biblioteca de préstamo f.

length [leŋθ] n longitud f, largo m; (*distance*) distancia f; (*space*) espacio m; (*piece*) pedazo m; (*length* v alargar; prolongar. **lengthy** adj largo; prolongado.

lenient ['liːniənt] adj indulgente, clemente. **leniency** n indulgencia f, clemencia f.

lens [lenz] n lente f; (*magnifying glass*) lupa f; (*photo*) objetivo m; (*eye*) cristalino m. **contact-lens** lente de contacto f.

lent [lent] V **lend**.

Lent [lent] n Cuaresma f.

lentil ['lentil] n lenteja f.

Leo ['liːou] n (*astrol*) León m.

leopard ['lepəd] n leopardo m.

leotard ['liːətaɪd] n leotardo m.

leper ['lepə] n leproso, -a m, f. **leprosy** n lepra f. **leprous** adj leproso.

lesbian ['lezbiən] nf, adj lesbiana. **lesbianism** n lesbianismo m.

less [les] adj menos; menor; inferior. adv, prep menos. n menor m, f. **less and less** cada vez menos. **lessen** v disminuir, reducir. **lesser** adj menor.

lesson ['lesn] n lección f; clase f.

lest [lest] conj de miedo que; para no.

*let [let] v permitir, dejar; (*rent*) alquilar. **let down** (*lower*) bajar, descender; (*disappoint*) fallar. **let-down** n decepción f. **let in** dejar entrar; hacer entrar. **let out** dejar salir; (*clothes*) ensanchar; ...

lethal ['liːθəl] adj mortífero.

lethargy ['leθədʒi] n letargo m. **lethargic** adj letárgico.

letter ['letə] n (*character*) letra f; (*message*) carta f. **letter-box** n buzón m.

lettuce ['letis] n lechuga f.

leukaemia [luːˈkiːmiə] n leucemia f.

level ['levl] adj horizontal; (*flat*) llano; (*even*) a nivel; (*equal*) igual; (*spoonful*) raso; uniforme. **be level with** al nivel de. **level crossing** paso a nivel m. **level-headed** adj juicioso. n nivel m. **on the level** (*coll*) honrado. v nivelar, allanar.

lever ['liːvə] n palanca f. **leverage** n apalancamiento m.

levy ['levi] n exacción f; impuesto m. v exigir; imponer.

lewd

lewd [luːd] *adj* lascivo.
liable ['laiəbl] *adj* sujeto; (*law*) responsable. **liable to** capaz de. **liability** *n* responsabilidad *f*; inconveniente *m*; (*nuisance*) estorbo *m*.
liaison [liː'eizon] *n* enlace *m*.
liar ['laiə] *n* mentiroso, -a *m*, *f*.
libel ['laibəl] *n* (*act*) difamación *f*; (*writing*) escrito difanatorio *m*. *v* difamar.
libellous *adj* difamatorio.
liberal ['libərəl] *adj* liberal; libre; generoso.
liberate ['libəreit] *v* liberar. **liberation** *n* liberación *f*.
liberty ['libəti] *n* libertad *f*. **at liberty** libre.
Libra ['liːbrə] *n* Libra *f*.
library ['laibrəri] *n* biblioteca *f*. **librarian** *n* bibliotecario, -a *m*, *f*.
libretto [li'bretou] *n* libreto *m*.
lice [lais] *V* **louse**.
licence ['laisəns] *n* licencia *f*, permiso *m*, autorización *f*; (*driving*) carnet de conducir *m*. **licence number** matrícula *f*. *v* conceder una licencia; autorizar. **licensed** *adj* autorizado. **licensee** *n* concesionario *m*.
lichen ['laikən] *n* liquen *m*.
lick [lik] *v* lamer. *n* lamedura *f*, lamido *m*.
lid [lid] *n* tapa *f*, tapadera *f*.
lie[1] [lai] *v* acostarse; echarse. **lie around** estar tirado. **lie down** acostarse. **lie in** quedarse en la cama.
lie[2] [lai] *n* mentira *f*. *v* mentir.
lieutenant [ləf'tenənt] *n* (*mil*) teniente *m*; (*deputy*) lugarteniente *m*.
life [laif] *n* vida *f*. **lifeless** *adj* sin vida, muerto.
lifebelt ['laifbelt] *n* cinturón salvavidas *m*.
lifeboat ['laifbout] *n* bote salvavidas *m*.
lifebuoy ['laifboi] *n* boya salvavidas *f*.
lifeguard ['laifgaɪd] *n* vigilante *m*.
life insurance *n* seguro de vida *m*.
life-jacket *n* chaleco salvavidas *m*.
lifelike ['laiflaik] *adj* natural; parecido.
lifeline ['laiflain] *n* (*diver's*) cordel de señales *m*; (*fig*) cordón umbilical *m*.
lifelong ['laiflɒŋ] *adj* de toda la vida.
life-size *adj* de tamaño natural.
lifetime ['laiftaim] *n* vida *f*.
lift [lift] *n* ascensor *m*; (*act of lifting*) levantamiento *m*; (*upward support*) empuje *m*. **give someone a lift** llevar en coche. *v* levantar; alzar; coger; elevar.
ligament ['ligəmənt] *n* ligamento *m*.

light[1] [lait] *v* (*set fire to*) encender; (*room, etc.*) iluminar. *n* luz *f*; lámpara *f*; (*mot*) faro *m*. *adj* claro; luminoso. **light bulb** bombilla *f*. **lighthouse** *n* faro *m*. **light meter** fotómetro *m*. **light-year** *n* año luz *m*. **lighten** *v* aclarar. **lighter** (*cigarette*) *n* mechero *m*. **lighting** *n* alumbrado *m*; iluminación *f*.
light[2] [lait] *adj* liviano; ligero. **light-headed** *adj* mareado; delirante. **light-hearted** *adj* alegre. **lightweight** *adj* ligero, de poco peso. **lighten** *v* alijerar; aliviar. **lightness** *n* ligereza *f*.
light[3] [lait] *v* **light upon** posarse.
lightning ['laitniŋ] *n* relámpago *m*. **lightning conductor** pararrayos *m invar*.
like[1] [laik] *adj* parecido; semejante; igual; mismo. *prep* como, igual que. **be** *or* **look like** parecerse a. **liken** *v* comparar. **likeness** *n* semejanza *f*; forma *f*; retrato *m*. **likewise** *adv* del mismo modo.
like[2] [laik] *v* gustarle (a uno); querer a; (*want*) querer. **likeable** *adj* amable, simpático. **liking** *n* cariño *m*; simpatía *f*; gusto *m*.
likely ['laikli] *adj* probable; posible; plausible. **be likely to** ser probable que. *adv* probablemente. **likelihood** *n* probabilidad *f*.
lilac ['lailək] *n* lila *f*; (*colour*) lila *m*. *adj* de color lila.
lily ['lili] *n* azucena *f*. **lily-of-the-valley** *n* lirio de los valles *m*.
limb [lim] *n* miembro *m*.
limbo ['limbou] *n* (*rel*) limbo *m*; (*fig*) olvido *m*.
lime[1] [laim] *n* cal *f*. **limestone** *n* piedra caliza *f*.
lime[2] [laim] *n* (*fruit*) lima *f*; (*tree*) limero *m*. **lime juice** jugo de lima *m*.
limelight ['laim,lait] *n* **in the limelight** en el candelero.
limerick ['limərik] *n* quintilla humorística *f*.
limit ['limit] *n* límite *m*. *v* limitar. **limitation** *n* limitación *f*. **limitless** *adj* ilimitado.
limousine ['limə,ziːn] *n* limusina *f*.
limp[1] [limp] *v* cojear.
limp[2] [limp] *adj* flácido. **limpness** *n* flojedad *f*.
limpet ['limpit] *n* lapa *f*.
line [lain] *n* línea *f*, rayo *m*, trazo *m*; (*wrinkle*) arruga *f*; (*row*) fila *f*; (*wire*) cable *m*; (*people*) cola *f*; (*of poem*) verso

m; (*rope*) cuerda *f*; (*flex*) cordón *m*; (*of communication*) via *f*; (*shipping*) compañia *f*. *v* rayar; arrugar; alinearse por; bordear; (*provide an inner layer*) forrar; (*brakes*) guarnecer. **line up** poner en fila.
linear *adj* lineal.
linen ['linin] *n* hilo *m*, lino *m*; (*sheets, etc.*) ropa blanca *f*. **linen basket** canasta de la ropa *f*.
liner ['lainə] *n* transatlántico *m*.
linger ['liŋgə] *v* (*person*) quedarse; (*memory, etc.*) persistir; (*dawdle*) rezagarse; (*loiter*) callejear.
lingerie ['lãʒəriː] *n* ropa interior *f*.
linguist ['liŋgwist] *n* lingüista *m*, *f*. **linguistic** *adj* lingüistico. **linguistics** *n* lingüistica *f*.
lining ['lainiŋ] *n* (*clothes*) forro *m*; (*brakes*) guarnición *f*.
link [liŋk] *n* (*chain*) eslabón *m*; (*cuff*) gemelos *m pl*; (*fig*) vínculo *m*. *v* unir; acoplar; conectar.
linoleum [li'nouliəm] *n also* **lino** linóleo *m*.
linseed ['lin,siːd] *n* linaza *f*. **linseed oil** aceite de linaza *m*.
lint [lint] *n* hilas *f pl*.
lion ['laiən] *n* león *m*. **lioness** *n* leona *f*.
lip [lip] *n* labio *m*; (*jug*) pico *m*; (*cup*) borde *m*. **lip-read** *v* leer en los labios.
lipstick *n* barra de labios *f*.
liqueur [li'kjuə] *n* licor *m*.
liquid ['likwid] *nm, adj* líquido. **liquidate** *v* liquidar. **liquidation** *n* liquidación *f*.
liquor ['likə] *n* bebida alcohólica *f*.
liquorice ['likəris] *n* regaliz *m*.
Lisbon ['lizbən] *n* Lisboa.
lisp [lisp] *n* ceceo *m*. *v* decir ceceando.
list[1] [list] *v* hacer una lista de; enumerar. *n* lista *f*; catálogo *m*.
list[2] [list] *v* (*naut*) escorar. *n* escora *f*.
listen ['lisn] *v* escuchar, oír. **listener** *n* oyente *m*, *f*.
listless ['listlis] *adj* decaído, apático.
lit [lit] *V* **light**.
litany ['litəni] *n* letania *f*.
literacy ['litərəsi] *n* capacidad de leer y escribir *f*. **be literate** saber leer y escribir.
literal ['litərəl] *adj* literal.
literary ['litərəri] *adj* literario.
literature ['litrətʃə] *n* literatura *f*; (*advertising matter*) folletos publicitarios *m pl*.
litigation [liti'geiʃən] *n* litigio *m*.
litre ['liːtə] *n* litro *m*.
litter ['litə] *n* basura *f*; desorden *m*; (*zool*)

camada *f*; (*bedding for animals*) pajaza *f*; (*stretcher*) camilla *f*. **litter-bin** *n* papelera *f*. *v* ensuciar; cubrir; desordenar.
little ['litl] *adj* (*small*) pequeño; (*quantity*) poco. *nm, adv* poco. **little by little** poco a poco.
liturgy ['litədʒi] *n* liturgia *f*. **liturgical** *adj* litúrgico.
live[1] [liv] *v* vivir. **live down** conseguir que se olvide. **live up to** cumplir con.
live[2] [laiv] *adj* vivo; (*broadcast*) en directo; (*coal*) en ascuas; (*elec*) cargado. *adv* en directo.
livelihood ['laivlihud] *n* sustento *m*.
lively ['laivli] *adj* vivo; enérgico; activo. **liveliness** *n* viveza *f*; animación *f*.
liven ['laivn] *v* **liven up** animar.
liver ['livə] *n* hígado *m*.
livestock ['laivstok] *n* ganado *m*.
livid ['livid] *adj* lívido; (*coll*) furioso.
living ['liviŋ] *adj* vivo, viviente. *n* vida *f*; vivos *m pl*. **living room** sala de estar *f*.
lizard ['lizəd] *n* lagarto *m*.
load [loud] *n* (*burden*) carga *f*; (*animals, vehicles*) cargamento *m*; (*fig*) peso *m*. *v* cargar. **loaded** *adj* cargado; (*coll: rich*) podrido de dinero.
loaf[1] [louf] *n* pan *m*.
loaf[2] [louf] *v* **loaf around** callejear. **loafer** *n* (*coll*) holgazán, -ana *m*, *f*.
loan [loun] *n* préstamo *m*. *v* prestar.
loathe [louð] *v* aborrecer. **loathing** *n* aborrecimiento *m*. **loathsome** *adj* asqueroso.
lob [lob] *v* volear. *n* volea alta *f*, lob *m*.
lobby ['lobi] *n* pasillo *m*; vestíbulo *m*; grupo de presión *m*. *v* ejercer presiones sobre.
lobe [loub] *n* lóbulo *m*.
lobster ['lobstə] *n* langosta *f*.
local ['loukəl] *adj* local; vecinal. *n* (*coll: pub*) bar del barrio *m*. **the locals** (*coll: people*) la gente del lugar *f*. **locality** *n* (*neighbourhood*) localidad *f*; (*place*) lugar *m*. **localize** *v* localizar. **locally** *adv* localmente; en el sitio.
locate [lə'keit] *v* (*find*) encontrar; (*look for and discover*) localizar; situar. **location** *n* localización *f*; colocación *f*; situación *f*; (*cinema*) exteriores *m pl*. **film on location** *v* rodar.
lock[1] [lok] *n* (*on door, box, etc.*) cerradura *f*; (*canal*) esclusa *f*. *v* cerrarse con llave; (*mech*) bloquearse. **lock away** guardar bajo llave. **lock in** encerrar. **lock out** cerrar la puerta a. **lock up** (*house*) cerrar;

lock

(*money*) dejar bajo llave; (*imprison*) encarcelar.

lock² [lok] *n* (*of hair*) mecha *f*, mechón *m*.

locker ['lokə] *n* (*shelf*) casillero *m*, (*cupboard*) armario *m*.

locket ['lokit] *n* relicario *m*.

locomotive [ˌloukə'moutiv] *n* locomotiva *f. adj* locomotor. **locomotion** *n* locomoción *f*.

locust ['loukəst] *n* langosta *f*.

lodge [lodʒ] *n* (*porter's*) portería *f*; (*caretaker's*) casa del guarda *f*; (*hunting*) pabellón *m*. *v* alojar; (*place*) colocar; presentar; (*appeal*) interponer. **lodger** *n* huésped, -a *m, f*. **lodgings** *pl n* habitación *f*. **board and lodging** pensión completa *f*.

loft [loft] *n* (*for hay*) pajar *m*; (*attic*) desván. **lofty** *adj* (*high*) alto; (*principles*) elevado; (*haughty*) arrogante.

log [log] *n* tronco *m*. **logbook** *n* (*naut*) cuaderno de bitácora *m*; (*aero*) diario de vuelo *m*. *v* anotar, apuntar.

logarithm ['logəriðəm] *n* logaritmo *m*.

loggerheads ['logəhedz] *pl n* **be at loggerheads** estar a mal.

logic ['lodʒik] *n* lógica *f*. **logical** *adj* lógico.

loins [loins] *pl n* lomos *m pl*.

loiter ['loitə] *v* callejear.

lollipop ['loliˌpop] *n* chupón *m*.

London ['lʌndən] *n* Londres.

lonely ['lounli] *adj* solo; aislado; solitario. **loneliness** *n* soledad *f*.

long¹ [loŋ] *adj* (*length*) largo; (*memory*) bueno; (*time*) mucho; (*long-lasting*) viejo. **as long as** mientras. **long-range** *adj* de larga distancia. **long-sighted** *adj* hipermétrope; (*having foresight*) previsor. **long-sleeved** *adj* de mangas largas. **long-standing** *adj* de muchos años. **long-term** *adj* a largo plazo. **long-winded** *adj* (*person*) prolijo; (*speech*) interminable.

long² [loŋ] *v* **long for** desear con ansia. **long to** tener muchas ganas de. **longing** *n* anhelo *m*.

longevity [lon'dʒevəti] *n* longevidad *f*.

longitude ['londʒitjuːd] *n* longitud *f*. **longitudinal** *adj* longitudinal.

loo [luː] *n* (*coll*) retrete *m*.

look [luk] *n* (*glance*) mirada *f*; (*inspection*) ojeada *f*; aspecto *m*. *v* mirar; parecer; representar. **look after** cuidar a, cuidar de; (*watch over*) vigilar. **look at** mirar. **look down on** mirar despectivamente.

look for buscar. **look forward to** esperar. **look out** tener cuidado. **look up** levantar los ojos; (*improve*) ponerse mejor; (*research*) consultar, buscar. **look up to** apreciar.

loom¹ [luːm] *v* perfilarse; surgir.

loom² [luːm] *n* telar *m*.

loop [luːp] *n* lazo *m*; (*belt*) presilla *f*. *v* hacer un lazo en.

loophole ['luːphoul] *v* (*fig*) escapatoria *f*.

loose [luːs] *adj* suelto; (*fitting*) holgado; (*knot*) flojo; (*translation*) libre; (*tooth*) que se mueve; **get loose** escaparse. **let loose** soltar. **loose change** dinero suelto *m*. **loose-leaf** *adj* de hojas sueltas. *v* (*free*) soltar; (*untie*) desatar. **loosely** *adv* sin apretar; aproximadamente; vagamente. **loosen** *v* aflojar, soltar.

loot [luːt] *n* botín *m*. **looter** *n* saqueador, -a *m, f*. **looting** saqueo *m*.

lop [lop] *v* cortar.

lopsided [ˌlop'saidid] *adj* ladeado; desequilibrado.

lord [loːd] *n* señor *m*.

lorry ['lori] *n* camión *m*. **lorry-driver** *n* camionero *m*.

***lose** [luːz] *v* perder; (*watch, clock*) atrasar. **loser** *n* perdedor, -a *m, f*. **lost property** objetos perdidos *m pl*.

loss [los] *n* pérdida *f*; (*damage*) daño *m*. (*defeat*) derrota *f*. **be at a loss** estar perdido. **sell at a loss** vender con pérdida.

lost [lost] *V* lose.

lot [lot] *n* destino *m*; porción *f*; (*auction*) lote *m*; (*ground*) parcela *f*. **a lot** mucho. **lots of** cantidades de. **quite a lot of** bastante.

lotion ['louʃən] *n* loción *f*.

lottery ['lotəri] *n* lotería *f*.

lotus ['loutəs] *n* loto *m*.

loud [laud] *adj* fuerte; alto; ruidoso; sonoro; (*colours*) chillón; vulgar. *adv* (*laugh*) estrepitosamente. **loud-hailer** *n* megáfono *m*. **loud-mouthed** *adj* fanfarrón, -ona *m, f*. **loudspeaker** *n* altavoz *m*. **loudly** *adv* en voz alta. **loudness** *n* fuerza *f*.

lounge [laundʒ] *n* salón *m*. **lounge suit** traje de calle *m*. *v* (*lazy posture*) repantigarse; (*idle*) gandulear. **lounger** *n* tumbona *f*.

louse [laus] *n, pl* **lice** piojo *m*. **lousy** *adj* piojoso; (*slang*) malísimo.

lout [laut] *n* bruto *m*. **loutish** *adj* bruto.
love [lʌv] *n* amor *m*; cariño *m*; pasión *f*;
(*tennis*) cero *m*. **fall in love with**
enamorarse de. **love affair** amorío *m*.
make love hacer el amor con. **with love
from** (*in letter*) abrazos *m pl. v* amar,
querer. **lovable** *adj* adorable. **lover** *n*
amante *m*, *f*; (*enthusiast*) aficionado, -a
m, *f*. **loving** *adj* cariñoso; amoroso.
lovely ['lʌvli] *adj* encantador; delicioso;
precioso.
low [lou] *adj* bajo; pequeño; (*scarce*)
escaso; (*weak*) débil; (*downhearted*)
desanimado. **lowland** *n* tierra baja *f*. **low-
lying** *adj* bajo. **low-paid** *adj* mal pagado.
low-priced *adj* barato. **lowly** *adj* humilde.
lower ['louə] *adj* inferior; más bajo. *v*
bajar. **lower oneself** rebajarse.
loyal ['loiəl] *adj* leal; fiel. **loyalty** *n* lealtad
f; fidelidad *f*.
lozenge ['lozindʒ] *n* pastilla *f*.
lubricate ['luːbrikeit] *v* lubrificar, lubricar.
lubricant *n* lubrificante *m*, lubricante *m*.
lubrication *n* lubrificación *f*, lubricación
f, engrase *m*.
lucid ['luːsid] *adj* lúcido; claro. **lucidity** *n*
lucidez *f*; claridad *f*.
luck [lʌk] *n* suerte *f*; destino *m*. **bad luck**
mala suerte *f*. **good luck** buena suerte *f*.
lucky *adj* afortunado; oportuno. **be lucky**
tener mucha suerte.
lucrative ['luːkrətiv] *adj* lucrativo.
ludicrous ['luːdikrəs] *adj* ridículo,
absurdo.
lug [lʌg] *v* arrastrar.
luggage ['lʌgidʒ] *n* equipaje *m*; maletas *f
pl*. **luggage label** etiqueta *f*. **luggage rack**
portaequipajes *m invar*. **luggage van**
furgón de equipajes *m*.
lukewarm ['luːkwoːm] *adj* tibio.
lull [lʌl] *n* (*in storm*) calma *f*; (*fig*) tregua
f. *v* sosegar.
lullaby ['lʌləˌbai] *n* canción de cuna *f*.
lumbago [lʌmˈbeigou] *n* lumbago *m*.
lumber[1] ['lʌmbə] *n* (*wood*) maderos *m pl*;
(*junk*) trastos viejos *m pl*. **lumberjack** *n*
leñador *m*. **lumber yard** depósito de
madera *m*. *v*. **lumber with** (*coll*) hacer que
cargue con.
lumber[2] ['lʌmbə] *v* moverse pesadamente.
luminous ['luːminəs] *adj* luminoso.
lump [lʌmp] *n* pedazo *m*, trozo *m*; (*mass*)
masa *f*; (*clay*) pella *f*; (*stone*) bloque *m*;
(*earth*, *sugar*) terrón *m*; (*med*) chichón.

lump sum cantidad total *f*. **lumpy** *adj* lleno de bultos.
lunar ['luːnə] *adj* lunar.
lunatic ['luːnətik] *n*, *adj* loco, -a *m*, *f*. **luna-
cy** *n* locura *f*.
lunch [lʌntʃ] *n* almuerzo *m*. *v* almorzar.
lunchtime *n* hora de comer *f*.
lung [lʌŋ] *n* pulmón *m*.
lunge [lʌndʒ] *v* embestir, lanzarse. *n*
embestida *f*.
lurch[1] [ləːtʃ] *v* dar bandazos. **lurch along**
ir dando bandazos. *n* bandazo *m*.
lurch[2] [ləːtʃ] *n* **leave in the lurch** dejar en
la estacada.
lure [luə] *v* atraer. *n* aliciente *m*; encanto
m; (*decoy*) cebo *m*.
lurid ['luərid] *adj* espeluznante; sensacional.
lurk [ləːk] *v* (*lie in wait*) estar al acecho;
(*be hidden*) esconderse; (*fig: be always
around*) rondar. **lurking** *adj* vago; oculto.
luscious ['lʌʃəs] *adj* exquisito; apetitoso;
voluptuoso.
lush [lʌʃ] *adj* lozano, exuberante.
lust [lʌst] *n* (*sexual*) lascivia *f*; (*for power*,
etc.) anhelo *m*. *v* **lust after** (*object*)
codiciar; (*person*) desear. **lusty** *adj* robusto, fuerte.
lustre ['lʌstə] *n* lustre *m*.
lute [luːt] *n* laúd *m*.
Luxembourg ['lʌksəmˌbəːg] *n* Luxemburgo *m*.
luxury ['lʌkʃəri] *n* lujo *m*. **luxuriant** *adj*
exuberante. **luxurious** *adj* lujoso.
lynch [lintʃ] *v* linchar.
lynx [links] *n* lince *m*.
lyre [laiə] *n* lira *f*.
lyrical ['lirikəl] *adj* lírico.
lyrics ['liriks] *pl n* letra *f sing*. **lyricist** *n*
autor de la letra de una canción *m*.

M

mac [mak] *n* (*coll*) impermeable *m*.
macabre [məˈkaːbr] *adj* macabro.
macaroni [makəˈrouni] *n* macarrones *m
pl*.
mace[1] [meis] *n* (*staff*) maza *f*.
mace[2] [meis] *n* (*spice*) macis *f*.
machine [məˈʃiːn] *n* máquina *f*. **machine-**

gun *n* ametralladora *f*. **machinery** *n* maquinaria *f*; mecanismo *m*.

mackerel ['makrəl] *n* caballa *f*.

mackintosh ['makin,tɒʃ] *n* impermeable *m*.

mad [mad] *adj* loco, demente; rabioso; (*angry*) furioso. **madden** *v* enloquecer; enfurecer. **maddening** *adj* desesperante. **madly** *adv* locamente; furiosamente. **madness** *n* locura *f*; rabia *f*; furia *f*. **madam** ['madəm] *n* señora *f*. **made** [meid] *V* **make**. **Madeira** [mə'diərə] *n* (*island*) Madera *f*; (*wine*) madera *m*.

magazine [,magə'ziːn] *n* (*publication*) revista *f*; (*warehouse*) almacén *m*; (*explosives store*) polvorín *m*; (*rifle*) recámara *f*.

maggot ['magət] *n* gusano *m*, cresa *f*. **maggoty** *adj* gusanoso.

magic ['madʒik] *n* magia *f*. *adj also* **magical** mágico. **magician** *n* ilusionista *m*, *f*.

magistrate ['madʒistreit] *n* magistrado *m*; juez municipal *m*.

magnanimous [mag'nanimɔs] *adj* magnánimo. **magnanimity** *n* magnanimidad *f*.

magnate ['magneit] *n* magnate *m*.

magnet ['magnət] *n* imán *m*. **magnetic** magnético; atractivo. **magnetism** *n* magnetismo *m*. **magnetize** *v* magnetizar; atraer.

magnificent [mag'nifisnt] *adj* magnífico. **magnificence** *n* magnificencia *f*.

magnify ['magnifai] *v* magnificar; aumentar; exagerar. **magnifying glass** lupa *f*. **magnification** *n* aumento *m*; exageración *f*.

magnitude ['magnitjuːd] *n* magnitud *f*.

magnolia [mag'nouliə] *n* magnolia *f*.

magpie ['magpai] *n* urraca *f*.

mahogany [mə'hogəni] *n* caoba *f*.

maid [meid] *n* (*servant*) criada *f*; muchacha *f*. **old maid** solterona *f*.

maiden ['meidən] *n* doncella *f*. *adj* virgen; soltera; inaugural. **maiden name** apellido de soltera *m*.

mail [meil] *n* (*letters*) correspondencia *f*; (*service*) correo *m*. **mailbag** *n* saca de correspondencia *f*. **mail order** pedido hecho por correo *m*.

maim [meim] *v* mutilar.

main [mein] *adj* principal. **main course** plato principal *m*. **mainland** *n* continente *m*. **main line** línea principal *f*. **main road** carretera general *f*. **mainstay** *n* estay

mayor *m*. *n* (*gas, water*) cañería principal *f*. **in the main** por lo general. **mains** *n* (*elec*) la red eléctrica *f*.

maintain [mein'tein] *v* mantener; conservar. **maintenance** *n* mantenimiento *m*; conservación *f*. **maintenance allowance** pensión alimenticia *f*.

maisonette [meizə'net] *n* casita *f*.

maize [meiz] *n* maíz *m*.

majesty ['madʒəsti] *n* majestad *f*. **majestic** *adj* majestuoso.

major ['meidʒə] *adj* mayor; principal. *n* (*mil*) comandante *m*.

majority [mə'dʒoriti] *n* mayoría *f*. **overwhelming majority** mayoría abrumadora *f*.

*make [meik] *v* hacer, efectuar; servir de; llegar a. *n* marca *f*; hechura *f*. **make-believe** *n* simulación *f*. **make out** (*draw up*) hacer; (*cheque*) extender. **make do with** arreglárselas con. **makeshift** *adj* improvisado. **make up** inventar; completar; recuperar; (*face*) maquillarse. **make-up** *n* maquillaje *m*; carácter *m*. **make up for** compensar. **maker** *n* fabricante *m*. **making** *n* fabricación *f*.

maladjusted [malə'dʒʌstid] *adj* inadaptado. **maladjustment** *n* inadaptación *f*.

malaria [mə'leəriə] *n* malaria *f*, paludismo *m*.

male [meil] *nm, adj* macho.

malevolent [mə'levələnt] *adj* malévolo. **malevolence** *n* malevolencia *f*.

malfunction [mal'fʌŋkʃən] *n* funcionamiento defectuoso *m*. *v* funcionar defectuosamente.

malice ['malis] *n* malicia *f*. **malicious** *adj* malicioso.

malignant [mə'lignənt] *adj* malvado; malo; (*med*) maligno. **malignancy** *n* maldad *f*; malignidad *f*.

malinger [mə'liŋgə] *v* fingirse enfermo.

mallet ['malit] *n* mazo *m*.

malnutrition [malnju'triʃən] *n* desnutrición *f*.

malt [mɔːlt] *n* malta *f*.

Malta ['mɔːltə] *n* Malta. **Maltese** *n, adj* maltés, -esa.

maltreat [mal'triːt] *v* maltratar. **maltreatment** *n* maltrato *m*.

mammal ['maməl] *n* mamífero *m*.

mammoth ['maməθ] *n* mamut *m*. *adj* gigantesco.

man [man] *n, pl* **men** hombre *m. v* armar; ocupar. **manhood** *n* virilidad *f.* **manly** *adj* masculino.

manage ['manidʒ] *v (business, affairs, etc.)* dirigir; *(instrument)* manejar; *(property)* administrar. **manage to** conseguir, arreglárselas. **manageable** *adj* manejable; *(undertaking)* factible; *(animal, person)* dócil. **management** *n* gestión *f,* administración *f,* dirección *f; (board of directors)* junta directiva *f.* **manager** *n* gerente *m,* director *m.* **managerial** *adj* directorial. **managing director** director gerente *m.*

mandarin ['mandərin] *n* mandarín *m. adj* mandarino. **mandarin orange** mandarina *f; (tree)* mandarino *m.*

mandate ['mandeit] *n* mandato *m.* **mandatory** *adj* obligatorio.

mandolin ['mandəlin] *n* mandolina *f.*

mane [mein] *n* crin *f,* crines *f pl.*

mange [meindʒ] *n* sarna *f.* **mangy** *adj* sarnoso; *(coll)* asqueroso.

manger ['meindʒə] *n* pesebre *m.*

mangle[1] ['maŋgl] *n (wringer)* escurridor *m. v* pasar por el escurridor.

mangle[2] ['maŋgl] *v* despedazar; *(fig)* deformar.

mango ['maŋgou] *n* mango *m.*

manhandle [man'handl] *v (person)* maltratar; *(goods)* manipular.

manhole ['manhoul] *n* registro *m.*

mania ['meiniə] *n* manía *f.* **maniac** *n* maníaco, -a *m, f; (fig)* fanático, -a *m, f.*

manicure ['manikjuə] *n* manicura *f. v* hacer la manicura a. **manicurist** *n* manicuro, -a *m, f.*

manifest ['manifest] *adj* manifiesto, evidente. *v* mostrar, manifestarse. **manifestation** *n* manifestación *f.*

manifesto [mani'festou] *n* manifiesto *m.*

manifold ['manifould] *adj* múltiple; diverso. *n* **exhaust manifold** *(mot)* colector de escape *m.*

manipulate [mə'nipjuleit] *v* manipular. **manipulation** *n* manipulación *f.*

mankind [man'kaind] *n* raza humana *f,* humanidad *f.*

man-made [man'meid] *adj* sintético, artificial.

manner ['manə] *n* manera *f,* modo *m;* clase *f;* aire *m.* **manners** *pl n* modales *m pl.*

mannerism ['manə,rizəm] *n* amaneramiento *m.*

manoeuvre [mə'nuɪvə] *n* maniobra *f. v* maniobrar.

manor ['manə] *n* señorío *m.* **manor house** casa solariega *f.*

manpower ['man,pauə] *n* mano de obra *f.*

mansion ['manʃən] *n (country)* gran casa de campo *f; (town)* palacete *m.*

manslaughter ['man,slɔɪtə] *n* homicidio sin premeditación *m.*

mantelpiece ['mantlpiɪs] *n* repisa de chimenea *f.*

mantle ['mantl] *n (cloak)* capa *f; (gas-lamp)* manguito *m.*

manual ['manjuəl] *nm, adj* manual. **manually** *adv* a mano.

manufacture [manju'faktʃə] *n (product)* producto manufacturado; *(act)* fabricación *f. v* manufacturar, fabricar. **manufacturer** *n* fabricante *m.*

manure [mə'njuə] *n* estiércol *m,* abono. *v* estercolar, abonar.

manuscript ['manjuskript] *nm* manuscrito.

many ['meni] *adj* muchos, mucho, un gran número de. *pron* muchos. **as many as** hasta. **how many?** ¿cuántos? ¿cuántas? **so many** tantos, tantas. **too many** demasiado.

map [map] *n* mapa *m; (town)* plano *m. v* levantar un mapa de. **map out** proyectar.

maple ['meipl] *n* arce *m.*

mar [maɪ] *v* estropear; frustrar.

marathon ['marəθən] *nm, adj* maratón.

marble ['maɪbl] *n* mármol *m; (toy)* bola *f. v* jaspear.

march [maɪtʃ] *v* marchar. *n* marcha *f.*

March [maɪtʃ] *n* marzo *m.*

marchioness [,maɪʃə'nes] *n* marquesa *f.*

mare [meə] *n* yegua *f.*

margarine [,maɪdʒə'riɪn] *n* margarina *f.*

margin ['maɪdʒin] *n* borde *m,* lado *m;* orilla *f;* margen *m.* **marginal** *adj* marginal. **marginally** *adv* por muy poco.

marguerite [,maɪgə'riɪt] *n* margarita *f.*

marigold ['marigould] *n* caléndula *f.*

marijuana [mari'waɪnə] *n* marijuana *f,* marihuana *f.*

marina [mə'riɪnə] *n* puerto deportivo *m.*

marinade [,mari'neid] *n* adobo *m. v* adobar.

marine [mə'riɪn] *adj* marino. *n (mil)* soldado de infantería de marina. **merchant marine** marina mercante *f.*

marital ['maritl] *adj* marital, matrimonial.

maritime ['maritaim] *adj* marítimo.
marjoram ['maɪdʒərəm] *n* mejorana *f*.
mark¹ [maɪk] *n* marca *f*, señal *f*, mancha *f*; (*school*) nota *f*; calificación *f*; (*trace*) huella *f*. **marksman** *n* tirador *m*. *v* marcar, señalar; calificar. **marked** *adj* marcado; pronunciado; sensible.
mark² [maɪk] *n* (*currency*) marco *m*.
market ['maɪkit] *n* mercado *m*; (*demand*) salida *f*. **market day** día de mercado *m*. **market place** plaza de mercado *f*. **market research** estudio de mercados *m*. **market value** valor corriente *m*. *v* poner en venta, vender. **marketing** *n* comercialización.
marmalade ['maɪməleid] *n* mermelada de naranja *f*.
maroon¹ [mə'ruːn] *adj* castaño.
maroon² [mə'ruːn] *v* abandonar.
marquee [maɪ'kiː] *n* gran tienda de campaña *f*.
marquess ['maɪkwis] *n* marqués *m*.
marquetry ['maɪkətri] *n* marquetería *f*.
marriage ['maridʒ] *n* matrimonio *m*; (*wedding*) boda *f*. **marriage certificate** partida de casamiento *f*.
marrow ['marou] *n* (*bone*) médula *f*. **vegetable marrow** calabacín *m*.
marry ['mari] *v* casar; (*get married*) casarse. **married** *adj* casado. **married couple** matrimonio *m*. **married name** apellido de casada *m*.
Mars [maɪz] *n* Marte *m*. **Martian** *n, adj* marciano, -a.
marsh [maɪʃ] *n* pantano *m*. **marshmallow** *n* (*bot*) malvavisco *m*; (*cookery*) melcocha *f*. **marshy** *adj* pantanoso.
marshal ['maɪʃəl] *n* (*mil*) mariscal *m*; (*organizer*) maestro de ceremonias *m*. *v* poner en orden; (*mil*) formar.
martial ['maɪʃəl] *adj* marcial.
martin ['maɪtin] *n* avión *m*.
martyr ['maɪtə] *n* mártir *m, f*. *v* martinizar. **martyrdom** *n* martirio *m*.
marvel ['maɪvəl] *n* maravilla *f*. *v* maravillarse. **marvellous** *adj* maravilloso.
marzipan [maɪzi'pan] *n* mazapán *m*.
mascara [ma'skaɪrə] *n* rimel *m*.
mascot ['maskət] *n* mascota *f*.
masculine ['maskjulin] *adj* masculino. **masculinity** *n* masculinidad *f*.
mash [maʃ] *v* machacar. *n* (*animal feed*) afrecho remojado *m*.
mask [maɪsk] *n* máscara *f*, careta *f*. *v* enmascarar.

masochist ['masəkist] *n* masoquista *m, f*. **masochism** *n* masoquismo *m*. **masochistic** *adj* masoquista.
mason ['meisn] *n* albañil *m*. **masonry** *n* albañilería.
masquerade [maskə'reid] *n* (*pretence*) mascarada *f*. *v* **masquerade as** hacerse pasar por.
mass¹ [mas] *n* masa *f*. **mass media** medios informativos *m pl*. **mass meeting** mitin popular *m*. **mass-produce** *v* fabricar en serie. **mass production** fabricación en serie *f*. *v* agrupar.
mass² [mas] *n* (*rel*) misa *f*.
massacre ['masəkə] *n* matanza *f*. *v* matar en masa.
massage ['masaɪʒ] *n* masaje *m*. *v* dar un masaje. **masseur, masseuse** *n* masajista *m, f*.
massive ['masiv] *adj* sólido; masivo.
mast [maɪst] *n* (*naut*) palo *m*, mástil *m*; (*radio, etc.*) poste *m*.
master ['maɪstə] *n* (*owner*) dueño *m*; (*college*) director *m*; (*secondary school*) profesor *m*; (*primary school*) maestro; (*graduate*) licenciado, -a *m, f*; (*household*) señor *m*; (*work force*) patrón *m*; (*ship*) capitán *m*. **master copy** original *m*. **master key** llave maestra *f*. **master of ceremonies** maestro de ceremonias *m*. **masterpiece** *n* obra maestra *f*. *v* (*passions, language*) dominar; (*an animal*) domar; (*difficulties*) vencer. **mastery** *n* dominio *m*; maestría *f*.
masturbate ['mastəbeit] *v* masturbarse. **masturbation** *n* masturbación *f*.
mat [mat] *n* (*floor*) estera *f*; (*door*) esterilla *f*; (*table*) salvamanteles *m invar*; (*doily*) tapete *m*. **matted** *adj* (*hair*) enmarañado.
match¹ [matʃ] *n* fósforo *m*, cerilla *f*. **matchbox** *n* caja de fósforos *or* cerillas *f*.
match² [matʃ] *n* (*sport*) partido *m*; (*equal*) igual *m*; (*pair*) pareja *f*. *v* igualar; (*colours*) casar; (*gloves, etc.*) parear; (*clothes, furnishings*) hacer juego con; (*fit*) encajar; corresponder. **matchless** *adj* sin igual.
mate [meit] *n* (*animals*) macho, hembra *m, f*; amigo, -a *m, f*; camarada *m, f*; (*spouse*) compañero, -a *m, f*. *v* acoplar; casar; (*chess*) dar jaque mate a.
material [mə'tiəriəl] *n* material *m*; (*cloth*) tela *f*. **materials** *pl n* (*building*) materiales *m pl*; (*teaching*) material *m*; artículos *m*

meditate

pl. adj material; esencial. **materialist** *n(m+f)*, *adj* materialista. **materialize** *v* materializar; realizar.
maternal [mə'tɜːnl] *adj* maternal; (*relation*) materno.
maternity [mə'tɜːnəti] *n* maternidad *f*. **maternity hospital** casa de maternidad *f*.
mathematics [maθə'matiks] *n* matemáticas *f pl*. **mathematical** *adj* matemático.
mathematician *n* matemático, -a *m, f*.
matinée ['matinei] *n* (*cinema*) primera sesión *f*; (*theatre*) función de la tarde *f*. **matinée idol** ídolo del público *m*.
matins ['matinz] *n* maitines *m pl*.
matriarch ['meitriɑːk] *n* mujer que manda *f*. **matriarchal** *adj* matriarcal.
matrimony ['matriməni] *n* matrimonio *m*. **matrimonial** *adj* matrimonial.
matrix ['meitriks] *n* matriz *f*.
matron ['meitrən] *n* matrona *f*; (*hospital*) enfermera jefe *f*; (*school*) ama de llaves *f*.
matt [mat] *adj* mate.
matter ['matə] *n* materia *f*; material *m*; asunto *m*; cuestión *f*; tema *m*. **as a matter of fact** en realidad. **matter-of-fact** *adj* prosaico. **what's the matter?** ¿qué pasa? *v* importar. **it doesn't matter** no importa.
mattress ['matris] *n* colchón *m*. **spring-mattress** *n* colchón de muelles *m*.
mature [mə'tjuə] *adj* maduro. *v* madurar. **maturity** *n* madurez *f*.
maudlin ['mɔːdlin] *adj* sensiblero.
maul [mɔːl] *v* maltratar; herir gravemente.
mausoleum [mɔːsə'liəm] *n* mausoleo *m*.
mauve [mouv] *nm, adj* malva.
maxim ['maksim] *n* máxima *f*.
maximum ['maksiməm] *nm, adj* máximo.
***may** [mei] *v* poder.
May [mei] *n* mayo *m*. **May Day** primero de mayo *m*.
maybe ['meibiː] *adv* quizás, quizá.
mayday ['meidei] *n* señal de socorro *f*.
mayonnaise [ˌmeiə'neiz] *n* mayonesa *f*.
mayor [meə] *n* alcalde *m*. **mayoress** *n* alcaldesa *f*.
maze [meiz] *n* laberinto *m*.
me [miː] *pron* me; (*after prep*) mí.
mead [miːd] *n* (*drink*) aguamiel *f*.
meadow ['medou] *n* prado *m*.
meagre ['miːgə] *adj* escaso, pobre.
meal¹ [miːl] *n* (*food*) comida *f*.
meal² [miːl] *n* (*flour*) harina *f*.
***mean¹** [miːn] *v* (*signify*) tener la intención de, querer decir.

mean² [miːn] *adj* (*humble*) humilde; (*petty*) mezquino; (*stingy*) agarrado; (*character*) vil; (*unkind*) malo. **meanness** *n* humildad *f*; mezquindad *f*; (*stinginess*) tacañería *f*; vileza *f*; maldad *f*.
mean³ [miːn] *n* (*average*) promedio; (*math*) media *f*. *adj* medio; mediano.
meander [mi'andə] *v* (*river*) serpentear; (*person*) vagar. *n* meandro *m*.
meaning ['miːnin] *n* significación *f*; sentido *m*; pensamiento *m*. **meaningful** *adj* significativo. **meaningless** *adj* sin sentido; insignificante.
means [miːnz] *n* (*way*) medio *m*, manera *f*; (*wealth*) fondos *m pl*. **by all means!** ¡por supuesto! **by means of** por medio de. **by no means** de ningún modo.
meanwhile ['miːnwail] *adv* mientras tanto.
measles ['miːzlz] *n* sarampión *m*.
measure ['meʒə] *v* medir. *n* medida *f*. **made to measure** hecho a medida. **measurement** *n* medida *f*.
meat [miːt] *v* carne *f*. **cold meat** fiambre *m*. **meatball** *n* albóndiga *f*. **meat pie** empanada *f*.
mechanic [mi'kanik] *n* mecánico *m*. **mechanical** *adj* mecánico. **mechanics** *n* mecánica *f sing*. **mechanism** *n* mecanismo *m*. **mechanize** *v* mecanizar.
medal ['medl] *n* medalla *f*. **medallion** *n* medallón *m*. **medallist** *n* condecorado con una medalla.
meddle ['medl] *v* **meddle in** meterse en; **meddle with** toquetear. **meddlesome** *adj* entrometido.
media ['miːdiə] *pl n* medios *m pl*.
mediate ['miːdieit] *v* ser mediador en; mediar. **mediation** *n* mediación *f*. **mediator** *n* mediador, -a *m, f*.
medical ['medikəl] *adj* médico; de medicina. **medical consultant** médico consultor *m*. **medical school** facultad de medicina *f*. **medicate** *v* medicinar. **medicated** *adj* medicinal.
medicine ['medsən] *n* (*art and drug*) medicina *f*; (*coll*) purga *f*. **medicine cabinet** botiquín *m*. **medicinal** *adj* medicinal.
medieval [medi'iːvəl] *adj* medieval.
mediocre [miːdi'oukə] *adj* mediocre. **mediocrity** *n* mediocridad *f*.
meditate ['mediteit] *v* meditar. **meditation** *n* meditación *f*. **meditative** *adj* meditativo.

Mediterranean [ˌmedItə'reinIən] *adj* mediterráneo. *n* Mediterráneo *m*.

medium ['miːdIəm] *n* (*environment*) medio ambiente *m*; (*means*) medio *m*; (*spiritualism*) médium *m, f*. **happy medium** justo medio *m*. *adj* mediano. **medium wave** (*radio*) onda media *f*.

medley ['medlI] *n* mezcla *f*; (*music*) popurrí *m*.

meek [miːk] *adj* dócil, manso; humilde. **meekness** *n* docilidad *f*, mansedumbre *f*.

meet [miːt] *v* (*encounter*) encontrar, encontrarse a; (*come together*) entrevistarse con; (*come across*) cruzarse con; (*roads*) desembocar en; (*correspond to*) empalmar con; satisfacer; (*requirement, engagement*) cumplir con; (*expenses*) costear; (*claims*) acceder a. **meet someone half-way** llegar a un arreglo con alguien. **pleased to meet you!** ¡mucho gusto! **meeting** *n* encuentro *m*; reunión *f*; sesión *f*; (*interview*) cita *f*; (*official*) entrevista *f*.

megaphone ['megəfoun] *n* megáfono *m*.

melancholy ['melənkəlI] *n* melancolía *f*. *adj also* **melancholic** melancólico.

mellow ['melou] *adj* (*ripe*) maduro; (*wine*) añejo; (*voice*) suave. *v* madurar; suavizar.

melodrama ['melədraImə] *n* melodrama *m*. **melodramatic** *adj* melodramático.

melody ['melədI] *n* melodía *f*. **melodious** *adj* melodioso.

melon ['melən] *n* melón *m*.

melt [melt] *v* fundir; derretir; (*fig*) ablandar. **melting** *n* fusión *f*, fundición *f*.

member ['membə] *n* miembro *m*. **membership** *n* calidad de miembro *f*. **membership fee** cuota de socio *f*.

membrane ['membrein] *n* membrana *f*. **membranous** *adj* membranoso.

memento [mə'mentou] *n* recuerdo *m*.

memo ['memou] *n* (*coll*) memorándum *m*.

memoirs ['memwaIz] *pl n* memorias *f pl*.

memorable ['memərəbl] *adj* memorable.

memorandum [memə'randəm] *n* memorándum *m*.

memory ['memərI] *n* memoria *f*; (*thing remembered*) recuerdo *m*. **memorize** *v* memorizar, aprender de memoria.

men [men] *V* **man**.

menace ['menis] *n* amenaza *f*. *v* amenazar.

menagerie [mi'nadʒərI] *n* casa de fieras *f*.

mend [mend] *v* remendar; reparar; (*improve*) mejorar. **be on the mend** (*coll*) estar mejorando.

menial ['miːnIəl] *adj* (*of a servant*) doméstico; (*mean*) bajo. *n* (*servant*) criado, -a *m, f*.

meningitis [ˌmenin'dʒaitis] *n* meningitis *f*.

menopause ['menəpoɪz] *n* menopausia *f*.

menstrual ['menstruəl] *adj* menstrual. **menstruate** *v* menstruar. **menstruation** *n* menstruación *f*.

mental ['mentl] *adj* mental; (*coll: mad*) chiflado. **mental arithmetic** cálculo mental *m*. **mental deficiency** deficiencia mental *f*. **mental home** *or* **hospital** manicomio *m*. **mentality** *n* mentalidad *f*. **mentally** *adj* mentalmente. **mentally handicapped** anormal.

menthol ['menθəl] *n* mentol *m*.

mention ['menʃən] *v* mencionar, hablar de. **don't mention it!** ¡de nada! ¡no hay de qué! **not to mention** por no decir nada de. *n* mención *f*.

menu ['menjuː] *n* carta *f*, lista de platos *f*.

mercantile ['məːkənˌtail] *adj* mercantil; mercante.

mercenary ['məːsinərI] *nm, adj* mercenario.

merchandise ['məːtʃəndaiz] *n* mercancías *f pl*. **merchandizing** *n* comercio mercantil *m*.

merchant ['məːtʃənt] *n* comerciante *m, f*, negociante *m, f*; (*shopkeeper*) tendero, -a *m, f*. **merchant navy** marina mercante *f*.

mercury ['məːkjurI] *n* mercurio *m*.

mercy ['məːsI] *n* misericordia *f*, merced *f*. **at the mercy of** a merced de. **merciful** *adj* clemente; misericordioso. **merciless** *adj* despiadado.

mere [miə] *adj* mero.

merge [məːdʒ] *v* (*parties, companies*) fusionar; (*join*) unir; (*colours*) fundir. **merger** *n* fusión *f*; unión *f*.

meridian [mə'ridIən] *nm, adj* meridiano.

meringue [mə'raŋ] *n* merengue *m*.

merit ['merit] *n* mérito *m*. *v* merecer.

mermaid ['məːmeid] *n* sirena *f*.

merry ['merI] *adj* alegre; divertido; (*coll: slightly drunk*) achispado. **merry-go-round** *n* tiovivo *m*. **merriment** *n* alegría *f*; diversión *f*.

mesh [meʃ] *n* malla *f*; (*gears*) engranaje *m*. *v* engranar (con).

mesmerize ['mezməraiz] *v* hipnotizar.

mess [mes] *n* confusión *f*, desorden *m*; (*dirt*) porquería *f*, suciedad *f*; (*awkward situation*) lío *m*; (*mil*) comedor de la tropa *m*. **make a mess of** desordenar;

ensuciar. **what a mess!** ¡qué asco! ¡qué porquería! ¡qué lío! **mess up** desordenar; ensuciar. **messy** *adj* confuso; desordenado; sucio.
message ['mesidʒ] *n* recado *m*; (*official communication*) mensaje *m*; (*errand*) encargo *m*. **messenger** *n* mensajero, -a *m, f.*
met [met] *V* **meet.**
metal ['metl] *n* metal *m. adj* de metal. **metallic** *adj* metálico. **metallurgist** *n* metalúrgico *m.* **metallurgy** *n* metalurgia *f.*
metamorphosis [metə'mɔɪfəsis] *n* metamorfosis *f.*
metaphor ['metəfə] *n* metáfora *f.* **metaphorical** *adj* metafórico.
metaphysics [metə'fiziks] *n* metafísica *f.* **metaphysical** *adj* metafísico. **metaphysician** *n* metafísico *m.*
meteor ['miɪtiə] *n* meteoro. **meteoric** *adj* meteórico. **meteorite** *n* meteorito *m.*
meteorology [miɪtiə'rolədʒi] *n* meteorología *f.* **meteorological** *adj* meteorológico. **meteorologist** *n* meteorologista *m, f.*
meter ['miɪtə] *n* contador *m.*
methane ['miɪθein] *n* metano *m.*
method ['meθəd] *n* método *m*; técnica *f.* **methodical** *adj* metódico.
Methodist ['meθədist] *n* metodista *m, f.* **Methodism** *n* metodismo *m.*
methylated spirits ['meθileitid] *pl n* alcohol desnaturalizado *m.*
meticulous [mi'tikjuləs] *adj* meticuloso.
metre ['miɪtə] *n* metro *m.* **metric** *adj* métrico.
metronome ['metrənoum] *n* metrónomo *m.*
metropolis [mə'tropəlis] *n* metrópoli *f.* **metropolitan** *adj* metropolitano.
Mexico ['meksikou] *n* Méjico, México. **Mexican** *n, adj* mejicano, -a, mexicano, -a.
mice [mais] *V* **mouse.**
microbe ['maikroub] *n* microbio *m.*
microfilm ['maikrə,film] *n* microfilm *m.*
microphone ['maikrəfoun] *n* micrófono *m.*
microscope ['maikrəskoup] *n* microscopio *m.* **microscopic** *adj* microscópico.
microwave ['maikrəweiv] *n* microonda *f.*
mid [mid] *adj* medio; mediados.
mid-air [,mid'eə] *n* **in mid-air** entre cielo y tierra.
midday [,mid'dei] *n* mediodía *m.*

middle ['midl] *n* medio *m*, centro *m*; mitad *f.* **in the middle** en el centro. *adj* central; mediano; de en medio; medio; intermedio. **middle-aged** *adj* de mediano edad. **the Middle Ages** Edad Media *f sing.* **middle-class** *adj* de la clase media; burgués. **Middle East** Oriente Medio *m.* **middleman** *n* intermediario *m.* **middle-of-the-road** *adj* centrista, moderado. **middleweight** *n* peso medio *m.* **middling** *adj* regular, mediano.
midge [midʒ] *n* mosca enana *f.*
midget ['midʒit] *n* enano, -a *m, f.*
midnight ['midnait] *n* medianoche *f.*
midriff ['midrif] *n* diafragua *m.*
midst [midst] *n* **in our midst** entre nosotros. **in the midst of** en medio de.
midstream [,mid'striːm] *n* **in midstream** en medio del río.
midsummer ['mid,sʌmə] *n* pleno verano *m.* **Midsummer Day** el día de San Juan *m.*
midway [,mid'wei] *adv, adj* a medio camino.
midweek [,mid'wiːk] *n* medio de la semana *m.*
midwife ['midwaif] *n* comadrona *f.* partera *f.* **midwifery** *n* obstetricia *f.*
midwinter [,mid'wintə] *n* pleno invierno *m.*
might[1] [mait] *V* **may.**
might[2] [mait] *n* poder *m*; fuerza *f.*
mighty ['maiti] *adj* poderoso; fuerte; enorme. *adv* (*coll*) muy.
migraine ['miːgrein] *n* migraña *f.*
migrate [mai'greit] *v* emigrar. **migration** *n* migración. *adj* migratoria.
mike [maik] *n* (*coll: microphone*) micro *m.*
mild [maild] *adj* (*person*) dulce, apacible; (*weather*) templado; (*wind*) suave; (*disease*) benigno. **mildness** *n* dulzura *f*; suavidad *f*; benignidad *f.*
mildew ['mildjuː] *n* moho *m*; (*vine*) mildeu *m*; (*plants*) tizón *m.*
mile [mail] *n* milla *f.* **mileage** recorrido en millas *m.* **milestone** *n* mojón *m*; (*fig*) jalón *m.*
militant ['militənt] *adj* belicoso; (*pol*) militante. *n* militante *m, f.*
military ['militəri] *adj* militar.
milk [milk] *n* leche *f.* **milk chocolate** *n* chocolate con leche *m.* **milkman** *n* lechero *m.* **milk of magnesia** *n* leche de magnesia *f.* *v* ordeñar; (*fig*) exprimir.

Milky Way

milkiness *n* aspecto lechoso *m*. **milking** *n* ordeño *m*. **milky** *adj* lechoso.
Milky Way *n* Vía Láctea *f*.
mill [mil] *n* molino *m*; (*grinder*) molinillo *m*; (*factory*) fábrica *f*. **millstone** *n* muela *f*; (*burden*) cruz *f*. *v* moler. **miller** *n* molinero, -a *m*, *f*.
millennium [mi'leniəm] *n* milenario *m*.
millet ['milit] *n* mijo *m*.
milligram ['mili,gram] *n* miligramo *m*.
millimetre ['mili,miitə] *n* milímetro *m*.
milliner ['milinə] *n* sombrerero, -a *m*, *f*. **milliner's** *n* sombrerería *f*. **millinery** *n* sombreros de señora *m pl*.
million ['miljən] *n* millón *m*. **millionaire** *n* millonario, -a *m*, *f*. **millionth** *n*, *adj* millonésimo, -a *m*, *f*.
mime [maim] *n* mimo *m*, pantomima *f*. *v* actuar de mimo.
mimic ['mimik] *adj* mímico; imitativo. *n* mimo *m*; imitador, -a *m*, *f*. *v* imitar, remedar. **mimicry** *n* mímica *f*; (*zool*) mimetismo *m*.
minaret [minə'ret] *n* minarete *m*.
mince [mins] *n* (*meat*) carne picada *f*. **mincemeat** *n* conserva de fruta picada y especias *f*. **mince pie** pastel con frutas picadas *m*. *v* picar; (*walk*) andar con pasos menuditos. **mince words** tener pelos en la lengua. **mincer** *n* máquina de picar carne *f*. **mincing** *adj* afectado.
mind [maind] *n* mente *f*. **bear in mind** tener en cuenta. **go out of one's mind** perder el juicio. **have a good mind to** tener ganas de. **keep in mind** acordarse de. **make up one's mind** decidirse. **read someone's mind** adivinar el pensamiento de alguien. **to my mind** a mi parecer. *v* (*look out*) tener cuidado; (*guard*) cuidar; (*rules*) cumplir; (*pay attention*) prestar atención. **do you mind?** ¿le importa? **I don't mind** a mí no me importa. **never mind** no se precocupe.
mine¹ [main] *pron* (el) mío, (la) mía, (lo) mío.
mine² [main] *n* mina *f*. **minefield** *n* campo de minas *m*. **mineshaft** *n* pozo de extracción *m*. **minesweeper** *n* dragaminas *m invar*. *v* minar; (*mil*) sembrar minas en. **miner** *n* minero *m*. **mining** *n* minería *f*. **mining engineer** ingeniero de minas *m*.
mineral ['minərəl] *nm*, *adj* mineral. **minerals** (*coll*: *drinks*) *pl n* gaseosas *f pl*.
mingle ['miŋgl] *v* mezclar.
miniature ['minitʃə] *nf*, *adj* miniatura.

minim ['minim] *n* mínima *f*, blanca *f*.
minimum ['miniməm] *nm*, *adj* mínimo. **minimal** *adj* mínimo. **minimize** *v* minimizar.
minister ['ministə] *n* ministro *m*. *v* **minister to** atender a. **ministerial** *adj* ministerial. **ministry** *n* ministerio *m*.
mink [miŋk] *n* visón *m*.
minor ['mainə] *adj* menor, más pequeño; secundario; de poca importancia. *n* menor de edad *m*, *f*.
minority [mai'noriti] *n* minoría *f*. **in the minority** en la minoría. *adj* minoritario.
minstrel ['minstrəl] *n* trovador.
mint¹ [mint] *n* (*bot*) menta *f*.
mint² [mint] *n* casa de la moneda *f*. *adj* nuevo. *v* acuñar.
minuet [minju'et] *n* minué *m*.
minus ['mainəs] *prep* menos. *adj* negativo. **minus sign** signo menos *m*.
minute¹ ['minit] *n* minuto *m*. **minutes** *pl n* actas *f pl*.
minute² [mai'njuit] *adj* (*tiny*) diminuto; (*detailed*) minucioso.
miracle ['mirəkl] *n* milagro *m*. **miraculous** *adj* milagroso.
mirage ['miraiʒ] *n* espejismo *m*.
mirror ['mirə] *n* espejo *m*; (*mot*) retrovisor *m*. *v* reflejar.
mirth [məiθ] *n* alegría *f*; hilaridad *f*.
misadventure [misəd'ventʃə] *n* desgracia *f*.
misanthropist [miz'anθrəpist] *n* misántropo *m*. **misanthropic** *adj* misantrópico. **misanthropy** *n* misantropía *f*.
misapprehension [misapri'henʃən] *n* malentendido *m*.
misbehave [misbi'heiv] *v* portarse mal. **misbehaviour** *n* mala conducta *f*.
miscalculate [mis'kalkjuleit] *v* calcular mal. **miscalculation** *n* cálculo erróneo *m*.
miscarriage [mis'karidʒ] *n* (*med*) aborto *m*; (*plans*, *etc*.) fracaso *m*. **miscarriage of justice** error judicial *m*.
miscellaneous [misə'leiniəs] *adj* diverso.
mischief ['mistʃif] *n* (*evil*) maldad *f*; (*of child*) travesura *f*; (*damage*) daño *m*. **get into mischief** hacer tonterías. **make mischief** sembrar la discordia. **mischievous** *adj* malo; travieso; dañino.
misconception [miskən'sepʃən] *n* concepto falso *m*.
misconduct [mis'kondʌkt] *n* (*misbehaviour*) mala conducta *f*; (*mismanagement*) mala administración *f*.

misconstrue [miskən'struɪ] v interpretar mal.

misdeed [mis'diːd] n delito m.

misdemeanour [misdi'miːnə] n (law) infracción f; (misbehaviour) mala conducta f.

miser ['maizə] n avaro, -a m, f. **miserly** adj mezquino.

miserable ['mizərəbl] adj (sad) triste; (sick) mal; (unfortunate) desgraciado; (wretched) miserable; (distressing) de pena.

misery ['mizəri] n tristeza f; (pain) dolor m; desgracia f; miseria f; (coll: person) aguafiestas m, f.

misfire [mis'faiə] v fallar; (mot) tener fallos. n fallo m.

misfit ['misfit] n inadaptado, -a m, f.

misfortune [mis'fɔːtʃən] n desgracia f.

misgiving [mis'giviŋ] n recelo m; inquietud f.

misguided [mis'gaidid] adj descaminado; poco afortunado.

mishap ['mishap] n contratiempo m.

misinterpret [misin'təɪprit] v interpretar mal. **misinterpretation** n interpretación errónea f.

misjudge [mis'dʒʌdʒ] v juzgar mal. **misjudgment** n estimación errónea f.

***mislay** [mis'lei] v extraviar.

***mislead** [mis'liːd] v engañar; equivocar. **misleading** adj engañoso.

misnomer [mis'noumə] n nombre inapropiado m.

misogynist [mi'sodʒənist] n misógino m.

misplace [mis'pleis] v colocar mal; (lose) extraviar.

misprint ['misprint] n errata f.

miss¹ [mis] v fallar; no dar en; (train, bus, etc.) perder; (a meeting) no asistir a; (long for) echar de menos. **miss out** omitir. n tiro errado m; (failure) fracaso m.

missing adj (lacking) que falta; perdido; ausente; desaparecido.

miss² [mis] n señorita.

misshapen [miʃʃeipən] adj (object) deformado; (person) deforme.

missile ['misail] n proyectil m. **guided missile** proyectil teledirigido m.

mission [miʃən] n misión f. **missionary** n, adj misionero, -a.

mist [mist] n (haze) calina f; (fog) neblina f; (at sea) bruma f; (on glasses) vaho m. **mist over** or **up** empañar. **misty** adj de niebla; brumoso; vago; empañado.

***mistake** [mi'steik] v (be wrong) equivocarse en; (the way) equivocarse de; (misunderstand) entender mal. n error m; equivocación f; falta f. **by mistake** sin querer. **make a mistake** equivocarse. **mistaken** adj equivocado; erróneo; mal comprendido. **be mistaken** estar equivocado.

mistletoe ['misltou] n muérdago m.

mistress ['mistris] n (of the house) señora f; (owner) dueña f; (lover) amante f; (teacher) profesora f.

mistrust [mis'trʌst] n desconfianza f; (suspicion) recelo m. v desconfiar de; recelar de. **mistrustful** adj desconfiado; receloso.

***misunderstand** [misʌndə'stand] v entender mal. **misunderstanding** n malentendido m.

misuse [mis'juːs; v mis'juːz] n mal uso m; abuso m; maltrato m; mal empleo m. v abusar de; maltratar; emplear mal.

mitigate ['mitigeit] v mitigar; aliviar; atemar. **mitigation** n mitigación f; alivio m; atenuación f.

mitre ['maitə] n (rel) mitra f; (carpentry) inglete m. v unir con ingletes.

mitten ['mitn] n mitón m.

mix [miks] v mezclar; (drinks) preparar; (salad) aliñar; (flour, cement, etc.) amasar. **mix up** mezclar; confundir. **mix-up** n lío m; confusión f. **mixed feelings** sentimientos contradictorios m pl. **mixed grill** plato combinado m. **mixer** n (elec) mezclador m; (cement) mezcladora f. **mixture** n mezcla f; (med) mixturia f.

moan [moun] v gemir; (coll: complain) quejarse. n gemido m; queja f.

moat [mout] n foso m.

mob [mob] n multitud f; (rabble) chusma f. v acosar.

mobile ['moubail] nm, adj móvil. **mobility** n movilidad f. **mobilize** v movilizar.

moccasin ['mokəsin] n mocasín m.

mock [mok] v burlarse de; ridiculizar. adj simulado; falso; imitado. **mockery** n burla f; simulacro m; imitación f. **mocking** adj burlón.

mode [moud] n modo m, manera f; (fashion) moda f.

model ['modl] n modelo m; (of a statue) maqueta f; (fashion) maniquí m; (dressmaking pattern) patrón m. v modelar; (dress) presentar.

moderate ['modərət; *v* 'modəreit] *n, adj* moderado, -a. *v* moderar; aplacar. **moderately** *adv* moderadamente; (*fairly*) mediocremente. **in moderation** con moderación.
modern ['modən] *adj* moderno. **modern languages** lenguas vivas *f pl.* **modernization** *n* modernisación *f.* **modernize** *v* modernizar.
modest ['modist] *adj* modesto; discreto. **modesty** *n* modestia *f.*
modify ['modifai] *v* modificar. **modification** *n* modificación *f.*
modulate ['modjuleit] *v* modular. **modulation** *n* modulación *f.*
module ['modjuːl] *n* módulo *m.*
mohair ['mouheə] *n* moer *m.*
moist [moist] *adj* húmedo. **moisten** *v* numedecer, mojar. **moisture** *n* humedad *f.* **moisturize** *v* humedecer. **moisturizing cream** crema hidratante *f.*
molasses [mə'lasiz] *n* melaza *f.*
mole¹ [moul] *n* (*on skin*) lunar *m.*
mole² [moul] *n* (*zool*) topo *m.* **molehill** *n* topera *f.*
molecule ['molikjuːl] *n* molécula *f.* **molecular** *adj* molecular.
molest [mə'lest] *v* molestar, importunar.
mollusc ['moləsk] *n* molusco *m.*
molten ['moultən] *adj* fundido.
moment ['moumənt] *n* momento *m.* **at the moment** de momento. **momentary** *adj* momentáneo. **momentarily** *adv* momentáneamente. **momentous** *adj* de gran importancia.
momentum [mə'mentəm] *n* momento *m*; impetu *m*; impulso *m.*
monarch ['monək] *n* monarca *m.* **monarchist** *n, adj* monárquico, -a. **monarchy** *n* monarquía *f.*
monastery ['monəstəri] *n* monasterio *m.* **monastic** *adj* monacal.
Monday ['mʌndi] *n* lunes *m.*
money ['mʌni] *n* dinero *m.* **get one's money's worth** sacar jugo al dinero. **moneylender** *n* prestamista *m, f.*
mongol ['moŋgəl] *n, adj* (*med*) mongol, -a. **mongolism** *n* mongolismo *m.*
mongrel ['mʌŋgrəl] *n* (*dog*) perro mestizo *m.*
monitor ['monitə] *n* monitor *m*; instructor *m*; (*tech*) radioescucha *m. v* controlar.
monk [mʌŋk] *n* monje *m.*

monkey ['mʌŋki] *n* mono *m.* **monkey around** entretenerse, perder el tiempo.
monogamy [mə'nogəmi] *n* monogamia *f.* **monogamous** *adj* monógamo.
monogram ['monəgram] *n* monograma *m.*
monologue ['monəlog] *n* monólogo *m.*
monopolize [mə'nopəlaiz] *v* monopolizar. **monopoly** *n* monopolio *m.*
monosyllable ['monəsiləbl] *n* monosílabo *m.* **monosyllabic** *adj* (*word*) monosílabo; (*statement*) monosilábico.
monotone ['monətoun] *n* monotonía *f.* **monotonous** *adj* monótono. **monotony** *n* monotonía *f.*
monsoon [mon'suːn] *n* monzón *m.*
monster ['monstə] *n* monstruo *m.* **monstrosity** *n* monstruosidad *f.* **monstrous** *adj* monstruoso.
month [mʌnθ] *n* mes *m.* **calendar month** mes civil *m.* **monthly** *n, adj* mensual. *adv* mensualmente.
monument ['monjument] *n* monumento *m.* **monumental** *adj* monumental; enorme.
mood¹ [muːd] *n* humor *m.* **moody** *adj* malhumorado; caprichoso.
mood² [muːd] *n* (*gramm*) modo *m.*
moon [muːn] *n* luna *f.* **crescent moon** media luna *f.* **full moon** luna llena *f.* **new moon** luna nueva *f.* **moonbeam** *n* rayo de luna *m.* **moonlight** *n* claro de luna *m.* **moonlighting** *n* (*coll*) pluriempleo *m.*
moor¹ [muə] *n* páramo *m.*
moor² [muə] *v* marrrar.
mop [mop] *n* (*floor*) fregona *f*; (*hair*) pelambrera *f. v* fregar. **mop up** limpiar.
mope [moup] *v* tener ideas negras.
moped ['mouped] *n* ciclomotor *m.*
moral ['morəl] *adj* moral; virtuoso. **moral support** apoyo moral *m. n* (*fable*) moraleja *f.* **morals** *pl n* moralidad *f sing.* **moralist** *n* moralista *m, f.* **moralize** *v* moralizar.
morale [mə'raɪl] *n* moral *f.*
morbid ['moːbid] *adj* mórbido.
more [moː] *adj* más; superior; mayor. *pron, adv* más. **all the more** aún más. **and what's more** y lo que es más. **even more** más aún. **more and more** cada vez más. **more than ever** más que nunca. **once more** una vez más.
moreover [moː'rouvə] *adv* además, también; por otra parte.
morgue [moɪg] *n* depósito de cadáveres *m.*

morning ['mɔɪnɪŋ] n mañana f. adj de la mañana. morning coat chaqué m. morning sickness náuseas f pl.

moron ['mɔɪron] n retrasado mental m; (coll) imbécil m, f. moronic adj retrasado mental; (coll) idiota.

morose [mə'rous] adj malhumorado.

morphine ['mɔɪfiɪn] n morfina f.

Morse code [mɔɪs] n morse m.

morsel ['mɔɪsəl] n bocado m.

mortal ['mɔɪtl] nm, adj mortal. mortality n mortalidad f.

mortar ['mɔɪtə] n mortero m.

mortgage ['mɔɪgidʒ] n hipoteca f.

mortify ['mɔɪtifai] v mortificar. mortification n mortificación f.

mortuary ['mɔɪtʃuəri] n depósito de cadáveres m.

mosaic [mə'zeiik] n mosaico m. adj de mosaico.

Moscow ['moskou] n Moscú.

mosque [mosk] n mezquita f.

mosquito [mə'skiɪtou] n mosquito m. mosquito bite picadura de mosquito f. mosquito net mosquitero m.

moss [mos] n musgo m. mossy adj musgoso.

most [moust] adj más; la mayoría de. pron la mayoría; la mayor parte; lo máximo. adv más; (very) de lo más. at most a lo sumo. make the most of sacar el mayor provecho de. mostly adv principalmente, sobre todo; en general.

motel [mou'tel] n motel m.

moth [moθ] n mariposa nocturna f. clothes moth polilla f. mothball bola de naftalina f. moth-eaten adj apohillado; (fig) anticuado.

mother ['mʌθə] n madre f. mother-in-law n suegra f. mother-of-pearl n madreperla f. Mothers' Day día de la Madre m. mother-to-be futura madre f. motherhood n maternidad f. motherly adj maternal.

motion ['mouʃən] n movimiento m; (signal) señas f pl; (indication) ademán m; (of a machine) mecanismo m; (med) deposición f; (at a meeting) moción f. set in motion poner en marcha. v indicar con la mano; hacer señas. motionless adj inmóvil.

motivate ['moutiveit] v motivar. motivation n motivo m.

motive ['moutiv] n (reason) motivo m; (law) móvil m. adj motor, motriz.

motor ['moutə] n motor m. motorbike n

(coll) moto f. motorboat n lancha motora f. motorcar n automóvil m, coche m. motorcyclist n motociclista m, f. motoring n automovilismo m. motorist n automovilista m, f. motorway n autopista f.

mottled ['motld] adj abigarrado.

motto ['motou] n lema m.

mould[1] [mould] n (container) molde m; (shape) forma f; (pattern) modelo m. v moldear; formar.

mould[2] [mould] n (fungus) moho m. mouldy adj mohoso. go mouldy enmohecerse.

moult [moult] v mudar. n muda f.

mound [maund] n (natural) montículo m; (artificial) terraplén m; (heap) montón m; (burial) túmulo m.

mount[1] [maunt] v subir; montar a caballo. mount up aumentar. n (horse) montura f; (base) soporte m; (phot) borde m; (drawing) fondo m.

mount[2] [maunt] n monte m.

mountain ['mauntən] n montaña f. mountaineer n montañero, -a m, f. mountaineering n montañismo m. mountainous adj montañoso.

mourn [mɔɪn] v lamentar. mournful adj triste; afligido. mourning n luto m, duelo m.

mouse [maus] n, pl mice ratón m. mousetrap n ratonera f. mousy adj (coll: hair) pardusco; (coll: shy) tímido.

mousse [muɪs] n crema batida f.

moustache [mə'staɪʃ] n bigote m.

mouth [mauθ] n boca f; (opening) abertura f; (entrance) entrada f; (bottle) gollete m; (river) desembocadura f. mouthpiece n (music) boquita f; (phone) micrófono m; (spokesman) portavoz m. mouthwash n enjuague m. mouth-watering adj muy apetitoso. v articular.

move [muɪv] v cambiar de; mudarse de; mover; transportar; (from one place to another) trasladar; poner en marcha; (emotionally) emocionar; (in debate) proponer. n (fig) paso m; marcha f; medida f; (house) mudanza f; (turn) turno m; (chess, etc.) jugada f. movable adj movible, móvil. movement n movimiento m; (gesture) ademán m; acto m; tendencia f; transporte m; traslado m; (vehicles) tráfico m; (tech) mecanismo m; (mil) maniobra f. moving adj móvil; en movimiento; (emotional) conmovedor.

movie ['muːvi] n (US) película f. go to the movies ir al cine.
*mow [mou] v (lawn) cortar, segar. mow down barrer.
Mr ['mistə] n señor m; Sr.
Mrs ['misiz] n señora f; Sra.
much [mʌtʃ] adj, adv, pron mucho. as much tanto (como). how much? ¿cuánto? much as por mucho que. so much tanto. too much demasiado.
muck [mʌk] n (manure) estiércol m; (dirt) suciedad f. v muck about (coll) perder el tiempo. mucky adj asqueroso.
mucus ['mjuːkəs] n mucosidad f. mucous adj mucoso.
mud [mʌd] n barro m; (thick mud) fango m. mudguard n guardabarros m invar. muddy adj fangoso.
muddle ['mʌdl] n desorden m; confusión f. v confundir, embrollar. muddle through salir del paso. muddleheaded adj atontado.
muff [mʌf] n manguito m.
muffle ['mʌfl] v amortiguar. muffle up embozar. muffler n bufanda f.
mug [mʌg] n tazón m; (slang: face) jeta f; (slang: fool) primo, -a m, f. v asaltar. mugging n asalto m.
muggy ['mʌgi] adj bochornoso.
mulberry ['mʌlbəri] n (fruit) mora f; (tree) morera f, moral m.
mule¹ [mjuːl] n (animal) mulo, -a m, f. mulish adj testarudo.
mule² [mjuːl] n (slipper) babucha f.
multicoloured [ˌmʌltiˈkʌləd] adj multicolor.
multilingual [ˌmʌltiˈliŋgwəl] adj poligloto.
multiple ['mʌltipl] adj múltiple. n múltiplo m. multiple sclerosis esclerosis en placas f.
multiply ['mʌltiplai] v multiplicar. multiplication n multiplicación f. multiplication table tabla de multiplicar f.
multiracial [ˌmʌltiˈreiʃəl] adj multiracial.
multitude ['mʌltitjuːd] n multitud f, muchedumbre f.
mumble ['mʌmbl] v mascullar. n refunfuño m.
mummy¹ ['mʌmi] n momia f. mummification n momificación f. mummify v momificar.
mummy² ['mʌmi] n (coll: mother) mamá f.
mumps [mʌmps] n paperas f pl.
munch [mʌntʃ] v mascar.
mundane [mʌnˈdein] adj mundano.

municipal [mjuˈnisipəl] adj municipal. municipality n municipio m.
mural ['mjuərəl] nm, adj mural.
murder ['məːdə] n homicidio m, asesinato m. murderer n asesino m. murderess n asesina f. murderous adj homicida, asesino.
murky ['məːki] adj oscuro; lóbrego.
murmur ['məːmə] v murmurar. n murmullo m.
muscle ['mʌsl] n músculo m. v muscle in (coll) meterse por fuerza en. muscular adj muscular; (person) musculoso.
muse [mjuːz] n musa f. v meditar, contemplar.
museum [mjuˈziəm] n museo m.
mushroom ['mʌʃrum] n hongo m, seta f; (food) champiñón m. v crecer como hongos.
music {'mjuːzik] n música f. music hall music-hall m. music stand atril m. musical adj de música; (ear) musical; (person) aficionado a la música. musical (comedy) n comedia musical f. musical instrument instrumento de música m. musician n músico, -a m, f.
musk [mʌsk] n almizcle m.
musket ['mʌskit] n mosquete m. musketeer n mosquetero m.
Muslim ['mʌzlim] n, adj musulmán, -ana.
muslin ['mʌzlin] n muselina f.
mussel ['mʌsl] n mejillón m.
*must [mʌst] v deber; tener que.
mustard ['mʌstəd] n mostaza f. mustard pot mostacera f.
muster ['mʌstə] v reunir; (mil) formar. n reunión f; asamblea f; (mil) revista f. pass muster ser aceptable.
musty ['mʌsti] adj mohoso. smell musty oler a cerrado.
mute [mjuːt] n, adj mudo, -a; (music) sordina f. v apagar; poner sordina a. muted adj sordo.
mutilate ['mjuːtileit] v mutilar. mutilation n mutilación f.
mutiny ['mjuːtini] n motín m, rebelión f. v amotinarse, rebelarse. mutinous adj amotinado; (fig) rebelde.
mutter ['mʌtə] v murmurar. n murmullo m. muttering n refunfuño m.
mutton ['mʌtn] n cordero m.
mutual ['mjuːtʃuəl] adj mutuo; común.
muzzle ['mʌzl] n (nose) hocico m; (device) bozal m; (gun) boca f. v abozalar.

my [mai] *adj* mi (*pl* mis), mío, mía (*pl* míos, mías).
myself [mai'self] *pron* (*reflexive*) me; (*emphatic*) yo mismo, -a; (*after prep*) mí. **by myself** (completamente) solo, -a.
mystery ['mistəri] *n* misterio *m*. **mysterious** *adj* misterioso.
mystic ['mistik] *n* iniciado, -a *m*, *f*; místico, -a *m*, *f*. *adj also* **mystical** místico; esotérico; oculto; sobrenatural.
mystify ['mistifai] *v* oscurecer; desconcertar; desorientar; (*deceive*) engañar. **mystification** *n* mistificación *f*; complejidad *f*; confusión *f*.
mystique [mi'stiːk] *n* mística *f*.
myth [miθ] *n* mito *m*. **mythical** *adj* mítico. **mythological** *adj* mitológico. **mythology** *n* mitología *f*.

N

nag [nag] *v* regañar. *n* (*horse*) rocín *m*.
nail [neil] *n* (*metal*) clavo *m*; (*anat*) uña *f*; (*claw*) garra *f*. **nailbrush** *n* cepillo de uñas *m*. **nail-file** *n* lima de uñas *f*. **nail polish** esmalte de uñas *m*. **nail-scissors** *n* tijeras para las uñas *f pl*. *v* clavar.
naive [nai'iːv] *adj* ingenuo. **naivety** *n* ingenuidad *f*.
naked ['neikid] *adj* desnudo. **nakedness** *n* desnudez *f*.
name [neim] *n* nombre *m*; (*surname*) apellido *m*; fama *f*; título *m*. **my name is ...** me llamo .... **namesake** *n* tocayo, -a *m*, *f*. **what's your name?** ¿cómo se llama? *v* llamar; nombrar. **nameless** *adj* sin nombre; anónimo. **namely** *adv* a saber.
nanny ['nani] *n* niñera *f*.
nap¹ [nap] *n* sueño ligero *m*. *v* dormitar. **be caught napping** estar desprevenido.
nap² [nap] *n* (*of cloth*) lanilla *f*.
nape [neip] *n* nuca *f*.
napkin ['napkin] *n* servilleta *f*.
nappy ['napi] *n* pañal *m*.
narcotic [naɪ'kotic] *nm*, *adj* narcótico.
narrate [nə'reit] *v* contar. **narration** *n* narración *f*. **narrator** *n* narrador, -a *m*, *f*.
narrative ['narətiv] *n* narrativa *f*. *adj* narrativo.
narrow ['narou] *adj* estrecho. **narrow-gauge** *adj* de vía estrecha. **narrow-minded** *adj* de miras estrechas. *v* estrechar. **narrow down** reducir. **narrowly** *adv* (*only just*) por muy poco; estrechamente. **narrowness** *n* estrechez *f*.
nasal ['neizəl] *adj* nasal. **nasalize** *v* nasalizar.
nasturtium [nə'stəːtʃəm] *n* capuchina *f*.
nasty ['naɪsti] *adj* sucio; repugnante; (*unfriendly*) antipático; grosero; desagradable.
nation ['neiʃən] *n* nación *f*. **national** *nm*, *adj* nacional. **national anthem** himno nacional *m*. **nationalism** *n* nacionalismo *m*. **nationalist** *n*(*m*+*f*), *adj* nacionalista. **nationality** *n* nacionalidad *f*. **nationalization** *n* nacionalización *f*. **nationalize** *v* nacionalizar.
native ['neitiv] *adj* (*country, town*) natal; (*inhabitant*) nativo; (*language*) materno; (*product*) del país. *n* natural *m*, *f*; nativo, -a *m*, *f*.
nativity [nə'tivəti] *n* nacimiento *m*.
natural ['natʃərəl] *adj* natural. **naturalism** *n* naturalismo *m*. **naturalist** *n* naturalista *m*, *f*. **naturally** *adv* naturalmente; por naturaleza.
nature ['neitʃə] *n* naturaleza *f*; (*character*) natural *m*; esencia *f*.
naughty ['noɪti] *adj* travieso; malvado. **naughtiness** *n* travesura *f*.
nausea ['noɪziə] *n* náusea *f*. **nauseate** *v* dar asco.
nautical ['noɪtikəl] *adj* marítimo, náutico.
naval ['neivəl] *adj* naval; de marina. **naval officer** oficial de marina *m*.
navel ['neivəl] *n* ombligo *m*. **navel orange** naranja navel *f*.
navigate ['navigeit] *v* navegar; (*steer*) gobernar. **navigable** *adj* navegable. **navigation** *n* navegación *f*. **navigator** *n* navegante *m*.
navy ['neivi] *n* marina *f*. **navy blue** azul marino *m*.
near [niə] *adv* cerca. *prep* cerca de. *adj* cercano. *v* acercarse a; aproximarse a. **the near future** el futuro próximo. **nearby** *adv* cerca. **nearly** *adv* casi. **not nearly** ni con mucho. **very nearly** casi casi.
neat [niːt] *adj* limpio; bien cuidado; ordenado; (*drink*) solo. **neaten** *v* limpiar; ordenar. **neatly** *adv* con cuidado; (*dress*) con gusto; (*skilfully*) hábilmente. **neatness** *n* limpieza *f*; orden *m*; gusto *m*.

necessary ['nesisəri] *adj* necesario. **if necessary** si es preciso. **it is necessary** es preciso. **necessitate** *v* necesitar. **necessity** *n* necesidad *f.*

neck [nek] *n* (*human, garment*) cuello *m*; (*animal*) pescuezo *m*; (*bottle*) gollete *m.* **neck and neck** parejos. **necklace** *n* collar *m.*

nectar ['nektə] *n* néctar *m.*

need [niːd] *n* necesidad *f*; (*lack*) carencia *f. v* necesitar; hacer falta a uno. **needless** *adj* innecesario; inútil. **needy** *adj* necesitado. *n* **the needy** los necesitados *m pl.*

needle ['niːdl] *n* aguja *f.* **darning needle** aguja de zurcir. **knitting needle** aguja de hacer punto. **needlework** *n* costura *f. v* (*coll*) pinchar.

negative ['negətiv] *adj* negativo. *n* (*gramm*) negación *f*; (*phot*) negativo *m*; (*reply*) contestación negativa *f.*

neglect [ni'glekt] *v* no cumplir con; dejar de; no observar; descuidar; abandonar. *n* negligencia *f*; abandono *m*; inobservancia *f*; dejadez *f.* **neglected** *adj* descuidado; abandonado.

negligée ['negliʒei] *n* negligé *m.*

negligence ['neglidʒəns] *n* negligencia *f*; descuido *m.* **negligent** *adj* negligente; descuidado.

negotiate [ni'gouʃieit] *v* negociar; (*obstacle*) franquear; (*hill*) subir; (*bend*) tomar. **negotiable** *adj* negociable; franqueable. **negotiation** *n* negociación *f.*

Negro ['niːgrou] *nm, adj* negro.

neigh [nei] *v* relinchar. *n* relincho *m.*

neighbour ['neibə] *n* vecino, -a *m, f.* **neighbourhood** *n* vecindad *f*; (*district*) barrio *m.* **neighbouring** *adj* vecino; (*near*) cercano. **neighbourly** *adj* de buena vecindad.

neither ['naiðə] *adv* tampoco. **neither ... nor ...** ni ... ni .... *conj* ni, tampoco. *pron* ninguno, -a *m, f. adj* ninguno de los dos.

neon ['niːon] *n* neón *m.*

nephew ['nefjuː] *n* sobrino *m.*

nepotism ['nepətizəm] *n* nepotismo *m.*

nerve [nəːv] *n* nervio *m*; valor *m*; (*coll: cheek*) cara *f.* **get on someone's nerves** crisparle los nervios a uno. **lose one's nerve** (*coll*) rajarse. **nerve-wracking** *adj* crispante; horribilante. **nerves** *pl* (*coll*) nerviosismo *m.* **nervous** *adj* nervioso;

(*apprehensive*) miedoso. **nervous breakdown** depresión nerviosa *f.*

nest [nest] *n* nido *m. v* anidar.

nestle ['nesl] *v* arrellanarse; acurrucarse.

net¹ [net] *n* red *f.* **net curtains** visillo *m sing.* **network** *n* red *f. v* coger.

net² [net] *adj* neto. **net weight** peso neto *m.*

Netherlands ['neðələndz] *pl n* Países Bajos *m pl.*

nettle ['netl] *n* ortiga *f.* **nettle rash** urticaria *f. v* irritar.

neuralgia [nju'raldʒə] *n* neuralgia *f.* **neuralgic** *adj* neurálgico.

neurosis [nju'rousis] *n* neurosis *f.* **neurotic** *n, adj* neurótico, -a.

neuter ['njuːtə] *nm, adj* neutro.

neutral ['njuːtrəl] *adj* neutro. *n* (*mot*) punto muerto *m.* **neutrality** *n* neutralidad *f.* **neutralize** *v* neutralizar.

never ['nevə] *adv* nunca, jamás. **never-ending** *adj* sin fin. **nevermore** *adv* nunca más.

nevertheless [nevəðə'les] *adv* sin embargo, no obstante.

new [njuː] *adj* nuevo; fresco.

newcomer ['njuːkʌmə] *n* recién llegado, -a *m, f.*

new-born ['njuːbɔːn] *adj* recién nacido, -a *m, f.*

new-fangled ['njuːˌfaŋgəld] *adj* recién inventado.

new-laid [njuː'leid] *adj* (*egg*) recién puesto.

newly-wed ['njuːliˌwed] *adj* recién casado, -a *m, f.*

news [njuːz] *n* noticias *f pl*; actualidad *f*; (*radio*) diario hablado *m*; (*TV*) telediario *m*; (*film*) noticiario *m.* **news agency** agencia de información *f.* **newsagent** *n* vendedor de periódicos *m.* **news flash** noticia de última hora *f.* **news item** noticia *f.* **newsletter** *n* boletín *m.* **newspaper** *n* periódico *m*, diario *m.* **newsstand** *n* quiosco de periódicos *m.*

newt [njuːt] *n* tritón *m.*

New Testament *n* Nuevo Testamento *m.*

New Year *n* Año Nuevo *m.* **Happy New Year!** ¡feliz Año Nuevo! **New Year's Eve** nochevieja *f.*

New Zealand [njuː'ziːlənd] *n* Nueva Zelanda *f*, Nueva Zelandia *f.* **New Zealander** neocelandés, -esa *m, f*, neozelandés, -esa *m, f.*

next [nekst] *adj* próximo; siguiente; que viene; (*adjoining*) vecino. *adv* luego, después; la proxima vez; ahora. *prep* junto a, cerca de. **the next day** el día siguiente *m*. **next-door** *adj* de al lado. **next to** al lado de. **next-of-kin** *n* pariente más cercano *m*. **who's next?** ¿a quién le toca?

nib [nib] *n* plumilla *f*.

nibble ['nibl] *v* mordiscar, mordisquear. *n* mordisqueo *m*.

nice [nais] *adj* (*kind*) amable; (*agreeable*) agradable; (*likeable*) simpático; (*pretty*) bonito; (*pleasant*) ameno; precioso; escrupuloso; (*weather*) bueno; (*point*) delicado. **nicely** *adv* amablemente; agradablemente; bien. **nicety** *n* precisión *f*; delicadeza *f*.

niche [nitʃ] *n* nicho *m*, hornacina *f*.

nick [nik] *n* (*notch*) muesca *f*. (*cut*) rasguño *m*. **in the nick of time** justo a tiempo. *v* hacer muescas; cortar; (*slang: steal*) birlar; (*slang: arrest*) pescar.

nickel ['nikl] *n* niquel *m*.

nickname ['nikneim] *n* apodo *m*. *v* apodar.

nicotine ['nikətiɪn] *n* nicotina *f*.

niece [niɪs] *n* sobrina *f*.

niggle ['nigl] *v* ocuparse de menudencias. **niggling** *adj* de poca monta; molesto.

night [nait] *n* noche *f*. **good night!** ¡buenas noches! **last night** anoche *f*. **tomorrow night** mañana por la noche *f*.

night cap *n* (*garment*) gorro de dormir; (*coll: drink*) bebida tomada antes de acostarse *f*.

nightclub ['naitklʌb] *n* night club *m*.

nightdress ['naitdres] *n* camisón *m*, camisa de dormir *f*.

nightfall ['naitfoɪl] *n* anochecer *m*.

nightingale ['naitiŋ,geil] *n* ruiseñor *m*.

night-life ['naitlaif] *n* vida nocturna *f*.

night-light ['naitlait] *n* lamparilla *f*.

nightly ['naitli] *adj* nocturno. *adv* por las noches; todas las noches.

nightmare ['naitmeə] *n* pesadilla *f*.

night-school ['nait,skuɪl] *n* escuela nocturna *f*.

nightshade ['naitʃeid] *n* **deadly nightshade** belladona *f*.

night shift *n* turno de noche *m*.

night-watchman [,nait'wotʃmən] *n* guarda nocturno *m*; sereno *m*.

nil [nil] *n* nada *f*; ninguno, -a *m, f*; (*sport*) cero *m*.

nimble ['nimbl] *adj* ágil; (*mind*) vivo. **nimbleness** *n* agilidad *f*; vivacidad *f*.

nine [nain] *nm, adj* nueve. **dressed up to the nines** de punta en blanco. **ninth** *n, adj* noveno, -a.

nineteen [nain'tiɪn] *nm, adj* diecinueve. **nineteenth** *n, adj* decimonoveno, -a.

ninety ['nainti] *nm, adj* noventa. **ninetieth** *n, adj* nonagésimo, -a.

nip¹ [nip] *v* (*pinch*) pellizcar; (*bite*) morder; (*coll: go quickly*) pegar un salto. **nip in the bud** cortar de raíz. *n* pellizco *m*; mordisco *m*. **nippy** *adj* rápido; (*chilly*) fresquito.

nip² [nip] *n* (*drop*) gota *f*; (*drink*) trago *m*.

nipple ['nipl] *n* (*female*) pezón *m*; (*male*) tetilla *f*; (*bottle*) tetina *f*.

nit [nit] *n* liendre *f*; (*coll*) papanatas *m invar*.

nitrogen ['naitrədʒən] *n* nitrógeno *m*.

no [nou] *adv* no. *adj* ninguno. **no longer or more** ya no. **no parking** prohibido aparcar. **no smoking** prohibido fumar. **no thoroughfare** calle sin salida.

noble ['noubl] *n(m+f)*, *adj* noble. **nobility** *n* nobleza *f*.

nobody ['noubodi] *pron* nadie.

nocturnal [nok'təɪnəl] *adj* nocturno.

nod [nod] *v* inclinar; asentir con la cabeza; saludar con la cabeza; (*sleepily*) dar cabezadas. *n* inclinación de cabeza *f*; saludo con, la cabeza *m*; cabezada *f*.

noise [noiz] *n* ruido *m*. **noiseless** *adj* silencioso. **noisy** *adj* ruidoso.

nomad ['noumad] *n* nómada *m, f*. **nomadic** *adj* nómada.

nominal ['nominl] *adj* nominal.

nominate ['nomineit] *v* (*appoint*) nombrar; (*propose*) designar. **nomination** *n* nombramiento *m*, designación *f*.

nonchalant ['nonʃələnt] *adj* imperturbable; indiferente. **nonchalance** *n* imperturbabilidad *f*; indiferencia *f*.

nonconformist [nonkən'foɪmist] *n(m+f)*, *adj* disidente.

nondescript ['nondiskript] *adj* indescriptible.

none [nʌn] *pron* nadie; ninguno, -a. *adv* de ningún modo, de ninguna manera.

nonentity [non'entəti] *n* nulidad *f*.

nonetheless [,nʌnðə'les] *adv* sin embargo, no obstante.

non-existent [nonig'zistənt] *adj* inexistente.

non-fiction [non'fikʃən] *n* literatura no novelesca *f*.

non-resident [non'rezidənt] *n(m+f)*, *adj* no residente.

nonsense ['nonsəns] *n* tonterías *f pl*. **nonsensical** *adj* disparatado.

non-stop [non'stop] *adj* directo; continuo; sin escalas. *adv* sin parar; directamente.

noodles ['nuːdlz] *pl n* fideos *m pl*.

noon [nuːn] *n* mediodía *m*.

no-one ['nouwʌn] *pron* nadie.

noose [nuːs] *n* nudo corredizo *m*; lazo *m*; (*hangman's*) soga *f*.

nor [noɪ] *conj* ni; tampoco.

norm [noɪm] *n* norma *f*.

normal ['noɪməl] *adj* normal. *n* lo normal *m*.

north [noɪθ] *n* norte *m*. *adj also* **northerly, northern** del norte, norteño; (*facing north*) que da al norte. *adv* hacia el norte. **northbound** *adj* de dirección norte. **north-east** *nm*, *adj* nordeste. **north-west** *nm*, *adj* noroeste.

Norway ['noɪwei] *n* Noruega *f*. **Norwegian** *n*, *adj* noruego, -a.

nose [nouz] *n* nariz *f*; (*sense of smell*) olfato *m*; (*aircraft, car*) morro *m*. **blow one's nose** sonarse. **have a nosebleed** sangrar por la nariz. **nosey** *adj* (*coll*) entremetido.

nostalgia [no'staldʒə] *n* nostalgia *f*. **nostalgic** *adj* nostálgico.

nostril ['nostrəl] *n* ventamilla de la nariz *f*; (*horse*) ollar *m*. **nostrils** *pl n* narices *f pl*.

not [not] *adv* no; ni; como no; sin. **certainly not!** ¡de ninguna manera! **not at all** (*acknowledging thanks*) no hay de qué.

notable ['noutəbl] *adj* notable. **notably** *adv* notablemente, señaladamente.

notary ['noutəri] *n* notario *m*.

notch [notʃ] *n* (*cut*) muesca *f*; (*degree*) grado *m*. *v* hacer una muesca en.

note [nout] *n* nota *f*; (*key of piano, organ*) tecla *f*; (*sound*) sonido *m*; (*money*) billete *m*; (*music*) tono *m*; (*renown*) renombre *m*; marca. **notebook** *n* cuaderno *m*. **notepaper** papel de escribir *m*. **noteworthy** *adj* notable. *v* tomar nota de; darse cuenta de; anotar, apuntar. **noted** *adj* notable; célebre.

nothing ['nʌθiŋ] *pron* nada; no ... nada. *n* cero *m*. **nothing but** sólo.

notice ['noutis] *n* (*advert*) anuncio *m*; (*poster*) cartel *m*; (*sign*) letrero *m*; atención *f*; (*warning*) aviso *m*; (*dismissal*) despido *m*; (*resignation*) dimisión *f*. **notice-board** *n* tablón de anuncios *m*. **at short notice** a corto plazo. **notice to quit** desahucio *m*. *v* darse cuenta de; fijarse en; observar; ver; prestar atención. **noticeable** *adj* notable; evidente.

notify ['noutifai] *v* avisar, notificar.

notion ['nouʃən] *n* idea *f*, concepto *m*.

notorious [nou'toɪriəs] *adj* notorio. **notoriety** *n* notoriedad *f*.

notwithstanding [notwiθ'standiŋ] *prep* a pesar de. *adv* sin embargo. *conj* por más que.

nougat ['nuːgaɪ] *n* turrón de almendras *m*.

nought [noɪt] *n* cero *m*.

noun [naun] *n* nombre *m*, sustantivo *m*.

nourish ['nʌriʃ] *v* alimentar. **nourishing** *adj* alimenticio. **nourishment** *n* alimento *m*.

novel[1] ['novəl] *n* novela *f*. **novelist** *n* novelista *m*, *f*.

novel[2] ['novəl] *adj* nuevo; original. **novelty** *n* novedad *f*.

November [nə'vembə] *n* noviembre *m*.

novice ['novis] *n* novicio, -a *m*, *f*.

now [nau] *adv* ahora; ya; ya ahora; actualmente; inmediatamente. **from now on** de ahora en adelante. **nowadays** *adv* hoy día. **now and again** de vez en cuando. **up to now** hasta ahora.

nowhere ['nouweə] *adv* por ninguna parte; en ninguna parte; a ninguna parte.

noxious ['nokʃəs] *adj* nocivo.

nozzle ['nozl] *n* boca *f*, boquilla *f*.

nuance ['njuːãs] *n* matiz *m*.

nuclear ['njuːkliə] *adj* nuclear.

nucleus ['njuːkliəs] *n* núcleo *m*.

nude ['njuːd] *nm*, *adj* desnudo. **nudism** *n* nudismo *m*. **nudist** *n(m+f)*, *adj* nudista. **nudity** *n* desnudez *f*.

nudge [nʌdʒ] *v* dar un codazo a. *n* codazo *m*.

nugget ['nʌgit] *n* pepita *f*.

nuisance ['njuːsns] *n* (*thing*) molestia *f*; (*person*) molesta *f*. **be a nuisance** ponerse pesado. **what a nuisance!** (*coll*) ¡qué pesadez!

null [nʌl] *adj* nulo. **null and void** nulo y sin valor.

numb [nʌm] *adj* entumecido; (*with fear*) petrificado. *v* entumecer; dejar helado.

numbness *n* entumecimiento *m*; parálisis *f*.

number ['nʌmbə] *n* número *m*. **number plate** (*mot*) matricula *f*. *v* numerar; contar.

numeral ['njuːmərəl] *n* número *m*, cifra *f*.

numeration [ˌnjuːmə'reiʃn] *n* numeración *f*. **numerator** *n* numerador *m*.

numerical [njuː'merikl] *adj* numérico.

numerous ['njuːmərəs] *adj* numeroso.

nun [nʌn] *n* monja *f*.

nurse [nəːs] *n* enfermera *f*; (*nanny*) niñera *f*. *v* (*the sick*) cuidar; (*suckle*) criar; (*cradle*) mecer; (*hopes*) abrigar; (*plans*) acariciar. **nursing home** clínica *f*.

nursery ['nəːsəri] *n* (*room*) habitación de los niños *f*; (*day nursery*) guardería infantil *f*; (*plants*) vivero *m*. **nursery rhyme** poesía infantil *f*. **nursery school** escuela de párvulos *f*.

nurture ['nəːtʃə] *v* nutrir, alimentar; (*rear*) criar.

nut [nʌt] *n* (*bot*) nuez *f*; (*tech*) tuerca *f*; (*person*) loco, -a *m, f*. **in a nutshell** en pocas palabras. **nutcracker** *n*,cascanueces *m invar*. **nutmeg** *n* nuez moscada *f*.

nutrient ['njuːtriənt] *n* alimento nutritivo *m*.

nutrition [nju'triʃən] *n* nutrición *f*. **nutritious** *adj* nutritivo.

nuzzle ['nʌzl] *v* hocicar.

nylon ['nailon] *n* nilón *m*.

nymph [nimf] *n* ninfa *f*.

O

oak [ouk] *n* roble *m*.

oar [oː] *n* remo *m*. **oarsman** *n* remero *m*.

oasis [ou'eisis] *n* oasis *m invar*.

oath [ouθ] *n* (*law*) juramento *m*; (*expletive*) blasfemia *f*. **take the oath** prestar juramento.

oats [outs] *pl n* avena *f sing*. **oatmeal** *n* harina de avena *f*.

obedient [ə'biːdiənt] *adj* obediente. **obedience** *n* obediencia *f*.

obese [ə'biːs] *adj* obeso. **obesity** *n* obesidad *f*.

obey [ə'bei] *v* obedecer.

obituary [ə'bitjuəri] *n* necrología *f*.

object ['obʒikt; *v* əb'ʒekt] *n* objeto *m*;

(*gramm*) complemento *m*; (*aim*) meta *f*. *v* oponerse; objetar; protestar. **objection** *n* objeción *m*; reparo *m*. **objectionable** *adj* censurable; desagradable. **objective** *nm, adj* objetivo.

oblige [ə'blaidʒ] *v* (*compel*) obligar; (*please*) complacer; (*assist*) hacer un favor. **be obliged to** (*have to*) verse obligado a; (*be grateful*) estar agradecido a. **obligation** *n* obligación *f*; (*comm*) compromiso *m*. **obligatory** *adj* obligatorio.

oblique [ə'bliːk] *adj* sesgado; indirecto.

obliterate [ə'blitəreit] *v* borrar; cancelar. **obliteration** *n* borrado *m*; cancelación *f*.

oblivion [ə'bliviən] *n* olvido *m*. **oblivious** *adj* olvidadizo; ignorante.

oblong ['oblon] *adj* oblongo. *n* cuadrilongo *m*.

obnoxious [əb'nokʃəs] *adj* ofensivo; execrable.

oboe ['oubou] *n* oboe *m*. **oboist** *n* oboe *m*, oboísta *m, f*.

obscene [əb'siːn] *adj* obsceno. **obscenity** *n* obscenidad *f*.

obscure [əb'skjuə] *adj* oscuro; confuso. *v* oscurecer; (*hide*) esconder. **obscurity** *n* oscuridad *f*.

observe [əb'zəːv] *v* observar; ver; decir. **observant** *adj* observador; atento. **observation** *n* (*remark*) observación *f*; (*of rules*) observancia *f*. **observatory** *n* observatorio *m*.

obsess [əb'ses] *v* obsesionar. **obsession** *n* obsesión *f*.

obsolescent [obsə'lesnt] *adj* que cae en desuso. **obsolescence** *n* caída en desuso *f*.

obsolete ['obsəliːt] *adj* anticuado.

obstacle ['obstəkl] *n* obstáculo *m*.

obstetrics [ob'stetriks] *n* obstetricia *f*. **obstetrician** *n* tocólogo *m*.

obstinate ['obstinət] *adj* obstinado; terco; rebelde. **obstinacy** *n* obstinación *f*; terquedad *f*.

obstruct [əb'strʌkt] *v* obstruir; (*hinder*) estorbar. **obstruction** *n* obstrucción *f*; estorbo *m*.

obtain [əb'tein] *v* obtener, lograr; (*acquire*) adquirir; (*extract*) sacar.

obtrusive [əb'truːsiv] *adj* importuno, molesto; (*meddlesome*) entrometido. **obtrusion** *n* intrusión *f*.

obtuse [əb'tjuːs] *adj* obtuso.

obverse ['obvəːs] *n* anverso *m*. *adj* del anverso.

obvious ['obviəs] *adj* obvio.
occasion [ə'keiʒən] *n* ocasión *f*, oportunidad *f*; (*cause*) motivo *m*; circunstancia *f*. *v* ocasionar; incitar. **occasional** *adj* ocasional. **occasionally** *adv* de vez en cuando.
occult ['okʌlt] *adj* oculto. *n* **the occult** ciencias ocultas *f pl*.
occupy ['okjupai] *v* ocupar; emplear. **occupant** *n* (*place*) ocupante *m, f*; (*position*) posesor, -a *m, f*. **occupation** *n* ocupación *f*; profesión *f*; trabajo *m*. **occupational** *adj* profesional. **occupational hazard** gajes del oficio *m pl*.
occur [ə'kəɪ] *v* (*happen*) ocurrir, acontecer; producirse; (*opportunity*) presentarse; (*take place*) tener lugar. **occurrence** *n* acontecimiento *m*; caso *m*.
ocean ['ouʃən] *n* océano *m*. **oceanic** *adj* oceánico.
ochre ['oukə] *n* ocre *m*.
o'clock [ə'klok] *adv* **one o'clock** la una. **two/three/etc. o'clock** las dos/tres/etc.
octagon ['oktəgən] *n* octágono *m*. **octagonal** *adj* octagonal.
octane ['oktein] *n* octano *m*.
octave ['oktiv] *n* octava *f*.
October [ok'toubə] *n* octubre *m*.
octopus ['oktəpəs] *n* pulpo *m*.
oculist ['okjulist] *n* oculista *m, f*.
odd [od] *adj* extraño, raro; (number) impar; (*left over*) sobrante; (*occasional*) alguno. **odd jobs** pequeños arreglos *m pl*. **oddity** *n* (*thing*) curiosidad *f*; (*quality*) singularidad *f*. **oddment** *n* saldo *m*. **odds** *pl n* (*betting*) apuesta *f sing*; (*chances*) posibilidades *f pl*. **be at odds with** estar peleado con uno. **it makes no odds** no importa. **odds and ends** pedazos *m pl*.
ode [oud] *n* oda *f*.
odious ['oudiəs] *adj* odioso.
odour ['oudə] *n* olor *m*; perfume *m*. **odourless** *adj* inodoro.
oesophagus [iː'sofəgəs] *n* esófago *m*.
of [ov] *prep* de.
off [of] *adj* (*substandard*) malo; (*fruit, vegetables, meat, fish*) pasado; (*wine*) agriado; (*cancelled*) suspendido; (*elec*) apagado; (*water*) cortado; (*brake*) suelto. *prep* de; fuera de; a ... de; desde; en.
offal ['ofəl] *n* asadura *f*.
off-chance [,of'tʃaɪns] *n* **on the off-chance** (*coll*) por si acaso.
off-colour [of'kʌlə] *adj* **be off-colour** (*coll*) encontrarse indispuesto.

offend [ə'fend] *v* ofender; escandalizar; (*eyes, ears*) herir. **offence** *n* ofensa *f*; escándalo *m*; (*law*) delito *m*. **take offence** ofenderse por. **offender** *n* ofensor, -a *m, f*; delincuente *m, f*. **offensive** *adj* ofensivo; chocante; insultante.
offer ['ofə] *v* ofrecer; (*proposal*) proponer; presentarse. *n* oferta *f*; propuesta *f*. **offering** *n* (*action*) oferta *f*; (*gift*) regalo *m*.
offhand [of'hand] *adj* improvisado; brusco. *adv* sin pensarlo; bruscamente.
office ['ofis] *n* (*place*) oficina *f*; (*service*) oficio *m*; (*public office*) cargo *m*; (*function*) funciones *f pl*. **take office** entrar en funciones. **officer** *n* (*mil*) oficial *m*; (*public appointee*) funcionario, -a *m, f*; (*police*) policía *f*.
official [ə'fiʃəl] *adj* oficial. *n* funcionario, -a *m, f*.
officious [ə'fiʃəs] *adj* oficioso.
offing ['ofiŋ] *n* **in the offing** en perspectiva.
off-licence ['oflaisns] *n* bodega *f*.
off-peak [of'piːk] *adj, adv* de menos tráfico; (*elec*) de menor consumo.
off-season [of'siːzn] *n* estación muerta *f*. *adv, adj* fuera de temporada.
offset [of'set; *n* 'ofset] *v* compensar; desviar. *n* (*printing*) offset *m*.
offshore ['ofʃoɪ] *adj* de la costa.
offside [of'said] *n* (*mot: right*) lado derecho *m*; (*mot: left*) lado izquierdo *m*; (*sport*) fuera de juego *m*.
offspring ['ofspriŋ] *n* progenitura *f*; (*fig*) fruto *m*.
offstage ['ofsteidʒ] *adv, adj* entre bastidores.
off-the-cuff [ofðə'kʌf] *adj* espontáneo. *adv* de proviso.
off-white [of'wait] *adj* blancuzco.
often ['ofn] *adv* a menudo. **as often as not** la mitad de las veces. **every so often** alguna que otra vez.
ogre ['ougə] *n* ogro *m*.
oil [oil] *n* aceite *m*; petróleo *m*; (*painting*) óleo *m*; fuel *m*. **oily** *adj* (*tech*) grasiento; (*food*) aceitoso; (*skin*) graso; (*fig: manner*) zalamero.
oilcan ['oilkan] *n* aceitera *f*; (*for storage*) bidón de aceite *m*.
oilcloth ['oilkloθ] *n* hule *m*.
oil colour *n* óleo *m*.

oilfield ['oilfiːld] *n* yacimiento pertrolífero *m*.

oil-fired [oil'faiəd] *adj* alimentado con mazut.

oilskin ['oilˌskin] *n* impermeable de hule *m*.

oil stove *n* estufa de mazut *f*.

oil tanker *n* petrolero *m*.

oil well *n* pozo de petróleo *m*.

ointment ['ointmənt] *n* ungüento *m*.

O.K. [ou'kei] *interj* ¡de acuerdo!

old [ould] *adj* viejo; antiguo; (*adult*) mayor; (*clothes*) usado; (*wine*) añejo; (*other food*) pasado; (*familiar*) conocido. **I am six years old** tengo seis años. **how old is he?** ¿cuántos años tiene? **old age** vejez *f*. **old-age pensioner** pensionista *m*, *f*. **old-fashioned** *adj* chapado a la antigua; pasado de moda. **old maid** solterona *f*.

olive ['oliv] *n* (*fruit*) aceituna *f*, oliva *f*; (*tree*) olivo *m*. **olive green** *nm*, *adj* verde oliva *m*. **olive oil** aceite de oliva *m*.

Olympic [ə'limpik] *adj* olímpico. **Olympic Games** juegos olímpicos *m pl*.

omelette ['omlit] *n* tortilla *f*.

omen ['oumən] *n* presagio *m*, augurio *m*.

ominous ['ominəs] *adj* amenazador.

omit [ou'mit] *v* omitir; suprimir. **omission** *n* omisión *f*; olvido *m*.

omnipotent [om'nipətənt] *adj* omnipotente. **omnipotence** *n* omnipotencia *f*.

on [on] *pron* en, sobre; a. **oncoming** *adj* venidero. **onlooker** *n* espectador, -a *m*, *f*. **onset** *n* principio *m*; ataque *m*. **onshore** *adj* hacia la tierra. **onslaught** *n* ataque violento *m*. **onward(s)** *adj*, *adv* hacia adelante. **from now onwards** de ahora en adelante.

once [wʌns] *adv* una vez; (*formerly*) antes, hace tiempo. *conj* una vez que. **at once** en seguida. **once again** una vez más. **once and for all** de una vez para siempre.

one [wʌn] *n*, *pron*, *adj* uno, -a *m*, *f*. **be one up on** marcar un tanto a costa de. **one by one** uno por uno. **one-sided** *adj* parcial; desigual. **one-way** *adj* de dirección única. **that one** ése *or* aquél, ésa *or* aquélla. **this one** éste, ésta. **which one?** ¿cuál?

oneself [wʌn'self] *pron* se; sí; sí mismo, -a; (*emphatic*) uno mismo, una misma. **by oneself** solo, -a.

onion ['ʌnjən] *n* cebolla *f*.

only ['ounli] *adj* solo; único. *adv* sólo, solamente. *conj* pero, sólo que.

onus ['ounəs] *n* responsabilidad *f*.

onyx ['oniks] *n* ónice *m*, *f*.

ooze [uːz] *v* rezumar; exudar.

opal ['oupəl] *n* ópalo *m*.

opaque [ə'paik] *adj* opaco; oscuro. **opacity** *n* opacidad *f*; oscuridad *f*.

open ['oupən] *v* abrir; (*exhibition*) inaugurar; iniciar. *adj* abierto; (*unfolded*) desplegado; (*frank*) franco; (*meeting*) público; (*unsolved*) pendiente; (*post*) vacante; (*free*) libre; (*sea*) alta. **open-air** *adj* al aire libre. **open-handed** *adj* generoso. **open-minded** *adj* imparcial. **open-mouthed** *adj*, *adv* boquiabierto.

opening ['oupəniŋ] *n* abertura *f*; inauguración *f*; oportunidad *f*; vacante *f*; principio *m*; (*act of opening*) apertura *f*; (*breach*) brecha *f*. *adj* inaugural. **opening night** noche de estreno *f*.

opera ['opərə] *n* ópera *f*. **opera glasses** prismáticos *m pl*. **opera house** ópera *f*. **opera singer** cantante de ópera *m*, *f*. **operatic** *adj* operístico. **operetta** *n* opereta *f*, zarzuela *f*.

operate ['opəreit] *v* (*machine*) manejar; (hacer) funcionar; (*direct*) dirigir; (*med*) operar. **operable** *adj* operable. **operating table** quirófano *m*. **operation** *n* funcionamiento *m*; manejo *m*; maniobra *f*; aplicación *f*; actividad *f*. **in operation** en vigor; en funcionamiento. **operational** *adj* operacional. **operative** *adj* en vigor; operativo; eficaz. **operator** *n* operario, -a *m*, *f*; maquinista *m*, *f*; telefonista *m*, *f*; (*tour*) agente de viajes; (*wireless*) radiotelegrafista *m*.

ophthalmic [ofˈθalmik] *adj* oftálmico.

opinion [ə'pinjən] *n* opinión *f*. **in my opinion** a mi parecer. **public opinion poll** sondeo de la opinión pública *m*.

opium ['oupiəm] *n* opio *m*.

opponent [ə'pounənt] *n* adversario, -a *m*, *f*; contrario, -a *m*, *f*.

opportune [opə'tjuːn] *adj* oportuno. **opportunism** *n* oportunismo *m*. **opportunist** *n*(*m*+*f*), *adj* oportunista.

opportunity [opə'tjuːnəti] *n* oportunidad *f*.

oppose [ə'pouz] *v* oponerse a. **opposed** *adj* opuesto. **be opposed to** oponerse a. **opposition** *n* oposición *f*; resistencia *f*.

opposite ['opəzit] *adj* opuesto; contrario. **the opposite sex** el otro sexo. *prep*

enfrente de, frente a. *n* lo opuesto, lo contrario.
oppress [ə'pres] *v* oprimir. **oppression** *n* opresión *f*. **oppressive** *adj* opresor, opresivo; (*heat*) sofocante; (*mentally*) agobiante. **oppressor** *n* opresor, -a *m, f*.
opt [opt] *v* **opt out of** no meterse. **opt to** optar por.
optical ['optikl] *adj* óptico. **optical illusion** ilusión óptica *f*. **optician** *n* óptico *m*.
optimism ['optimizəm] *n* optimismo *m*. **optimist** *n* optimista *m, f*. **optimistic** *adj* optimista.
optimum ['optiməm] *adj* óptimo. *n* lo óptimo.
option ['opʃən] *n* opción *f*; posibilidad *f*; elección *f*. **optional** *adj* facultativo.
opulent ['opjulənt] *adj* opulento; abundante. **opulence** *n* opulencia *f*.
or [oɪ] *conj* o; (*negative*) ni. **or else** si no. **or not** o no.
oracle ['orəkl] *n* oráculo *m*.
oral ['oɪrəl] *nm, adj* oral.
orange ['orindʒ] *n* (*fruit*) naranja *f*; (*tree*) naranjo *m*; (*colour*) naranja *m*. *adj* naranja. **orangeade** *n* naranjada *f*.
orator ['orətə] *n* orador, -a *m, f*. **orate** *v* perorar. **oration** *n* oración *f*. **oratory** *n* oratoria *f*.
orbit ['oɪbit] *n* órbita *f*. *v* estar en órbita; dar vueltas.
orchard ['oɪtʃəd] *n* huerto *m*; (*apple*) manzanal *m*; (*pear*) peral *m*.
orchestra ['oɪkəstrə] *n* orquesta *f*. **orchestral** *adj* orquestal. **orchestrate** *v* orquestar. **orchestration** *n* orquestación *f*.
orchid ['oɪkid] *n* orquídea *f*.
ordain [oɪ'dein] *v* (*rel*) ordenar; (*fate*) destinar. **ordination** *n* ordenación *f*.
ordeal [oɪ'diːl] *n* sufrimiento *m*.
order ['oɪdə] *n* orden *m*; (*rel*) orden *f*; (*comm*) pedido *m*; (*medal*) condecoración *f*. **in order** (*correct*) en regla. **in order to** para. **out of order** no funcionar. *v* ordenar; organizar; clasificar; pedir; mandar.
orderly ['oɪdəli] *adj* ordenado; metódico; disciplinado. *n* (*mil*) ordenanza *m*.
ordinal ['oɪdinl] *adj* ordinal.
ordinary ['oɪdənəri] *adj* corriente, usual; (*mediocre*) ordinario; simple; (*average*) medio. *n* lo corriente, lo ordinario. **out of the ordinary** extraordinario, excepcional.
ore [oɪ] *n* mineral *m*.
oregano [ori'gaɪnou] *n* orégano *m*.

organ ['oɪgən] *n* órgano *m*. **organist** *n* organista *m, f*.
organic [oɪ'ganik] *adj* orgánico.
organism ['oɪgənizəm] *n* organismo *m*.
organize ['oɪgənaiz] *v* organizar. **organization** *n* organización *f*. **organizer** *n* organizador, -a *m, f*.
orgasm ['oɪgazəm] *n* orgasmo *m*.
orgy ['oɪdʒi] *n* orgía *f*.
oriental [oɪri'entl] *n(m+f)*, *adj* oriental.
orientate ['oɪriənteit] *v* orientar. **orientation** *n* orientación *f*.
orifice ['orifis] *n* orificio *m*.
origin ['oridʒin] *n* origen *m*. **originate** *v* originar, provocar; comenzar. **originate from** ser descendiente de. **originator** *n* autor, -a *m, f*; creador, -a *m, f*.
original [ə'ridʒinl] *adj* original; (*first*) primero. *n* original *m*. **originally** *adv* al principio; con originalidad.
ornament ['oɪnəmənt] *n* ornamento *m*, adorno *m*. *v* ornamentar, adornar. **ornamental** *adj* ornamental, de adorno.
ornate [oɪ'neit] *adj* recargado.
ornithology [oɪni'θolədʒi] *n* ornitología *f*. **ornithological** *adj* ornitológico. **ornithologist** *n* ornitólogo *m*.
orphan ['oɪfən] *n, adj* huérfano, -a. *v* dejar huérfano. **orphanage** *n* orfanato *m*.
orthodox ['oɪθədoks] *adj* ortodoxo. **orthodoxy** *n* ortodoxia *f*.
orthopaedic [oɪθə'piːdik] *adj* ortopédico.
oscillate ['osileit] *v* oscilar; fluctuar. **oscillation** *n* oscilación *f*; fluctuación *f*.
ostensible [o'stensəbl] *adj* aparente. **ostensibly** *adv* aparentemente.
ostentatious [osten'teiʃəs] *adj* ostentoso. **ostentation** *n* ostentación *f*.
osteopath ['ostiəpaθ] *n* osteópata *m, f*.
ostracize ['ostrəsaiz] *v* condenar al ostracismo. **ostracism** *n* ostracismo *m*.
ostrich ['ostritʃ] *n* avestruz *m*.
other ['ʌðə] *pron, adj* otro, -a. **other than** de otra manera que.
otherwise ['ʌðəwaiz] *adj* distinto. *adv* de otra manera; a parte de eso.
otter ['otə] *n* nutria *f*.
***ought** [oɪt] *v* deber; tener que.
our [auə] *pron* nuestro, -a; el nuestro, la nuestra. *adj* nuestro.
ours [auəz] *pron* nuestro, -a; el nuestro, la nuestra.
ourselves [auə'selvz] *pron* nos; nosotros, nosotras; (*emphatic*) nosotros mismos,

nosotras mismas. **by ourselves** solos, solas.

oust [aust] *v* expulsar, echar.

out [aut] *adj* fuera; (*light, fire, etc.*) apagado; (*games*) eliminado. **out loud** en voz alta. **out of** fuera de; (*through*) por; (*from*) de; (*without*) no tener, sin.

outboard ['autbɔɪd] *adj* fuera borda, fuera bordo.

outbreak ['autbreik] *n* (*start*) comienzo *m*; (*disease*) epidemia *f*; (*spots*) erupción *f*; (*violence, crime*) ola *f*; (*revolution*) motín *m*; (*temper*) arrebato *m*.

outbuilding ['autbildiŋ] *n* dependencia *f*.

outburst ['autbɜɪst] *n* explosión *f*; (*applause*) salvo *m*; (*temper*) arrebato *m*.

outcast ['autkaɪst] *n* proscrito, -a *m, f*; paria *m, f*.

outcome ['autkʌm] *n* resultado *m*; consecuencias *f pl*.

outcry ['autkrai] *n* (*noise*) alboroto *m*; protesta *f*.

*outdo [aut'duɪ] *v* superar.

outdoor ['autdɔɪ] *adj* al aire libre; (*clothes*) de calle. **outdoors** *adv* fuera; al aire libre.

outer ['autə] *adj* externo, exterior. **outer space** espacio exterior *m*.

outfit ['autfit] *n* (*gear*) equipo *m*; (*clothes*) ropa *f*; (*lady's costume*) conjunto *m*.

outgoing ['autgouiŋ] *adj* saliente; (*manner*) sociable. **outgoings** *pl n* gastos *m pl*.

*outgrow [aut'grou] *v* crecer más que; (*lose*) perder con la edad. **outgrowth** *n* excrecencia *f*.

outing ['autiŋ] *n* excursión *f*; paseo *m*.

outlandish [aut'landiʃ] *adj* extraño; apartado.

outlaw ['autlɔɪ] *n* proscrito, -a *m, f*. *v* proscribir; declarar ilegal.

outlay ['autlei] *n* gastos *m pl*.

outlet ['autlit] *n* salida *f*; (*drain*) desaguadero *m*; (*elec*) toma *f*; (*comm*) mercado *m*.

outline ['autlain] *n* contorno *m*; perfil *m*; silueta *f*; (*draft*) bosquejo *m*; (*summary*) resumen *m*; (*map*) trazado *m*; (*sketch*) esbozo *m*. *v* perfilar; bosquejar; resumir; trazar.

outlive [aut'liv] *v* sobrevivir.

outlook ['autluk] *n* vista *f*; punto de vista *m*.

outlying ['autlaiiŋ] *adj* exterior; remoto.

outnumber [aut'nʌmbə] *v* exceder en número.

out-of-date [autəv'deit] *adj* anticuado; pasado de moda.

outpatient ['autpeiʃənt] *n* paciente no internado *m*.

outpost ['autpoust] *n* puesto avanzado *m*.

output ['autput] *n* producción *f*; (*tech*) rendimiento *m*; (*power*) potencia *f*.

outrage ['autreidʒ] *n* ultraje *m*; desafuero *m*. *v* ultrajar.

outrageous [aut'reidʒəs] *adj* ultrajante; escandaloso.

outright [aut'rait; *adj* 'autrait] *adv* francamente; (*entirely*) en su totalidad; (*at once*) en el acto. *adj* completo; absoluto; categórico; franco.

outset ['autset] *n* principio *m*. **at the outset** al principio.

outside [aut'said; *adj* 'autsaid] *adv* fuera, afuera. *prep* fuera de; más allá de. *n* exterior *m*. *adj* exterior, externo; al aire libre; remoto; independiente. **outsider** *n* (*to a group*) intruso, -a *m, f*; (*to a place*) forastero, -a *m, f*; (*horse racing*) caballo no favorito *m*.

outsize ['autsaiz] *adj* de talla muy grande.

outskirts ['autskɜɪtz] *pl n* afueras *f pl*; cercanías *f pl*.

outspoken [aut'spoukən] *adj* franco. **outspokenness** *n* franqueza *f*.

outstanding [aut'standiŋ] *adj* destacado, notable; (*features*) sobresaliente; (*success*) excepcional; (*debt*) pendiente; (*still to be done*) por hacer.

outstrip [aut'strip] *v* dejar atrás.

outward ['autwəd] *adj* exterior; (*journey*) de ida. **outward bound** que sale. **outwardly** *adv* exteriormente; aparentemente. **outwards** *adv* hacia fuera.

outweigh [aut'wei] *v* pesar más que; (*value*) valer más que.

outwit [aut'wit] *v* burlar.

oval ['ouvəl] *adj* oval, ovalado. *n* óvalo *m*.

ovary ['ouvəri] *n* ovario *m*.

ovation [ou'veiʃən] *n* ovación *f*.

oven ['ʌvn] *n* horno *m*. **ovenproof** *adj* de horno.

over ['ouvə] *adv* encima, por encima; (*too much*) demasiado; al otro lado. *adj* (*finished*) terminado. *prep* sobre, encima de; al otro lado de; superior a; durante.

overall ['ouvərɔɪl] *adj* de conjunto; total. *adv* en conjunto; por todas partes. **overalls** *pl n* guardapolvo *m sing*.

overbalance [ouvə'baləns] *v* (hacer) perder el equilibrio.

overbearing [ouvə'beəriŋ] *adj* dominante, autoritario.

overboard ['ouvəbɔɪd] *adv* (*fall*) por la borda. **go overboard** (*coll*) pasarse de la raya. **man overboard!** ¡hombre al agua!

overcast [ouvə'kaɪst] *adj* nublado.

overcharge [ouvə'tʃaɪdʒ] *v* cobrar un precio excesivo; (*overload*) sobrecargar.

overcoat ['ouvəkout] *n* abrigo *m*, sobretodo *m*.

***overcome** [ouvə'kʌm] *v* vencer; triunfar. **be overcome by** estar muerto de.

overcrowded [ouvə'kraudid] *adj* atestado; superpoblado. **overcrowding** *n* atestamiento *m*; superpoblación *f*.

***overdo** [ouvə'duɪ] *v* exagerar; (*exhaust*) fatigarse demasiado.

overdose ['ouvədous] *n* dosis excesiva *f*.

overdraft ['ouvədraɪft] *n* giro en descubierto *m*.

***overdraw** [ouvə'drɔɪ] *v* girar en descubierto. **be overdrawn** *adj* tener un descubierto en su cuenta.

overdue [ouvə'djuɪ] *adj* (*train*, *etc*.) atrasado; (*comm*) vencido y sin pagar.

overestimate [ouvə'estimeit] *v* sobreestimar.

overexpose [ouvəik'spouz] *v* (*phot*) sobreexponer.

overflow [ouvə'flou; *n* 'ouvəflou] *v* (*flow over*) derramarse; (*flood*) inundar. *n* desbordamiento *m*; derrame *m*; inundación *f*; (*pipe*) cañería de desagüe *f*.

overgrown [ouvə'groun] *adj* cubierto de hierba; (*too big*) demasiado crecido para su edad.

***overhang** [ouvə'haŋ; *n* 'ouvəhaŋ] *v* sobresalir. *n* saliente *m*. **overhanging** *adj* saliente, sobresaliente.

overhaul [ouvə'hɔɪl] *v* investigar; revisar. *n* examen *m*, revisión *f*; arreglo *m*.

overhead [ouvə'hed] *adv* arriba. *adj* de arriba. **overheads** *pl n* gastos generales *m pl*.

***overhear** [ouvə'hiə] *v* oír (por casualidad); sorprender.

overheat [ouvə'hiɪt] *v* recalorar; (*fig*) acalorar.

overjoyed [ouvə'dʒɔid] *adj* contentísimo.

overland [ouvə'land] *adv* por vía terrestre. *adj* terrestre.

overlap [ouvə'lap; *n* 'ouvəlap] *v* traslapar. *n* traslapo *m*.

***overlay** [ouvə'lei; *n* 'ouvəlei] *v* revestir. *n* revestimiento *m*; cubierta *f*.

overleaf [ouvə'liɪf] *adv* a la vuelta.

overload [ouvə'loud; *n* 'ouvəloud] *v* sobrecargar. *n* sobrecarga *f*.

overlook [ouvə'luk] *v* (*miss*) no notar; (*ignore*) no darse cuenta de; (*excuse*) perdonar; (*command a view*) dar a; dominar.

overnight [ouvə'nait] *adv* (*during the night*) por la noche; (*suddenly*) de la noche a la mañana. **stay overnight** pasar la noche. *adj* (*journey*) de noche; (*stay*) por una noche.

overpower [ouvə'pauə] *v* subyugar; (*smell*, *etc*.) trastornar; dominar. **overpowering** *adj* (*desire*) irresistible; abrumador.

overrated [ouvə'reitid] *adj* sobreestimado.

***override** [ouvə'raid] *v* (*ride over*) pasar por encima de; dominar; (*fig*) anular, rechazar. **overriding** *adj* principal.

overrule [ouvə'ruɪl] *v* denegar, no admitir.

***overrun** [ouvə'rʌn] *v* (*exceed*) rebasar; (*overflow*) derramarse; (*invade*) invadir; (*flood*) inundar; (*infest*) plagar.

overseas [ouvə'siɪz] *adv* en ultramar. *adj* de ultramar; (*foreign*) extranjero; (*comm*) exterior.

overseer [ouvə'siə] *n* capataz *m*; inspector, -a *m, f*.

overshadow [ouvə'ʃadou] *v* sombrear; (*fig*) eclipsar.

***overshoot** [ouvə'ʃuɪt] *v* ir más allá de.

oversight ['ouvəsait] *n* descuido *m*; omisión *f*. **through an oversight** por descuido.

***oversleep** [ouvə'sliɪp] *v* dormir demasiado.

overspill ['ouvəspil] *n* exceso *m*.

overt [ou'vəɪt] *adj* abierto; manifiesto. **overtly** *adv* evidentemente.

***overtake** [ouvə'teik] *v* (*pass*) adelantar; (*catch up*) alcanzar.

***overthrow** [ouvə'θrou; *n* 'ouvəθrou] *v* (*overturn*) volcar; (*plans*) desbaratar; (*government*) derrocar; (*empire*) derrumbar. *n* desbaratamiento *m*; derrocamiento *m*; derrumbamiento *m*.

overtime ['ouvətaim] *n* horas extraordinarias *f pl*.

overtone ['ouvətoun] *n* (*music*) armónico *m*; (*fig*) alusión *f*.

overture ['ouvətjuə] *n* (*music*) obertura *f*; (*proposal*) propuesta *f*.

overturn [ouvə'təɪn] v (*car*) volcar; (*government, etc.*) derrocar.
overweight [ouvə'weit] adj **be overweight** pesar demasiado.
overwhelm [ouvə'welm] v (*conquer*) vencer; (*with grief*) postrar; (*work*) inundar; (*in argument*) confundir; (*joy*) rebosar. **overwhelming** adj (*desire*) irresistible; (*defeat*) aplastante; (*work*) abrumador.
overwork [ouvə'wəɪk] v usar demasiado; hacer trabajar demasiado. n exceso de trabajo m.
overwrought [ouvə'rɔɪt] adj sobreexcitado, nerviosísimo.
ovulation [ovju'leiʃn] n ovulación f.
owe [ou] v deber; tener deudas. **owing** adj que se debe. **owing to** debido a.
owl [aul] n lechuza f.
own [oun] v tener, poseer; (*acknowledge*) reconocer. **own up** confesar. adj propio. **get one's own back** desquitarse. **on one's own** solo, sola. **owner** n dueño, -a m, f; poseedor, -a m, f. **ownership** n propiedad f; posesión f.
ox [oks] n, pl **oxen** buey m. **oxtail** n rabo de buey m.
oxygen ['oksidʒən] n oxígeno m. **oxygen tent** cámara de oxígeno f.
oyster ['oistə] n ostra f.

P

pace [peis] n paso m; (*gait*) andar m; (*horse*) andadura f; (*speed*) velocidad f. **keep pace with** ajustarse al paso de; (*events*) mantenerse al corriente de. v andar; recorrer. **pace up and down** dar vueltas.
pacific [pə'sifik] adj pacífico.
Pacific Ocean n Océano Pacífico m.
pacifism ['pasifizəm] n pacifismo m. **pacifist** n(m+f), adj pacifista.
pacify ['pasifai] v pacificar; calmar.
pack [pak] n (*gang*) partida f; (*hounds*) jauría f; (*cards*) baraja f; (*bundle*) bulto m; (*med*) paño m, compresa f. **packhorse** n caballo de carga m. v embalar; envasar; (*suitcase*) hacer; (*cram*) apretar. **pack it in** (*coll*) dejarlo. **packing** n embalaje m; envase m.

package ['pakidʒ] n paquete m; (*bundle*) fardo m. adj (*deal*) acuerdo global m; (*holiday, tour*) viaje todo comprendido m. v embalar; envasar.
packet ['pakit] n paquete m; (*tea, etc.*) sobre m; (*cigarettes*) cajetilla f.
pact [pakt] n pacto m.
pad[1] [pad] n (*paper*) bloc m; (*blotting*) carpeta f; (*ink*) tampón m; (*cushion*) almohadilla f; (*launching*) plataforma de lanzamiento f. v acolchar; rellenar. **pad out** (*coll*) meter paja en. **padding** n acolchado m; relleno m; (*fig*) paja f.
pad[2] [pad] v andar a pasos quedos.
paddle[1] ['padl] n (*oar*) canalete m; (*waterwheel*) álabe m. **paddle boat** or **steamer** vapor de ruedas m. v remar con canalete.
paddle[2] ['padl] n (*wade*) chapotear.
paddock ['padək] n paddock m.
padlock ['padlok] n candado m. v cerrar con candado.
paediatric [piɪdi'atrik] adj pediátrico.
paediatrician n pediatra m, pediatra m.
paediatrics n pediatría f.
pagan ['peigən] n, adj pagano, -a.
page[1] [peidʒ] n (*book*) página f.
page[2] [peidʒ] n also **page-boy** (*hotel*) botones m invar; (*court, wedding*) paje m. v (*person*) hacer llamar por un paje.
pageant ['padʒənt] n desfile histórico m. **pageantry** n aparato m, pompa f.
paid [peid] V **pay**.
pail [peil] n cubo m.
pain [pein] n dolor m. **painkiller** n calmante m. **pains** pl n (*effort*) esfuerzo m. **painstaking** adj concienzudo; cuidadoso. v doler; afligir. **painful** adj doloroso; (*embarrassing*) difícil. **painless** adj sin dolor; (*easy*) fácil.
paint [peint] n pintura f. **paintbox** n caja de pinturas f. **paintbrush** (*artist*) pincel m; (*house painter*) brocha f. **paint roller** rodillo m. v pintar; (*fig*) describir. **painter** n pintor, -a m, f. **painting** n pintura f; (*picture*) cuadro m.
pair [peə] n (*objects*) par m; (*people, animals*) pareja f; (*oxen*) yunta f; (*horses*) tronco m. v (*socks, etc.*) emparejar; (*mate*) aparearse. **pair off** (*people*) formar pareja.
pal [pal] n (*coll*) amigote m; camarada m, f.
palace ['paləs] n palacio m. **palatial** adj magnífico; suntuoso.

palate ['palit] *n* paladar *m*. **palatable** *adj* sabroso; (*fig*) agradable.
pale [peil] *adj* pálido. *v* palidecer. **paleness** *n* palidez *f*.
palette ['palit] *n* paleta *f*.
pall¹ [poːl] *v* perder el sabor; aburrirse (de).
pall² [poːl] *n* paño mortuorio *m*; (*smoke*) cortina *f*; (*snow*) capa *f*.
pallid ['palid] *adj* pálido.
palm¹ [paːm] *n* (*hand*) palma *f*. **palm off** (*coll*) colar. **palmist** *n* quiromántico, -a *m*, *f*. **palmistry** *n* quiromancia *f*.
palm² [paːm] *n* (*tree*) palma *f*, palmera *f*.
palpitate ['palpiteit] *v* palpitar. **palpitation** *n* palpitación *f*.
paltry ['poːltri] *adj* miserable.
pamper ['pampə] *v* mimar.
pamphlet ['pamflit] *n* folleto *m*.
pan [pan] *n* cacerola *f*.
Panama [panə'maː] *n* Panamá *m*. **Panama City** *n* Panamá.
pancake ['pankeik] *n* pancake *m*. **Pancake Tuesday** martes de carnaval.
pancreas ['paŋkriəs] *n* páncreas *m*. **pancreatic** *adj* pancreático.
panda ['pandə] *n* panda *m*.
pandemonium [pandi'mouniəm] *n* pandemonio *m*.
pander ['pandə] *v* **pander to** complacer.
pane [pein] *n* vidrio *m*, cristal *m*.
panel ['panl] *n* (*door*) panel *m*; (*wall*) lienzo *m*; (*dress*) paño *m*; (*control*) tablero *m*; (*experts*) grupo *m*; (*judges*) jurado *m*. *v* revestir con paneles; artesonar. **panelist** *n* miembro del jurado *m*. **panelling** *n* revestimiento de madera *m*; artesonado *m*.
pang [paŋ] *n* (*pain, hunger*) punzada *f*; (*jealousy*) angustia *f*; (*love*) herida *f*; (*conscience*) remordimiento *m*.
panic ['panik] *n* pánico *m*. **panic-stricken** *adj* preso de pánico. *v* asustarse.
panorama [,panə'raːmə] *n* panorama *m*. **panoramic** *adj* panorámico.
pansy ['panzi] *n* pensamiento *m*.
pant [pant] *v* jadear. *n* jadeo *m*.
panther ['panθə] *n* pantera *f*.
pantomime ['pantəmaim] *n* (*mime*) pantomima *f*.
pantry ['pantri] *n* despensa *f*.
pants [pants] *pl n* (*underpants*) calzoncillos *m pl*; (*coll: trousers*) pantalones *m pl*.
papal ['peipl] *adj* papal.

paper ['peipə] *n* papel *m*; (*news*) periódico *m*, diario *m*; (*blotting*) papel secante *m*; (*brown*) papel de estraza *m*; (*carbon*) papel carbón *m*; (*drawing*) papel de dibujo *m*; (*greaseproof*) papel vegetal *m*; (*tissue*) papel de seda *m*; (*toilet*) papel higiénico *m*; (*writing*) papel de escribir *m*; (*identity*) documentación *f*. *v* (*walls*) empapelar.
paperback ['peipəbak] *n* libro en rústica *m*.
paper bag *n* saco de papel *m*.
paper-boy *n* repartidor de periódicos *m*.
paper-clip *n* sujetapapeles *m invar*.
paper-knife *n* cortapapeles *m invar*.
paper-mill *n* fábrica de papel *f*.
paper shop *n* (*coll*) vendedor de periódicos *m*.
paperweight ['peipəweit] *n* pisapapeles *m invar*.
paperwork ['peipəwəːk] *n* papeleo *m*.
paprika ['paprikə] *n* paprika *f*.
par [paː] *n* igualdad *f*; (*comm*) par *f*; (*golf*) recorrido normal *m*. **be on a par with** correr parejas con. **feel below par** (*coll*) no sentirse bien.
parable ['parəbl] *n* parábola *f*.
parachute ['parəʃuːt] *n* paracaídas *m invar*. *v* saltar con paracaídas. **parachutist** *n* paracaidista *m*, *f*.
parade [pə'reid] *n* alarde *m*; (*mil*) desfile *m*; (*promenade*) paseo público *m*. *v* (*display*) hacer alarde de; hacer desfilar; (*placard*) pasear.
paradise ['parədais] *n* paraíso *m*.
paradox ['parədoks] *n* paradoja *f*. **paradoxical** *adj* paradójico.
paraffin ['parəfin] *n* (*solid*) parafina *f*; (*fuel*) petróleo *m*.
paragraph ['parəgraːf] *m* párrafo *m*. **new paragraph** punto y aparte.
parallel ['parəlel] *adj* paralelo. *n* paralela *f*. **parallelogram** *n* paralelogramo *m*.
paralyse ['parəlaiz] *v* paralizar. **paralysis** *n* parálisis *f*. **paralytic** *n*, *adj* paralítico, -a. *adj* (*coll: drunk*) como una cuba.
paramilitary [,parə'militəri] *adj* paramilitar.
paramount ['parəmaunt] *adj* supremo.
paranoia [,parə'noiə] *n* paranoia *f*. **paranoid** *n*, *adj* paranoico, -a.
parapet ['parəpit] *n* parapeto *m*.
paraphernalia [,parəfə'neiliə] *n* avíos *m pl*.

paraphrase ['parəfreiz] *n* paráfrasis *f. v* parafrasear.
paraplegic [ˌparə'pliːdʒik] *n, adj* parapléjico, -a.
parasite ['parəsait] *n* parásito *m.* **parasitic** *adj* parasito.
parasol ['parəsol] *n* parasol *m.*
paratrooper ['parəˌtruːpə] *n* soldado paracaidista *m.*
parcel ['paɪsəl] *n* paquete *m;* (*portion*) parcela *f.* **parcel office** despacho de paquetes *m.* **parcel post** servicio de paquetes *m. v also* **parcel up** empaquetar.
parch [paɪtʃ] *v* (*land*) resecar; (*person*) abrasar; **be parched with thirst** abrasarse de sed.
parchment ['paɪtʃmənt] *n* pergamino *m.*
pardon ['paɪdn] *n* perdón *m;* (*law*) indulto *m;* (*rel*) indulgencia *f. v* perdonar; disculpar; indultar. **pardon?** ¿cómo? **I beg your pardon** dispénseme.
pare [peə] *v* reducir; (*vegetables*) pelar; (*fruit*) mondar.
parent ['peərənt] *n* padre, madre *m, f.* **parents** *pl n* padres *m pl.* **parental** *adj* de los padres. **parenthood** *n* paternidad *f,* maternidad *f.*
parenthesis [pə'renθəsis] *n* paréntesis *m invar.* **in parentheses** entre paréntesis.
Paris ['paris] *n* París.
parish ['pariʃ] *n* parroquia *f;* (*civil*) municipio *m.* **parish church** iglesia parroquial *f.* **parishioner** *n* parroquiano, -a *m, f.*
parity ['pariti] *n* paridad *f.*
park [paɪk] *n* parque (público) *m.* **car park** aparcamiento de coches *m. v* aparcar. **parking** *n* estacionamiento *m.* **parking meter** parcómetro *m.* **parking ticket** multa por aparcamiento indebido *f.*
parliament ['paɪləmənt] *n* parlamento *m.* **parliamentary** *adj* parlamentario.
parlour ['paɪlə] *n* salón *m;* sala de recibir *f.*
parochial [pə'roukiəl] *adj* parroquial; (*derog*) pueblerino.
parody ['parədi] *n* parodia *f. v* parodiar.
parole [pə'roul] *n* libertad bajo palabra *f.*
paroxysm ['parəksizəm] *n* paroxismo *m;* (*joy, anger, etc.*) ataque *m.*
parrot ['parət] *n* loro *m.* **parrot fashion** como un loro.
parsley ['paɪsli] *n* perejil *m.*
parsnip ['paɪsnip] *n* pastinaca *f.*

parson ['paɪsn] *n* (*priest*) cura *m;* (*Protestant*) pastor *m.* **parsonage** *n* casa del cura *f.*
part [paɪt] *n* parte *f;* (*role*) papel *m;* (*tech*) pieza *f.* **on my part** di mi parte. **part exchange** cambio de un objeto por otro pagando la diferencia. **part-time** *adv* a media jornada; *adj* de media jornada. *v* dividir; separar; (*leave*) despedirse. **part one's hair** hacerse la raya. **part with** tener que separarse de. **parting** *n* separación *f;* despedida *f;* (*hair*) raya *f.* **partly** *adv* en parte.
*** partake** [paɪteik] *v* **partake of** compartir.
partial ['paɪʃəl] *adj* parcial. **be partial to** ser aficionado a. **partiality** *n* parcialidad *f;* inclinación *f.*
participate [paɪ'tisipeit] *v* participar. **participant** *n* partícipe *m, f.* **participation** *n* participación *f.*
participle ['paɪtisipl] *n* participio *m.*
particle ['paɪtikl] *n* partícula *f;* (*dust, etc.*) grano *m;* (*fig*) pizca *f.*
particular [pə'tikjulə] *adj* particular; detallado; exigente. *n* detalle *m.* **in particular** particularmente. **I'm not particular** me da igual. **full particulars** información completa *f.*
partisan [paɪti'zan] *n* partidario, -a *m, f;* (*mil*) guerrillero *m.* **partisanship** *n* partidismo *m.*
partition [paɪ'tiʃən] *n* división *f;* (*section*) parte *f. v* dividir; repartir.
partner ['paɪtnə] *n* (*comm*) asociado, -a *m, f,* socio, -a *m, f;* (*dancing*) pareja *f;* (*cards, etc.*) compañero, -a *m, f;* (*marriage*) cónyuge *m, f. v* asociarse con; ser pareja de. **partnership** *n* asociación *f;* (*firm*) sociedad *f.* **go into partnership with** asociarse con.
partridge ['paɪtridʒ] *n* perdiz *f.*
party ['paɪti] *n* (*pol*) partido *m;* (*law*) parte *f;* (*reception*) fiesta *f;* (*gathering*) reunión *f.* **party line** (*phone*) línea telefónica compartida entre abonados *f;* (*pol*) línea política del partido *f.*
pass [paɪs] *v* pasar; (*exam*) aprobar; (*be acceptable*) aceptarse. **pass away** *or* **on** (*die*) pasar a mejor vida. **pass out** (*faint*) desmayarse. **pass round** (*detour*) dar la vuelta a; (*distribute*) pasar de mano en mano. **pass up** (*decline*) rechazar. *n* (*permit*) pase *m;* (*exam*) aprobado *m;* (*mountain*) desfiladero *m;* (*sport*) pase *m.*

passage ['pasidʒ] n (way) pasaje m; (alley) callejón m; (house) corredor m; (time) paso m; (literature) trozo m; (bill) aprobación f; (sea voyage) travesía f.

passenger ['pasindʒə] n pasajero, -a m, f.

passer-by [ˌpaɪsəˈbai] n transeúnte m, f.

passion ['paʃən] n pasión f; (anger) cólera f. **passionate** adj apasionado; colérico.

passive ['pasiv] adj pasivo. n (gramm) voz pasiva f. **passiveness** also **passivity** n pasividad f.

Passover ['paɪsouvə] n pascua (de los Judíos) f.

passport ['paɪspoɪt] n pasaporte m.

password ['paɪswɔɪd] n contraseña f.

past [paɪst] nm, adj pasado. prep por delante de; (beyond) más allá de; (time) más de. **twenty past nine** las nueve y veinte. **go past** pasar.

pasta ['pastə] n pastas f pl.

paste [peist] n (meat) pasta f; (glue) engrudo m; (jewellery) estrás m. v pegar.

pastel ['pastəl] n pastel m.

pasteurize ['pastʃəraiz] v pasteurizar. **pasteurization** n pasteurización f.

pastime ['paɪstaim] n pasatiempo m.

pastoral ['paɪstərəl] adj pastoril; (rel) pastoral.

pastry ['peistri] n (dough) pasta f; (cakes) pasteles m pl. **puff pastry** hojaldre m. **pastry-cook** n pastelero m.

pasture ['paɪstʃə] n (grass) pasto m; (field) prado m. v apacentar.

pasty¹ ['peisti] adj pastoso; (face) pálido.

pasty² ['pasti] n empanada f.

pat [pat] v dar palmaditas; (a pet) acariciar. n palmadita f; caricia f; (of butter) porción f. adj adecuado. adv oportunamente.

patch [patʃ] n (clothes) pieza f, remiendo m; (for puncture, wound, etc.) parche m; (land) parcela f. **patchwork** n labor de retazos m. v remendar; poner un parche. **patchy** adj desigual.

patent ['peitənt] adj patente, evidente; patentado. **patent leather** charol m. v patentar. n patente f. **patently** adv evidentemente.

paternal [pəˈtɔɪnl] adj paterno, paternal. **paternity** n paternidad f.

path [paɪθ] n (way) camino m, sendero m; (star, sun) curso m.

pathetic [pəˈθetik] adj patético.

pathology [pəˈθolədʒi] n patología f. **pathological** adj patológico. **pathologist** n patólogo m.

patient ['peiʃənt] adj paciente. n enfermo, -a m, f. **patience** n paciencia f; (game) solitario m.

patio ['patiou] n patio m.

patriarchal ['peitriaɪkəl] adj patriarcal.

patriot ['patriət] n patriota m, f. **patriotic** adj patriótico. **patriotism** n patriotismo m.

patrol [pəˈtroul] n patrulla f. **patrol car** coche patrulla m. v patrullar.

patron ['peitrən] n patrocinador, -a m, f; (saint) patrón, -ona m, f, patrono m; (arts) mecenas m; (customer) cliente m, f. **patronage** n (sponsorship) patrocinio m; (royal) patronato m. **patronize** v (comm) patrocinar; (arts) fomentar; (artist) proteger; (be condescending) tratar con condescencia. **patronizing** adj de superioridad.

patter¹ ['patə] v (rain) repiquetear; (footsteps) corretear. n golpecitos m pl; repiqueteo m.

patter² ['patə] n (salesman) charlatanería f. v chapurrear.

pattern ['patən] n (design) dibujo m; (needlework) patrón m; (sample) muestra f; (example) ejemplo m. v diseñar; (cloth) estampar. **patterned** adj adornado con dibujos.

paunch [poɪntʃ] n panza f, barriga f.

pauper ['poɪpə] n pobre m, f.

pause [poɪz] n pausa f; silencio m. v hacer una pausa; descansar; vacilar; pararse.

pave [peiv] v empedrar, enlosar. **pave the way for** facilitar el paso de. **pavement** n acera f. **paving** n pavimento m. **paving stone** adoquín m.

pavilion [pəˈviljən] n pabellón m.

paw [poɪ] n pata f; (cat) garra f. v tocar con la pata; (coll) manosear.

pawn¹ [poɪn] v empeñar. n prenda f. **pawnbroker** n prestanista m, f. **pawnshop** n casa de empeños f.

pawn² [poɪn] n peón m.

***pay** [pei] v pagar; dar; (compliment, visit) hacer; (attention) prestar. **pay back** (money) reembolsar; (avenge) devolver. **pay in** ingresar. **pay off** (debt) saldar; (creditor) reembolsar; (mortgage) redimir; (be worthwhile) merecer la pena; (be fruitful) dar resultado. n paga f;

salario *m*. **pay-as-you-earn** *n* deducción del sueldo para los impuestos *f*. **payday** *n* día de paga *m*. **pay rise** aumento de sueldo *m*. **pay-roll** *n* nómina *f*. **pay-slip** *n* hoja de paga *f*. **payable** *adj* pagadero. **payee** *n* beneficiario, -a *m*, *f*. **payment** *n* pago *m*; recompensa *f*.

pea [piː] *n* guisante *m*.

peace [piːs] *n* paz *f*. **peacemaker** *n* pacificador, -a *m*, *f*. **peace offering** sacrificio propiciatorio *m*. **peaceful** *adj* pacífico.

peach [piːtʃ] *n* (*fruit*) melocotón *m*; (*tree*) melocotonero *m*.

peacock ['piːkok] *n* pavo real *m*.

peak [piːk] *n* punta *f*; peñasco *m*; (*cap*) visera *f*. **peak hours** horas punta *f pl*.

peal [piːl] *n* (*bells*) ripiqueteo *m*; (*laughter*) carcajada *f*; (*thunder*) trueno *m*. *v* repiquetear; (*thunder*) retumbar; (*laugh*) resonar.

peanut ['piːnʌt] *n* cacahuete *m*.

pear [peə] *n* (*fruit*) pera *f*; (*tree*) peral *m*.

pearl [pəːl] *n* perla *f*. **pearly** *adj* nacarado.

peasant ['peznt] *n*, *adj* campesino, -a.

peat [piːt] *n* turba *f*.

pebble ['pebl] *n* guijarro *m*. **pebbly** *adj* guijarroso.

peck [pek] *v* picotear; picar. *n* picotazo *m*; (*coll: kiss*) besito *m*.

peckish ['pekiʃ] *adj* **feel peckish** (*coll*) tener gazuza.

peculiar [pi'kjuːljə] *adj* raro; extraño; característico; propio; especial. **peculiarity** *n* particularidad *f*; rareza *f*; característica *f*.

pedal ['pedl] *n* pedal *m*. *v* pedalear.

pedantic [pi'dantik] *adj* pedante.

peddle ['pedl] *v* vender de puerta en puerta.

pedestal ['pedistl] *n* pedestal *m*.

pedestrian [pi'destriən] *n* peatón *m*. **pedestrian crossing** paso de peatones *m*. **pedestrian precinct** zona reservada para peatones *f*. *adj* (*style*) prosaico.

pedigree ['pedigriː] *n* (*ancestry*) linaje *m*; (*animals*) pedigrí *m*. **pedigree animal** animal de raza *m*.

pedlar ['pedlə] *n* vendedor ambulante *m*.

peel [piːl] *v* pelar. **peel off** quitar, despegar. *n* (*potatoes, oranges*) monda *f*, cáscara *f*; (*candied*) piel confitada *f*. **potato-peeler** *n* pelapatatas *m invar*. **peelings** *pl n* peladuras *f pl*.

peep [piːp] *n* ojeada *f*. *v* echar una ojeada (a). **peeping Tom** mirón *m*. **peep out** asomar.

peer¹ [piə] *v* entornar los ojos. **peer into** mirar dentro de.

peer² [piə] *n* (*nobility*) par *m*; (*equal*) igual *m*. **peerage** *n* pares *m pl*. **peerless** *adj* sin par.

peevish ['piːviʃ] *adj* displicente; enojadizo.

peg [peg] *n* (*hats, coats*) percha *f*; (*clothes*) pinza *f*; (*tent*) estaca *f*. **off the peg** *adj* de confección. *v* enclavijar; (*prices*) estabilizar.

pejorative [pə'dʒorətiv] *adj* pejorativo.

Peking [ˌpiː'kiŋ] *n* Pekín, Pequín.

pelican ['pelikən] *n* pelicano *m*.

pellet ['pelit] *n* bolita *f*; (*gun*) perdigón *m*; (*med*) píldora *f*.

pelmet ['pelmit] *n* galería *f*.

pelt¹ [pelt] *v* tirar, arrojar; (*with questions*) acribillar; (*rain*) llover a cántaros; (*coll: run*) ir a todo correr. **at full pelt** a toda mecha.

pelt² [pelt] *n* pellejo *m*, piel *f*.

pelvis ['pelvis] *n* pelvis *f*. **pelvic** *adj* pélvico.

pen¹ [pen] *n* pluma *f*. **penknife** *n* cortaplumas *m invar*. **pen-name** *n* seudónimo *m*.

pen² [pen] *n* (*farm animals*) corral *m*; (*sheep*) redil *m*; (*pigs*) pocilga *f*. *v* scorralar.

penal ['piːnl] *adj* penal. **penal colony** penal *m*. **penalize** *v* penar, castigar. **penalty** *n* pena *f*; (*football*) penalty *m*; (*fig*) castigo *m*.

penance ['penəns] *n* penitencia *f*.

pencil ['pensl] *n* lápiz *m*. **pencil-sharpener** *n* sacapuntas *m invar*. *v* escribir con lápiz.

pendant ['pendənt] *n* colgante *m*.

pending ['pendiŋ] *adj* pendiente. *prep* hasta; durante.

pendulum ['pendjuləm] *n* péndulo *m*.

penetrate ['penitreit] *v* penetrar. **penetrable** *adj* penetrable. **penetration** *n* penetración *f*.

penguin ['peŋgwin] *n* pingüino *m*.

penicillin [peni'silin] *n* penicilina *f*.

peninsula [pə'ninsjulə] *n* península *f*. **peninsular** *adj* peninsular.

penis ['piːnis] *n* pene *m*.

penitent ['penitənt] *n(m+f)*, *adj* penitente. **penitence** *n* penitencia *f*.

pennant ['penənt] *n* (*small flag*) banderín *m*; (*naut*) gallardete *m*.

penniless ['penilis] *adj* sin dinero.

pension ['penʃən] *n* (*old age, retirement*) jubilación *f*; (*allowance*) pensión *f*. **pension fund** caja de jubilaciones *f*. *v* pensionar. **pension off** jubilar. **pensioner** *n* pensionista *m, f*.

pensive ['pensiv] *adj* pensativo.

pentagon ['pentəgən] *n* pentágono *m*. **pentagonal** *adj* pentagonal.

penthouse ['penthaus] *n* ático *m*.

pent-up [pent'ʌp] *adj* reprimido.

penultimate [pi'nʌltimət] *adj* penúltimo.

people ['piːpl] *n* personas *f pl*; gente *f sing*; (*nation*) nación *f sing*; pueblo *m sing*; habitantes *m pl*; (*coll*) familia *f sing*. *v* poblar.

pepper ['pepə] *n* (*spice*) pimienta *f*; (*vegetable*) pimiento *m*. **peppercorn** *n* grano de pimiento *m*. **peppermint** *n* (*plant*) hierbabuena *f*; (*flavour*) menta *f*; (*sweet*) pastilla de menta *f*. **pepper-pot** *n* pimentero *m*. *v* sazonar con pimienta. **peppery** *adj* picante.

per [pəː] *prep* por. **per cent** por ciento. **percentage** *n* porcentaje *m*.

perceive [pə'siːv] *v* percibir; (*notice*) notar.

perceptible [pə'septibl] *adj* perceptible; sensible. **perceptibly** *adv* sensiblemente.

perception [pə'sepʃən] *n* percepción *f*; sensibilidad *f*. **perceptive** *adj* perceptivo; perspicaz.

perch [pəːtʃ] *n* percha *f*. *v* (*bird*) posarse; encaramar.

percolate ['pəːkəleit] *v* filtrar. **percolator** *n* cafetera de filtro *f*.

percussion [pə'kʌʃən] *n* percusión *f*.

perennial [pə'reniəl] *adj* perenne. *n* planta perenne.

perfect ['pəːfikt; *v* pə'fekt] *adj* perfecto; absoluto. *n* (*gramm*) pretérito perfecto *m*. *v* perfeccionar. **perfection** *n* perfección *f*; (*perfecting*) perfeccionamiento *m*. **perfectionist** *n*(*m*+*f*), *adj* perfeccionista.

perforate ['pəːfəreit] *v* perforar. **perforation** *n* perforación *f*.

perform [pə'foːm] *v* llevar a cabo, ejecutar; (*duty*) cumplir; (*functions*) desempeñar; (*act*) representar. **performance** *n* ejecución *f*; cumplimiento *m*; desempeño *m*; representación *f*; (*machine*) funcionamiento *m*; *m*; celebración *f*; (*sport*) actuación *f*.

perfume ['pəːfjuːm] *n* perfume *m*. *v* perfumar.

perhaps [pə'haps] *adv* quizá, quizás, tal vez.

peril ['peril] *n* peligro *m*. **perilous** *adj* peligroso.

perimeter [pə'rimitə] *n* perímetro *m*.

period ['piəriəd] *n* período *m*; época *f*; edad *f*; tiempo *m*; (*school*) clase *f*; (*menstrual*) regla *f*. **periodic** *adj* periódico. **periodical** *nm, adj* periódico.

peripheral [pə'rifərəl] *adj* periférico. **periphery** *n* periferia *f*.

periscope ['periskoup] *n* periscopio *m*.

perish ['periʃ] *v* perecer. **perishable** *adj* perecedero.

perjure ['pəːdʒə] *v* **perjure oneself** perjurarse. **perjurer** *n* perjuro, -a *m, f*. **perjury** *n* perjurio *m*. **commit perjury** jurar en falso.

perk [pəːk] *v* **perk up** animarse. **perky** *adj* descarado; fresco.

perm [pəːm] *n* (*coll*) permanente *f*. **have a perm** hacerse la permanente.

permanent ['pəːmənənt] *adj* permanente. **permanence** *n* permanencia *f*. **permanently** *adv* permanentemente, para siempre.

permeate ['pəːmieit] *v* penetrar; (*soak*) impregnar. **permeable** *adj* permeable.

permit [pə'mit; *n* 'pəːmit] *v* permitir; dar permiso; tolerar. *n* permiso *m*; licencia *f*; pase *m*. **permissible** *adj* permisible. **permission** *n* permiso *m*; licencia *f*. **permissive** *adj* permisivo; tolerante.

permutation [pəːmju'teiʃən] *n* permutación *f*.

pernicious [pə'niʃəs] *adj* (*med*) pernicioso; (*evil*) funesto.

perpendicular [ˌpəːpen'dikjulə] *nf, adj* perpendicular.

perpetrate ['pəːpitreit] *v* perpetrar; cometer. **perpetration** *n* perpetración *f*; comisión *f*. **perpetrator** *n* (*law*) perpetrador, -a *m, f*; (*author*) autor, -a *m, f*.

perpetual [pə'petʃuəl] *adj* perpetuo.

perpetuate [pə'petʃueit] *v* perpetuar. **perpetuation** *n* perpetuación *f*.

perplex [pə'pleks] *v* dejar perplejo, confundir. **perplexed** *adj* perplejo; confuso. **perplexing** *adj* confuso; complicado; difícil. **perplexity** *n* perplejidad *f*; confusión *f*.

persecute ['pəːsikjuːt] *v* perseguir; molestar. **persecution** *n* persecución *f*.

persevere [,pɔɪsi'viɔ] v perseverar. **perseverance** n perseverancia f. **persevering** adj perseverante.
persist [pɔ'sist] v persistir. **persistence** n persistencia f. **persistent** adj persistente; continuo.
person ['pɔɪsn] n persona f. **personal** adj personal; en persona. **personality** n personalidad f. **personally** adv personalmente.
personify [pɔ'sonifai] v personificar. **personification** n personificación f.
personnel [pɔɪsɔ'nel] n personal m.
perspective [pɔ'spektiv] n perspectiva f.
perspire [pɔ'spaiɔ] v transpirar, sudar. **perspiration** n transpiración f, sudor m.
persuade [pɔ'sweid] v persuadir. **persuasion** n persuasión f. **persuasive** adj persuasivo; convincente.
pert [pɔɪt] adj impertinente; alegre; animado.
pertain [pɔ'tein] v pertenecer; ser propio de. **pertinent** adj pertinente. **pertinent to** relacionado con.
perturb [pɔ'tɔɪb] v perturbar. **perturbation** perturbación f.
Peru [pɔ'ruɪ] n Perú m.
peruse [pɔ'ruɪz] v leer atentamente; examinar. **perusal** n lectura atenta f; examen m.
pervade [pɔ'veid] v penetrar; saturar.
perverse [pɔ'vɔɪs] adj obstinado; contrario; (wicked) perverso. **perversity** n obstinación f; perversidad f.
pervert [pɔ'vɔɪt] n 'pɔɪvɔɪt] v (person) pervertir; (facts) desnaturalizar. n pervertido (-a) sexual m, f. **perversion** n perversión f; desnaturalización f.
pessimism ['pesimizɔm] n pesimismo m. **pessimist** n pesimista m, f. **pessimistic** adj pesimista.
pest [pest] n animal or insecto mocivo m; (coll: person) lata f. **pesticide** n pesticida m.
pester ['pestɔ] v importunar, molestar.
pet [pet] n animal doméstico m; (person) preferido, -a m, f. my pet! ¡mi cielo! adj mimado. **pet hate** pesadilla f. **pet name** nombre cariñoso m. **pet subject** tema preferido m. v minar; (caress) acariciar.
petal ['petl] n pétalo m.
petition [pɔ'tiʃɔn] n petición f. v suplicar; pedir.
petrify ['petrifai] v petrificarse; quedarse seco.

petrol ['petrɔl] n gasolina f; (S.Am.) nafta f. **petrol pump** surtidor de gasolina m. **petrol station** gasolinera f. **petrol tank** depósito de gasolina m.
petroleum [pɔ'trouliɔm] n petróleo m.
petticoat ['petikout] n enaguas f pl, enagua f.
petty ['peti] adj pequeño; insignificante. **petty cash** dinero suelto m. **petty-minded** mezquino. **petty officer** contramaestre m.
pettiness n pequeñez f; insignificancia f.
petulant ['petjulɔnt] adj malhumorado, irritable. **petulance** n mal humor m, irritabilidad f.
pew [pjuɪ] n banco de iglesia m.
pewter ['pjuɪtɔ] n estaño m, peltre m.
phantom ['fantɔm] n fantasma m.
pharmacy ['faɪmɔsi] n farmacia f. **pharmaceutical** adj farmacéutico. **pharmacist** n farmacéutico, -a m, f.
pharynx ['farinks] n faringe f. **pharyngitis** n faringitis f.
phase [feiz] n fase f. **phase in** introducir progresivamente. **phase out** reducir progresivamente.
pheasant ['feznt] n faisán m.
phenomenon [fɔ'nomɔnɔn] n, pl -ena fenómeno m. **phenomenal** adj fenomenal.
phial ['faiɔl] n frasco m.
philanthropy [fi'lanθrɔpi] n filantropía f. **philanthropic** adj filantrópico. **philanthropist** n filántropo, -a m, f.
philately [fi'latɔli] n filatelia f. **philatelic** adj filatélico. **philatelist** n filatelista m, f.
philosophy [fi'losɔfi] n filosofía f. **philosopher** n filósofo, -a m, f. **philosophical** adj filosófico. **philosophize** v filosofar.
phlegm [flem] n flema f. **phlegmatic** adj flemático.
phobia ['foubiɔ] n fobia f.
phone [foun] n (coll) teléfono m. v telefonear.
phonetic [fɔ'netik] adj fonético. **phonetics** n fonética f.
phoney ['founi] adj (coll) falso, espurio.
phosphate ['fosfeit] n fosfato m.
phosphorescence [fosfɔ'resɔns] n fosforescencia f. **phosphorescent** adj fosforescente.
phosphorus ['fosfɔrɔs] n fósforo m. **phosphorous** adj fosforoso.
photo ['foutou] n (coll) foto f.
photocopy ['foutou,kopi] n fotocopia f. v fotocopiar. **photocopier** n fotocopiadora f. **photocopying** n fotocopiaje m.

photogenic [,foutou'dʒenik] *adj* fotogénico.
photograph ['foutəgraɪf] *n* fotografía *f*. **photograph album** álbum de fotografías *m*. *v* fotografiar. **photographer** *n* fotógrafo, -a *m,f*. **photographic** *adj* fotográfico. **photography** *n* fotografía *f*.
phrase [freiz] *n* frase *f*, expresión *f*; (*gramm*) locusión *f*. **phrase-book** *n* repertorio de expresiones *m*. *v* expresar.
physical ['fizikəl] *adj* físico; *n* (*coll*) reconocimiento médico *m*.
physician [fi'ziʃən] *n* médico *m*.
physics ['fiziks] *n* física *f*. **physicist** *n* físico *m*.
physiology [,fizi'olədʒi] *n* fisiología *f*. **physiological** *adj* fisiológico. **physiologist** *n* fisiólogo, -a *m, f*.
physiotherapy [,fiziou'θerəpi] *n* fisioterapia *f*. **physiotherapist** *n* fisioterapeuta *m, f*.
physique [fi'ziːk] *n* constitución *f*; (*appearance*) físico *m*.
piano [pi'anou] *n* piano *m*. **pianist** *n* pianista *m, f*.
pick¹ [pik] *n* elección *f*, selección *f*. **take one's pick** elegir a su gusto. *v* escoger; seleccionar; (*fruit*) recoger; (*flowers*) coger; (*lock*) abrir con ganzúa. **pick at** (*food*) picar (la comida). **pick-me-up** *n* (*coll*) tónico. *m*. **pick out** escoger; distinguir; (*highlight*) hacer resaltar. **pickpocket** *n* ratero, -a *m, f*. **pick up** levantar; recoger; (*improve*) mejorarse; (*learn*) aprender; (*arrest*) detener.
pick² [pik] *n* (*tool*) piqueta *f*; (*music*) plectro *m*.
picket ['pikit] *n* piquete *m*; (*person*) huelguista *m, f*. *v* estar de guardia.
pickle ['pikl] *v* conservar en vinagre. *n* encurtido *m*.
picnic ['piknik] *n* merienda campestre *f*. *v* merendar en el campo.
pictorial [pik'toɪriəl] *adj* pictórico, ilustrado.
picture ['piktʃə] *n* ilustración *f*; (*portrait*) retrato *m*; (*painting*) cuadro *m*; (*film*) película *f*. **picture frame** marco *m*. **picture gallery** museo de pintura *m*. **pictures** *n* (*coll*) cine *m*. *v* describir; imaginarse.
picturesque [piktʃə'resk] *adj* pintoresco.
pidgin ['pidʒən] *n* lengua macarrónica *f*.
pie [pai] *n* (*fruit*) pastel *m*; (*meat*) pastel de carne *m*.

piece [piːs] *n* pedazo *m*, trozo *m*; parte *f*; (*material*) pieza *f*. **piecemeal** *adv* hecho por partes. **piecework** *n* trabajo a destajo *m*. *v* **piece together** juntar.
pier [piə] *n* malecón *m*; (*landing-stage*) muelle *m*.
pierce [piəs] *v* penetrar; perforar; (*go through*) traspasar. **piercing** *adj* penetrante; (*wind*) cortante.
piety ['paiəti] *n* piedad *f*.
pig [pig] *n* puerco *m*, cerdo *m*. **pigskin** *n* piel de cerdo *f*. **pigsty** *n* pocilga *f*. **pigtail** *n* coleta *f*.
pigeon ['pidʒən] *n* paloma *f*. **pigeonhole** *n* casilla *f*.
pigment ['pigmənt] *n* pigmento *m*.
pike [paik] *n* (*fish*) lucio *m*.
pilchard ['piltʃəd] *n* sardina arenque *f*.
pile¹ [pail] *n* (*heap*) pila *f*, montón *m*. *v* amontonar. **pile up** acumular. **pile-up** *n* accidente múltiple *m*.
pile² [pail] *n* (*post*) poste *m*.
pile³ [pail] *n* (*of carpet, etc.*) pelo *m*.
piles [pailz] *pl n* (*med*) hemorroides *f pl*.
pilfer ['pilfə] *v* (*coll*) sisar. **pilferage** *n* sisa *f*.
pilgrim ['pilgrim] *n* peregrino, -a *m, f*. **pilgrimage** *n* peregrinación *f*.
pill [pil] *n* píldora *f*.
pillage ['pilidʒ] *n* saqueo *m*. *v* saquear.
pillar ['pilə] *n* pilar *m*, columna *f*. **pillar-box** *n* buzón *m*.
pillion ['piljən] *n* grupa *f*. **ride pillion** ir a la grupa.
pillow ['pilou] *n* almohada *f*. **pillowcase** *n* funda de almohada *f*.
pilot ['pailət] *n* piloto *m*. **pilot-light** *n* piloto *m*. *v* guiar; conducir.
pimento [pi'mentou] *n* pimienta de Jamaica *f*.
pimp [pimp] *n* chulo *m*.
pimple ['pimpl] *n* espinilla *f*. **pimply** *adj* espinilloso.
pin [pin] *n* alfiler *m*; (*hairpin*) horquilla *f*; (*safety pin*) imperdible *m*; (*tech*) pezonera *f*; (*bolt*) perno *m*. **pincushion** *n* almohadilla *f*. **pin-money** *n* alfileres *m pl*; **pinpoint** *v* localizar con toda precisión. **pins and needles** hormigueo *m*. **pinstripe** *n* raya muy fina *f*. *v* prender con alfileres. **pin down** (*fix*) sujetar; (*find*) encontrar; (*enemy*) inmovilizar. **pin up** (*notice*) fijar.
pinafore ['pinəfoɪ] *n* (*apron*) delantal *m*. **pinafore dress** falda con peto *f*.

pincers ['pinsəz] *pl n* (*tool*) tenazas *f pl*; (*zool*) pinzas *f pl*.

pinch [pintʃ] *n* pellizco *m*; (*salt, etc.*) pizca *f*. **at a pinch** en caso de necesidad. **feel the pinch** empezar a pasar apuros. *v* pellizcar; (*shoes, etc.*) apretar; (*coll: steal*) mangar.

pine[1] [pain] *n* pino. *m*. **pine-cone** *n* piña *f*.

pine[2] [pain] *v* languidecer. **pine for** anhelar.

pineapple ['painapl] *n* ananás *m*, piña *f*.

ping-pong ['piŋpoŋ] *n* ping-pong *m*, tenis de mesa *m*.

pinion ['pinjən] *n* ala *f*. *v* maniatar.

pink [piŋk] *n* (*colour*) rosa *m*; (*flower*) clavel *m*. *adj* rosa.

pinnacle ['pinəkl] *n* pináculo *m*.

pioneer [ˌpaiə'niə] *n* pionero *m*, iniciador *m*.

pious ['paiəs] *adj* pío, devoto.

pip[1] [pip] *n* (*seed*) pepita *f*.

pip[2] [pip] *n* (*phone, etc.*) señal *f*.

pipe [paip] *n* (*gas, water, etc.*) tubo *m*, tubería *f*, cañería *f*; (*tobacco*) pipa *f*; (*music*) caramillo *m*. **pipe-cleaner** limpiapipas *m invar*. **pipeline** *n* (*oil*) oleoducto *m*; (*gas*) gasoducto *m*; (*water*) tubería *f*. *v* conducir por tubería; transportar por oleoducto. **pipe down** (*coll*) callarse. **piping** *n* (*music*) sonido de la gaite *m*; (*sewing*) ribete; tubería *f*.

piquant ['piːkənt] *adj* picante. **piquancy** *n* picante *m*.

pique [piːk] *n* pique *m*. *v* picar; herir.

pirate ['paiərət] *n* pirata *m*. *v* piratear. **piracy** *n* piratería *f*.

pirouette [piru'et] *n* pirueta *f*. *v* hacer piruetas.

Pisces ['paisiːz] *n* Piscis *m*.

piss [pis] *n* (*impol*) meada *f*. *v* mear. **piss off!** ¡vete al cuerno! **pissed** *adj* (*drunk*) trompa. **be pissed off** estar furioso (con).

pistachio [pi'staːʃiou] *n* pistacho *m*.

pistol ['pistl] *n* pistola *f*.

piston ['pistən] *n* émbolo *m*, pistón *m*.

pit [pit] *n* (*hole*) pozo *m*, hoyo; mina; (*orchestra*) foso de la orquesta *m*; (*of the stomach*) boca *f*; *v* llenar de hojitos; (*oppose*) oponer. **pit oneself against** medirse con.

pitch[1] [pitʃ] *n* (*throw*) lanzamiento *m*; (*sport*) campo *m*; (*music*) tono *m*; (*gradient*) grado de inclinación *m*; (*of a ship*) cabezada *f*. *v* lanzar, echar; entonar; (*of a ship*) cabecear; (*tent*) armar; (*fall*)

pitchfork *n* horca *f*. *v* (*fig*) catapultar.

pitch[2] [pitʃ] *n* pez *f*, brea *f*. **pitch-black** *adj* negro como el carbón.

pitfall ['pitfoil] *n* escollo *m*; trampa *f*.

pith [piθ] *n* médula *f*; (*fig*) meollo *m*. **pithy** *adj* conciso, expresivo.

pittance ['pitəns] *n* miseria *f*.

pituitary [pi'tjuːitəri] *n* glándula pituitaria *f*.

pity ['piti] *n* compasión *f*; lástima *f*. **take pity on** tener lástima de. **what a pity!** ¡qué lástima! *v* compadecese de. **pitiful** *adj* lastimoso; (*bad*) lamentable. **pitiless** *adj* despiadado.

pivot ['pivət] *n* pivote *m*; eje *m*. *v* girar sobre su eje.

placard ['plakaɪd] *n* cartel *m*. *v* fijar carteles.

placate [plə'keit] *v* aplacar. **placatory** *adj* placativo.

place [pleis] *n* sitio *m*, lugar *m*; (*post*) puesto *m*; local *m*; posición *f*. **all over the place** por todas partes. **in place** en su sitio. **in place of** en lugar de. **out of place** fuera de lugar. **take place** suceder, ocurrir. **take the place of** sustituir a. *v* colocar; poner; situar; (*an order*) hacer. **be well placed** estar en buena posición.

placenta [plə'sentə] *n* placenta *f*.

placid ['plasid] *adj* plácido. **placidity** *n* placidez *f*.

plagiarize ['pleidʒəraiz] *v* plagiar. **plagiarism** *n* plagio *m*. **plagiarist** *n* plagiario, -a *m, f*.

plague [pleig] *n* (*disease*) peste *f*; (*social scourge*) plaga *f*; (*nuisance*) molestia *f*. *v* importunar.

plaice [pleis] *n* platija *f*.

plaid [plad] *n* tartán *m*. *adj* escocés.

plain [plein] *adj* (*clear*) claro; simple; puro; completo; (*frank*) franco; natural; (*unattractive*) sin atractivo. **plain-clothes** *adj* en traje de calle. **make plain** poner de manifiesto. *n* llanura *f*.

plaintiff ['pleintif] *n* demandante *m, f*.

plaintive ['pleintiv] *adj* quejumbroso.

plait [plat] *n* (*fold*) pliegue *m*; (*hair*) trenza *f*. *v* plisar; trenzar.

plan [plan] *n* (*map*) plano *m*; (*scheme*) plan *m*, proyecto *m*. *v* (*for the future*) hacer planes para; (*holidays*) hacer el plan de; (*design*) hacer el plano de; (*action*) planear; (*production*) planificar. **planning** *n* planificación *f*.

plane 150

plane¹ [plein] *n* plano *m*; (*coll*: *aeroplane*) avión *m*. *adj* plano.
plane² [plein] *n* (*tool*) cepillo *m*. *v* cepillar.
plank [plaŋk] *n* tabla *n*.
plankton ['plaŋktən] *n* plancton *m*.
plant [plaɪnt] *n* (*bot*) planta *f*; (*tech*) maquinaria *f*; (*factory*) fábrica *f*; (*installation*) instalación *f*. *v* plantar. plantation *n* plantación *f*; hacienda *f*.
plaque [plaɪk] *n* placa *f*.
plasma ['plazmə] *n* plasma *m*.
plaster ['plaɪstə] *n* (*walls*) yeso *m*; (*for wounds*) emplasto *m*. plaster of Paris yeso blanco *m*. *v* enyesar; cubrir. plasterer yesero *m*.
plastic ['plastik] *nm*, *adj* plástico. plastic surgery cirugía plástica *f*.
plate [pleit] *n* (*dish*) plato *m*; (*of metal*) chapa *f*; (*tableware*) vajilla *f*; (*in book*) lámina *f*. *v* chapar; (*silver*) platear; (*gold*) dorar. plateful *n* plato *m*.
plateau ['platou] *n* meseta *f*.
platform ['platfoɪm] *n* plataforma *f*; (*rail*) andén *m*; (*stage*) estrado *m*; (*builders*) andamio *m*; (*pol*) programa *m*. platform ticket billete de andén *m*.
platinum ['platinəm] *n* platino *m*.
platonic [plə'tonik] *adj* platónico.
platoon [plə'tuɪn] *n* (*mil*) pelotón *m*.
plausible ['ploɪzəbl] *adj* plausible; (*person*) convincente. plausibility *n* plausibilidad *f*.
play [plei] *n* juego *m*, diversión *f*. (*theatre*) obra de teatro *f*; (*manoeuvre*) jugada *f*. *v* jugar. player *n* jugador, -a *m*, *f*; (*music*) intérprete *m*, *f*; (*theatre*) actor, actriz *m*, *f*. playful *adj* juguetón. playfulness *n* carácter juguetón *m*.
playback ['pleibak] *n* reproducción *f*. play back *v* volver a poner.
playground ['pleigraund] *n* campo de juegos *m*.
playhouse ['pleihaus] *n* teatro *m*.
playing card *n* carta *f*, naipe *m*.
playing field *n* campo de deportes *m*.
plaything ['pleiθiŋ] *n* juguete *m*.
playwright ['pleirait] *n* autor de teatro *m*.
plea [pliɪ] *n* suplica *f*; petición *f*; (*law*) alegato *m*.
plead [pliɪd] *v* suplicar; implorar; intervenir; hacer un alegato.
pleasant ['pleznt] *adj* agradable.
please [pliɪz] *v* gustar, agradar. if you please por favor. pleased *adj* contento.
pleasing *adj* agradable.

pleasure ['pleʒə] *n* placer *m*, gusto *m*. pleasurable *adj* grato.
pleat [pliɪt] *n* pliegue *m*. *v* plisar.
plectrum ['plektrəm] *n* plectro *m*.
pledge [pledʒ] *n* prenda *f*; promesa *f*. *v* dar en prenda; prometer.
plenty ['plenti] *n* abundancia *f*; cantidad *f*. plenty of bastante. plentiful *adj* abundante, copioso.
pleurisy ['pluərisi] *n* pleuresía *f*.
pliable ['plaiəbl] *adj* flexible; (*person*) dócil. pliability *n* flexibilidad *f*; docilidad *f*.
pliers ['plaiəz] *pl n* alicates *m pl*.
plight [plait] *n* aprieto *m*; crisis *f*.
plimsolls ['plimsəlz] *pl n* zapatos de tenis *m pl*.
plod [plod] *v* andar con paso pesado; (*coll*: *work*) trabajar con ahinco. plodder *n* empollón, -ona *m*, *f*.
plonk [ploŋk] *n* (*coll*) pirriaque *m*.
plop [plop] *n* plaf *m*. *v* hacer plaf.
plot¹ [plot] *n* (*story, etc.*) argumento *m*; (*conspiracy*) conspiración *f*; *v* tramar, maquinar; (*route*) trazar.
plot² [plot] *n* (*land*) terreno *m*; (*garden*) cuadro *m*.
plough [plau] *n* arado *m*. *v* arar. plough one's way through abrirse paso. ploughman *n* arador.
pluck [plʌk] *n* valor *m*; (*music*) plectro *m*; (*pull*) tirón *m*. *v* (*pull*) arrancar; (*music*) puntear; (*fruit*) coger; (*fowl*) desplumar; (*eyebrows*) despilarse. pluck out arrancar. pluck up courage armarse de valor. plucky *adj* valiente.
plug [plʌg] *n* (*stopper*) taco *m*; (*sink, bath*) tapón *m*; (*elec*) enchufe *m*; (*mot*) bujía *f*. *v* taponar; tapar; enchufar; (*block up*) atascar; (*coll*: *advertise*) dar publicidad a. plug away at perseverar en. plug in enchufar.
plum [plʌm] *n* (*fruit*) ciruela *f*; (*tree*) ciruelo *m*.
plumage ['pluɪmidʒ] *n* plumaje *m*.
plumb [plʌm] *n* plomada *f*, plomo *m*. plumbline *n* cuerda de plomada *f*; (*in water*) sonda *f*. *adj* vertical. *adv* a plomo. *v* aplomar; sondar. plumber *n* fontanero *m*. plumbing *n* fontanería *f*; instalación de cañerías *f*.
plume [pluɪm] *n* (*feather*) pluma *f*; (*smoke*) penacho *m*. *v* emplumar.

plummet ['plʌmit] *n* plomo *m*. *v* (*bird, aircraft*) caer en picado; (*person, thing*) caer a plomo; (*prices*) caer verticalmente.
plump¹ [plʌmp] *adj* (*person*) rellenito; (*animal*) gordo. **plumpness** *n* gordura *f*.
plump² [plʌmp] *v* caer de golpe. **plump for** decidirse por.
plunder ['plʌndə] *v* saquear; robar. *n* saqueo *m*; (*loot*) botin *m*. **plunderer** *n* saqueador *m*. **plundering** *n* saqueo *m*.
plunge [plʌndʒ] *n* (*fall*) caida *f*; (*short dive*) zambullida *f*; (*high dive*) salto *m*. **take the plunge** aventurarse. *v* (*knife, etc*.) meter; sumergir; (*into despair*) hundirse; (*launch oneself*) lanzarse; (*fall*) caer.
pluperfect [pluɪ'pəfikt] *n* pluscuamperfecto *m*.
plural ['pluərəl] *nm, adj* plural.
plus [plʌs] *prep* más. *n* cantidad positiva *f*; (*sign*) signo más *m. adj* positivo.
plush [plʌʃ] *adj* afelpado; (*fig*) lujoso. *n* felpa *f*.
ply¹ [plai] ´v (*tool*) manejar; (*trade*) ejercer; (*questions*) acosar; (*ship, etc*.) hacer el trayecto de. **ply between** hacer el servicio entre.
ply² [plai] *n* (*wood*) chapa *f*; (*wool*) cabo *m*; (*fabric*) capa *f*. **plywood** *n* contrapachado *m*.
pneumatic [njuˈmatik] *adj* neumático. **pneumatic drill** barreno neumático *m*.
pneumonia [njuˈmouniə] *n* pulmonía *f*.
poach¹ [poutʃ] *v* cazar *or* pescar en vedado. **poacher** *n* cazador *or* pescador furtivo *m*. **poaching** *n* caza *or* pesca furtiva *f*.
poach² [poutʃ] *v* (*egg*) escalfar.
pocket ['pokit] *n* bolsillo *m*. **pocket-money** *n* dinero de bolsillo *m*. *v* embolsarse.
pod [pod] *n* vaina *f*.
podgy ['podʒi] *adj* (*coll*) gordo.
poem ['pouim] *n* poema *m*.
poet ['pouit] *n* poeta *m*. **poetess** *n* poetisa *f*. **poetic** *adj* poético. **poetry** *n* poesía *f*.
poignant ['poinjənt] *adj* conmovedor.
point [point] *n* punto *m*; (*sharp end*) punta *f*; (*decimal*) coma *f*; (*elec*) contacto *m*; (*meaning*) sentido *m*; motivo; (*headland*) cabo *m*. **points** *pl n* (*railway*) agujas *f pl*. **beside the point** que no viene al caso. **come** *or* **get to the point** ir al grano. **make a point of** insistir en. **point-blank** *adv* (*shoot*) a quema ropa;

(*demand*) sin rodeos; (*refuse*) categóricamente. **what's the point?** ¿para qué sirve? *v* señalar; (*a weapon*) apuntar. **point out** señalar; advertir. **pointed** *adj* (*sharpened*) afilado; (*shape*) puntiagudo; (*remark*) directo. **pointless** *adj* inútil.
poise [poiz] *n* equilibrio *m*; (*bearing*) porte *m*; elegancia *f*; serenidad *f*. *v* poner en equilibrio; preparar. **be poised** estar en equilibrio; estar preparado.
poison ['poizən] *n* veneno *m*. *v* envenenar. **poisoning** *n* envenenamiento *m*. **poisonous** *adj* venenoso; tóxico.
poke [pouk] *n* empujón con el dedo; (*with elbow*) codazo *m*; (*fig*) hurgonada *f*. *v* dar con la punta del dedo; dar un codazo; hurgar. **poker** *n* hurgón *m*.
poker ['poukə] *n* (*cards*) póker *m*. **pokerfaced** *adj* de cara inmutable.
Poland ['poulənd] *n* Polonia *f*. **Pole** *n* polaco, -a *m, f*. **Polish** *nm, adj* polaco.
polar ['poulə] *adj* polar. **polar bear** oso blanco. **polarize** *v* polarizar.
pole¹ [poul] *n* (*wood*) palo *m*; (*metal*) barra *f*; (*telegraphs*) poste *m*; (*flag*) asta *f*. **pole-vault** *n* salto de pértiga *m*.
pole² [poul] *n* (*geog, elec*) polo *m*. **pole star** estrella polar *f*.
police [pəˈliɪs] *n* policía *f*. **the police force** el cuerpo de policía *m*. **policeman** *n* policía *m*, guardia *m*. **police station** comisaría de policía *f*. **policewoman** *n* mujer policía *f*.
policy¹ ['poləsi] *n* (*government*) política *f*; principio *m*; táctica *f*.
policy² ['poləsi] *n* (*insurance*) póliza *f*.
polio ['pouliou] *n* polio *f*.
polish ['poliʃ] *n* (*shine*) brillo *m*; (*act*) pulimento *m*; (*furniture*) cera *f*; (*shoes*) betún *m*; (*nails*) esmalte *m*; (*fig*) elegancia *f*. *v* (*shoes*) limpiar; (*metal*) pulir; (*floors*) encerar. **polish off** zampar. **polish up** dar brillo a; (*improve*) perfeccionar.
polite [pəˈlait] *adj* cortés. **politeness** *n* cortesía *f*.
politics ['politiks] *n* polítca *f*. **political** *adj* político. **politician** *n* político.
polka ['polkə] *n* polca *f*.
poll [poul] *n* votación *f*; elecciones *f pl*; (*survey*) sondeo *m*. *v* obtener; sondear. **polling booth** cabina electoral *f*; **polling day** día de elecciones *m*. **polling station** central electoral *m*.
pollen ['polən] *n* polen *m*. **pollen count**

índice de polen *m*. **pollinate** *v* polinizar.
pollination *n* polinización *f*.
pollute [pə'luɪt] *v* contaminar. **pollution** *n*
contaminación *f*.
polo ['poulou] *n* polo *m*. **water polo** polo
acuático *m*. **polo-neck** *n* cuello vuelto *m*.
polyester [ˌpoli'estə] *n* poliéster *m*.
polygamy [pə'ligəmi] *n* poligamia *f*.
polygon ['poligən] *n* poligono *m*.
polystyrene [ˌpoli'staɪəriɪn] *n* poliestireno
m.
polytechnic [ˌpoli'teknik] *n* escuela
politécnica *f*.
polythene ['poliθiɪn] *n* polietileno *m*.
pomegranate ['pomigranit] *n* (*fruit*) granada *f*; (*tree*) granado *m*.
pomp [pomp] *n* pompa *f*. **pompous** *adj*
pomposo.
pond [pond] *n* charca *f*; (*artificial*) estanque *m*.
ponder ['pondə] *v* considerar; meditar.
pony ['pouni] *n* poney *m*. **pony-tail** *n* cola
de caballo *f*.
poodle ['puɪdl] *n* perro de lanas *m*.
poof [puɪf] *n* (*derog*) marica *m*.
pool[1] [puɪl] *n* (*liquid*) charco *m*; (*swimming*) piscina *f*.
pool[2] [puɪl] *n* (*money*) banca *f*; (*things*)
recursos comunes *m pl*; (*reserve*) reserva
f; (*comm*) fondos comunes *m pl*; (*typing*)
servicio de mecanografía *m*. **pools** *pl n*
(*football*) quinielas *f pl*. *v* aunar; reunir;
poner en un fondo común.
poor [puə] *adj* pobre; mediocre.
poorly ['puəli] *adj* pobremente; mal. **be
poorly** estar malo.
pop[1] [pop] *n* taponazo *m*; (*drink*) gaseosa
f. **popcorn** *n* rosetas de maíz *f pl*. *v*
pinchar; (*cork*) hacer saltar; (*put*) meter.
pop in entrar un momento.
pop[2] [pop] *adj* popular. **pop music** música
pop *f*.
pope [poup] *n* papa *m*.
poplar ['poplə] *n* álamo *m*.
poplin ['poplin] *n* popelina *f*.
poppy ['popi] *n* amapola *f*.
popular ['popjulə] *adj* popular. **popularity**
n popularidad *f*. **popularize** *v* popularizar.
population [ˌpopju'leiʃən] *n* población *f*.
populate *v* poblar.
porcelain ['poɪslin] *n* porcelana *f*.
porch [poɪtʃ] *n* pórtico *m*.
porcupine ['poɪkjupain] *n* puerco espú *m*.

pore[1] [poɪ] *n* (*anat*) poro *m*.
pore[2] [poɪ] *v* **pore over** estar absorto en.
pork [poɪk] *n* cerdo *m*.
pornography [poɪ'nogrəfi] *n* pornografía
f. **pornographic** *adj* pornográfico.
porous ['poɪrəs] *adj* poroso.
porpoise ['poɪpəs] *n* marsopa *f*.
porridge ['poridʒ] *n* gachas de avena *f pl*.
port[1] [poɪt] *n* (*harbour*) puerto *m*.
port[2] [poɪt] *n* (*naut: left*) babor *m*.
port[3] [poɪt] *n* (*wine*) oporto *m*.
portable ['poɪtəbl] *adj* portátil.
portent ['poɪtent] *n* presagio *m*.
porter ['poɪtə] *n* (*attendant*) mozo *m*;
(*doorman*) portero; (*in government build-
ings*) conserje *m*.
portfolio [poɪt'fouliou] *n* (*folder*) carpeta
f; (*pol*) cartera *f*.
porthole ['poɪthoul] *n* portilla *f*.
portion ['poɪʃən] *n* porción *f*; parte *f*.
portrait ['poɪtrət] *n* retrato *m*.
portray [poɪ'trei] *v* retratar; representar.
portrayal *n* retrato *m*; representación *f*.
Portugal ['poɪtjugl] *n* Portugal *m*. **Portuguese** *nm, adj* portugués. **the Portuguese**
los portugueses.
pose [pouz] *n* postura *f*; afectación *f*. *v*
colocar; (*question*) formular; (*problem*)
plantear. **pose as** dárselas de.
posh [poʃ] *adj* elegante, de lujo; afectado.
position [pə'ziʃən] *n* posición *f*; sitio *m*;
situación *f*; opinión *f*; (*job*) empleo *m*. *v*
situar, disponer.
positive ['pozətiv] *adj* seguro; categórico;
verdadero; afirmativo; positivo.
possess [pə'zes] *v* poseer. **possession** *n*
posesión *f*. **possessive** *nm, adj* posesivo.
possible ['posəbl] *adj* posible. **possibility** *n*
posibilidad *f*. **possibly** *adv* (*perhaps*) tal
vez.
post[1] [poust] *n* (*pole*) poste *m*. *v* pegar.
post[2] [poust] *n* (*sentry, job*) puesto *m*. *v* (*a
sentry*) apostar; (*mil: send*) destinar.
post[3] [poust] *n* (*mail*) correo *m*; (*letters*)
cartas *f pl*. *v* mandar, enviar; echar. **postage** *n* franqueo *m*. **postage stamp** sello *m*.
postal *adj* postal. **postal order** giro postal
m.
postbox ['pousboks] *n* buzón *m*.
postcard ['pouskaɪd] *n* tarjeta postal *f*.
post-code *n* código postal *m*.
poster ['poustə] *n* cartel *m*.
poste restante [poust'restãt] *n* lista de
correos *f*.

posterior [po'stiəriə] *adj* posterior. *n* (*coll*) trasero *m*.
posterity [po'sterəti] *n* posteridad *f*.
postgraduate [poust'grædjuit] *n*, *adj* postgraduado, -a.
post-haste *adv* a toda prisa.
posthumous ['postjuməs] *adj* póstumo.
postman ['pousmən] *n* cartero *m*.
postmark ['pousmɑːk] *n* matasellos *m invar*. *v* matasellar.
postmaster ['pousmɑːstə] *n* administrador de correos *m*. **postmistress** *n* administradora de correos *f*.
post-mortem *n* autopsia *f*.
post office *n* correos *m pl*.
postpone [pous'poun] *v* aplazar. **postponement** *n* aplazamiento *m*.
postscript ['pousskript] *n* posdata *f*.
postulate ['postjuleit; *n* 'postjulət] *v* postular. *n* postulado *m*.
posture ['postʃə] *n* postura *f*, actitud *f*.
pot [pot] *n* (*cooking*) olla *f*; (*flowers*) tiesto *m*; (*preserves*) tarro *m*. **pot roast** carne asada *f*. **pots and pans** batería de cocina *f*. *v* (*plant*) poner en tiesto.
potassium [pə'tasjəm] *n* potasio *m*.
potato [pə'teitou] *n* patata *f*.
potent ['poutənt] *adj* poderoso; (*drink*) fuerte.
potential [pə'tenʃəl] *adj* posible; (*phys*) potencial. *n* posibilidad *f*; (*phys*) potencial *m*; (*elec*) voltaje *m*.
pot-hole ['pothoul] *n* (*in road*) bache *m*; (*underground*) cueva *f*. **pot-holer** *n* espeleólogo *m*. **pot-holing** *n* espeleología *f*.
potion ['pouʃən] *n* dosis *f*, poción *f*.
potter¹ ['potə] *v* (*coll*) **potter about** *or* **around** no hacer nada de particular.
potter² ['potə] *n* alfarero *m*. **potter's wheel** torno de alfarero *m*.
pottery ['potəri] *n* (*shop, craft*) alfarería *f*; (*pots*) cacharros de barro *m pl*.
potty ['poti] *n* (*coll: baby's*) orinal *m*. *adj* (*coll: crazy*) chiflado.
pouch [pautʃ] *n* bolsa *f*; (*tobacco*) petaca *f*.
poultice ['poultis] *n* cataplasma *f*.
poultry ['poultri] *n* aves de corral *f pl*.
pounce [pauns] *v* saltar. *n* salto *m*, ataque *m*.
pound¹ [paund] *v* aporrear; martillear; azotar.
pound² [paund] *n* libra *f*.
pour [poː] *v* verter; echar; servir; (*rain*)

diluviar; (*flow*) fluir; (*people*) salir en tropel.
pout [paut] *n* mala cara *f*. *v* poner mala cara.
poverty ['povəti] *n* pobreza *f*.
powder ['paudə] *n* polvo *m*; (*cosmetic*) polvos *m pl*; (*gun*) pólvora *f*. **powder puff** borla *f*. **powder room** cuarto tocador *m*. *v* pulverizar. **powdery** *adj* en polvo; pulverizado.
power ['pauə] *n* poder *m*; (*elec*) potencia *f*; (*tech*) fuerza *f*; (*energy*) energía *f*. **power station** central eléctrica *f*. *v* accionar, impulsar. **powerful** *adj* poderoso; potente. **powerless** *adj* impotente; sin autoridad.
practicable ['praktikəbl] *adj* practicable; utilizable; realizable. **practicability** *n* practicabilidad *f*.
practical ['praktikəl] *adj* práctico. **practical joke** broma pesada *f*.
practice ['praktis] *n* práctica *f*; (*music*) ejercicios *m pl*; (*training*) entrenamiento *m*; (*profession*) ejercicio *m*.
practise ['praktis] *v* practicar; (*professionally*) ejercer; (*exercise*) ejercitarse; (*patience, etc.*) tener; (*music*) hacer ejercicios en.
practitioner [prak'tiʃənə] *n* (*med*) médico *m*. **general practitioner** internista *m*.
pragmatic [prag'matik] *adj* pragmático; dogmático.
Prague [prɑːg] *n* Praga.
prairie ['preəri] *n* llanura *f*, pradera *f*.
praise [preiz] *n* alabanza *f*, elogio *m*. *v* alabar, elogiar. **praiseworthy** *adj* laudable.
pram [pram] *n* cochecito de niño *m*.
prance [prɑːns] *v* caracolear, encabritarse.
prank [praŋk] *n* (*joke*) broma *f*; (*mischief*) travesura *f*.
prattle ['pratl] *v* (*chatter*) charlar; (*of a child*) balbucear. *n* chácara *f*; balbuceo *m*.
prawn [proːn] *n* gamba *f*.
pray [prei] *v* orar, rezar. **prayer** *n* oración *f*, rezo *m*. **prayer book** devocionario *m*.
preach [priːtʃ] *v* predicar. **preacher** *n* predicador, -a *m*, *f*. **preaching** *n* predicación *f*.
precarious [pri'keəriəs] *adj* precario.
precaution [pri'koːʃən] *n* precaución *f*. **take precautions** tomar precauciones.
precede [pri'siːd] *v* preceder, anteceder.

precedence *n* precedencia *f*; prioridad *f*.
precedent *n* precedente *m*.
precinct ['priːsiŋkt] *n* recinto *m*; frontera *f*; zona *f*. **shopping precinct** zona comercial *f*.
precious ['preʃəs] *adj* precioso.
precipice ['presipis] *n* precipicio *m*.
precipitate [pri'sipiteit; *adj* pri'sipitət] *v* (*throw*) precipitar, arrojar; (*hasten*) acelerar; (*cause*) causar. *adj* precipitado.
precipitation *n* precipitación *f*.
précis ['preisi] *n* resumen *m*.
precise [pri'sais] *adj* preciso; exacto. **precision** *n* precisión *f*; exactitud *f*.
preclude [pri'kluːd] *v* excluir; evitar; impedir.
precocious [pri'kouʃəs] *adj* precoz. **precociousness** *or* **precocity** *n* precocidad *f*.
preconceive [ˌpriːkən'siːv] *v* preconcebir. **preconception** *n* preconcepción *f*.
precursor [ˌpriː'kəːsə] *n* precursor, -a *m, f*.
predator ['predətə] *n* animal de rapiña *m*; (*person*) depredador, -a *m, f*.
predecessor ['priːdisesə] *n* predecesor, -a *m, f*.
predestine [pri'destin] *v* predestinar. **predestination** *n* predestinación *f*.
predicament [pri'dikəmənt] *n* situación difícil *f*.
predicate ['predikət] *n* predicado *m*. *v* afirmar; implicar.
predict [pri'dikt] *v* predecir. **predictable** *adj* previsible. **prediction** *n* predicción *f*.
predominate [pri'domineit] *v* predominar. **predominance** *n* predominio *m*. **predominant** *adj* predominante.
pre-eminent [priː'eminənt] *adj* preeminente. **pre-eminence** *n* preeminencia *f*.
preen [priːn] *v* limpiar. **preen oneself** pavonearse.
prefabricate [priː'fabrikeit] *v* prefabricar. **prefabrication** *n* prefabricación *f*. **prefab** *n* (*coll*) casa prefabricada *f*.
preface ['prefis] *n* prólogo *m*. *v* (*introduce*) introducir.
prefect ['priːfekt] *n* (*school*) alumno/alumna responsable de disciplina *m, f*.
prefer [pri'fəː] *v* preferir. **preferable** *adj* preferible. **preference** *n* preferencia *f*. **preferential** *adj* preferente.
prefix ['priːfiks] *n* prefijo *m*. *v* poner un prefijo; anteponer.
pregnant ['pregnənt] *adj* (*woman*)

embarazada, encinta; (*animal*) preñada.
pregnancy *n* embarazo *m*.
prehistoric [ˌpriːhi'storik] *adj* prehistórico.
prejudice ['predʒədis] *n* prejuicio *m*; parcialidad *f*. *v* predisponer; (*damage*) perjudicar. **prejudiced** *adj* predispuesto; parcial. **prejudicial** *adj* perjudicial.
preliminary [pri'liminəri] *adj* preliminar. **preliminaries** *pl n* preliminares *m pl*.
prelude ['preljuːd] *n* preludio *m*.
premarital [priː'maritl] *adj* premarital.
premature [premə'tʃuə] *adj* prematuro.
premeditate [priː'mediteit] *v* premeditar. **premeditation** *n* premeditación *f*.
premier ['premiə] *adj* primero. *n* primer ministro *m*.
première ['premieə] *n* estreno *m*.
premise ['premis] *n* premisa *f*. **premises** *pl n* local *m sing*; edificio *m sing*.
premium ['priːmiəm] *n* (*comm*) prima *f*; (*award*) premio *m*. **at a premium a** premio.
premonition [ˌpremə'niʃən] *n* premonición *f*.
preoccupied [priː'okjupaid] *adj* preocupado. **preoccupation** *n* preocupación *f*.
prepare [pri'peə] *v* preparar, disponer. **preparation** *n* preparación *f*. **preparations** *pl n* preparativos *m pl*. **preparatory** *adj* preparatorio; preliminar. **preparatory school** escuela preparatoria *f*.
preposition [ˌprepə'ziʃən] *n* preposición *f*.
preposterous [pri'postərəs] *adj* ridículo, absurdo.
prerogative [pri'rogətiv] *n* prerrogativa *f*.
prescribe [pri'skraib] *v* prescribir; (*med*) recetar. **prescription** *n* (*med*) receta *f*, prescripción *f*.
presence ['prezns] *n* presencia *f*.
present[1] ['preznt] *adj* presente. *n* presente *m*, actualidad *f*. **at present** ahora, en la actualidad. **those present** los presentes. **presently** *adv* luego.
present[2] [pri'zent; *n* 'preznt] *v* presentar; regalar; (*a problem*) plantear; (*an argument*) exponer. *n* regalo *m*. **presentable** *adj* presentable. **presentation** *n* presentación *f*; (*gift*) regalo *m*; (*ceremony*) entrega *f*.
preserve [pri'zəːv] *v* (*food*) conservar; (*protect*) preservar. **preserved** *adj* en conserva. **preserves** *pl n* conservas *f pl*; (*jam*) confitura *f*. **preservation** *n* conservación

f; (*protection*) preservación *f*. **preservative** *n* producto de conservación *m*.
preside [pri'zaid] *v* presidir.
president ['prezidənt] *n* presidente, -a *m*, *f*. **presidency** *n* presidencia *f*. **presidential** *adj* presidencial.
press [pres] *n* (*newspapers*) prensa *f*; (*printing*) imprenta *f*. **press conference** rueda de prensa *f*. **press cutting** recorte de periódico *m*. *v* (*mechanical*) prensar; (*push*) apretar; (*iron*) planchar; (*button*) dar a; (*squeeze*) estrucar; (*urge*) urgir. **press for** pedir con insistencia. **pressing** *adj* urgente.
pressure ['preʃə] *n* presión *f*; (*weight*) peso *m*; (*strength*) fuerza *f*; (*elec, med*) tensión *f*. **pressure cooker** olla de presión *f*. **pressure gauge** manómetro *m*. **pressurize** *v* (*cabin, etc.*) presurizar; (*coll: force*) acozar.
prestige [pre'stiːʒ] *n* prestigio *m*.
presume [pri'zjuːm] *v* suponer; permitirse. **presumption** *n* presunción *f*; (*daring*) atrevimiento *m*. **presumptuous** *adj* presuntuoso; atrevido.
pretend [pri'tend] *v* fingir; (*claim*) pretender; (*imagine*) suponer. **pretence** *n* fingimiento *m*; pretensión *f*; pretexto *m*; apariencia *f*. **pretension** *n* pretensión *f*. **pretentious** *adj* pretencioso; (*showy*) presumido.
pretext ['priːtekst] *n* pretexto *m*.
pretty ['priti] *adj* bonito, lindo. *adv* bastante.
prevail [pri'veil] *v* prevalecer, triunfar; predominar. **prevail upon** convencer. **prevailing** *adj* (*wind*) predominante, reinante; (*present*) actual. **prevalent** *adj* predominante; (*present-day*) actual; (*common*) común; extendido.
prevent [pri'vent] *v* impedir; (*avoid*) evitar. **prevention** *n* prevención *f*; impedimento *m*. **preventive** *adj* preventivo.
preview ['priːvjuː] *n* preestreno *m*. *v* ver antes que los demás.
previous ['priːviəs] *adj* anterior. **previously** *adv* antes.
prey [prei] *n* presa *f*; víctima *f*. **be a prey to** ser víctima de. *v* **prey on** (*animals*) alimentarse de. **prey on one's mind** preocupar mucho.
price [prais] *n* precio *m*. **fixed price** precio fijo *m*. **full price** precio fuerte *m*. **price list** tarifa *f*. **sale price** precio de venta *m*.

v poner precio a; valorar. **priceless** *adj* inestimable.
prick [prik] *n* pinchazo *m*. *v* pinchar. **prick up one's ears** aguzar el oído.
prickle ['prikl] *n* espina. *v* picar. **prickly** *adj* espinoso.
pride [praid] *n* orgullo *m*; dignidad *f*. **pride oneself on** enorgullecerse de.
priest [priːst] *n* sacerdote *m*. **priesthood** *n* (*office*) sacerdocio *m*; (*clergy*) clero *m*.
prim [prim] *adj* (*fussy*) remilgado; (*demure*) recatado.
primary ['praiməri] *adj* primario; básico; primero.
primate ['praimət] *n* (*zool*) primate *m*; (*rel*) primado *m*.
prime [praim] *adj* primero; principal; original; selecto; (*math*) primo. **prime minister** primer ministro *m*. *v* preparar; (*person*) informar. **primer** *n* (*book*) cartilla *f*. **primer coat** primera mano *f*.
primitive ['primitiv] *adj* primitivo.
primrose ['primrouz] *n* primavera *f*.
prince [prins] *n* príncipe *m*. **princely** *adj* principesco. **princess** *n* princesa *f*.
principal ['prinsəpəl] *adj* principal. *n* (*school*) director, -a *m*, *f*.
principle ['prinsəpəl] *n* principio *m*. **on principle** por principio.
print [print] *n* (*finger*) huella *f*; (*impression*) marca *f*; (*phot*) prueba *f*; (*edition*) tirada *f*; (*type*) tipo *m*; (*picture*) grabado *m*. **out of print** agotado. *v* imprimir; (*phot*) sacar. **printed matter** impresos *m pl*. **printer** *n* impresor *m*. **printing** *n* impresión *f*; (*phot*) tiraje *m*. **printing press** prensa *f*.
prior ['praiə] *adj* anterior; preferente. **prior to** antes de. **priority** *n* prioridad *f*.
prise [praiz] *v* **prise off/open** abrir; levantar por fuerza.
prism ['prizm] *n* prisma *m*.
prison ['prizn] *n* cárcel *f*. **prisoner** *n* preso, -a *m*, *f*.
private ['praivət] *adj* privado; personal; reservado; (*house, car, lessons, etc.*) particular; confidencial. *n* soldado raso *m*. **privacy** *n* intimidad *f*; aislamiento *m*. **privately** *adv* en privado; personalmente.
privet ['privət] *n* alheña *f*.
privilege ['privəlidʒ] *n* privilegio *m*. **privileged** *adj* privilegiado.
privy ['privi] *n* letrina *f*.
prize [praiz] *n* premio *m*. **prizewinner** *n*

premiado, -a *m*, *f*. *adj* premiado. *v* estimar.

probable ['prɔbəbl] *adj* probable; (*credible*) verosímil. **probability** *n* probabilidad *f*. **probably** *adv* probablemente.

probation [prə'beiʃən] *n* (*law*) libertad vigilada *f*; (*trial period*) período de prueba *m*. **on probation** a prueba. **probationary** *adj* de prueba.

probe [proub] *n* (*act*) sondeo *m*; (*med*) sonda *f*. *v* sondear; explorar.

problem ['prɔbləm] *n* problema *m*. **problematic** *adj* problemático.

proceed [prə'siːd] *v* seguir; proceder; avanzar. **proceed to** ponerse a. **procedure** *n* procedimiento *m*. **proceedings** *pl n* debates *m pl*; (*law*) proceso *m sing*.

process ['prouses] *n* proceso *m*; procedimiento *m*; método *m*. **in the process of** en curso de. *v* tratar; (*phot*) revelar.

procession [prə'seʃən] *n* processión *f*, desfile *m*.

proclaim [prə'kleim] *v* proclamar; declarar. **proclamation** *n* proclamación *f*; declaración *f*.

procreate ['proukrieit] *v* procrear. **procreation** *n* procreación *f*.

procure [prə'kjuə] *v* conseguir.

prod [prod] *n* golpecito *m*. *v* punzar; (*urge*) estimular.

prodigal ['prodigəl] *adj* pródigo.

prodigy ['prodidʒi] *n* prodigio *m*. **prodigious** *adj* prodigioso.

produce [prə'djuːs; *n* 'prodjuːs] *v* producir; (*manufacture*) fabricar; causar. *n* productos *m pl*. **producer** *n* productor, -a *m*, *f*; (*theatre*) escenógrafo *m*. **product** *m* producto *m*. **production** *n* producción *f*; fabricación *f*; presentación *f*; (*theatre*) dirección *f*. **productive** *adj* productivo; fecundo. **productivity** *n* productividad *f*.

profane [prə'fein] *adj* profano. *v* profanar. **profanity** *n* lo profano; impiedad *f*.

profess [prə'fes] *v* (*state*) declarar; (*claim*) pretender; (*affirm*) afirmar.

profession [prə'feʃən] *n* profesión *f*. **professional** *n*(*m*+*f*), *adj* profesional.

professor [prə'fesə] *n* catedrático, -a *m*, *f*. **professorship** *n* cátedra *f*.

proficient [prə'fiʃənt] *adj* competente; experto. **proficiency** *n* competencia *f*; pericia *f*.

profile ['proufail] *n* perfil *m*; (*biography*) reseña *f*.

profit ['profit] *n* (*financial*) ganancia *f*; (*fig*) provecho *m*. **profit-making** *adj* productivo. *v* **profit by** *or* **from** beneficiarse de. **profitable** *adj* provechoso.

profound [prə'faund] *adj* profundo. **profoundly** *adv* profundamente.

profuse [prə'fjuːs] *adj* profuso; abundante. **profusely** *adv* profusamente. **profusion** *n* profusión *f*; abundancia *f*.

programme ['prougram] *n* programa *m*. *v* programar. **programmer** *n* programador, -a *m*, *f*. **programming** *n* programación *f*.

progress ['prougres] *n* progreso *m*. **in progress** en curso. **make progress** hacer progresos. *v* progresar, avanzar, hacer progresos. **progression** *n* progresión *f*. **progressive** *adj* progresivo; (*political, social*) progresista.

prohibit [prə'hibit] *v* prohibir; impedir. **prohibition** *n* prohibición *f*.

project ['prodʒekt; *v* prə'dʒekt] *n* proyecto *m*. *v* proyectar; (*protrude*) hacer resaltar. **projectile** *n* proyectil *m*. **projecting** *adj* saliente. **projection** *n* proyección *f*; saliente *m*. **projector** *n* proyector *m*; (*planner*) proyectista *m*, *f*.

proletarian [proulə'teəriən] *n*, *adj* proletario, -a. **proletariat** *n* proletariado *m*.

proliferate [prə'lifəreit] *v* proliferar. **proliferation** *n* proliferación *f*.

prolific [prə'lifik] *adj* prolífico.

prologue ['proulog] *n* prólogo *m*.

prolong [prə'lon] *v* prolongar. **prolongation** *n* prolongación *f*.

promenade [promə'naid] *n* paseo *m*. *v* pasear, pasearse.

prominent ['prominənt] *adj* prominente; saliente; preeminente. **prominence** *n* prominencia *f*; importancia *f*.

promiscuous [prə'miskjuəs] *adj* promiscuo; (*person*) libertino. **promiscuity** *n* promiscuidad *f*.

promise ['promis] *n* promesa *f*. *v* prometer. **promising** *adj* que promete.

promontory ['promən təri] *n* promontorio *m*.

promote [prə'mout] *v* promover, ascender; (*comm*) promocionar; (*encourage, stir up*) fomentar; financiar. **promotion** *n* ascenso *m*; promoción *f*; fomento *m*.

prompt [prompt] *adj* pronto; rápido; inmediato; puntual. *v* incitar; inspirar;

sugerir; (*theatre*) apuntar. **prompter** *n* apuntador, -a *m, f.*

prone [proun] *adj* propenso; (*lying*) boca abajo.

prong [proŋ] *n* diente *m*, púa *f.*

pronoun ['prounaun] *n* pronombre *m.*

pronounce [prə'nauns] *v* pronunciar; declarar. **pronouncement** *n* declaración *f.* **pronunciation** *n* pronunciación *f.*

proof [pruːf] *n* prueba *f*; (*alcohol*) graduación normal *f.* *adj* resistente (a); al abrigo de. **proof-read** *v* corregir pruebas. **proof-reading** *n* corrección de pruebas *f.*

prop[1] [prop] *n* puntal *m*; (*fig*) sostén *m*, apoyo *m.* *v* (*lean*) apoyar; (*support*) mantener.

prop[2] [prop] *n* (*coll: theatre*) accesorio *m.*

propaganda [propə'gandə] *n* propaganda *f.*

propagate ['propəgeit] *v* propagar. **propagation** *n* propagación *f.*

propel [prə'pel] *v* propulsar, impulsar. **propeller** *n* propulsor *m*; (*aircraft, ship*) hélice *f.* **propelling pencil** portaminas *m invar.*

proper ['propə] *adj* propio; correcto; decente; formal; justo; (*suitable*) apto; (*true*) verdadero; (*characteristic*) peculiar. **proper noun** nombre propio *m.* **properly** *adv* propiamente; bien; decentemente; correctamente.

property ['propəti] *n* (*estate*) hacienda *f*; (*possessions*) bienes *m pl*, propiedad *f.* (*quality*) cualidad *f.*

prophecy ['profəsi] *n* profecía *f.* **prophesy** *v* profetizar. **prophet** *n* profeta *m.* **prophetic** *adj* profético.

proportion [prə'poːʃən] *n* proporción *f*; parte *f.* **out of proportion** desproporcionado. *v* proporcionar; distribuir. **proportional** *adj* proporcional, en proporción.

propose [prə'pouz] *v* proponer; (*marriage*) declararse; (*toast*) brindar; (*intend*) intentar. **proposal** *n* proposición *f*; (*marriage*) oferta de matrimonio *f*; (*plan*) proyecto *m.* **proposition** *n* proposición *f*; proyecto *m.*

proprietor [prə'praiətə] *n* propietario, -a *m, f*; dueño *m, f.*

propriety [prə'praiəti] *n* decoro *m*; conveniencia *f*; oportunidad *f*; corrección *f.*

propulsion [prə'pʌlʃən] *n* propulsión *f.*

prose [prouz] *n* prosa *f.*

prosecute ['prosikjuːt] *v* proseguir; (*law*)

procesar. **prosecution** *n* (*of duty*) cumplimiento *m*; (*continuation*) continuación *f*; (*action of prosecuting*) procesamiento *m*; (*trial*) proceso *m*; (*party*) parte acusadora *f.*

prospect ['prospekt; *v* prə'spekt] *n* perspectiva *f*; vista *f.* **prospects** *pl n* (*of a job, etc.*) perspectivas *f pl.* *v* prospectar. **prospective** *adj* eventual; futuro.

prospectus [prə'spektəs] *n* prospecto *m.*

prosper ['prospə] *v* prosperar. **prosperity** *n* prosperidad *f.* **prosperous** *adj* próspero.

prostitute ['prostitjuːt] *n* prostituta *f.* *v* prostituir. **prostitution** *n* prostitución *f.*

prostrate ['prostreit; *v* pro'streit] *adj* (*lying down*) boca abajo; (*exhausted*) postrado. *v* postrar. **prostrate oneself** postrarse. **prostration** *n* prostración *f*; prosternación *f.*

protagonist [prou'tagənist] *n* protagonista *m, f*

protect [prə'tekt] *v* proteger. **protection** *n* protección *f.* **protective** *adj* protector.

protégé ['protəʒei] *n* protegido *m.* **protégée** *n* protegida *f.*

protein ['proutiin] *n* proteína *f.*

protest ['proutest; *v* prə'test] *n* protesta *f*; *v* protestar. **protester** *n* (*on march*) manifestador, -a *m, f.*

Protestant ['protistənt] *n*(*m+f*), *adj* protestante.

protocol ['proutəkol] *n* protocolo *m.*

prototype ['proutətaip] *n* prototipo *m.*

protractor [prə'traktə] *n* transportador *m.*

protrude [prə'truːd] *v* sacar; sobresalir. **protruding** *adj* saliente, sobresaliente.

proud [praud] *adj* orgulloso; soberbio.

prove [pruːv] *v* probar; demostrar; (*show*) mostrar.

proverb ['provəːb] *n* proverbio *m.* **proverbial** *adj* proverbial.

provide [prə'vaid] *v* proveer; dar; preparar (por); proporcionar medios de vida (a). **provided that** si siempre que.

provident ['providənt] *adj* próvido. **providence** *n* providencia *f.* **providential** *adj* providencial.

province ['provins] *n* provincia *f*; esfera *f.* **the provinces** la provincia *f.* **provincial** *adj* provincial.

provision [prə'viʒən] *n* (*supply*) suministro *m*; (*providing*) provisión *f*; (*of treaty, law, etc.*) disposición *f.* **make provision for** prever. **provisions** *pl n* provisiones *f pl.* **provisional** *adj* provisional.

proviso [prə'vaizou] *n* condición *f*; estipulación *f*.
provoke [prə'vouk] *v* provocar. **provocation** *n* provocación *f*. **provocative** *adj* provocador.
prow [prau] *n* proa *f*.
prowess ['prauis] *n* valor *m*; proeza *f*.
prowl [praul] *v* rondar. **prowler** *n* rondador, -a *m*, *f*.
proximity [prok'siməti] *n* proximidad *f*.
proxy ['proksi] *n* poder *m*, procuración *f*. **by proxy** por poderes.
prude [pruɪd] *n* mojigato, -a *m*, *f*. **prudish** *adj* mojigato.
prudent ['pruɪdənt] *adj* prudente. **prudence** *n* prudencia *f*.
prune¹ [pruɪn] *n* (*fruit*) ciruela pasa *f*.
prune² [pruɪn] *v* podar; cortar; reducir.
pry [prai] *v* fisgar, fisgonear. **pry into** entrometerse en. **prying** *adj* fisgón.
psalm [saɪm] *n* salmo *m*.
pseudonym ['sjuɪdənim] *n* pseudónimo *m*.
psychedelic [,saikə'delik] *adj* psiquedélico.
psychiatry [sai'kaiətri] *n* psiquiatría *f*.
psychic ['saikik] *adj* psíquico. *n* medium *m*.
psychoanalysis [,saikouə'naləsis] *n* psicoanálisis *m*. **psychoanalyse** *v* psicoanalizar. **psychoanalyst** *n* psicoanalista *m*, *f*.
psychology [sai'kolədʒi] *n* psicología *f*. **psychological** *adj* psicológico. **psychologist** *n* psicólogo, -a *m*, *f*.
psychopath ['saikəpaθ] *n* psicópata *m*, *f*. **psychopathic** *adj* psicopático.
psychosis [sai'kousis] *n* psicosis *f*. **psychotic** *adj* psicopático. *n* psicópata *m*, *f*.
psychosomatic [,saikəsə'matik] *adj* psicosomático.
psychotherapy [,saikə'θerəpi] *n* psicoterapia *f*.
pub [pʌb] *n* taberna *f*. **pub crawl** chateo *m*.
puberty ['pjuɪbəti] *n* pubertad *f*.
pubic ['pjuɪbik] *adj* púbico.
public ['pʌblik] *nm*, *adj* público.
publication [,pʌbli'keiʃən] *n* publicación *f*.
publicity [pʌb'lisəti] *n* publicidad *f*.
publicize ['pʌblisaiz] *v* publicar.
public library *n* biblioteca de préstamo *f*.
public relations *n* colegio privado de enseñanza media *m*.

public-spirited *adj* de espíritu cívico.
public transport *n* servicio de transportes *m*.
publish ['pʌbliʃ] *v* publicar. **publisher** *n* editor, -a *m*, *f*. **publishing** *n* publicación *f*. **publishing house** casa editora *f*.
pucker ['pʌkə] *v* (*wrinkle*) arrugar; (*pleat*) fruncir. *n* (*pleat*) frunce *m*.
pudding ['pudiŋ] *n* pudín *m*, budín *m*.
puddle ['pʌdl] *n* charco *m*.
puerile ['pjuərail] *adj* pueril.
Puerto Rico [,pwəɪtou'riɪkou] *n* Puerto Rico.
puff [pʌf] *n* (*breath*) resoplido *m*; (*air*) soplo *m*; (*wind*) ráfaga *f*; (*smoke*) bocanada *f*; *v* (*blow*) soplar; (*pant*) jadear; (*smoke*) echar bocanadas. **puff out** *or* **up** hinchar. **puffy** *adj* hinchado.
pull [pul] *n* tracción *f*; (*tide*) arrastre *m*; esfuerzo *m*; (*influence*) enchufe *m*; atracción *f*. *v* (*open*) tirar de; (*drag*) arrastrar; (*uproot*) arrancar; (*tooth*) sacar; (*trigger*) apretar; (*attract*) atraer. **pull ahead** destacarse. **pull away** separar, apartar. **pull down** bajar; echar abajo. **pull in** entrar; llegar. **pull oneself together** serenarse. **pull out** (*mot*) salirse; sacar; arrancar; (*mil*) retirarse. **pull through** sacar de un apuro. **pull together** aunar sus esfuerzos. **pull up** (*mot*) parar; (*socks*) subirse; (*a chair*) acercar.
pulley ['puli] *n* polea *f*.
pullover ['puḷouvə] *n* jersey *m*.
pulp [pʌlp] *n* pulpa *f*. *v* reducir a pulpa.
pulpit ['pulpit] *n* púlpito *m*.
pulsate [pʌl'seit] *v* palpitar; vibrar; brillar. **pulsation** *n* pulsación *f*; vibración *f*.
pulse [pʌls] *n* (*med*) pulso *m*; (*phys*) pulsación *f*. *v* latir; vibrar.
pulverize ['pʌlvəraiz] *v* pulverizar. **pulverization** *n* pulverización *f*.
pump [pʌmp] *n* bomba *f*; (*petrol*) surtidor *m*; (*plimsoll*) zapato de lona *m*. *v* bombear; sacar. **pump up** inflar.
pumpkin ['pʌmpkin] *n* calabaza *f*.
pun [pʌn] *n* retruécano *m*.
punch¹ [pʌntʃ] *n* puñetazo *m*; golpe *m*. *v* dar um puñetazo.
punch² [pʌntʃ] *n* (*drink*) ponche *m*.
punch³ [pʌntʃ] *n* (*tool*) sacabocados *m invar*; perforadora *f*. *v* taladrar; perforar; picar.
punctual ['pʌŋktʃuəl] *adj* puntual. **punctuality** *n* puntualidad *f*.

punctuate ['pʌŋktʃueit] *v* puntuar. **punctuation** *n* puntuación *f*.
puncture ['pʌŋktʃə] *n* (*tyre*) pinchazo *m*; (*leather, skin*) perforación *f*. **have a puncture** tener un pinchazo. *v* pinchar; perforar.
pungent ['pʌndʒənt] *adj* (*smell*) acre; (*taste*) picante. **pungency** *n* acritud *f*; lo picante; mordazidad *f*.
punish ['pʌniʃ] *v* castigar. **punishment** *n* castigo *m*.
punt[1] [pʌnt] *n* (*boat*) batea *f*.
punt[2] [pʌnt] *v* (*bet*) apostar. **punter** *n* jugador *m*.
puny ['pjuːni] *adj* escuchimizado.
pupil[1] ['pjuːpl] *n* alumno, -a *m, f*.
pupil[2] ['pjuːpl] *n* (*eye*) pupila *f*.
puppet ['pʌpit] *n* títere *m*; marioneta *f*.
puppy ['pʌpi] *m* cachorro *m*.
purchase ['pəːtʃəs] *n* compra *f*. **purchase tax** impuesto sobre la venta *m*. *v* comprar.
pure ['pjuə] *adj* puro. **purify** *v* purificar. **purist** *n* purista *m, f*. **purity** *n* pureza *f*.
purée ['pjuərei] *n* puré *m*.
purgatory ['pəːgətəri] *n* purgatorio *m*.
purge [pəːdʒ] *v* purgar; purificar. *n* purga *f*. **purgative** *nm, adj* purgante.
puritan ['pjuəritən] *n, adj* puritano, -a. **puritanical** *adj* puritano.
purl [pəːl] *v* ribetear; hacer al revés. *n* (*on lace*) puntilla *f*; (*thread*) hilo de oro o de plata *m*.
purple ['pəːpl] *nm, adj* morado.
purpose ['pəːpəs] *n* propósito *m*, objetivo *m*; destino *m*; determinación *f*; uso *m*; utilidad *f*. **on purpose** a propósito. **purposeful** *adj* decidido; (*person*) resuelto; útil.
purr [pəː] *v* ronronear. *n* ronroneo *m*.
purse [pəːs] *n* monedero *m*, portamonedas *m invar*; (*prize*) premio *m*. *v* **purse one's lips** apretar los labios.
purser ['pəːsə] *n* contador *m*.
pursue [pə'sjuː] *v* perseguir. **pursuer** *n* perseguidor, -a *m, f*. **pursuit** *n* persecución *f*; profesión *f*; ocupación *f*; pasatiempo *m*.
pus [pʌs] *n* pus *m*.
push [puʃ] *n* empujón *m*; (*force*) empuje *m*. *v* empujar; presionar; (*notice on doors*) empujen. **be pushed for time** tener prisa. **pushing** *adj* ambicioso.
*put [put] *v* poner; meter; echar; (*question*) hacer; (*state*) decir. **put away**

guardar; (*money*) ahorrar. **put back** volver a poner; (*clock*) atrasar. **put down** bajar; (*in writing*) apuntar; (*repress*) reprimir; (*kill*) sacrificar. **put off** (*postpone*) aplazar; (*disgust*) censar; (*revolt*) asquear; disuadir. **put on** (*clothes*) ponerse; (*a show*) representar; (*pretend*) fingir. **put up** levantar; (*hang*) colgar; (*resistance*) oponer; (*build*) construir. **put up with** aguantar; conformarse con. **put upon** engañar.
putrid ['pjuːtrid] *adj* pútrido; podrido.
putt [pʌt] *n* put *m*. *v* tirar al hoyo. **putter** *n* putter *m*.
putty ['pʌti] *n* masilla *f*.
puzzle ['pʌzl] *n* enigma *f*; (*game*) rompecabezas *m invar*. *v* dejar perplejo. **puzzle out** resolver; descifrar. **puzzling** *adj* enigmático; misterioso.
pyjamas [pə'dʒɑːməz] *pl n* pijama *m sing*.
pylon ['pailən] *n* poste *m*.
pyramid ['pirəmid] *n* pirámide *f*.
python ['paiθən] *n* pitón *m*.

Q

quack[1] [kwak] *n* (*duck*) graznido *m*. *v* graznar.
quack[2] [kwak] *n* charlatán *m*.
quadrangle ['kwodraŋgl] *n* (*courtyard*) patio *m*; (*math*) cuadrángulo *m*.
quadrant ['kwodrənt] *n* cuadrante *m*.
quadrilateral [kwodrə'latərəl] *nm, adj* cuadrilátero.
quadruped ['kwodruped] *nm, adj* cuadrúpedo.
quadruple [kwod'ruːpl] *adj* cuádruple.
quadruplets [kwo'druːplits] *pl n* cuatrillizos, -as *m, f pl*.
quagmire ['kwagmaiə] *n* pantano *m*.
quail[1] [kweil] *n* (*zool*) codorniz *f*.
quail[2] [kweil] *v* acobardarse.
quaint [kweint] *adj* pintoresco; excéntrico.
quake [kweik] *v* estremecerse. *n* estremecimiento. **quake with fear** temblar de miedo.
qualify ['kwolifai] *v* (*entitle*) capacitar; calificar; modificar; limitar. **qualification** *n* reserva *f*; aptitud *f*; requisito *m*. **qualifications** *pl n* títulos *m pl*. **qualified** *adj*

competente; capacitado; titulado; con reservas.
quality ['kwolɔti] n (attribute) cualidad f; calidad f.
qualm [kwaɪm] n escrúpulo m.
quandary ['kwondɔri] n incertidumbre f, dilema m.
quantify ['kwontifai] v determinar la cantidad de.
quantity ['kwontɔti] n cantidad f.
quarantine ['kworɔntiɪn] n cuarentena f. v someter a cuarentena.
quarrel ['kworɔl] n disputa f, pelea f. v disputar, pelear. **quarrelsome** adj peleador.
quarry[1] ['kwori] n (stone, etc.) cantera f. v explotar una cantera.
quarry[2] ['kwori] n presa f.
quarter ['kwoɪtɔ] n cuarto m; cuarta parte f; (of year) trimestre m; (district) barrio m. **quarter-final** n cuarto de final m. **quartermaster** n (naut) cabo de la marina m. **quarter past four** las cuatro y quince. **quarters** pl n (mil) cuartel m sing. **at close quarters** de cerca. **quarter to four** las cuatro menos cuarto. v dividir en cuatros; (mil) acuartelar. **quarterly** adj trimestral.
quartet [kwoɪ'tet] n cuarteto m.
quartz [kwoɪts] n cuarzo m.
quash [kwoʃ] v amular; ahogar; (rebellion) reprimir.
quaver ['kweivɔ] n (music) corchea f; temblor m. v temblar.
quay [kiɪ] n muelle m.
queasy ['kwiɪzi] adj (sick) mareado; (upset) delicado. **queasiness** n náuseas f pl.
queen [kwiɪn] n reina f; (cards) dama f. **Queen Mother** reina madre f.
queer [kwiɔ] adj raro; curioso; (unwell) indispuesto; (slang: homosexual) maricón. n (slang) maricón m, marica f.
quell [kwel] v reprimir.
quench [kwentʃ] v (flames) apagar; (thirst) aplacar; (desire) sofocar.
query ['kwiɔri] n pregunta f; duda f. v preguntar; dudar (de).
quest [kwest] n búsqueda f.
question ['kwestʃɔn] n pregunta f; cuestión f; problema m. **begging the question** petición de principio f. **beside the question** que no viene al caso. **out of the question** imposible. **question mark** signo de interrogación m. **without question** sin

duda. v preguntar; interrogar; poner en duda. **questionable** adj dudoso; discutible. **questioning** n interrogatorio m. **questionnaire** n cuestionario m.
queue [kjuɪ] n cola f. v hacer cola.
quibble ['kwibl] n pega f; subterfugio m. v sutilizar; (find fault) ser quisquilloso.
quick [kwik] adj rápido; (reply) pronto; (lively) vivo; (clever) agudo; (on feet) ligero. **quicksand** n avena movediza f. **quick-tempered** adj irascible. **quick-witted** adj agudo. **quicken** v acelerar; estimular.
quickly adv rápidamente.
quid [kwid] n (coll) libra f.
quiet ['kwaiɔt] adj silencioso; callado; (step) ligero; tranquilo; (dress) sobrio. n also **quietness** tranquilidad f; silencio m; reposo m. **quieten** v callar; calmar. **quietly** adv silenciosamente; tranquilamente.
quill [kwil] n (feather) pluma f; (pen) cálamo m; (porcupine) púa f.
quilt [kwilt] n colcha f; (eiderdown) edredón m. v acolchar.
quince [kwins] n membrillo m.
quinine [kwi'niɪn] n quinina f.
quinsy ['kwinzi] n angina f.
quintet [kwin'tet] n quinteto m.
quirk [kwɔɪk] n peculiaridad f.
quit [kwit] v (job) abandonar; (place) dejar; (leave) irse de.
quite [kwait] adv completamente, enteramente; exactamente; verdaderamente; (fairly) bastante.
quiver[1] ['kwivɔ] v tremblar; estremecerse. n temblor m; estremecimiento m.
quiver[2] ['kwivɔ] n (for arrows) aljaba f.
quiz [kwiz] n (inquiry) encuesta f; (questioning) interrogatorio m; examen m. v interrogar.
quizzical ['kwizikl] adj curioso; (bantering) burlón.
quota ['kwoutɔ] n cupo m; (share) cuota f.
quote [kwout] v citar; dar; (comm) cotizar. **quotation** n cita f; (comm) cotización f. **quotation marks** comillas f pl.

R

rabbi ['rabai] *n* rabino *m*.
rabbit ['rabit] *n* conejo *m*.
rabble ['rabl] *n* gentío *m*; (*derog*) populacho *m*.
rabies ['reibiɪz] *n* rabia *f*. **rabid** *adj* rabioso.
race[1] [reis] *n* carrera *f*; (*yacht*) regata *f*. **racehorse** *n* caballo de carreras *m*. *v* (*person*) competir con; (*horse*) hacer correr; (*pulse*) latir a ritmo acelerado.
race[2] [reis] *n* raza *f*; familia *f*. **racial** *adj* racial. **racialism** *n* *also* **racism** racismo *m*. **racialist** *n*(*m*+*f*), *adj* *also* **racist** racista.
rack [rak] *n* (*shelf*) estante *m*; (*coats, etc.*) percha *f*; (*plates*) escurreplatos *m* *invar*; (*car roof*) baca *f*; (*torture*) potre *m*. *v* atormentar. **rack one's brains** devanarse los sesos.
racket[1] ['rakit] *n* (*sport*) raqueta *f*.
racket[2] ['rakit] *n* (*noise*) alboroto *m*, barullo *m*; (*coll: crime*) tráfico *m*; timo *m*.
radar ['reidaɪ] *n* radar *m*.
radial ['reidiəl] *adj* radial. **radial tyre** neumático radial *m*.
radiant ['reidiənt] *adj* resplandeciente. **radiance** *n* resplandor *m*.
radiate ['reidieit] *v* (*heat*) irradiar; (*rays*) emitir; (*spread*) difundir. **radiation** *n* radiación *f*. **radiator** *n* radiador *m*.
radical ['radikəl] *nm, adj* radical.
radio ['reidiou] *n* radio *f*. **radio beacon** radiofaro *m*. **radio contact** radiocomunicación *f*. **radio control** teledirección *f*. **radio station** emisora *f*. **radio wave** onda *f*. *v* transmitir por radio.
radioactive [reidiou'aktiv] *adj* radioactivo. **radioactivity** *n* radioactividad *f*.
radiography [reidi'ogrəfi] *n* radiografía *f*. **radiographer** *n* radiógrafo *m*.
radiology [reidi'olədʒi] *n* radiología *f*. **radiologist** *n* radiólogo *m*.
radiotherapy [reidiou'θerəpi] *n* radioterapia *f*.
radish ['radiʃ] *n* rábano *m*.
radium ['reidiəm] *n* radio *m*.
radius ['reidiəs] *n* radio *m*.
raffia ['rafiə] *n* rafia *f*.
raffle ['rafl] *n* rifa *f*. *v* rifar.
raft [raɪft] *n* balsa *f*.
rafter ['raɪftə] *n* viga *f*.
rag[1] [rag] *n* (*waste piece*) harapo *m*; (*cleaning*) trapo *m*; (*derog: newspaper*) periodicucho *m*. **ragamuffin** *n* golfo *m*.

ragged *adj* (*clothes*) hecho jirones; (*edge*) mellado.
rag[2] [rag] *v* (*coll*) tomar el pelo a. *n* payasadas *f* *pl*. **ragtime** *n* música sincopada *f*.
rage [reidʒ] *n* (*anger*) cólera *f*, rabia *f*; (*of elements*) furia *f*; (*fashion*) moda *f*. **be all the rage** hacer furor. *v* (*be angry*) estar furioso; (*wind, fire, beasts*) bramar; (*sea*) alborotarse. **raging** *adj* (*person*) furioso; (*pain*) muy fuerte; (*storm*) encrespado.
raid [reid] *n* (*mil*) correría *f*; (*aerial*) ataque *m*; (*police*) redada *f*; (*robbery*) asalto *m*. *v* hacer una redada; asaltar. **raider** *n* invasor *m*; (*thief*) ladrón *m*.
rail [reil] *n* (*stairs*) barandilla *f*; (*bridge*) antepecho *m*; (*balcony*) baranda *f*; (*bar*) barra *f*; (*fence*) cerco *m*; (*train, tram*) via férrea *f*. **by rail** por ferrocarril. **railway** *or* US **railroad** *n* ferrocarril *m*.
railings ['reiliɪz] *pl* *n* barandilla *f* *sing*.
rain [rein] *n* lluvia *f*. **rainbow** *n* arco iris *m*. **raincoat** *n* impermeable *m*. **raindrop** *n* gota de lluvia *f*. **rainfall** *n* precipitación *f*; **rainwater** *n* agua de lluvia *f*. *v* llover. **rainy** *adj* lluvioso.
raise [reiz] *v* alzar, levantar; (*increase*) aumentar; provocar; (*problem*) plantar; (*animals*) criar.
raisin ['reizən] *n* pasa *f*.
rake [reik] *n* rastro *m*. *v* rastrillar. **rake together** reunir a duras penas.
rally ['rali] *n* reunión *f*; (*pol*) mitin político *m*; (*mot*) rallye *m*; (*tennis*) peloteo *m*. *v* reunir; (*recover*) recuperarse. **rally round** tomar el partido de.
ram [ram] *n* carnero *m*; (*battering ram*) ariete *m*. *v* (*earth, etc.*) apisonar; (*fist, head*) dar con; (*pack*) meter a la fuerza.
ramble ['rambl] *n* excursión *f*. *v* pasear; (*fig*) divagar.
ramp [ramp] *n* rampa *f*.
rampage ['rampeidʒ] *n* **be on the rampage** alborotar.
rampant ['rampənt] *adj* (*plant*) exuberante; (*heraldry*) rampante; (*aggressive*) violento. **be rampant** estar difundido.
rampart ['rampaɪt] *n* terraplén *m*, muralla *f*.
ramshackle ['ramʃakl] *adj* desvenajado.
ran [ran] *V* **run**.
ranch [raɪntʃ] *n* rancho *m*; hacienda *f*.
rancid ['ransid] *adj* rancio.
rancour ['raŋkə] *n* rencor *m*.

random ['randəm] *n* **at random** al azar. *adj* hecho al azar. **random sample** muestra cogida al azar *f.*

rang [raŋ] *V* **ring.**

range [reindʒ] *n* (*row*) fila *f;* (*mountains*) sierra *f;* (*area*) extensión *f;* (*distance*) alcance *m;* (*of an aircraft*) autonomía *f;* (*mil: firing*) campo de tiro *m;* (*voice*) registro *m;* (*colours, prices*) gama *f;* (*subjects*) variedad *f;* (*grazing land*) dehesa *f;* (*cooking stove*) cocina económica *f. v* (*place*) colocar; (*put in a row*) alinear; clasificar; (*wander*) recorrer.

rank¹ [raŋk] *n* fila *f;* grado *m;* categoría *f.* **the rank and file** la tropa *f;* (*ordinary people*) gente del montón *f. v* (*estimate*) situar, poner; figurar; (*mil*) alinear.

rank² [raŋk] *adj* lozano; rancio.

rankle ['raŋkl] *v* escocer.

ransack ['ransak] *v* saquear; (*search*) registrar.

ransom ['ransəm] *n* rescate *m.* **hold to ransom** exigir rescate. *v* rescatar.

rap [rap] *v* golpear. *n* golpecito *m.*

rape [reip] *n* violación *f. v* violar. **rapist** *n* violador *m.*

rapid ['rapid] *adj* rápido. **rapids** *pl n* rápidos *m pl.* **rapidity** *n* rapidez *f.*

rapier ['reipiə] *n* estoque *m.*

rapport [ra'poɪ] *n* relación *f;* armonía *f.*

rapture ['raptʃə] *n* éxtasis *m invar.* **go into raptures over** extasiarse por.

rare¹ ['reə] *adj* raro. **rarity** *n* rareza *f.*

rare² ['reə] *adj* (*cookery*) poco hecho.

rascal ['raɪskəl] *n* bribón *m,* pícaro *m.*

rash¹ [raʃ] *adj* temerario. **rashness** *n* temeridad *f.*

rash² [raʃ] *n* (*med*) erupción *f.*

rasher ['raʃə] *n* loncha *f.*

raspberry ['raɪzbəri] *n* (*fruit*) frambuesa *f;* (*bush*) frambueso *m.*

rat [rat] *n* rata *f.* **rat poison** matarratas *m invar.* **rat race** competencia *f.*

rate [reit] *n* proporción *f;* índice *m;* velocidad *f;* ritmo *m;* precio; (*discount, interest*) tipo *m;* (*pulse*) frecuencia *f.* **at any rate** de todos modos. **ratepayer** *n* contribuyente *m, f.* **rates** *pl n* contribución municipal *f sing. v* valorar; considerar; clasificar; estimar. **rateable** *adj* valorable.

rather ['raɪðə] *adv* más bien; bastante; (*fairly*) algo. **I would rather ...** prefiero ....

ratify ['ratifai] *v* ratificar. **ratification** *n* ratificación *f.*

ratio ['reiʃiou] *n* razón *f,* relación *f.*

ration ['raʃən] *n* ración *f. v* racionar. **rationing** *n* racionamiento *m.*

rational ['raʃnl] *adj* racional; razonable; lógico. **rationale** *n* razón fundamental *f.* **rationalize** *v* racionalizar.

rattle ['ratl] *n* (*toy*) sonajero *m;* (*football fan's*) carraca *f;* ruido de sonajero; (*train noise*) traqueteo *m;* (*chains*) ruido metálico *m;* (*door, window*) golpe *m;* (*teeth*) castañeteo *m;* (*machine gun*) tableteo *m; v* hacer sonar; traquetear; hacer un ruido metálico; golpetear; castañetear; tabletear; (*put off*) desconcertar.

raucous ['rɔɪkəs] *adj* ronco.

ravage ['ravidʒ] *n* estrago *m. v* asolar.

rave [reiv] *v* delirar, desvariar. **rave over** entusiasmarse por. **raving** *adj* delirante.

raven ['reivən] *n* cuervo *m.*

ravenous ['ravənəs] *adj* hambriento. **be ravenous** tener um hambre canina.

ravine [rə'viɪn] *n* desfiladero *m.*

ravish ['raviʃ] *v* violar; raptar. **ravishing** *adj* encantador.

raw [rɔɪ] *adj* (*uncooked*) crudo; (*unrefined*) bruto; (*inexperienced*) novato; (*nerves*) a flor de piel; (*flesh*) vivo; (*weather*) frío y húmedo. **raw deal** (*coll*) injusticia *f.* **raw materials** materias primas *f pl.* **rawness** *n* crudeza *f.*

ray [rei] *n* rayo *m;* (*line, fish*) raya *f.*

rayon ['reion] *n* rayón *m.*

razor ['reizə] *n* navaja *f;* (*safety*) maquinilla de afeitar *f;* (*elec*) máquina de afeitar eléctrica *f.* **razor blade** hoja de afeitar *f.*

reach [riɪtʃ] *v* (*arrive at*) llegar a; (*achieve*) lograr; (*stretch out*) extender; alcanzar. *n* alcance *m;* poder *m;* capacidad *f.* **out of reach** fuera del alcance. **within reach** al alcance.

react [ri'akt] *v* reaccionar. **reaction** *n* reacción *f.* **reactionary** *n, adj* reaccionario, -a. **reactor** *n* reactor *m.*

*read [riɪd] *v* leer; estudiar; (*public address*) decir; (*riddle*) interpretar; (*meter, etc.*) marcar. **reader** *n* lector, -a *m, f;* (*university*) profesor, -a *m, f;* (*book*) libro de lectura *m.* **reading** *n* lectura *f;* estudio *m;* interpretación *f.* **reading-glass** *n* lente para leer *m.* **reading-lamp** lámpara de sobremesa *f.*

readjust [riːəˈdʒʌst] *v* reajustar. **readjustment** *n* reajuste *m*.
ready [ˈredi] *adj* listo; pronto; a mano. **get ready** prepararse. **ready cash** dinero contante *m*. **ready-made** *adj* hecho. **readily** *adv* fácilmente; en seguida. **readiness** *n* prontitud *f*; facilidad *f*.
real [riəl] *adj* real, verdadero. **realism** *n* realismo *m*. **realist** *n* realista *m*, *f*. **reality** *n* realidad *f*, verdad *f*. **really** *adv* realmente, en verdad. **really?** ¿de veras?
realize [ˈriəlaiz] *v* (*understand*) darse cuenta de; (*achieve*) llevar a cabo; (*make real*) realizar. **realization** *n* comprensión *f*; realización *f*.
realm [relm] *n* reino *m*; (*fig*) esfera *f*.
reap [riːp] *v* segar; (*fig*) cosechar. **reaping** *n* siega *f*; cosecha *f*. **reaping machine** segadora mecánica *f*.
reappear [riːəˈpiə] *v* reaparecer. **reappearance** *n* reaparición *f*.
rear[1] [riə] *adj* posterior, de atrás. **rear-admiral** *n* contraalmirante *m*. **rearguard** *n* retaguardia *f*. **rear-view mirror** retrovisor *m*. *n* parte posterior *f*, parte de atrás *f*; (*of a column*) cola *f*. **bring up the rear** cerrar la marcha.
rear[2] [riə] *v* (*family*) criar; (*lift up*) alzar, levantar; (*horse, etc.*) empinarse.
rearrange [riːəˈreindʒ] *v* arreglar de otra manera; volver a arreglar. **rearrangement** *n* nuevo arreglo *m*.
reason [ˈriːzn] *n* razón *f*. *v* razonar. **reasonable** *adj* razonable. **reasoning** *n* razonamiento *m*.
reassure [riːəˈʃuə] *v* asegurar de nuevo; confortar. **reassurance** *n* confianza restablecida *f*. **reassuring** *adj* tranquilizador.
rebate [ˈriːbeit] *n* rebaja *f*, descuento *m*.
rebel [ˈrebl] *n*(*m*+*f*), *adj* rebelde. *v* rebelarse. **rebellion** *n* rebelión *f*. **rebellious** *adj* rebelde.
rebound [riˈbaund; *n* ˈriːbaund] *v* rebotar. *n* rebote *m*.
rebuff [riˈbʌf] *v* rechazar. *n* desaire *m*.
*****rebuild** [riːˈbild] *v* reedificar.
rebuke [riˈbjuːk] *n* censura *f*, reproche *m*. *v* censurar, reprochar.
recall [riˈkɔːl] *v* llamar; recordar. *n* llamada *f*; (*dismissal*) destitución *f*.
recant [riˈkant] *v* retractar.
recap [ˈriːkap] *v* (*coll*) recapitular. *n* recapitulación *f*.
recapture [riˈkaptʃə] *v* reconquistar; (*recreate*) hacer revivir. *n* reconquista *f*.

recede [riˈsiːd] *v* retroceder; (*tide*) descender.
receipt [rəˈsiːt] *n* (*act of receiving*) recepción *f*; (*slip of paper*) recibo *m*.
receive [rəˈsiːv] *v* recibir; aceptar. **receiver** *n* (*of loot*) recibidor, -a *m*, *f*; (*law*) síndico *m*; (*phone*) auricular *m*.
recent [ˈriːsnt] *adj* reciente. **recently** *adv* recientemente.
receptacle [rəˈseptəkl] *n* receptáculo *m*.
reception [rəˈsepʃən] *n* recepción *f*; acogida *f*. **receptionist** *n* recepcionista *m*, *f*. **receptive** *adj* receptivo.
recess [riˈses] *n* (*hollow*) hueco *m*; (*niche*) nicho *m*; (*parliament*) período de clausura *m*; (*rest*) descanso *m*.
recession [rəˈseʃən] *n* (*comm*) recesión *f*; (*retreat*) retroceso *m*.
recharge [riˈtʃɑːdʒ] *v* recargar.
recipe [ˈresəpi] *n* receta *f*.
recipient [rəˈsipiənt] *n* (*receiver*) receptor, -a *m*, *f*; (*cheque, letter, etc.*) destinatario, -a *m*, *f*.
reciprocate [rəˈsiprəkeit] *v* corresponder; intercambiar. **reciprocating engine** motor alternativo *m*. **reciprocal** *adj* recíproco.
recite [rəˈsait] *v* recitar. **recital** *n* (*a relating*) relato *m*; (*music*) recital *m*. **recitation** *n* relato *m*; recitación *f*.
reckless [ˈrekləs] *adj* temerario; audaz. **recklessness** *n* temeridad *f*; audacia *f*.
reckon [ˈrekən] *v* calcular; contar; considerar; (*coll*) creer. **reckoning** *n* cálculo *m*; cuenta *f*; (*fig*) retribución *f*.
reclaim [riˈkleim] *v* (*land*) ganar; (*reform*) reformar; (*by-product*) regenerar. **reclamation** *n* (*claiming back*) reclamación *f*; (*moral*) enmienda *f*; (*land*) aprovechamiento *m*; regeneración *f*.
recline [rəˈklain] *v* apoyar; recostar.
recluse [rəˈkluːs] *n* recluso, -a *m*, *f*.
recognize [ˈrekəgnaiz] *v* reconocer; confesar. **recognition** *n* reconocimiento *m*. **recognizable** *adj* identificable.
recoil [rəˈkoil; *n* ˈriːkoil] *v* echarse atrás; (*gun*) dar culatazo; (*spring*) aflojarse. *n* culatazo *m*; aflojamiento *m*; (*repugnance*) asco *m*.
recollect [rekəˈlekt] *v* acordarse de. **recollection** *n* recuerdo *m*.
recommence [rekəˈmens] *v* empezar de nuevo.
recommend [rekəˈmend] *v* recomendar; aconsejar. **recommendation** *n* recomendación *f*.

recompense ['rekəmpens] *n* recompensa *f*; (*law*) compensación *f*. *v* recompensar; compensar.

reconcile ['rekənsail] *v* (*dispute*) arreglar; (*individuals*) reconciliar; (*ideas*) conciliar. **reconcile oneself to** resignarse a. **reconciliation** *n* arreglo *m*; reconciliación *f*; conciliación *f*.

reconstruct [riːkən'strʌkt] *v* (*building*) reconstruir; (*crime*) reconstituir. **reconstruction** *n* reconstrucción *f*; reconstitución *f*.

record [rə'koɪd; *n* 'rekoɪd] *v* registrar; tomar nota de; (*sound*) grabar. *n* registro *m*; anotación *f*; grabación *f*; disco *m*; (*account*) relación *f*; (*minutes*) actas *f pl*; (*personal history*) historial *m*; (*sport*) récord *m*. **long-playing record** disco de larga duración *m*. **record-player** *n* tocadiscos *m invar*. **recorded** *adj* grabado; registrado. **recorded delivery** entrega registrada *f*. **recorder** *n* archivista *m*, *f*; (*music*) flauta *f*. **recording** *n* (*music*) grabación *f*.

recount [riˈkaunt; *n* 'riːkaunt] *v* contar. *n* recuento *m*.

recoup [riˈkuːp] *v* (*recover*) recuperar; (*compensate*) indemnizar.

recover [rə'kʌvə] *v* (*get back*) recuperar; (*get well*) recobrar; ganar; obtener. **recovery** *n* recuperación *f*; (*med*) restablecimiento *m*.

recreation [rekri'eiʃən] *n* recreación *f*; (*school break*) recreo *m*.

recrimination [rəkrimi'neiʃən] *n* recriminación *f*. **recriminate** *v* recriminar.

recruit [rə'kruːt] *n* recluta *m*. *v* reclutar. **recruitment** *n* reclutamiento *m*.

rectangle ['rektaŋgl] *n* rectángulo *m*. **rectangular** *adj* rectangular.

rectify ['rektifai] *v* rectificar.

rectum ['rektəm] *n* recto *m*.

recuperate [rə'kjuːpəreit] *v* recuperar; (*health*) recobrar. **recuperation** *n* recuperación *f*; (*health*) restablecimiento *m*.

recur [riˈkəɪ] *v* volver; repetirse. **recurrence** *n* vuelta *f*; repetición *f*; reaparición *f*. **recurrent** *adj also* **recurring** periódico; que vuelve; (*med*) recurrente.

red [red] *n* rojo *m*, colorado *m*. **in the red** deber dinero. *adj* rojo, colorado. **go red** ruborizarse. **Red Cross** Cruz Roja *f*. **redcurrant** grosella *f*. **red-handed** *adv* con las manos en la masa. **redhead** *n* pelirrojo, -a *m*, *f*. **red-hot** *adj* al rojo; ardiente. **red-letter day** día memorable

m. **red-light district** barrio de mala fama *m*. **red tape** (*coll*) papeleo *m*. **redness** *n* color rojo *m*.

redeem [rə'diːm] *v* (*promise*) cumplir; (*mortgage*) amortizar; (*pawn*) desempeñar; (*fault*) expiar; (*rescue*) rescatar. **redemption** *n* cumplimiento *m*; amortización *f*; desempeño *m*; expiación *f*; rescate *m*; (*rel*) redención *f*. **beyond redemption** sin redención, irremediable.

redirect [riːdai'rekt] *v* (*letter, etc.*) remitir al destinatario.

redress [rə'dres] *v* rectificar. *n* reparación *f*.

reduce [rə'djuːs] *v* reducir; rebajar; (*slim*) adelgazar. **reduction** *n* reducción *f*; (*length*) acortamiento *m*; (*width*) estrechamiento; (*weight*) adelgazamiento *m*; (*rank*) degradación *f*; (*prices*) disminución *f*; (*discount*) rebaja *f*; (*temperature*) baja *f*.

redundant [rə'dʌndənt] *adj* excesivo, superfluo. **be made redundant** perder su empleo. **redundancy** *n* desempleo *m*.

reed [riːd] *n* caña *f*; (*of wind instrument*) lengüeta *f*.

reef [riːf] *n* arrecife *m*.

reek [riːk] *v* apestar. *n* tufo *m*.

reel[1] [riːl] *n* (*cotton*) carrete *m*, bobina *f*; (*film*) cinta *f*; (*fishing*) carretel *m*. **reel off** (*recite*) recitar de un tirón.

reel[2] [riːl] *v* (*sway*) hacer eses, dar vueltas.

refectory [rə'fektəri] *n* refectorio *m*.

refer [rə'fəɪ] *v* remitir; enviar; (*date, event*) situar; atribuir. **reference** *n* referencia *f*; alusión *f*; relación *f*; (*source of information*) fuente *f*; (*person*) fiador *m*. **reference book** libro de consulta *m*. **reference library** biblioteca de consulta *f*. **reference number** número de referencia *m*. **terms of reference** mandato *m*. **make reference to** referirse a. **without reference to** sin consultar. **with reference to** en cuanto a.

referee [refəˈriː] *n* árbitro *m*; (*guarantor of character*) garante *m*. *v* arbitrar.

referendum [refəˈrendəm] *n* referéndum *m*.

refill [riːˈfil; *n* 'riːfil] *v* rellenar. *n* recambio *m*; carga *f*.

refine [rə'fain] *v* refinar; purificar; (*technique*) perfeccionar; (*style*) pulir. **refinement** *n* (*person*) refinamiento *m*; (*manners*) finura *f*; (*sugar, oil*) refinado *m*;

(*metal*) purificación *f*; (*technique*) perfeccionamiento *m*; (*style*) elegancia *f*. **refinery** *n* refinería *f*.
reflect [rə'flekt] *v* reflejar; (*think*) reflexionar. **reflection** *n* (*image*) reflejo *m*; (*act*) reflexión; meditación *f*; crítica *f*.
reflex ['riːfleks] *nm, adj* reflejo. **reflexive** *adj* reflexivo.
reform [rə'fɔːm] *v* reformar; formar de nuevo. *n* reforma *f*. **reformation** *n* reformación *f*. **reformed** *adj* reformado.
refract [rə'frakt] *v* refractar. **refraction** *n* refracción *f*.
refrain¹ [rə'frein] *v* abstenerse.
refrain² [rə'frein] *n* estribillo *m*.
refresh [rə'freʃ] *v* refrescar. **refresher course** cursillo de repaso *m*. **refreshing** *adj* refrescante. **refreshments** *pl n* refrescos *m pl*.
refrigerator [rə'fridʒəreitə] *n* refrigerador *m*, nevera *f*. **refrigerate** *v* refrigerar. **refrigeration** *n* refrigeración *f*.
refuel [riː'fjuːəl] *v* repostar(se).
refuge ['refjuːdʒ] *n* refugio *m*; asilo *m*. **take refuge** refugiarse en. **refugee** *n* refugiado, -a *m, f*.
refund [ri'fʌnd; *n* 'riːfʌnd] *v* reembolsar. *n* reembolso *m*.
refuse¹ [rə'fjuːz] *v* negar. **refusal** *n* negativa *f*; (*rejection*) rechazo *m*.
refuse² ['refjuːs] *n* basura *f*, desecho *m*, desperdicios *m pl*.
refute [ri'fjuːt] *v* refutar.
regain [ri'gein] *v* recobrar; (*return to*) volver a.
regal ['riːgəl] *adj* real, regio.
regard [rə'gaːd] *v* mirar; observar; considerar. **as regards** con respecto a. *n* mirada *f*; atención *f*; respeto *m*; aprecio *m*. **regards** *pl n* (*in a letter*) saludos *m pl*. **regarding** *prep* con respecto a. **regardless** *adv* a pesar de todo. **regardless of** sin tener en cuenta.
regatta [rə'gatə] *n* regata *f*.
regent ['riːdʒənt] *n* regente *m, f*. **regency** *n* regencia *f*.
regime [rei'ʒiːm] *n* régimen *m*.
regiment ['redʒimənt] *n* regimiento *m*. **regimental** *adj* del regimiento.
region ['riːdʒən] *n* región *f*. **regional** *adj* regional.
register ['redʒistə] *n* registro *m*; lista *f*. *v* registrar; (*a complaint*) presentar; (*luggage*) facturar; (*letter*) certificar; (*birth*,

death) declarar. **registrar** *n* registrador *m*; (*med*) doctor, -a *m, f*. **registration** *n* (*trademark*) registro *m*; inscripción *f*; declaración *f*; certificación *f*; facturación *f*; matrícula *f*. **registration number** número de matrícula *m*. **registration plate** placa de matrícula *f*. **registry office** registro civil *m*.
regress [ri'gres] *v* retroceder. **regression** *n* regresión *f*.
regret [rə'gret] *v* sentir, lamentar. *n* sentimiento *m*; pesar *m*; arrepentimiento *m*; excusas *f pl*. **regrettable** *adj* lamentable; doloroso.
regular ['regjulə] *adj* regular; normal; habituado. *n* (*mil*) regular; (*bar*) asiduo, -a *m, f*. **regularity** *n* regularidad *f*.
regulate ['regjuleit] *v* regular; ajustar.
regulation [regju'leiʃən] *n* regulación *f*; regla *f*. *adj* reglamentario.
rehabilitate [riːhə'biliteit] *v* (*reputation*) rehabilitar; (*for work*) restaurar. **rehabilitation** *n* reconstrucción *f*; (*med*) reeducación *f*.
rehearse [rə'həːs] *v* ensayar. **rehearsal** *n* ensayo *m*.
reign [rein] *n* reinado *m*; dominio *m*. *v* reinar.
reimburse [riːim'bəːs] *v* reembolsar. **reimbursement** *n* reembolso *m*.
rein [rein] *n* rienda *f*; (*fig*) riendas *f pl*.
reincarnation [riːinkaː'neiʃən] *n* reencarnación *f*.
reindeer ['reindiə] *n* reno *m*.
reinforce [riːin'fɔːs] *v* reforzar. **reinforcement** *n* refuerzo *m*. **reinforced concrete** hormigón armado *m*.
reinstate [riːin'steit] *v* reinstalar; restablecer. **reinstatement** *n* reintegración *f*, restablecimiento *m*.
reinvest [riːin'vest] *v* reinvertir. **reinvestment** *n* reinversión *f*.
reissue [riː'iʃuː] *v* (*book*) reeditar; (*shares, stamps*) volver a emitir.
reject [rə'dʒekt; *n* 'riːdʒekt] *v* rechazar. *n* cosa defectuosa *f*. **rejection** *n* rechazamiento *m*; (*a reject*) cosa rechazada *f*.
rejoice [rə'dʒois] *v* alegrar, regocijar. **rejoicing** *n* alegría *f*, regocijo *m*.
rejoin [rə'dʒoin] *v* (*reply*) replicar; (*club, society, etc.*) reincorporarse a; (*friends*) reunirse con; (*two objects*) volver a unirse a.

rejuvenate [rə'dʒuɪvəneit] *v* rejuvenecer. **rejuvenation** *n* rejuvenecimiento *m*.

relapse [rə'laps] *n* recaída *f*; (*med*) recidiva *f*. *v* recaer; reincidir.

relate [rə'leit] *v* (*tell*) contar; (*be connected*) relacionar. **related** *adj* (*subjects*) relacionado; (*by birth or marriage*) emparentado. **relating to** lo que tiene que ver con.

relation [rə'leiʃn] *n* (*account*) narración *f*; (*relative*) pariente, -a *m*, *f*; (*connection*) relación *f*. **relationship** *n* relación *f*; (*kinship*) parentesco *m*.

relative ['relətiv] *adj* relativo. *n* pariente, -a *m*, *f*. **relatively** *adv* relativamente. **relativity** *n* relatividad *f*.

relax [rə'laks] *v* relajar; (*loosen*) aflojar. **relaxation** *n* relajación *f*; descanso *m*; distracción *f*. **relaxing** *adj* relajante.

relay [ri'lei; *n* 'riːlei] *v* transmitir. *n* relevo *m*. **relay race** carrera de relevos *f*.

release [rə'liːs] *n* liberación *f*; (*exemption*) exención *f*; (*film, record*) salida *f*; (*information*) anuncio *m*; (*gas, steam*) escape *m*. *v* liberar; (*film, record*) estrenar; anunciar; (*let go*) soltar; (*mechanism*) disparar.

relegate ['religeit] *v* relegar. **relegation** *n* relegación *f*.

relent [rə'lent] *v* ceder; enternecerse. **relentless** *adj* inexorable.

relevant ['reləvənt] *adj* pertinente; relativo; aplicable. **relevance** *n* pertinencia *f*; aplicabilidad *f*.

reliable [ri'laiəbl] *adj* de confianza; seguro. **reliability** *n* seguridad *f*; formalidad *f*.

reliance [rə'laiəns] *n* dependencia *f*; (*trust*) confianza *f*.

relic ['relik] *n* reliquia *f*; vestigio *m*.

relief [rə'liːf] *n* alivio *m*; (*aid*) socorro *m*; (*for the poor*) auxilio *m*; (*substitute worker*) relevo *m*; (*geog, art*) relieve *m*. *adj* suplementario.

relieve [rə'liːv] *v* aliviar; liberar; (*replace*) relevar; (*help*) socorrer.

religion [rə'lidʒən] *n* religión *f*. **religious** *adj* religioso.

relinquish [rə'liŋkwiʃ] *v* renunciar.

relish ['reliʃ] *v* (*food*) saborear; (*enjoy*) disfrutar. *n* gusto *m*; atracción *f*; entusiasmo *m*; (*food*) condimento *m*.

relive [riː'liv] *v* volver a vivir, revivir.

reluctant [rə'lʌktənt] *adj* maldispuesto.

reluctance *n* resistencia *f*. **reluctantly** *adv* de mala gana.

rely [rə'lai] *v* **rely on** contar con, confiar en.

remain [rə'mein] *v* quedarse. **remainder** *n* residuo *m*; resto *m*. **remains** *pl n* restos *m pl*; ruinas *f pl*.

remand [rə'maind] *v* reencarcelar. *n* reencarcelamiento *m*. **be on remand** estar detenido.

remark [rə'maik] *n* observación *f*; comentario *m*. *v* observar, notar; hacer una observación. **remarkable** *adj* notable.

remarry [riː'mari] *v* volver a casarse. **remarriage** *n* segundas nupcias *f pl*.

remedy ['remədi] *n* remedio *m*. *v* remediar. **remedial** *adj* remediador; reparador.

remember [ri'membə] *v* recordar, acordarse de. **remembrance** *n* recuerdo *m*.

remind [rə'maind] *v* recordar. **reminder** *n* advertencia *f*; (*comm*) notificación *f*.

reminiscence [remə'nisens] *n* reminiscencia *f*. **reminisce** *v* recordar el pasado. **reminiscent** *adj* evocador. **be reminiscent of** recordar.

remiss [rə'mis] *adj* descuidado.

remission [rə'miʃn] *n* remisión *f*, perdón *m*; exoneración *f*.

remit [rə'mit] *v* (*send*) remitir; (*forgive*) perdonar; (*return to a lower court*) devolver a un tribunal inferior. **remittance** *n* remesa *f*.

remnant ['remnənt] *n* resto *m*; (*fabric*) retal *m*.

remorse [rə'mois] *n* remordimiento *m*. **remorseful** *adj* arrepentido. **remorseless** *adj* sin remordimientos.

remote [rə'mout] *adj* (*distant*) lejano; (*in time or space*) remoto; (*slight*) ligero; (*out-of-the-way*) retirado; (*stand-offish*) distante. **remote control** mando a distancia *m*.

remove [rə'muːv] *v* quitar; sacar; separar; (*move house*) mudar. **removal** *n* mudanza *f*; (*transfer*) traslado *m*; (*from office*) despido *m*.

remunerate [rə'mjuːnəreit] *v* remunerar. **remuneration** *n* remuneración *f*. **remunerative** *adj* remunerador.

renaissance [rə'neisəns] *n* renacimiento *m*.

rename [riː'neim] *v* poner un nuevo nombre a.

render ['rendə] v (*comm*) rendir; dar; (*a service*) hacer; (*assistance*) prestar; interpretar; (*fat*) derretir. **rendering** n also **rendition** interpretación f.
rendezvous ['rondivuɪ] n cita f. v reunir.
renegade ['renigeid] n, adj renegado, -a.
renew [rə'njuɪ] v renovar; (*extend*) prorogar; (*efforts*) reanudar. **renewal** n renovación f; prórroga f; (*continuation after interruption*) reanudación f.
renounce [ri'nauns] v renunciar. **renunciation** n renunciación f.
renovate ['renəveit] v renovar; reformar. **renovation** n renovación f; reforma f.
renown [rə'naun] n renombre m, fama f. **renowned** adj renombrado, afamado.
rent [rent] n alquiler m. **rent-free** sin pagar alquiler. v alquilar. **rental** n alquiler m.
reopen [riɪ'oupən] v volver a abrir. **reopening** n reapertura f.
reorganize [riɪ'ɔɪgənaiz] v reorganizar. **reorganization** n reorganización f.
rep [rep] n (*coll*) viajante m.
repair [ri'peə] v reparar; componer. n reparación f; compostura f; arreglo m. **beyond repair** no tener arreglo. **closed for repairs** cerrado por reformas.
repartee [repaɪ'tiɪ] n respuesta aguda f; (*coll*) dimes y diretes m pl.
repatriate [riɪ'patrieit] v repatriar. **repatriation** n repatriación f.
***repay** [ri'pei] v (*money*) devolver; (*debt*) liquidar; (*a person*) compensar; (*return*) corresponder a. **repayment** n devolución f, pago m; (*reward*) recompensa f.
repeal [rə'piɪl] v revocar, abrogar. n revocación f, abrogación f.
repeat [rə'piɪt] v repitir; recitar. n repetición f.
repel [rə'pel] v repeler; rechazar. **repellent** adj repelente.
repent [rə'pent] v arrepentirse de. **repentance** n arrepentimiento m. **repentant** adj arrepentido.
repercussion [riɪpə'kʌʃən] n repercusión f.
repertoire ['repətwaɪ] n also **repertory** repertorio m.
repetition [repə'tiʃn] n repetición f. **repetitive** adj reiterativo.
replace [rə'pleis] v (*substitute*) sustituir; (*put back*) reponer. **replacement** n repuesto m; (*person*) sustituto, -a m, f.
replay [riɪ'plei; n 'riɪplei] v (*sport*) volver a

jugar; (*music*) volver a tocar. n (*sport*) repetición de un partido f; (*television*) repetición f.
replenish [rə'pleniʃ] v rellenar. **replenishment** n relleno m.
replica ['replikə] n réplica f, copia f.
reply [rə'plai] v responder, contestar. n respuesta f, contestación f.
report [rə'poɪt] n (*spoken account*) relato m; (*piece of news*) noticia f; (*official*) informe m; (*newspaper or broadcast story*) reportaje m; (*reputation*) fama f; (*school*) boletín m; (*explosion*) estampido m. v relatar; (*for a newspaper*) hacer la crónica de; (*message*) repetir; (*denounce*) denunciar; presentar un informe. **reporter** n reportero m, periodista m, f.
repose [rə'pouz] n reposo m, descanso m. v reposar, descansar.
represent [reprə'zent] v representar. **representation** n representación f.
representative [reprə'zentətiv] adj representativo. n representante m, f.
repress [rə'pres] v reprimir. **repression** n represión f. **repressive** adj represivo.
reprieve [rə'priɪv] n (*law*) indulto m; (*fig: relief*) alivio m. v indultar; aliviar.
reprimand ['reprimaɪnd] n reprimenda f. v reprender.
reprint ['riɪprint; v riɪ'print] n reimpresión f. v reimprimir.
reprisal [rə'praizəl] n represalia f.
reproach [rə'proutʃ] v reprochar. n reproche m. **reproachful** adj reprensor, acusador.
reproduce [riɪprə'djuɪs] v reproducir. **reproduction** n reproducción f. **reproductive** adj reproductor.
reprove [rə'pruɪv] v reprobar, censurar. **reproof** n reprobación f, censura f.
reptile ['reptail] n reptil m.
republic [rə'pʌblik] n república f. **republican** n, adj republicano, -a.
repudiate [rə'pjuɪdieit] v (*person*) repudiar; (*reject*) rechazar; (*contract*) negarse a cumplir. **repudiation** n repudiación f; rechazo m; desconocimiento m.
repugnant [rə'pʌgnənt] adj repugnante. **repugnance** n repugnancia f.
repulsion [rə'pʌlʃn] n repulsión f. **repulsive** adj repulsivo. **repulsiveness** n carácter repulsivo m.
repute [rə'pjuɪt] n reputación f. **reputable** adj acreditado. **reputation** n reputación f. **reputed** adj supuesto.

request [ri'kwest] *n* ruego *m*; demanda *f*. **at the request of** a petición de. *v* rogar, pedir. **request stop** parada discrecional *f*.
requiem ['rekwiəm] *n* requiem *m*.
require [rə'kwaiə] *v* (*need*) requerir; (*demand*) exigir; (*desire*) desear. **requirement** *n* requisito *m*; necesidad *f*.
requisite ['rekwizit] *adj* necesario, indispensable.
requisition [‚rekwi'ziʃən] *n* demanda *f*; pedido *m*. *v* requisar.
*reread [riː'riːd] *v* releer.
re-route [riː'ruːt] *v* cambiar el itinerario de.
*rerun [riː'rʌn; *n* 'riːrʌn] *v* (*film*) reestrenar; (*race*) correr de nuevo. *n* reestreno *m*.
resale [riː'seil] *n* reventa *f*.
rescue ['reskjuː] *n* rescate *m*. **rescue operations** operaciones de salvamento *f pl*. **go to the rescue of** ir en auxilio de. *v* rescatar, salvar. **rescuer** *n* rescatador, -a *m, f*; salvador, -a *m, f*.
research [ri'səːtʃ] *n* investigación *f*. *v* investigar. **researcher** *n* investigador, -a *m, f*.
*resell [riː'sel] *v* revender.
resemble [rə'zembl] *v* parecerse a. **resemblance** *n* parecido *m*.
resent [ri'zent] *v* tomar a mal; ofenderse por. **resentful** *adj* resentido; ofendido. **resentment** *n* resentimiento *m*.
reserve [rə'zəːv] *v* reservar. *n* reserva *f*; (*mil*) reservista *m*. **reservation** *n* reserva *f*. **reserved** *adj* reservado.
reservoir ['rezəvwaː] *n* represa *f*, embalse *m*.
reside [rə'zaid] *v* residir. **residence** *n* (*building*) residencia *f*; (*stay*) permanencia *f*. **resident** *n*(*m*+*f*), *adj* residente. **residential** *adj* residencial.
residue ['rezidjuː] *n* residuo *m*. **residual** *adj* residual.
resign [rə'zain] *v* renunciar; (*hand over*) ceder. **resign oneself to** resignarse a. **resignation** *n* renuncia *f*; (*from a post*) dimisión *f*; resignación *f*. **resigned** *adj* resignado.
resilient [rə'ziliənt] *adj* elástico; (*human body*) resistente; (*person*) de carácter fuerte. **resilience** *n* elasticidad *f*; resistencia *f*; fuerza moral *f*.
resin ['rezin] *n* resina *f*.
resist [rə'zist] *v* resistir; (*bear*) aguantar;

(*impede*) impedir. **resistance** *n* resistencia *f*; aguante *f*. **resistant** *adj* resistente.
*resit [riː'sit] *v* (*exam*) representarse.
resolute ['rezəluːt] *adj* resuelto.
resolve [rə'zolv] *v* resolverse. **resolution** *n* resolución *f*.
resonant ['rezənənt] *adj* resonante. **resonance** *n* resonancia *f*. **resonate** *v* resonar.
resort [rə'zoːt] *n* estación *f*; centro *m*; recurso *m*. **as a last resort** como último recurso. *v* **resort to** recurrir a.
resound [rə'zaund] *v* resonar; (*fig*) tener resonancias. **resounding** *adj* resonante; sonoro; (*fig*) tremendo.
resource [rə'zois] *n* recurso *m*; expediente *m*. **resourceful** *adj* ingenioso, inventivo. **resourcefulness** *n* ingenio *m*, inventiva *f*.
respect [rə'spekt] *n* respeto *m*; consideración *f*; (*aspect*) aspecto *m*. **pay one's respects to** presentar sus respetos a. **with respect to** con respecto a. *v* respetar. **respectable** *adj* respetable; decente. **respectful** *adj* respetuoso. **respective** *adj* respectivo.
respiration [respə'reiʃn] *n* respiración *f*.
respite ['respait] *n* respiro *m*.
respond [rə'spond] *v* contestar; responder; reaccionar. **response** *n* respuesta *f*. **responsive** *adj* sensible.
responsible [rə'sponsəbl] *adj* responsable. **responsibility** *n* responsabilidad *f*.
rest[1] [rest] *n* descanso *m*; reposo *m*; (*music*) pausa *f*; tranquilidad *f*; (*support*) apoyo *m*. *v* descansar; (*stop*) pararse; (*stay*) quedar; (*decision*) depender de; (*lean*) apoyar. **restful** *adj* descansado; tranquilo. **restive** *adj* inquieto. **restless** *adj* desasosegado.
rest[2] [rest] *n* (*remainder*) resto *m*. **the rest** lo demás.
restaurant ['restront] *n* restaurant(e) *m*, restorán *m*. **restaurant car** coche restaurante *m*.
restore [rə'stoː] *v* restaurar; restablecer; (*return*) restituir; (*repair*) reformar; (*to former rank*) rehabilitar. **restoration** *n* restauración *f*; restablecimiento *m*; (*returning*) restituición *f*.
restrain [rə'strein] *v* impedir; limitar; (*repress*) contener. **restraint** *n* restricción *f*; limitación *f*; (*feelings*) represión *f*; moderación *f*.
restrict [rə'strikt] *v* restringir. **restricted** *adj* restringido; (*outlook*) estrecho.

restriction *n* restricción *f*. **restrictive** *adj* restrictivo.
result [rə'zʌlt] *n* resultado *m*. *v* resultar. **result from** derivarse de. **result in** tener por resultado. **resultant** *adj* resultante.
resume [rə'zjuːm] *v* reanudar. **resumption** *n* reanudación *f*.
résumé ['reizumei] *n* resumen *m*.
resurgence [ri'səɪdʒəns] *n* resurgimiento *m*.
resurrect [rezə'rekt] *v* resucitar. **resurrection** *n* resurrección *f*.
resuscitate [rə'sʌsəteit] *v* resucitar. **resuscitation** *n* resucitación *f*.
retail ['riːteil] *n* venta al por menor. *adj, adv* al por menor. *v* vender al por menor; (*relate*) contar. **retailer** *n* vendedor al por menor.
retain [rə'tein] *v* (*keep*) quedarse con; conservar; retener.
retaliate [rə'talieit] *v* vengarse. **retaliation** *n* venganza *f*. **in retaliation** para vengarse.
retard [rə'taɪd] *v* retardar, retrasar. **retarded** *adj* atrasado.
reticent ['retisənt] *adj* reservado. **reticence** *n* reserva *f*.
retina ['retinə] *n* retina *f*.
retinue ['retinjuː] *n* comitiva *f*.
retire [rə'taiə] *v* (*from work*) jubilarse; (*draw back*) retirarse; (*go to bed*) cogerse. **retired** *adj* (*trader, soldier*) retirado; (*civilian*) jubilado. **retirement** *n* retiro *m*; jubilación *f*.
retort[1] [rə'toɪt] *v* replicar. *n* réplica *f*.
retort[2] [rə'toɪt] *n* (*chem*) retorta *f*.
retrace [ri'treis] *v* volver a trazar; repasar. **retrace one's steps** desandar lo andado.
retract [rə'trakt] *v* retractar. **retraction** *n* retractación *f*, retracción *f*.
retreat [rə'triːt] *v* retirarse; retroceder. *n* retirada *f*; (*place*) retiro *m*.
retrial [riː'traiəl] *n* nuevo juicio *m*.
retrieve [rə'triːv] *v* recuperar; (*from ruin*) salvar; (*hunting*) cobrar. **retrieval** *n* recuperación *f*. **retriever** *n* (*dog*) perro cobrador *m*.
retrograde ['retrəgreid] *adj* a retrógrado.
retrospect ['retrəspekt] *n* **in retrospect** retrospectivamente. **retrospective** *adj* retrospectivo.
return [rə'təɪn] *v* devolver; (*refund*) reembolsar; (*lost or stolen property*) restituir; (*investment*) dar; (*elect*) elegir; (*come*

back) volver. **return a call** devolver una visita. *n* vuelta *f*, retorno *m*; (*reward*) recompensa *f*; restitución *f*; (*profit*) ganancias *f pl*; (*interest*) interés *m*; (*tax*) declaración *f*; (*ballot*) resultados *m pl*. **many happy returns!** ¡feliz cumpleaños! **return ticket** billete de ida y vuelta *m*. **in return** en recompensa. **on sale or return** en depósito.
reunite [riːju'nait] *v* reunir. **reunion** *n* reunión *f*.
rev [rev] (*mot*) *n* revolución *f*. **rev counter** cuentarrevoluciones *m invar*. **rev up** acelerar.
reveal [rə'viːl] *v* revelar, descubrir. **revealing** *adj* revelador. **revelation** *n* revelación *f*.
revel ['revl] *v* jaranear, ir de juerga. *n* jarana *f*, juerga *f*. **revelry** *n* jolgorio *m*.
revenge [rə'vendʒ] *n* venganza *f*. *v* vengar. **take revenge for** vengarse de.
revenue ['revinjuː] *n* (*from taxes*) rentas públicas *f pl*; (*income*) entrada *f*.
reverberate [rə'vəɪbəreit] *v* reverberar, reflejar. **reverberation** *n* reverberación *f*.
reverence ['revərəns] *n* reverencia *f*, veneración *f*. **revere** *v* reverenciar, venerar. **reverent** *adj* reverente, respetuoso.
reverse [rə'vəɪs] *n* lo contrario; (*cloth*) revés *m*; (*coin*) cruz *f*; (*printed form*) dorso *m*; (*mot: gear*) marcha atrás *f*. *adj* opuesto; contrario; inverso. *v* invertir; (*turn the other way round*) volver al revés; (*decision*) revocar; (*car*) dar marcha atrás. **reverse the charges** (*phone*) poner una conferencia a cobro revertido. **reversal** *n* inversión *f*. **reversible** *adj* reversible.
revert [rə'vəɪt] *v* volver; revertir.
review [rə'vjuː] *n* examen *m*; crítica *f*; (*mil, theatre*) revista *f*. *v* examinar; volver a examinar; hacer una crítica de. **reviewer** *n* crítico, -a *m, f*.
revise [rə'vaiz] *v* revisar; corregir. **revision** *n* repaso *m*; corrección *f*.
revive [rə'vaiv] *v* (*med*) reanimar, resucitar; (*trade*) reactivar; (*play*) reponer; (*custom*) restablecer; (*interest*) renovar; (*hopes*) despertar. **revival** *n* reanimación *f*; resucitación *f*; reactivación *f*; restablecimiento *m*; (*interest*) renacimiento *m*.
revoke [rə'vouk] *v* revocar; (*withdraw*) suspender.

revolt [rə'voult] *n* rebelión *f*. *v* (*offend*) dar asco a; rebelarse. **revolting** *adj* asqueroso.
revolution [revə'luːʃən] *n* revolución *f*. **revolutionary** *n*, *adj* revolucionario, -a. **revolutionize** *v* revolucionar.
revolve [rə'volv] *v* girar. **revolver** *n* revólver *m*. **revolving door** puerta giratoria *f*.
revue [rə'vjuː] *n* revista *f*.
revulsion [rə'vʌlʃən] *n* repulsión *f*.
reward [rə'woːd] *n* premio *m*, recompensa *f*. *v* premiar, recompensar.
***rewind** [riː'waind] *v* (*film, tape*) rebobinar. **rewinding** *n* rebobinado *m*.
***rewrite** [riː'rait] *v* volver a escribir; volver a redactar.
rhesus ['riːsəs] *n* macaco de la India *m*. **rhesus factor** factor Rhesus *m*.
rhetoric ['retərik] *n* retórica *f*. **rhetorical** *adj* retórico.
rheumatism ['ruːmətizəm] *n* reumatismo *m*. reúma *m*. **rheumatic** *adj* reumático.
rhinoceros [rai'nosərəs] *n* rinoceronte *m*.
rhododendron [roudə'dendrən] *n* rododendro *m*.
rhubarb ['ruːbaːb] *n* ruibarbo *m*.
rhyme [raim] *n* rima *f*. *v* rimar.
rhythm ['riðəm] *n* ritmo *m*. **rhythmic** *adj* rítmico.
rib [rib] *n* costilla *f*; (*umbrella*) varilla *f*; (*knitting*) cordoncillo *m*.
ribbon ['ribən] *n* cinta *f*. **in ribbons** hecho jirones.
rice [rais] *n* arroz *m*.
rich [ritʃ] *adj* rico. **riches** *pl n* riqueza *f sing*. **richness** *n* abundancia *f*; fertilidad *f*.
rickety ['rikəti] *adj* tambaleante.
***rid** [rid] *v* librar, desembarazar. **get rid of** deshacerse de. **riddance** *n* libramiento *m*. **good riddance!** ¡menudo alivio!
riddle¹ ['ridl] *n* enigma *m*; acertijo *m*.
riddle² ['ridl] *v* cribar.
***ride** [raid] *v* montar; (*horse*) montar a caballo. **ride a bicycle/motorbike** montar en bicicleta/motocicleta. *n* vuelta *f*, paseo *m*; (*journey*) viaje *m*. **rider** *n* (*horse*) jinete *m*; (*addition*) cláusula adicional *f*. **riding** *n* equitación *f*.
ridge [ridʒ] *n* (*hills*) cadena *f*; (*crest*) cumbre *f*; (*surface*) ondulación *f*; (*roof*) caballete *m*.
ridicule ['ridikjuːl] *n* ridículo *m*. *v* ridiculizar. **ridiculous** *adj* ridículo.
rife [raif] *adj* abundante.

rifle¹ ['raifl] *n* fusil *m*. **rifle range** campo de tiro *m*.
rifle² ['raifl] *v* saquear.
rift [rift] *n* (*fissure*) grieta *f*; (*in clouds*) claro *m*; (*fig*) ruptura *f*.
rig [rig] *n* (*naut*) aparejo *m*. *v* (*mast*) enjarciar; preparar; arreglar; equipar; (*election*) amañar. **rig out** ataviar. **rig up** improvisar. **rigging** *n* aparejo *m*; montaje *m*; equipo *m*.
right [rait] *adj* (*not left*) derecho; bueno; bien; justo; correcto; exacto. **be right** tener razón. *adv* a la derecha; (*straight*) derecho; bien; correctamente; exactamente; inmediatamente. *n* bien *m*; justicia *f*; (*divine, to the throne, etc.*) derecho *m*; (*right hand*) derecha *f*. **civil rights** *pl n* derechos civiles *m pl*. **right angle** ángulo recto *m*. **right-handed** *adj* que usa la mano derecha. **right-of-way** *n* (*public*) servidumbre de paso *m*; (*roads*) prioridad *f*. **right-wing** *adj* (*pol*) derechista.
righteous ['raitʃəs] *adj* justo, honrado.
rightful ['raitfəl] *adj* legítimo.
rigid ['ridʒid] *adj* rígido; severo. **rigidity** *n* rigidez *f*; severidad *f*.
rigmarole ['rigməroul] *n* (*coll*) galimatías *m invar*.
rigour ['rigə] *n* rigor *m*; severidad *f*. **rigorous** *adj* riguroso; severo.
rim [rim] *m* (*cup*) borde *m*; (*wheel*) llanta *f*.
rind [raind] *n* (*fruit*) cáscara *f*; (*cheese, bacon*) corteza *f*.
ring¹ [riŋ] *n* (*finger*) anillo *m*, sortija *f*; círculo *m*; (*napkin*) aro *m*; (*keys*) llavero *m*. *v* formar círculo. **ringleader** *n* cabecilla *m*. **ring road** carretera de circunvalación *f*.
***ring²** [riŋ] *v* (*bell*) sonar; llamar (por teléfono); (*ears*) zumbar. **ring off** (*phone*) colgar. **ring up** (*phone*) llamar (por teléfono); (*curtain*) subir. *n* (*phone*) llamada *f*; (*sound*) sonido *m*; (*large bell*) campaneo *m*; (*electric bell*) toque *m*; (*alarm clock*) timbre *m*; (*laughter*) cascabeleo *m*.
rink [riŋk] *n* (*ice-skating*) pista de hielo *f*; (*roller-skating*) pista de patinaje *f*.
rinse [rins] *v* aclarar. *n* aclarado *m*.
riot ['raiət] *n* revuelta *f*. **run riot** desmandarse. *v* alborotarse. **rioter** *n* alborotador, -a *m*, *f*. **riotous** *adj* alborotado.

rip [rip] v rasgar. **rip off** *or* **out** arrancar. n rasgón m, rasgadura f.

ripe [raip] adj maduro. **ripen** v madurar. **ripeness** n madurez f.

ripple ['ripl] n rizo m; (*sound of water*) chapoteo m; (*conversation*) murmullo m. v rizar.

*rise [raiz] v (*get up*) levantarse; (*in the air*) elevarse; (*temperature, slope*) subir; (*in rank*) ascender; salir; crecer; desarrollarse; (*revolt*) sublevarse. **rising** adj naciente; ascendente; creciente. n (*sun, moon*) salida f; (*tide*) flujo m; (*water level*) crecida f; (*slope, temperature, curtain*) subida f; (*hill*) elevación f; (*development*) desarrollo m; (*prices, rate, pressure*) aumento m. **give rise to** provocar.

risk [risk] n riesgo m, peligro m. **at risk** a riesgo. v arriesgar. **risky** adj arriesgado.

rissole ['risoul] n croqueta f.

rite [rait] n rito m.

ritual ['ritʃuəl] nm, adj ritual.

rival ['raivəl] n(m+f), adj rival. v competir con. **rivalry** n rivalidad f, competencia f.

river ['rivə] n río m. **riverside** n ribera f. **River Plate** n Río de la Plata m.

rivet ['rivit] n remache m, roblón m. v (*tech*) remachar; (*fig*) fijar; (*fig*) cautivar. **rivetting** adj cautivador.

road [roud] n camino m; carretera f; (*in town*) calle f. **road-block** n barricada f. **road-side** n borde de la carretera m. **road sign** señal de tráfico f. **roadway** n calzada f. **roadworks** pl n obras f pl.

roam [roum] v rondar, vagar por.

roar [roɪ] v (*lion*) rugir; (*bull, sea, wind*) bramar; (*engine*) zumbar; (*shout*) vociferar. **roar with anger** rugir de cólera. **roar with laughter** reirse a carcajadas. n rugido m; bramido m; zumbido m; (*crowd*) clamor m; vociferaciones f pl.

roast [roust] v (*meat*) asar; (*coffee*) tostar. nm, adj asado.

rob [rob] v robar, hurtar. **robber** n ladrón, -ona m, f. **robbery** n robo m, hurto m.

robe [roub] n (*judge's*) toga f; (*dressing gown*) bata f; (*costume*) traje m; (*monk's*) hábito m. v vestir.

robin ['robin] n petirrojo m.

robot ['roubot] n robot m.

robust [rə'bʌst] adj robusto, vigoroso.

rock¹ [rok] n roca f; (*in the sea*) peña f; (*stone*) piedra f; (*sweet*) pirulí m.

rock² [rok] v (*cradle*) mecer; (*move*) balancear; (*shake*) sacudir. n (*music*) rock m. **rocking chair** mecedora f. **rocking-horse** n caballito de balancín m.

rocket ['rokit] n cohete m. v (*prices*) subir vertiginosamente.

rod [rod] n (*pole*) barra f; (*fishing*) caña f; (*curtain*) varilla f.

rode [roud] V **ride**.

rodent ['roudənt] n roedor m.

roe [rou] n (*fish eggs*) hueva f. **soft roe** lechas f pl.

rogue [roug] n granuja m, pícaro m. **roguish** adj pícaro, picaresco. **roguishness** n picardía f.

role [roul] n papel m.

roll [roul] n (*paper, film, butter, tobacco*) rollo m; (*bread*) panecillo m; (*cloth*) pieza f; (*register*) registro m; (*list of names*) nómina f; (*thunder*) fragor m; (*drum*) redoble m. **roll-call** n lista f. **roll of honour** lista de honor f. v hacer rodar; (*cigarettes*) liar; (*waves*) arrastrar. **roll along** rodar por. **roll over** dar una vuelta. **roller** n (*lawn*) rodillo m. **roller-coaster** n montaña rusa f. **roller-skate** n patín de ruedas m. **rolling-pin** n rodillo m.

romance [rou'mans] n (*love*) amores m pl; aventura amorosa f; (*story*) novela romántica f. adj (*language*) romance. v fantasear. **romantic** n, adj romántico, -a.

Rome [roum] n Roma. **Roman** n, adj romano, -a. **Roman Catholic** n, adj católico romano, católica romana. **Roman numeral** número romano m.

romp [romp] n retozo m. v retozar.

roof [ruːf] n, pl **roofs** (*building*) tejado m; (*cave, car, etc.*) techo m. **roof of the mouth** cielo de la boca m. **roof rack** baca f.

rook [ruk] n (*bird*) grajo m; (*chess*) torre f.

room [ruːm] n cuarto m; (*public*) sala f; (*hotel*) habitación de hotel f; (*space*) sitio m; (*accommodation*) alojamiento m. **double room** habitación de matrimonio f. **make room for** dejar sitio. **room and board** cama y comida f, pensión completa f. **room-mate** n compañero/compañera de habitación m, f. **room service** servicio de habitaciones m. **single room** habitación individual f. **roomy** adj espacioso.

roost [ruːst] n percha f; gallinero m. v posarse. **rooster** n gallo m.

root¹ [ruɪt] *n* raíz *f*; origen *m*. *v* echar raíces; (*become fixed*) arraigar.

root² [ruɪt] *v* (*pigs*) hozar.

rope [roup] *n* cuerda *f*; (*pearls*) sarta *f*. **know the ropes** estar al tanto. **learn the ropes** ponerse al tanto. *v* (*tie*) amarrar; (*lasso*) coger con lazo. **rope off** acordonar. **ropy** *adj* (*coll*) malo.

rosary ['rouzəri] *n* rosario *m*.

rose¹ [rouz] *n* rosa *f*. **rose-bush** *n* rosal *m*. **rose garden** rosaleda *f*. **rosewood** *n* palisandro *m*. **rosy** *adj* rosado.

rose² [rouz] *V* rise.

rosemary ['rouzməri] *n* romero *m*.

rosette [rou'zet] *n* escarapela *f*.

***rot** [rot] *v* pudrirse. *n* putrefacción *f*; (*substance*) podredumbre *f*; (*coll: rubbish*) bobadas *f pl*. **rotten** *adj* podrido; (*coll: bad*) pésimo; (*coll: ill*) fatal.

rota ['routə] *n* lista *f*.

rotate [rou'teit] *v* (hacer) girar, (hacer) dar vueltas; (*crops*) alternar. **rotary** *adj* rotatorio, rotativo. **rotation** *n* giro *m*; revolución *f*.

rouge [ruɪʒ] *n* colorete *m*.

rough [rʌf] *adj* (*surface*) áspero; (*coarse*) tosco; duro; brutal; (*draft*) aproximado. **rough-and-ready** *adj* improvisado. **rough copy** *or* **draft** borrador *m*. *v* **rough it** (*coll*) vivir sin comodidades. **roughly** *adv* más o menos. **roughness** *n* aspereza *f*; tosquedad *f*; brutalidad *f*; dureza *f*.

roulette [ruɪ'let] *n* ruleta *f*.

round [raund] *adj* redondo. *prep* alrededor de. *n* círculo *m*; esfera *f*; (*slice*) rodaja *f*; (*patrol, drinks*) ronda *f*; (*ammunition*) andanada *f*; (*applause*) salva *f*. *v* redondear; dar la vuelta; doblar. **round off** acabar. **round up** acorralar; reunir; (*figure*) redondear.

roundabout ['raundəbaut] *n* (*mot*) plaza circular *f*; (*fair*) tiovivo *m*. *adj* indirecto.

rouse [rauz] *v* despertar; animar.

route [ruɪt] *n* ruta *f*, itinerario *m*.

routine [ruɪ'tiɪn] *adj* rutinario. *n* rutina *f*.

rove [rouv] *v* vagar, errar.

row¹ [rou] *n* (*file*) fila *f*; (*knitting*) vuelta *f*.

row² [rou] *v* (*boat*) remar; (*a person*) llevar a remo. **rowing** *n* remo *m*. **rowing boat** *n* bote de remos *m*.

row³ [rau] *n* (*quarrel*) bronca *f*; (*fuss*) jaleo *m*; (*noise*) alboroto *m*. *v* reñir.

rowdy ['raudi] *n*(*m*+*f*), *adj* camorrista. **rowdiness** *n* alboroto *m*; ruido *m*.

royal ['roiəl] *adj* real, regio. **royalist** *n* monárquico, -a *m*, *f*. **royalties** *pl n* derechos de autor *m pl*. **royalty** *n* realeza *f*.

rub [rʌb] *n* frotamiento *m*. *v* frotar. **rubbing** *n* (*brass, etc.*) frotamiento *m*.

rubber ['rʌbə] *n* caucho *m*, goma *f*; (*eraser*) goma de borrar *f*. **rubber band** goma *f*. **rubber stamp** sello de goma *m*. **rubber tree** gomero *m*. **rubbery** *adj* parecido a la goma.

rubbish ['rʌbiʃ] *n* (*refuse*) basura *f*; (*waste*) desperdicios *m pl*; (*derog*) porquería *f*; (*nonsense*) tonterías *f pl*.

rubble ['rʌbl] *n* escombros *m pl*.

ruby ['ruɪbi] *n* rubí *m*.

rucksack ['rʌksak] *n* mochila *f*.

rudder ['rʌdə] *n* timón *m*.

rude [ruɪd] *adj* (*coarse*) grosero; (*impolite*) descortés; (*rough*) tosco; (*hard*) duro; (*painful*) penoso; (*health*) robusto. **rudeness** *n* grosería *f*; descortesía *f*; indecencia *f*.

rudiment ['ruɪdimənt] *n* rudimento *m*. **rudimentary** *adj* rudimentario.

rueful ['ruɪfəl] *adj* contrito; vergonzoso; triste. **ruefully** *adv* tristemente. **ruefulness** *n* tristeza *f*, aflicción *f*.

ruff [rʌf] *n* (*dress*) gorguera *f*; (*on animals*) collarín *m*.

ruffian ['rʌfiən] *n* rufián *m*.

ruffle ['rʌfl] *v* (*disturb*) agitar; (*hair*) desgreñar; (*feathers*) erizar; (*cloth*) fruncir; (*wrinkle*) arrugar; (*worry*) perturbar.

rug [rʌg] *n* (*carpet*) alfombra *f*; (*small carpet*) tapete *m*; (*blanket*) manta de viaje *f*.

rugged ['rʌgid] *adj* (*rock*) escarpado; (*ground*) accidentado; (*character*) desabrido; (*face*) duro; (*climate*) riguroso. **ruggedness** *n* lo escarpado; lo accidentado; desabrimiento *m*; dureza *f*.

ruin ['ruɪin] *n* ruina *f*. *v* arruinar. **ruinous** *adj* ruinoso.

rule [ruɪl] *n* regla *f*; mando *m*, gobierno *m*. **as a rule** por regla general. **rule of the road** reglamento del tráfico *m*. **rules and regulations** reglamento *m sing*. *v* mandar, gobernar; (*lines*) tirar (una línea). **rule out** excluir. **ruler** *n* gobernante *m*, *f*; soberano, -a *m*, *f*; (*measuring*) regla *f*. **ruling** *n* (*law*) decisión *f*.

rum [rʌm] *n* ron *m*.

rumble ['rʌmbl] *n* nido sordo *m*; (*stomach*) borborigmo *m*. *v* retumbar; (*stomach*) sonar.

rummage ['rʌmidʒ] *v* revolver. **rummage sale** venta de prendas usadas *f*.
rumour ['ruːmə] *n* rumor *m*. **it is rumoured (that)** se rumorea (que).
rump [rʌmp] *n* (*quadruped*) ancas *f pl*; (*person*) trasero *m*; (*cookery*) cuarto trasero *m*.
*****run** [rʌn] *v* correr; circular; (*theatre*) estar en cartel; (*leak*) salirse; (*car*) marchar; (*machine*) funcionar; (*melt*) derretirse; (*colours*) desteñirse; (*road*) pasar; (*stockings*) hacirse una carrerilla. *n* (*race*) carrera *f*; (*short trip*) paseo *m*; (*of a train, etc.*) trayecto *m*; (*series*) serie *f*; (*ski*) pista *f*; (*print*) tirada *f*. **in the long run** a la larga.
run away *v* escaparse. **runaway** *nm, adj* fugitivo.
run down *v* (*knock over*) atropellar; (*criticize*) poner por los suelos. **run-down** *adj* (*exhausted*) agotado. **rundown** *n* informe detallado *m*.
rung[1] [rʌŋ] *V* ring.
rung[2] [rʌŋ] *n* peldaño *m*.
run in *v* (*mot*) rodar; (*arrest*) detener.
runner ['rʌnə] *n* (*athlete*) corredor, -a *m, f*; (*sledge*) patín *m*. **runner bean** judía escarlata *f*. **runner-up** *n* subcampeón, -ona *m, f*.
run out *v* acabarse.
run over *v* (*hit*) pillar; (*rehearse*) volver a ensayar; (*text*) echar un vistazo a; (*overflow*) rebosar.
run up *v* (*make quickly*) hacer rápidamente; (*flag*) izar. **run up against** tropezar con.
runway ['rʌnwei] *n* pista *f*.
rupture ['rʌptʃə] *n* ruptura *f*; (*med*) hernia *f*. *v* romper.
rural ['ruərəl] *adj* rural, campestre.
ruse [ruːz] *n* ardid *m*.
rush[1] [rʌʃ] *n* ímpetu *m*; prisa *f*; carrera precipitada *f*. *v* hacer precipitadamente; meter prisa. **rush hour** hora punta *f*.
rush[2] [rʌʃ] *n* (*bot*) junco *m*.
rusk [rʌsk] *n* galleta dura *f*.
Russia ['rʌʃə] *n* Rusia *f*. **Russian** *n, adj* ruso, -a.
rust [rʌst] *n* orín *m*, herrumbre *f*. *v* oxidar. **rusty** *adj* oxidado.
rustic ['rʌstik] *adj* rústico.
rustle ['rʌsl] *v* (*leaves*) susurrar; (*paper*) crujir. *n* susurro *m*; crujido *m*.
rut [rʌt] *n* rodera *f*.

ruthless ['ruːθlis] *adj* despiadado, implacable.
rye [rai] *n* centeno *m*.

S

sabbatical [sə'batikəl] *adj* sabático. **sabbatical year** año de permiso *m*.
sable ['seibl] *n* cebellina *f*.
sabotage ['sabətaːʒ] *n* sabotaje *m*. *v* sabotear. **saboteur** *n* saboteador, -a *m, f*.
sabre ['seibə] *n* sable *m*.
saccharin ['sakərin] *n* sacarina *f*. *adj* sacarino.
sachet ['saʃei] *n* saquito *m*.
sack [sak] *n* saco *m*. **get the sack** (*coll*) recibir el pasaporte. *v* (*coll*) despedir.
sacrament ['sakrəmənt] *n* sacramento *m*.
sacred ['seikrid] *adj* sagrado.
sacrifice ['sakrifais] *n* sacrificio *m*. *v* sacrificar.
sacrilege ['sakrəlidʒ] *n* sacrilegio *m*. **sacrilegious** *adj* sacrílego.
sad [sad] *adj* triste. **sadden** *v* entristecer. **sadly** *adv* tristemente; (*unfortunately*) desgraciadamente. **sadness** *n* tristeza *f*.
saddle ['sadl] *n* (*horse*) silla *f*; (*bicycle*) sillín *m*. **saddle-bag** *n* (*horse*) alforja *f*; (*bicycle*) cartera *f*. **saddle with** cargar con. **saddler** *n* guarnicionero *m*. **saddlery** *n* guarnicones *f pl*.
sadism ['seidizəm] *n* sadismo *m*. **sadist** *n* sádico, -a *m, f*. **sadistic** *adj* sádico.
safari [sə'faːri] *n* safari *m*. **safari park** reserva *f*.
safe [seif] *adj* (*unhurt*) sano y salvo; (*undamaged*) intacto; (*secure*) seguro; (*harmless*) inofensivo; (*trustworthy*) de fiar. *n* caja de caudales *f*. **safekeeping** *n* custodia *f*. **be on the safe side** para mayor seguridad. **safely** *adv* a buen puerto; sin peligro. **safety** *n* seguridad *f*; salvamento *m*. **safety belt** cinturón de seguridad *m*. **safety pin** imperdible *m*.
safeguard ['seifgaːd] *n* salvaguardia *f*. *v* salvaguardar.
saffron ['safrən] *n* azafrán *m*. *adj* azafranado.
sag [sag] *v* doblegarse; flaquear. *n* hundimiento *m*; flexión *f*.

saga ['saɪgə] *n* saga *f.*
sage¹ [seɪdʒ] *nm. adj* sabio.
sage² [seɪdʒ] *n* (*bot*) salvia *f.*
Sagittarius [sadʒi'teəriəs] *n* Sagitario *m.*
said [sed] *V* say.
sail [seil] *n* vela *f*; (*trip*) paseo *m*; (*windmill*) brazo *m.* **sailcloth** *n* lona *f.* **set sail** hacerse a la mar. *v* (*leave*) salir; (*cross*) atravesar; (*boat*) navegar. **sail through** (*coll*) hacer muy fácilmente. **sailing** *n* (*navigation*) navegación *f*; (*departure*) salida *f.* **sailing boat** barco de vela *m.* **sailor** *n* marinero *m.*
saint [seint] *n* santo, -a *m, f.*
sake [seik] *n* **for the sake of** por; para; por amor de.
salad ['saləd] *n* ensalada *f.* **salad cream** mayonesa *f.* **salad dressing** vinagreta *f.*
salami [sə'laɪmi] *n* salchichón *m.*
salary ['saləri] *n* sueldo *m.*
sale [seil] *n* venta *f*; (*reductions*) liquidación *f.* **for** *or* **on sale** en venta. **sale-room** *n* sala de subasta *f.* **salesman** *n* (*shop*) dependiente *m*; (*rep*) representante *m.* **salesmanship** *n* arte de vender *m.*
saline ['seilain] *adj* salino. **salinity** *n* salinidad *f.*
saliva [sə'laivə] *n* saliva *f.* **salivary** *adj* salival. **salivate** *v* salivar.
sallow ['salou] *adj* cetrino.
salmon ['samən] *n* salmón *m.*
salon ['salon] *n* salón *m.*
saloon [sə'luɪn] *n* salón *m*; sala *f.* **saloon bar** salón interior *m.* **saloon car** coche salón *m.*
salt [soɪlt] *n* sal *f.* **salt-cellar** *n* salero *m.* *v* salar. **salty** *adj* salado.
salute [sə'luɪt] *n* saludo *m*; (*gun*) salva *f.* *v* saludar.
salvage ['salvidʒ] *n* salvamento *m*; objetos salvados *m pl.* *v* salvar.
salvation [sal'veiʃən] *n* salvación *f.*
same [seim] *adj* mismo; igual. *pron* el mismo, la misma. *adv* de la misma forma. **all the same** sin embargo. **at the same time** al mismo tiempo.
sample ['saimpl] *n* muestra *f*; prueba *f*; ejemplo *m.* *v* probar; (*drinks*) catar.
sanatorium [sanə'toɪriəm] *n* sanatorio *m.*
sanctify ['saŋktifai] *v* santificar. **sanctification** *n* santificación *f.*
sanctimonious [saŋkti'mouniəs] *adj* santurrón.
sanction ['saŋkʃən] *n* sanción *f.* *v* sancionar; autorizar.

sanctity ['saŋktəti] *n* santidad *f*; inviolabilidad *f.*
sanctuary ['saŋktʃuəri] *n* santuario *m*; (*refuge*) refugio *m*; (*animal*) reserva *f.*
sand [sand] *n* arena *f.* **sandbag** *n* saco terrero *m.* **sand dune** duna *f.* **sandpaper** *n* papel de lija *m.* *v* (*with sandpaper*) lijar. **sandy** *adj* (*beach*) arenoso; (*hair*) rubio rojizo.
sandal ['sandl] *n* sandalia *f.*
sandwich ['sanwidʒ] *n* bocadillo *m.* *v* intercalar.
sane [sein] *adj* sano; razonable. **sanity** *n* juicio *m*; (*sensibleness*) sensatez *f.*
sang [saŋ] *V* sing.
sanitary ['sanitəri] *adj* sanitario; higiénico. **sanitary towel** paño higiénico *m.*
sank [saŋk] *V* sink.
sap [sap] *n* savia *f.*
sapphire ['safaiə] *n* zafiro *m.*
sarcasm ['saɪkazəm] *n* sarcasmo *m.*
sardine [saɪ'diɪn] *n* sardina *f.*
Sardinia [saɪ'dinjə] *n* Cerdeña *f.* **Sardinian** *n, adj* sardo, -a *m, f.*
sardonic [saɪ'donik] *adj* sardónico.
sash¹ [saʃ] *n* faja *f*; (*chest ribbon*) banda *f*; (*waist*) fajín *m.*
sash² [saʃ] *n* (*frame*) marco *m.* **sash window** ventana de guillotina *f.*
sat [sat] *V* sit.
Satan ['seitən] *n* Satán *m*, Satanás *m.* **satanic** *adj* satánico.
satchel ['satʃəl] *n* cartera *f.*
satellite ['satəlait] *n* satélite *m.*
satin ['satin] *n* raso *m.*
satire ['sataiə] *n* sátira *f.* **satirical** *adj* satírico. **satirize** *v* satirizar.
satisfy ['satisfai] *v* satisfacer; convencer. **satisfaction** *n* satisfacción *f.* **satisfactory** *adj* satisfactorio.
saturate ['satʃəreit] *v* saturar; (*soak*) empapar. **saturation** *n* saturación *f.* **reach saturation point** llegar al punto de saturación.
Saturday ['satədi] *n* sábado *m.*
sauce [sois] *n* salsa *f*; (*slang*) insolencia *f.* **saucy** *adj* descarado; coquetón.
saucepan ['soispən] *n* cacerola *f.*
saucer ['soisə] *n* platillo *m.* **flying saucer** platillo volante *m.*
sauerkraut ['sauəkraut] *n* sauerkraut *m.*
sauna [soɪnə] *n* sauna *f.*
saunter [soɪntə] *v* pasearse. *n* paso lento *m*; paseo *m.*

sausage ['sosidʒ] *n* salchicha *f.* **sausage-meat** *n* carne de salchicha *f.* **sausage roll** empanadilla de salchicha *f.*
savage ['savidʒ] *adj* (*fierce*) feroz; (*primitive*) salvaje; cruel; violento. *n* salvaje *m*, *f. v* embestir. **savagery** *n* salvajada *f*; ferocidad *f.*
save[1] [seiv] *v* salvar; (*put aside*) ahorrar; (*keep till later*) quardar; (*protect*) proteger; (*goal*) parar. **savings** *pl n* ahorros *m pl.* **savings bank** caja de ahorros *f.*
save[2] [seiv] *prep* salvo, excepto. *conj* a no ser que.
saviour ['seivjə] *n* salvador, -a *m*, *f.*
savoir-faire [ˌsavwaɪ'feə] *n* desparpajo *m*; sentido común *m.*
savour ['seivə] *v* saborear; tener sabor de. *n* sabor *m*, gusto *m.* **savoury** *adj* sabroso; salado. *n* entremés salado *m.*
saw[1] [soɪ] *V* see.
*saw[2] [soɪ] *n* (*tool*) sierra *f*; (*proverb*) refrán *m.* **sawdust** *n* aserrín *m.* **sawmill** *n* aserradero *m. v* aserrar.
saxophone ['saksəfoun] *n* saxofón *m.*
*say [sei] *v* decir; recitar. *n* **have no say** no tener ni voz ni voto. **saying** *n* (*act*) decir *m*; (*maxim*) refrán *m.*
scab [skab] *n* costra *f*, postilla *f*; (*derog: blackleg*) esquirol *m.*
scaffold ['skafəld] *n* (*platform*) tarina *f*; (*gallows*) cadalso *m.* **scaffolding** *n* andamio *m.*
scald [skoɪld] *v* escaldar; (*instruments*) esterilizar. *n* escaldadura *f.* **scalding** *adj* hirviendo, hirviente.
scale[1] [skeil] *n* (*fish, etc.*) escama *f*; (*tartar*) sarro *m.* **scaly** *adj* escamoso; sarroso.
scale[2] [skeil] *n* (*music, measurement*) escala *f*; (*damage, etc.*) amplitud *f.* **scale drawing** dibujo hecho a escala *m. v* (*climb*) escalar. **scale down** reducir a escala.
scales [skeilz] *pl n* balanza *f sing.*
scallop ['skaləp] *n* (*zool*) venera *f*; (*cookery*) escalope *m*; (*sewing*) festón *m.* **scallop shell** concha *f. v* festonear.
scalp [skalp] *n* cuero cebelludo *m. v* escalpar.
scalpel ['skalpəl] *n* escalpelo *m.*
scamper ['skampə] *v* corretear.
scampi ['skampi] *n* gamba grande *f.*
scan [skan] *v* recorrer con la mirada; escrutar; (*tech*) explorar; (*poetry*) escandir.
scandal ['skandl] *n* escándalo *m*; (*gossip*)

chismorreo *m*; (*law*) difamación *f.* **scandalize** *v* escandalizar. **scandalous** *adj* escandaloso.
Scandinavia [ˌskandi'neivjə] *n* Escandinavia *f.* **Scandinavian** *n*, *adj* escandinavo, -a.
scant [skant] *adj also* **scanty** insuficiente. **scantily** *adv* muy ligeramente.
scapegoat ['skeipgout] *n* cabeza de turco *f.*
scar [skaɪ] *n* cicatriz *f. v* cicatrizar; (*fig*) marcar.
scarce [skeəs] *adj* escaso; insuficiente; raro. **scarcely** *adv* apenas; casi. **scarcity** *n* escasez *f.*
scare [skeə] *n* susto *m*; alarma *f. v* asustar, espantar. **be scared** tener miedo. **scarecrow** *n* espantapájaros *m invar.*
scarf [skaɪf] *m* (*woollen*) bufanda *f*; (*light*) pañuelo *m.*
scarlet ['skaɪlit] *adj* escarlato. **scarlet fever** escarlatina *f.*
scathing ['skeiðiŋ] *adj* cáustico, mordaz.
scatter ['skatə] *v* esparcir; (*sprinkle*) salpicar; (*put to flight*) derrotar; dispersar; (*squander*) desparramar. **scatter-brained** *adj* atolondrado.
scavenge ['skavindʒ] *v* recoger; buscar entre. **scavenger** *n* barrendero *m*; animal que se alimenta de carroña *m.*
scene [siɪn] *n* escena *f*; (*place*) lugar *m*; espectáculo *m*; vista *f.* **scenic** *adj* escénico; pintoresco.
scenery ['siɪnəri] *n* (*landscape*) paisaje *m*; (*theatre*) decorado *m.*
scent [sent] *n* perfume *m*; (*smell*) olor *m*; (*track*) rastro *m. v* perfumar; (*smell*) oler.
sceptic ['skeptik] *n* escéptico, -a *m*, *f.* **sceptical** *adj* escéptico. **scepticism** *n* escepticismo *m.*
sceptre ['septə] *n* cetro *m.*
schedule ['ʃedjuɪl] *n* programa *m*; (*timetable*) horario *m. v* programar; fijar.
scheme [skiɪm] *n* plan *m*; proyecto *m*, esquema *m*; (*plot*) intriga *f. v* proyectar; intrigar, conspirar.
schizophrenia [ˌskitsə'friɪniə] *n* esquizofrenia *f.* **schizophrenic** *n*, *adj* esquizofrénico, -a.
scholar ['skolə] *n* (*learned person*) erudito, -a *m*, *f*; (*schoolchild*) colegial, -a *m*, *f*, alumno, -a *m*, *f*; (*student*) estudiante *m*, *f.* **scholarly** *adj* erudito. **scholarship** *n* (*award*) beca *f*; erudición *f.*

scholastic [skə'lastik] *adj* escolar, escolástico.

school[1] [skuːl] *n* escuela *f*; (*private or secondary*) colegio *m*. **schoolboy** *n* alumno *m*, colegial *m*. **schoolgirl** *n* alumna *f*, colegiala *f*. **schooling** *n* educación *f*, enseñanza *f*. **schoolmaster** *n* (*primary*) maestro *m*; (*secondary*) profesor *m*. **schoolmistress** *n* maestra *f*; profesora *f*. **school-room** *n* clase *f*; sala de clase *f*.

school[2] [skuːl] *n* (*of fish*) banco *m*.

schooner ['skuːnə] *n* goleta *f*.

sciatica [sai'atikə] *n* ciática *f*. **sciatic** *adj* ciático.

science ['saiəns] *n* ciencia *f*. **science fiction** ciencia ficción *f*. **scientific** *adj* científico. **scientist** *n* científico, -a *m*, *f*.

scintillating ['sintileitiŋ] *adj* relumbrante; (*fig*) brillante.

scissors ['sizəz] *pl n* tijeras *f pl*.

scoff[1] [skof] *v* burlarse.

scoff[2] [skof] *v* (*coll: eat*) zamparse.

scold [skould] *v* reñir, reprender. *n* virago *f*. **scolding** *n* reprensión *f*.

scone [skon] *n* bollo *m*.

scoop [skuːp] *n* pala de mano *f*; (*press*) éxito periodístico *m*. *v* sacar con pala; (*dig*) excavar.

scooter ['skuːtə] *n* (*motor*) scooter *m*; (*child's*) patinete *m*.

scope [skoup] *n* (*range*) alcance *m*; (*opportunity*) libertad *f*; (*field of action*) esfera *f*.

scorch [skoːtʃ] *n* quemadura *f*. *v* quemar; (*singe*) chamuscar.

score [skoi] *n* (*number of points*) tanteo *m*; (*result*) resultado *m*; (*test marks*) calificación *f*; (*twenty*) veintena *f*; (*music*) partitura *f*; (*notch*) muesca *f*. **scoreboard** *n* marcador *m*. *v* (*point, goal*) marcar; orquestar; hacer una muesca en. **scorer** *n* (*scorekeeper*) tanteador *m*; (*football*) goleador *m*.

scorn [skoin] *n* desdén *m*, desprecio *m*. *v* desdeñar, despreciar. **scornful** *adj* desdeñoso, despreciativo.

Scorpio ['skoːpiou] *n* Escorpión *m*.

scorpion ['skoːpiən] *n* escorpión *m*.

Scotland ['skotlənd] *n* Escocia *f*. **Scot** *n* escocés, -esa *m*, *f*. **Scotch** *n* whisky escocés *m*. **Scots** *nm*, *adj* escocés. **Scottish** *adj* escocés.

scoundrel ['skaundrəl] *n* sinvergüenza *m*.

scour[1] [skauə] *v* (*clean*) fregar. **scourer** *n* (*pad*) estropajo *m*.

scour[2] [skauə] *v* (*search*) recorrer, batir.

scout [skaut] *n* explorador *m*. **scoutmaster** *n* jefe de exploradores *m*.

scowl [skaul] *v* fruncir el entrecejo. *n* ceño *m*.

scramble ['skrambl] *v* (*climb*) trepar; (*struggle*) pelearse; (*mix*) mezclar; (*eggs*) revolver. *n* lucha *f*, pelea *f*.

scrap [skrap] *n* (*piece*) trozo *m*; (*metal*) chatarra *f*; (*coll: fight*) pelea *f*. **scrapbook** *n* álbum de recortes *m*. papel para apuntes *m*. **scraps** *pl n* restos *m pl*, sobras *f pl*. *v* desechar; (*coll*) pelear.

scrape [skreip] *n* (*noise*) chirrido *m*; (*act*) raspado *m*; (*mark*) arañazo *m*; (*graze*) rasguño *m*; (*coll: trouble*) apuro *m*. *v* raspar; (*graze*) arañar; (*drag*) arrastrar.

scratch [skratʃ] *n* arañazo *m*; raya *f*; rasguño *m*; cero *m*.

scrawl [skroil] *v* garabatear. *n* garabato *m*.

scream [skriːm] *n* grito *m*, chillido *m*. *v* gritar, chillar.

screech [skriːtʃ] *v* chillar, gritar; (*brakes*) chirriar. *n* chillido *m*, grito *m*; chirrido *m*.

screen [skriːn] *n* (*TV, film*) pantalla *f*; (*folding*) biombo *m*; (*fig*) cortina *f*. **screen-play** *n* guión *m*. **screen test** prueba cinematográfica *f*. *v* (*film*) proyectar; (*shelter*) proteger; (*sift*) tamizar.

screw [skruː] *n* tornillo *m*; (*propeller*) hélice *f*. **screwdriver** *n* destornillador *m*. *v* atornillar. **screw up** (*paper*) arrugar.

scribble ['skribl] *v* garabatear. *n* garabato *m*.

script [skript] *n* (*film*) guión *m*; (*theatre*) argumento *m*; (*writing*) escritura *f*.

scripture ['skriptʃə] *n* (*school*) religión *f*; (*holy*) Sagrada Escritura *f*.

scroll [skroul] *n* rollo *m*; (*arch*) voluta *f*.

scrounge [skraundʒ] (*coll*) *v* sablear; gorronear. **scrounger** *n* sablista *m*, *f*; gorrón, -ona *m*, *f*.

scrub[1] [skrʌb] *n* fregado *m*; fricción *f*. *v* fregar; restregar; (*coll: cancel*) cancelar. **scrubbing brush** cepillo de fregar *m*.

scrub[2] [skrʌb] *n* matorral *m*; maleza *f*.

scruff [skrʌf] *n* **by the scruff of the neck** por el cogote.

scruffy ['skrʌfi] *adj* desaliñado. **scruffiness** *n* desaliño *m*.

scrum [skrʌm] *n* melée *f*.
scruple ['skruːpl] *n* escrúpulo *m*. **scrupulous** *adj* escrupuloso.
scrutiny ['skruːtəni] *n* escrutinio *m*. **scrutinize** *v* escudriñar.
scuffle ['skʌfl] *n* pelea *f*, refriega *f*. *v* pelear, reñir.
scull [skʌl] *n* remo *m*.
scullery ['skʌləri] *n* trascocina *f*.
sculpt [skʌlpt] *v* esculpir. **sculptor** *n* escultor, -a *m*, *f*. **sculpture** *n* escultura *f*.
scum [skʌm] *n* espuma *f*; (*derog*) escoria *f*.
scurf [skəːf] *n* caspa *f*.
scurvy ['skəːvi] *n* escorbuto *m*.
scuttle[1] ['skʌtl] *n* (*coal*) cubo del carbón *m*.
scuttle[2] ['skʌtl] *v* (*naut*) barrenar.
scuttle[3] ['skʌtl] *v* escabullirse.
scythe [saið] *n* guadaña *f*. *v* guadañar.
sea [siː] *n* mar *m*, *f*.
sea-bed *n* fondo del mar *m*.
seaborne ['siːboːn] *adj* transportado por mar.
seafood ['siːfuːd] *n* mariscos *m pl*.
seafront ['siːfrʌnt] *n* paseo marítimo *m*.
seagoing ['siːgouiŋ] *adj* (*ship*) de alta mar; (*person*) marinero.
seagull ['siːgʌl] *n* gaviota *f*.
seahorse ['siːhoːs] *n* caballo de mar *m*.
seal[1] [siːl] *n* sello *m*. *v* sellar; (*close*) cerrar; (*fate*) decidir. **sealing wax** lacre *m*.
seal[2] [siːl] *n* (*zool*) foca *f*. **sealskin** *n* piel de foca *f*.
sea-level *n* nivel del mar *m*.
sea-lion *n* león marino *m*.
seam [siːm] *n* (*sewing*) costura *f*; (*coal*) vena *f*; (*geol*) capa *f*. **seamy** *adj* (*fig*) sórdido.
seaman ['siːmən] *n pl* **seamen** marinero *m*.
séance ['seiãs] *n* sesión de espiritismo *f*.
sear [siə] *v* (*scorch*) abrasar; (*wither*) marchitar. **searing** *adj* (*pain*) punzante.
search [səːtʃ] *n* investigación *f*; (*to find something*) búsqueda *f*; (*house, car*) registro *m*. **searchlight** *n* reflector *m*. **search-party** *n* equipo de salvamento *m*. **search warrant** *n* mandamiento de registro *m*. *v* buscar; registrar; investigar. **searching** *adj* (*look*) penetrante; (*examination*) minucioso.
sea shell *n* concha marina *f*.
seashore ['siːʃoː] *n* playa *f*; costa *f*.

seasick ['siːsik] *adj* be **seasick** marearse. **sea sickness** mareo *m*.
seaside ['siːsaid] *n* playa *f*; costa *f*. **seaside resort** estación balnearia *f*.
season ['siːzn] *n* estación *f*; temporada *f*; época *f*. **season ticket** abono *m*. *v* (*food*) sazonar; (*wood*) secar. **seasonal** *adj* estacional; (*work*) temporal. **seasoning** *n* condimento *m*.
seat [siːt] *n* asiento *m*; silla *f*; localidad *f*; centro *m*. **seat-belt** *n* cinturón de seguridad *m*. *v* sentar; colocar; tener cabida para.
seawater ['siːˌwoːtə] *n* agua de mar *f*.
seaweed ['siːwiːd] *n* alga *f*.
seaworthy ['siːwəːði] *adj* marinero. **seaworthiness** *n* navegabilidad *f*.
secluded [si'kluːdid] *adj* retirado; aislado. **seclusion** *n* reclusión *f*; soledad *f*.
second[1] ['sekənd] *n* (*time*) segundo *m*. **second hand** segundero *m*.
second[2] ['sekənd] *n* segundo, -a *m*, *f*. (*gear*) segunda *f*. **seconds** *pl n* artículos de segunda clase *m pl*. *adj* segundo. **on second thoughts** pensándolo bien. **second-class** *adj* de segunda clase. **travel second-class** viajar en segunda. **second-hand** *adj* de segunda mano, usado. **second-rate** *adj* de segunda categoría. *v* (*in debate*) apoyar. **secondly** *adv* en segundo lugar.
secondary ['sekəndəri] *adj* secundario. **secondary school** instituto de enseñanza media *m*.
secret ['siːkrit] *nm*, *adj* secreto. **secrecy** *n* secreto *m*. **secretive** *adj* reservado; callado. **secretly** *adv* en secreto.
secretary ['sekrətəri] *n* secretario, -a *m*, *f*. **secretarial** *adj* de secretario.
secrete [si'kriːt] *v* (*hide*) esconder; (*med*) secretar. **secretion** *n* secreción *f*.
sect [sekt] *n* secta *f*. **sectarian** *adj* sectario.
section ['sekʃən] *n* sección *f*; parte *f*.
sector ['sektə] *n* sector *m*.
secular ['sekjulə] *adj* profano; secular; laico.
secure [si'kjuə] *adj* seguro. *v* asegurar; cerrar firmemente; garantizar; conseguir; reservar; consolidar. **security** *n* seguridad *f*; (*for loan*) garantía *f*.
sedate [si'deit] *adj* sosegado; tranquilo. **sedation** *n* sedación *f*. **sedative** *nm*, *adj* sedante.

sediment ['sedimənt] n (geol) sedimento m; (liquid) poso m.

seduce [si'djuːs] v seducir. **seduction** n seducción f. **seductive** adj seductor.

*see[1] [siː] v ver; comprender; mirar; visitar; recibir. **see off** ir a despedir. **see through** (not be deceived) calar. **see to** ocuparse de. **see you later!** ¡hasta luego!

see[2] [siː] n (rel) obispado m.

seed [siːd] n semilla f; (fruit) pepita f; (sperm) semen m. **seedless** adj sin semillas; sin pepitas. **seedling** n plantón m.

seedy adj granado; (coll: ill) pachucho.

*seek [siːk] v buscar; tratar; solicitar.

seem [siːm] v parecer. **seeming** adj aparente. **seemingly** adv al parecer, por lo visto.

seep [siːp] v rezumarse. **seepage** n filtración f.

seesaw ['siːsɔː] n columpio m, subibaja m. v columpiarse.

seethe [siːð] v borbotar. **seething** adj (coll) bufando de cólera.

segment ['segmənt] n segmento m; (orange, etc.) gajo m.

segregate ['segrigeit] v segregar. **segregation** n segregación f.

seize [siːz] v tomar; (grab firmly) agarrar; (a person) detener. **seize up** (tech) agarrotarse. **seizure** n asimiento m; detención f; (property) embargo m; (in war) toma f; (med) ataque m.

seldom ['seldəm] adv raramente.

select [sə'lekt] v escoger, elegir. adj escogido; (exclusive) selecto. **selection** n selección f. **selective** adj selectivo.

self [self] n sí mismo m, sí misma f; personalidad f.

self-addressed adj con su propia dirección.

self-adhesive adj autoadhesivo.

self-assured adj seguro de sí mismo. **self-assurance** n confianza en sí mismo f.

self-centred adj egocéntrico.

self-confident adj seguro de sí mismo. **self-confidence** n seguridad en sí mismo f.

self-conscious adj cohibido. **self-consciousness** n turbación f.

self-contained adj independiente.

self-control n dominio de sí mismo m. **self-controlled** adj sereno.

self-defence n (technique) autodefensa f; (law) legítima defensa f.

self-determination n autodeterminación f.

self-discipline n autodisciplina f.

self-educated adj autodidacto.

self-employed adj que trabaja por cuenta propia.

self-esteem n amor propio m.

self-evidence adj patente, manifiesto.

self-explanatory adj que se explica por sí mismo.

self-expression n expresión de la propia personalidad f.

self-interest n interés propio m.

selfish ['selfiʃ] adj egoísta. **selfishness** n egoísmo m.

selfless ['selflis] adj desinteresado.

self-made adj **self-made man** hijo de sus propias obras m.

self-opinionated adj obstinado.

self-pity n lástima de sí mismo f.

self-portrait n autorretrato m.

self-possessed adj seguro de sí mismo.

self-respect n dignidad f.

self-righteous adj farisaico. **self-righteousness** n fariseísmo m.

self-rule n autonomía f.

self-sacrifice n sacrificio de sí mismo m.

selfsame ['selfseim] adj mismísimo m.

self-satisfied adj satisfecho de sí mismo.

self-service n autoservicio m.

self-sufficient adj independiente. **self-sufficiency** n independencia f.

self-willed adj obstinado.

self-winding adj de cuerda automática.

*sell [sel] v vender(se); hacer vender. **sell off** liquidar. **seller** n vendedor, -a m, f; (dealer) comerciante m.

semantic [sə'mantik] adj semántico. **semantics** n semántica f.

semaphore ['seməfɔː] n semáforo m.

semblance ['sembləns] n apariencia f.

semen ['siːmən] n semen m.

semibreve ['semibriːv] n semibreve f.

semicircle ['semisɜːkl] n semicírculo m. **semicircular** adj semicircular.

semicolon [,semi'koulən] n punto y coma m.

semiconscious [semi'konʃəs] adj semiconsciente.

semi-detached house n casa doble f.

semifinal [semi'fainl] n semifinal f.

seminar ['seminɑː] n seminario m.

semi-precious adj fino; semiprecioso.

semiquaver ['semikweivə] n semicorchea f.

semitone ['semitoun] *n* semitono *m*.
semolina [,semə'liːnə] *n* sémola *f*.
senate ['senit] *n* senado *m*. **senator** *n* senador *m*.
***send** [send] *v* enviar, mandar; remitir; echar; transmitir. **send back** devolver. **send for** llamar a; (*mail-order*) escribir pidiendo.
senile ['siːnail] *adj* senil. **senility** *n* senilidad *f*.
senior ['siːnjə] *adj* (*age*) mayor; (*rank*) superior. *n* (*school*) mayor *m*, *f*. **seniority** *n* antigüedad *f*.
sensation [sen'seiʃən] *n* sensación *f*. **sensational** *adj* sensacional.
sense [sens] *n* sentido *m*; significado *m*; sensación *f*; sentimiento *m*; (*consensus*) sentir *m*. **senses** *pl n* (*reason*) juicio *m sing*; (*consciousness*) sentido *m*. *v* sentir. **senseless** *adj* (*unconscious*) sin sentido; (*silly*) insensato.
sensible ['sensəbl] *adj* sensato; razonable; (*clothes*) práctico.
sensitive ['sensitiv] *adj* sensible; (*easily hurt*) susceptible. **sensitivity** *n* sensibilidad *f*; susceptibilidad *f*.
sensual ['sensjuəl] *adj* sensual. **sensuality** *n* sensualidad *f*.
sensuous ['sensjuəs] *adj* sensual.
sent [sent] *V* send.
sentence ['sentəns] *n* (*gramm*) frase *f*; (*law*) sentencia *f*. *v* sentenciar, condenar.
sentiment ['sentimənt] *n* sentimiento *m*; (*sentimentality*) sentimentalismo *m*; opinión *f*. **sentimental** *adj* sentimental.
sentry ['sentri] *n* centinela *m*.
separate ['sepərət] *v* 'sepəreit] *adj* separado; distinto; independiente; (*room*) particular. *v* separar; dividir; distinguir entre. **separation** *n* separación *f*.
September [sep'tembə] *n* septiembre *m*, setiembre *m*.
septic ['septik] *adj* séptico.
sequel ['siːkwəl] *n* consecuencia *f*; secuela *f*.
sequence ['siːkwəns] *n* sucesión *f*; serie *f*; orden *m*.
sequin ['siːkwin] *n* lentejuela *f*.
serenade [serə'neid] *n* serenata *f*. *v* dar una serenata a.
serene [sə'riːn] *adj* sereno. **serenity** *n* serenidad *f*.
serf [səːf] *n* siervo, -a *m*, *f*.

sergeant ['saːdʒənt] *n* (*mil*) sargento *m*; (*police*) cabo *m*. **sergeant-major** *n* sargento mayor *m*.
serial ['siəriəl] *n* serial *m*. *adj* de serie; seriado. **serialize** *v* publicar por entregas.
series ['siəriːz] *n* serie *f*.
serious ['siəriəs] *adj* serio; grave. **seriousness** *n* seriedad *f*; gravedad *f*.
sermon ['səːmən] *n* sermón *m*.
serpent ['səːpənt] *n* serpiente *f*.
serrated [sə'reitid] *adj* serrado; dentado.
servant ['səːvənt] *n* criado, -a *m*, *f*; sirviente, -a *m*, *f*; empleado, -a *m*, *f*; funcionario, -a *m*, *f*.
serve [səːv] *v* servir; atender. **it serves you right** te está bien empleado. *n* (*tennis*) saque *m*.
service ['səːvis] *n* servicio *m*; favor *m*; (*mot*) revisión *f*; (*tea*) juego *m*; (*tennis*) saque *m*. **service charge** servicio *m*. **serviceman** *n* militar *m*. **service station** (*mot*) estación de servicio *f*. *v* (*check*) revisar; (*maintain*) mantener. **serviceable** *adj* utilizable; práctico.
serviette [,səːvi'et] *n* servilleta *f*.
servile ['səːvail] *adj* servil. **servility** *n* servilismo *m*.
session ['seʃən] *n* sesión *f*; junta *f*.
***set** [set] *v* poner; colocar; fijar; (*clock*) regular; (*bones*) reducir; (*type*) componer; (*to music*) poner en música; (*sun*) ponerse. **set about** ponerse (a). **setback** *n* revés *m*; contratiempo *m*. **set off** (*leave*) partir; (*explode*) hacer estallar; (*cause*) hacer. **set out** partir; disponer. **set up** erigir; montar; establecer. *n* grupo *m*; (*tools, china, etc.*) juego *m*; (*kitchen implements*) batería *f*; (*books*) colección *f*; (*people*) clase *f*; (*clothes*) caída *f*; (*sun, etc.*) puesta *f*; (*radio, etc.*) aparato *m*; (*tennis*) set *m*; (*theatre*) decorado *m*. *adj* fijo; inmóvil; asignado; establecido. **setting** *n* (*adjustment*) ajuste *m*; (*theatre*) decorado *m*.
settee [se'tiː] *n* canapé *m*.
settle ['setl] *v* (*solve*) resolver; calmar; (*country*) colonizar. **settle down** instalarse; calmarse. **settle up** (*bill*) pagar. **settlement** *n* colonización *f*; arreglo *m*; liquidicación *f*; satisfacción *f*.
seven ['sevn] *nm, adj* siete. **seventh** *n, adj* séptimo, -a..
seventeen [sevn'tiːn] *nm, adj* diecisiete. **seventeenth** *n, adj* decimoséptimo, -a.

seventy ['sevnti] *nm, adj* setenta. **seventi-eth** *n, adj* septuagésimo, -a.
sever ['sevə] *v* cortar.
several ['sevrəl] *adj, pron* varios.
severe [sə'viə] *adj* severo; duro; (*pain*) agudo; (*illness*) grave. **severity** *n* severidad *f*; gravedad *f*; (*weather*) inclemencia *f*.
*****sew** [sou] *v* coser. **sewing** *n* costura *f*. **sewing machine** máquina de coser *f*.
sewage ['sjuidʒ] *n* aguas residuales *f pl*.
sewer ['sjuə] *n* alcantarilla *f*, albañal *m*.
sex [seks] *n* sexo *m*. **sexual** *adj* sexual. **sexual intercourse** relaciones sexuales *f pl*. **sexuality** *n* sexualidad *f*. **sexy** *adj* provocativo.
sextet [seks'tet] *n* sexteto *m*.
shabby ['ʃabi] *adj* andrajoso; (*behaviour*) mezquino.
shack [ʃak] *n* choza *f*.
shade [ʃeid] *n* sombra *f*; (*lamp*) pantalla *f*; (*colour*) tono *m*; (*meaning*) matiz *m*. *v* dar sombra; (*art*) sombrear. **shady** *adj* sombreado; (*person*) dudoso.
shadow ['ʃadou] *n* sombra *f*. **shadow cabinet** gabinete fantasma *m*. *v* (*follow*) seguir. **shadowy** *adj* indistinto; misterioso.
shaft [ʃaift] *n* (*handle*) mango *m*; (*lift*) hueco *m*; (*light*) rayo *m*; (*ventilation*) pozo de ventilación *m*; (*mine*) pozo *m*; (*spear*) asta *f*.
shaggy ['ʃagi] *adj* peludo.
*****shake** [ʃeik] *v* sacudir; (*bottle*) agitar; (*head*) menear; (*brandish*) esgrimir. **shake hands** darse la mano. **shake off** librarse de. *n* sacudida *f*; meneo *m*; movimiento *m*; temblor *m*. **shaky** *adj* tembloroso; (*weak*) poco sólido.
shall [ʃal] *aux translated by future tense*.
shallot [ʃə'lot] *n* chalote *m*.
shallow ['ʃalou] *adj* poco profundo; superficial.
sham [ʃam] *adj* fingido, simulado; falso. *n* (*person*) impostor, -a *m, f*; (*object*) impostura *f*. *v* fingir, simular.
shame [ʃeim] *n* vergüenza *f*; deshonra *f*; pena *f*. *v* avergonzar; deshonrar. **shame-faced** *adj* avergonzado; tímido. **shameful** *adj* vergonzoso. **shameless** *adj* desvergonzado; sinvergüenza.
shampoo [ʃam'puɪ] *n* champú *m*. *v* dar un champú a.
shamrock ['ʃamrok] *n* trébol *m*.
shandy ['ʃandi] *n* cerveza con gaseosa *f*.

shanty[1] ['ʃanti] *n* (*hut*) chabola *f*. **shanty town** barrio de las latas *m*.
shanty[2] ['ʃanti] *n* (*music*) saloma *f*.
shape [ʃeip] *n* forma *f*; figura *f*; aspecto *m*. *v* dar forma a; labrar; cortar; (*idea*) formular. **shapeless** *adj* informe. **shapely** *adj* bien proporcionado.
share [ʃeə] *n* parte *f*; (*comm*) acción *f*. **shareholder** *n* accionista *m, f*. *v* compartir.
shark [ʃaɪk] *n* tiburón *m*.
sharp [ʃaɪp] *adj* (*edge*) afilado; (*point*) punzante; (*bend*) brusco; (*phot*) nítido; (*outline*) definido; (*pain*) agudo; (*taste*) picante; (*clever*) vivo. *n* (*music*) sostenido *m*. **sharpen** *v* (*knife*) afilar; (*pencil*) sacar punta a. **sharpness** *n* lo afilado; agudeza *f*; (*clarity*) nitidez *f*.
shatter ['ʃatə] *v* destrozar; (*health*) quebrantar; (*fig*) echar por tierra. **shattered** *adj* destrozado; roto; quebrantado. **shattering** *adj* demoledor; fulgurante.
shave [ʃeiv] *v* afeitarse. **shaving** *n* (*of wood, metal*) viruta *f*. **shaving brush** brocha de afeitar *f*. **shaving cream** crema de afeitar *f*.
shawl [ʃoɪl] *n* chal *m*.
she [ʃiɪ] *pron* ella. **she who** la que, aquella que, quien.
sheaf [ʃiɪf] *n* (*corn*) gavilla *f*; (*arrows*) haz *m*; (*papers*) fajo *m*.
*****shear** [ʃiə] *v* esquilar. **shears** *pl n* tijeras *f pl*.
sheath [ʃiɪθ] *n* (*umbrella, knife, etc.*) funda *f*; (*sword*) vaina *f*. **sheathe** *v* envainar; cubrir.
*****shed**[1] [ʃed] *v* (*drop*) deshacerse de.
shed[2] [ʃed] *n* cobertizo *m*; barraca *f*.
sheen [ʃiɪn] *n* brillo *m*; (*silk*) viso *m*.
sheep [ʃiɪp] *n* oveja *f*. **sheepdog** *n* perro pastor *m*. **sheepskin** *n* piel de carnero *f*. **sheepish** *adj* vergonzoso.
sheer[1] [ʃiə] *adj* completo; total; puro; (*cliff*) cortado a pico; (*stockings*) diáfano.
sheer[2] [ʃiə] *v* (*naut*) guiñar.
sheet [ʃiɪt] *n* (*bed*) sábana *f*; (*paper, glass*) hoja *f*; (*ice*) capa *f*; (*metal*) chapa *f*; (*water*) extensión *f*. **sheet lightning** fucilazo *m*. **sheet music** música en hojas sueltas *f*.
sheikh [ʃeik] *n* jeque *m*.
shelf [ʃelf] *n* estante *m*.
shell [ʃel] *n* concha *f*; (*crustacean*) caparazón *m*; (*egg, nut*) cáscara *f*; (*pea*) vaina *f*; (*cannon*) proyectil *m*. **shellfish** *pl*

n mariscos *m pl. v* (*mil*) bombardear; (*peas, shrimps*) pelar; (*nuts*) descascarar.
shelter ['ʃeltə] *n* abrigo *m*; asilo *m. v* abrigar; proteger; dar asilo.
shelve [ʃelv] *v* (*project*) dar carpetazo a. **shelving** *n* estantería *f.*
shepherd ['ʃepəd] *n* pastor *m.*
sheriff ['ʃerif] *n* sheriff *m.*
sherry ['ʃeri] *n* jerez *m.*
shield [ʃiːld] *n* escudo *m*; (*fig*) defensa *f. v* escudar; proteger.
shift [ʃift] *n* cambio *m*; movimiento *m*; (*work*) turno *m*. **shift key** tecla de mayúsculas *f.* **shift work** trabajo por turnos *m. v* cambiar; mover. **shifty** *adj* furtivo.
shimmer ['ʃimə] *v* relucir. *n* luz trémula *f.*
shin [ʃin] *n* espinilla *f.*
*shine [ʃain] *v* brillar. *n* brillo *m*, lustre *m*. **shiny** *adj* lustroso, brillante.
shingle ['ʃiŋgl] *n* (*pebbles*) guijarros *m pl.* **shingles** *n* (*med*) herpes *m, f pl.*
ship [ʃip] *n* barco *m*, navío *m*, buque *m.* **shipshape** *adj* en buen orden. **shipwreck** *n* naufragio *m. v* embarcar; transportar; (*send*) enviar. **shipment** *n* cargamento *m.* **shipping** *n* barcos *m pl*, buques *m pl.*
shirk [ʃəːk] *v* esquivar. **shirker** *n* gandul, -a *m, f.*
shirt [ʃəːt] *n* camisa *f.* **in one's shirt sleeves** en mangas de camisa. **shirt-tail** *n* faldón *m.*
shit [ʃit] *nf, interj* (*vulgar*) mierda. *v* cagar.
shiver ['ʃivə] *v* temblar; estremecerse. *n* temblor *m*; estremecimiento *m.*
shoal [ʃoul] *n* (*fish*) banco *m.*
shock [ʃok] *n* choque *m*; (*elec*) descarga *f.* **shock absorber** amortiguador *m.* **shockproof** *adj* a prueba de choques. *v* conmocionar; escandalizar. **shocking** *adj* escandaloso; espantoso; (*news*) aterrador.
shoddy ['ʃodi] *adj* inferior. **shoddiness** *n* fabricación inferior *f.*
*shoe [ʃuː] *v* (*horse*) herrar. *n* zapato *m.* **shoelace** *n* cordón *m.* **shoemaker** *n* zapatero *m.* **shoe repairer's** zapatería de viejo *f.* **shoe shop** zapatería *f.*
shone [ʃon] *V* **shine.**
shook [ʃuk] *V* **shake.**
*shoot [ʃuːt] *v* (*fire*) lanzar, tirar; (*kill*) matar; (*wound*) herir; (*film*) filmar; (*hunt*) cazar. *n* (*bot*) brote *m.* **shooting** *n* tiro *m pl*; (*hunting*) caza *f.*
shop [ʃop] *n* tienda *f*; (*larger*) almacén *m.*

shop assistant *n* dependiente, -a *m, f.*
shopkeeper ['ʃopkiːpə] *n* comerciante *m, f.*
shoplifter ['ʃopliftə] *n* ratero, -a *m, f.* **shoplifting** *n* ratería *f.*
shopper ['ʃopə] *n* comprador, -a *m, f.*
shopping ['ʃopiŋ] *n* compras *f pl.* **go shopping** ir de compras. **shopping bag** bolsa de la compra *f.* **shopping centre** centro comercial *m.* **shopping trolley** carrito *m.*
shop steward *n* enlace sindical *m.*
shore [ʃoː] *n* (*beach*) playa *f*; (*edge of sea*) orilla *f*; (*coast*) costa *f.*
short [ʃoːt] *adj* corto; pequeño; (*not tall*) bajo; (*brusque*) seco; (*temper*) vivo. **in short** en resumen. **shortage** *n* falta *f*, escasez *f.* **shorten** *v* acortar; disminuir; abreviar. **shortly** *adv* dentro de poco.
shortbread ['ʃoːtbred] *n* mantecada *f.*
short-circuit *n* cortocircuito. *v* ponerse en cortocircuito.
shortcoming ['ʃoːtkʌmiŋ] *n* defecto *m.*
short cut *n* atajo *m.*
shorthand ['ʃoːthand] *n* taquigrafía *f.* **shorthand typist** taquimecanógrafo, -a *m, f.*
short list *n* lista de los posibles *f.*
short-lived *adj* efímero.
shorts [ʃoːts] *pl n* pantalones cortos *m pl.*
short-sighted *adj* miope.
short story *n* novela corta *f.*
short-tempered *adj* de mal genio.
short-term *adj* de corto plazo.
short wave *n* onda corta *f. adj* de onda corta.
shot[1] [ʃot] *V* **shoot.**
shot[2] [ʃot] *n* bala *f*; tiro *m*; tirador, -a *m, f*; (*sport*) peso *m*; (*med*) inyección *f.* **shotgun** *n* escopeta *f.*
should[1] [ʃud] *v* deber, tener que.
should[2] [ʃud] *aux translated by conditional tense.*
shoulder ['ʃouldə] *n* hombro *m.* **shoulderblade** *n* omóplato *m*; (*animal*) paletilla *f. v* llevar al hombro.
shout [ʃaut] *n* grito *m. v* gritar.
shove [ʃʌv] *n* empujón *m. v* empujar.
shovel ['ʃʌvl] *n* pala *f. v* traspalar.
*show [ʃou] *v* mostrar; descubrir; revelar; exhibir; indicar; demostrar; probar. *n* exposición *f*; espectáculo *m*; (*appearance*) apariencia *f*; (*ostentation*) pompa *f.*
show business *n* mundo del espectáculo *m.*

shower ['ʃauə] n (rain) chubasco m; (bath) ducha f. v llover; ducharse; (pour) derramar.
show in v hacer pasar.
show jumping n concurso hípico m.
show off v (coll) darse pisto.
showpiece ['ʃoupiːs] n modelo m; obra maestra f.
showroom ['ʃourum] n sala de muestras f.
show up v (coll: arrive) aparecer; (embarrass) poner en evidencia.
showy ['ʃoui] adj ostentoso.
shrimp [ʃrimp] n camarón m.
shrine [ʃrain] n capilla f; santuario m; altar m.
***shrink** [ʃriŋk] v (clothes) encoger. **shrink from** repugnarse de. **shrinkage** n encogimiento m.
shrivel ['ʃrivl] v secar, marchitar. **shrivel up** apergaminarse.
shroud [ʃraud] n sudario m, mortaja f; (fig) velo m. v amortajar; (fig) envolver.
Shrove Tuesday [ʃrouv] n martes de carnaval m.
shrub [ʃrʌb] n arbusto m. **shrubbery** n arbustos m pl, matorrales m pl.
shrug [ʃrʌg] v encogimiento de hombros m. v encogerse de hombros.
shudder ['ʃʌdə] n repeluzno m; (engine) vibración f. v estremecerse.
shuffle ['ʃʌfl] n arrastramiento de los pies m; (cards) barajada f. v arrastrar; barajar.
shun [ʃʌn] v evitar, rehuir.
shunt [ʃʌnt] v (trains) desviar.
***shut** [ʃʌt] v cerrar. **shut in** encerrar. **shut out** no admitir. **shut up** (coll) callarse; hacer callar.
shutter ['ʃʌtə] n (window) postigo m; (phot) obturador m.
shuttle ['ʃʌtl] n lanzadera f. **shuttlecock** n volante m. **shuttle service** servicio regular de ida y vuelta m.
shy [ʃai] adj tímido. v (horse) espantarse. **shyness** n timidez f.
Siamese [ˌsaiə'miːz] adj (cat, twin) siamés.
sick [sik] adj enfermo. **be sick** vomitar. **be sick of** (coll) estar harto de. **feel sick** tener náuseas. **sickbed** n lecho de enfermo m. **sick benefit** subidio de enfermedad m. **sicken** v poner enfermo. **sickening** adj nauseabundo; (distressing) deprimente. **sickly** adj (person) enfermizo; (taste) empalagoso. **sickness** n enfermedad f; (sea, air) mareo m.

sickle ['sikl] n hoz f.
side [said] n lado m; (edge) borde; (team) equipo m. **side with** ponerse de parte de. adj lateral; secundario; indirecto.
sideboard ['saidbɔːd] n aparador m.
sideburns ['saidbəːnz] pl n patillas f pl.
sidecar ['saidkaː] n sidecar m.
side effects pl n efectos secundarios m pl.
sidelight ['saidlait] n (mot) luz de posición f.
sideline ['saidlain] n negocio accesorio m; (sport) banquillo m.
sidelong ['saidloŋ] adj, adv de reojo.
side-splitting adj divertidísimo.
side-step v evitar.
side street n calle lateral f.
side-track v despistar.
sideways ['saidweiz] adv oblicuamente. adj de lado.
siding ['saidiŋ] n (rail) vía muerta f.
sidle ['saidl] v avanzar furtivamente. **sidle up to** acercarse furtivamente.
siege [siːdʒ] n sitio m, asedio m.
sieve [siv] n tamiz m, scolador m. v tamizar.
sift [sift] v tamizar; (sprinkle) espolvorear; (evidence) examinar cuidadosamente. **sift out** encontrar; seleccionar. **sifter** cedazo m.
sigh [sai] n suspiro m. v suspirar.
sight [sait] n vista f; espectáculo m. **sightseeing** n turismo m. v avistar; (aim) apuntar.
sign [sain] n señal f; indicio m; (notice) anuncio m; muestra f. **signpost** n letrero m. v firmar.
signal ['signəl] n señal f. v hacer señales; indicar.
signature ['signətʃə] n firma f.
signify ['signifai] v significar. **significance** n significado m. **significant** adj significativo.
silence ['sailəns] n silencio m. v callar; hacer callar. **silencer** (mot, gun) n silenciador m. **silent** adj silencioso; callado.
silhouette [silu'et] n silueta f. **be silhouetted against** destacarse contra.
silk [silk] n seda f. **silkworm** n gusano de seda m. **silky** adj (fabric) sedoso; (voice, manner) suave.
sill [sil] n antepecho m, alféizar m.
silly ['sili] adj tonto, bobo. **silliness** n tontería f, bobería f.

silt [silt] *n* cieno *m*, limo *m*. **silt up** encenagar.

silver ['silvə] *n* plata *f*; (*coll*: *change*) suelto *m*. *adj* de plata; (*like silver*) plateado. **silver plate** baño de plata *m*. **silversmith** *n* platero *m*. *v* platear. **silvery** *adj* plateado; (*voice*) argentino.

similar ['similə] *adj* semejante, parecido. **similarity** *n* semejanza *f*.

simile ['siməli] *n* símil *m*.

simmer ['simə] *v* hervir a fuego lento; (*fig*) germentar. **simmer down** calmarse.

simple ['simpl] *adj* sencillo; natural; fácil; simple; puro; inocente; (*simple-minded*) necio. **simpleton** *n* simplón, -ona *m*, *f*. **simplicity** *n* sencillez *f*; simpleza *f*. **simplify** *v* simplificar. **simply** *adv* sencillamente; meramente.

simulate ['simjuleit] *v* similar. **simulation** *n* simulación *f*.

simultaneous [ˌsiməl'teinjəs] *adj* simultáneo.

sin [sin] *n* pecado *m*. *v* pecar. **sinful** *adj* (*person*) pecador; pecaminoso. **sinner** *n* pecador, -a *m*, *f*.

since [sins] *adv* desde entonces. *prep* desde. *conj* desde que; (*because*) ya que.

sincere [sin'siə] *adj* sincero. **sincerity** *n* sinceridad *f*.

sinew ['sinjuɪ] *n* tendón *m*.

*sing [siŋ] *v* cantar. **singer** *n* cantor, -a *m*, *f*, cantante *m*, *f*. **singing** *n* canto *m*.

singe [sindʒ] *v* chamuscar. *n* chamusquina *f*.

single ['siŋgl] *adj* solo; único; (*copy*) suelto; (*not double*) individual; (*unmarried*) soltero. **single bed** cama individual *f*. **single file** fila de a uno *f*. **single-handed** *adv* sin ayuda. **single-minded** *adj* resuelto. **single room** habitación individual *f*. **single (ticket)** billete de ida *m*. **singles** *n* (*sport*) individual *m*. **single out** separar, distinguir.

singular ['siŋgjulə] *nm*, *adj* singular.

sinister ['sinistə] *adj* siniestro.

*sink [siŋk] *v* hundir, sumergir; (*mine*) cavar; (*voice*) bajar; (*collapse*) dejarse caer; (*go down*) descender. **sink in** (*idea*, *etc*.) darse cuenta de. *n* (*kitchen*) fregadero; (*bathroom*, *bedroom*) lavabo *m*.

sinuous ['sinjuəs] *adj* sinuoso.

sinus ['sainəs] *n* seno *m*. **sinusitis** *n* sinusitis *f*.

sip [sip] *n* sorbo *m*. *v* sorber, beber a sorbos.

siphon ['saifən] *n* sifón *m*. *v* trasegar con sifón. **siphon off** sacar con un sifón.

sir [səɪ] *n* señor *m*, caballero *m*.

siren ['saiərən] *n* sirena *f*.

sirloin ['səɪloin] *n* solomillo *m*.

sister ['sistə] *n* hermana *f*; (*hospital*) enfermera *f*; (*nun*) monja *f*; (*religious title*) sor *f*. **sister-in-law** *n* cuñada *f*.

*sit [sit] *v* sentar; (*exam*) presentarse a; (*committee*) ser miembro. **baby-sit** *v* cuidar niños. **sit down** sentarse. **sit up** incorporarse; (*stay up*) no acostarse. **sitting** *n* sentada *f*; sesión *f*; (*meal*) servicio *m*. **sittingroom** *n* sala de estar *f*.

site [sait] *n* lugar *m*, sitio *m*; (*building*) solar *m*; camping *m*.

situation [sitju'eiʃən] *n* situación *f*; (*job*) empleo *m*. **situate** *v* situar.

six [siks] *nm*, *adj* seis. **sixth** *n*, *adj* sexto, -a; (*date*) seis *m*.

sixteen [siksˈtiɪn] *nm*, *adj* dieciséis. **sixteenth** *n*, *adj* decimosexto, -a.

sixty ['siksti] *nm*, *adj* sesenta. **sixtieth** *n*, *adj* sexagésimo, -a.

size [saiz] *n* tamaño *m*; (*person*, *clothes*) talla *f*; (*gloves*, *shoes*) número *m*. **size up** evaluar, juzgar. **sizeable** *adj* grande; considerable.

sizzle ['sizl] *v* chisporrotear. *n* chisporroteo *m*.

skate[1] [skeit] *n* patín *m*. *v* patinar. **skateboard** *n* skateboard *m*. **skater** *n* patinador, -a *m*, *f*. **skating** *n* patinaje *m*. **skating-rink** *n* pista de patinaje *f*.

skate[2] [skeit] *n* (*fish*) raya *f*.

skeleton ['skelitn] *n* esqueleto *m*. *adj* (*staff*, *etc*.) muy reducido. **skeleton key** llave maestra *f*.

sketch [sketʃ] *n* dibujo *m*; (*rough*) croquis *m*; (*theatre*) sketch *m*. *v* dibujar; hacer un croquis de. **sketch-book** *n* bloc de dibujo *m*. **sketchy** *adj* incompleto; impreciso.

skewer ['skjuə] *n* brocheta *f*. *v* espetar.

ski [skiɪ] *n* esquí *m*. **ski-lift** telesquí *m*. *v* esquiar. **skier** *n* esquiador, -a *m*, *f*. **skiing** *n* esquí *m*.

skid [skid] *n* patinazo *m*. *v* patinar.

skill [skil] *n* habilidad *f*; destreza *f*. **skilful** *adj* hábil; diestro. **skilled** diestro; experto; (*worker*) cualificado.

skim [skim] *v* (*milk*) desnatar; (*surface*) rozar. **skim through** hojear.

skimp [skimp] v escatimar; chapucear.
skimpy adj escaso; pequeño; corto.
skin [skin] n piel f; (face) cutis m; (milk)
nata f. **skin-diving** n natación submarina
f. **skin-tight** adj muy ajustado. v (an
animal) despellejar. **skinny** adj flaco,
descarnado.
skip [skip] n pequeño salto m, brinco m.
v saltar, brincar; saltar a la comba;
(miss) saltarse.
skipper ['skipə] n capitán m.
skirmish ['skə:miʃ] n escaramuza f. v
escaramuzar.
skirt [skə:t] n falda f. v dar la vuelta a.
skirting board zócalo m.
skittle ['skitl] n bolo m. **skittles** n juego
de bolos m.
skull [skʌl] n cráneo m. **skull and cross-
bones** calavera f.
skunk [skʌŋk] n mofeta f.
sky [skai] n cielo m. **sky-blue** nm, adj azul
celeste. **skylark** n alondra f. **skylight** n
claraboya f. **skyline** n horizonte m. **skyscraper** n rascacielos m invar.
slab [slab] n (lump) trozo m; (cake) porción f; (block) bloque m; (stone) losa f;
(metal) plancha f; (chocolate) tableta f.
slack [slak] adj (loose) flojo; (lazy) perezoso; (trade) encalmado. **slacken** v
aflojar; disminuir.
slacks [slaks] pl n pantalones m pl.
slag [slag] n escoria f. **slag heap** escorial
m.
slam [slam] n golpe m; (door) portazo m;
(bridge) slam m. v hacer golpear; cerrar
de un golpe. **slam on the brakes** dar un
frenazo.
slander ['slamdə] n calumnia f; (law)
difamación f. v calumniar; difamar. **slan-
derous** adj calumnioso; difamatorio.
slang [slaŋ] n germanía f, argot m; jerga
f.
slant [slaint] n inclinación f, sesgo m. v
inclinar. **slanting** adj inclinado, al sesgo.
slap [slap] n palmada f; (on face)
bofetada f. v pegar con la mano; (put)
poner violentamente. **slapdash** adj (person) descuidado; (work) chapucero. **slap-
stick** n payasada f.
slash [slaʃ] n (knife) cuchillada f; (whip)
latigazo m. v acuchillar; dar latigazos a;
(coll: prices) sacrificar.
slat [slat] n tablilla f.
slate [sleit] n pizarra f. v empizarrar.

slaughter [slo:tə] n matanza f. **slaughter-
house** n matadero m. v matar;
exterminar.
slave [sleiv] n esclavo, -a m, f. v trabajar
como un negro. **slavery** n esclavitud f.
sledge [sledʒ] n trineo m.
sledgehammer ['sledʒhamə] n almádena
f.
sleek [sli:k] adj liso; pulcro.
*****sleep** [sli:p] v dormir; (spend the night)
pasar la noche. n sueño m. **go to sleep**
dormirse. **sleeper** (rail) traviesa f.
sleeping-bag n saco de dormir m. **sleep-
ing-pill** n somnífero m. **sleepless night**
noche en blanco f. **sleepy** adj soñoliento.
sleet [sli:t] n aguanieve f. v caer
aguanieve.
sleeve [sli:v] n manga f; (record) funda f.
sleeveless adj sin manga.
sleigh [slei] n trineo m.
slender ['slendə] adj (thin) delgado, fino;
(light and graceful) esbelto; (resources)
escaso; (excuse) pobre; (hopes) ligero.
slice [slais] n tajada f; (bread) rebanada f;
(fruit) raja f; (implement) pala f. v cortar;
partir en tajadas/rebanadas/rajas.
slick [slik] adj (derog) astuto; resbaladizo.
n (oil) capa de aceite f.
*****slide** [slaid] v deslizar; hacer resbalar. n
(children's) tobogán m; (act of sliding)
deslizamiento m; (microscope)
portaobjeto m; (phot) diapositiva f. **slide-
rule** n regla de cálculo f. **sliding** adj
(door) corredera; (roof) corredizo; (scale)
móvil.
slight [slait] adj pequeño; insignificante;
(person) débil; frágil. v despreciar. n
desprecio m. **slightest** adj lo más
mínimo. **slightly** adv ligeramente.
slim [slim] adj delgado; esbelto. v adelgazar. **slimming** adj (diet, etc.) que no
engorda, para adelgazar.
slime [slaim] n limo m; (fig) cieno m.
slimy adj limoso; (person) rastrero.
*****sling** [sliŋ] v lanzar; suspender. n (med)
cabestrillo m; (weapon) honda f.
*****slink** [sliŋk] v slink away escurrirse.
slip [slip] n (error) falta f; (oversight)
inadvertencia f; (skid) patinazo m;
(stumble) traspiés m; (moral lapse) desliz
m; (petticoat) combinación f; (pillow)
funda f; (paper) trozo m. **slip of the tongue
or pen** lapsus m. v resbalar; pasar;
poner; descorrer; escurrirse.

slipper ['slipə] n zapatilla f.
slippery ['slipəri] adj resbaladizo; (person) escurridizo.
*slit [slit] v cortar; rasgar. n cortadura f; resquicio m.
slither ['sliðə] v resbalar; deslizarse.
slobber ['slobə] v babosear. n baba f.
sloe [slou] n endrina f.
slog [slog] n (coll) pesadez f. v (coll) sudar tinta.
slogan ['slougən] n slogan m.
slop [slop] v (splash) salpicar; (pour) derramar.
slope [sloup] n inclinación f; (hill) falda f. v inclinarse. sloping adj inclinado; (shoulders) caídos.
sloppy ['slopi] adj (food) aguoso; (garment) muy ancho; (careless) capucero; (sentimental) sensiblero. sloppiness n (sentiment) sensibleria f.
slot [slot] n ranura f, muesca f. v encajar; hacer una ranura.
slouch [slautʃ] v andar cabizbajo.
slovenly ['slʌvnli] adj desaliñado.
slow [slou] adj despacio; lento; (clock) atrasado; (stupid) tardo; (boring) aburrido. in slow motion a cámara lenta. slow down ir más despacio.
slug [slʌg] n (zool) babosa f; (bullet) posta f.
sluggish ['slʌgiʃ] adj perezoso; lento.
sluice [sluis] n esclusa f. v regar; lavar.
slum [slʌm] n barrio bajo m. the slums tugurios m pl.
slumber ['slʌmbə] n sueño tranquilo m. v dormir tranquilo.
slump [slʌmp] n (fig) baja f; (comm) baja repentina f; depresión económica f. v desplomarse.
slung [slʌŋ] V sling.
slunk [slʌŋk] V slink.
slur [sləi] n baldón m; borrón m; (music) ligado m. v articular mal.
slush [slʌʃ] n nieve sucia y deshecha f.
slut [slʌt] n marrana f.
sly [slai] adj astuto; disimulado.
smack¹ [smak] n golpe m; bofetada f; (sound) chasquido m; v dar una bofetada; dar una palmada; pegar con la mano.
smack² [smak] v smack of saber a; (fig) oler a.
small [smoil] adj pequeño; poco; chico; escaso. small change dinero suelto m.

smallpox n viruela f. small talk charla f. n the small of the back región lumbar f.
smart [smait] adj vivo; rápido; (clever) listo; de moda; majo. v picar. smarten up ponerse elegante. smartness n viveza f; elegancia f.
smash [smaʃ] n (sound) estrépito m; accidente m; (blow) puñetazo m; ruina f. v quebrar, romper; destruir; aplastar; chocar con. smashing adj (slang) estupendo.
smear [smiə] n mancha f; (med) frotis m; (fig) calumnia f. v manchar; (bread) untar; calumniar.
*smell [smel] v oler; tener olor. n olor m; (sense) olfato m. smelly adj maloliente.
smile [smail] n sonrisa f. v sonreír.
smirk [smɜik] n sonrisa afectada f. v sonreír afectadamente.
smock [smok] n blusa f.
smog [smog] n niebla espesa con humo f.
smoke [smouk] n humo m. smoke-screen n cortina de humo f. v humear; (tobacco) fumar. smoker n fumador, -a m, f. no smoking se prohibe fumar. smoky adj que huele a humo.
smooth [smuið] adj liso; suave; llano; uniforme; (person) suavón. v alisar; suavizar. smooth over exculpar. smoothly adv lisamente; con suavidad.
smother ['smʌðə] v sofocar; apagar.
smoulder ['smouldə] v arder sin llama.
smudge [smʌdʒ] n mancha f; tiznón m. v manchar; tiznar.
smug [smʌg] adj pagado de sí mismo.
smuggle ['smʌgl] v pasar de contrabando; matutear. smuggler n contrabandista m, f. smuggling n contrabando m.
snack [snak] n bocado m, tentempié m. snack bar cafetería f.
snag [snag] n pega f, obstáculo m. v enganchar; estorbar.
snail [sneil] n caracol m.
snap [snap] n (fingers) castañeteo m; (bones, teeth, mouth) crujido m; (breaking wood) chasquido m; (bite) mordisco m; (phot) instantánea f. adj instantáneo; rápido. snapdragon n dragón m. snapshot n instantánea f. v (bones) romper; (branch) partir; (joints) hacer crujir; (dog) intentar morder; (person) regañar.
snare [sneə] n trampa f, lazo m. v atrapar.
snarl [snail] n gruñido m. v gruñir.

snatch [snatʃ] n fragmento m; (theft) robo m. v agarrar; tomar.

sneak [sniːk] v hacer furtivamente. sneak in/out entrar/salir furtivamente. n (slang) chivato, -a m, f.

sneer [sniə] v decir con desprecio. n desprecio m. sneering adj burlón.

sneeze [sniːz] n estornudo m. v estornudar.

sniff [snif] n aspiración f; inhalación f. v (smell) oler; aspirar.

snigger ['snigə] n risa disimulada f. reírse por lo bajo.

snip [snip] v cortar de un tijeretazo. n (coll: bargain) ganga f.

snipe [snaip] n agachadiza f. v snipe at (mil) tirotear. sniper n paco m.

snivel ['snivl] v lloriquear. snivelling adj llorón; mocoso.

snob [snob] n snob m, esnob m. snobbish adj snob, esnob.

snooker ['snuːkə] n snooker m.

snoop [snuːp] v fisgonear; entrometerse.

snooty ['snuːti] adj (coll) presumido.

snooze [snuːz] n siesta f; sueñecito m. v dormitar.

snore [snoː] n ronquido m. v roncar. snoring n ronquido m.

snorkel ['snoːkəl] n (swimmer's) tubo de respiración m; (submarine's) esnórquel m.

snort [snoːt] n resoplido m. v resoplar.

snout [snaut] n hocico m.

snow [snou] n nieve f. v nevar. be snowed under with estar abrumado de. snowy adj nevoso.

snowball ['snoubɔːl] n bola de nieve f. v tirar bolas de nieve; acumularse.

snowbound ['snoubaund] adj bloqueado por la nieve.

snowdrift ['snoudrift] n ventisquero m.

snowdrop ['snoudrop] n campanilla blanca f.

snowfall ['snoufɔːl] n nevada f.

snowflake ['snoufleik] n copo de nieve m.

snowstorm ['snoustɔːm] n tormenta de nieve f.

snub [snʌb] n repulsa f. v repulsar.

snuff [snʌf] n rapé m. snuff-box n tabaquera f. v (extinguish) despabilar.

snug [snʌg] adj cómodo; abrigadito.

snuggle ['snʌgl] v arrimarse; apretarse.

so [sou] adv así; tan; también; tanto; por lo tanto. conj así que, de modo que, de

manera que. and so on y así sucesivamente. if so de ser así. is that so? ¿de veras? ... or so a poco más o menos ... . so as to de manera que. so-called adj llamado. so much or many tanto, tantos. so-so adj (coll) así así. so that para que. so what? ¿y qué?

soak [souk] v empapar. soak in penetrar en. soak up absorber. soaking n remojo m. soaking wet calado hasta los huesos.

soap [soup] n jabón m. soap dish jabonera f. soap powder jabón en polvo m. soapsuds pl n jabonaduras f pl. v jabonar. soapy adj jabonoso.

soar [soː] v remontarse; (fig) elevarse.

sob [sob] n sollozo m. v sollozar.

sober ['soubə] adj moderado; serio; (not drunk) sobrio. v sober up serenarse.

soccer ['sokə] n fútbol m.

sociable ['souʃəbl] adj sociable.

social ['souʃəl] adj social; (friendly) amistoso. social science sociología f. social security seguridad social f. socialism n socialismo m. socialist n(m+f), adj socialista. socialize v socializar.

society [sə'saiəti] n sociedad f.

sociology [sousi'olədʒi] n sociología f. sociological adj sociológico. sociologist n sociólogo, -a m, f.

sock [sok] n calcetín m.

socket ['sokit] n hueco m; (elec) enchufe m.

soda ['soudə] n (chem) sosa f; (water) agua de seltz f.

sodden ['sodn] adj empapado, saturado.

sofa ['soufə] n sofá m.

soft [soft] adj blando; suave; (low) bajo. soft-boiled adj (egg) pasado por agua. soften v ablandar; suavizar; bajar; softness n blandura f; suavidad f; dulzura f; debilidad f; estupidez f.

soggy ['sogi] adj empapado; (bread) pastoso.

soil¹ [soil] n tierra f.

soil² [soil] v ensuciar.

solar ['soulə] adj solar.

sold [sould] V sell.

solder ['soldə] n soldadura f. v soldar. soldering-iron n soldador m.

soldier ['souldʒə] n soldado m.

sole¹ [soul] adj solo, único.

sole² [soul] n (of shoe) suela f; (of foot) planta f. v solar.

sole³ [soul] n (fish) lenguado m.

solemn ['soləm] *adj* solemne. **solemnity** *n* solemnidad *f.*

solicitor [sə'lisitə] *n* abogado, -a *m, f.*

solicitude [sə'lisitjuɪd] *n* solicitud *f.*

solid ['solid] *adj* sólido; firme; continuo. *n* sólido *m.* **solids** *pl n* alimentos sólidos *m pl.* **solidarity** *n* solidaridad *f.* **solidify** *v* solidificarse; congelarse.

solitary ['solitəri] *adj* solitario; solo, único.

solitude ['solitjuɪd] *n* soledad *f.*

solo ['soulou] *nm, adj* solo. **soloist** *n.* solista *m, f.*

solstice ['solstis] *n* solsticio *m.*

soluble ['soljubl] *adj* soluble.

solution [sə'luɪʃən] *n* solución *f.*

solve [solv] *v* resolver; acertar.

solvent ['solvənt] *adj* (*finance*) solvente. *n* (*chem*) disolvente *m.* **solvency** *n* solvencia *f.*

sombre ['sombə] *adj* sombrío.

some [sʌm] *adj* algún, alguno, algunos; unos, varios. *pron* algunos; unos; un poco; parte. *adv* bestante; unos. **somebody** *or* **someone** *pron* alguien. **somehow** *adv* de algún modo; por alguna razón. **something** *pron* algo. **sometime** *adv* alguna vez, algún día. **sometimes** *adv* a veces, de vez en cuando. **somewhat** *adv* algo, algún tanto. **somewhere** *adv* en alguna parte. **somewhere else** en alguna otra parte.

somersault ['sʌməsɔɪlt] *n* salto mortal *m.* *v* dar un salto mortal.

son [sʌn] *n* hijo *m.* **son-in-law** *n* yerno *m.*

sonata [sə'naɪtə] *n* sonata *f.*

song [soŋ] *n* (*art*) canto *m;* (*composition*) canción *f.*

sonic ['sonik] *adj* sónico.

sonnet ['sonit] *n* soneta *m.*

soon [suɪn] *adv* pronto, dentro de poco; (*early*) temprano. **as soon as** tan pronto como. **sooner or later** tarde o temprano.

soot [sut] *n* hollín *m.*

soothe [suɪð] *v* tranquilizar, calmar. **soothing** *adj* tranquilizador, calmante.

sophisticated [sə'fistikeitid] *adj* sofisticado; mundano; (*machinery*) complejo.

sopping ['sopiŋ] *adj* empapadísimo.

soprano [sə'praɪnou] *n* soprano *m, f.*

sordid ['sɔɪdid] *adj* sórdido.

sore [sɔɪ] *adj* malo; dolorido; (*fig*) doloroso. **sore point** tema delicado *m.* **sorely** *adv* (*bitterly*) profundamente; (*very*) muy. **soreness** *n* dolor *m.*

sorrow ['sorou] *n* pesar *m;* tristeza *f.* *v* afligirse. **sorrowful** *adj* afligido; triste.

sorry ['sori] *adj* afligido; triste; apenado; lastimoso. **feel sorry for** compadecer. *interj* ¡perdóneme! ¡disculpe!

sort [sɔɪt] *n* clase *f;* especie *f;* tipo *m;* modo *m;* persona *f.* *v* separar de; clasificar. **sort out** apartar; (*problems*) arreglar. **sorting office** sala de batalla *f.*

soufflé ['suɪflei] *n* soufflé *m.*

sought [sɔɪt] *V* **seek.**

soul [soul] *n* alma *f.* **soulful** *adj* expresivo; conmovedor.

sound[1] [saund] *n* (*noise*) sonido *m,* ruido *m.* **sound barrier** barrera del sonido *f.* **sound effects** efectos sonoros *m pl.* **soundproof** *adj* insonoro. **sound-track** *n* pista sonora *f.* *v* sonar, resonar; (*seem*) parecer.

sound[2] [saund] *adj* sano; (*reasonable*) lógico; (*argument*) válido; (*policy*) prudente; (*investment*) seguro; (*comm*) solvente. **be sound asleep** estar profundamente dormido.

sound[3] [saund] *v* (*depth*) sondar; (*opinion*) sondear.

soup [suɪp] *n* sopa *f.* **clear soup** consomé *m.* **thick soup** puré *m.* **soup plate** plato sopero *m.* **soup spoon** cuchara sopera *f.*

sour [sauə] *adj* ácido, agrio. *v* agriar. **sourness** *n* acidez *f,* agrura *f.*

source [sɔɪs] *n* fuente *f;* origen *m.*

south [sauθ] *n* sur *m.* *adj* *also* **southerly, southern** del sur. *adv* hacia el sur. **southbound** *adj* con rumbo al sur. **south-east** *nm, adj* sudeste. **south-west** *nm, adj* sudoeste.

South America *n* Sudamérica *f,* América del Sur *f.* **South American** sudamericano, -a *m, f.*

souvenir [suɪvə'niə] *n* recuerdo *m.*

sovereign ['sovrin] *n, adj* soberano, -a.

*sow[1] [sou] *v* sembrar; esparcir.

sow[2] [sau] *n* cerda *f,* puerca *f.*

soya ['soiə] *n* soja *f.* **soya bean** soja *f.* **soy sauce** salsa picante de soja *f.*

spa [spaɪ] *n* balneario *m;* manantial mineral *m.*

space [speis] *n* espacio *m;* (*place*) sitio *m;* (*time*) temporada *f.* **spaceman** *n* astronauta *m,* cosmonauta *m.* **spaceship** *n* nave espacial *f.* *v* espaciar. **spacious** *adj* espacioso; amplio.

spade [speid] *n* pala *f*.
spades [speidz] *pl n* (*cards*) picos *m pl*; (*Spanish cards*) espadas *f pl*.
spaghetti [spə'geti] *n* espaguetis *m pl*.
Spain [spein] *n* España *f*. **Spaniard** *n* español, -a *m, f*. **Spanish** *nm, adj* español.
span [span] *n* (*time*) espacio *m*, duración *f*; (*wings*) envergadura *f*; (*space*) distancia *f*; (*bridge*) tramo *m*. *v* atravesar; medir.
spaniel ['spanjəl] *n* perro de aguas *m*; (*cocker*) sabueso *m*.
spank [spaŋk] *v* dar una azotaina. **spanking** *n* azotaina *f*.
spanner ['spanə] *n* llave *f*.
spare [speə] *adj* de reserva; de sobra; disponible. **spare part** (*mot*) recambio *m*.
spare-ribs *pl n* (*cookery*) costillas de cerdo *f pl*. **spare room** cuarto de los invitados *m*. **spare time** ratos libres *m pl*. **spare tyre** neumático de repuesto *m*. *v* (*do without*) pasarse sin; (*avoid*) evitar; (*expense*) escatimar. **sparing** *adj* (*words*) parco; limitado; escaso; frugal.
spark [spaɪk] *n* chispa *f*. *v* chispear. **spark off** provocar. **sparking-plug** *n* bujía *f*.
sparkle ['spaɪkl] *n* centelleo *m*; (*fig*) brillo *m*. *v* centellear; (*fig*) brillar. **sparkling** *adj* (*drink*) espumoso.
sparrow ['sparou] *n* gorrión *m*.
sparse [spaɪs] *adj* escaso, poco denso. **sparsely** *adv* escasamente.
spasm ['spazəm] *n* espasmo *m*; (*fit*) ataque *m*. **spasmodic** *adj* espasmódico.
spastic ['spastik] *n, adj* espástico, -a.
spat [spat] *V* **spit**.
spatial ['speiʃl] *adj* espacial.
spatula ['spatjulə] *n* espátula *f*.
spawn [spoɪn] *n* (*fish*) freza *f*, hueva *f*; (*frog*) huevos *m pl*. *v* frezar; depositar.
***speak** [spiɪk] *v* decir; hablar. **speak up** hablar más fuerte. **speak up for** hablar en favor de. **speaker** *n* orador, -a *m, f*; (*loudspeaker*) altavoz *m*.
spear [spiə] *n* lanza *f*. *v* traspasar. **spearhead** *n* vanguardia *f*.
special ['speʃəl] *adj* especial; particular; extraordinario. **specialist** *n* especialista *m, f*. **speciality** *n* especialidad *f*. **specialize** *v* especializar.
species ['spiɪʃɪz] *n* especie *f*.
specify ['spesifai] *v* especeficar. **specific** *adj* específico. **specification** *n* especificación *f*; estipulación *f*; requisito *m*.

specimen ['spesimin] *n* (*biol*) espécimen *m*; modelo *m*; (*sample*) muestra *f*; (*example*) ejemplar *m*.
speck [spek] *n* manchita *f*; pizca *f*. **speckle** *v* motear.
spectacle ['spektəkl] *n* espectáculo *m*. **spectacles** *pl n* gafas *f pl*. **spectacular** *adj* espectacular.
spectator [spek'teitə] *n* espectador, -a *m, f*.
spectrum ['spektrəm] *n* espectro *m*.
speculate ['spekjuleit] *v* especular; conjeturar. **speculation** *n* especulación *f*; conjetura *f*. **speculative** *adj* especulativo; conjetural.
speech [spiɪtʃ] *n* (*address*) discurso *m*; (*faculty*) habla *f*; (*lecture*) conferencia *f*; conversación *f*; pronunciación *f*. **speechless** *adj* mudo.
***speed** [spiɪd] *v* (*mot*) ir a toda velocidad. **speed along** apresurarse. **speed up** acelerar. **speeding** *n* exces de velocidad *m*. **speedy** *adj* veloz. *n* prisa *f*; velocidad *f*; rapidez *f*. **speedboat** *n* lancha motora *f*. **speed limit** velocidad máxima *f*. **speedometer** *n* velocímetro *m*.
***spell**[1] [spel] *v* escribir; deletrear; significar. **spelling** *n* ortografía *f*.
spell[2] [spel] *n* (*magic*) hechizo *m*, encanto *m*. **spellbound** *adj* encantado.
spell[3] [spel] *n* período *m*; turno *m*.
***spend** [spend] *v* (*money*) gastar; (*time*) pasar. **spending** *n* gasto *m*. **spending money** dinero para gastos menudos *m*.
sperm [spəɪm] *n* esperma *f*.
spew [spjuɪ] *v* vomitar.
sphere [sfiə] *n* esfera *f*; (*province*) competencia *f*. **spherical** *adj* esférico.
spice [spais] *n* especia *f*. *v* especiar. **spicy** *adj* especiado, picante; (*fig*) sabroso.
spider ['spaidə] *n* araña *f*. **spider's web** telaraña *f*.
spike [spaik] *n* escarpia *f*.
***spill** [spil] *v* derramar. *n* (*coll: fall*) caida *f*.
***spin** [spin] *v* girar, dar vueltas; dar efecto a; (*cotton, silk, etc.*) hilar; (*web*) tejer; (*fig: a yarn*) contar. **spin-dryer** *n* secador centrifugo *m*. **spin out** prolongar. **spinning** *n* hilado *m*. **spinning wheel** rueca *f*. *n* giro *m*.
spinach ['spinidʒ] *n* espinaca *f*.
spindle ['spindl] *n* (*axle, shaft*) eje *m*; (*of a lathe*) mandril *m*; (*of a spinning wheel*) huso *m*. **spindly** *adj* larguirucho.

spine [spain] *n* (*anat*) espina dorsal *f*; (*zool*) púa *f*; (*book*) lomo *m*. **spinal** *adj* espinal. **spiny** *adj* espinoso.

spinster ['spinstə] *n* soltera *f*.

spiral ['spaiərəl] *adj* espiral. *n* espiral *f*. *v* dar vueltas en espiral.

spire ['spaiə] *n* aguja *f*.

spirit ['spirit] *n* espíritu *m*, alma *f*; (*ghost*) fantasma *m*; (*courage*) valor *m*; (*liveliness*) ánimo; (*mood*) humor *m*; alcohol *m*. **spirited** *adj* animado, vigoroso. **spirited** *adj* espiritual. **spiritualism** *n* espiritualismo *m*. **spiritualist** *n*(*m*+*f*), *adj* espiritualista.

****spit**[1] [spit] *v* escupir. *n* saliva *f*, escupitajo *m*.

spit[2] [spit] *n* (*cookery*) espetón *m*, asador *m*; (*geog*) lengua de tierra *f*.

spite [spait] *n* rencor *m*, malevolencia *f*. **in spite of** a pesar de. *v* mortificar. **spiteful** *adj* rencoroso.

splash [splaʃ] *n* salpicadura *f*; (*sound*) chapoteo; (*mark*) mancha *f*. *v* salpicar.

spleen [spliːn] *n* (*anat*) bazo *m*; (*fig*) mal humor *m*.

splendid ['splendid] *adj* espléndido; excelente. **splendour** *n* resplandor *m*.

splice [splais] *v* empalmar; (*coll: marry*) unir, casar.

splint [splint] *n* férula *f*.

splinter ['splintə] *n* (*wood*) astilla *f*; (*bomb*) casco *m*; (*bone*) esquirla *f*; (*piece*) fragmento *m*. *v* astillar.

****split** [split] *v* hender, partir; rajar; dividir; separar; (*atom*) desintegrar. *n* partido *m*, hendido *m*; división *f*; (*in cloth*) rasgón *m*; (*quarrel*) ruptura *f*. **split second** fracción de segundo *f*.

splutter ['splʌtə] *v* (*person*) farfullar; (*flame*) chisporrotear. *n* farfulla *f*; chisporroteo *m*.

****spoil** [spoil] *v* estropear, echar a perder; (*child*) minar; (*damage*) dañar. **spoilsport** *n* aguafiestas *m*, *f invar*. **spoils** *pl n* botín *m sing*.

spoke[1] [spouk] *V* **speak**.

spoke[2] [spouk] *n* reyo *m*.

spokesman ['spouksmən] *n* portavoz *m*.

sponge [spʌndʒ] *n* esponja *f*; (*cake*) bizcocho esponjoso *m*. **sponge bag** esponjera *f*. *v* limpiar con esponja; (*coll: cadge*) sacar de gorra. **spongy** *adj* esponjoso.

sponsor ['sponsə] *n* (*for financial support*) patrocinador, -a *m*, *f*; (*warrantor*) fiador, -a *m*, *f*; (*for club membership*) padrino, -a *m*, *f*. *v* patrocinar; fiar; apadrinar. **sponsorship** *n* patrocinio *m*.

spontaneous [spon'teinjəs] *adj* espontáneo. **spontaneity** *n* espontaneidad *f*.

spool [spuːl] *n* bobina *f*.

spoon [spuːn] *n* cuchara *f*. **spoonful** *n* cucharada *f*.

sporadic [spə'radik] *adj* esporádico.

sport [spoːt] *n* deporte *m*; (*plaything*) juguete *m*; (*amusement*) bula *f*. **sports car** coche deportivo *m*. **sports jacket** chaqueta de sport *f*. **sportsman/woman** *n* deportista *m*, *f*. *v* llevar; ostentar. **sporting** *adj* deportista; caballeroso. **sportive** *adj* juguetón; bromista.

spot [spot] *n* (*med*) grano *m*; espinilla *f*; (*mark*) mancha *f*; (*pattern*) lunar *m*; (*place*) sitio *m*; (*liquid*) gota *f*; parte *f*; punto *m*; (*coll*) poco *m*. **on the spot** en el momento; en el acto. **spot check** inspección repentina *f*. **spotlight** *n* foco *m*. *v* manchar; reconocer; notar. **spotless** *adj* inmaculado. **spotted** *adj* (*speckled*) moteado; con manchas; de lunares. **spotty** *adj* espinilloso.

spouse [spaus] *n* esposo, -a *m*, *f*.

spout [spaut] *n* (*teapot*) pitorro *m*; (*jug*) pico *m*; (*rainwater pipe*) caño *m*; (*jet*) chorro *m*; (*waterspout*) tromba *f*. *v* echar; (*coll*) soltar.

sprain [sprein] *n* torcedura *f*. *v* torcer.

sprawl [sproːl] *n* postura desgarbada *f*. *v* extender.

spray[1] [sprei] *n* (*water*) rociada *f*; (*sea*) espuma *f*; (*sprayer*) pulverizador *m*. *v* (*sprinkle*) rociar; pulverizar; (*crops*) fumigar; vaporizarse.

spray[2] [sprei] *n* (*flowers*) ramo *m*, ramillete *m*.

****spread** [spred] *v* extender; (*on the ground*) exponer; (*marmalade, butter, etc.*) untar; propagar; difundir; (*wings*) desplegar. **spread out** esparcir. *n* propagación *f*, difusión *f*; (*town*) extensión *f*; (*span*) envergadura *f*; (*range*) gama *f*.

spree [spriː] *n* juerga *f*.

sprig [sprig] *n* ramito *m*.

sprightly ['spraitli] *adj* despierto, vivo.

****spring** [spriŋ] *v* saltar. **spring up** brotar; surgir. *n* (*season*) primavera *f*; (*leap*) salto *m*, brinco *m*; (*water*) fuente *f*; (*coil*) muelle *m*. **springboard** *n* trampolín *m*. **spring-cleaning** *n* limpieza general *f*.

spring onion cebolleta *f*. **springy** *adj* elástico.

sprinkle ['sprɪŋkl] *v* (*water*) rociar; (*sugar, salt, etc.*) salpicar. **sprinkler** *n* regadera *f*; (*fire*) extintor *m*.

sprint [sprint] *n* sprint *m*, esprint *m*. *v* sprintar, esprintar.

sprout [spraut] *n* brote *m*, retoño *m*. **Brussels sprouts** coles de Bruselas *f pl*.

spruce [spruːs] *n* (*bot*) pícea *f*. *adj* elegante. **spruce up** acicalar.

spun [spʌn] *V* **spin**.

spur [spəː] *n* espuela *f*; (*fig*) estímulo *m*. **on the spur of the moment** sin pensarlo. *v* espolear. **spur on** estimular.

spurious ['spjuəriəs] *adj* espurio, falso.

spurn [spəːn] *v* desdeñar, rechazar.

spurt [spəːt] *n* (*water*) chorro *m*; (*energy*) gran esfuerzo *m*. *v* chorrear; hacer un gran esfuerzo; acelerar.

spy [spai] *n* espía *m*, *f*. *v* espiar; observar. **spying** *n* espionaje *m*.

squabble ['skwobl] *n* riña *f*. *v* disputar.

squad [skwod] *n* escuadra *f*; (*mil*) pelotón *m*.

squadron ['skwodrən] *n* (*mil*) escuadrón *m*; (*naut*) escuadra *f*; (*aero*) escuadrilla *f*.

squalid ['skwolid] *adj* mugriento; escuálido; miserable. **squalor** *n* mugre *f*; miseria *f*.

squall [skwoːl] *n* ráfaga *f*.

squander ['skwondə] *v* malgastar.

square [skweə] *n* (*shape*) cuadrado *m*; (*pattern*) cuadro *m*; (*chessboard*) casilla *f*; (*in a town*) plaza *f*. *adj* cuadrado; rectangular; (*coll: old-fashioned*) anticuado. *v* cuadrar; (*settle*) arreglar.

squash [skwoʃ] *n* (*sport*) juego de pelota *m*; (*drink*) limonada *f*, naranjada *f*; (*crushing*) aplastamiento *m*. *v* (*crush*) aplastar; (*squeeze*) apretar.

squat [skwot] *n* posición en cuchillas *f*. *adj* rechoncho. *v* agacharse. **squatter** *n* persona que ocupe ilegalmente un sitio *f*.

squawk [skwoːk] *n* graznido *m*. *v* graznar.

squeak [skwiːk] *n* (*mice, etc.*) chillido *m*; (*hinge*) chirrido *m*. *v* chillar; chirriar.

squeal [skwiːl] *n* chillido *m*. *v* chillar.

squeamish ['skwiːmiʃ] *adj* remilgado; delicado.

squeeze [skwiːz] *n* presión *f*; (*hug*) abrazo *m*; (*hand*) apretón *m*; (*crowd*) gentío *m*. *v* abrazar; apretar; (*extract*) exprimir.

squid [skwid] *n* calamar *m*.

squint [skwint] *n* (*med*) estrabismo *m*;

(*coll: glance*) ojeada *f*. *v* entrecerrar los ojos.

squirm [skwəːm] *v* retorcerse.

squirrel ['skwirəl] *n* ardilla *f*.

squirt [skwəːt] *n* chorro *m*. *v* lanzar; chorrear.

stab [stab] *n* puñalada. *v* apuñalar.

stabilize ['steibilaiz] *v* estabilizar. **stabilizer** *n* estabilizador *m*.

stable[1] ['steibl] *n* cuadra *f*.

stable[2] ['steibl] *adj* estable; fijo. **stability** *n* estabilidad *f*; firmeza *f*.

staccato [stə'kaːtou] *adv* staccato. *adj* (*voice, style, etc.*) entrecortado.

stack [stak] *n* (*hay, etc.*) almiar *m*; (*pile*) montón *m*; (*chimney*) cañón *m*. **stacks of** (*coll*) un montón de *m sing*. *v* hacinar; amontonar.

stadium ['steidiəm] *n* estadio *m*.

staff [staːf] *n* vara *f*; palo *m*; (*flag*) asta *f*; personal *m*. **staff-room** *n* (*school*) sala de profesores *f*. *v* proveer de personal.

stag [stag] *n* venado *m*, ciervo *m*. **stag party** reunión de hombres *f*.

stage [steidʒ] *n* (*theatre*) escenario *m*; (*platform*) estrado *m*; (*point*) etapa *f*; (*phase*) fase *f*. **stage manager** regidor de escena *m*. *v* representar; efectuar; organizar.

stagger ['stagə] *n* tambaleo *m*. *v* tambalearse; (*amaze*) asombrar; (*payments, etc.*) escalonar. **staggering** *adj* asombroso.

stagnant ['stagnənt] *adj* estancado. **stagnate** *v* estancarse. **stagnation** *n* estancamiento *m*.

staid [steid] *adj* serio; formal.

stain [stein] *n* mancha *f*; tinte *m*. **stain remover** quitamanchas *m invar*. *v* manchar; (*wood*) teñir. **stained-glass window** vidriera *f*.

stair [steə] *n* escalón *m*. **staircase** *n also* **stairs** *pl n* escalera *f sing*.

stake[1] [steik] *n* (*post*) poste *m*; estaca *f*; (*for plants*) rodrigón *m*; (*for execution*) hoguera *f*. *v* estacar.

stake[2] [steik] *n* (*bet*) apuesta *f*; (*investment*) intereses *m pl*. **at stake** en juego. *v* apostar.

stale [steil] *adj* (*bread*) duro; (*egg*) poco fresco; (*food*) rancio; (*air*) viciado. **staleness** *n* ranciedad *f*.

stalemate ['steilmeit] *n* (*chess*) ahogado *m*; (*fig*) punto muerto *m*.

stalk¹ [stɔːk] n (*stem*) tallo m.
stalk² [stɔːk] v acechar. **stalk in/out** entrar/salir con paso airado.
stall¹ [stɔːl] n (*market*) puesto m; (*theatre*) butaca f; (*exhibition*) caseta f. v (*engine*) parar.
stall² [stɔːl] v (*delay*) andar con rodeos. **stall off** dar largas a.
stallion ['staljən] n semental m.
stamina ['staminə] n vigor m; aguante m.
stammer ['stamə] n tartamudez f. v tartamudear.
stamp [stamp] n sello m, timbre m; marca f; impresión f; (*with foot*) zapatazo m.
stamp-collecting n filatelia f. v estampar; sellar; imprimir; (*one's foot*) patear.
stampede [stam'piːd] n desbocamiento m; desbandada f. v provocar la desbandada de.
*stand [stand] v (*on feet*) estar de pie; (*place*) poner; resistir; soportar; (*trial*) someterse a; (*remain*) permanecer; (*pay for*) sufragar. n posición f; plataforma f; (*coats, hats*) percha f; (*fig*) postura f. **stand for** significar; representar. **stand out** sobresalir. **standstill** n parada f. **come to a standstill** pararse. **stand up for** defender.
standard ['standəd] n (*weight, length, money*) patrón m; (*of living*) nivel m; modelo m; criterio m. adj normal; oficial; legal; (*comm*) standard. **standard lamp** lámpara de pie f. **standardize** v estandardizar; normalizar.
standing ['standiŋ] adj de pie; vertical; clásico; fijo. **standing order** (*bank*) pedido regular m. n posición f; situación f; reputación f; duración f.
stank [staŋk] V stink.
stanza ['stanzə] n estancia f, estrofa f.
staple¹ ['steipl] n (*papers*) grapa f; (*of wool, cotton*) fibra f. v sujetar con una grapa.
staple² [steipl] adj básico; principal.
star [staɪ] n (*astron, cinema*) estrella f; asterisco m. **stars** pl n (*astrol*) astros m pl. **starfish** n estrella de mar f. v estrellar; ser protagonista. **stardom** n estrellato m.
starry adj estrellado.
starboard ['staɪbəd] n estribor m.
starch [staɪtʃ] n almidón m. v almidonar. **starchy** adj almidonado.
stare [steə] n mirada fija f. v mirar fijamente.
stark [staɪk] adj (*bleak*) desolado; (*stiff*)

rígido; completo; puro; absoluto. **stark naked** completamente desnudo.
starling ['staɪliŋ] n estornino m.
start [staɪt] n comienzo m; (*of a race*) salida f; (*jump*) sobresalto m; (*fright*) susto m. v comenzar, empezar; (*clock*) poner en marcha; (*car*) arrancar; (*establish*) fundar; (*rumour*) lanzar; provocar; sobresaltar. **starter** n (*mot*) arranque m; (*meal*) entremés m.
startle ['staɪtl] v asustar. **startling** adj sorprendente; alarmante.
state [steit] n estado m; condición f; (*luxury*) lujo m; gran pompa f. **statesman** n estadista m. v afirmar, declarar; dar; decir; consignar; exponer. **stately** adj majestuoso. **statement** n declaración f; informe m; comunicado m; (*bank*) balance mensual m.
static ['statik] adj estático. n (*radio*) parásitos m pl.
station ['steiʃən] n (*rail, radio*) estación f; (*position*) puesto m; (*place*) lugar m; (*social*) posición f. v apostar; estacionar.
stationary ['steiʃənəri] adj estacionario; inmóvil.
stationer ['steiʃənə] n papelero m. **stationer's** n papelería f. **stationery** n objetos de escritorio m pl; papel de escribir y sobres m.
statistics [stə'tistiks] n (*science*) estadística f. pl n (*data*) estadísticas f pl. **statistical** adj estadístico.
statue ['statjuː] n estatua f.
stature ['statʃə] n estatura f; (*fig*) talla f.
status ['steitəs] n (*standing*) categoría f; (*state*) condición f; (*social standing*) posición f.
statute ['statjuːt] n estatuo m. **statutory** adj establecido por la ley.
staunch¹ [stɔːntʃ] adj fiel; inquebrantable.
staunch² [stɔːntʃ] v restañar.
stay [stei] n estancia f; (*support*) apoyo m. v (*remain*) quedarse; (*postpone*) aplazar; (*endure*) resistir; (*support*) apoyar.
steadfast ['stedfaɪst] adj constante; fijo.
steady ['stedi] adj constante; firme; regular; continuo. v estabilizar; calmar; sostener. **steadily** adv firmemente; regularmente; sin parar. **steadiness** n firmeza f; estabilidad f; uniformidad f; regularidad f.
steak [steik] n (*beefsteak*) bistec m; (*of other meat or fish*) filete m.

*steal [stiːl] v robar. **stealing** n robo m.
stealthy ['stelθi] adj furtivo.
steam [stiːm] n vapor m. **let off steam**
(coll) desahogarse. v echar vapor;
(cookery) cocinar al vapor.
steel [stiːl] n acero m. **steel wool**
estropajo m. **steelworks** pl n acería f sing.
steely adj acerado; inflexible.
steep¹ [stiːp] adj escarpado.
steep² [stiːp] v empapar.
steeple ['stiːpl] n aguja f. **steeplechase** n
carrera de obstáculos f. **steeplejack** n
reparador de chimeneas m.
steer [stiə] v (ship) gobernar; (vehicle)
dirigir; (bicycle) llevar; (course) seguir;
(car) manejar. **steering** n (naut) gobierno
m; (mot) conducción f. **steering-wheel** n
volante m.
stem¹ [stem] n tallo m; (glass) pie m.
stem from derivarse de.
stem² [stem] v (stop) detener, contener.
stench [stentʃ] n tufo m.
stencil ['stensl] n estarcido m. v (typing)
cliché de multicopista m.
step [step] n paso m; (stairs, ladder)
peldaño m; (doorway) umbral m;
(degree) escalón m; (measure) medida f.
stepladder n escalera de tijera f. v dar un
paso; ir. **step up** subir; aumentar.
stepbrother ['stepbrʌðə] n hermanastro
m.
stepdaughter ['stepdɔːtə] n hijastra f.
stepfather ['stepfɑːðə] n padrastro m.
stepmother ['stepmʌðə] n madrastra f.
stepsister ['stepsistə] n hermanastra f.
stepson ['stepsʌn] n hijastro m.
stereo ['steriou] nf, adj estéreo. **stereophonic** adj estereofónico.
stereotype ['steriətaip] n estereotipo m. v
estereotipar.
sterile ['sterail] adj estéril. **sterility** n
esterilidad f. **sterilization** esterilización f.
sterilize v esterilizar.
sterling ['stəːliŋ] n libra esterlina f. adj
(silver) plata de ley f; (character)
excelente.
stern¹ [stəːn] adj severo.
stern² [stəːn] n (naut) popa f.
stethoscope ['steθəskoup] n estetoscopio
m.
stew [stjuː] n estofado m. v (meat)
estofar; guisar; (fruit) cocer.
steward ['stjuəd] n camarero m; despen-
sero m. **shop steward** enlace sindical m.

stewardess n (ship) camarera f; (air)
azafata f.
stick¹ [stik] n madero m; estaca f; palo
m; (club) garrote m; (walking) bastón m.
*stick² [stik] v fijar; (thrust) clavar; (penetrate) pinchar; (glue) pegar; (stay)
quedarse. **stick out** sacar; sobresalir.
stick up for (coll) defender. **sticky** adj
pegajoso; (coll) difícil.
stickler ['stiklə] n **be a stickler for** dar
mucha importancia a.
stiff [stif] adj rígido; (manner) distante;
(person) severo. **stiffen** v atiesarse;
endurecerse. **stiffness** n rigidez f; frialdad
f; obstinación f.
stifle ['staifl] v ahogar, sofocar; (smile,
etc.) suprimir. **stifling** adj sofocante.
stigma ['stigmə] n estigma m.
stile [stail] n portilla con escalones f.
still¹ [stil] adv todavía, aún; (always)
siempre; (nevertheless) sin embargo; (sit,
stand) quieto. adj tranquilo; inmóvil;
silencioso. **stillborn** adj nacido muerto.
still life bodegón m. n calma f; (phot)
vista fija f.
still² [stil] n alambique m; destilería f.
stilt [stilt] n zanco m. **stilted** adj
campanudo.
stimulus ['stimjuləs] n, pl -li estímulo m;
incentivo m. **stimulant** nm, adj estimulante. **stimulate** v estimular. **stimulation** n
estímulo m.
*sting [stiŋ] v picar; herir; (coll: overcharge) clavar. n (insect) aguijón m;
(wound) picadura f; (pain) escozor m.
*stink [stiŋk] v heder, oler mal. n hedor
m.
stint [stint] n sesión de trabajo f. v escatimar; limitar.
stipulate ['stipjuleit] v estipular. **stipulation** n estipulación f.
stir [stəː] n agitación f; sensación f; conmoción f. v (tea, etc.) revolver; mezclar;
(move) mover; excitar. **stir up** provocar;
fomentar.
stirrup ['stirəp] n estribo m.
stitch [stitʃ] n (sewing) puntada f; (knitting) punto m; (med) punto de sutura m;
(pain) dolor de costado m. v coser; (med)
suturar.
stoat [stout] n armiño m.
stock [stok] n (supply) reserva f; (farm)
ganado m; (cookery) caldo m; (lineage)
linaje m; (race) raza f; (tree) tronco m.
stockbroker n corredor de Bolsa m. **stock**

exchange Bolsa *f.* **stockpile** *n* reservas *f pl.* **stocktaking** *n* inventario *m.* *v* surtir, abastecer.
Stockholm ['stokhoum] *n* Estocolmo.
stocking ['stokiŋ] *n* media *f.*
stocky ['stoki] *adj* rechoncho.
stodge [stodʒ] *n* (*coll*) comida indigesta *f.*
stodgy *adj* indigesto.
stoical ['stouikl] *adj* estoico.
stoke [stouk] *v* alimentar.
stole[1] [stoul] *V* **steal.**
stole[2] [stoul] *n* estola *f.*
stomach ['stʌmək] *n* estómago *m.* **stomach-ache** *n* dolor de estómago *m.* *v* soportar.
stone [stoun] *n* piedra *f*; (*fruit*) hueso *m*; (*med*) cálculo *m.* **stone-cold** *adj* helado. *v* (*throw*) apedrear. **stony** *adj* pedregoso.
stood [stud] *V* **stand.**
stool [stuɪl] *n* taburete *m.*
stoop [stuɪp] *n* espaldas encorvadas *f pl.* *v* encorvarse; agacharse. **stoop to** rebajarse a.
stop [stop] *n* parada *f*; cesación *f*; suspensión *f*; (*stay*) estancia *f*; (*gramm*) punto *m.* *v* parar; impedir; interrumpir; evitar; dejar de; (*a hole*) tapar; (*a gap*) rellenar; cesar. **stop-watch** *n* cronómetro *m.* **stoppage** *n* (*blockage*) obstrucción *f*; (*strike*) huelga *f.* **stopper** *n* tapón *m.*
store [stoɪ] *n* (*supply*) provisión *f*; (*warehouse*) depósito *m*; (*large shop*) almacén *m*; (*smaller shop*) tienda *f.* *v* (*keep*) guardar; almacenar; (*supply*) suministrar. **storage** *n* almacenaje *m.*
storey ['stoɪri] *n* piso *m.*
stork [stoɪk] *n* cigüeña *f.*
storm [stoɪm] *n* tempestad *f*; (*thunderstorm*) tormenta *f.* *v* (*mil*) asaltar; (*wind*) ser tempestuoso; (*fig*) fabiar. **stormy** *adj* tempestuoso; violento.
story ['stoɪri] *n* historia *f*; cuento *m.*
stout [staut] *adj* fuerte; intrépido; gordo; grueso. *n* cerveza negra *f.*
stove [stouv] *n* (*cooker*) cocina *f*; (*heater*) estufa *f.*
stow [stou] *v* colocar, meter. **stow away** guardar; esconder. **stowaway** *n* polizón *m.*
straddle ['stradl] *v* estar a caballo sobre; montar a horcajadas.
straggle ['stragl] *v* (*leg*) rezagarse; (*spread*) desparramarse. **straggler** *n* rezagado, -a *m, f.*
straight [streit] *adj* derecho; recto; en

orden; (*hair*) lacio. *adv* derecho; directamente. **straight ahead** todo recto. **straight away** en seguida. **straightforward** *adj* sincero; (*simple*) sencillo. **straighten** *v* enderezar; arreglar.
strain[1] [strein] *n* tensión *f*; esfuerzo *m*; (*med*) torcedura *f.* *v* (*stretch*) estirar; forzar; (*sprain*) torcer; (*filter*) filtrar; (*cookery*) colar. **strainer** *n* colador *m.*
strain[2] [strein] *n* raza *f*; tendencia *f.*
strait [streit] *n* estrecho *m.*
strand[1] [strand] *n* (*hair*) trenza *f*; (*rope*) cabo *m*; (*thread*) hebra *f.*
strand[2] [strand] *n* (*shore*) playa *f*; (*river*) ribera *f.* *v* (*ship*) encallar. **be stranded** hallarse abandonado.
strange [streindʒ] *adj* extraño; raro; inesperado; (*unknown*) desconocido. **stranger** *n* desconocido, -a *m, f.*
strangle ['straŋgl] *v* estrangular. **stranglehold** *n* collar de fuerza *m.* **strangler** *n* estrangulador, -a *m, f.*
strap [strap] *n* correa *f*; (*on garment*) tirante *m.* *v* atar con correa; (*med*) vendar. **strapping** *adj* robusto.
strategy ['stratədʒi] *n* estrategia *f.* **strategic** *adj* estratégico.
stratum ['straɪtəm] *n, pl* **-ta** estrato *m*, capa *f.*
straw [stroɪ] *n* paja *f.* **it's the last straw!** ¡es el colmo!
strawberry ['stroɪbəri] *n* (*plant and fruit*) fresa *f.*
stray [strei] *n* animal extraviado *m.* *adj* perdido; extraviado; aislado. *v* errar; desviarse; perderse.
streak [striɪk] *n* raya *f*; vena *f*; (*light*) rayo *m.* *v* rayar; ir como un rayo. **streaky** *adj* rayado.
stream [striɪm] *n* río *m*; arroyo *m*; corriente *f.* **streamlined** *adj* aerodinámico; (*mot*) carenado; (*efficient*) eficaz. *v* correr, fluir. **streamer** *n* serpentina *f.*
street [striɪt] *n* calle *f.*
strength [streŋθ] *n* fuerza *f.* **strengthen** *v* fortalecer; reforzar; confirmar.
strenuous ['strenjuəs] *adj* arduo; enérgico.
stress [stres] *n* tensión *f*; presión *f*; (*gramm*) acento tónico *m.* *v* (*emphasize*) subrayar; insistir en; acentuar.
stretch [stretʃ] *n* (*scope*) alcance *m*; (*of arms, distance*) extensión *f*; (*time*) período *m*; (*of road*) trecho *m.* **home**

stretch última etapa *f. v* estirar; tender; extender. **stretcher** *n* camilla *f.*
stricken ['strikən] *adj* afligido.
strict [strikt] *adj* severo; exacto. **strictly** *adv* severamente; exactamente. **strictly speaking** en realidad. **strictness** *n* severidad *f;* exactitud *f.*
*stride [straid] *v* dar zancadas; andar a pasos largos. *n* zancada *f;* tranco *m.*
strident ['straidənt] *adj* estridente; llamativo.
strife [straif] *n* disputa *f,* lucha *f.*
*strike [straik] *n* (*industry*) huelga *f;* (*hit*) golpe *m;* (*oil, etc.*) descubrimiento *m. v* (*hit*) golpear; pegar; declararse en huelga; (*clock*) sonar; (*a bargain*) cerrar; descubrir; (*a match*) encender. **striker** *n* huelguista *m, f.* **striking** *adj* impresionante; en huelga.
*string [striŋ] *v* (*beads*) ensartar; (*hang*) enristrar. *n* cuerda *f;* (*of cars*) fila *f.* **string bean** judía verde *f.* **string quartet** cuarteto de cuerdas *m.* **stringy** *adj* fibroso.
stringent ['strindʒənt] *adj* estricto, riguroso.
strip¹ [strip] *v* quitar; (*undress*) desnudar; (*bed*) deshacer.
strip² [strip] *n* (*of land*) zona *f;* (*of wood*) listón *m;* (*tatter, scrap*) tira *f.*
stripe [straip] *n* raya *f;* azote *m.* **striped** *adj* con rayas.
*strive [straiv] *v* esforzarse (a).
strode [stroud] *V* **stride**.
stroke¹ [strouk] *n* golpe *m,* choque *m;* (*swimming*) braza *f;* (*clock*) campanada *f;* (*mark*) trazo *m;* (*med*) ataque *m;* (*lightning*) rayo *m.*
stroke² [strouk] *v* acariciar. *n* caricia *f.*
stroll [stroul] *n* vuelta *f,* paseo *m. v* dar un paseo, pasearse.
strong [stroŋ] *adj* fuerte; robusto. *adv* muy bien. **stronghold** *n* fortaleza *f;* (*fig*) baluarte *m.* **strong-minded** *adj* resuelto. **strong-room** *n* cámara acorazada *f.*
struck [strʌk] *V* **strike**.
structure ['strʌktʃə] *n* estructura *f;* construcción *f.* **structural** *adj* estructural; de construcción.
struggle ['strʌgl] *n* lucha *f. v* luchar; (*to escape*) forcejear. **struggle in/out** entrar/salir penosamente.
strum [strʌm] *v* (*guitar*) rasguear; (*other instruments*) rascar. *n* (*guitar*) rasgueo *m.*
strung [strʌŋ] *V* **string**.

strut¹ [strʌt] *v* pavonearse.
strut² [strʌt] *n* (*arch*) puntal *m;* (*aero*) montante *m.*
stub [stʌb] *n* (*tree*) tocón *m;* (*cigarette*) colilla *f;* (*cheque*) talón *m;* (*ticket*) resguardo *m;* (*pencil, candle*) cabo *m. v* (*toe*) tropezar con. **stub out** apagar.
stubble ['stʌbl] *n* rastrojo *m;* (*chin*) barba *f.*
stubborn ['stʌbən] *adj* terco; inflexible. **stubbornness** *n* terquedad *f;* tenacidad *f.*
stuck [stʌk] *V* **stick**.
stud¹ [stʌd] *n* (*collar*) botón de camisa *m;* (*boot*) taco *m;* (*nail, rivet*) tachón *m. v* tachonar. **studded with** sembrado de, lleno de.
stud² [stʌd] *n* (*place*) cuadra *f;* (*animal*) semental *m.* **stud horse** caballo padre *m.*
student ['stjuidənt] *n* estudiante *m, f;* (*pupil*) alumno, -a *m, f.*
studio ['stjuidiou] *n* estudio *m.*
study ['stʌdi] *n* estudio *m;* (*room*) gabinete *m. v* estudiar; examinar. **studious** *adj* estudioso; solícito.
stuff [stʌf] *n* material *m,* materia *f;* cosas *f pl;* (*cloth*) tejido *m. v* llenar; (*cram*) atestar; (*cookery*) rellenar. **stuffing** *n* (*furniture*) rehenchimiento *m;* (*cookery*) relleno *m;* (*padding*) paja *f.* **stuffy** *adj* mal ventilado; (*person*) pomposo.
stumble ['stʌmbl] *v* tropezar.
stump [stʌmp] *n* (*tree*) tocón *m;* (*limb*) muñón *m;* (*pencil, etc.*) cabo *m;* (*cricket*) poste *m. v* (*fig*) dejar perplejo.
stun [stʌn] *v* aturdir; (*amaze*) pasmar. **stunning** *adj* aturdidor; (*coll*) fenomenal.
stung [stʌŋ] *V* **sting**.
stunk [stʌŋk] *V* **stink**.
stunt¹ [stʌnt] *v* impedir el crecimiento de. **stunted** *adj* atrofiado.
stunt² [stʌnt] *n* hazania *f;* truco publicitario *m.* **stunt man** doble especial *m.*
stupid ['stjuipid] *adj* estúpido. **stupidity** *n* estupidez *f.*
stupor ['stjuipə] *n* estupor *m.*
sturdy ['stəidi] *adj* robusto, vigoroso. **sturdiness** *n* robustez *f;* vigor *m.*
sturgeon ['stəidʒən] *n* esturión *m.*
stutter ['stʌtə] *n* tartamudeo *m. v* tartamudear.
sty [stai] *n* (*pig*) pocilga *f;* (*med*) orzuelo *m.*
style [stail] *n* estilo *m;* (*kind*) tipo *m;* manera *f;* (*fashion*) moda *f;* (*clothes*)

hechura *f*; (*hair*) peinado *m*. *v* (*design*) diseñar. **stylish** *adj* elegante.

stylus ['stailəs] *n* (*tool*) estilete *m*; (*record player*) aguja *f*.

suave [swaɪv] *adj* afable, urbano.

subconscious [sʌb'konʃəs] *nm, adj* subconsciente.

subcontract [sʌbkən'trakt] *v* subcontratar. **subcontractor** *n* subcontratista *m*.

subdivide [sʌbdi'vaid] *v* subdividir(se). **subdivision** *n* subdivisión *f*.

subdue [səb'djuɪ] *v* (*riot, etc.*) sojuzgar; (*sound, light*) atenuar; (*voice*) bajar; (*pain*) aliviar; (*feelings*) contener. **subdued** *adj* sojuzgado; atenuado; bajo; aliviado; contenido.

subject ['sʌbdʒikt; *v* səb'dʒekt] *n* sujeto *m*; (*school*) asignatura *f*; (*theme*) tema *m*; motivo *m*; (*people*) súbdito, -a *m, f*. **subject to** sujeto a; propenso a. *v* sojuzgar; (*to an examination*) someter. **subjection** *n* sujeción *f*. **subjective** *adj* subjetivo.

subjunctive [səb'dʒʌŋktiv] *nm, adj* subjuntivo.

sublet [sʌb'let] *v* subarrendar.

sublime [sə'blaim] *adj* sublime. *n* lo sublime.

submarine ['sʌbməriːn] *n* submarino *m*.

submerge [səb'məɪdʒ] *v* sumergir. *n* sumersión *f*.

submit [səb'mit] *v* someter. **submission** *n* sumisión *f*. **submissive** *adj* sumiso.

subnormal [sʌb'noɪməl] *adj* subnormal.

subordinate [sə'boɪdinət] *adj* (*gramm*) subordinado; subalterno. *n* subordinado, -a *m, f*; subalterno, -a *m, f*. *v* subordinar. **subordination** *n* subordinación *f*.

subscribe [səb'skraib] *v* **subscribe to** aprobar; (*newspaper*) subscribirse a. **subscriber** *n* suscriptor, -a *m, f*; abonado, -a *m, f*. **subscription** *n* suscripción *f*; abono *m*; (*membership fee*) cuota *f*.

subsequent ['sʌbsikwənt] *adj* subsiguiente; posterior.

subservient [səb'səɪviənt] *adj* subordinado; servil.

subside [səb'said] *v* (*land*) hundirse; (*flood*) bajar; (*excitement*) calmarse; (*wind*) amainar. **subsidence** *n* hundimiento *m*.

subsidiary [səb'sidiəri] *adj* subsidiario; secundario; (*comm*) afiliado. *n* (*comm*) filial *f*.

subsidize ['sʌbsidaiz] *v* subvencionar. **subsidy** *n* subvención *f*.

subsist [səb'sist] *v* subsistir. **subsistence** *n* subsistencia *f*.

substance ['sʌbstəns] *n* sustancia *f*. **substantial** *adj* sustancial; sustancioso; importante.

substandard [sʌb'standəd] *adj* inferior.

substitute ['sʌbstitjuɪt] *n* (*person*) sustituto, -a *m, f*, substituto, -a *m, f*; (*thing*) sucedáneo *m*. *v* sustituir, reemplazar. **substitution** *n* sustitución *f*.

subtitle ['sʌbtaitl] *n* subtítulo *m*. *v* subtitular.

subtle ['sʌtl] *adj* sutil; delicado. **subtlety** *n* sutileza f; delicadeza *f*.

subtract [səb'trakt] *v* restar, sustraer. **subtraction** *n* resta *f*, sustracción *f*.

suburb ['sʌbəɪb] *n* suburbio *m*. **the suburbs** las afueras *f pl*. **suburban** *adj* suburbano.

subvert [səb'vəɪt] *v* derribar; corromper. **subversion** *n* subversión *f*. **subversive** *adj* subversivo.

subway ['sʌbwei] *n* pasaje subterráneo *m*; (*US*) metro *m*.

succeed [sək'siːd] *v* triunfar; (*follow*) suceder; (*inherit*) heredar. **succeeding** *adj* sucesivo; venidero. **success** *n* éxito *m*; triunfo *m*. **successful** *adj* que tiene éxito; próspero. **successfully** *adv* con éxito. **succession** *n* sucesión *f*; herencia *f*. **successive** *adj* sucesivo. **successor** *n* sucesor, -a *m, f*.

succinct [sək'siŋkt] *adj* sucinto.

succulent ['sʌkjulənt] *adj* suculento; (*plant*) carnoso. *n* planta carnosa *f*.

succumb [sə'kʌm] *v* sucumbir.

such [sʌtʃ] *adj* tal; semejante, parecido; tan, tanto. **such as** como. *adv* tan, tanto. *pron* los que, las que; lo que; todo lo que; esto, éste, ésta. **as such** en sí.

suck [sʌk] *v* chupar; (*baby*) mamar. **suck up to** (*slang*) dar coba a.

sucker ['sʌkə] *n* (*bot*) chupón *m*; (*device*) émbolo *m*; (*slang: simpleton*) primo *m*.

suction ['sʌkʃən] *n* succión *f*.

sudden ['sʌdən] *adj* súbito; inesperado; repentino. **all of a sudden** de repente.

suds [sʌdz] *pl n* jabonaduras *f pl*.

sue [suɪ] *v* proceder contra.

suede [sweid] *n* ante *m*.

suet ['suɪt] *n* sebo *m*.

suffer ['sʌfə] *v* sufrir, padecer; tolerar; dejar; (*undergo*) aguantar. **suffering** *n* sufrimiento *m*, padecimiento *m*; dolor *m*.

sufficient [sə'fiʃənt] *adj* suficiente: bastante. **suffice** *v* ser suficiente, bastar. **sufficiently** *adv* suficientemente, bastante.

suffix ['sʌfiks] *n* sufijo *m*.

suffocate ['sʌfəkeit] *v* ahogar, sofocar. **suffocation** *n* ahogo *m*: asfixia *f*.

sugar ['ʃugə] *n* azúcar *m*. **sugar bowl** azucarero *m*. **sugar cane** caña de azúcar *f*. **sugar lump** terrón de azúcar *m*.

suggest [sə'dʒest] *v* sugerir: indicar. **suggestion** *n* sugerencia *f*: indicación *f*. **suggestive** *adj* sugestivo: evocador.

suicide ['suːisaid] *n* (*act*) suicidio *m*: (*person*) suicida *m*, *f*. **commit suicide** suicidarse. **suicidal** *adj* suicida.

suit [suːt] *n* traje *m*: (*woman's*) conjunto *m*: (*law*) pleito *m*: (*cards*) palo *m*. **suitcase** *n* maleta *f*. *v* convenir: venir bien a. **suitable** *adj* conveniente: apropiado.

suite [swiːt] *n* (*in hotel*) suite *f*: (*furniture*) juego *m*.

sulk [sʌlk] *v* enfurruñarse. *n* enfurruñamiento *m*. **sulky** *adj* enfurruñado.

sullen ['sʌlən] *adj* taciturno: malhumorado. **sullenness** *n* taciturnidad *f*: mal humor *m*.

sulphur ['sʌlfə] *n* azufre *m*. **sulphuric** *adj* sulfúrico.

sultan ['sʌltən] *n* sultán *m*.

sultana [sʌl'taːnə] *n* pasa de Esmirna *f*.

sultry ['sʌltri] *adj* (*weather*) sofocante: (*person*) sensual.

sum [sʌm] *n* suma *f*; cantidad *f*: cálculo *m*. *v* **sum up** recapitular: resumir: (*person*) evaluar.

summarize ['sʌməraiz] *v* resumir, recapitular. **summary** *n* resumen *m*: *adj* sumario.

summer ['sʌmə] *n* verano *m*. **summer holidays** vacaciones de verano *f pl*. **summerhouse** *n* cenador *m*.

summit ['sʌmit] *n* cumbre *f*, cima *f*: (*fig*) apogeo *m*.

summon ['sʌmən] *v* llamar, convocar: mandar: hacer venir. **summon up** evocar.

summons ['sʌmənz] *pl n* llamamiento *m*: (*law*) citación *f*. *v* citar.

sumptuous ['sʌmptʃuəs] *adj* suntuoso.

sun [sʌn] *n* sol *m*. **sunny** *adj* bañado de sol.

sunbathe ['sʌnbeið] *v* tomar el sol. **sunbathing** *n* baños de sol *m pl*.

sunbeam ['sʌnbiːm] *n* rayo de sol *m*.

sunburn ['sʌnbəːn] *n* (*tan*) bronceado *m*:

(*pain*) quemadura del sol *f*. **sunburnt** *adj* bronceado: quemado por el sol.

Sunday ['sʌndi] *n* domingo *m*.

sundial ['sʌndaiəl] *n* reloj de sol *m*.

sundry ['sʌndri] *adj* varios. **all and sundry** todo el mundo. **sundries** *pl n* artículos diversos *m pl*.

sunflower ['sʌnˌflauə] *n* girasol *m*.

sun-glasses ['sʌnglaːsiz] *pl n* gafas de sol *f pl*.

sunk [sʌŋk] *V* **sink.**

sunlight ['sʌnlait] *n* luz del sol *f*.

sunrise ['sʌnraiz] *n* salida del sol *f*.

sunset ['sʌnset] *n* puesta del sol *f*.

sunshine ['sʌnʃain] *n* sol *m*.

sunstroke ['sʌnstrouk] *n* insolación *f*.

sun-tan ['sʌntan] *n* bronceado *m*. **sun-tan lotion** loción bronceadora *f*.

super ['suːpə] *adj* (*coll*) estupendo: formidable.

superannuation [ˌsuːpəranjuˈeiʃən] *n* jubilación *f*.

superb [suːˈpəːb] *adj* soberbio: magnífico.

supercilious [ˌsuːpəˈsiliəs] *adj* altanero: desdeñoso.

superficial [ˌsuːpəˈfiʃəl] *adj* superficial.

superfluous [suːˈpəːfluəs] *adj* superfluo.

superhuman [suːpəˈhjuːmən] *adj* sobrehumano.

superimpose [ˌsuːpərimˈpouz] *v* sobreponer. **superimposed** *adj* (*photo, etc.*) superpuesto.

superintendent [ˌsuːpərinˈtendənt] *n* superintendente *m*, *f*: director, -a *m*, *f*: (*police*) subjefe de la policía *m*.

superior [suːˈpiəriə] *n*, *adj* superior, -a. **superiority** *n* superioridad *f*.

superlative [suːˈpəːlətiv] *adj* superlativo: supremo. (*gramm*) *nm*, *adj* superlativo.

supermarket ['suːpəˌmaːkit] *n* supermercado *m*.

supernatural [ˌsuːpəˈnatʃərəl] *adj* sobrenatural. *n* lo sobrenatural.

supersede [ˌsuːpəˈsiːd] *v* sustituir, reemplazar.

supersonic [ˌsuːpəˈsonik] *adj* supersónico.

superstition [suːpəˈstiʃən] *n* superstición *f*. **superstitious** *adj* supersticioso.

supervise ['suːpəvaiz] *v* supervisar: vigilar. **supervision** *n* superintendencia *f*. **supervisor** *n* supervisor, -a *m*, *f*: director, -a *m*, *f*.

supper ['sʌpə] *n* cena *f*.

supple ['sʌpl] *adj* flexible, elástico. **suppleness** *n* flexibilidad *f*.

supplement ['sʌpləmənt] *n* suplemento *m*. *v* suplir, complementar. **supplementary** *adj* suplementario.

supply [sə'plai] *n* (*stock*) surtido *m*; provisión *f*; (*act of supplying*) suministro *m*. **supplies** *pl n* material *m* *sing*; provisiones *f pl*; (*stores*) viveres *m pl*. *v* alimentar; proveer; abastecer; presentar.

support [sə'poɪt] *n* apoyo *m*; sostén *m*; soporte *m*. *v* apoyar; sostener; defender; (*financially*) mantener. **supporter** *n* partidario, -a *m, f*; (*sport*) aficionado, -a.

suppose [sə'pouz] *v* suponer. **supposed** *adj* supuesto. **be supposed to** deber. **supposedly** *adv* según se supone. **supposing** *conj* si, suponiendo (que). **supposition** *n* suposición *f*.

suppress [sə'pres] *v* suprimir; (*yawn, laugh, etc.*) contener; (*passion*) dominar; (*fact*) disimular; (*revolt*) sofocar; (*publication*) prohibir; (*news*) ocultar. **suppression** *n* supresión *f*; dominio *m*; represión *f*; prohibición *f*; ocultación *f*.

supreme [su'priːm] *adj* supremo. **supremacy** *n* supremacía *f*.

surcharge ['səɪtʃaɪdʒ] *n* sobrecarga *f*.

sure [ʃuə] *adj* seguro, cierto. **sure enough** efectivamente. **sure-footed** *adj* de pie firme. **surely** *adv* seguramente; sin duda.

surety ['ʃuərəti] *n* garantía *f*, fianza *f*.

surf [səɪf] *n* resaca *f*; (*foam*) espuma *f*. **surf-board** *n* tabla hawaiana *f*. **surfing** *n* surf *m*.

surface ['səɪfis] *n* superficie *f*. **on the surface** en apariencia. *v* (*road*) revestir; (*swimmer*) salir a la superficie; (*submarine*) sacar a la superficie.

surfeit ['səɪfit] *n* exceso *m*.

surge [səɪdʒ] *n* oleada *f*; (*anger*) ola *f*. *v* (*sea*) levantarse; (*crowd*) bullir.

surgeon ['səɪdʒən] *n* cirujano *m*. **surgery** *n* (*skill*) cirugía *f*; (*place*) consultorio *m*.

surgical *adj* quirúrgico.

surly ['səɪli] *adj* malhumormado.

surmount [sə'maunt] *v* vencer, superar.

surname ['səɪneim] *n* apellido *m*.

surpass [sə'paɪs] *v* superar, sobrepasar.

surplus ['səɪpləs] *n* excedente *m*. *adj* sobrante.

surprise [sə'praiz] *n* sorpresa *f*. *adj* de sorpresa. *v* sorprender.

surrealism [sə'riəlizəm] *n* surrealismo *m*. **surrealist** *n*(*m+f*), *adj* surrealista. **surrealistic** *adj* surrealista.

surrender [sə'rendə] *v* rendir; (*give up*) ceder; entregar. *n* rendición *f*; capitulación *f*.

surreptitious [,sʌrəp'tiʃəs] *adj* subrepticio.

surround [sə'raund] *v* cercar, rodear. *n* borde *m*. **surrounding** *adj* circundante. **surroundings** *pl n* (*environment*) medio ambiente *m*; (*environs*) alrededores *m pl*.

survey ['səɪvei; *v* sə'vei] *n* inspección *f*; (*report*) informe *m*; (*of a question*) examen *m*; panorama *m*; (*land*) medición *f*. *v* inspeccionar; estudiar; examinar; contemplar; medir. **surveying** *n* inspección *f*; agrimensura *f*. **surveyor** *n* (*land*) agrimensor *m*; (*house*) inspector *m*.

survive [sə'vaiv] *v* sobrevivir a. **survival** *n* supervivencia *f*. **survivor** *n* sobreviviente *m, f*.

susceptible [sə'septəbl] *adj* susceptible; sensible.

suspect ['sʌspekt; *v* sə'spekt] *n, adj* sospechoso, -a. *v* sospechar.

suspend [sə'spend] *v* suspender. **suspender** *n* liga *f*. **suspense** *n* incertidumbre *f*; (*book, film*) suspense *m*. **in suspense** pendiente. **suspension** *n* suspensión *f*. **suspension bridge** puente colgante *m*.

suspicion [sə'spiʃən] *n* sospecha *f*. **suspicious** *adj* (*suspecting*) suspicaz; (*suspected*) sospechoso.

sustain [sə'stein] *v* sostener; mantener; apoyar; (*suffer*) recibir.

swab [swob] *n* (*mop*) estropajo *m*; (*med*: *pad*) tapón *m*. *v* fregar con estropajo; limpiar con tapón.

swagger ['swagə] *n* pavoneo *m*. *v* pavonearse; darse importancia.

swallow¹ ['swolou] *v* tragar. **swallow up** tragarse. *n* trago *m*; (*amount*) bocado *m*.

swallow² ['swolou] *n* (*bird*) golondrina *f*.

swam [swam] *V* swim.

swamp [swomp] *n* pantano *m*; marisma *f*. *v* sumergir; inundar. **swampy** *adj* pantanoso.

swan [swon] *n* cisne *m*.

swank [swaŋk] (*coll*) *n* fanfarronada *f*; (*person*) fanfarrón, -ona *m, f*. *v* fanfarronear. **swanky** *adj* fanfarrón.

swap *or* **swop** [swop] *n* cambio *m*, treque *m*. *v* cambiar, trocar.

swarm [swoɪm] *n* (*bees*) enjambre *m*; (*fig*) multitud *f*. *v* enjambrar; (*fig*) pulular.

swarthy ['swoɪði] *adj* moreno.

swat [swot] *v* aplastar.

sway [swei] *n* balanceo *m*; oscilación *f*; dominio *m*. *v* balancearse; oscilar; (*influence*) influir.

*swear** [sweə] *v* jurar. **swear in** tomar juramento a. **swear-word** *n* palabrota *f*.

sweat [swet] *n* sudor *m*. *v* sudar.

sweater *n* suéter *m*.

swede [swiɪd] *n* naba *f*.

Sweden ['swiɪdn] *n* Suecia *f*. **Swede** *n* sueco, -a *m*, *f*. **Swedish** *nm*, *adj* sueco.

*sweep** [swiɪp] *v* deshollinar; barrer; explorar. **sweep in/out** entrar/salir rápidamente. **sweep through** difundirse. *n* (*chimney*) deshollinador *m*; (*a cleaning*) barrido *m*; (*curve*) curva *f*. **make a clean sweep** llevárselo todo. **sweeping** *adj* aplastante; demasiado general. **sweeping statement** declaración demasiado general *f*.

sweet [swiɪt] *adj* (*taste*) dulce; (*air, breath, etc.*) fresco; (*smell*) bueno; (*friendly*) encantador; (*kind*) bondadoso. *n* (*toffee*) caramelo *m*; (*dessert*) postre *m*. **sweetbread** *n* mollejas *f pl*. **sweet corn** maíz tierno *m*. **sweetheart** *n* novio, -a *m*, *f*. **sweet potato** patata boniato *f*. **sweetshop** *n* confitería *f*. **sweeten** *v* azucarar, endulzar. **sweetly** *adv* dulcemente; (*sound*) melodiosamente. **sweetness** *n* dulzor *m*; (*character*) dulzura *f*.

*swell** [swel] *v* hinchar; inflarse. *n* inflado *m*; hinchazón *m*; curvatura *f*. **swelling** *n* inflamiento *m*.

swelter ['sweltə] *v* sofocarse de calor. **sweltering** *adj* sofocante.

swerve [swɜɪv] *v* desviar; (*vehicle*) dar un viraje. *n* viraje *m*.

swift [swift] *adj* rápido; pronto. *n* (*bird*) vencejo *m*. **swiftness** rapidez *f*; prontitud *f*.

swill [swil] *v* lavar con much agua; (*drink*) beber a tragos. *n* (*for pigs*) bazofia *f*.

*swim** [swim] *v* nadar. *n* baño *m*. **swimmer** *n* nadador, -a *m*, *f*. **swimming** *n* natación *f*. **swimming baths** *or* **pool** piscina *f*. **swimming costume** traje de baño *m*.

swindle ['swindl] *n* estafa *f*. *v* estafar. **swindler** *n* estafador, -a *m*, *f*.

swine [swain] *n* cerdo *m*, puerco *m*; (*impol*) canalla *m*, *f*.

*swing** [swiŋ] *v* hacer girar; balancear; oscilar; virar. *n* (*amusement*) columpio *m*; oscilación *f*; impulso *m*; (*pol*) viraje *m*. **in full swing** a toda velocidad.

swipe [swaip] (*coll*) *n* golpetazo *m*. *v* golpear con fuerza; (*steal*) afanar.

swirl [swɜɪl] *n* remolino *m*. *v* arremolinarse.

swish [swiʃ] *n* silbo *m*; (*of water*) susurro *m*; (*of garment*) crujido *m*. *v* (*cane*) blandir; (*tail*) menear.

Swiss [swis] *n*, *adj* suizo, -a. **Swiss roll** brazo de gitano *m*.

switch [switʃ] *n* (*elec*) interruptor *m*, conmutador *m*; (*change*) paso *m*; (*stick*) varilla *f*. **switchboard** *n* centralita de teléfonos *f*. *v* (*opinion, policy*) cambiar de; (*places*) cambiar; (*a train*) desviar. **switch off** desconectar. **switch on** encender.

Switzerland ['switsələnd] *n* Suiza *f*.

swivel ['swivl] *n* pivote *m*. *v* girar sobre un eje; dar una vuelta.

swollen ['swoulən] *V* **swell**.

swoop [swuɪp] *n* calada *f*; redada *f*. **at one fell swoop** de un solo golpe. *v* calarse, abatirse.

swop *V* **swap**.

sword [soɪd] *n* espada *f*. **swordfish** *n* pez espada *m*.

sworn [swoɪn] *V* **swear**.

swot [swot] (*coll*) *n* empollón, -ona *m*, *f*. *v* empollar **swotting** *n* estudio *m*.

swum [swʌm] *V* **swim**.

swung [swʌŋ] *V* **swing**.

sycamore ['sikəmoɪ] *n* sicomoro *m*.

syllable ['siləbl] *n* sílaba *f*. **syllabic** *adj* silábico.

syllabus ['siləbəs] *n* programa *m*.

symbol ['simbl] *n* símbolo *m*, emblema *m*. **symbolic** *adj* simbólico. **symbolism** *n* simbolismo *m*. **symbolize** *v* simbolizar.

symmetry ['simitri] *n* simetría *f*. **symmetrical** *adj* simétrico.

sympathy ['simpəθi] *n* pésame *m*; compasión *f*. **sympathetic** *adj* compasivo; comprensivo; favorable. **sympathize with** compadecerse de.

symphony ['simfəni] *n* sinfonía *f*. **symphonic** *adj* sinfónico.

symposium [sim'pouziəm] *n* simposio *m*.

symptom ['simptəm] *n* síntoma *m*. **symptomatic** *adj* sintomático.

synagogue ['sinəgog] *n* sinagoga *f*.

synchromesh ['siŋkroumeʃ] *n* sincronizador.

synchronize ['siŋkrənaiz] *v* sincronizar. **synchronization** *n* sincronización *f*.

syncopate ['siŋkəpeit] n sincopar. syncopation n síncopa f.

syndicate ['sindikit] n sindicato m.

syndrome ['sindroum] n síndrome m.

synonym ['sinənim] n sinónimo m. synonymous adj sinónimo.

synopsis [si'nopsis] n, pl -ses sinopsis f invar.

syntax ['sintaks] n sintaxis f.

synthesis ['sinθisis] n, pl -ses síntesis f invar. synthesize v sintetizar.

syphilis ['sifilis] n sífilis f.

syringe [si'rindʒ] n jeringa f. v jeringar.

syrup ['sirəp] n (med) jarabe m; (fruit) almíbar m. syrupy adj almibarado.

system ['sistəm] n sistema m; método m. systematic adj sistemático.

T

tab [tab] n etiqueta f. keep tabs on (coll) tener controlado.

tabby ['tabi] n gato atigrador m.

table ['teibl] n mesa f. table-cloth n mantel m. table-mat n salvamanteleo m invar. table-napkin n servilleta f. tablespoon n cucharón m. tablespoonful cucharada f. table tennis tenis de mesa m. clear the table levantar la mesa. set the table poner la mesa.

table d'hôte [taɪblə'dout] n menú m.

tablet ['tablit] n (med, soap) pastilla f; (stone, chocolate) tableta f; (writing-paper) bloc m.

taboo [ta'buɪ] nm, adj tabú.

tabulate ['tabjuleit] v tabular.

tacit ['tasit] adj tácito.

taciturn ['tasitəɪn] adj taciturno.

tack [tak] n (nail) tachuela f; (sewing) hilván m; (naut: change of direction) virada f; (distance sailed) bordada f. v clavar con tachuelas; hilvanar; virar de bordo.

tackle ['takl] n (ropes) jarcias f pl; (rigging) aparejo m; (equipment) trastos m pl; (sport) placaje m. v placar; (seize) agarrar; (fig) abordar, emprender.

tact [takt] n tacto m. tactful adj con tacto, discreto. tactless adj falto de tacto, indiscreto.

tactics ['taktiks] pl n táctica f sing. tactical adj táctico.

tadpole ['tadpoul] n renacuajo m.

taffeta ['tafitə] n tafetán m.

tag [tag] n etiqueta f; (shoelace) herrete m; (game) pillapilla m. tag along (coll) seguir.

tail [teil] n cola f; rabo m; (coat, shirt) faldón m. tail-end n zaga f, rabera f. tails pl n (coin) cruz f sing. v (coll) seguir.

tailor ['teilə] n sastre m. v entallar; (fig) adaptar.

taint [teint] v (stain) manchar; (food) corromper; (air) viciar; (fig) mancillar. n mancha f; corrupción f; contaminación f.

*take [teik] v tomar; llevarse; (carry) cargarse; (phot) sacar; (shoe size) calzar; (occupy) ocupar; (responsibility) asumir; (bear) aguantar; (suppose) suponer. take after parecerse a. take along llevarse. take away quitar; (subtract) restar. take back (return) devolver; (retract) retirar. take down (pictures, curtains) descolgar; (from a shelf) bajar; (write) apuntar. take someone down a peg (coll) bajarle los humos a alguien. take in acoger; (situation) entender; (clothes) achicar; (coll: deceive) engañar. take off (clothes) quitarse; (aero) despegar. take-off n despegue m; (coll) imitamonos m invar. take on (employ) contratar; (challenge) competir con. take-over (comm) adquisición f.

talcum powder ['talkəm] n talco m.

tale [teil] n cuento m. fairy tales cuentos de hadas m pl. tell tales (coll) contar chismes.

talent ['talənt] n talento m. talented adj talentoso, talentudo.

talk [toɪk] n conversación f; charla f; (lecture) conferencia f; (speech) discurso m. v decir; hablar. talk back replicar. talk down to ponerse al alcance de. talk into convencer para que. talk over discutir. talkative adj hablador. talking n conversación f. talking point tema de conversación m.

tall [toɪl] adj alto; grande. tallboy n cómoda alta f. tallness n altura f; lo alto.

tally ['tali] n tarja f; cuenta f. v tarjar; cuadrar.

talon ['talən] n garra f.

tambourine [tambə'riɪn] n pandereta f, pandero m.

tame [teim] *adj* manso; domesticado; (*not exciting*) aburrido. *v* domesticar; amansar.

tamper ['tampə] *v* **tamper with** (*text*) amañar; (*spoil*) estropear.

tampon ['tampon] *n* tapón *m*.

tan [tan] *n* bronceado *m*, color tostado *m*. *adj* bronceado, tostado. (*hide*) curtir; (*sun*) broncear, tostar.

tandem ['tandəm] *n* tándem *m*.

tangent ['tandʒənt] *nf, adj* tangente. **go off at a tangent** salirse por la tangente.

tangerine [tandʒə'riɪn] *n* (*fruit*) mandarina *f*.

tangible ['tandʒəbl] *adj* tangible.

tangle ['taŋgl] *v* enmarañar; enredar. *n* maraña *f*; enredo *m*.

tank [taŋk] *n* tanque *m*, cisterna *f*, depósito *m*; (*mil*) tanque *m*. **tanker** *n* (*lorry*) camión cisterna *m*; (*ship*) petrolero *m*.

tankard ['taŋkəd] *n* jarro *m*.

tantalize ['tantəlaiz] *v* atormentar. **tantalizing** *adj* que atormenta.

tantamount ['tantəmaunt] *adj* **be tantamount to** ser equivalente a.

tantrum ['tantrəm] *n* berrinche *m*, rabieta *f*. **fly into a tantrum** coger una rabieta.

tap¹ [tap] *n* golpecito *m*. **tap-dance** *n* zapateado *m*. *v* golpear ligeramente.

tap² [tap] *n* (*water*) grifo *m*; (*barrel*) espita *f*. *v* poner una espita a; (*phone*) interceptar; (*fig: draw on*) utilizar.

tape [teip] *n* cinta *f*; (*recording*) cinta magnetofónica *f*. **tape-measure** *n* cinta métrica *f*. **tape-recorder** *n* magnetófono *m*. **tapeworm** *n* tenia *f*. *v* (*record*) grabar; (*fasten*) atar con cinta.

taper ['teipə] *n* (*candle*) vela *f*; (*narrowing*) estrachamiento *m*. *v* estrechar. **tapering** *adj* cónico.

tapestry ['tapəstri] *n* tapiz *m*.

tapioca [tapi'oukə] *n* tapioca *f*.

tar [taɪ] *n* alquitrán *m*. *v* alquitranar.

tarantula [tə'rantjulə] *n* tarántula *f*.

target ['taɪgit] *n* blanco *m*; (*fig*) objeto *m*.

tariff ['tarif] *n* tarifa *f*.

tarmac ['taɪmak] *n* superficie alquitranada *f*.

tarnish ['taɪniʃ] *v* deslustrar. *n* deslustre *m*.

tarpaulin [taɪ'poɪlin] *n* lona alquitranada *f*.

tarragon ['tarəgən] *n* estragón *m*.

tart¹ [taɪt] *adj* agrio; ácido.

tart² [taɪt] *n* tarta *f*; (*slang*) fulana *f*.

tartar ['taɪtə] *n* (*chem*) tártaro *m*; (*on teeth*) sarro *m*.

task [taɪsk] *n* tarea *f*. **taskmaster** *n* capataz *m*.

tassel ['tasəl] *n* borla *f*.

taste [teist] *n* (*sense*) gusto *m*; sabor *m*. *v* probar; saber. **taste of** saber a. **tasteful** *adj* de buen gusto. **tasteless** *adj* insípido; (*in bad taste*) de mal gusto. **tasty** *adj* sabroso.

tattered ['tatəd] *adj* andrajoso.

tattoo¹ [tə'tuɪ] *n* (*on skin*) tatuaje *m*. *v* tatuar.

tattoo² [tə'tuɪ] *n* (*mil*) desfile militar *m*; (*drumming*) repiqueteo *m*.

tatty ['tati] *adj* (*coll*) en mal estado.

taunt [toɪnt] *v* mofarse de. *n* mofa *f*. **taunting** *adj* burlón; provocante.

Taurus ['toɪrəs] *n* Tauro *m*.

taut [toɪt] *adj* tenso, tirante. **tautness** *n* tensión *f*, tirantez *f*.

tavern ['tavən] *n* (*bar*) taberna *f*; (*inn*) venta *f*.

tawny ['toɪni] *adj* leonado.

tax [taks] *n* impuesto *m*, contribución *f*. **tax-free** *adj* exento de impuestos. **tax evasion** evasión fiscal *f*. **tax haven** refugio fiscal *m*. **taxpayer** *n* contribuyente *m, f*. **tax return** declaración de renta *f*. *v* gravar con un impuesto; imponer contribuciones; (*try*) poner a prueba. **taxable** *adj* imponible. **taxation** *n* impuestos *m pl*; (*system*) sistema tributario *m*.

taxi ['taksi] *n* taxi *m*. **taxi-driver** *n* taxista *m, f*. **taximeter** *n* taxímetro *m*. **taxi rank** parada de taxis *f*. *v* (*aero*) rodar por la pista.

tea [tiɪ] *n* té *m*; (*snack*) merienda *f*. **teacup** *n* tasa de té *f*. **teapot** *n* tetera *f*. **teaspoon** *n* cucharilla *f*. **teaspoonful** *n* cucharadita *f*. **tea towel** trapo de cocina *m*.

***teach** [tiɪtʃ] *v* enseñar. **teacher** *n* (*primary*) maestro, -a *m, f*; (*secondary*) profesor, -a *m, f*. **teaching** *n* enseñanza *f*.

teak [tiɪk] *n* teca *f*.

team [tiɪm] *n* (*yoked animals*) yunta *f*; (*horses*) tronco *m*; (*people*) equipo *m*. **team-mate** *n* compañero de equipo *m*. **team spirit** espíritu de equipo *m*. **teamwork** *n* trabajo de equipo *m*. *v* **team up** agruparse.

*tear¹ [teə] *v* desgarrar; (*snatch*) arrancar. **tear along/out** ir a toda velocidad. **tear down** demoler. **tear off** (*coupon*) cortar. *n* rasgón *m*.

tear² [tiə] *n* lágrima *f*. **tear gas** gas lacrimógeno *m*. **tear-jerker** (*coll*) *n* obra sentimental *f*. **tearful** *adj* lloroso.

tease [tiːz] *v* provocar. *n* broma *f*; (*person*) bromista *m*, *f*. **teasing** *n* bromas *f pl*.

teat [tiːt] *n* pezón *m*; (*animals*) teta *f*.

technique [tek'niːk] *n* técnica *f*. **technical** *adj* técnico. **technicality** *n* detalle técnico *m*. **technician** *n* técnico, -a *m*, *f*. **technological** *adj* tecnológico. **technology** *n* tecnología *f*.

teddy bear ['tediˌbeə] *n* osito de felpa *m*.

tedious ['tiːdiəs] *adj* latoso. **tediousness** *n also* **tedium** pesadez *f*, tedio *m*.

tee [tiː] *n* tee *m*. *v* **tee off** dar el primer golpe.

teem [tiːm] *v* pulular, hormiguear.

teenage ['tiːneidʒ] *adj* adolescente. **teenager** *n* adolescente *m*, *f*. **teens** *pl n* adolescencia *f sing*.

teeth [tiːθ] *V* tooth.

teethe [tiːð] *v* echar los dientes. **teething** *n* dentición *f*.

teetotaller [tiː'toutələ] *n* abstemio, -a *m*, *f*.

telecommunications [ˌtelikəmjuːni'keiʃənz] *pl n* telecomunicaciones *f pl*.

telegram ['teligram] *n* telegrama *m*.

telegraph ['teligraːf] *n* telégrafo *m*. **telegraph pole** poste telegráfico *m*. *v* telegrafiar. **telegraphic** *adj* telegráfico.

telepathy [tə'lepəθi] *n* telepatía *f*. **telepathic** *adj* telepático.

telephone ['telifoun] *n* teléfono *m*. **telephone box** *or* **kiosk** cabina telefónica *f*. **telephone call** llamada telefónica *f*. **telephone directory** guía de teléfonos *f*. **telephone exchange** central telefónica *f*. **telephone number** número de teléfono *m*. **telephone operator** *or* **telephonist** telefonista *m*, *f*. *v* telefonear a.

telescope ['teliskoup] *n* telescopio *m*. **telescopic** *adj* telescópico.

television ['teliviʒən] *n* televisión *f*. **television set** televisor *m*. **televise** *v* televisar.

telex ['teleks] *n* télex *m*.

*tell [tel] *v* decir; (*story*) contar; comunicar; mandar; (*identify*) reconocer; (*distinguish*) distinguir; (*deduce*) deducir;

(*observe*) notar. **tell against** perjudicar. **tell of** hablar de. **tell off** (*coll*) regañar. **tell on** afectar a. **telltale** *adj* revelador.

temper ['tempə] *n* (*anger*) cólera *f*; temperamento *m*; humor *m*. **lose one's temper** enfadarse. *v* templar.

temperament ['tempərəmənt] *n* temperamento *m*. **temperamental** *adj* caprichoso.

temperate ['tempərət] *adj* templado.

temperature ['temprətʃə] *n* temperatura *f*; (*med*) fiebre *f*.

tempestuous [tem'pestjuəs] *adj* tempestuoso.

temple¹ ['templ] *n* (*rel*) templo *m*.

temple² ['templ] *n* (*anat*) sien *f*.

tempo ['tempou] *n* (*music*) tiempo *m*; (*fig*) ritmo *m*.

temporary ['tempərəri] *adj* temporal, provisional. **temporary worker** temporario, -a *m*, *f*.

tempt [tempt] *v* tentar; seducir. **temptation** *n* tentación *f*.

ten [ten] *nm*, *adj* diez. **tenth** *n*, *adj* décimo, -a.

tenacious [tə'neiʃəs] *adj* tenaz. **tenaciousness** *also* **tenacity** *n* tenacidad *f*.

tenant ['tenənt] *n* habitante *m*, *f*, ocupante *m*, *f*. **tenancy** *n* alquiler *m*, arrendamiento *m*.

tend¹ [tend] *v* tender, tener tendencia a. **tendency** *n* tendencia *f*.

tend² [tend] *v* (*look after*) cuidar; manejar.

tender¹ ['tendə] *adj* tierno; delicado; (*kind*) cariñoso; compasivo; (*sensitive*) sensible; (*painful*) dolorido. **tenderize** *v* ablandar. **tenderness** *n* (*affection*) ternura *f*; (*meat*) lo tierno.

tender² ['tendə] *v* ofertar, hacer una oferta. *n* oferta *f*. **legal tender** moneda corriente *f*.

tendon ['tendən] *n* tendón *m*.

tendril ['tendril] *n* zarcillo *m*.

tenement ['tenəmənt] *n* casa de vecindad *f*.

tennis ['tenis] *n* tenis *m*. **tennis ball** pelota de tenis *f*. **tennis court** campo de tenis *m*. **tennis player** tenista *m*, *f*. **tennis shoes** zapatos de tenis *m pl*.

tenor ['tenə] *n* (*music*) tenor *m*; (*sense*) significado *m*; (*course*) curso *m*.

tense¹ [tens] *adj* tenso; estirado. *v* tensar. **tension** *n* tensión *f*.

tense² [tens] *n* tiempo *m*.

tent [tent] *n* tienda de campaña *f*. **pitch a tent** armar una tienda de campaña.

tentacle ['tentəkl] *n* tentáculo *m*.

tentative ['tentətiv] *adj* provisional; de tanteo; indeciso.

tenterhooks ['tentəhuks] *pl n* **be on tenterhooks** estar sobre ascuas.

tenuous ['tenjuəs] *adj* tenue; delgado.

tepid ['tepid] *adj* templaducho; *(fig)* tibio.

tepidness *n also* tepidity tibieza *f*.

term [təɪm] *n* período *m*; *(comm)* plazo *m*; *(school)* trimestre *m*; curso *m*; *(end)* término *m*. **terms** *pl n* condiciones *f pl*; *(terminology)* términos *m pl*; *(comm)* tarifa *f sing*; *(relationship)* relaciones *f pl*. **come to terms with** llegar a un acuerdo con. **on good/bad terms with** en buenas/malas relaciones con. **terms of reference** mandato *m sing*. *v* llamar, calificar.

terminal ['təɪminəl] *adj* terminal, final. *n* final de línea *m*; *(extremity)* extremidad *f*; *(elec)* borne *m*.

terminate ['təɪmineit] *v* terminar, concluir. **termination** *n* terminación *f*.

terminology [təɪmi'nolədʒi] *n* terminología *f*.

terminus ['təɪminəs] *n* término *m*.

terrace ['terəs] *n* terraza *f*; *(houses)* hilera de casas *f*.

terrain [tə'rein] *n* terreno *m*.

terrestrial [tə'restriəl] *adj* terrestre.

terrible ['terəbl] *adj* terrible; atroz; horrible. **terribly** *adv* terriblemente. **terribly bad** malísimo. **terribly good** buenísimo.

terrier ['teriə] *n* terrier *m*.

terrify ['terifai] *v* aterrorizar. **terrific** *adj* *(coll: excellent)* estupendo; *(coll: extreme)* terrible; enorme.

territory ['teritəri] *n* territorio *m*. **territorial** *adj* territorial.

terror ['terə] *n* terror *m*. **terrorism** *n* terrorismo *m*. **terrorist** *n(m +f)*, *adj* terrorista. **terrorize** *v* aterrorizar, aterrar.

terse [təɪs] *adj* conciso.

terylene ® ['terəliɪn] *n* terylene ® *m*.

test [test] *n* prueba *f*; examen *m*; *(med)* análisis *m*. **test case** *(law)* juicio que hace jurisprudencia *m*. **test match** partido internacional *m*. **test paper** examen *m*. **test pilot** piloto de pruebas *m*. **test tube** tubo de ensayo *m*. *v* probar; poner un examen a; analizar; *(sight)* graduar; *(weight)* comprobar.

testament ['testəmənt] *n* testamento *m*.

the New Testament el Nuevo Testamento *m*. **the Old Testament** el Antiguo Testamento *m*.

testicle ['testikl] *n* testículo *m*.

testify ['testifai] *v* testificar; dar testimonio.

testimony ['testiməni] *n* testimonio *m*.

testimonial *n* testimonio *m*; recomendación *f*.

tetanus ['tetənəs] *n* tétanos *m*.

tether ['teðə] *n* traba *f*, atadura *f*. **at the end of one's tether** hartísimo. *v* trabar, atar.

text [tekst] *n* texto *m*. **textbook** *n* libro de texto *m*. **textual** *adj* textual.

textile ['tekstail] *nm*, *adj* textil.

texture ['tekstjuə] *n* textura *f*.

than [ðən] *conj* que; de; cuando; del que.

thank [θaŋk] *v* agradecer. **thank you** gracias. **thanksgiving** *n* acción de gracias *f*. **thanks to** gracias a. **thankful** *adj* agradecido. **thankless** *adj* desagradecido; ingrato.

that [ðat] *adj* ese, esa; aquel, aquella; el, la. *pron* ése, ésa; aquél, aquélla; *(neuter)* eso; *(neuter: farther away)* aquello; *(before relative pron or of)* el, la, lo; *(who, which)* que; el que, la que; quien; el cual, la cual; *(neuter)* lo que. *adv* así de; tan; tanto. *conj* que; de que; para que; porque.

thatch [θatʃ] *n* *(straw)* paja *f*; *(roof)* techo de paja *m*. *v* cubrir con un tejado de paja.

thaw [θɔɪ] *n* *(ice)* deshielo *m*; *(snow)* derretimiento *m*. *v* deshelar; derretir.

the [ðə] *art* el, la *(pl* los, las); *(neuter)* lo.

theatre ['θiətə] *n* teatro *m*. **theatrical** *adj* teatral, de teatro.

theft [θeft] *n* hurto, robo.

their [ðeə] *adj* su, sus; suyo, suya.

theirs [ðeəz] *pron* el suyo, la suya.

them [ðem] *pron* ellos, ellas; *(direct object)* los, las; *(indirect object)* les.

theme [θiɪm] *n* tema *m*. **thematic** *adj* temático.

themselves [ðəm'selvz] *pl pron* se; ellos mismos, ellas mismas; sí mismos, sí mismas. **by themselves** solos.

then [ðen] *adv* *(that time)* entonces; *(afterwards)* después, luego; *(furthermore)* además; *(despite that)* a pesar de eso; *(consequently)* por lo tanto. *n* entonces; ese momento. *conj* en ese caso; entonces.

theology [θi'olədʒi] *n* teología *f*. **theologian** *n* teólogo, -a *m*, *f*. **theological** *adj* teológico.

theorem ['θiərəm] *n* teorema *m*.

theory ['θiəri] *n* teoría *f*. **theoretical** *adj* teórico.

therapy ['θerəpi] *n* terapia *f*. **therapeutic** *adj* terapéutico. **therapist** *n* terapeuta *m*, *f*.

there [ðeə] *adv* ahí; allí; allá. *thereabouts adv* (*place*) por ahí, por allí; (*degree*) más o menos. **thereafter** *adv* después, más tarde. **thereby** *adv* por eso, por ello. **therefore** *adv* por lo tanto. **therein** *adv* allí dentro; en eso. **there is** *or* **are** hay. **thereof** *adv* de eso; su. **thereto** *adv* a eso, a ello. **thereupon** *adv* immediatamente después; sobre eso. **therewith** *adv* con eso. **there you are** eso es.

thermal ['θəɪməl] *adj* termal; (*tech*) térmico. *n* corriente de aire caliente que sube.

thermodynamics [θəɪmoudai'namiks] *n* termodinámica *f*.

thermometer [θə'momitə] *n* termómetro *m*.

thermonuclear [θəɪmou'njukliə] *adj* termonuclear.

Thermos ® ['θəɪməs] *n* termo ® *m*, termos ® *m*.

thermostat ['θəɪməstat] *n* termostato *m*. **thermostatic** *adj* termostático.

these [ðiɪz] *pl adj* estos, estas. *pl pron* éstos, éstas.

thesis ['θiɪsis] *n*, *pl* **-ses** tesis *f invar*.

they [ðei] *pl pron* ellos, ellas.

thick [θik] *adj* grueso; espeso; denso; (*coll*) torpe. **thick-skinned** *adj* (*fig*) insensible. **thicken** *v* espesar(se). **thickness** *n* espesor *m*.

thief [θiɪf] *n* ladrón, -ona *m*, *f*.

thigh [θai] *n* muslo *m*.

thimble ['θimbl] *n* dedal *m*.

thin [θin] *adj* (*person*) flaco; delgado; fino; (*hair*) ralo; (*audience*) escaso; (*air*) enrarecido; (*beer*) aguado; (*voice*) débil; (*liquid*) claro; (*excuse*) flojo. *v* adelgazar; (*dilute*) diluir. **thinness** *n* delgadez *f*, flaqueza *f*.

thing [θiŋ] *n* cosa *f*; objeto *m*; artículo *m*; (*coll*) chisme *m*. **things** *pl n* (*affairs*, *belongings*) cosas *f pl*.

*****think** [θiŋk] *v* pensar; meditar; imaginar. **I think so** creo que sí. **think about** pensar en. **think over** pensar bien.

third [θəɪd] *adj* tercero. *n* tercero, -a *m*, *f*; (*fraction*) tercio *m*; (*music*) tercera *f*. **third-party insurance** seguro contra tercera persona *m*. **third-rate** *adj* de poca calidad.

thirst [θəɪst] *n* sed *f*. *v* tener sed. **be thirsty** tener sed.

thirteen [θəɪ'tiɪn] *nm*, *adj* trece. **thirteenth** *n*, *adj* decimotercero, -a *m*, *f*.

thirty ['θəɪti] *nm*, *adj* treinta. **thirtieth** *n*, *adj* trigesimo, -a *m*, *f*.

this [ðis] *adj* este, esta. *pron* éste, ésta. *adv* tan; así de.

thistle ['θisl] *n* cardo *m*.

thong [θoŋ] *n* correa *f*.

thorn [θoɪn] *n* espina *f*. **thorny** *adj* espinoso.

thorough ['θʌrə] *adj* (*search*, *etc.*) minucioso; (*person*) concienzudo; a fondo; completo. **thoroughbred** *n* pura sangre *m*, *f*. **thoroughfare** *n* vía pública *f*. **thoroughly** *adv* a fondo; completamente. **thoroughness** *n* minuciosidad *f*.

those [ðouz] *adj* esos, esas; aquellos, aquellas. *pron* ésos, ésas; aquéllos, aquéllas.

though [ðou] *conj* aunque. *adv* sin embargo. **as though** como si.

thought [θoɪt] *n* pensamiento *m*; idea *f*; consideración *f*; intención *f*; opinión *f*. **thoughtful** *adj* pensativo; serio; (*mindful*) cuidadoso; (*considerate*) solícito. **thoughtless** *adj* irreflexivo; descuidado; desconsiderado.

thousand ['θauzənd] *nm*, *adj* mil. **thousandth** *adj* milésimo. *n* (*fraction*) milésima parte *f*; (*position*) número mil *m*.

thrash [θraʃ] *v* dar una paliza a. **thrash about** revolcarse. **thrash out** discutir a fondo. **thrashing** *n* paliza *f*.

thread [θred] *n* hilo *m*; (*screw*) rosca *f*, filete *m*. *v* ensartar, enhebrar. **threadbare** *adj* raido, gastado.

threat [θret] *n* amenaza *f*. **threaten** *v* amenazar.

three [θriɪ] *nm*, *adj* tres. **three-cornered** *adj* triangular. **three-dimensional** *adj* tridimensional. **threefold** *adj* triple. **three-legged** *adj* de tres patas. **three-piece suite** tresillo *m*. **three-ply** *adj* contrapachado. **three-quarter** *adj* tres cuartos.

thresh [θreʃ] *v* trillar. **threshing machine** *n* trilladora *f*.

threshold ['θreʃould] *n* umbral *m*.
threw [θruː] *V* throw.
thrift [θrift] *n* economía *f*. **thrifty** *adj* económico.
thrill [θril] *n* emoción *f*; (*quiver*) estremecimiento *m*. *v* estremecer. **thriller** *n* novela *or* película escalofriante *f*. **thrilling** *adj* emocionante; escalofriante.
thrive [θraiv] *v* crecer; desarrollarse; tener buena salud; prosperar. **thriving** *adj* lozano; próspero.
throat [θrout] *n* garganta *f*. **clear one's throat** aclararse la voz. **throaty** *adj* gutural.
throb [θrob] *n* (*heart*) latido *m*, palpitación *f*; (*engine*) zumbido *m*; (*pulse*) pulsación *f*; (*pain*) punzada *f*. *v* latir; pulsar; zumbar; dar punzadas.
thrombosis [θrom'bousis] *n* trombosis *f* invar.
throne [θroun] *n* trono *m*.
throng [θroŋ] *n* multitud *f*, muchedumbre *f*. *v* atestar; afluir.
throttle ['θrotl] *v* estrangular. *n* (*tech*) regulador *m*; (*mot*) acelerador.
through [θruː] *adj* directo; continuo. *adv* de parte a parte; completamente. *prep* (*via*) por; (*time*) durante; (*place*) a través de. **no through road** calle sin salida *f*. **through traffic** tránsito *m*. **throughout** *prep* (*place*) por todo, en todo; (*time*) durante todo. *adv* hasta el final.
*****throw** [θrou] *n* tiro *m*, lanzamiento *m*; (*wrestling*) tumbado *m*. *v* lanzar, tirar, arrojar; (*a blow*) dar; (*light*) proyectar. **throw away** tirar; (*get rid of*) desechar; (*money*) despilfarrar. **throw off** (*a habit*) renunciar a; (*the scent*) despistar. **throw out** expulsar, echar; rechazar. **throw up** (*job*) dejar; (*vomit*) devolver.
thrush [θrʌʃ] *n* tordo *m*.
*****thrust** [θrʌst] *v* empujar; clavar; meter; poner. *n* empujón *m*; (*stab*) estocada *f*.
thud [θʌd] *n* ruido sordo *m*. *v* caer con un ruido sordo.
thumb [θʌm] *n* pulgar *m*. *v also* **thumb through** hojear. **thumb a lift** (*coll*) hacer autostop. **thumb index** uñeros *m pl*.
thump [θʌmp] *n* (*blow*) porrazo *m*; (*noise*) ruido sordo *m*. *v* (*strike*) golpear; (*heart*) latir con fuerza.
thunder ['θʌndə] *n* trueno *m*; (*fig*) estruendo *m*. **thunderstorm** *n* tormenta *f*. **thunderstruck** *adj* atónito. *v* tronar.

Thursday ['θəːzdi] *n* jueves *m*.
thus [ðʌs] *adv* así; de este modo.
thwart [θwɔːt] *v* frustrar, impedir.
thyme [taim] *n* tomillo *m*.
thyroid ['θairoid] *n* tiroides *f* invar. *adj* tiroideo.
tiara [ti'aːrə] *n* tiara *f*.
tick[1] [tik] *n* (*mark*) marca *f*; (*sound*) tictac *m*. **tick off** (*coll*) reprender.
tick[2] [tik] *n* (*zool*) garrapata *f*.
ticket ['tikit] *n* (*price*) etiqueta *f*; (*entrance*) entrada *f*; (*transport*) billete *m*; (*permit*) pase *m*. **cloakroom ticket** número del guardarropa *m*. **complimentary ticket** entrada de favor *f*. **parking ticket** multa por aparcamiento indebido *f*. **return ticket** billete de ida y vuelta *m*. **single ticket** billete de ida *m*. **ticket agency** agencia de venta de billetes *f*. **ticket office** taquilla *f*.
tickle ['tikl] *v* hacer cosquillas a. *n* cosquilleo *m*. **ticklish** *adj* cosquilloso.
tide [taid] *n* marea *f*. **tide-mark** *n* línea de la marea alta *f*; (*coll*) lengua del aqua *f*. *v* **tide over** sacar de apuro.
tidy ['taidi] *adj* ordenado; (*appearance*) arreglado; (*clean*) limpio. *v* ordenar; limpiar. **tidily** *adv* bien; aseadamente. **tidiness** *n* orden *m*; aseo *m*.
tie [tai] *v* atar; (*lace*) lacear; (*knot*) hacer; (*unite*) unir; (*link*) ligar; (*sport*) empatar. *n* (*neck*) corbata *f*; (*knot*) nudo *m*; (*bond*) lazo *m*; (*sport*) empate *m*; (*fig*) atadura *f*.
tier [tiə] *n* grada *f*; (*row*) fila *f*; (*cake*) piso *m*.
tiger ['taigə] *n* tigre *m*.
tight [tait] *adj* (*bolt, knot, etc.*) apretado; (*clothes*) ajustado; (*taut*) tirante; (*control*) estricto; (*seal*) hermético; (*bend*) cerrado; (*coll: drunk*) borracho; (*coll: mean*) agarrado. **tight-fisted** *adj* tacaño. **tight-lipped** *adj* callado. **tightrope** *n* cuerda de volatinero *f*. *adv also* **tightly** bien; herméticamente. **hold tight!** ¡agárrense bien! **tighten** (*screw, etc.*) apretar; (*rope, etc.*) tensar; (*control*) estrechar. **tighten one's belt** (*coll*) apretarse el cinturón.
tights *pl n* mallas *f pl*.
tile [tail] *n* (*roof*) teja *f*; (*floor*) baldosa *f*. *v* tejar; embaldosar.
till[1] [til] *V* until.
till[2] [til] *n* caja *f*.
till[3] [til] *v* labrar, cultivar.

tiller ['tilǝ] *n* (*naut*) caña del timón *f*.
tilt [tilt] *n* inclinación *f*. **at full tilt** en toda mecha. *v* inclinar. **tilt at** arremeter contra.
timber ['timbǝ] *n* madera de construcción *f*. **timbered** (*house*) enmaderado.
time [taim] *n* tiempo *m*, momento *m*; época *f*; periodo *m*; (*season*) estación *f*; (*clock*) hora *f*; (*occasion*) vez *f*; (*fixed time period*) plazo *m*: (*music*) duración *f*; (*music: tempo*) compás *m*; (*sport*) final *m*. **a long time** mucho tiempo. **a short time** poco tiempo. **at the same time** al mismo tiempo. **from time to time** de vez en cuando. **in time** a tiempo. **on time** a la hora. **timeless** *adj* eternal. **timely** *adj* oportuno.
time exposure *n* exposición *f*.
time limit *n* límite de tiempo *m*.
timepiece ['taimpiːs] *n* reloj *m*.
timesaving ['taim,seiviŋ] *adj* que ahorra tiempo.
time signal *n* señal horaria *f*.
timetable ['taimteibl] *n* horario *m*; (*transport*) guía *f*.
time zone *n* huso horario *m*.
timid ['timid] *adj* tímido. **timidity** *n* timidez *f*.
tin [tin] *n* estaño *m*; (*tinplate*) hojalata *f*; (*can*) lata *f*; (*baking*) molde *m*. **tinfoil** *n* papel de estaño *m*. **tin-opener** *n* abrelatas *m invar*. **tinny** *adj* (*sound, taste*) metálico.
tinge [tindʒ] *n* tinte *m*. *v* teñir.
tingle ['tiŋgl] *v* sentir hormigueo. *n* hormigueo *m*.
tinker ['tiŋkǝ] *n* calderero *m*. *v* componer, arreglar. **tinker with** jugar con.
tinkle ['tiŋkl] *n* tintineo *m*. *v* hacer tintinear.
tinsel ['tinsǝl] *n* oropel *m*.
tint [tint] *n* (*hair*) tinte *m*; tono *m*; matiz *m*. *v* teñir; matizar.
tiny ['taini] *adj* diminuto.
tip[1] [tip] *n* punta *f*; (*cigarette*) filtro *m*. **on tiptoe** de puntillas.
tip[2] [tip] *v* (*tilt*) inclinar; (*pour*) verter; (*upset*) volcar.
tip[3] [tip] *n* (*hint*) consejo *m*, información *f*; (*money*) propina *f*. *v* dar una propina a. **tip-off** *n* (*coll*) información *f*.
tipsy ['tipsi] *adj* (*coll*) achispado.
tire[1] ['taiǝ] *v* cansar(se). **tire out** agotar. **tired** *adj* cansado. **be tired of** estar harto de. **tiredness** *n* cansancio *m*. **tiresome** *adj* pesado.

tire[2] *V* tyre.
tissue ['tiʃuː] *n* (*anat*) tejido *m*; (*cloth*) tisú *m*; (*handkerchief*) pañuelo de papel *m*. **tissue paper** papel de seda *m*.
title ['taitl] *n* título *m*; derecho *m*. **title deed** título de propiedad *m*. **title page** portada *f*. *v* titular. **titled** *adj* con título de nobleza.
titter ['titǝ] *n* risita *f*. *v* reírse nerviosamente.
to [tu] *prep* a; (*direction*) hacia; (*as far as*) hasta; (*time*) menos; (*destination, purpose*) para; (*according to*) según; (*in juxtaposition*) contra; (*compared with*) en comparación con; (*in*) por; (*in memory of*) en honor a. **to-do** *n* (*coll*) follón *m*.
toad [toud] *n* sapo *m*. **toadstool** *n* hongo venenoso *m*.
toast [toust] *n* pan tostado *m*; (*speech*) brindis *m invar*. **toast-rack** *n* portatostadas *m invar*. *v* tostar. **toaster** *n* tostador *m*.
tobacco [tǝ'bakou] *n* tabaco *m*. **tobacconist's** *n* estanco *m*.
toboggan [tǝ'bogǝn] *n* tobogán *m*. *v* deslizarse en tobogán.
today [tǝ'dei] *nm, adj* hoy.
toddler ['todlǝ] *n* niño pequeño *m*; niña pequeña *f*.
toe [tou] *n* dedo del pie. **big toe** dedo gordo *m*. **toenail** *n* uña (del dedo del pie) *f*. **toe the line** (*coll*) conformarse.
toffee ['tofi] *n* caramelo *m*. **toffee-apple** *n* manzana garrapiñada *f*.
together [tǝ'geðǝ] *adv* juntos; (*at the same time*) a la vez; (*agreed*) de acuerdo. **togetherness** *n* solidaridad *f*.
toil [toil] *n* trabajo agotador *m*. *v* trabajar duro.
toilet ['toilit] *n* (*lavatory*) retrete *m*; (*washing, etc.*) arreglo *m*. **toilet paper** papel higiénico *m*. **toilet soap** jabón de tocador *m*. **toilet water** agua de Colonia *f*.
token ['toukǝn] *n* (*sign*) muestra *f*, prueba *f*; (*symbol*) símbolo *m*; (*keepsake*) recuerdo *m*; (*disc*) ficha *f*; (*book, record*) vale *m*. **as a token of** como prueba de. *adj* simbólico.
told [tould] *V* tell.
tolerate ['tolǝreit] *v* tolerar, soportar; admitir; respetar. **tolerable** *adj* tolerable; (*fair*) mediano. **tolerance** *n also* **toleration** tolerancia *f*. **tolerant** *adj* tolerante.

toll¹ [toul] *n* (*road*) peaje *m*; (*bridge*) pontaje *m*; (*victims*) bajas *f pl*. **toll-gate** *n* barrera de peaje *f*.

toll² [toul] *v* tocar, tañar.

tomato [tə'maɪtou] *n* tomate *m*.

tomb [tuɪm] *n* tumba *f*. **tombstone** *n* piedra sepulcral *f*.

tomorrow [tə'morou] *nm, adv* mañana. **the day after tomorrow** pasado mañana *m*.

ton [tʌn] *n* tonelada *f*.

tone [toun] *n* tono *m*; estilo *m*. *v* (*colour*) matizar. **tone down** atenuarse.

tongs [toŋz] *pl n* (*coal*) tenazas *f pl*; (*sugar*) tenacillas *f pl*.

tongue [tʌŋ] *n* lengua *f*. **tongue-tied** *adj* mudo.

tonic ['tonik] *adj* tónico. *n* (*med*) tónico *m*; (*music*) tónica *f*.

tonight [tə'nait] *n, adv* esta noche.

tonsil ['tonsil] *n* amígdala *f*. **tonsillitis** *n* amigdalitis *f*.

too [tuɪ] *adv* demasiado; (*also*) también; (*moreover*) además.

took [tuk] *V* take.

tool [tuɪl] *n* herramienta *f*; utensilio *m*. **toolshed** *n* cobertizo para herramientas *m*.

tooth [tuɪθ] *n, pl* teeth diente *m*; (*back tooth*) muela *f*. **toothache** *n* dolor de muelas *m*. **tooth-brush** *n* cepillo de dientes *m*. **toothpaste** *n* pasta dentífrica *f*. **toothpick** *n* palillo de dientes *m*. **toothless** *adj* desdentado.

top¹ [top] *n* parte de arriba *f*, lo alto *m*; (*of mountain*) cima *f*; (*of tin, pan, bottle, etc.*) tapa *f*; (*of page*) cabeza *f*; (*of the head*) coronilla *f*; (*surface*) superficie *f*. *adj* de arriba; (*best*) mejor; (*first*) primero. *v* (*cover*) cubrir; (*exceed*) superar. **top up** llenar completamente.

top² [top] *n* (*toy*) peón *m*, trompo *m*.

topaz ['toupaz] *n* topacio *m*.

topcoat ['topkout] *n* abrigo *m*.

topdressing ['top,dresiŋ] *n* abono *m*.

top hat *n* chistera *f*.

top-heavy *adj* inestable.

topic ['topik] *n* tema *m*, asunto *m*. **topical** *adj* de actualidad.

topography [tə'pogrəfi] *n* topografía *f*. **topographical** *adj* topográfico.

topple ['topl] *v* derribar, volcar, hacer caer.

top-secret *adj* confidencial.

topsoil ['topsoil] *n* tierra vegetal *f*.

topsy-turvy [topsi'təɪvi] *adj* revuelto.

torch [toɪtʃ] *n* (*electric*) linterna *f*; (*burning*) antorcha *f*.

tore [toɪ] *V* tear.

torment ['toɪment; *v* toɪ'ment] *n* tormento *m*, suplicio *m*. *v* atormentar.

tornado [toɪ'neidou] *n* tornado *m*.

torpedo [toɪ'piɪdou] *n* torpedo *m*. *v* torpedear.

torrent ['torənt] *n* torrente *m*. **torrential** *adj* torrencial.

torso ['toɪsou] *n* torso *m*.

tortoise ['toɪtəs] *n* tortuga *f*. **tortoise-shell** *n* carey *m*.

tortuous ['toɪtʃuəs] *adj* tortuoso.

torture ['toɪtʃə] *n* tortura *f*. *v* torturar. **torturer** *n* torcionario *m*.

toss [tos] *v* (*throw*) lanzamiento *m*; (*fall*) caída *f*; (*head*) sacudida *f*; (*coin*) sorteo a cara o cruz *m*; (*bull*) cogida *f*. *v* lanzar; sacudir; (*coin*) echar a cara o cruz; (*salad*) dar vueltas a.

tot¹ [tot] *n* (*child*) nene *m*; (*drink*) trago *m*.

tot² [tot] *v* tot up sumar.

total ['toutəl] *nm, adj* total. *v* (*add up*) sumar; (*add up to*) totalizar. **totalitarian** *n, adj* totalitario, -a.

totter ['totə] *v* bambolearse.

touch [tʌtʃ] *n* (*sense*) tacto *m*; (*contact*) contacto *m*; (*light stroke*) toque *m*; (*tap*) golpe ligero *m*; (*brush*) roce *m*. *v* tocar; rozar; (*reach*) alcanzar; (*affect*) afectar; (*move*) enternecer; (*food*) tomar. **touchy** *adj* susceptible.

tough [tʌf] *adj* (*hard*) duro; resistente; (*character*) tenaz; (*job*) difícil. **toughen** *v* endurecer. **toughness** *n* dureza *f*; resistencia *f*; dificultad *f*.

toupee ['tuɪpei] *n* tupé *m*.

tour [tuə] *n* excursión *f*; visita *f*; viaje *m*; (*theatre*) gira *f*. **package tour** viaje todo comprendido *m*. **tour of duty** turno de servicio *m*. *v* recorrer. **touring** *n* also **tourism** turismo *m*. **tourist** *n* turista *m, f*. **tourist agency** agencia de viajes *f*.

tournament ['tuənəmənt] *n* torneo *m*.

tousled ['tauzld] *adj* (*hair*) despeinado.

tow [tou] *n* remolque *m*. *v* remolcar; (*from towpath*) sirgar. **towpath** *n* camino de sirga *m*. **tow-rope** *n* remolque *m*.

towards [tə'woɪdz] *prep* hacia; (*for*) para; (*with*) con; (*with regard to*) con respecto a.

towel ['tauəl] *n* toalla *f*; (*bath*) toalla de baño *f*; (*sanitary*) paño higiénico *m*. **towel-rail** *n* toallero *m*. **towelling** *n* felpa *f*.
tower ['tauə] *n* torre *f*. **control tower** torre de control *f*. **tower over** dominar. **towering** *adj* sobresaliente.
town [taun] *n* (*large*) ciudad *f*; (*small*) pueblo *m*. **new town** pueblo nuevo *m*. **town hall** ayuntamiento *m*. **town planning** urbanismo *m*.
toxic ['toksik] *adj* tóxico.
toy [toi] *n* juguete *m*. *adj* de juguete. *v* **toy with** toquetear; (*idea*) acariciar.
trace [treis] *n* (*trail*) rastro *m*; (*indication*) indicio *m*; (*a little*) pizca *f*. *v* (*plan*) trazar; (*through paper*) calcar; (*trail*) rastrear; (*find*) encontrar. **tracing** *n* calco *m*. **tracing paper** papel de calcar *m*.
track [trak] *n* (*of animals, people*) huella *f*; (*of things*) rastro *m*; (*path*) sendero *m*; (*rail*) via *f*; (*course*) curso *m*; (*racing*) pista *f*; (*tank, tractor*) oruga *f*. **tracksuit** *n* mono de entrenamiento *m*. *v* (*hunt*) rastrear; (*pursue*) seguir la pista de. **track down** acorralar. **tracker** *n* perseguidor *m*.
tract¹ [trakt] *n* (*region*) trecho *m*; (*anat*) aparato *m*.
tract² [trakt] *n* (*pamphlet*) folleto *m*.
tractor ['traktə] *n* tractor *m*.
trade [treid] *n* comercio *m*; (*job*) ramo *m*. **trademark** *n* marca de fábrica *f*. **tradesman** *n* comerciante *m*. **trade union** sindicato *m*. **trade unionist** sindicalista *m*, *f*. *v* comerciar; negociar; cambiar. **trade in** tomar como entrada. **trader** *n* comerciante *m*, *f*; negociante *m*, *f*.
tradition [trə'diʃən] *n* tradición *f*. **traditional** *adj* tradicional.
traffic ['trafik] *n* (*mot*) circulación *f*, tráfico *m*; (*tourist*) tránsito *m*; (*trade*) comercio *m*. **traffic jam** embotellamiento *m*. **traffic-light** *n* semáforo *m*. **traffic warden** guardián del tráfico *m*.
tragedy ['tradʒədi] *n* tragedia *f*. **tragic** *adj* trágico.
trail [treil] *n* (*path*) camino *m*, sendero; (*person or animal*) huellas *f pl*; (*smoke*) estela *f*; (*blood*) reguero *m*. *v* (*drag*) arrastrar; (*chase*) perseguir; (*an animal*) rastrear; (*lag*) ir detrás de; (*hang down*) colgar. **trailer** *n* (*mot*) remolque *m*; (*film*) trailer *m*.
train [trein] *n* (*railway*) tren *m*; (*procession*) desfile *m*; (*series*) serie *f*; (*dress*) cola *f*. *v* (*teach*) educar; (*someone for a*

job) formar, capacitar; (*animal*) amaestrar; (*horse*) domar; (*sport*) entrenar.
trainee *n* aprendiz, -a *m*, *f*. **trainer** *n* (*sport*) entrenador, -a *m*, *f*; (*boxing*) cuidador *m*; (*animals*) amaestrador, -a *m*, *f*; (*horses*) domador, -a *m*, *f*.
trait [treit] *n* rasgo *m*.
traitor ['treitə] *n* traidor, -a *m*, *f*.
tram [tram] *n* tranvía *m*.
tramp [tramp] *n* (*person*) vagabundo, -a *m*, *f*; (*hike*) caminata *f*; (*sound*) ruido de pasos *m*. *v* patear; vagabundear.
trample ['trampl] *v* pisotear, pisar.
trampoline ['trampəliːn] *n* cama elástica *f*.
trance [trɑːns] *n* trance *m*.
tranquil ['traŋkwil] *adj* tranquilo. **tranquillity** *n* tranquilidad *f*. **tranquillize** *v* tranquilizar. **tranquillizer** *n* tranquilizante *m*.
transact [tran'zakt] *v* (*negotiate*) tratar; (*perform*) llevar a cabo. **transaction** *n* (*business*) negociación *f*; (*deal*) transacción *f*.
transcend [tran'send] *v* exceder, superar. **transcendental** *adj* trascedental.
transcribe [tran'skraib] *v* transcribir. **transcription** *n* trascripción *f*.
transept ['transept] *n* transepto *m*.
transfer [trans'fəː; *n* 'transfəː] *v* trasladar; transferir. *n* traslado *m*; (*law*) cesión *f*; (*picture*) calcomanía *f*. **transferable** *adj* transferible. **not transferable** (*right*) inalienable; (*ticket*) intransferible.
transfix [trans'fiks] *v* traspasar.
transform [trans'fɔːm] *v* transformar. **transformation** *n* transformación *f*. **transformer** *n* (*elec*) transformador *m*.
transfuse [trans'fjuːz] *v* transfundir. **transfusion** *n* transfusión *f*.
transient ['tranziənt] *adj* transitorio.
transistor [tran'zistə] *n* transistor *m*. **transistorize** *v* transistorizar.
transit ['transit] *n* tránsito *m*. **in transit** de tránsito.
transition [tran'ziʃən] *n* transición *f*. **transitional** *adj* transitorio.
transitive ['transitiv] *adj* transitivo.
transitory ['transitəri] *adj* transitorio.
translate [trans'leit] *v* traducir. **translation** *n* traducción *f*. **translator** *n* traductor, -a *m*, *f*.
translucent [trans'luːsnt] *adj* translúcido. **translucence** *n* translucidez *f*.

transmit [tranz'mit] v transmitir, trasmitir. **transmission** n transmisión f, trasmisión f. **transmitter** n (apparatus) transmisor m; (station) emisora f.

transparent [trans'peərənt] adj transparente. **transparency** n transparencia f; (phot) transparente m.

transplant [trans'plaint; n 'transplaint] v trasplantar. n trasplante m.

transport ['transpoit; v trans'poit] n transporte m. v transportar. **transportation** n transporte m; (convicts) deportación f.

transpose [trans'pouz] v transponer; (music) transportar. **transposition** n transposición f; transporte m.

transverse ['tranzvəis] adj transverso.

transvestite [tranz'vestait] n travestido m.

trap [trap] n trampa f; (mice, rats) ratonera f; (vehicle) cabriolé m; (tech) sifón de depósito m; (theatre) escotillón m. **trapdoor** n trampa f. v coger; coger en una trampa; rodear; pillar; bloquear.

trapeze [trə'piiz] n trapecio m. **trapeze artist** trapecista m, f.

trash [traʃ] n basura f; (coll) cachivaches m pl.

trauma ['troimə] n trauma f. **traumatic** adj traumático.

travel ['travl] v recorrer; viajar por. **travels** pl n viajes m pl. **travel agency** agencia de viajes f. **travel-sickness** n mareo m. **traveller** n viajero, -a m, f; (comm) viajante de comercio m. **traveller's cheque** cheque de viaje m.

travesty ['travəsti] n parodia f.

trawler ['troilə] n barco rastreador m. **trawling** n pesca a la rastrea f.

tray [trei] n bandeja f.

treachery ['tretʃəri] n traición f. **treacherous** adj (person) traidor; (action) traicionero.

treacle ['triikl] n melaza f.

*tread [tred] v pisar; (walk) andar por. **tread on** (crush) pisotear. n paso m; (step of a staircase) huella f; (tyre) banda de rodadura f.

treason ['triizn] n traición f.

treasure ['treʒə] n tesoro m. v valorar; guardar en la memoria. **treasurer** n tesorero, -a m, f. **treasury** n tesorería f.

treat [triit] v tratar; tomar; (a patient) atender; (pay for) invitar, comprar. n invitación f; placer m. **treatment** n trato m; (med) tratamiento m.

treatise ['triitiz] n tratado m.

treaty ['triiti] n tratado m; acuerdo m.

treble ['trebl] n (music) tiple m, soprano m. adj triple; (music) de tiple. v triplicar. adv tres veces.

tree [trii] n árbol m.

trek [trek] v caminar trabajosamente. n expedición f; caminata f.

trellis ['trelis] n enrejado m; espaldera f. v poner un enrejado.

tremble ['trembl] v temblar. n temblor m.

tremendous [trə'mendəs] adj tremendo, enorme; extraordinario; (coll: excellent) formidable.

tremor ['tremə] n temblor m.

trench [trentʃ] n zanja f; (mil) trinchera f.

trend [trend] n tendencia f; dirección f; orientación f. **trendy** adj (coll) modernísimo.

trespass ['trespəs] n entrada ilegal f. v violar; abusar; invadir. **trespasser** n intruso, -a m, f. **trespassers will be prosecuted** prohibido el paso.

trestle ['tresl] n caballete m. **trestle table** mesa de caballete f.

trial ['traiəl] n (law) juicio m; (experiment) prueba f, ensayo m; (annoyance) molestia f; (hardship) dificultad f. adj de prueba.

triangle ['traiaŋgl] n triángulo m. **triangular** adj triangular.

tribe [traib] n tribu f. **tribal** adj tribal. **tribesman** n miembro de una tribu m.

tribunal [trai'bjuinl] n tribunal m.

tributary ['tribjutəri] n afluente m. adj tributario.

tribute ['tribjuit] n tributo m.

trick [trik] n (stratagem) truco m; (ruse) astucia f; (practical joke) broma f; (cards) baza f. **trick photography** trucaje m. **trick question** pega f. v engañar. **trickery** n engaño m; astucia f. **tricky** adj difícil; delicado.

trickle ['trikl] n hilo m, chorrito m. v verter poco a poco; gotear.

tricycle ['traisikl] n triciclo m.

trifle ['traifl] n nadería f. v **trifle with** jugar con. **trifling** adj insignificante.

trigger ['trigə] n gatillo m. v accionar. **trigger off** provocar.

trigonometry [trigə'nomətri] n trigonometría f.

trill [tril] n trino m. v trinar.

trim [trim] adj aseado; (neat) arreglado; elegante. v arreglar; (reduce) cercenar; (hair) entresacar; (nails) recortar; (hedge)

podar; (*sails*) orientar. **trimmings** *pl n*
recortes *m pl*; accesorios *m pl*.
trinket ['trɪŋkɪt] *n* dije *m*.
trio ['triːou] *n* trío *m*.
trip [trip] *n* (*voyage, effect of drugs*) viaje
m; (*stumble*) tropezón *m*. *v* dar un traspié; tropezar; (*make someone fall*) echar
la zancadilla.
tripe [traip] *n* callos *m pl*; (*coll*) bobadas *f
pl*.
triple ['tripl] *nm, adj* triple. *v* triplicar. *adv*
tres veces.
triplet ['triplit] *n* (*music*) tresillo *m*; (*poetry*) terceto *m*; (*person*) trillizo, -a *m, f*.
tripod ['traipod] *n* trípode *m*.
trite [trait] *adj* trillado, trivial. **triteness** *n*
lo trillado; trivialidad *f*.
triumph ['traiʌmf] *n* triunfo *m*. *v* triunfar.
triumphant *adj* triunfante. **triumphantly**
adv triunfantemente.
trivial ['triviəl] *adj* trivial. **trivia** *pl n also*
trivialities trivialidades *f pl*.
trod [trod] *V* **tread**.
trolley ['troli] *n* (*shopping*) carretilla *f*;
(*tea*) carrito *m*; (*in mines*) vagoneta *f*.
trombone [trom'boun] *n* trombón *m*.
troop [truːp] *n* (*people*) banda *f*, grupo *m*;
(*animals*) manada *f*. **troops** *pl n* (*mil*)
tropas *f pl*. *v* **troop in/out** entrar/salir en
tropel.
trophy ['troufi] *n* trofeo *m*.
tropic ['tropik] *n* trópico *m*. **Tropic of
Cancer** Trópico de Cáncer. **Tropic of
Capricorn** Trópico de Capricornio. **tropical** *adj* tropical.
trot [trot] *n* trote *m*. **on the trot** (*coll*)
seguidos, seguidas. *v* trotar. **trotter** *n*
mano *f*.
trouble ['trʌbl] *n* (*worry*) preocupación *f*;
apuro *m*; pena *f*; (*misfortune*) desgracia
f; problema *m*; disturbios *m pl*. **be in
trouble** estar en un apuro. **look for trouble** buscar camorra. **what's the trouble?**
¿qué pasa? **troublemaker** *n* alborotador,
-a *m, f*. **troublesome** *adj* molesto. *v* preocupar; pertubar; afectar; molestar.
trough [trof] *n* (*food*) pesebre *m*; (*drinking*) abrevadero *m*; (*depression*) depresión *f*.
trousers ['trauzəz] *pl n* pantalón *m sing*.
trout [traut] *n* trucha *f*.
trowel ['trauəl] *n* palustre *m*; (*gardening*)
desplantador *m*.
truant ['truːənt] *n* **play truant** hacer novillos. **truancy** *n* rabona *f*.

truce [truːs] *n* tregua *f*. **call a truce**
acordar una tregua.
truck [trʌk] *n* camión *m*; (*rail*) batea *f*.
truck driver conductor de camión *m*.
trudge [trʌdʒ] *v* andar con dificultad.
true [truː] *adj* verdadero; (*faithful*) fiel;
legítimo; (*real*) auténtico; (*accurate*)
exacto. **true to life** conforme a la
realidad. **truly** *adv* verdaderamente.
truffle ['trʌfl] *n* trufa *f*.
trump [trʌmp] *n* (*cards*) triunfo *m*. *v* fallar. **trump up** inventar.
trumpet ['trʌmpit] *n* trompeta *f*. *v* (*elephant*) barritar. **trumpeter** *n* trompetista
m, f.
truncate [trʌŋ'keit] *v* truncar.
truncheon ['trʌntʃən] *n* matraca *f*; (*police*)
porra *f*.
trunk [trʌŋk] *n* (*anat, bot*) tronco *m*; (*elephant*) trompa *f*; (*case*) baúl *m*. **trunk call**
conferencia telefónica *f*. **trunk road** carretera principal *f*. **trunks** *pl n* calzoncillos
cortos *m pl* ; (*mot*) maleta.
truss [trʌs] *n* (*hay*) haz *m*; (*fruit*) racimo
m; (*med*) braguero *m*. *v* atar.
trust [trʌst] *n* confianza *f*; (*law*)
fideicomiso *m*; (*comm*) trust *m*; (*expectation*) esperanza *f*. **trustworthy** *adj* digno
de confianza; fidedigno. *v* tener confianza en; confiar; esperar; creer. **trustee** *n*
guardián *m*; (*law*) fideicomisario, -a *m, f*.
trusting *adj* confiado. **trusty** *adj* leal,
seguro.
truth [truːθ] *n* verdad *f*. **truthful** *adj* veraz;
verdadero. **truthfulness** *n* veracidad *f*.
try [trai] *n* tentativa *f*, prueba *f*; (*rugby*)
ensayo *m*. *v* probar; intentar; ensayar;
(*law*) ver; (*strain*) poner a prueba;
(*annoy*) molestar; (*tire*) cansar; (*afflict*)
hacer sufrir. **try on** (*garment*) probarse.
try it on (*coll*) intentar dar el pego. **trying**
adj molesto.
tsar [zaɪ] *n* zar *m*.
T-shirt ['tiːʃəɪt] *n* camiseta *f*.
tub [tʌb] *n* tina *f*; (*bath*) bañera *f*.
tuba ['tjuːbə] *n* tuba *f*.
tube [tjuːb] *n* tubo *m*; (*coll: underground*)
metro *m*. **tubeless** *adj* (*tyre*) sin cámara.
tuber ['tjuːbə] *n* tubérculo *m*.
tuberculosis [tjubəɪkjuˈlousis] *n* tuberculosis *f*.
tuck [tʌk] *n* (*sewing*) alforza *f*; (*food*)
comida *f*; (*sweets*) cucherías *f pl*. *v*
meter; (*sheets*) remeter; (*fold*) alforzar.
tuck up (*in bed*) arropar.

Tuesday ['tjuːzdi] n martes m.
tuft [tʌft] n (plants) mata f; (feathers) penacho m; (hair) mechón m.
tug [tʌg] n tirón m; (boat) remolcador m.
tug-of-war n juego de la cuerda m. v (pull) tirar; (tow) remolcar; (drag) arrastrar.
tuition [tjuˈiʃən] n enseñanza f.
tulip ['tjuːlip] n tulipán m.
tumble ['tʌmbl] n caída f; (acrobatics) voltereta f. v caerse; dar volteretas; (knock over) derribar. **tumbledown** adj ruinoso. **tumble-dryer** n secadora al aire caliente f. **tumbler** n (glass) vaso m; (acrobat) voltalinero, -a m, f.
tummy ['tʌmi] n (coll) barriga f.
tumour ['tjuːmə] n tumor m.
tumult ['tjuːmʌlt] n tumulto m. **tumultuous** adj tumultuoso.
tuna ['tjuːnə] n atún m.
tune [tjuːn] n aire m. **in tune** afinado. **out of tune** desafinado. v (music) afinar; (mot) poner a punto. **tune in to** (radio) sintonizar con. **tuneful** adj melodioso. **tuneless** adj discordante. **tuner** n (person) afinador m; (radio) sintonizador m. **tuning** afinación f; sintonización f; puesta a punto f. **tuning fork** diapasón m.
tunic ['tjuːnik] n túnica f.
tunnel ['tʌnl] n túnel m. v hacer un túnel en; (dig) cavar.
turban ['təːbən] n turbante m.
turbine ['təːbain] n turbina f.
turbot ['təːbət] n rodaballo m.
turbulent ['təːbjulənt] adj turbulento. **turbulence** n turbulencia f.
tureen [təˈriːn] n sopera f.
turf [təːf] n cesped m; (sport) turf m. v encespedar. **turf out** (coll) echar.
turkey ['təːki] n pavo m.
Turkish ['təːkiʃ] nm, adj turco. **Turkish bath** baño turco m.
turmeric ['təːmərik] n cúrcuma f.
turmoil ['təːmoil] n desorden m; agitación f; alboroto m.
turn [təːn] n vuelta f; (road) curva f; (body) movimiento m; (opportunity) turno m; (change) cambio m; (change in situation) viraje m; (fright) susto m. **take turns at** turnarse en. v dar vueltas; dar la vuelta a; (body) volver; (corner) doblar; (page) pasar; cambiar. **turn down** (lower) bajar; (reject) rechazar. **turn off** cerrar; (light) apagar; (engine) parar. **turn on**

(light, radio) encender; (current) conectar; (coll: excite) excitar. **turn out** (end up) resultar; (light) apagar. **turnover** n (comm) volumen de negocios m. **turnstile** n torniquete m. **turntable** n (record-player) plato giratorio m. **turn up** presentarse; (appear) aparecer. **turning** n vuelta f; curva f; (side road) bocacalle f. **turning point** momento crucial m.
turnip ['təːnip] n nabo m.
turpentine ['təːpəntain] n trementina f.
turquoise ['təːkwoiz] n (stone) turquesa f; (colour) azul turquesa m.
turret ['tʌrit] n torreón m; (mil) torreta f.
turtle ['təːtl] n tortuga de mar f. **turtleneck** n (jumper collar) cuello que sube ligeramente m.
tusk [tʌsk] n defensa f.
tussle ['tʌsl] n pelea f; lucha f. v pelearse.
tutor ['tjuːtə] n (private) profesor particular m; (university) tutor m. v dar clases privadas.
tuxedo [tʌkˈsiːdou] n smoking m.
tweed [twiːd] n tweed m.
tweezers ['twiːzəz] pl n pinzas f pl.
twelve [twelv] nm, adj doce. **twelfth** n, adj duodécimo, -a.
twenty ['twenti] nm, adj veinte. **twentieth** n, adj vigésimo, -a.
twice [twais] adv dos veces.
twiddle ['twidl] v dar vueltas a. **twiddle one's thumbs** estar mano sobre mano.
twig [twig] n ramita f.
twilight ['twailait] n crepúsculo m.
twin [twin] n, adj gemelo, -a. **twin beds** camas gemelas f pl.
twine [twain] n bramante m. v (twist) retorcer; (interlace) trenzar; (embrace) rodear con.
twinge [twindʒ] n (pain) punzada f; (fig) arrebato m.
twinkle ['twiŋkl] n centelleo m; (brightness) brillo m. v centellear; (eyes) brillar.
twirl [twəːl] v dar vueltas a. n vuelta f.
twist [twist] v torcer; retorcer. n torcimiento m, torsión f; (tobacco) rollo m; vuelta f; deformación f; contorsión f; inclinación f; (warp) abarquillamiento m; (ankle) torcedura f; (swindle) trampa f.
twit [twit] n (slang) imbécil m, f.
twitch [twitʃ] n (pull) tirón m; (med) tic m. v tirar bruscamente de; (nervously) crispar.

twitter ['twitə] v gorjear. n gorjeo m.
two [tuː] nm, adj dos. two-faced adj falso.
two-legged adj bípedo.
tycoon [tai'kuːn] n magnate m.
type [taip] n (sort) tipo m, clase f; (print)
carácter m, tipo m. typesetting n composición f. typewriter n máquina de
escribir f. v escribir a máquina. typical
adj típico. typing n mecanografía f. typist
n mecanógrafo, -a m, f.
typhoid ['taifoid] n fiebre tifoidea f.
typhoon [tai'fuːn] n tifón m.
tyrant ['tairənt] n tirano m. tyrannical adj
tiránico. tyranny n tiranía f.
tyre or US tire ['taiə] n neumático m.

U

ubiquitous [ju'bikwitəs] adj ubicuo.
udder ['ʌdə] n ubre f.
ugly ['ʌgli] adj feo; repugnante. ugliness n
fealdad f.
ulcer ['ʌlsə] n úlcera f.
ulterior [ʌl'tiəriə] adj ulterior. ulterior
motive segunda intención f.
ultimate ['ʌltimət] adj último; fundamental. ultimately adv por fin, al final;
esencialmente. ultimatum n ultimátum
m.
ultraviolet [ʌltrə'vaiələt] adj ultravioleta.
umbilical [ʌm'bilikəl] adj umbilical.
umbilical cord cordón umbilical m.
umbrage ['ʌmbridʒ] n resentimiento m,
enfado m. take umbrage at ofenderse
por.
umbrella [ʌm'brelə] n paraguas m invar.
umpire ['ʌmpaiə] n árbitro m. v arbitrar.
umpteen [ʌmp'tiːn] (coll) adj muchísimos.
umpteenth adj enésimo.
unable [ʌn'eibl] adj incapaz. be unable to
(physical) ser incapaz de; (due to circumstances) no poder hacer.
unabridged [ʌnə'bridʒd] adj íntegro.
unacceptable [ʌnək'septəbl] adj inaceptable.
unaccompanied [ʌnə'kumpənid] adj solo,
sin compañía; (music) sin acompañamiento.
unaided [ʌn'eidid] adj sin ayuda, solo.
unadulterated [ʌnə'dʌltəreitid] adj no
adulterado, sin mezcla.

unanimous [ju'nanimǝs] adj unánime.
unanimity n unanimidad f.
unarmed [ʌn'aimd] adj (person) sin
armas; desarmado.
unattached [ʌnə'tatʃt] adj (loose) suelto;
libre; independiente.
unattractive [ʌnə'traktiv] adj poco
atrayente, desagradable.
unauthorized [ʌn'oiθəraizd] adj no
autorizado.
unavoidable [ʌnə'voidəbl] adj inevitable.
unaware [ʌnə'weə] adj inconsciente;
ignorante. be unaware of ignorar. unawares adv sin querer; de improviso.
unbalanced [ʌn'balənst] adj desequilibrado; (mentally) trastornado.
unbearable [ʌn'beərəbl] adj insoportable,
intolerable, insufrible.
unbelievable [ʌnbi'liːvəbl] adj increíble.
*unbend [ʌn'bend] v (straighten)
desencorvar; (fig) relajar. unbending adj
inflexible.
unbiased [ʌn'baiəst] adj imparcial.
unbreakable [ʌn'breikəbl] adj irrompible.
unbridled [ʌn'braidld] adj (fig) desenfrenado.
unbutton [ʌn'butn] v desabrochar; (fig)
desahogarse.
uncalled-for [ʌn'koildfoi] adj innecesario;
injustificado; gratuito.
uncanny [ʌn'kani] adj extraño; misterioso.
uncertain [ʌn'səitn] adj incierto. uncertainty n incertidumbre f.
uncle ['ʌŋkl] n tío m.
uncomfortable [ʌn'kʌmfətəbl] adj
incómodo; (anxious) inquieto; (awkward) difícil.
uncommon [ʌn'komən] adj poco común,
raro.
uncompromising [ʌn'komprəmaiziŋ] adj
inflexible; irreconciliable.
unconditional [ʌnkən'diʃənl] adj incondicional.
unconscious [ʌn'konʃəs] adj (med) inconsciente; (unaware) ignorante.
unconventional [ʌnkən'venʃənl] adj poco
convencional.
uncooked [ʌn'kukt] adj no cocido, crudo.
uncouth [ʌn'kuːθ] adj grosero.
uncover [ʌn'kʌvə] v descubrir; (reveal)
revelar; (take the lid off) destapar.
uncut [ʌn'kʌt] adj no cortado.

undecided [ʌndi'saidid] *adj* indeciso; irresoluto.

undeniable [ʌndi'naiəbl] *adj* incontestable.

under ['ʌndə] *adv* debajo; abajo; más abajo; (*insufficient*) insuficiente; (*for less*) para menos. *prep* debajo de; bajo; por debajo de; menos de; (*age*) menor de; (*lower in rank*) por debajo de; (*repair, construction, etc.*) en; (*according to*) según; conforme a.

underarm ['ʌndəraim] *adj, adv* por debajo del brazo; sobacal.

undercharge [ʌndə'tʃaidʒ] *v* cobrar menos de lo debido.

underclothes ['ʌndəklouðz] *pl n* ropa interior *f sing*.

undercoat ['ʌndəkout] *n* (*paint*) primera capa *f*.

undercover [ʌndə'kʌvə] *adj* secreto; clandestino.

undercut [ʌndə'kʌt] *v* vender más barato que.

underdeveloped [ʌndədi'veləpt] *adj* de desarrollo atrasado; (*phot*) no revelado lo suficiente.

underdog ['ʌndədog] *n* desvalido *m*.

underdone [ʌndə'dʌn] *adj* (*meat*) poco hecho.

underestimate [ʌndə'estimeit] *v* tasar en menos; menospreciar. *n also* **underestimation** infravaloración *f*; menosprecio *m*.

underfoot [ʌndə'fut] *adv* debajo de los pies.

*****undergo** [ʌndə'gou] *v* sufrir, pasar por.

undergraduate [ʌndə'gradjuət] *n* estudiante no licenciado, -a *m, f*.

underground ['ʌndəgraund; *adv* ʌndə'graund] *adj* subterráneo; oculto, secreto. *adv* bajo tierra; clandestinamente.

undergrowth ['ʌndəgrouθ] *n* maleza *f*.

underhand [ʌndə'hand] *adj* bajo mano; secreto.

*****underlie** [ʌndə'lai] *v* estar debajo de; servir de base a. **underlying** *adj* básico, fundamental.

underline [ʌndə'lain] *v* subrayar. **underlining** *n* subrayado *m*.

undermine [ʌndə'main] *v* socavar, minar.

underneath [ʌndə'niːθ] *prep* bajo, debajo de. *adv* debajo, por debajo. *adj* inferior, de abajo.

underpaid [ʌndə'peid] *adj* mal pagado.

underpants ['ʌndəpants] *pl n* calzoncillos *m pl*.

underpass ['ʌndəpais] *n* paso subterráneo *m*.

underprivileged [ʌndə'privilidʒd] *adj* menesteroso.

underrate [ʌndə'reit] *v* subestimar.

underskirt ['ʌndəskəit] *n* enaguas *f pl*.

understaffed [ʌndə'staift] *adj* falto de personal.

*****understand** [ʌndə'stand] *v* entender, comprender; (*believe*) creer. **understandable** *adj* comprensible. **understanding** *n* entendimiento *m*; comprensión *f*; (*reason*) razón *f*; interpretación *f*; (*knowledge*) conocimientos *m pl*; (*agreement*) acuerdo *m*.

understate *v* quitar importancia a. **make an understatement** describir sin énfasis. **that's an understatement!** ¡y usted que lo diga!

understudy ['ʌndəstʌdi] *n* suplente *m, f*. *v* suplir, doblar.

*****undertake** [ʌndə'teik] *v* emprender; prometer. **undertaker** *n* empresario de pompas funebres *m*. **undertaking** *n* empresa *f*; compromiso *m*.

undertone ['ʌndətoun] *n* **in an undertone** en voz baja.

underwater [ʌndə'woitə] *adj* submarino.

underwear ['ʌndəweə] *n* ropa interior *f*.

underweight [ʌndə'weit] *adj* de peso insuficiente.

underworld ['ʌndəwəild] *n* (*criminal*) hampa *f*; (*hell*) infierno *m*.

*****underwrite** [ʌndə'rait] *v* (*sign, bonds*) subscribir; (*guarantee*) garantizar; (*insure*) asegurar.

undesirable [ʌndi'zaiərəbl] *adj* no deseable; pernicioso. *n* indeseable *m, f*.

*****undo** [ʌn'dui] *v* (*open*) abrir; (*knot*) desatar; (*a tie*) desanudar; (*button*) desabrochar; (*parcel*) deshacer; (*zip*) bajar; (*ruin*) arruinar. **undoing** *n* ruina *f*. **come undone** desatarse.

undoubted [ʌn'dautid] *adj* indudable.

undress [ʌn'dres] *v* desnudar(se).

undue [ʌn'djui] *adj* excesivo; impropio. **unduly** *adv* excesivamente; impropiamente.

undulate ['ʌndjuleit] *v* ondular. **undulating** *adj* ondulante. **undulation** *n* ondulación *f*.

unearth [ʌn'ɔːθ] v desenterrar; descubrir.
unearthly adj sobrenatural; misterioso; espantoso. **unearthly hour** (coll) hora intempestiva f.
uneasy [ʌn'iːzi] adj inquieto; molesto; agitado; preocupado.
uneducated [ʌn'edjukeitid] adj ineducado.
unemployed [ʌnem'ploid] adj parado, desempleado. **the unemployed** los parados m pl. **unemployment** n paro m, desempleo m.
unenthusiastic [ʌnenθjuːzi'astik] adj sin entusiasmo.
unequal [ʌn'iːkwəl] adj desigual; (inadequate) inadecuado; (med) irregular.
uneven [ʌn'iːvn] adj accidentado; (unequal) designal; (number) impar.
uneventful [ʌni'ventfəl] adj sin acontecimientos.
unexpected [ʌneks'pektid] adj inesperado.
unfailing [ʌn'feiliŋ] adj infalible; (inexhaustible) inagotable; (unceasing) constante.
unfair [ʌn'feə] adj injusto. **unfairness** n injusticia f.
unfaithful [ʌn'feiθfəl] adj infiel. **unfaithfulness** n infidelidad f.
unfamiliar [ʌnfə'miljə] adj desconocido; extraño.
unfasten [ʌn'fɑːsn] v (open) abrir; (dress, button) desabrochar; (knot) desatar; (set free) soltar; (loosen) aflojar.
unfavourable [ʌn'feivərəbl] adj desfavorable, adverso.
unfinished [ʌn'finiʃt] adj inacabado, no terminado.
unfit [ʌn'fit] adj incapaz; no apto; incompetente; impropio; (ill) enfermo, malo.
unfold [ʌn'fould] v desplegar; (plans) revelar; (thoughts) desarrollarse.
unforeseen [ʌnfɔː'siːn] adj imprevisto.
unforgivable [ʌnfə'givəbl] adj imperdonable.
unfortunate [ʌn'fɔːtʃənət] adj desafortunado; desgraciado.
unfounded [ʌn'faundid] adj infundado, sin fundamento.
unfriendly [ʌn'frendli] adj hostil; desfavorable.
unfurnished [ʌn'fɜːniʃd] adj desamueblado.
ungainly [ʌn'geinli] adj desgarbado.

ungrateful [ʌn'greitfəl] adj ingrato.
unhappy [ʌn'hapi] adj infeliz; triste. **unhappiness** n infelicidad f.
unhealthy [ʌn'helθi] adj (person) enfermo; (place) malsano.
unheard-of [ʌn'hɜːdov] adj inaudito; sin precedente.
unhoped-for [ʌn'houptfɔː] adj inesperado.
unhurt [ʌn'hɜːt] adj indemne, ileso.
unhygienic [ʌnhai'dʒiːnik] adj antihigiénico.
unicorn ['juːnikɔːn] n unicornio m.
unidentified flying object [ʌnai'dentifaid] n also **UFO** objeto volador no identificado m, OVNI m.
uniform ['juːnifɔːm] nm, adj uniforme. **uniformity** n uniformidad f.
unify ['juːnifai] v unificar. **unification** n unificación f.
unilateral [juːni'latərəl] adj unilateral.
unimaginative [ʌni'madʒinətiv] adj poco imaginativo.
unimportant [ʌnim'pɔːtnt] adj poco importante.
uninhabited [ʌnin'habitid] adj inhabitado.
uninhibited [ʌnin'hibitid] adj sin inhibición.
unintentional [ʌnin'tenʃənl] adj involuntario.
uninterested [ʌn'intristid] adj indiferente; desinteresado. **uninteresting** adj poco interesante.
union ['juːnjən] n unión f; (trade) sindicato m.
unique [juː'niːk] adj único.
unisex ['juːniˌseks] adj (coll) unisexo invar.
unison ['juːnisn] n unisonancia. **in unison** al unísono.
unite [juː'nait] v unir; reunir; juntarse. **united** adj unido. **United Kingdom** Reino Unido m. **United Nations** Naciones Unidas f pl. **United States of America** Estados Unidos de América m pl.
unity ['juːniti] m unidad f.
universe ['juːnivɜːs] m universo m. **universal** adj universal.
university [juːni'vɜːsəti] n universidad f. adj universitario.
unjust [ʌn'dʒʌst] adj injusto.
unkempt [ʌn'kempt] adj descuidado; (hair) despeinado.
unkind [ʌn'kaind] adj poco amable; severo; cruel. **unkindness** n falta de amabilidad f; severidad f; crueldad f.

unknown [ʌn'noun] *n, adj* desconocido, -a.

unlawful [ʌn'lɔɪfəl] *adj* ilegal; ilegítimo.

unless [ʌn'les] *conj* a no ser que, a menos que.

unlike [ʌn'laik] *adj* diferente, distinto. *prep* a diferencia de.

unlikely [ʌn'laikli] *adj* improbable; (*unexpected*) inverosímil.

unlimited [ʌn'limitid] *adj* ilimitado.

unload [ʌn'loud] *v* descargar; (*get rid of*) deshacerse de.

unlock [ʌn'lok] *v* abrir.

unlucky [ʌn'lʌki] *adj* desgraciado; (*day, number, etc.*) funesto.

unmarried [ʌn'marid] *adj* soltero.

unnatural [ʌn'natʃərəl] *adj* antinatural; anormal; artificial.

unnecessary [ʌn'nesəsəri] *adj* innecesario, inútil.

unnerving [ʌn'nərviŋ] *adj* desconcertante.

unnoticed [ʌn'noutist] *adv* inadvertido; desapercibido. **go** *or* **pass unnoticed** pasar desapercibido.

unobtainable [ʌnəb'teinəbl] *adj* que no se puede conseguir.

unobtrusive [ʌnəb'truɪsiv] *adj* discreto, modesto.

unoccupied [ʌn'okjupaid] *adj* (*at leisure*) desocupado; (*untenanted*) deshabitado; (*seat*) libre.

unofficial [ʌnə'fiʃəl] *adj* no oficial.

unorthodox [ʌn'ɔɪθədoks] *adj* poco ortodoxo.

unpack [ʌn'pak] *v* (*box*) desembalar; (*suitcase*) deshacer.

unpaid [ʌn'peid] *adj* impagado; (*bill*) por pagar; (*worker*) no retribuido.

unpleasant [ʌn'pleznt] *adj* (*weather*) desagradable; (*unfriendly*) antipático; (*annoying*) molesto.

unpopular [ʌn'popjulə] *adj* impopular.

unprecedented [ʌn'presidentid] *adj* sin precedentes.

unpredictable [ʌnprə'diktəbl] *adj* que no se puede prever; (*capricious*) antojadizo.

unqualified [ʌn'kwolifaid] *adj* sin título; (*without reservation*) sin reserva.

unravel [ʌn'ravəl] *v* (*wool*) deshacer; (*untangle*) desenredar; (*mystery*) desembrollar.

unreal [ʌn'riəl] *adj* irreal.

unreasonable [ʌn'riːzənəbl] *adj* irrazonable; extravagante; excesivo.

unrelenting [ʌnri'lentiŋ] *adj* implacable.

unreliable [ʌnri'laiəbl] *adj* (*character*) inconstante; (*person*) poco seguro; (*machine*) poco fiable; (*service*) dudoso.

unrest [ʌn'rest] *n* desasosiego *m*, agitación *f*.

unruly [ʌn'ruːli] *adj* ingobernable; rebelde.

unsafe [ʌn'seif] *adj* inseguro; peligroso.

unsatisfactory [ʌnsatis'faktəri] *adj* poco satisfactorio.

unscrew [ʌn'skruː] *v* destornillar.

unscrupulous [ʌn'skruːpjuləs] *adj* poco escrupuloso.

unselfish [ʌn'selfiʃ] *adj* desinteresado; generoso.

unsettle [ʌn'setl] *v* pertubar; (*mentally*) desequilibrar. **unsettled** *adj* perturbado; agitado; desequilibrado; (*weather*) incierto.

unsightly [ʌn'saitli] *adj* feo, repugnante.

unskilled [ʌn'skild] *adj* no cualificado; no especializado. **unskilled worker** obrero no cualificado *m*.

unsound [ʌn'saund] *adj* (*unhealthy*) enfermizo; (*mentally*) demente; (*morally*) corrompido; (*goods*) imperfecto; (*foundations*) poco sólido; (*business*) poco seguro; (*argument, opinion*) falso.

unspeakable [ʌn'spiːkəbl] *adj* indecible.

unspecified [ʌn'spesifaid] *adj* no especificado.

unstable [ʌn'steibl] *adj* inestable.

unsteady [ʌn'stedi] *adj* inestable; inconstante.

unstuck [ʌn'stʌk] *adj* **come unstuck** despegarse; (*hopes, plans*) fracasar.

unsuccessful [ʌnsək'sesfəl] *adj* sin éxito; (*person, attempt, etc.*) fracasado; (*candidate*) suspendido. **be unsuccessful** fracasar. **unsuccessfully** *adv* sin éxito; infructuosamente.

unsuitable [ʌn'suːtəbl] *adj* inapropiado; inconveniente; inoportuno.

untangle [ʌn'taŋgl] *v* desenmarañar.

untidy [ʌn'taidi] *adj* desarreglado; (*person*) desordenado. **untidiness** *n* desorden *m*.

untie [ʌn'tai] *v* desatar.

until [ən'til] *prep* hasta. *conj* hasta que.

untoward [ʌntə'wɔɪd] *adj* insumiso; adverso; desafortunado.

untrue [ʌn'truː] *adj* falso, mentiroso; imaginario; infiel.

unusual [ʌnˈjuːʒuəl] *adj* desacostumbrado; extraño; excepcional.
unwanted [ʌnˈwɒntid] *adj* no deseado; superfluo.
unwell [ʌnˈwel] *adj* indispuesto, enfermo.
***unwind** [ʌnˈwaind] *v* desenrollar; (*relax*) descansar.
unwise [ʌnˈwaiz] *adj* imprudente; indiscreto.
unworthy [ʌnˈwɜːði] *adj* indigno.
unwrap [ʌnˈrap] *v* desenvolver; (*parcel*) deshacer.
up [ʌp] *adv* arriba; hacia arriba; al aire; en el aire; (*louder*) más fuerte; (*out of bed*) levantado; (*standing*) de pie, en pie. **be up to** ser capaz de. *prep* arriba; en; contra; en el fondo de. **walk up and down** pasearse a lo largo y a lo ancho. **ups and downs** los altibajos *m pl*. **up-and-coming** *adj* joven y prometedor.
upbringing [ˈʌpbrɪŋɪŋ] *n* educación *f*.
update [ʌpˈdeit] *v* (*bring up to date*) poner al día; (*modernize*) modernizar.
upheaval [ʌpˈhiːvl] *n* (*geol*) levantamiento *m*; (*fig*) agitación *f*.
uphill [ʌpˈhil] *adj* ascendente; (*struggle*) arduo.
***uphold** [ʌpˈhould] *v* sostener; defender; confirmar.
upholster [ʌpˈhoulstə] *v* entapizar. **upholstery** *n* (*material*) tapicería *f*; (*filling*) relleno *m*.
upkeep [ˈʌpkiːp] *n* mantenimiento *m*.
uplift [ʌpˈlift] *n* (*geol*) elevación *f*; (*fig*) inspiración.
upon [əˈpɒn] *prep* sobre, encima de.
upper [ˈʌpə] *adj* alto; superior. **upper-class** *adj* de la clase alta. **upper hand** dominio *m*. **uppermost** *adj* más alto; predominante.
upright [ˈʌprait] *adj* vertical; derecho; (*fig*) recto. *adv* en posición vertical.
uprising [ˈʌpraizɪŋ] *n* sublevación *f*.
uproar [ˈʌprɔː] *n* alboroto *m*, tumulto *m*.
uproarious *adj* tumultuoso; ruidoso.
uproot [ʌpˈruːt] *v* desarraigar; (*fig*) arrancar.
***upset** [ʌpˈset; *n* ˈʌpset] *v* (*knock over*) volcar; (*spill*) derramar; (*plans, etc.*) trastornar; desconcertar; (*displease*) enfadar. *adj* (*worried*) preocupado; (*ill*) indispuesto; (*nerves*) desquiciado; enfadado; (*stomach*) trastornado. *n* vuelco *m*; trastorno *m*; (*illness*) malestar *m*; dificultad *f*; (*trouble*) molestia *f*.

upshot [ˈʌpʃɒt] *n* resultado *m*.
upside down [ʌpsaiˈdaun] *adv*, *adj* al revés.
upstairs [ʌpˈsteəz] *adv* arriba. **go upstairs** subir. *adj* de arriba.
upstream [ʌpˈstriːm] *adv* río arriba, aguas arriba; (*swim*) a contracorriente.
up-to-date *adj* moderno.
upward [ˈʌpwəd] *adj* ascendente. **upwards** *adv* hacia arriba.
uranium [juˈreiniəm] *n* uranio *m*.
urban [ˈɜːbən] *adj* urbano.
urchin [ˈɜːtʃɪn] *n* pilluelo *m*.
urge [ɜːdʒ] *v* incitar; exhortar; requerir. *n* vivo deseo *m*; impulso *m*.
urgent [ˈɜːdʒənt] *adj* urgente; insistente. **urgency** *n* urgencia *f*; insistencia *f*.
urine [ˈjuːrin] *n* orina *f*. **urinate** *v* orinar.
urn [ɜːn] *n* urna *f*.
Uruguay [ˈjuːrəgwai] *n* Uruguay *m*. **Uruguayan** *n*, *adj* uruguayo, -a.
us [ʌs] *pron* nos; nosotros.
usage [ˈjuːzidʒ] *n* (*custom*) usanza *f*; (*treatment*) tratos *m pl*; (*gramm*) uso *m*.
use [juːs; *v* juːz] *n* uso *m*; empleo *m*; (*tool*) manejo *m*. **it's no use** es inútil. **what's the use?** ¿para qué? *v* usar, emplear; consumir; tomar; utilizar. **use up** agotar. **used** de segunda mano. **be used for** servir para. **be used to** estar acostumbrado a. **get used to** habituarse a. **useful** *adj* útil. **useless** *adj* inútil. **user** *n* usuario, -a *m*, *f*.
usher [ˈʌʃə] *n* (*law*) ujier *m*; (*theatre*) acomodador *m*. *v* **usher in** anunciar; hacer pasar. **usherette** *n* acomodadora *f*.
usual [ˈjuːzuəl] *adj* normal; habitual; acostumbrado. **as usual** como siempre. **usually** *adv* normalmente.
usurp [juˈzɜːp] *v* usurpar.
utensil [juˈtensl] *n* utensilio *m*.
uterus [ˈjuːtərəs] *n* útero *m*.
utility [juˈtiləti] *n* utilidad *f*. *adj* utilitario.
utilize [ˈjuːtilaiz] *v* utilizar.
utmost [ˈʌtmoust] *adj* mayor; supremo; extremo; más lejano. *n* máximo *m*. **do one's utmost** hacer todo lo posible.
utter[1] [ˈʌtə] *v* decir; (*cries*) lanzar; (*sigh*) dar; (*sentiments*) expresar.
utter[2] [ˈʌtə] *adj* absoluto; completo.
U-turn [ˈjuːtɜːn] *n* media vuelta *f*.

V

vacant *adj* (*empty*) vacío; deshabitado; (*free*) libre; (*absent-minded*) distraído; vago; estúpido. **vacancy** (*job*) vacante *f*; (*room*) habitación libre *f*. **no vacancies** completo.
vacate *v* dejar vacío.
vacation *n* vacaciones *f pl*.
vaccine *n* vacuna *f*. **vaccinate** *v* vacunar. **vaccination** *n* vacunación *f*.
vacillate *v* vacilar; oscilar. **vacillation** *n* vacilación *f*.
vacuum *n* vacío *m*. **vacuum cleaner** aspiradora *f*. **vacuum flask** termo *m*. *v* pasar la aspiradora en.
vagina *n* vagina *f*.
vagrant *n*, *adj* vagabundo, -a. **vagrancy** *n* vagabundeo *m*.
vague *adj* vago, indistinto; incierto.
vain *adj* vano, inútil; (*conceited*) vanidoso. **in vain** en vano.
valiant *adj* valeroso.
valid *adj* válido. **validity** *n* validez *f*.
valley *n* valle *m*.
value *n* valor *m*; precio *m*; importancia *f*. *v* (*appraise*) valorar, tasar; estimar; apreciar. **valuable** *adj* valioso; precioso; costoso. **valuables** *pl n* objetos de valor *m pl*. **valuation** *n* valuación *f*; estimación *f*.
valve *n* válvula *f*.
vampire *n* vampiro *m*.
van *n* (*road*) camión *m*; (*removal*) carro de mudanzas *m*; (*guard's*) furgón de equipajes *m*; (*leading section*) vanguardia *f*.
vandal *n* vándalo, -a *m*, *f*. **vandalism** *n* vandalismo *m*. **vandalize** *v* destrozar.
vanilla *n* vainilla *f*.
vanish *v* desaparecer.
vanity *n* vanidad *f*. **vanity case** neceser *m*.
vapour *n* vapor *m*. **vapourize** *v* vaporizar.
varicose veins *pl n* varices *f pl*.
variety *n* variedad *f*; diversidad *f*. **variety show** función de variedades *f*.
various *adj* diverso; vario.
varnish *n* barniz *m*. *v* barnizar.
vary *v* variar; cambiar; modificar. **vary from** diferenciarse de. **variable** *nf*, *adj* variable. **variant** *nf*, *adj* variante. **variation** *n* variación *f*.

vase *n* vaso *m*; jarrón *m*.
vasectomy *n* vasectomía *f*.
vast *adj* vasto. **vastness** *n* inmensidad *f*.
vat *n* tinaja *f*.
Vatican *n* Vaticano *m*. **Vatican City** Ciudad del Vaticano *f*.
vault[1] *n* (*cellar*) sótano *m*; (*arch*) bóveda *f*; (*tomb*) panteón *m*; (*bank*) cámara acorzada *f*.
vault[2] *v* saltar. *n* salto *m*. **vaulting horse** potro *m*.
veal *n* ternera *f*.
veer *v* (*wind*) girar; (*ship*) virar; (*fig*) cambiar.
vegetable *n* (*bot*) vegetal *m*; (*cookery*) verdura *f*, legumbre *f*. *adj* vegetal. **vegetable garden** huerto *m*, huerta *f*. **vegetarian** *n*, *adj* vegetariano, -a. **vegetation** *n* vegetación *f*.
vehement *adj* vehemente; violento. **vehemence** *n* vehemencia *f*; violencia *f*. **vehemently** *adj* con vehemencia.
vehicle *n* vehículo *m*.
veil *n* velo *m*. *v* velar.
vein *n* vena *f*.
velocity *n* velocidad *f*.
velvet *n* terciopelo *m*. *adj* de terciopelo. **velvety** *adj* aterciopelado.
vending machine *n* distribuidor automático *m*.
veneer *n* chapa *f*; (*fig: gloss*) barniz *m*. *v* chapear.
venerate *v* venerar. **venerable** *adj* venerable. **veneration** *n* veneración *f*.
venereal disease *n* enfermedad venérea *f*.
Venetian blind *n* persiana veneciana *f*.
Venezuela [,veni'zweilə] *n* Venezuela *f*. **Venezuelan** *n*, *adj* venezolano, -a.
vengeance *n* venganza *f*. **with a vengeance** (*coll*) de verdad.
venison *n* venado *m*.
venom *n* veneno *m*. **venomous** *adj* venenoso.
vent *n* (*hole*) agujero *m*, abertura *f*; (*air-hole*) respiradero *m*; (*tube*) conducto de ventilación *m*. **give vent to** dar libre curso a. *v* desahogar.
ventilate *v* ventilar. **ventilation** *n* ventilación *f*.
ventriloquist *n* ventrílocuo, -a *m*, *f*. **ventriloquism** *n* ventriloquia *f*.
venture *n* aventura *f*, empresa arriesgada *f*. *v* aventurar; arriesgar.
venue *n* lugar de reunión *m*.

veranda n also **verandah** veranda f, galería f.
verb n verbo. **verbal** adj verbal.
verdict n veredicto m.
verge n margen m, borde m; (lake) orilla f. **on the verge of** (fig) a punto de, a dos dedos de. v **verge on** rayar en.
verify v verificar. **verification** n verificación f.
vermin n (rats, mice, etc.) bichos m pl; (fleas, people) sabandijas f pl. **verminous** adj (lousy) piojoso.
vermouth n vermut m.
vernacular adj vernáculo. n lenguaje vulgar m.
versatile adj de talentos variados; (mind) flexible. **versatility** n diversos talentos m pl; flexibilidad f.
verse n (poetry) poesía f; (stanza) estrofa f; (Bible) versículo m.
version n versión f.
versus prep contra.
vertebra n, pl -brae vértebra f. **vertebral** adj vertebral. **vertebrate** nm, adj vertebrado.
vertical nf, adj vertical.
vertigo n vértigo m.
very adv muy; mucho, mucha. **very much** mucho, muchísimo. adj mismo; propio; (real) verdadero; puro.
vessel n (container) vasija f; (ship) nave f.
vest n camiseta f.
vestibule n vestíbulo m.
vestige n vestigio m, rastro m.
vestry n vestuario m, sacristía f.
vet n (coll) veterinario m. v (coll) corregir, revisar.
veteran nm, adj veterano. **veteran troops** tropas aguerridas f pl.
veterinary surgeon n veterinario m.
veto n veto m. v vetar, poner el veto.
vex v molestar; enfadar. **vexation** n molestia f; disgusto m.
via prep por, por la vía de.
viable adj viable. **viability** n viabilidad f.
viaduct n viaducto m.
vibrate v vibrar. **vibration** n vibración f.
vicar n vicario m; (of a parish) cura m. **vicarage** n casa del cura f.
vicarious adj vicario.
vice[1] n (evil) vicio m; (defect) defecto m.
vice[2] n (tool) tornillo de banco m.
vice-chancellor n rector m.
vice-consul n vicecónsul m.

vice-president n vicepresidente m.
vice versa adv viceversa.
vicinity n vecindad f; (nearness) cercanía f.
vicious adj (of vice) vicioso; (bad) malo; (depraved) pervertido; (taste) corrompido; (life) disoluto; (crime) atroz. **vicious circle** círculo vicioso m. **viciousness** n lo vicioso; maldad f; perversidad f.
victim n víctima f. **victimize** v perseguir; tomar como víctima. **victimization** n persecución f.
victory n victoria f. **victorious** adj victorioso.
video-tape n cinta magnética video f. v grabar programas de televisión.
vie v competir, rivalizar.
Vienna n Viena f.
view n vista f; panorama m; inspección f; idea f. **viewfinder** n visor m. **viewpoint** punto de vista m. v mirar; visitar; considerar. **viewer** n (TV) telespectador, -a m, f; (onlooker) espectador, -a m, f; (for slides) visionadora f.
vigil n vela f, vigilia f. **vigilance** n vigilancia f. **vigilant** adj vigilante.
vigour n vigor m. **vigorous** adj vigoroso.
vile adj vil; horrible.
villa n chalet m; (country house) casa de campo f.
village n aldea f, pueblo m. **villager** n aldeano, -a m, f.
villain n canalla m. **villainy** n villanía f.
vindictive adj vengativo.
vine n vid f; parra f. **vineyard** n viña f.
vinegar n vinagre m.
vintage adj (season) vendimia f; (crop) cosecha f. **vintage wine** vino añejo m.
vinyl n vinilo m.
viola n (music) viola f.
violate v (ravish) violar; (desecrate) profanar; (infringe) contravenir. **violation** n violación f; profanación f; contravención f.
violence n violencia f. **violent** adj violento.
violet n (flower, colour) violeta. adj violado.
violin n violín m. **violinist** n violinista m, f.
viper n víbora f.
virgin nf, adj virgen. **virginity** n virginidad f.

Virgo n Virgo m.
virile adj viril. **virility** n virilidad f.
virtually adv virtualmente; prácticamente.
virtue n virtud f; (advantage) ventaja f. **by virtue of** debido a. **virtuous** adj virtuoso.
virus n virus m.
visa n visado m.
viscount n vizconde m. **viscountess** vizcondesa f.
visible adj visible. **visibility** n visibilidad f.
vision n (sight, apparition) visión f; (capacity to see) vista f; (dream) sueño m.
visionary n, adj visionario, -a m, f.
visit n visita f. v (go to, call on) visitar; (stay in) pasar una temporada en. **visitor** n visitante m, f; visita f.
visor n visera f.
visual adj visual. **visualize** v imaginarse.
vital adj vital. **vitality** n vitalidad f. **vitally** adv vitalmente.
vitamin n vitamina f.
vivacious adj vivo; vivaracho. **vivaciousness** n also **vivacity** viveza f, vivacidad f.
vivid adj vivo; (description) gráfico. **vividness** n (colour) viveza f, intensidad f; (style) fuerza f.
vivisection n vivisección f.
vixen n zorra f, raposa f.
vocabulary n vocabulario m.
vocal adj vocal; (fig) ruidoso. **vocalist** n cantante m, f.
vocation n vocación f. **vocational** adj profesional.
vociferous adj ruidoso.
vodka n vodca m.
voice n voz f. v hablar; expresar.
void n vacío m. adj (empty) vacío; (job) vacante; (law) nulo.
volatile adj (chem) volátil; (fig) voluble.
volcano n volcán m. **volcanic** adj volcánico.
volley n (bullets) andanada f; (arrows, stones) lluvia f; (applause) salva f; (sport) voleo m. v (missile) lanzar; (sport) volear.
volt n voltio m. **voltage** n voltaje m.
volume n (space, sound) volumen m; (book) tomo m, volumen m. **voluminous** adj voluminoso; abundante.
volunteer nm, adj voluntario. v ofrecer; (remark) hacer; (information) dar.
voluptuous adj voluptuoso. **voluptuousness** n voluptuosidad f.
vomit n vómito m. v vomitar.

voodoo n vodú m.
voracious adj voraz. **voraciousness** n also **voracity** voracidad f.
vote n voto m; (action) votación f. **vote of confidence** voto de confianza f. **vote of thanks** voto de gracias m. v votar; elegir; proponer; declarar. **voter** n votante m, f; elector, -a m, f.
vouch v **vouch for** (thing) responder de, garantizar; (person) responder por.
voucher n (comm) bono m, vale m. **luncheon voucher** vale de comida m.
vow n voto m; promesa solemne f. v jurar; prometer.
vowel n vocal f.
voyage n viaje m. v viajar (por mar).
vulgar adj común; ordinario; grosero. **vulgarity** n vulgaridad f; grosería f.
vulnerable adj vulnerable.
vulture n buitre m.

W

wad n (bung) tapón m; (notes) rollo m; (cotton wool) bolita f. **wadding** n (cotton wool) guata f; (filling) relleno m.
waddle v anadear. n anadeo m.
wade v vadear. **wade through** (book, etc.) estudiar detenidamente.
wafer n (for ices) barquillo m. **wafer-thin** adj finísimo.
waft v llevar por el aire; flotar. n ráfaga f.
wag v agitar; (tail) menear. n (tail) coleada f; movimiento m; (joker) bromista m, f.
wage n salario m, paga f. v **wage war** hacer guerra.
wager n apuesta f. v apostar.
waggle v menear, agitar. n meneo m.
wagon n carro m; carreta f; (rail) vagón m.
waif n niño abandonado m.
wail n lamento m, gemido. v lamentarse, gemir.
waist n cintura f, talle m. **waistband** n pretina f. **waistcoat** n chaleco m. **waistline** n cintura f.
wait n espera f. **lie in wait for** acechar. v esperar; (at table) atender. **waiter** n mozo m, camarero m. **waiting** n espera f; servicio m. **waiting-list** n lista de espera f.

waiting-room *n* sala de espera *f.* **waitress** *n* camarera *f.*

waive *v* renunciar a; desitir de.

wake[1] *n* velatorio *m.*

***wake**[2] *v also* wake up despertar(se).

Wales *n* el País de Gales.

walk *n* paseo *m*; camino *m*; (*gait*) andar *m*; (*pace*) paso *m*. *v* (*go on foot*) recorrer a pie; (*distance*) hacer a pie; (*take out*) pasear; (*escort*) acompañar. **walkout** *n* huelga *f.* **walkover** *n* victoria fácil *f.* **walker** *n* paseante *m, f.* **walking** *n* andar m. **walking-stick** *n* bastón *m.*

wall *n* pared *f*; muro *m. v* murar; amurallar.

wallet *n* cartera *f.*

wallflower *n* alhelí *m.* **be a wallflower** quedarse en el poyete.

wallop (*coll*) *n* golpazo *m*, trompazo *m. v* zurrar. **walloping** *n* paliza *f.*

wallow *v* revolcarse.

wallpaper *n* papel pintado *m. v* empapelar.

walnut *n* (*nut*) nuez *f*; (*tree, wood*) nogal *m.*

walrus *n* morsa *f.*

waltz *n* vals *m. v* valsar.

wan *adj* macilento.

wand *n* (*magic*) varita *f*; vara *f.*

wander *v* vagar por; (*stroll*) pasearse; (*mentally*) desvariar.

wane *v* (*moon*) menguar; (*fig*) decaer.

wangle *v* conseguir con trampas. (*coll*) *n* trampa *f.*

want *n* (*lack*) falta *f*; (*need*) necesidad *f*; (*poverty*) miseria *f*; (*wish*) deseo *m*; (*gap*) vacío *m.* **for want of** por falta de. *v* querer; desear; necesitar; (*ask*) pedir; (*look for*) buscar. **wanted** *adj* buscado (por la policía). **wanting** *adj* (*absent*) ausente; (*lacking*) deficiente.

wanton *adj* lascivo; (*promiscuous*) libertino; (*senseless*) sin sentido. **wantonness** *n* libertinaje *f*; crueldad *f*; exuberancia *f*; (*lack of moderation*) desenfreno *m.*

war *n* guerra *f.* **be on the warpath** (*coll*) estar buscando guerra. **warfare** *n* guerra *f.* **warhead** *n* cabeza de guerra *f.* **war memorial** monumento a los Caídos *m.* **War Office** Ministerio de la Guerra *m.* **warship** *n* buque de guerra *m.* **wartime** *n* tiempo de guerra *m.*

warble *v* gorjear, trinar. *n* gorjeo *m*, trino *m.*

ward *n* (*hospital*) sala *f*; (*pol*) distrito electoral *m*; (*law: guardianship*) custodia *f*; (*minor*) pupilo *m. v* **ward off** evitar.

warden *n* guarda *m*; vigilante *m*; director *m.*

warder *n* carcelero *m*; guardián *m.*

wardrobe *n* guardarropa *m*; (*theatre*) vestuario *m.*

warehouse *n* almacén *m. v* almacenar.

warm *adj* tibio; caliente; (*climate*) cálido; (*fire*) acogedor; (*welcome*) caluroso; (*kind*) cariñoso. *v* calentar; acalorar. **warm up** calentar; (*reheat*) recalentar. **warming-pan** *n* calentador de cama *m.* **warmth** *n* calor *m*; cordialidad *f.*

warn *v* advertir; aconsejar; (*rebuke*) amonestar. **warning** *n* advertencia *f*, aviso *m*; alarma *f*; ejemplo *m*; amonestación *f.* **warning light** lámpara indicadora *f.*

warp *v* (*wood*) alabear; (*yarn*) urdir; (*fig*) deformar. *n* alabeo *m*; urdimbre *f*; deformación *f.*

warrant *n* (*police*) orden *f*; (*law*) autorización legal *f*; justificación *f*; garantía *f. v* autorizar; justificar; garantizar. **warranty** *n* garantía *f.*

warren *n* (*rabbit*) conejal *m*; (*fig*) colmena *f.*

warrior *n* guerrero *m.*

Warsaw ['wɔɪsɔɪ] *n* Varsovia.

wart [wɔɪt] *n* verruga *f.*

wary ['weəri] *adj* cauto, precavido.

was [woz] *V* be.

wash [woʃ] *v* lavar; (*dishes*) fregar. **wash away** quitar. **wash down** (*swallow*) tragar. **wash up** fregar. **washable** *adj* lavable. **wash-and-wear** *adj* de lava y pon. **washbasin** *n* lavabo *m.* **washboard** *n* tabla de lavar *f.* **washer** *n* arandela *f.* **washing** *n* lavado *m*; colada *f*; fregado *m.* **washing machine** lavadora *f.* **washing powder** jabón en polvo *m.* **washing-up bowl** barreño *m.* **washout** *n* (*slang*) desastre *m.*

wasp [wosp] *n* avispa *f.*

waste [weist] *n* pérdida *f*; (*food*) desperdicios *m pl*; (*rubbish*) basura *f.* **waste disposal unit** vertedero de basuras *m.* **waste land** yermo *m*; erial *m.* **waste paper** papel usado *m.* **waste-paper basket** papelera *f. v* malgastar, despilfarrar; perder; (*use up*) consumir; (*by disuse*) desperdiciar. **waste away** consumirse. **wasteful** *adj* (*person*) despilfarrador, -a *m, f;* ruinoso. **waster** *n also* **wastrel** derrochador, -a *m, f.*

watch [wotʃ] *n* (*wrist*) reloj de la pulsera *m*; (*pocket*) reloj de bolsillo *m*; (*naut*) guardia *f*; vigilancia *f.* **keep watch** estar de guardia. **watch chain** cadena de reloj *f.* **watchdog** *n* perro guardián *m.* **watchmaker** *n* relojero *m.* **watchman** *n* vigilante *m.* **watch spring** muelle *m.* **watch strap** correa de reloj *f.* **watchword** *n* consigna *f. v* mirar, ver, observar; (*pay attention to*) fijarse en; (*keep an eye on*) vigilar. **watchful** *adj* atento; vigilante.

water ['wɔitə] *n* agua *f. v* (*wet*) humedecer; (*soak*) mojar; (*plants*) regar; (*eyes*) llorar. **water down** moderar. **watery** *adj* acuoso; aguado, insípido.

water-biscuit *n* galleta de harina y agua *f.*

water-closet *n* retrete *m,* wáter *m.*

water-colour *n* acuarela *f.*

watercress ['wɔitəkres] *n* berro *m.*

waterfall ['wɔitəfɔil] *n* cascada *f*; catarata *f.*

water-ice *n* sorbete *m.*

watering-can *n* regadera *f.*

water lily *n* nenúfar *m.*

waterline ['wɔitəlain] *n* línea de flotación *f.*

waterlogged ['wɔitəlogd] *adj* (*wood*) empapado; (*med*) inundado.

water main *n* cañería principal *f.*

watermark ['wɔitəmaik] *n* filigrana *f*; (*tide*) marca del nivel de agua *f.*

watermelon ['wɔitəmelən] *n* sandía *f.*

waterproof ['wɔitəpruf] *nm, adj* impermeable. *v* impermeabilizar.

watershed ['wɔitəʃed] *n* (*fig*) momento decisivo *m*; (*geog*) línea divisoria de las aguas *f.*

water-ski *v* hacer esquí acuático. **water-skiing** *n* esquí acuático *m.*

water softener *n* ablandador del agua *m.*

watertight ['wɔitətait] *adj* estanco; hermético; (*fig*) perfecto.

waterway ['wɔitəwei] *n* vía navegable *f.*

waterworks ['wɔitəwɔiks] *n* sistema de abastecimiento de agua *m.*

watt [wot] *n* vatio *m.*

wave [weiv] *n* (*sea*) ola *f*; (*hair*) ondulación *f*; (*physics, radio, etc.*)onda *f*; (*hand*) señal *f.* **permanent wave** permanente *f.* **waveband** *n* banda de ondas *f.* **wavelength** *n* longitud de onda *f. v* agitar; (*hair*) ondular. **wavy** *adj* ondulado.

waver ['weivə] *v* vacilar; (*falter*) flaquear; (*totter*) titubear. **wavering** *adj* vacilante; tembloroso.

wax[1] [waks] *n* cera *f.* **waxwork** *n* figura de cera *f.* **waxworks** *n* museo de figuras de cera *m. v* encerar. **waxy** *adj* ceroso.

wax[2] [waks] *v* crecer.

way [wei] *n* camino *m*; paso *m*; ruta *f*; senda *f*; dirección *f*; rumbo *m*; distancia *f*; (*journey*) viaje *m*; progreso *m*; modo *m*, manera *f*; (*means*) medio *m.* **be in the way** estar de por medio. **by the way** a propósito. **give way** ceder. **on the way** en camino. **this way** por aquí. **under way** en marcha; en preparación. **way in** entrada *f.* **way out** salida *f.*

*****waylay** [wei'lei] *v* abordar.

wayside ['weisaid] *n* borde del camino *m. adj* al borde del camino.

wayward ['weiwəd] *adj* voluntarioso; díscolo.

we [wii] *pron* nosotros, -as.

weak [wiik] *adj* débil; flaco; flojo. **weaken** *v* debilitar. **weakling** *n* persona débil *f*; cobarde *m.* **weakness** *n* debilidad *f*; (*point*) punto flaco *m.*

wealth [welθ] *n* riqueza *f*; abundancia *f.* **wealthy** *adj* rico.

wean [wiin] *v* (*baby*) destetar. **wean from** apartar de.

weapon ['wepən] *n* arma *f.*

*****wear** [weə] *v* llevar; poner; gastar. **wear off** pasar(se). **wear out** usarse, consumirse. *n* uso *m*; gasto *m*; deterioro *m.* **wear and tear** desgaste *m.*

weary ['wiəri] *adj* fatigado, cansado, aburrido. *v* fatigar, causar; aburrir. **wearily** *adv* cansadamente. **weariness** *n* fatiga *f.*

weasel ['wiizl] *n* comadreja *f.*

weather ['weðə] *n* tiempo *m.* **weatherbeaten** *adj* curtido. **weather chart** mapa meteorológico *m.* **weathercock** *n* veleta *f.* **weather forecast** boletín meteorológico *m. v* (*survive*) superar.

*****weave** [wiiv] *v* tejer; entrelazar; (*through traffic, etc.*) zigzaguear.

web [web] *n* (*spider*) tela de araña *f*; (*fabric*) tejido *m*; (*on feet*) membrana *f*; (*network*) red *f*; (*fig*) sarta *f.* **web-footed** *adj* palmípedo.

wed [wed] *v* casarse con; casar. **wedding** *n* boda *f*, casamiento *m.* **wedding dress** traje de novia *m.* **wedding ring** alianza *f*

wedge [wedʒ] *n* cuña *f*, calzo *m*. *v* encajar; (*jam*) apretar.
Wednesday ['wenzdi] *n* miércoles *m*.
weed [wiːd] *n* mala hierba *f*. **weed-killer** *n* herbicida *m*. *v* desherbar. **weeding** *n* escarda *f*.
week [wiːk] *n* semana *f*. **a week today/tomorrow** hoy/mañana en ocho.
weekday *n* dia de trabajo *m*. **weekend** *n* fin de semana *m*. **weekly** *adv* semanal. **weekly** *n* semanario *m*.
*weep** [wiːp] *v* llorar, lamentar. **weeping willow** sauce llorón *m*.
weigh [wei] *v* pesar. **weigh down** doblar bajo un peso. **weight** *n* peso *m*. **pull one's weight** poner de su parte. **weightlifting** *n* halterofilia *f*. **weightlessness** *n* ingravidez *f*.
weird [wiəd] *adj* extraño; misterioso; fantástico. **weirdness** *n* misterio *m*; lo sobrenatural.
welcome ['welkəm] *adj* bienvenido; grato. **be welcome** ser oportuno. **you're welcome!** ¡eres el bienvenido!; (*after thanks*) ¡no hay de que! *n* bienvenida *f*. *v* dar la bienvenida a; recibir; alegrarse por.
weld [weld] *v* soldar. **welder** *n* soldador *m*. **welding** *n* soldadura *f*.
welfare ['welfeə] *n* bienestar *m*, bien *m*. **welfare state** estado benefactor *m*.
well¹ [wel] *n* pozo *m*. **well up** brotar.
well² [wel] *adj*, *adv* bien. **as well** también.
well-advised *adj* juicioso.
well-behaved *adj* bien educado.
well-being *n* bienestar *m*.
well-born *adj* de buena familia.
well-bred *adj* (*person*) bien educado; (*animal*) de raza pura.
well-built *adj* bien hecho.
well-dressed *adj* bien vestido.
well-informed *adj* muy documentado.
wellington ['weliŋtən] *n* bota de agua *f*.
well-kept *adj* (*secret*) bien guardado; (*garden*) bien cuidado.
well-known *adj* bien conocido.
well-made *adj* bien hecho.
well-off *adj* rico.
well-paid *adj* bien pagado.
well-read *adj* leído.
well-spent *adj* (*time*) bien empleado.
well-spoken *adj* bienhablado.
well-timed *adj* oportuno.
well-to-do *adj* rico.
well-trodden *adj* trillado.

well-worn *adj* gastado.
Welsh [welʃ] *adj* galés. *n* (*language*) galés *m*; (*person*) galés, -esa *m*, *f*.
went [went] *V* go.
wept [wept] *V* weep.
were [wəi] *V* be.
west [west] *n* oeste *m*. **the West** el Mundo Occidental *m*. *adj also* **westerly** del oeste, occidental. *adv* al oeste, hacia el oeste. **westbound** *adj* con rumbo al oeste. **western** *adj* occidental, del oeste. *n* (*film*) western *m*.
wet [wet] *adj* mojado; húmedo; (*weather*) lluvioso; (*paint*) fresco. **wet blanket** aguafiestas *m*, *f invar*. **wet suit** traje de buzo *m*. *n* lluvia *f*. *v* mojar; humedecer.
whack [wak] *n* golpe *m*. *v* golpear, pegar.
whale [weil] *n* ballena *f*.
wharf [woːf] *n* muelle *m*.
what [wot] *pron* lo que; (*interrog, interj*) qué, cuál, cómo, cúanto. *adj* el que, la que, lo que; qué.
whatever [wot'evə] *pron* todo lo que; lo que; cualquier cosa que. *adj* cualquiera. **nothing/whatever** nada en absoluto.
wheat [wiːt] *n* trigo *m*.
wheel [wiːl] *n* rueda *f*; (*steering*) volante *m*. **wheelbarrow** *n* carretilla *f*. **wheelchair** *n* sillón de ruedas *m*. *v* hacer rodar; empujar; dar una vuelta.
wheeze [wiːz] *n* respiración dificultosa *f*. *v* respirar con dificultad. **wheezy** *adj* asmático.
whelk [welk] *n* buccino *m*.
when [wen] *adv* cuándo, a qué hora. *conj* cuando; en que; (*as soon as*) en cuanto. **whenever** *conj* cuando; cada vez que.
where [weə] *interrog adv* dónde; adónde; de dónde; por dónde; (*in what respect*) en qué. *relative adv* donde; en donde, en que, en el cual, en la cual; adonde, a donde, al que, al cual, a la cual. *conj* donde. **whereabouts** *adv* dónde, por dónde; *n* paradero *m*. **whereas** *conj* mientras, en tanto que. **whereupon** *adv* después de lo cual. **wherever** *conj* dondequiera que; a dondequiera que.
whether ['weðə] *conj* si.
which [witʃ] *interrog pron* cuál; qué. *relative pron* que; el cual, la cual, el que, la que; lo cual, lo que. *adj* qué; cuál; cuyo; cómo. **of which** del que, de la que; del cual; de la cual. **whichever** *pron* el que, la que; cualquiera que; *adj* cualquier.

whiff [wif] *n* soplo *m*; olorcillo *m*.
while [wail] *conj* mientras; (*although*) aunque. *n* rato *m*, tiempo *m*. **while away** pasar.
whim [wim] *n* capricho *m*.
whimper ['wimpə] *n* quejido *m*, gemido *m*. *v* quejarse, gemir.
whimsical ['wimzikl] *adj* caprichoso; fantástico.
whine [wain] *n* (*animal*) gañido *m*; (*complaint*) queja *f*; (*pain*) quejido *m*; (*engine*) zumbido *m*. *v* gañir; quejarse; zumbar.
whip [wip] *n* azote *m*; (*riding*) látigo *m*. **whiplash** *n* latigazo *m*. **whip-round** *n* (*coll*) colecta *f*. *v* azotar; (*cookery*) batir. **whip up** avivar. **whipping** *n* azotamiento *m*.
whippet ['wipit] *n* lebrel *m*.
whirl [wəil] *n* vuelta *f*, giro *m*; (*fig*) torbellino *m*. *v* dar vueltas, girar. **whirlpool** *n* remolino *m*.
whirr [wəi] *n* (*wings*) batir *m*; (*engine*) zumbido *m*. *v* girar; zumbar.
whisk [wisk] *n* (*cookery*) batidor. *v* batir.
whisker ['wiskə] *n* pelo del bigote *m*. **whiskers** *pl n* bigotes *m pl*.
whisky ['wiski] *n* whisky *m*.
whisper ['wispə] *n* cuchicheo *m*. *v* cuchichear.
whistle ['wisl] *n* pito *m*; (*sound*) silbido *m*; pitido *m*. *v* silbar.
white [wait] *adj* blanco. **white elephant** (*fig*) objeto costoso e inútil *m*. *n* blanco *m*; (*person*) blanco, -a *m*, *f*. **whiten** *v* blanquear. **whiteness** *n* blancura *f*.
whitewash ['waitwoʃ] *n* cal *f*. *v* encalar; (*fig: cover up*) encubrir.
whiting ['waitiŋ] *n* pescadilla *f*.
whittle ['witl] *v* tallar. **whittle down** reducir poco a poco.
whizz [wiz] *n* zumbido *m*. **whizz-kid** *n* (*coll*) promesa *f*. **whizz past** pasar como un rayo.
who [huı] *relative pron* quien, el quel la que; que, el cual, la cual; que, a quien. *interrog pron* quién. **whoever** *pron* quienquiera que, cualquiera que, el que, la que, quien.
whole [houl] *adj* todo, completo, entero, total; íntegro, intacto. *n* todo *m*, total *m*, totalidad *f*. **on the whole** en general. **wholehearted** *adj* sin reservas. **wholeheartedly** *adv* incondicionalmente. **wholemeal** *adj* integral. **wholesome** *adj* saludable.

wholesale ['houlseil] *n* venta al por mayor *f*. *adj, adv* al por mayor; en masa.
whom [huım] *relative pron* que, quien, a quien. *interrog pron* quién, a quién. **of whom** del cual, de la cual, de quien.
whooping cough ['huıpiŋ] *n* tos ferina *f*.
whore [hoı] *n* (*derog*) puta *f*.
whose [huız] *relative pron* cuyo, cuya. *interrog pron* de quién.
why [wai] *adv* (*interrog*) por qué; (*on account of which*) por el cual, por la cual, por lo cual. *interj* ¡vaya! ¡toma! ¡pues bien!
wick [wik] *n* mecha *f*.
wicked ['wikid] *adj* malo, perverso, malicioso. **wickedness** *n* maldad *f*, perversidad *f*.
wicker ['wikə] *n* mimbre *m*. **wickerwork** *n* cestería *f*.
wicket ['wikit] *n* (*cricket*) palos *m pl*.
wide [waid] *adj* ancho; vasto; grande. *adv* lejos; mucho. **wide awake** completamente despierto. **widespread** *adj* general. **widely** *adv* muy; mucho; generalmente.
widow ['widou] *n* viuda *f*. **be widowed** quedar viuda. **widower** *n* viudo *m*.
width [widθ] *n* anchura *f*.
wield [wiıld] *v* (*tool*) manejar; (*weapon*) blandir; (*power*) ejercer.
wife [waif] *n* mujer *f*, esposa *f*.
wig [wig] *n* peluca *f*.
wiggle ['wigl] *v* menear. *n* meneo *m*. **wiggly** *adj* (*line*) ondulante.
wild [waild] *adj* (*animal, person*) salvaje; (*plant*) silvestre; (*bull*) bravo; (*character*) violento. **like wildfire** como un reguero de pólvora. **wildlife** *n* fauna *f*. **wildly** *adv* violentamente; locamente; frenéticamente; disolutamente.
wilderness ['wildənəs] *n* desierto *m*; soledad *f*.
wilful ['wilfəl] *adj* (*stubborn*) obstinado; (*headstrong*) voluntarioso; deliberado.
will¹ [wil] *aux translated by future tense.*
will² [wil] *n* voluntad *f*; testamento *m*. *v* disponer; desear; (*bequeath*) legar. **against one's will** de mal grado. **willpower** *n* fuerza de voluntad *f*. **willing** *adj* de buena voluntad; (*obliging*) complaciente. **be willing to** estar dispuesto a. **willingly** *adv* de buena gana. **willingness** *n* buena voluntad *f*.
willow ['wilou] *n* sauce *m*. **willowy** *adj* esbelto.

wilt [wilt] *v* marchitar(se); (*person*) languidecer.

wily ['waili] *adj* astuto, chuzón.

*win [win] *n* victoria *f*; (*amount won*) ganancia *f*. *v* ganar; conquistar; triunfar. **winner** *n* ganador, -a *m*, *f*; vencedor, -a *m*, *f*. **winning** *adj* ganador; (*smile, etc.*) encantador. **winnings** *pl n* ganancias *f pl*.

wince [wins] *v* hacer muecas. *n* mueca de dolar *f*.

winch [wintʃ] *n* torno *m*. *v* guindar.

wind[1] [wind] *n* viento *m*; (*breath*) aliento *m*; respiración *f*; (*med*) gases *m pl*. *v* dejar sin aliento. **windy** *adj* (*place*) expuesto al viento; (*day, night*) ventoso.

*wind[2] [waind] *v* devanar; envolver; enrollar; (*bend*) torcer; (*road*) serpentear; (*watch*) dar cuerda a. **wind up** terminar; (*comm*) liquidar. **winding** *adj* sinuoso; tortuoso.

wind-break *n* protección contra el viento *f*.

windfall ['windfɔːl] *n* fruta caída *f*; (*fig*) ganancia inesperada *f*.

wind instrument *n* instrumento de viento *m*.

windlass ['windləs] *n* torno *m*.

windmill ['wind,mil] *n* molino de viento *m*.

window ['windou] *n* ventana *f*; (*car*) ventanilla *f*; (*cashier's*) taquilla *f*; (*shop*) escaparate *m*. **window blind** persiana *f*. **window-box** *n* jardinera *f*. **window cleaner** limpiacristales *m invar*. **window-sill** *n* antepecho *m*. **window-shopping** *n* contemplación de escaparates *f*.

windpipe ['windpaip] *n* tráquea *f*.

windproof ['windpruːf] *adj* a prueba de viento.

windshield ['windʃiːld] *n* parabrisas *m invar*. **windshield wiper** limpiaparabrisas *m invar*.

wind-sock *n* manga de aire *f*.

windswept ['windswept] *adj* (*hair*) despeinado.

wind tunnel *n* túnel aerodinámico *m*.

wine [wain] *n* vino *m*. **wineglass** *n* copa *f*. **wine list** lista de vinos *f*. **wine-taster** *n* catavinos *m invar*. **wine waiter** bodeguero *m*.

wing [wiŋ] *n* ala *f*. **wing chair** sillón de orejas *m*. **wing commander** teniente coronel *m*. **wing-mirror** *n* retrovisor *m*. **wing nut** palometa *f*. **wings** *pl n* (*theatre*) bastidores *m pl*. **wingspan** *n* envergadura *f*.

wink [wiŋk] *n* guiño *m*; (*light*) parpadeo *m*. *v* guiñar; (light) parpadear.

winkle ['wiŋkl] *n* bígaro *m*. *v* **winkle out** sacar con dificultad.

winter ['wintə] *n* invierno *m*. *v* invernar. **wintry** *adj* de invierno; (*fig*) frío.

wipe [waip] *v* limpiar; (*mop*) enjugar; (*dry*) secar. **wipe out** destruir. *n* limpieza *f*.

wire [waiə] *n* alambre *m*; (*elec*) cordón *m*, cable *m*; hilo *m*; (*piano*) cuerda *f*; telegrama *m*. **barbed wire** alambrada *f*. **wire-brush** *n* cepillo metálico *m*. **wire-cutters** *pl n* cortaalambres *m invar*. **wireless** *n* radio *f*. *v* telegrafiar; (*a house*) poner la instalación eléctrica de. **wiry** *adj* (*hair*) tieso; (*person*) enjuto y fuerte.

wise [waiz] *adj* sabio; juicioso; (*informed*) enterado. **wisdom** *n* sabiduría *f*; juicio *m*. **wisdom tooth** muela del juicio *f*.

wish [wiʃ] *v* querer; desear; gustar. *n* deseo *m*. **wishbone** *n* espoleta *f*. **wishful** *adj* deserso. **wishful thinking** ilusiones *f pl*.

wisp [wisp] *n* (*straw*) manojo *m*; (*hair*) mechón *m*; (*smoke*) voluta *f*; (*trace*) vestigio *m*. **wispy** *adj* fino.

wistful ['wistfəl] *adj* triste; ansioso; pensativo. **wistfully** *adv* tristemente; con ansia.

wit [wit] *n* inteligencia *f*; agudeza *f*; (*humour*) gracia *f*; (*person*) persona aguda *f*. **be at one's wits' end** no saber qué hacer.

witch [witʃ] *n* bruja *f*. **witchcraft** *n* brujería *f*. **witch-doctor** *n* hechicero *m*. **witch-hunt** *n* persecución *f*.

with [wið] *prep* con; junto con; en manos de; más; en compañiá de; (*because of*) de.

*withdraw [wið'drɔː] *v* quitar; apartar; retirar; sacar. **withdrawal** *n* retirada *f*; (*bank*) salida *f*; renuncia *f*; retractación *f*; abandono *m*. **withdrawn** *adj* ensimismado.

wither ['wiðə] *v* (*plant*) marchitar(se); (*weaken*) debilitar. **withered** *adj* marchito; seco. **withering** *adj* (*look*) fulminante; (*remark*) mordaz.

*withhold [wið'hould] *v* (*refuse*) negar; (*hold back*) retener; (*hide*) ocultar.

within [wi'ðin] *adv* dentro; (*at home*) en casa. *prep* dentro de; en; al alcance de; (*less than*) a menos de.

without [wi'ðaut] *prep* sin; (*outside*) fuera de. *adv* fuera.

*****withstand** [wið'stand] *v* resistir, aguantar; oponerse a.

witness ['witnis] *n* (*person*) testigo *m*; (*evidence*) prueba *f*; (*testimony*) testimonio *m*. *v* (*be present at*) asistir a; (*document*) firmar como testigo. **witness to** atestiguar.

witty ['witi] *adj* salado, gracioso. **witticism** *n* rasgo de ingenio *m*, agudeza *f*.

wizard ['wizəd] *n* mago *m*.

wobble ['wobl] *v* tambalearse. *n* tambaleo *m*. **wobbly** *adj* tambaleante.

woke [wouk] *V* **wake**.

wolf [wulf] *n* lobo *m*. **wolfhound** *n* perro lobo *m*. **wolf-whistle** *n* silbido de admiración *m*. *v* **wolf down** (*coll*) zamparse.

woman ['wumən] *n*, *pl* **women** mujer *f*. **Women's Lib** (*coll*) Movimiento de la Liberación de la Mujer *m*. **womanhood** *n* mujeres *f pl*; femenidad *f*. **womanly** *adj* femenino.

womb [wuːm] *n* matriz *f*, útero *m*.

won [wʌn] *V* **win**.

wonder ['wʌndə] *n* maravilla *f*; milagro *m*; admiración *f*. **no wonder** no es de extrañar. *v* preguntarse; pensar; asombrarse. **wonderful** *adj* maravilloso; (*astonishing*) asombroso.

woo [wuː] *v* cortejar; (*fig*) solicitar. **wooing** *nm*, *adj* galanteo.

wood [wud] *n* (*forest*) bosque *m*; (*material*) madera *f*; (*stick*) palo *m*; (*firewood*) leña *f*. **wooden** *adj* de madera; (*stiff*) estirado. **woody** *adj* arbolado; (*stem*) leñoso.

woodcock ['wudkok] *n* chocha *f*, becada *f*.

woodcut ['wudkʌt] *n* grabado en madera *m*. **woodcutter** *n* (*forester*) leñador *m*.

woodland ['wudlənd] *n* bosque *m*.

woodpecker ['wudpekə] *n* pájaro carpintero *m*.

wood-pigeon *n* paloma torcaz *f*.

woodshed ['wudʃed] *n* leñera *f*.

woodwind ['wudwind] *n* (*music*) instrumentos de viento de madera *m pl*.

woodwork ['wudwəːk] *n* carpintería *f*.

woodworm ['wudwəːm] *n* carcoma *f*.

wool [wul] *n* lana *f*. **woollen** *adj* de lana. **woolly** *adj* lanoso; de lana; (*ideas*) borroso.

word [wəːd] *n* palabra *f*; (*gramm*) vocablo *m*. **in other words** en otras palabras; es

decir. *v* expresar; redactar. **wording** *n* redacción *f*; términos *m pl*. **wordy** *adj* verboso.

wore [woː] *V* **wear**.

work [wəːk] *n* trabajo *m*, obra *f*. **men at work** obras *f pl*. **out of work** parado. -a. *v* trabajar. **work out** resolver. **workable** *adj* (*plan*) realizable.

worker ['wəːkə] *n* trabajador, -a *m*, *f*; obrero, -a *m*, *f*.

work-force *n* mano de obra *f*.

working ['wəːkiŋ] *n* trabajo *m*; funcionamiento *m*; manejo *m*; cultivo *m*. **working-class** *adj* de la clase obrera. **workings** *pl n* excavaciones *f pl*.

workman ['wəːkmən] *n* trabajador *m*; obrero *m*. **workmanship** *n* (*skill*) artesanía *f*; ejecución *f*.

work permit *n* permiso de trabajo *m*.

workshop ['wəːkʃop] *n* taller *m*.

work-to-rule *n* trabajo a ritmo lento *m*.

world [wəːld] *n* mundo *m*. **world-wide** *adj* mundial. **worldly** *adj* mundano; material.

worm [wəːm] *n* guzano *m*; (*earthworm*) lombriz *f*.

worn [woːn] *V* **wear**.

worry ['wʌri] *n* preocupación *f*. *v* preocupar(se); molestar. **don't worry!** ¡no te ocupes! **worried** *adj* preocupado.

worse [wəːs] *adj*, *adv* peor. **get worse or worsen** empeorar. **to make matters worse** para empeorar las cosas. *n* lo peor.

worship ['wəːʃip] *n* culto *m*; (*fig*) adoración *f*. *v* venerar; (*fig*) adorar.

worst [wəːst] *adj*, *adv* peor. *n* el peor *m*, la peor *f*, lo peor. **at worst** en el peor de los casos.

worsted ['wustid] *n* estambre *m*.

worth [wəːθ] *n* valor *m*; mérito *m*; valía *f*; fortuna *f*. **be worth** valer. **be worth it** merecer la pena. **worthless** *adj* sin valor; inútil. **worthwhile** *adj* que vale la pena; útil.

would [wud] *aux translated by conditional or imperfect tense*.

wound¹ [waund] *V* **wind²**.

wound² [wuːnd] *n* herida *f*. *v* herir.

wove [wouv] *V* **weave**.

wrangle ['raŋgl] *n* disputa *f*. *v* discutir.

wrap [rap] *v* envolver; cubrir. **wrap up** abrigarse. *n* (*shawl*) chal *m*. **wrapper** *n* envoltura *f*; (*book*) sobrecubierta *f*. **wrapping** *n* envoltura *f*. **wrapping-paper** *n* papel de envolver *m*.

wreath [riːθ] *n* guirnalda *f*; (*funeral*) corona *f*. **wreathe** *v* enguirnaldar; (*wind*) enroscar.

wreck [rek] *n* (*ship*) naufragio *m*; (*train, car, plane*) restos *m pl*; (*accident*) accidente *m*; (*person*) ruina *f*. *v* (*ship*) hundir; (*building*) destruir; destrozar; (*hopes*) estropear. **wreckage** *n* restos *m pl*; (*building*) escombros *m pl*.

wren [ren] *n* reyezuelo *m*.

wrench [rentʃ] *n* (*tool*) llave inglesa *f*; (*pull*) tirón *m*; (*emotional*) dolor *m*. *v* arrancar; (*med*) torcer.

wrestle ['resl] *v* luchar con *or* contra. **wrestler** *n* luchador, -a *m*, *f*. **wrestling** *n* lucha *f*.

wretch [retʃ] *n* desgraciado, -a *m*, *f*; miserable *m*, *f*. **wretched** *adj* desgraciado; (*weather*) miserable; horrible.

wriggle ['rigl] *v* menear; agitar; (*fish*) colear. *n* meneo *m*; serpenteo *m*.

*wring [rin] *v* retorcer. **wringer** *n* escurridor *m*. **wringing wet** chorreando.

wrinkle ['riŋkl] *n* arruga *f*. *v* arrugar.

wrist [rist] *n* muñeca *f*.

writ [rit] *n* (*law*) orden *f*, mandato *m*. **issue a writ against someone** demandar a alguien en juicio.

*write [rait] *v* escribir; redactar. **writer** *n* escritor, -a *m*, *f*; autor, -a *m*, *f*. **writing** *n* el escribir *m*; (*handwriting*) escritura *f*; (*something written*) escrito *m*. **in writing** por escrito. **writing-pad** *n* bloc de papel de escribir *m*. **writing-paper** *n* papel de escribir *m*.

writhe [raið] *v* retorcerse; angustiarse.

wrong [ron] *adj* malo; mal; (*incorrect*) equivocado; impropio; falso; erróneo. **be wrong** tener la culpa; (*mistaken*) estar equivocado. *adv* mal. *n* mal *m*; error *m*; daño *m*; injusticia *f*. **wrongful** *adj* injusto; ilegal.

wrote [rout] *V* **write**.

wrought iron [ˌroɪt'aiən] *n* hierro forjado *m*.

wry [rai] *adj* torcido; doblado; (*smile*) forzado.

X

xenophobia *n* xenofobia *f*. **xenophobic** *adj* xenófobo.

Xerox ® *n* (*machine*) Xérox ® *m*, fotocopiadora *f*; (*copy*) xerografía *f*. *v* fotocopiar.

Xmas *V* **Christmas**.

X-ray *n* (*photo*) radiografía *f*. **X-rays** *pl n* rayos X *m pl*. *v* radiografiar.

xylophone *n* xilófono *m*.

Y

yacht *n* yate *m*. **yachting** *n* navegación a vela *f*.

yank *n* tirón *m*. *v* dar un tirón.

yap *n* ladrido *m*. *v* ladrar.

yard *n* patio *m*; (*site*) depósito *m*; (*repair*) taller *m*; (*rail*) estación *f*.

yarn *n* hilo *m*; (*tale*) cuento *m*.

yawn *v* bostezar; (*hole*) abrirse. *n* bostezo *m*.

year *n* año *m*. **yearbook** *n* anuario *m*. **yearly** *adj* anual.

yearn *v* anhelar, ansiar. **yearning** *n* anhelo *m*, ansia *f*.

yeast *n* levadura *f*; (*fig*) fermento *m*.

yell *n* grito *m*. *v* gritar.

yellow *nm*, *adj* amarillo. *v* volver amarillo.

yelp *n* gañido *m*. *v* gañir.

yes *nm*, *adv* sí.

yesterday *nm*, *adv* ayer. **the day before yesterday** anteayer.

yet *adv* todavía, aún; (*already*) ya. *conj* sin embargo, no obstante; (*but*) pero.

yew *n* tejo *m*.

yield *v* producir; entregar; dar; ceder; (*interest*) devengar. *n* producción *f*; (*crop*) cosecha *f*; (*interest*) rédito *m*.

yodel *n* canción tirolesa *f*. *v* cantar a la tirolesa.

yoga *n* yoga *m*.

yoghurt *n* yogur *m*.

yoke *n* (*animals*) yugo *m*; (*oxen*) yunta *f*; (*dress*) canesú *m*. *v* **yoke together** trabajar juntos.

yolk *n* yema *f*.

yonder *adv* allá, a lo lejos.

you *pron* (*subject: fam*) tú *sing*; (*subject: fam*) vosotros, vosotras *pl*; (*after prep*) ti; (*direct and indirect object*) te *sing*; (*direct and indirect object*) os *pl*; (*subject and after prep: polite*) usted, ustedes; (*direct object*) le, la; (*indirect object*) le; (*indirect object with direct object pron*) se *sing, pl.*

young *adj* joven. *pl n* (*people*) los jóvenes *m pl*; (*of an animal*) cría *f sing*. **youngster** *n* joven *m, f.*

your *adj* (*fam*) tu *sing*, vuestro *pl*; (*polite*) su, sus, de usted, de ustedes. **yours** *pron* (*fam*) el tuyo, la tuya, los tuyos, las tuyas, el vuestro, la vuestra, los vuestros, las vuestras; (*polite*) el suyo, la suya, el de usted, la de usted.

yourself *pron* (*fam*) tú mismo *m*, tú misma *f*; (*after prep*) ti *m, f*; (*polite*) usted mismo *m*, usted misma *f*. **by yourself** tú solo, usted solo. **yourselves** *pl pron* (*fam*) vosotros mismos *m pl*; vosotras mismas *f pl*; (*polite*) ustedes mismos *m pl*, ustedes mismas *f pl.*

youth *n* juventud *f*; (*boy*) joven *m*. **youth hostel** albergue de juventud *m.*

Yugogslavia [juɪgəˈslaɪvɪə] *n* Yugoslavia *f.*

Yugoslav *n, adj* yugoslavo, -a. **Yugoslavian** *n, adj* yugoslavo, -a.

Z

zany *adj* (*coll*) estrafalario.

zeal *n* celo *m*. **zealous** *adj* celoso.

zebra *n* cebra *f*. **zebra crossing** paso de peatones *m.*

zero *n* cero *m*. **zero hour** hora H *f*, momento decisivo *m.*

zest *n* ánimo *m*; brío *m*; sabor *m*. **zestful** *adj* animado; sabroso.

zigzag *n* zigzag *m*. *v* zigzaguear.

zinc *n* cinc *m*, zinc *m.*

zip *n* cremallera *f*. **zip code** (*US*) código postal *m*. *v* **zip up** subir la cremallera de.

zodiac *n* zodíaco *m.*

zone *n* zona *f*. *v* dividir en zonas.

zoo *n* zoo *m*, parque zoológico *m.*

zoology *n* zoología *f*. **zoological** *adj* zoológico. **zoologist** *n* zoólogo, -a *m, f.*

zoom *n* zumbido *m*. **zoom lens** zoom *m*. *v* zumbar. **zoom past** (*coll*) pasar zumbando.

Spanish—Inglés

A

a [a] *prep* to, at; on, in; by, by means of.
abacero [aβa'θero] *sm* grocer. **abacería** *sf* grocery.
abad [a'βaδ] *sm* abbot. **abadesa** *sf* abbess. **abadía** *sf* abbey.
abadejo [aβa'δexo] *sm* codfish.
abajo [a'βaxo] *adv* underneath, below, down. ¡**abajo** ... ! *interj* down with ... ! **de abajo** *adj* lower.
abalanzar [aβalan'θar] *v* balance; hurl. **abalanzarse a** rush at.
abandonar [aβando'nar] *v* abandon; leave. **abandonarse** *v* give way; lose heart. **abandonado** *adj* abandoned; slovenly. **abandono** *sm* abandonment; neglect.
abanicar [aβani'kar] *v* fan. **abanico** *sm* fan.
abarcar [aβar'kar] *v* take in; comprise; undertake.
abarrotar [aβarro'tar] *v* stow; fill up; overload.
*****abastecer** [aβaste'θer] *v* supply, provide with. **abastecimiento** *sm* supply. **abasto** *sm* supply of provisions.
abatir [aβa'tir] *v* knock down; kill; humble. **abatido** *adj* dejected; depressed; dismayed. **abatimiento** *sm* depression; discouragement.
abdicar [aβδi'kar] *v* abdicate. **abdicación** *sf* abdication.
abdomen [aβ'δomen] *sm* abdomen.
abedul [aβe'δul] *sm* birch-tree.
abeja [a'βexa] *sf* bee. **abeja machiega** honey bee.
aberración [aβerra'θjon] *sf* aberration.
abertura [aβer'tura] *sf* aperture, opening; gap.
abeto [a'βeto] *sm* fir.

abierto [a'βjerto] *adj* open; candid.
abigarrar [aβigar'rar] *v* variegate; fleck. **abigarrado** *adj* flecked; mottled; variegated.
abismo [a'βismo] *sm* abyss. **abismal** *adj* abysmal.
abjurar [aβxu'rar] *v* abjure, forswear. **abjuración** *sf* abjuration.
ablandar [aβlan'dar] *v* soften. **ablandarse** *v* mellow; relent.
*****abnegarse** [aβne'garse] *v* deny oneself; renounce.
abobado [aβo'βaδo] *adj* stupid, silly; stupefied.
abocarse [aβo'karse] *v* approach; meet by appointment.
abochornar [aβotʃor'nar] *v* overheat; (*fig*) shame. **abochornarse** *v* blush.
abofetear [aβofete'ar] *v* slap.
abogar [aβo'gar] *v* plead; advocate.
abolengo [aβo'lengo] *sm* ancestry; inheritance.
abolir [aβo'lir] *v* abolish.
abollar [aβo'ʎar] *v* dent. **abolladura** *sf* dent. **abollonar** *v* emboss.
abominar [aβomi'nar] *v* abominate. **abominable** *adj* abominable. **abominación** *sf* abomination.
abonar [aβo'nar] *v* guarantee; stand surety for; subscribe to; improve; (*agr*) manure. **abonado** *adj* safe; sure; trustworthy. *sm* subscriber; season-ticket holder. **abono** *sm* guarantee; subscription; fertilizer.
abordar [aβor'δar] *v* approach; (*mar*) board ship; (*mar*) put into port.
aborigen [aβo'rixen] *s(m+f)*, *adj* aborigine, aboriginal.
*****aborrecer** [aβorre'θer] *v* hate. **aborrecimiento** *sm* hatred.
abortar [aβor'tar] *v* abort. **aborto** *sm* (*med*) abortion; (*fig*) failure.

abotonar [aβoto'nar] *v* button up.

abovedado [aβoβe'ðaðo] *adj* arched. **abovedar** *v* arch.

abrasar [aβra'sar] *v* burn; dry up. **abrasarse (de, en)** *v* (*de, en amor*) burn with. **abrasivo** *adj* abrasive.

abrazar [aβra'θar] *v* embrace, hug. **abrazo** *sm* embrace.

abrelatas [aβre'latas] *sm invar* tin-opener.

abreviar [aβre'βjar] *v* abbreviate; speed up. **abreviatura** *sf* abbreviation.

abrigar [aβri'gar] *v* shelter; wrap up. **abrigo** *sm* shelter; overcoat.

abril [a'βril] *sm* April.

abrir [a'βrir] *v* open; extend; unfold; reveal.

abrochar [aβro'tʃar] *v* fasten; button.

abrogar [aβro'gar] *v* repeal. **abrogación** *sf* repeal.

abrumar [aβru'mar] *v* oppress; weigh down; overwhelm; annoy. **abrumarse** *v* become foggy. **abrumador** *adj* overwhelming; annoying.

abrupto [a'βrupto] *adj* rugged; steep; abrupt.

absceso [aβs'θeso] *sm* abscess.

ábside ['aβsiðe] *sm* apse.

absolución [aβsolu'θjon] *sf* (*rel*) absolution; (*jur*) acquittal.

absoluto [aβso'luto] *adj* absolute; complete; (*fig*) overbearing. **en absoluto** absolutely.

*absolver [aβsol'βer] *v* absolve; acquit.

absorber [aβsor'βer] *v* absorb. **absorbente** *adj* absorbent. **absorción** *sf* absorption. **absorto** *adj* absorbed; amazed.

abstemio [aβs'temjo] *adj* abstemious.

*abstenerse [aβste'nerse] *v* abstain. **abstinencia** *sf* abstinence.

abstracto [aβs'trakto] *adj* abstract. **abstracción** *sf* abstraction. ***abstraer** *v* abstract; refrain from; become thoughtful. **abstraer de** exclude; do without. **abstraído** *adj* retired; preoccupied; absent-minded.

absurdo [aβ'surðo] *adj* absurd.

abuelo [a'βuelo] *sm* grandfather. **abuela** *sf* grandmother.

abultar [aβul'tar] *v* enlarge; increase; be bulky. **abultado** *adj* bulky; exaggerated. **abultamiento** *sm* bulkiness; exaggeration.

abundar [aβun'dar] *v* abound. **abundancia** *sf* abundance. **abundante** *adj* abundant.

aburrir [aβur'rir] *v* bore; (*fam*) spend time/money; grow bored; grow weary.

aburrido *adj* boring; weary. **aburrimiento** *sm* boredom; wearisomeness.

abusar [aβu'sar] *v* abuse; impose upon; go too far. **abuso** *sm* abuse; misuse.

abyecto [a'βjecto] *adj* abject. **abyección** *sf* degradation; misery.

acá [a'ka] *adv* here; now. **acá y allá** here and there.

acabar [aka'βar] *v* end; complete; kill; be destroyed. **acabar de** have just. **acabarse** *v* run out. **acabado** *adj* finished; perfect. *sm* finish.

academia [aka'ðemja] *sf* academy. **académico** *adj* academic.

*acaecer [akae'θer] *v* happen. **acaecimiento** *sm* happening.

acalorar [akalo'rar] *v* make warm; (*fig*) excite. **acalorarse** *v* become heated. **acalorado** *adj* hot.

acallar [aka'ʎar] *v* quieten; silence; (*fig*) ease.

acampar [akam'par] *v* camp.

acantilado [akanti'laðo] *adj* steep; rocky. *sm* cliff.

acaparar [akapa'rar] *v* monopolize; hoard. **acaparador** *adj* monopolistic; (*fig*) acquisitive.

acariciar [akari'θjar] *v* caress, fondle, stroke; (*fig*) cherish. **acariciador** *adj* caressing.

acarrear [akarre'ar] *v* transport; carry; (*fig*) cause; bring about.

acaso [a'kaso] *sm* chance. *adv* perhaps. **por si acaso** just in case.

acatar [aka'tar] *v* respect; heed; observe. **acatable** *adj* worthy of respect. **acatador** *adj* respectful. **acatamiento** *sm* respect.

acaudalar [akauða'lar] *v* accumulate, hoard. **acaudalado** *adj* wealthy.

acaudillar [akauði'ʎar] *v* lead, command. **acaudillamiento** *sm* leadership.

acceder [akθe'ðer] *v* accede, consent. **acceder a** agree to. **accesión** *sf* agreement.

acceso [ak'θeso] *sm* access; (*med*) fit.

accidente [akθi'ðente] *sm* accident. **accidental** *adj* accidental.

acción [ak'θjon] *sf* action. **acciones** *s pl* shares *pl*, stock *sing*. **accionar** *v* work, actuate. **accionista** *s(m+f)* shareholder.

acebo [a'θeβo] *sm* holly.

acechar [aθe'tʃar] *v* spy on; watch; ambush; stalk. **acecho** *sm* observation; lying in wait.

aceite [a'θeite] *sm* oil. **aceite de motor** engine oil. **aceitoso** *adj* oily. **aceituna** *sf* olive.

acelerar [aθele'rar] *v* accelerate; quicken. **acelerarse** *v* hurry. **acelerador** *sm* accelerator.

acendrar [aθen'drar] *v* (*metales*) refine; (*fig*) purify.

acentuar [aθen'twar] *v* accentuate; stress. **acento** *sm* accent; stress.

aceptar [aθep'tar] *v* accept. **aceptable** *adj* acceptable, passable. **aceptación** *sf* acceptance.

acequia [a'θekja] *sf* irrigation ditch; drain.

acera [a'θera] *sf* pavement.

acerbo [a'θerβo] *adj* harsh; sharp; sour; (*fig*) severe.

acerar [aθe'rar] *v* harden with steel; strengthen; (*fig*) fortify.

acerca de [a'θerka ðe] *adv* about.

acercar [aθer'kar] *v* approach; bring near. **acercarse** *v* approach, draw near. **acercamiento** *sm* approach; approximation; reconciliation.

acero [a'θero] *sm* steel.

acérrimo [a'θerrimo] *adj* very strong; extremely tenacious; stalwart.

***acertar** [aθer'tar] *v* (*el blanco*) hit; guess; be right; find; succeed. **acertado** *adj* correct; apt.

acertijo [aθer'tixo] *sm* riddle.

aciago [a'θjago] *adj* unlucky; ill-fated.

acicalar [aθika'lar] *v* polish; bedeck; groom; (*fam*) spruce oneself up. **acicalado** *adj* spruce; dapper; polished. **acicaladura** *sf also* **acicalamiento** *sm* polishing; grooming; dressing up.

ácido ['aθiðo] *sm, adj* acid.

acierto [a'θjerto] *sm* success; good idea; skill.

aclamar [akla'mar] *v* acclaim; applaud. **aclamación** *sf* acclamation.

aclarar [akla'rar] *v* explain, clarify; (*color*) lighten; thin out; (*dudas*) remove; (*la ropa*) rinse. **aclaración** *sf* explanation. **aclarado** *sm* rinse.

aclimatizar [aklimati'θar] *v* acclimatize.

acné [ak'ne] *sm* acne.

acobardar [akoβar'ðar] *v* frighten; discourage.

acoger [ako'xer] *v* welcome; receive; shelter; accept. **acogerse** *v* take refuge. **acogedor** *adj* (*persona*) welcoming; (*ambiente*) friendly. **acogida** *sf* welcome.

acolchar [akol'tʃar] *v* pad; upholster; (*fig*) muffle. **acolchado** *adj* padded.

acólito [a'kolito] *sm* acolyte.

acometer [akome'ter] *v* attack; undertake; fill; occur to. **acometida** *sf* attack.

acomodar [akomo'ðar] *v* arrange; settle; accommodate; adjust; adapt; prepare; (*fig*) reconcile. **acomodación** *sf* arrangement; preparation. **acomodamente** *adv* conveniently; easily. **acomodadizo** *adj* accommodating; adaptable. **acomodado** *adj* convenient; prepared; well-to-do. **acomodador** *sm* usher. **acomodamiento** *sm* convenience; arrangement; preparation.

acompañar [akompa'ɲar] *v* accompany; escort. **acompañamiento** *sm* accompaniment; escort; (*cortejo*) funeral procession.

acondicionar [akondiθjo'nar] *v* set up; fix; prepare; improve. **acondicionarse** *v* condition oneself. **acondicionado** *adj* equipped. **aire acondicionado** air-conditioning.

acongojar [akongo'xar] *v* sadden; distress.

aconsejar [akonse'xar] *v* advise. **aconsejarse** *v* seek advice.

***acontecer** [akonte'θer] *v* happen. **acontecimiento** *sm* event.

acopiar [ako'pjar] *v* store; collect. **acopiamiento** *sm* stock.

acoplar [ako'plar] *v* fit; connect; couple; (*animales*) mate. **acoplarse** *v* become friends again. **acoplado** *adj* well-matched. **acoplamiento** *sm* connection; coordination.

acorazar [akora'θar] *v* armour. **acorazado** *adj* armoured; (*fig*) hardened.

***acordar** [akor'ðar] *v* agree; decide; remind. **acordarse** *v* remember; agree. **acordado** *adj* agreed to; wise.

acordeón [akorðe'on] *sm* accordion.

acordonar [akorðo'nar] *v* cordon off; (*los zapatos*) lace. **acordonado** *adj* cordoned off; ribbed.

acorralar [akorra'lar] *v* enclose; corner; round up.

acortar [akor'tar] *v* shorten; reduce. **acortarse** *v* become shorter; (*intimidarse*) be shy. **acortamiento** *sm* shortening; reduction.

acosar [ako'sar] *v* hound; pursue; harass; pester. **acoso** *sm* pursuit.

*acostar [akos'tar] *v* lay down; put to bed. **acostarse** *v* lie down; go to bed.

acostumbrar [akostum'brar] *v* accustom; be in the habit of. **acostumbrarse a** *v* become used to. **acostumbrado** *adj* usual.

acotar [ako'tar] *v* (*terreno*) demarcate; enclose; delimit; outline; accept. **acotado** *adj* enclosed. **acotamiento** *sm* demarcation; boundary mark; outline.

acre[1] ['akre] *adj* acrid; bitter.

acre[2] ['akre] *sm* acre.

*acrecentar [akreθen'tar] *v* increase. **acrecentamiento** *sm* increase; growth.

acreditar [akreði'tar] *v* accredit; prove; vouch for; authorize; (*com*) credit. **acreditado** *adj* reputable.

acreedor [akree'ðor] *s(m+f)* creditor. *adj* worthy.

acribillar [akriβi'ʎar] *v* riddle with holes.

acróbata [a'kroβata] *s(m+f)* acrobat.

acta ['akta] *sf* minutes of a meeting; official document.

actitud [akti'tud] *sf* posture, attitude.

activar [akti'βar] *v* speed up; stimulate; (*quim*) activate. **actividad** *sf* activity.

activo [ak'tiβo] *adj* active. *sm* (*com*) assets *pl.*

acto ['akto] *n* act, deed; ceremony; (*teatro*) act. **salón de actos** *sm* assembly hall. **actor** *sm* actor. **actriz** *sf* actress. **actual** *adj* present; topical; of this month. **actualmente** *adv* at present; nowadays.

actuar [ak'twar] *v* act; perform; behave. **actuación** *sf* action; performance; conduct. **actuario** *sm* (*jur*) clerk of the court.

acuarela [akwa'rela] *sf* watercolour.

acuario [a'kwario] *sm* aquarium.

acuático [a'kwatiko] *adj* aquatic.

acuciar [aku'θjar] *v* urge; pester; (*anhelar*) long for. **acucioso** *adj* urgent; diligent; desirous.

acuclillarse [akukʎi'ʎarse] *v* crouch, squat.

acuchillar [akutʃi'ʎar] *v* knife, stab, hack. **acuchillado** *adj* knifed; (*fig*) experienced.

acudir [aku'ðir] *v* come; go; (*a una cita*) keep; answer; attend; help; (*al médico*) consult.

acueducto [akwe'ðukto] *sm* aqueduct.

acuerdo [a'kwerðo] *sm* agreement. **¡de acuerdo!** O.K.! **ponerse de acuerdo** come to an agreement.

acumular [akumu'lar] *v* accumulate; pile; store. **acumulación** *sf* accumulation.

acuñar [aku'ɲar] *v* (*monedas*) mint; (*poner cuñas*) wedge.

acuoso [aku'oso] *adj* watery. **acuosidad** *sf* wateriness.

acurrucarse [akurru'karse] *v* curl up.

acusar [aku'sar] *v* (*jur*) accuse; charge; blame; denounce; reveal; (*com*) acknowledge. **acusación** *sf* accusation. **acusado** *sm* (*jur*) defendant.

acústico [a'kustiko] *adj* acoustic. **acústica** *sf* acoustics.

achacar [atʃa'kar] *v* attribute.

achatar [atʃa'tar] *v* flatten.

achicar [atʃi'kar] *v* reduce; (*mar*) bale; (*fig*) humiliate. **achicado** *adj* childish.

achicoria [atʃi'korja] *sf* chicory.

achicharrar [atʃitʃar'rar] *v* burn; (*molestar*) annoy. **achicharradero** *sm* furnace.

achispado [atʃis'paðo] *adj* tipsy. **achispar** *v* make tipsy.

adalid [aða'lið] *sm* leader.

adaptar [aðap'tar] *v* adapt; adjust. **adaptabilidad** *sf* adaptability. **adaptable** *adj* adaptable. **adaptación** *sf* adaptation; (*tecn*) fitting.

adecuado [aðe'kwaðo] *adj* adequate; suitable.

adefesio [aðe'fesjo] (*fam*) *sm* nonsense; (*traje*) ridiculous garment; (*persona*) ridiculously dressed person.

adelantar [aðelan'tar] *v* advance; (*reloj*) put forward; speed up; gain; (*auto*) overtake. **prohibido adelantar** no overtaking. **adelantarse** *v* go forward. **adelantado** *adj* advanced. **adelantamiento** *sm* also **adelanto** advance. **adelante** *adv* ahead, forward. **¡adelante!** come in! **de hoy en adelante** in future.

adelgazar [aðelga'θar] *v* make thin; slim. **adelgazador** *adj* slimming. **adelgazamiento** *sm* slimming. **régimen de adelgazamiento** diet.

ademán [aðe'man] *sm* expression; gesture. **ademanes** *s pl* manners.

además [aðe'mas] *adv* besides, furthermore. **además de** as well as.

adentro [a'ðentro] *adv* within, inside. **¡adentro!** come in! **mar adentro** out to sea. **tierra adentro** inland.

adepto [a'ðepto] *s(m+f)* adept; supporter.

adestrar *V* adiestrar.

aderezar [aðere'θar] *v* adorn; (*culin*) prepare; guide. **aderezo** *sm* adornment; cooking; seasoning; (*de ensalada*) dressing.

adeudar [aðeu'ðar] *v* owe; (*com*) charge; run into debt. **adeudado** *adj* owing; (*persona*) in debt. **adeudo** *sm* (*deuda*) debt; (*com*) charge.

***adherir** [aðe'rir] *v* adhere, stick. **adherirse** adhere to. **adherencia** *sf* (*acción de pegar*) adherence. **adhesión** *sf* adhesion; (*apoyo*) support. **adhesivo** *sm*, *adj* adhesive.

adición [aði'θyon] *sf* addition. **adicional** *adj* additional. **adicionar** *v* add.

adicto [a'ðikto] *adj* devoted. *s(m+f)* supporter; addict.

adiestrar [aðjes'trar] *v* train, teach. **adiestrador, -a** *sm*, *sf* trainer. **adiestramiento** *sm* training.

adinerado [aðine'raðo] *adj* wealthy. **adinerado, -a** *sm*, *sf* rich person. **adinerarse** *v* (*fam*) make one's fortune.

adiós [a'ðjos] *interj*, *sm* goodbye.

adivinar [aðiβi'nar] *v* foretell; guess; (*el pensamiento*) read. **adivinable** *adj* foreseeable. **adivinación** *sf also* **adivinamiento** *sm* divination; guessing. **adivinador, -a** *sm*, *sf* fortune-teller.

adjetivo [aðxe'tiβo] *sm* adjective.

adjudicar [aðxuði'kar] *v* award; adjudicate.

adjuntar [aðxun'tar] *v* attach; enclose; give.

adjunto [að'xunto] *adj* attached; enclosed. *sm* assistant.

administrar [aðminis'trar] *v* administer, control; (*fam*) hand out. **administración** *sf* administration. **administrativo** *adj* administrative.

admirar [aðmi'rar] *v* admire. **admirarse** *v* surprise, astonish. **admirable** *adj* admirable. **admiración** *sf* admiration.

admirador [að'miraðor], **-a** *sm*, *sf* admirer. *adj* admiring.

admitir [aðmi'tir] *v* admit; accept; allow; acknowledge. **admisible** *adj* admissible. acceptable. **admisión** *sf* admission; acceptance.

adobar [aðo'βar] *v* pickle; season; cook.

***adolecer** [aðole'θer] *v* fall ill. **adolecer de** suffer from.

adolescencia [aðoles'θenθja] *sf* adolescence. **adolescente** *s(m+f)*, *adj* adolescent.

adonde ['aðonde] *adv* where. **¿adónde?** where?

adoptar [aðop'tar] *v* adopt; assume. **adopción** *sf* adoption. **adoptivo** *adj* adoptive.

adoquín [aðo'kin] *sm* paving-stone; (*fam*) dunce. **adoquinar** *v* pave.

adorar [aðo'rar] *v* adore; worship; pray. **adorable** *adj* adorable. **adoración** *sf* adoration; worship.

***adormecer** [aðorme'θer] *v* make sleepy. **adormecerse** fall asleep. **adormecerse en** give oneself up to.

adormidera [aðormi'ðera] *sf* poppy.

adornar [aðor'nar] *v* adorn, decorate; (*trajes*) trim; (*coc*) garnish; (*fig*) embellish. **adornarse** *v* dress up. **adorno** *sm* decoration; trimming; garnish.

***adquirir** [aðki'rir] *v* acquire, obtain. **adquisición** *sf* acquisition; (*compra*) purchase. **adquisitivo** *adj* acquisitive.

adrede [að'rede] *adv* on purpose.

adscribir [aðskri'βir] *v* attribute, ascribe; assign. **adscripción** *sf* attribution; assignment. **adscripto** *adj* attributed; assigned.

aduana [a'ðwana] *sf* customs *pl*. **derechos de aduana** *sm pl* customs duty *sing*. **aduanero** *sm* customs officer.

***aducir** [aðu'θir] *v* (*razones*) allege; (*un texto*) quote; (*pruebas*) offer as proof.

adueñarse [aðwe'narse] *v* appropriate.

adular [aðu'lar] *v* flatter. **adulación** *sf* flattery.

adulterar [aðulte'rar] *v* adulterate; commit adultery. **adulterio** *sm* adultery. **adúltero, -a** *sm*, *sf* adulterer, adulteress.

adulto [a'ðulto], **-a** *s*, *adj* adult.

adusto [a'ðusto] *adj* very hot; (*fig*) harsh.

advenedizo [aðβene'ðiθo], **-a** *s*, *adj* upstart.

advenimiento [aðβeni'mjento] *sm* advent; coming.

adverbio [að'βerβjo] *sm* adverb.

adversario [aðβer'sarjo] *sm* adversary. **adversidad** *sf* adversity. **adverso** *adj* adverse; opposing.

***advertir** [aðβer'tir] *v* warn; recommend; (*señalar*) point out; tell; (*comprender*) realize. **advertido** *adj* informed; experienced. **advertencia** *sf also* **advertimiento** *sm* warning.

adyacente [aðja'θente] *adj* adjacent.

aéreo [a'ereo] *adj* aerial.

aerodinámica [aeroði'namika] *sf* aerodynamics. **aerodinámico** *adj* aerodynamic.

aeronáutica [aero'nautika] *sf* aeronautics. **aeronáutico** *adj* aeronautical.

aeroplano [aero'plano] *sm* aeroplane.

aeropuerto [aero'pwerto] *sm* airport.
aerosol [aero'sol] *sm* aerosol.
afable [a'faβle] *adj* pleasant; genial.
afabilidad *sf* affability.
afamado [afa'maðo] *adj* famous.
afán [a'fan] *sm* (*trabajo penoso*) toil; (*deseo*) desire; (*entusiasmo*) zeal; (*preocupación*) anxiety. **afanador** *adj* enthusiastic. **afanar** *v* work hard; (*fig: robar*) steal. **afanarse** *v* exert oneself. **afanoso** *adj* laborious; hectic.
afección [afek'θjon] *sf* (*cariño*) affection; (*med*) complaint. **afeccionarse** *v* grow fond.
afectar [afek'tar] *v* affect; pretend; adopt; (*atañer*) concern; (*dañar*) damage. **afectado** *adj* spoiled; unnatural; upset.
afecto [a'fekto] *adj* dear. **afecto a** fond of. *sm* affection.
afeitar [afei'tar] *v* shave. **afeitarse** *v* shave; make up one's face. **afeite** *sm* make-up, cosmetics *pl*.
afeminado [afemi'naðo] *adj* effeminate. *sm* effeminate person.
***aferrar** [afer'rar] *v* seize; (*mar*) moor. **aferrarse** *v* cling.
afianzar [afjan'θar] *v* reinforce; establish; restore; guarantee; seize; support. **afianzarse** *v* steady oneself; become strong. **afianzamiento** *sm* surety; guarantee; establishment.
afición [afi'θjon] *sf* inclination; fondness; (*interés*) hobby. **la afición** *sf* the fans *pl*.
aficionado [afiθjo'naðo], **-a** *sm*, *sf* fan. *adj* amateur; keen.
afilar [afi'lar] *v* sharpen; grind. **afilado** *adj* sharp. **afilador** *sm* (*persona*) knife-grinder; (*correa*) strop. **afilamiento** *sm* (*la nariz*) pointedness; (*los dedos*) slenderness.
afiliar [afi'ljar] *v* affiliate. **afiliación** *sf* affiliation.
afín [a'fin] *adj* adjacent; similar; related. **afinidad** *sf* similarity, affinity.
afinar [afi'nar] *v* polish; perfect; (*música*) tune. **afinarse** *v* become slimmer. **afinadura** *sf also* **afinamiento** *sm* tuning; (*fig*) refinement.
afirmar [afir'mar] *v* affirm; strengthen. **afirmarse** *v* steady oneself. **afirmación** *sf* statement; strengthening. **afirmativo** *adj* affirmative.
aflicción [aflik'θjon] *sf* affliction, grief. **afligido** *adj* distressed; (*por una muerte*) bereaved. **afligir** *v* grieve; distress; afflict.

aflojar [aflo'xar] *v* loosen, slacken; relax; (*fiebre*) abate; (*fam*) fork out, cough up.
aflojamiento *sm* loosening, slackening; abatement; relaxation.
afluencia [aflu'enθja] *sf* crowd; (*tropel*) rush; influx; abundance.
***afluir** [aflu'ir] *v* flow.
afónico [af'oniko] *adj* hoarse, voiceless. **afonía** *sf* loss of voice.
***aforar** [afo'rar] *v* gauge, measure; appraise. **aforo** *sm* measurement; appraisal.
aforrar [afor'rar] *v* (*ropa, etc.*) line. **aforrarse** *v* wrap oneself up.
afortunado [afortu'naðo] *adj* fortunate, happy.
afrenta [a'frenta] *sf* insult; disgrace. **afrentar** *v* insult. **afrentarse** *v* be ashamed. **afrentador** *adj also* **afrentoso** insulting; offensive.
África ['afrika] *sf* Africa. **africano, -a** *s*, *adj* African.
afrontar [afron'tar] *v* confront; bring face to face. **afrontamiento** *sm* confrontation.
afuera [a'fwera] *adv* out, outside. ¡**afuera**! get out! **afueras** *s pl* suburbs *pl*.
agachar [aga'tʃar] *v* lower, bend. **agacharse** *v* bend over; crouch; (*para evitar algo*) duck. **agachada** *sf* (*fam*) trick.
agalla [a'gaʎa] *sf* gill; (*fam*) pluck. **agallas** *s pl* tonsils *pl*.
agarrar [agar'rar] *v* seize, clutch; (*comprender*) grasp; get; take; win; (*fam*) stick. **agarro** *sm* hold, grasp. **agarradero** *sm* handle.
agarrotar [agarro'tar] *v* tighten; strangle. **agarrotarse** *v* (*motor*) seize up; (*músculo*) go numb. **agarrotado** *adj* bound; stiff; seized up.
agasajar [agasa'xar] *v* welcome warmly; entertain. **agasajo** *sm* gift; welcome. **agasajos** *sm pl* hospitality *sing*.
agazapar [agaθa'par] *v* (*fam*) nab, catch. **agazaparse** *v* crouch; duck.
agencia [a'xenθja] *sf* agency; office. **agencia de prensa** news agency. **agencia de turismo** *or* **viajes** travel agency. **agenciar** *v* get; (*fam*) wangle. **agente** *sm* agent; policeman. **agente de bolsa** stockbroker. **agente inmobiliario** estate agent.
agenda [a'xenda] *sf* diary.
ágil ['axil] *adj* agile. **agilidad** *sf* agility.
agitar [axi'tar] *v* wave; shake; upset; stir up. **agitarse** *v* sway; fidget. **agitación** *sf* waving; shaking; movement; excitement.

agitado *adj* agitated; rough. **agitador, -a** *sm*, *sf* agitator.

aglomerar [aglome'rar] *v* form a crowd; amass. **aglomeración** *sf* mass. **aglomeración de tráfico** traffic jam.

agobiar [ago'βjar] *v* weigh down; overwhelm; humiliate; depress. **agobiado** *v* bent down; overwhelmed; exhausted. **agobio** *sm* burden.

agolparse [agol'parse] *v* crowd together; amass. **agolpamiento** *sm* crowd; (*cosas*) pile.

agonía [ago'nia] *sf* (*muerte*) death; desire; agony. **agonizar** *v* be dying; suffer; annoy.

***agorar** [ago'rar] *v* predict. **agorero, -a** *sm*, *sf* fortune-teller.

agosto [a'gosto] *sm* August.

agotar [ago'tar] *v* drain; exhaust. **agotador** *adj* exhausting. **agotamiento** *sm* exhaustion.

agraciar [agra'θjar] *v* adorn; award; pardon. **agraciado** *adj* pretty; graceful.

agradar [agra'ðar] *v* please. **agradable** *adj* pleasant.

***agradecer** [agraðe'θer] *v* thank; be grateful for; be welcome. **agradecido** *adj* grateful. ¡**muy agradecido!** much obliged! **agradecimiento** *sm* gratitude.

agrado [agra'ðo] *sm* pleasure; liking.

agrandar [agran'ðar] *v* make larger; exaggerate. **agrandamiento** *sm* enlargement.

agravar [agra'βar] *v* aggravate; worsen. **agravación** *sf* also **agravamiento** *sm* aggravation. **agravante** *adj* aggravating.

agraviar [agra'βjar] *v* offend; insult; wrong; take offence. **agravio** *sm* insult; affront; wrong.

***agredir** [agre'ðir] *v* assault.

agregado [agre'gaðo] *sm* aggregate; assistant; attaché; addition. **agregar** join; incorporate. **agregarse** *v* be added; be incorporated.

agricultura [agrikul'tura] *sf* agriculture. **agrícola** *adj* agricultural.

agrietar [agrje'tar] *v* crack; chap.

agrio ['agrjo] *adj* sour; (*carácter*) bitter. *sm* (*sabor*) sourness.

agrupar [agru'par] *v* group; gather together. **agruparse** *v* come together.

agua [a'gwa] *sf* water. **agua abajo/arriba** down-/upstream. **agua dulce** fresh water. **entre dos aguas** sitting on the fence. **hacer agua** leak. **irse al agua** fall through.

aguacate [agwa'kate] *sm* avocado pear.

aguacero [agwa'θero] *sm* shower, downpour.

aguantar [agwan'tar] *v* tolerate, bear; (*sostener*) support; (*esperar*) wait, await; (*durar*) last. **aguante** *sm* patience; endurance.

aguar [a'gwar] *v* dilute; spoil. **aguarse** be ruined. **aguado** *adj* watered down.

aguardar [agwar'ðar] *v* wait for.

aguardiente [agwar'ðjente] *sm* liquor.

aguarrás [agwar'ras] *sm* turpentine.

aguazal [agwa'θal] *sm* mire.

agudeza [agu'deθa] *sf* (*de los sentidos*) sharpness; (*del dolor*) acuteness; (*ingenio*) wit. **agudizar** *v* sharpen; worsen. **agudo** *adj* sharp; acute; witty.

agüero [a'gwero] *sm* omen. **de buen agüero** lucky.

aguijar [agi'xar] *v* goad; hurry. **aguijón** *sm* (*de un insecto*) sting; stimulus. **aguijonada** *sf* sting; prick. **aguijonear** *v* goad; spur on.

águila ['agila] *sf* eagle. **águila ratonera** buzzard.

aguinaldo [agi'nalðo] *sm* Christmas present.

aguja [a'guxa] *sf* needle; (*reloj*) hand; (*arq*) spire. **agujas** *s pl* points *pl*.

agujero [agu'xero] *sm* hole; (*alfiletero*) pincushion.

agujetas [agu'xetas] *sf pl* stiffness *sing*. **lleno de agujetas** stiff all over.

aguzar [agu'θar] *v* sharpen; (*estimular*) encourage; (*el apetito*) whet. **aguzado** *adj* sharp; sharpened. **aguzador** *adj* sharpening.

ahí [a'i] *adv* there. **de ahí** thus, so. **por ahí** that way; thereabouts. ¡**ahí es nada!** fancy that!

ahijada [ai'xaða] *sf* goddaughter; protégée. **ahijado** *sm* godson; protégé.

ahincar [ain'kar] *v* urge. **ahincarse** *v* hurry. **ahincadamente** *adv* tenaciously. **ahincado** *adj* insistent; eager. **ahínco** *sm* effort.

ahogar [ao'gar] *v* drown; flood; stifle; overwhelm. **ahogarse** *v* drown, be drowned. **ahogadero** *sm* Turkish bath. **ahogado** *adj* drowned; (*por el gas*) asphyxiated; strangled; (*grito*) muffled. **ahogador** *adj* suffocating. **ahogo** *sm* breathlessness; (*angustia*) distress.

ahora [a'ora] *adv* now. *conj* now, now then. **ahora bien** come now. **ahora mismo** right away.

ahorcar [aor'kar] *v* hang. **ahorcarse** *v* hang oneself. **ahorcadura** *sf* hanging.

ahorrar [aor'rar] *v* save; free; avoid. **ahorrador** *adj* thrifty. **ahorro** *sm* saving; thrift.

ahuecar [awe'kar] *v* hollow. **¡ahueca!** (*fam*) scram!

ahumar [au'mar] *v* (*culin*) smoke; (*llenar de humo*) fill with smoke. **ahumarse** *v* taste smoky; (*fam: emborracharse*) become tipsy. **ahumado** *adj* smoky; smoked; (*fam*) tipsy.

ahuyentar [aujen'tar] *v* frighten off; keep at bay; (*fig*) dismiss. **ahuyentarse** *v* flee.

airado [ai'raðo] *adj* vexed; immoral.

aire ['aire] *sm* air; (*parecido*) likeness; (*aspecto*) appearance; (*porte*) bearing; (*música*) time; (*auto: estrangulador*) choke. **hace aire** it's windy. **aire acondicionado** air conditioning. **aireación** *sf* ventilation. **airear** *v* ventilate. **airoso** *adj* ventilated; windy; (*fig*) graceful.

aislar [ai'slar] *v* isolate; (*elec*) insulate. **aislado** *adj* alone; remote; insulated. **aislador** *adj* insulating. **cinta aisladora** *sf* insulating tape. **aislamiento** *sm* isolation; insulation.

ajar [a'xar] *v* crumple; wrinkle; fade; (*fig*) age.

ajedrez [axe'ðreθ] *sm* chess.

ajeno [a'xeno] *adj* of other people; alien; free; detached; irrelevant.

ajetreo [axe'treo] *sm* rush; activity; bustle; exhaustion. **ajetreado** *adj* busy. **ajetrearse** *v* be busy; rush; exhaust oneself.

ajo ['axo] *sm* garlic. **ajo cebollino** chive. **ajo porro** leek. **diente de ajo** clove of garlic. **soltar ajos** swear.

ajuar [a'xwar] *sm* (*de novia*) trousseau; (*de casa*) furnishings *pl*.

ajustar [axus'tar] *v* adjust; arrange; tighten. **ajuste** *sm* adjustment; fitting.

ajusticiar [axusti'θjar] *v* execute.

al [al] *contraction of* **a** **el**.

ala ['ala] *sf* wing; hat brim.

alabar [ala'βar] *v* praise. **alabarse** *v* (*jactarse*) boast. **alabanza** *sf* praise.

alabastro [ala'βastro] *sm* alabaster.

alacena [ala'θena] *sf* larder; cupboard.

alacrán [ala'kran] *sm* scorpion.

alambicar [alambi'kar] *v* distil; complicate; (*precio*) minimize. **alambicado** *adj* elaborate; (*estilo*) subtle; affected; minimized. **alambique** *sm* still. **pasar algo por**

el **alambique** examine something very carefully.

alambre [a'lambre] *sm* wire. **alambrada** *sf* (*de la guerra*) barbed wire; (*reja*) wire netting.

alameda [ala'meða] *sf* (*avenida*) tree-lined walk; (*de álamos*) poplar grove.

álamo ['alamo] *sm* poplar. **álamo temblón** aspen.

alano [a'lano] *sm* mastiff.

alarde [a'larðe] *sm* parade; display. **alardear** *v* boast. **alardeo** *sm* boasting.

alargar [alar'gar] *v* lengthen, increase, enlarge; (*posponer*) defer; (*dar*) reach, hand; (*la mano*) stretch. **alargarse** *v* get longer. **alargado** *adj* elongated. **alargamiento** *sm* lengthening; extension.

alarido [ala'riðo] *sm* yell, shriek.

alarmar [alar'mar] *v* alarm; alert. **alarmarse** *v* be frightened. **alarma** *sf* alarm.

alba ['alβa] *sf* dawn.

albañil [alβa'ɲil] *sm* bricklayer.

albaricoque [alβari'koke] *sm* apricot.

albatros [alβa'tros] *sm* albatross.

albedrío [alβe'ðrio] *sm* will; (*capricho*) whim; custom. **libre albedrío** free will.

albergar [alβer'gar] *v* shelter; accommodate; (*fig*) cherish. **albergue** *sm* lodgings *pl*; (*refugio*) shelter; (*posada*) hostel.

albóndiga [al'βondiga] *sf* rissole.

albor [al'βor] *sm* dawn; (*blancura*) whiteness.

albornoz [alβor'noθ] *sm* bathrobe.

alborotar [alβoro'tar] *v* make a noise; disturb. **alborotarse** *v* (*perturbarse*) become upset; get excited; (*una muchedumbre*) riot. **alborotado** *adj* excited; (*fig*) eventful. **alborotador** *adj* noisy; rebellious. **alboroto** *sm* disturbance, uproar.

alborozar [alβoro'θar] *v* gladden; produce laughter. **alborozarse** *v* rejoice. **alborozado** *adj* overjoyed.

álbum ['alβum] *sm* album.

alcachofa [alka'tʃofa] *sf* artichoke.

alcahuete [alka'wete] *sm* pimp; (*chismoso*) gossip. **alcahueta** *sf* procuress; gossip.

alcalde [al'kalðe] *sm* mayor. **alcaldesa** *sf* mayoress. **alcaldía** *sf* mayorship; (*oficina*) mayor's office.

alcance [al'kanθe] *sm* reach; (*sonido, arma de fuego, etc.*) range; scope; importance. **al alcance** within reach. **dar alcance a** catch up with. **alcanzar** *v*

reach; catch up; understand; hit; affect;
succeed; be enough; (durar) last.

alcantarilla [alkanta'riʎa] sf sewer; drain.

alcázar [al'kaθar] sm palace; fortress;
(mar) quarterdeck.

alcoba [al'koβa] sf bedroom.

alcohol [alko'ol] sm alcohol. **alcohólico, -a**
s, adj alcoholic.

alcornoque [alkor'noke] sm cork tree;
(fig) nitwit.

aldaba [al'ðaβa] sf door knocker; (pestillo) latch, bolt. **tener buenas aldabas**
(fam) have influential friends.

aldea [al'ðea] sf village.

aleación [alea'θjon] sf alloy.

alegar [ale'gar] v allege; state; emphasize;
quote; (jur) plead, claim. **alegato** sm declaration; plea.

alegoría [alego'ria] sf allegory. **alegórico**
adj allegorical.

alegrar [ale'grar] v gladden; make merry;
be pleasing to; excite. **alegrarse** v be
happy; (fam) become tipsy. **alegre** adj
happy; bright; good; (fam) tipsy;
(atrevido) daring. **alegría** sf joy; happiness. **¡qué alegría!** great!

alejar [ale'xar] v move away; keep away;
avert. **alejarse** v go away. **alejado** adj far
away; aloof. **alejamiento** sm removal;
absence.

Alemania [ale'manja] sf Germany.
alemán, -ana sm, sf German (person).
alemán sm (idioma) German (language).

***alentar** [alen'tar] v breathe; (fig) glow;
(animar) encourage. **alentado** adj
encouraged; (orgulloso) proud; (valiente)
brave. **alentador** adj encouraging.

alerce [a'lerθe] sm larch.

alergia [a'lerxja] sf allergy. **alérgico** adj
allergic.

alero [a'lero] sm eaves pl. **estar en el alero**
hang in the balance.

alerta [a'lerta] sm alert. adv on the alert.
¡alerta! look out! **alertar** v alert, warn.
alerto adj alert.

aleta [a'leta] sf (peces) fin; (foca) flipper.

aleve [a'leβe] adj also **alevoso** treacherous.
alevosía sf treachery. **alevoso, -a** sm, sf
traitor.

alfabeto [alfa'βeto] sm alphabet. **alfabético** adj alphabetical. **por orden alfabético**
in alphabetical order. **alfabetizado** adj literate.

alfarero [alfa'rero] sm potter. **alfarería** sf
pottery (art and workshop).

alférez [al'fereθ] sm (mil) second lieutenant.

alfil [al'fil] sm (ajedrez) bishop.

alfiler [alfi'ler] sm pin; brooch. **alfiler de
la ropa** clothes-peg. **alfilerar** v pin. **alfiler-
azo** sm pinprick.

alfombra [al'fombra] sf carpet; rug.
alfombrar v carpet.

alforja [al'forxa] sf rucksack.

alga ['alga] sf seaweed.

algarabía [algara'βia] sf Arabic; (fig) gibberish; (ruido) noise, row.

algazara [alga'θara] sf hubbub, uproar.

álgebra ['alxebra] sf algebra. **algebráico**
adj also **algébrico** algebraic.

álgido ['alxiðo] adj icy cold; (fig) decisive.

algo ['algo] pron something; anything. adv
rather, quite. sm something; (comida)
snack.

algodón [algo'ðon] sm cotton. **algodón
hidrófilo** cotton wool.

alguacil [algwa'θil] sm sheriff; city governor.

alguien ['algjen] pron someone, somebody; (interrog) anybody.

algún [al'gun] adj some, any. **algún tanto**
a little.

alguno [al'guno] adj some, any. pron one,
some; someone. **algunos ms pl** some, a
few.

alhaja [al'axa] sf jewel; treasure.

alhelí [ale'li] sm, pl -líes wallflower.

alheña [a'leɲa] sf privet; blight, mildew.
alheñar v (secarse) wither; become
mildewed.

alhucema [alu'θema] sf lavender.

aliaga [ali'aga] sf gorse.

aliar [ali'ar] v ally. **aliado, -a** sm, sf ally.
alianza sf alliance.

alicaído [alika'iðo] adj depressed; weak.

alicates [ali'kates] sm pl pliers, pincers pl.

aliciente [ali'θjente] sm lure; interest;
encouragement.

alienar [alje'nar] v alienate. **alienación** sf
alienation. **alienado** adj insane.

aliento [a'ljento] sm breath; (fig) courage.
cobrar aliento catch one's breath.

aligerar [alixe'rar] v lighten; shorten; alleviate. **aligerarse** v get a move on.

alimentar [alimen'tar] v feed; supply;
(promover) foster. **alimentación** sf food;
feeding. **alimenticio** adj nourishing.
alimento sm food.

alinear [aline'ar] *v* line up. **alinearse en** join. **alineación** *sf also* **alineamiento** *sm* alignment.

aliñar [ali'ɲar] *v* adorn; (*culin*) season; prepare. **aliño** *sm* adornment; seasoning; preparation.

alisar [ali'sar] *v* smooth; polish; level. **alisaduras** *sf pl* shavings *pl*.

alistar [alis'tar] *v* list; recruit; prepare. **alistado** *adj* enlisted. **alistamiento** *sm* enlistment.

aliviar [ali'βjar] *v* lighten; alleviate; help; console. **aliviarse** *v* feel better, recover. **alivio** *sm* lightening; relief. **... de alivio** (*fam*) a hell of a ....

alma ['alma] *sf* soul; spirit; person. **con el alma en la boca** at death's door.

almacén [alma'θen] *sm* warehouse; department store. **almacenaje** *sm* storage. **almacenero** *sm* storekeeper.

almanaque [alma'nake] *sm* almanac; diary.

almeja [al'mexa] *sf* clam.

almendra [al'mendra] *sf* almond. **almendro** *sm* almond tree.

almiar [al'mjar] *sm* haystack.

almíbar [al'miβar] *sm* syrup.

almidón [almi'ðon] *sm* starch.

almirante [almi'rante] *sm* admiral. **almirantazgo** *sm* admiralty.

almohada [almo'aða] *sf* pillow; cushion; (*funda*) pillowslip.

almoneda [almo'neða] *sf* auction; (*a bajo precio*) clearance sale.

almorranas [almor'ranas] *sf pl* haemorrhoids *pl*, piles *pl*.

***almorzar** [almor'θar] *v* lunch. **almuerzo** *sm* lunch.

alojar [alo'xar] *v* lodge, accommodate. **alojarse** *v* put up, stay. **alojamiento** *sm* accommodation, lodgings *pl*.

alondra [a'londra] *sf* lark.

alpargata [alpar'gata] *sf* rope-soled shoe. **alpargatería** *sf* shoe factory *or* shop.

Alpes ['alpes] *sm pl* Alps *pl*.

alpinismo [alpi'nismo] *sm* mountaineering. **alpinista** *s(m+f)* climber.

alpiste [al'piste] *sm* canary seed; (*fam*) drink; (*fam*) money.

alquería [alke'ria] *sf* farm; (*aldea*) village.

alquilar [alki'lar] *v* rent; hire; charter. **alquilarse** *v* be for hire; to be let. **se alquila** (*casa*) to rent; (*coche*) for hire. **alquiler** *sm* renting; letting; hiring.

alquileres *sm pl* rent *sing*. **exento de alquiler** rent-free.

alquimia [al'kimja] *sf* alchemy.

alquitrán [alki'tran] *sm* tar. **alquitranado** *adj* tarred.

alrededor [alreðe'ðor] *adv* round, around. **alrededor de** about, around. **alrededores** *sm pl* environs *pl*, outskirts *pl*.

alta ['alta] *sf* (*del hospital*) discharge; (*ingreso*) enrolment. **dar de alta** pass as fit. **darse de alta** enrol.

altanero [alta'nero] *adj* haughty, arrogant.

altar [al'tar] *sm* altar.

altavoz [alta'βoθ] *sm* loudspeaker.

alterar [alte'rar] *v* change, alter; disturb; (*estropear*) spoil. **alterarse** *v* go sour; change; be disturbed; get excited. **alteración** *sf* alteration; (*altercado*) quarrel.

altercar [alter'kar] *v* argue, quarrel. **altercación** *sf* argument, quarrel.

alternar [alter'nar] *v* alternate; be sociable. **alterno** *adj* alternating; alternate.

alternativa [alterna'tiβa] *sf* alternative choice; (*trabajo*) shift-work; (*rotación de cosechas*) rotation. **tomar la alternativa** qualify as a bullfighter.

alto¹ ['alto] *adj* tall; high; upper; (*fuerte*) loud; advanced; noble. **lo alto** the top. *adv* high; high up; out loud. *sm* (*elevación*) hill; (*altura*) height. **alteza** *sf* height; (*título*) highness; grandeur. **altitud** *sf* altitude; (*geog*) elevation.

alto² *sm, interj* halt. **hacer alto** stop.

alubia [a'luβja] *sf* French bean.

alucinación [aluθina'θjon] *sf* hallucination.

alud [a'luð] *sm* avalanche.

aludir [alu'ðir] *v* allude, mention. **aludido** *adj* in question. **no darse por aludido** turn a deaf ear.

alumbrar [alum'brar] *v* light; illuminate; give light; (*descubrir*) find; (*parir*) give birth; (*brillar*) shine. **alumbrarse** *v* (*fam*) become tipsy. **alumbramiento** *sm* lighting; illumination. **alumbrante** *adj* illuminating; (*fig*) enlightening.

aluminio [alu'minjo] *sm* aluminium.

alumno [a'lumno] *sm* pupil, student.

alzar [al'θar] *v* raise; lift. **alzarse** *v* rise; stand out. **alza** *sf* raise. **¡alza!** bravo! **alzamiento** *sm* increase; uprising.

allá [a'ʎa] *adv* there; long ago. **más allá** farther on. **vamos allá** let's go.

allanar [aʎa'nar] *v* level, flatten, smooth. **allanar el terreno** clear the way.

allegar [aʎe'gar] v collect, reap; add; unite. **allegar fondos** raise funds. **allegarse** v arrive; approach. **allegarse a** become attached to.

allegado [aʎe'gaðo], **-a** sm, sf relative; close friend. adj related, close. **allegamiento** sm collection; gathering; union; friendship; relationship.

allende [a'ʎende] adv beyond; besides. **allende el mar** overseas.

allí [a'ʎi] adv there; then. **aquí y allí** here and there. **por allí** over there.

ama ['ama] sf mistress of the house; (patrona) landlady.

amable [a'maβle] adj kind. **amabilidad** sf kindness.

amaestrar [amaes'trar] v train.

amagar [ama'gar] v threaten; show signs of. **amagarse** v (fam) hide.

amainar [amai'nar] v lessen; moderate. **amainarse** v yield.

amalgamar [amalga'mar] v amalgamate. **amalgamación** sf amalgamation.

amamantar [amaman'tar] v suckle, nurse. **amamantador** adj suckling. **amamantamiento** sm suckling.

*amanecer [amane'θer] v dawn; arrive at break of day. sm dawn, daybreak.

amansar [aman'sar] v break in; tame; (fig: dolor) ease.

amante [a'mante] sm, sf lover. adj fond.

amañado [ama'ɲaðo] adj skilful; (falso) fake. **amañar** v fix; fake.

amapola [ama'pola] sf poppy.

amar [a'mar] v love.

amargar [amar'gar] v embitter; be or taste bitter. **amargo** adj bitter. **amargor** sm also **amargura** sf bitterness.

amarillo [ama'riʎo] adj yellow.

amarrar [amar'rar] v fasten; tie; moor. **amarradero** sm moorings pl. **amarro** sm fastening.

amartelar [amarte'lar] v (enamorar) make lovesick; (dar celos) make jealous. **amartelarse de** (fam) get a crush on.

amartillar [amarti'ʎar] v hammer.

amasar [ama'sar] v knead; mix; prepare; (med) massage; (fam) cook up; (fig) amass. **amasijo** sm (harina) dough; (fam) mixture, hotchpotch; plot.

amatista [ama'tista] sf amethyst.

ámbar ['ambar] sm amber.

ambición [ambi'θjon] sf ambition. **ambicioso** adj ambitious.

ambiente [am'bjente] sm atmosphere; environment. adj surrounding.

ambiguo [am'bigwo] adj ambiguous. **ambigüedad** sf ambiguity.

ámbito ['ambito] sm (recinto) enclosure; (alcance) scope; sphere; (extensión) expanse.

ambos ['ambos] adj, pron both.

ambulancia [ambu'lanθja] sf ambulance.

ambulante [ambu'lante] adj travelling; walking.

amedrentar [ameðren'tar] v frighten.

amenazar [amena'θar] v threaten. **amenaza** sf threat. **amenazador** adj threatening.

amenguar [amen'gwar] v lessen; (deshonrar) dishonour.

amenizar [ameni'θar] v make pleasant. **amenidad** sf pleasantness; amenity. **ameno** adj pleasant, delightful.

América [a'merika] sf America. **América del Norte/Sur** North/South America. **América Latina** Latin America. **americano, -a** s, adj American.

ametralladora [ametraʎa'ðora] sf machine gun.

amianto [a'mjanto] sm asbestos.

amígdala [a'migðala] sf tonsil. **amigdalitis** sf tonsillitis.

amigo [a'migo] sm friend; boyfriend. **amiga** sf friend; girlfriend; mistress. **amigo por correspondencia** pen friend. **amigo** adj friendly.

amilanar [amila'nar] v frighten, terrify. **amilanarse** v become terrified.

aminorar [amino'rar] v lessen, reduce. **aminoración** sf lessening.

amistad [amis'tað] sf friendship. **amistades** sf pl friends pl. **hacer las amistades** make up. **amistar** v reconcile. **amistoso** adj friendly.

amnesia [am'nesja] sf amnesia.

amnistía [amnis'tia] sf amnesty. **amnistiar** v grant an amnesty to.

amo ['amo] sm master; overseer; employer; proprietor; (fam) boss.

amodorrarse [amoðor'rarse] v become drowsy. **amodorrado** adj drowsy.

amohinar [amoi'nar] v irritate; fret. **amohinarse** v become irritated or peevish.

*amolar [amo'lar] v (cuchillo) grind, sharpen; (fam: fastidiar) annoy.

amoldar [amol'ðar] v mould; fit; shape. **amoldarse** v adapt oneself.

amonestar [amones'tar] *v* warn; advise; admonish; (*anuncio de bodas*) publish the banns of. **amonestación** *sf* warning, admonition. **correr las amonestaciones** publish the banns.

amontonar [amonto'nar] *v* pile up; accumulate. **amontonarse** *v* crowd together; heap up; (*fam*) become angry.

amor [a'mor] *sm* love; devotion. **amor interesado** love of money. **amor propio** self-esteem. **amoroso** *adj* affectionate.

amoratar [amora'tar] *v* (*frio*) make purple; (*golpes*) bruise. **amoratado** *adj* purple; black and blue.

amordazar [amorða'θar] *v* gag; (*un perro*) muzzle; (*fig*) gag, silence.

amorfo [a'morfo] *adj* amorphous.

amortiguar [amorti'gwar] *v* (*luz*) dim; (*ruido*) deaden; (*fuego*) damp; (*golpe*) cushion; (*fig*) mitigate. **amortiguación** *sf* also **amortiguamiento** *sm* dimming; deadening; mitigation.

amortiguador [amortigwa'ðor] *sm* (*auto*) shock absorber. *adj* dimming; deadening; mitigating.

amortizar [amorti'θar] *v* amortize; (*una máquina*) depreciate.

amotinar [amoti'nar] *v* incite to revolt; (*fig*) disturb. **amotinarse** *v* mutiny. **amotinado** *adj* also **amotinador** mutinous, rebellious. **amotinamiento** *sm* mutiny.

amparar [ampa'rar] *v* shelter; protect; (*ayudar*) help. **ampararse** *v* seek help *or* protection. **amparo** *sm* aid; protection; refuge.

ampliar [am'pljar] *v* enlarge; lengthen; expand; increase. **amplio** *adj* wide, full; spacious. **amplitud** *sf* width; fullness; spaciousness; extent.

amplificar [amplifi'kar] *v* amplify. **amplificación** *sf* amplification. **amplificador** *sm* amplifier; *adj* amplifying.

ampolla [am'poʎa] *sf* blister; (*redoma*) phial; (*frasco*) flask. **ampollar** *v* blister.

amputar [ampu'tar] *v* amputate. **amputación** *sf* amputation.

amueblar [amwe'βlar] *v* furnish.

amuleto [amu'leto] *sm* amulet.

anacronismo [anakro'nismo] *sm* anachronism.

anales [a'nales] *sm pl* annals *pl*. **analista** *s(m + f)* annalist.

analfabeto [analfa'βeto], **-a** *s*, *adj* illiterate.

análisis [a'nalisis] *sm invar* analysis. **analista** *s(m + f)* analyst. **analítico** *adj* analytical. **analizar** *v* analyse.

analogía [analo'xia] *sf* analogy. **análogo** *adj* analogous, similar.

ananás [ana'nas] *sm* pineapple.

anaquel [ana'kel] *sm* shelf. **anaquelería** *sf* shelving.

anarquía [anar'kia] *sf* anarchy. **anarquismo** *sm* anarchism. **anarquista** *s(m + f)*, *adj* anarchist.

anatomía [anato'mia] *sf* anatomy. **anatómico** *adj* anatomical.

anca ['anka] *sf* haunch; rump. **ancas** *sf pl* (*fam*) bottom *sing*.

anciano [an'θjano] *adj* old. *sm* old man. **ancianidad** *sf* old age.

ancla ['ankla] *sf* anchor. **anclar** *v* also **echar anclas** anchor.

ancho ['antʃo] *adj* wide, broad; thick; (*fig*) relieved. *sm* width. **a sus anchas** at ease. **anchura** *sf* width; fullness; (*media*) measurement; (*fig: frescura*) cheek.

anchoa [an'tʃoa] *sf* anchovy.

Andalucía [andalu'θia] *sf* Andalusia. **andaluz, -a** *s*, *adj* Andalusian.

andamio [an'damjo] *sm* scaffold; platform. **andamios** *sm pl* scaffolding *sing*.

***andar** [an'dar] *v* walk; go; come; (*máquina*) work; (*correr*) run. ¡**anda!** go on! **andar en** be engaged in; rummage in. *sm* walk, gait.

andas ['andas] *sf pl* (*para una imagen*) portable platform *sing*; (*féretro*) bier *sing*; (*para enfermo*) stretcher *sing*.

andén [an'den] *sm* station platform; (*de autopista*) hard shoulder.

Andorra [an'dorra] *sf* Andorra. **andorrano, -a** *s*, *adj* Andorran.

andrajo [an'draxo] *sm* rag. **estar hecho un andrajo** be in rags. **andrajoso** *adj* ragged, tattered.

anécdota [a'nekðota] *sf* anecdote. **anecdótico** *adj* anecdotal.

anegar [ane'gar] *v* flood; drown. **anegación** *sf* drowning; flooding.

anejo [a'nexo] *adj* joined, attached. *sm* annexe.

anemia [a'nemja] *sf* anaemia. **anémico** *adj* anaemic.

anestésico [anes'tesiko] *sm*, *adj* anaesthetic. **anestesista** *s(m + f)* anaesthetist.

anexar [anek'sar] *v* annex. **anexión** *sf* annexation.

anfibio [an'fiβjo] *sm* amphibian. *adj* amphibious.

anfiteatro [anfite'atro] *sm* amphitheatre; (*universidad*) lecture theatre; (*teatro*) gallery.

anfitrión [anfitri'on], **-ona** *sm, sf* host, hostess.

ángel ['anxel] *sm* angel. **tener ángel** be charming. **angelical** *adj also* **angélico** angelic. **angelito** *sm* cherub.

angina [an'xina] *sf* angina.

anglicano [angli'kano], **-a** *s, adj* Anglican.

angosto [an'gosto] *adj* narrow. **angostura** *sf* narrowness.

anguila [an'gila] *sf* eel.

ángulo ['angulo] *sm* angle; bend. **anguloso** *adj* angular.

angustiar [angus'tjar] *v* distress; worry. **angustia** *sf* anguish. **angustiado** *adj* distressed; miserable. **angustioso** *adj* distressing; anguished.

anhelar [ane'lar] *v* pant, gasp; (*desear*) yearn for, crave. **anhelo** *sm* panting; desire.

anidar [ani'ðar] *v* nest; (*fig*) shelter.

anillo [a'niʎo] *sm* ring. **anillo de boda** wedding ring. **anillo de compromiso** *or* **pedida** engagement ring. **anillar** *v* ring.

ánima ['anima] *sf* soul.

animal [ani'mal] *sm* animal, beast. *adj* animal. **animalada** *sf* stupid thing to do *or* say; (*grosería*) bad language.

animar [ani'mar] *v* animate; entertain; encourage; comfort. **animarse** *v* cheer up. **animación** *sf* animation. **animado** *adj* lively. **animador, -a** *sm, sf* entertainer; master of ceremonies; *adj* entertaining; encouraging.

ánimo ['animo] *sm* soul; spirit; mind; courage; intention. **¡ánimo!** come on! **animoso** *adj* spirited; courageous.

aniquilar [aniki'lar] *v* annihilate.

anís [a'nis] *sm* aniseed.

aniversario [aniβer'sarjo] *sm* anniversary.

ano ['ano] *sm* anus.

anoche [a'notʃe] *adv* last night.

*****anochecer** [anotʃe'θer] *v* grow dark. *sm* nightfall.

anomalía [anoma'lia] *sf* anomaly. **anómalo** *adj* anomalous.

anónimo [a'nonimo] *adj* anonymous. *sm* anonymous person.

anormal [anor'mal] *adj* abnormal. **anormalidad** *sf* abnormality.

anotar [ano'tar] *v* note, jot down. **anotación** *sf* note.

ansiar [an'sjar] *v* long for. **ansia** *sf* longing; (*pena*) anguish; (*fervor*) eagerness. **ansias** *sf pl* retching *sing*. **ansiedad** *sf* longing; anxiety; eagerness. **ansioso** *adj* anxious; eager; longing.

antagonismo [antago'nismo] *sm* antagonism. **antagonista** *adj* antagonistic. **antagonizar** *v* antagonize.

antaño [an'taɲo] *adv* last year; formerly.

antártico [an'tartico] *adj* antarctic. *sm* the Antarctic. **Antártica** *sf* Antarctica.

ante¹ ['ante] *prep* before; in the presence of; with regard to. **ante todo** to begin with.

ante² ['ante] *sm* suede.

anteanoche [antea'notʃe] *adv* the night before last.

anteayer [antea'jer] *adv* the day before yesterday.

antecedente [anteθe'ðente] *sm* antecedent. *adj* previous. **antecedencia** *sf* lineage. **anteceder** *v* precede.

antecesor [anteθe'sor], **-a** *sm, sf* predecessor; ancestor. *adj* antecedent.

antelación [antela'θjon] *sf* preference. **con antelación** in advance.

antemano [ante'mano] *adv* **de antemano** beforehand.

antena [an'tena] *sf* (*radio*) aerial; (*insecto*) antenna.

antenatal [antena'tal] *adj* antenatal.

anteojo [ante'oxo] *sm* small telescope. **anteojos** *sm pl* spectacles *pl*.

antepasado [antepa'saðo] *adj* previous. *sm* ancestor.

antepecho [ante'petʃo] *sm* (*de escalera*) handrail; (*de ventana*) window sill.

*****anteponer** [antepo'ner] *v* prefer. **anteponerse** *v* push forward.

anterior [ante'rjor] *adj* preceding, former; front.

antes ['antes] *adv* before, formerly; first; rather. **antes de** before. **antes que** rather than. **cuanto antes** as soon as possible.

antiaéreo [antja'ereo] *adj* anti-aircraft.

antibiótico [anti'bjotiko] *sm, adj* antibiotic.

anticiclón [antiθi'klon] *sm* anticyclone.

anticipar [antiθi'par] *v* anticipate; advance. **anticiparse a** (*con infinitivo*) to ... before. **anticipación** *sf* anticipation. **con anticipación** in advance. **anticipado**

adj early, premature. **anticipo** *sm* advance payment; foretaste.

anticoncepcional [antikonθepθjo'nal] *sm*, *adj* contraceptive. **anticonceptivo** *adj* contraceptive.

anticuado [anti'kwaðo] *adj* out of date; old-fashioned.

anticuario [anti'kwarjo], **-a** *sm*, *sf* antiquarian.

antídoto [an'tiðoto] *sm* antidote.

antieconómico [antieko'nomiko] *adj* uneconomic.

antiguo [an'tigwo] *adj* ancient, antique; senior; former. **de antiguo** of old. **antigualla** *sf* antique; (*persona*) old fogey; (*noticia*) stale news. **antiguamente** *adv* formerly. **antigüedad** *sf* antiquity; seniority.

antílope [an'tilope] *sm* antelope.

Antillas [an'tiʎas] *sf pl* West Indies.

antipatía [antipa'tia] *sf* antipathy; dislike; unfriendliness. **antipático** *adj* disagreeable; unfriendly; nasty.

antisemítico [antise'mitiko] *adj* anti-Semitic. **antisemitismo** *sm* anti-Semitism.

antiséptico [anti'septiko] *sm*, *adj* antiseptic.

antisocial [antiso'θjal] *adj* antisocial.

antítesis [an'titesis] *sf* antithesis.

antojarse [anto'xarse] *v* seem; imagine; fancy; take a fancy to. **antojársele a uno** take it into one's head to.

antojo [an'toxo] *sm* whim; (*lunar*) birthmark. **antojos** *sm pl* craving *sing*. **antojadizo** *adj* capricious.

antología [antolo'xia] *sf* anthology.

antorcha [an'tortʃa] *sf* torch.

antro ['antro] *sm* cave, den; (*fam: tasca*) low dive.

antropófago [antro'pofago], **-a** *sm*, *sf* cannibal. *adj* cannibalistic. **antropofagia** *sf* cannibalism.

antropología [antropolo'xia] *sf* anthropology. **antropológico** *adj* anthropological. **antropólogo**, **-a** *sm*, *sf* anthropologist.

anual [a'nwal] *adj* annual. **anualidad** *sf* annuity. **anuario** *sm* yearbook.

anublar [anu'βlar] *v* cloud over, obscure. **anublarse** *v* become cloudy; fade away.

anudar [anu'ðar] *v* knot; join; tie; (*empezar*) begin. **anudarse** become knotted; (*plantas*) wither. **anudadura** *sf* also **anudamiento** *sm* knotting; withering.

anular [anu'lar] *v* (*cheque*) cancel; (*ley*) repeal; (*fig: dominar*) overshadow. **anularse** *v* (*fig: renunciar*) give up everything. **anulación** *sf* cancellation; abrogation; repeal. **anulador** *adj* repealing.

anunciar [anun'θjar] *v* announce, proclaim; notify; (*hacer publicidad*) advertise; (*predecir*) foretell. **anunciador**, **-a** *sm*, *sf* announcer; advertiser; *adj* announcing; advertising. **anuncio** *sm* announcement; advertisement; omen; sign.

anzuelo [an'θwelo] *sm* fish-hook; (*fig: aliciente*) lure.

añadir [aɲa'ðir] *v* add; increase. **añadido** *sm* addition. **añadidura** *sf* addition; extra. **por añadidura** furthermore, besides.

añejo [a'ɲexo] *adj* mature; (*carne*) cured; very old.

añicos [a'ɲikos] *sm pl* pieces, bits. **hacerse añicos** wear oneself out.

añil [a'ɲil] *sm* indigo plant; indigo dye.

año ['aɲo] *sm* year. **al año** yearly. **tener ... años** be ... years old. **todos los años** every year.

añorar [aɲo'rar] *v* long for; be homesick. **añoranza** *sf* homesickness; nostalgia; yearning.

*apacentar [apaθen'tar] *v* graze. **apacentadero** *sm* pasture. **apacentador**, **-a** *sm*, *sf* herdsman/woman.

apacible [apa'θiβle] *adj* mild; gentle; peaceful. **apacibilidad** *sf* mildness; peacefulness.

apaciguar [apaθi'gwar] *v* pacify; appease. **apaciguarse** *v* calm down. **apaciguador**, **-a** *sm*, *sf* peace-maker. **apaciguamiento** *sm* pacification; appeasement.

apagar [apa'gar] *v* (*fuego*) extinguish; switch off; muffle; (*sed*) quench; (*dolor*) soothe; (*disturbio*) calm down. **apagado** *adj* extinguished; dull; lifeless; muffled. **apagaincendios** *sm invar* fire-extinguisher.

apalear [apale'ar] *v* beat; (*grano*) thresh; (*maltratar*) thrash. **apaleo** *sm* beating; winnowing; thrashing.

apañar [apa'ɲar] *v* fix; arrange; repair; (*ataviar*) dress up; (*coger*) grab; (*fam: robar*) swipe; (*fam: preparar*) get ready. **apañado** *adj* handy; dressed up.

aparador [apara'ðor] *sm* sideboard; (*escaparate*) shop window.

aparato [apa'rato] *sm* apparatus; machine; ceremony.

*aparecer [apare'θer] *v* appear. **aparecido** *sm* ghost.

aparejar [apare'xar] *v* prepare; (*caballos*) harness, saddle; (*cuadro*) prime. **aparejador** *sm* quantity surveyor. **aparejo** *sm* preparation; equipment; harness.

aparentar [aparen'tar] *v* pretend; feign.

aparente [apa'rente] *adj* apparent; evident; (*adecuado*) suitable.

aparición [apari'θjon] *sf* appearance; (*visión*) apparition; publication.

apariencia [apari'enθja] *sf* appearance; aspect; probability.

apartamento [aparta'mento] *sm* flat.

apartar [apar'tar] *v* separate; (*quitar*) remove; (*clasificar*) sort; (*poner a un lado*) put aside. **apartarse** *v* turn aside; (*irse*) leave. **apartado** *adj* separated; distant; *sm* paragraph; (*habitación*) spare room. **apartado de correos** post-office box. **apartamiento** *sm* separation; remoteness. **aparte** *adv* apart (from); aside.

apasionar [apasjo'nar] *v* rouse, stir. **apasionarse** *v* become excited. **apasionado** *adj* madly in love; passionate; (*ardiente*) fervent. **apasionamiento** *sm* passion.

apatía [apa'tia] *sf* apathy. **apático** *adj* apathetic.

apear [ape'ar] *v* get down; dismount. **apearse** *v* alight, get off.

apedrear [apeðre'ar] *v* stone. **apedrearse** *v* hail. **apedreo** *sm* stoning.

apelar [ape'lar] *v* appeal. **apelar a** appeal to. **apelar de** appeal against.

apellido [ape'ʎiðo] *sm* surname; (*apodo*) nickname. **apellido de soltera** maiden name.

apenar [ape'nar] *v* grieve.

apenas [a'penas] *adv* scarcely; no sooner than.

apéndice [a'penðiθe] *sm* appendix; supplement. **apendicitis** *sf* appendicitis.

apercibir [aperθi'βir] *v* prepare; (*proveer*) equip; (*advertir*) warn. **apercibirse de** equip oneself with. **apercibimiento** *sm* preparation; advice; (*jur*) summons.

aperitivo [aperi'tiβo] *sm* appetizer; apéritif. *adj* appetizing.

apero [a'pero] *sm* equipment; tools *pl*.

apertura [aper'tura] *sf* opening.

apesadumbrar [apesadum'brar] *v* grieve, afflict. **apesadumbrarse** *v* be upset.

apestar [apes'tar] *v* infect; (*fig*) vex; (*fam*) stink. **apestado** *adj* (*olor*) foul; (*que tiene peste*) plague-ridden; infested.

*apetecer [apete'θer] *v* have a hankering for, fancy; (*bienvenido*) be welcome. **apetecible** *adj* desirable, tempting. **apetencia** *sf* desire; appetite.

apetito [ape'tito] *sm* appetite.

apiadarse [apja'ðarse] *v* have pity on.

ápice ['apiθe] *sm* apex; jot, iota.

apiñar [api'ɲar] *v* squeeze together. **apiñarse** *v* crowd, throng. **apiñadura** *sf* also **apiñamiento** *sm* congestion; throng.

apio ['apjo] *sm* celery.

apisonadora [apisona'ðora] *sf* steam roller. **apisonar** *v* flatten. **apisonamiento** *sm* flattening.

aplacar [apla'kar] *v* appease; calm. **aplacable** *adj* appeasable. **aplacamiento** *sm* appeasement. **aplacador** *adj* appeasing.

aplanar [apla'nar] *v* level, flatten; (*fam*) make dejected. **aplanador** *adj* levelling. **aplanadora** *sf* leveller. **aplanamiento** *sm* levelling, flattening; (*fam*) dejection.

aplastar [aplas'tar] *v* crush, flatten.

aplaudir [aplau'ðir] *v* applaud. **aplauso** *sm* applause.

aplazar [apla'θar] *v* postpone; (*convocar*) summon. **aplazamiento** *sm* postponement; summons.

aplicar [apli'kar] *v* apply; attach; (*recursos, dinero*) assign. **aplicarse** *v* apply oneself; be applicable. **aplicación** *sf* application. **aplicado** *adj* studious.

aplomo [a'plomo] *sm* aplomb, self-confidence. **aplomado** *adj* self-assured.

apocar [apo'kar] *v* lessen; belittle. **apocarse** *v* become cowed. **apocado** *adj* spineless, timid. **apocamiento** *sm* timidity.

apodar [apo'ðar] *v* nickname. **apodo** *sm* nickname.

apoderar [apoðe'rar] *v* authorize. **apoderarse de** take possession of. **apoderado** *sm* agent; sports manager.

apogeo [apo'xeo] *sm* climax; summit.

apolillarse [apoli'ʎarse] *v* become moth-eaten. **apolilladura** *sf* moth-hole.

apoplejía [apople'xia] *sf* apoplexy. **apoplético, -a** *s, adj* apoplectic.

aportar [apor'tar] *v* bring, contribute; arrive. **aportación** *sf* contribution.

aposentar [aposen'tar] *v* lodge; give lodging to. **aposentarse** *v* take lodgings. **aposentamiento** *sm* lodging. **aposento** *sm* room; lodging.

*apostar [apos'tar] *v* bet. **apostarse** *v* bet; take up one's post. **apostador, -a** *sm, sf* punter.

apóstol [a'postol] *sm* apostle. **apostólico** *adj* apostolic.

apóstrofo [a'postrofo] *sm* (*gram*) apostrophe.

apoyar [apo'jar] *v* support; back up; lean; rest. **apoyar en** lean against. **apoyarse en** lean on. **apoyo** *sm* support.

apreciar [apre'θjar] *v* appreciate; value. **apreciar en mucho** value highly. **apreciable** *adj* appreciable; estimable; (*ruido*) audible. **apreciación** *sf* appreciation; (*valoración*) appraisal. **apreciativo** *adj* appreciative. **aprecio** *sm* appraisal; esteem.

aprehender [apreen'der] *v* seize; understand. **aprehensible** *adj* understandable. **aprehensión** *sf* capture, arrest; understanding.

apremiar [apre'mjar] *v* press, urge; (*obligar*) force; (*dar prisa*) hurry. **apremiador** *adj* urgent. **apremio** *sm* urgency; compulsion.

aprender [apren'der] *v* learn. **aprendiz, -a** *sm, sf* apprentice. **aprendizaje** *sm* apprenticeship.

aprensión [apren'sjon] *sf* apprehension, fear. **aprensivo** *adj* apprehensive.

apresar [apre'sar] *v* seize, arrest. **apresamiento** *sm* seizure.

aprestar [apres'tar] *v* prepare; (*telas*) size. **aprestarse** *v* get ready. **apresto** *sm* preparation.

apresurar [apresu'rar] *v* hurry, quicken. **apresuradamente** *adv* hastily. **apresurado** *adj* hurried. **apresuramiento** *sm* haste.

*apretar [apre'tar] *v* squeeze; grip; tighten; (*botón*) press; (*la mano*) shake; (*dolor*) get worse; (*comprimir*) press down. **apretarse** *v* crowd together; huddle together. **apretado** *adj* tight; (*colchón*) hard; cramped; cluttered; difficult; (*tacaño*) miserly. **apretón** *sm* squeeze; (*fam: aprieto*) tight spot; (*fam: accesidad natural*) call of nature. **aprieto** *sm* awkward situation.

aprisa [a'prisa] *adv* quickly.

aprisionar [aprisjon'ar] *v* imprison.

*aprobar [apro'βar] *v* approve; approve of; (*examen*) pass. **aprobación** *sf* approval; pass. **aprobado** *adj* approved. *sm* pass.

apropiar [apro'pjar] *v* appropriate; adapt.

apropriarse de algo appropriate something. **apropiado** *adj* appropriate, suitable.

aprovechar [aproβe'tʃar] *v* profit by; be useful; make progress. **aprovecharse de** take advantage of. **aprovechado** *adj* thrifty; (*apañado*) resourceful; studious; (*egoísta*) selfish. **aprovechamiento** *sm* profit; exploitation; benefit.

aproximar [aproksi'mar] *v* bring nearer. **aproximarse** *v* approach. **aproximación** *sf* approximation; nearness. **aproximado** *adj* approximate.

aptitud [apti'tuð] *sf* aptitude; capacity. **apto** *adj* apt; suitable.

apuesta [a'pwesta] *sf* bet.

apuesto [a'pwesto] *adj* smart, spruce.

apuntar [apun'tar] *v* (*señalar*) point at; (*arma*) aim; (*sugerir*) point out; (*anotar*) make a note of; (*demostrar*) display; (*sacar punta*) sharpen; (*jugar*) bet; (*teatro*) prompt. **apuntarse** *v* put one's name down; (*fam*) enrol. **apuntado** *adj* pointed. **apunte** *sm* (*nota*) note; (*puesta*) stake; prompter; (*teatro*) cue; (*dibujo*) sketch.

apuñalar [apuɲa'lar] *v* stab.

apurar [apu'rar] *v* purify; (*acabar*) exhaust; (*vaciar*) drain; examine in detail; (*dar prisa*) rush, hurry. **apurarse** *v* (*preocuparse*) worry; hurry up. **apuradamente** *adv* with difficulty; (*ser indigente*) in want; (*fam*) exactly. **apurado** *adj* (*pobre*) hard up; (*agotado*) worn out; (*avergonzado*) embarrassed. **apuro** *sm* (*dificultad*) tight spot; embarrassment.

aquejar [ake'xar] *v* afflict. **aquejoso** *adj* afflicted.

aquel, aquella [a'kel, a'keʎa] *adj* that. **aquellos, aquellas** *pl* those. **aquél, aquélla** *pron* that; the one; the former.

aquí [a'ki] *adv* here. **de aquí en adelante** from now on. **heme aquí** here I am. **por aquí** this way.

aquietar [akje'tar] *v* quieten.

aquilatar [akila'tar] *v* test, examine closely.

Arabia [a'raβja] *sf* Arabia. **árabe** *adj* Arab, Arabian, Arabic; *sm, sf* Arab, Arabian; *sm* (*lengua*) Arabic. **arábico** *adj* also **arábigo** Arabic.

arancel [aran'θel] *sm* tariff, duty.

araña [a'raɲa] *sf* spider; (*luz*) chandelier.

arañar [ara'ɲar] *v* scratch. **arañada** *sf* scratch. **arañador** *adj* scratching, scraping. **arañazo** *sm* scratch.

arar [a'rar] *v* plough. **arado** *sm* plough.
arbitrar [arβi'trar] *v* arbitrate; referee.
arbitraje *sm* arbitration. **arbitrario** *adj*
arbitrary. **árbitro** *sm* referee, umpire.
arbitrio [ar'βitrjo] *sm* (*voluntad*) will;
(*recurso*) means; (*jur*) judgment. **arbitrios**
sm pl taxes *pl*.
árbol ['arβol] *sm* tree; (*tecn*) shaft; (*palo*)
mast. **árbol de Navidad** Christmas tree.
arboleda *sf* wood, spinney.
arbusto [ar'βusto] *sm* bush.
arca ['arka] *sf* box, chest. **arca de agua**
reservoir.
arcada [ar'kaða] *sf* arcade. **arcadas** *sf pl*
nausea *sing*.
arcaico [ar'kaiko] *adj* archaic. **arcaísmo**
sm archaism.
arce ['arθe] *sm* maple.
arcilla [ar'θiʎa] *sf* clay.
arco ['arko] *sm* arc; arch; (*arma, música*)
bow. **arco iris** rainbow.
archiduque [artʃi'ðuke] *sm* archduke.
archiduquesa *sf* archduchess.
archipiélago [artʃi'pjelago] *sm* archipelago.
archivo [ar'tʃiβo] *sm* file; archives *pl*.
archivador *sm* filing cabinet. **archivar** *v*
file. **archivero, -a** *sm, sf also* **archivista**
s(m + f) archivist.
arder [ar'ðer] *v* burn; (*estiércol*) rot; (*fig*)
seethe. **arderse** *v* burn up. **ardiente** *adj*
ardent, burning; feverish.
ardid [ar'ðið] *sm* trick, ruse.
ardilla [ar'ðiʎa] *sf* squirrel.
ardor [ar'ðor] *sm* ardour; (*quemazón*)
burn; (*fig*) enthusiasm. **ardorosamente**
adv ardently. **ardoroso** *adj* burning;
feverish; fervent.
arduo ['arðuo] *adj* arduous, difficult.
área ['area] *sf* area.
arena [a'rena] *sf* sand; (*en el circo*) arena;
(*ruedo*) bullring. **arena movediza** quicksand. **arenal** *sm* stretch of sand. **arenar** *v*
sand.
arengar [aren'gar] *v* harangue. **arenga** *sf*
harangue.
arenque [a'renke] *sm* herring.
argamasa [arga'masa] *sf* mortar.
argamasar *v* mortar.
Argentina [arxen'tina] *sf* Argentina.
argentino *adj* (*de plata*) silvery; Argentinian. **argentino, -a** *sm, sf* Argentine,
Argentinian.
argolla [ar'goʎa] *sf* large metal ring,
hoop.

argucia [ar'guθja] *sf* fallacy; subtlety.
*argüir [ar'gwir] *v* (*alegar*) argue; indicate; demonstrate; (*delatar*) accuse;
infer.
aria ['arja] *sf* aria.
argumento [argu'mento] *sm* argument;
(*cuento*) plot. **argumentador** *adj* argumentative.
aridez [ari'ðeθ] *sf* dryness. **aridecer** *v* dry
up. **aridecerse** *v* become dry. **árido** *adj*
arid. **medida de áridos** *sf* dry measure.
arisco [a'risko] *adj* (*tímido*) shy; (*huraño*)
unfriendly; (*animales*) wild.
aristocracia [aristo'kraθja] *sf* aristocracy.
aristócrata *s(m + f)* aristocrat. **aristocrático** *adj* aristocratic.
aritmética [arit'metika] *sf* arithmetic.
aritmético *adj* arithmetic, arithmetical.
armada [ar'maða] *sf* navy, fleet.
armar [ar'mar] *v* arm; prepare; reinforce;
(*proveer*) provide; organize. **armarse** *v*
arm oneself; prepare oneself; (*estallar*)
break out. **arma** *sf* weapon. **armado** *adj*
armed. **armadura** *sf* armour; framework.
armamento *sm* armament.
armario [ar'marjo] *sm* cupboard; (*para
ropa*) wardrobe.
armazón [arma'θon] *sm* (*anat*) skeleton. *sf*
(*conjunto de piezas*) framework.
armería [arme'ria] *sf* gunsmiths; (*heráldica*) heraldry.
armisticio [armis'tiθjo] *sm* armistice.
armonía [armo'nia] *sf* harmony. **armónico**
adj also **armonioso** harmonious.
armónica [ar'monika] *sf* harmonica.
aro ['aro] *sm* (*argolla*) iron ring; (*de tonel*)
hoop.
aroma [a'roma] *sm* aroma. **aromático** *adj*
aromatic, fragrant. **aromatizante** *adj*
flavouring. **aromatizar** *v* flavour.
arpa ['arpa] *sf* harp. **arpista** *s(m + f)* harpist.
arpón [ar'pon] *sm* harpoon.
arquear [arke'ar] *v* arch, curve. **arqueo** *sm*
arching.
arqueología [arkeolo'xia] *sf* archaeology.
arqueológico *adj* archaeological. **arqueólogo** *sm* archaeologist.
arquero [ar'kero] *sm* archer; (*com*) cashier.
arquitectura [arkitek'tura] *sf* architecture.
arquitecto *sm* architect.
arrabal [arra'βal] *sm* suburb. **arrabales** *sm
pl* outskirts *pl*.

arraigar [arrai'gar] v take root. **arraigarse** v settle down. **arraigado** adj deep-rooted. **arraigo** sm roots pl; influence.

arrancar [arran'kar] v root up, tear out, force out; (las flemas) expectorate; (suspiro) heave; (agarrar) snatch; (auto) start. **arrancarse** v begin. **arrancada** sf sudden start; jerk. **arrancado** adj uprooted; (fam) broke. **arrancadura** sf pulling; uprooting; (dientes) extraction. **arranque** sm (auto) starting; (carretera) beginning; (energía) burst; origin.

arrasar [arra'sar] v (llenar) fill to the brim; (edificio) demolish; (allanar) level. **arrasarse** v clear up. **arrasadura** sf levelling. **arrasamiento** sm levelling; demolition.

arrastrar [arras'trar] v pull, haul, drag; (viento) blow away; (provocar) give rise to; attract. **arrastrarse** v crawl, creep. **arrastre** sm dragging; haulage. **ser de mucho arrastre** be highly influential.

arrebatar [arreβa'tar] v snatch; (viento) blow away; carry away; (arrancar) rip off; enrage; captivate. **arrebatarse** v get overcooked. **arrebatadamente** adv hurriedly. **arrebatadizo** adj short-tempered. **arrebatamiento** sm seizure; (éxtasis) rapture. **arrebato** sm (furor) rage; rapture.

arrebujarse [arreβu'xarse] v wrap oneself up.

arreciar [arre'θjar] v grow worse or stronger; increase in intensity.

arrecife [arre'θife] sm reef.

arreglar [arre'glar] v organize, regulate; (poner en orden) tidy; (disponer) arrange; (componer) mend; get ready; (rectificar) put right. **arreglarse** v be content; (vestirse) dress; (ponerse de acuerdo) agree; (ir tirando) get by. **arreglado** adj regulated; tidy; (bien vestido) smart; reasonable; (conducta) good. **arreglo** sm agreement; arrangement; repair.

arremeter [arreme'ter] v attack. **arremetida** sf assault.

*__arrendar__ [arren'dar] v let; (alquilar) rent. **arrendador** sm landlord; (que toma en alquiler) tenant. **arrendadora** sf landlady; tenant. **arrendamiento** sm letting; rent.

arreo [ar'reo] sm adornment. **arreos** sm pl harness sing.

*__arrepentirse__ [arrepen'tirse] v repent. **arrepentimiento** sm repentance.

arrestar [arres'tar] v arrest. **arrestarse** v rush boldly. **arrestado** adj imprisoned; (audaz) bold. **arresto** sm arrest; imprisonment. **arrestos** sm pl boldness sing.

arriar [ar'rjar] v (vela, bandera) strike, lower; (cable) slacken. **arriarse** v (inundarse) be flooded.

arriba [ar'riβa] adv up; upstairs; above. **de arriba abajo** from head to foot. ¡mano arriba! hands up! **arriba** prep above.

arribar [arri'βar] v arrive. **arribar a** reach. **arribada** sf arrival.

arriendo [ar'rjendo] sm letting; renting; hiring.

arriesgar [arrjes'gar] v risk. **arriesgarse** v take a risk. **arriesgarse en** venture on. **arriesgado** adj dangerous.

arrimar [arri'mar] v (acercar) get near or close; put away. **arrimarse** v draw up; gather together; live together.

arrinconar [arrinko'nar] v corner; (desechar) discard; (fam: vivir solo) live in isolation. **arrinconado** adj (olvidado) forgotten; (abandonado) forsaken.

arroba [ar'roβa] sf weight of 11.5 kg.

arrobar [arro'βar] v entrance. **arrobado** adj in ecstasy. **arrobador** adj bewitching. **arrobamiento** sm also **arrobo** ecstasy, rapture.

arrodillarse [arroði'ʎarse] v kneel. **arrodillamiento** sm kneeling.

arrogancia [arro'ganθja] sf arrogance. **arrogante** adj arrogant.

arrojar [arro'xar] v throw, hurl; emit. **arrojarse** v hurl oneself. **arrojado** adj bold. **arrojo** sm boldness, daring.

arrollar [arro'ʎar] v (enrollar) roll up; (llevarse) sweep away; (atropellar) run over; (aniquilar) crush.

arropar [arro'par] v (abrigarse) wrap up; (en una cama) tuck up; cover.

arrostrar [arros'trar] v face up to, confront.

arroyo [ar'roʎo] sm stream; (calle) gutter.

arroz [ar'roθ] sm rice.

arrugar [arru'gar] v wrinkle; (ropa) crease. **arruga** sf wrinkle; crease.

arruinar [arrui'nar] v ruin; destroy.

arrullar [arru'ʎar] v lull to sleep; (paloma) coo. **arrullo** sm cooing.

arrumbar [arrum'bar] v discard; (fig) ignore.

arrurruz [arrur'ruθ] sm arrowroot.

arsenal [arse'nal] sm arsenal; (astillero) shipyard.

arsénico [ar'seniko] *sm* arsenic.
arte ['arte] *sm, sf* art; (*hechura*) workmanship; (*astucia*) cunning. **no tener arte ni parte en** have nothing to do with. **por buenas o malas artes** by fair means or foul.
artefacto [arte'fakto] *sm* device, appliance.
artejo [ar'texo] *sm* knuckle.
arteria [ar'terja] *sf* artery.
artesano [arte'sano] *sm* craftsman. **artesanía** *sf* craftsmanship.
ártico ['artiko] *adj* arctic. **Ártico** *sm* the Arctic. **Círculo Polar Ártico** *sm* Arctic Circle.
articular [artiku'lar] *v* articulate, join together. **articulación** *sf* articulation.
artículo [ar'tikulo] *sm* article; item; (dictionary) entry. **artículos** *sm pl* goods *pl*.
artificial [artifi'θjal] *adj* artificial.
artificio [arti'fiθjo] *sm* device; skill; (*truco*) trick.
artillería [artiʎe'ria] *sf* artillery. **artillero** *sm* gunner.
artimaña [arti'maɲa] *sf* (*trampa*) trap; (*astucia*) trick.
artista [ar'tista] *s(m+f)* artist; actor, actress. **artístico** *adj* artistic.
artritis [ar'tritis] *sf* arthritis.
arzobispo [arθo'βispo] *sm* archbishop.
as [as] *sm* ace.
asa ['asa] *sf* handle.
asado [a'saðo] *sm* (*culin*) roast (meat). *adj* roast, roasted. **asador** *sm* spit. **asar** *v* roast; (*fam*) pester.
asalariado [asala'rjaðo], **-a** *sm, sf* wage-earner. *adj* paid, wage-earning.
asaltar [asal'tar] *v* assault, attack; (*banco*) raid; (*fig: idea*) cross one's mind. **asalto** *sm* attack; (*boxeo*) round.
asamblea [asam'blea] *sf* assembly, meeting.
asbesto [as'βesto] *sm* asbestos.
ascendencia [asθen'denθja] *sf* ancestry; origin; (*predominio*) influence.
***ascender** [asθen'der] *v* ascend; (*subir a*) add up; (*empleo*) be promoted; promote. **ascendiente** *sm* influence. **ascendientes** *sm pl* ancestors *pl*, ancestry *sing*. **ascensión** *sf* ascent; promotion. **ascensor** *sm* elevator.
asco ['asko] *sm* disgust, loathing. **dar asco** disgust. **hacer asco** turn one's nose up.
ascua ['askwa] *sf* ember. **estar sobre ascuas** be on tenterhooks.

asear [ase'ar] *v* clean; wash; decorate; (*arreglar*) tidy up. **asearse** *v* have a wash; spruce oneself up. **aseado** *adj* clean; tidy. **aseo** *sm* cleanliness; tidiness.
asechar [ase'tʃar] *v* ambush. **asecho** *sm* trap.
asediar [ase'ðjar] *v* besiege; (*fig*) bother. **asedio** *sm* siege.
asegurar [asegu'rar] *v* secure; safeguard; (*consolidar*) strengthen; (*confortar*) reassure; insure; assure. **asegurarse** *v* make sure. **asegurado** *adj* insured; assured. **asegurador** *sm* underwriter. **aseguramiento** *sm* securing; insurance; assurance.
asemejarse [aseme'xarse] *v* resemble, be alike.
***asentar** [asen'tar] *v* place; seat; (*cimientos*) lay; (*polvo*) settle; (*campamento*) pitch; (*establecer*) found; (*afilar*) sharpen; (*convenir*) agree; (*acalmar*) calm down; (*ir bien*) be suitable. **asentarse** *v* sit down; settle down.
***asentir** [asen'tir] *v* agree, assent. **asentimiento** *sm* assent.
asequible [ase'kiβle] *adj* reasonable; (*alcanzable*) obtainable; affable.
***aserrar** [aser'rar] *v* saw. **aserradero** *sm* sawmill. **aserrado** *adj* serrated. **aserrín** *sm* sawdust.
aserto [a'serto] *sm* assertion.
asesinar [asesi'nar] *v* murder; assassinate. **asesinato** *sm* murder; assassination. **asesino** *adj* murderous.
asesorar [aseso'rar] *v* advise; take advice. **asesoramiento** *sm* advising; opinion.
asestar [ases'tar] *v* (*arma*) aim; (*golpe*) strike. **asestadura** *sf* aiming.
asfalto [as'falto] *sm* asphalt. **asfaltado** *adj* covered with asphalt. **asfaltar** *v* asphalt.
asfixiar [asfik'sjar] *v* suffocate. **asfixia** *sf* suffocation.
así [a'si] *adv* so, thus, in this way, in that way. **así así** so-so. **así como** just as; as well as. **así que** as soon as; therefore. **así sea** so be it.
Asia ['asja] *sf* Asia. **asiático, -a** *s, adj* Asiatic, Asian.
asidero [asi'ðero] *sm* handle; (*fig*) excuse.
asiduo [a'siðwo] *adj* assiduous, hardworking; frequent.
asiento [a'sjento] *sm* seat, chair; place; (*de botellas, etc.*) base, bottom; (*tratado*) treaty; note; stability; (*sentido común*) common sense. **asientos** *sm pl* seat *sing*,

bottom *sing*. **asiento de estómago** attack of indigestion. **tomar asiento** sit down.
asignar [asig'nar] *v* assign; attribute; allocate. **asignación** *sf* (*atribución*) allocation; (*cita*) appointment; (*subsidio*) grant; (*sueldo*) wages.
asignatura [asigna'tura] *sf* (scholastic) subject.
asilo [a'silo] *sm* asylum; refuge; home; shelter.
asimilar [asimi'lar] *v* assimilate; compare. **asimilarse** *v* be assimilated; (*asemejarse*) resemble. **asimilación** *sf* assimilation; comparison.
asimismo [asi'mismo] *adv* in like manner, in the same way.
*asir [a'sir] *v* grasp; grip; (*plantas*) take root. **asirse de** hang on to.
asistir [asis'tir] *v* help; attend; be present; (*testigo*) witness. **asistencia** *sf* assistance; attendance; (*teatro, etc*.) audience; (*muchedumbre*) crowd; (*médica*) care; presence. **asistencias** *sf pl* maintenance *sing*. **asistenta** *sf* charlady; (*hotel*) chambermaid. **asistente** *sm* assistant; (*mil*) orderly; member of an audience.
asma ['asma] *sf* asthma.
asno ['asno] *sm* donkey, ass; (*fig*) idiot.
asociar [aso'θjar] *v* associate; (*com*) enter into partnership. **asociarse** *v* associate oneself; share. **asociación** *sf* association; (*com*) partnership. **asociado** *sm* member.
asolar [aso'lar] *v* destroy; (*arrasar*) flatten; (*calor*) parch. **asalador** *adj* devastating. **asolamiento** *sm* devastation.
asolear [asole'ar] *v* put in the sun. **asolearse** *v* sunbathe.
asomar [aso'mar] *v* show, appear. **asomarse** *v* lean out; (*fam: archisparse*) become tipsy. **asomada** *sf* brief appearance. **asomo** *sm* appearance; (*sombra*) shadow; (*indicio*) hint.
asombrar [asom'brar] *v* astonish; (*dar sombra*) shade; (*color*) darken. **asombrador** *adj* astonishing. **asombramiento** *sm also* **asombro** *sm* astonishment; (*fam: aparecido*) ghost. **asombroso** *adj* astonishing; stupefying.
aspecto [as'pekto] *sm* aspect; appearance.
áspero ['aspero] *adj* (*tosco*) rough; (*agrio*) sour; (*persona*) gruff; (*voz*) harsh; (*clima*) hard; (*terreno*) rugged. **aspereza** *sf* roughness; sourness; harshness.
aspersión [asper'sjon] *sf* sprinkling; spraying. **asperjar** *v* sprinkle.

aspirar [aspi'rar] *v* inhale; (*fig*) aspire. **aspiración** *sf* inhalation; aspiration. **aspiradora** *sf* vacuum cleaner.
aspirina [aspi'rina] *sf* aspirin.
asqueroso [aske'roso] *adj* disgusting; vile; dirty; repulsive. **asquerosidad** *sf* filth; obscenity.
asta ['asta] *sf* (*arma*) spear; (*palo*) shaft; (*de la bandera*) staff; (*cuerno*) horn. **a media asta** at half mast.
asterisco [aste'risko] *sm* asterisk.
astil [as'til] *sm* handle; (*pluma*) quill.
astillar [asti'ʎar] *v* splinter; smash.
astillero [asti'ʎero] *sm* shipyard.
astringir [astrin'xir] *v* constrict; (*sujetar*) blind. **astringente** *sm, adj* astringent.
astro ['astro] *sm* star.
astrología [astrolo'xia] *sf* astrology. **astrólogo** *sm* astrologer.
astronauta [astro'nauta] *s(m+f)* astronaut. **astronáutica** *sf* astronautics.
astronomiá [astrono'mia] *sf* astronomy. **astronómico** *adj* astronomical. **astrónomo** *sm* astronomer.
astucia [as'tuθja] *sf* (*habilidad*) cleverness; (*ingenio*) cunning. **astuto** *adj* clever; cunning.
asumir [asu'mir] *v* assume.
asunto [a'sunto] *sm* (*tema*) subject; (*cosa*) affair; (*negocio*) business; (*caso*) fact; (*cuestión*) matter. **asuntos a tratar** *pl* agenda *sing*. **asuntos exteriores** foreign affairs.
asustar [asus'tar] *v* frighten.
atacar [ata'kar] *v* attack; (*recalcar*) stuff; (*un botón*) fasten. **atacador, -a** *sm, sf* assailant. **ataque** *sm* attack; (*med*) fit. **ataque cardíaco** heart attack. **ataque fulminante** (*med*) stroke.
atado [a'taðo] *sm* bundle. *adj* shy.
atajar [ata'xar] *v* intercept; (*detener*) check; (*impedir*) obstruct; (*tomar el camino más corto*) take a short cut. **atajador, -a** *sm, sf* interceptor. **atajo** *sm* short cut.
atar [a'tar] *v* tie; lace; bind. **loco de atar** raving mad. **atarse** *v* become confused. **atador** *adj* binding. **atadura** *sf* binding; (*cuerda*) rope; (*fig: vínculo*) bond.
*atardecer [ataрðe'θer] *v* get late; grow dark. *sm* dusk.
atareado [atare'aðo] *adj* very busy. **atarear** *v* load with work.

atascar [atas'kar] *v* plug, stop (a leak); obstruct. **atascadero** *sm* mire; (*fig*) stumbling-block. **atasco** *sm* obstruction.

ataúd [ata'uð] *sm* coffin.

ataviar [ata'βjar] *v* dress up, adorn. **ataviarse en** *or* **de** dress oneself up in. **atavío** *sm* attire.

ateísmo [ate'ismo] *sm* atheism. **ateísta** *s*(*m* + *f*) atheist. **ateo, -a** *sm, sf* atheist.

atemorizar [atemori'θar] *v* frighten.

atención [aten'θjon] *sf* attention; courtesy; interest; (*cariño*) kindness. **prestar atención** pay attention. **atenciones** *sf pl* business affairs. **atento** *adj* attentive; kind; careful; special; (*consciente*) aware.

*****atender** [aten'der] *v* attend to; (*cuidar*) look after; serve; (*una máquina*) service; (*un aviso*) listen to.

*****atenerse** [ate'nerse] *v* abide, adhere; (*a una persona*) rely on.

atentar [aten'tar] *v* attempt; offend.

atenuar [ate'nwar] *v* attenuate; lessen; (*la luz*) dim. **atenuación** *sf* attenuation.

*****aterrar**[1] [ater'rar] *v* demolish.

aterrar[2] [ater'rar] *v* frighten, terrify. **aterrador** *adj* terrifying.

aterrizar [aterri'θar] *v* (*aviac*) land. **aterrizaje** *sm* landing.

aterrorizar [aterrori'θar] *v* terrify; terrorize. **aterrorizador** *adj* terrifying.

atesorar [ateso'rar] *v* hoard; (*fig*) possess. **atesoramiento** *sm* hoarding.

*****atestar** [ates'tar] *v* (*llenar*) stuff; (*un tren*) crowd, pack; (*desordenar*) clutter up. **atestado** *adj* full up; packed.

atestiguar [atesti'gwar] *v* testify.

ático ['atiko] *sm* attic.

atisbar [atis'βar] *v* (*mirar*) spy on; (*vislumbrar*) distinguish; (*vigilar*) watch for. **atisbo** *sm* spying; (*fig*) hint.

atizar [ati'θar] *v* (*el fuego*) poke, stir; (*fig*) stir up, incite. **atizador** *sm* poker.

Atlántico [at'lantiko] *sm* Atlantic. **atlántico** *adj* Atlantic.

atlas ['atlas] *sm* atlas.

atleta [at'leta] *s*(*m* + *f*) athlete. **atlético** *adj* athletic. **atletismo** *sm* athletics.

atmósfera [at'mosfera] *sf* atmosphere. **mala atmosfera** atmospherics *pl*. **atmosférico** *adj* atmospheric.

atolondrar [atolon'drar] *v* confuse; (*aturdir*) stun. **atolondrarse** *v* lose one's head. **atolondradamente** *adv* recklessly. **atolondramiento** *sm* recklessness; confusion.

atolladero [atoʎa'ðero] *sm* bog; (*fig*) impasse. **atollarse** *v* get bogged down.

átomo ['atomo] *sm* atom. **atómico** *adj* atomic.

atónito [a'tonito] *adj* astonished.

atontar [aton'tar] *v* (*golpe*) stun, daze; (*dejar sin habla*) dumbfound; (*embrutecer*) deaden; (*drogas*) make stupid. **atontado** *adj* stunned; bewildered; dumbfounded; stupid.

atormentar [atormen'tar] *v* torment; torture. **atormentador** *sm* tormentor; torturer.

atornillar [atorni'ʎar] *v* screw in/on/down.

atosigar [atosi'gar] *v* poison; (*molestar*) pester. **atosigarse** *v* toil. **atosigador** *adj* poisoning; pestering. **atosigamiento** *sm* poisoning; pestering.

atracar [atra'kar] *v* (*robar*) hold up; moor; (*fam*) gorge. **atracarse** *v* gorge oneself. **atracada** *sf* docking; (*pelea*) scuffle. **atracador** *sm* bandit.

atracción [atrak'θjon] *sf* attraction. **atracciones** *sf pl* entertainment *sing*. **atractivo** *adj* attractive.

*****atraer** [atra'er] *v* attract. **attracción** *sf* attraction. **atracciones** *sf pl* entertainment *sing*.

atrancar [atran'kar] *v* (*puerta*) bar; block up. **atrancarse** *v* become blocked/stuck/jammed.

atrapar [atra'par] *v* catch, trap.

atrás [a'tras] *adv* behind; in the rear; back; backwards; previously. **¡atrás!** get back! **atrasado** *adj* late; behind; in arrears; (*reloj*) slow; backward; in debt. **atrasar** *v* (*diferir*) postpone; put back; slow down; lose (time). **atrasarse** lag behind; be late; be slow. **atraso** *sm* delay; backwardness; slowness.

*****atravesar** [atraβe'sar] *v* (*poner*) place *or* put across; (*traspasar*) pierce; penetrate; cross; (*apostar*) bet. **atravesarse** *v* stand *or* lie across; get stuck; interfere; quarrel. **atravesado** *adj* lying across; pierced; (*fig*) wicked.

atreverse [atre'βerse] *v* dare; venture; be insolent. **atrevido, -a** *sm, sf* daredevil; cheeky person. **atrevimiento** *sm* boldness; effrontery.

*****atribuir** [atriβu'ir] *v* attribute. **atribución** *sf* attribution. **atributo** *sm* attribute.

atrocidad [atroθi'ðað] *sf* atrocity. **atroz** *adj* atrocious. **atrozmente** *adv* atrociously.

atrófia [a'trofja] *sf* atrophy. **atrofiar** *v* atrophy.

atropellar [atrope'ʎar] *v* knock down; (*pisotear*) trample on; (*ultrajar*) offend; (*agraviar*) bully; (*trabajo*) rush. **atropellar por** ignore. **atropellarse** *v* hurry. **atropelladamente** *adv* hurriedly. **atropellado** *adj* hasty. **atropellador** *adj* precipitate. **atropello** *sm* jostling, pushing; accident; outrage.

atún [a'tun] *sm* tunny, tuna.

aturdir [atur'ðir] *v* stun, daze; (*marear*) make dizzy; bewilder. **aturdido** *adj* dazed; (*imprudente*) thoughtless. **aturdidor** *adj* deafening. **aturdimiento** *sm* daze; giddiness; amazement.

aturrullar [aturru'ʎar] *v* confuse, bewilder. **aturrullarse** *v* become confused; panic.

atusar [atu'sar] *v* (*cortar*) trim; (*alisar*) smooth; (*acariciar*) stroke. **atusarse** *v* spruce oneself up.

audacia [au'ðaθja] *sf* audacity. **audaz** *adj* audacious.

audible [au'ðiβle] *adj* audible. **audibilidad** *sf* audibility.

audición [auði'θjon] *sf* hearing; (*prueba*) audition.

audiencia [au'ðjenθja] *sf* audience; hearing; (*tribunal*) court.

audífono [au'ðifono] *sm* hearing aid.

audiovisual [auðjoβi'swal] *adj* audiovisual.

auge ['auxe] *sm* peak; progress.

augurar [augu'rar] *v* predict. **augurio** *sm* augury, omen.

aula ['aula] *sf* lecture hall; (*escuela*) classroom. **aula magna** assembly hall.

aullar [au'ʎar] *v* howl. **aullido** *sm* howl.

aumentar [aumen'tar] *v* increase; (*sueldo*) raise; magnify; (*mejorar*) get better; (*empeorar*) get worse. **aumento** *sm* increase; rise; magnification.

aun [a'un] *adv* even. **aun así** even so. **aun cuando** although. **aún** *adv* still, yet. **aún no** not yet.

aunque [a'unke] *conj* even though, although.

áureo ['aureo] *adj* gold(en).

aureola [aure'ola] *sf* halo.

auricular [auriku'lar] *adj* of the ear, aural.

sm (*dedo*) little finger; (*teléfono*) telephone receiver. **auriculares** *sm pl* headphones *pl.*

aurora [au'rora] *sf* dawn.

ausencia [au'senθja] *sf* absence. **ausente** *adj* absent; missing.

auspicio [aus'piθjo] *sm* auspice, omen; (*patrocinio*) patronage.

austero [aus'tero] *adj* austere. **austeridad** *sf* austerity.

austral [aus'tral] *adj* southern.

Australia [aus'tralja] *sf* Australia. **australiano, -a** *s, adj* Australian.

Austria ['austrja] *sf* Austria. **austriaco, -a** *s, adj* Austrian.

auténtico [au'tentiko] *adj* authentic. **autenticar** *v* authenticate. **autenticidad** *sf* authenticity.

autístico [au'tistiko] *adj* autistic.

auto¹ ['auto] *sm* (*fam*) car. **auto de choque** dodgem car.

auto² *sm* (*jur*) sentence; (*de un pleito*) judgment. **autos** *sm pl* proceedings *pl.*

autobiografía [autoβjogra'fia] *sf* autobiography. **autobiográfico** *adj* autobiographical.

autobús [auto'βus] *sm* bus.

autocar [auto'kar] *sm* motor coach.

autodominio [autoðo'minjo] *sm* self-control.

autoescuela [autoes'kwela] *sf* driving school.

autoexpresión [autoekspre'sjon] *sf* self-expression.

autógrafo [au'tografo] *sm, adj* autograph.

automata [au'tomata] *sm* robot.

automático [auto'matiko] *adj* automatic. **automización** *sf* automation.

automóvil [auto'moβil] *sm* motorcar. **automovilista** *s(m+f)* motorist.

autonomía [autono'mia] *sf* autonomy. **autónomo** *adj* autonomous.

autopista [auto'pista] *sf* expressway.

autopsia [au'topsja] *sf* autopsy, post-mortem.

autor [au'tor], **-a** *sm, sf* author; creator.

autorizar [autori'θar] *v* authorize; approve. **autoridad** *sf* authority. **autoritario** *adj* authoritarian. **autorización** *sf* authorization. **autorizado** *adj* authorized, official; (*seguro*) reliable.

autorretrato [autorre'trato] *sm* self-portrait.

autoservicio [autoser'βiθjo] *sm* self-service restaurant; supermarket.

autostop [auto'stop] *sm* hitchhiking. **hacer el autostop** hitchhike. **autostopista** *s(m+f)* hitchhiker.

auxiliar [auksi'ljar] *v* help; attend. *sm, adj* assistant; auxiliary.

avalancha [aβa'lantʃa] *sf* avalanche.

avalorar [aβalo'rar] *v* (*realzar*) enhance; (*fig*) inspire.

avaluar [aβalu'ar] *v* value, appraise.

avanzar [aβan'θar] *v* advance, progress. **avance** *sm* advance; (*com*) balance. **avanzada** *sf* (*mil*) outpost.

avaricia [aβa'riθja] *sf* avarice. **avaricioso** *adj* greedy; miserly. **avaro** *adj* miserly, mean.

avasallar [aβasa'ʎar] *v* subjugate; dominate. **avasallarse** *v* submit.

ave ['aβe] *sf* bird. **aves de corral** *pl* poultry *sing*.

avecinarse [aβeθi'narse] *v* approach.

avellana [aβe'ʎana] *sf* hazelnut.

avena [a'βena] *sf sing* oats *pl*.

avenencia [aβe'nenθja] *sf* agreement; (*arreglo*) compromise.

avenida [aβe'niδa] *sf* avenue.

*****avenir** [aβe'nir] *v* reconcile, bring together; (*suceder*) happen. **avenirse** *v* agree; adapt; correspond to. **avenimiento** *sm* agreement.

aveñtajar [aβenta'xar] *v* lead; come in front of; (*sobresalir*) surpass; prefer. **aventajado** *adj* outstanding; favourable.

aventura [aβen'tura] *sf* adventure; (*riesgo*) risk; (*amor*) affair. **aventurado** *adj* risky. **aventurar** *v* risk; venture. **aventurero** *adj* adventurous.

*****avergonzar** [aβergon'θar] *v* shame; (*poner en un apuro*) embarrass. **avergonzarse** *v* be ashamed. **avergonzado** *adj* ashamed; embarrassed.

avería¹ [aβe'ria] *sf* aviary.

avería² [aβe'ria] *sf* (*coche*) breakdown; (*daño*) damage. **averiar** *v* damage; break down.

averiguar [aβeri'gwar] *v* investigate; (*examinar*) verify. **averiguación** *sf* investigation; verification. **averiguador** *adj* investigating; inquiring.

aversión [aβer'sjon] *sf* aversion.

avestruz [aβes'truθ] *sm* ostrich.

aviación [aβja'θjon] *sf* aviation; air force. **aviador, -a** *sm, sf* aviator.

ávido ['aβiδo] *adj* avid; (*con ganas*) eager. **avidez** *sf* avidity; eagerness.

avinagrar [aβina'grar] *v* sour, make bitter. **avinagrado** *adj* sour; (*fam*) peevish.

avión¹ [a'βjon] *sm* aircraft. **avión a reacción** jet plane. **por avión** by airmail.

avión² *sm* swift; martin.

avisar [aβi'sar] *v* inform; advise; admonish. **avisado** *adj* prudent. **mal avisado** rash. **avisador, -a** *sm, sf* adviser; informer; messenger. **aviso** *sm* notice; announcement; advice; (*advertencia*) warning; prudence.

avispa [a'βispa] *sf* wasp.

avivar [aβi'βar] *v* enliven; (*acelerar*) hasten; revive. **avivador** *adj* hastening; enlivening.

ay ['ai] *interj* alas!

aya ['aja] *sf* governess.

ayer [a'jer] *adv* yesterday; (*fig*) formerly, lately. *sm* the recent past. **de ayer acá** since yesterday.

ayo ['ajo] *sm* tutor.

ayudar [aju'δar] *v* help. **ayudarse** *v* help each other; make use of. **ayuda** *sf* help. **ayudante, -a** *sm, sf* assistant.

ayunar [aju'nar] *v* fast. **ayuno** *sm* fast, fasting.

ayuntamiento [ajunta'mjento] *sm* union; joint; (*cópula*) copulation; (*institución*) town council; (*edificio*) town hall.

azada [a'θaδa] *sf* hoe; spade.

azafata [aθa'fata] *sf* air hostess.

azafrán [aθa'fran] *sm* saffron.

azahar [aθa'ar] *sm* orange blossom; lemon blossom.

azar [a'θar] *sm* chance, accident; (*desgracia*) misfortune. **al azar** at random.

azogue [a'θoge] *sm* mercury.

azorar [aθo'rar] *v* upset, embarrass. **azorarse** *v* become flustered. **azoramiento** *sm* embarrassment; (*miedo*) fear.

azotar [aθo'tar] *v* beat; (*a un niño*) spank; (*látigo*) whip. **azote** *sm* whip; spanking; (*fig: verdugo*) scourge.

azotea [aθo'tea] *sf* flat roof.

azúcar [a'θukar] *sm or sf* sugar. **azúcar en terrón** lump sugar. **azúcar extra fina** castor sugar. **azúcar morena** brown sugar. **azucarado** *adj* sugary. **azucarero, -a** *sm, sf* sugar bowl.

azucena [aθu'θena] *sf* white lily.

azufre [a'θufre] *sm* sulphur.

azul [a'θul] *sm, adj* blue. **azul marino** navy blue. **azulado** *adj* blue, bluish.

azulejo [aθu'lexo] *sm* tile.
azuzar [aθu'θar] *v* (*fig*) incite; urge; cause trouble. **azuzador, -a** *sm, sf* trouble-maker.

B

baba ['baβa] *sf* saliva, spit. **babero** *sm* bib.
Babia ['baβja] *sf* **estar en Babia** have one's head in the clouds.
babor [ba'βor] *sm* (*mar*) port side.
babosa [ba'βosa] *sf* slug.
bacalao [baka'lao] *sm* cod.
bacía [ba'θia] *sf* (*de barbero*) shaving-bowl; (*recipiente*) metal basin.
bacteria [bak'teria] *sf* germ. **bacterias** *sf pl* bacteria *pl*.
bache ['batʃe] *sm* pothole.
bachiller [batʃi'ʎer] *s(m+f)* holder of a school-leaving certificate; (*universidad*) holder of a bachelor's degree. **bachillerato** *sm* school-leaving certificate; bachelor's degree.
bagaje [ba'gaxe] *sm* (*mil*) baggage; (*animal*) beast of burden.
bahía [ba'ia] *sf* bay.
bailar [bai'lar] *v* dance. **bailarín, -ina** *sm, sf* ballet dancer. **baile** *sm* dancing; dance; ball. **baile de disfraces** *or* **trajes** fancy-dress ball.
bajamar [baxa'mar] *sf* low tide.
bajar [ba'xar] *v* get down; lower; let down; take *or* bring down. **baja** *sf* fall, drop. **bajada** *sf* (*caida*) drop; (*pendiente*) slope; (*descendimiento*) descent.
bajo ['baxo] *adj* (*estatura*) short; low; lowered; (*sonido*) soft; (*conducta*) disgraceful. *adv* low; below; quietly, softly. *prep* under. **bajeza** *sf* base act; lowness.
bajón [ba'xon] *sm* (*música*) bassoon; (*bajada*) fall.
bala ['bala] *sf* (*proyectil*) bullet; (*algodón*) bale. **balazo** *sm* (*tiro*) shot; (*herida*) wound.
balada [ba'laða] *sf* ballad.
baladí [bala'ði] *adj* trivial, unimportant.
baladrón [bala'ðron], **-ona** *sm, sf* boaster, braggart. *adj* boastful.
balancear [balanθe'ar] *v* balance; (*barco*)

roll; (*vacilar*) hesitate. **balancearse** *v* roll; (*en un columpio*) swing. **balance** *sm* (*com*) balance sheet; (*inventario*) stocktaking. **balanceo** *sm* balancing; (*oscilación*) swaying. **balanza** *sf* scales *pl*.
balar [ba'lar] *v* bleat.
balaustrada [balau'straða] *sf* balustrade.
balbucear [balβuθe'ar] *v* stammer, stutter. **balbuceo** *sm* stammer.
balcón [bal'kon] *sm* balcony.
baldar [bal'ðar] *v* cripple; (*naipes*) trump; (*molestar*) inconvenience. **baldarse** *v* wear oneself out. **baldado, -a** *sm, sf* cripple.
baldadura *sf* infirmity.
balde¹ ['balðe] *sm* bucket.
balde² *adv* **de balde** free of charge. **en balde** in vain.
baldío [bal'ðio] *sm* wasteland. *adj* uncultivated; (*fig*) useless.
baldón [bal'ðon] *sm* (*afrenta*) affront; (*deshonra*) disgrace.
baldosa [bal'ðosa] *sf* paving tile.
balneario [balne'arjo] *sm* spa.
balón [ba'lon] *sm* ball, football; (*com*) bale. **baloncesto** *sm* basketball. **balonvolea** *sm* volleyball.
balsa¹ ['balsa] *sf* balsa.
balsa² *sf* raft.
balsa³ *sf* (*agua*) pond.
bálsamo ['balsamo] *sm* balsam; (*fig*) balm.
Báltico ['baltiko] *sm* Baltic Sea. **báltico** *adj* Baltic.
ballena [ba'ʎena] *sf* whale.
ballesta [ba'ʎesta] *sf* crossbow. **ballestero** *sm* archer.
ballet [ba'le] *sm* ballet.
bambolear [bambole'ar] *v* sway.
bambolla [bam'boʎa] *sf* show, ostentation. **darse bambolla** show off.
bambú [bam'bu] *sm* bamboo.
banana [ba'nana] *sf* banana. **banano** *sm* banana tree.
banasta [ba'nasta] *sf* large basket.
banca ['banka] *sf* (*asiento*) bench; (*com*) banking.
bancarrota [bankar'rota] *sf* bankruptcy. **hacer bancarrota** go bankrupt.
banco ['banko] *sm* bench; (*iglesia*) pew; (*colegio*) desk; (*com*) bank.
banda ['banda] *sf* group; (*pandilla*) gang; (*faja*) sash; (*cinta*) ribbon; (*lado*) side; (*orilla*) river bank. **bandada** *sf* flock.
bandeja [ban'dexa] *sf* tray.

bandera [ban'dera] *sf* flag, banner. **a banderas desplegadas** openly. **banderilla** *sf* bullfighter's dart. **banderillero** *sm* one who thrusts banderillas into the bull.
bandido [ban'diðo] *sm* bandit.
bando ['bando] *sm* proclamation; (*facción*) faction; party; (*pez*) shoal (of fish).
bandolero [bando'lero], **-a** *sm*, *sf* bandit.
banjo ['banxo] *sm* banjo.
banquete [ban'kete] *sm* banquet, feast.
bañar [ba'ɲar] *v* bathe. **bañarse** *v* (*en la bañera*) have a bath; (*en el mar*) bathe. **bañera** *sf* bathtub. **bañero** *sm* lifeguard. **bañista** *s*(*m*+*f*) bather. **baño** *sm* bath; (*en el agua*) dip, swim; (*cubierta*) coating. **cuarto de baño** bathroom.
baquetear [bakete'ar] *v* (*incomodar*) bother; (*maltratar*) treat harshly. **baquetazo** *sm* blow, knock. **baqueteo** *sm* (*traqueteo*) jolting; (*molestia*) bother.
bar [bar] *sm* bar.
baraja [ba'raxa] *sf* pack of cards. **barajar** *v* shuffle.
barandilla [baran'diʎa] *sf* rail, railing.
barato [ba'rato] *adj* cheap. **dar de barato** take for granted. **baratear** *v* undersell. **baratija** *sf* trinket. **baratijas** *sf pl* junk *sing*. **baratura** *sf* cheapness.
baraúnda [bara'unda] *sf* (*alboroto*) uproar; (*confusión*) chaos.
barba ['barβa] *sf* beard. **barba a barba** face to face. **barbado** *adj* bearded. **barbería** *sf* barber's shop. **barbero** *sm* barber. **barbudo** *adj* having a full beard.
bárbaro ['barβaro], **-a** *sm*, *sf* barbarian; (*fig*) lout. *adj* barbarous, barbaric; (*bruto*) rough; (*fam*) fantastic. **barbaridad** *sf* barbarity; (*ultraje*) outrage. **¡qué barbaridad!** fancy that! how terrible!
barbecho [bar'βetʃo] *sm* fallow land. **barbechar** *v* leave fallow.
barbilla [bar'βiʎa] *sf* chin.
barca ['barka] *sf* boat. **barca de pasaje** ferry boat.
barco ['barko] *sm* ship, boat. **ir en barco** go by boat.
barnizar [barni'θar] *v* (*madera*) varnish; (*cerámica*) glaze. **barniz** *sm* varnish; glaze.
barómetro [ba'rometro] *sm* barometer. **barométrico** *adj* barometric.
barón [ba'ron] *sm* baron. **baronesa** *sf* baroness. **baronet** *sm* baronet.
barquillo [bar'kiʎo] *sm* thin sweet wafer.

barra ['barra] *sf* (*metal, madera, chocolate, jabón, etc.*) bar; (*vara*) rod; (*joya*) pin; (*palanca*) lever; (*pan*) loaf; (*jur*) dock; (*mar*) tiller.
barraca [bar'raka] *sf* cabin, hut; (*feria*) stall.
barranco [bar'ranko] *sm* ravine, gully; (*fig*) obstacle.
barrenar [barre'nar] *v* drill, bore; (*leyes*) violate; (*una empresa*) foil. **barrena** *sf* drill.
barrer [bar'rer] *v* sweep.
barrera [bar'rera] *sf* barrier; obstacle; gate. **barrera de peaje** tollgate.
barricada [barri'kada] *sf* barricade.
barriga [bar'riga] *sf* belly.
barril [bar'ril] *sm* barrel.
barrio ['barrjo] *sm* district, quarter.
barro ['barro] *sm* mud. **barroso** *adj* muddy.
barroco [bar'roko] *sm* baroque period. *adj* baroque.
barruntar [barrun'tar] *v* have a feeling; (*suponer*) suppose. **barruntador** *adj* prophetic. **barrunte** *or* **barrunto** *sm* feeling; supposition; (*indicio*) sign.
bártulos ['bartulos] *sm pl* belongings, odds and ends. **liar los bártulos** pack one's bags.
barullo [ba'ruʎo] *sm* confusion; (*alboroto*) row. **a barullo** galore.
basar [ba'sar] *v* found; base. **basarse en** be based on. **base** *sf* base, basis. **a base de** by. **alimento base** staple food. **básico** *adj* basic, essential.
bastante [bas'tante] *adj* enough. *adv* enough, sufficiently; (*algo*) rather, fairly. **bastar** *v* suffice. **¡basta!** that's enough!
bastardo [bas'tardo], **-a** *s*, *adj* bastard. **bastardear** *v* degenerate. **bastardilla** *sf* italics *pl*. **bastardillo** *adj* italic.
bastidor [basti'ðor] *sm* frame; (*ventana*) sash. **entre bastidores** behind the scenes.
basto[1] ['basto] *adj* coarse, crude.
basto[2] *sm* (*arnés*) pack-saddle.
basto[3] *sm* (*naipes*) ace of clubs. **bastos** *sm pl* clubs.
bastón [bas'ton] *sm* cane, stick.
basura [ba'sura] *sf* rubbish, litter. **basurero** *sm* dustman.
bata ['bata] *sm* (*de cama*) dressing gown; (*de médico, etc.*) overall.
batalla [ba'taʎa] *sf* battle. **campo de batalla** battlefield.

batata [ba'tata] *sf* sweet potato.

batea [ba'tea] *sf* (*barco*) punt; (*bandeja*) tray; (*vagón*) open wagon.

batería [bate'ria] *sf* battery; (*teatro*) footlights; (*música*) percussion. **batería de cocina** kitchen utensils *pl*.

batir [ba'tir] *v* (*huevos*) beat; (*las manos*) clap; (*vencer*) defeat; (*derribar*) knock down; (*culin*) whisk. **batirse** *v* fight. **batido** *sm* (*leche*) milk shake; (*culin*) batter. **batidor** *sm* whisk.

batuta [ba'tuta] *sf* (*música*) baton. **llevar la batuta** rule the roost.

baúl [ba'ul] *sm* trunk.

bautizar [bauti'θar] *v* baptize, christen; (*fam: vino, etc.*) water down. **bautismo** *sm* baptism, christening. **bautista** *sm* Baptist.

baya ['baja] *sf* berry.

bayeta [ba'jeta] *sf* baize; floorcloth; rag.

bayoneta [bajo'neta] *sf* bayonet.

baza ['baθa] *sf* (*naipes*) trick. **meter baza** intervene.

bazar [ba'θar] *sm* bazaar.

bazo ['baθo] *sm* spleen. *adj* brownish yellow.

beato [be'ato] *adj* pious; blessed; (*fam*) sanctimonious.

beber [be'βer] *v* drink. **beberse** *v* drink up. **bebida** *sf* drink.

beca ['beka] *sf* grant; scholarship.

becerro [be'θerro] *sm* yearling calf.

bedel [be'ðel] *sm* porter; beadle.

befar [be'far] *v* mock, taunt. **befa** *sf* jeer, taunt.

béisbol ['beisβol] *sm* baseball.

Belén [be'len] *s* Bethlehem. **belén** *sm* Nativity scene; (*fam*) bedlam.

Bélgica ['belxika] *sf* Belgium. **belga** *s(m+f)*, *adj* Belgian.

bélico ['beliko] *adj* warlike. **belicosidad** *sf* bellicosity. **belicoso** *adj* bellicose.

beligerante [belixe'rante] *s(m+f)*, *adj* belligerent. **beligerancia** *sf* belligerence.

bellaco [be'ʎako], **-a** *sm*, *sf* rogue. *adj* cunning; wicked.

belleza [be'ʎeθa] *sf* beauty. **bellísimo** *adj* gorgeous. **bello** *adj* beautiful; noble.

bellota [be'ʎota] *sf* acorn.

bemol [be'mol] *sm*, *adj* (*música*) flat.

bencina [ben'θina] *sf* benzine.

*****bendecir** [benðe'θir] *v* bless; praise. **bendición** *sf* benediction; grace. **bendito** *adj* blessed; saintly; (*fam*) wretched.

beneficiar [benefi'θjar] *v* benefit; profit. **benefactor, -a** *sm*, *sf also* **beneficiador, -a** benefactor. **beneficencia** *sf* charity; welfare. **beneficiado, -a** *sm*, *sf also* **beneficiario, -a** beneficiary. **beneficio** *sm* benefit; gain. **beneficioso** *adj* beneficial.

benemérito [bene'merito] *adj* worthy, well-deserving.

beneplácito [bene'plaθito] *sm* consent, approval.

benevolencia [benevo'lenθja] *sf* benevolence. **benevolente** *or* **benévolo** *adj* benevolent.

benignidad [benigni'daθ] *sf* kindness; (*clima*) mildness. **benigno** *adj* kind; mild.

beodo [be'oðo], **-a** *sm*, *sf* drunkard. *adj* drunk.

berberecho [berβe'retʃo] *sm* cockle.

berenjena [beren'xena] *sf* eggplant.

bermejo [ber'mexo] *adj* vermilion; (*cabellos*) ginger.

bermellón [berme'ʎon] *sm* vermilion.

berrear [berre'ar] *v* bellow; yell. **berrearse** *v* (*fam*) spill the beans. **berrido** *sm* bellow; yell.

berrinche [ber'rintʃe] *sm* (*fam*) tantrum.

berro ['berro] *sm* watercress.

berza ['berθa] *sf* cabbage.

besar [be'sar] *v* kiss. **beso** *sm* kiss.

bestia ['bestja] *sf* beast, animal. *sm* (*persona*) beast; idiot. **bestial** *adj* bestial; beastly; (*fam*) smashing; enormous. **bestialidad** *sf* bestiality; beastliness.

betún [be'tun] *sm* shoe polish; bitumen.

biblia ['biβlia] *sf* Bible. **bíblico** *adj* biblical.

bibliografía [biβliogra'fia] *sf* bibliography. **bibliográfico** *adj* bibliographic(al). **bibliógrafo, -a** *sm*, *sf* bibliographer.

biblioteca [biβlio'teka] *sf* library. **bibliotecario, -a** *sm*, *sf* librarian.

bíceps ['biθeps] *sm invar* biceps.

bicicleta [biθi'kleta] *sf* bicycle.

bicho ['bitʃo] *sm* small animal; insect; (*fam*) odd character; (*fam*) ugly person.

bieldo ['bjelðo] *sm* pitchfork.

bien [bjen] *adv* well; right; properly; very; fully; easily; gladly. **ahora bien** nevertheless. **o bien** or else. **¿y bien?** so what? *sm* good; welfare; advantage; gain; darling. **bien que** *conj also* **si bien** although. **no bien** no sooner. **bienes** *sm pl* property *sing*, riches. **bienes inmuebles** real estate *sing*.

bienal [bje'nal] *sf, adj* biennial.
bienaventurado [bjenaβentu'raðo] *adj* happy; blessed; (*fig*) naïve.
bienestar [bjenes'tar] *sm* well-being; comfort.
bienhechor [bjene'tʃor], **-a** *sm, sf* benefactor.
bienio ['bjenjo] *sm* period of two years.
bienvenida [bjenβe'niða] *sf* welcome. **dar la bienvenida a** welcome.
biftec [bif'tek] *sm* steak.
bifurcarse [bifur'karse] *v* fork; branch off. **bifurcación** *sf* fork; junction.
bigamia [bi'gamja] *sf* bigamy. **bígamo, -a** *sm, sf* bigamist.
bigote [bi'gote] *sm* moustache.
bilingüe [bi'lingwe] *adj* bilingual.
bilis ['bilis] *sf* bile; (*fig*) bad temper.
billar [bi'ʎar] *sm* billiards. **billar ruso** snooker.
billete [bi'ʎete] *sm* ticket; (*dinero*) banknote; (*carta*) letter. **billete de abono** season ticket. **billete de ida** single ticket. **billete de ida y vuelta** return ticket. **sacar un billete** buy a ticket.
billón [bi'ʎon] *sm* billion.
binóculo [bi'nokulo] *sm* binoculars *pl*.
biografía [biogra'fia] *sf* biography. **biográfico** *adj* biographical. **biógrafo, -a** *sm, sf* biographer.
biología [biolo'xia] *sf* biology. **biológico** *adj* biological. **biólogo** *sm* biologist.
biombo ['bjombo] *sm* folding screen.
bióxido [bi'oksido] *sm* dioxide. **bioxido de carbono** carbon dioxide.
biplano [bi'plano] *sm* biplane.
birlar [bir'lar] *v* (*fam: robar*) pinch, swipe; (*fam: matar*) bump off.
bisabuela [bisa'βwela] *sf* great-grandmother. **bisabuelo** *sm* great-grandfather.
bisagra [bi'sagra] *sf* hinge.
bisiesto [bi'sjesto] *adj* **año bisiesto** leap year.
bisoño [bi'soɲo], **-a** *sm, sf* greenhorn, novice; (*mil*) rookie.
bizarría [biθar'ria] *sf* (*valor*) bravery; generosity.
bizcar [biθ'kar] *v* squint. **bizco** *adj* cross-eyed. **dejar bizco** (*fam*) dumbfound.
bizcocho [biθ'kotʃo] *sm* sponge cake. **bizcocho borracho** rum baba.
bizma ['biθma] *sf* poultice.
blanco ['blanko], **-a** *adj* white; blank; (*fam*) cowardly. *sm, sf* white man/woman; white colour; *sm* (*de tiro*)

target. **blanca** *sf* (*música*) minim. **no tener blanca** be completely broke. **blancura** *sf* whiteness. **dar en el blanco** be on target. **quedarse en blanco** be disappointed. **blanquear** *v* whiten; whitewash. **blanquecer** *v* whitewash; bleach.
blandir [blan'dir] *v* flourish, brandish.
blando ['blando] *adj* soft; mild; gentle. *adv* softly; gently. **blandura** *sf* softness; tenderness; (*carácter*) weakness.
blasfemar [blasfe'mar] *v* blaspheme; (*fig*) curse. **blasfemia** *sf* blasphemy; curse. **blasfemo, -a** *sm, sf* blasphemer.
blasón [bla'son] *sm* heraldry; (*escudo*) coat of arms. **hacer blasón de** boast about.
blindaje [blin'daxe] *sm* armour. **blindado** *adj* armoured; armour-plated.
bloquear [bloke'ar] *v* block; obstruct; (*mil*) blockade. **bloque** *sm* block; bloc. **bloqueo** *sm* blockade.
blusa ['blusa] *sf* blouse; (*guardapolvo*) overall.
boa ['boa] *sf* boa constrictor.
boato [bo'ato] *sm* pomp; show.
bobada [bo'baða] *sf* nonsense; foolish thing. **bobería** *sf* stupidity. **bobo, -a** *sm, sf* fool, idiot.
bobina [bo'bina] *sf* reel, spool.
boca ['boka] *sf* mouth; opening. **a boca de jarro** point-blank. **a boca de noche** at dusk. **boca abajo/arriba** face down/up. **¡punto en boca!** mum's the word!
bocacalle [boka'kaʎe] *sf* intersection.
bocadillo [boka'ðiʎo] *sm* sandwich; snack. **bocado** *sm* mouthful; bite.
boceto [bo'θeto] *sm* (*dibujo*) sketch; (*escrito*) draft.
bocina [bo'θina] *sf* trumpet; (*aut*) horn, hooter.
bochorno [bo'tʃorno] *sm* sultry weather; (*vergüenza*) embarrassment; (*mareo*) giddiness. **sufrir un bochorno** feel embarrassed. **bochornoso** *adj* sultry; thundery; embarrassing.
boda ['boða] *sf* wedding, marriage.
bodega [bo'ðega] *sf* wine cellar; wine shop; bar.
bofetada [bofe'taða] *sf* slap; blow.
boga ['boga] *sf* (*mar*) rowing; (*fig*) vogue. **estar en boga** be in fashion. **bogador, -a** *sm, sf* rower.
bohemio [bo'emjo], **-a** *s, adj* Bohemian; (*gitano*) gipsy.

boicotear [boikote'ar] *v* boycott. **boicot** *or* **boicoteo** *sm* boycott.

boina ['boina] *sf* beret.

bola ['bola] *sf* ball; *(canica)* marble; *(betún)* shoe polish; *(del mundo)* globe; *(fig)* fib. **bola de naftalina** mothball. **bolear** *v* fib; throw.

boleta [bo'leta] *sf* ticket; pass; *(vale)* voucher; *(votación)* ballot paper.

boleto [bo'leto] *sm* lottery ticket; betting slip; *(fam)* fib. **boletín** *sm* bulletin. **boletín de noticias** news bulletin. **boletín de precios** price list. **boletín meteorológico** weather forecast.

bolígrafo [bo'ligrafo] *sm* ballpoint pen.

Bolivia [bo'liβja] *sf* Bolivia. **boliviano, -a** *s, adj* Bolivian.

bolsa ['bolsa] *sf* bag; purse. **bolsillo** *sm* pocket.

bollo ['boʎo] *sm* roll, bun, small loaf.

bomba ['bomba] *sf* pump, bomb. **bomba de gasolina** petrol pump.

bombardear [bombarðe'ar] *v* bombard.

bombilla [bom'biʎa] *sf* (*elec*) light bulb; *(tecn)* small pump; glass tube.

bombo ['bombo] *sm* big drum; great praise. *adj* surprised.

bombón [bom'bon] *sm* sweet, chocolate.

bonachón [bona'tʃon] *adj* *(fam)* genial.

bondad [bon'dað] *sf* goodness; kindness. **tenga la bondad de ...** please ... . **bondadoso** *adj* warm-hearted; good.

bonete [bo'nete] *sm* academic cap. **gran bonete** important person.

bonito [bo'nito] *adj* pretty, nice, graceful.

bono ['bono] *sm* voucher; certificate; bond. **bono postal** money-order.

boquear [boke'ar] *v* gasp; utter; be dying. **boqueada** *sf* gasp.

boquerón [boke'ron] *sm* large opening; anchovy; whitebait. **boquete** *sm* small hole; gap.

boquiabierto [bokja'βjerto] *adj* open-mouthed; gaping.

boquilla [bo'kiʎa] *sf* mouthpiece; nozzle; pipe stem.

borboll(e)ar [borβo'ʎar] *v* bubble. **borbolleo** *sm* bubbling. **borbollón** *sm* bubble.

borbotar [borβo'tar] *v* bubble; boil; gush. **borbotón** *sm* bubbling; boiling.

bordar [bor'ðar] *v* embroider. **bordado** *sm* embroidery.

borde ['borðe] *sm* border, edge; rim. **bordear** *v* skirt, edge round.

bordillo [bor'ðiʎo] *sm* kerb.

bordo ['borðo] *sm* *(mar)* side of a ship; tack. **a bordo** on board. **de alto bordo** ocean-going.

boreal [bore'al] *adj* northern.

bornear [borne'ar] *v* bend, turn, twist; warp.

borra ['borra] *sf* coarse wool; nap; waste; *(fam)* idle chatter.

borracho [bor'ratʃo] *adj* drunk; *(fam)* crazy. **borrachera** *or* **borrachería** *sf* drunkenness; drunken spree.

borrador [borra'ðor] *sm* rough copy; blotter; scribbling pad.

borrar [bor'rar] *v* cross out; erase; blot. **goma de borrar** rubber. **borrable** *adj* erasable.

borrasca [bor'raska] *sf* storm; squall. **borrascoso** *adj* stormy; squally; *(fig)* boisterous.

borrico [bor'riko] *sm* ass. **puesto en el borrico** hellbent.

borrón [bor'ron] *sm* blot, smudge; blemish; stain. **borronear** *v* scribble (on). **borroso** *adj* blurred; smudged; stained; illegible.

bosque ['boske] *sm* forest, wood.

bosquejar [boske'xar] *v* make a rough sketch of. **bosquejo** *sm* outline; sketch.

bostezar [boste'θar] *v* yawn. **bostezo** *sm* yawn.

bota¹ ['bota] *sf* boot. **ponerse las botas a** do justice to (something).

bota² *sf* wineskin.

botánica [bo'tanika] *sf* botany. **botánico** *adj* botanical. **botanista** *s(m+f)* botanist.

botar [bo'tar] *v* throw, fling; launch.

bote¹ ['bote] *sm* thrust; blow; jump; bounce.

bote² *sm* jar; can.

bote³ *sm* boat. **bote salvavidas** lifeboat.

botella [bo'teʎa] *sf* bottle.

botica [bo'tika] *sf* chemist's shop; medicine chest; medicines *pl*; shop, store. **hay de todo como en botica** there is everything under the sun. **boticario** *sm* chemist.

botija [bo'tixa] *sf* earthenware pot. **botijo** *sm* earthenware jug.

botín [bo'tin] *sm* booty, loot.

botón [bo'ton] *sm* button; *(flor)* bud; *(puerta)* knob. **botonar** *v* bud.

bóveda ['boβeða] *sf* vault. **bóveda de jardín** bower.

bovino [bo'βino] *adj* bovine.

boxear [bokse'ar] *v* box. **boxeador** *sm* boxer. **boxeo** *sm* boxing.

boya ['boja] *sf* buoy. **boyante** *adj* buoyant.

bozal [bo'θal] *sm* muzzle. *s(m+f)* (*fam*) greenhorn. *adj* (*fam*) stupid; foolish; untamed.

bracero [bra'θero], **-a** *sm, sf* hired hand; labourer.

braga ['braga] *sf* (*cuerda*) guy-rope; (*de mujer*) knickers *pl*; (*de niño*) nappy. **calzarse las bragas** wear the trousers.

bramar [bra'mar] *v* roar, bellow. **bramido** *sm* roar, bellow.

brasa ['brasa] *sf* live coal. **estar en brasas** be on edge. **brasero** *sm* brazier.

Brasil [bra'sil] *sm* Brazil. **brasileño, -a** *s, adj* Brazilian.

bravío [bra'βio] *adj* wild; fierce. *sm* fierceness.

bravo ['braβo] *adj* brave; fierce; (*fam*) rough; (*fam*) rude; (*fam*) luxurious. **mar bravo** rough sea. **¡bravo!** *interj* bravo! well done! **bravura** *sf* ferocity; courage; manliness.

brazada [bra'θaða] *sf* arm movement; stroke. **brazado** *sm* armful.

brazalete [braθa'lete] *sm* bracelet.

brazo ['braθo] *sm* arm; branch; (*fig*) strength, power. **brazo a brazo** hand to hand. **a brazo partido** with bare fists. **brazo derecho** right-hand man. **tener brazo** be tough.

brea ['brea] *sf* pitch, tar.

brebaje [bre'βaxe] *sm* concoction, potion.

brecol ['brekol] *sm* broccoli.

brecha ['bretʃa] *sf* breach, opening.

bregar¹ [bre'gar] *v* struggle; fight. **brega** *sf* struggle; quarrel. **andar a la brega** (*fig*) slog away.

bregar² *v* (*amasar*) knead.

Bretaña [bre'taɲa] *sf* Britain; Brittany. **Gran Bretaña** Great Britain. **bretón, -ona** *s, adj* Breton.

breve ['breβe] *adj* brief, short. **en breve** before long. *sf* (*música*) breve. **brevedad** *sf* brevity.

brezal [bre'θal] *sm* heath. **brezo** *sm* heather.

bribón [bri'βon], **-ona** *sm, sf* rascal; rogue; vagabond. *adj* rascally.

brida ['briða] *sf* bridle; rein; horsemanship. **a toda brida** hell for leather.

brigada [bri'gaða] *sf* brigade; gang; squad. *sm* sergeant-major.

brillar [bri'ʎar] *v* shine; sparkle; gleam. **brillante** *adj* brilliant; shining; glossy. **brillo** *sm* brilliance; brightness; glitter.

brincar [brin'kar] *v* bounce; jump; hop. **brinco** *sm* jump; hop; skip; bounce.

brindar [brin'ðar] *v* offer; drink someone's health. **brindis** *sm invar* toast.

brío ['brio] *sm* spirit; vigour; determination. **brioso** *adj* spirited; vigorous; determined; elegant.

brisa ['brisa] *sf* breeze.

británico [bri'taniko], **-a** *sm, sf* Briton. *adj* British. **los británicos** the British.

brocha ['brotʃa] *sf* paintbrush; (*afeitar*) shaving brush.

broche ['brotʃe] *sm* brooch; clasp, clip. **broche de oro** finishing touch.

broma ['broma] *sf* joke; fun; trick. **broma pesada** practical joke. **en broma** as a joke. **sin broma** joking apart. **bromear** *v* joke. **bromista** *s(m+f)* practical joker; funny person.

bromuro [bro'muro] *sm* bromide.

bronca ['bronka] *sf* (*fam*) row; brawl; ticking off. **echar una bronca** tick off.

bronce ['bronθe] *sm* bronze. **bronceado** *adj* bronzed; sun-tanned.

bronco ['bronko] *adj* rough; brittle; (*voz*) harsh; (*carácter*) hard, rude.

bronquial [bronki'al] *adj* bronchial. **bronquitis** *sf* bronchitis.

brotar [bro'tar] *v* grow; bud; germinate; spring forth. **brote** *sm* bud; shoot; (*agua*) gushing; (*fiebre*) rise; (*fig*) outbreak.

bruja ['bruxa] *sf* witch. **brujo** *sm* sorcerer.

brújula ['bruxula] *sf* compass. **perder la brújula** lose one's grip.

bruma ['bruma] *sf* mist. **brumoso** *adj* misty.

bruno ['bruno] *adj* dark brown.

bruñir [bru'ɲir] *v* polish. **bruñido** *sm* shine, polish. **bruñidor** *sm* polisher.

brusco ['brusko] *adj* brusque; abrupt; rough.

Bruselas [bru'selas] *sf* Brussels.

bruto ['bruto] *adj* coarse; brutish; rough; gross. *sm* brute; beast. **en bruto** gross; rough; uncut. **brutal** *adj* brutal; savage. **brutalidad** *sf* brutality; brutishness.

bucear [buθe'ar] *v* dive; swim underwater. **buceo** *sm* dive; diving; skin diving.

bucle ['bukle] *sm* curl; ringlet.

buche ['butʃe] *sm* craw; crop; stomach; (*fam*) belly; (*fam*) bosom, breast.
budismo [bu'ðismo] *sm* Buddhism. **budista** *s*(*m*+*f*), *adj* Buddhist.
buenaventura [bwenaβen'tura] *sf* good luck, fortune.
bueno ['bweno] *adj also* **buen** good; right; sound; fine; (*fam*) funny; (*fam*) amazing. *interj, conj* well; all right. **a buenas** of one's own accord. **buena voluntad** goodwill. **de buena gana** willingly. **¡buenas!** hello! **buenas noches** good night. **buenas tardes** good afternoon; good evening. **buenos días** good morning. **de buenas a primeras** without warning; at first sight; straight away. **estar de buenas** be in a good mood.
buey [bwej] *sm* ox. **a paso de buey** at a snail's pace.
búfalo ['bufalo] *sm* buffalo.
bufanda [bu'fanda] *sf* scarf, muffler.
bufar [bu'far] *v* spit; snort; puff and blow.
bufete [bu'fete] *sm* (*mesa*) writing-desk; (*despacho*) solicitor's office; clientele.
buhardilla [bwar'ðiʎa] *sf* attic, garret; skylight.
búho ['buo] *sm* owl; (*fam*) recluse.
buhonero [bwo'nero] *sm* pedlar, hawker. **buhonería** *sf* hawking, peddling.
buitre ['bwitre] *sm* vulture.
bujía [bu'xia] *sf* candle; candlepower; (*aut*) sparking-plug.
bulbo ['bulβo] *sm* (*bot*) bulb. **bulboso** *adj* bulbous.
Bulgaria [bul'garja] *sf* Bulgaria. **búlgaro, -a** *s, adj* Bulgarian.
bulto ['bulto] *sm* bulk, size; shape, form; bale, package; piece of luggage; (*med*) lump, swelling. **a bulto** approximately. **de bulto** obvious. **escoger a bulto** pick at random.
bulla ['buʎa] *sf* noise; bustle. **meter bulla** kick up a racket.
bullir [bu'ʎir] *v* boil; swarm; stir; bustle; abound; itch. **bullicio** *sm* bustle; uproar. **bullicioso** *adj* lively; noisy; bustling.
buñuelo [bu'ɲwelo] *sm* fritter; doughnut; (*fam*) mess.
buque ['buke] *sm* ship, vessel. **buque de guerra** warship. **buque cargero** freighter.
burbujear [burβuxe'ar] *v* bubble. **burbuja** *sf* bubble.
burdel [bur'ðel] *sm* brothel.
burdo ['burðo] *adj* clumsy; coarse; crude.

burgués [bur'ges] *adj* bourgeois, middle-class. **burguesía** *sf* bourgeoisie, middle class.
burla ['burla] *sf* hoax; joke; trick; taunt. **burlar** *v* hoax; trick; mock. **burlarse de** make fun of. **burlería** *sf* fun; artifice; deceit; ridicule.
burocracia [buro'kraθja] *sf* bureaucracy. **burócrata** *s*(*m*+*f*) bureaucrat. **burocrático** *adj* bureaucratic.
burro ['burro] *sm* donkey; (*fam*) fool. **burro cargado de letras** pompous ass.
buscar [bus'kar] *v* search for, look for. **busca** *sf* search. **en busca de** in search of. **buscador, -a** *sm, sf* seeker. **búsqueda** *sf* search.
busto ['busto] *sm* bust.
butaca [bu'taka] *sf* theatre seat; armchair.
buzo ['buθo] *sm* diver. **campana de buzo** diving-bell.
buzón [bu'θon] *sm* pillar box, letter box; plug, bung.

C

cabal [ka'βal] *adj* exact; complete; perfect. *adv* exactly; perfectly.
cábala ['kaβala] *sf* (*fig*) intrigue; divination.
cabalgar [kaβal'gar] *v* ride. **cabalgada** *sf* raid; cavalcade. **cabalgador** *sm* horseman.
caballa [ka'βaʎa] *sf* mackerel.
caballero [kaβa'ʎero] *sm* horseman; gentleman; knight. **caballeresco** *adj* chivalrous. **caballería** *sf* cavalry.
caballete [kaβa'ʎete] *sm* ridge; trestle; easel; bridge of the nose.
caballo [ka'βaʎo] *sm* horse; (*ajedrez*) knight; (*naipes*) queen. **a caballo** on horseback. **caballo de vapor** horsepower. **caballo entero** stallion. **caballito** *sm* pony.
cabaña [ka'βaɲa] *sf* cabin; herd, flock.
cabaret [kaβa're] *sm* cabaret; nightclub.
cabecear [kaβeθe'ar] *v* nod; shake one's head. **cabecera** *sf* (*de mesa, cama, etc.*) head; river's source.
cabello [ka'βeʎo] *sm* hair. **traído por los cabellos** far-fetched. **cabelludo** *adj* hairy; shaggy; downy.

*caber [ka'βer] *v* fit, find room; befall; be possible. **no cabe duda** there is no doubt.
cabestro [ka'βestro] *sm* halter; leading ox. **llevar del cabestro** lead by the nose.
cabestrillo *sm* arm sling.
cabeza [ka'βeθa] *sf* head; chief; summit; capital. **cabeza de turco** scapegoat. **cabeza torcida** hypocrite. **cabezudo** *adj* big-headed.
cabida [ka'βiða] *sf* capacity, space. **dar cabida a** make room for. **tener cabida** be appropriate.
cabildo [ka'βilðo] *sm* town council; (*rel*) chapter.
cabina [ka'βina] *sf* cabin; telephone kiosk.
cabizbajo [kaβiθ'βaxo] *adj* downcast.
cable ['kaβle] *sm* cable, rope; cable(gram). **cablegrafiar** *v* cable. **cablegrama** *sm* cable(gram).
cabo ['kaβo] *sm* cape, headland; end; stump; handle; rope; corporal; bit, piece. **al cabo de** at the end of. **llevar a cabo** carry out.
cabotaje [kaβo'taxe] *sm* coastal navigation.
cabra ['kaβra] *sf* goat.
cabria ['kaβrja] *sf* crane, hoist.
cabriola [ka'βrjola] *sf* gambol; hop; jump. **cabriolar** *v* jump; caper.
cacahuete [kaka'wete] *sm* peanut.
cacao [ka'kao] *sm* cocoa; cacao.
cacarear [kakare'ar] *v* crow, cackle; boast. **cacareo** *sm* crowing, cackling; boasting.
cacería [kaθe'ria] *sf* hunting; hunt.
cacerola [kaθe'rola] *sf* saucepan.
cacique [ka'θike] *sm* political boss; tyrant.
caco ['kako] *sm* pickpocket; thief; (*fam*) coward.
cacto ['kakto] *sm* cactus.
cacharrería [katʃarre'ria] *sf* crockery. **cacharro** *sm* earthenware vessel; thing; piece of junk. **lavar los cacharros** do the washing-up.
cachemir [katʃe'mir] *sm* cashmere.
cachete [ka'tʃete] *sm* blow, slap; cheek; swollen cheek. **cachetear** *v* slap.
cachivache [katʃi'βatʃe] *sm* pot; thing; utensil; bauble.
cacho ['katʃo] *sm* piece, chunk, slice.
cachorro [ka'tʃorro], **-a** *sm, sf* pup; cub; kitten.

cada ['kaða] *adj invar* each, every. **cada vez más** more and more.
cadáver [ka'ðaβer] *sm* corpse.
cadena [ka'ðena] *sf* chain. **cadena perpetua** life imprisonment. **estar en cadena** be in prison.
cadencia [ka'ðenθja] *sf* cadence, rhythm.
cadera [ka'ðera] *sf* hip.
cadete [ka'ðete] *sm* cadet.
caducar [kaðu'kar] *v* expire, lapse; become senile. **caduco** *adj* senile; in decline.
*caer [ka'er] *v* fall, drop, tumble; decline; fall due; fade; fit, suit; realize, understand; be located, lie. **caer en** *or* **sobre** fall upon. **caer en la cuenta** understand. **caer en saco roto** fall on deaf ears. **caída** *sf* fall; downfall; lapse.
café [ka'fe] *sm* coffee; café. **café con leche** white coffee. **café solo** black coffee. **cafeína** *sf* caffeine. **cafetera** *sf* coffee pot. **cafetería** *sf* coffee bar.
caimán [kai'man] *sm* alligator.
caja ['kaxa] *sf* box, case; safe; coffin; frame; hole, slot; cash box; cashier's office; cash; (*música*) drum; (*auto*) body. **caja de ahorros** savings bank. **cajero, -a** *sm, sf* cashier. **cajetilla** *sf* packet; small box. **cajón** *sm* large box; crate, chest; drawer; coffin.
cal [kal] *sm* lime.
calabaza [kala'βaθa] *sf* pumpkin; gourd; (*fam*) fool. **dar calabazas a** (*examen*) fail; jilt. **llevar calabazas** be jilted. **calabazada** *sf* (*fam*) blow on the head.
calabozo [kala'βoθo] *sm* prison cell; pruning knife.
calamar [kala'mar] *sm* squid.
calambre [ka'lambre] *sm* cramp.
calamidad [kalami'ðað] *sf* calamity.
calar [ka'lar] *v* soak; perforate; slice; size up; (*fam*) pick pockets. **calarse hasta los huesos** get soaked to the skin.
calavera [kala'βera] *sf* skull. **calaverada** *sf* wild escapade, tomfoolery. **calaverear** *v* act recklessly; live it up.
calcar [kal'kar] *v* trace; copy; trample upon. **calco** *sm* tracing; copy.
calce ['kalθe] *sm* (*de rueda*) rim; wedge.
calceta [kal'θeta] *sf* stocking; fetter. **hacer calceta** knit. **calcetero, -a** *sm, sf* hosier. **calcetín** *sm* sock.
calcinar [kalθi'nar] *v* burn, blacken.
calcio ['kalθjo] *sm* calcium.

calcular [kalku'lar] *v* calculate. **calculación** *sf* calculation. **calculadora** *sf* calculating machine. **cálculo** *sm* calculation; estimate; (*med*) gallstone.

calda ['kalða] *sf* heating. **caldas** *sf pl* thermal springs *pl*.

caldera [kal'ðera] *sf* cauldron, boiling pan. **calderilla** *sf* small change.

caldo ['kalðo] *sm* broth; soup; salad dressing. **caldos** *sm pl* liquid foodstuffs *pl*; wines *pl*.

calefacción [kalefak'θjon] *sf* heating. **calefacción central** central heating.

calendario [kalen'darjo] *sm* calendar.

*calentar [kalen'tar] *v* heat, warm; (*fam*) thrash. **calentarse** *v* warm oneself; become excited. **calentador** *sm* heater. **calentura** *sf* fever. **caliente** *adj* hot, warm.

caletre [ka'letre] *sm* (*fam*) good sense, sound judgment.

calibrar [kali'βrar] *v* calibrate; gauge, measure. **calibre** *sm* calibre; gauge; (*fig*) importance.

calidad [kali'ðað] *sf* quality; (*med*) fever. **calidades** *sf pl* conditions *pl*; rules *pl*. **a calidad de que** on condition that. **en calidad de** in the capacity of.

cálido ['kaliðo] *adj* hot, warm.

calificar [kalifi'kar] *v* qualify; judge; distinguish; prove worthy. **calificarse** *v* give proof of nobility. **calificación** *sf* appreciation; distinction; judgment. **calificado** *adj* distinguished; suitable.

calina [ka'lina] *sf* mist, fog.

cáliz ['kaliθ] *sm* chalice, cup.

calmante [kal'mante] *adj* soothing. *sm* sedative.

calmar [kal'mar] *v* calm; be calm. **calmarse** *v* quieten down. **calma** *sf* calm, lull. **calmoso** *adj* calm.

calor [ka'lor] *sm* heat, warmth; fervour; fever. **hacer calor** (*temperatura*) be hot. **tener calor** (*persona*) be hot. **caluroso** *adj* hot, warm; (*fig*) ardent.

caloría [kalo'ria] *sf* calorie.

calvo ['kalβo] *adj* bald; bare; threadbare. **calvez** *sf* also **calvicie** baldness.

calzar [kal'θar] *v* put shoes on; wear (shoes, gloves, spurs); wedge. **calza** *sf* chock; (*fam*) stocking. **calzada** *sf* roadway.

calzón [kal'θon] *sm* trousers *pl*; safety belt. **calzones** *sm pl* trousers *pl*. **calzoncillos** *sm pl* underpants *pl*.

callar [ka'ʎar] *v* be silent; shut up. **callado** *adj* silent; reserved; secret. **de callado** quietly.

calle ['kaʎe] *sf* street, road. **dejar en la calle** leave penniless. **hacer calle** clear the way. **callejón** *sm* alley. **callejón sin salida** cul-de-sac. **callejuela** *sf* back street; (*fig*) loophole.

callo ['kaʎo] *sm* (*med*) corn, callus. **callos** *sm pl* tripe *sing*. **calloso** *adj* hard, callous.

cama ['kama] *sf* bed; litter; floor. **caer en cama** fall ill. **cama de campaña/matrimonio/soltero** camp/double/single bed.

camafeo [kama'feo] *sm* cameo.

camaleón [kamale'on] *sm* chameleon.

camandulero [kamandu'lero] *adj* (*fam*) sly; hypocritical.

cámara ['kamara] *sf* room; loft; chamber; cine *or* TV camera; inner tube. **ayuda de cámara** *sf* valet. **música de cámara** *sf* chamber music.

camarada [kama'raða] *sm* comrade; colleague.

camarero [kama'rero] *sm* waiter; steward. **camarera** *sf* waitress; stewardess; chambermaid.

camarilla [kama'riʎa] *sf* clique; parliamentary lobby.

camarón [kama'ron] *sm* shrimp.

camarote [kama'rote] *sm* cabin.

cambiar [kam'bjar] *v* change; exchange. **cambiante** *sm* moneychanger. **cambio** *sm* change; alteration; small change. **a cambio de** in exchange for. **en cambio** on the other hand.

camelar [kame'lar] *v* (*fam*) flatter; woo. **cameleo** *sm* (*fam*) flattery.

camello [ka'meʎo] *sm* camel.

camilla [ka'miʎa] *sf* stretcher; litter; couch.

caminar [kami'nar] *v* walk; travel; move along. **caminante** *s*(*m*+*f*) traveller. **camino** *sm* path; road; route; way. **abrirse camino** make one's way. **camino adelante** straight on. **ponerse en camino** set out.

camión [ka'mjon] *sm* truck. **camión de bomberos** fire engine.

camisa [ka'misa] *sf* shirt; fruit skin; casing; lining; dust jacket; paper wrapper. **camisa de dormir** nightdress. **camisa de fuerza** straightjacket. **dejar sin camisa** ruin (someone). **camiseta** *sf* vest. **camisón** *sm* nightdress; nightshirt.

camorra [ka'morra] *sf* (*fam*) quarrel, fight. **buscar camorra** look for trouble.
campamento [kampa'mento] *sm* camp. **campar** *v* camp; excel.
campana [kam'pana] *sf* bell; mantelpiece; parish (church); curfew.
campante [kam'pante] *adj* proud; pleased; (*fam*) relaxed, cool.
campaña [kam'paɲa] *sf* plain; campaign.
campechano [kampe'tʃano] *adj* (*fam*) genial; frank. **campechanía** *sf* good nature; frankness.
campeón [kampe'on], **-ona** *sm, sf* champion. **campeón de venta** bestseller. **campeonato** *sm* championship. **de campeonato** (*fig, fam*) fantastic.
campo ['kampo] *sm* field; countryside; camp; pitch; background. **campo de aviación** airfield. **campo raso** open country. **campesino, -a** *s, adj* peasant, rustic.
can [kan] *sm* dog; trigger.
cana ['kana] *sf* white *or* grey hair. **peinar canas** be getting old.
Canadá [kana'ða] *sm* Canada. **canadiense** *s(m+f), adj* Canadian.
canal [ka'nal] *sm* canal; channel; ditch; tube. *sf* carcass. **canalón** *sm* drainpipe; gutter.
canalla [ka'naʎa] *sf* rabble, mob. *sm* swine, scoundrel.
canapé [kana'pe] *sm* couch, sofa; (*culin*) canapé.
Canarias [ka'narjas] *sf pl* Canary Islands *pl*. **canario, -a** *sm, sf* inhabitant of the Canary Islands.
canario [ka'narjo] *sm* canary.
canasta [ka'nasta] *sf* basket.
cancelar [kanθe'lar] *v* cancel, annul. **cancelación** *sf* cancellation.
cáncer ['kanθer] *sm* (*med*) cancer.
Cáncer *sm* (*astron*) Cancer.
canciller [kanθi'ʎer] *sm* chancellor.
canción [kan'θjon] *sf* song; tune; rhyme. **mudar de canción** change one's tune. **cancionero** *sm* song-book.
cancha ['kantʃa] *sf* football ground; tennis court; racecourse.
candado [kan'daðo] *sm* padlock.
candela [kan'dela] *sf* candle; candlestick; fire; blossom; (*fam*) light. **candelero** *sm* candlestick; oil lamp. **poner en el candelero** make popular.
candente [kan'dente] *adj* red-hot, burning.

candidato [kandi'ðato] *sm* candidate. **candidatura** *sf* candidature.
cándido ['kandiðo] *adj* innocent, pure; gullible; candid. **candidez** *sf* candour; gullibility; stupid remark.
candil [kan'ðil] *sm* oil lamp.
candor [kan'dor] *sm* innocence; candour; simplicity. **candoroso** *adj* ingenuous; innocent; frank.
canela [ka'nela] *sf* cinnamon.
canelón [kane'lon] *sm* gutter; spout; icicle.
cangrejo [kan'grexo] *sm* crab.
canguro [kan'guro] *sm* kangaroo.
caníbal [ka'niβal] *s(m+f), adj* cannibal. **canibalismo** *sm* cannibalism.
canilla [ka'niʎa] *sf* (*tecn*) bobbin, spool; (*med*) shinbone; tap, spout.
canino [ka'nino] *adj* canine. **hambre canina** ravenous hunger.
canjear [kanxe'ar] *v* exchange. **canje** *sm* exchange.
cano ['kano] *adj* white-haired, grey-haired; (*fig*) ancient.
canoa [ka'noa] *sf* canoe.
canon ['kanon] *sm* rule; levy; perfect example; (*rel, música*) canon.
canónigo [ka'nonigo] *sm* (*rel*) canon. **canónico** *adj* canonical. **canonización** *sf* canonization. **canonizar** *v* canonize.
cansar [kan'sar] *v* tire, fatigue. **cansado** *adj* tired, weary; tiresome. **vista cansada** weak eyesight. **cansancio** *sm* weariness, fatigue.
cantar [kan'tar] *v* sing; chant; praise; (*fam*) squeal, confess. *sm* song; tune; poem. **cantante** *s(m+f)* singer.
cántara ['kantara] *sf* pitcher; liquid measure.
cántaro ['kantaro] *sm* pitcher. **llover a cántaros** rain cats and dogs.
cantera [kan'tera] *sf* quarry; (*fig*) breeding ground, source. **cantería** *sf* masonry; building made of hewn stone. **cantero** *sm* stonemason; crust of bread; strip of land.
cantidad [kanti'ðað] *sf* quantity, amount.
cantimplora [kantim'plora] *sf* siphon; water bottle.
cantina [kan'tina] *sf* buffet; canteen; wine cellar; picnic basket.
canto¹ ['kanto] *sm* song; singing. **cantor, -a** *sm, sf* singer.
canto² *sm* edge; border; crust; corner;

pebble. **al canto** (*fam*) in support. **de canto** edgeways.

caña ['kaɲa] *sf* cane; reed; walking stick; beer glass; shin bone. **caña de azúcar** sugar-cane. **caña de pescar** fishing-rod.

cañada [ka'ɲada] *sf* glen, ravine.

cáñamo ['kaɲamo] *sm* hemp.

caño ['kaɲo] *sm* pipe; sewer. **cañería** *sf* drain; piping.

cañón [ka'ɲon] *sm* canyon; cannon, gun; gun barrel; pipe, tube.

caoba [ka'oβa] *sf* mahogany.

caos ['kaos] *sm* chaos. **caótico** *adj* chaotic.

capa ['kapa] *sf* cloak; cape; covering; lid.

capacidad [kapaθi'ðað] *sf* capacity; ability; opportunity.

capacha [ka'patʃa] *sf* also **capacho** *sm* shopping basket.

capar [ka'par] *v* castrate; (*fam*) reduce.

capataz [kapa'taθ] *sm* foreman; overseer.

capaz [ka'paθ] *adj* capable; able; spacious.

capellán [kape'ʎan] *sm* chaplain.

capilar [kapi'lar] *sm, adj* capillary.

capilla [ka'piʎa] *sf* chapel; choir; hood. **estar en capilla** (*fam*) be in suspense.

capital [kapi'tal] *sm* (*com*) capital. *sf* capital city. *adj* principal.

capitán [kapi'tan] *sm* captain, leader. **capitanear** *v* command; lead.

capitular [kapitu'lar] *v* capitulate; make an agreement. **capitulación** *sf* capitulation; agreement.

capítulo [ka'pitulo] *sm* (*libro*) chapter; town council meeting; (*rel*) chapter.

capón [ka'pon] *sm* capon; eunuch; gelding; bundle of sticks.

capote [ka'pote] *sm* cape; greatcoat. **capotear** *v* (*fig, fam*) shirk.

capricho [ka'pritʃo] *sm* caprice, whim. **caprichoso** *adj* capricious.

cápsula ['kapsula] *sf* capsule; cartridge case; metal cap.

captar [kap'tar] *v* win over; gain; grasp.

capturar [kaptu'rar] *v* capture; arrest. **captura** *sf* capture.

capucha [ka'putʃa] *sf* hood; circumflex accent.

capuchina [kapu'tʃina] *sf* nasturtium.

capullo [ka'puʎo] *sm* cocoon; bud. **en capullo** in embryo.

cara ['kara] *sf* face; appearance; surface. **cara adelante/atrás** forwards/backwards. **cara o cruz** heads or tails. **dar la cara** face the music. **hacer cara a** face up to. **tener cara de** look like.

carabina [kara'βina] *sf* carbine; rifle. **carabinero** *sm* rifleman.

caracol [kara'kol] *sm* snail; spiral.

carácter [ka'rakter] *sm* character; nature; condition; sign, mark. **característica** *sf* characteristic. **característico** *adj* characteristic. **caracterización** *sf* characterization; (*teatro*) make-up. **caracterizar** *v* characterize; confer an honour on; (*teatro*) make up.

¡caramba! [ka'ramba] *interj* damn it!

caramelo [kara'melo] *sm* sweet, toffee; caramel.

carapacho [kara'patʃo] *sm* shell, carapace.

carátula [ka'ratula] *sf* mask; (*fam*) theatre, stage.

caravana [kara'βana] *sf* caravan; group, crowd.

carbohidrato [karβoi'ðrato] *sm* carbohydrate.

carbón [kar'βon] *sm* coal; charcoal; carbon; carbon paper. **carbonera** *sf* coal cellar; coal scuttle; charcoal burner. **carbonería** *sf* coalyard. **carbono** *sm* carbon.

carbunclo [kar'βunklo] *sm* also **carbunco** (*med*) carbuncle.

carburador [karβura'ðor] *sm* carburettor.

carcajada [karka'xaða] *sf* burst of laughter.

cárcel ['karθel] *sf* prison. **carcelero, -a** *sm, sf* jailer, warder.

carcomer [karko'mer] *v* corrode, eat away; undermine.

cardar [kar'ðar] *v* (*tecn*) card, comb. **carda** *sf* (*tecn*) card, carding; (*fam*) reprimand.

cardenal [karðe'nal] *sm* cardinal; bruise.

cardíaco [kar'ðiako] *adj* cardiac.

cardinal [karði'nal] *adj* principal; cardinal.

cardo ['karðo] *sm* thistle.

carear [kare'ar] *v* confront; compare; come face to face. **carearse** *v* meet.

*****carecer** [kare'θer] *v* lack, need. **carencia** *sf* lack, shortage; deficiency.

carestía [kares'tia] *sf* shortage, scarcity; high price.

careta [ka'reta] *sf* mask. **careta antigás** gasmask.

carey [ka'rej] *sm* turtle; tortoiseshell.

cargar [kar'gar] *v* load; burden; charge; tax; blame; attack; (*fam*) vex; lean, incline. **cargarse de** become full; be overburdened; (*fam*) be fed up; (*cielo*) become dark. **carga** *sf* load, burden; charge; tax; pressure. **cargadero** *sm* loading bay. **cargador** *sm* freighter; loader; carrier. **cargamento** *sm* cargo, load.

cargo ['kargo] *sm* post; accusation; responsibility; (*com*) charge; freighter. **cuenta a cargo** *sf* charge account.

cariarse [ka'rjarse] *v* decay. **caries** *sf invar* caries.

caribe [ka'riβe] *s(m+f)*, *adj* Caribbean. **Mar Caribe** *sm* Caribbean Sea.

caricatura [karika'tura] *sf* caricature.

caricia [ka'riθja] *sf* caress. **caricioso** *adj* caressing.

caridad [kari'ðað] *sf* charity. **caritativo** *adj* charitable.

cariño [ka'riɲo] *sm* love, affection. **cariñoso** *adj* affectionate, loving.

cariz [ka'riθ] *sm* appearance, aspect.

carmesí [karme'si] *sm*, *adj* crimson.

carmín [kar'min] *sm*, *adj* carmine.

carnada [kar'naða] *sf* bait.

carnaval [karna'βal] *sm* carnival.

carne ['karne] *sf* meat, flesh. **carne magra** lean meat. **carnal** *adj* carnal. **carnicería** *sf* butcher's shop. **carnicero** *sm* butcher.

carnero [kar'nero] *sm* sheep; ram; mutton; cemetery.

carpa ['karpa] *sf* carp.

caro ['karo] *adj* expensive; dear, beloved.

carpeta [kar'peta] *sf* folder, file; portfolio; briefcase; tablecloth. **dar carpetazo a** shelve.

carpintería [karpinte'ria] *sf* carpentry; carpenter's shop. **carpintero** *sm* carpenter, joiner.

carrera [kar'rera] *sf* race; road; career; course; line; (*media*) ladder. **de carrera** swiftly. **hacer carrera** succeed.

carreta [kar'reta] *sf* cart, wagon. **carretear** *v* cart, haul.

carrete [kar'rete] *sm* reel, spool, bobbin.

carretera [karre'tera] *sf* road, highway. **carretera de circunvalación** by-pass.

carril [kar'ril] *sm* furrow, rut; narrow road; rail.

carro ['karro] *sm* cart; car; typewriter carriage. **carro blindado** armoured car. **carro de mudanzas** removal van.

carroña [kar'roɲa] *sf* carrion.

carroza [kar'roθa] *sf* carriage; state coach; float.

carta ['karta] *sf* letter; chart; map; playing card; charter, document. **carta certificada** registered letter. **carta de venta** bill of sale. **tomar cartas en** (*fam*) take part in.

cartel [kar'tel] *sm* placard, poster. **cartelera** *sf* hoarding.

cartera [kar'tera] *sf* wallet; purse; briefcase; notebook; portfolio; office of a cabinet minister.

cartero [kar'tero] *sm* postman.

cartílago [kar'tilago] *sm* cartilage.

cartón [kar'ton] *sm* cardboard; carton; cartoon.

cartucho [kar'tutʃo] *sm* cartridge; paper cone.

casa ['kasa] *sf* house, home; household; business; building; flat. **casa de empeños** pawnshop. **casa de huéspedes** boarding-house. **casa pública** brothel. **casa y comida** board and lodging. **en casa** at home. **un amigo de casa** a friend of the family.

casar [ka'sar] *v* give in marriage; join. **casarse con** marry, get married. **casamiento** *sm* marriage.

cascabel [kaska'βel] *sm* small bell. **serpiente de cascabel** *sf* rattlesnake. **cascabelada** *sf* (*fam*) foolish action.

cascada [kas'kaða] *sf* waterfall.

cascar [kas'kar] *v* crack; burst; split; break; (*fam*) beat up; (*fam*) cough up; (*fam*) chatter; (*fam*) kick the bucket.

cáscara ['kaskara] *sf* shell; peel; rind; husk; bark.

cascarón [kaska'ron] *sm* egg-shell.

casco ['kasko] *sm* skull; helmet; skin; segment; shrapnel. **cascotes** *sm pl* rubble *sing*.

caserío [kase'rio] *sm* group of houses; settlement; country house.

casero [ka'sero] *adj* home-made; familiar; informal; (*fam*) domestic. *sm* landlord; tenant; caretaker.

casi ['kasi] *adv* nearly, almost.

casilla [ka'siʎa] *sf* hut, cabin; lodge; pigeonhole; section.

caso ['kaso] *sm* case, matter; event; chance; occasion. **el caso es** the fact is. **en tal caso** in such a case. **en todo caso** in any case. **hacer caso a** pay attention to.

caspa ['kaspa] *sf* dandruff.

casta ['kasta] *sf* caste; breed; class.

castaño [kas'taɲo] *sm* chestnut-tree;

chestnut brown. *adj* chestnut. **castaña** *sf* chestnut; hair bun.

castañuela [kastaˈɲwela] *sf* castanet.

castellano [kasteˈʎano], **-a** *s, adj* Castilian. *sm* (*lengua*) Castilian.

castidad [kastiˈðað] *sf* chastity.

castigar [kastiˈgar] *v* punish, chastise. **castigo** *sm* punishment.

Castilla [kasˈtiʎa] *sf* Castile.

castillo [kasˈtiʎo] *sm* castle.

castizo [kasˈtiθo] *adj* pure; pure-blooded; traditional.

casto [ˈkasto] *adj* chaste, pure.

castor [kasˈtor] *sm* beaver.

castrar [kasˈtrar] *v* castrate; (*agr*) prune. **castrado** *sm* eunuch.

castrense [kasˈtrense] *adj* military.

casual [kaˈswal] *adj* chance, coincidental. **casualidad** *sf* chance; coincidence; accident. **por casualidad** by chance.

casucha [kaˈsutʃa] *sf also* **casuca** hovel.

cataclismo [kataˈklismo] *sm* cataclysm.

catacumbas [kataˈcumbas] *sf pl* catacombs *pl*.

catadura¹ [kataˈðura] *sf* tasting. **catador** *sm* taster, sampler. **catar** *v* taste, sample.

catadura² *sf* (*fam*) expression, look.

catalejo [kataˈlexo] *sm* telescope.

catálogo [kaˈtalogo] *sm* catalogue. **catalogar** *v* catalogue; classify.

Cataluña [kataˈluɲa] *sf* Catalonia.

cataplasma [kataˈplasma] *sf* poultice.

catarata [kataˈrata] *sf* waterfall; (*med*) cataract.

catarro [kaˈtarro] *sm* catarrh, common cold. **catarro pradial** hay fever. **coger un catarro** catch cold.

catástrofe [kaˈtastrofe] *sf* catastrophe. **catastrófico** *adj* catastrophic.

catecismo [kateˈθismo] *sm* catechism.

cátedra [ˈkateðra] *sf* lecture room; senior teaching post; (*puesto*) chair.

catedral [kateˈðral] *sf* cathedral.

categoría [kategoˈria] *sf* category; class; rank. **categórico** *adj* categorical; strict.

caterva [kaˈterβa] *sf* crowd; heap.

cátodo [ˈkatoðo] *sm* cathode.

católico [kaˈtoliko], **-a** *s, adj* (Roman) Catholic. **catolicismo** *sm* (Roman) Catholicism.

catorce [kaˈtorθe] *sm, adj* fourteen. **catorceno** *adj* fourteenth.

catre [ˈkatre] *sm* camp-bed; cot.

cauce [ˈkauθe] *sm* river bed; ditch.

caución [kauˈθjon] *sf* caution; pledge; bail.

caucho [ˈkautʃo] *sm* rubber.

caudal [kauˈðal] *sm* wealth; abundance.

caudillo [kauˈðiʎo] *sm* leader, chief.

causar [kauˈsar] *v* cause, create, occasion. **causa** *sf* cause, reason, motive; (*jur*) trial. **a causa de** owing to. **causa pública** public welfare.

cáustico [ˈkaustiko] *adj* caustic, burning; scathing.

cautela [kauˈtela] *sf* care, caution; cunning. **cauteloso** *adj* cautious; cunning. **cauto** *adj* cautious, wary.

cautivar [kautiˈβar] *v* capture; captivate; charm. **cautividad** *sf* captivity. **cautivo, -a** *sm, sf* captive.

cavar [kaˈβar] *v* dig; excavate; (*agr*) dress; ponder. **cava** *sf* cultivation. **cavadura** *sf* digging; dressing.

caverna [kaˈβerna] *sf* cavern, cave. **cavernoso** *adj* cavernous; (*fig*) deep.

cavidad [kaβiˈðað] *sf* cavity.

cavilar [kaβiˈlar] *v* think deeply, meditate. **caviloso** *adj* pensive; worried.

cayado [kaˈjaðo] *sm* shepherd's crook; walking-stick.

cazar [kaˈθar] *v* hunt; chase; shoot; catch. **caza** *sf* hunt; chase; game. **cazador, -a** *sm, sf* hunter.

cazo [ˈkaθo] *sm* ladle; saucepan; gluepot. **cazo eléctrico** electric kettle.

cazoleta [kaθoˈleta] *sf* small pan; pipe bowl.

cazuela [kaˈθwela] *sf* casserole; (*teatro*) the gods.

cebada [θeˈβaða] *sf* barley. **cebadar** *v* feed (animals).

cebar [θeˈβar] *v* feed, fatten up; prime, charge; penetrate; long for. **cebarse en** vent one's rage on; gloat over.

cebolla [θeˈβoʎa] *sf* onion; flower bulb. **cebollana** *sf* chive. **cebolleta** *sf* leek.

cebra [ˈθeβra] *sf* zebra. **paso de cebra** *sm* zebra crossing.

cecear [θeθeˈar] *v* lisp. **ceceo** *sm* lisp. **ceceoso** *adj* lisping.

ceder [θeˈðer] *v* give up; yield; sag.

cedro [ˈθeðro] *sm* cedar.

cédula [ˈθeðula] *sf* charter; certificate; form; patent.

*cegar [θeˈgar] *v* blind; go blind; block up; cover. **cegador** *adj* blinding. **cegarra** *adj* (*fam*) short-sighted. **cegarrita** *adj* (fam) peering. **ceguedad** or **ceguera** sf blindness.

ceja ['θexa] sf eyebrow; mountain top; rim; cloud-cap. **fruncir las cejas** knit one's brows. **quemarse las cejas** burn the midnight oil. **tener entre ceja y ceja** (fam) concentrate on.

celada [θe'laδa] sf helmet; trick; ambush.

celar [θe'lar] v check on; watch; conceal; protect. **celador** sm watchman.

celda ['θelδa] sf cell.

celebrar [θele'βrar] v celebrate; praise; acclaim; conduct; (rel) say mass. **celebrarse** v take place. **celebración** sf celebration; acclamation. **celebrante** sm celebrant priest. **célebre** adj famous. **celebridad** sf fame; celebration.

celeridad [θeleri'δaδ] sf speed.

celeste [θe'leste] adj heavenly.

celibato [θeli'βato] sm celibacy; (fam) bachelor. **célibe** s(m+f) single person; bachelor; spinster.

celo ['θelo] sm zeal; heat, rut. **celos** sm pl jealousy sing. **dar celos a** make jealous. **tener celos** be jealous. **celosía** sf window lattice; venetian blind; jealousy. **celoso** adj zealous; jealous.

celta ['θelta] s(m+f) Celt. sm (lengua) Celtic.

célula ['θelula] sf cell.

celuloide [θelu'lojδe] sm celluloid.

celulosa [θelu'losa] sf cellulose.

cementerio [θemen'terjo] sm cemetery.

cemento [θe'mento] sm cement. **cemento armado** reinforced concrete.

cenagal [θena'gal] sm marsh, swamp; (fam) tight spot, mess.

cenar [θe'nar] v dine on, have for supper/dinner. **cena** sf evening meal, supper, dinner.

cenefa [θe'nefa] sf border; edging; frieze.

ceniza [θe'niθa] sf ash, cinder. **convertir en cenizas** reduce to ashes. **cenicero** sm ashtray.

censo ['θenso] sm census; tax; annuity; pension; ground rent; (fig) burden. **censar** v take a census of. **censor** sm censor; auditor.

censurar [θensu'rar] v censor; censure; condemn. **censura** sf censoring; censorship. **censurable** adj blameworthy. **censurador** sm censor. **censurista** s(m+f) critic; fault-finder.

centellear [θenteʎe'ar] v also **centellar**

sparkle; flash; twinkle; flicker. **centella** sf flash; spark. **centelleo** sm gleam; glitter; sparkle.

centavo [θen'taβo] sm cent.

centena [θen'tena] sf hundred. **centenada** sf also **centenar** sm hundred. **a** or **por centenares** by the hundred. **centenario** sm centenary.

centeno[1] [θen'teno] sm rye.

centeno[2] adj hundred.

centésimo [θen'tesimo] adj hundredth. sm cent.

centígrado [θen'tigraδo] adj centigrade.

centímetro [θen'timetro] sm centimetre.

céntimo ['θentimo] adj hundredth. sm cent.

centinela [θenti'nela] s(m+f) guard, sentry.

centrar [θen'trar] v centre. **central** adj central. **central** sf head office; headquarters; power station; switchboard. **centro** sm centre, middle; aim, goal, objective.

centrífugo [θen'trifugo] adj centrifugal.

centroamérica [θentroa'merika] sf Central America. **centroamericano** adj Central American.

centuria [θen'turja] sf century.

*****ceñir** [θe'ɲir] v gird, surround, encircle; crown; frame; shorten, take in; be a tight fit for. **ceñirse** v limit; adapt oneself to; cling. **ceñido** adj tight-fitting. **ceñidor** sm belt.

ceño ['θeɲo] sm frown. **fruncir el ceño** frown. **ceñudo** adj frowning.

cepa ['θepa] sf tree stump; stock; root; origin.

cepillar [θepi'ʎar] v brush; plane. **cepillarse** v (fam) fail an exam; (fam) polish off. **cepillo** sm brush; plane.

cepo ['θepo] sm branch; stocks pl; collecting box; (tecn) clamp, socket.

cera ['θera] sf wax.

cerámico [θe'ramiko] adj ceramic. **cerámica** sf ceramics; pottery.

cerca ['θerka] adv near, close, nearby. **cerca de** close by; almost; about. **de cerca** closely. **cercanía** sf nearness. **cercamás** sf pl vicinity sing, neighbourhood sing. **cercano** adj near, close.

cercar [θer'kar] v enclose; fence; surround. **cerca** sf enclosure, wall, fence. **cercado** sm enclosure.

cerco ['θerko] sm ring; circle; enclosure; frame; siege.

cerda [ˈθerda] *sf* (*zool*) sow; bristle. **cerdear** *v* (*animales*) be lame, limp. **cerdo** *sm* pig; pork. **cerdoso** *adj* bristly.

Cerdeña [θerˈðeɲa] *sf* Sardinia.

cereal [θereˈal] *sm, adj* cereal.

cerebro [θeˈreβro] *sm* brain. **cerebral** *adj* cerebral.

ceremonia [θereˈmonja] *sf* ceremony. **ceremonial** *adj* ceremonial. **ceremonioso** *adj* ceremonious.

cereza [θeˈreθa] *sf* cherry. **cerezo** *sm* cherry tree.

cerilla [θeˈriʎa] *sf* match.

***cerner** [θerˈner] *v* sift; sieve; examine carefully; drizzle. **cernerse** *v* sway; waddle; hover; threaten.

cero [ˈθero] *sm* zero, nothing.

***cerrar** [θerˈrar] *v* shut, close. **cerrarse** *v* close up; stand firm; heal; cloud over. **cerrar con llave** lock. **cerrar la boca** shut up. **cerrar la marcha** bring up the rear. **cerrado** *adj* closed; secretive; obtuse; overcast. **cerradura** *sf* lock; locking up. **cerraje** *sm* lock.

cerril [θerˈril] *adj* rough, rocky; wild; illbred.

cerro [ˈθerro] *sm* hill, ridge; animal's neck.

cerrojo [θerˈroxo] *sm* bolt.

certeza [θerˈteθa] *sf also* **certidumbre** certainty.

certificar [θertifiˈkar] *v* certify; register; guarantee. **certificado** *sm* certificate; registered letter.

cervato [θerˈβato] *sm* (*zool*) fawn.

cerveza [θerˈβeθa] *sf* beer.

cerviz [θerˈβiθ] *sf* nape of the neck, cervix. **bajar la cerviz** bow one's head.

cesar [θeˈsar] *v* cease, stop; leave one's job. **cesación** *sf* cessation, stoppage. **cesante** *adj* out of office, unemployed. **cesantía** *sf* suspension from office.

cesión [θeˈsjon] *sf* transfer; assignment; conveyance; resignation.

césped [ˈθespeð] *sf* turf, lawn. **césped inglés** lawn.

cesta [ˈθesta] *sf* basket, hamper. **cestería** *sf* basketwork, wickerwork. **cesto** *sm* basket.

cetro [ˈθetro] *sm* sceptre; (*fig*) power.

cheque [tʃek] *s* check

cianuro [θjaˈnuro] *sm* cyanide.

ciática [ˈθjatika] *sf* sciatica. **ciático** *adj* sciatic.

cicatería [θikateˈria] *sf* stinginess.

cicatriz [θikaˈtriθ] *sf* scar.

ciclismo [θiˈklismo] *sm* cycling. **ciclista** *s*(*m+f*) cyclist.

ciclo [ˈθiklo] *sm* cycle. **cíclico** *adj* cyclical.

ciclón [θiˈklon] *sm* cyclone.

cidra [ˈθiðra] *sf* citron. **cidro** *sm* citron tree.

ciego [ˈθjego], **-a** *sm, sf* blind person. *adj* blind.

cielo [ˈθjelo] *sm* sky; heaven; ceiling; climate. **¡cielos!** good heavens!

ciempiés [θjemˈpjes] *sm invar* centipede.

ciénaga [ˈθjenaga] *sf* bog, marsh, swamp.

ciencia [ˈθjenθja] *sf* science; knowledge, learning. **ciencia ficción** science fiction.

científico [θjenˈtifiko], **-a** *sm, sf* scientist. *adj* scientific.

cieno [ˈθjeno] *sm* mud. **cienoso** *adj* muddy.

ciento [ˈθjento] *sm, adj also* **cien** hundred.

cierre [ˈθjerre] *sm* closing; fastening; lock.

cierto [ˈθjerto] *adj* certain. *adv* certainly. **de cierto** certainly. **por cierto** of course.

ciervo [ˈθjerβo] *sm* deer; stag. **cierva** *sf* hind.

cierzo [ˈθjerθo] *sm* north wind.

cifra [ˈθifra] *sf* number, figure; cipher; code; abbreviation. **en cifra** in short. **cifrar** *v* summarize; cipher; enclose. **cifrar las esperanzas en** set one's hopes on.

cigarro [θiˈgarro] *sm* cigar. **cigarillo** *sm* cigarette.

cigüeña [θiˈgweɲa] *sf* stork.

cilindro [θiˈlindro] *sm* cylinder. **cilíndrico** *adj* cylindrical.

cima [ˈθima] *sf* top; summit. **dar cima a** finish off. **por cima** at the top; superficially.

címbalo [ˈθimbalo] *sm* cymbal.

cimbrar [θimˈbrar] *v also* **cimbrear** vibrate; bend; sway.

***cimentar** [θimenˈtar] *v* found; establish. **cimiento** *sm* foundation.

cinc [θink] *sm* zinc.

cincel [θinˈθel] *sm* chisel. **cincelador** *sm* engraver; stonecutter.

cinco [ˈθinko] *sm, adj* five.

cincuenta [θinˈkwenta] *sm, adj* fifty.

cinchar [θinˈtʃar] *v* girth; fasten with hoops. **cincha** *sf* girth, cinch. **cincho** *sm* belt; hoop.

cine [ˈθine] *sm* cinema.

cínico ['θinico], **-a** *sm.* *sf* cynic. *adj* cynical; shameless. **cinismo** *sm* cynicism.

cínife ['θinife] *sm* mosquito.

cinta ['θinta] *sf* ribbon; strip; tape; tape-measure. **cinteado** *adj* beribboned.

cintura [θin'tura] *sf* waist; belt. **meter a uno en cintura** make someone behave. **cinturón** *sm* belt; zone; circle. **cinturón de seguridad** safety belt.

ciprés [θi'pres] *sm* cypress.

circo ['θirko] *sm* circus.

circuito [θir'kwito] *sm* circuit.

circular [θirku'lar] *v* circulate; circularize; move. *adj* round, circular. **circulación** *sf* circulation; traffic.

circuncidar [θirkunθi'ðar] *v* circumcise. **circuncisión** *sf* circumcision. **circunciso** *adj* circumcised.

circundar [θirkun'dar] *v* surround, encircle.

circunferencia [θirkunfe'renθja] *sf* circumference.

circunflejo [θirkun'flexo] *sm* circumflex.

circunscribir [θirkunskri'βir] *v* circumscribe.

circunspecto [θirkun'spekto] *adj* circumspect. **circunspección** *sf* circumspection.

circunstancia [θirkun'stanθja] *sf* circumstance; condition; incident. **circunstancial** *adj* circumstantial. **circunstante** *adj* surrounding; present.

circunvecino [θirkunβe'θino] *adj* neighbouring.

ciruela [θi'rwela] *sf* plum. **ciruelo** *sm* plum-tree.

cirugía [θiru'xia] *sf* surgery. **cirujano** *sm* surgeon.

cisco ['θisko] *sm* coal dust; (*fam*) hubbub.

cisma ['θisma] *sm* schism; discord.

cisne ['θisne] *sm* swan.

cisterna [θis'terna] *sf* cistern, water tank.

cita ['θita] *sf* citation; appointment; quotation. **citar** *v* make an appointment; quote; (*jur*) summons.

ciudad [θju'ðað] *sf* city. **ciudadanía** *sf* citizenship. **ciudadano, -a** *sm, sf* citizen. **ciudadela** *sf* citadel.

cívico ['θiβiko] *adj* civic; patriotic.

civilizar [θiβili'θar] *v* civilize. **civil** *adj* civil. **civilización** *sf* civilization.

cizalla [θi'θaʎa] *sf* shears *pl*; metal shavings *pl*.

clamar [kla'mar] *v* cry out; beseech.

clamor [kla'mor] *sm* shout; cry. **clamorear**

v cry out for; beseech. **clamoroso** *adj* noisy.

clandestino [klandes'tino] *adj* secret.

clara ['klara] *sf* white of egg; bald patch. **claraboya** [klara'βoja] *sf* skylight.

clarear [klare'ar] *v* clear; dawn; grow light; be transparent; (*fam*) reveal secrets.

clarete [kla'rete] *sm* claret.

clarificar [klarifi'kar] *v* clarify. **clarificación** *sf* clarification.

clarín [kla'rin] *sm* bugle.

clarinete [klari'nete] *sm* clarinet.

claro ['klaro] *adj* light; clear; distinct. *adv* clearly. *sm* opening; space; clearing. **claro que** of course. **claro que sí** certainly. **claridad** *sf* clarity; light; brightness.

clase ['klase] *sf* class, type; lesson; classroom. **clase media** middle class. **clase particular** private lesson.

clásico ['klasiko] *adj* classic(al). *sm* classic.

clasificar [klasifi'kar] *v* classify. **clasificación** *sf* classification.

claudicar [klauði'kar] *v* limp; (*fam*) yield; (*fig*) shirk; (*fig*) falter. **claudicación** *sf* limping; yielding; shirking.

claustro ['klaustro] *sm* cloister; teaching staff. **claustral** *adj* cloistered.

claustrofobia [klaustro'foβja] *sf* claustrophobia.

cláusula ['klausula] *sf* clause.

clavar [kla'βar] *v* nail; fasten, fix; (*fam*) cheat. **clava** *sf* club, cudgel. **clavado en la cama** bed-ridden. **clavija** *sf* peg, pin. **clavo** *sm* nail; spike.

clave ['klaβe] *sf* key; clue; clef. *sm* harpsichord.

clavel [kla'βel] *sm* carnation.

clavícula [kla'βikula] *sf* collar bone.

clemencia [kle'menθja] *sf* mercy. **clemente** *adj* merciful.

clérigo ['klerigo] *sm* clergyman, priest. **clerical** *adj* clerical. **clericato** *sm* also **clero** clergy.

cliente ['kljente], **-a** *sm, sf* client, customer; patient. **clientela** *sf* clients *pl*, customers *pl*; practice.

clima ['klima] *sm* climate. **climático** *adj* climatic.

clínica ['klinika] *sf* clinic. **clínico** *adj* clinical.

clisé [kli'se] *sm* (*foto*) negative; (*fig*) cliché.

cloaca [klo'aka] *sf* sewer, drain.
cloro ['kloro] *sm* chlorine.
clorofila [kloro'fila] *sf* chlorophyll.
cloroformo [kloro'formo] *sm* chloroform.
cloroformar *v* chloroform.
club [kluβ] *sm* club. **club de noche** night-club.
coacción [koak'θjon] *sf* coercion. **coactivo** *adj* coercive.
coagular [koagu'lar] *v* coagulate; curdle; clot. **coagulación** *sf* coagulation; clotting.
coalición [koali'θjon] *sf* coalition.
coartada [koar'taða] *sf* alibi.
coartar [koar'tar] *v* hinder; prevent; limit; restrict.
cobarde [ko'βarðe] *s(m+f)* coward. *adj* cowardly. **cobardía** *sf* cowardice.
cobertizo [koβer'tiθo] *sm* garage; shed.
cobertura [koβer'tura] *sf* covering.
cobijar [koβi'xar] *v* cover, shelter. **cobijo** *sm* shelter.
cobrar [ko'βrar] *v* charge; earn; gain. **cobrarse** *v* (*med*) recover. **cobradero** *adj* recoverable. **cobrador, -a** *sm, sf* collector; conductor; receiver. **cobranza** *sf* collection; receipt.
cobre ['koβre] *sm* copper. **batirse el cobre** (*fam*) get on with it. **cobres** *sm pl* (*música*) brass.
*cocer [ko'θer] *v* cook. **cocido** *sm* stew.
cocinar [koθi'nar] *v* cook. **cocina** *sf* kitchen; cookery. **cocinero, -a** *sm, sf* cook.
coco ['koko] *sm* coconut; coconut palm; grub, larva; (*fam*) face; (*fam*) head. **hacer cocos** make faces.
cocodrilo [koko'ðrilo] *sm* crocodile.
cóctel ['koktel] *sm* cocktail.
coche ['kotʃe] *sm* car; coach; carriage. **coche cama** sleeper. **coche de alquiler** self-drive car. **coche fúnebre** hearse.
cochino [ko'tʃino], **-a** *sm, sf* pig, swine. *adj* (*fam*) rotten; filthy; disgusting. **cochinada** *sf* filth; filthy thing. **cochinera** *sf* pigsty.
codear [koðe'ar] *v* nudge, elbow. **codearse** *v* rub shoulders with. **codazo** *sm* nudge. **codo** *sm* elbow; bend.
codeína [koðe'ina] *sf* codeine.
codelincuente [koðelin'kwente] *s(m+f)* accomplice. **codelincuencia** *sf* complicity.
códice ['koðiθe] *sm* codex.
codiciar [koði'θjar] *v* covet. **codicia** *sf* greed. **codicioso** *adj* greedy.
codificar [koðifi'kar] *v* codify. **codificación** *sf* codification.

código ['koðigo] *sm* code. **código de carreteras** highway code.
codillo [ko'ðiʎo] *sm* forearm; (*culin*) shoulder.
codorniz [koðor'niθ] *sf* quail.
coercer [koer'θer] *v* coerce. **coerción** *sf* coercion.
coexistir [koeksis'tir] *v* coexist. **coexistencia** *sf* coexistence.
cofia ['kofja] *sf* coif; hair-net.
cofradía [kofra'ðia] *sf* fraternity; society.
cofre ['kofre] *sm* chest.
coger [ko'xer] *v* get; take; catch; seize; fit; collect. **cogida** *sf* gathering; (*tauromaquia*) goring. **cogido** *sm* fold, pleat.
cogote [ko'gote] *sm* nape of the neck. **ser tieso de cogote** be stiff-necked.
cohete [ko'ete] *sm* rocket.
cohibir [koi'βir] *v* inhibit; embarrass. **cohibidor** *adj* inhibiting. **cohibición** *sf* inhibition. **cohibido** *adj* restricted.
cohombrillo [koom'briʎo] *sm* gherkin. **cohombro** *sm* cucumber.
coincidencia [koinθi'ðenθja] *sf* coincidence. **coincidente** *adj* coincidental.
cojear [koxe'ar] *v* limp; hobble; (*fig*) waver; (*fig*) lapse. **cojera** *sf* lameness. **cojo** *adj* lame; lopsided.
cojín [ko'xin] *sm* cushion. **cojinete** *sm* small pillow; pad; (*tecn*) bearing. **cojinete de bolas** ball-bearing.
cok [kok] *sm* coke.
col [kol] *sf* cabbage. **coles de Bruselas** Brussels sprouts *pl*.
cola ['kola] *sf* tail; end; (*vestido*) train; queue; glue. **hacer cola** form a queue.
colaborar [kolaβo'rar] *v* collaborate. **colaboración** *sf* collaboration. **colaborador, -a** *sm, sf* collaborator.
colapso [ko'lapso] *sm* collapse, breakdown.
*colar [ko'lar] *v* strain; filter; wash; confer; (*fig, fam*) slip through. **colarse** *v* slip; gatecrash; jump the queue; err. **colada** *sf* washing. **coladero** *sm* colander, sieve.
colcha ['koltʃa] *sf* bedspread.
colchón [kol'tʃon] *sm* mattress.
colear [kole'ar] *v* wag the tail.
colección [kolek'θjon] *sf* collection. **colectivo** *adj* collective. **colectividad** *sf* collectivity; community.
colega [ko'lega] *sm* colleague.
colegio [ko'lexjo] *sm* college, school. **colegial** *sm* schoolboy.

colegir [kole'xir] v infer. conclude.

cólera ['kolera] sf anger. sm cholera.
colérico adj angry.

coleta [ko'leta] sf pigtail: postscript.

***colgar** [kol'gar] v hang. hang up. hang out. **colgadero** sm hook: peg: hanger. **puente colgante** sm suspension bridge.

coliflor [koli'flor] sf cauliflower.

colilla [ko'liʎa] sf cigarette stub.

colina [ko'lina] sf hill.

colindar [kolin'dar] v adjoin. **colindante** adj adjacent.

colisión [koli'sjon] sf collision.

colmar [kol'mar] v fill to overflowing. **colmado** adj plentiful.

colmena [kol'mena] sf beehive.

colmillo [kol'miʎo] sm tooth: fang: tusk. **enseñar los colmillos** (fam) threaten.

colmo ['kolmo] sm highest point: limit.

colocar [kolo'kar] v place: put in position: arrange: find employment for. **colocarse** v get a job. **colocación** sf employment: position: investment.

Colombia [ko'lombja] sf Colombia. **colombiano, -a** s. adj Colombian.

colonia [ko'lonja] sf colony. **colonial** adj colonial: imported. **colonialismo** sm colonialism. **colonización** sf colonization. **colonizar** v colonize. **colono** sm colonist. colonial.

coloquio [ko'lokjo] sm conversation.

color [ko'lor] sm colour: dye: paint: complexion. **colorado** sm. adj coloured: red. **ponerse colorado** blush. **colorar** v colour. dye. **colorear** v colour. dye: grow red: ripen. **colorete** sm rouge. **colorido** sm colour. colouring. **colorín** sm goldfinch: (fam) measles.

colosal [kolo'sal] adj colossal.

columbrar [kolum'brar] v glimpse: (fig) suspect.

columna [ko'lumna] sf column. pillar.

columpiar [kolum'pjar] v swing. **columpiarse** v sway: (fam) waddle: blunder. **columpio** sm swing.

collado [ko'ʎaðo] sm hill: fell.

collar [ko'ʎar] sm necklace: collar.

coma¹ ['koma] sf (gram) comma.

coma² sm (med) coma.

comadre [ko'maðre] sf midwife: godmother: (fam) neighbour. friend. **comadrear** v gossip. **comadreo** sm gossip.

comadreja [koma'ðrexa] sf weasel.

comadrona [koma'ðrona] sf midwife.

comandante [koman'dante] sm commander. **comandar** v command.

comandita [koman'dita] sf sleeping partnership. **socio comanditario** sm sleeping partner.

comarca [ko'marka] sf region. district.

comba ['komba] sf bend. curve: camber: sag. **combadura** sf curvature: camber.

combatir [komba'tir] v combat. fight. **combate** sm combat. battle. struggle. **combatiente** sm fighter: soldier.

combinar [kombi'nar] v combine: plan. arrange. **combinación** sf combination: project: permutation. **combinatorio** adj combining.

combustible [kombus'tiβle] adj combustible. sm fuel.

comedero [kome'ðero] adj edible. sm dining-room: feeding-trough.

comedia [ko'meðja] sf play: comedy: theatre. **comediante, -a** sm. sf actor/actress.

comediar [kome'ðjar] v divide into equal shares.

comedido [kome'ðiðo] adj polite. courteous: moderate. **comedir** v prepare. **comedirse** v restrain oneself.

comedor [kome'ðor] sm dining-room.

comensal [komen'sal] sm table companion.

comentar [komen'tar] v comment on: discuss. **comentario** sm commentary. **comentarista** s(m+f) commentator. **comento** sm comment.

***comenzar** [komen'θar] v commence. **comienzo** sm beginning.

comer [ko'mer] v eat: corrode: erode. **no tener qué comer** have nothing to eat. **ser de buen comer** have a good appetite. **comerse** v swallow: eat up. **comestible** adj edible. **comestibles** sm pl food sing: groceries pl. **comida** sf food: meal: lunch.

comercio [ko'merθjo] sm commerce: trade: shop. **comercio al por mayor/menor** wholesale/retail trade. **comerciante** sm shopkeeper: merchant: tradesman. **comerciar** v trade.

cometa [ko'meta] sf kite. sm comet.

cometer [kome'ter] v commit. **cometido** sm task: assignment: mission.

comezón [kome'θon] sf itch: itching.

cómico ['komiko] adj comic(al). sm comedian.

comilón [komi'lon], **-ona** sm. sf glutton. adj gluttonous. sf feast.

comillas [ko'miʌas] *sf pl* inverted commas *pl.*

comisaría [komisa'ria] *sf* police station. **comisario** *sm* commissary; commissioner; police inspector.

comisión [komi'sjon] *sf* commission; mission; committee.

comiso [ko'miso] *sm* (*jur*) confiscation.

comité [komi'te] *sm* committee.

comitiva [komi'tiβa] *sf* retinue.

como ['komo] *adv* how; as; as if; why; when; so that; about, approximately. *conj* as, since, because; if. **así como** as soon as; in the same way that. **como quiera que sea** in one way or another. **tan pronto como** as soon as. **¿cómo?** *adv* how? why? in what way? **¡cómo!** *interj* what! why! eh! **el cómo y el porqué** the how and the why.

cómoda ['komoða] *sf* chest of drawers.

cómodo ['komoðo] *adj* convenient; comfortable. **comodidad** *sf* convenience, comfort. **a su comodidad** at your earliest convenience.

compacto [kom'pakto] *adj* compact, close.

***compadecer** [kompaðe'θer] *v* pity. **compadecerse** *v* sympathize; agree.

compadre [kom'paðre] *sm* godfather; pal, crony.

compaginar [kompaxi'nar] *v* arrange; combine; join; match; agree.

compañero [kompa'ɲero], -a *sm, sf* companion, partner; one of a pair. **compañerismo** *sm* fellowship. **compañiá** *sf* company, society.

comparar [kompa'rar] *v* compare. **comparación** *sf* comparison. **comparativo** *adj* comparative.

***comparecer** [kompare'θer] *v* appear in court. **orden de comparecer** *sm* summons.

compartimiento [komparti'mjento] *sm* compartment; section; division. **compartir** *v* divide; share.

compás [kom'pas] *sm* (*mar*) compass; (*mat*) pair of compasses; rhythm; pattern, standard. **llevar el compás** beat time. **compasado** *adj* orderly, moderate. **compasar** *v* measure; regulate.

compasión [kompa'sjon] *sf* compassion. **compasivo** *adj* compassionate.

compatible [kompa'tiβle] *adj* compatible. **compatibilidad** *sf* compatibility.

compatriota [kompa'trjota] *s(m+f)* compatriot.

compeler [kompe'ler] *v* compel.

compendio [kom'pendjo] *sm* compendium; summary, précis. **en compendio** briefly. **compendir** *v* summarize.

compensar [kompen'sar] *v* compensate; offset; make amends. **compensación** *sf* compensation. **compensatorio** *adj* compensatory.

***competir** [kompe'tir] *v* compete; contest. **competencia** *sf* competition; concern; competence. **competente** *adj* competent; able. **competición** *sf* competition. **competidor**, -a *sm, sf* competitor.

compilar [kompi'lar] *v* compile. **compilación** *sf* compilation.

compinche [kom'pintʃe] *s(m+f)* pal, chum; accomplice.

***complacer** [kompla'θer] *v* please; oblige; humour. **complacerse** *v* be pleased, be glad (to). **complacencia** *sf* pleasure; indulgence. **complaciente** *adj* helpful; obliging.

complejo [kom'plexo] *adj*, *sm* complex. **complejidad** *sf* complexity.

complementario [komplemen'tarjo] *adj* complementary. **complemento** *sm* complement.

completar [komple'tar] *v* complete. **completo** *adj* complete.

complicar [kompli'kar] *v* complicate; be complicated *or* confused. **complicarse** *v* become confused *or* complicated. **complicación** *sf* complication. **complicado** *adj* complicated.

cómplice ['kompliθe] *s(m+f)* accomplice. **complicidad** *sf* complicity.

complot [kom'plot] *sm* plot; intrigue; (*fam*) understanding.

***componer** [kompo'ner] *v* compose; form; repair; adjust; write. **componerse** *v* compose oneself; tidy oneself up; dress up; agree. **componerse de** consist of. **componedor**, -a *sm, sf* compositor; repairer; arbitrator. **componente** *sm* component; ingredient. **componible** *adj* adjustable.

comportar [kompor'tar] *v* tolerate; involve. **comportarse** *v* behave. **comportamiento** *sm* behaviour. **comporte** *sm* behaviour; bearing.

composición [komposi'θjon] *sf* composition; mixture; agreement; settlement. **compositor**, -a *sm, sf* composer.

compostura [kompos'tura] *sf* composition, structure; repair; neatness; adornment; agreement; composure; adjustment.

compota [kom'pota] *sf* (*culin*) compote.

comprar [kom'prar] *v* buy; bribe. **compra** *sf* purchase. **comprador, -a** *sm, sf* shopper.

comprender [kompren'der] *v* understand; include. **comprensibilidad** *sf* intelligibility. **comprensible** *adj* understandable. **comprensión** *sf* understanding; inclusion. **comprensivo** *adj* understanding; comprising.

comprimir [kompri'mir] *v* squeeze, compress. **comprimirse** *v* control oneself.

compresa *sf* compress; sanitary towel. **compresión** *sf* compression.

*comprobar [kompro'βar] *v* verify, check. **comprobación** *sf* verification. **comprobante** *adj* verifying. *sm* voucher; receipt.

comprometer [komprome'ter] *v* risk; compromise; commit. **comprometido** *adj* embarrassing; committed; implicated. **compromiso** *sm* commitment; agreement; compromise.

compuesto [kom'pwesto] *sm* compound. *adj* compound; repaired; dressed-up.

compunción [kompun'θjon] *sf* compunction; contrition.

computar [kompu'tar] *v* compute, calculate. **computadora** *sf* computer.

comulgar [komul'gar] *v* give/take communion; (*fig*) share.

común [ko'mun] *adj* common; ordinary; vulgar. *sm* community, public toilet. **por lo común** generally. **comunal** *adj* communal.

comunicar [komuni'kar] *v* communicate; convey; transmit; (*dos cuartos*) connect. **comunicarse** *v* spread; keep in touch with; exchange. **comunicación** *sf* communication; message. **comunicativo** *adj* talkative; catching.

comunidad [komuni'ðað] *sf* community.

comunión [komu'njon] *sf* communion.

comunismo [komu'nismo] *sm* communism. **comunista** *s(m+f), adj* communist.

con [kon] *prep* with; by; in spite of; to, towards. **con que** *conj* whereupon; and so. **con tal que** provided that.

cóncavo ['konkaβo] *adj* concave. **concavidad** *sf* hollow, cavity.

*concebir [konθe'βir] *v* conceive; imagine; understand; take; (*med*) conceive.

concebible *adj* conceivable, imaginable. **concepción** *sf* conception, idea; (*med*) conception. **concepto** *sm* concept; idea; opinion; witticism.

conceder [konθe'ðer] *v* concede, grant; allow; spare; award. **concesión** *sf* concession; grant.

concejo [kon'θexo] *sm* council. **concejal** *sm* councillor. **concejil** *adj* municipal.

concentrar [konθen'trar] *v* concentrate. **concentración** *sf* concentration.

concerniente [konθer'njente] *adj* concerning, regarding. **concernir** *v* concern.

*concertar [konθer'tar] *v* harmonize; agree; adjust; compare. **concertado** *adj* concerted.

conciencia [kon'θjenθja] *sf* conscience; consciousness; mind; conscientiousness. **concienzudo** *adj* conscientious.

concierto [kon'θjerto] *sm* concert; concerto; agreement; (*fig*) harmony. **de concierto** in agreement.

conciliar [konθi'ljar] *v* conciliate; reconcile; gain. *adj* of a council. *sm* councillor. **concilio** *sm* councillor; council.

conciso [kon'θiso] *adj* concise.

concitar [konθi'tar] *v* stir up.

*concluir [konklu'ir] *v* conclude; deduce; settle; convince. **conclusión** *sf* conclusion.

*concordar [konkor'ðar] *v* agree. **concordancia** *sf* agreement. **concorde** *adj* in agreement. **concordia** *sf* harmony.

concretar [konkre'tar] *v* bring together; limit; specify; state explicitly. **concretarse** *v* confine oneself; be definite; keep; take shape. **concreto** *adj* concrete, specific. **en concreto** in brief.

concubina [konku'βina] *sf* concubine.

concurrir [konkur'rir] *v* meet; attend; go; coincide; contribute; concur; compete. **concurrido** *adj* popular; crowded. **concurso** *sm* meeting; cooperation; help; competition.

concusión [konku'sjon] *sf* concussion.

concha ['kontʃa] *sf* shell.

condado [kon'daðo] *sm* earldom; county. **conde** *sm* earl. **condesa** *sf* countess.

condecorar [kondeko'rar] *v* (*persona*) decorate. **condecoración** *sf* medal, decoration.

condenar [konde'nar] *v* condemn; sentence; block up. **condena** *sf* sentence; conviction. **cumplir condena** serve a sentence. **condenación** *sf* condemnation;

damnation. **condenado, -a** *sm, sf* condemned person; wretch.

condensar [konden'sar] *v* condense. **condensación** *sf* condensation. **condensador** *sm* condenser.

***condescender** [kondesθen'der] *v* condescend; yield; comply. **condescendencia** *sf* condescension; compliance. **condescendiente** *adj* condescending; obliging.

condicionar [kondiθjo'nar] *v* condition; determine. **condición** *sf* condition; quality; temperament.

condimentar [kondimen'tar] *v* season. **condimento** *sm* seasoning, condiment.

condolerse [kondo'lerse] *v* condole, sympathize. **condolencia** *sf* condolence.

condonar [kondo'nar] *v* pardon, condone; (*deuda*) cancel. **condonación** *sf* pardon.

***conducir** [kondu'θir] *v* conduct; transport; guide; manage; (*auto*) drive; be suitable. **conducirse** *v* behave. **conducción** *sf* transport; guidance; direction, management. **conducción a izquierda** left-hand drive. **permiso de conducción** *sm* driving licence. **conducta** *sf* transport; conduct; direction; behaviour.

conducto [kon'dukto] *sm* conduit; pipe. **conductor** *sm* (*tecn*) conductor.

conectar [konek'tar] *v* connect; switch on. **conectador** *sm* connector. **conexión** *sf* connection.

conejo [ko'nexo] *sm* rabbit.

confabularse [konfaβu'larse] *v* plot. **confabulación** *sf* conspiracy.

confeccionar [konfekθjon'ar] *v* make, make up. **confección** *sf* making; tailoring; clothing. **confeccionado** *adj* ready-made, ready-to-wear.

confederar [konfeðe'rar] *v* confederate. **confederación** *sf* confederation, confederacy.

conferenciar [konferen'θjar] *v* talk, discuss. **conferencia** *sf* conference; lecture; telephone call. **conferencia a cobro revertido** reverse-charge call. **conferencia en la cumbre** summit conference. **conferencia interurbana** trunk call.

***conferir** [konfe'rir] *v* confer, consult; award, grant.

***confesar** [konfe'sar] *v* confess, admit. **confesar de plano** own up. **confesión** *sf* confession.

confeti [kon'feti] *sm pl* confetti *sing*.

confiar [kon'fjar] *v* entrust; trust; rely. **confiable** *adj* trustworthy. **confiado** *adj* confident; trusting. **confianza** *sf* confidence; reliability; informality.

confidencia [konfi'ðenθja] *sf* secret; confidence. **confidencial** *adj* confidential. **confidente** *adj* faithful.

confinar [konfi'nar] *v* confine; banish. **confinar con** border on. **confín** *sm* border, limit.

confirmar [konfir'mar] *v* confirm. **confirmarse** *v* be confirmed. **confirmación** *sf* confirmation.

confiscar [konfis'kar] *v* confiscate. **confiscación** *sf* confiscation.

confitar [konfi'tar] *v* coat with sugar; preserve in syrup. **confite** *sm* sweet. **confitería** *sf* sweet-shop. **confitura** *sf* candied fruit.

conflicto [kon'flikto] *sm* conflict.

***confluir** [konflu'ir] *v* converge, meet.

conformar [konfor'mar] *v* conform. **conformarse** *v* resign oneself. **conforme** *adj* in agreement; alike; according. **conforme a** in accordance with. **según y conforme** it all depends.

confortar [konfor'tar] *v* comfort; encourage. **confortable** *adj* comfortable. **conforte** *sm* solace, comfort.

confrontar [konfron'tar] *v* confront; compare. **confrontar con** border on; confront. **confrontación** *sf* confrontation.

confundir [konfun'dir] *v* confuse; mistake. **confusión** *sf* confusion. **confuso** *adj* confused; embarrassed.

congelar [konxe'lar] *v* freeze; congeal. **congelación** *sf* freezing. **congelación de salarios** wage freeze. **congelador** *sm* freezer.

congénito [kon'xenito] *adj* congenital.

congestionar [konxestjo'nar] *v* congest. **congestión** *sf* congestion.

conglomerarse [konglome'rarse] *v* conglomerate. **conglomeración** *sf* conglomeration.

congoja [kon'goxa] *sf* agony; distress.

congratular [kongratu'lar] *v* congratulate. **congratularse** *v* be delighted. **congratulación** *sf* congratulation; delight.

congregar [kongre'gar] *v* congregate. **congregación** *sf* congregation.

congreso [kon'greso] *sm* congress; assembly; conference.

congrio ['kongrjo] *sm* conger eel.

congruente [kongru'ente] *adj* congruent; suitable. **congruencia** *sf* congruence; suitability.

cónico ['koniko] *adj* conical.

conífero [ko'nifero] *adj* coniferous. **conífera** *sf* conifer.

conjeturar [konxetu'rar] *v* conjecture, guess. **conjetura** *sf* conjecture, guess.

conjugar [konxu'gar] *v* combine; (*gram*) conjugate. **conjugación** *sf* conjugation.

conjunto [kon'xunto] *sm* whole. *adj* joint. **en conjunto** as a whole. **conjunción** *sf* (*gram*) conjunction.

conjurar [konxu'rar] *v* bind by oath; implore; ward off; conspire; exorcise. **cónjura** *sf* *also* **conjuración** conspiracy. **conjurador** *sm* exorcist. **conjuro** *sm* exorcism; entreaty.

conmemorar [konmemo'rar] *v* commemorate. **conmemoración** *sf* commemoration. **conmemorativo** *adj* commemorative.

conmigo [kon'migo] *pron* with me, with myself.

conminar [konmi'nar] *v* threaten; warn. **conminativo** *adj* threatening; compulsory.

conmiseración [konmisera'θjon] *sf* commiseration.

conmoción [konmo'θjon] *sf* commotion; upheaval; shock. **conmoción cerebral** concussion.

conmover [konmo'βer] *v* disturb; touch. **conmoverse** *v* be moved. **conmovedor** *adj* moving, touching.

conmutar [konmu'tar] *v* exchange. **conmutador** *sm* switch.

connivencia [konni'βenθja] *sf* connivance.

connotar [konno'tar] *v* imply. **connotación** *sf* connotation.

cono ['kono] *sm* cone.

*conocer [kono'θer] *v* know; understand; recognize. **conocer de** know about. **conocer de** *or* **en** (*jur*) try (a case). **conocer de nombre** know by name. **conocerse** *v* meet; be acquainted with. **se conoce que** it is clear that. **conocedor, -a** *s, adj* expert. **conocido, -a** *sm, sf* acquaintance. **conocimiento** *sm* knowledge; good sense; consciousness; (*com*) bill of lading; proof of identity. **perder el conocimiento** lose consciousness.

conque ['konke] *conj* so. *sm* (*fam*) condition. **conqué** *sm* (*fam*) means.

conquistar [konkis'tar] *v* conquer; win;

win over. **conquista** *sf* conquest. **conquistador, -a** *sm, sf* conqueror.

consabido [konsa'βiðo] *adj* traditional; well known; aforementioned.

consagrar [konsa'grar] *v* consecrate; dedicate. **consagración** *sf* consecration; dedication.

consanguíneo [konsan'gineo] *adj* related by blood. **consanguinidad** *sf* blood relationship.

consciente [kons'θjente] *adj* conscious.

consecuencia [konse'kwenθja] *sf* consequence; outcome; consistency. **en** *or* **por consecuencia** consequently. **ser de consecuencia** be of importance. **traer como consecuencia** result in. **consecuente** *adj* consequent; consistent.

consecutivo [konseku'tiβo] *adj* consecutive.

*conseguir [konse'gir] *v* get; attain; procure; bring about; manage. **dar por conseguido** take for granted.

consejo [kon'sexo] *sm* advice, counsel; council. **consejo de guerra** court-martial. **entrar en consejo** begin consultation. **consejero** *sm* adviser; member of board of directors.

*consentir [konsen'tir] *v* allow; believe; tolerate; spoil; agree. **consentir en** consent to. **consentirse** *v* begin to crack; come loose. **consentido** *adj* pampered.

conserje [kon'serxe] *sm* porter, doorkeeper.

conservar [konser'βar] *v* conserve; preserve. **conservarse** *v* last, wear well. **conserva** *sf* preserved food; jam; pickles *pl*. **conservación** *sf* conservation; preserving. **conservador, -a** *sm, sf* (*pol*) Conservative; (*museo*) curator.

considerar [konsiðe'rar] *v* consider. **considerable** *adj* considerable; substantial. **consideración** *sf* consideration. **por consideración a** out of respect for. **ser de consideración** be important. **tener** *or* **guardar consideraciones** show consideration.

consignar [konsig'nar] *v* consign; assign; deposit; send. **consignación** *sf* consignment. **consigna** *sf* left-luggage office; password; slogan.

consigo [kon'sigo] *pron* with him/her/you/one.

consiguiente [konsi'gjente] *adj* consequent.

consistir [konsis'tir] *v* consist. **consistir en** consist of. **consistencia** *sf* consistency. **consistente** *adj* consistent.

consolar [konso'lar] *v* console. **consolación *sf* consolation.

consolidar [konsoli'ðar] *v* consolidate; strengthen. **consolidación** *sf* consolidation.

consonante [konso'nante] *sm* consonant. *adj* rhyming; harmonious. **consonancia** *sf* rhyme; harmony. **consonar** *v* rhyme; harmonize.

consorte [kon'sorte] *s(m+f)* consort; accomplice; companion. **consorcio** *sm* association; fellowship; consortium.

conspicuo [kons'pikwo] *adj* conspicuous.

conspirar [konspi'rar] *v* conspire, plot. **conspiración** *sf* conspiracy, plot.

constante [kons'tante] *adj* constant. **constancia** *sf* constancy.

constar [kons'tar] *v* be clear; be evident; be on record. **constar de** consist of. **constar en** appear; be recorded.

constelación [konstela'θjon] *sf* constellation; climate.

consternarse [konster'narse] *v* be dismayed. **consternación** *sf* consternation, dismay.

constiparse [konsti'parse] *v* catch a cold. **constipación** *sf* cold. **estar constipado** have a cold.

constituir [konstitu'ir] *v* constitute; establish; compose. **constitución *sf* constitution.

constreñir [konstre'nir] *v* constrain; force; constipate. **constreñimiento** *sm* constraint. **constricción** *sf* constriction.

construir [konstru'ir] *v* construct. **construcción *sf* construction. **constructor, -a** *sm, sf* builder, constructor.

consuelo [kon'swelo] *sm* consolation.

cónsul ['konsul] *sm* consul. **consulado** *sm* consulate.

consultar [konsul'tar] *v* consult. **consulta** *sf* consultation.

consumado [konsu'maðo] *adj* consummate; accomplished. **consumación** *sf* consummation; completion. **consumar** *v* accomplish; complete.

consumir [konsu'mir] *v* consume. **consumirse** *v* languish; be uneasy. **consumido** *adj* consumed; (*fam*) lean; (*fam*) timid. **consumo** *sm* consumption.

contabilidad [kontaβili'ðað] *sf* accounting; bookkeeping. **contable** *sm* bookkeeper; accountant.

contacto [kon'takto] *sm* contact.

contagiar [konta'xjar] *v* infect, contaminate; corrupt. **contagio** *sm* contagion. **contagioso** *adj* contagious.

contaminar [kontami'nar] *v* contaminate. **contaminación** *sf* contamination.

contar [kon'tar] *v* count; relate. **contar con count on; expect; possess. **contado** *adj* counted, limited. **al contado** cash down. **de contado** immediately. **por de contado** certainly. **contador** *sm* counter; cashier; (*tecn*) meter. **contador de aparcamiento** parking meter.

contemplar [kontem'plar] *v* contemplate. **contemplación** *sf* contemplation. **contemplativo** *adj* contemplative.

contemporáneo [kontempo'raneo], **-a** *s, adj* contemporary.

contender [konten'der] *v* contend; struggle; argue. **contención *sf* contention. **contencioso** *adj* contentious. **contendedor** *sm* contender, antagonist. **contendiente** *s(m+f)* litigant. **contienda** *sf* contest; dispute.

**contener [konte'ner] *v* contain; control; suppress; stop.

contenido [konte'niðo] *adj* reserved; moderate; contained. *sm* contents *pl*.

contentar [konten'tar] *v* satisfy, content. **contentarse** *v* be pleased. **contentamiento** *sm* contentment. **contento** *adj* content, satisfied.

contestar [kontes'tar] *v* answer; confirm; agree. **contestable** *adj* questionable. **contestación** *sf* reply; dispute.

contexto [kon'teksto] *sm* context.

contigo [kon'tigo] *pron* (*fam*) with you.

contiguo [kon'tigwo] *adj* contiguous; adjoining. **contigüidad** *sf* contiguity.

continente [konti'nente] *sm* continent; bearing; container. *adj* containing; continent. **continencia** *sf* continence. **continental** *adj* continental.

contingente [kontin'xente] *adj* contingent, accidental. *sm* contingent. **contingencia** *sf* contingency.

continuar [konti'nwar] *v* continue; remain; endure. **continuación** *sf* continuation. **a continuación de** following. **continuo** *adj* continuous.

contorno [kon'torno] *sm* contour, outline.

contornos *sm pl* environs *pl*. en contorno round about.

contra ['kontra] *prep* against; opposite; facing. el pro y el contra the pros and cons. en contra de in opposition to.

contrabajo [kontra'βaxo] *sm* double bass.

contrabando [kontra'βando] *sm* contraband; smuggling.

contracción [kontrak'θjon] *sf* contraction.

*contradecir [kontraðe'θir] *v* contradict. contradicción *sf* contradiction.

*contraer [kontra'er] *v* contract; enter into; be infected with. contraer matrimonio con marry.

contrafuerte [kontra'fwerte] *sm* buttress.

*contrahacer [kontraa'θer] *v* counterfeit; copy. contrahacerse *v* feign.

contrahecho [kontra'etʃo] *adj* deformed.

contramaestre [kontrama'estre] *sm* foreman; (*mar*) boatswain.

contramandar [kontraman'dar] *v* countermand.

contrapelo [kontra'pelo] *adv* a contrapelo against the grain.

contrapesar [kontrape'sar] *v* counterpoise, counterbalance; offset. contrapeso *sm* counterpoise.

contraponer [kontrapo'ner] *v* set against; oppose; contrast.

contrapunto [kontra'punto] *sm* counterpoint.

contrariar [kontra'rjar] *v* oppose. contrariedad *sf* opposition; setback; annoyance.

contrario [kon'trarjo], -a *sm, sf* opponent. al contrario on the contrary. de lo contrario otherwise. *adj* contrary, opposite.

contrarrestar [kontrarres'tar] *v* counteract; oppose; resist; (*la pelota*) return.

contrarrevolución [kontrarreβolu'θjon] *sf* counter-revolution. contrarrevolucionario, -a *s, adj* counter-revolutionary.

contrasentido [kontrasen'tiðo] *sm* contradiction; nonsense; mistranslation; misinterpretation.

contraseña [kontra'seɲa] *sf* countersign; password.

contrastar [kontras'tar] *v* contrast; resist; inspect. contraste *sm* contrast; opposition; hallmark; inspector. en contraste con in contrast to.

contrato [kon'trato] *sm* contract; covenant.

contraveneno [kontraβe'neno] *sm* antidote.

*contravenir [kontraβe'nir] *v* contravene. contravención *sf* contravention.

*contribuir [kontri'βwir] *v* contribute; pay tax. contribución *sf* contribution; tax. contribuyente *s(m+f)* tax-payer.

contrición [kontri'θjon] *sf* contrition.

contrincante [kontrin'kante] *sm* competitor; rival.

controversia [kontro'βersja] *sf* controversy. controvertible *adj* controversial. controvertir *v* dispute, argue.

contumacia [kontu'maθja] *sf* stubbornness, obstinacy; (*jur*) contempt of court. contumaz *adj* stubborn; perverse.

conturbar [kontur'βar] *v* perturb; disturb. conturbación *sf* perturbation.

contusión [kontu'sjon] *sf* contusion, bruise. contusionar *v* bruise.

*convalecer [konβale'θer] *v* convalesce. convalecencia *sf* convalescence.

convecino [konβe'θino] *adj* neighbouring.

convencer [konβen'θer] *v* convince. convencedor *adj* convincing. convencimiento *sm* conviction.

*convenir [konβe'nir] *v* agree, be agreed; arrange; be convenient; be advisable. me conviene it suits me. convención *sf* convention; agreement; assembly. convencional *adj* conventional. convenible *adj* docile. conveniencia *sf* convenience; conformity; usefulness; advantage. conveniente *adj* convenient; expedient; proper. convenio *sm* agreement; compact.

convento [kon'βento] *sm* convent.

converger [konβer'xer] *v also* convergir converge; (*fig*) agree. convergencia *sf* convergence. convergente *adj* convergent.

conversar [konβer'sar] *v* converse. conversar con talk to. conversar sobre talk about. conversador *adj* sociable. conversación *sf* conversation.

*convertir [konβer'tir] *v* convert. convertirse *v* become, turn into. conversión *sf* conversion. convertible *adj* convertible.

convexo [kon'βekso] *adj* convex. convexidad *sf* convexity.

convicción [konβik'θjon] *sf* conviction. convicto *adj* convicted.

convidar [konβi'ðar] *v* invite. convidarse *v* offer one's services. convidada *sf* (*fam*) invitation to a drink. pagar la convidada (*fam*) treat to a drink. convidado, -a *sm*, *sf* guest. **convidador, -a** *sm, sf* host/hostess.

convincente [konβin'θente] *adj* convincing.

convivir [konβi'βir] *v* coexist. **convivencia** *sf* coexistence.

convocar [konβo'kar] *v* convoke. **convocación** *sf* convocation. **convocador, -a** *sm, sf* convener. **convocatoria** *sf* summons.

convoy [kon'βoj] *sm* convoy. **convoyar** *v* convoy.

convulsión [konβul'sjon] *sf* convulsion. **convulsivo** *adj* convulsive.

conyugal [konju'gal] *adj* conjugal. **cónyuge** *s(m+f)* spouse.

coñac [ko'ɲak] *sm* cognac, brandy.

cooperar [koope'rar] *v* cooperate. **cooperación** *sf* cooperation. **cooperativa** *sf* cooperative.

coordinar [koorði'nar] *v* coordinate. **coordinación** *sf* coordination.

copa ['kopa] *sf* glass; cup; goblet. **sombrero de copa** top-hat. **tomar una copa** have a drink. **copas** *sf pl* (*naipes*) hearts. **copado** *adj* (*árbol*) bushy. **copera** *sf* cupboard; sideboard.

Copenhague [kope'nage] *sf* Copenhagen.

copete [ko'pete] *sm* tuft of hair; bun; (*pájaro*) crest; summit; (*fig*) haughtiness. **de alto copete** aristocratic.

copiar [ko'pjar] *v* copy; record. **copia** *sf* copy; duplicate; image; abundance. **copiador, -a** *sm, sf* copier. **copiante** *s(m+f)* copyist.

copla ['kopla] *sf* verse; song; ballad. **coplas de ciego** doggerel.

copo ['kopo] *sm* flake; ball of wool; clot; lump.

coque ['koke] *sm* coke.

coquetear [kokete'ar] *v* flirt. **coqueta** *sf* flirt. **coqueteo** *sm* flirtation. **coquetón** *sm* (*fam*) philanderer.

coraje [ko'raxe] *sm* courage; anger. **corajinoso** *adj* irate.

coral [ko'ral] *sm* coral. *adj* choral.

coraza [ko'raθa] *sf* armour.

corazón [kora'θon] *sm* heart. **de corazón** sincerely.

corbata [kor'βata] *sf* necktie.

corcovado [korko'βaðo], **-a** *sm, sf* hunchback. *adj* hunchbacked.

corchea [kor'tʃea] *sf* (*música*) quaver.

corchete [kor'tʃete] *sm* clasp.

corcho ['kortʃo] *sm* cork.

cordel [kor'ðel] *sm* thin rope, line. **a cordel** in a straight line.

cordero [kor'ðero] *sm* lamb.

cordial [kor'ðjal] *adj* invigorating, stimulating; cordial, friendly. **dedo cordial** *sm* middle finger. **cordialidad** *sf* cordiality.

cordillera [korði'ʎera] *sf* mountain range.

cordón [kor'ðon] *sm* string; cord; braid.

cordura [kor'ðura] *sf* prudence; discretion.

coreografía [koreogra'fia] *sf* choreography.

cornada [kor'nada] *sf* goring. **cornear** *v* gore.

corneja [kor'nexa] *sf* crow.

corneta [kor'neta] *sf* bugle; hunting horn. **corneta de llaves** cornet.

cornudo [kor'nuðo] *adj* horned; cuckolded. *sm* cuckold.

coro ['koro] *sm* chorus.

coronar [koro'nar] *v* crown. **corona** *sf* crown. **coronación** *sf* coronation.

coronel [koro'nel] *sm* colonel.

coronilla [koro'niʎa] *sf* crown of the head.

corporal [korpo'ral] *adj* corporal. **corporación** *sf* corporation. **corpóreo** *adj* corporeal. **corpulencia** *sf* corpulence. **corpulento** *adj* corpulent.

corpúsculo [kor'puskulo] *sm* corpuscle.

corral [kor'ral] *sm* yard; courtyard; corral; enclosure.

correa [kor'rea] *sf* leather strap; belt. **correa de ventilador** fan belt.

corredor [korre'ðor] *sm* corridor: runner; (*com*) broker.

***corregir** [korre'xir] *v* correct. **corregirse** *v* reform oneself. **corrección** *sf* correction; punishment. **correccional** *adj* reformatory. **correctivo** *sm, adj* corrective. **correcto** *adj* correct; well-bred.

correo [kor'reo] *sm* mail, post; post office; courier. **correo certificado** registered post. **a vuelta de correo** by return of post.

correr [kor'rer] *v* run; flow; pass; sail; cover; travel over. **correrse** *v* move; (*fam*) talk too much.

corresponder [korrespon'der] *v* correspond; concern; reply; repay; be grateful; belong to; match; suit; fit. **a quien corresponda** to whom it may concern. **corresponderse** *v* correspond; agree; like

each other. **correspondencia** *sf* correspondence, letters *pl*; agreement; reciprocation. **corresponsal** *s(m+f)* newspaper correspondent.
corrida [kor'riða] *sf* sprint. **corrida de toros** bullfight.
corrido [kor'riðo] *adj* abashed; experienced; over the specified weight.
corriente [kor'rjente] *sf* current, flow. *adj* current; running; everyday; standard; fluent. **agua corriente** running water. **al corriente** informed, up-to-date. **corriente alterna/continua** alternating/direct current. **corriente de aire** draught.
corroborar [korroβo'rar] *v* corroborate; strengthen. **corroboración** *sf* corroboration.
*****corroer** [korro'er] *v* corrode. **corrosión** *sf* corrosion.
corromper [korrom'per] *v* corrupt; ruin; bribe. **corromperse** *v* putrefy; be corrupted. **corrupción** *sf* corruption; stink; bribery.
corsé [kor'se] *sm* corset.
cortabolsas [korta'bolsas] *sm invar* (*fam*) pickpocket.
cortaplumas [korta'plumas] *sm invar* penknife.
cortar [kor'tar] *v* cut; cut short; break in on; stop; switch off. **cortarse** *v* cut oneself; become embarrassed. **cortante** *adj* cutting; sharp. **corte** *sm* cut; cutting edge.
corte ['korte] *sf* (royal) court.
cortejar [korte'xar] *v* court; accompany. **cortejo** *sm* courtship; accompaniment; homage.
cortesía [korte'sia] *sf* courtesy. **cortés** *adj* courteous.
corteza [kor'teθa] *sf* bark; rind; crust.
cortijo [kor'tixo] *sm* farmhouse and farm.
cortina [kor'tina] *sf* curtain; screen; dregs *pl*. **cortina de hierro** iron curtain. **cortina de humo** smokescreen.
corto ['korto] *adj* short; defective; stupid; timid. **corto circuito** *sm* short circuit. **corto de vista** short-sighted.
corvo ['korβo] *adj* curved; bent; crooked.
cosa ['kosa] *sf* thing; something; affair. **cosa de oir/ver** something worth listening to/seeing. **no sea cosa que** lest.
cosecha [ko'setʃa] *sf* harvest. **cosechar** *v* reap, harvest.
coser [ko'ser] *v* sew; stitch; join. **coserse la boca** (*fam*) keep mum.

cosquillas [kos'kiʎas] *sf* tickling; ticklishness. **hacer cosquillas a** tickle. **cosquillear** *v* tickle. **cosquilloso** *adj* ticklish.
costa[1] ['kosta] *sf* coast. **costear** *v* sail along the coast. **costera** *sf* slope, hill. **costero** *adj* coastal.
costa[2] *sf* cost; expense. **a toda costa** at all costs. **costar** *v* cost; cause. **coste** *sm* cost, price.
costado [kos'taðo] *sm* side. **costados** *sm pl* lineage *sing*.
costilla [kos'tiʎa] *sf* rib; chop, cutlet. **costillas** *sf pl* shoulders *pl*.
costra ['kostra] *sf* scab; crust; (*fam*) filthiness.
costumbre [kos'tumbre] *sf* custom. **de costumbre** usual; usually.
costura [kos'tura] *sf* sewing; seam; dressmaking. **costurera** *sf* seamstress.
cotejar [kote'xar] *v* compare. **cotejo** *sm* comparison.
cotidiano [koti'ðjano] *adj* daily.
coto ['koto] *sm* enclosure; reserve; limit. **coto de caza** hunting reserve.
cotorra [ko'torra] *sf* parrot; magpie; (*fam*) chatterbox.
coyuntura [konjun'tura] *sf* joint; opportunity.
coz [koθ] *sf* recoil; kick.
cráneo ['kraneo] *sm* skull.
cráter ['krater] *sm* crater.
crear [kre'ar] *v* create; make; invent; found. **creación** *sf* creation. **creador, -a** *sm, sf* creator; inventor. **creativo** *adj* also **creador** creative.
*****crecer** [kre'θer] *v* grow. **crecerse** *v* become conceited; take courage. **creces** *sf pl* increase *sing*. **con creces** amply, with interest. **crecido** *adj* grown; high; large; in flood. **crecimiento** *sm* growth; increase; flooding.
credenciales [kreðen'θjales] *sf pl* credentials *pl*.
crédito ['kreðito] *sm* credit; credence; reputation. **carta de crédito** *sf* credit card.
credo ['kreðo] *sm* creed.
crédulo ['kreðulo] *adj* credulous.
*****creer** [kre'er] *v* believe; think. **¡créamelo!** believe me! **¡ya lo creo!** of course! **creíble** *adj* credible.
crema ['krema] *sf* cream; custard.
cremación [krema'θjon] *sf* cremation.

cremallera [krema'ʎera] *sf* zip-fastener.

crepúsculo [kre'puskulo] *sm* twilight.

crespo ['krespo] *adj* crispy; fuzzy; crinkled; (*fig*) obscure; (*fig*) angry.

cresta ['kresta] *sf* crest, comb; tuft.

creta ['kreta] *sf* chalk.

criar [kri'ar] *v* breed; create; beget. **criarse** *v* grow up; be raised *or* reared. **cría** *sf* act of breeding; litter; brood; young. **criada** *sf* maid. **criadero** *sm* (*plants*) nursery. **criado** *sm* manservant. **crianza** *sf* breeding; nursing. **buena/mala crianza** good/bad upbringing. **criatura** *sf* creature; infant.

cribar [kri'βar] *v* sieve; sift. **criba** *sf* sieve; screen.

crimen ['krimen] *sm* crime. **criminal** *sm*, *adj* criminal.

criollo [kri'oʎo], **-a** *s*, *adj* Creole.

cripta ['kripta] *sf* crypt.

crisálida [kri'saliða] *sf* chrysalis.

crisantemo [krisan'temo] *sm* chrysanthemum.

crisis ['krisis] *sf invar* crisis (*pl* -ses).

crisol [kri'sol] *sm* crucible.

crispar [kris'par] *v* cause to contract *or* twitch; contort; irritate. **crisparse** *v* twitch.

cristal [kirs'tal] *sm* crystal; glass; window; mirror. **cristal de contacto** contact lens. **cristal tallado** cut glass. **cristal trasero** (*auto*) rear window. **cristalería** *sf* glassworks; glassware. **cristalero, -a** *sm*, *sf* glazier; glassblower. **cristalino** *adj* crystalline; (*fig*) limpid.

Cristo ['kristo] *sm* Christ. **cristiandad** *sf* Christianity. **cristianismo** *sm* Christianity. **cristiano, -a** *s*, *adj* Christian.

criterio [kri'terjo] *sm* criterion (*pl* -a); point of view; opinion.

criticar [kriti'kar] *v* criticize. **crítica** *sf* criticism; review.

crítico ['kritiko] *sm* critic. *adj* critical.

cromo ['kromo] *sm* chromium, chrome; picture card.

crónica ['kronika] *sf* chronicle; report. **cronista** *sm* chronicler; correspondent.

crónico ['kroniko] *adj* chronic.

cronología [kronolo'xia] *sf* chronology. **cronológico** *adj* chronological.

cronómetro [kro'nometro] *sm* chronometer; stopwatch.

croqueta [kro'keta] *sf* croquette.

croquis ['krokis] *sm invar* sketch, rough draft.

crucero [kru'θero] *sm* cruiser; cruise; crossroads *pl*.

crucificar [kruθifi'kar] *v* crucify. **crucifijo** *sm* crucifix. **crucifixión** *sf* crucifixion.

crucigrama [kruθi'grama] *sm* crossword puzzle.

crudo ['kruðo] *adj* crude; raw; immature; (*fam*) boastful.

cruel [kru'el] *adj* cruel. **crueldad** *sf* cruelty.

cruento [kru'ento] *adj* bloody.

crujir [kru'xir] *v* creak; rustle; crackle. **crujido** *sm* creak; rustle; crackle.

crustáceo [krus'taθeo] *sm*, *adj* crustacean.

cruz [kruθ] *sf* cross. **en cruz** crosswise. **cruzada** *sf* crusade; crossroads *pl*. **cruzado** *sm* crusader; knight. **cruzar** *v* cross; cross oneself; pass *or* place across; dub. **cruzarse** *v* pass each other; exchange.

cuaderno [kwa'ðerno] *sm* notebook; exercise book; (*fam*) pack of cards.

cuadra ['kwaðra] *sf* stable; hut; large hall; hospital ward.

cuadragésimo [kwaðra'xesimo] *adj* fortieth.

cuadrante [kwa'ðrante] *adj* squaring. *sm* quadrant.

cuadrar [kwa'ðrar] *v* square. **cuadrado** *adj* square; stocky; perfect.

cuadrilla [kwa'ðriʎa] *sf* gang. **cuadrillero** *sm* foreman.

cuadro ['kwaðro] *sm* square; picture; sight, scene. **en cuadro** in a square.

cuadrúpedo [kwa'ðrupeðo] *sm*, *adj* quadruped.

cuajar [kwa'xar] *v* coagulate; congeal; clot; settle; fill with; (*fam*) catch on. **cuajado** *adj* curdled; congealed; (*fig*) dumbfounded. **cuajadura** *sf* curdling; congealing; coagulation.

cual [kwal] *pron* which; who. *adv* such as. **a cual más** equally. **¿cuál?** *pron interrog* which? what?

cualidad [kwali'ðað] *sf* quality.

cualquier [kwal'kjer] *adj* (*con sustantivo*) any. **cualquiera** *pron*, *pl* **cualesquiera** any; anyone; anybody.

cuan [kwan] *adv* how; as.

cuando ['kwando] *adv* when. **de vez en cuando** from time to time. **hasta cuando** until. **¿cuándo?** *adv interrog* when?

cuantía [kwan'tia] *sf* quantity.

cuanto ['kwanto] *adj* as much as; all; whatever. *adv* **en cuanto** as soon as. **en**

cuanto a as to. **¿cuánto?** *pron interrog* how much? how long?

cuarenta [kwaˈrenta] *sm, adj* forty.

cuaresma [kwaˈresma] *sf* Lent.

cuartear [kwarteˈar] *v* quarter; cut into joints. **cuartearse** *v* crack.

cuartel [kwarˈtel] *sm* quarter; barracks.

cuarto [ˈkwarto] *adj* fourth. *sm* quarter; room. **cuarto de baño** bathroom. **cuarto de estar** livingroom.

cuarzo [ˈkwarθo] *sm* quartz.

cuatro [ˈkwatro] *sm, adj* four.

cuba [ˈkuba] *sf* barrel; tub; drunkard. **estar como una cuba** (*fam*) be drunk.

Cuba *sf* Cuba. **cubano, -a** *s, adj* Cuban.

cúbico [ˈkuβiko] *adj* cubic. **raíz cubica** *sf* cube root.

cubículo [kuˈβikulo] *sm* cubicle.

cubo [ˈkuβo] *sm* bucket.

cubrir [kuˈβrir] *v* cover; drown; repay. **cubrirse** *v* cover oneself; put on one's hat; cloud over. **cubierta** *sf* cover; roof; tyre; bedspread; (*mar*) deck. **cubierto** *sm* cover; place-setting; menu. **bajo cubierto** under cover. **precio del cubierto** *sm* cover charge.

cucaracha [kukaˈratʃa] *sf* cockroach.

cuclillas [kuˈkliʎas] *adv* **en cuclillas** squatting, on one's haunches.

cuclillo [kuˈkliʎo] *sm* cuckoo; cuckold.

cuchara [kuˈtʃara] *sf* spoon; ladle; trowel. **cucharada** *sf* spoonful. **cucharadita** *sf* teaspoonful. **cucharita** *sf* teaspoon; coffeespoon. **cucharón** *sm* ladle; scoop.

cuchichear [kutʃitʃeˈar] *v* whisper. **cuchicheo** *sm* whisper; whispering.

cuchilla [kuˈtʃiʎa] *sf* kitchen knife; chopper; razor blade; range of mountains. **patines de cuchilla** *sm pl* ice skates *pl*. **cuchillada** *sf* slash; stab; knifing. **andar a cuchilladas** be at daggers drawn. **cuchillería** *sf* cutlery; cutlery shop. **cuchillo** *sm* knife.

cuello [ˈkweʎo] *sm* collar; neck; throat. **cuello de pico** V-neck. **cuello vuelto** polo neck.

cuenca [ˈkwenka] *sf* wooden bowl; eye socket; (*geog*) basin.

cuenta [ˈkwenta] *sf* account; bill; count; report. **a cuenta** on account. **¿a cuenta de qué?** why? **tener en cuenta** bear in mind.

cuento [ˈkwento] *sm* tale; fib; fuss. **cuento chino** nonsense.

cuerda [ˈkwerða] *sf* cord; rope; string;

chain; (*anat*) chord. **cuerdas vocales** vocal chords *pl*.

cuerdo [ˈkwerðo], **-a** *sm, sf* sane person. *adj* sane.

cuerno [ˈkwerno] *sm* horn; antler; feeler.

cuero [ˈkwero] *sm* skin; hide; leather.

cuerpo [ˈkwerpo] *sm* body; piece, section; stage; corps. **cuerpo de casa** housework. **cuerpo entero** full-length. **cuerpo muerto** (*mar*) mooring buoy.

cuervo [ˈkwerβo] *sm* raven.

cuesta [ˈkwesta] *sf* slope; hill. **a cuestas** on one's back. **cuesta abajo/arriba** down/uphill.

cuestión [kwesˈtjon] *sf* question, issue; dispute. **cuestionar** *v* question; argue.

cueva [ˈkweβa] *sf* cave; cellar; den.

cuidar [kwiˈðar] *v* take care of; pay attention to. **cuidar de que** take care that. **no cuidarse de** take no notice of. **cuidado** *sm* care; carefulness; affair; worry. **¡cuidado!** beware! **cuidador** *adj* careful.

cuita [ˈkwita] *sf* worry; sorrow. **cuitado** *adj* worried; bashful.

culebra [kuˈleβra] *sf* snake; (*fam*) practical joke. **culebrear** *v* wriggle; zigzag.

culinario [kuliˈnarjo] *adj* culinary.

culminar [kulmiˈnar] *v* culminate. **culminación** *sf* culmination. **culminante** *adj* culminating.

culo [ˈkulo] *sm* (*fam*) bottom, arse. **ir de culo** go downhill.

culpar [kulˈpar] *v* blame. **culparse** *v* take the blame. **culpa** *sm* blame; fault; guilt. **echar la culpa a** lay the blame on. **culpabilidad** *sf* culpability. **culpable** *adj* guilty.

cultivar [kultiˈβar] *v* cultivate; grow; develop. **cultivador, -a** *sm, sf* farmer; grower; *sf* (*máquina*) cultivator. **cultivación** *sf* cultivation; culture. **cultivo** *sm* cultivation; culture.

culto [ˈkulto] *adj* cultivated; cultured; civilized. *sm* worship; cult. **rendir culto a** worship. **cultura** *sf* culture, learning.

cumbre [ˈkumbre] *sf* peak, summit.

cumpleaños [kumpleˈaɲos] *sm invar* birthday. **feliz cumpleaños** happy birthday.

cumplir [kumˈplir] *v* fulfil; reach; end; do one's duty. **cumplirse** *v* be realized. **cumplir años** have a birthday. **por cumplir** as a matter of form. **cumplido** *adj* plentiful;

faultless; polite. **cumplimentar** *v* compliment; fulfil. **cumplimentero** *adj* excessively formal. **cumplimiento** *sm* compliment; fulfilment; politeness.

cúmulo ['kumulo] *sm* heap; large amount; (*nube*) cumulus.

cuna ['kuna] *sf* cradle; (*fig*) origin; birthplace.

cundir [kun'dir] *v* spread; increase; grow.

cuneta [ku'neta] *sf* ditch; gutter; hard shoulder.

cuña ['kuɲa] *sf* wedge; chock. **tener cuña** (*fam*) have friends at court.

cuñado [ku'ɲado] *sm* brother-in-law

cuño ['kuɲo] *sm* die; die-stamp; (*fig*) impression.

cuota ['kwota] *sf* quota; contribution; dues *pl*.

cupón [ku'pon] *sm* coupon; ticket.

cúpula ['kupula] *sf* dome.

cura[1] ['kura] *sm* priest. **cura párroco** parish priest.

cura[2] *sf* cure; healing; remedy; treatment; dressing. **primera cura** first aid. **curación** *sf* cure. **curador, -a** *sm, sf* guardian; tutor; curator. **curativo** *adj* healing.

curioso [ku'rjoso] *adj* curious; neat; attentive. *sm* bystander. **curiosidad** *sf* curiosity.

cursar [kur'sar] *v* attend; study; frequent. **cursado** *adj* skilled. **cursante** *s(m+f)* student.

cursi ['kursi] *adj* pretentious; affected; vulgar. *s(m+f)* pretentious person; snob.

curso ['kurso] *sm* course; direction; school year. **curso acelerado** crash course.

curtir [kur'tir] *v* tan; harden. **curtirse** *v* become tanned; become hardened; accustom oneself. **curtidor** *sm* tanner. **curtiduría** *sf* tannery. **curtimiento** *sm* tanning.

curva ['kurβa] *sf* curve; bend. **curvar** *v* curve; bend. **curvatura** *sf* curvature. **curvo** *adj* curved; bent.

cúspide ['kuspiðe] *sf* peak; summit.

custodiar [kusto'ðjar] *v* take care of; guard; defend. **custodia** *sf* custody. **custodio** *sm* custodian.

cutis ['kutis] *sm invar* skin; complexion.

cuyo ['kujo] *pron* whose; of which; of whom.

CH

chabacano [tʃaβa'kano] *adj* vulgar; common. **chabacanería** *sf* vulgarity; vulgar remark.

chacal [tʃa'kal] *sm* jackal.

chafar [sʃa'far] *v* flatten; crush; crease; (*en una discusión*) stump.

chal [tʃal] *sm* shawl.

chalado [tʃa'laðo] *adj* (*fam*) crazy; dotty.

chalán [tʃa'lan] *sm* horse dealer; shady businessman.

chaleco [tʃa'leko] *sm* waistcoat.

chalupa [tʃa'lupa] *sf* canoe; launch.

chambelán [tʃambe'lan] *sm* chamberlain.

champaña [tʃam'paɲa] *sm* champagne.

champú [tʃam'pu] *sm* shampoo.

chamuscar [tʃamus'kar] *v* singe; scorch.

chancear [tʃanθe'ar] *v* joke. **chancearse** *v* make fun of. **chanza** *sf* joke.

chanchullo [tʃan'tʃuʎo] *sm* (*fam*) crooked deal.

chantaje [tʃan'taxe] *sm* blackmail. **chantajista** *s(m+f)* blackmailer.

chapa ['tʃapa] *sf* metal sheet; rouge; (*fam*) common sense.

chaparro [tʃa'parro] *adj* (*fam*) tubby.

chaparrón [tʃapar'ron] *sm* downpour, cloudburst.

chapón [tʃa'pon] *sm* ink blot.

chapotear [tʃapote'ar] *v* sponge; moisten; splash. **chapoteo** *sm* sponging; moistening; splashing.

chapucero [tʃapu'θero] **, -a** *sm, sf* bungler; liar. *adj* crude, clumsy. **chapucear** *v* botch, bungle.

chapuzar [tʃapu'θar] *v* duck, plunge into water.

chaqueta [tʃa'keta] *sf* jacket.

charca ['tʃarka] *sf* pool.

charco ['tʃarko] *sm* puddle.

charlar [tʃar'lar] *v* (*fam*) chat, chatter; gossip. **charla** *sf* (*fam*) chatter, talk. **charlador, -a** *sm, sf also* **charlatán, -ana** *sm, sf* chatterbox. **charladuría** *sf* chatter; gossip.

charol [tʃa'rol] *sm* varnish; patent leather. **darse charol** boast. **charolar** *v* varnish.

charro ['tʃarro] *adj* (*fam*) churlish; illbred; tawdry. **charrada** *sf* boorishness.

chasquear [tʃaske'ar] v trick; disappoint. chasco sm trick; disappointment.

chato ['tʃato] adj flat-nosed; flat. sm small glass.

chaval [tʃa'βal] sm (fam) lad; kid. chavala sf (fam) lass; girl.

Checoslovaquia [tʃekoslo'βakja] sf Czechoslovakia. checoslovaco, -a s, adj Czechoslovak(ian).

cheque ['tʃeke] sm cheque. cheque de viajero traveller's cheque.

chicle ['tʃikle] sm chewing gum.

chico ['tʃiko] adj small. sm boy. chica sf girl.

chichón [tʃi'tʃon] sm lump, bump.

chiflar [tʃi'flar] v whistle; hiss; (fam) swig. chiflarse por be crazy about. chifla sf whistle; hissing. chiflado, -a sm, sf (fam) crackpot; (fam: aficionado) fan; adj (fam) crazy.

chile ['tʃile] sm chili, chilli.

Chile ['tʃile] sm Chile. chileno, -a s, adj Chilean.

chillar [tʃi'ʎar] v scream; howl; squeak; blare. chillador adj screaming; shrieking. chillería sf screaming; scolding. chillido sm scream; howl; squeak.

chimenea [tʃime'nea] sf chimney; fireplace.

chimpancé [tʃimpan'θe] sm chimpanzee.

china ['tʃina] sf porcelain; china.

China sf China. chino, -a s, adj Chinese.

chinche ['tʃintʃe] sf bedbug.

chingar [tʃin'gar] v (fam) drink; (fam) pester.

Chipre ['tʃipre] sm Cyprus. chipriota s(m+f), adj Cypriot.

chiripa [tʃi'ripa] sf fluke, lucky accident.

chirriar [tʃirri'ar] v creak; squeak; chatter. chirrido sm creaking; squeaking; chattering.

chisme ['tʃisme] sm gadget; contrivance; knick-knack. chismes sm pl gossip sing. chismear v gossip. chismería sf tittle-tattle. chismoso adj gossiping.

chispear [tʃispe'ar] v spark; sparkle; drizzle. chispa sf spark; little bit. chispeante adj sparkling.

chisporrotear [tʃisporrote'ar] v spark; sizzle. chisporroteo sm sparking; sizzling.

chistar [tʃis'tar] v speak; open one's lips. no chistar say not a word. ¡chite! interj hush!

chiste ['tʃiste] sf joke. tener chiste be funny. chistoso adj funny; joking.

chivo ['tʃiβo], -a sm, sf (zool) kid.

chocar [tʃo'kar] v surprise; shock; collide. choque sm shock; jolt; crash; dispute.

chocolate [tʃoko'late] sm chocolate. chocolatería chocolate shop.

chochear [tʃotʃe'ar] v be in one's dotage. chochera sf dotage. chocho adj doddering.

chofer ['tʃofer] sm chauffeur.

chorizo [tʃo'riθo] sm spicy sausage.

chorrear [tʃorre'ar] v gush; spout; drip. chorreo sm gushing; spouting; dripping. chorro sm jet; gush; flow; stream.

choza ['tʃoθa] sf hut, hovel.

chubasco [tʃu'βasko] sm shower; squall; (fig) setback.

chuleta [tʃu'leta] sf chop, cutlet; (fam) slap.

chulo ['tʃulo] sm pimp; (fam) ruffian; (fam) spiv. adj cheeky; flashy; insolent. chulada sf cheek; vulgar thing; funny thing. chulear v get cheeky with.

chungar [tʃun'gar] v (fam) tease; tell jokes. chunga sf banter, fun.

chupar [tʃu'par] v suck; absorb. chuparse v become worn to a shadow. chupada sf suck, sucking. chupadero also chupador adj sucking; absorbent. chupete sm (para niños) dummy. chupetear v suck at.

churro ['tʃurro] sm deep-fried batter; (fam) dead loss.

chusco ['tʃusko], -a sm, sf wag, wit. adj funny.

chusma ['tʃusma] sf rabble, riffraff.

chuzo ['tʃuθo] sm (arma) pike. llover a chuzos pour down.

D

dactilógrafo [dakti'lografo], -a sm, sf typist. dactilografía sf typing.

dádiva ['daðiβa] sf gift. dadivoso adj generous.

dado ['daðo] sm die (pl dice).

daga ['daga] sf dagger.

dama ['dama] sf lady; mistress; (ajedrez) queen; (juego de damas) king. damas sf pl draughts.

damasco [da'masko] sm damask.

damnificar [damnifi'kar] v injure, harm.
danés [da'nes], **-esa** sm, sf Dane. sm
(lengua) Danish. adj Danish.
danzar [dan'θar] v dance. **danza** sf dance,
dancing. **danzante, -a** sm, sf dancer.
dañar [da'ɲar] v harm; damage; spoil.
dañino adj destructive. **daño** sm injury;
damage; loss.
*****dar** [dar] v give; grant; yield; (reloj)
strike; (naipes) deal. **dar a** face; overlook. **dar como** or **por** declare; consider.
dar con meet. **lo mismo da** it makes no
difference. **darse** v regard oneself; devote
oneself; matter; occur. **darse cuenta** realize.
dardo ['darðo] sm dart.
dársena ['darsena] sm dock.
dátil ['datil] sm (fruto) date.
dato ['dato] sm fact; piece of information.
de [de] prep of; from.
debajo [de'βaxo] adv underneath. **debajo
de** prep under, beneath, below.
debatir [deβa'tir] v debate, discuss.
debate sm debate.
deber [de'βer] v owe; must; ought. sm
duty; debt. **debidamente** adv fittingly.
debido adj fitting; just. **debido a** due to.
débito sm debt.
debilitar [deβili'tar] v weaken. **débil** adj
weak. **debildad** sf weakness.
*****decaer** [deka'er] v decline; decay.
decadencia sf decadence; decline.
decadente adj decadent.
decano [de'kano] sm dean.
decapitar [dekapi'tar] v decapitate.
decapitación sf decapitation.
decena [de'θena] sf unit of ten.
decencia [de'θenθja] sf decency; modesty;
cleanliness. **decente** adj decent; modest;
clean.
decenio [de'θenjo] sm decade.
decepción [deθep'θjon] sf disappointment.
decidir [deθi'ðir] v decide. **decidirse** v
make up one's mind. **decisión** sf decision. **decisivo** adj decisive.
décima ['deθima] sf tenth; tithe. **decimal**
adj decimal. **décimo** adj tenth.
decimoctavo adj eighteenth.
decimocuarto adj fourteenth. **decimonono**
or **decimonoveno** adj nineteenth. **decimoquinto** adj fifteenth. **decimoséptimo** adj
seventeenth. **decimosexto** adj sixteenth.
decimotercio adj thirteenth.

*****decir** [de'θir] v say; tell; speak; call.
¿diga? (teléfono) hello!
declamar [dekla'mar] v declaim; speak
out; recite. **declamación** sf declamation;
oration. **declamador, -a** sm, sf orator.
declarar [dekla'rar] v declare; state;
explain. **declararse** v declare oneself;
(fuego, etc.) break out; (amor) propose.
declaración sf declaration.
declinar [dekli'nar] v decay; fade; depart;
(gram) decline. **declinación** sf decline;
(gram) declension.
declive [de'kliβe] sm slope; (com) slump.
decorar [deko'rar] v decorate. **decoración**
sf decoration. **decorador, -a** sm, sf decorator. **decorativo** adj decorative.
decoro [de'koro] sm decorum; dignity;
respect.
*****decrecer** [dekre'θer] v decrease. **decre-
mento** sm diminution.
decrépito [de'krepito] adj decrepit.
decretar [dekre'tar] v decree. **decreto** sm
decree.
dedal [de'ðal] sm thimble.
dédalo ['deðalo] sm maze.
dedicar [deði'kar] v dedicate, devote.
dedicación sf dedication. **dedicatoria** sf
(libro) dedication.
dedillo [de'ðiʎo] sm **al dedillo** at one's
fingertips.
dedo ['deðo] sm finger; toe. **dedo del
corazón** middle finger. **dedo índice** forefinger. **dedo meñique** little finger. **dedo
pulgar** thumb.
*****deducir** [deðu'θir] v deduce; allege;
deduct. **deducción** sf deduction. **deduc-
tivo** adj deductive.
defectible [defek'tiβle] adj fallible; defective. **defecto** sm defect. **defectuoso** adj
defective.
*****defender** [defen'der] v defend; prohibit;
oppose. **defendible** adj defensible.
defendido, -a sm, sf (jur) defendant.
defensa sf defence; shelter. **defensa
pasiva** civil defence. **defensivo** adj defensive. **defensor, -a** sm, sf protector; counsel.
deferencia [defe'renθja] sf deference.
deferente adj deferential.
*****deferir** [defe'rir] v defer; delegate.
deficiencia [defi'θjenθja] sf deficiency.
deficiente adj deficient.
definir [defi'nir] v define. **definición** sf definition. **definido** adj definite. **definitivo**
adj definitive. **en definitiva** in short.

deformar [defor'mar] *v* deform; disfigure. **deformación** *sf* deformation; distortion. **deforme** *adj* deformed; abnormal. **deformidad** *sf* deformity; (*fig*) perversion. **defraudar** [defrau'dar] *v* defraud; evade; disappoint; frustrate. **defraudar al fisco** evade taxes. **defraudación** *sf* fraud; deceit. **defraudador, -a** *sm, sf* tax evader; swindler.

defunción [defun'θjon] *sf* decease.

degenerar [dexene'rar] *v* degenerate. **degeneración** *sf* degeneration.

deglutir [deglu'tir] *v* swallow. **deglución** *sf* swallowing.

*degollar [dego'ʎar] *v* cut the throat of; behead; (*fig*) ruin. **degollación** *sf* throat-cutting; decapitation. **degolladero** *sm* slaughter-house; scaffold. **degollador, -a** *sm, sf* executioner.

degradar [degra'ðar] *v* degrade. **degradación** *sf* degradation.

degustación [degusta'θion] *sf* tasting; sampling.

dehesa [de'esa] *sf* pasture.

deificar [deifi'kar] *v* deify. **deidad** *sf* deity. **deificación** *sf* deification.

dejar [de'xar] *v* leave; yield; drop; let, allow. **dejar de** leave off, stop; fail to. **dejarse** *v* neglect oneself. **dejarse vencer** give in to. **dejarse de** cease to.

del [del] *contraction of* **de el**.

delantal [delan'tal] *sm* apron.

delante [de'lante] *adv* before, in front, ahead. **delante de** before, in front of. **delantera** *sf* front; advantage; lead. **delantero** *adj* front; foremost.

delatar [dela'tar] *v* denounce; betray. **delator, -a** *sm, sf* informer.

delegar [dele'gar] *v* delegate. **delegación** *sf* delegation. **delegado** *adj* delegated.

deleitar [delei'tar] *v* delight; please. **deleitarse** *v* take delight. **deleite** *sm* delight; pleasure. **deleitoso** *adj* delightful.

deletrear [deletre'ar] *v* spell out; interpret. **deletreo** *sm* spelling out; decipherment.

deleznable [deleθ'naβle] *adj* brittle; fragile; frail.

delfín [del'fin] *sm* dolphin.

delgado [del'gaðo] *adj* thin; delicate; ingenious. **delgadez** *sf* thinness.

deliberar [deliβe'rar] *v* deliberate, consider. **deliberación** *sf* deliberation. **deliberado** *adj* deliberate.

delicado [deli'kaðo] *adj* delicate; tender; touchy. **delicadez** *sf* delicacy; tenderness; touchiness; frailty; squeamishness.

delicioso [deli'θjoso] *adj* delicious; delightful. **delicia** *sf* delight.

delimitar [delimi'tar] *v* delimit. **delimitación** *sf* delimitation.

delincuencia [delin'kwenθja] *sf* delinquency. **delincuente** *s(m+f)* delinquent; criminal.

delinear [deline'ar] *v* delineate; outline; sketch. **delineación** *sf* delineation. **delineante** *sm* draughtsman.

delirar [deli'rar] *v* be delirious; rave. **delirio** *sm* delirium.

delito [de'lito] *sm* crime.

delta ['delta] *sm* delta.

demacrarse [dema'krarse] *v* waste away. **demacración** *sf* emaciation. **demacrado** *adj* emaciated.

demagogia [dema'goxja] *sf* demagogy. **demagogo** *sm* demagogue.

demandar [deman'dar] *v* request; desire; (*jur*) sue. **demanda** *sf* demand; appeal; petition; question. **demandado, -a** *sm, sf* (*jur*) defendant. **demandante** *s(m+f)* (*jur*) plaintiff.

demarcar [demar'kar] *v* demarcate. **demarcación** *sf* demarcation.

demás [de'mas] *adj* other; rest; remaining. **los demás, las demás** the others. **estar demás** be unwanted. **y demás** etcetera. **demasía** *sf* excess; outrage; insolence. **demasiado** *adj, adv* too much.

demencia [de'menθja] *sf* insanity. **demente** *adj* insane.

democracia [demo'kraθja] *sf* democracy. **demócrata** *adj* democratic. *s(m+f)* democrat. **democrático** *adj* democratic.

*demoler [demo'ler] *v* demolish. **demolición** *sf* demolition.

demonio [de'monjo] *sm* demon. **demoniaco** *adj* demoniac.

demorar [demo'rar] *v* delay; remain. **demora** *sf* delay.

*demostrar [demos'trar] *v* demonstrate; prove. **demostrable** *adj* demonstrable. **demostración** *sf* demonstration. **demostrativo** *adj* demonstrative.

*denegar [dene'gar] *v* deny, refuse. **denegación** *sf* denial, refusal.

denigrar [deni'grar] *v* denigrate; slander; insult. **denigración** *sf* denigration; disgrace.

denominar [denomi'nar] *v* name. **denominación** *sf* denomination.

denotar [deno'tar] *v* denote; indicate.

denso ['denso] *adj* dense. **densidad** *sf* density.

dentado [den'taðo] *adj* toothed; jagged; (*tecn*) cogged. **dentadura** *sf* set of teeth. **dental** *adj* dental. **dentar** *v* furnish with teeth; cut one's teeth. **dentellar** *v* (*dientes*) chatter. **dentallear** *v* bite. **dentífrico** *sm* toothpaste. **dentista** *s(m+f)* dentist.

dentro ['dentro] *adv* inside, within. **dentro de poco** shortly.

denudar [denu'ðar] *v* denude.

denunciar [denun'θjar] *v* denounce; inform; accuse. **denuncia** *sf* denunciation; accusation.

departamento [departa'mento] *sm* department.

depender [depen'der] *v* depend. **dependencia** *sf* dependence; reliance. **dependiente, -a** *sm, sf* shop assistant. **dependiente de** dependent on.

deplorar [deplo'rar] *v* deplore; regret. **deplorable** *adj* deplorable.

*deponer [depo'ner] *v* lay down; lay aside; remove from office; depose; (*jur*) give evidence; defecate. **deponente** *s(m+f)* witness.

deportar [depor'tar] *v* deport. **deportación** *sf* deportation.

deporte [de'porte] *sm* sport. **deportismo** *sm* sport; enthusiasm for sport. **deportista** *s(m+f)* sportsman/woman. **coche deportivo** sports car.

depositar [deposi'tar] *v* deposit. **depósito** *sm* deposit; store; tank; tip.

depravar [depra'βar] *v* deprave; corrupt. **depravación** *sf* depravity. **depravado** *adj* depraved.

depreciar [depre'θjar] *v* depreciate, lessen in value. **depreciación** *sf* depreciation.

deprimir [depri'mir] *v* depress. **depresión** *sf* depression. **depresivo** *adj* depressing.

depurar [depu'rar] *v* purify. **depuración** *sf* purification.

derecha [de'retʃa] *sf* right; right hand. **a la derecha** on the right. **derecho** *sm* law; *adj* right; straight; upright.

derivar [deri'βar] *v* derive. **derivación** *sf* derivation.

derogar [dero'gar] *v* repeal; abolish; cancel. **derogación** *sf* repeal; abolition.

derramar [derra'mar] *v* spill; overflow;

scatter; spread. **derramarse** *v* be scattered; overflow. **derrame** *sm* spilling; leakage; overflow; slope.

*derretir [derre'tir] *v* melt; dissipate. **derretirse** *v* be deeply in love; (*fam*) be impatient. **derretimiento** *sm* melting; (*fam*) consuming passion.

derribar [derri'βar] *v* tear down; knock down; throw down. **derribarse** *v* fall down. **derribo** *sm* demolition. **derribos** *sm pl* rubble *sing*.

derrocar [derro'kar] *v* hurl down; ruin.

derrochar [derro'tʃar] *v* squander. **derrochador, -a** *s, adj* prodigal; spendthrift.

derrotar [derro'tar] *v* defeat; ruin; put to flight. **derrota** *sf* defeat; failure. **derrotado** *adj* defeated; shabby.

derrumbar [derrum'bar] *v* knock down, hurl down, pull down. **derrumbarse** *v* collapse. **derrumbo** *sm* collapse; overthrow; demolition.

desabotonar [desaβoto'nar] *v* unbutton; blossom. **desabotonarse** *v* come undone.

desabrigar [desaβri'gar] *v* uncover; leave without shelter; take off clothing. **desabrigado** *adj* uncovered; unprotected; exposed. **desabrigo** *sm* uncovering; exposure.

desabrochar [desaβro'tʃar] *v* unfasten; undo. **desabrocharse** *v* come undone.

desacatar [desaka'tar] *v* be disrespectful; disobey. **desacato** *sm* disrespect; contempt.

*desacertar [desaθer'tar] *v* be wrong; act foolishly. **desacertado** *adj* mistaken; ill-advised; unsuccessful; unfortunate; clumsy. **desacierto** *sm* mistake, blunder.

desacomodar [desakomo'ðar] *v* inconvenience; dismiss. **desacomodarse** *v* lose one's job. **desacomodado** *adj* poor; inconvenient; unemployed. **desacomodamiento** *sm* also **desacomodo** *sm* discomfort; inconvenience.

desaconsejado [desakonse'xaðo] *adj* ill-advised. **desaconsejar** *v* advise against.

*desacordar [desakor'ðar] *v* put out of tune. **desacordarse** *v* get out of tune; be forgetful. **desacordado** *adj* discordant.

desacostumbrar [desakostum'brar] *v* break a habit. **desacostumbrado** *adj* unusual.

desacreditar [desakreði'tar] *v* discredit.

desacuerdo [desa'kwerðo] *sm* discord; disagreement; unconsciousness.

desafecto [desa'fekto] *adj* disaffected; indifferent; adverse.

desafinar [desafi'nar] *v* be out of tune; (*fig*) speak out of turn.

desafio [desa'fio] *sm* challenge.

desagradar [desagra'ðar] *v* displease; be unpleasant. **desagradable** *adj* unpleasant.

desagradecido [desagraðe'θiðo], **-a** *sm*, *sf* ingrate. *adj* ungrateful.

desagraviar [desagra'βjar] *v* make amends for. **desagravio** *sm* indemnity; compensation.

desaguar [desa'gwar] *v* drain. **desaguadero** *sm* drain; channel. **desagüe** *sm* drainage; outlet.

desahogar [desao'gar] *v* ease; console. **desahogarse** *v* recover; free oneself; speak one's mind; get out of debt. **desahogado** *adj* impudent; well-off; spacious; uncluttered. **desahogo** *sm* ease; comfort; relief.

desahuciar [desau'θjar] *v* evict; despair of. **desahucio** *sm* eviction.

desairar [desai'rar] *v* disregard; snub. **desairado** *adj* spurned; unattractive; awkward. **desaire** *sm* snub; rebuff; gracelessness.

desajustar [desaxus'tar] *v* disarrange. **desajustarse** *v* break down. **desajuste** *sm* breakdown.

desalado [desa'laðo] *adj* impatient; hasty; unsalted.

*desalentar [desalen'tar] *v* make breathless; discourage. **desalentarse** *v* lose heart.

desaliñar [desali'ɲar] *v* disturb; ruffle. **desaliñado** *adj* slovenly. **desaliño** *sm* slovenliness; uncleanness; negligence.

desalojar [desalo'xar] *v* remove; eject. **desalojarse** *v* move out. **desalojamiento** *sm* ejection.

desalquilado [desalki'laðo] *adj* vacant. **desalquilar** *v* vacate.

desamor [desa'mor] *sm* indifference; ingratitude.

desamparar [desampa'rar] *v* abandon. **desamparo** *sm* abandonment; helplessness.

desangrar [desan'grar] *v* bleed; impoverish. **desangrarse** *v* lose much blood.

desanimar [desani'mar] *v* discourage. **desanimarse** *v* become discouraged. **desánimo** *sm* discouragement.

desanudar [desanu'ðar] *v* untie; disentangle.

desapacible [desapa'θiβle] *adj* disagreeable. **desapacibilidad** *sf* unpleasantness.

*desaparecer [desapare'θer] *v* disappear; hide; wear off. **desaparecido** *adj* missing. **desaparecimiento** *sm* disappearance.

desapegarse [desape'garse] *v* lose interest in. **desapego** *sm* lack of interest; coldness.

desapercibido [desaperθi'βiðo] *adj* unnoticed. **coger desapercibido** catch unawares.

desapoderar [desapoðe'rar] *v* dispossess; dismiss.

*desapretar [desapre'tar] *v* loosen.

*desaprobar [desapro'βar] *v* disapprove of. **desaprobación** *sf* disapproval.

desaprovechar [desaproβe'tʃar] *v* waste; lose ground. **desaprovechado** *adj* unprofitable; backward. **desaprovechamiento** *sm* waste; misuse.

desapuntar [desapun'tar] *v* unstitch.

desarmar [desar'mar] *v* disarm; disband; dismantle; calm. **desarme** *sm* disarmament.

desarraigar [desarrai'gar] *v* uproot. **desarraigado** *adj* uprooted; rootless.

desarreglar [desarre'glar] *v* upset; disarrange. **desarreglado** *adj* slovenly; faulty. **desarreglo** *sm* disorder; untidiness; trouble.

desarrollar [desarro'ʎar] *v* unfold; develop. **desarrollo** *sm* development.

desarrugar [desarru'gar] *v* smooth out.

desasear [desase'ar] *v* soil; disarrange. **desaseo** *sm* dirtiness; disorder.

*desasir [desa'sir] *v* loosen, undo. **desasirse de** get rid of.

*desasosegar [desasose'gar] *v* disturb. **desasosiego** *sm* disquiet; restlessness.

desastre [de'sastre] *sm* disaster. **desastrado** *adj* unlucky; dirty; disorderly. **desastroso** *adj* disastrous.

desatar [desa'tar] *v* undo; unravel. **desatarse** *v* break out; lose all reserve. **desatadura** *sf* untying.

*desatender [desaten'der] *v* ignore; slight. **desatención** *sf* inattention; discourtesy. **desatentado** *adj* absent-minded. **desatento** *adj* discourteous.

desatinar [desati'nar] *v* bewilder; rave; blunder. **desatinado** *adj* silly; rash. **desatino** *sm* absurdity; blunder; tactlessness.

*desavenir [desaβe'nir] *v* cause to quarrel. **desavenirse** *v* quarrel. **desavenido** *adj* incompatible.

desaventajado [desaβenta'xaðo] *adj* unfavourable; inferior.

desaviar [desa'βjar] *v* lead astray; deprive of necessities; inconvenience. **desavío** *sm* inconvenience; lack of means.

desayunar [desaju'nar] *v* breakfast. **desayuno** *sm* breakfast.

desazonar [desaθo'nar] *v* render tasteless; displease. **desazón** *sm* insipidity; displeasure. **desazonado** *adj* tasteless; displeased.

desbandarse [desβan'darse] *v* disband; disperse.

desbarajustar [desβaraxus'tar] *v* confuse. **desbarajuste** *sm* confusion.

desbaratar [desβara'tar] *v* ruin; spoil; waste; talk rubbish. **desbaratarse** *v* fall apart; get carried away. **desbaratado** *adj* wrecked; dissipated. **desbaratamiento** *sm* waste; disorder; wrecking.

desbordar [desβor'ðar] *v* flood; overflow; (*fig*) lose one's self-control. **desbordamiento** *sm* overflow.

descabezar [deskaβe'θar] *v* behead. **descabezarse** *v* rack one's brains. **descabezado** *adj* headless; rash.

descalabrar [deskala'βrar] *v* wound (in the head); maltreat; defeat. **descalabro** *sm* setback; defeat.

descalificar [deskalifi'kar] *v* disqualify. **descalificación** *sf* disqualification.

descalzar [deskal'θar] *v* take off one's shoes. **descalzo** *adj* barefoot.

descamisado [deskami'saðo] *adj* destitute. *sm* tramp.

descansar [deskan'sar] *v* rest; sleep; lean; depend. **descansado** *adj* rested. **descanso** *sm* rest; repose.

descarado [deska'raðo] *adj* brazen; cheeky; blatant.

descargar [deskar'gar] *v* unload; discharge; free; absolve. **descarga** *sf* discharge; unloading. **descargado** *adj* (*bateria*) flat. **descargo** *sm* unloading; discharge of debt. **descargue** *sm* unloading of goods.

descartar [deskar'tar] *v* discard; leave out. **descartarse** *v* get out of. **descarte** *sm* discarding; rejection.

*descender [desθen'der] *v* descend; flow; lower. **descendencia** *sf* lineage. **descendiente** *s(m+f)* descendant. **descenso** *sm* descent; fall; decline.

descentralizar [desθentrali'θar] *v* decentralize.

descifrar [desθi'frar] *v* decipher. **decifrable** *adj* decipherable.

*descolgar [deskol'gar] *v* lower; (*teléfono*) pick up; take down. **descolgarse** *v* come down; slip; drop; surprise.

descolorar [deskolo'rar] *v* discolour. **descolorido** *adj* discoloured.

descomedido [deskome'ðiðo] *adj* immoderate; disproportionate; rude. **descomedirse** *v* go too far.

*descomponer [deskompo'ner] *v* decompose; disturb. **descomponerse** *v* rot; become upset. **descomposición** *sf* decomposition. **descompuesto** *adj* broken; faulty; insolent.

*desconcertar [deskonθer'tar] *v* disconcert; damage. **desconcierto** *sm* disorder; confusion.

desconectar [deskonek'tar] *v* disconnect.

desconfiar [deskon'fjar] *v* lack confidence. **desconfiar de** distrust. **desconfiado** *adj* distrustful. **desconfianza** *sf* mistrust, suspicion.

desconformar [deskonfor'mar] *v* disagree, dissent.

*desconocer [deskono'θer] *v* fail to recognize; ignore; deny; disown. **desconocido** *adj* unknown; unrecognized; ungrateful. **desconocimiento** *sm* ignorance; ingratitude; repudiation.

desconsiderado [deskonside'raðo] *adj* inconsiderate.

*desconsolar [deskonso'lar] *v* grieve, distress. **desconsolado** *adj* disconsolate. **desconsuelo** *sm* grief; affliction.

*descontar [deskon'tar] *v* discount; deduct; take for granted.

descontento [deskon'tento] *adj* dissatisfied.

descontinuar [deskontinu'ar] *v* discontinue.

descorazonar [deskorazo'nar] *v* discourage.

descorchar [deskor'tʃar] *v* uncork. **descorchador** *sm* corkscrew.

descortés [deskor'tes] *adj* discourteous. **descortesía** *sf* discourtesy.

descreer [deskre'er] *v* disbelieve; discredit. **descrédito** *sm* discredit.

describir [deskri'βir] *v* describe. **descripción** *sf* description. **descriptivo** *adj* descriptive.

descuajar [deskwa'xar] *v* liquefy; uproot; dishearten.

descubrir [desku'βrir] *v* discover; uncover; publish. **descubierto** *adj* exposed; manifest; hatless. **descubridor, -a** *sm, sf* discoverer. **descubrimiento** *sm* discovery.

descuento [des'kwento] *sm* discount.

descuidar [deskwi'ðar] *v* neglect; release; distract. **descuidar de** forget to. **¡descuida!** don't worry! **descuidarse** *v* be careless; neglect one's health. **descuidado** *adj* neglectful; careless; casual. **descuido** *sm* negligence; carelessness; thoughtlessness.

desde ['desðe] *prep* from; since; after. **desde luego** of course; immediately.

*****desdecir** [desðe'θir] *v* gainsay; be unworthy of. **desdecirse** *v* retract.

desdeñar [desðe'ɲar] *v* disdain; scorn. **desdén** *sm* disdain; scorn. **al desdén** nonchalantly. **desdeñoso** *adj* disdainful.

desdicha [des'ðitʃa] *sf* misfortune; misery. **desdichado** *adj* unfortunate; wretched.

desdoblar [desðo'βlar] *v* unfold; split.

desdorar [desðo'rar] *v* tarnish. **desdoro** *sm* stain; dishonour.

desear [dese'ar] *v* wish, desire. **deseable** *adj* desirable. **deseo** *sm* desire. **deseoso** *adj* desirous.

desecar [dese'kar] *v* dry up.

desechar [dese'tʃar] *v* refuse; reject. **desecho** *sm* residue; rubbish; contempt.

desembalar [desemba'lar] *v* unpack.

desembarazar [desembara'θar] *v* clear; extricate; vacate. **desembarazarse** *v* get rid of. **desembarazo** *sm* freedom; naturalness.

desembarcar [desembar'kar] *v* unload; disembark. **desembarcadero** *sm* landing-stage. **desembarco** *sm* disembarkation; landing.

desembocar [desembo'kar] *v* flow; empty. **desembocadura** *sf* mouth; outlet; opening.

desembolsar [desembol'sar] *v* pay out. **desembolso** *sm* payment. **desembolsos** *sm pl* expenses *pl*.

desembragar [desembra'gar] *v* disengage; release; (*auto*) declutch. **desembrague** *sm* disengaging; (*auto*) declutching; (*auto*) clutch pedal.

desembrollar [desembro'ʎar] *v* disentangle; sort out.

desempate [desem'pate] *sm* (*fútbol*) play-off.

desempeñar [desempe'ɲar] *v* (*teatro*) play a role; release from debt. **desempeño** *sm* redemption of a pledge; freedom from an obligation.

desempleado [desemple'aðo] *adj* unemployed. **desempleo** *sm* unemployment.

desencantar [desenkan'tar] *v* disillusion. **desencanto** *sm* disillusionment.

desenfadar [desenfa'ðar] *v* appease. **desenfadarse** *v* calm down. **desenfadado** *adj* free, unencumbered. **desenfado** *sm* freedom; naturalness.

desenfrenar [desenfre'nar] *v* unbridle. **desenfrenarse** *v* give way to passion. **desenfrenado** *adj* unbridled. **desenfreno** *sm* licentiousness.

desenganchar [desengan'tʃar] *v* unfasten, unhook.

desengañar [desenga'ɲar] *v* disabuse, disillusion. **desengaño** *sm* disillusionment.

desenlace [desen'laθe] *sm* dénouement; outcome.

desenredar [desenre'ðar] *v* disentangle; straighten out. **desenredo** *sm* disentanglement.

desenrollar [desenro'ʎar] *v* unroll; unwind.

*****desentenderse** [desenten'derse] *v* pretend to be ignorant (of); take no part in.

*****desenterrar** [desenter'rar] *v* disinter; unearth; recall. **desenterramiento** *sm* disinterment; recollection.

desentonar [desento'nar] *v* be out of tune; humiliate; behave badly. **desentono** *sm* discord; bad behaviour.

desentrañar [desentra'ɲar] *v* disembowel; (*fig*) unravel.

desenvainar [desenβai'nar] *v* unsheath; (*fig*) bring into the open.

*****desenvolver** [desenβol'βer] *v* unwrap; unwind; develop; expand. **desenvolverse** *v* become unwrapped; fend for oneself; prosper. **desenvoltura** *sf* naturalness; cheerfulness; eloquence.

deseo [de'seo] *V* desear.

desequilibrar [desekili'βrar] *v* unbalance. **desequilibrado** *adj* off balance; mentally unbalanced. **desequilibrio** *sm* imbalance.

desertar [deser'tar] *v* desert. **desertor, -a** *sm, sf* deserter.

desesperar [desespe'rar] *v* (cause to) despair; exasperate. **desesperación** *sf* desperation; despair; anger. **desesperado** *adj* desperate; hopeless. **desesperanza** *sf* despair.

desestimar [desesti'mar] *v* undervalue; reject. **desestima** *sf* lack of esteem.

desfachatado [desfatʃa'taðo] *adj* brazen; shameless. **desfachatez** *sf* brazenness; impudence.

desfalcar [desfal'kar] *v* embezzle. **desfalco** *sm* embezzlement.

*****desfallecer** [desfaʎe'θer] *v* faint; weaken. **desfallecido** *adj* faint; weak. **desfallecimiento** *sm* weakness; faintness.

desfavorable [desfaβo'raβle] *adj* unfavourable.

desfigurar [desfigu'rar] *v* disfigure; disguise; distort. **desfiguramiento** *sm* disfigurement; distortion.

desfilar [desfi'lar] *v* parade. **desfiladero** *sm* gorge, defile. **desfile** *sm* parade. **desfile de modas** fashion show.

desgajar [desga'xar] *v* tear off; break off.

desganar [desga'nar] *v* spoil the appetite of. **desganarse** *v* lose one's appetite. **desgana** *sf* loss of appetite; reluctance. **desganado** *adj* lacking appetite; reluctant.

desgarbado [degar'βaðo] *adj* gawky; ungainly.

desgarrar [degar'rar] *v* rend; tear; (*fig: corazón*) break. **desgarrado** *adj* dissolute. **desgarro** *sm* tear; impudence.

desgastar [desgas'tar] *v* wear away; corrode; ruin. **desgaste** *sm* wear; corrosion; ruin.

desgraciar [desgra'θjar] *v* displease; prevent; spoil. **desgraciarse** *v* fail; lose favour. **desgracia** *sf* misfortune; accident; grief; disgrace; unfriendliness. **por desgracia** unfortunately. **desgraciado** *adj* unlucky; unhappy; in disgrace.

deshabitado [desaβi'taðo] *adj* uninhabited.

*****deshacer** [desa'θer] *v* undo; cancel; destroy; frustrate. **deshacerse** *v* get rid of; break; go to pieces. **deshacerse por** strive to.

*****deshelar** [dese'lar] *v* thaw; melt. **deshelamiento** *sm* de-icing. **deshielo** *sm* thawing; melting.

desheredar [desere'ðar] *v* disinherit. **desheredado** *adj* disinherited; underprivileged. **desheredamiento** *sm* disinheritance.

deshidratar [desiðra'tar] *v* dehydrate. **deshidratación** *sf* dehydration.

deshilar [desi'lar] *v* unravel. **deshilado** *adj* unravelled; frayed.

deshilvanado [desilβa'naðo] *adj* (*fig: discurso*) disjointed; disconnected.

deshinchar [desin'tʃar] *v* deflate; give vent to. **deshincharse** *v* go down; go flat; (*fig*) come off one's high horse. **deshinchado** *adj* flat; deflated. **deshinchadura** *sf* deflation.

deshojar [deso'xar] *v* defoliate.

deshollinar [desoʎi'nar] *v* sweep chimneys. **deshollinador** *sm* chimney-sweep.

deshonesto [deso'nesto] *adj* dishonest; indecent.

deshonrar [deson'rar] *v* dishonour. **deshonra** *sf* dishonour; affront. **deshonroso** *adj* shameful, disgraceful.

deshora [des'ora] *adv* **a deshora** at an inconvenient time.

deshuesar [deswe'sar] *v* (*carne*) bone; (*fruta*) stone.

desidia [de'siðja] *sf* carelessness; inertia. **desidioso** *adj* lazy.

desierto [de'sjerto] *sm* desert. *adj* deserted.

designar [desig'nar] *v* designate. **designación** *sf* designation. **designio** *sm* intention, idea.

desigual [desi'gwal] *adj* unequal; uneven; changeable; different. **desigualdad** *sf* inequality.

desilusionar [desilusjo'nar] *v* disillusion. **desilusión** *sf* disillusionment.

desinfectar [desinfek'tar] *v* disinfect. **desinfección** *sf* disinfection. **desinfectante** *sm, adj* disinfectant.

desinflar [desin'flar] *v* deflate.

desinterés [desinte'res] *sm* disinterest. **desinteresado** *adj* disinterested.

desistir [desis'tir] *v* desist.

desleal [desle'al] *adj* disloyal. **deslealtad** *sf* disloyalty.

deslenguado [deslen'gwado] *adj* foulmouthed; shameless. **deslenguarse** *v* (*fam*) use foul language.

desligar [desli'gar] *v* loosen; untie; (*fig*) absolve. **desligarse** *v* break away.

deslindar [deslin'dar] *v* define the limits of. **deslinde** *sm* delimitation.

deslizar [desli'θar] *v* slip; glide; slide. **desliz** *sm* skid; (*fig*) indiscretion. **deslizadero** *sm* slippery place.

*****deslucir** [deslu'θir] *v* tarnish.

deslumbrar [deslum'βrar] *v* dazzle; (*fig*) bewilder. **deslumbrador** *adj* dazzling. **deslumbramiento** *sm* dazzle; glare.

desmán [des'man] *sm* excess; misconduct; outrage.
desmandar [desman'dar] *v* countermand. **desmandarse** *v* stray; get out of hand.
desmantelar [desmante'lar] *v* dismantle.
desmayar [desma'jar] *v* falter; discourage. **desmayarse** *v* faint. **desmayado** *adj* faint, fainting. **desmayo** *sm* swoon.
*desmedirse [desme'ðirse] *v* forget oneself; lose self-control. **desmedido** *adj* excessive.
desmejorar [desmexo'rar] *v* weaken; impair. **desmejorarse** *v* deteriorate.
*desmembrar [desmem'brar] *v* dismember; divide. **desmembración** *sf* dismemberment.
*desmentir [desmen'tir] *v* contradict; deny; belie. **desmentirse** *v* go back on one's word.
desmenuzar [desmenu'θar] *v* crumble; sift.
desmerecer [desmere'θer] *v* be unworthy of; be inferior. **desmerecimiento** *sm* demerit.
desmesurado [desmesu'raðo] *adj* disproportionate; excessive. **desmesurarse** *v* go too far.
desmontar [desmon'tar] *v* clear; level; (*árbol*) fell; dismantle.
desmoralizar [desmorali'θar] *v* demoralize. **desmoralización** *sf* demoralization.
desmoronar [desmoro'nar] *v* cause to crumble away. **desmoronarse** *v* crumble.
desnatar [desna'tar] *v* (*leche*) skim; (*fig*) take the best of.
desnivel [des'niβel] *sm* unevenness; gradient; difference of level.
desnudar [desnu'ðar] *v* strip, denude. **desnudez** *sf* nakedness. **desnudo** *adj* naked.
*desobedecer [desoβeðe'θer] *v* disobey. **desobediencia** *sf* disobedience. **desobediente** *adj* disobedient.
desocupar [desoku'par] *v* vacate. **desocuparse** *v* leave work; retire. **desocupación** *sf* leisure; unemployment. **desocupado** *adj* idle; unemployed; free.
desolar [deso'lar] *v* lay waste; afflict. **desolarse** *v* grieve. **desolación** *sf* desolation. **desolado** *adj* desolate; disconsolate.
desodorante [desoðo'rante] *sm. adj* deodorant.
desorden [des'orden] *sm* disorder. **desordenado** *adj* disordered.

desorganizar [desorgani'θar] *v* disorganize. **desorganización** *sf* disorganization.
desorientar [desorjen'tar] *v* mislead; (*fig*) confuse. **desorientarse** *v* lose one's bearings. **desorientación** *sf* disorientation; perplexity.
despabilado [despaβi'laðo] *adj* wide awake; alert. **despabilarse** *v* wake up.
despacio [des'paθjo] *adv* slowly; gradually.
despachar [despa'tʃar] *v* dispatch; attend to; dismiss. **despacharse** *v* get rid of; finish; hurry. **despacho** *sm* dispatch; customs clearance; study; office; warrant; telegram.
despachurrar [despatʃur'rar] *v* (*fam*) crush; squash; (*fig*) make a mess of.
desparpajo [despar'paxo] *sm* self-assurance; nonchalance. **desparpajado** *adj* self-assured. **desparpajar** *v* disarrange; (*fam*) prattle.
desparramar [desparra'mar] *v* scatter; squander.
despavorido [despaβori'ðo] *adj* terrified.
despectivo [despek'tiβo] *adj* contemptuous, scornful.
despechar [despe'tʃar] *v* drive to despair; slight; enrage; (*fam*) wean. **despecharse** *v* despair. **despecho** *sm* despair. **a despecho de** in spite of.
despedazar [despeða'θar] *v* tear to pieces; smash.
*despedir [despe'ðir] *v* dismiss; see off; give off; escort. **despedirse** *v* say goodbye. **despedida** *sf* dismissal; farewell.
despegar [despe'gar] *v* unstick. **despegarse** *v* become detached; become indifferent. **despegado** *adj* unstuck; (*fig*) cold.
despeinar [despei'nar] *v* disarrange the hair.
despejar [despe'xar] *v* free from obstructions. **despejarse** *v* be free and easy. **despejado** *adj* bright; clear. **despejo** *sm* brightness; self-confidence.
despellejar [despeʎe'xar] *v* skin, flay.
despensa [des'pensa] *sf* pantry; store of food.
despeñadero [despeɲa'ðero] *sm* precipice; (*fam*) risk. **despeñadizo** *adj* steep. **despeñar** *v* precipitate. **despeño** *sm* fall.
desperdiciar [desperði'θjar] *v* waste. **desperdiciador, -a** *sm. sf* squanderer.
desperezarse [despere'θarse] *v* stretch oneself; rouse oneself.

*despertar [desper'tar] v awaken. despertarse v wake up. despertador sm alarm clock; warning. despertamiento sm awakening. despierto adj awake; watchful.

despiadado [despja'ðaðo] adj cruel, pitiless.

despilfarrar [despilfar'rar] v squander. despilfarrado adj wasteful; shabby. despilfarro sm waste; slovenliness.

despintar [despin'tar] v take paint off; fade.

despistar [despis'tar] v throw off the scent. despistarse v get lost. despiste sm absent-mindedness.

*desplegar [desple'gar] v unfold; reveal; display. desplegadura sf unfolding.

desplomarse [desplo'marse] v tilt; collapse; drop. desplomo sm (pared, etc.) bulge.

despojar [despo'xar] v deprive; dispossess. despojarse v divest oneself. despojo sm plunder. despojos sm pl scraps pl, leavings pl.

desposado [despo'saðo] adj newly-wed. desposanda sf bride. desposando sm bridegroom. desposar v marry. desposarse v become engaged; get married.

desposeer [despose'er] v dispossess.

déspota ['despota] sm despot. despótico adj despotic. despotismo sm despotism.

despreciar [despre'θjar] v reject; ignore; despise. despreciarse de not deign to. despreciable adj despicable. desprecio sm scorn; contempt; snub.

desprender [despren'der] v separate, remove; give off. desprenderse v withdraw; renounce; be deduced. desprendimiento sm disinterestedness; generosity; separation. desprendimiento de tierras landslide.

desprevenido [despreβe'niðo] adj unprepared. desprevención sf lack of foresight.

desproporción [despropor'θjon] sf disproportion. desproporcionado adj disproportionate.

después [des'pwes] adv afterwards, after; next, later; since. después de after. después que after.

desquiciar [deski'θjar] v unhinge; disconnect. desquiciarse v lose control. desquiciado adj off balance; (fam) crazy.

desquitar [deski'tar] v compensate.

desquitarse v recoup; get one's revenge. desquite sm compensation; revenge.

destacar [desta'kar] v (mil) detach; stand out. destacarse v be conspicuous. destacado adj outstanding.

destajo [des'taxo] sm piecework. destajar v settle the terms for a job.

destapar [desta'par] v uncover. destaparse v reveal oneself.

destartalado [destarta'laðo] adj (casa) tumbledown; rambling.

destello [des'teʎo] sm sparkling. destellar v sparkle.

destemplar [destem'plar] v disconcert. destemplarse v get out of tune; lose one's temper. destemplado adj out of tune; inharmonious.

*desteñir [deste'nir] v discolour; fade.

*desterrar [dester'rar] v banish; (fig) discard. desterrarse v go into exile. destierro sm exile.

destilar [desti'lar] v distil; filter; ooze. destilación sf distillation. destilador sm still.

destinar [desti'nar] v destine; assign. destino sm destiny; destination; job. con destino a bound for. destinario sm addressee.

*destituir [desti'twir] v dismiss; deprive of. destitución sf removal; dismissal.

destornillar [destorni'ʎar] v unscrew. destornillarse v (fam) go crazy. destornillador sm screwdriver.

destreza [des'treθa] sf skill, dexterity.

destronar [destro'nar] v dethrone; depose. destronamiento sm dethronement.

destrozar [destro'θar] v destroy; squander. destrozo sm destruction.

*destruir [destru'ir] v destroy. destruirse v (mat) cancel out. destrucción sf destruction. destructivo adj destructive. destructor adj destructive.

desunir [desu'nir] v separate; disunite. desunión sf separation.

desusar [desu'sar] v be unaccustomed to. desusarse v become obsolete. desusado adj obsolete. desuso sm disuse.

desvalido [desβa'liðo] adj helpless; destitute.

desvalijar [desβali'xar] v rifle; rob.

desván [des'βan] sm attic.

*desvanecer [desβane'θer] v make disappear; remove. desvanecerse v evaporate; disappear; faint. desvanecido adj smug.

vain; (*med*) faint. **desvanecimiento** *sm*
disappearance; smugness; faint.

desvariar [desβa'rjar] *v* rave. **desvarío** *sm*
delirium.

desvelar [desβe'lar] *v* stop from sleeping.
desvelarse *v* stay awake; (*fig*) dedicate
oneself. **desvelo** *sm* insomnia; effort;
devotion. **gracias a mis desvelos** thanks
to my efforts.

desventaja [desβen'taxa] *sf* disadvantage.
desventajoso *adj* disadvantageous.

desventura [desβen'tura] *sf* misfortune.
desventurado *adj* unfortunate; faint-
hearted.

desvergonzado [desβergon'θaðo], **-a** *sm*,
sf shameless person. *adj* shameless.

desviar [des'βjar] *v* deviate; turn aside.
desviarse *v* branch off. **desvío** *sm* detour;
deviation.

desvirtuar [desβir'twar] *v* impair;
decrease in strength *or* merit.

desvivirse [desβi'βirse] *v* long for; go out
of one's way to.

detallar [deta'ʎar] *v* (*com*) retail; tell in
detail. **detalle** *sm* detail; nice gesture.
vender al detalle sell retail. **detalladamente** *adv* in detail. **detallista** *s*(*m*+*f*)
retailer.

detective [detek'tiβe] *s*(*m*+*f*) detective.

***detener** [dete'ner] *v* detain. **detenerse** *v*
linger. **detención** *sf* arrest; delay; thoroughness. **detenido** *adj* under arrest;
careful.

detergente [deter'xente] *sm*, *adj* detergent.

deteriorar [deterjo'rar] *v* deteriorate;
damage. **deterioración** *sf also* **deterioro**
sm deterioration.

determinar [determi'nar] *v* determine.
determinarse *v* make up one's mind.
determinación *sf* determination; decision. **determinado** *adj* determined; decided; definite.

detestar [detes'tar] *v* detest. **detestable** *adj*
detestable. **detestación** *sf* detestation.

detonar [deto'nar] *v* detonate. **detonación**
sf detonation.

detractar [detrak'tar] *v* defame. **detrac-
ción** *sf* defamation.

***detraer** [detra'er] *v* denigrate; withdraw.

detrás [de'tras] *adv* behind. **detrás de** *prep*
behind. **por detrás de uno** behind someone's back.

detrimento [detri'mento] *sm* detriment;

damage. **en detrimento de** to the detriment of.

deuda ['deuða] *sf* debt; trespass. **deudor,
-a** *sm*, *sf* debtor.

deudo ['deuðo], **-a** *sm*, *sf* relative. *sm* relationship.

devanar [deβa'nar] *v* wind, coil.
devanarse los sesos (*fam*) rack one's
brains.

devanear [deβane'ar] *v* rave. **devaneo** *sm*
delirium; flirtation.

devastar [deβas'tar] *v* devastate. **devastación** *sf* devastation.

devengar [deβen'gar] *v* have due; (*intereses*) yield.

devoción [deβo'θjon] *sf* devotion. **devocionario** *sm* prayer book.

***devolver** [deβol'βer] *v* return. **devolución**
sf return; refund.

devorar [deβo'rar] *v* devour.

devoto [de'βoto], **-a** *sm*, *sf* devotee. *adj*
devout; devoted.

día ['dia] *sm* day. **¡buenos días!** good
morning! **del día** fresh. **ocho días** a week.
todos los días every day.

diablo ['djaβlo] *sm* devil. **diabólico** *adj*
diabolical.

diafragma [dja'fragma] *sm* diaphragm.

diagnosticar [diagnosti'kar] *v* diagnose.
diagnosis *sf invar* diagnosis. **diagnóstico**
adj diagnostic.

diagonal [diago'nal] *sf*, *adj* diagonal.

diagrama [dia'grama] *sm* diagram.

dialecto [dia'lekto] *sm* dialect.

diálogo [di'alogo] *sm* dialogue.

diamante [dia'mante] *sm* diamond.

diámetro [di'ametro] *sm* diameter. **diame-
tral** *adj* diametric.

diario [di'arjo] *sm* daily newspaper; diary.
diario hablado news bulletin. *adj* daily.
de diario for everyday use.

diarrea [diar'rea] *sf* diarrhoea.

dibujar [diβu'xar] *v* draw. **dibujante**
s(*m*+*f*) artist; designer; cartoonist;
draughtsman. **dibujo** *sm* drawing;
sketch; design.

dicción [dik'θjon] *sf* diction; word.

diccionario [dikθjo'narjo] *sm* dictionary.

diciembre [di'θjembre] *sm* December.

dictado [dik'taðo] *sm* dictation; title.
dictados *sm pl* dictates *pl*. **dictador** *sm*
dictator. **dictadura** *sf* dictatorship. **dictar**
v dictate.

dictamen [dik'tamen] *sm* opinion; advice;
report.

dicha ['ditʃa] *sf* happiness; good luck. **por dicha** luckily. **dichoso** *adj* happy; lucky; (*fam*) boring.

dicho ['ditʃo] *V* **decir**. *sm* saying; remark; proverb. **dicho y hecho** no sooner said than done.

diente ['djente] *sm* tooth.

diestra ['djestra] *sf* right hand. **diestro** *adj* right; skilful; sly.

dieta ['djeta] *sf* diet.

diez [djeθ] *sm*, *adj* ten. **diecinueve** *sm*, *adj* nineteen. **dieciocho** *sm*, *adj* eighteen. **dieciséis** *sm*, *adj* sixteen. **diecisiete** *sm*, *adj* seventeen. **diezmar** *v* decimate.

difamar [difa'mar] *v* defame, slander. **difamación** *sf* defamation. **difamatorio** *adj* defamatory.

diferencia [dife'renθja] *sf* difference. **a diferencia de** unlike. **diferenciar** *v* differentiate; differ. **diferenciarse** be different. **diferente** *adj* different.

***diferir** [dife'rir] *v* defer; differ.

difícil [di'fiθil] *adj* difficult. **dificultad** *sf* difficulty. **dificultar** *v* make difficult; hinder.

difidente [difi'ðente] *adj* mistrustful. **difidencia** *sf* mistrust.

difundir [difun'dir] *v* diffuse; broadcast; divulge; spread. **difusión** *sf* spread; broadcast; diffusion.

difunto [di'funto] *adj* dead. *sm* deceased person.

***digerir** [dixe'rir] *v* digest; (*fig*) endure. **digestible** *adj* digestible. **digestión** *sf* digestion.

dignarse [dig'narse] *v* deign, condescend. **dignidad** [digni'ðað] *sf* dignity; rank. **dignitario** *sm* dignitary. **digno** *adj* worthy.

digresión [digre'sjon] *sf* digression.

dilación [dila'θjon] *sf* delay.

dilatar [dila'tar] *v* dilate; expand; delay. **dilatarse** *v* speak at great length. **dilatación** *sf* extension; delay. **dilatado** *adj* numerous; long-winded. **dilatorio** *adj* dilatory.

dilema [di'lema] *sm* dilemma.

diligencia [dili'xenθja] *sf* diligence; (*fam*) job.

dilucidar [diluθi'ðar] *v* elucidate; solve.

diluir [dilu'ir] *v* dilute. **dilución** *sf* dilution.

diluvio [di'luβjo] *sm* deluge.

dimanar [dima'nar] *v* arise from; flow.

dimensión [dimen'sjon] *sf* dimension.

diminutivo [diminu'tiβo] *adj* diminutive. **diminuto** *adj* tiny.

dimitir [dimi'tir] *v* resign. **dimisión** *sf* resignation.

Dinamarca [dina'marka] *sf* Denmark. **dinamarqués, -esa** *sm*, *sf* Dane; *adj* Danish.

dinamita [dina'mita] *sf* dynamite.

dínamo ['dinamo] *sm* dynamo. **dinámico** *adj* dynamic.

dinastía [dinas'tia] *sf* dynasty.

dinero [di'nero] *sm* money. **de dinero** rich. **dinero suelto** loose change. **estar mal de dinero** be hard up.

dintel [din'tel] *sm* lintel.

dio [djo] *V* **dar**.

diócesi(s) [di'oθesi(s)] *sf invar* diocese.

dios [djos] *sm* god, idol. **diosa** *sf* goddess.

diploma [di'ploma] *sf* diploma.

diplomacia [diplo'maθja] *sf* diplomacy. **diplomático** *sm* diplomat; *adj* diplomatic.

diputado [dipu'taðo] *sm* deputy, delegate, representative.

dique ['dike] *sm* dike; dam; dry dock.

dirigir [diri'xir] *v* direct; govern; steer; regulate. **dirigirse** *v* go; speak; write. **dirección** *sf* direction; directorship; management; postal address. **directivo** *adj* directive; guiding. **directo** *adj* direct; straight. **director, -a** *sm*, *sf* director; editor. **directorio** *sm* directory.

***discernir** [disθer'nir] *v* discern. **discernimiento** *sm* discernment.

disciplina [disθip'lina] *sf* discipline; doctrine; obedience. **disciplinar** *v* discipline; train.

discípulo [dis'θipulo], **-a** *sm*, *sf* disciple; pupil.

disco ['disko] *sm* disc; record; discus.

disconforme [diskon'forme] *adj* in disagreement. **disconformidad** *sf* disagreement.

discontinuar [disconti'nwar] *v* discontinue. **discontinuación** *sf* discontinuation. **discontinuo** *adj* discontinuous.
discordia [dis'korðja] *sf* discord. **discordante** *adj also* **discorde** discordant.
discoteca [disko'teka] *sf* disco; record library.
discreción [diskre'θjon] *sf* discretion. **a discreción** optional, at will.
discrepancia [diskre'panθja] *sf* discrepancy.
discreto [dis'kreto] *adj* discreet; moderate; sober; witty.
disculpar [diskul'par] *v* excuse; forgive. *v* apologize. **disculpa** *sf* excuse; apology.
discurrir [diskur'rir] *v* ponder; speak; roam; invent.
discurso [dis'kurso] *sm* discourse; reasoning; passage of time. **discursivo** *adj* discursive.
discutir [disku'tir] *v* discuss; debate. **discusión** *sf* discussion; argument. **discutido** *adj* controversial.
disecar [dise'kar] *v* dissect. **disección** *sf* dissection.
diseminar [disemi'nar] *v* scatter. **diseminarse** *v* spread. **diseminación** *sf* dissemination.
disentería [disente'ria] *sf* dysentery.
*disentir [disen'tir] *v* dissent; differ. **disensión** *sf* dissent; disagreement; quarrel.
diseñar [dise'par] *v* sketch; design. **diseñador, -a** *sm, sf* designer. **diseño** *sm* sketch; design.
disfrazar [disfra'θar] *v* disguise. **disfraz** *sm* disguise; fancy dress.
disfrutar [disfru'tar] *v* possess; enjoy; receive. **disfrute** *sm* enjoyment.
disgregar [disgre'gar] *v* disintegrate; separate. **disgregación** *sf* disintegration; separation.
disgustar [disgus'tar] *v* upset; displease. **disgustarse** *v* become angry. **disgustado** *adj* annoyed; displeased; disappointed. **disgusto** *sm* annoyance; displeasure; repugnance; trouble.
disidente [disi'ðente] *s(m+f)*, *adj* dissident. **disidir** *v* dissent.
disimular [disimu'lar] *v* pretend; dissemble; hide; tolerate. **disimulable** *adj* excusable. **disimulo** *sm* concealment; indulgence.
disipar [disi'par] *v* dissipate. **disiparse** *v* disperse; vanish; clear up. **disipación** *sf* dissipation. **disipado** *adj* dissipated.

dislocar [dislo'kar] *v* dislocate. **dislocación** *sf* dislocation.
*disminuir [disminu'ir] *v* diminish. **diminución** *sf* decrease; reduction.
disociar [diso'θjar] *v* dissociate. **disociación** *sf* dissociation.
*disolver [disol'βer] *v* dissolve. **disoluble** *adj* dissoluble. **disolución** *sf* dissolution; (*fig*) dissoluteness. **disoluto** *adj* dissolute.
*disonar [diso'nar] *v* disagree; be inharmonious. **disonancia** *sf* discord. **disonante** *adj* discordant.
disparar [dispa'rar] *v* fire; shoot; throw. **dispararse** *v* explode; fly off; race. **disparadamente** *adv* hurriedly; foolishly. **disparo** *sm* firing; shot; attack.
disparatado [dispara'taðo] *adj* absurd. **disparatar** *v* talk nonsense; act foolishly. **disparate** *sm* absurdity.
disparidad [dispari'ðað] *sf* disparity.
dispensar [dispen'sar] *v* dispense; pardon. **dispense usted** forgive me. **dispensa** *sf* dispensation; exemption. **dispensable** *adj* dispensable. **dispensario** *sm* dispensary.
dispersar [disper'sar] *v* disperse. **dispersión** *sf* dispersal. **disperso** *adj* dispersed, scattered.
*disponer [dispo'ner] *v* dispose; arrange; decide; prepare. **disponer de** dispose of; have. **disponerse a** get ready. **disponible** *adj* disposable; available. **disposición** *sf* disposition; instruction; inclination; determination. **tomar disposiciones** take steps. **ultima disposición** last will and testament. **dispuesto** *adj* arranged; disposed; ready; willing.
disputar [dispu'tar] *v* dispute; debate. **disputa** *sf* dispute, argument.
distancia [dis'tanθja] *sf* distance. **distante** *adj* distant.
distinguir [distin'gir] *v* distinguish; esteem. **distinción** *sf* distinction; politeness. **distinguido** *adj* distinguished. **distintivo** *adj* distinctive. **distinto** *adj* distinct; different.
*distraer [distra'er] *v* distract; entertain. **distracción** *sf* distraction. **distraído** *adj* absent-minded; entertaining.
*distribuir [distriβu'ir] *v* distribute; deliver; allot. **distribución** *sf* distribution. **cuadro de distribución** *sm* switchboard. **distribuidor** *sm* (*auto*) distributor; agent. **distribuidor automático** slot machine.

distrito [dis'trito] *sm* district.
disturbar [distur'βar] *v* disturb. **disturbio** *sm* disturbance.
disuadir [diswa'ðir] *v* dissuade.
diurno [di'urno] *adj* daily.
divagar [diβa'gar] *v* digress; roam. **divagación** *sf* digression.
diván [di'βan] *sm* divan.
divergir [diβer'xir] *v* diverge; disagree. **divergencia** *sf* divergence. **divergente** *adj* divergent.
diverso [di'βerso] *adj* diverse. **diversos** *adj pl* various; many. **diversidad** *sf* diversity.
*divertir [diβer'tir] *v* entertain; divert. **divertido** *adj* amusing; entertaining.
dividir [diβi'ðir] *v* divide; split. **división** *sf* division; (*gram*) hyphen, dash. **divisor** *sm* divider. **divisorio** *adj* dividing.
divino [di'βino] *adj* divine. **divinidad** *sf* divinity.
divisa [di'βisa] *sf* emblem; (*com*) currency. **divisas** *sf pl* (*com*) foreign exchange *sing*. **control de divisas** (*com*) exchange control.
divisar [diβi'sar] *v* distinguish, discern.
divorciar [diβor'θjar] *v* divorce. **divorciarse** *v* get divorced. **divorciado, -a** *sm, sf* divorcee. **divorcio** *sm* divorce.
divulgar [diβul'gar] *v* divulge; circulate; spread. **divulgarse** *v* come out. **divulgación** *sf* disclosure.
doblar [do'βlar] *v* double; fold; bend; (*fig*) persuade; (*fig*) submit. **doblarse** *v* fold; buckle; stoop; yield. **dobladillo** *sm* hem; trouser turn-up. **dobladura** *sf* crease, fold. **doble** *adj also* **doblado** double; dual; stocky; deceitful. **el doble** twice as much.
doce ['doθe] *sm, adj* twelve. **docena** *sf* dozen.
docente [do'θente] *adj* educational. **personal docente** teaching staff.
dócil ['doθil] *adj* docile; obedient. **docilidad** *sf* docility.
doctor [dok'tor], **-a** *sm, sf* doctor. **docto** *adj* learned. **doctorado** *sm* doctorate.
doctrina [dok'trina] *sf* doctrine. **doctrinal** *adj* doctrinal.
documentar [dokumen'tar] *v* document. **documentación** *sf* documentation; identity papers *pl*.
dogal [do'gal] *sm* halter.
dogma ['dogma] *sm* dogma. **dogmático** *adj* dogmatic. **dogmatismo** *sm* dogmatism.

dogo ['dogo] *sm* bulldog.
*doler [do'ler] *v* hurt; ache; grieve. **dolerse de** feel the effects of; regret; pity. **dolor** *sm* pain; grief; repentance. **dolorido** *adj* in pain; grief-stricken. **doloroso** *adj* painful; pitiful; sorrowful.
domar [do'mar] *v* tame; train. **doma** *sf* training.
doméstico [do'mestiko], **-a** *sm, sf* servant. *adj* domestic. **domesticar** *v* domesticate. **domesticidad** *sf* domesticity.
domiciliar [domiθi'ljar] *v* domicile. **domiciliarse** *v* take up residence. **domiciliado** *adj* resident. **domicilio** *sm* home.
dominar [domi'nar] *v* dominate; master. **dominación** *sf* domination; authority. **dominador** *adj* dominating. **dominante** *adj* dominating; dominant. **dominio** *sm* dominion; authority; supremacy.
domingo [do'mingo] *sm* Sunday. **hacer domingo** take a day off.
dominó [domi'no] *sm* (*juego*) dominoes *pl*.
don¹ [don] *sm* (*con nombre de pila*) Mr.
don² *sm* gift; talent. **donación** *sf* donation. **donador, -a** *sm, sf* donor. **donar** *v* give, bestow. **donativo** *sm* offering.
donaire [do'naire] *sm* charm, grace; wit. **donairoso** *adj* graceful; witty.
donde ['donðe] *adv* where. **dondequiera** *adv* wherever. **¿dónde?** where? **¿por dónde?** which way?
doña ['doɲa] *sf* (*con el nombre de pila de una señora o una viuda*) Mrs.
dorar [do'rar] *v* gild; (*culin*) brown. **dorado** *adj* gilt; golden.
*dormir [dor'mir] *v* sleep. **dormirse** *v* go to sleep. **dormilón, -ona** *sm, sf* sleepyhead. **dormitorio** *sm* dormitory.
dorso ['dorso] *sm* back. **dorsal** *adj* dorsal.
dos [dos] *sm, adj* two. **dos veces** twice. **las dos** two o'clock. **los dos** both.
dosis ['dosis] *sf invar* dose. **dosificación** *sf* dosage. **dosificar** *v* dose.
dotar [do'tar] *v* endow; equip; staff. **dotación** *sf* endowment; foundation; personnel. **dotado** *adj* endowed; gifted. **dotador, -a** *sm, sf* donor. **dote** *sf* dowry. **dotes** *sf pl* endowments *pl*, talents *pl*.
draga ['draga] *sf* dredge. **dragado** *sm* dredging. **dragar** *v* dredge; (*minas*) sweep.

dragón [dra'gon] *sm* dragon.
drama ['drama] *sm* drama. **dramática** *sf* dramatic art. **dramático** *adj* dramatic. **dramatizar** *v* dramatize. **dramaturgo, -a** *sm, sf* playwright.
drenaje [dre'naxe] *sm* drainage. **drenar** *v* drain.
droga ['droga] *sf* drug. (*fam, fig*) trick, practical joke, fib. **drogadicto, -a** *s, adj* drug addict. **drogar** *v* drug, dope.
dual [dwal] *adj* dual. **dualidad** *sf* duality. **dualismo** *sm* dualism.
ducado [du'kaðo] *sm* duchy.
dúctil ['duktil] *adj* ductile; malleable.
ducha ['dutʃa] *sf* shower. **ducharse** *v* have *or* take a shower.
dudar [du'ðar] *v* doubt. **duda** *sf* doubt. **sin duda** doubtless. **dudoso** *adj* doubtful; dubious.
duelo¹ ['dwelo] *sm* sorrow; mourning.
duelo² *sm* duel.
duende ['dwende] *sm* imp; goblin; elf.
dueño ['dweɲo], **-a** *sm, sf* owner; master/mistress; landlord/landlady.
dulce ['dulθe] *sm* sweet. *adj* sweet; mild; gentle; soft; (*agua*) fresh. **dulcería** *sf* confectionery. **dulzura** *sf* sweetness; mildness.
dúo ['duo] *sm* duet.
duodécimo [duo'ðeθimo] *sm, adj* twelfth.
duplicar [dupli'kar] *v* duplicate. **duplicarse** *v* double. **duplicación** *sf* duplication; doubling. **duplicado** *sm, adj* duplicate. **duplicador** *sm* duplicator.
duplicidad [dupliθi'ðað] *sf* duplicity.
duque ['duke] *sm* duke. **duquesa** *sf* duchess.
durar [du'rar] *v* last, endure. **durable** *adj* durable. **duración** *sf* duration. **durante** *adv* during.
durazno [du'raθno] *sm* peach; peach tree.
durmiente [dur'mjente] *adj* sleeping.
duro ['duro] *adj* hard; firm. **dureza** *sf* hardness; severity.

E

e [e] *conj* and.
ébano ['eβano] *sm* ebony.
ebrio ['eβrjo] *adj* drunk.

eclesiástico [ekle'sjastiko] *adj, sm* ecclesiastic.
eclipse [e'klipse] *sm* eclipse. **eclipsar** *v* eclipse.
eco ['eko] *sm* echo.
economía [ekono'mia] *sf* economy. **económico** *adj* economical. **economista** *s(m+f)* economist. **economizar** *v* economize.
ecuador [ekwa'ðor] *sm* equator.
ecuestre [e'kwestre] *adj* equestrian.
echar [e'tʃar] *v* throw; emit; (*naipes*) deal/pour out; dismiss; begin; perform. **echar a** start to. **echar abajo** demolish. **echar a perder** spoil. **echar de ver** notice. **echarse** *v* lie down.
edad [e'ðað] *sf* age. **edad madura** middle age.
edicto [e'ðikto] *sm* edict.
edificar [eðifi'kar] *v* build; (*fig*) edify. **edificio** *sm* edifice.
editar [eði'tar] *v* publish. **edición** *sf* edition. **editor, -a** *sm, sf* publisher.
edredón [eðre'ðon] *sm* eiderdown.
educar [eðu'kar] *v* educate; bring up; train. **educación** *sf* education; upbringing. **educado** *adj* educated; well-mannered.
efectivo [efek'tiβo] *adj* effective; real. **dinero efectivo** *sm* cash. **efecto** *sm* effect; result; (*com*) document. **efectos** *sm pl* effects *pl*, assets *pl*. **efectos en cartera** holdings *pl*. **efectuar** *v* carry out.
efervescencia [eferβes'θenθja] *sf* effervescence. **efervescente** *adj* effervescent.
eficacia [efi'kaθja] *sf* efficacy; efficiency. **eficaz** *adj* efficacious; efficient. **eficiencia** *sf* efficiency. **eficiente** *adj* efficient.
efigie [e'fixje] *sf* effigy.
efímero [e'fimero] *adj* ephemeral.
efusión [efu'sjon] *sf* effusion.
Egipto [e'xipto] *sm* Egypt. **egipcio, -a** *s, adj* Egyptian.
egoísmo [ego'ismo] *sm* egoism. **egoísta** *s(m+f)* egoist. **egotismo** *sm* egotism. **egotista** *s(m+f)* egotist.
egregio [e'grexjo] *adj* eminent.
eje ['exe] *sm* axis; axle; (*fig*) core, hub. **eje del mundo** earth's axis.
ejecutar [exeku'tar] *v* execute; put to death; seize; perform. **ejecución** *sf* execution. **ejecutivo** *sm, adj* executive. **ejecutor, -a** *sm, sf* executor; executioner.
ejemplar [exem'plar] *sm* copy; model;

specimen; example. *adj* exemplary. **ejemplificar** *v* exemplify. **ejemplo** *sm* example. **dar ejemplo** set an example. **sin ejemplo** unprecedented.

ejercer [exer'θer] *v* practise; exercise. **ejercicio** *sm* exercise.

ejército [e'xerθito] *sm* army.

el [el] *art m* the.

él [el] *pron* he, it.

elaborar [elaβo'rar] *v* elaborate; make; manufacture. **elaboración** *sf* elaboration. **elaborado** *adj* elaborate.

elástico [e'lastiko] *sm, adj* elastic. **elasticidad** *sf* elasticity.

elección [elek'θjon] *sf* election; choice, selection. **elector, -a** *sm, sf* elector. **electorado** *sm* electorate. **electoral** *adj* electoral.

eléctrico [e'lektriko] *adj* electric(al). **electricidad** *sf* electricity. **electrizar** *v* electrify. **electrocutar** *v* electrocute. **electrodo** *sm* electrode. **electrónico** *adj* electronic.

elefante [ele'fante] *sm* elephant.

elegancia [ele'ganθja] *sf* elegance. **elegante** *adj* elegant.

***elegir** [ele'xir] *v* elect, choose. **elegible** *adj* eligible.

elemental [elemen'tal] *adj* elementary. **elemento** *sm* element. **elementos** *sm pl* elements; rudiments.

elevar [ele'βar] *v* elevate, lift, raise. **elevarse** *v* rise; soar; be elated. **elevación** *sf* elevation; rapture; pride. **elevado** *adj* lofty; sublime.

eliminar [elimi'nar] *v* eliminate. **eliminación** *sf* elimination.

elocución [eloku'θjon] *sf* elocution. **elocuencia** *sf* eloquence. **elocuente** *adj* eloquent.

elogiar [elo'xjar] *v* praise. **elogio** *sm* praise. **elogioso** *adj* laudatory.

elucidar [eluθi'ðar] *v* elucidate. **elucidación** *sf* elucidation.

eludir [elu'ðir] *v* elude.

ella ['eʎa] *pron* she, it.

ello ['eʎo] *pron* it.

emanar [ema'nar] *v* emanate. **emanación** *sf* emanation.

emancipar [emanθi'par] *v* emancipate. **emancipación** *sf* emancipation.

embajada [emba'xaða] *sf* embassy; (*fig*) errand. **embajador** *sm* ambassador.

embalar [emba'lar] *v* pack, bale. **embalaje** *sm* packing; bale.

embarazar [embara'θar] *v* embarrass; hinder; make pregnant. **embarazarse** *v* become pregnant. **embarazada** *adj* pregnant. **embarazo** *sm* embarrassment; obstacle; pregnancy. **embarazoso** *adj* embarrassing; awkward.

embarcar [embar'kar] *v* embark; ship; (*fam*) involve. **embarcarse** *v* go on board. **embarcación** *sf* boat; embarkation; voyage. **embarcadero** *sm* landing-stage. **embarco** *sm* embarkation.

embargar [embar'gar] *v* (*jur*) seize; (*fig*) overcome; blunt. **embargo** *sm* embargo. **sin embargo** nevertheless.

embarque [em'barke] *sm* shipment.

embarrar [embar'rar] *v* smear; cover with mud. **embarrarse** *v* get dirty.

embeber [embe'βer] *v* absorb, soak up; shrink. **embebecerse** *v* (*fig*) immerse oneself.

***embellecer** [embeʎe'θer] *v* embellish.

***embestir** [embes'tir] *v* attack; charge. **embestida** *sf* onslaught; charge.

emblema [em'blema] *sm* emblem. **emblemático** *adj* emblematic.

embobar [embo'βar] *v* stupefy; fascinate.

embocar [embo'kar] *v* put in the mouth; enter; (*fig*) swallow. **embocadura** *sf* mouth of a river; (*vino*) taste; (*caballo*) bit.

embolsar [embol'sar] *v* pocket.

emborrachar [emborra'tʃar] *v* intoxicate. **emborracharse** *v* get drunk.

emboscar [embos'kar] *v* ambush. **emboscarse** *v* lie in ambush. **emboscada** *sf* ambush.

embotar [embo'tar] *v* blunt, dull; pack in a jar. **embotarse** *v* become enervated. **embotadura** *sf* also **embotamiento** *sm* bluntness, dullness.

embotellar [embote'ʎar] *v* bottle. **embotellarse** *v* learn by heart. **embotellado** *adj* bottled; jammed. **embotellamiento** *sm* bottling; traffic jam.

embozar [embo'θar] *v* muffle; wrap up. **embozadamente** *adv* secretly. **embozo** *sm* fold; (*fig*) disguise. **quitarse el embozo** bare one's face.

embragar [embra'gar] *v* (*auto*) engage the clutch. **embrague** *sm* (*auto*) clutch.

embriagarse [embrja'garse] *v* get drunk. **embriagado** *adj* drunk.

embrión [em'brjon] *sm* embryo. **embriología** *sf* embryology.

embrollar [embro'ʎar] *v* muddle, confuse. **embrollarse** *v* get mixed up. **embrollo** *sm* confusion.

embrujar [embru'xar] *v* bewitch.

***embrutecer** [embrute'θer] *v* brutalize; stupefy.

embudo [em'buðo] *sm* funnel; crater; (*fig*) trick.

embuste [em'buste] *sm* lie; trick. **embustear** *v* lie; cheat. **embustería** *sf* deceit; imposture. **embustero, -a** *sm, sf* liar; cheat; *adj* lying; deceitful.

embutir [embu'tir] *v* stuff; cram; (*tecn*) inlay. **embutido** *sm* sausage.

emergencia [emer'xenθja] *sf* emergence; emergency. **emergente** *adj* emergent; resultant. **emerger** *v* emerge.

emigrar [emi'grar] *v* emigrate; migrate. **emigración** *sf* emigration; migration. **emigrado, -a** *sm, sf* emigrant. **emigrante** *s(m + f), adj* emigrant.

eminencia [emi'nenθja] *sf* eminence; height. **eminente** *adj* eminent.

emisario [emi'sarjo], **-a** *sm, sf* emissary.

emitir [emi'tir] *v* emit; broadcast; transmit. **emisión** *sf* emission; broadcast; programme. **emisor** *sm* transmitter. **emisora** *sf* radio station.

emoción [emo'θjon] *sf* emotion; thrill. **emocionante** *adj* moving; exciting.

empachar [empa'tʃar] *v* satiate; give indigestion; sicken; conceal; (*fig*) hinder. **empacharse** *v* have indigestion; become confused; get fed up. **empachado** *adj* clumsy; sick; fed up. **empacho** *sm* indigestion; (*fig*) embarrassment.

empadronar [empaðro'nar] *v* register. **empadronamiento** *sm* census.

empalagar [empala'gar] *v* cloy; vex. **empalagarse** *v* get fed up. **empalagoso** *adj* cloying.

empalar [empa'lar] *v* impale.

empalizada [empali'θaða] *sf* stockade. **empalizar** *v* fence.

empalmar [empal'mar] *v* splice; couple, join. **empalme** *sm* joint; junction.

empanada [empa'naða] *sf* meat pie.

empañar [empa'par] *v* tarnish; swathe; obscure. **empañarse** *v* cloud over. **empañado** *adj* misty.

empapar [empa'par] *v* soak; drench. **empapamiento** *sm* soaking.

empapelar [empape'lar] *v* paper; wrap in paper.

empaquetar [empake'tar] *v* pack, package. **empaque** *sm* packing.

emparejar [empare'xar] *v* match; pair; draw level; catch up. **emparejadura** *sf* matching; levelling.

empastar [empas'tar] *v* paste; fill. **empastado** *adj* filled; (*libro*) clothbound.

empatar [empa'tar] *v* (*juegos*) tie, draw. **empate** *sm* tie, draw.

***empedernir** [empeðer'nir] *v* harden. **empedernido** *adj* hardened; inveterate.

***empedrar** [empe'ðrar] *v* pave. **empedrado** *adj* paved; cobbled.

empeine [em'peine] *sm* groin; instep; (*med*) impetigo.

empeñar [empe'par] *v* pawn, pledge; commit; get involved. **empeñarse** *v* start; strive; get into debt. **empeñado** *adj* insistent. **empeño** *sm* pledge; contract; insistence; yearning. **casa de empeño** *sf* pawnshop. **en empeño** in pawn.

empeorar [empeo'rar] *v* make worse; worsen. **empeoramiento** *sm* deterioration.

***empequeñecer** [empekepe'θer] *v* dwarf; belittle.

emperador [empera'ðor] *sm* emperor. **emperatriz** *sf* empress.

***empezar** [empe'θar] *v* begin.

empinar [empi'nar] *v* straighten; exalt. **empinarse** *v* rear up; stand on tiptoe; tower. **empinado** *adj* erect; on tiptoe; haughty.

empírico [em'piriko] *adj* empirical. **empirismo** *sm* empiricism.

emplazar [empla'θar] *v* summon; locate. **emplazamiento** *sm* (*jur*) summons.

emplear [emple'ar] *v* employ; use; invest; spend. **empleado, -a** *sm, sf* employee. **empleador, -a** *sm, sf* employer. **empleo** *sm* employment; job; use.

***empobrecer** [empoβre'θer] *v* impoverish. **empobrecimiento** *sm* impoverishment.

empollar [empo'ʎar] *v* hatch; (*fam*) swot, mug up.

emponzoñar [empoŋθo'par] *v* poison. **emponzoñamiento** *sm* poisoning.

empotrar [empo'trar] *v* embed. **empotramiento** *sm* embedding.

emprender [empren'der] *v* undertake; start; attack. **emprender con** accost. **emprendedor** *adj* enterprising.

empresa [em'presa] *sf* enterprise; (*com*) company; management. **empresario, -a** *sm, sf* impresario; contractor.

empréstito [em'prestito] *sm* loan.

empujar [empu'xar] *v* push; press; (*fig*) urge. empuje *sm* push; enterprise. a empujes by fits and starts.

empuñar [empu'nar] *v* seize; take up. empuñadura *sf* hilt.

emular [emu'lar] *v* emulate.

emulsión [emul'sjon] *sf* emulsion. emulsionar *v* emulsify.

en [en] *prep* on; in; into; onto. en casa at home. en donde where. en tren by train.

enaguas [e'nagwas] *sf pl* petticoat *sing*.

enajenar [enaxe'nar] *v* alienate; transfer; drive mad; enrapture. enajenarse *v* lose one's self-control. enajenación *sf also* enajenamiento *sm* alienation; absent-mindedness; rapture; panic.

enamorar [enamo'rar] *v* court; win the love of. enamorarse *v* fall in love. enamorado, -a *sm, sf* sweetheart.

enano [e'nano], -a *sm, sf* dwarf.

enarbolar [enarβo'lar] *v* hoist. enarbolarse *v* rear; lose one's temper.

*enardecer [enarðe'θer] *v* inflame. enardecerse *v* become excited.

encabestrar [enkaβes'trar] *v* put a halter on.

encabezar [enkaβe'θar] *v* lead; head; take a census of; put a title to. encabezamiento *sm* headline; heading; census.

encadenar [enkaðe'nar] *v* chain, shackle. encadenamiento *sm* chaining; (*fig*) linking.

encajar [enka'xar] *v* fit; join; bear; pocket; drop; land. encajarse *v* get stuck; squeeze in. encajadura *sf* (*hueso*) setting; socket. encaje *sm* joint; setting; socket; lace.

encallar [enka'ʎar] *v* run aground. encallarse *v* harden. encalladero *sm* sandbank; reef.

encaminar [enkami'nar] *v* direct; guide. encaminarse *v* set out for.

encandilar [enkandi'lar] *v* dazzle; stimulate. encandilarse *v* (*ojos*) sparkle.

encantar [enkan'tar] *v* enchant; charm. encantado *adj* charmed; haunted. ¡encantado! pleased to meet you! encantador *adj* charming. encanto *sm* charm; delight.

encapotar [enkapo'tar] *v* cover with a cloak. encapotarse *v* cloak oneself; look sullen; cloud over. encapotado *adj* overcast.

encapricharse [enkapri'tʃarse] *v* set one's mind on. encapricharse por *or* con become infatuated with.

encarar [enka'rar] *v* face up to; aim; confront. encaramiento *sm* encounter.

encarcelar [enkarθe'lar] *v* imprison. encarcelamiento *sm* imprisonment.

*encarecer [enkare'θer] *v* raise the price of; praise; urge. encarecidamente *adv* earnestly. encarecido *adj* highly recommended. encarecimiento *sm* price increase; emphasis; recommendation.

encargar [enkar'gar] *v* (*com*) order; commission; entrust; charge; advise. encargarse de take charge of. encargado *sm* agent. encargo *sm* errand; job; order.

encarnar [enkar'nar] *v* personify; heal; pierce the flesh; bait. encarnarse *v* mix, join in. encarnación *sf* incarnation. encarnado *adj* incarnate; red; (*uña*) ingrowing.

encarnizar [enkarni'θar] *v* infuriate. encarnizarse *v* devour. encarnizado *adj* inflamed; bloody.

encasillar [enkasi'ʎar] *v* classify.

encauzar [enkau'θar] *v* channel; direct. encauzamiento *sm* channelling; (*fig*) guidance.

*encender [enθen'der] *v* light; set on fire; turn on; arouse. encendedor *sm* lighter. encendido *adj* lit; burning; flushed. encendimiento *sm* burning; ardour.

*encerrar [enθer'rar] *v* shut up; enclose; contain. encerrarse *v* live in seclusion. encerramiento *sm* enclosure; lock-up. encierro *sm* enclosure; prison.

encía [en'θia] *sf* (*anat*) gum.

enciclopedia [enθiklo'peðja] *sf* encyclopaedia. enciclopédico *adj* encyclopaedic.

encima [en'θima] *adv* above; overhead. por encima over; quickly; superficially. encima de on top of.

encina [en'θina] *sf* ilex, holm oak.

encinta [en'θinta] *adj* pregnant.

enclavar [enkla'βar] *v* locate; nail; pierce. enclave *sm* enclave; situation.

enclenque [en'klenke] *adj* sickly; feeble; skinny.

encoger [enko'xer] *v* shrink. encogerse de hombros shrug one's shoulders. encogido *adj* shrunk; (*fig*) timid. encogimiento *sm* shrinkage; shyness.

encolar [enko'lar] *v* glue. encolamiento *sm* gluing.

*encomendar [enkomen'ðar] v entrust.
encomendarse v commend oneself.
encomienda sf assignment; tribute; land concession.
encomiar [enko'mjar] v praise.
encomiador adj laudatory.
enconar [enko'nar] v inflame; infect.
enconarse v become inflamed; become infected; get angry.
encontrar [enkon'trar] v find; meet.
encontrarse v find oneself; quarrel.
encontrado adj opposed.
encopetado [enkope'taðo] adj of noble birth; aristocratic; presumptuous.
encorvar [enkor'βar] v curve. encorvarse v become bent; (caballo) buck. encorvado adj bent; stooped. encorvamiento sm bend; stoop.
encrespar [enkres'par] v curl; make rough; excite; irritate. encresparse v curl; become rough; become entangled.
encrucijada [enkruθi'xaða] sf crossroads pl.
encuadernar [enkwaðer'nar] v (libro) bind. encuadernación sf bookbinding.
encuadrar [enkwa'ðrar] v frame; insert. encuadre sm frame.
*encubrir [enku'βrir] v conceal; (jur) receive stolen goods. encubierto adj concealed. encubrimiento sm concealment.
encuentro [en'kwentro] sm encounter; collision.
encumbrar [enkum'brar] v raise; ascend; exalt. encumbrado adj high, lofty. encumbramiento sm height; praise.
enchufar [entʃu'far] v plug in; connect. enchufado, -a sm, sf (fam) wirepuller. enchufe sm electric plug; joint; (fam) cushy job. enchufismo sm (fam) wirepulling.
endeble [en'deβle] adj frail. endeblez sf frailty.
endémico [en'demiko] adj endemic.
enderezar [endere'θar] v straighten; guide; put right. enderezarse v stand up straight. enderezado adj favourable.
endeudarse [endeu'ðarse] v get into debt.
endiablado [endja'βlaðo] adj devilish. endiablar v bedevil.
endiosar [endjo'sar] v deify. endiosarse v be conceited. endiosado adj deified; conceited.
endosar [endo'sar] v also endorsar endorse. endoso sm also endorso sm endorsement.

endulzar [endul'θar] v sweeten. endulzadura sf sweetening.
*endurecer [endure'θer] v harden. endurecido adj hardened. endurecimiento sm hardening.
enebro [e'neβro] sm juniper.
enemigo [ene'migo], -a sm, sf enemy. adj hostile. enemistar v make an enemy of.
energía [ener'xia] sf energy. enérgico adj energetic; vigorous; drastic.
enero [e'nero] sm January.
enfadar [enfa'ðar] v anger. enfado sm anger; annoyance. enfadoso adj annoying.
énfasis ['enfasis] s(m or f) emphasis. enfático adj emphatic.
enfermar [enfer'mar] v make ill; fall ill. enfermedad sf illness. enfermedad profesional occupational disease. enfermería sf infirmary. enfermera, -o sf, sm nurse. enfermo adj ill.
enfilar [enfi'lar] v line up.
*enflaquecer [enflake'θer] v weaken; make thin; grow thin. enflaquecimiento sm weakening; emaciation.
enfocar [enfo'kar] v focus; approach, tackle. enfoque sm focus; approach.
enfrascar [enfras'kar] v bottle. enfrascarse v become involved; become engrossed.
enfrentar [enfren'tar] v confront; face; resist. enfrentarse v face up to. enfrente adv opposite. enfrente de prep opposite.
enfriar [enfri'ar] v cool. enfriarse v cool down. enfriadero sm coldroom. enfriamiento sm cooling.
*enfurecer [enfure'θer] v infuriate. enfurecerse v rage. enfurecimiento sm fury.
enganchar [engan'tʃar] v hook; hitch; hang up; harness. enganche sm hook; coupling; harnessing; enlistment.
engañar [enga'ɲar] v deceive. engaño sm deceit. engañoso adj deceitful.
engatusar [engatu'sar] v coax; flatter. engatusamiento sm coaxing.
engendrar [enxen'drar] v engender; breed. engendrador adj generating. engendramiento sm generating. engendro sm foetus; abortion; monster; brainchild.
englobar [englo'βar] v include; embrace.
engordar [engor'ðar] v fatten; gain weight. engorde sm (animales) fattening up.

engorro [en'gorro] *sm* nuisance. **engorroso** *adj* troublesome.

engranar [engra'nar] *v* put in gear, mesh, interlock. **engranaje** *sm* gear; cogs; connection.

*__engrandecer__ [engrande'θer] *v* enlarge; exaggerate; promote. **engrandecimiento** *sm* enlargement; increase; exaggeration.

engrasar [engra'sar] *v* grease. **engrase** *sm* greasing.

engreído [engre'iðo] *adj* conceited. **engreimiento** *sm* conceit. **engreir** *v* make conceited.

*__engrosar__ [engro'sar] *v* fatten; thicken; increase. **engrosarse** *v* enlarge. **engrosamiento** *sm* fattening; thickening.

*__engullir__ [engu'ʎir] *v* gobble; gulp down.

enhiesto [e'njesto] *adj* erect; upright. **enhestar** *v* erect. **enhestarse** *v* rise; straighten oneself up.

enhorabuena [enora'βwena] *sf* congratulations *pl*. **dar la enhorabuena** congratulate. **enhoramala** *adv* inopportunely.

enigma [e'niɣma] *sm* enigma. **enigmático** *adj* enigmatic.

enjabonar [enxaβo'nar] *v* soap. **enjabonadura** *sf* lathering.

enjambre [en'xambre] *sm* swarm. **enjambrar** *v* swarm.

enjaular [enxau'lar] *v* cage.

enjuagar [enxwa'gar] *v* rinse. **enjuague** *sm* rinse, rinsing; (*fig*) plot.

enjugar [enxu'gar] *v* dry; wipe; cancel. **enjugador** *sm* clothes-drier.

enjuiciar [enxwi'θjar] *v* (*jur*) sue; try; prosecute; judge. **enjuiciamiento** *sm* trial; lawsuit; judgment.

enlace [en'laθe] *sm* link; connection; liaison; marriage. **enlazar** *v* join; connect; relate. **enlazarse** *v* marry.

*__enloquecer__ [enloke'θer] *v* madden. **enloquecido** *adj* mad. **enloquecimiento** *sm* madness.

enlosar [enlo'sar] *v* tile; pave. **enlosado** *sm* tiling; paving.

*__enlucir__ [enlu'θir] *v* plaster; polish. **enlucido** *sm* plaster. **enlucimiento** *sm* plastering; polishing.

enlutar [enlu'tar] *v* dress in mourning; (*fig*) sadden. **enlutado** *adj* in mourning.

enmarañar [enmara'nar] *v* entangle; muddle; confuse. **enmarañamiento** *sm* tangle; confusion.

enmascarar [enmaska'rar] *v* mask. **enmascararse** *v* go in disguise. **enmascaramiento** *sm* camouflage.

*__enmendar__ [enmen'dar] *v* amend; correct; reform. **enmendadura** *sf* correction. **enmienda** *sf* rectification; repair; amendment.

*__enmohecer__ [enmoe'θer] *v* rust; make mouldy. **enmohecerse** *v* get rusty; grow mouldy. **enmohecimiento** *sm* rusting; mouldering.

*__enmudecer__ [enmuðe'θer] *v* silence. **enmudecerse** *v* fall silent; become dumb.

ennoblecer [ennoβle'θer] *v* ennoble; do honour to. **ennoblecimiento** *sm* ennobling.

enojar [eno'xar] *v* annoy; offend. **enojarse** *v* get cross. **enojado** *adj* angry. **enojo** *sm* annoyance; anger.

*__enorgullecer__ [enorguʎe'θer] *v* make proud. **enorgullecerse** *v* grow proud. **enorgullecerse de** pride oneself on. **enorgullecimiento** *sm* pride.

enorme [e'norme] *adj* enormous. **enormidad** *sf* hugeness; enormity.

*__enrarecer__ [enrare'θer] *v* make rare; rarefy. **enrarecerse** *v* become scarce. **enrarecido** *adj* rarefied. **enrarecimiento** *sm* scarcity.

enredar [enre'ðar] *v* catch; entangle; compromise; involve. **enredarse** *v* become involved. **planta enredadera** *sf* climbing plant. **enredador** *adj* mischievous. **enredo** *sm* tangle; mess; love affair. **enredoso** *adj* complicated; mischievous.

enrevesado [enreβe'saðo] *adj* complicated, involved.

*__enriquecer__ [enrike'θer] *v* enrich.

*__enrojecer__ [enroxe'θer] *v* redden; cause to blush. **enrojecerse** *v* blush. **enrojecimiento** *sm* glowing; blush.

enrollar [enro'ʎar] *v* coil up. **enrollamiento** *sm* rolling up; coiling.

*__enronquecer__ [enronke'θer] *v* make hoarse. **enronquecimiento** *sm* hoarseness.

enroscar [enros'kar] *v* twist, curl. **enroscarse** *v* curl up. **enroscadura** *sf* twisting, curling.

ensalada [ensa'laða] *sf* salad.

ensalmar [ensal'mar] *v* (*huesos*) set; cure. **ensalmador, -a** *sm*, *sf* quack; bonesetter. **ensalmado** *sm* quack remedy.

ensalzar [ensal'θar] *v* praise. **ensalzarse** *v* boast. **ensalzamiento** *sm* praise.

ensamblar [ensam'blar] *v* assemble; join.

ensamblado *sm* joint. ensamblador *sm* joiner. ensamblaje *sm* joining; joint.
ensanchar [ensan'tʃar] *v* grow broader; enlarge; stretch. ensancharse *v* put on airs. ensanche *sm* enlargement; extension; new suburb.
ensañar [ensa'ɲar] *v* infuriate. ensañarse *v* be merciless.
ensayar [ensa'jar] *v* test; try; rehearse. ensayarse *v* practise; rehearse. ensayo *sm* test; trial; essay; rehearsal. ensayo general dress rehearsal.
ensenada [ense'naða] *sf* cove; inlet.
enseñar [ense'ɲar] *v* show; teach. bien/mal enseñado well/ill-bred. enseñanza *sf* teaching; education.
enseres [en'seres] *sm pl* goods and chattels; equipment *sing*.
ensillar [ensi'ʎar] *v* saddle.
ensimismarse [ensimis'marse] *v* become lost in thought. ensimismado *adj* lost in thought. ensimismamiento *sm* pensiveness.
*ensordecer [ensorðe'θer] *v* deafen. ensordecerse *v* grow deaf. ensordecedor *adj* deafening. ensordecimiento *sm* deafness.
ensuciar [ensu'θjar] *v* dirty. ensuciador *adj* dirtying. ensuciamiento *sm* dirtiness, dirt.
ensueño [en'sweɲo] *sm* dream; fantasy. ¡ni por ensueño! not likely!
entablar [enta'βlar] *v* begin; open; establish; board up; put in a splint; (*juegos*) set up. entablado *sm* planking; wooden floor.
entallar [enta'ʎar] *v* carve; notch; engrave; fit to the body. entalladura *sf* notch; mortise; carving.
ente ['ente] *sm* entity; (*fam*) fellow.
*entender [enten'der] *v* understand; believe; mean. entenderse *v* make oneself understood. entendedor, -a *sm, sf* expert. entendidamente *adv* cleverly. entendido *adj* understood; well informed; clever. ¡entendido! O.K.!
enterar [ente'rar] *v* inform; instruct. enterarse *v* become aware. enterado *adj* aware.
*enternecer [enterne'θer] *v* soften. enternecerse *v* be moved; relent.
entero [en'tero] *adj* entire, whole; perfect; pure; strong. por entero completely. enteramente *adv* entirely.
*enterrar [enter'rar] *v* bury. entarrador

sm gravedigger. entierro *sm* burial; funeral.
entidad [enti'ðað] *sf* society; company; significance; entity.
entonar [ento'nar] *v* tune; intone; sing in tune. entonación *sf* intonation. entonado *adj* in tune; haughty.
entonces [en'tonθes] *adv* then; in that case; and so.
entornar [entor'nar] *v* (*ojos, puerta*) half close; tilt.
*entorpecer [entorpe'θer] *v* benumb; obstruct. entorpecimiento *sm* numbness; sluggishness; obstruction.
entrada [en'traða] *sf* entrance; doorway; admission; (*deporte*) gate; ticket; income; takings *pl*. derechos de entrada *sm pl* import duty *sing*. de entrada to begin with. entrar *v* enter; flow into; fit; join; introduce; invade. el año que entra the coming year.
entrambos [en'trambos] *pl adj* both.
entraña [en'traɲa] *sf* essence; core; disposition. entrañas *sf pl* entrails, bowels. no tener entrañas be heartless. entrañable *adj* dear, beloved. entrañar *v* bury deep; involve. entrañarse *v* penetrate to the core.
entre ['entre] *prep* between; among. entre semana on weekdays. entretanto *adv* meanwhile.
entreabierto [entrea'βjerto] *adj* half-open.
entrecejo [entre'θexo] *sm* frown.
entregar [entre'gar] *v* deliver; surrender. entrega *sf* delivery; (*fascículo*) instalment.
entrelazar [entrela'θar] *v* entwine.
entremés [entre'mes] *sm* (*culin*) hors d'oeuvre; (*teatro*) short farce.
entremeter [entreme'ter] *v* also entrometer mix; insert. entremeterse *also* entrometerse *v* interfere. entremetido, -a *sm, sf also* entrometido, -a busybody.
entrenar [entre'nar] *v* train; coach. entrenador, -a *sm, sf* trainer; coach. entrenamiento *sm* training; coaching.
entresacar [entresa'kar] *v* select; prune; thin out.
entresuelo [entre'swelo] *sm* mezzanine.
entretejer [entrete'xer] *v* interweave.
*entretener [entrete'ner] *v* entertain; delay; maintain. entretenerse *v* pass the time. entretenido *adj* entertaining; busy. entretenimiento *sm* entertainment; pastime; delaying.

*entrever [entre'βer] *v* make out; foresee.
entrevista [entre'βista] *sf* interview.
entrevistar *v* interview. **entrevistarse** *v* hold an interview.
*entristecer [entriste'θer] *v* sadden. **entristecerse** *v* grow sad. **entristecimiento** *sm* sadness.
*entumecer [entume'θer] *v* numb. **entumecerse** *v* go numb; (*mar*) surge. **entumecido** *adj* numb. **entumecimiento** *sm* numbness.
enturbiar [entur'βjar] *v* make cloudy; muddy. **enturbiarse** *v* be in disorder.
entusiasmar [entusjas'mar] *v* fill with enthusiasm. **entusiasmarse** *v* be very keen. **entusiasmo** *sm* enthusiasm. **entusiasta** *s(m+f)* enthusiast; *adj* enthusiastic. **entusiástico** *adj* enthusiastic.
enumerar [enume'rar] *v* enumerate. **enumeración** *sf* enumeration.
enunciar [enun'θjar] *v* enunciate, state. **enunciación** *sf* statement, enunciation.
envainar [enβai'nar] *v* sheathe.
*envanecer [enβane'θer] *v* make vain. **envanecimiento** *sm* vanity.
envasar [enβa'sar] *v* pack; wrap; bottle. **envasador** *sm* packer; large funnel. **envase** *sm* packing; bottling; container.
*envejecer [enβexe'θer] *v* age. **envejecerse** *v* grow old. **envejecido** *adj* aged. **envejecimiento** *sm* ageing.
envenenar [enβene'nar] *v* poison. **envenenador** *adj* poisonous. **envenenamiento** *sm* poisoning; pollution.
envergadura [enβerga'ðura] *sf* wingspan; (*fig*) scope.
enviar [en'βjar] *v* send. **enviado, -a** *sm, sf* messenger; representative; envoy.
envidiar [enβi'ðjar] *v* envy. **envidia** *sf* envy. **envidioso** *adj* envious.
*envilecer [enβile'θer] *v* debase. **envilecimiento** *sm* debasement; degradation.
envío [en'βio] *sm* dispatch; shipment; remittance.
*envolver [enβol'βer] *v* envelop; wrap up; involve; imply; (*mil*) encircle. **envoltura** *sf* wrapping; envelope.
enzarzar [enθar'θar] *v* cover with brambles; set at odds. **enzarzarse** *v* get caught up in brambles; (*fig*) squabble.
enzima [en'θima] *sf* enzyme.
épico ['epiko] *adj* epic.
epidemia [epi'ðemja] *sf* epidemic. **epidémico** *adj* epidemic.

epígrafe [e'pigrafe] *sm* epigraph.
epílogo [e'pilogo] *sm* epilogue.
episcopado [episko'paðo] *sm* bishopric; episcopate. **episcopal** *adj* episcopal.
episodio [epi'soðjo] *sm* episode.
epitafio [epi'tafjo] *sm* epitaph.
época ['epoka] *sf* epoch.
equidad [eki'ðað] *sf* equity; fairness.
equilibrar [ekili'βrar] *v* balance. **equilibrio** *sm* equilibrium; balance; poise. **equilibrismo** *sm* acrobatics. **equilibrista** *s(m+f)* acrobat.
equinoccio [eki'nokθjo] *sm* equinox. **equinoccial** *adj* equinoctial.
equipar [eki'par] *v* equip. **equipaje** *sm* luggage; equipment. **equipo** *sm* team; equipment; trousseau.
equitación [ekita'θjon] *sf* riding; horsemanship.
equitativo [ekita'tiβo] *adj* fair, equitable.
equivalencia [ekiβa'lenθja] *sf* equivalence. **equivalente** *adj* equivalent. **equivaler** *v* be equivalent.
equivocar [ekiβo'kar] *v* mistake. **equivocarse** *v* be mistaken. **equivocación** *sf* mistake. **equívoco** *adj* ambiguous.
era¹ ['era] *sf* era.
era² ['era] *V* ser.
eremita [ere'mita] *sm* also **ermitaño** *sm* hermit.
eres ['eres] *V* ser.
*erguir [er'gir] *v* raise, erect. **erguirse** *v* straighten up. **erguimiento** *sm* raising.
erigir [eri'xir] *v* erect; build; establish. **erigirse** *v* set oneself up. **erección** *sf* erection; establishment. **erecto** *adj* erect.
erizar [eri'θar] *v* bristle. **erizarse** *v* bristle; (*pelo*) stand on end. **erizado** *adj* bristly.
erizo [e'riθo] *sm* hedgehog.
erradicar [erraði'kar] *v* eradicate; uproot. **erradicación** *sf* eradication.
*errar [er'rar] *v* miss; fail; wander. **errarse** *v* be mistaken. **erradizo** *adj* wandering. **errado** *adj* mistaken. **errante** *adj* wandering; nomadic. **erróneo** *adj* erroneous, mistaken. **error** *sm* error.
eructar [eruk'tar] *v* belch. **eructo** *sm* belch.
erudición [eruði'θjon] *sf* erudition. **erudito, -a** *sm, sf* scholar; *adj* erudite.
erupción [erup'θjon] *sf* eruption; (*med*) rash. **eruptivo** *adj* eruptive.
esbelto [es'βelto] *adj* slim. **esbeltez** *sf* slimness.

esbozar [esβo'θar] *v* sketch. **esbozo** *sm* sketch.

escabechar [eskaβe'tʃar] *v* (*culin*) pickle; (*fam*) fail an exam; (*fam*) bump off. **escabeche** *sm* pickle.

escabroso [eska'βroso] *adj* rough; crude; harsh; (*fig*) difficult. **escabro** *sm* (*med*) scab. **escabrosidad** *sf* roughness; crudity; harshness.

***escabullirse** [eskaβu'ʎirse] *v* sneak away *or* out.

escala [es'kala] *sf* ladder; scale; port of call. **en gran escala** on a large scale. **escala franca** free port. **hacer escala en** put in at. **escalar** *v* climb; escalate. **escalamiento** *sm* escalation.

escaldar [eskal'ðar] *v* scald; make red hot. **escaldado** *adj* scalded; cautious.

escalera [eska'lera] *sf* stairs *pl*. **escalera móvie** escalator.

escalfar [eskal'far] *v* (*culin*) poach. **escalfado** *adj* poached. **escalfador** *sm* poacher.

escalofrío [eskalo'frio] *sm* shiver. **escalofriante** *adj* bloodcurdling.

escalón [eska'lon] *sm* rung; step. **escalonar** *v* space; stagger. **escalonado** *adj* spread out; staggered. **escalonamiento** *sm* spacing; staggering.

escalonia [eska'lonja] *sf* *also* **escaloña** shallot.

escalpelo [eskal'pelo] *sm* scalpel.

escama [es'kama] *sf* (*jabón*) flake; (*animal*) scale. **escamado** *adj* (*fam*) suspicious. **escamar** *v* scale; (*fam*) make suspicious. **escamarse** *v* (*fam*) become suspicious. **escamoso** *adj* scaly; (*fam*) suspicious.

escamot(e)ar [eskamo't(j)ar] *v* make disappear; shirk. **escamoteo** *sm* (*fam*) swindle. **escamoteador, -a** *sm, sf* conjurer; (*fam*) swindler.

escampar [eskam'par] *v* clear out; stop raining. **escampada** *sf* clear spell.

escándalo [es'kandalo] *sm* scandal; uproar; viciousness. **dar un escándalo** make a scene. **escandalizar** *v* scandalize. **escandalizar** *v* be shocked. **escandaloso** *adj* scandalous; turbulent.

escaño [es'kaɲo] *sm* bench; seat in Parliament.

escapar [eska'par] *v* escape. **escaparse** *v* escape; leak. **escapada** *sf* escape; escapade. **escape** *sm* escape; leakage. **a**

escape at full speed. **tubo de escape** exhaust pipe.

escaparate [eskapa'rate] *sm* shop window.

escarabajo [eskara'βaxo] *sm* beetle; (*fam*) dwarf.

escaramuza [eskara'muθa] *sf* skirmish. **escaramucear** *v* skirmish.

escarbar [eskar'βar] *v* scratch; scrape; pry into. **escarbo** *sm* scraping; scratching.

escarcha [es'kartʃa] *sf* frost.

escarlata [eskar'lata] *sf, adj* scarlet.

***escarmentar** [eskarmen'tar] *v* punish; learn from experience; be warned. **escarmiento** *sm* punishment; warning.

***escarnecer** [eskarne'θer] *v* mock. **escarnecimiento** *sm* scorn; derision.

escarola [eska'rola] *sf* endive.

escarpa [es'karpa] *sf* slope.

escasear [eskase'ar] *v* skimp; be scarce. **escasamente** *adv* scantily. **escasez** *sf* scarcity. **escaso** *adj* scarce; skimpy.

escena [es'θena] *sf* scene; stage. **poner en escena** stage. **escénico** *adj* scenic.

escéptico [es'θeptiko] *s, adj* sceptic(al). **esceptisismo** *sm* scepticism.

***esclarecer** [esklare'θer] *v* brighten; clear; dawn. **esclarecido** *adj* illustrious. **esclarecimiento** *sm* illumination; splendour; dawn.

esclavitud [esklaβi'tuð] *sf* slavery. **esclavizar** *v* enslave. **esclavo, -a** *sm, sf* slave.

esclusa [es'klusa] *sf* lock; floodgate. **esclusa de aire** airlock.

escoba [es'koβa] *sf* broom, brush. **escobar** *v* sweep, brush.

***escocer** [esko'θer] *v* smart, sting. **escocerse** *v* chafe. **escocedor** *adj* painful. **escocedura** *sf* sting.

escoger [esko'xer] *v* choose. **escogido** *adj* chosen, choice. **escogimiento** *sm* choice, selection.

escolar [esko'lar] *s(m+f)* schoolboy/girl. *adj* scholastic. **escolástica** *sf* scholasticism. **escolástico** *adj* scholastic.

escolta [es'kolta] *sf* escort. **escoltar** *v* escort.

escollo [es'koʎo] *sm* reef; difficulty; danger.

escombro [es'kombro] *sm* mackerel; débris; rubbish.

esconder [eskon'der] *v* hide. **esconderse** *v* conceal oneself. **escondidamente** *adv* secretly. **escondite** *sm* hiding place; (*juego*) hide-and-seek.

escopeta [esko'peta] *sf* shotgun; rifle. **escopeta de aire comprimido** airgun.

escoplo [es'koplo] *sm* chisel. **escoplear** *v* chisel; gouge.

escoria [es'korja] *sf* slag; dross; (*fig*) scum. **escorial** *sm* slag heap.

escorpión [eskor'pjon] *sf* scorpion.

escotado [esko'taðo] *adj* (*vestido*) low-cut. **escotar** *v* lower the neckline; scoop out.

escotilla [esko'tiʎa] *sf* (*mar*) hatch.

escribano [eskri'βano] *sm* clerk; notary.

***escribir** [eskri'βir] *v* write. **escribir a máquina** type. **escribirse** *v* spell. **escribido** *adj* (*fam*) well read. **escribiente** *s(m+f)* clerk. **escrito a mano** handwritten. *sm* writing; document; letter. **escritor, -a** *sm, sf* writer. **escritorio** *sm* bureau; office. **escritura** *sf* writing; script; (*jur*) deed.

escrúpulo [es'krupulo] *sm* scruple; conscientiousness. **escrupuloso** *adj* scrupulous.

escrutinio [eskru'tinjo] *sm* scrutiny. **escrutar** *v* scrutinize.

escuadra [es'kwaðra] *sf* carpenter's square; (*mil*) squad; (*mil*) corporal; (*mar*) squadron; (*fig*) gang. **a escuadra** at right angles. **escuadrar** *v* square.

escuálido [es'kwaliðo] *adj* squalid; weak; skinny. **escualidez** *sf* squalor; weakness; emaciation.

escuchar [esku'tʃar] *v* listen to; hear. **escucharse** *v* pay too much attention to oneself. **escucha** *sf* listening; sentry; chaperone. **a la escucha** on the alert. **escuchador, -a** *sm, sf* listener.

escudero [esku'ðero] *sm* squire; page. **escudar** *v* shield. **escudo** *sm* shield.

escudriñar [eskuðri'ɲar] *v* scrutinize. **escudriñador** *adj* examining; curious. **escudriñamiento** *sm* investigation; search.

escuela [es'kwela] *sf* school.

esculpir [eskul'pir] *v* sculpture; engrave. **escultor. -a** *sm, sf* sculptor. **escultura** *sf* sculpture.

escupir [esku'pir] *v* spit. **escupidura** *sf* spittle.

escurrir [eskur'rir] *v* drain; wring out; drip; slip; ooze. **escurrirse** *v* drain; sneak off. **escurridizo** *adj* slippery. **escurridor** *sm* plate rack; colander; draining board; wringer. **escurriduras** *sf pl* dregs *pl*. **escurrimiento** *sm* draining; dripping.

ese ['ese] *adj also* **esa** that.

ése ['ese] *pron also* **ésa** that one; the former.

esencia [e'senθja] *sf* essence. **esencial** *adj* essential.

esfera [es'fera] *sf* sphere. **esférico** *adj* spherical.

esfinge [es'finxe] *sf* sphinx.

***esforzar** [esfor'θar] *v* invigorate; strengthen; encourage. **esforzarse** *v* make an effort. **esforzado** *adj* vigorous. **esfuerzo** *sm* effort.

esgrimir [esgri'mir] *v* brandish; fence. **esgrima** *sf* fencing. **esgrimidor, -a** *sm, sf* fencer.

eslabón [esla'βon] *sm* link. **eslabonamiento** *sm* linking. **eslabonar** *v* link.

esmaltar [esmal'tar] *v* enamel; (*las uñas*) varnish. **esmalte** *sm* varnish.

esmerado [esme'raðo] *adj* careful, painstaking. **esmerar** *v* polish; take great pains.

esmeralda [esme'ralða] *sf* emerald.

esnórquel [es'norkel] *sm* snorkel.

eso ['eso] *pron* that, that thing. **en eso** at that moment. **eso es** that's right. **eso mismo** just so. **por eso** because of that. **esos** *adj pl also* **esas** those. **ésos** *pron pl also* **ésas** those; the former.

espabilar [espaβi'lar] *v* (*vela*) snuff. **espabilarse** *v* (*fam*) look sharp.

espaciar [espa'θjar] *v* space out; spread. **espaciarse** *v* expatiate; enjoy oneself. **espacial** *adj* space. **nave espacial** spaceship. **espaciamiento** *sm* spacing. **espacio** *sm* space. **espacioso** *adj* spacious.

espada [es'paða] *sf* sword; swordsman. *sm* matador. **pez espada** swordfish.

espalda [es'palða] *sf* shoulder; back. **a espaldas** behind someone's back. **volver las espaldas** turn tail.

espantapájaros [espanta'paxaros] *sm invar* scarecrow.

espantar [espan'tar] *v* scare. **espantarse** *v* take fright. **espanto** *sm* fright; terror. **espantoso** *adj* frightful; amazing.

España [es'paɲa] *sf* Spain.

español [espa'ɲol], **-a** *sm, sf* Spaniard. *sm* (*lengua*) Spanish. *adj* Spanish.

***esparcir** [espar'θir] *v* scatter; spread. **esparcirse** *v* amuse oneself. **esparcidamente** *adv* separately. **esparcido** *adj* cheerful; amusing; scattered. **esparcimiento** *sm* scattering; pastime.

espárrago [es'parrago] *sm* asparagus.
espasmo [es'pasmo] *sm* spasm. espasmódico *adj* spasmodic.
especia [es'peθja] *sf* spice.
especial [espe'θjal] *adj* special; particular. en especial especially. especialidad *sf* speciality. especialista *s(m+f). adj* specialist. especializarse *v* specialize.
especie [es'peθje] *sf* species; kind; affair; appearance.
específico [espe'θifiko] *adj* specific. *sm* (*med*) patent medicine. especificación *sf* specification. especificación normalizada standard specification. especificar *v* specify.
espectáculo [espek'takulo] *sm* spectacle; entertainment. espectacular *adj* spectacular. espectador, -a *sm, sf* spectator.
espectro [es'pektro] *sm* spectre.
espejo [es'pexo] *sm* mirror. espejo retrovisor (*auto*) rear-view mirror. espejismo *sm* mirage.
esperar [espe'rar] *v* hope; expect; await. esperar a que wait until. espera *sf* waiting; expectation; delay. sala de espera waiting room. esperanza *sf* hope. esperanzador *adj* encouraging.
esperpento [esper'pento] *sm* fright; grotesqueness; absurdity.
espesar [espe'sar] *v* thicken; tighten. espeso *adj* thick; greasy. espesamiento *sm* thickening.
espetar [espe'tar] *v* (*culin*) skewer; pierce. espetarse *v* be pompous.
espía [es'pia] *s(m+f)* spy. espiar *v* spy upon. espionaje *sm* espionage.
espiga [es'piga] *sf* (*bot*) ear, spike. espigado *adj* gone to seed. espigar *v* glean.
espín [es'pin] *sm* porcupine.
espina [es'pina] *sf* thorn; spine; splinter; fishbone. espina dorsal backbone.
espinaca [espi'naka] *sf* spinach.
espiral [espi'ral] *sf, adj* spiral.
espíritu [es'piritu] *sm* spirit; soul; ghost; wit; breathing. espiritado *adj* possessed; (*fam*) skinny. espiritismo *sm* spiritualism. espiritista *s(m+f)* spiritualist. espirituoso *adj* spirited. espiritual *adj* spiritual. espiritualidad *sf* spirituality.
espléndido [es'plendiðo] *adj* splendid; magnificent. esplendor *sm* splendour.
espliego [es'pljego] *sm* lavender.
esplín [es'plin] *sm* spleen.
espolear [espole'ar] *v* spur. spur on. espoleo *sm* spurring.

esponja [es'ponxa] *sf* sponge. esponjar *v* make spongy; puff up. esponjarse *v* become spongy; (*fig*) become puffed up with pride; glow with health.
esponsales [espon'sales] *sm pl* betrothal *sing*.
espontáneo [espon'taneo] *adj* spontaneous. espontaneidad *sf* spontaneity.
esporádico [espo'raðiko] *adj* sporadic.
esposa [es'posa] *sf* wife. esposas *sf pl* handcuffs. esposado *adj* newly married; handcuffed.
espuela [es'pwela] *sf* spur. echar la espuela have one for the road.
espuma [es'puma] *sf* foam; froth; lather. espumadera *sf* strainer. espumajear *v* foam at the mouth. espumajoso *adj* foaming; frothy. espumar *v* skim; froth; lather; sparkle. espumoso *adj* frothy; sparkling.
esquela [es'kela] *sf* note; short letter; obituary.
esqueleto [eske'leto] *sm* skeleton.
esquema [es'kema] *sm* scheme. esquemático *adj* schematic.
esquí [es'ki] *sm, pl* esquíes *or* esquís ski. esquiador, -a *sm, sf* skier. esquiar *v* ski.
esquilar [eski'lar] *v* shear, clip. sin esquilar unshorn.
esquimal [eski'mal] *sm, adj* Eskimo.
esquina [es'kina] *sf* (*afuera*) corner. doblar la esquina turn the corner. esquinar *v* form a corner with.
esquirol [eski'rol] *sm* (*fam*) strike-breaker, blackleg.
esquivar [eski'βar] *v* avoid, shun; disappear. esquivarse *v* shy away. esquivo *adj* unsociable.
estabilidad [estaβili'ðað] *sf* stability. estabilizar *v* stabilize. estable *adj* stable.
*establecer [estaβle'θer] *v* establish. establecerse *v* settle down; set up. establecido *adj* established. establecimiento *sm* establishment.
establo [es'taβlo] *sm* cowshed.
estaca [es'taka] *sf* stake, post. estacada *sf* fence; stockade. estacar *v* fence; stake out.
estación [esta'θjon] *sf* station; season. estacionamiento *sm* parking. estacionar *v* park.
estadio [es'taðjo] *sm* stadium; (*med*) phase.

estado [es'taðo] *sm* state: status: order: estate: statement. **estado de ánimo** state of mind. **estar en estado** be pregnant. **hombre de estado** statesman.

Estados Unidos [es'taðos u'niðos] *sm pl* United States (of America). **estadounidense** *s(m+f)*, *adj* American.

estafa [es'tafa] *sf* swindle. **estafador. -a** *sm*, *sf* swindler. **estafar** *v* swindle.

estafeta [esta'feta] *sf* courier: sub-post office.

estallar [esta'ʎar] *v* explode: burst: erupt. **estallido** *sm* explosion: crash.

estampar [estam'par] *v* stamp: print: imprint. **estampa** *sf* print: engraving: impression: footprint.

estampida [estam'piða] *sf* stampede: explosion. bang. **estampido** *sm* explosion, bang.

estancar [estan'kar] *v* stem: block: delay: monopolize. **estancarse** *v* stagnate. **estancación** *sf* stagnation. **estancado** *adj* stagnant: blocked. **estanco** *sm* monopoly: state tobacco shop. **estanquero, -a** *sm*, *sf* tobacconist.

estandarte [estan'darte] *sm* banner.

estanque [es'tanke] *sm* reservoir: ornamental pond.

estante [es'tante] *sm* shelf. **estantería** *sf* shelving: bookcase.

estaño [es'taɲo] *sm* tin. **estañar** *v* solder.

*estar [es'tar] *v* be. **está bien** (it's) all right. **estar para** be about to. **no está** he *or* she is not at home. **ya que estamos** while we're at it.

estático [es'tatiko] *adj* static.

estatua [es'tatwa] *sf* statue.

estatura [esta'tura] *sf* stature, height.

estatuto [esta'tuto] *sm* statute. **estatuario** *adj* statutory.

este¹ ['este] *adj* also **esta** this; the latter.

este² *sm*, *adj* east.

éste ['este] *pron* also **ésta** this.

estela [es'tela] *sf* (*mar*) wake: trail.

estelar [este'lar] *adj* stellar.

estepa [es'tepa] *sf* steppe.

estera [es'tera] *sf* matting.

estereofónico [estereo'foniko] *adj* stereophonic.

estereotipo [estereo'tipo] *sm* stereotype.

estéril [es'teril] *adj* sterile: pointless. **esterelizar** *v* sterilize.

esterlina [ester'lina] *adj* sterling. **libra esterlina** pound sterling.

estético [es'tetiko] *adj* aesthetic. **estética** *sf* aesthetics.

estetoscopio [esteto'skopjo] *sm* stethoscope.

estiércol [es'tjerkol] *sm* manure.

estigma [es'tigma] *sm* stigma. **estigmatizar** *v* stigmatize.

estilar [esti'lar] *v* be accustomed: (*documento*) draw up: be in use: be in fashion. **estilístico** *adj* stylistic. **estilizado** *adj* stylized. **estilo** *sm* style: type: fashion.

estimar [esti'mar] *v* esteem: estimate. **estima** *sf* esteem. **estimable** *adj* estimable. **estimación** *sf* estimate: estimation.

estimular [estimu'lar] *v* stimulate. **estimulante** *adj* stimulating: *sm* (*med*) stimulant. **estimulo** *sm* stimulus.

estipular [estipu'lar] *v* stipulate. **estipulación** *sf* stipulation.

estirar [esti'rar] *v* stretch: extend. **estirado** *adj* affected: miserly. **estirón** *sm* jerk.

estirpe [es'tirpe] *sf* lineage: stock.

esto ['esto] *pron* this. **en esto** whereupon.

estofa [es'tofa] *sf* (*fig*) quality: class: brocade. **estofado** *adj* quilted: (*culin*) stewed. **estofar** *v* quilt: stew.

estoico [es'toiko], **-a** *s*, *adj* stoic. **estoicismo** *sm* stoicism.

estómago [es'tomago] *sm* stomach. **estomagar** *v* give indigestion.

estorbar [estor'βar] *v'* hinder: be in the way. **estorbo** *sm* hindrance: obstruction.

estornino [estor'nino] *sm* starling.

estornudar [estornu'ðar] *v* sneeze. **estornudo** *sm* sneeze.

estoy [es'toi] *V* estar.

estrafalario [estrafa'larjo] *adj* outlandish; extravagant; slovenly.

estrada [es'traða] *sf* road, highway.

estragar [estra'gar] *v* corrupt: destroy. **estrago** *sm* ruin, havoc. **hacer estragos** wreak havoc.

estrangular [estrangu'lar] *v* strangle. **estrangulación** *sf* strangulation. **estrangulador** *sm* strangler: (*auto*) choke.

estratagema [estrata'xema] *sf* stratagem. **estrategia** *sf* strategy. **estratégico** *adj* strategic.

estrechar [estre'tʃar] *v* make smaller; tighten; bring closer together. **estrecharse** *v* become narrower; squeeze together; shake hands; make economies. **estrechamente** *adv* narrowly. **estrechamiento** *sm* narrowing; taking-in;

tightening; handshake. **estrecho** *adj* narrow; cramped; tight; strict.
estrella [es'treʎa] *sf* star. **estrellado** *adj* starry.
estrellar [estre'ʎar] *v* smash (to pieces).
***estremecer** [estreme'θer] *v* shake; startle. **estremecerse** *v* shudder; tremble.
estremecimiento *sm* shake; shudder; tremble.
estrenar [estre'nar] *v* wear for the first time; (*teatro*) perform for the first time. **estreno** *sm* inauguration; first night; dress rehearsal.
estrenuo [es'trenwo] *adj* strong; courageous.
estreñido [estre'ɲiðo] *adj* constipated. **estreñimiento** *sm* constipation.
estrépito [es'trepito] *sm* noise, din; fuss. **estrepitoso** *adj* noisy; resounding.
estribo [es'triβo] *sm* stirrup; step; running-board. **perder los estribos** lose one's head.
estribor [estri'βor] *sm* (*mar*) starboard.
estricto [es'trikto] *adj* strict.
estridente [estri'ðente] *adj* strident.
estropajo [estro'paxo] *sm* scourer; rubbish. **estropajoso** *adj* thick; stringy; slovenly.
estropear [estrope'ar] *v* spoil; break; maim; age.
estructura [estruk'tura] *sf* structure; framework. **estructural** *adj* structural. **estructurar** *v* organize; construct.
estruendo [estru'endo] *sm* din; uproar; bustle; pomp. **estruendoso** *adj* noisy.
estrujar [estru'xar] *v* squeeze; crush. **estrujadura** *sf* pressure. **estrujón** *sm* squeeze.
estuario [es'twarjo] *sm* estuary.
estuche [es'tutʃe] *sm* box; case; casket; sheath.
estudiar [estu'ðjar] *v* study. **estudiante** *s(m+f)* student. **estudio** *sm* study; research; studio. **estudioso** *adj* studious.
estufa [es'tufa] *sf* stove; fire; hothouse.
estupefacto [estupe'fakto] *adj* stupefied; astonished. **estupefacción** *sf* stupefaction; astonishment.
estupefaciente [estupefa'θjente] *adj* stupefying; astonishing. *sm* (*med*) narcotic.
estupendo [estu'pendo] *adj* stupendous.
estúpido [es'tupiðo] *adj* stupid. **estupidez** *sf* stupidity. **estupor** *sm* stupor.
esturión [estu'rjon] *sm* sturgeon.

etapa [e'tapa] *sf* (*de un viaje*) stage; period.
éter ['eter] *sm* ether. **etereo** *adj* ethereal.
eternidad [eterni'ðað] *sf* eternity. **eternal** *adj* eternal. **eternizar** *v* perpetuate.
ética ['etika] *sf* ethics. **ético** *adj* ethical.
etimología [etimolo'xia] *sf* etymology. **etimológico** *adj* etymological.
etiqueta [eti'keta] *sf* etiquette; label; tag. **etiquetero** *adj* formal.
eucalipto [euka'lipto] *sm* eucalyptus.
eufemismo [eufe'mismo] *sm* euphemism. **eufemístico** *adj* euphemistic.
eunuco [eu'nuko] *sm* eunuch.
Europa [eu'ropa] *sf* Europe. **europeo, -a** *s, adj* European.
eutanasia [euta'nasja] *sf* euthanasia.
evacuar [eβa'kwar] *v* evacuate; fulfil. **evacuación** *sf* evacuation. **evacuado, -a** *sm, sf* evacuee.
evadir [eβa'ðir] *v* evade. **evadirse** *v* escape. **evadido, -a** *sm, sf* fugitive. **evasión** *sf* escape; flight. **evasivo** *adj* evasive.
evaluar [eβa'lwar] *v* evaluate; value. **evaluación** *sf* evaluation.
evangélico [eβan'xeliko] *adj* evangelical. **evangelio** *sm* gospel. **evangelista** *sm* evangelist.
evaporar [evapo'rar] *v* evaporate. **evaporación** *sf* evaporation.
evento [e'βento] *sm* (unforeseen) event. **eventual** [even'twal] *adj* temporary; possible; accidental. **eventualidad** *sf* contingency.
evidencia [evi'ðenθja] *sf* certainty; proof; evidence. **evidenciar** *v* make evident. **evidente** *adj* evident.
evitar [eβi'tar] *v* avoid. **evitable** *adj* avoidable.
evocar [evo'kar] *v* evoke. **evocación** *sf* evocation. **evocativo** *adj* evocative.
evolución [evolu'θjon] *sf* evolution. **evolucionar** *v* evolve. **evolutivo** *adj* evolutionary.
exacerbar [eksaθer'βar] *v* exacerbate; exasperate. **exacerbación** *sf* exacerbation.
exactitud [eksakti'tuð] *sf* exactitude; accuracy. **exacto** *adj* exact; correct.
exagerar [eksaxe'rar] *v* exaggerate. **exagerado** *adj* exaggerated. **exageración** *sf* exaggeration.
exaltar [eksal'tar] *v* exalt; raise; praise. **exaltarse** *v* get worked up; get heated. **exaltación** *sf* exaltation. **exaltado** *adj* hotheaded.

examinar [eksami'nar] *v* examine; inspect; test. **examinarse** *v* take an examination. **examen** *sm* examination; inquiry; investigation. **examen de conductor** driving test. **examinador, -a** *sm, sf* examiner.

exangüe [ek'sangwe] *adj* bloodless; weak.

exánime [ek'sanime] *adj* lifeless; unconscious; weak. **caer exánime** fall in a faint.

exasperar [eksaspe'rar] *v* exasperate; vex. **exasperarse** *v* become annoyed. **exasperación** *sf* exasperation. **exasperante** *adj* exasperating.

excavar [ekska'βar] *v* excavate; dig. **excavación** *sf* excavation.

exceder [eksθe'ðer] *v* exceed. **excederse** *v* forget oneself. **excedente** *adj* exceeding; excessive.

excelencia [eksθe'lenθja] *sf* excellence. **excelente** *adj* excellent; first-rate.

excéntrico [eks'θentriko] *adj, sm* eccentric. **excentricidad** *sf* eccentricity.

excepción [eksθep'θjon] *sf* exception. **a excepción de** with the exception of. **estado de excepción** state of emergency. **excepcional** *adj* exceptional. **excepto** *prep* excepting.

excerpta [ek'θerpta] *sf* excerpt.

excesivo [eksθe'siβo] *adj* excessive. **exceso** *sm* excess; surplus. **exceso de equipaje** excess luggage.

excitar [eksθi'tar] *v* excite; stir up. **excitabilidad** *sf* excitability. **excitable** *adj* excitable. **excitante** *adj* exciting.

exclamar [ekskla'mar] *v* exclaim. **exclamarse contra** protest against. **exclamación** *sf* exclamation. **exclamativo** *adj* exclamatory.

*excluir [eksklu'ir] *v* exclude. **exclusivo** *adj* exclusive. **exclusión** *sf* exclusion.

excomulgar [ekskomul'gar] *v* excommunicate. **excomulgación** *sf* excommunication. **excomulgado** *adj* excommunicated; (*fam*) accused.

excreción [ekskre'θjon] *sf* excretion. **excremento** *sm* excrement. **excretar** *v* excrete.

excursión [ekskur'sjon] *sf* excursion. **excursión a pie** hike. **ir de excursión** go on an outing. **excursionista** *s(m + f)* tripper; hiker.

excusar [eksku'sar] *v* excuse; avoid; exempt. **excusarse** *v* apologize. **excusa** *sf* excuse; apology. **excusable** *adj* pardonable. **excusadamente** *adv* unnecessarily. **excusado** *adj* excused; unnecessary; exempt; concealed; private. **excusado es decir** needless to say. **excusado** *sm* toilet.

exentar [eksen'tar] *v* exempt. **exención** *sf* exemption. **exento** *adj* exempt.

exequias [ek'sekjas] *sf pl* funeral rites.

exhalar [eksa'lar] *v* exhale; emit; utter. **exhalación** *sf* exhalation; vapour; shooting star; lightning flash.

exhausto [ek'sausto] *adj* exhausted. **exhaustivo** *adj* exhaustive.

exhibir [eksi'βir] *v* exhibit. **exhibición** *sf* exhibition. **exhibicionismo** *sm* exhibitionism. **exhibicionista** *s(m + f)* exhibitionist.

exhortar [eksor'tar] *v* exhort. **exhortación** *sf* exhortation.

exigir [eksi'xir] *v* demand. **exigencia** *sf* demand; requirement. **exigente** *adj* exacting.

exiguo [ek'sigwo] *adj* scanty. **exigüidad** *sf* scantiness.

eximir [eksi'mir] *v* exempt; excuse. **eximente** *adj* exempting.

existir [eksis'tir] *v* exist. **existencia** *sf* existence. **en existencia** in stock. **existente** *adj* existent; extant; in stock.

éxito ['eksito] *sm* success; result. **tener éxito** be successful.

éxodo ['eksoðo] *sm* exodus, emigration.

exonerar [eksone'rar] *v* exonerate; relieve; dismiss. **exoneración** *sf* exoneration; relief.

exorbitante [eksorβi'tante] *adj* exorbitant, excessive.

exorcizar [eksorθi'θar] *v* exorcize. **exorcismo** *sm* exorcism. **exorcista** *sm* exorcist.

exótico [ek'sotiko] *adj* exotic.

expansión [ekspan'sjon] *sf* expansion; recreation. **expansionarse** *v* give vent to one's feelings. **expansivo** *adj* expansive.

expatriar [ekspatri'ar] *v* exile. **expatriación** *sf* banishment.

expectación [ekspekta'θjon] *sf* expectation. **expectante** *adj* expectant.

expedición [ekspeði'θjon] *sf* expedition; party; shipment; dispatch; speed.

*expedir [ekspe'ðir] *v* send, dispatch; issue. **expediente** *sm* (*jur*) proceedings *pl*; dossier; inquiry; record. **expediente** *adj* expedient.

expendedor [ekspenðe'ðor], **-a** *sm, sf*

dealer; retailer; ticket agent. *adj* spending.

experiencia [ekspe'rjenθja] *sf* experience; experiment.

experimentar [eksperimen'tar] *v* experiment; test; feel. **experimentado** *adj* experienced. **experimental** *adj* experimental. **experimento** *sm* experiment.

experto [eks'perto] *sm, adj* expert.

expiar [eks'pjar] *v* atone for. **expiación** *sf* atonement.

expirar [ekspi'rar] *v* expire; die; die down. **expiración** *sf* expiration.

explanar [ekspla'nar] *v* level; (*fig*) explain. **explanación** *sf* levelling; (*fig*) explanation.

explicar [ekspli'kar] *v* explain; justify; lecture. **explicarse** *v* speak plainly; understand. **explicación** *sf* explanation. **explicativo** *adj* explanatory.

explícito [eks'pliθito] *adj* explicit.

explorar [eksplo'rar] *v* explore, investigate. **exploración** *sf* exploration. **explorador** *sm* explorer; (*mil*) scout; boy scout; *adj* exploratory.

explosión [eksplo'sjon] *sf* explosion. **explosivo** *sm, adj* explosive.

explotar [eksplo'tar] *v* exploit; develop; cultivate; explode. **explotación** *sf* exploitation; operation; development; cultivation.

***exponer** [ekspo'ner] *v* expose; set out; explain. **exponerse** *v* lay oneself open. **exponente** *s(m + f)* exponent; example; proof.

exportar [ekspor'tar] *v* export. **exportación** *sf* export. **exportador, -a** *sm, sf* exporter.

exposición [exposi'θjon] *sf* exhibition; display; statement; explanation; risk; (*foto*) exposure. **sala de exposición** showroom.

exprés [eks'pres] *sm* (*tren*) express; (*café*) espresso.

expresar [ekspre'sar] *v* express, convey. **expresarse** *v* express oneself; state. **expresamente** *adv* specifically; explicitly. **expresión** *sf* expression. **expresiones** *sf pl* greetings; regards. **expresivamente** *adv* expressively; affectionately. **expresivo** *adj* expressive; affectionate. **expreso** *adj* expressed; express.

exprimir [ekspri'mir] *v* squeeze; exploit. **exprimidor** *sm* squeezer.

expuesto [eks'pwesto] *adj* on display; exposed; explained.

expulsar [ekspul'sar] *v* expel, throw out.

exquisito [ekski'sito] *adj* exquisite; delightful; refined.

éxtasis ['ekstasis] *sm invar* ecstasy.

***extender** [eksten'der] *v* extend; spread. **extenderse** *v* spread; range; enlarge. **extendido** *adj* extended; widespread; outstretched. **extensamente** *adv* at length. **extensible** *adj* extending. **extensión** *sf* extension; expanse; extent; area. **extensivo** *adj* extendible. **extenso** *adj* extensive; large; widespread; full.

extenuar [ekste'nwar] *v* weaken; exhaust. **extenuación** *sf* emaciation; extenuation.

exterior [ekste'rjor] *adj* exterior, external; foreign. **asuntos exteriores** *sm pl* foreign affairs. *sm* outside, exterior; appearance. **al exterior** outside. **del exterior** from abroad.

exterminar [ekstermi'nar] *v* exterminate. **exterminación** *sf* extermination. **exterminador, -a** *sm, sf* exterminator.

externo [eks'terno], **-a** *sm, sf* day pupil. *adj* external; outward. **externado** *sm* day school.

extinguir [ekstin'gir] *v* extinguish; wipe out; put down. **extinguirse** *v* die out. **extinción** *sf* extinction. **extinto** *adj* extinct. **extintor** *sm* fire extinguisher.

extirpar [ekstir'par] *v* uproot; remove. **extirpación** *sf* uprooting; extraction.

extra ['ekstra] *adj invar* extra; best-quality. *sm* (*cine, teatro*) extra.

***extraer** [ekstra'er] *v* extract; release. **extracción** *sf* extraction; birth. **extracto** *sm* extract; excerpt; abstract.

extranjero [ekstran'xero], **-a** *sm, sf* foreigner; foreign countries *pl. adj* foreign.

extrañar [ekstra'nar] *v* be surprised; surprise; be shy; banish. **extrañarse** *v* go into exile. **extrañamiento** *sm* surprise; banishment. **extrañeza** *sf* strangeness; surprise. **extraño, -a** *sm, sf* stranger. **extraño** *adj* strange; peculiar; foreign.

extraordinario [ekstraorði'narjo] *adj* extraordinary. *sm* (*diario*) special edition.

extravagancia [ekstraβa'ganθja] *sf* extravagance; strangeness. **extravagante** *adj* extravagant; eccentric.

extraviar [ekstra'βjar] *v* lose; mislay; mislead. **extraviarse** *v* get lost; be missing; go astray.

extremar [ekstre'mar] v take to extremes.
extremarse v do one's best.
extremo [ek'stremo] adj extreme, last. **en caso extremo** as a last resort. sm extreme; end; point. **al extremo de** to the point of. **de extremo a extremo** from end to end. **Extremo Oriente** Far East.
extremidad sf extremity; end; limit.
exuberancia [eksuβe'ranθja] sf exuberance; abundance. **exuberante** adj exuberant.
exudar [eksu'ðar] v exude. **exudación** sf exudation.
exultar [eksul'tar] v exult. **exultación** sf exultation.

F

fábrica ['faβrika] sf factory; manufacture. **fabricación** sf manufacture. **de fabricación casera** home-made. **fabricación en serie** mass production. **fabricante** s(m+f) manufacturer. **fabricar** v manufacture; make; build.
fábula ['faβula] sf fable; story; gossip. **fabuloso** adj fabulous; incredible.
facción [fak'θjon] sf faction; gang. **facciones** sf pl features.
faceta [fa'θeta] sf facet.
facial [fa'θjal] adj facial.
fácil ['faθil] adj easy; simple; likely; well-behaved. **facilidad** sf facility; ease; fluency; gift. **facilitar** v facilitate; supply; provide; arrange. **fácilmente** adv easily.
facsímil [fak'simil] sm, adj also **facsímile** facsimile.
factible [fak'tiβle] adj feasible.
factor [fak'tor] sm factor; agent.
facturar [faktu'rar] v invoice; (ferrocarril) register luggage. **factura** sf invoice. **facturación** sf invoicing.
facultad [fakul'tað] sf faculty; authority; school. **facultar** v commission; authorize. **facultativo** adj optional.
facha ['fatʃa] sf (fam) appearance, looks; (fam) mess.
fachada [fa'tʃaða] sf façade.
faena [fa'ena] sf task; (fam) dirty trick. **estar de faena** be at work. **faenas domésticas** housework.
fagot [fa'got] sm bassoon.

faisán [fai'san] sm pheasant.
faja ['faxa] sf bandage; sash; belt; wrapper; strip of land. **fajar** v wrap; bandage.
falaz [fa'laθ] adj fallacious; deceitful.
falda ['falda] sf skirt; side of a hill; hat brim; lap.
falsear [false'ar] v falsify. **falseador, -a** sm, sf forger; counterfeiter. **falseamiento** sm misrepresentation. **falsedad** sf falsity. **falseo** sm bevelling. **falso** adj false; treacherous; sham.
falsificar [falsifi'kar] v falsify; forge; adulterate. **falsificación** sf falsification; adulteration.
falta ['falta] sf lack, want, need; shortage; failure; (deporte) foul. **faltar** v be lacking; fail; be absent; be untrue. **falto** sm shortage; deficiency; fault. **falto** adj short; deficient; incomplete.
fallar [fa'ʎar] v (jur) judge; sentence; fail; (naipes) trump. **no falla** it's always the same. **sin falla** without fail.
*****fallecer** [faʎe'θer] v die. **fallecido** adj deceased. **fallecimiento** sm death.
fallido [fa'ʎiðo] sm bankrupt. adj bankrupt; unsuccessful. **fallo** sm (jur) sentence, judgment; failure; fault; (naipes) trump.
fama ['fama] sf fame; reputation. **es fama que** it is rumoured that. **famoso** adj famous.
familia [fa'milja] sf family; household. **familiar** adj family; familiar; simple. **familiar** sm friend; relative. **familiaridad** sf familiarity. **familiarizar** v familiarize.
fanático [fa'natiko] adj, sm fanatic(al). **fanatismo** sm fanaticism.
fanfarrón [fanfar'ron], **-ona** sm, sf bully; braggart. adj boastful. **fanfarronear** v brag.
fango ['fango] sm mire, mud. **fangal** sm quagmire. **fangoso** adj muddy.
fantasía [fanta'sia] sf fantasy; fancy; whim. **joyas de fantasía** imitation jewellery.
fantasma [fan'tasma] sm ghost. **fantasmal** adj ghostly.
fantástico [fan'tastiko] adj fantastic; wonderful; vain.
fantoche [fan'totʃe] sm puppet; foolish figure.
fardo ['farðo] sm bundle, pack; burden.
fariseo [fari'seo] sm Pharisee; (fam) hypocrite. **farisaico** adj (fam) hypocritical.

farmacia [far'maθja] *sf* chemist's shop. **farmacia de guardia** all-night chemist's. **farmacéutico** *adj* pharmaceutical.
faro ['faro] *sm* lighthouse; beacon; (*auto*) headlamp.
farol [fa'rol] *sm* lantern; lamp; street lamp; (*fam*) swank.
farsa ['farsa] *sf* farce; humbug. **farsante** *sm* charlatan.
fas [fas] *adv* (*fam*) **por fas o por nefas** rightly or wrongly; by hook or by crook.
fascinar [fasθi'nar] *v* fascinate. **fascinación** *sf* fascination. **fascinador** *adj* fascinating.
fascismo [fas'θismo] *sm* fascism. **fascista** *s, adj* fascist.
fase ['fase] *sf* phase.
fastidiar [fasti'ðjar] *v* annoy; bore; upset. ¡**no fastidies!** don't talk rot! **fastidio** *sm* annoyance; nuisance. **fastidioso** *adj* annoying; tedious.
fastuoso [fas'twoso] *adj* magnificent, grand, splendid.
fatal [fa'tal] *adj* fatal; inevitable; (*fam*) awful. **fatalidad** *sf* fatality; bad luck; destiny; disaster. **fatalista** *s(m+f)* fatalist. **fatalismo** *sm* fatalism.
fatigar [fati'gar] *v* weary; annoy. **fatigarse** *v* get tired. **fatiga** *sf* fatigue. **fatigas** *sf pl* troubles. **fatigoso** *adj* tiring; tiresome; laboured.
fatuidad [fatwi'ðað] *sf* fatuity; vanity.
fausto ['fausto] *adj* lucky; happy. *sm* display; pomp.
favor [fa'βor] *sm* favour; gift; grace; help. **a favor de** in favour of. **de favor** complimentary. **hacer el favor de** be so kind as to. **por favor** please. **favorable** *adj* favourable. **favorecer** *v* favour; help. **favoritismo** *sm* favouritism. **favorito, -a** *s, adj* favourite.
faz [faθ] *sf* face; obverse.
fe [fe] *sf* faith; faithfulness; trust; witness; certificate. **a fe de** on the word of. **dar fe de** certify. **prestar fe a** believe in.
fealdad [feal'ðað] *sf* ugliness.
febrero [fe'βrero] *sm* February.
febril [fe'βril] *adj* feverish; (*fig*) anxious.
fecundar [fekun'dar] *v* fertilize. **fecundación** *sf* fertilization. **fecundidad** *sf* fertility; fruitfulness. **fecundizar** *v* fertilize. **fecundo** *adj* fertile; fruitful; prolific. **fecundo en** full of.
fecha ['fetʃa] *sf* date. **hasta la fecha** to date. **fechar** *v* date.
federación [feðera'θjon] *sf* federation.

federal *adj* federal. **federalismo** *sm* federalism. **federar** *v* federate. **federativo** *adj* federative.
fehaciente [fea'θjente] *adj* (*jur*) authentic; irrefutable; reliable.
felicidad [feliθi'ðað] *sf* happiness; success. ¡**felicidades!** congratulations! **feliz** *adj* happy; fortunate.
felicitar [feliθi'tar] *v* congratulate. **felicitación** *sf* congratulation; compliment.
feligrés [feli'gres], **-esa** *sm, sf* parishioner. **feligresía** *sf* parish.
felino [fe'lino] *sm, adj* feline.
felpa ['felpa] *sf* plush; towelling; (*fam*) beating. **felpar** *v* cover with plush. **felpudo** *adj* plushy.
femenino [feme'nino] *adj* feminine; female. **feminismo** *sm* feminism. **feminista** *s, adj* feminist.
***fenecer** [fene'θer] *v* die; end. **fenecimiento** *sm* death; end.
fenómeno [fe'nomeno] *sm* phenomenon; freak. *adj* fantastic.
feo ['feo] *adj* ugly.
féretro ['feretro] *sm* coffin; bier.
feria ['ferja] *sf* fair; show; festival; holiday. **feria de muestras** trade fair.
fermentar [fermen'tar] *v* ferment; agitate. **fermentación** *sf* fermentation.
ferocidad [feroθi'ðað] *sf* ferocity; fury. **feroz** *adj* savage; wild; fierce.
férreo ['ferreo] *adj* iron; ferrous; (*fig*) stern. **ferretería** *sf* ironmonger's shop; hardware shop. **ferretero** *sm* ironmonger.
ferrocarril [ferrokar'ril] *sm* railway. **ferroviario** *adj* railway.
fértil ['fertil] *adj* fertile; abundant. **fertilidad** *sf* fertility. **fertilizante** *sm* fertilizer. **fertilizar** *v* fertilize.
ferviente [fer'βjente] *adj* fervent. **fervor** *sm* fervour. **fervoroso** *adj* fervid, ardent.
festejar [feste'xar] *v* entertain; feast; celebrate; woo. **festejo** *sm* entertainment; celebration; courtship.
festival [festi'βal] *sm* festival. *adj* festive. **festividad** *sf* festivity. **festivo** *adj* festive.
fétido ['fetiðo] *adj* fetid, stinking.
feto ['feto] *sm* foetus. **fetal** *adj* foetal.
feudal [feu'ðal] *adj* feudal. **feudalismo** *sm* feudalism.
fiado ['fjaðo] *sm* trust. **comprar al fiado** buy on credit. **fiador, -a** *sm, sf* guarantor. **fiador** *sm* press stud; pin; bracket; tumbler; safety catch. **salir fiador de** go bail for. **fianza** *sf* deposit; guarantor; surety.

libertad bajo fianza release on bail. **fiar** *v* guarantee; go bail for; sell on credit; trust. **no se fia** no credit given.

fiambre ['fjambre] *sm* cold cooked meat; (*coll*) corpse.

fiasco [fi'asko] *sm* fiasco; flop.

fibra ['fiβra] *sf* fibre; (*fig*) vigour. **fibra de vidrio** fibreglass.

ficción [fik'θjon] *sf* fiction; invention. **ficticio** *adj* fictitious.

ficha ['fitʃa] *sf* counter, chip; (*juegos*) piece; filing card.

fidedigno [fiδe'δigno] *adj* trustworthy. **fidelidad** *sf* loyalty, fidelity. **alta fidelidad** hi-fi.

fideos [fi'δeos] *sm pl* noodles.

fiebre ['fjeβre] *sf* fever. **tener fiebre** be feverish.

fiel [fjel] *adj* faithful; true; accurate; reliable; honourable. *sm* good Christian; inspector; scale pointer.

fieltro ['fjeltro] *sm* (*tejido*) felt; felt hat.

fiera ['fjera] *sf* wild beast; (*persona*) brute. **casa de fieras** menagerie. **fiero** *adj* wild.

fiesta ['fjesta] *sf* feast day; holiday; party. **estar de fiesta** be in high spirits. **hacer fiestas a uno** make a fuss over someone.

figurar [figu'rar] *v* shape; adorn; figure; pretend. **figurarse** *v* imagine, seem. **figura** *sf* shape; figure; face; (*música*) note; (*naipes*) court card; (*fig*) personality; (*fam*) unpleasant person. **figurado** *adj also* **figurativo** figurative.

fijar [fi'xar] *v* fasten; fix; stick; secure; draw up. **fijarse** *v* settle; take notice; look. **¡fijate!** just think! **¡fijamos en esto!** that's settled! **fijación** *sf* setting; fixing; sticking. **fijador** *sm* fixative. **fijeza** *sf* fixity; certainty; firmness. **fijo** *adj* fixed; permanent; steady.

fila ['fila] *sf* row; line; file; column. **en fila india** in single file.

filantropía [filantro'pia] *sf* philanthropy. **filantrópico** *adj* philanthropic. **filántropo, -a** *sm, sf* philanthropist.

filete [fi'lete] *sm* sirloin; fillet; (*ropa*) edging; (*tecn*) screw thread.

filiación [filja'θjon] *sf* filiation; relationship; association; personal description. **filial** [fi'ljal] *adj* filial. *sf* subsidiary.

filigrana [fili'grana] *sf* filigree work; watermark; delicate object.

filo ['filo] *sm* cutting edge; dividing line. **dar un filo a** sharpen. **por filo** exactly.

filón [fi'lon] *sm* (*mineral*) vein, seam; (*fam*) cushy job.

filosofía [filoso'fia] *sf* philosophy. **filosofar** *v* philosophize. **filósofo, -a** *sm, sf* philosopher. **filósofe** *adj* philosophic(al).

filtrar [fil'trar] *v* filter; strain. **filtrarse** *v* seep through. **filtración** *sf* filtration; (*fig*) leak. **filtrador** *sm* filter. **filtro** *sm* filter; strainer; love potion.

fin [fin] *sm* end; death; aim. **a fin de** in order to. **a fines de** at the end of. **al fin y al cabo** when all is said and done. **por fin** at last.

final [fi'nal] *adj* final. *sm* end. **al final de** at the end of. **finalidad** *sf* aim; purpose; finality. **finalizar** *v* finalize.

financiar [finan'θjar] *v* finance. **financiero** *sm* financier. **financiero** *adj* financial. **finanzas** *sf pl* finances.

finca ['finka] *sf* property; estate; farm.

fineza [fi'neθa] *sf* refinement; kindness; gift.

fingir [fin'xir] *v* pretend; sham. **fingirse** *v* pretend to be. **fingimiento** *sm* pretence; deceit.

Finlandia [fin'landja] *sf* Finland. **finlandés, -esa** *s, adj* Finn(ish).

fino ['fino] *adj* fine; refined; delicate; sharp; shrewd; elegant; precious; select; pure.

firmar [fir'mar] *v* sign. **firma** *sf* signature; (*negocio*) firm.

firme ['firme] *adj* firm; steady; rigid; hard; settled. *sm* firm ground; foundation; roadbed. **de firme** steadily. **oferta en firme** firm offer. **¡firmes!** (*mil*) attention! **firmeza** *sf* firmness; steadfastness.

fiscal [fis'kal] *adj* fiscal; tax. *sm* treasury official; (*jur*) public prosecutor. **fiscalizar** *v* control; criticize; pry into. **fisco** *sm* exchequer.

física ['fisika] *sf* physics. **físico** *sm* physician; physique. **físico** *adj* physical. **físico, -a** *sm, sf* physicist.

fisiología [fisjolo'xia] *sf* physiology. **fisiológico** *adj* physiological. **fisiólogo, -a** *sm, sf* physiologist.

fisionomía [fisjono'mia] *sf* physiognomy.

fisioterapia [fisjote'rapja] *sf* physiotherapy. **fisioterapeuta** *s(m+f)* physiotherapist.

flaco ['flako] *adj* thin; weak; (*memoria*) short. *sm* weak point. **flaquear** *v* weaken; slacken; flag; fail. **flaqueza** *sf* thinness; frailty.

flagrante [fla'grante] *adj* flagrant, blatant. **en flagrante** in the act.

flamante [fla'mante] *adj* blazing; brand-new.

flamenco[1] [fla'menko] *adj* Flemish; gypsy; flamenco.

flamenco[2] *sm* flamingo.

flanco ['flanko] *sm* flank. **coger por el flanco** catch unawares.

flauta ['flauta] *sf* flute. **flautista** *s(m+f)* flautist.

fleco ['fleko] *sm* fringe.

flecha ['fletʃa] *sf* arrow. **flecha de dirección** traffic indicator. **flecha de mar** squid. **subir en flecha** shoot up. **flechar** *v* shoot with an arrow; (*fam*) inspire love at first sight; (*fam*) rush. **flechero** *sm* archer.

fletar [fle'tar] *v* charter; hire. **fletamento** *also* **fletamiento** *sm* charter. **flete** *sm* freight.

flexible [flek'siβle] *adj* flexible. *sm* flex. **flexibilidad** *sf* flexibility. **flexión** *sf* flexing; (*gram*) inflexion.

flojo ['floxo] *adj* loose; weak; meagre; lazy. **flojear** *v* slacken; grow weak. **flojedad** *sf* slackness; weakness; carelessness.

flor [flor] *sf* flower. **a flor de tierra** at ground level. **echar flores** flatter. **en flor** in bloom. **flor de lis** lily. **floral** *adj* floral. **florar** *v* flower. **florecer** *v* flourish; flower. **florescerse** *v* mildew. **florería** *sf* florist's shop. **florero** *sm* vase. **florido** *adj* flowery; florid. **florista** *s(m+f)* florist.

flotar [flo'tar] *v* float; flutter; stream. **flota** *sf* fleet. **flotable** *adj* buoyant. **flotación** *sf* floatation; fluttering. **flotante** *adj* floating; flowing. **flote** *sm* floatation. **a flote** afloat.

fluctuar [fluk'twar] *v* fluctuate. **fluctuación** *sf* fluctuation.

***fluir** [flu'ir] *v* flow. **fluente** *adj* fluid; flowing. **fluidez** *sf* fluidity; fluency. **flúido** *sm, adj* fluid. **flujo** *sm* stream; flow; rising tide. **flujo de vientre** diarrhoea.

fluorescencia [fluores'θenθja] *sf* fluorescence. **fluorescente** *adj* fluorescent.

fluoruro [flwo'ruro] *sm* fluoride.

fobia ['foβja] *sf* phobia.

foca ['foka] *sf* (*zool*) seal.

foco ['foko] *sm* focus; centre; source. **focal** *adj* focal.

fogata [fo'gata] *sf* blaze; bonfire.

fogón [fo'gon] *sm* fireplace; stove.

fogoso [fo'goso] *adj* fiery; impetuous.

follaje [fo'ʎaxe] *sm* foliage; excessive decoration.

folletín [foʎe'tin] *sm* serial story; newspaper article. **folleto** *sm* pamphlet. **folletista** *s(m+f)* pamphleteer.

follón [fo'ʎon] *adj* lazy; arrogant; blustering; cowardly. **follón, -ona** *sm, sf* good-for-nothing; coward; loafer.

fomentar [fomen'tar] *v* foment; warm; incubate; (*fig*) encourage.

fonda ['fonda] *sf* inn, boarding house.

fondear [fonde'ar] *v* anchor; sound; search.

fondo ['fondo] *sm* bottom; depth; essence; capital; fund; character; disposition. **a fondo** thoroughly. **artículo de fondo** leading article. **en el fondo** at heart. **estar en fondos** be well off.

fontanero [fonta'nero] *sm* plumber. **fontanar** *sm* spring. **fontanería** *sf* plumbing.

forajido [fora'xiðo], **-a** *sm, sf* outlaw; fugitive.

forastero [foras'tero], **-a** *sm, sf* stranger; alien. *adj* strange.

forcejear [forθexe'ar] *v* struggle, strive. **forcej(e)o** *sm* struggle.

forense [fo'rense] *adj* forensic; strange.

forjar [for'xar] *v* forge; beat into shape; invent. **forja** *sf* forge; forging.

formal [for'mal] *adj* formal; regular; methodical; serious; steady; reliable. **formalidad** *sf* formality; seriousness; orderliness; propriety. **formalismo** *sm* formalism. **formalizar** *v* formulate; legalize. **formalizarse** *v* take seriously.

formar [for'mar] *v* form; educate; train. **formarse** *v* be trained; develop. **forma** *sf* form; shape; manner; convention; mould. **de forma que** so that. **tener buenas formas** be polite.

formidable [formi'ðaβle] *adj* formidable; tremendous. **¡formidable!** great!

fórmula ['formula] *sf* formula; (*med*) prescription.

fornicar [forni'kar] *v* fornicate. **fornicación** *sf* fornication. **fornicador, -a** *sm, sf* fornicator.

fornido [for'niðo] *adj* robust, husky.

foro ['foro] *sm* forum; legal profession; leasehold; (*teatro*) back.

forraje [for'raxe] *sm* fodder; forage; (*fam*) hodgepodge. **forrajeador** *sm* forager. **forrajear** *v* forage.

forrar [for'rar] *v* line; pad; put a cover on. forrarse *v* line one's pockets. forro *sm* lining; cover.

*fortalecer [fortale'θer] *v* strengthen; encourage. fortalecimiento *sm* fortification; strengthening. fortaleza *sf* fortress; fortitude; vigour. fortificación *sf* fortification. fortificar *v* fortify; strengthen. fortificarse *v* gain strength.

fortuito [for'twito] *adj* fortuitous; accidental.

fortuna [for'tuna] *sf* fortune, wealth; good luck; happiness; fate. por fortuna luckily. probar fortuna try one's luck.

*forzar [for'θar] *v* force; rape. forzadamente *adv* forcibly. forzado *adj* forced; hard; far-fetched. forzosamente *adv* unavoidably. forzoso *adj* unavoidable; necessary.

fosa ['fosa] *sf* grave; (*anat*) cavity.

fosfato [fos'fato] *sm* phosphate. fosforescencia *sf* phosphorescence. fosforescente *adj* phosphorescent. fósforo *sm* phosphorus; match.

fósil ['fosil] *sm* fossil. fosilizarse *v* fossilize.

foso ['foso] *sm* hole; ditch; (*teatro*) pit; (*mil*) trench.

fotocopiar [fotoko'pjar] *v* photocopy. fotocopia *sf* photocopy. fotocopiadora *sf* copier.

fotografía [fotogra'fia] *sf* photography; photograph. fotografiar *v* photograph. fotográfico *adj* photographic. fotógrafo, -a *sm, sf* photographer.

frac [frak] *sm* dress coat, tails *pl*.

fracasar [fraka'sar] *v* fail. fracaso *sm* failure.

fracción [frak'θjon] *sf* (*mat*) fraction; portion; fragment. fraccionamiento *sm* breaking-up. fraccionar *v* break up; divide.

fractura [frak'tura] *sf* (*med*) fracture. robo con fractura *sm* burglary. fracturar *v* fracture.

fragancia [fra'ganθja] *sf* fragrance. fragante *adj* fragrant; flagrant.

fragata [fra'gata] *sf* frigate.

frágil ['fraxil] *adj* fragile; weak. fragilidad *sf* fragility; weakness.

fragmento [frag'mento] *sm* fragment. fragmentar *v* fragment. fragmentario *adj* fragmentary.

fragor [fra'gor] *sm* row, noise. fragoroso *adj* deafening.

fraguar [fra'gwar] *v* (*hierro*) forge; concoct; (*cemento*) harden. fragua *sf* forge. fraguador, -a *sm, sf* schemer, plotter.

fraile ['fraile] *sm* friar, monk.

frambuesa [fram'bwesa] *sf* raspberry. frambueso *sm* raspberry bush.

Francia ['franθja] *sf* France. francés, -esa *sm, sf* Frenchman/woman. francés *sm, adj* French.

francmasón [frankma'son] *sm* freemason. francmasonería *sf* freemasonry.

franco ['franko] *adj* frank, open; generous; free; (*com*) post *or* duty free.

franela [fra'nela] *sf* flannel.

franja ['franxa] *sf* fringe; border. franjar *v* fringe, trim.

franquear [franke'ar] *v* free; clear; exempt; grant. franquearse *v* open one's heart. franqueo *sm* franking, stamping; postage.

franqueza [fran'keθa] *sf* frankness; generosity; freedom.

frasco ['frasko] *sm* flask.

frase ['frase] *sf* (*gram*) sentence; phrase; expression. frase hecha cliché. fraseología *sf* phraseology.

fraternal [frater'nal] *adj* fraternal. fraternidad *sf* fraternity. fraternizar *v* fraternize. fraterno *adj* fraternal.

fraude ['frauðe] *sm* fraud; deception. fraudulencia *sf* dishonesty. fraudulento *adj* fraudulent.

fray [fraj] *sm* (*rel*) friar, brother.

frecuencia [fre'kwenθja] *sf* frequency. con frecuencia often. frecuentar *v* frequent. frecuente *adj* frequent.

*fregar [fre'gar] *v* rub; scrub; wash up. fregadero *sm* sink. fregado *sm* rubbing; scrubbing; washing; (*fam*) intrigue. fregador, -a *sm, sf* dishwasher; *sm* sink, dishcloth.

*freír [fre'ir] *v* fry; (*fam*) bother. freidura *sf* frying. freiduría *sf* fish shop.

fréjol ['frexol] *sm* kidney bean.

frenar [fre'nar] *v* brake; check. freno *sm* brake; bridle. freno de mano handbrake. poner/soltar el freno apply/release the brake.

frenesí [frene'si] *sm* frenzy.

frente ['frente] *sm* front; face; façade. al frente at the head. de frente forward. en frente opposite. *sf* forehead; head. frente a frente face to face.

fresa ['fresa] *sf* strawberry.
fresco ['fresko] *adj* cool; fresh; new; calm. **frescura** *sf* coolness; freshness; fertility; calmness; indifference; (*fam*) insolence.
fresno ['fresno] *sm* (*bot*) ash.
fricción [frik'θjon] *sf* friction; (*med*) massage. **friccionar** *v* rub; massage.
frigidez [frixi'ðeθ] *sf* frigidity. **frígido** *adj* frigid. **frigorífico** *sm* refrigerating; refrigerator.
frijón [fri'xon] *sm* bean.
frío ['frio] *adj* cold; cool; indifferent. *sm* cold. **coger frío** catch cold. **tener frío** be cold. **frialdad** *sf* coldness; indifference; impotence.
friolera [frjo'lera] *sf* triviality, trifle.
frisar [fri'sar] *v* frizz, curl. **frisar en** (*edad*) border on.
frito ['frito] *V* **freír**. *adj* fried. **estar frito** be fed up. **patatas fritas** chips. **quedarse frito** (*fam*) nod off.
frívolo ['friβolo] *adj* frivolous. **frivolidad** *sf* frivolity.
frondoso [fron'doso] *adj* leafy; lush. **frondosidad** *sf* leafiness; lushness.
frontera [fron'tera] *sf* frontier.
frotar [fro'tar] *v* rub; (*cerilla*) strike. **frotación** *sf* rubbing; friction. **frote** *sm* rub.
fructífero [fruk'tifero] *adj* fruit-bearing; fruitful.
frugal [fru'gal] *adj* frugal. **frugalidad** *sf* frugality.
fruncir [frun'θir] *v* wrinkle; gather; pleat. **fruncir el ceño** frown. **fruncido** *adj* gathered; wrinkled. **fruncimiento** *sm* gathering; wrinkling.
frustrar [frus'trar] *v* frustrate. **frustrarse** *v* fail.
fruta ['fruta] *sf* fruit. **fruta de sartén** fritter. **frutal** *adj* fruit. **frutería** *sf* fruiterer's. **frutero, -a** *sm, sf* fruiterer. **fruto** *sm* fruit; product; result; offspring; profit. **frutos civiles** (*jur*) unearned income.
fue¹ ['fue] *V* **ir**.
fue² ['fue] *V* **ser**.
fuego ['fwego] *sm* fire; light; burner; heat; rash; passion; zeal. **apagar el fuego** put out the fire. **arma de fuego** firearm. **cocer a fuego lento/vivo** cook slowly/quickly. **fuegos artificiales** fireworks. **prender fuego a** set fire to.
fuelle ['fweʎe] *sm* bellows.
fuente ['fwente] *sf* fountain; spring; source; serving dish.

fuera ['fwera] *adv* outside; out; abroad. **aquí/allí fuera** out here/there. **estar fuera** be away. **¡fuera!** get out! **ir fuera** go outside. **por fuera** on the outside.
fuero ['fwero] *sm* law; code of laws; jurisdiction.
fuerte ['fwerte] *adj* strong; large; heavy; concentrated. **precio fuerte** full price. *sm* (*mil*) fort; stronghold. **fuerza** *sf* strength; loudness; power; effort; electric current. **fuerza pública** police force.
fugarse [fu'garse] *v* run away; escape. **fuga** *sf* escape; elopement; (*gas, etc.*) leak; (*música*) fugue. **ponerse en fuga** take flight. **fugaz** *adj* fleeting. **fugitivo, -a** *s, adj* fugitive.
fulano [fu'lano] *sm* so-and-so, what's-his-name. **fulana** *sf* whore.
fulcro ['fulkro] *sm* fulcrum.
fulgor [ful'gor] *sm* glow; sparkle; brilliance. **fulgente** *also* **fúlgido** *adj* brilliant. **fulgir** *v* shine. **fulgurante** *adj* shining; glowing. **fulgurar** *v* flash; shine; glow.
fulminante [fulmi'nante] *adj* explosive; thundering; (*med*) grave; (*med*) mortal. **fulminar** *v* strike (by lightning); thunder; explode.
fumar [fu'mar] *v* smoke. **prohibido fumar** no smoking. **fumarse** *v* squander. **fumada** *sf* (*de humo*) puff.
fumigar [fumi'gar] *v* fumigate. **fumigación** *sf* fumigation. **fumigador** *sm* fumigator.
funcionar [funθjo'nar] *v* function, work, go. **no funciona** out of order. **función** *sf* function; performance; party; duty. **funcional** *adj* functional. **funcionamiento** *sm* functioning; operation; performance. **funcionario, -a** *sm, sf* public official.
funda ['funda] *sf* case, cover. **funda de almohada** pillowcase.
fundar [fun'dar] *v* found; establish; base. **fundarse** *v* be based. **fundación** *sf* foundation. **fundado** *adj* founded; justified. **fundamental** *adj* fundamental. **fundamento** *sm* foundation; basis; reason; reliability.
fundir [fun'dir] *v* cast; smelt; melt; merge. **fundición** *sf* melting; smelting; foundry.
fúnebre ['funeβre] *adj* funeral; mournful. **coche fúnebre** hearse.
funesto [fu'nesto] *adj* ill-fated; disastrous; fatal.

furgón [fur'gon] *sm* wagon; truck; van. **furgón de cola** guard's van. **furgoneta** *sf* van. **furgoneta familiar** station wagon.

furia ['furja] *sf* fury; violence; frenzy. **furioso** *adj* furious; raging; enormous. **furor** *sm* fury; passion; fever. **con furor** furiously. **hacer furor** be all the rage.

furtivo [fur'tiβo] *adj* furtive; sly.

furúnculo [fu'runkulo] *sm* (*med*) boil.

fusible [fu'siβle] *adj* fusible. *sm* fuse.

fusil [fu'sil] *sm* rifle.

fusión [fu'sjon] *sf* fusion; melting; thawing. **fusionar** *v* fuse; merge. **fusionamiento** *sm* merger.

fuste ['fuste] *sm* wood; (*fig*) importance. **gente de fuste** people of consequence.

fútbol ['futβol] *sm* football. **futbolista** *sm* footballer.

fútil ['futil] *adj* futile, trivial. **futilidad** *sf* futility; triviality.

futuro [fu'turo] *sm*, *adj* future. **futurista** *adj* futuristic.

G

gabán [ga'βan] *sm* overcoat.

gabardina [gaβar'ðina] *sf* raincoat.

gabinete [gaβi'nete] *sm* (*pol*) cabinet; study; studio.

gacela [ga'θela] *sf* gazelle.

gaceta [ga'θeta] *sf* gazette; journal. **gacetero** *sm* journalist; **gacetilla** *sf* gossip column.

gachas ['gatʃas] *sf pl* porridge *sing*; slops *pl*.

gacho ['gatʃo] *adj* drooping.

gafas ['gafas] *sf pl* spectacles. **gafas de sol** sunglasses.

gajo ['gaxo] *sm* (*de horcas*) prong; (*de naranja*) segment; (*de frutas*) cluster.

gala ['gala] *sf* full dress; pomp; elegance. **de gala** in full dress. **hacer gala de** show off. **tener a gala** pride oneself in.

galán [ga'lan] *sm* gallant; suitor; handsome man; (*teatro*) leading man. **galante** *adj* gallant; flirtatious. **galantear** *v* woo; flirt; flatter. **galanteo** *sm* flirtation; courting; flattery. **galantería** *sf* gallantry; elegance.

galardón [galar'ðon] *sm* reward. **galardonar** *v* reward.

galeón [gale'on] *sm* galleon.

galera [ga'lera] *sf* (*mar*) galley; wagon.

galería [gale'ria] *sf* gallery.

Gales ['gales] *sm* Wales. **galés, -esa** *sm, sf* Welshman/woman. **galés** *sm* (*lengua*) Welsh.

galgo ['galgo] *sm* greyhound.

galón¹ [ga'lon] *sm* braid; (*mil*) stripe. **quitar los galones** demote.

galón² *sm* gallon.

galopar [galo'par] *v* gallop. **galope** *sm* gallop. **a medio galope** at a canter.

galvanizar [galβani'θar] *v* galvanize.

gallardo [ga'ʎarðo] *adj* elegant; gallant. **gallardía** *sf* elegance; charm. **gallardear** *v* behave gracefully.

galleta [ga'ʎeta] *sf* biscuit.

gallina [ga'ʎina] *sf* hen, chicken. **gallo** *sm* cock, rooster.

gamuza [ga'muθa] *sf* chamois; (*trapo*) duster.

gana ['gana] *sf* desire; wish; appetite. **de buena/mala gana** willingly/unwillingly. **tener ganas de** want to.

ganadería [ganaðe'ria] *sf* cattle-raising; cattle farm; cattle; breed. **ganadero, -a** *sm, sf* cattle-raiser; stockbreeder. **ganado** *sm* cattle; livestock.

ganar [ga'nar] *v* gain, get; earn; take; surpass. **ganar en peso** put on weight. **ganancia** *sf* profit. **ganancias** *sf pl* earnings; winnings.

gancho ['gantʃo] *sm* hook; (*fam*) decoy; (*fam*) pimp; (*fam*) sex appeal.

ganga ['ganga] *sf* (*fam*) bargain; (*fam*) cushy job.

gangrena [gan'grena] *sf* gangrene. **gangrenoso** *adj* gangrenous.

ganso ['ganso] *sm* goose, gander; (*fam*) boor. **gansada** *sf* (*fam*) stupid thing.

garabatear [garaβate'ar] *v* scribble; (*fam*) beat about the bush. **garabateo** *sm* scribbling. **garabato** *sm* scribble.

garaje [ga'raxe] *sm* garage.

garantizar [garanti'θar] *v* guarantee. **garantía** *sf* guarantee.

garbanzo [gar'βanθo] *sm* chickpea.

garbo ['garβo] *sm* grace; generosity; jauntiness. **garboso** *adj* graceful; generous; jaunty.

garganta [gar'ganta] *sf* throat. **tener buena garganta** have a good voice. **gargantear** *v* warble.

gargarizar [gargari'θar] *v* gargle. **gárgara** *sf* gargle.

gárgola ['gargola] *sf* gargoyle.

garita [ga'rita] *sf* sentry box; lavatory; porter's lodge. **garita de señales** signal-box.

garra ['garra] *sf* claw.

garrafa [gar'rafa] *sf* decanter.

garrapata [garra'pata] *sf* (*zool*) tick.

garrote [gar'rote] *sm* stick, club; garotte; (*med*) tourniquet. **dar garrote a** execute.

garza ['garθa] *sf* heron.

gas [gas] *sm* gas. **a todo gas** flat out.

gasa ['gasa] *sf* gauze.

gaseosa [gase'osa] *sf* lemonade.

gasolina [gaso'lina] *sf* gasoline. **gasolinera** *sf* gasoline pump.

gastar [gas'tar] *v* spend; waste; wear out or away. **gasto** *sm* expense; outlay. **gastos** *sm pl* expenses; costs. **gastos generales** overheads.

gatillo [ga'tiʎo] *sm* trigger; dentist's forceps; (*tecn*) jack.

gato ['gato] *sm* cat; (*tecn*) jack; (*fam*) hoard. **a gatas** on all fours. **gatear** *v* clamber; (*fam*) crawl. **gatearse** *v* scratch.

gavilán [gaβi'lan] *sm* hawk; (*pluma*) nib; (*bot*) thistle.

gavilla [ga'βiʎa] *sf* sheaf; bundle; (*fam*) gang.

gaviota [ga'βjota] *sf* seagull.

gazapo [ga'θapo] *sm* young rabbit; slip of the tongue; blunder; misprint.

gazpacho [gaθ'patʃo] *sm* cold vegetable soup.

gelatina [xela'tina] *sf* gelatine.

gelignita [xelig'nita] *sf* gelignite.

gemelo [xe'melo] *sm*, *adj* twin. *sm pl* cuff-links; opera glasses.

*****gemir** [xe'mir] *v* groan. **gemido** *sm* groan; wail.

genealogía [xenealo'xia] *sf* genealogy. **genealógico** *adj* genealogical. **árbol genealógico** family tree.

generación [xenera'θjon] *sf* generation. **generador** *sm* (*tecn*) generator. **generar** *v* generate.

generalizar [xenerali'θar] *v* generalize. **general** *adj* general. **general** *sm* (*mil*) general. **generalidad** *sf* majority. **generalización** *sf* generalization.

genérico [xe'neriko] *adj* generic. **género** *sm* race; kind; style; material; article; gender. **géneros** *sm pl* goods, merchandise *sing*.

generoso [xene'roso] *adj* generous. **generosidad** *sf* generosity.

genética [xe'netika] *sf* genetics. **genético** *adj* genetic.

genial [xe'njal] *adj* brilliant; outstanding; pleasant. **genio** *sm* genius; character. **estar de mal genio** be in a bad temper.

genital [xeni'tal] *adj* genital. **genitales** *sm pl* genitals.

gente ['xente] *sf* people. **gente baja** lower classes. **gente menuda** children.

gentil [xen'til] *adj* charming; genteel; civil; gentile; heathen. *sm* gentile; heathen; pagan. **gentileza** *sf* grace; elegance; gentility; civility.

gentío [xen'tio] *sm* crowd.

genuino [xe'nwino] *adj* genuine.

geografía [xeogra'fia] *sf* geography. **geográfico** *adj* geographic(al). **geógrafo** *sm* geographer.

geología [xeolo'xia] *sf* geology. **geológico** *adj* geological. **geólogo** *sm* geologist.

geometría [xeome'tria] *sf* geometry. **geométrico** *adj* geometric.

geranio [xe'ranjo] *sm* geranium.

gerencia [xe'renθa] *sf* management. **gerente** *sm* manager.

germinar [xermi'nar] *v* germinate. **germen** *sm* germ.

gesticular [xestiku'lar] *v* gesticulate. **gesticulación** *sf* gesticulation; grimace.

gestión [xes'tjon] *sf* arrangement; measure; management. **gestionar** *v* negotiate; get hold of.

gesto ['xesto] *sm* expression; countenance; gesture.

geyser ['xejser] *sm* geyser.

gigante [xi'gante] *sm* giant. *adj* gigantic.

gimnasia [xim'nasja] *sf* gymnastics. **gimnasio** *sm* gymnasium. **gimnasta** *s(m+f)* gymnast.

ginebra [xi'neβra] *sf* gin.

ginecología [xinekolo'xia] *sf* gynaecology. **ginecólogo, -a** *sm*, *sf* gynaecologist.

gira ['xira] *sf* tour; excursion; picnic.

giralda [xi'ralδa] *sf* weathercock.

girar [xi'rar] *v* turn; swivel; send; (*com*) draw. **girar dinero** remit money. **giratorio** *adj* gyratory. **puerta giratoria** revolving door. **giro** *sm* turn; (*com*) draft. **giro postal** *sm* postal order; money order.

girasol [xira'sol] *sm* sunflower.

gitano [xi'tano], **-a** *s*, *adj* gypsy.

glacial [gla'θjal] *adj* freezing.
glaciar [gla'θjar] *sm* glacier.
gladio ['glaðjo] *sm* (*bot*) gladiolus.
glándula ['glandula] *sf* gland. **glandular** *adj* glandular.
glicerina [gliθe'rina] *sf* glycerine.
global [glo'βal] *adj* global; comprehensive; total. **globo** *sm* globe, sphere. **en globo** all in all. **globo ocular** eyeball. **globular** *adj* globular. **glóbulo** *sm* globule.
gloriarse [glo'rjarse] *v* boast; glory. **gloria** *sf* glory; (*culin*) custard tart. **glorificación** *sf* glorification. **glorificar** *v* glorify. **glorioso** *adj* glorious; conceited.
glosar [glo'sar] *v* annotate. **glosa** *sf* annotation. **glosario** *sm* glossary.
glotón [glo'ton], **-ona** *sm, sf* glutton. *adj* gluttonous.
glucosa [glu'kosa] *sf* glucose.
*gobernar [goβer'nar] *v* govern; control; manage. **gobernación** *sf* government. **gobernador** *sm* governor. **gobierno** *sm* (*pol*) government; guidance.
goce ['goθe] *sm* enjoyment.
gol [gol] *sm* (*deporte*) goal. **golear** *v* score a goal.
golfo ['golfo] *sm* gulf; (*geog*) bay; guttersnipe.
golondrina [golon'drina] *sf* (*zool*) swallow.
golosina [golo'sina] *sf* sweet; delicacy; (*fig*) desire; (*fig*) greed. **goloso** *adj* sweettoothed; appetizing; greedy.
golpear [golpe'ar] *v* strike, hit. **golpe** *sm* blow; coup; large amount; attack. **golpe de estado** coup d'état. **golpe de gracia** coup de grâce.
goma ['goma] *sf* rubber; gum; rubber band; elastic. **goma de borrar** eraser. **goma espuma** foam rubber.
gordo ['gorðo] *sm, adj* fat. **gordura** *sf* fatness, obesity.
gorila [go'rila] *sf* gorilla.
gorjear [gorxe'ar] *v* chirp, trill; twitter. **gorjeo** *sm* chirping; trilling; twittering.
gorra ['gorra] *sf* peaked cap; bonnet; (*fam*) sponger. **de gorra** free. **vivir de gorra** sponge.
gorrión [gor'rjon] *sf* sparrow.
gorro ['gorro] *sm* cap.
gotear [gote'ar] *v* drip; trickle; leak. **gota** *sf* drop. **gotera** *sf* leak; gutter. **goteras** *sf pl* (*fig*) aches and pains.
gótico ['gotiko] *adj* Gothic.

gozar [go'θar] *v* enjoy; possess. **gozarse** *v* rejoice. **gozo** *sm* joy. **gozoso** *adj* joyful.
gozne ['goθne] *sm* hinge.
grabar [gra'βar] *v* engrave; carve; imprint; record. **grabado** *sm* engraving; picture; recording. **grabador de cinta** *sm* tape recorder.
gracia ['graθja] *sf* grace; favour; charm; joke. **me hace gracia** it amuses me. **tener gracia** be amusing.
gracias ['graθjas] *sf pl* thanks. **acción de gracias** thanksgiving. **dar gracias** thank. **muchas gracias** many thanks.
gracioso [gra'θjoso] *adj* graceful; amusing; gracious. *sm* (*teatro*) buffoon.
grada ['graða] *sf* step; stair. **gradería** *sf* flight of steps; row of seats.
grado ['graðo] *sm* grade; degree; rank; pleasure. **de grado** willingly. **graduación** *sf* graduation. **gradual** *adj* gradual. **graduando, -a** *sm, sf* undergraduate. **graduar** *v* graduate; award a degree to. **graduarse** *v* gain a degree.
gráfico ['grafiko] *adj* graphic. *sm* graph; diagram.
grajo ['graxo] *sm* (*zool*) rook.
gramática [gra'matika] *sf* grammar. **gramático** *adj* grammatical.
gramo ['gramo] *sm* gramme.
gramófono [gra'mofono] *sm* gramophone.
gran [gran] *V* grande.
grana[1] ['grana] *sf* small seed; seeding time.
grana[2] *sf, adj* scarlet.
granada [gra'naða] *sf* pomegranate.
grande ['grande] *adj also* gran large, big, great. **grandeza** *sf* greatness; size. **grandioso** *adj* grandiose; grand.
granel [gra'nel] *adv* **a granel** in bulk.
granero [gra'nero] *sm* granary.
granito [gra'nito] *sm* granite.
granizar [grani'θar] *v* hail. **granizo** *sm* hail.
granja ['granxa] *sf* farm. **granja avícola** poultry farm. **granjero, -a** *sm, sf* farmer.
grano ['grano] *sm* grain; bean; pimple. **ir al grano** come to the point. **granoso** *adj* granular.
grapa ['grapa] *sf* clamp; staple; dowel.
grasa ['grasa] *sf* grease; fat. **grasera** *sf* dripping pan. **grasiento** *adj* greasy; oily; filthy. **graso** *adj* fatty.
gratificar [gratifi'kar] *v* gratify; reward; tip. **gratificación** *sf* reward; gratuity; bonus; gratification.

gratis ['gratis] *adv* free.

gratitud [grati'tuð] *sf* gratitude.

grato ['grato] *adj* pleasing; pleasant; welcome. **me es grato** ... I am pleased ....

gratuito [gra'twito] *adj* free; gratuitous.

gravamen [gra'βamen] *sm* charge; obligation; burden; tax. **gravar** *v* burden; oppress. **gravar impuestos a** *or* **sobre** tax.

grave ['graβe] *adj* grave, serious; weighty. **ponerse grave** become gravely ill. **gravedad** *sf* gravity, seriousness.

gravitar [graβi'tar] *v* gravitate. **gravitación** *sf* gravitation, gravity.

graznar [graθ'nar] *v* croak; cackle. **graznido** *sm* croak; cackle.

Grecia ['greθja] *sf* Greece. **griego** *s, adj* Greek. **griego** *sm* (*idioma*) Greek; (*fam*) gibberish.

greda ['greða] *sf* clay. **gredoso** *adj* clayey.

gregario [gre'garjo] *adj* gregarious.

gremio ['gremjo] *sm* guild; fraternity; union. **gremio obrero** trade union.

greña ['grenja] *sf* tangled hair. **andar a la greña** (*fam*) squabble.

grey [grej] *sf* congregation; flock, herd.

grieta ['grjeta] *sf* crack.

grifo ['grifo] *sm* tap. **al grifo** on draught.

grillo ['griʎo] *sm* (*zool*) cricket. **grillos** *sm pl* shackles, fetters.

gringo ['gringo], **-a** *sm, sf* (*fam*) foreigner.

gripe ['gripe] *sf* (*med*) influenza, flu.

gris [gris] *adj* grey.

gritar [gri'tar] *v* shout, scream, yell. **grito** *sm* shout, scream, yell. **el último grito** the latest fashion.

grosella [gro'seʎa] *sf* currant. **grosella espinosa/negra/roja** gooseberry/ blackcurrant/redcurrant.

grosería [grose'ria] *sf* vulgarity. **grosero** *adj* vulgar.

grotesco [gro'tesko] *adj* grotesque; absurd.

grúa ['grua] *sf* (*tecn*) crane.

grueso [gru'eso] *adj* thick; large; heavy; dull; slow; coarse. *sm* thickness; heaviness. **gruesa** *sf* (*número*) gross.

grulla ['gruʎa] *sf* (*zool*) crane.

grumete [gru'mete] *sm* cabin boy.

*gruñir [gru'nir] *v* growl. **gruñido** *sm* growl.

grupo ['grupo] *sm* group. **grupo sanguíneo** blood group.

gruta ['gruta] *sf* grotto; cave.

guadaña [gwa'ðana] *sf* scythe.

guante ['gwante] *sm* glove. **guantear** *v* slap.

guapo ['gwapo] *adj* handsome; pretty; flashy. *sm* boaster; bully; (*fam*) lover.

guardar [gwar'ðar] *v* guard; keep; protect; respect. **guarda** *s(m+f)* guard; keeper. **guarda** *sf* custody; protection.

guardacostas *sm invar* coastguard.

guardafuego *sm* hearth fender.

guardapolvo *sm* dust-cover. **guardarropa** *sm* wardrobe; cloakroom. **guardia** *sf* guard; police force. **guardia civil** Civil Guard.

guardián [gwar'ðjan], **-a** *sm, sf* guardian; keeper; caretaker.

guardilla [gwar'ðiʎa] *sf* attic.

guarida [gwa'riða] *sf* den, lair; haunt; shelter.

*guarnecer [gwarne'θer] *v* equip; provide; furnish; adorn; garnish; plaster. **guarnición** *sf* adornment; provision; (*mil*) garrison. **guarnicionar** *v* garrison.

guasa ['gwasa] *sf* joke. **sin guasa** seriously. **guasearse** *v* (*fam*) joke; tease. **guaseo** *sm* leg-pull.

gubernamental [guβernamen'tal] *adj* governmental.

guerra ['gerra] *sf* war. **guerra mundial** world war. **guerrear** *v* wage war. **guerrero, -a** *sm, sf* warrior. **guerrilla** *sf* guerrilla band; guerrilla warfare. **guerrillero** *sm* guerrilla fighter.

guiar [gi'ar] *v* guide; steer; drive. **guía** *sm* (*persona*) guide. **guía** *sf* (*libro*) guide, guidebook. **guía sonora** soundtrack.

guija ['gixa] *sf* pebble.

guillotina [giʎo'tina] *sf* guillotine. **guillotinar** *v* guillotine.

guiñar [gi'nar] *v* wink. **guiño** *sm* wink.

guión [gi'on] *sm* hyphen; film script; outline; subtitle.

guisa ['gisa] *sf* way, manner. **a guisa de** like. **de tal guisa** in such a manner.

guisado [gi'saðo] *sm* stew. **guisar** *v* cook; prepare. **guiso** *sm* cooked dish; stew.

guisante [gi'sante] *sm* pea. **guisante de olor** sweet pea.

guitarra [gi'tarra] *sf* guitar. **guitarrista** *s(m+f)* guitarist.

gula ['gula] *sf* greed.

gusano [gu'sano] *sm* worm; maggot; caterpillar. **gusano de seda** silkworm.

gustar [gus'tar] *v* please; like; taste; try. **gustar de** enjoy. **¡así me gusta!** that's what I like! **gusto** *sm* pleasure; fancy;

style; taste; flavour. **de buen/mal gusto**
in good/bad taste. **con mucho gusto** with
great pleasure. **¡mucho gusto!** how do
you do? **gustoso** *adj* tasty; pleasant.
gutural [gutu'ral] *adj* guttural.

H

haba ['aβa] *sf* broad bean; swelling;
bruise.
***haber** [a'βer] *v* have. **haber de** have to.
hay que one must. **no hay de que** don't
mention it. **haberes** *sm pl* assets; property *sing*; income *sing*.
habichuela [aβi'tʃwela] *sf* bean. **habichuela verde** French bean.
hábil ['aβil] *adj* clever; able. **habilidad** *sf*
cleverness; ability.
habilitar [aβili'tar] *v* qualify; enable.
habilitación *sf* qualification.
habitar [aβi'tar] *v* inhabit. **habitable** *adj*
habitable. **habitación** *sf* habitation;
room; lodgings *pl*. **habitante** *s(m+f)*
inhabitant.
hábito ['aβito] *sm* habit; attire. **habitual**
adj habitual. **habituar** *v* accustom.
habituarse *v* become accustomed to.
hablar [a'βlar] *v* speak, talk. **¿quién
habla?** (*al teléfono*) who's speaking? **se
habla español** Spanish spoken. **habla** *sf*
language; speech. **hablador, -a** *sm, sf*
chatterbox. **hablilla** *sf* rumour; gossip.
hacedero [aθe'ðero] *adj* feasible. **hacedor,
-a** *sm, sf* creator.
hacendado [aθen'daðo] *sm* landowner.
***hacer** [a'θer] *v* do; make; perform; pro-
duce. **hacer calor/frío** be hot/cold. **hacer
fiesta** take a holiday. **hace mucho tiempo
que** it is a long time since. **hacer para**
make an effort to. **hacerse** *v* become.
hacia ['aθja] *prep* towards; about. **hacia
atrás** backwards.
hacienda [a'θjenda] *sf* estate; ranch.
hacina [a'θina] *sf* stack, rick. **hacinar** *v*
stack; amass.
hacha ['atʃa] *sf* axe.
hada ['aða] *sf* fairy. **hada madrina** fairy
godmother. **cuento de hadas** *sm* fairy
tale.
hado ['aðo] *sm* fate.

halagar [ala'gar] *v* flatter. **halago** *sm*
flattery. **halagüeño** *adj* flattering.
halcón [al'kon] *sm* falcon. **halconería** *sf*
falconry.
hálito ['alito] *sm* breath.
hallar [a'ʎar] *v* find; find out. **hallarse** *v*
be situated. **hallarse bien con** be pleased
with. **hallazgo** *sm* discovery.
hamaca [a'maka] *sf* hammock.
hambre ['ambre] *sf* hunger; starvation.
pasar hambre go hungry. **tener hambre**
be hungry. **hambriento** *adj* hungry.
hamburguesa [ambur'gesa] *sf* hamburger.
haragán [ara'gan] *adj* lazy. **haraganear** *v*
idle.
harapiento [ara'pjento] *adj* ragged.
harapo *sm* rag.
harina [a'rina] *sf* flour. **harinero** *adj also*
harinoso floury.
hartar [ar'tar] *v* stuff; gorge; weary; bore.
harto *adj* satiated. **hartura** *sf* satiety.
hasta ['asta] *prep* until; up to; as much
as; as far as. *adv* even. **hasta ahora** up to
now. **hasta aquí** so far. **hasta luego**
(*interj*) so long, good-bye. **hasta que**
until.
hastío [as'tio] *sm* disgust; weariness. **has-
tiar** *v* disgust; bore.
hato ['ato] *sm* herd; flock; gang.
hay [aj] there is; there are. **hay que** one
must.
haya ['aja] *sf* beech.
haz¹ [aθ] *sm* bunch; bundle; sheaf.
haz² *sf* face; surface. **a sobre haz** on the
surface.
hazaña [a'θaɲa] *sf* deed; feat; exploit.
hazmerreír [aθmerre'ir] *sm* laughing-
stock.
hebilla [e'βiʎa] *sf* buckle; clasp.
hebra ['eβra] *sf* fibre; thread; (*de madera*)
grain.
hebreo [e'βreo] *s, adj* Hebrew. *sm*
(*lengua*) Hebrew.
hechicero [etʃi'θero] *sm* sorcerer; wizard.
hechicera *sf* sorceress; witch. **hechicería**
sf witchcraft; sorcery; enchantment.
hechizar *v* bewitch. **hechizo** *sm* magic
spell.
hecho ['etʃo] *V* hacer. *adj* mature;
finished; cooked. **hecho y derecho** in
every sense of the word. **muy/poco
hecho** overdone/underdone. *sm* fact;
deed; feat; matter; event. **de hecho** in
fact. **hechura** *sf* making; making-up;
shape; workmanship.

hediondo [e'ðjondo] adj stinking; repulsive. heder v stink; vex. hedor sm stink.

*helar [e'lar] v freeze. helada sf frost. helado sm ice cream.

helecho [e'letʃo] sm fern.

hélice ['eliθe] sf helix; spiral; propeller.

helicóptero [eli'koptero] sm helicopter.

hembra ['embra] sf female; clasp; socket; (de tornillo) nut.

hemisferio [emis'ferjo] sm hemisphere. hemisférico adj hemispheric, hemispherical.

hemorragia [emor'raxja] sf haemorrhage.

hemorroides [emor'rojðes] sf pl haemorrhoids.

*henchirse [en'tʃirse] v swell up; stuff oneself. henchidura sf filling.

*hender [en'der] v split. hendidura sf split; crack.

heno ['eno] sm hay.

heraldo [e'raldo] sm herald. heráldica sf heraldry. adj heraldic.

herbaje [er'βaxe] sm pasture. herbario adj herbal. herbicida sm weedkiller. herbívoro, -a sm, sf herbivore. herbívoro adj herbivorous. herbolario sm herbalist. herboso adj grassy.

heredar [ere'ðar] v inherit. heredad sf estate. heredero, -a sm, sf heir/heiress. hereditario adj hereditary.

hereje [e'rexe] s(m+f) heretic. herejía sf heresy. herético adj heretic.

herencia [e'renθja] sf inheritance; heredity.

*herir [e'rir] v wound. herida sf wound. herido sm casualty.

hermano [er'mano] sm brother. hermana sf sister. hermandad sf brotherhood. hermanastro, -a sm, sf stepbrother/stepsister.

hermético [er'metiko] adj hermetic.

hermoso [er'moso] adj beautiful; handsome. hermosura sf beauty; handsomeness.

héroe ['eroe] sm hero. heroico adj heroic. heroína sf heroine. heroísmo sm heroism.

heroína [ero'ina] sf heroin.

herramienta [erra'mjenta] sf tool; implement.

*herrar [er'rar] v (caballo) shoe. herradura sf horseshoe. camino de herradura bridle path. herrería sf smithy, forge. herrero sm blacksmith.

herrumbre [er'rumbre] sf rust. herrumbrar v rust. herrumbroso adj rusty.

*hervir [er'βir] v boil. hervidero sm boiling; bubbling; (fig) swarm, crowd; hotbed. hervidor sm kettle. hervor sm boiling; fervour.

hesitar [esi'tar] v hesitate. hesitación sf hesitation.

hez [eθ] sf, pl heces dregs pl; scum.

hibernar [iβer'nar] v hibernate. hibernación sf hibernation.

híbrido ['iβriðo] sm, adj hybrid. hibridación sf hybridization. hibridizar v hybridize.

hidalgo [i'ðalgo] sm nobleman. adj noble. hidalguía sf nobility.

hidráulico [i'ðrauliko] adj hydraulic. freno hidráulico sm hydraulic brake.

hidroala [iðro'ala] sf hovercraft.

hidroavión [iðroa'βjon] sm seaplane.

hidroeléctrico [iðroe'lektriko] adj hydroelectric.

hidrofobia [iðro'foβja] sf hydrophobia.

hidrógeno [i'ðroxeno] sm hydrogen.

hidropesía [idrope'sia] sf dropsy.

hiedra ['jeðra] sf ivy.

hielo ['jelo] sm ice.

hiena ['jena] sf hyena.

hierba ['jerβa] sf grass; herb. mala hierba weed.

hierbabuena [jerβa'βwena] sf mint.

hierro ['jerro] sm iron. hierro colado cast iron. hierro forjado wrought iron.

hígado ['igaðo] sm liver.

higiene [i'xjene] sf hygiene. higiénico adj hygienic. paños higiénicos sm pl sanitary towels.

higo ['igo] sm fig. higuera sf fig-tree.

hijo ['ixo] sm son. hijos sm pl children. hija sf daughter. hijo/hija político, -a son/daughter-in-law.

hilar [i'lar] v spin; infer. hiladora sf spinning wheel. hilandería sf spinning. hilandero, -a sm, sf (persona) spinner.

hilarante [ila'rante] adj hilarious. hilaridad sf hilarity.

hilera [i'lera] sf row; rank; file.

hilo ['ilo] sm thread; yarn; wire. hilo de coser sewing thread. hilo de perlas string of pearls. telegrafía sin hilos sf wireless telegraphy.

himno ['imno] sm hymn; anthem. himno nacional national anthem. himnario sm hymn book.

hincapié [inka'pje] sm foothold; emphasis. hacer hincapié en insist on.

hincar [in'kar] v drive in; sink; plunge. **hincarse de rodillas** kneel down.

hinchar [in'tʃar] v inflate; swell. **hincharse** v puff up; (fam) become bigheaded.

hinchazón sm (med) swelling; arrogance.

hinojo [i'noxo] sm fennel. **hinojos** sm pl knees.

hípico ['ipiko] adj equine. **hipismo** sm show-jumping. **hipódromo** sm race course.

hipnosis [ip'nosis] sm hypnosis. **hipnótico** adj hypnotic. **hipnotismo** sm hypnotism. **hipnotizador, -a** sm, sf hypnotist. **hipnotizar** v hypnotize.

hipo ['ipo] sm hiccup; longing; grudge. **tener hipo** have the hiccups.

hipocondría [ipokon'dria] sf hypochondria. **hipocondríaco, -a** sm, sf hypochondriac.

hipocresía [ipokre'sia] sf hypocrisy. **hipócrita** adj hypocritical. **hipócrita** s(m+f) hypocrite.

hipodérmico [ipo'ðermiko] adj hypodermic.

hipopótamo [ipo'potamo] sm hippopotamus.

hipotecar [ipote'kar] v mortgage. **hipoteca** sf mortgage.

hipótesis [i'potesis] sf hypothesis. **hipotético** adj hypothetical.

hirsuto [ir'suto] adj hairy.

hirviente [ir'βjente] adj boiling.

hispánico [is'paniko] adj Hispanic.

hispanoamericano [ispanoameri'kano] s, adj Spanish American.

histerectomía [isterekto'mia] sf hysterectomy.

histeria [i'sterja] sf hysteria. **histérico** adj hysterical.

historia [is'torja] sf history; story; fib; gossip; trouble. **armar historias** (fam) make trouble. **historiador, -a** sm, sf historian. **histórico** adj historical; historic.

hogar [o'gar] sm hearth; home.

hoguera [o'gera] sf bonfire.

hoja ['oxa] sf leaf; petal; sheet; layer; flake; blade; newspaper; (formulario) form. **hoja de afeitar** razor blade. **hoja de paga** payroll.

hojalata [oxa'lata] sf tinplate; tin.

hojear [oxe'ar] v leaf through.

Holanda [o'landa] sf Holland. **holandés** adj Dutch. **holandés** sm Dutchman; (lengua) Dutch. **holandesa** sf Dutchwoman.

*holgar [ol'gar] v rest; be idle; be unnecessary. **holgarse** v enjoy oneself. **holgazán** adj idle. **holgazanear** v idle. **holgura** sf roominess; comfort.

*hollar [o'ʎar] v tread; trample down.

hollín [o'ʎin] sm soot. **hollimiento** adj sooty.

hombre ['ombre] sm man. **hombre bueno** arbiter. **hombre de negocios** businessman. **¡hombre!** good heavens, man! **hombrear** v act the man.

hombro ['ombro] sm (anat) shoulder. **echarse al hombro** shoulder.

homenaje [ome'naxe] sm homage. **homenajear** v pay homage to.

homeópata [ome'opata] s(m+f) homeopath. adj homeopathic. **homeopatía** sf homeopathy.

homicida [omi'θiða] s(m+f) murderer. adj homicidal. **homicidio** sm murder.

homogéneo [omo'xeneo] adj homogeneous. **homogeneidad** sf homogeneity, homogeneousness.

homólogo [o'mologo] adj corresponding; synonymous.

honda ['onda] sf catapult; sling.

hondo ['ondo] adj deep. sm bottom. **hondonada** sf depression; hollow. **hondura** sf depth.

honesto [o'nesto] adj honest; modest; chaste. **honestidad** sf honesty; modesty; chastity.

hongo ['ongo] sm mushroom; bowler hat.

honor [o'nor] sm honour. **honorable** adj honourable. **honorario** adj honorary. **honorario** sm honorarium. **honra** sf honour; reputation; dignity; respect. **tener a mucha honra** be very proud of. **honradez** sf honesty; uprightness. **honrado** adj honest; upright. **honrar** v honour; be a credit to. **honrarse** v be honoured. **honroso** adj honourable.

hora ['ora] sf hour. **pedir hora** make an appointment. **¿qué hora es?** what time is it? **horario** adj hour. **horario** sm hours of work; timetable.

horca ['orka] sf gallows pl; pitchfork. **horcado** adj forked.

horda ['orða] sf horde.

horizonte [ori'θonte] sm horizon. **horizontal** adj horizontal.

hormiga [or'miga] sf ant; itch. **hormigoso** adj ant-eaten; itchy. **hormiguear** v swarm; creep; itch. **hormigueo** sm itching; swarming. **hormiguero** *sm* anthill; swarm.

hormigón [ormi'gon] *sm* concrete. **hormigón armado** reinforced concrete.

hormona [or'mona] *sf* hormone.

hornero [or'nero], **-a** *sm, sf* baker. **hornear** *v* bake. **hornería** *sf* baking.

horno ['orno] *sm* oven; furnace. **hornillo** *sm* stove, cooker; gas or electric ring.

horóscopo [o'roskopo] *sm* horoscope.

horquilla [or'kiʎa] *sf* pitchfork; hairpin; rowlock.

horrible [or'riβle] *adj* horrible.

horror [or'ror] *sm* horror. **horrendo** *adj* hideous; horrible. **horrífico** *adj* horrific, horrifying. **horrorizar** *v* horrify. **horroroso** *adj* horrid, horrible.

hortaliza [orta'liθa] *sf* green vegetable. **hortelano, -a** *sm, sf* gardener. **hortelano** *adj* market-gardening.

horticultura [ortikul'tura] *sf* horticulture. **hortícula** *adj* horticultural.

hosco ['osko] *adj* grim; surly; gloomy. **hoscoso** *adj* bristly.

hospedar [ospe'ðar] *v* lodge, put up. **hospedarse** *v* have lodgings. **hospedaje** *sf* lodging. **hospedería** *sf* inn, hostelry.

hospicio [os'piθjo] *sm* orphanage; poorhouse.

hospital [ospi'tal] *sm* hospital. **hospitalario** *adj* hospitable. **hospitalidad** *sf* hospitality. **hospitalización** *sf* hospitalization. **hospitalizar** *v* hospitalize.

hostelero [oste'lero], **-a** *sm, sf* innkeeper. **hostería** *sf* inn.

hostia ['ostja] *sf* (*rel*) wafer; (*fam*) bashing.

hostigar [osti'gar] *v* whip; harass; molest. **hostigamiento** *sm* harassing; molesting; lashing. **hostigo** *sm* lash.

hostil [os'til] *adj* hostile. **hostilidad** *sf* hostility.

hotel [o'tel] *sm* hotel; villa. **hotelería** *sf* hotel-keeping. **hotelero, -a** *sm, sf* hotelkeeper.

hoy [oj] *adv* today; now. **de hoy en adelante** from now on. **hoy en día** nowadays. **hoy por hoy** for the time being.

hoya ['oja] *sf* hole; valley.

hoyo ['ojo] *sm* pit; hole; dent; grave. **hoyuelo** *sm* small hole; dimple.

hoz [oθ] *sf* sickle; ravine.

hueco ['weko] *adj* hollow; empty; vain; resonant. *sm* hollow; gap; cavity; vacancy.

huelga ['welga] *sf* (*de obreros*) strike. **huelgista** *s*(*m+f*) striker.

huelgo ['welgo] *sm* breath; (*tecn*) play.

huella ['weʎa] *sf* footprint; tread; impression. **huella digital** fingerprint. **huella de sonido** soundtrack.

huérfano ['werfano], **-a** *sm, sf* orphan.

huerta ['werta] *sf* vegetable garden; orchard; irrigated land. **huerto** *sm* orchard; kitchen garden.

hueso ['weso] *sm* bone; stone; pip; (*fam*) drudgery. **dar con sus huesos** end up. **estar en los huesos** be very thin. **huesudo** *adj* bony.

huésped ['wespeð], **-a** *sm, sf* guest; lodger. **casa de huéspedes** boarding house.

hueva ['weβa] *sf* roe. **huevas** *sf pl* spawn.

huevo ['weβo] *sm* egg. **huevo de Pascua** Easter egg. **huevo duro** hard-boiled egg. **huevo escalfado** poached egg. **huevo frito** fried egg. **huevo pasado por agua** soft-boiled egg. **huevo revuelto** scrambled egg.

*****huir** [wir] *v* flee. **huida** *sf* flight; escape.

hule[1] ['ule] *sm* oilskin; rubber.

hule[2] *sm* (*cornada*) goring.

hulla ['uʎa] *sf* coal.

humano [u'mano] *adj* human; humane. *sm* human being. **humanar** *v* humanize. **humanidad** *sf* humanity. **humanismo** *sm* humanism. **humanista** *s*(*m+f*) humanist. **humanitario, -a** *s, adj* humanitarian.

húmedo ['umeðo] *adj* humid, damp, moist. **humedad** *sf* humidity, dampness. **humedecer** *v* dampen, moisten.

humillar [umi'ʎar] *v* humiliate; shame. **humildad** *sf* humility. **humilde** *adj* humble. **humillación** *sf* humiliation.

humo ['umo] *sm* smoke; fumes *pl*. **vender humos** boast. **humear** *v* smoke. **humoso** *adj* smoky.

humor [u'mor] *sm* humour; temper; mood. **buen/mal humor** good/bad temper. **humorada** *sf* witticism. **humorista** *s*(*m+f*) humorist. **humorístico** *adj* humorous.

hundir [un'dir] *v* sink; drive in; crush. **hundirse** *v* go under; collapse. **hundimiento** *sm* sinking; collapse.

Hungría [un'gria] *sf* Hungary. **húngaro** *s, adj* Hungarian.

huracán [ura'kan] *sm* hurricane.

hurgar [ur'gar] *v* poke; stir; pick. **hurgón** *sm* poker.

hurón [u'ron] *sm* ferret. **huronear** *v* hunt with a ferret; (*fam*) pry.
hurtadillas [urta'ðiʎas] *adv* **a hurtadillas** slyly, stealthily.
hurtar [ur'tar] *v* steal; remove; cheat. **hurtar el cuerpo** dodge. **hurtador, -a** *sm, sf* thief. **hurto** *sm* theft; thing stolen.
husmear [usme'ar] *v* scent; track; (*fam*) pry; (*fam: carne*) smell high. **husmeo** *sm* scenting; smelling; prying.
huso ['uso] *sm* spindle; (*avión*) fuselage.

I

íbice ['iβiθe] *sm* ibex.
ictericia [ikte'riθja] *sf* jaundice.
ida ['iða] *sf* departure; journey. **idas y venidas** coming and going.
idea [i'ðea] *sf* idea; intention. **tener idea de** intend to. **ideal** *adj* ideal; imaginary. **idealismo** *sm* idealism. **idealista** *s, adj* idealist. **idealizar** *v* idealize. **idear** *v* imagine; plan.
idéntico [i'ðentiko] *adj* identical. **identidad** *sf* identity. **identificación** *sf* identification. **identificar** *v* identify.
ideología [iðeolo'xia] *sf* ideology. **ideológico** *adj* ideological.
idilio [i'ðiljo] *sm* idyll. **idílico** *adj* idyllic.
idioma [i'ðjoma] *sm* language. **idiomático** *adj* idiomatic; linguistic.
idiosincrasia [iðjosin'krasja] *sf* idiosyncrasy. **idiosincrásico** *adj* idiosyncratic.
idiota [i'ðjota] *s(m+f)* idiot. *adj* idiotic. **idiotez** *sf* idiocy. **idiótico** *adj* idiotic.
ídolo ['iðolo] *sm* idol. **idólatra** *s(m+f)* idolater. **idólatra** *adj* idolatrous. **idolatrar** *v* idolize. **idolatría** *sf* idolatry.
idóneo [i'ðoneo] *adj* apt, fit. **idoneidad** *sf* aptness, fitness.
iglesia [i'glesja] *sf* church.
ignición [igni'θjon] *sf* ignition. **ignito** *adj* ignited.
ignominia [igno'minja] *sf* ignominy. **ignominioso** *adj* ignominious.
ignorar [igno'rar] *v* be unaware of; refuse to know. **ignorancia** *sf* ignorance. **ignorante** *adj* ignorant.
igual [i'gwal] *adj* same; equal; even. **por**

igual evenly. **es igual** it makes no difference. **igualar** *v* equalize. **igualación** *sf* equalization. **igualdad** *sf* equality.
ijada [i'xaða] *sf* flank. **ijadear** *v* pant.
ilegal [ile'gal] *adj* illegal. **ilegalidad** *sf* illegality.
ilegible [ile'xiβle] *adj* illegible.
ilegítimo [ile'xitimo] *adj* illegitimate. **ilegitimidad** *sf* illegitimacy.
ileso [i'leso] *adj* unharmed.
ilícito [i'liθito] *adj* illicit.
ilógico [i'loxiko] *adj* illogical.
iluminar [ilumi'nar] *v* illuminate. **iluminación** *sf* illumination.
ilusión [ilu'sjon] *sf* illusion; delusion; expectation. **ilusionado** *adj* eager. **ilusionar** *v* fascinate. **ilusionarse** *v* delude oneself; build up hopes. **ilusionismo** *sm* conjuring trick. **ilusionista** *s(m+f)* conjurer. **iluso** *adj* deceived; deluded. **ilusorio** *adj* illusory.
ilustrar [ilu'strar] *v* illustrate. **ilustración** *sf* illustration; enlightenment. **ilustrador, -a** *sm, sf* illustrator.
imaginar [imaxi'nar] *v* imagine. **imagen** *sf* image. **imaginación** *sf* imagination. **imaginario** *adj* imaginary. **imaginativo** *adj* imaginative.
imán [i'man] *sm* magnet **imanar** *v* also **imantar** magnetize. **imantación** *sf* magnetization.
imbécil [im'βeθil] *adj* imbecile. **imbecilidad** *sf* imbecility.
imborrable [imbor'raβle] *adj* unforgettable.
***imbuir** [imbu'ir] *v* imbue.
imitar [imi'tar] *v* imitate, copy. **imitable** *adj* imitable. **imitación** *sf* imitation. **imitador, -a** *sm, sf* imitator. **imitativo** *adj* imitative.
impaciente [impa'θjente] *adj* impatient. **impaciencia** *sf* impatience. **impacientarse** *v* become impatient.
impacto [im'pakto] *sm* impact.
impar [im'par] *adj* (*mat*) odd. **número impar** odd number.
imparcial [impar'θjal] *adj* impartial. **imparcialidad** *sf* impartiality.
impartir [impar'tir] *v* impart.
impasible [impa'siβle] *adj* impassive. **impasibilidad** *sf* impassivity.
impávido [im'paβiðo] *adj* fearless, dauntless. **impavidez** *sf* fearlessness, dauntlessness.

impecable [impe'kaβle] *adj* impeccable. impecabilidad *sf* impeccability.
*impedir [impe'ðir] *v* impede; prevent. impediente *adj* obstructing. impedimento *sm* impediment.
impeler [impe'ler] *v* impel; drive; propel.
impenetrable [impene'traβle] *adj* impenetrable.
impenitente [impeni'tente] *adj* impenitent.
imperar [impe'rar] *v* rule; prevail. imperativo *adj* imperative; commanding.
imperceptible [imperθep'tiβle] *adj* imperceptible.
imperdible [imper'ðiβle] *sm* safety pin.
imperdonable [imperðo'naβle] *adj* unforgivable.
imperfecto [imper'fekto] *adj* imperfect. imperfección *sf* imperfection.
imperio [im'perjo] *sm* empire. imperial *adj* imperial. imperialismo *sm* imperialism. imperialista *s, adj* imperialist.
impermeable [imperme'aβle] *adj* waterproof. *sm* mackintosh.
impersonal [imperso'nal] *adj* impersonal.
impertinente [imperti'nente] *adj* impertinent. impertinencia *sf* impertinence.
imperturbable [impertur'βaβle] *adj* imperturbable. imperturbabilidad *sf* imperturbability.
ímpetu ['impetu] *sm* impetus. impetuosidad *sf* impetuosity.
impío [im'pio] *adj* godless, impious. impiedad *sf* impiety.
implacable [impla'kaβle] *adj* implacable. implacabilidad *sf* implacability.
implantar [implan'tar] *v* implant.
implicar [impli'kar] *v* imply; implicate; entail. implicación *sf* implication; contradiction. implicatorio *adj* contradictory.
implícito [im'pliθito] *adj* implicit.
implorar [implo'rar] *v* implore, beg. imploración *sf* entreaty.
*imponer [impo'ner] *v* impose; inflict; acquaint; inspire; deposit; impute falsely. imponerse *v* dominate. imponente *adj* imposing; striking; (*fam*) sensational, smashing.
impopular [impopu'lar] *adj* unpopular. impopularidad *sf* unpopularity.
importante [impor'tante] *adj* important. importancia *sf* importance. importar *v* matter, concern. no importa it doesn't matter.
importunar [importu'nar] *v* importune,

pester. importunidad *sf* importunity. importuno *adj* importunate, pestering.
imposible [impo'siβle] *adj* impossible. imposibilidad *sf* impossibility. imposibilitar *v* make impossible.
imposición [imposi'θjon] *sf* imposition; tax.
impostor [impos'tor], -a *sm, sf* impostor.
impotente [impo'tente] *adj* impotent; powerless. impotencia *sf* impotence.
impracticable [imprakti'kaβle] *adj* impracticable.
imprecar [impre'kar] *v* curse. imprecación *sf* curse. imprecatorio *adj* abusive.
impreciso [impre'θiso] *adj* imprecise. imprecisión *sf* imprecision.
impregnar [impreg'nar] *v* impregnate; saturate. impregnable *adj* absorbent. impregnación *sf* impregnation.
imprescindible [impresθin'diβle] *adj* indispensable.
impreso [im'preso] *adj* printed. imprenta *sf* press; printing. impresión *sf* impression; imprint; stamp; print; printing; edition. impresionable *adj* impressionable. impresionar *v* impress; shock. impresionarse *v* be deeply moved. impresionismo *sm* impressionism. impresionista *s(m + f)* impressionist. impresor *sm* printer.
imprevisto [impre'βisto] *adj* unexpected.
imprimir [impri'mir] *v* print; implant.
improbable [impro'βaβle] *adj* improbable. improbabilidad *sf* improbability.
ímprobo ['improβo] *adj* wicked; arduous. improbidad *sf* dishonesty.
improcedente [improθe'ðente] *adj* improper; inappropriate; (*jur*) inadmissible. improcedencia *sf* impropriety; inappropriateness; (*jur*) inadmissibility.
improductivo [improduk'tiβo] *adj* unproductive.
impropio [im'propjo] *adj* improper; unbecoming. impropiedad *sf* impropriety.
improvido [im'proβiðo] *adj* improvident. improvidencia *sf* improvidence.
improvisar [improβi'sar] *v* improvise. improvisación *sf* improvisation.
improvisto [impro'βisto] *adj* unforeseen. a la improvista without warning.
imprudente [impru'ðente] *adj* imprudent. imprudencia *sf* imprudence.
impúdico [im'puðiko] *adj* shameless, immodest.

impuesto [im'pwesto] *sm* tax; duty.
impugnar [impug'nar] *v* impugn; oppose; refute.
impulsar [impul'sar] *v* impel; drive; move. **impulsión** *sf* impulse; impetus.
impulso *sm* impulse; drive; momentum.
impune [im'pune] *adj* unpunished.
impunidad *sf* impunity.
impuro [im'puro] *adj* impure; lewd.
impureza *sf* impurity; lewdness. **impurificación** *sf* defilement. **impurificar** *v* defile.
imputar [impu'tar] *v* impute; ascribe.
imputable *adj* chargeable. **imputación** *sf* imputation; accusation.
inacabable [inaka'βaβle] *adj* endless.
inaccesible [inakθe'siβle] *adj* inaccessible.
inaccesibilidad *sf* inaccessibility.
inaceptable [inaθep'taβle] *adj* unacceptable.
inacostumbrado [inakostum'braðo] *adj* unaccustomed.
inactivo [inak'tiβo] *adj* inactive. **inactividad** *sf* inactivity.
inadecuado [inaðe'kwaðo] *adj* inadequate.
inadecuación *sf* inadequacy.
inadmisible [inaðmi'siβle] *adj* inadmissible.
inadvertido [inaðβer'tiðo] *adj* inadvertent.
inadvertencia *sf* inadvertence, carelessness.
inagotable [inago'taβle] *adj* inexhaustible.
inaguantable [inagwan'taβle] *adj* unbearable.
inajenable [inaxe'naβle] *adj* inalienable.
inalterable [inalte'raβle] *adj* unalterable; imperturbable. **inalterabilidad** *sf* immutability; imperturbability. **inalterado** *adj* unchanged.
inanición [inani'θjon] *sf* starvation; weakness; exhaustion.
inanimado [inani'maðo] *adj* inanimate, lifeless.
inapagable [inapa'gaβle] *adj* unquenchable.
inaplicable [inapli'kaβle] *adj* inapplicable.
inaplicado *adj* indolent.
inapreciable [inapre'θjaβle] *adj* priceless; invaluable.
inapto [in'apto] *adj* unsuitable; incapable.
inasequible [inase'kiβle] *adj* unattainable.
inaudible [inau'ðiβle] *adj* inaudible.
inaudito [inau'ðito] *adj* unheard of; outrageous.
inaugurar [inaugu'rar] *v* inaugurate.
inauguración *sf* inauguration.

incalculable [inkalku'laβle] *adj* incalculable.
incandescente [inkandes'θente] *adj* incandescent. **incandescencia** *sf* incandescence.
incansable [inkan'saβle] *adj* indefatigable, untiring.
incapacitar [inkapaθi'tar] *v* incapacitate; disable; disqualify. **incapacidad** *sf* incapacity; incompetence; disability. **incapaz** *adj* unfit; incompetent.
incautarse [inkau'tarse] *v* (*jur*) confiscate.
incautación *sf* confiscation.
incauto [in'kauto] *adj* incautious; gullible.
incendiar [inθen'djar] *v* set on fire.
incendiarse *v* catch fire. **incendiario, -a** *sm, sf* arsonist. **incendiario** *adj* incendiary. **incendio** *sm* fire. **incendio provocado** arson.
incentivo [inθen'tiβo] *sm* incentive. **incentivar** *v* incite.
incertidumbre [inθerti'ðumbre] *sf* uncertainty.
incesante [inθe'sante] *adj* incessant.
incesto [in'θesto] *sm* incest. **incestuoso** *adj* incestuous.
incidente [inθi'ðente] *sm* incident. *adj* incidental. **incidencia** *sf* incident; incidence. **incidental** *adj* incidental.
incienso [in'θjenso] *sm* incense.
incierto [in'θjerto] *adj* uncertain; untrue.
incinerar [inθine'rar] *v* incinerate; cremate. **incineración** *sf* incineration; cremation.
incipiente [inθi'pjente] *adj* incipient.
incisivo [inθi'siβo] *adj* incisive; cutting. *sm* (*diente*) incisor. **incisión** *sf* incision, cut. **inciso** *adj* cut.
incitar [inθi'tar] *v* incite; instigate. **incitación** *sf* incitement; enticement. **incitador, -a** *sm, sf* instigator.
incivil [inθi'βil] *adj* uncivil, impolite.
inclemente [inkle'mente] *adj* inclement; harsh. **inclemencia** *sf* inclemency; harshness.
inclinar [inkli'nar] *v* incline; lean; influence; induce; lower. **inclinarse** *v* feel disposed; bow; stoop. **inclinación** *sf* inclination; leaning; slope; dip. **inclinado** *adj* inclined; sloping.
*incluir [inklu'ir] *v* include. **inclusión** *sf* inclusion. **inclusivo** *adj* inclusive. **incluso** *adj* included; enclosed. **incluso** *adv* even.

incógnito [in'kognito] *adj* unknown. **de incógnito** incognito.
incoherente [inkoe'rente] *adj* incoherent. incoherencia *sf* incoherence.
incoloro [inko'loro] *adj* colourless.
incombustible [inkombus'tiβle] *adj* incombustible, fireproof.
incomodar [inkomo'ðar] *v* disturb, annoy, molest. incomodidad *sf* inconvenience; discomfort. incómodo *adj* uncomfortable; annoying.
incomparable [inkompa'raβle] *adj* incomparable.
incompatible [inkompa'tiβle] *adj* incompatible. incompatibilidad *sf* incompatibility.
incompetente [inkompe'tente] *adj* incompetent. incompetencia *sf* incompetence.
incompleto [inkom'pleto] *adj* incomplete. incompletamente *adv* incompletely.
incomprensible [inkompren'siβle] *adj* incomprehensible. incomprensibilidad *sf* incomprehensibility. incomprensión *sf* lack of understanding.
incomunicado [inkomuni'kaðo] *adj* isolated. incomunicable *adj* incommunicable. incomunicación *sf* isolation. incomunicar *v* isolate.
inconcebible [inkonθe'βiβle] *adj* inconceivable.
inconcluso [inkon'kluso] *adj* unfinished; inconclusive.
incondicional [inkondiθjo'nal] *adj* unconditional. *s(m+f)* staunch supporter.
inconfundible [inkonfun'diβle] *adj* unmistakable.
incongruente [inkongru'ente] *adj* incongruous; incongruent. incongruencia *sf* incongruousness; incongruity.
inconmensurable [inkonmensu'raβle] *adj* immeasurable.
inconmovible [inkonmo'βiβle] *adj* unshakable; firm.
inconsciente [inkons'θjente] *adj* unconscious; unaware; thoughtless. inconsciencia *sf* unconsciousness; unawareness; thoughtlessness.
inconsecuente [inkonse'kwente] *adj* inconsequential; inconsistent. inconsecuencia *sf* inconsistency.
inconsiderado [inkonsiðe'raðo] *adj* ill-considered. inconsideración *sf* inconsiderateness.
inconstante [irikon'stante] *adj* inconstant,

fickle. inconstancia *sf* inconstancy, fickleness.
incontable [inkon'taβle] *adj* innumerable.
incontestable [inkontes'taβle] *adj* incontestable, indisputable.
incontinente [inkonti'nente] *adj* incontinent. incontinencia *sf* incontinence.
inconveniente [inkonβe'njente] *adj* inconvenient, impolite. *sm* objection; trouble; obstacle. inconveniencia *sf* inconvenience; impropriety; unsuitability.
incorporar [inkorpo'rar] *v* incorporate. incorporarse *v* sit up; become a member. incorporación *sf* incorporation. incorporado *adj* incorporated.
incorrecto [inkor'rekto] *adj* incorrect. incorrección *sf* inaccuracy. incorregibilidad *sf* incorrigibility. incorregible *adj* incorrigible.
incorrupto [inkor'rupto] *adj* incorrupt, pure. incorruptible *adj* incorruptible.
incrédulo [in'kreðulo] *adj* incredulous, sceptical. incredulidad *sf* incredulity, scepticism. increíble *adj* incredible.
incremento [inkre'mento] *sm* increase.
increpar [inkre'par] *v* reproach; rebuke. increpación *sf* rebuke.
incriminar [inkrimi'nar] *v* incriminate; exaggerate. incriminación *sf* incrimination.
incrustar [inkrus'tar] *v* encrust. incrustación *sf* encrustation.
incubar [inku'βar] *v* incubate; (*med*) be sickening for. incubación *sf* incubation. incubadora *sf* incubator.
inculcar [inkul'kar] *v* inculcate. inculcarse *v* be obstinate. inculcación *sf* inculcation.
inculpable [inkul'paβle] *adj* blameless. inculpabilidad *sf* blamelessness.
inculto [in'kulto] *adj* uncouth; uneducated. incultura *sf* lack of culture.
incumbencia [inkum'benθja] *sf* responsibility, duty. incumbir *v* be incumbent upon.
incurable [inku'raβle] *adj* incurable.
incurrir [inkur'rir] *v* incur; fall; commit.
incursión [inkur'sjon] *sf* incursion, raid.
indagar [inda'gar] *v* investigate. indagación *sf* investigation. indagador, -a *sm*, *sf* investigator.
indebido [inde'βiðo] *adj* unjust; improper.
indecente [inde'θente] *adj* indecent; foul; wretched. indecencia *sf* indecency; obscenity.

indecible [inde'θiβle] *adj* indescribable; unspeakable.

indecifrable [indeθi'fraβle] *adj* indecipherable.

indecisión [inde'θisjon] *sf* indecision. **indeciso** *adj* indecisive.

indecoroso [indeco'roso] *adj* indecorous. **indecoro** *sm* lack of propriety.

indefectible [indefek'tiβle] *adj* unfailing.

indefenso [inde'fenso] *adj* defenceless. **indefendible** *adj* indefensible.

indefinible [indefi'niβle] *adj* indefinable. **indefinido** *adj* indefinite.

indeleble [inde'leβle] *adj* indelible.

indelicado [indeli'kaðo] *adj* indelicate. **indelicadeza** *sf* indelicacy.

indemne [in'demne] *adj* unhurt. **indemnidad** *sf* indemnity. **indemnización** *sf* compensation. **indemnizar** *v* indemnify, compensate.

independencia [indepen'denθja] *sf* independence. **independiente** *adj* independent.

indescriptible [indescrip'tiβle] *adj* indescribable.

indeseable [indese'aβle] *adj* undesirable.

indestructible [indestruk'tiβle] *adj* indestructible. **indestructibilidad** *sf* indestructibility.

indeterminado [indetermi'naðo] *adj* indeterminate; undetermined.

India ['indja] *sf* India. **indio, -a** *s, adj* Indian.

indicar [indi'kar] *v* indicate; show; suggest. **indicación** *sf* indication. **indicado** *adj* suitable; recommended. **indicador** *sm* pointer; gauge. **indicativo** *adj* indicative. *sm* (*gram*) indicative.

índice ['indiθe] *sm* index.

indicio [in'diθjo] *sm* sign; trace. **indicios** *sm pl* (*jur*) evidence *sing*.

indiferencia [indife'renθja] *sf* indifference. **indiferente** *adj* indifferent.

indígena [in'dixena] *s(m+f), adj* native.

indigestión [indixes'tjon] *sf* indigestion. **indigestible** *adj* indigestible.

indignar [indig'nar] *v* anger, annoy. **indignarse** *v* become indignant. **indignación** *sf* indignation. **indignidad** *sf* indignity. **indigno** *adj* unworthy; disgraceful.

indirecta [indi'rekta] *sf* innuendo. **indirecto** *adj* indirect.

indisciplina [indisθi'plina] *sf* indiscipline. **indisciplinado** *adj* undisciplined.

indiscreción [indiskre'θjon] *sf* indiscretion. **indiscreto** *adj* indiscreet.

indisculpable [indiskul'paβle] *adj* inexcusable.

indiscutible [indisku'tiβle] *adj* unquestionable.

indisoluble [indiso'luβle] *adj* indissoluble.

indispensable [indispen'saβle] *adj* indispensable.

***indisponer** [indispo'ner] *v* upset; render unfit. **indisponerse** *v* become ill. **indisposición** *sf* indisposition. **indispuesto** *adj* indisposed, poorly.

indisputable [indispu'taβle] *adj* indisputable.

indistinto [indis'tinto] *adj* indistinct; vague.

individual [indiβi'ðwal] *adj* individual. **individualidad** *sf* individuality. **individualismo** *sm* individualism. **individualista** *s(m+f)* individualist. **individualizar** *v* individualize. **individuo, -a** *sm, sf* individual.

indivisible [indiβi'siβle] *adj* indivisible. **indiviso** *adj* undivided.

índole ['indole] *sf* nature.

indolente [indo'lente] *adj* indolent; painless. **indolencia** *sf* indolence; painlessness.

indómito [in'domito] *adj* untamed; indomitable.

indubitable [induβi'taβle] *adj* indubitable.

***inducir** [indu'θir] *v* persuade; lead; infer. **inducción** *sf* induction. **inducimiento** *sm* inducement.

indudable [indu'ðaβle] *adj* unquestionable.

indulgente [indul'xente] *adj* indulgent. **indulgencia** *sf* indulgence.

indultar [indul'tar] *v* pardon; excuse. **indulto** *sm* mercy; reprieve; exemption.

indumento [indu'mento] *sm* apparel.

industria [in'dustrja] *sf* industry; business; ingenuity. **de industria** on purpose. **industrial** *adj* industrial. **industrial** *sm* industrialist. **industrialismo** *sm* industrialism. **industrializar** *v* industrialize. **industrioso** *adj* industrious.

inédito [i'neðito] *adj* unpublished.

inefable [ine'faβle] *adj* ineffable.

ineficaz [inefi'kaθ] *adj* inefficient. **ineficacia** *sf* inefficiency.

ineludible [inelu'ðiβle] *adj* inevitable.

inepto [i'nepto] *adj* inept. **ineptitud** *sf* ineptitude.

inequívoco [ine'kiβoko] *adj* unmistakable.
inercia [i'nerθja] *sf* inertia; lifelessness.
inerme [i'nerme] *adj* unarmed.
inerte [i'nerte] *adj* inert.
inesperado [inespe'raðo] *adj* unexpected, unforeseen.
inestable [ines'taβle] *adj* unstable. **inestabilidad** *sf* instability.
inestimable [inesti'maβle] *adj* invaluable.
inevitable [ineβi'taβle] *adj* inevitable.
inexacto [inek'sakto] *adj* inaccurate. **inexactitud** *sf* inaccuracy.
inexcusable [ineksku'saβle] *adj* inexcusable; essential.
inexorable [inekso'raβle] *adj* inexorable.
inexperto [ineks'perto] *adj* inexperienced.
inexplicable [inekspli'kaβle] *adj* inexplicable.
infalible [infa'liβle] *adj* infallible. **infalibilidad** *sf* infallibility.
infamar [infa'mar] *v* dishonour. **infamación** *sf* defamation. **infame** *adj* infamous. **infamia** *sf* infamy.
infante [in'fante] *sm, adj* infant. *sm* prince. **infancia** *sf* infancy. **infantil** *adj* infantile.
infantería [infante'ria] *sf* infantry.
infatigable [infati'gaβle] *adj* indefatigable.
infausto [in'fausto] *adj* ill-omened; ill-famed.
infectar [infek'tar] *v* infect. **infección** *sf* infection. **infeccioso** *adj* infectious.
infeliz [infe'liθ] *adj* unhappy. *s(m+f)* luckless person.
inferior [infe'rjor] *adj* inferior; lower. *sm* inferior. **inferioridad** *sf* inferiority.
***inferir** [infe'rir] *v* infer; inflict. **inferirse** *v* follow.
infernal [infer'nal] *adj* infernal.
infestar [infes'tar] *v* infest; overrun. **infestación** *sf* infestation.
infiel [in'fjel] *adj* unfaithful. *s(m+f)* infidel.
infierno [in'fjerno] *sm* hell.
ínfimo ['infimo] *adj* lowest; vilest.
infinito [infi'nito] *adj* infinite. **infinidad** *sf* infinity. **infinitivo** *sm* (*gram*) infinitive.
inflamar [infla'mar] *v* inflame. **inflamable** *adj* inflammable. **inflamación** *sf* inflammation.
inflar [in'flar] *v* inflate. **inflación** *sf* inflation; swelling.
inflexible [inflek'siβle] *adj* inflexible. **inflexibilidad** *sf* inflexibility.
infligir [infli'xir] *v* inflict.

***influir** [influ'ir] *v* influence; affect.
influencia *sf* influence; authority. **influente** *adj also* **influyente** influential. **influjo** *sm* influence; flood.
informal [infor'mal] *adj* informal; unreliable. **informalidad** *sf* informality; unreliability.
informar [infor'mar] *v* inform; notify. **informarse** *v* find out. **información** *sf* information; judicial inquiry. **informador, -a** *sm, sf* informant. **informe** *sm* report; testimonial. **informe** *adj* shapeless.
infortunio [infor'tunjo] *sm* misfortune. **infortunado** *adj* unfortunate.
infracción [infrak'θjon] *sf* breach; infringement. **infractor, -a** *sm, sf* transgressor.
infranqueable [infranke'aβle] *adj* impassable; insurmountable.
infringir [infrin'xir] *v* infringe; violate.
infructuoso [infruk'twoso] *adj* fruitless.
infundado [infun'daðo] *adj* unfounded.
infundir [infun'dir] *v* instil. **infusión** *sf* inspiration.
ingeniería [inxenje'ria] *sf* engineering. **ingeniero** *sm* engineer.
ingenio [in'xenjo] *sm* talent; wit; ingenuity; device. **ingeniosidad** *sf* ingenuity. **ingenioso** *adj* ingenious.
ingenuo [in'xenwo] *adj* naïve; frank; simple. **ingenuidad** *sf* frankness; credulity.
***ingerir** [inxe'rir] *v* (*comida*) consume. **ingerirse** *v* meddle. **ingerencia** *sf* interference.
Inglaterra [ingla'terra] *sf* England. **inglés** *adj* English; *sm* Englishman; (*idioma*) English. **inglesa** *sf* Englishwoman.
ingrato [in'grato] *adj* ungrateful; unpleasant. **ingratitud** *sf* ingratitude.
ingrediente [ingre'ðjente] *sm* ingredient.
ingresar [ingre'sar] *v* enter; join; (*hospital*) be admitted; (*dinero*) deposit. **ingreso** *sm* entrance; (*com*) deposit; admission. **derecho de ingreso** *sm* entrance fee.
inhábil [i'naβil] *adj* incompetent; tactless. **día inhábil** non-working day. **inhabilidad** *sf* incompetence; inability. **inhabilitar** *v* disqualify; disable.
inhabitable [inaβi'taβle] *adj* uninhabitable. **inhabitado** *adj* uninhabited.
inhalar [ina'lar] *v* inhale. **inhalación** *sf* inhalation.

inherente [ine'rente] *adj* inherent. **inherencia** *sf* inherence.
inhibir [ini'βir] *v* inhibit. **inhibirse** *v* refrain. **inhibición** *sf* inhibition. **inhibitorio** *adj* inhibitive.
inhospitalario [inospita'larjo] *adj* inhospitable. **inhospitalidad** *sf* inhospitableness.
inhumano [inu'mano] *adj* inhuman. **inhumanidad** *sf* inhumanity.
inhumar [inu'mar] *v* bury.
inicial [ini'θjal] *adj, sf* initial. **iniciación** *sf* initiation. **iniciado, -a** *sm, sf* initiate. **iniciador, -a** *sm, sf* initiator. **iniciar** *v* initiate. **iniciativa** *sf* initiative.
inicuo [i'nikwo] *adj* wicked. **iniquidad** *sf* iniquity.
injertar [inxer'tar] *v* graft. **injerto** *sm* graft, grafting.
injuriar [inxuri'ar] *v* insult; damage; injure. **injuria** *sf* offence; harm. **injuriador** *adj* offensive. **injurioso** *adj* insulting.
injusticia [inxus'tiθja] *sf* injustice. **injusto** *adj* unjust.
inmediato [inme'ðjato] *adj* immediate. **de inmediato** immediately.
inmejorable [inmexo'raβle] *adj* unsurpassable.
inmemorial [inmemo'rjal] *adj* immemorial.
inmenso [in'menso] *adj* immense.
inmerecido [inmere'θiðo] *adj* undeserved.
inmigrar [inmi'grar] *v* immigrate. **inmigración** *sf* immigration. **inmigrante** *s(m+f), adj* immigrant.
inminente [inmi'nente] *adj* imminent. **inminencia** *sf* imminence.
inmoderado [inmoðe'raðo] *adj* excessive. **inmoderación** *sf* excess.
inmodestia [inmodes'tia] *sf* immodesty. **inmodesto** *adj* immodest.
inmolar [inmo'lar] *v* sacrifice. **inmolación** *sf* sacrifice.
inmoral [inmo'ral] *adj* immoral. **inmoralidad** *sf* immorality.
inmortal [inmor'tal] *adj, s(m+f)* immortal. **inmortalidad** *sf* immortality. **inmortalizar** *v* immortalize.
inmóvil [in'moβil] *adj* motionless. **inmovible** *adj* immovable. **inmovilidad** *sf* immobility. **inmovilizar** *v* immobilize.
inmueble [in'mweβle] *sm* property; real estate.
inmundo [in'mundo] *adj* filthy; impure. **inmundicia** *sf* filth; impurity.

inmune [in'mune] *adj* immune; exempt.
inmunidad *sf* immunity; exemption.
inmunización *sf* immunization. **inmunizar** *v* immunize.
inmutar [inmu'tar] *v* change. **inmutarse** *v* change one's expression. **inmutabilidad** *sf* immutability. **inmutable** *adj* immutable.
innato [in'nato] *adj* innate.
innecesario [inneθe'sarjo] *adj* unnecessary.
innegable [in'negaβle] *adj* undeniable.
innoble [in'noβle] *adj* ignoble.
innocuo [in'nokwo] *adj also* **inocuo** innocuous.
innovar [inno'βar] *v* innovate. **innovación** *sf* innovation. **innovador, -a** *sm, sf* innovator. **innovador** *adj* innovative. **innovamiento** *sm* innovation.
innumerable [innume'raβle] *adj* innumerable.
inobediente [inoβe'ðjente] *adj* disobedient. **inobediencia** *sf* disobedience.
inocente [ino'θente] *adj* innocent. **innocencia** *sf* innocence.
inocular [inoku'lar] *v* inoculate; contaminate. **inoculación** *sf* inoculation.
inodoro [ino'ðoro] *adj* odourless.
inofensivo [inofen'siβo] *adj* harmless.
inolvidable [inolβi'ðaβle] *adj* unforgettable.
inoperable [inope'raβle] *adj* inoperable.
inopinado [inopi'naðo] *adj* unexpected.
inoportuno [inopor'tuno] *adj* inopportune.
inoxidable [inoksi'ðaβle] *adj* rustless; stainless. **acero inoxidable** *sm* stainless steel.
inquebrantable [inkeβran'taβle] *adj* unbreakable; unyielding.
inquietar [inkje'tar] *v* disturb; disquiet. **inquietador** *adj* disquieting. **inquietante** *adj* disquieting. **inquieto** *adj* restless. **inquietud** *sf* restlessness.
inquilino [inki'lino], **-a** *sm, sf* tenant. **inquilinato** *sm* lease.
✦inquirir [inki'rir] *v* investigate; examine. **inquiridor, -a** *sm, sf* inquirer. **inquisición** *sf* inquisition; inquiry. **inquisidor** *sm* inquisitor. **inquisitivo** *adj* inquisitive.
insciable [insa'θjaβle] *adj* insatiable.
insalubre [insa'luβre] *adj* unhealthy. **insalubridad** *sf* unhealthiness.
insanable [insa'naβle] *adj* incurable.

insano [in'sano] *adj* insane; unhealthy.
insania *sf* insanity.
inscribir [inskri'βir] *v* inscribe; register.
inscripción *sf* inscription; registration.
insecto [in'sekto] *sm* insect. **insecticida** *sm*
insecticide. **insectólogo, -a** *sm, sf* ento-
mologist.
inseguro [inse'guro] *adj* insecure; unsafe;
uncertain. **inseguridad** *sf* insecurity;
uncertainty.
insensato [insen'sato] *adj* senseless; wild.
insensatez *sf* folly.
insensible [insen'siβle] *adj* insensible;
insensitive; imperceptible. **insensibilidad**
sf insensibility; insensitiveness.
insertar [inser'tar] *v* insert. **inserto** *sm*
insertion.
inservible [inser'βiβle] *adj* useless.
insidioso [insi'ðjoso] *adj* insidious.
insigne [in'signe] *adj* illustrious, distinguished.
insignia [in'signja] *sf* badge; banner.
insignias *sf pl* insignia.
insignificante [insignifi'kante] *adj* insignificant. **insignificancia** *sf* insignificance.
insincero [insin'θero] *adj* insincere.
insinceridad *sf* insincerity.
insinuar [insinu'ar] *v* insinuate, suggest.
insinuarse *v* work one's way (into); make
advances. **insinuación** *sf* insinuation;
suggestiveness. **insinuante** *adj* insinuat-
ing; suggestive.
insípido [in'sipiðo] *adj* insipid, tasteless.
insipidez *sf* tastelessness.
insistir [insis'tir] *v* insist; persist. **insistencia** *sf* insistence; persistence. **insistente** *adj* insistent; persistent.
insociable [inso'θjaβle] *adj* unsociable.
insociabilidad *sf* unsociability, unsocia-
bleness.
insolación [insola'θjon] *sf* sunstroke. **inso-
lar** *v* expose to the sun. **insolarse** *v* get
sunstroke.
insolente [inso'lente] *adj* insolent.
insolencia *sf* insolence.
insólito [in'solito] *adj* unusual.
insolvente [insol'βente] *adj* insolvent,
penniless. **insoluble** *adj* insoluble.
insolvencia *sf* insolvency.
insomne [in'somne] *s(m+f), adj* insomniac. **insomnio** *sm* insomnia.
insondable [inson'daβle] *adj* unfathom-
able.
insoportable [insopor'taβle] *adj* intolerable.

inspeccionar [inspekθjo'nar] *v* inspect.
inspección *sf* inspection. **inspector, -a** *sm,
sf* inspector.
inspirar [inspi'rar] *v* inhale; inspire.
inspiración *sf* inhalation; inspiration.
inspirador *adj* inspirational.
instable [in'staβle] *adj* unstable.
instabilidad *sf* instability.
instalar [insta'lar] *v* install; establish.
instalación *sf* installation; (*fábrica*) plant.
instalador *sm* fitter.
instancia [instan'θja] *sf* petition; application form.
instante [in'stante] *sm* instant; moment.
adj insistent. **instantánea** *sf* snapshot.
instantáneo *adj* instantaneous. **instante-
mente** *adv* insistently.
instaurar [instau'rar] *v* set up; restore.
instauración *sf* restoration. **instaurativo**
adj restorative.
instigar [insti'gar] *v* instigate; incite. **instigación** *sf* instigation. **instigador, -a** *sm, sf*
instigator.
instintivo [instin'tiβo] *adj* instinctive.
instinto *sm* instinct.
*****instituir** [institu'ir] *v* institute. **institución**
sf institution. **instituto** *sm* institute; state
secondary school.
*****instruir** [instru'ir] *v* instruct. **instrucción**
sf instruction; education; knowledge.
instructivo *adj* instructive. **instructor, -a**
sm, sf instructor. **instruido** *adj* educated.
instrumento [instru'mento] *sm* instrument. **instrumentación** *sf* orchestration.
instrumental *adj* instrumental. **instru-
mentar** *v* orchestrate. **instrumentista**
s(m+f) instrumentalist; instrument-
maker.
insubordinar [insuβorði'nar] *v* incite to
rebellion. **insubordinarse** *v* rebel.
insubordinación *sf* insubordination.
insubordinado *adj* insubordinate.
insubstancial [insuβstan'θjal] *adj* insub-
stantial.
insuficiente [insufi'θjente] *adj* insufficient;
inadequate. **insuficiencia** *sf* insufficiency;
inadequacy.
insufrible [insu'friβle] *adj* insufferable.
insular [insu'lar] *adj* insular.
insulso [in'sulso] *adj* dull; tasteless. **insul-
sez** *sf* tastelessness.
insultar [insul'tar] *v* insult. **insultador** *adj*
also **insultante** insulting. **insulto** *sm*
insult.

insuperable [insupe'raβle] *adj* insuperable.
insurgente [insur'xente] *s(m+f)* rebel. *adj*
rebellious. **insurrección** *sf* rebellion.
insurreccionarse *v* rebel. **insurrecto, -a** *s*,
adj insurgent.
intacto [in'takto] *adj* intact.
intachable [inta'tʃaβle] *adj* irreproachable.
intangible [intan'xiβle] *adj* intangible.
intangibilidad *sf* intangibility.
integrar [inte'grar] *v* integrate; compose;
complete; repay. **integración** *sf* integration. **integral** *adj* integral. **pan integral** *sm*
wholemeal bread. **integrante** *adj* integral.
integridad *sf* integrity. **integro** *adj* entire,
whole.
intelecto [inte'lekto] *sm* intellect. **intelectual** *s(m+f)*, *adj* intellectual. **intelectu-
alidad** *sf* intelligentsia. **intelectualismo** *sm*
intellectualism.
inteligente [inteli'xente] *adj* intelligent.
inteligencia *sf* intelligence; knowledge;
comprehension. **inteligibilidad** *sf* intelligibility. **inteligible** *adj* intelligible.
intemperante [intempe'rante] *adj* intem-
perate. **intemperancia** *sf* intemperance.
intemperie [intem'perje] *sf* bad weather.
estar a la intemperie be out in the open.
intempestivo [intempes'tiβo] *adj* inopportune.
intención [inten'θjon] *sf* intention.
primera intención frankness. **segunda
intención** duplicity. **intencionadamente**
adv deliberately. **intencionado** *adj* deliberate. **intencional** *adj* intentional.
intenso [in'tenso] *adj* intense. **intensidad**
sf intensity. **intensificar** *v* intensify. **inten-
sión** *sf* intensity. **intensivo** *adj* intensive.
intentar [inten'tar] *v* try. **intento** *sm*
attempt.
intercalar [interka'lar] *v* insert.
intercambio [inter'kambjo] *sm*
interchange. **intercambiar** *v* interchange,
exchange. **intercambiable** *adj* interchangeable.
interceder [interθe'ðer] *v* intercede.
intercesión *sf* intercession.
interceptar [interθep'tar] *v* intercept;
block. **intercepción** *sf* interception.
interdecir [interðe'θir] *v* prohibit.
interdicción *sf also* **interdicto** *sm* prohibition.
interesar [intere'sar] *v* interest. **interés** *sm*

interest. **llevar interés** bear interest. **interesante** *adj* interesting.
*****interferir** [interfe'rir] *v* interfere.
interferencia *sf* interference.
intertin ['interin] *sm* interim. **interino** *adj*
provisional; acting.
interior [inte'rjor] *adj* interior; internal;
inner; home. *sm* interior; inside; inland.
interjección [interxek'θjon] *sf* interjection.
intermedio [inter'meðjo] *sm* interval;
interlude. *adj* intermediate. **intermediar** *v*
mediate. **intermediario, -a** *s*, *adj* intermediary.
interminable [intermi'naβle] *adj* interminable.
intermisión [intermi'sjon] *sf* intermission.
intermitente [intermi'tente] *adj* intermittent.
internacional [internaθjo'nal] *adj* international. **internacionalismo** *sm* internation-
alism. **internacionalista** *s(m+f)* interna-
tionalist.
internar [inter'nar] *v* intern; confine.
internarse *v* penetrate; intrude.
internamiento *sm* internment. **interno** *adj*
internal; domestic. **escuela interna** *sf*
boarding school.
interpelar [interpe'lar] *v* appeal to,
implore. **interpelación** *sf* appeal.
*****interponer** [interpo'ner] *v* interpose.
interponerse *v* intervene. **interposición** *sf*
intervention; (*jur*) lodging of an appeal.
interpretar [interpre'tar] *v* interpret.
interpretación *sf* interpretation. **intérprete** *s(m+f)* interpreter.
interrogar [interro'gar] *v* question. **interrogación** *sf* question; question mark.
interrogativo *adj* interrogative. **interrogatorio** *sm* interrogation.
interrumpir [interrum'pir] *v* interrupt.
interrupción *sf* interruption. **interruptor**
sm electrical switch.
intervalo [inter'βalo] *sm* interval; gap.
*****intervenir** [interβe'nir] *v* intervene;
interfere; participate; happen; control;
(*med*) operate on; (*com*) audit. **intervención** *sf* intervention; control; operation;
audit. **interventor** *sm* auditor; inspector;
supervisor.
intestado [intes'taðo] *adj* intestate.
intestino [intes'tino] *adj* internal. *sm*
intestine. **intestinal** *adj* intestinal.
intimar [inti'mar] *v* intimate; become
close friends. **intimación** *sf* declaration.

intimidad sf intimacy. **en la intimidad** privately. **íntimo** adj intimate.
intimidar [intimi'ðar] v intimidate. **intimidación** sf intimidation.
intolerable [intole'raβle] adj intolerable. **intolerancia** sf intolerance. **intolerante** adj intolerant.
intoxicar [intoksi'kar] v poison. **intoxicación** sf poisoning.
intraducible [intraðu'θiβle] adj untranslatable.
intranquilo [intran'kilo] adj restless. **intranquilidad** sf restlessness.
intransigente [intransi'xente] adj intransigent. **intransigencia** sf intransigence.
intransitable [intransi'taβle] adj impassable.
intransitivo [intransi'tiβo] adj (gram) intransitive.
intratable [intra'taβle] adj intractable; unsociable.
intrépido [in'trepiðo] adj brave. **intrepidez** sf valour.
intrigar [intri'gar] v intrigue. **intriga** sf intrigue. **intrigante** adj intriguing.
intrincado [intrin'kaðo] adj intricate; entangled.
intrínseco [in'trinseko] adj intrinsic.
*__introducir__ [introðu'θir] v introduce. **introducción** sf introduction. **introductor** adj introductory.
intruso [in'truso], -a sm, sf intruder. adj intrusive. **intrusarse** v intrude. **intrusión** sf intrusion.
intuición [intwi'θjon] sf intuition. **intuir** v feel; sense. **intuitivo** adj intuitive.
inundar [inun'dar] v flood. **inundación** sf flood. **inundante** adj flooding.
inusitado [inusi'taðo] adj unusual.
inútil [i'nutil] adj useless. **inutilidad** sf uselessness. **inutilizar** v render useless.
invadir [inβa'ðir] v invade. **invasión** sf invasion. **invasor**, -a sm, sf invader.
invalidar [inβali'ðar] v invalidate. **invalidación** sf invalidity. **inválido**, -a sm, sf invalid. adj invalid, void.
invariable [inva'rjaβle] adj invariable.
invencible [inβen'θiβle] adj invincible. **invencibilidad** sf invincibility.
inventar [inβen'tar] v invent. **invención** sf invention. **inventivo** adj inventive. **invento** sm invention. **inventor**, -a sm, sf inventor.
inventario [inβen'tarjo] sm inventory.

invernáculo [inβer'nakulo] sm also **invernadero** greenhouse, hothouse.
*__invernar__ [inβer'nar] v winter; hibernate. **invernada** sf winter; hibernation. **invernal** adj wintry.
inverosímil [inβero'simil] adj improbable. **inverosimilitud** sf improbability.
invertebrado [inβerte'βraðo] sm, adj invertebrate.
*__invertir__ [inβer'tir] v invert; (com) invest. **inversión** sf inversion; investment. **inverso** adj inverse, inverted. **por la inversa** the other way round.
investigar [inβesti'gar] v investigate. **investigación** sf investigation. **investigador**, -a sm, sf investigator; researcher.
*__investir__ [inβes'tir] v invest; confer upon. **investidura** sf investiture.
inveterado [inβete'raðo] adj inveterate, confirmed.
invicto [in'βikto] adj undefeated.
invierno [in'βjerno] sm winter.
inviolable [inβjo'laβle] adj inviolable. **inviolado** adj inviolate.
invisible [inβi'siβle] adj invisible. **invisibilidad** sf invisibility.
invitar [inβi'tar] v invite; call on. **invitar a una copa** stand a drink. **invitación** sf invitation. **invitado**, -a sm, sf guest.
invocar [inβo'kar] v invoke. **invocación** sf invocation.
involuntario [inβolun'tarjo] adj involuntary.
invulnerable [inβulne'raβle] adj invulnerable. **invulnerabilidad** sf invulnerability.
inyectar [injek'tar] v inject. **inyección** sf injection. **inyectado** adj congested.
*__ir__ [ir] v go; walk; come; suit. **irse** v go away. **ir a medias** go halves. **ir tirando** get by.
ira ['ira] sf anger. **iracundia** sf wrath. **iracundo** adj wrathful.
iris ['iris] sm (anat) iris. **arco iris** sm rainbow.
Irlanda [ir'landa] sf Ireland. **irlandés** adj Irish. sm Irishman; (idioma) Irish. **irlandesa** sf Irishwoman.
ironía [iro'nia] sf irony. **irónico** adj ironic(al).
irracional [irraθjo'nal] adj irrational. **irracionalidad** sf irrationality.
irradiar [irra'ðjar] v irradiate, radiate. **irradiación** sf irradiation.
irrazonable [irraθo'naβle] adj unreasonable.

irreal [irre'al] *adj* unreal. **irrealidad** *sf* unreality.

irreconciliable [irrekonθi'ljaβle] *adj* irreconcilable.

irrecuperable [irrekupe'raβle] *adj* irretrievable.

irreemplazable [irreempla'θaβle] *adj* irreplaceable.

irreflexión [irreflek'sjon] *sf* hastiness; thoughtlessness. **irreflexivo** hasty; thoughtless.

irrefrenable [irrefre'naβle] *adj* uncontrollable.

irrefutable [irrefu'taβle] *adj* irrefutable.

irregular [irregu'lar] *adj* irregular. **irregularidad** *sf* irregularity.

irreligioso [irreli'xjoso] *adj* irreligious.

irremediable [irreme'ðjaβle] *adj* incurable.

irreprimible [irrepri'miβle] *adj* irrepressible.

irresistible [irresis'tiβle] *adj* irresistible.

irresoluto [irreso'luto] *adj* irresolute. **irresoluble** *adj* unsolvable. **irresolución** *sf* irresolution, indecision.

irrespetuoso [irrespe'twoso] *adj* disrespectful.

irresponsable [irrespon'saβle] *adj* irresponsible. **irresponsabilidad** *sf* irresponsibility.

irrigar [irri'gar] *v* irrigate. **irrigación** *sf* irrigation. **irrigador** *sm* sprinkler.

irritable [irri'taβle] *adj* irritable. **irritabilidad** *sf* irritability. **irritación** *sf* irritation. **irritante** *sm, adj* irritant. **irritar** *v* irritate.

isla ['isla] *sf* island. **en isla** isolated. **isleño, -a** *sm, sf* islander.

Islandia [is'landja] *sf* Iceland. **islandés, -esa** *sm, sf* Icelander; *sm* (*idioma*) Icelandic. **islandés** *adj* Icelandic.

istmo ['istmo] *sm* isthmus.

Italia [i'talja] *sf* Italy. **italiano, -a** *s, adj* Italian.

itinerario [itine'rarjo] *sm* itinerary.

izar [i'θar] *v* hoist.

izquierda [iθ'kjerða] *sf* left; left hand; left wing. **mantenerse a la izquierda** keep left. **izquierdo** *adj* left; left-handed.

J

jabalí [xaβa'li] *sm* wild boar.

jabalina [xaβa'lina] *sf* javelin; (*zool*) wild sow.

jabón [xa'βon] *sm* soap. **jabón de tocador** toilet soap. **jabonar** *v* soap. **jabonera** *sf* soap-dish. **jabonoso** *adj* soapy.

jaca ['xaka] *sf* pony.

jacinto [xa'θinto] *sm* hyacinth.

jactarse [xak'tarse] *v* boast. **jactancia** *sf* boasting. **jactancioso** *adj* boastful.

jadear [xaðe'ar] *v* pant. **jadeante** *adj* panting. **jadeo** *sm* pant; panting.

jalear [xale'ar] *v* urge on. **jaleo** *sm* row, din. **armar un jaleo** start a row.

jamás [xa'mas] *adv* never. **nunca jamás** never ever.

jamón [xa'mon] *sm* ham. **jamón serrano** cured ham.

Japón [xa'pon] *sm* Japan. **japonés** *s(m+f)*, *adj* Japanese.

jaque ['xake] *sm* (*ajedrez*) check.

jaqueca [xa'keka] *sf* migraine. **dar jaqueca a** (*fam*) pester.

jarabe [xa'raβe] *sm* syrup.

jarana [xa'rana] *sf* spree; rumpus; trick. **dar jarabe a uno** (*fam*) butter someone up.

jardín [xar'ðin] *sm* garden. **jardinería** *sf* gardening. **jardinero, -a** *sm, sf* gardener.

jarra ['xarra] *sf* jug, pitcher. **jarro** *sm* jug; jar. **jarrón** *sm* vase.

jaula ['xaula] *sf* cage; crate; playpen.

jazmín [xaθ'min] *sm* jasmine.

jefe ['xefe] *sm* chief; head; leader. **jefa** *sf* head; manageress. **jefatura** *sf* leadership; managership; chieftaincy. **jefatura de policía** police headquarters.

jengibre [xen'xiβre] *sm* ginger.

jeque ['xeke] *sm* sheikh.

jerarquía [xerar'kia] *sf* hierarchy. **jerárquico** *adj* hierarchical.

jerez [xe'reθ] *sm* sherry.

jerga ['xerga] *sf also* **jerigonza** jargon.

jeringa [xe'ringa] *sf* syringe. **jeringar** *v* syringe; (*fam*) annoy.

jeroglífico [xero'glifiko] *s, adj* hieroglyphic.

jersey [xer'sei] *sm* jersey.

jesuita [xesu'ita] *sm, adj* Jesuit. **jesuítico** *adj* jesuitical.

jeta ['xeta] *sf* snout; thick lips; (*fam*) face, mug. **poner jeta** pull a face.

jilguero [xil'gero] *sm* goldfinch.

jinete [xi'nete] *sm* horseman; saddle horse; thoroughbred horse. **jinetear** *v* ride on horseback.

jirafa [xi'rafa] *sf* giraffe.

jocoso [xo'koso] *adj* amusing. **jocosidad** *sf* humour.

jofaina [xo'faina] *sf* washbowl.

jornada [xor'naða] *sf* journey; working day; session; expedition; (*teatro*) act. **al fin de la jornada** at the end of the day. **jornal** *sm* day's wage. **jornalero** *sm* day labourer.

joroba [xo'roβa] *sf* hump; (*fam*) pest. **jorobado, -a** *s, adj* hunchback.

jota ['xota] *sf* letter *j*; jot; Spanish dance.

joven ['xoβen] *adj* young. **jovenes** *s(m+f) pl* youth.

joya ['xoja] *sf* jewel. **joyería** *sf* jewellery. **joyero** *sm* jeweller.

jubilar [xuβi'lar] *v* retire; pension off. **jubilarse** *v* retire; rejoice. **jubilación** *sf* pension; retirement; jubilation.

jubileo [xuβi'leo] *sm* jubilee; comings and goings *pl*.

júbilo ['xuβilo] *sm* jubilation, rejoicing. **jubiloso** *adj* jubilant.

judía [xu'ðia] *sf* bean. **judía blanca** haricot bean. **judía escarlata** runner bean. **judía verde** French bean.

judicial [xuði'θjal] *adj* judicial. **judicatura** *sf* judicature.

judío [xu'ðio], **-a** *sm, sf* Jew. *adj* Jewish. **judaico** *adj* Jewish. **judaismo** *sm* Judaism.

juego ['xwego] *sm* game; sport; gambling; play; (*platos, tazas, etc.*) set; service.

juerga ['xwerga] *sf* (*fam*) spree, binge. **juergista** *s(m+f)* reveller.

jueves ['xweβes] *sm* Thursday.

juez [xweθ] *sm* judge, justice. **juez de hecho** juror.

*jugar [xu'gar] *v* play; bet; gamble. **jugarse** *v* bet; risk. **jugada** move; throw; stroke; shot; play. **mala jugada** dirty trick. **jugador, -a** *sm, sf* player; gambler.

juglar [xu'glar], **-a** *sm, sf* minstrel.

jugo ['xugo] *sm* juice; sap. **jugoso** *adj* juicy.

juguete [xu'gete] *sm* toy; plaything. **juguetear** *v* frolic. **jugueteo** *sm* frolicking. **juguetería** *sf* toyshop.

juicio ['xwiθjo] *sm* (*jur*) trial; judgment;

opinion; sense. **a juicio de** in the opinion of. **perder el juicio** lose one's mind. **juicioso** *adj* judicious.

julio ['xuljo] *sm* July.

jumento [xu'mento] *sm* ass.

junco¹ ['xunko] *sm* (*bot*) reed.

junco² *sm* (*mar*) junk.

jungla ['xungla] *sf* jungle.

junio ['xunjo] *sm* June.

junquera [xun'kera] *sf* (*bot*) rush.

junquillo [xun'kiʎo] *sm* (*bot*) jonquil.

juntar [xun'tar] *v* join; assemble; unite; collect. **juntarse** *v* meet; join; gather; live together. **junta** *sf* meeting; session; board; council; junta. **junto** *adj* joined, united, together. *adv* **junto a** near. **muy junto** very close.

juramentar [xuramen'tar] *v* swear in. **juramentarse** *v* take an oath. **jura** *sf* oath; swearing. **jurado** *adj* sworn; *sm* jury. **jurado de cuentas** chartered accountant. **juramento** *sm* oath; curse. **juramento falso** perjury. **jurar** *v* swear. **jurar al cargo** take the oath of office.

jurídico [xu'riðiko] *adj* juridical, legal.

jurisconsulto [xuriskon'sulto] *sm* legal expert. **jurisdicción** *sf* jurisdiction. **jurisprudencia** *sf* jurisprudence. **jurista** *sm* jurist, lawyer.

justa ['xusta] *sf* joust; contest.

justificar [xustifi'kar] *v* justify. **justificarse** *v* clear oneself. **justamente** *adv* justly; exactly; **¡justamente!** precisely! **justicia** *sf* justice; execution. **justiciable** *adj* actionable. **justiciero** *adj* just. **justificable** *adj* justifiable. **justificación** *sf* justification. **justificado** *adj* justified.

justo ['xusto] *adj* just; lawful; precise. *adv* exactly; tightly.

juvenil [xuβe'nil] *adj* youthful. *s(m+f)* junior. **juventud** *sf* youth.

juzgar [xuθ'gar] *v* judge; consider. **juzgar mal** misjudge. **juzgado** *sm* court.

K

kaki ['kaki] *sm, adj* khaki.

kilo ['kilo] *sm* kilo.

kilogramo [kilo'gramo] *sm* kilogramme.

kilolitro [kilo'litro] *sm* kilolitre.

kilómetro [ki'lometro] *sm* kilometre.
kilométrico *adj* kilometric.
kilovatio [kilo'βatjo] *sm* kilowatt.
kiosco ['kjosko] *sm* kiosk.

L

la [la] *art f* the. *pron* her, it.
laberinto [laβe'rinto] *sm* labyrinth; maze.
labio ['laβjo] *sm* lip. **labial** *adj* labial.
labor [la'βor] *sf* work; labour. **laborador** *sm* worker; farmer. **laborar** *v* work; till.
laborear *v* work; till; mine. **laboreo** *sm* working; tilling; mining. **laborioso** *adj* industrious; laborious. **laborismo** *sm* (*pol*) Labour party. **laborista** *s(m+f)* Labour-party member.
laboratorio [laβora'torjo] *sm* laboratory.
labrar [la'βrar] *v* fashion; carve; work; cultivate; build; bring about. **labradero** *adj* workable; arable. **labrador, -a** *sm, sf* peasant. **labranza** *sf* farming; farmland.
labriego *sm* peasant; farmhand.
laburno [la'βurno] *sm* laburnum.
laca ['laka] *sf* lacquer, varnish.
lacayo [la'kajo] *sm* lackey.
lacerar [laθe'rar] *v* lacerate; harm; (*fruta*) damage. **laceración** *sf* laceration; damage.
lacio ['laθjo] *adj* limp; lank; withered.
lacónico [la'koniko] *adj* laconic.
lacrar¹ [la'krar] *v* infect; damage. **lacra** *sf* blemish.
lacrar² *v* seal. **lacre** *sm* sealing wax.
lacrimoso [lakri'moso] *adj* tearful.
lácteo ['lakteo] *adj* milky. **vía láctea** *sf* Milky Way. **productos lácteos** *sm pl* dairy products. **lactante** *adj* suckling, nursling. **lactar** *v* suckle.
ladear [laðe'ar] *v* tip, tilt, overturn; deviate; skirt. **ladeo** *sm* tipping, tilting.
ladera [la'ðera] *sf* slope; hillside.
ladino [la'ðino] *adj* multilingual; crafty.
lado ['laðo] *sm* side; way; space; direction; protection. **al lado** close. **al lado de** beside. **por el lado de** in the direction of.
ladrar [la'ðrar] *v* bark. **ladrido** *sm* bark; barking.
ladrillo [la'ðriʎo] *sm* brick, tile.
ladrón [la'ðron], **-a** *sm, sf* thief, robber. *sm* sluice gate; multiple socket.

lagarto [la'garto] *sm* lizard.
lago ['lago] *sm* lake.
lágrima ['lagrima] *sf* tear; drop. **verter lágrimas** shed tears. **lagrimoso** *adj* tearful.
laguna [la'guna] *sf* lagoon; pond; gap.
laico ['laiko] *adj* lay, secular.
lamentar [lamen'tar] *v* lament; regret; grieve. **lamentarse** *v* complain. **lamentable** *adj* deplorable. **lamentación** *sf* lamentation, lament. **lamento** *sm* lament; mourning. **lamentoso** *adj* lamentable, mournful.
lamer [la'mer] *v* lick.
lámina ['lamina] *sf* metal sheet; picture; engraving. **laminar** *v* laminate.
lámpara ['lampara] *sf* lamp; light; valve.
lana ['lana] *sf* wool; fleece. **lana de vidrio** fibreglass. **lanudo** *adj* woolly; shaggy.
lance ['lanθe] *sm* throw; event; move; stroke. **lance de fortuna** chance. **de lance** second-hand.
lanceta [lan'θeta] *sf* lancet.
lancha ['lantʃa] *sf* launch; flagstone. **lancha salvavidas** lifeboat. **lanchero** *sm* boatman.
langosta [lan'gosta] *sf* lobster; locust.
*languidecer [langiðe'θer] *v* languish. **languidez** *sf* languor. **lánguido** *adj* languid.
lanza ['lanθa] *sf* spear; lance; pike; nozzle.
lanzar [lan'θar] *v* throw; fling; evict. **lanzarse** *v* spring. **lanzamiento** *sm* launching.
lápida ['lapiða] *sf* stone slab; tablet.
lápiz ['lapiθ] *sm* pencil. **lapicero** *sm* pencil-holder.
lapso ['lapso] *sm* lapse.
lar [lar] *sm* hearth; home.
largar [lar'gar] *v* loosen; free. **largarse** *v* go away.
largo ['largo] *adj* long; (*fam*) generous. *sm* length. **a lo largo de** the length of. **dar largas a** delay. **largueza** *sf* length; generosity.
laringe [la'rinxe] *sf* larynx.
larva ['larβa] *sf* larva.
lascivo [las'θiβo] *adj* lascivious. **lascivia** *sf* lasciviousness.
laso ['laso] *adj* weary. **lasitud** *sf* lassitude.
lástima ['lastima] *sf* pity; complaint. **¡qué lástima!** what a pity! **lastimar** *v* hurt. **lastimarse** *v* pity; complain. **lastimoso** *adj* pitiable, pitiful.

lastre ['lastre] *sm* ballast.

lata ['lata] *sf* tin, can; (*fam*) nuisance. **dar la lata** (*fam*) pester.

latente [la'tente] *adj* latent.

lateral [late'ral] *adj* lateral, side.

látigo ['latigo] *sm* whip. **latigazo** *sm* whiplash.

latín [la'tin] *sm* Latin. **latinoamericano, -a** *s, adj* Latin American.

latir [la'tir] *v* beat; throb. **latido** *sm* heartbeat; throb.

latitud [lati'tuð] *sf* latitude; breadth. **lato** *adj* broad.

latón [la'ton] *sm* brass.

latoso [la'toso] *adj* (*fam*) annoying; boring.

latrocinio [latro'θinjo] *sm* theft.

laúd [la'uð] *sm* lute.

laudable [lau'ðaβle] *adj* praiseworthy.

laurel [lau'rel] *sm* laurel; laurel wreath. **laureado** *adj* laureate. **laurear** *v* honour; reward. **lauro** *sm* (*fig*) glory.

lava ['laβa] *sf* lava.

lavar [la'βar] *v* wash. **lavable** *adj* washable. **lavabo** *sm* wash-basin. **lavación** *sf* lotion; wash. **lavadero** *sm* washing-place. **lavado** *sm* wash; washing. **lavadora** *sf* washing machine. **lavandería** *sf* laundry.

laxante [lak'sante] *sm* laxative. **laxidad** *sf* laxity.

lazo ['laθo] *sm* lasso; loop; bow; knot; snare; link.

leal [le'al] *adj* loyal. **lealdad** *sf* loyalty.

lebrel [le'βrel] *sm* greyhound.

lección [lek'θjon] *sf* lesson. **lector, -a** *sm, sf* reader; lecturer. **lectura** *sf* reading matter.

leche ['letʃe] *sf* milk. **lechería** *sf* dairy. **lechero** *sm* milkman.

lecho ['letʃo] *sm* bed; layer.

lechuga [le'tʃuga] *sf* lettuce.

lechuza [le'tʃuθa] *sf* owl.

*leer [le'er] *v* read.

legación [lega'θjon] *sf* legation. **legado** *sm* legacy; ambassador.

legal [le'gal] *adj* legal; lawful. **legalidad** *sf* legality. **legalización** *sf* legalization. **legalizar** *v* legalize.

legar [le'gar] *v* bequeath; depute.

legendario [lexen'darjo] *adj* legendary.

legible [le'xiβle] *adj* legible.

legión [le'xjon] *sf* legion.

legislar [lexis'lar] *v* legislate. **legislación** *sf* legislation. **legislador, -a** *sm, sf* legislator.

legislativo *adj* legislative. **legislatura** *sf* legislature.

legitimar [lexiti'mar] *v* prove; justify. **legitimidad** *sf* legitimacy. **legítimo** *adj* legitimate.

lego ['lego] *adj* lay. *sm* layman.

legua ['legwa] *sf* league.

legumbre [le'gumbre] *sf* vegetable.

lejía [le'xia] *sf* bleach.

lejos ['lexos] *adv* far away. **a lo lejos** in the distance. *sm* perspective; background. **lejanía** *sf* distance. **lejano** *adj* far-away.

lema ['lema] *sf* motto.

lencería [lenθe'ria] *sf* linen goods; lingerie.

lengua ['lengwa] *sf* tongue; language. **trabarse la lengua** become tongue-tied. **lenguaje** *sm* language; speech; style.

lenguado [len'gwaðo] *sm* (*zool*) sole.

lengüeta [len'gweta] *sf* (*de zapato*) tongue.

lenidad [leni'ðað] *sf* lenience; mildness.

lente ['lente] *s(m+f)* lens. **lente de aumento** magnifying glass. **lentes** *pl* glasses, spectacles. **lentes de contacto** contact lenses.

lenteja [len'texa] *sf* lentil.

lento ['lento] *adj* slow. **lentitud** *sf* slowness.

leña ['leɲa] *sf* firewood.

león [le'on] *sm* lion. **leona** *sf* lioness. **leonino** *adj* leonine.

lepra ['lepra] *sf* leprosy. **leproso** *adj* leprous.

lesión [le'sjon] *sf* injury. **lesionar** *v* injure. **lesivo** *adj* injurious.

letanía [leta'nia] *sf* litany; long list.

letargo [le'targo] *sm* lethargy. **letárgico** *adj* lethargic.

letra ['letra] *sf* letter; handwriting; lyric; (*com*) draft. **Letras** *sf pl* literature; Arts. **letra mayúscula** capital letter. **letra minúscula** lower-case letter. **letrado** *sm* lawyer. **letrero** *sm* label; sign.

leva ['leβa] *sf* (*tecn*) cam; lever. **árbol de levas** camshaft.

levadizo [leβa'ðiθo] *adj* that can be lifted. **puente levadizo** *sm* drawbridge.

levadura [leβa'ðura] *sf* leaven, yeast.

levantar [leβan'tar] *v* lift; raise; erect. **levantarse** *v* rise, get up. **levantamiento** *sm* raising; insurrection. **levantado** *adj* raised; lofty.

leve ['leβe] *adj* slight; trifling. **levedad** *sf* lightness; slightness.

léxico ['leksiko] *adj* lexical. *sm* dictionary; vocabulary.

ley [lej] *sf* law; loyalty; standard. **a toda ley** according to rule. **tener ley a** be very fond of.

leyenda [le'jenda] *sf* legend.

liar [ljar] *v* bind; tie up; (*fam*) involve. **liarlas** *v* (*fam*) clear off. **liarse** *v* (*fam*) join; start an affair; get involved.

libélula [li'βelula] *sf* dragonfly.

liberal [liβe'ral] *adj* generous. **liberalidad** *sf* generosity.

libertar [liβer'tar] *v also* **liberar** liberate, free. **libertad** *sf* freedom; independence. **libertador, -a** *sm, sf* liberator.

libertinaje [liβerti'naxe] *sm* licentiousness. **libertino, -a** *s, adj* libertine.

libra ['liβra] *sf* (*peso*) pound. **libra esterlina** pound sterling.

librar [li'βrar] *v* free; exempt; deliver; despatch; expedite; (*com*) draw; pass sentence. **librador, -a** *sm, sf* liberator. **libramiento** *sm* delivery; rescue; (*com*) draft. **libranza** *sf* (*com*) draft. **libre** *adj* free; vacant; isolated; loose.

librería [liβre'ria] *sf* bookshop; bookselling; bookcase. **librero, -a** *sm, sf* bookseller.

libreta [li'βreta] *sf* notebook; cashbook; one-pound loaf.

libro ['liβro] *sm* book. **libro diario** journal. **libro mayor** ledger.

licenciar [liθen'θjar] *v* license. **licenciarse** *v* graduate. **licencia** *sf* licence; degree; (*mil*) leave. **licenciado, -a** *sm, sf* graduate; *sm* lawyer; discharged soldier. **licenciatura** *sf* Bachelor's degree.

licencioso [liθen'θjoso] *adj* licentious.

liceo [li'θeo] *sm* lyceum; secondary school.

licitar [liθi'tar] *v* (*subasta*) bid. **licitación** *sf* bid. **licitador, -a** *sm, sf* bidder.

lícito ['liθito] *adj* authorized.

licor [li'kor] *sm* liquor; liqueur.

líder ['liðer] *sm* leader.

lidiar [li'ðjar] *v* (*toros*) fight. **lidia** *sf* bullfight. **lidiador** *sm* bullfighter.

liebre ['ljeβre] *sf* hare. **coger una liebre** (*fam*) come a cropper.

lienzo ['ljenθo] *sm* canvas; linen.

liga ['liga] *sf* garter; league; alloy. **ligadura** *sf* ligature; bond. **ligamento** *sm* ligament; bond. **ligar** *v* bind; tie; unite; alloy. **ligarse** *v* join; band together.

ligero [li'xero] *adj* light; swift; frivolous.

ligereza *sf* lightness; swiftness; frivolousness.

lija ['lixa] *sf* sandpaper; (*zool*) dogfish. **lijar** *v* sandpaper.

lila ['lila] *sf* (*bot*) lilac. *sm* (*color*) lilac. *adj* (*fam*) foolish.

lima¹ ['lima] *sf* file; polish. **limar** *v* file; polish; undermine. **limadura** *sf* filing.

lima² *sf* lime; lime tree.

limaza [li'maθa] *sf* slug.

limitar [limi'tar] *v* limit. **limitación** *sf* limitation. **límite** *sm* limit; boundary.

limón [li'mon] *sm* lemon; lemon tree. **limonada** *sf* lemonade. **limonero** *sm* lemon tree.

limosna [li'mosna] *sf* alms *pl*.

limpiabotas [limpja'βotas] *sm invar* bootblack.

limpiadera [limpja'ðera] *sf* clothes brush.

limpiadientes [limpja'ðjentes] *sm invar* toothpick.

limpiar [lim'pjar] *v* clean; clear; wipe; prune; weed. **limpiador, -a** *sm, sf* cleaner. **limpiadura** *sf* cleaning. **limpieza** *sf* cleanness. **limpio** *adj* clean; clear; pure. **jugar limpio** play fair. **poner en limpio** copy out.

linaje [li'naxe] *sm* lineage. **linaje humano** mankind.

linaza [li'naθa] *sf* linseed.

lince ['linθe] *sm* lynx.

linchar [lin'tʃar] *v* lynch. **linchamiento** *sm* lynching.

lindar [lin'dar] *v* **lindar con** border; adjoin. **linde** *sf* boundary. **lindero** *sm* limit.

lindo ['lindo] *adj* pretty; handsome; nice. **de lo lindo** a great deal. **lindeza** *sf* beauty; niceness. **lindura** *sf* prettiness.

línea ['linea] *sf* line; boundary; class. **línea aérea** airline. **lineal** *adj* linear.

lingüista [lin'gwista] *s(m+f)* linguist. **lingüística** *sf* linguistics. **lingüístico** *adj* linguistic.

linimento [lini'mento] *sm* liniment.

lino ['lino] *sm* linen.

linóleo [li'noleo] *sm* linoleum.

linterna [lin'terna] *sf* lantern; lamp; torch; lighthouse.

lío ['lio] *sm* parcel; trouble; mess. **armar un lío** raise a rumpus.

liquidar [liki'ðar] *v* liquefy; liquidate, settle up. **liquidez** *sf* fluidity. **líquido** *sm, adj* liquid; (*com*) net. **líquido imponible** net taxable amount.

lira ['lira] *sf* lyre; inspiration.
lírica ['lirika] *sf* lyric poetry. **lírico** *adj* lyric.
lirio ['lirjo] *sm* lily.
lirón [li'ron] *sm* dormouse. **dormir como un lirón** sleep like a log.
lisiar [li'sjar] *v* cripple. **lisiado** *adj* crippled.
liso ['liso] *adj* smooth.
lisonjear [lisonxe'ar] *v* flatter. **lisonja** *sf* flattery. **lisonjero** *adj* flattering.
lista ['lista] *sf* list; stripe; band. **a listas** striped. **lista de correos** poste restante. **lista de platos** menu.
listo ['listo] *adj* ready; finished; clever.
litera [li'tera] *sf* berth; bunk; (*cama*) litter.
literato [lite'rato], **-a** *sm, sf* literary person. *adj* literary. **literatura** *sf* literature.
litigar [liti'gar] *v* go to law, litigate. **litigación** *sf* litigation. **litigio** *sm* lawsuit. **litigioso** *adj* contentious.
litografía [lito'grafja] *sf* lithograph; lithography. **litográfico** *adj* lithographic.
litoral [lito'ral] *adj* coastal. *sm* shore.
litro ['litro] *sm* litre.
liturgia [litur'xia] *sf* liturgy. **litúrgico** *adj* liturgical.
liviano [li'βjano] *adj* light; trivial; lewd. **liviandad** *sf* lightness; triviality; lewdness.
lívido ['liβiðo] *adj* livid.
lo [lo] *art m* him, it; that, what.
loable [lo'aβle] *adj* praiseworthy. **loa** *sf* praise. **loador** *adj* praising. **loar** *v* praise.
lobo ['loβo] *sm* wolf. **lobo marino** seal. **lobero** *adj* wolfish.
lóbrego ['loβrego] *adj* gloomy, murky. **lobreguecer** *v* darken; grow dark. **lobreguez** *sf* gloom; murk.
lóbulo ['loβulo] *sm* lobe.
local [lo'kal] *adj* local. *sm* place. **localidad** *sf* locality; (*teatro*) seat. **sacar localidades** get tickets. **localizar** *v* localize.
loción [lo'θjon] *sf* lotion.
loco ['loko], **-a** *adj* mad; excessive. *sm, sf* mad person. **volverse loco** go mad. **locura** *sf* madness; folly. **hacer locuras** act madly.
locomoción [lokomo'θjon] *sf* locomotion. **locomotora** *sf* locomotive.
locuaz [lo'kwaθ] *adj* talkative. **locuacidad** *sf* talkativeness.
locutor [loku'tor], **-a** *sm, sf* radio announcer; commentator.

lodo ['loðo] *sm* mud. **lodoso** *adj* muddy.
lógica ['loxika] *sf* logic. **lógico** *adj* logical. **lógicamente** *adv* logically; naturally. **logística** *sf* logistics.
lograr [lo'grar] *v* get; achieve. **lograrse** *v* succeed. **logrería** *sf* profiteering. **logro** *sm* success; profit; usury.
loma ['loma] *sf* hill; slope.
lombriz [lom'briθ] *sf* worm; earthworm. **lombriz solitaria** tapeworm.
lomo ['lomo] *sm* (*carne*) loin; (*animal*) back; (*libro*) spine.
lona ['lona] *sf* canvas.
Londres ['londres] *sm* London.
longaniza [longa'niθa] *sf* pork sausage.
longevidad [lonxeβi'ðað] *sf* longevity.
longitud [lonxi'tuð] *sf* longitude. **longitudinal** *adj* longitudinal.
lonja ['lonxa] *sf* (*de carne*) slice; grocer's shop; strap; church porch.
loro ['loro] *sm* parrot.
losa ['losa] *sf* stone slab; tile.
lote ['lote] *sm* (*com*) lot; share; prize.
loza ['loθa] *sf* crockery; pottery.
lozano [lo'θano] *adj* luxuriant; lush; robust; sprightly. **lozanía** *sf* luxuriance.
lubrificar [luβrifi'kar] *v also* **lubricar** lubricate. **lubricación** *sf also* **lubrificación** lubrication. **lubricante** *sm, adj also* **lubrificante** lubricant.
lúcido ['luθiðo] *adj* lucid; shining. **lucidez** *sf* lucidity; brilliance.
luciérnaga [lu'θjernaga] *sf* glow-worm.
***lucir** [lu'θir] *v* shine; gleam; excel; show off. **lucirse** *v* be successful; dress up.
lucro ['lukro] *sm* profit, gain. **lucros y daños** profit and loss.
luchar [lu'tʃar] *v* fight, struggle. **lucha** *sf* fight, struggle. **lucha libre** all-in wrestling. **luchador, -a** *sm, sf* fighter.
luego ['lwego] *adv* then; next; later; presently. *conj* as; therefore. **luego que** as soon as. **desde luego** of course. **hasta luego** so long.
lugar [lu'gar] *sm* place; occasion; chance; opportunity. **en lugar de** instead of. **tener lugar** take place.
lugarteniente [lugarte'njente] *sm* lieutenant.
lúgubre ['luguβre] *adj* lugubrious.
lujo ['luxo] *sm* luxury. **de lujo** de luxe. **lujoso** *adj* luxurious.
lujuria [lu'xurja] *sf* lust; lechery. **lujuriar** *v* lust. **lujurioso** *adj* lustful; lecherous.

lumbago [lum'bago] *sm* lumbago.
lumbre ['lumbre] *sf* fire; brightness; light; skylight. **echar lumbres** spark. **lumbrera** *sf* luminary; skylight; air vent; (*fig*) leading light.
luminoso [lumi'noso] *adj* bright; luminous.
luna ['luna] *sf* moon. **luna de miel** honeymoon. **lunar** *adj* lunar. **lunático, -a** *s, adj* lunatic.
lunar [lu'nar] *sm* mole; beauty spot; blemish.
lunes ['lunes] *sm* Monday.
lupa ['lupa] *sf* magnifying glass.
lupanar [lupa'nar] *sm* brothel.
lustrar [lus'trar] *v* polish; purify. **lustre** *sm* lustre; gloss; splendour.
luto ['luto] *sm* mourning; bereavement. **ir de luto** be in mourning.
Luxemburgo [luksem'burgo] *sm* Luxembourg.
luz [luθ] *sf* light; daylight; window. **a todas luces** clearly. **dar la luz** put the light on.

LL

llaga ['ʎaga] *sf* ulcer; sore; wound. **llagar** *v* ulcerate; wound.
llama¹ ['ʎama] *sf* (*fuego*) flame. **estar en llamas** burst into flames. **llamear** *v* blaze.
llama² *sf* (*pantano*) swamp.
llama³ *sf* (*zool*) llama.
llamar [ʎa'mar] *v* call; appeal to; name; attract. **llamarse** *v* be called. **¿cómo se llama?** what is your name? **llamado** *adj* so-called. **llamada** *sf* call; summons. **llamador, -a** *sm, sf* caller; messenger.
llana ['ʎana] *sf* trowel.
llano ['ʎano] *adj* flat; plain; straightforward. **número llano** Roman numeral. *sm* plain; flatness. **llanura** *sf* evenness; flat land.
llanta ['ʎanta] *sf* iron hoop; rim.
llanto ['ʎanto] *sm* lament; crying.
llave ['ʎaβe] *sf* key; spanner. **llave maestra** skeleton key. **llave inglesa** adjustable spanner.
llegar [ʎe'gar] *v* arrive; reach; suffice;

happen. **llegarse** *v* come *or* go round. **llegar a** end up at. **llegar a sev** become. **llegada** *sf* arrival. **a la llegada** on arrival.
llenar [ʎe'nar] *v* fill; be satisfied. **lleno** *adj* full; covered; complete. **de lleno** completely. **llenura** *sf* abundance.
llevar [ʎe'βar] *v* take; carry; wear; deal with; sever; charge; manage; (*tiempo*) spend. **llevar a cabo** carry out. **llevarse** *v* take away. **llevarse bien con** get on well with.
llorar [ʎo'rar] *v* weep, cry; mourn. **llorón, -ona** *adj* weepy. **lloroso** *adj* tearful.
llover [ʎo'βer] *v* rain. **llover a cántaros** pour down. **lloverse** *v* (*tejado*) leak. **lloviznar** *v* drizzle. **llovizna** *sf* drizzle. **lluvia** *sf* rain. **lluvioso** *adj* rainy.

M

macabro [ma'kaβro] *adj* macabre.
macarrón [makar'ron] *sm* macaroon. **macarrones** *sm pl* macaroni *sing*.
macanudo [maka'nuðo] *adj* (*fam*) terrific.
maceta [ma'θeta] *sf* flowerpot.
macilento [maθi'lento] *adj* lean; wan.
macizo [ma'θiθo] *adj* solid. *sm* mass; flowerbed. **macizar** *v* fill up.
mácula ['makula] *sf* spot, stain. **macular** *v* spot, stain.
machacar [matʃa'kar] *v* pound; crush; bombard; (*fig*) harp on. **machacón, -ona** *sm, sf* bore; swot. **machaconería** *sf* tiresomeness. **machaqueo** *sm* pounding; crushing; harping.
machete [ma'tʃete] *sm* machete; hunting-knife.
macho ['matʃo] *adj* male; masculine; virile. *sm* (*fam*) he-man; sledgehammer; he-mule. **machismo** *sm* virility.
machucar [matʃu'kar] *v* beat; pound; bruise.
madeja [ma'ðexa] *sf* skein; mop of hair.
madera [ma'ðera] *sf* wood, timber; horn. **tener madera de** have the makings of. **maderería** *sf* timber yard. **madero** *sm* beam; log.
madrastra [ma'ðrastra] *sf* stepmother.
madre ['maðre] *sf* mother. **madre política** mother-in-law.

madreselva [maðre'selβa] *sf* honeysuckle.
madriguera [maðri'gera] *sf* den; warren.
madrina [ma'ðrina] *sf* godmother; patroness. **madrina de boda** bridesmaid.
madrugar [maðru'gar] *v* rise early. **madrugada** *sf* early morning. **madrugador, -a** *sm, sf* early riser.
madurar [maðu'rar] *v* mature, ripen.
madurez *sf* maturity; wisdom. **maduro** *adj* ripe; middle-aged.
maestría [maes'tria] *sf* mastery. **maestrar** *v* direct; conduct; domineer. **maestra** *sf* mistress; schoolmistress. **maestro** *sm* master; teacher; *adj* master, main, chief.
magistral *adj* masterly.
magia ['maxja] *sf* magic. **mágico** *adj* magic(al). **magico** *sm* magician.
magistrado [maxi'straðo] *sm* magistrate. **magistratura** *sf* judicature.
magnánimo [mag'nanimo] *adj* magnanimous. **magnanimidad** *sf* magnanimity.
magnético [mag'netiko] *adj* magnetic. **magnetismo** *sm* magnetism. **magnetizar** *v* magnetize.
magnetofón [magneto'fon] *sm also* **magnetófono** tape recorder. **cinta magnetofónica** recording tape.
magnífico [mag'nifiko] *adj* magnificent. **magnificencia** *sf* magnificence.
magnitud [magni'tuð] *sf* size, magnitude.
mago ['mago] *sm* magician, wizard.
magro ['magro] *adj* thin, lean. *sm* lean meat.
magullar [magu'ʎar] *v* bruise. **magulladura** *sf* bruise.
maíz [ma'iθ] *sm* maize. **harina de maíz** *sf* cornflour.
majadero [maxa'ðero] *adj* silly; boring. *sm* pestle. **majadería** *sf* nonsense. **majadura** *sf* crushing, pounding. **majar** *v* crush, pound.
majestad [maxes'tað] *sf* majesty; royalty; grandeur. **majestuoso** *adj* majestic; stately; solemn.
majo ['maxo], **-a** *sm, sf* dandy. *adj* sporty; swaggering; genial.
mal [mal] *adj V* **malo**. *adv* badly; poorly; wrongly. *sm* wrong; evil; illness; harm. **de mal en peor** from bad to worse. **echar a mal** despise; waste. **llevar a mal** take offence at. **mal que bien** somehow or other.
malaconsejado [malakonse'xaðo] *adj* ill-advised.

malacostumbrado [malakostum'braðo] *adj* spoiled.
malaventura [malaβen'tura] *sf* misfortune. **malaventurado** *adj* unlucky.
malbaratar [malβara'tar] *v* squander; undersell.
malcontento [malkon'tento], **-a** *sm, sf* malcontent. *adj* discontented.
malcriado [malkri'aðo] *adj* ill-bred. **malcriar** *v* spoil.
maldad [mal'ðað] *sf* wickedness.
***maldecir** [malðe'θir] *v* curse. **maldecir de** speak ill of. **maldición** *sf* curse. **maldito** *adj* accursed.
maleable [male'aβle] *adj* malleable. **maleabilidad** *sf* malleability.
malear [male'ar] *v* damage; spoil. **malearse** *v* go wrong.
maleficio [male'fiθjo] *sm* injury; witchcraft. **maleficiar** *v* hurt; bewitch.
malestar [males'tar] *sm* uneasiness.
maleta [ma'leta] *sf* suitcase; (*auto*) trunk. **hacer la maleta** pack up.
malévolo [ma'leβolo] *adj* malevolent. **malevolencia** *sf* malevolence.
maleza [ma'leθa] *sf* thicket; weeds *pl*.
malgastar [malgas'tar] *v* squander, waste. **malgastador, -a** *s, adj* spendthrift.
malhablado [mala'βlaðo] *adj* foulmouthed.
malhechor [male'tʃor], **-a** *sm, sf* wrongdoer. **malhecho** *sm* misdeed.
malhumorado [malumo'raðo] *adj* ill-tempered.
malicia [ma'liθja] *sf* malice; slyness; mischievousness. **maliciable** *adj* suspicious. **maliciarse** *v* go bad. **malicioso** *adj* malicious; shrewd; sly.
maligno [ma'ligno] *adj* malignant; malicious. **maliguidad** *sf* malignity; malice.
malintencionado [malintenθjo'naðo] *adj* ill-disposed.
malo ['malo] *adj also* **mal** bad; evil; wrong; poor; difficult; sick. **estar malo** be ill. **mala fama** ill fame. **venir de malas** have bad intentions.
malograr [malo'grar] *v* waste; miss. **malograrse** *v* fail; fall through. **malogrado** *adj* abortive. **malogro** *sm* failure.
***malquerer** [malke'rer] *v* hate. **malquerencia** *sf* ill-will; hatred.
malsano [mal'sano] *adj* unhealthy; sick; insanitary.

malta ['malta] *sf* malt.

Malta ['malta] *sf* Malta. **maltés, -esa** *s, adj* Maltese; *sm* (*idioma*) Maltese.

maltratar [maltra'tar] *v* ill-treat. **maltraer** *v* hurt; abuse. **maltrato** *sm* ill-treatment.

malva ['malβa] *sf* mallow. **malva real** hollyhock.

malvado [mal'βaðo], **-a** *sm, sf* evildoer. *adj* wicked.

malla ['maʎa] *sf* mesh; network; (*de metal*) mail. **mallas** *sf pl* tights.

mallo ['maʎo] *sm* mallet.

mamá [ma'ma] *sf also* **mama** mum(my), mother.

mamar [ma'mar] *v* suck; acquire. **mamarse** *v* get drunk; fiddle, wangle. **mamoso** *adj* sucking.

mamífero [ma'mifero] *sm* mammal.

mampostería [mamposte'ria] *sf* masonry. **mampuesto** *sm* rubble.

manada [ma'naða] *sf* herd, flock; crowd. **manadero** *sm* herdsman; shepherd.

manantial [manan'tjal] *sm* spring; source, origin. **manar** *v* flow; issue.

mancebo [man'θeβo] *sm* youth; shop assistant; bachelor.

manco ['manko] *adj* one-handed; one-armed; crippled; faulty. **mancar** *v* cripple.

mancomunar [mankomu'nar] *v* join, unite. **mancomún** *adv* jointly. **mancomunarse** *v* merge. **mancomunidad** *sf* association, confederation.

manchar [man'tʃar] *v* stain; mark. **mancha** *sf* stain; mark; dishonour.

mandar [man'dar] *v* order; command; send; bequeath. **mandarse** *v* manage by oneself. **mandadero, -a** *sm, sf* messenger. **mandado** *sm* order; errand. **mandamiento** *sm* commandment, order.

mandatario [manda'tarjo] *sm* attorney; agent; mandatary. **mandato** *sm* commandment; mandate. **mandato judicial** writ.

mandíbula [man'diβula] *sf* jawbone.

mando ['mando] *sm* command; power; authority.

manejar [mane'xar] *v* operate; handle; manage. **manejable** *adj* manageable. **manejo** *sm* operation; handling; control; stratagem.

manera [ma'nera] *sf* manner; mode; way; fashion. **a manera de** by way of. **de ninguna manera** by no means. **de todas**

maneras by all means. **manera de ver** outlook.

manga ['manga] *sf* sleeve; hosepipe; waterspout. **manga de agua** shower. **manga de viento** whirlwind. **manguera** *sf* garden hose.

mango[1] ['mango] *sm* (*bot*) mango.

mango[2] *sm* handle; stock.

manía [ma'nia] *sf* mania, craze. **maníaco** *adj, sm* maniac.

maniatar [manja'tar] *v* manacle.

manicomio [mani'komjo] *sm* lunatic asylum.

***manifestar** [manifes'tar] *v* show; declare; manifest. **manifestación** *sf* manifestation. **manifestante** *s(m+f)* demonstrator. **manifiesto** *adj* clear, evident. **manifiesto** *sm* manifesto.

maniobrar [manjo'βrar] *v* manoeuvre; operate; manipulate; plot. **maniobra** *sf* manoeuvre; stratagem; handling.

manipular [manipu'lar] *v* manipulate. **manipulación** *sf* manipulation. **manipulador, -a** *sm, sf* manipulator.

maniquí [mani'ki] *sm* tailor's dummy; puppet. *sf* mannequin; model.

manivela [mani'βela] *sf* (*auto*) crank.

mano ['mano] *sf* hand; paw; (*pintura*) coat; (*juego*) hand, round, turn. **a mano** by hand. **a mano salva** without risk. **de segunda mano** secondhand. **darse las manos** shake hands. **mano a mano** in a friendly way. **manojo** *sm* handful.

manosear [manose'ar] *v* handle; paw; fondle. **manoseado** *adj* hackneyed.

mansión [man'sjon] *sf* mansion.

manso ['manso] *adj* tame; gentle; meek. **mansedumbre** *sf* tameness; meekness.

manta ['manta] *sf* blanket; rug; (*fam*) thrashing.

manteca [man'teka] *sf* grease; lard; butter; cream. **mantecada** *sf* slice of bread and butter.

mantecado [mante'kaðo] *sm* ice-cream; bun.

mantel ['mantel] *sm* tablecloth.

***mantener** [mante'ner] *v* maintain; hold; defend; feed; sustain. **mantenimiento** *sm* maintenance.

mantequilla [mante'kiʎa] *sf* butter. **mantequera** *sf* churn; butter-dish. **mantequería** *sf* dairy.

mantilla [man'tiʎa] *sf* mantilla, shawl.

manto ['manto] *sm* cloak. **mantón** *sm* shawl.

manual [ma'nwal] *sm* handbook. *adj* manual.
manubrio [manu'βrio] *sm* handle; crank.
manufactura [manufak'tura] *sf* manufacture; factory. **manufacturado** *adj* manufactured. **manufacturar** *v* manufacture.
manuscrito [manu'skrito] *sm* manuscript.
manzana [man'θana] *sf* apple; block of flats. **manzano** *sm* apple tree.
maña ['maɲa] *sf* skill; bad habit; cunning. **mañoso** *adj* clever; crafty.
mañana [ma'ɲana] *sf* morning. *sm, adv* tomorrow. **de mañana** early. **hasta mañana** see you tomorrow. **pasado mañana** the day after tomorrow.
mapa ['mapa] *sm* map; chart.
máquina ['makina] *sf* machine; locomotive; engine; car; bicycle. **a toda máquina** at full speed. **máquina de coser** sewing machine. **máquina de escribir** typewriter. **máquina registradora** cash register.
maquinación [makina'θjon] *sf* machination; plotting. **maquinal** *adj* automatic; mechanical. **maquinar** *v* plot.
mar [mar] *s(m+f)* sea. **alta mar** high seas. **baja mar** low tide.
maraña [ma'raɲa] *sf* thicket; tangle; perplexity. **marañar** *v* tangle. **marañoso** *adj* entangling.
maravillar [maraβi'ʎar] *v* wonder; amaze. **maravilla** *sf* marvel; wonder. **maravilloso** *adj* wonderful.
marcar [mar'kar] *v* mark; brand; show; dial; score. **marca** *sf* mark; make; gauge; label. **marca registrada** registered trademark.
marcial [mar'θjal] *adj* martial; warlike.
marco ['marko] *sm* frame; setting; (*moneda*) mark.
marchar [mar'tʃar] *v* march; go; run; work; depart. **marcharse** *v* go away. **marcha** *sf* march; course; movement; departure. **poner en marcha** set in motion.
marchitar [martʃi'tar] *v* fade; wither; shrivel. **marchitable** *adj* perishable. **marchito** *adj* faded.
marea [ma'rea] *sf* tide; light breeze; dew. **marea creciente/menguante** flood/ebb tide.
marearse [mare'arse] *v* feel (sea) sick. **mareado** *adj* (sea) sick; dizzy. **mareo** *sm* sickness; (*fam*) nuisance.
marfil [mar'fil] *sm* ivory.
margarina [marga'rina] *sf* margarine.

margarita [marga'rita] *sf* daisy; pearl.
margen [mar'xen] *sm* border; margin; verge; shoulder; fringe. **al margen de** in addition to. *sf* river bank; seashore.
marica [ma'rika] *sf* magpie. *sm* (*fam*) sissy. **maricón** *sm* homosexual.
marido [ma'riðo] *sm* husband.
mariguana [mari'gwana] *sf also* **marihuana** marijuana.
marina [ma'rina] *sf* navy; shore; seamanship. **marinero** *sm* sailor. **marinero** *adj* seafaring; seaworthy. **marino** *sm* sailor. **marino** *adj* marine.
mariposa [mari'posa] *sf* butterfly.
mariquita [mari'kita] *sf* ladybird.
mariscal [maris'kal] *sm* marshal. **mariscal de campo** field marshal.
marisco [ma'risko] *sm* seafood; shellfish.
marítimo [ma'ritimo] *adj* maritime.
marmita [mar'mita] *sf* stewpot.
mármol ['marmol] *sm* marble. **marmóreo** *adj* marble.
marqués [mar'kes] *sm* marquis. **marquesa** *sf* marchioness.
marrano [ma'rrano] *sm* pig. *adj* filthy.
marrón [ma'rron] *adj* brown; maroon. *sm* (*color*) chestnut.
marsopa [mar'sopa] *sf* porpoise.
martes ['martes] *sm invar* Tuesday.
martillar [marti'ʎar] *v* hammer. **martillo** *sm* hammer.
martín pescador [mar'tin peska'ðor] *sm* kingfisher.
mártir ['martir] *s(m+f)* martyr. **martirio** *sm* martyrdom.
marxista [mark'sista] *s(m+f)* Marxist. **marxismo** *sm* Marxism.
marzo ['marθo] *sm* March.
mas [mas] *conj* but; yet. **mas que** although.
más [mas] *adv* more; most. **nada más** nothing else. **es más** moreover. **más bien** rather. **por más que** however much. *sm* plus.
masa ['masa] *sf* mass; volume; dough; mortar.
masaje [ma'saxe] *sm* massage. **masajista** *s(m+f)* masseur, masseuse.
mascar [mas'kar] *v* chew; (*fam*) mumble. **mascadura** *sf* chewing.
máscara ['maskara] *sf* mask. **mascarada** *sf* masquerade.
masculino [masku'lino] *adj* masculine, male. *sm* (*gram*) masculine. **masculinidad** *sf* masculinity.

masón [ma'son] sm freemason. masonería sf freemasonry.

masoquismo [maso'kismo] sm masochism. masoquista s(m+f) masochist. masoquista adj masochistic.

masticar [masti'kar] v chew. masticación sf mastication.

mástil ['mastil] sm (mar) mast; pole; post.

mastín [mas'tin] sm mastiff. mastín danés Great Dane.

masturbación [masturβa'θjon] sf masturbation. masturbarse v masturbate.

mata ['mata] sf bush; shrub; grove; mop of hair.

matafuego [mata'fwego] sm fire extinguisher.

matar [ma'tar] v kill, slaughter; tire out; put out. matadero sm slaughterhouse. matador sm bullfighter. matanza sf slaughter.

matamoscas [mata'moskas] sm invar flyswatter.

matarratas [matar'ratas] sm invar rat poison.

mate¹ ['mate] sm (check)mate.

mate² adj mat, dull.

matemáticas [mate'matikas] sf mathematics. matemático, -a sm, sf mathematician. matemático adj mathematical.

materia [ma'terja] sf matter; stuff; subject. materia prima raw material. en materia de as regards. material adj material. material sm stuff, material. materiales de derribo rubble sing. materialismo sm materialism. materialista s(m+f) materialist. materialista adj materialistic. materializar v materialize.

maternal [mater'nal] adj maternal. maternidad sf maternity. casa de maternidad maternity hospital. materno adj maternal.

matinal [mati'nal] adj morning.

matiz ['matiθ] sm tint; hue; shade; shade of meaning. matizado adj variegated. matizar v blend; shade.

matorral [mator'ral] sm bush; thicket; scrubland.

matricular [matriku'lar] v enrol; register; matriculate. matricularse v register; (contienda) enter. matrícula sf register; enrolment; matriculation; (auto) licence plate.

matrimonio [matri'monjo] sm matrimony, marriage; (fam) married couple.

matriz [ma'triθ] sf matrix; womb. adj mother; chief. casa matriz headquarters.

matrona [ma'trona] sf matron; midwife.

matute [ma'tute] sm smuggling; contraband. matutear v smuggle. matutero, -a sm, sf smuggler.

matutino [matu'tino] adj also matutinal morning.

maullar [mau'ʎar] v mew. maullido sm mewing.

mausoleo [mauso'leo] sm mausoleum.

máxima ['maksima] sf maxim.

máxime ['maksime] adv especially; principally. máximo adj, sm maximum.

maya ['maja] sf daisy.

mayo ['majo] sm May; maypole.

mayonesa [majo'nesa] sf mayonnaise.

mayor [ma'jor] sm head, chief. adj older, elder; major, main; larger; adult. calle mayor high street. al por mayor wholesale. mayoral sm foreman; farm manager.

mayorazgo [majo'raθgo] sm primogeniture; first born son; entailed estate.

mayordomo [major'ðomo] sm butler; steward.

mayoría [majo'ria] sf majority; coming of age.

mayorista [majo'rista] sm wholesaler. adj wholesale.

mayúscula [ma'juskula] sf capital letter.

maza ['maθa] sf mace; club; butt. mazada sf blow with a club.

mazapán [maθa'pan] sm marzipan.

mazmorra [maθ'morra] sf dungeon.

me [me] pron me, myself.

mear [me'ar] v (vulgar) piss. mearse v wet oneself. meadero sm urinal.

mecánica [me'kanika] sf mechanics; machinery. mecánico sm mechanic; driver. mecanismo sm mechanism. mecanizar v mechanize.

mecanógrafo [meka'nografo], -a sm, sf typist. mecanografía sf typewriting. mecanografiar v type.

mecer [me'θer] v rock; swing; shake; stir. mecador sm swing. mecedora sf rocking-chair.

mecha ['metʃa] sf wick; fuse; match.

mechera [me'tʃera] sf (fam) shoplifter.

mechero [me'tʃero] sm cigarette lighter; gas burner.

medalla [me'ðaʎa] sf medal.

media ['meðja] sf stocking.

mediado [me'ðjaðo] adj half-full; halfway through; half-finished. a mediados de in or about the middle of.

mediano [me'ðjano] *adj* medium; average; mediocre. **medianero** *adj* intermediate; interceding.

medianoche [meðja'notʃe] *sf* midnight.

mediante [me'ðjante] *adj* intervening. *prep* by means of. **mediar** *v* intervene; mediate; elapse.

medicina [meði'θina] *sf* medicine. **medicación** *sf* medication. **medicamento** *sm* medicament. **medicar** *v* medicate. **medicinal** *adj* medicinal. **médico** *sm* doctor. **médico** *adj* medical.

medio ['meðjo] *sm* middle; half; medium; way. **de medio a medio** completely. **medios** *sm pl* means, resources. *adv* half; partly. **medidas a medias** half-measures. *adj* half; middle; average; medium. **de medio cuerpo** half-length.

mediocre [me'ðjokre] *adj* mediocre. **mediocridad** *sf* mediocrity.

mediodía [meðjo'ðia] *sm* midday, noon; south.

medioeval [meðjoe'βal] *adj* medieval.

***medir** [me'ðir] *v* measure; scan. **medirse** *v* act prudently. **medida** *sf* measure(ment); step; moderation. **a medida que** according as.

meditar [meði'tar] *v* meditate (on). **meditabundo** *adj* pensive. **meditación** *sf* meditation.

mediterráneo [meðiter'raneo] *adj* Mediterranean.

medrar [me'ðrar] *v* prosper, thrive; grow. **medra** *sf* prosperity; growth. **medro** *sm* progress; improvement.

medroso [me'ðroso] *adj* fearful; timid; frightening.

médula ['meðula] *sf also* **medula** marrow; (*fig*) essence.

medusa [me'ðusa] *sf* jellyfish.

megáfono [me'gafono] *sm* megaphone.

megalómano [mega'lomano], **-a** *sm, sf* megalomaniac. **megalomanía** *sf* megalomania.

mejilla [me'xiʎa] *sf* cheek.

mejor [me'xor] *adj* better; best. *adv* better; best; rather. **a lo mejor** probably. **mejor que mejor** better still. **tanto mejor** so much the better. **mejora** *sf* improvement. **mejorar** *v* improve; surpass. **mejorarse** *v* get better.

melancólico [melan'koliko] *adj* melancholy. **melancolía** *sf* melancholy.

melandro [me'landro] *sm* badger.

melaza [me'laθa] *sf* molasses; treacle.

melena [me'lena] *sf* mane; long hair.

melindroso [melin'droso] *adj* finicky; squeamish.

melocotón [meloko'ton] *sm* peach; peach tree.

melodía [melo'ðia] *sf* melody; tune. **melodioso** *adj* melodious.

melodrama [melo'ðrama] *sm* melodrama. **melodramático** *adj* melodramatic.

melón [me'lon] *sm* melon.

meloso [me'loso] *adj* honeyed; mild; sickly.

mella ['meʎa] *sf* notch; dent; impression. **hacer mella a** make a deep impression on.

mellizo [me'ʎiθo], **-a** *s, adj* twin.

membrana [mem'brana] *sf* membrane.

membrillo [mem'briʎo] *sm* quince; quince tree.

memorable [memo'raβle] *adj* memorable. **memorar** *v* remember. **memoria** *sf* memory; record. **de memoria** by heart. **memorial** *sm* memorial; petition.

mencionar [menθjo'nar] *v* mention, name. **mención** *sf* mention.

mendigar [mendi'gar] *v* beg. **mendicación** *sf* begging. **mendicante** *adj* begging. **mendigante** *sm* beggar. **mendigo, -a** *sm, sf* beggar.

menear [mene'ar] *v* stir; shake; sway; manage; run. **meneo** *sm* wag; shake; rearranging.

menester [menes'ter] *sm* need; want; occupation. **ser menester** be necessary. **menesteroso** *adj* needy.

menguar [men'gwar] *v* lessen; decline. **mengua** *sf* lessening; decline. **menguado** *adj* impaired; diminished; wretched.

menopausia [meno'pausja] *sf* menopause.

menor [me'nor] *adj* minor; lesser; least; younger; youngest; smaller; smallest. **al por menor** retail.

menos ['menos] *adj* less, fewer. *adv* less; minus; except. **al, a lo** *or* **por lo menos** at least. **echar de menos** miss.

menoscabar [menoska'βar] *v* lessen; impair; discredit. **menoscabo** *sm* reduction; impairment.

menospreciar [menospre'θjar] *v* underrate; despise. **menospreciable** contemptible. **menosprecio** *sm* contempt; scorn; disrespect; undervaluation.

mensaje [men'saxe] *sm* message. **mensajero, -a** *sm, sf* messenger.

menstruar [menstru'ar] v menstruate.
menstruación sf menstruation. menstrual adj menstrual.
mensual [men'swal] adj monthly. mensualidad sf monthly salary.
mensurar [mensu'rar] v measure. mensura sf measure. mensural adj measuring.
menta ['menta] sf mint; peppermint.
mental [men'tal] adj mental; intellectual. mentalidad sf mentality. mente sf mind. irse de la mente slip one's mind.
mentecato [mente'kato], -a sm, sf simpleton. adj foolish; half-witted.
*mentir [men'tir] v lie. mentir con disagree. mentira sf lie; error. parece mentira it's hard to believe.
menudear [menuðe'ar] v repeat frequently; happen often. menudencia sf detail; minuteness; pettiness. menudencias sf pl or menudas sm pl offal sing. menudo adj small, tiny; petty. a menudo often.
meñique [me'ɲike] sm little finger. adj tiny.
meollo [me'oʎo] sm (anat) marrow; brains pl; (fig) essence.
meple ['meple] sm maple.
mercado [mer'kaðo] sm market. Mercado Común Common Market. mercadear v trade. mercader sm merchant. mercadería sf merchandise. mercancía sf goods pl. mercante adj merchant. mercantil adj mercantile.
merced [mer'θeð] sf mercy; favour. merced a thanks to.
mercenario [merθe'narjo], -a s, adj mercenary.
mercero [mer'θero], -a sm, sf haberdasher. mercería sf haberdashery.
mercurio [mer'kurjo] sm mercury. mercurial adj mercurial.
*merecer [mere'θer] v deserve; be worthy of. merecer la pena be worthwhile. merecimiento sm merit.
*merendar [meren'dar] v take afternoon tea; have an afternoon snack. merendarse a get the better of. merendero sm open-air café. merienda sf afternoon snack.
merengue [me'renge] sm meringue.
meridiano [meri'ðjano] sm, adj meridian. meridiana sf couch. meridional adj southern.
mérito ['merito] sm merit; value. hacer mérito de mention. meritorio adj meritorious.

merla ['merla] sf blackbird.
merluza [mer'luθa] sf hake.
mermar [mer'mar] v decrease, reduce. merma sf reduction; wastage; loss.
mermelada [merme'laða] sf marmalade; jam.
mero ['mero] adj mere, pure.
merodear [meroðe'ar] v maraud. merodeador, -a sm, sf marauder.
mes [mes] sm month. al mes per month.
mesa ['mesa] sf table; desk. mesa de cambios bank. alzar la mesa clear the table.
meseta [me'seta] sf plateau; staircase landing.
mesón [me'son] sm inn, hostelry. mesonero, -a sm, sf innkeeper.
mestizo [mes'tiθo], -a s, adj half-caste.
mesura [me'sura] sf dignity; politeness; moderation.
meta ['meta] sf goal; aim; destination. guardameta sm goalkeeper.
metabolismo [metabo'lismo] sm metabolism.
metafísica [meta'fiska] sf metaphysics. metafísico adj metaphysical.
metáfora [me'tafora] sf metaphor. metafórico adj metaphorical.
metal [me'tal] sm metal; (música) brass; (voz) timbre. metálico adj metallic. metalurgía sf metallurgy.
meteoro [mete'oro] sm meteor. meteórico adj meteoric. meteorito sm meteorite. meteorología sf meteorology.
meter [me'ter] v insert, put in; smuggle; produce; reduce. meterse v interfere; intervene. meterse a turn to. meterse con quarrel with. metido adj compressed.
meticuloso [metiku'loso] adj meticulous.
metodista [meto'ðista] s(m+f), adj Methodist. metodismo sm Methodism.
método ['metoðo] sm method, manner. metódico adj methodical.
métrico ['metriko] adj metric(al). metro sm metre; underground railway.
metrónomo [me'tronomo] sm metronome.
metrópoli [me'tropoli] sf metropolis. metropolitano adj metropolitan.
mezclar [meθ'klar] v mix; blend. mezclarse v mingle; intermarry. mezcla sf mixture, medley. mezcladora sf mixer, blender. mezcolanza sf hotchpotch.

mezquino [meθ'kino] *adj* mean. **mezquindad** *sf* meanness.
mezquita [meθ'kita] *sf* mosque.
mi [mi] *adj* my. **mí** *pron* me.
miaja ['mjaxa] *sf* crumb; bit.
mico ['miko] *sm* monkey.
microbio [mi'kroβjo] *sm* microbe. **microbiología** *sf* microbiology.
micrófono [mi'krofono] *sm* microphone.
microscopio [mikro'skopjo] *sm* microscope. **microscópico** *adj* microscopic.
miedo [mi'eðo] *sm* fear. **dar miedo a** frighten. **tener miedo** be afraid. **miedoso** *adj* frightened.
miel [mi'el] *sf* honey. **miel de caña** molasses.
miembro ['mjembro] *sm* member; limb.
miente ['mjente] *sf* mind; thought. **caer en mientes** come to mind. **¡ni por mientes!** not on your life! **parar mientes en** consider.
mientras ['mjentras] *adv, conj* while; meanwhile; so long as. **mientras tanto** meanwhile.
miércoles [mi'erkoles] *sm* Wednesday. **miércoles de ceniza** Ash Wednesday.
mierda ['mjerða] *sf* (*fam*) shit; muck. **¡váyase a la mierda!** go to hell!
mies [mjes] *sf* corn. **mieses** *sf pl* cornfield.
miga ['miga] *sf* crumb; substance. **hacer buenas migas con** get on well with.
migración [migra'θjon] *sf* migration. **migratorio** *adj* migratory.
migraña [mi'graɲa] *sf* migraine.
mil [mil] *sm, adj* thousand. **milésimo** *adj* thousandth. **miles de** masses of.
milagro [mi'lagro] *sm* miracle; wonder. **milagroso** *adj* miraculous.
milano [mi'lano] *sm* (*ave*) kite.
mildeu [mil'deu] *sm* mildew.
milicia [mi'liθja] *sf* militia; military service. **militar** *adj* military. *sm* soldier.
miligramo [mili'gramo] *sm* milligramme.
milla ['miʎa] *sf* mile.
millar [mi'ʎar] *sm* thousand. **a millares in** thousands.
millón [mi'ʎon] *sm* million. **millonésimo** *adj* millionth. **millonario, -a** *sm, sf* millionaire.
mimar [mi'mar] *v* spoil; pamper.
mimbre ['mimbre] *s(m + f)* wicker.
minar [mi'nar] *y* mine. **mina** *sf* mine; store; pencil lead. **minador** *sm* miner; (*mar*) minelayer. **minero** *sm* miner; mine-owner.

minarete [mina'rete] *sm* minaret.
mineral [mine'ral] *sm, adj* mineral. **mineralogía** *sf* mineralogy.
miniatura [minja'tura] *sf* miniature.
mínimo ['minimo] *sm, adj* minimum.
ministerio [mini'sterjo] *sm* ministry; office. **ministerial** *adj* ministerial. **ministrador** *sm* administrator. **ministrar** *v* minister; administer. **ministro** *sm* minister; judge. **primer ministro** prime minister.
minoría [mino'ria] *sf* minority. **minorar** *v* diminish.
minucioso [minu'θjoso] *adj* meticulous; minute.
minué [minu'e] *sm* minuet.
minúscula [mi'nuskula] *sf* small letter.
minuta [mi'nuta] *sf* memo; menu; list. **minutar** *v* make notes on.
minutía [minu'tia] *sf* carnation.
minuto [mi'nuto] *sm* minute.
mío ['mio] *adj, pron pers* mine.
miope [mi'ope] *adj* shortsighted. **miopía** *sf* myopia.
miosotis [mjo'sotis] *sm* forget-me-not.
mirar [mi'rar] *v* look; consider. **mira** *sf* sight. **estar a la mira** be on the lookout. **con miras a** with a view to. **mirada** *sf* look; glance. **miradero** *sm* centre of attention; vantage point. **mirado** *adj* circumspect. **mirador** *sm* bay window. **miramiento** *sm* look; consideration; respect.
mirasol [mira'sol] *sm* sunflower.
mirlo ['mirlo] *sm* blackbird.
mirra ['mirra] *sf* myrrh.
mirto ['mirto] *sf* mass. **misal** *sm* missal.
miserable [mise'raβle] *adj* wretched, miserable. **miseria** *sf* misery; poverty. **misericordia** *sf* mercy; compassion. **misericordioso** *adj* merciful; compassionate. **mísero** *adj* wretched.
misión [misi'on] *sf* mission.
mismo ['mismo] *adj* same; own; very; just; right. **aquí mismo** right here. **lo mismo con** the same goes for. **yo mismo** I myself.
misterio [mis'terjo] *sm* mystery. **misterioso** *adj* mysterious. **misticismo** *sm* mysticism. **místico, -a** *s, adj* mystic. **mistificación** *sf* falsification; trick. **mistificar** *v* falsify; deceive.
mitad [mi'tað] *sf* half; middle.
mítico ['mitiko] *adj* mythical. **mito** *m* myth. **mitología** *sf* mythology. **mitológico** *adj* mythological.

mitigar [miti'gar] *v* mitigate; relieve. **mitigación** *sf* mitigation. **mitigante** *adj* mitigating.

mitin ['mitin] *sm* political rally.

mitón [mi'ton] *sm* mitten.

mitra ['mitra] *sf* mitre.

mixto ['miksto] *adj* mixed. *sm* compound. **mixtura** *sf* mixture. **mixturar** *v* mix.

mobiliario [moβili'arjo] *sm* furniture.

mocasín [moka'sin] *sm* moccasin.

mocero [mo'θero] *adj* sensual. **mocear** *v* act like a youngster. **mocedad** *sf* youth; youthful prank.

moción [mo'θjon] *sf* motion.

moco ['moko] *sm* mucus. **mocoso** *adj* mucous.

mochila [mo'tʃila] *sf* rucksack.

mocho ['motʃo] *adj* shorn; lopped; (*sin cuernos*) hornless.

moda ['moða] *sf* fashion. **de moda** in fashion. **pasado de moda** old-fashioned.

modales [mo'ðales] *sm pl* manners.

modelo [mo'ðelo] *sm, adj* model. **modela** *sf* fashion model. **modelar** *v* model.

moderar [moðe'rar] *v* moderate; restrain. **moderación** *sf* moderation. **moderado** *adj* moderate. **moderador, -a** *sm, sf* moderator. **moderativo** *adj* moderating.

moderno [mo'ðerno] *adj* modern. **modernidad** *sf* modernity. **modernizar** *v* modernize. **modernizarse** *v* get up-to-date.

modesto [mo'ðesto] *adj* modest. **modestia** *sf* modesty.

módico ['moðiko] *adj* moderate. **modicidad** *sf* moderateness.

modificar [moðifi'kar] *v* modify. **modificación** *sf* modification.

modismo [mo'ðismo] *sm* idiom.

modista [mo'ðista] *sf* dressmaker.

modo ['moðo] *sm* mode; manner; method. **de modo que** so that. **de todos modos** in any case.

modorra [mo'ðorra] *sf* drowsiness. **modorro** *adj* drowsy.

modular [moðu'lar] *v* modulate. **modulación** *sf* modulation.

mofar [mo'far] *v* scoff; mock. **mofarse de** jeer at. **mofa** *sf* mockery. **mofador** *adj* mocking.

mohín [mo'in] *sm* grimace. **mohíno** *adj* sulky.

moho ['moo] *sm* mould; rust. **mohoso** *adj* mouldy; rusty. **ponerse mohoso** go mouldy; rust.

mojar [mo'xar] *v* wet; moisten; soak. **mojado** *adj* wet; damp.

mojigato [moxi'gato], **-a** *sm, sf* hypocrite; prude. *adj* hypocritical; prudish.

mojón [mo'xon] *sm* landmark.

moldar [mol'ðar] *v also* **moldear** mould. **molde** *sm* mould. **moldura** *sf* moulding.

molécula [mo'lekula] *sf* molecule. **molecular** *adj* molecular.

****moler** [mo'ler] *v* grind; crush; (*fig*) bore, weary. **moledura** *sf* grinding; milling; exhaustion.

molestar [moles'tar] *v* annoy; bother; disturb. **molestarse** *v* worry. **no se moleste** don't bother. **molestia** *sf* trouble. **molesto** *adj* tiresome; embarrassing.

molinero [moli'nero] *sm* miller. **molino** *sm* mill.

molusco [mo'lusko] *sm* mollusc.

mollera [mo'ʎera] *sf* crown of the head; (*fig*) brains. **cerrado de mollera** dense; obstinate.

momentáneo [momen'taneo] *adj* momentary. **momento** *sm* moment; momentum. **al momento** immediately.

momia ['momja] *sf* (*cadáver*) mummy. **momificación** *sf* mummification. **momificar** *v* mummify.

monada [mo'naða] *sf* kindness; flattery, dirty trick. **¡qué monada!** how lovely!

monarca [mo'narka] *sm* monarch. **monarquía** *sf* monarchy. **monárquico** *adj* monarchic(al).

monasterio [monas'terjo] *sm* monastery. **monástico** *adj* monastic.

mondar [mon'dar] *v* clean; prune; strip; trim; peel. **monda** *sf* pruning; trimming; cleaning. **mondadientes** *m invar* toothpick. **mondador, -a** *sm, sf* pruner; peeler; cleaner. **mondo** *adj* pure; bare; clean.

moneda [mo'neða] *sf* money; coin. **monedero** *sm* purse. **monedero falso** counterfeiter.

monitor ['monitor], **-a** *sm, sf* monitor.

monja ['monxa] *sf* nun. **monje** *sm* monk.

mono¹ ['mono] *sm* monkey; ape.

mono² *adj* lovely; cute.

monólogo [mo'nologo] *sm* monologue.

monopolizar [monopoli'θar] *v* monopolize. **monopolio** *sm* monopoly.

monosílabo [mono'silaβo] *sm* monosyllable.

monótono [mo'notono] *adj* monotonous. **monotonía** *sf* monotony.

monstruo ['monstruo] *sm* monster. **monstruosidad** *sf* monstrosity. **monstruoso** *adj* monstrous.

monta ['monta] *sf* mounting; amount.

montacargas *sm invar* service lift.

montaje *sm* mounting.

montaña [mon'taɲa] *sf* mountain. **montañés** *adj* of mountains. **montañismo** *sm* mountaineering. **montañoso** *adj* mountainous. **monte** *sm* mountain; mount.

montar [mon'tar] *v* mount; ride; assemble; establish. **montura** *sf* mount; saddle; frame; mounting.

montera [mon'tera] *sf* cloth cap; bullfighter's hat; skylight. **montero** *sm* hunter.

montón [mon'ton] *sm* heap, pile. **a montones** lots of.

monumento [monu'mento] *sm* monument; memorial. **monumental** *adj* monumental.

moño ['moɲo] *sm* bun, topknot. **ponerse moños** put on airs.

mora¹ ['mora] *sf* blackberry; mulberry.

mora² *sf* delay.

morada [mo'raða] *sf* abode; sojourn. **morar** *v* dwell.

morado [mo'raðo] *adj* purple; violet. **ponerse morado** stuff oneself.

moral [mo'ral] *adj* moral. **morales** *sf pl* morals. **moraleja** *sf* (*de un cuento*) moral. **moralidad** *sf* morality. **moralista** *s(m+f)* moralist. **moralizar** *v* moralize.

mórbido ['morβiðo] *adj* morbid; delicate. **morbidez** *sf* tenderness. **morbilidad** *sf* morbidity. **morboso** *adj* morbid; diseased.

morcilla [mor'θiʎa] *sf* black pudding.

mordaz [mor'ðaθ] *adj* mordant; pungent.

mordaza [mor'ðaθa] *sf* (*en la boca*) gag.

*morder [mor'ðer] *v* bite. **mordedura** *sf* bite. **mordiente** *adj* biting. **mordiscar** *v* nibble. **mordiscón** *sm* nibble; mouthful.

moreno [mo'reno] *adj* brown; tanned; dark.

morera [mo'rera] *sf* mulberry tree.

morfina [mor'fina] *sf* morphine.

moribundo [mori'βundo] *adj* moribund.

*morir [mo'rir] *v* die; end; fade. **morirse por** crave.

mormón [mor'mon], **-a** *sm, sf* Mormon. **mormonismo** *sm* Mormonism.

moro ['moro], **-a** *sm, sf* Moor. *adj* Moorish.

moroso [mo'roso] *adj* slow; sluggish; late. **morosidad** *sf* slowness; inactivity.

morralla [mor'raʎa] *sf* rubbish; (*fig*) rabble.

morriña [mor'riɲa] *sf* nostalgia; homesickness.

mortaja [mor'taxa] *sf* shroud.

mortal [mor'tal] *adj* mortal; lethal; awful. *s(m+f)* mortal. **mortalidad** *sf* mortality.

mortero [mor'tero] *sm* mortar.

mortífero [mor'tifero] *adj* deadly, fatal.

mortificar [mortifi'kar] *v* mortify. **mortificación** *sf* mortification.

mosca ['moska] *sf* fly. **papar moscas** gape. **moscarda** *sf* bluebottle. **moscardón** *sm* blowfly; hornet.

mosquete [mos'kete] *sm* musket. **mosquetero** *sm* musketeer.

mosquito [mos'kito] *sm* mosquito; gnat. **mosquitero** *sm* mosquito net.

mostaza [mos'taθa] *sf* mustard.

*mostrar [mos'trar] *v* show; exhibit; point out. **mostrable** *adj* demonstrable. **mostrador** *sm* (*reloj*) dial; (*tienda*) counter.

mote ['mote] *sm* nickname. **motejar** *v* label; name.

motín [mo'tin] *sm* uprising; mutiny.

motivar [moti'βar] *v* cause, give rise to; justify; explain. **motivación** *sf* motivation. **motivo** *sm* motive; grounds *pl*. **con motivo de** owing to.

motocicleta [motoθi'kleta] *sf* motor cycle. **motociclista** *s(m+f)* motor-cyclist.

motor ['motor] *sm* motor; engine. **motorista** *s(m+f)* motor-cyclist. **motorizar** *v* motorize.

motriz [mo'triθ] *adj* motive.

mover [mo'βer] *v* move; shake; stir; incite. **moverse** *v* get a move on. **movedizo** *adj* movable; inconstant. **movible** *adj* mobile. **móvil** *adj* mobile; fickle. **movilidad** *sf* mobility. **movilizar** *v* mobilize. **movilización** *sf* mobilization. **movimiento** *sm* movement; motion; activity.

mozo ['moθo] *sm* youth, lad; waiter. **moza** *sf* girl; servant.

mucoso [mu'koso] *adj* mucous. **mucosidad** *sf* mucus.

muchacho [mu'tʃatʃo] *sm* boy; chap. **muchacha** *sf* girl; servant.

muchedumbre [mutʃe'ðumbre] *sf* crowd; (*fig*) a lot.

mucho ['mutʃo] *adj* a lot of; much; great; many. *pron* many; a lot. *adv* much; a lot; a long time. **con mucho** by far. **por mucho que** however much.

mudar [mu'ðar] *v* change; remove; shed. **mudarse** *v* move house; change one's clothes. **muda** *sf* change; moulting. **mudable** *adj* changeable; variable. **mudanza** *sf* change; removal. **camión de mundanzas** *sm* removal van.

mudo ['muðo] *adj* dumb, mute. **mudez** *sf* dumbness.

mueble ['mweβle] *sm* piece of furniture. **muebles** *sm pl* furniture *sing*.

mueca ['mweka] *sf* grimace.

muela ['mwela] *sf* molar. **muela del juicio** wisdom tooth.

muelle ['mweʎe] *adj* soft; luxurious. *sm* wharf; embankment; spring.

muérdago [mu'erðago] *sm* mistletoe.

muerte ['mwerte] *sf* death; murder. **de mala muerte** (*fam*) rotten, lousy.

muerto ['mwerto] *V* **morir**. *adj* dead. *sm* corpse.

muestra ['mwestra] *sf* sample, example; specimen; sign.

mugir [mu'xir] *v* roar; bellow; low. **mugido** *sm* roar; bellow; lowing.

mujer [mu'xer] *sf* woman; wife.

muleta [mu'leta] *sf* crutch; bullfighter's cape.

mulo ['mulo] *sm* mule.

multar [mul'tar] *v* fine. **multa** *sf* fine.

múltiple ['multiple] *adj* multiple; many. **multiplicación** *sf* multiplication. **multiplicar** *v* multiply, increase.

multitud [multi'tuð] *sf* multitude, crowd.

***mullir** [mu'ʎir] *v* beat; break up; loosen. **mullido** *adj* soft; fluffy.

mundo ['mundo] *sm* world; (*fam*) crowd. **todo el mundo** everybody. **mundanal** *adj* worldly. **mundanería** *sf* worldliness. **mundial** *adj* world; worldwide. **mundovisión** *sm* broadcasting by satellite.

municipal [muniθi'pal] *adj* municipal. *sm* policeman. **municipalidad** *sf* municipality. **municipio** *sm* town council.

munífico [mu'nifiko] *adj* munificent; liberal. **munificencia** *sf* munificence; liberality.

muñeca [mu'ɲeka] *sf* doll; dressmaker's dummy; wrist.

muralla [mu'raʎa] *sf* wall; rampart. **mural** *adj, sm* mural. **murar** *v* wall. **muro** *sm* wall.

murciélago [mur'θielago] *sm* (*zool*) bat.

murmullo [mur'muʎo] *sm* murmur; whisper; rustle.

murmurar [murmu'rar] *v* murmur; whisper; mutter; gossip. **murmuración** *sf* gossiping. **murmurio** *sm* murmuring.

músculo ['muskulo] *sm* muscle. **muscular** *adj* muscular.

muselina [muse'lina] *sf* muslin.

museo [mu'seo] *sm* museum; art gallery.

musgo ['musgo] *sm* moss.

música ['musika] *sf* music. **musical** *adj* musical. **músico, -a** *sm, sf* musician. **musicología** *sf* musicology.

muslo ['muslo] *sm* thigh.

mustio ['mustjo] *adj* withered; sad. **mustiarse** *v* wither.

mutación [muta'θjon] *sf* mutation; change. **mutabilidad** *sf* mutability. **mutante** *sm, adj* mutant.

mutilar [muti'lar] *v* mutilate; cripple. **mutilación** *sf* mutilation. **mutilado, -a** *sm, sf* cripple.

mutual ['mutwal] *adj* mutual. **mutuo** *adj* mutual; joint.

muy [mwi] *adv* very; quite; too; much. **muy señor mío** (*carta*) Dear Sir.

N

nabo ['naβo] *sm* turnip.

nácar ['nakar] *sm* mother-of-pearl.

***nacer** [na'θer] *v* be born; originate. **nacido** *adj* born. **naciente** *adj* growing. **nacimiento** *sm* birth; origin.

nación [na'θjon] *sf* nation. **nacional** *adj* national. *s(m+f)* national; native. **nacionalidad** *sf* nationality. **nacionalismo** *sm* nationalism. **nacionalizar** *v* nationalize.

nada ['naða] *sf* nothing. *adv* by no means. **de nada** don't mention it. **nada más** only.

nadar [na'ðar] *v* swim. **nadador, -a** *sm, sf* swimmer.

nadie ['naðje] *pron* nobody, no one.

naipe ['naipe] *sm* playing-card.

nalga ['nalga] *sf* buttock.

naranja [na'ranxa] *sf* orange. **naranjada** *sf* orangeade. **naranjo** *sm* orange tree.

narciso [nar'θiso] *sm* narcissus. **narcisismo** *sm* narcissism.

narcótico [nar'kotiko] *sm, adj* narcotic.

nariz [na'riθ] *sf, pl* **narices** nose.

narrar [nar'rar] *v* narrate. **narración** *sf* narration. **narrador, -a** *sm, sf* narrator. **narrativa** *sf* narrative.

nasal [na'sal] *adj* nasal.

nata ['nata] *sf* cream; curd; (*fig*) the best. **natillas** *sf pl* custard *sing*.

natación [nata'θjon] *sf* swimming.

natal [na'tal] *adj* natal; native. *sm* birth; birthday. **natalidad** *sf* birthrate.

nativo [na'tiβo], **-a** *s, adj* native. **natividad** *sf* nativity. **nato** *adj* born.

natural [natu'ral] *s(m+f)* native; citizen. *sm* nature. *adj* natural. **naturaleza** *sf* nature; nationality. **naturalidad** *sf* naturalness; citizenship.

naufragar [naufra'gar] *v* sink; be shipwrecked. **naufragio** *sm* shipwreck. **náufrago** *adj* shipwrecked.

náusea ['nausea] *sf* nausea. **nauseabundo** *adj* nauseous; nauseating.

náutico ['nautiko] *adj* nautical. **náutica** *sf* navigation.

navaja [na'βaxa] *sf* penknife; razor. **navajada** *sf* stab; gash.

naval [na'βal] *adj* naval. **nave** *sf or* **navío** *sm* ship. **navegable** *adj* navigable. **navegación** *sf* navigation; sailing. **navegante** *sm* navigator.

neblina [ne'βlina] *sf* mist, fog. **nebulosidad** *sf* nebulosity; haziness. **nebuloso** *adj* nebulous.

necedad [neθe'ðað] *sf* foolishness; nonsense. **necio** *adj* foolish.

necesario [neθe'sarjo] *adj* necessary. **necesidad** *sf* necessity; poverty. **necesitado** *adj* needy. **necesitar** *v* need.

néctar ['nektar] *sm* nectar.

nefario [ne'farjo] *adj* nefarious.

nefasto [ne'fasto] *adj* ill-omened; unlucky.

*****negar** [ne'gar] *v* deny; refuse. **negarse** *v* decline. **negación** *sf* negation. **negativa** *sm* (*foto*) negative; *sf* refusal.

negligencia [negli'xenθja] *sf* negligence. **negligente** *adj* negligent.

negociar [nego'θjar] *v* trade; negotiate. **negociable** *adj* negotiable. **negociación** *sf* transaction; negotiation. **negociado** *sm* bureau; divison. **negociador, -a** *sm, sf* negotiator; agent. **negociante** *sm* businessman; merchant. **negocio** *sm* business; trade; negotiation.

negro ['negro], **-a** *s, adj* black. **negrura** *sf* blackness.

nene ['nene], **-a** *sm, sf* baby.

nenúfar [ne'nufar] *sm* waterlily.

neón [ne'on] *sm* neon.

nepotismo [nepo'tismo] *sm* nepotism.

nervio ['nerβjo] *sm* nerve; (*de una hoja*) rib; sinew. **crisparle los nervios a uno** get on someone's nerves. **tener los nervios en punta** be on edge. **nerviosidad** *sf* nervousness. **nervioso** *adj* nervous. **crisis nerviosa** *sf* nervous breakdown.

neto ['neto] *adj* pure; clear; (*com*) net.

neumático [neu'matiko] *sm* tyre. *adj* pneumatic.

neumonía [neumo'nia] *sf* pneumonia.

neuralgia [neu'ralxja] *sf* neuralgia. **neurálgico** *adj* neuralgic.

neurótico [neu'rotiko] *adj* neurotic. **neurosis** *sf* neurosis.

neutro ['neutro] *adj* neutral; (*gram*) neuter. **neutral** *s(m+f)*, *adj* neutral. **neutralidad** *sf* neutrality. **neutralizar** *v* neutralize.

*****nevar** [ne'βar] *v* snow. **nevada** *sf* snow storm. **nevasca** *sf* snowfall. **nevera** *sf* refrigerator. **nevisca** *sf* light snowfall. **neviscar** *v* snow lightly. **nevoso** *adj* snowy.

nexo ['nekso] *sm* link, tie.

ni [ni] *conj* neither; nor; or; not even. **ni uno ni otro** neither one nor the other.

nicotina [niko'tina] *sf* nicotine.

nicho ['nitʃo] *sm* niche.

nido ['niðo] *sm* nest. **cunas de nido** pull-out beds. **nidada** *sf* brood; clutch. **nidal** *sm* nest; nest egg.

niebla [ni'eβla] *sf* fog; mist; mildew.

nieto [ni'eto] *sm* grandson. **nieta** *sf* granddaughter.

nieve [ni'eβe] *sf* snow.

nilón [ni'lon] *sm* nylon.

ninfa ['ninfa] *sf* nymph.

ninguno [nin'guno] *adj also* **ningún** no; not one. **de ninguna manera** in no way. *pron* nobody.

niña ['niɲa] *sf* little girl; (*del ojo*) pupil. **niñada** *sf* childishness. **niñera** *sf* nanny. **niñez** *sf* childhood. **niño** *sm* little boy; child. **desde niño** from childhood.

níquel ['nikel] *sm* nickel. **niquelar** *v* nickel-plate.

níspero ['nispero] *sm* medlar tree. **níspola** *sf* medlar.

nítido ['nitiðo] *adj* clear; bright. **nitidez** *sf* brightness; neatness.

nitrógeno [ni'troxeno] *sm* nitrogen. **nitrato** *sm* nitrate. **nítrico** *adj* nitric. **nitro** *sm* nitre; saltpetre. **nitroso** *adj* nitrous.

nivelar [niβe'lar] *v* level; balance. **nivelarse** *v* become level. **nivelarse con** get even with. **nivel** *sm* level; standard. **nivel de aire** spirit-level. **nivel de vida** standard of living. **paso a nivel** level-crossing. **nivelación** *sf* levelling.

no [no] *adv* no; not. **no bien** no sooner. **no más** only. **no obtante** in spite of. **que no** if only.

noble ['noβle] *adj* noble. *sm* nobleman. **nobleza** *sf* nobility.

noción [no'θjon] *sf* notion; idea. **nociones** *sf pl* smattering *sing*; rudiments.

nocivo [no'θiβo] *adj* noxious; harmful.

nocturno [nok'turno] *adj* nocturnal; night. **noctámbulo, -a** *sm, sf* sleepwalker.

noche ['notʃe] *sf* night; evening. **por la noche** at night. **Nochebuena** *sf* Christmas Eve.

nódulo ['noðulo] *sm* nodule.

nogal [no'gal] *sm also* **noguera** *sf* walnut tree.

nómada ['nomaða] *s(m+f)* nomad. *adj* nomadic.

nombrar [nom'brar] *v* name; nominate; mention. **nombradía** *sf* reputation. **nombramiento** *sm* naming; nomination. **nombre** *sm* name; title. **nombre de pila** Christian name. **nomenclatura** *sf* nomenclature; terminology; catalogue. **nómina** *sf* list; payroll. **nominación** *sf* nomination. **nominal** *adj* nominal. **nominativo** *sm* (*gram*) nominative.

non [non] *adj* (*mat*) odd. *sm* odd number. **nonagésimo** [nona'xesimo] *adj* ninetieth. **nonagenario, -a** *s, adj* nonagenarian.

norabuena [nora'βwena] *sf* congratulations *pl*. *adv* by good fortune. **noramala** *adv* unfortunately.

nordeste [nor'ðeste] *sm* north-east; (*viento*) northeaster. *adj* north-east.

noria [no'ria] *sf* waterwheel.

norma ['norma] *sf* norm; rule. **normal** *adj* normal. **normalidad** *sf* normality. **normalizar** *v* normalize.

noroeste [noro'este] *sm* north-west; (*viento*) northwesterly. *adj* north-west.

norte ['norte] *sm, adj* north. **perder el norte** lose one's bearings. **norteño** *adj* northern.

Noruega [nor'wega] *sf* Norway. **noruego, -a** *sm, sf* (*persona*) Norwegian; *sm* (*idioma*) Norwegian.

nos [nos] *pron* us, ourselves.

nosotros [no'sotros] *pron* we; us, ourselves.

nostalgia [nos'talxja] *sf* nostalgia. **nostálgico** *adj* nostalgic; homesick.

notar [no'tar] *v* note; notice; note down. **nota** *sf* (*música, etc.*) note; mark; report; repute. **notabilidad** *sf* notability. **notable** *adj* notable. **notación** *sf* notation.

notario [no'tarjo] *sm* notary. **notaría** *sf* notary's office.

noticiar [noti'θjar] *v* notify. **noticia(s)** *sf* (*pl*) news *sing*. **noticiario** *sm* news bulletin. **noticiero, -a** *sm, sf* reporter. **notición** *sm* (*fam*) big news. **noticioso** *adj* well-informed. **notificación** *sf* notification.

notorio [no'torjo] *adj* notorious. **notoriedad** *sf* notoriety.

novato [no'βato], **-a** *s, adj* novice.

novecientos [noβe'θjentos] *adj, s* nine hundred.

novedad [nove'ðað] *sf* novelty; change. **novedades** *sf pl* latest models.

novela [no'βela] *sf* novel. **novelista** *s(m+f)* novelist.

noveno [no'βeno] *adj* ninth. **noventa** *adj* ninety.

novia ['noβja] *sf* girlfriend; fiancée; bride. **traje de novia** wedding dress. **novio** *sm* boyfriend; fiancé; bridegroom.

novicio [no'βiθjo] *sm* beginner; apprentice. **noviciado** *sm* novitiate; apprenticeship.

noviembre [no'βjembre] *sm* November.

novilla [no'βiʎa] *sf* heifer. **novillada** *sf* bullfight with young bulls. **novillero** *sm* novice bullfighter. **novillo** *sm* young bull. **hacer novillos** play truant.

nube ['nuβe] *sf* cloud. **estar por las nubes** (*precios*) be sky-high. **poner por las nubes** praise to the skies. **nublado** *adj* overcast. **nublar** *v* cloud over. **nubloso** *adj* cloudy; ill-fated.

núcleo ['nukleo] *sm* nucleus; core; (*bot*) stone. **nuclear** *adj* nuclear.

nudillo [nu'ðiʎo] *sm* knuckle.

nudo¹ ['nuðo] *sm* knot; bond; tumour.

nudo² *adj* nude.

nuera ['nwera] *sf* daughter-in-law.
nuestro ['nwestro] *adj* our. *pron* ours.
nueva ['nweβa] *sf* news. **nuevo** *adj* new.
de nuevo again. **nuevo flamante** brand
new.
nueve ['nweβe] *adj*, *sm* nine.
nuez [nweθ] *sf* nut; walnut. **nuez de la
garganta** Adam's apple.
nulo ['nulo] *adj* null; void; (*fig*) hopeless.
numerar [nume'rar] *v* number. **numeral**
sm, *adj* numeral. **numérico** *adj* numerical. **número** *sm* number; size; quantity.
numeroso *adj* numerous.
nunca ['nunka] *adv* never; ever. **casi nunca** hardly ever.
nuncio ['nunθjo] *sm* nuncio; (*fig*) omen.
nupcial [nup'θjal] *adj* nuptial. **nupcias** *sf
pl* nuptials.
nutria [nu'tria] *sf also* **nutra** *sf* otter.
nutrir [nu'trir] *v* nourish. **nutrición** *sf*
nutrition. **nutrimento** *sm* nutriment.

Ñ

ñaque ['pake] *sm* odds and ends.
ñoño ['popo] *adj* insipid; prudish; fussy.
ñoñeria *sf also* **ñoñez** *sf* insipidity; prud-
ery; fussiness.
ñu [pu] *sm* gnu.

O

o [o] *conj* or. **o ... o** either ... or. **o sea**
in other words.
obcecar [oβθe'kar] *v* blind; deceive. **obce-
carse** *v* become blind; be dazzled. **obce-
cado** *adj* blind; obdurate.
obduración [oβðura'θjon] *sf* obduracy;
obstinacy.
***obedecer** [oβeðe'θer] *v* obey. **obediencia**
sf obedience. **obediente** *adj* obedient.
obertura [oβer'tura] *sf* (*música*) overture.
obesidad [oβesi'ðað] *sf* obesity. **obeso** *adj*
obese.
obispo [o'βispo] *sm* bishop. **obispado** *sm*
bishopric.
obituario [oβi'twarjo] *sm* obituary.

objetar [oβxe'tar] *v* object (to). **objeción**
sf objection. **objetivo** *sm* objective. **objeto**
sm object.
oblicuo [o'βlikwo] *adj* oblique. **oblicuar** *v*
slant.
obligar [oβli'gar] *v* oblige; force. **verse
obligado a** be forced to. **obligación** *sf*
obligation. **obligado** *adj* essential. **obligatorio** *adj* compulsory.
obliterar [oβlite'rar] *v* obliterate;
obstruct.
oblongo [o'βlongo] *adj* oblong.
obrar [o'βrar] *v* work; operate; make;
build; behave. **obra** *sf* work. **obra maestra** masterpiece. **obrero, -a** *sm*, *sf* worker.
obsceno [oβs'θeno] *adj* obscene.
obscenidad *sf* obscenity.
***obscurecer** [oβskure'θer] *v* *also*
oscurecer obscure, darken. **obscuridad** *sf*
obscurity. **obscuro** *adj* obscure.
obsequiar [oβseki'ar] *v* entertain; treat;
present. **obsequio** *sm* courtesy; gift. **obse-
quioso** *adj* obsequious; attentive.
observar [oβser'var] *v* observe. **observación** *sf* observation. **observador, -a** *sm*, *sf*
observer. **observancia** *sf* observance.
observante *adj* observant. **observatorio**
sm observatory.
obsesión [oβse'sjon] *sf* obsession. **obsesionante** *adj* obsessive. **obseso** *adj*
obsessed.
obsoleto [oβso'leto] *adj* obsolete.
obstáculo [oβ'stakulo] *sm* obstacle.
obstante [oβ'stante] *prep* in spite of. *adv*
no obstante notwithstanding; nevertheless. **obstar** *v* hinder; oppose.
obstetricia [oβste'triθja] *sf* obstetrics.
obstétrico *adj* obstetric.
obstinarse [oβsti'narse] *v* be obstinate;
persist. **obstinación** *sf* obstinacy.
obstinado *adj* obstinate.
***obstruir** [oβstru'ir] *v* obstruct. **obstruc-
ción** *sf* obstruction. **obstructivo** *adj*
obstructive.
***obtener** [oβte'ner] *v* obtain. **obtención** *sf*
attainment.
obturar [obtu'rar] *v* stop up, plug. **obturación** *sf* plugging; sealing. **velocidad de
obturación** (*foto*) shutter speed.
obturador *sm* plug; (*foto*) shutter.
obtuso [oβ'tuso] *adj* obtuse.
obús [o'βus] *sm* howitzer.
obvio ['oββjo] *adj* obvious. **obviar** *v* obvi-
ate.

oca ['oka] *sf* goose.
ocasión [oka'sjon] *sf* occasion; opportunity; reason. **ocasional** *adj* occasional; chance. **ocasionalmente** *adv* occasionally; accidentally. **ocasionar** *v* cause.
ocaso [o'kaso] *sm* sunset; decline; west.
occidental [okθiðen'tal] *adj* western, occidental. **occidente** *sm* west.
océano [o'θeano] *sm* ocean.
ocio ['oθjo] *sm* leisure; idleness. **ociosidad** *sf* idleness. **ocioso** *adj* idle.
ocre ['okre] *sm* ochre.
octágono [ok'tagono] *adj* octagonal. *sm* octagon.
octava [ok'taβa] *sf* octave. **octavo** *adj* eighth. **octogenario, -a** *sm, sf* octogenarian. **octogésimo** *adj* eightieth.
octubre [ok'tuβre] *sm* October.
ocular [oku'lar] *adj* ocular. **testigo ocular** eyewitness. *sm* eyepiece. **oculista** *s(m+f)* oculist.
ocultar [okul'tar] *v* hide. **ocultación** *sf* concealment; dissimulation. **oculto** *adj* secret; hidden; occult.
ocupar [oku'par] *v* occupy; employ; take over. **ocuparse (de)** look after; do; employ. **ocupación** *sf* occupation. **ocupado** *adj* occupied; taken; engaged. **ocupante** *s(m+f)* occupant.
occurrir [okur'rir] *v* occur. **ocurrencia** *sf* occurrence; (*fig*) witticism; idea. **ocurrente** *adj* witty.
ochenta [o'tʃenta] *sm, adj* eighty. **ocho** *sm, adj* eight.
oda ['oða] *sf* ode.
odiar [o'ðjar] *v* hate. **odio** *sm* hate, hatred. **tener odio a uno** hate someone. **odiosidad** *sf* hatefulness; odiousness. **odioso** *adj* odious; hateful.
odorífero [oðo'rifero] *adj* odoriferous, fragrant.
oeste [o'este] *sm* west.
ofender [ofen'der] *v* offend; insult. **ofenderse** *v* resent. **ofensa** *sf* offence; insult. **ofensiva** *sf* attack. **ofensivo** *adj* offensive; insulting. **ofensor, -a** *sm, sf* offender.
oferta [o'ferta] *sf* offer; bid; tender; gift. **ley de la oferta y la demanda** law of supply and demand.
oficial [ofi'θjal] *adj, sm* official. **oficialía** *sf* clerkship. **oficina** *sf* office; agency; laboratory. **oficio** *sm* job; appointment; calling. **oficioso** *adj* diligent; meddlesome.

*ofrecer [ofre'θer] *v* offer. **ofrecerse** *v* volunteer. **¿qué se le ofrece a usted?** may I help you? **ofrecimiento** *sm* offer. **ofrendar** *v* contribute. **ofrenda** *sf* offer.
ofuscar [ofus'kar] *v* bewilder; dazzle.
ogro ['ogro] *sm* ogre.
oigo [o'igo] *V* oír.
*oír [o'ir] *v* hear; listen to. **oírse** *v* be heard. **oír decir que** hear that. **oída** *sf* hearing. **oíble** *adj* audible. **oído** *sm* hearing; ear. **dolor de oídos** earache.
ojal [o'xal] *sm* buttonhole.
ojalá [oxa'la] *interj* let's hope so! would to God! *conj* if only.
ojear[1] [oxe'ar] *v* look at. **ojeada** *sf* glance.
ojear[2] *v* (*en la caza*) start game; (*espantar*) scare off.
ojo ['oxo] *sm* eye; opening; hole; keyhole; (*puente*) span. **¡ojo!** look out!
ola ['ola] *sf* wave. **ola de calor** heatwave.
olé [o'le] *interj* bravo!
oleandro [ole'andro] *sm* oleander.
óleo ['oleo] *sm* oil. **pintura al óleo** *sf* oil painting. **oleoducto** *sm* pipeline. **oleosidad** *sf* oiliness. **oleoso** *adj* oily.
*oler [o'ler] *v* smell. **oler bien/mal** smell good/bad. **olfatear** *v* smell; sniff; sniff out. **olfato** *sm* sense of smell. **olfatorio** *adj* olfactory. **oliente** *adj* smelling. **olor** *sm* smell. **oloroso** *adj* fragrant.
oligarquía [oligar'kia] *sf* oligarchy.
olímpico [o'limpiko] *adj* Olympic. **juegos olímpicos** Olympic games.
oliva [o'liβa] *sf* olive; olive tree. **olivar** *sm* olive grove. **olivo** *sm* olive tree.
olmo ['olmo] *sm* elm tree. **olmeda** *sf* elm grove.
olvidar [olβi'ðar] *v* forget. **olvidadizo** *adj* forgetful. **olvido** *sm* forgetfulness.
olla ['oʎa] *sf* pot; kettle; stew; (*remolino*) eddy. **olla exprés** pressure cooker. **olla podrida** hotpot.
ombligo [om'bligo] *sm* navel; (*fig*) core.
ominoso [omi'noso] *adj* ominous.
omitir [omi'tir] *v* omit; neglect. **omisión** *sf* omission. **omiso** *adj* careless. **hacer caso omiso de** ignore; overlook.
ómnibus ['omniβus] *sm* omnibus.
omnipotencia [omnipo'tenθja] *sf* omnipotence. **omnipotente** *adj* omnipotent.
omnisciencia [omni'sθjenθja] *sf* omniscience. **omniscio** *adj* omniscient.
omnívoro [om'niβoro] *adj* omnivorous.
once ['onθe] *sm, adj* eleven.

onda ['onda] *sf* wave; ripple. **onda corta/larga/media** short/long/medium wave. **onda luminosa** light wave. **onda sonora** sound wave. **ondear** *v* wave. **ondearse** *v* swing. **ondulación** *sf* undulation. **ondulado** *adj* wavy. **ondulante** *adj* undulating. **ondular** *v* undulate; wriggle.

oneroso [one'roso] *adj* onerous.

ónice ['oniθe] *sm also* **ónique, ónix** onyx.

onza ['onθa] *sf* (*peso y animal*) ounce.

opaco [o'pako] *adj* opaque; dull. **opacidad** *sf* opacity.

opción [op'θjon] *sf* option. **opcional** *adj* optional.

ópera ['opera] *sf* opera.

operar [ope'rar] *v* operate. **operación** *sf* operation. **operador, -a** *sm, sf* operator; surgeon; projectionist. **operante** *adj* operative. **operario, -a** *sm, sf* operative, worker. **operativo** *adj* operative.

opinar [opi'nar] *v* think; judge. **opinión** *sf* opinion.

opio ['opjo] *sm* opium.

***oponer** [opo'ner] *v* oppose; hinder; contradict. **oponerse a** compete for. **oposición** *sf* opposition. **opositor, -a** *sm, sf* opponent; competitor.

oportunidad [oportuni'ðað] *sf* opportunity. **oportunista** *adj* opportunist. **oportuno** *adj* opportune.

oprimir [opri'mir] *v* oppress; depress. **opresión** *sf* oppression. **opresivo** *adj* oppressive. **opresor, -a** *sm, sf* oppressor.

oprobio [o'proβio] *sm* opprobium, disgrace. **oprobioso** *adj* disgraceful.

optar [op'tar] *v* opt, choose.

óptico ['optiko] *adj* optic, optical. *sm* optician.

optimismo [opti'mismo] *sm* optimism. **optimista** *s(m+f)* optimist.

óptimo ['optimo] *adj* optimum, best.

opuesto [o'pwesto] *adj* opposed; against.

opulento [opu'lento] *adj* opulent. **opulencia** *sf* opulence.

oquedad [oke'ðað] *sf* hole; hollow.

ora ['ora] *conj* now.

oráculo [o'rakulo] *sm* oracle.

orangután [orangu'tan] *sm* orangutan.

orar [o'rar] *v* pray; plead; make a speech. **oración** *sf* oration; prayer. **partes de la oración** parts of speech. **orador, -a** *sm, sf* orator. **orador sagrado** preacher. **oral** *adj* oral.

orbe [or'βe] *sm* orb, globe.

órbita ['orβita] *sf* orbit. **orbitar** *v* orbit.

ordenar [orðe'nar] *v* order, command; tidy; direct; ordain. **ordenarse** *v* become ordained. **orden** *sm* order, sequence. **por su orden** successively. **ordenación** *sf* arrangement; ordination. **ordenanza** *sf* arrangement; ordinance.

ordeñar [orðe'nar] *v* milk.

ordinal [orði'nal] *adj* ordinal.

ordinario [orði'narjo] *adj* ordinary; common. **de ordinario** usually.

orear [ore'ar] *v* air, ventilate. **orearse** *v* get a breath of fresh air.

oreja [o'rexa] *sf* ear. **bajar las orejas** knuckle under.

orfebre [or'feβre] *sm* goldsmith; silversmith. **orfebrería** *sf* goldwork; silverwork.

orfeón [orfe'on] *sm* choral society.

orgánico [or'ganiko] *adj* organic. **organismo** *sm* organism. **organista** *s(m+f)* organist. **organización** *sf* organization. **organizador, -a** *sm, sf* organizer. **organo** *sm* organ.

orgasmo [or'gasmo] *sm* orgasm.

orgía [or'xia] *sf* orgy.

orgulloso [orgu'loso] *adj* proud. *sm* pride.

orientarse [orjen'tarse] *v* find one's bearings. **orientación** *sf* orientation. **oriental** *adj* oriental, eastern. **oriente** *sm* orient, east. **Extremo Oriente** Far East. **Oriente Medio** Middle East.

orificio [ori'fiθjo] *sm* orifice, hole.

origen [o'rixen] *sm* origin; native country. **original** *adj* original. **originalidad** *sf* originality. **originar** *v* originate. **originarse** *v* arise.

orilla [o'riʎa] *sf* edge; bank; shore. **a orillas de** on the banks of.

orín [o'rin] *sm* rust.

orina [o'rina] *sf* urine. **orinal** *sm* chamber pot. **orinar** *v* urinate.

oriundo [o'rjundo] *adj* native of.

orlar [or'lar] *v* border, edge. **orla** *sf* border, trimming.

ornamentar [ornamen'tar] *v* adorn, decorate. **ornamentación** *sf* ornamentation. **ornamental** *adj* ornamental. **ornamento** *sm* ornament. **ornar** *v* adorn. **ornato** *sm* adornment.

ornitología [ornitolo'xia] *sf* ornithology. **ornitólogo** *sm* ornithologist.

oro ['oro] *sm* gold. **oro batido** gold leaf. **oro en bruto** bullion. **oropel** *sm* tinsel.

orquesta [or'kesta] *sf* orchestra. **orquestación** *sf* orchestration. **orquestar** *v* orchestrate.

orquídea [or'kiðea] *sf* orchid.

ortega [or'tega] *sf* grouse.

ortodoxo [orto'ðokso] *adj* orthodox. **ortodoxia** *sf* orthodoxy.

ortografía [ortogra'fia] *sf* orthography, spelling.

ortopédico [orto'peðiko], **-a** *sm, sf* orthopedist. *adj* orthopedic.

oruga [o'ruga] *sf* caterpillar.

os [os] *pron pl* you.

osa ['osa] *sf* she-bear. **oso** bear. **oso blanco** polar bear.

osar [o'sar] *v* dare. **osadía** *sf* daring. **osado** *adj* daring.

oscilar [osθi'lar] *v* oscillate, swing. **oscilación** *sf* oscillation.

oscuro [os'kuro] *adj* dark, obscure. **oscurecer** *v* darken; confuse. **oscuridad** *sf* obscurity.

ostensible [osten'siβle] *adj* ostensible; apparent. **ostentación** *sf* ostentation. **ostentar** *v* show off. **ostentativo** *adj also* **ostentoso** ostentatious.

ostra ['ostra] *sf* oyster.

otear [ote'ar] *v* make out; watch; scan.

otoño [o'toɲo] *sm* autumn. **otoñada** *sf* autumn season. **otoñal** *adj* autumnal. **otoñarse** *v* be seasoned.

otorgar [otor'gar] *v* grant; award; confer. **otorgamiento** *sm* granting; authorization.

otro ['otro] *adj* other; another. **otra vez** again. **otro tanto** the same (again). *pron* another. **algún otro** some other.

ovación [oβa'θjon] *sf* ovation. **ovacionar** *v* give an ovation to.

óvalo ['oβalo] *sm* oval; ellipse. **oval** *adj* oval.

ovario [o'βarjo] *sm* ovary.

oveja [o'βexa] *sf* ewe; sheep.

ovillo [o'βiʎo] *sm* (*de lana*) ball; heap.

oxidar [oksi'ðar] *v* oxidize. **óxido** *sm* oxide. **oxígeno** *sm* oxygen.

oye ['oje] *V* **oír**.

oyente [o'jente] *adj* hearing. *s(m + f)* listener.

ozono [o'θono] *sm* ozone.

P

pabellón [paβe'ʎon] *sm* pavilion; bell tent; summerhouse; hospital block; flag.

***pacer** [pa'θer] *v* graze, pasture.

paciencia [pa'θjenθja] *sf* patience. **paciente** *s(m + f)*, *adj* patient. **pacienzudo** *adj* long-suffering.

pacificar [paθifi'kar] *v* pacify. **pacificación** *sf* pacification. **pacificador** *adj* pacifying. **pacífico** *adj* pacific, peaceful. **Oceano Pacífico** Pacific Ocean. **pacifismo** *sm* pacifism. **pacifista** *s(m + f)* pacifist.

pacotilla [pako'tiʎa] *sf* inferior goods *pl*. **de pacotilla** shoddy.

pactar [pak'tar] *v* make a pact, agree. **pacto** *sm* pact, agreement.

pachorra [pa'tʃorra] *sf* sluggishness; indolence.

***padecer** [paðe'θer] *v* suffer; endure. **padecer de** suffer from. **padecimiento** *sm* suffering; ailment.

padre ['paðre] *sm* father. **padres** *sm pl* parents. **padrastro** *sm* stepfather. **Padre Nuestro** Lord's Prayer. **padrino** *sm* godfather; second; sponsor. **padrino de boda** best man.

padrón [pa'ðron] *sm* census; pattern; memorial; (*fam*) indulgent father.

pagano [pa'gano], **-a** *sm, sf, adj* pagan.

pagar [pa'gar] *v* pay. **pagarse de** take a liking to. **paga** *sf* payment; salary. **pagadero** *adj* payable. **pagador, -a** *sm, sf* payer. **pagaduría** *sf* pay office. **pagaré** *sm* IOU. **pago** *sm* payment; reward.

página ['paxina] *sf* page.

país [pa'is] *sm* country. **paisaje** *sm* landscape; countryside. **paisanaje** *sm* peasantry. **paisano, -na** *sm, sf* compatriot; peasant.

Paises Bajos [pa'ises'βaxos] *sm pl* The Netherlands.

paja ['paxa] *sf* straw. **echar pajas** draw lots. **pajita** *sf* drinking straw.

pájaro ['paxaro] *sm* bird. **pajarera** *sf* birdcage.

paje ['paxe] *sm* (*niño*) page.

pala ['pala] *sf* shovel; spade; scoop; dustpan; bat. **palazo** *sm* blow with a stick.

palabra [pa'laβra] *sf* word. **de palabra** by word of mouth. **faltar a la palabra** break one's word. **palabreo** *sm* verbiage.

palabrista *s(m+f)* chatterbox. **palabrota** *sf* swear word.
palacio [pa'laθjo] *sm* palace; mansion. **en palacio** at court.
paladar [pala'ðar] *sm* palate. **paladear** *v* taste, relish.
palanca [pa'lanka] *sf* crowbar; lever; (*fam*) influence.
palangana [palan'gana] *sf* washbasin.
palco ['palko] *sm* (*teatro*) box.
paleta [pa'leta] *sf* shovel; trowel; (*de pintor*) palette; (*de hélice*) blade; (*anat*) shoulder blade.
paliar [pali'ar] *v* alleviate. **paliativo** *adj* palliative.
*palidecer [paliðe'θer] *v* become pale. **palidez** paleness. **pálido** *adj* pale.
palillo [pa'liʎo] *sm* toothpick; small stick.
paliza [pa'liθa] *sf* beating, hiding.
palma ['palma] *sf* palm tree; (*anat*) palm. **palmada** *sf* slap; applause. **palmar** *adj* clear, obvious. **palmatoria** *sf* candlestick; cane. **palmear** *v* clap hands. **palmera** *sf* palm tree.
palmo ['palmo] *sm* (*medida*) span, handbreadth. **palmotear** *v* applaud. **palmoteo** *sm* applause.
palo ['palo] *sm* stick; pole; handle; blow with a stick; mast. **dar de palos** thrash.
paloma [pa'loma] *sf* dove; pigeon. **palomar** *sm* dovecote. **palomino** *sm* young pigeon.
palpable [pal'paβle] *adj* palpable.
palpar [pal'par] *v* feel, touch. **palparse** *v* grope.
palpitar [palpi'tar] *v* palpitate, throb. **palpitación** *sf* palpitation. **palpitante** *adj* palpitating, throbbing.
paludismo [palu'ðismo] *sm* malaria.
palurdo [pa'lurðo] *sm, adj* rustic.
palustre¹ [pa'lustre] *adj* marshy.
palustre² *sm* trowel.
pan [pan] *sm* bread; loaf; dough. **pan ácimo** unleavened bread. **panadería** *sf* bread shop. **panadero, -a** *sm, sf* baker.
pana ['pana] *sf* corduroy. **pana lisa** velvet.
panal [pa'nal] *sm* honeycomb.
panamá [pana'ma] *sm* Panama hat.
panamericano [panameri'kano] *adj* pan-American.
pancarta [pan'karta] *sf* placard.
pandereta [pande'reta] *sf* tambourine.
pandilla [pan'diʎa] *sf* gang; clique.
panfleto [pan'fleto] *sm* pamphlet. **panfletista** *s(m+f)* pamphleteer.

pánico ['paniko] *sm, adj* panic.
pantalón [panta'lon] *sm also* **pantalones** trousers.
pantalla [pan'taʎa] *sf* lampshade; screen.
pantano [pan'tano] *sm* marsh; bog. **pantanal** *sm* marshland. **pantanoso** *adj* swampy.
panteísta [pante'ista] *s(m+f)* pantheist. **panteísmo** *sm* pantheism.
pantera [pan'tera] *sf* panther.
pantomima [panto'mima] *sf* pantomime.
pantorrilla [pantor'riʎa] *sf* (*anat*) calf.
pantufla [pan'tufla] *sf or* **pantuflo** *sm* slipper.
panza ['panθa] *sf* belly. **panzada** *sf* bellyful.
pañal [pa'ɲal] *sm* nappy.
pañería [paɲe'ria] *sf* drapery. **pañero** *sm* draper. **pañete** *sm* light cloth. **paño** *sm* cloth. **paños menores** underclothes. **pañuelo** *sm* handkerchief.
papa¹ ['papa] *sm* pope. **papado** *sm* papacy. **papal** *adj* papal.
papa² *sf* potato.
papá [pa'pa] *sm* daddy.
papada [pa'paða] *sf* double chin.
papagayo [papa'gajo] *sm* parrot.
papar [pa'par] *v* eat; gulp. **papamoscas** *m invar* flycatcher; (*fig*) simpleton. **papar moscas** gape.
papel [pa'pel] *sm* paper. **papel de forrar** brown paper. **papel de fumar** cigarette paper. **papeleo** *sm* paper work; (*fam*) red tape. **papelera** *sf* wastepaper basket. **papelería** *sf* stationer's.
papera [pa'pera] *sf* goitre. **paperas** *sf pl* mumps *sing*.
papiro [pa'piro] *sm* papyrus.
paquete [pa'kete] *sm* packet.
par [par] *sm* pair. *adj* equal. **sin par** matchless.
para ['para] *prep* for; towards. **para mañana** by tomorrow. **¿para qué?** why?
parábola [pa'raβola] *sf* parable; parabola.
parabrisas [para'βrisas] *sm invar* windshield.
paracaídas [paraka'iðas] *sm invar* parachute. **paracaidista** *s(m+f)* parachutist.
parochoques [para'ʃtokes] *sm invar* (*auto*) bumper.
parada [pa'raða] *sf* stop; stopping; (*taxi*) rank; pause; parade; dam. **paradero** *sm* whereabouts; destination; home. **parado** *adj* motionless; unemployed.

paradoja [para'ðoxa] *sf* paradox. **paradójico** *adj* paradoxical.

parador [para'ðor] *sm* tourist hotel.

parafina [para'fina] *sf* paraffin.

paráfrasis [pa'rafrasis] *sf invar* paraphrase. **parafrasear** *v* paraphrase.

paraguas [pa'ragwas] *sm invar* umbrella.

paraíso [para'iso] *sm* paradise; (*teatro*) gallery.

paralela [para'lela] *sf* parallel. **paralelas** *sf pl* parallel bars. **paralelo** *sm, adj* parallel.

parálisis [pa'ralisis] *sf* paralysis. **paralítico** *sm, adj* paralytic. **paralizar** *v* paralyse.

páramo ['paramo] *sm* wilderness; bleak plateau. **paramera** *sf* desert.

parangón [paran'gon] *sm* comparison. **parangonar** *v* compare.

parapeto [para'peto] *sm* parapet; railing.

parar [pa'rar] *v* stop; check. **pararse** *v* stay; end up. **parar en mal** come to a bad end.

pararrayos [parar'rajos] *sm invar* lightning conductor.

parásito [pa'rasito] *sm* parasite. *adj* parasitic.

parasol [para'sol] *sm* parasol.

parcela [par'θela] *sf* (*de tierra*) plot. **parcelar** *v* parcel out.

parcial [par'θjal] *adj* partial. **parcialidad** *sf* partiality.

parco ['parko] *adj* frugal; mean; sparing.

parche ['partʃe] *sm* plaster; patch; drumhead.

pardo ['parðo] *adj* dark; brown.

parear [pare'ar] *v* match, pair.

***parecer** [pare'θer] *v* seem; appear. **parecerse** *v* resemble. **parecido** *adj* similar. **bien parecido** good-looking.

pared [pa'reð] *sf* wall. **paredón** *sm* large wall.

pareja [pa'rexa] *sf* pair; couple. **parejo** *adj* even; equal.

parentela [paren'tela] *sf* kindred. **parentesco** *sm* kinship.

paréntesis [pa'rentesis] *sm* parenthesis; bracket.

paridad [pari'ðað] *sf* comparison; parity.

pariente [pa'rjente] *sm* relation.

parir [pa'rir] *v* give birth to.

París [pa'ris] *s* Paris.

parla ['parla] *sf* gossip; chatter. **parlador, -a** *sm, sf* talker. **parlanchín** *adj* talkative. **parlante** *adj* chattering. **parlar** *v* chatter. **parleta** *sf* small talk.

parlamento [parla'mento] *sm* parliament. **parlamentario** *adj* parliamentary.

paro ['paro] *sm* stoppage; unemployment.

parodiar [paro'ðjar] *v* parody. **parodia** *sf* parody.

paroxismo [parok'sismo] *sm* paroxysm.

parpadear [parpaðe'ar] *v* blink; wink. **parpadeo** *sm* blinking; winking. **párpado** *sm* eyelid.

parque ['parke] *sm* park.

parra ['parra] *sf* vine. **hoja de parra** figleaf. **parra virgen** Virginia creeper.

párrafo ['parrafo] *sm* paragraph.

parricida [parri'θiða] *s(m+f)* (*criminal*) parricide. **parricidio** *sm* (*crimen*) parricide.

parrilla [par'riʎa] *sf* grill; gridiron; grate; grillroom.

párroco ['parroko] *sm* parish priest. **parroquia** *sf* parish; parish church. **parroquial** *adj* parochial. **parroquiano, -a** *sm, sf* parishioner; regular customer.

parsimonia [parsi'monja] *sf* parsimony; frugality; calmness.

parte ['parte] *sf* part; share; point; side; way; party; role; actor. **en otra parte** elsewhere. **por todas partes** everywhere. **por una parte y por otra** on the one hand and on the other.

partera [par'tera] *sf* midwife.

partición [parti'θjon] *sf* partition; division. **partible** *adj* divisible.

participar [partiθi'par] *v* participate; partake; invest; inform; announce. **participación** *sf* participation; share; announcement. **participante** *s(m+f)* participant; informant; competitor. **partícipe** *s(m+f)* participant.

participio [parti'θipjo] *sm* (*gram*) participle.

partícula [par'tikula] *sf* particle.

particular [partiku'lar] *adj* particular; peculiar; individual; personal. **casa particular** private house. *sm* matter; individual; civilian. **particularidad** *sf* peculiarity. **particularizar** *v* specify; distinguish; prefer. **particularizarse** *v* stand out. **particularamente** *adv* in particular.

partida [par'tiða] *sf* departure; certificate; (*com*) entry; item; party; game. **partida de campo** picnic. **partida doble** double entry. **partidario, -a** *sm, sf* follower; partisan.

partido [par'tiðo] *sm* (*deporte*) match;

(*pol*) party. *adj* divided. **darse a partido** give in. **sacar partido** benefit from.

partir [par'tir] *v* leave, depart; divide; share. **a partir de hoy** from today on. **partirse** *v* differ in opinion; depart. **partidor** *sm* distributor.

partitura [parti'tura] *sf* (*música*) score.

parto ['parto] *sm* childbirth; delivery; (*fig*) brainchild.

parvo ['parβo] *adj* little. **párvulo** *adj* very small.

pasa ['pasa] *sf* raisin. **pasa de Corinto** currant.

pasada [pa'saða] *sf* passage; (*aves*) flight. **de pasada** in passing. **mala pasada** dirty trick. **pasadero** *adj* tolerable.

pasado [pa'saðo] *sm, adj* past. **lo pasado, pasado** let bygones be bygones. **pasado mañana** the day after tomorrow.

pasador [pasa'ðor], -a *sm, sf* smuggler. *sm* filter; colander; bolt; pin; fastener. **pasadores** *sm pl* cufflinks *pl*.

pasaje [pa'saxe] *sm* passage; fare; ticket; voyage; passengers *pl*. **pasajero**, -a *sm, sf* passenger.

pasamano [pasa'mano] *sm* bannister; handrail.

pasapasa [pasa'pasa] *sm* sleight-of-hand.

pasaporte [pasa'porte] *sm* passport.

pasar [pa'sar] *v* pass; give; spend; take; send; run; cross; penetrate. **pasar de moda** be out of fashion. **pasarlo bien/mal** have a good/bad time. **pasar por** be considered. **pasar por alto** overlook. **¿qué pasa?** what's up? **pasarse** pass off; be over; miss. **pasarse de** be too. **pasarse por** call in at.

pasarela [pasa'rela] *sf* footbridge; gangway.

pasatiempo [pasa'tjempo] *sm* pastime, amusement.

pascua ['paskwa] *sf* (*rel*) feast; Christmas; Easter; Epiphany; Passover. **¡felices pascuas y próspero año nuevo!** merry Christmas and a happy New Year!

pase ['pase] *sm* invitation; permission; (*autorización*) pass.

pasear [pase'ar] *v* go for a walk; take for a walk; go for a ride. **paseo** *sm* walk; drive; ride.

pasillo [pa'siʎo] *sm* corridor, passage.

pasión [pasi'on] *sf* passion. **pasional** *adj* passionate.

pasivo [pa'siβo] *adj* passive. *sm* (*com*) liabilities *pl*. **pasividad** *sf* passivity.

pasmar [pas'mar] *v* chill; stun; amaze. **pasmo** *sm* amazement; convulsion. **pasmoso** *adj* wonderful.

paso ['paso] *sm* step; pace; walk; passage; situation. **paso a nivel** level-crossing. **paso a paso** step by step. **salir del paso** get out of a difficulty.

pasta ['pasta] *sf* pasta; dough; paste. **pastas** *sf pl* noodles.

pastar [pas'tar] *v* graze, pasture.

pastel [pas'tel] *sm* cake, pastry; (*color*) pastel. **pastel de carne** meat pie. **pastelería** *sf* cake shop; cakes *pl*; confectionery. **pastelero**, -a *sm, sf* pastrycook.

pastilla [pas'tiʎa] *sf* bar; piece; tablet.

pastinaca [pasti'naka] *sf* (*bot*) turnip; (*zool*) stingray.

pasto ['pasto] *sm* grass; pasture. **a pasto** galore. **pastor** *sm* shepherd; pastor. **pastoral** *adj* pastoral. **pastorear** *v* pasture.

pastura [pas'tura] *sf* pasture; fodder.

pata ['pata] *sf* (*de animal*) foot; leg; paw. **meter la pata** (*fam*) put one's foot in it. **tener mala pata** (*fam*) be unlucky. **patada** *sf* kick; stamp. **patalear** *v* stamp; kick about. **pataleo** *sm* kicking.

patán [pa'tan] *sm* lout. *adj* churlish. **patanería** *sf* boorishness.

patata [pa'tata] *sf* potato. **patatas fritas** french fries.

patear [pate'ar] *v* kick; stamp.

patente [pa'tente] *sm* (*com*) patent. *adj* obvious.

paternal [pater'nal] *adj* paternal. **paternidad** *sf* paternity. **paterno** *adj* paternal.

patético [pa'tetiko] *adj* pathetic.

patíbulo [pa'tiβulo] *sm* gallows *pl*.

patillas [pa'tiʎas] *sf pl* whiskers *pl*, sideboards *pl*.

patín [pa'tin] *sm* skate. **patín de ruedas** roller skate. **patinadero** *sm* skating rink. **patinador**, -a *sm, sf* skater. **patinaje** *sm* skating. **patinar** *v* skate; skid. **patinazo** *sm* skid; (*fam*) blunder. **patinete** *sm* child's scooter.

patio ['patjo] *sm* patio; yard.

pato ['pato] *sm* duck. **pagar el pato** (*fam*) carry the can.

patochada [pato'tʃaða] *sf* blunder.

patología [patolo'xia] *sf* pathology. **patológico** *adj* pathological. **patólogo** *sm* pathologist.

patraña [pa'traɲa] *sf* cock-and-bull story; fib.

patria ['patrja] *sf* native land. **patriota** *s(m + f)* patriot. **patriótico** *adj* patriotic. **patriotismo** *sm* patriotism.

patriarca [pa'trjarka] *sm* patriarch. **patriarcal** *adj* patriarchal.

patricio [pa'triθjo], **-a** *sm, sf, adj* patrician.

patrimonio [patri'monjo] *sm* patrimony, birthright. **patrimonial** *adj* patrimonial.

patrocinar [patroθi'nar] *v* patronize; sponsor. **patrocinador, -a** *sm, sf* patron; sponsor. **patrocinio** *sm* patronage; sponsorship.

patrón [pa'tron] *sm* patron; owner; landlord; pattern. **patronato** *sm* patronage; board of trustees; society.

patrono [pa'trono] *sm* boss; patron saint; owner.

patrulla [pa'truʎa] *sf* patrol. **patrullar** *v* patrol.

paulatino [paula'tino] *adj* slow, gradual. **paulatinamente** *adj* gradually; little by little.

pausa ['pausa] *sf* pause; (*música*) rest. **pausado** *adj* slow; deliberate. **pausar** *v* pause; interrupt.

pauta ['pauta] *sf* rule; model; lines *pl*. **pautar** *v* rule; give instructions. **papel pautado** ruled paper.

pávido ['paβiðo] *adj* timid.

pavimentar [paβimen'tar] *v* pave; surface. **pavimento** *sm* pavement.

pavo ['paβo] *sm* turkey. **pavo real** peacock. **pavonear** *v* show off.

pavor [pa'βor] *sm* terror; dread. **pavorido** *adj* terror-stricken. **pavoroso** *adj* dreadful; awful. **pavura** *sf* fear; dread.

payaso [pa'jaso] *sm* clown. **payasada** *sf* clowning.

paz [paθ] *sf* peace. **hacer las paces** make it up. **¡paz!** hush!

peaje [pe'axe] *sm* toll. **peajero** *sm* toll-collector.

peatón [pea'ton] *sm* pedestrian.

peca ['peka] *sf* spot; freckle. **pecoso** *adj* freckled.

pecar [pe'kar] *v* sin. **pecado** *sm* sin. **pecador, -a** *sm, sf* sinner. **pecaminoso** *adj* sinful.

pécora ['pekora] *sf* sheep; (*fam*) slut.

peculiar [peku'ljar] *adj* peculiar; special. **peculiaridad** *sf* peculiarity. **peculiarmente** peculiarly.

pechera [pe'tʃera] *sf* bib; shirt-front.

pecho ['petʃo] *sm* chest; bosom; breast; courage; tax. **dar el pecho** suckle. **enfermo del pecho** consumptive. **pechuga** *sf* (*de ave*) breast.

pedagogía [peðago'xia] *sf* pedagogy. **pedagógico** *adj* teaching. **pedagogo** *sm* teacher.

pedal [pe'ðal] *sm* pedal. **pedalear** *v* pedal.

pedante [pe'ðante] *s(m + f)* pedant. *adj* pedantic. **pedantería** *sf* pedantry.

pedazo [pe'ðaθo] *sm* piece. **hacerse pedazos** be smashed to bits.

pedernal [peðer'nal] *sm* flint.

pedestal [peðe'stal] *sm* pedestal.

pedestre [pe'ðestre] *adj* pedestrian.

pediatría [peðja'tria] *sf* paediatrics. **pediatra** or **pediatra** *sm* paediatrician.

pedicuro [peði'kuro], **-a** *sm, sf* chiropodist. *sf* chiropody.

***pedir** [pe'ðir] *v* ask; ask for; order. **pedir limosna** beg. **pedir prestado** borrow. **pedido** *sm* demand; (*com*) order. **pedimento** *sm* petition.

pedo ['peðo] *sm* (*vulgar*) fart.

pedregal [peðre'gal] *sm* stony ground. **pedrea** *sf* stoning; hailstorm. **pedregoso** *adj* stony. **pedrería** *sf* jewels *pl*. **pedrero** *sm* stone-cutter. **pedrisco** *sm* hailstorm.

pegar [pe'gar] *v* hit; glue; (*med*) infect; take effect; give; let out; fire; sew on. **pegar fuego** a set fire to. **pegar un tiro** fire a shot. **pega** *sf* difficulty; hoax; snag. **poner pegas a** find fault with. **pegajoso** *adj* sticky; infectious.

peinar [pei'nar] *v* comb. **peinado** *sm* coiffure. **peinador, -a** *sm, sf* hairdresser; *sm* bathrobe. **peine** *sm* comb.

pelar [pe'lar] *v* cut; peel; shear; skin; shell. **pelar la pava** woo. **pelado** *adj* shorn; peeled; bare. **pelaje** *sm* fur. **pelambre** *sm* (*de animales*) hair. **pelambrera** *sf* fleece.

peldaño [pel'ðaɲo] *sm* stair; step.

pelear [pele'ar] *v* fight. **pelearse con alguien** fight somebody. **pelea** *sf* fight. **peleador** *sm* fight.

pelele [pe'lele] *sm* puppet; dummy.

peliagudo [pelja'guðo] *adj* (*fig*) difficult, tough.

pelícano [pe'likano] *sm* pelican.

película [pe'likula] *sf* film.

peligro [pe'ligro] *sm* danger. **peligrarse** *v* be in danger. **peligroso** *adj* dangerous.

pelmazo [pel'maθo] *sm also* **pelma** *sf* bore; crushed mass.

pelo ['pelo] *sm* hair; (*en madera*) grain; nap. **de medio pelo** low-class. **soltarse el pelo** show one's true colours. **pelón** *adj* bald.

pelota [pe'lota] *sf* ball. **echarse la pelota** pass the buck. **en pelota** naked.

pelotón [pelo'ton] *sm* platoon; squad.

peltre ['peltre] *sm* pewter.

peluca [pe'luka] *sf* wig.

peludo [pe'luðo] *adj* hairy.

peluquero [pelu'kero], **-a** *sm, sf* hairdresser. **peluquería** *sf* hairdresser's.

pelusa [pe'lusa] *sf* down; fuzz; (*fam*) jealousy.

pelleja [pe'ʎexa] *sf also* **pellejo** *sm* hide, skin. **jugarse el pellejo** risk one's neck.

pellizcar [peʎiθ'kar] *v* nip, pinch. **pellizco** *sm* nip, pinch.

pello ['peʎo] *sm* fur jacket.

pena ['pena] *sf* pain; grief; hardship; penalty; effort. **pena capital** capital punishment. **¡qué pena!** what a shame! **penable** *adj* punishable. **penado** *adj* painful. **penal** *adj* penal. **penalidad** *sf* penalty. **penar** *v* punish; suffer. **penarse** *v* grieve.

pender [pen'der] *v* hang; (*jur*) be pending. **pendiente** *adj* hanging; pending. **estar pendiente de** depend on.

péndulo ['pendulo] *sm* pendulum.

pene ['pene] *sm* penis.

penetrar [pene'trar] *v* penetrate; comprehend. **penetrarse** *v* become aware of; imbibe. **penetrable** *adj* penetrable. **penetración** *sf* penetration. **penetrante** *adj* penetrating.

penicilina [peniθi'lina] *sf* penicillin.

península [pe'ninsula] *sf* peninsula. **peninsular** *adj* peninsular.

penique [pe'nike] *sm* penny.

penitencia [peni'tenθja] *sf* penitence. **hacer penitencia** (*fam*) take pot-luck. **penitencial** *adj* penitential. **penitenciaria** *sf* penitentiary. **penitente** *adj* penitent.

penoso [pe'noso] *adj* painful; difficult.

***pensar** [pen'sar] *v* think; think over; intend. **pensar en** think about. **pensado** *adj* deliberate. **de pensado** on purpose. **pensador, -a** *sm, sf* thinker. **pensamiento** *sm* thought. **pensativo** *adj* thoughtful.

pensión [pensi'on] *sf* pension; boarding house; hardship. **pensionado, -a** *sm, sf* pensioner. **pensionar** *v* pension. **pensionista** *s(m+f)* pensioner; boarder.

pentágono [pen'tagono] *sm* pentagon.

penúltimo [pe'nultimo] *adj* penultimate.

penumbra [pe'numβra] *sf* half-light.

penuria [pe'nurja] *sf* penury; shortage.

peña ['peɲa] *sf* crag; rock; cliff; group of friends. **peñasco** *sm* large rock. **peñascoso** *adj* rocky. **peñón** *sm* rocky mountain. **el Peñón de Gibraltar** the Rock of Gibraltar.

peón [pe'on] *sm* unskilled labourer; pedestrian; foot-soldier; (*ajedrez*) pawn.

peonía [peo'nia] *sf* peony.

peor [pe'or] *adj, adv* worse; worst. **peoría** *sf* worsening.

pepino [pe'pino] *sm* cucumber. **no valer un pepino** not be worth a damn. **pepinillo** *sm* gherkin.

pepita [pe'pita] *sf* seed, pip; (*oro*) nugget.

pequeño [pe'keɲo] *adj* small; humble. **pequeñez** *sf* smallness; pettiness.

pera ['pera] *sf* pear; light-switch; (*barba*) goatee; sinecure. **peral** *sm* pear tree.

perca ['perka] *sf* (*zool*) perch.

percance [per'kanθe] *sm* mishap; profit.

percatarse [perka'tarse] *v* notice.

percibir [perθi'βir] *v* perceive; collect. **percepción** *sf* perception; collection. **perceptible** *adj* perceptible. **perceptivo** *adj* perceptive. **perceptor, -a** *sm, sf* perceiver. **percibo** *sm* collecting.

percusión [perku'sjon] *sf* percussion.

percha ['pertʃa] *sf* perch; pole; hat-stand; coat-rack.

***perder** [per'ðer] *v* lose; spoil; waste. **perderse por** be inordinately fond of. **perdición** *sf* loss; perdition. **pérdida** *sf* damage; waste. **perdido** *adj* lost; dissolute.

perdiz [per'ðiθ] *sf* partridge.

perdonar [perðo'nar] *v* pardon; excuse. **pardón** *sm* pardon; mercy. **con perdón** by your leave. **perdonable** *adj* pardonable. **perdonavidas** *m invar* (*fam*) bully.

perdurar [perðu'rar] *v* endure. **perdurable** *adj* everlasting.

***perecer** [pere'θer] *v* perish. **perecerse por** crave. **perecedero** *adj* perishable.

peregrinar [peregri'nar] *v* travel; go on a pilgrimage. **peregrinación** *sf* pilgrimage. **peregrino, -a** *sm, sf* pilgrim.

perejil [pere'xil] *sm* parsley.

perenne [pe'renne] *adj* perennial.

perentorio [peren'torjo] *adj* peremptory; urgent.

perezoso [pere'θoso] *adj* lazy. **pereza** *sf* laziness.

perfecto [per'fekto] *adj* perfect. **perfección** *sf* perfection. **perfeccionamiento** *sm* improvement; perfection. **perfeccionar** *v* perfect; improve.

pérfido ['perfiðo] *adj* perfidious. **perfidia** *sf* perfidy.

perfilar [perfi'lar] *v* outline. **perfil** *sm* profile; outline.

perforar [perfo'rar] *v* perforate; drill; puncture. **perforación** *sf* perforation. **perforadora** *sf* drill.

perfumar [perfu'mar] *v* perfume. **perfume** *sm* perfume. **perfumería** *sf* perfume shop.

perfunctorio [perfunk'torjo] *adj* perfunctory.

pericial [peri'θjal] *adj* expert. **pericia** *sf* skill.

perico [pe'riko] *sm* parakeet; toupee.

periferia [peri'ferja] *sf* periphery.

perímetro [pe'rimetro] *sm* perimeter.

periódico [peri'oðiko] *sm* periodical; newspaper. *adj* periodic. **periodicidad** *sf* recurrence. **periodismo** *sm* journalism. **periodista** *s(m+f)* journalist. **periodístico** *adj* journalistic. **período** *or* **periodo** *sm* period. **período de prácticas** probationary period.

peripecia [peri'peθja] *sf* vicissitude; incident; adventure.

periscopio [peris'kopjo] *sm* periscope.

perjudicar [perxuði'kar] *v* prejudice; harm. **perjudicial** *adj* harmful. **perjuicio** *sm* prejudice; damage.

perjurar [perxu'rar] *v* perjure oneself. **perjurio** *sm* perjury. **perjuro, -a** *sm, sf* perjurer.

perla ['perla] *sf* pearl. **de perlas** perfectly.

*permanecer [permane'θer] *v* stay, remain. **permanencia** *sf* stay; permanence. **permanente** *adj* permanent.

permitir [permi'tir] *v* permit. ¿me **permite?** may I? **permisible** *adj* permissible. **permisivo** *adj* permissive. **permiso** *sm* permission; permit; leave; licence. **con permiso** if I may.

permutar [permu'tar] *v* permute; exchange. **permuta** *sf* exchange; permutation. **permutación** *sf* permutation.

perniabierto [pernia'βjerto] *adj* bandy-legged.

pernicioso [perni'θjoso] *adj* pernicious.

pernoctar [pernok'tar] *v* spend the night.

pero[1] ['pero] *conj* but; yet. ¡**pero bueno!** why!

pero[2] *sm* pear tree.

perogrullada [perogru'ʎaða] *sf* platitude.

perorar [pero'rar] *v* make a speech. **peroración** *sf* peroration.

peróxido [per'oksiðo] *sm* peroxide.

perpendicular [perpendiku'lar] *sf, adj* perpendicular.

perpetrar [perpe'trar] *v* perpetrate. **perpetración** *sf* perpetration.

perpetuar [perpe'twar] *v* perpetuate. **perpetuación** *sf* perpetuation. **perpetuidad** *sf* perpetuity. **perpetuo** *adj* perpetual.

perplejo [per'plexo] *adj* perplexed; perplexing. **perplejidad** *sf* perplexity.

perro ['perro] *sm* dog; (*fam*) penny. **perra** *sf* bitch. **perrera** *sf* kennel; dog pound; dogcatcher's wagon. **perrero** *sm* dogcatcher.

*perseguir [perse'gir] *v* pursue; persecute. **persecución** *sf* pursuit; persecution. **perseguidor, -a** *sm, sf* pursuer; persecutor.

perseverar [perseβe'rar] *v* persevere. **perseverancia** *sf* perseverance. **perseverante** *adj* persevering.

persiana [per'sjana] *sf* slatted shutter. **persiana veneciana** venetian blind.

persistir [persis'tir] *v* persist. **persistencia** *sf* persistence. **persistente** *adj* persistent.

persona [per'sona] *sf* person. **persona a persona** man to man. **personaje** *sm* personage; (*teatro*) character. **personal** *adj* personal. **personalidad** *sf* personality. **personalismo** *sm* partiality. **personalizar** *v* personalize. **personarse** *v* appear in person. **personificar** *v* personify.

perspectiva [perspek'tiβa] *sf* perspective; outlook.

perspicaz [perspi'kaθ] *adj* perspicacious. **perspicacia** *sf* perspicacity.

persuadir [perswa'ðir] *v* persuade. **persuasión** *sf* persuasion. **persuasivo** *adj* persuasive.

*pertenecer [pertene'θer] *v* belong. **perteneciente** *adj* belonging. **pertenencia** *sf* ownership; property; membership.

pértiga ['pertiga] *sf* pole. **salto de pértiga** pole vault.

pertiguero [perti'gero] *sm* verger.

pertinaz [perti'naθ] *adj* pertinacious. **pertinacia** *sf* pertinacity.

pertinente [perti'nente] *adj* pertinent. **pertinencia** *sf* pertinence.

pertrechar [pertre'tʃar] *v* supply; equip.
pertrechos *sm pl* equipment *sing*; munitions *pl*.
perturbar [pertur'βar] *v* perturb. **perturbación** *sf* perturbation. **perturbador** *adj* perturbing.
***pervertir** [perβer'tir] *v* pervert. **perversidad** *sf* perversity. **perversión** *sf* perversion. **perverso** *adj* perverse.
pesa ['pesa] *sf* weight. **pesas y medidas** weights and measures. **pesadez** *sf* heaviness; drowsiness; hardship.
pesadilla [pesa'ðiʎa] *sf* nightmare.
pesado [pe'saðo] *adj* heavy; sluggish. *sm* bore. **pesadumbre** *sf* grief.
pésame ['pesame] *sm* condolence.
pesar [pe'sar] *v* weigh. **a pesar de** in spite of. **me pesa mucho** I'm very sorry.
pescar [pes'kar] *v* fish. **pesca** *sf* fishing. **pescada** *sf* hake. **pescadería** *sf* fish shop; fish market. **pescadero** *sm* fishmonger. **pescado** *sm* fish. **pescador** *sm* fisherman. **pescador de caña** angler.
pescuezo [pes'kweθo] *sm* neck.
pesebre [pe'seβre] *sm* crib; manger.
pesimista [pesi'mista] *s(m+f)* pessimist. *adj* pessimistic. **pesimismo** *sm* pessimism.
pésimo ['pesimo] *adj* worthless.
peso ['peso] *sm* weight; balance; scales *pl*; peso. **en peso** bodily. **peso específico** specific gravity.
pesquisa [pes'kisa] *sf* inquiry.
pestañear [pestaɲe'ar] *v* blink. **pestaña** *sf* eyelash; fringe; hem. **pestañeo** *sm* blink.
peste ['peste] *sf* plague; corruption; poison. **echar pestes** curse. **pesticida** *sf* pesticide. **pestilencia** *sf* pestilence. **pestilente** *adj* pestilent; stinking.
pestillo [pes'tiʎo] *sm* bolt; latch.
petaca [pe'taka] *sf* tobacco pouch; cigarette case.
pétalo ['petalo] *sm* petal.
petardo [pe'tarðo] *sm* firework; (*fam*) swindle.
petición [peti'θjon] *sf* petition; plea. **peticionario, -a** *sm, sf* petitioner.
petirrojo [petir'roxo] *sm* robin.
peto ['peto] *sm* bib; breastplate.
petrificar [petrifi'kar] *v* petrify. **pétreo** *adj* stony.
petróleo [pe'troleo] *sm* petroleum. **petrolero** *sm* oil-tanker.
petulante [petu'lante] *adj* petulant; insolent. **petulancia** *sf* petulance; insolence.

peyorativo [pejora'tiβo] *adj* pejorative.
pez [peθ] *sm* fish. *sf* pitch, tar.
pezón [pe'θon] *sm* (*bot*) stalk; (*anat*) nipple.
pezuña [pe'θuɲa] *sf* hoof.
piadoso [pja'ðoso] *adj* pious; merciful.
piano ['pjano] *sm* piano. **pianista** *s(m+f)* pianist.
piar [pjar] *v* chirp.
piara ['pjara] *sf* herd.
pica ['pika] *sf* lance, pike; goad; pick; magpie.
picadillo [pika'ðiʎo] *sm* minced meat.
picante [pi'kante] *adj* hot; spicy; pungent; biting.
picaporte [pika'porte] *sm* door handle; latch; knocker; latch-key.
picar [pi'kar] *v* prick, pierce; sting; burn; punch; bite, eat; chop up. **picado** *adj* bitten; stung; minced; sour; bad. **picadura** *sf* bite; sting; peck.
picardear [pikar'ðear] *v* corrupt; get up to mischief. **picardía** *sf* dirty trick; craftiness; mischief. **picaresco** *adj* roguish. **pícaro, -a** *sm, sf* rogue.
pico ['piko] *sm* beak; peak; pickaxe. **darse el pico** kiss. **pico carpintero** woodpecker. **son las cuatro y pico** it is just after four.
picotear [pikote'ar] *v* peck; chatter. **picotearse** *v* wrangle. **picotada** *sf* also **picotazo** *sm* peck. **picotero, -a** *sm, sf* chatterbox.
pichón [pi'tʃon] *sm* pigeon. **pichona** *sf* (*fam*) darling.
pie [pje] *sm* foot; base; stem. **a cuatro pies** on all fours. **dar pie a** give cause for. **de pies a cabeza** from head to foot.
piedad [pje'ðað] *sf* piety; pity.
piedra ['pjeðra] *sf* stone.
piel [pjel] *sf* skin.
pienso ['pjenso] *sm* fodder. **ni por pienso** not likely.
pierna ['pjerna] *sf* leg.
pieza ['pjeθa] *sf* piece; part; room. **dejar de una pieza** leave speechless.
pífano ['pifano] *sm* fife.
pigmento [pig'mento] *sm* pigment.
pigmeo [pig'meo], **-a** *s, adj* pygmy.
pijama [pi'xama] *sm* pyjamas *pl*.
pila¹ ['pila] *sf* heap; battery.
pila² *sf* basin; trough; font. **nombre de pila** Christian name.
pilar [pi'lar] *sm* pillar; pier; milestone; basin.

píldora ['pilðora] *sf* pill.

pilón [pi'lon] *sm* basin; trough; mortar; pylon.

piloto [pi'loto] *sm* pilot; (*auto*) rear light, parking light.

piltrafa [pil'trafa] *sf* gristly meat. **piltrafas** *sf pl* scraps *pl*.

pillar [pi'ʎar] *v* pillage; get; run over; (*fam*) catch. **pillaje** *sm* pillage.

pillo ['piʎo], -a *sm*, *sf* scoundrel. *adj* villainous. **pillastre** *sm* or **pillastron** *sm* rogue. **pillería** *sf* gang of villains; knavery.

pimienta [pi'mjenta] *sf* pepper. **pimiento** *sm* (*planta*) pepper. **pimentón** *sm* paprika.

pimpollo [pim'poʎo] *sm* sprout; sapling; (*fam*) handsome boy, pretty girl.

pináculo [pi'nakulo] *sm* pinnacle.

pinar [pi'nar] *sm* pine forest.

pincel [pin'θel] *sm* paintbrush. **pincelada** *sf* brush-stroke. **pincelar** *v* paint.

pinchar [pin'tʃar] *v* puncture. **pincharse** *v* have a puncture. **pinchazo** *sm* puncture. **pincho** *sm* point; prickle; spine.

pingo ['pingo] *sm* rag; devil. **pingos** *sm pl* (*fam*) togs.

pingüe ['pingwe] *adj* fatty; abundant.

pingüino [pin'gwino] *sm* penguin.

pino ['pino] *sm* pine tree. **pinocha** *sf* pine needle.

pintar [pin'tar] *v* paint. **pintarse** *v* make oneself up. **pinta** *sf* spot. **tener buena/mala pinta** look good/bad. **pintor, -a** *sm*, *sf* painter. **pintoresco** *adj* picturesque. **pintorrear** *v* (*fam*) daub. **pintura** *sf* painting; picture.

pinzas ['pinθas] *sf pl* tweezers; pincers; forceps; tongs; clothes pegs.

pinzón [pin'θon] *sm* finch.

piña ['piɲa] *sf* pineapple; pine cone.

piñón [pi'ɲon] *sm* pinion.

pío¹ ['pio] *sm* chirp.

pío² *adj* pious; merciful.

piojo ['pjoxo] *sm* louse. **piojoso** *adj* lousy.

pipa ['pipa] *sf* pipe; pip.

pique ['pike] *sm* pique; resentment. **echar a pique** sink; ruin.

piqueta [pi'keta] *sf* pickaxe.

piquete [pi'kete] *sm* picket; squad; sting; hole.

piragua [pi'ragwa] *sf* canoe.

pirámide [pi'ramiðe] *sf* pyramid. **piramidal** *adj* pyramidal.

pirata [pi'rata] *sm*, *adj* pirate.

Pirineos [piri'neos] *sm pl* Pyrenees *pl*.

piropear [pirope'ar] *v* (*fam*) compliment. **piropo** *sm* compliment.

pirotecnia [piro'teknja] *sf* fireworks *pl*.

pirueta [pi'rweta] *sf* pirouette. **piruetear** *v* pirouette.

pisar [pi'sar] *v* tread; trample. **pisada** *sf* footprint; step. **pisapapeles** *sm invar* paperweight.

piscina [pis'θina] *sf* swimming pool.

piscolabis [pisko'laβis] *sm invar* (*fam*) snack.

piso ['piso] *sm* floor; storey; flat. **piso bajo** ground floor.

pisotear [pisote'ar] *v* trample. **pisoteo** *sm* trampling.

pista ['pista] *sf* track; trail; runway; court; ring; rink. **pista de baile** dance floor.

pistola [pis'tola] *sf* pistol. **pistolera** *sf* holster. **pistolero** *sm* gunman.

pistón [pis'ton] *sm* piston.

pitar [pi'tar] *v* whistle at; blow a whistle; boo, hiss. **pitada** *sf* whistle.

pitón [pi'ton] *sm* python.

pizarra [pi'θarra] *sf* blackboard; slate.

pizca ['piθka] *sf* (*fam*) crumb; drop; pinch.

placa ['plaka] *sf* plate; badge; plaque. **placa de matrícula** (*auto*) number plate.

*placer [pla'θer] *v* please. *sm* pleasure. **a placer** at one's leisure.

plácido ['plaθiðo] *adj* placid; pleasant.

plagar [pla'gar] *v* plague. **plaga** *sf* plague.

plagiar [pla'xjar] *v* plagiarize. **plagio** *sm* plagiarism.

plan [plan] *sm* plan; project.

plana ['plana] *sf* (*imprenta*) page; (*llanura*) plain.

planchar [plan'tʃar] *v* iron, press. **mesa de planchar** *sf* ironing board. **plancha** *sf* iron. **planchado** *sm* ironing.

planear [plane'ar] *v* plan; glide. **planeo** *sm* gliding.

planeta [pla'neta] *sf* planet. **planetario** *sm* planetarium.

planincie [pla'niθje] *sf* plain; plateau.

planificar [planifi'kar] *v* plan. **planificación** *sf* planning.

plano ['plano] *adj* flat; level; smooth. *sm* map; plan; plane. **de plano** directly. **plano acotado** contour map. **primer plano** close-up.

plantar [plan'tar] v plant; erect. **plantarse** v stop; settle; stand firm. **planta** sf plant; (pie) sole; plan; floor. **plantación** sf plantation. **plante** sm strike; mutiny. **plantío** sm field; vegetable plot. **plantón** sm seedling.

plantear [plante'ar] v expound; create; institute; introduce. **planteamiento** sm exposition; introduction; layout.

plantel [plan'tel] sm (bot) nursery.

plantilla [plan'tiʎa] sf model, pattern; sole (of shoe); (com) payroll.

plasma ['plasma] sm plasma.

plasmar [plas'mar] v mould. **plasmarse** v materialize.

plástico ['plastiko] sm, adj plastic. **plasticidad** sf plasticity.

plata ['plata] sf silver; (fig) money. **hablar en plata** speak frankly.

plataforma [plata'forma] sf platform; flatcar; oilrig. **plataforma de lanzamiento** launching pad.

plátano ['platano] sm banana; banana tree; plane tree.

platea [pla'tea] sf (teatro) stalls pl.

platear [plate'ar] v silverplate. **platero** sm silversmith.

plática ['platika] sf chat; sermon.

platija [pla'tixa] sf plaice.

platillo [pla'tiʎo] sm saucer. **platillo volante** flying saucer.

platino [pla'tino] sm platinum.

plato ['plato] sm plate; course; dish. **hacer plato** serve a meal.

platónico [pla'toniko] adj platonic.

plausible [plau'siβle] adj plausible; praiseworthy. **plausibilidad** sf plausibility; praiseworthiness.

playa ['plaja] sf beach; seaside.

plaza ['plaθa] sf town square; market; town; position. **¡plaza!** make way!

plazo ['plaθo] sm time limit; instalment. **comprar a plazos** buy on hire-purchase.

pleamar [plea'mar] sf high tide.

plebe ['pleβe] sf common people pl. **plebeye** adj plebeian.

plebiscito [pleβis'θito] sm plebiscite.

*plegar [ple'gar] v fold; bend; pleat. **plegable** adj folding; collapsible; pliable. **plegadera** sf paper-knife. **pliegue** sm crease; tuck; pleat.

pleitear [pleite'ar] v litigate; plead. **pleito** sm lawsuit.

pleno ['pleno] adj complete; full. **plenamente** adv fully. **plenitud** sf fullness; abundance.

pliego ['pljego] sm sheet of paper; sealed letter. **pliego de condiciones** specifications pl.

plomo ['plomo] sm lead; fuse. **a plomo** straight down. **plomada** sf lead pencil; plumb line. **plomería** sf plumbing. **plomero** sm plumber.

pluma ['pluma] sf feather; pen. **pluma estilográfica** fountain pen. **plumaje** sm plumage.

plural [plu'ral] sm, adj plural. **pluralidad** sf majority.

plus [plus] sm bonus. **plus de carestía de vida** cost-of-living bonus.

pluscuamperfecto [pluskwamper'fekto] sm pluperfect.

plusmarca [plus'marka] (deporte) sm record. **plusmarquista** s(m+f) record-holder.

*poblar [po'βlar] v populate; inhabit; stock; colonize; plant. **poblarse** v bud; leaf. **población** sf population; town. **poblado** sm town; village. **poblador, -a** sm, sf settler.

pobre ['poβre] adj poor. sm pauper. **¡pobre de tí!** you poor thing! **pobrete** adj wretched. **pobretón** adj very poor. **pobreza** sf poverty.

pocilga [po'θilga] sf pigsty.

poción [po'θjon] sf potion.

poco ['poko] adj (cantidad) little; small. adv little; not very; not long. **un poco a** little. **pocos** adj pl few. **poco antes** shortly before. **poco a poco** little by little. **por poco** nearly.

podar [po'ðar] v prune. **poda** sf pruning. **podadera** sf pruning shears.

podenco [po'ðenko] sm hound.

*poder¹ [po'ðer] v can, be able to; be possible. **hasta más no poder** as much as one can. **no poder más** be exhausted. **puede ser** perhaps.

poder² sm power; capacity; possession. **casarse por poderes** marry by proxy. **hacer un poder** make an effort. **poder disuasivo** deterrent. **poderío** sm authority; wealth. **poderoso** adj powerful.

poema [po'ema] sm poem. **poesía** sf poetry. **poeta** sm poet. **poético** adj poetic. **poetisa** sf poetess.

*podrir V **pudrir**.

polaco [po'lako] *adj* Polish. *sm* Pole; (*idioma*) Polish.

polar [po'lar] *adj* polar. **polaridad** *sf* polarity. **polarizar** *v* polarize.

polea [po'lea] *sf* pulley.

polémica [po'lemika] *sf* polemic; polemics *pl*. **polémico** *adj* polemical.

polen [po'len] *sm* pollen.

policía [poli'θja] *sf* police force. *sm* policeman. **policiaco** *adj* police. **novela policiaca** detective novel.

poligamia [poli'gamja] *sf* polygamy. **polígamo** *adj* polygamous.

polígono [po'ligno] *sm* polygon. **polígono industrial** industrial estate. **poligonal** *adj* polygonal.

polilla [po'liʎa] *sf* moth.

pólipo ['polipo] *sm* polyp.

política [po'litika] *sf* politics; policy. **político** *sm* politician. **padre político** father-in-law.

póliza ['poliθa] *sf* policy; contract; stamp. **póliza de seguros** insurance policy.

polizón [poli'θon] *sm* stowaway.

polo ['polo] *sm* (*geog*) pole; (*tecn*) terminal; (*deporte*) polo; ice lolly. **polo acuático** water polo. **Polo Norte/Sur** North/South Pole.

Polonia [po'lonja] *sf* Poland. **polonesa** *sf* polonaise.

poltrona [pol'trona] *sf* easy chair. **poltrón** *adj* lazy.

polvo ['polβo] *sm* powder; dust. **café en polvo** instant coffee. **polvos** *sm pl* powder *sing*. **polvos de talco** talcum powder. **polvareda** *sf* dust cloud; (*fig*) to-do. **polvera** *sf* powder compact. **pólvora** *sf* gunpowder.

polla ['poʎa] *sf* pullet. **pollo** *sm* chicken. **polluelo** *sm* chick.

pómez ['pomeθ] *sf* pumice.

pomo ['pomo] *sm* pommel; doorknob.

pompa ['pompa] *sf* pomp; bubble; display. **pomposidad** *sf* pomposity. **pomposo** *adj* pompous.

pómpulo ['pompulo] *sm* cheekbone.

ponche ['pontʃe] *sm* (*bebida*) punch.

poncho ['pontʃo] *sm* poncho. *adj* listless.

ponderar [ponde'rar] *v* weigh up; praise highly. **ponderable** *adj* praiseworthy. **ponderación** *sf* weighing up; exaggerated praise. **ponderado** *adj* measured; prudent. **ponderativo** *adj* excessive; deliberative.

ponente [po'nente] *sm* reporter. **ponencia** *sf* report.

***poner** [po'ner] *v* put; set. **poner al día** bring up to date. **poner casa** move (house). **poner de comer** feed. **ponerse** *v* turn oneself; dress; get down to; arrive. **ponerse bueno** recover. **ponerse guapo** smarten oneself up.

poniente [po'njente] *sm* west.

pontificado [pontifi'kaðo] *sm* papacy. **pontifical** *adj* pontifical. **pontífice** *sm* pope.

pontón [pon'ton] *sm* (*puente*) pontoon.

ponzoña [pon'θoɲa] *sf* poison. **ponzoñoso** *adj* poisonous.

popa ['popa] *sf* stern. **a popa** astern.

popelina [pope'lina] *sf* poplin.

populacho [popu'latʃo] *sm* rabble.

popular [popu'lar] *adj* popular. **popularidad** *sf* popularity. **popularizar** *v* popularize.

por [por] *prep* for; by; through; during; in exchange for. **por ciento** per cent. **por más que** however. **por si acaso** in case. **por supuesto** of course.

porcelana [porθe'lana] *sf* porcelain.

porcentaje [porθen'taxe] *sm* percentage.

porción [por'θjon] *sf* portion.

porche ['portʃe] *sm* porch.

pordiosero [porðjo'sero], **-a** *sm, sf* beggar.

porfiar [por'fjar] *v* insist; persist; argue. **porfía** *sf* insistence. **porfiado** *adj* stubborn.

pormenor [porme'nor] *sm* detail. **al pormenor** retail.

pornografía [pornogra'fia] *sf* pornography.

poro ['poro] *sm* pore. **poroso** *adj* porous.

porque ['porke] *conj* because.

porqué [por'ke] *sm* reason.

porquería [porke'ria] *sf* disgusting mess; muck.

porra ['porra] *sf* club; truncheon. **porrazo** *sm* blow.

porro ['porro] *sm* leek.

porrón [por'ron] *adj* dull, stupid. **a porrones** (*fam*) galore.

portador [porta'ðor] *sm* (*com*) bearer. **portar** *v* bear, carry. **portarse** *v* behave oneself. **portátil** *adj* portable.

portal [por'tal] *sm* entrance hall, portal.

portamonedas [portamo'neðas] *sm invar* wallet.

portavoz [porta'βoθ] *sm* megaphone; spokesman.

portazgo [por'taθgo] *sm* toll.
portazo [por'taθo] *sm* slam. **dar un portazo** slam the door.
porte ['porte] *sm* transport; carriage; conduct.
portento [por'tento] *sm* marvel. **portentoso** *adj* marvellous.
portería [porte'ria] *sf* porter's lodge. **portero, -a** *sm, sf* porter.
portezuela [porte'θwela] *sf* (*auto*) door.
pórtico ['portiko] *sm* portico.
portilla [por'tiʎa] *sf* porthole.
Portugal [portu'gal] *sm* Portugal. **portugués, -esa** *s, adj* Portuguese; *sm* (*idioma*) Portuguese.
porvenir [porβe'nir] *sm* future. **sin porvenir** without prospects.
pos [pos] *adj* **en pos de** behind.
posada [po'saða] *sf* inn; lodging. **posadero, -a** *sm, sf* innkeeper.
posar [po'sar] *v* alight; pose; lodge; lay down. **posarse** *v* settle; land.
*poseer [pose'er] *v* possess; hold; master. **posesión** *sf* possession. **posesiones** *sf pl* property *sing*.
posible [po'siβle] *adj* possible. **posibilidad** *sf* possibility. **posibilitar** *v* facilitate.
posición [posi'θjon] *sf* position.
positivo [posi'tiβo] *adj*, *sm* positive.
*posponer [pospo'ner] *v* postpone; value less.
postal [pos'tal] *adj* postal. *sf* postcard. **giro postal** *sm* money order; postal order.
postdata [post'ðata] *sf* postscript.
poste ['poste] *sm* pole; pillar; post. **poste indicador** signpost.
postergar [poster'gar] *v* pass over; postpone; adjourn. **postergación** *sf* postponement; adjournment.
posteridad [posteri'ðað] *sf* posterity. **posterior** *adj* posterior; subsequent; later.
postizo [pos'tiθo] *adj* false; artificial; assumed. *sm* hairpiece. **pierna postiza** *sf* artificial leg.
postrar [pos'trar] *v* prostrate. **postrarse** *v* kneel down; weaken. **postración** *sf* prostration. **postrado** *adj* prostrate.
postre ['postre] *sm* dessert.
postremo [pos'tremo] *adj* last. **postrimería** *sf* end, death.
postular [postu'lar] *v* postulate; request; apply for; collect. **postulación** *sf* collection. **postulado** *sm* postulate. **postulante, -a** *sm, sf* collector; applicant.

póstumo ['postumo] *adj* posthumous.
postura [pos'tura] *sf* posture; attitude.
potable [po'taβle] *adj* drinkable.
potaje [po'taxe] *sm* stew; soup.
potasio [po'tasjo] *sm* potassium.
pote ['pote] *sm* jar; jug.
potencia [po'tenθja] *sf* power; ability; potential. **potencial** *adj* potential. **potentado** *sm* potentate. **potente** *adj* powerful.
potestad [potes'tað] *sf* authority; power.
potro ['potro] *sm* colt; instrument of torture.
pozo ['poθo] *sm* hole; well; shaft; bilge.
práctica ['praktika] *sf* practice; method. **practicabilidad** *sf* practicability. **practicable** *adj* practicable. **practicante** *s(m+f)* nurse; practitioner. **practicar** *v* practise; play; perform. **práctico** *adj* practical; experienced.
pradera [pra'ðera] *sf* meadow; prairie. **prado** *sm* field, meadow.
pragmático [prag'matiko] *adj* pragmatic. **pragmatismo** *sm* pragmatism.
preámbulo [pre'ambulo] *sm* preamble.
precario [pre'karjo] *adj* precarious. **precariedad** *sf* precariousness.
precaución [prekau'θjon] *sf* precaution. **con precaución** cautiously. **precaver** *v* forestall. **precaverse** *v* be on one's guard (against).
preceder [preθe'ðer] *v* precede. **precedencia** *sf* precedence; preference. **precedente** *sm* precedent.
precepto [pre'θepto] *sm* precept; regulation. **preceptivo** *adj* compulsory.
preciar [pre'θjar] *v* value. **preciarse** *v* boast. **preciado** *adj* prized; boastful. **precio** *sm* price; esteem. **preciosidad** *sf* excellence. **precioso** *adj* precious; witty.
precipicio [preθi'piθjo] *sm* precipice.
precipitar [preθipi'tar] *v* precipitate. **precipitarse** *v* rush. **precipitación** *sf* precipitation; haste. **precipitado** *adj* also **precipitoso** hasty, rash.
precisar [preθi'sar] *v* need; be necessary; define; fix. **precisamente** *adv* precisely; necessarily. **precisión** *sf* precision; necessity. **preciso** *adj* precise; necessary.
*preconcebir [prekonθe'βir] *v* preconceive. **preconcebido** *adj* preconceived.
preconizar [prekoni'θar] *v* praise; recommend; suggest. **preconización** *sf* recommendation; praise.

precoz [pre'koθ] *adj* precocious. **precocidad** *sf* precocity.

precursor [prekur'sor] *sm* forerunner.

predecesor [preðeθe'sor], **-a** *sm, sf* predecessor.

*predecir [preðe'θir] *v* predict. **predicción** *sf* prediction.

predestinar [preðesti'nar] *v* predestine. **predestinación** *sf* predestination.

prédica ['preðika] *sf* sermon; preaching. **predicación** *sf* preaching. **predicaderas** *sf pl* (*fam*) eloquence *sing*. **predicador, -a** *sm, sf* preacher. **predicar** *v* preach.

predicado [preði'kaðo] *sm* (*gram*) predicate.

predicamento [preðika'mento] *sm* predicament; prestige.

predilección [preðilek'θjon] *sf* predilection.

*predisponer [preðispo'ner] *v* predispose. **predisponer contra** prejudice against. **predisposición** *sf* predisposition.

predominar [preðomi'nar] *v* predominate. **predominancia** *sf* predominance. **predominante** *adj* predominant.

preeminente [preemi'nente] *adj* pre-eminent. **preeminencia** *sf* pre-eminence.

prefabricar [prefaβri'kar] *v* prefabricate. **prefabricación** *sf* prefabrication.

prefacio [pre'faθjo] *sm* preface.

prefecto [pre'fekto] *sm* prefect. **prefectura** *sf* prefecture.

*preferir [prefe'rir] *v* prefer. **preferencia** *sf* preference. **preferente** *adj* preferential; preferable. **preferible** *adj* preferable. **preferido** *adj* favourite.

prefigurar [prefigu'rar] *v* prefigure, foreshadow. **prefiguración** *sf* prefiguration.

prefijo [pre'fixo] *adj* prefixed. *sm* prefix. **prefijar** *v* prefix; prearrange.

pregonar [prego'nar] *v* proclaim, announce. **pregón** *sm* proclamation. **pregonero** *sm* town crier.

preguntar [pregun'tar] *v* ask; query; inquire. **preguntarse** *v* wonder. **pregunta** *sf* question. **preguntador, -a** *sm, sf* questioner.

prehistórico [preis'toriko] *adj* prehistoric.

prejuicio [pre'xwiθjo] *sm* prejudice. **prejuzgar** *v* prejudge.

prelado [pre'laðo] *sm* prelate.

preliminar [prelimi'nar] *adj, sm* preliminary. **preliminarios** *sm pl* preliminaries *pl*.

preludio [pre'luðjo] *sm* prelude.

prematuro [prema'turo] *adj* premature.

premeditar [premeði'tar] *v* premeditate. **premeditación** *sf* premeditation.

premiar [pre'mjar] *v* reward. **premio** *sm* reward; prize; (*com*) premium. **premio gordo** first prize.

premisa [pre'misa] *sf* premise, assumption.

premonición [premoni'θjon] *sf* premonition.

premura [pre'mura] *sf* urgency; tightness.

prenda ['prenda] *sf* pledge; (*com*) security; garment; darling. **en prenda** as a token of. **prendar** *v* pledge; pawn; please. **prendarse de** fall in love with. **prendería** *sf* second-hand shop. **prendero, -a** *sm, sf* second-hand dealer; pawnbroker.

prensa ['prensa] *sf* press; printing press. **dar a la prensa** publish. **prensar** *v* press.

prensil [pren'sil] *adj* prehensile.

preñado [pre'ɲaðo] *adj* pregnant; bulging; full. **preñar** *v* become pregnant; impregnate. **preñez** *sf* pregnancy.

preocupar [preoku'par] *v* preoccupy; worry; get worried. **¡no se preocupe!** don't worry! **preocupación** *sf* preoccupation; prejudice; worry. **preocupado** *adj* preoccupied; worried.

preparar [prepa'rar] *v* prepare. **preparación** *sf* preparation. **preparativo** *adj* also **preparatorio** preparatory.

preponderar [preponde'rar] *v* preponderate, prevail. **preponderancia** *sf* preponderance. **preponderante** *adj* preponderant.

preposición [preposi'θjon] *sf* (*gram*) preposition.

prerrogativa [prerroga'tiβa] *sf* prerogative.

presa[1] ['presa] *sf* capture; prey; victim; quarry; seizure. **presas** *sf pl* fangs *pl*; talons *pl*. **ave de presa** *sf* bird of prey.

presa[2] *sf* dam; weir. **presa de contención** reservóir.

presagiar [presa'xjar] *v* presage. **presagio** *sm* omen.

présbita ['presβita] *adj* also **présbite** longsighted. **presbicia** *sf* longsightedness.

presbítero [pres'βitero] *sm* priest. **presbiterado** *sm* priesthood.

prescindir [presθin'dir] *v* do without. **prescindible** *adj* dispensable.

prescribir [preskri'βir] *v* prescribe; determine. **prescripción** *sf* prescription. **prescrito** *adj* prescribed.

presenciar [presen'θjar] *v* attend; witness.
presencia *sf* presence; appearance.
presencia de ánimo presence of mind.
presentar [presen'tar] *v* present; introduce; submit; propose; tender. **le presento a** may I introduce you to.
presentarse *v* present oneself; arise; turn up; report; apply. **presentable** *adj* presentable. **presentación** *sf* presentation; introduction. **presente** *adj* present. **mejorando lo presente** present company excepted.
*presentir [presen'tir] *v* have forebodings of. **presentimiento** *sm* presentiment.
preservar [preser'βar] *v* preserve; protect. **preservación** *sf* preservation; protection. **preservador** *adj* preservative. **preservativo** *sm* condom.
presidencia [presi'ðenθja] *sf* presidency. **presidente** *sm* president.
presidiario [presi'ðjarjo] *sm* convict. **presidio** *sm* prison; penal servitude.
presidir [presi'ðir] *v* preside over; dominate.
presilla [pre'siʎa] *sf* loop; fastener.
presión [pre'sjon] *sf* pressure.
preso ['preso] *sm* prisoner. *adj* captured.
prestar [pres'tar] *v* lend. **prestación** *sf* lending. **prestado** *adj* loaned. **dar/pedir prestado** lend/borrow. **prestador, -a** *sm, sf* lender. **prestamista** *s(m+f)* moneylender. **préstamo** *sm* loan. **prestario, -a** *sm, sf* borrower.
presteza [pres'teθa] *sf* promptness.
prestidigitador [prestiðixita'ðor] *sm* conjurer; magician. **prestidigitación** *sf* conjuring; magic.
prestigio [pres'tixjo] *sm* prestige; trick. **prestigiado** *adj also* **prestigioso** prestigious.
presto ['presto] *adj* prompt; ready. *adv* promptly.
presumir [presu'mir] *v* presume, assume. **según cabe presumir** presumably. **presumirse** *v* swank; be presumptuous. **presumible** *adj* presumable. **presunción** *sf* assumption; presumptuousness. **presunto** *adj* presumed. **presuntuosidad** *sf* conceit. **presuntuoso** *adj* conceited.
*presuponer [presupo'ner] *v* presuppose; budget. **presupuesto** *sm* budget; reason; supposition.
presura [pre'sura] *sf* promptness; persistence. **presuroso** *adj* prompt; hasty.

pretender [preten'der] *v* claim; aspire to; seek; want; apply for; allege; pretend. **pretendiente** *sm* pretender; claimant; suitor. **pretensión** *sf* pretension; claim.
pretérito [pre'terito] *sm* (*gram*) past.
pretexto [pre'teksto] *sm* pretext.
*prevalecer [preβale'θer] *v* prevail. **prevaleciente** *adj* prevailing.
prevaricar [preβari'kar] *v* prevaricate. **prevaricación** *sf* prevarication; breach of trust. **prevaricador, -a** *sm, sf* prevaricator.
*prevenir [preβe'nir] *v* prevent; warn; prepare; foresee. **prevención** *sf* prevention; warning; preparation; prejudice; police station. **prevenido** *adj* prepared; forewarned. **bien prevenido** full. **preventivo** *adj* preventive.
*prever [pre'βer] *v* foresee; anticipate. **previsión** *sf* foresight; forecast. **caja de previsión** *sf* social security.
previo ['preβjo] *adj* previous. **previo pago** after payment.
prieto ['prjeto] *adj* dark; mean.
prima ['prima] *sf* premium; bonus.
primado [pri'maðo] *sm* (*rel*) primate.
primario [pri'marjo] *adj* primary.
primavera [prima'βera] *sf* spring.
primer [pri'mer] *adj* first. **primeramente** *adv* first; mainly. **primero** *adj* first; best; principal. **de primera** first-class.
primitivo [primi'tiβo] *adj* primitive; original.
primo ['primo] *adj* prime. *sm* cousin.
primogénito [primo'xenito] *adj* first-born.
primor [pri'mor] *sm* beauty; delicacy; skill. **primoroso** *adj* exquisite; skilful.
princesa [prin'θesa] *sf* princess.
principal [prinθi'pal] *adj, sm* principal.
príncipe ['prinθipe] *sm* prince.
principiar [prinθi'pjar] *v* start. **principiante** *s(m+f)* novice. **principio** *sm* beginning.
pringar [prin'gar] *v* stain with grease; wound; involve; slander. **pringarse** *v* embezzle. **pringón** *adj* greasy. **pringoso** *adj* fatty, greasy. **pringue** *s(m+f)* grease stain; dripping.
prior [pri'or] *sm* (*rel*) prior. *adj* prior. **priora** *sf* prioress. **priorato** *sm* priory. **prioridad** *sf* priority.
prisa ['prisa] *sf* hurry. **darse prisa** hurry. **tener prisa** be in a hurry.
prisión [pri'sjon] *sf* prison; imprisonment. **prisionero, -a** *sm, sf* prisoner.

prisma 368

prisma ['prisma] *sm* prism. **prismático** *adj* prismatic.
privar¹ [pri'βar] *v* deprive; prohibit. **privación** *sf* deprivation. **privado** *adj* private.
privar² *v* be in favour; be popular.
privilegiar [priβile'xjar] *v* grant a favour to. **privilegio** *sm* privilege.
pro [pro] *sm* benefit, profit. **en pro de** on behalf of. **hombre de pro** *sm* honest man.
proa ['proa] *sf* (*mar*) prow, bow, bows *pl*. **mascarón de proa** *sm* figurehead.
probable [pro'βaβle] *adj* probable. **probabilidad** *sf* probability.
*probar [pro'βar] *v* test; try; taste; prove. **probarse** *v* try on. **probador** *sm* fitting-room. **probanza** *sf* proof. **probeta** *sf* test tube.
probidad [proβi'ðað] *sf* probity, integrity.
problema [pro'βlema] *sm* problem.
proceder [proθe'ðer] *v* proceed; behave; originate. **procedencia** *sf* origin; port of departure. **procedente** *adj* originating; reasonable; proper. **procedimiento** *sm* process.
procesar [proθe'sar] *v* prosecute. **procesado, -a** *sm, sf* accused. **procesal** *adj* procedural. **procesamiento** *sm* prosecution.
procesión [proθe'sjon] *sf* procession.
proclamar [prokla'mar] *v* proclaim. **proclama** *sf also* **proclamación** proclamation.
procrear [prokre'ar] *v* procreate. **procreación** *sf* procreation. **procreador, -a** *sm, sf* procreator.
procurar [proku'rar] *v* cause; attempt; obtain; succeed; give. **procura** *sf* power of attorney. **procurador, -a** *sm, sf* lawyer.
prodigar [proði'gar] *v* squander; lavish. **prodigalidad** *sf* prodigality.
prodigio [pro'ðixjo] *sm* prodigy. **prodigioso** *adj* prodigious.
pródigo ['proðigo] *adj* prodigal; wasteful.
*producir [proðu'θir] *v* produce. **producirse** *v* happen. **producción** *sf* production. **productivo** *adj* productive. **producto** *sm* product. **productor, -a** *sm, sf* producer.
proeza [pro'eθa] *sf* deed; feat.
profanar [profa'nar] *v* profane. **profanación** *sf* profanation. **profano** *adj* profane.
profecía [profe'θia] *sf* prophecy. **profeta** *sm* prophet. **profético** *adj* prophetic. **profetisa** *sf* prophetess. **profetizar** *v* prophesy.
*proferir [profe'rir] *v* utter.

profesar [profe'sar] *v* profess; manifest; practise a profession. **profesión** *sf* profession. **profesional** *adj* professional. **profesor, -a** *sm, sf* professor, teacher. **profesorado** *sm* professorship; teaching staff.
prófugo ['profugo], **-a** *s, adj* fugitive.
profundizar [profundi'θar] *v* deepen. **profundidad** *sf* depth. **profundo** *adj* deep.
profusión [profu'sjon] *sf* profusion. **profuso** *adj* profuse.
progenie [pro'xenje] *sf* progeny. **progenitor** *sm* progenitor. **progenitores** *sm pl* ancestors *pl*; parents *pl*. **progenitura** *sf* offspring.
programa [pro'grama] *sm* programme.
progresar [progre'sar] *v* progress. **progresión** *sf* progression. **progresivo** *adj* progressive. **progreso** *sm* progress.
prohibir [proi'βir] *v* prohibit. **se prohibe fumar** no smoking. **prohibición** *sf* prohibition. **prohibitivo** *adj* prohibitive.
prohijar [proi'xar] *v* adopt. **prohijamiento** *sm* adoption.
prójimo ['proximo] *sm* fellow man; neighbour; (*fam*) bloke.
prole ['prole] *sf* offspring.
prolapso [pro'lapso] *sm* prolapse.
proletario [prole'tarjo], **-a** *s, adj* proletarian.
prolífico [pro'lifiko] *adj* prolific.
prolijo [pro'lixo] *adj* tedious; long-winded. **prolijidad** *sf* long-windedness.
prólogo ['prologo] *sm* prologue.
prolongar [prolon'gar] *v* prolong. **prolongación** *sf* prolongation. **prolongado** *adj* prolonged.
promediar [prome'ðjar] *v* bisect; average out; mediate. **promedio** *sm* middle; average.
promesa [pro'mesa] *sf* promise. **prometer** *v* promise. **prometerse** *v* expect; become engaged. **prometérselas felices** have high hopes. **prometida** *sf* fiancée. **prometido** *sm* fiancé.
prominencia [promi'nenθja] *sf* prominence; projection; bulge. **prominente** *adj* prominent.
promiscuo [pro'miskwo] *adj* promiscuous; ambiguous.
promontorio [promon'torjo] *sm* promontory.
*promover [promo'βer] *v* promote. **promoción** *sf* promotion. **promotor, -a** *sm, sf* promoter.

promulgar [promul'gar] *v* promulgate.
promulgación *sf* promulgation.
pronombre [pro'nombre] *sm* pronoun.
pronosticar [pronosti'kar] *v* prognosticate. **pronosticación** *sf* prognostication, forecast. **pronóstico** *sm* prediction.
prontitud [pronti'tuð] *sf* promptness. **pronto** *adv* quickly, at once. ¡hasta pronto! see you soon!
pronunciar [pronun'θjar] *v* pronounce. **pronunciarse** *v* rebel. **pronunciación** *sf* pronunciation. **pronunciamiento** *sm* rising; (*jur*) pronouncement.
propagar [propa'gar] *v* propagate. **propagación** *sf* propagation. **propaganda** *sf* propaganda.
propalar [propa'lar] *v* publish; divulge.
propenso [pro'penso] *adj* prone. **propender** *v* incline. **propensión** *sf* inclination.
propicio [pro'piθjo] *adj* propitious. **propiciación** *sf* propitiation. **propiciar** *v* propitiate.
propiedad [propje'ðað] *sf* property; ownership; propriety; resemblance. **propietario, -a** *sm, sf* landlord/lady.
propina [pro'pina] *sf* (*dinero*) tip.
propio ['propjo] *adj* proper; own; particular. **nombre propio** *sm* proper noun. **ser propio de** be typical of. **sus propias palabras** his very words. **propiamente** *adv* properly.
***proponer** [propo'ner] *v* propose. **proponente** *s(m+f)* proposer. **proposición** *sf* proposition; proposal.
proporción [propor'θjon] *sf* proportion. **proporcionado** *adj* proportionate. **bien proporcionado** well proportioned. **proporcional** *adj* proportional. **proporcionar** *v* supply; cause; adapt.
propósito [pro'posito] *sm* purpose; intention. **a propósito** by the way. **a propósito de** with regard to. **de propósito** on purpose.
propuesta [pro'pwesta] *sf* proposal.
propulsar [propul'sar] *v* propel. **propulsión** *sf* propulsion. **propulsor** *sm* propeller.
prorrata [pro'rrata] *sf* quota. **a prorrata** pro rata.
prórroga ['prorroga] *sf* prorogation, extension. **prorrogar** *v* prorogue, adjourn.
prorrumpir [prorrum'pir] *v* break out.
prosa ['prosa] *sf* prose. **prosaico** *adj* prosaic.

proscribir [proskri'βir] *v* proscribe, ban. **proscripción** *sf* proscription, prohibition. **proscrito** *adj* outlawed, banished.
prosecución [proseku'θjon] *sf* pursuit; continuation. **proseguir** *v* pursue; continue.
prosélito [pro'selito] *sm* proselyte.
prospecto [pros'pekto] *sm* prospectus.
prosperar [prospe'rar] *v* prosper. **prosperidad** *sf* prosperity. **próspero** *adj* prosperous.
prosternarse [proster'narse] *v* prostrate oneself.
***prostituir** [prostitu'ir] *v* prostitute. **prostíbulo** *sm* brothel. **prostitución** *sf* prostitution. **prostituta** *sf* prostitute.
protagonista [protago'nista] *s(m+f)* protagonist.
proteger [prote'xer] *v* protect. **protección** *sf* protection. **protector** *adj* protective. **protegido** *sm* protégé.
proteína [prote'ina] *sf* protein.
protestar [protes'tar] *v* protest. **protesta** *sf* protest. **protestación** *sf* protestation. **protestante** *s(m+f)*, *adj* Protestant. **protestantismo** *sm* Protestantism.
protocolo [proto'kolo] *sm* protocol.
prototipo [proto'tipo] *sm* prototype.
protuberancia [protuβe'ranθja] *sf* protuberance. **protuberante** *adj* protuberant.
provecho [pro'βetʃo] *sm* advantage; profit. **de provecho** useful. **sacar provecho de** benefit from. **provechoso** *adj* profitable.
proveer [proβe'er] *v* provide; deal with; decide; fill. **proveedor, -a** *sm, sf* supplier.
***provenir** [proβe'nir] *v* originate. **proveniente** *adj* originating.
proverbio [pro'βerβjo] *sm* proverb. **proverbial** *adj* proverbial.
providencia [proβi'ðenθja] *sf* providence; foresight. **providencial** *adj* providential. **provídente** *adj* provident.
provincia [pro'βinθja] *sf* province. **provincial** *adj* provincial. **provincialismo** *sm* provincialism.
provisión [proβisi'on] *sf* provision. **provisional** *adj* provisional. **provisionalmente** *adv* provisionally. **provisor** *sm* purveyer. **provisto** *adj* supplied.
provocar [proβo'kar] *v* provoke; cause. **provocación** *sf* provocation. **provocador** *adj* provocative. **provocante** *adj* provoking.

próximo ['proksimo] *adj* next; neighbouring. **la semana próxima** next week. **proximamente** *adv* closely; soon. **proximidad** *sf* proximity.

proyectar [projek'tar] *v* project; plan; throw. **proyección** *sf* projection. **proyectil** *sm* projectile. **proyecto** *sm* project. **proyector** *sm* projector; searchlight; spotlight.

prudencia [pru'ðenθja] *sf* prudence. **prudencial** *adj* (*fam*) moderate. **prudente** *adj* prudent.

prueba ['prweβa] *sf* test; proof; tasting; (*deporte*) event. **a prueba** on trial. **a prueba de** proof against.

prurito [pru'rito] *sm* itch; urge.

psicoanálisis [psikoa'nalisis] *sm invar* psychoanalysis. **psicoanalista** *s(m + f)* psychoanalyst. **psicoanalizar** *v* psychoanalyse.

psicología [psikolo'xia] *sf* psychology. **psicológico** *adj* psychological. **psicólogo, -a** *sm*, *sf* psychologist.

psiquiatría [psikja'tria] *sf* psychiatry. **psiquiatra** *s(m + f)* psychiatrist. **psiquiátrico** *adj* psychiatric.

púa ['pua] *sf* prong; barb; thorn; sharp point.

pubertad [puβer'tað] *sf* puberty.

publicar [puβli'kar] *v* publish. **publicación** *sf* publication. **publicidad** *sf* publicity; advertising. **público** *sm*, *adj* public. **dar al público** publish.

puchero [pu'tʃero] *sm* stew; cooking-pot. **ganarse el puchero** earn one's daily bread.

pucho ['putʃo] *sm* cigarette *or* cigar end; fag-end.

púdico ['puðiko] *adj* chaste; modest. **pudicia** *sf* chastity; modesty.

pudiente [pu'ðjente] *adj* rich.

pudín [pu'ðin] *sm* pudding.

pudor [pu'ðor] *sm* modesty; shame. **pudoroso** *adj* modest.

pudrir [pu'ðrir] *v* rot, decay. **pudrición** *sf* putrefaction. **pudrimiento** *sm* rotting.

pueblo ['pweβlo] *sm* people; town; village. **de pueblos** from the country.

puente ['pwente] *sm* bridge. **puente colgante** suspension bridge.

puerco ['pwerko] *sm* pig. *adj* filthy. **puerca** *sf* sow. **puerco espín** porcupine.

pueril [pue'ril] *adj* childish. **puerilidad** *sf* childishness.

puerro ['pwerro] *sm* leek.

puerta ['pwerta] *sf* door; entrance. **puerta principal** front door. **puerta trasera** back door.

puerto ['pwerto] *sm* port; harbour; mountain pass.

pues [pwes] *adv, conj* then; since; because; well; so; yes. **pues bien** OK. **¡pues claro!** of course! **¿pues qué?** so what?

puesta ['pwesta] *sf* (*del sol*) setting; bet; putting. **puesta en escena** staging.

puesto ['pwesto] *sm* small shop; place; stall; job. **puesto de periódicos** newspaper stand.

pugnar [pug'nar] *v* fight; struggle. **pugna** *sf* fight. **pugnaz** *adj* pugnacious.

pujar [pu'xar] *v* strain; strive; outbid. **pujante** *adj* strong. **pujanza** *sf* strength.

pulcritud [pulkri'tuð] *sf* neatness; care. **pulcro** *adj* neat, tidy.

pulga ['pulga] *sf* flea. **pulgoso** *adj* flea-ridden.

pulgada [pul'gaða] *sf* inch. **pulgar** *sm* thumb.

pulir [pu'lir] *v* polish; adorn. **pulidez** *sf* polish; neatness. **pulido** *adj* polished; smooth; neat. **pulidor** *sm* polisher. **pulimentar** *v* polish. **pulimento** *sm* polish, shine.

pulmón [pul'mon] *sm* lung. **pulmonía** *sf* pneumonia.

pulpa ['pulpa] *sf* pulp.

púlpito ['pulpito] *sm* pulpit.

pulpo ['pulpo] *sm* octopus.

pulsar [pul'sar] *v* pulsate. **pulso** *sm* pulse; wrist; steady hand.

pulsera [pul'sera] *sf* bracelet; watch strap. **reloj de pulsera** *sm* wristwatch.

pulverizar [pulβeri'θar] *v* pulverize; spray. **pulverización** *sf* pulverization. **pulverizador** *sm* spray; atomizer.

pulla ['puʎa] *sf* taunt; obscenity.

punción [pun'θjon] *sf* (*med*) puncture.

punición [puni'θjon] *sf* punishment. **punible** *adj* punishable. **punitivo** *adj* punitive.

punta ['punta] *sf* point; tip; head; end; nail. **horas punta** *sf pl* rush hours *pl*. **sacar punta a** sharpen. **velocidad punta** *sf* top speed.

puntada [pun'taða] *sf* stitch.

puntapié [punta'pje] *sm* kick. **echar a puntapiés** kick out.

Q

puntear [punte'ar] *v* stitch; tick off; perforate. **punteado** *sm* (*música*) plucking.

puntería [punte'ria] *sf* aim; marksmanship. **puntero** *adj* outstanding.

puntilla [pun'tiʎa] *sf* tack; nib; fine lace. **de puntillas** on tiptoe.

punto ['punto] *sm* point; full stop; stitch; mark; honour; matter; item. **al punto** at once. **dos puntos** colon. **en punto** on the dot. **¡punto en boca!** mum's the word!

puntual [puntu'al] *adj* punctual; reliable. **puntualidad** *sf* punctuality; reliability.

puntualizar [puntwali'θar] *v* arrange; determine; perfect; settle.

puntuar [pun'twar] *v* punctuate. **puntuación** *sf* punctuation. **signos de puntuación** *sm pl* punctuation marks *pl*.

punzar [pun'θar] *v* pierce. **punzada** *sf* prick; twinge. **punzante** *adj* sharp. **punzón** *sm* awl, punch.

puñado [pu'ɲaðo] *sm* handful. **puñada** *sf* also **puñetazo** *sm* blow, clout. **puño** *sm* fist; cuff. **de propio puño** in one's own handwriting.

puñal [pu'ɲal] *sm* dagger. **puñalada** *sf* stab.

pupila [pu'pila] *sf* (*anat*) pupil.

pupilaje [pupi'laxe] *sm* boarding-house; tutelage.

pupitre [pu'pitre] *sm* desk.

puré [pu're] *sm* purée. **puré de patatas** mashed potatoes *pl*.

pureza [pu'reθa] *sf* purity. **purificación** *sf* purification. **purificar** *v* purify. **purista** *s*(*m+f*) purist. **puro** *adj* pure; simple.

purgar [pur'gar] *v* purge; purify. **purgante** *sm* purgative. **purgativo** *adj* purgative. **purgatorio** *sm* purgatory.

puritano [puri'tano], **-a** *s, adj* puritan. **puritanismo** *sm* puritanism.

púrpura ['purpura] *sf* purple.

pus [pus] *sm* pus, matter.

pusilánime [pusi'lanime] *adj* cowardly. **pusilanimidad** *sf* cowardliness.

pústula ['pustula] *sf* (*med*) pustule, pimple.

puta ['puta] *sf* (*fam*) whore, prostitute. **puto** *sm* (*fam*) bugger.

putrefacción [putrefak'θjon] *sf* putrefaction. **putrefacto** *adj* rotten. **pútrido** *adj* putrid.

puya ['puja] *sf* goad; (*fig*) gibe.

que [ke] *pron* who; whom; that; which. *conj* that; because; than. **que sí** of course. **más que** more than.

qué [ke] *pron, adj* what. **¿qué pasa?** what's going on? **¡qué miedo!** what a fright! **¡qué raro!** how extraordinary!

***quebrar** [ke'βrar] *v* break; go bankrupt. **quebrado** *adj* broken; bankrupt. **quebradura** *sf* crack; gap. **quebrantar** *v* shatter. **quebranto** *sm* exhaustion.

queda ['keða] *sf* curfew.

quedar [ke'ðar] *v* stay; remain; sojourn. **quedarse** *v* stay behind. **quedar en nada** come to nothing.

quedo ['keðo] *adj* quiet; still. *adv* quietly.

quehaceres [kea'θeres] *sm pl* chores; duties.

quejarse [ke'xarse] *v* complain; moan. **queja** *sf* complaint. **quejido** *sm* groan. **quejoso** *adj* plaintive; complaining.

quemar [ke'mar] *v* burn; scorch. **quema** *sf* burning; fire. **quemadura** *sf* burn; scald. **quemante** *adj* burning. **quemazón** *sf* burning; burn.

querella [ke'reʎa] *sf* quarrel; (*jur*) complaint. **querellarse** *v* lodge a complaint.

***querer** [ke'rer] *v* love; want; try; determine. *sm* affection. **querido** *adj* dear.

queso ['keso] *sm* cheese. **queso rallado** grated cheese.

quiá [ki'a] *interj* never! surely not!

quicio ['kiθjo] *sm* hinge. **fuera de quicio** out of order.

quiebra [ki'eβra] *sf* bankruptcy; slump; fissure.

quien [ki'en] *pron* who; whom; whoever. **quién** *pron interrog* who. **¿quién sabe?** who knows? **quienquiera** *pron* whoever, whosoever.

quieto [ki'eto] *adj* still, quiet. **quietud** *sf* stillness.

quijote [ki'xote] *sm* quixotic person; idealist.

quilate [ki'late] *sm* carat.

quilla ['kiʎa] *sf* keel.

quimera [ki'mera] *sf* hallucination; quarrel. **quimérico** *adj* fantastic.

química ['kimika] *sf* chemistry.

quincalla [kin'kaʎa] *sf* hardware; ironmongery. **quincallero, -a** *sm, sf* ironmonger.

quince ['kinθe] *sm, adj* fifteen. **quincena** *sf* fortnight. **quincuagésima** *adj* fiftieth. **quinientos** *adj invar* five hundred.
quinta ['kinta] *sf* country house; conscription; (*música*) fifth.
quintal [kin'tal] *sm* hundredweight.
quinto ['kinto] *adj* fifth.
quiosco [ki'osko] *sm* kiosk.
quirúrgico [ki'rurxiko] *adj* surgical.
quisquilla [kis'kiʎa] *sf* quibble; trifle; (*zool*) shrimp.
quiste ['kiste] *sm* (*med*) cyst.
quitamanchas [kita'mantʃas] *sm invar* stain-remover.
quitar [ki'tar] *v* remove; take off; take away. **quitarse** *v* get rid of; withdraw; abstain. **de quita y pon** easily detachable.
quitasol [kita'sol] *sm* parasol, sunshade.
quizá(s) [ki'θa(s)] *adv* perhaps, maybe.

R

rábano ['raβano] *sm* radish.
rabiar [ra'βjar] *v* rave, rage. **rabiar por** long for. **rabia** *sf* rage, fury; (*med*) rabies. **rabioso** *adj* rabid.
rabino [ra'βino] *sm* rabbi.
rabo ['raβo] *sm* tail; stalk. **hacer rabona** play truant.
racial [ra'θjal] *adj* racial.
racimo [ra'θimo] *sm* bunch; cluster.
raciocinar [raθoθi'nar] *v also* **racionar** ration. **ración** *sf* portion, ration.
racional [raθjo'nal] *adj* rational. **racionalidad** *sf* rationality. **racionalista** *adj* rationalist.
racista [ra'θista] *s(m+f)* racist.
racha ['ratʃa] *sf* gust of wind; streak of luck; split.
radiactivo [raðjak'tiβo] *adj* radioactive. **radioactividad** *sf* radioactivity.
radiar [ra'ðjar] *v* radiate; broadcast. **radiación** *sf* radiation; broadcasting. **radiador** *sm* radiator. **radiante** *adj* radiant.
radicar [raði'kar] *v* take root; settle. **radicación** *sf* taking root.
radical [raði'kal] *adj* radical, fundamental. **radicalismo** *sm* radicalism.
radio¹ ['raðjo] *sm* radius.

radio² *sm* radium.
radio³ *sf* radio. **radiodifusión** *sf* broadcasting. **radiomisora** *sf* radio station. **radioyente** *s(m+f)* listener.
***raer** [ra'er] *v* scrape; erase.
raíz [ra'iθ] *sf* root. **bienes raíces** real estate *sing*.
rajar [ra'xar] *v* slit; crack; slice. **raja** *sf* crack; slice.
ralea [ra'lea] *sf* sort; breed.
rallar [ra'ʎar] *v* grate. **rallador** *sm* grater. **rallo** *sm* rasp.
rama ['rama] *sf* (*bot*) branch, bough.
rambla ['rambla] *sf* avenue; gully.
ramificarse [ramifi'karse] *v* branch out. **ramificación** *sf* ramification.
ramillete [rami'ʎete] *sm* bunch of flowers, posy; cluster.
ramo ['ramo] *sm* (*bot*) branch; cluster; bouquet.
rampa ['rampa] *sf* ramp.
ramplón [ram'plon] *adj* coarse, vulgar.
rana ['rana] *sf* frog.
rancio ['ranθjo] *adj* rancid, rank, stale.
rancho ['rantʃo] *sm* (*comida*) mess; farm; ranch. **ranchero** *sm* rancher.
rango ['rango] *sm* class, rank.
ranura [ra'nura] *sf* groove.
rapaz [ra'paθ] *adj* rapacious. **rapacidad** *sf* rapacity.
rapé [ra'pe] *sm* snuff.
rápido [ra'piðo] *adj* rapid. **rapidez** *sf* speed.
rapiña [ra'piɲa] *sf* robbery with violence.
rapsodia [rap'soðja] *sf* rhapsody.
raptar [rap'tar] *v* carry off, abduct; kidnap. **rapto** *sm* abduction. **raptor, -a** *sm, sf* kidnapper.
raquero [ra'kero] *sm* beachcomber.
raqueta [ra'keta] *sf* racket.
raro ['raro] *adj* rare. **rareza** *sf* rarity.
ras [ras] *sm* level. **a ras de tierra** at ground level.
rascacielos [raska'θjelos] *sm invar* skyscraper.
rascar [ras'kar] *v* scratch; scrape. **rascadura** *sf* scratching.
rasgar [ras'gar] *v* tear; rip; slash.
rasgo ['rasgo] *sm* feature; feat; (*de pluma*) stroke.
raso ['raso] *adj* flat; level; smooth.
raspar [ras'par] *v* rasp. **raspa** *sf* rasp. **raspadura** *sf* rasping.
rastra ['rastra] *sf* trail; trace; sledge.

rastrear [rastre'ar] *v* trace; track; rake.
rastrillar [rastri'ʎar] *v* rake. **rastrillo** *sm* rake.
rastro ['rastro] *sm* track; trail.
rastrojo [ras'troxo] *sm* stubble.
rasurar [rasu'rar] *v* shave. **rasura** *sf* shaving.
rata ['rata] *sf* rat.
ratería [rate'ria] *sf* larceny, petty thieving. **ratero, -a** *sm, sf* petty thief.
ratificar [ratifi'kar] *v* ratify. **ratificación** *sf* ratification.
rato ['rato] *sm* a little while, short period of time. **al poco rato** shortly after.
ratón [ra'ton] *sm* mouse. **ratonera** *sf* mousetrap.
rayar [ra'jar] *v* rule; draw lines on; underline. **raya** *sf* line; stripe; limit. **a raya** within bounds. **rayado** *adj* lined; striped.
rayo ['rajo] *sm* beam, ray of light; flash of lightning.
raza ['raθa] *sf* race; lineage; breed.
razón [ra'θon] *sf* reason; rationale. **tener razón** be right. **razonable** *adj* reasonable. **razonar** *v* reason; justify.
reacción [reak'θjon] *sf* reaction. **reaccionar** *v* react. **reaccionario** *s(m+f)* reactionary. **reactor** *sm* reactor.
reacio [re'aθjo] *adj* obstinate.
real¹ [re'al] *adj* real.
real² *adj* royal.
realce [re'alθe] *sm* (*arte*) relief; highlight; importance.
realizar [reali'θar] *v* realize; make; perform.
realzar [real'θar] *v* raise; emboss; dignify.
reanimar [reani'mar] *v* revive; encourage.
reanudar [reanu'ðar] *v* renew. **reanudarse** *v* start again.
*reaparecer [reapare'θer] *v* reappear. **reaparición** *sf* reappearance.
rebajar [reβa'xar] *v* lessen, reduce; lower; allow discount; (*bebida*) weaken. **rebaja** *sf* reduction.
rebanada [reβa'naða] *sf* slice. **rebanar** *v* slice.
rebaño [re'βaɲo] *sm* flock; herd.
rebasar [reβa'sar] *v* go beyond, exceed; overtake; overflow.
rebatir [reβa'tir] *v* rebut, refute; repel. **rebato** *sm* (*mil*) alarm, call to arms; surprise attack.
rebeca [re'βeka] *sf* cardigan.

rebelarse [reβe'larse] *v* rebel. **rebelde** *adj* rebellious. **rebeldía** *sf* rebelliousness. **rebelión** *sf* rebellion.
rebosar [reβo'sar] *v* overflow. **rebosadura** *sf* overflowing.
rebotar [reβo'tar] *v* bend back; rebound; bounce. **rebotación** *sf* bouncing. **rebote** *sm* bounce.
rebozar [reβo'θar] *v* muffle. **rebozo** *sm* muffler. **sin rebozo** openly.
rebuscar [reβus'kar] *v* search for. **rebusca** *sf* search. **rebuscado** *adj* elaborate.
rebuznar [reβuθ'nar] *v* bray. **rebuzno** *sm* bray.
recado {re'kaðo] *sm* errand; message. **recadista** *s(m+f)* messenger.
*recaer [reka'er] *v* relapse. **recaída** *sf* relapse.
recalcar [rekal'kar] *v* cram; pack; stress. **recalcadura** *sf* pressing; packing.
recalcitrante [ɾekalθi'trante] *adj* recalcitrant.
*recalentar [rekalen'tar] *v* reheat; rekindle. **recalentarse** *v* overheat.
recambio [re'kambjo] *sm* re-exchange. **piezas de recambio** *sf pl* spare parts.
recargar [rekar'gar] *v* reload; overload; increase; recharge. **recarga** *sf* refill. **recargable** *adj* refillable. **recargo** *sm* additional load; surcharge.
recatarse [reka'tarse] *v* be cautious. **recatar** *v* cover up. **recatado** *adj* prudent. **recato** *sm* prudence.
recaudar {rekau'ðar] *v* collect. **recaudación** *sf* collection. **recaudador** *sm* tax collector. **a buen recaudo** in safe keeping.
recelar [reθe'lar] *v* suspect; fear. **recelo** *sm* mistrust. **receloso** *adj* suspicious.
recepción [reθep'θjon] *sf* reception; receipt; admission.
receptáculo [reθep'takulo] *sm* receptacle.
receptor [reθep'tor] *sm* recipient, receiver.
recesión [reθe'sjon] *sf* recession.
receta [re'θeta] *sf* formula; recipe; prescription.
recibir [reθi'βir] *v* receive. **recibidor, -a** *sm, sf* receiver. **recibo** *sm* reception; (*com*) receipt. **acusar recibo** (*com*) acknowledge receipt.
recién [re'θjen] *adv* recently, lately, just. **recién llegado** *sm* newcomer. **reciente** *adj* recent, new.
recinto [re'θinto] *sm* enclosure; precinct, district.

recio ['reθjo] *adj* tough, strong. *adv* loudly.

recipiente [reθi'pjente] *sm* receptacle; recipient.

reciprocar [reθipro'kar] *v* reciprocate. **recíproco** *adj* reciprocal.

recitar [reθi'tar] *v* recite. *sm* recital. **recitación** *sf* recitation.

reclamar [rekla'mar] *v* claim; demand; appeal. **reclamación** *sf* claim; protest. **reclamo** *sm* call; advertisement.

reclinar [rekli'nar] *v* lean, recline. **reclinación** *sf* leaning.

reclusión [reklu'sjon] *sf* seclusion; imprisonment. **recluso, -a** *sm, sf* recluse; convict.

recluta [re'kluta] *sm* recruit; conscript. **reclutamiento** *sm* recruitment. **reclutar** *v* recruit; conscript.

recobrar [reko'βrar] *v* recover; recuperate; regain. **recobro** *sm* recovery.

recoger [reko'xer] *v* pick up; gather; collect; confiscate; take in; shrink. **recogerse** *v* withdraw within oneself. **recogida** *sf* collection; harvest; withdrawal. **recogido** *adj* short; small; secluded. **recogimiento** *sm* withdrawal.

recolección [rekolek'θjon] *sf* gathering; harvest; recollection; compilation. **recolectar** *v* harvest.

*recomendar [rekomen'dar] *v* recommend; commend. **recomendación** *sf* recommendation. **recomendado, -a** *sm, sf* protégé/protégée.

recompensar [rekompen'sar] *v* recompense, reward. **recompenso** *sf* compensation; recompense.

reconciliarse [rekonθi'ljarse] *v* reconcile oneself. **reconciliación** *sf* reconciliation.

recóndito [re'kondito] *adj* secret; obscure.

*reconocer [rekono'θer] *v* recognize; acknowledge; examine closely. **reconocible** *adj* recognizable. **recononcimiento** *sm* recognition; acknowledgement; examination.

reconquista [rekon'kista] *sf* reconquest. **reconquistar** *v* reconquer.

reconsiderar [rekonsiðe'rar] *v* reconsider.

*reconstituir [rekonstitu'ir] *v* reconstitute. **reconstitución** *sf* reconstitution.

*reconstruir [rekonstru'ir] *v* reconstruct.

*reconvenir [rekonβe'nir] *v* reproach; rebuke. **reconvención** *sf* reproach.

recopilar [rekopi'lar] *v* compile; summarize. **recopilación** *sf* compilation; summary. **recopilador** *sm* compiler.

*recordar [rekor'ðar] *v* remember; commemorate; remind. **recordarse** *v* wake up. **para recordar** in memory. **recordable** *adj* memorable. **recordativo** *adj* reminiscent.

recorrer [rekor'rer] *v* go over; traverse; examine; survey; repair. **recorrido** *sm* journey; run; revision.

recortar [rekor'tar] *v* cut out; cut down; clip; trim; stand out. **recorte** *sm* cutting; outline.

recoveco [reko'βeko] *sm* bend; nook; recess.

recrearse [rekre'arse] *v* amuse oneself. **recreación** *sf* recreation. **recreo** *sm* recreation; amusement.

recriminar [rekrimi'nar] *v* recriminate. **recriminación** *sf* recrimination.

*recrudecer [rekruðe'θer] *v* recur; break out again.

rectángulo [rek'tangulo] *sm* rectangle. **rectangular** *adj* rectangular.

rectificar [rektifi'kar] *v* rectify; correct. **rectificación** *sf* rectification.

rectitud [rekti'tuð] *sf* rectitude; rightness. **recto** *adj* right; just; straight.

rector [rek'tor] *sm* rector; principal; governor. **rectoría** *sf* rectory.

recua ['rekwa] *sf* drove, herd; (*fig*) gang.

recuento [re'kwento] *sm* recount; calculation; inventory.

recuerdo [re'kwerðo] *sm* recollection; memory. **recuerdos** *sm pl* regards *pl*.

recular [reku'lar] *v* recoil. **reculada** *sf* recoil.

recuperar [rekupe'rar] *v* recuperate. **recuperación** *sf* recovery.

recurrir [rekur'rir] *v* revert; resort (to). **recurrir a** have recourse to. **recurso** *sm* recourse; appeal.

recusar [reku'sar] *v* refuse; reject. **recusación** *sf* refusal; rejection.

rechazar [retʃa'θar] *v* repel; deny. **rechazamiento** *sm* repulsion. **rechazo** *sm* rebound; rejection.

rechinar [retʃi'nar] *v* creak; squeak; (*los dientes*) gnash. **rechinamiento** *sm* creaking; squeaking.

rechoncho [re'tʃontʃo] *adj* squat; chubby.

red [reð] *sf* net; grid; grille; grating; snare. **caer en la red** fall into the trap. **red ferroviaria** railway system.

redactar [reðak'tar] *v* edit. **redacción** *sf* editing; journalism. **redactor. -a** *sm, sf* editor; writer.

redención [reðen'θjon] *sf* redemption; help; salvation. **redentor. -a** *sm, sf* redeemer.

redimir [reði'mir] *v* redeem; ransom. **redimible** *adj* redeemable.

rédito ['reðito] *sm* income. **rédito imponible** taxable income.

redoblar [reðo'βlar] *v* double; redouble; repeat. **redobladura** *sf* redoubling.

redondear [reðonde'ar] *v* round; round off. **redondo** *adj* round; spherical. **negocio redondo** *sm* square deal.

*****reducir** [reðu'θir] *v* reduce; lessen; compress; scale down **reducción** *sf* reduction. **reducido** *adj* reduced; abridged.

redundar [reðun'dar] *v* redound; overflow.

reembolsar [reembol'sar] *v* reimburse, repay. **reembolso** *sm* reimbursement; refund. **contra reembolso** cash on delivery.

reemplazar [reempla'θar] *v* replace. **reemplazable** *adj* replaceable. **reemplazo** *sm* replacement.

referencia [refe'renθja] *sf* reference; account; allusion. **referente** *adj* referring. **referido** *adj* aforementioned; in question.

referéndum [refe'rendum] *sm* referendum.

*****referir** [refe'rir] *v* refer; narrate; describe.

refinar [refi'nar] *v* refine; polish; perfect. **refinación** *sf* refinement. **refinado** *adj* refined; slick. **refinadura** *sf* refinement. **refinería** *sf* refinery.

reflectar [reflek'tar] *v* reflect. **reflector** *sm* reflector; searchlight.

reflejar [refle'xar] *v* reflect; show. **refleja** *sf* reflection. **reflejo** *sm* reflection; reflex; glare.

reflexión [refle'ksjon] *sf* reflection. **reflexionar** *v* reflect. **reflexivo** *adj* (*gram*) reflexive.

reflujo [re'fluxo] *sm* ebb.

reformar [refor'mar] *v* reform; amend; remake; improve; repair. **reforma** *sf* reform, reformation. **reformación** *sf* reformation. **reformador. -a** *sm, sf* reformer. **reformativo** *adj* reformative. **reformatorio** *sm* reformatory.

*****reforzar** [refor'θar] *v* reinforce; strengthen; encourage; boost. **reforzado** *adj* reinforced.

refractario [refrak'tarjo] *adj* refractory. **refracción** *sf* refraction. **refractar** *v* refract.

refrán [re'fran] *sm* proverb, saying.

*****refregar** [refre'gar] *v* rub; scour; scold. **refregadura** *sf* rubbing, friction.

refrenar [refre'nar] *v* curb, control. **refrenamiento** *sm* restraint.

refrescar [refres'kar] *v* refresh; cool; repeat; revise. **refrescadura** *sf* refreshing. **refrescante** *adj* refreshing; cooling. **refresco** *sm* refreshment; cold drink.

refuerzo [re'fwerθo] *sm* reinforcement; backing; help.

refugiarse [refu'xjarse] *v* shelter. **refugio** *sm* refuge. **refugio de peatones** traffic island. **refugiado. -a** *sm, sf* refugee.

refulgir [reful'xir] *v* shine, gleam. **refulgencia** *sf* brilliance. **refulgente** *adj* brilliant.

refundir [refun'dir] *v* recast; adapt; refurbish. **refundición** *sf* recasting; adaptation.

refunfuñar [refunfu'par] *v* grumble, grouse. **refunfuñadura** *sf* also **refunfuño** *sm* grumbling.

refutar [refu'tar] *v* refute. **refutable** *adj* refutable. **refutación** *sf* refutation.

regadera [rega'ðera] *sf* watering-can; channel; irrigation ditch. **regadero** *sm* irrigation ditch. **regadío** *sm* irrigated land. **regadizo** *adj* irrigable. **regadura** *sf* irrigation. **regar** *v* water; irrigate; sprinkle.

regalar [rega'lar] *v* give; treat; regale; entertain. **regalador. -a** *sm, sf* entertainer. **regalo** *sm* gift; pleasure; treat; entertainment.

regaliz [rega'liθ] *sm* liquorice.

regañar [rega'par] *v* scold; quarrel; growl; grumble. **regaño** *sm* scolding; quarrel; growl; grumble.

regata [re'gata] *sf* regatta.

regatear [regate'ar] *v* haggle; bargain; retail; begrudge; dodge. **regate** *sm* dodge. **regateo** *sm* haggling. **regatería** *sf* retail. **regatero. -a** *sm, sf* retailer.

regazo [re'gaθo] *sm* lap.

regencia [re'xenθja] *sf* regency.

regenerar [rexene'rar] *v* regenerate. **regeneración** *sf* regeneration. **regenerativo** *adj* regenerative.

regentar [rexen'tar] *v* manage; govern; boss. **regente** *sm* regent; director; professor. **regentear** *v* domineer.

régimen ['reximen] *sm* regime; system; rate; diet; performance.

regimiento [rexi'mjento] *sm* regiment; administration; government; town council. **regimentación** *sf* regimentation. **regimental** *adj* regimental. **regimentar** *v* regiment.

región [re'xjon] *sf* region; territory; area; space. **regional** *adj* regional.

***regir** [re'xir] *v* govern; manage; control; obtain; prevail; steer.

registrar [rexis'trar] *v* register; inspect; record; search; show. **registración** *sf* registration. **registrado** *adj* registered; examined. **registrador** *sm* registrar; inspector. **registradora** *sf* cash register. **registro** *sm* register; registry; inspection.

reglar [re'glar] *v* rule; regulate; control. **reglarse** *v* conform; reform. **regla** *sf* rule; method; discipline; menstruation. **a regla** by rule. **regla de cálculo** slide rule. **regladamente** *adv* regularly. **reglado** *adj* regular; regulated; temperate. **reglamentación** *sf* regulation. **reglamentar** *v* regulate. **reglamentario** *adj* statutory. **reglamento** *sm* statute; rules and regulations *pl*.

regocijar [regoθi'xar] *v* rejoice; gladden. **regocijarse** *v* rejoice; exult. **regocijador** *adj* cheering. **regocijo** *sm* joy, gladness.

regresar [regre'sar] *v* return.

regular [regu'lar] *adj* regular; average; ordinary. **por lo regular** as a rule. *v* regulate; control; adjust. **regulación** *adj* regulation; control. **regulación a distancia** remote control. **regulado** *adj* regulated; regular. **regulador** *sm* regulator; throttle. **regulador de volumen** volume control. **regularidad** *sf* regularity; ordinariness. **regularización** *sf* regularization. **regularizar** *v* regularize.

rehabilitar [reaβili'tar] *v* rehabilitate. **rehabilitación** *sf* rehabilitation.

***rehacer** [rea'θer] *v* remake; recover; renovate; repair. **rehacerse** *v* recuperate. **rehecho** *adj* remade; squat.

rehén [re'en] *sm* hostage.

***rehuir** [re'wir] *v* flee; shrink from; avoid; shirk. **rehuida** *sf* flight.

rehusar [reu'sar] *v* refuse; reject.

reimprimir [reimpri'mir] *v* reprint. **reimpresión** *sf* reprint. **reimpreso** *adj* reprinted.

reinar [rei'nar] *v* reign; prevail. **reina** *sf* queen. **reinante** *adj* reigning. **reinado** *sm* reign. **reino** *sm* kingdom, reign. **reino animal** animal kingdom.

reincidir [reinθi'ðir] *v* backslide; relapse into; reiterate. **reincidencia** *sf* backsliding; reiteration. **reincidente** *adj* backsliding; relapsing; reiterating.

reintegrar [reinte'grar] *v* reintegrate; reimburse; recover. **reintergrarse** *v* recoup oneself. **reintegrable** *adj* reimbursable. **reintegración** *sf* reintegration; restoration. **reintegro** *sm* recovery; reimbursement.

***reír** [re'ir] *v* laugh. **reírse de** make fun of.

reiterar [reite'rar] *v* reiterate. **reiteración** *sf* reiteration.

reivindicar [reiβindi'kar] *v* reclaim; claim; rehabilitate. **reivindicación** *sf* claim; recovery.

reja ['rexa] *sf* grating; grille; ploughshare; lattice. **rejado** *sm* grating; railing. **rejería** *sf* ornamental ironwork. **rejilla** *sf* small grating; (*tren*) luggage rack.

***rejuvenecer** [rexuβene'θer] *v* rejuvenate. **rejuvenecimiento** *sm* rejuvenation.

relación [rela'θjon] *sf* relation; connection; report; narrative; intercourse; relationship. **relaciones** *sf pl* courtship *sing*; engagement *sing*. **relacionado** *adj* related. **relacionar** *v* relate; report; connect. **relacionarse** *v* be related; be connected.

relajar [rela'xar] *v* relax; remit; loosen; debauch. **relajación** *sf* relaxation; loosening; laxity; rupture. **relajadamente** *adv* loosely, dissolutely. **relajado** *adj* lax; ruptured. **relajador** *adj* relaxing.

relámpago [re'lampago] *sm* lightning. **relámpago difuso** sheet lightning.

relatar [rela'tar] *v* report; relate; tell. **relatador, -a** *sm, sf* narrator.

relatividad [relatiβi'ðað] *sf* relativity.

relevar [rele'βar] *v* relieve; absolve; replace; free; emboss. **relevación** *sf* relief; liberation; remission. **relevante** *adj* outstanding. **relevo** *sm* relay race. **relieve** *sm* relief; prominence. **en relieve** embossed.

relicario [reli'karjo] *sm* reliquary; shrine; locket.

religión [reli'xjon] *sf* religion; faith; creed.
religioso [reli'xjoso] *sm* friar, monk; religious person. *adj* religious.
reliquia [re'likja] *sf* relic; memento; ailment. **reliquia de familia** heirloom.
reloj [re'lox] *sm* clock; watch. **reloj de caja** grandfather clock. **reloj de cuclillo** cuckoo clock. **reloj despertador** alarm clock. **reloj pulsera** wristwatch. **relojería** *sf* watchmaker's shop. **relojero** *sm* watchmaker.
*relucir [relu'θir] *v* shine; excel. **sacar a relucir** show off. **reluciente** *adj* gleaming.
reluctante [reluk'tante] *adj* reluctant.
relumbrar [relum'brar] *v* dazzle; glare. **relumbrante** *adj* dazzling. **relumbre** *sm* sparkle; flash. **relumbro** *sm* glare; tinsel. **relumbroso** *adj* dazzling.
rellenar [reʎe'nar] *v* refill; fill; stuff; cram. **rellenable** *adj* refillable. **relleno** *sm* filling; stuffing; packing.
remachar [rema'tʃar] *v* rivet; stress. **remachado** *adj* riveted; (*fam*) quiet. **remache** *sm* rivet.
remanente [rema'nente] *sm* remains *pl*.
remanso [re'manso] *sm* backwater; sluggishness.
remar [re'mar] *v* row; toil.
rematar [rema'tar] *v* finish; kill; knock down at auction. **rematado** *adj* completely ruined. **rematante** *sm* highest bidder. **remate** *sm* end; finishing touch; highest bid.
remediar [reme'ðjar] *v* remedy; help; prevent. **remediable** *adj* remediable. **remedio** *sm* remedy. **no hay remedio** it can't be helped.
*remendar [remen'dar] *v* repair; patch; darn. **remendado** *adj* spotty; patched. **remendón, -ona** *sm, sf* mender; repairer. **remiendo** *sm* repair; patch. **echar un remiendo a** put a patch on.
remero [re'mero] *sm* oarsman.
remesa [re'mesa] *sf* remittance; consignment; shipment. **remesar** *v* remit; ship.
remilgado [remil'gaðo] *adj* mincing; prim; squeamish. **remilgarse** *v* simper. **remilgo** *sm* smirk; primness.
reminiscencia [remini'sθenθja] *sf* reminiscence.
remirado [remi'raðo] *adj* considerate; cautious; discreet. **remirar** *v* review. **remirarse** *v* take great pains; enjoy looking over.

remisión [remi'sjon] *sf* remission; pardon; reference. **remisible** *adj* pardonable. **remiso** *adj* remiss.
remitir [remi'tir] *v* send; pardon; adjourn; abate. **remitirse a** quote from. **remitido** *sm* dispatch.
remo ['remo] *sm* oar; paddle; rowing. **remos** *sm pl* limbs *pl*.
remojar [remo'xar] *v* soak; steep. **remojo** *sm* soaking; steeping.
remolcha [remo'latʃa] *sf* beetroot.
remolcar [remol'kar] *v* tow; haul. **remolcador** *sm* tug.
remolino [remo'lino] *sm* whirlwind; whirlpool; (*fig*) throng. **remolinar** *v* eddy.
remontar [remon'tar] *v* remount; mend; go back in time; raise; frighten. **remonte** *sm* repair; remounting; rising.
remordimiento [remorði'mjento] *sm* remorse.
remoto [re'moto] *adj* remote; improbable.
*remover [remo'βer] *v* remove; move; stir; discharge. **removimiento** *sm* removal.
remunerar [remune'rar] *v* remunerate. **remuneración** *sf* remuneration. **remunerativo** *adj* remunerative.
*renacer [rena'θer] *v* be reborn; recover. **renacimiento** *sm* rebirth; renaissance.
renacuajo [rena'kwaxo] *sm* tadpole.
rencilla [ren'θiʎa] *sf* squabble; feud. **rencilloso** *adj* quarrelsome.
rencor [ren'kor] *sm* rancour. **rencoroso** *adj* rancorous.
*rendir [ren'dir] *v* conquer; yield; surrender. **rendirse** *v* wear oneself out. **rendición** *sf* surrender; (*com*) profit. **rendido** *adj* submissive. **rendimiento** *sm* humility; weariness; output.
*renegar [rene'gar] *v* disown; detest; curse. **renegado, -a** *sm, sf* renegade. **renegador, -a** *sm, sf* blasphemer.
renglón [ren'glon] *sm* written or printed line. **leer entre renglones** read between the lines.
reno ['reno] *sm* reindeer.
renombre [re'nombre] *sm* renown; surname. **renombrado** *adj* renowned.
*renovar [reno'βar] *v* renovate; renew. **renovable** *adj* renewable. **renovación** *sf* renovation; renewal. **renuevo** *sm* renewal; sprout.
rentar [ren'tar] *v* yield an income or prof, it. **renta** *sf* income; profit. **rentero, -a** *sm,*

sf tenant farmer. **rentista** *s(m+f)* stockholder. **rentístico** *adj* financial.
renunciar [renun'θjar] *v* renounce; resign. **renuncia** *sf* renunciation; resignation.
*reñir [re'ɲir] *v* scold; quarrel. **reñido** *adj* on bad terms. **reñidor** *adj* quarrelsome.
reo ['reo], **-a** *sm, sf* defendant. *adj* guilty.
reojo [re'oxo] *sm* **mirar de reojo** look askance.
reorganizar [reorgani'θar] *v* reorganize. **reorganización** *sf* reorganization.
reparar [repa'rar] *v* repair; restore; correct; make amends for; observe; parry. **reparable** *adj* noteworthy. **reparador, -a** *sm, sf* repairer; faultfinder. **reparo** *sm* repair; remedy; observation; protection.
repartir [repar'tir] *v* share; distribute. **repartición** *sf* distribution. **repartidor, -a** *sm, sf* distributor. **reparto** *sm* distribution; (*teatro*) cast.
repasar [repa'sar] *v* revise; review; retrace. **repaso** *sm* review; (*fam*) reprimand.
repatriar [repa'trjar] *v* repatriate. **repatriación** *sf* repatriation. **repatriado, -a** *sm, sf* repatriate.
repeler [repe'ler] *v* repel. **repelente** *adj* repellent.
repente [re'pente] *sm* sudden impulse. **de repente** suddenly.
repercutir [reperku'tir] *v* re-echo; rebound. **repercusión** *sf* repercussion; reverberation.
repertorio [reper'torjo] *sm* repertory; repertoire.
*repetir [repe'tir] *v* repeat; recite. **repetición** *sf* repetition; recital.
repisa [re'pisa] *sf* shelf; ledge; bracket. **repisa de chimenea** mantelpiece. **repisa de ventana** window sill.
*replegar [reple'gar] *v* refold; (*mil*) retreat. **replegable** *adj* folding. **repliegue** *sm* fold; crease; retreat.
repleto [re'pleto] *adj* replete; plump.
réplica [re'plika] *sf* answer; replica. **replicar** *v* argue; answer back. **replicato** *sm* argument; answer.
repoblación [repoβla'θjon] *sf* repopulation; restocking; reforestation. **repoblar** *v* repopulate; restock; reforest.
repollo [re'poʎo] *sm* cabbage.
*reponer [repo'ner] *v* replace; restore. **reponerse** *v* recover.
reportar [repor'tar] *v* restrain; obtain; bring. **reportarse** *v* contain oneself. **reportamiento** *sm* restraint.
reposar [repo'sar] *v* rest; lie down; settle; lie buried. **reposo** *sm* repose.
repostería [reposte'ria] *sf* pastry shop; pantry. **repostero, -a** *sm, sf* pastrycook; confectioner.
reprender [repren'der] *v* reprimand. **reprensible** *adj* reprehensible. **reprensor** *adj* reproachful.
represalia [repre'salja] *sf* reprisal.
representar [represen'tar] *v* represent; signify; describe; express; perform; appear to have. **representarse** *v* imagine. **representable** *adj* representable; performable. **representación** *sf* representation; performance. **representante** *s(m+f)* representative; actor, actress. **representativo** *adj* representative.
represión [repre'sjon] *sm* repression; control. **represivo** *adj* repressive.
reprimenda [repri'menda] *sf* reprimand.
reprimir [repri'mir] *v* repress; suppress. **reprimible** *adj* repressible.
*reprobar [repro'βar] *v* reprove; condemn; (*examen*) fail. **reprobable** *adj* reprehensible. **reprobación** *sf* reproof; failure. **reprobado, -a** *sm, sf* also **réprobo, -a** *sm, sf* reprobate.
reprochar [repro't∫ar] *v* reproach; challenge. **reprochable** *adj* reproachable; reproachful. **reprochador, -a** *sm, sf* reproacher.
*reproducir [reproδu'θir] *v* reproduce. **reproducible** *adj* reproducible. **reproducción** *sf* reproduction. **reproductor, -a** *sm, sf* breeder.
reptil [rep'til] *sm* reptile.
república [re'puβlika] *sf* republic. **republicanismo** *sm* republicanism. **republicano, -a** *sm, sf* republican.
repudiar [repu'δjar] *v* repudiate. **repudiación** *sf* repudiation.
repuesto [re'pwesto] *sm* supply; store; sideboard. **de repuesto** spare, extra. *adj* replaced; secluded; recovered.
repugnar [repug'nar] *v* contradict; object to; be repugnant. **repugnarse** *v* conflict. **repugnacia** *sf* repugnance; opposition. **repugnante** *adj* repugnant.
repulsivo [repul'siβo] *adj* repulsive. **repulsa** *sf* refusal; rebuke. **repulsar** *v* reject; refuse. **repulsión** *sf* rejection; refusal.

reputar [repu'tar] *v* repute: consider: esteem. **reputación** *sf* reputation. **reputado** *adj* reputed.

***requebrar** [reke'βrar] *v* woo: flatter: flirt with. **requebrador, -a** *sm, sf* flirt.

requemar [reke'mar] *v* scorch: inflame: overcook. **requemarse** *v* smoulder: become tanned. **requemado** *adj* burnt: tanned. **requemamiento** *sm* bite: sting. **requemante** *adj* burning: stinging.

***requerir** [reke'rir] *v* request: require: urge: notify: summon: examine. **requeriente** *adj* requiring. **requerimiento** *sm* requisition: summons: notification: request.

requesón [reke'son] *sm* curd: cottage cheese.

requisar [reki'sar] *v* requisition. **requisa** *sf* tour of inspection: requisition. **requisición** *sf* requisition. **requisito** *adj* requisite.

res [res] *sf* head of cattle: animal.

resabio [re'saβjo] *sm* bad habit: unpleasant aftertaste. **resabiado** *adj* crafty: wicked: spoiled. **resabiar** *v* pervert: become vicious. **resabiarse** *v* become annoyed.

resaca [re'saka] *sf* undertow: surf: surge.

resaltar [resal'tar] *v* rebound, stand out. **resalte** *sm* projection. **resalto** *sm* rebound.

resarcir [resar'θir] *v* compensate. **resarcirse de** make up for. **resarcimiento** *sm* compensation.

resbalar [resβa'lar] *v* slide: skid: slip. **resbaladero** *also* **resbaladizo, resbalante** *adj* slippery. **resbalador** *adj* sliding. **resbaldura** *sf* skid mark. **resbalón** *sm* slide: slip: skid.

rescatar [reska'tar] *v* rescue: recover: save: ransom: make up for. **rescate** *sm* redemption: rescue: ransom.

rescindir [resθin'dir] *v* rescind. **rescisión** *sf* annulment.

rescoldo [res'kolðo] *sm* misgiving: embers *pl*.

resecar [rese'kar] *v* dry thoroughly. **reseco** *adj* desiccated.

***resentirse** [resen'tirse] *v* feel the effects: be weakened.

reseñar [rese'ɲar] *v* review: outline. **reseña** *sf* review: outline.

reservar [reser'βar] *v* reserve: preserve: conceal. **reserva** *sf* reserve: reservation. **a reserva de** with the intention of. **reserva de asiento** reservation. **sin reserva** frankly. **reservado** *adj* reserved: discreet.

resfriar [resfri'ar] *v* cool: turn cold. **resfriarse** *v* catch cold. **resfriado** *m* (*med*) cold.

resguardar [resgwar'ðar] *v* defend: preserve. **resguardarse** *v* protect oneself. **resguardo** *sm* defence: protection: guarantee. **reguardo de correos** postal receipt.

residencia [resi'ðenθja] *sf* residence: boarding house. **residencial** *adj* residential. **residente** *s(m+f)* resident. **residir** *v* reside.

residuo [re'siðwo] *sm* residue. **residuos** *sm pl* refuse *sing*. **residual** *adj* residual.

resignar [resig'nar] *v* resign: renounce. **resignarse** *v* resign oneself. **resigna** *sf* renunciation. **resignación** *sf* resignation.

resina [re'sina] *sf* resin.

resistir [resis'tir] *v* resist: refuse. **resistencia** *sf* resistance: stamina. **resistente** *adj* resistant.

resolución [resolu'θjon] *sf* resolution: decision. **resoluto** *adj* resolute: skilled.

***resolver** [resol'βer] *v* resolve: decide: analyse. **resolverse** *v* make up one's mind.

***resollar** [reso'ʎar] *v* pant: puff: snort.

***resonar** [reso'nar] *v* resound. **resonancia** *sf* resonance. **resonante** *adj* resonant.

resoplar [reso'plar] *v* snort: puff. **resoplido** *sm* snort: puff.

resorte [re'sorte] *sm* resort: means: motive: (*mec*) spring: elasticity.

respaldar [respal'ðar] *v* back: support: endorse. **respaldarse** *v* lean. **respaldo** *sm* chair back: support.

respecto [re'spekto] *sm* respect. **con respecto a** with regard to.

respetar [respe'tar] *v* respect. **respetabilidad** *sf* respectability. **respetable** *adj* respectable. **respetador** *adj* respectful. **respeto** *sm* respect. **respetuoso** *adj* respectful.

respirar [respi'rar] *v* breathe. **respiración** *sf* respiration. breath. **respiro** *sm* breathing. **respiradero** *sm* ventilator.

***resplandecer** [resplanðe'θer] *v* glitter. **resplandeciente** *adj* glittering. **resplandor** *sm* glitter.

responder [respon'der] *v* respond. **responder por** vouch for. **respondón** *adj* saucy. **responsivo** *adj* responsive. **respuesta** *sf* reply: refutation.

responsable [respon'saβle] *adj* responsible. **responsabilidad** *sf* responsibility.

*resquebrajar [reskeβra'xar] *v also* **resquebrar** split; crack. **resquebra(ja)dura** *sf* crack.

resquemar [reske'mar] *v* sting the tongue. *sm* sting in the mouth; remorse; resentment.

resquicio [res'kiθjo] *sm* crack; chink; (*fig*) slight chance.

*restablecer [restaβle'θer] *v* re-establish. **restablecerse** *v* recover from illness. **restablecimiento** *sm* re-establishment; recovery.

restallar [resta'ʎar] *v* crack; crackle.

restante [re'stante] *adj* remaining. *sm* remainder.

restar [res'tar] *v* subtract; remain.

restaurante [restau'rante] *sm* restaurant. **restauración** *sf* restoration. **restaurar** *v* restore; recover; repair.

*restituir [restitu'ir] *v* restore; pay back. **restituirse** *v* return. **restituición** *sf* restitution.

resto ['resto] *sm* rest, remainder.

*restregar [restre'gar] *v* rub; scrub; wipe. **restregón** *sm* rubbing; scrubbing; wiping.

restricción [restrik'θjon] *sf* restriction. **restrictivo** *adj* restrictive.

restringir [restrin'xir] *v* restrict.

resucitar [resuθi'tar] *v* resuscitate. **resucitación** *sf* resuscitation.

resuello [re'sweʎo] *sm* breathing.

resuelto [re'swelto] *adj* resolute; resolved; firm.

resultar [resul'tar] *v* result; happen; turn out; go. **resulta** *sf* result, effect. **resultado** *sm* result. **resultante** *adj* resultant.

resumir [resu'mir] *v* summarize; abbreviate. **resumen** *sm* summary. **en resumen** in brief. **resumido** *adj* summarized.

retablo [re'taβlo] *sm* altarpiece.

retaguardia [reta'gwarðja] *sf* rearguard.

retal [re'tal] *sm* remnant.

retama [re'tama] *sf* (*bot*) broom.

retardar [retar'ðar] *v* retard, delay; (*reloj*) put back. **retardación** *sf* delay. **retardo** *sm* delay.

retén [re'ten] *sm* spare, reserve.

*retener [rete'ner] *v* retain; deduct; detain; arrest. **retención** *sf* retention; deduction; detention. **retentiva** *sf* memory. **retentivo** *adj* retentive.

retina [re'tina] *sf* retina.

retintín [retin'tin] *sm* jingle.

retirar [reti'rar] *v* withdraw. **retirarse** *v* go into seclusion. **retirada** *sf* retreat. **retirado** *adj* retired; remote. **retiro** *sm* retirement; retreat.

reto ['reto] *sm* challenge.

retocar [reto'kar] *v* retouch. **retoque** *sm* retouching.

*retorcer [retor'θer] *v* twist; distort. **retorcerse** *v* writhe. **retorcimiento** *sm* contortion.

retórica [re'torika] *sf* rhetoric. **retórico** *adj* rhetorical.

retornar [retor'nar] *v* return. **retorno** *sm* return; remuneration.

retractar [retrak'tar] *v* retract. **retracción** *sf* retraction. **retractable** *adj also* **retráctil** retractable.

*retraer [retra'er] *v* dissuade; bring again. **retraerse** *v* shelter; retreat. **retraído** *adj* retiring; unsociable. **retraimiento** *sm* retirement; retreat.

retrasar [retra'sar] *v* delay; put back; (*reloj*) be slow. **retrasarse** *v* be late. **retraso** *sm* delay; lateness.

retratar [retra'tar] *v* portray. **retratista** *s(m+f)* portrait painter. **retrato** *sm* portrait.

retrete [re'trete] *sm* lavatory.

*retribuir [retriβu'ir] *v* recompense; repay. **retribuición** *sf* retribution; recompense.

retroceder [retroθe'ðer] *v* recede; fall back. **retroceso** *sm* retreat; (*com*) slump. **retrogresión** *sf* retrogression.

retruécano [retru'ekano] *sm* pun.

retumbar [retum'bar] *v* resound. **retumbante** *adj* resounding. **retumbo** *sm* rumble.

reuma ['reuma] *sm* rheumatism. **reumático** *adj* rheumatic. **reumatismo** *sm* rheumatism.

reunir [reu'nir] *v* reunite; unite; gather; reconcile. **reunión** *sf* meeting.

revalidar [reβali'ðar] *v* ratify; confirm. **revalidación** *sf* ratification.

revancha [re'βantʃa] *sf* revenge.

revelar [reβe'lar] *v* reveal; (*foto*) develop. **revelación** *sf* revelation. **revelador** *adj* revealing.

revendedor [reβende'ðor], **-a** *sm, sf* retailer. **revender** *v* retail.

*reventar [reβen'tar] *v* burst. **reventarse** *v* blow up. **reventón** *sm* burst; blowout.

reverberar [reβerβe'rar] *v* reverberate. **reverberación** *sf* reverberation. **reverbero** *sm* reverberation; reflector.

*reverdecer [reβerðe'θer] *v* grow green again; revive.
reverenciar [reβeren'θjar] *v* reverence, venerate. **reverencia** *sf* reverence. **reverendo** *adj* reverend. **reverente** *adj* reverent.
reversión [reβer'sjon] *sf* reversion. **reversible** *adj* revertible. **reverso** *adj* reverse.
revés [re'βes] *sm* reverse; back; setback. **al revés** upside down; inside out; back to front. **revesado** *adj* complicated; unruly.
revisar [reβi'sar] *v* revise; review. **revisión** *sf* revision; review; (*com*) audit. **revista** *sf* review; journal.
revivir [reβi'βir] *v* revive. **revivicar** *v* revive.
revocar [reβo'kar] *v* revoke; dissuade.
*revolcar [reβol'kar] *v* knock down; defeat; (*fam*) fail an exam. **revolcarse** *v* wallow.
revoltillo [reβol'tiʎo] *sm also* **revoltijo** jumble; mess.
revoltoso [reβol'toso] *adj* mischievous; unruly.
revolución [reβolu'θjon] *sf* revolution. **revolucionario, -a** *sm, sf* revolutionary.
*revolver [reβol'βer] *v* revolve; stir; disturb. **revolverse** *v* turn round.
revólver [re'βolβer] *sm* revolver.
revoque [re'βoke] *sm* plaster; stucco; whitewash.
revuelta [re'βwelta] *sf* revolt; turn; bend; change. **revuelto** *adj* difficult; unruly; upside down; disturbed.
rey [rej] *sm* king.
reyerta [re'jerta] *sf* quarrel; brawl.
rezagar [reθa'gar] *v* defer; postpone; leave behind. **rezagarse** *v* straggle. **rezagado** *sm* (*mil*) straggler. **rezago** *sm* remainder.
rezar [re'θar] *v* pray, pray for. **rezo** *sm* prayer; prayers *pl*.
rezumarse [reθu'marse] *v* ooze, drip; leak out.
riachuelo [rja'tʃwelo] *sm* brook. **ría** *sf* estuary.
ribera [ri'βera] *sf* river bank; shore.
ribete [ri'βete] *sm* (*de ropa*) border, edging; trimmings *pl*. **ribetear** *v* border; edge.
ricino [ri'θino] *sm* castor-oil plant. **aceite de ricino** *sm* castor oil.
rico ['riko], **-a** *sm, sf* rich person. *adj* rich; handsome; tasty.

ridiculizar [riðikuli'θar] *v* ridicule. **ridículo** *adj* ridiculous.
riego ['rjego] *sm* irrigation.
riel [rjel] *sm* ingot; (*ferro*) rail.
rienda ['rjenda] *sf* rein. **a rienda suelta** at full speed. **llevar las riendas** be in control.
riesgo ['rjesgo] *sm* risk.
rifar [ri'far] *v* raffle. **rifa** *sf* raffle.
rifle ['rifle] *sm* rifle.
rígido ['rixiðo] *adj* rigid. **rigidez** *sf* rigidity.
rigor [ri'gor] *sm* severity; rigour. **rigorismo** *sm* austerity. **riguroso** *adj* rigorous.
rimar [ri'mar] *v* rhyme. **rima** *sf* rhyme.
rimbombante [rimbom'bante] *adj* grandiloquent; bombastic. **rimbombancia** *sf* grandiloquence.
rincón [rin'kon] *sm* corner. **rinconada** *sf* corner table.
rinoceronte [rinoθe'ronte] *sm* rhinoceros.
riña ['riɲa] *sf* brawl; fight; quarrel.
riñón [ri'ɲon] *sm* kidney.
río ['rio] *sm* river. **río arriba** upstream.
ripio ['ripjo] *sm* rubble; refuse; residue. **no perder ripio** not to miss a trick.
riqueza [ri'keθa] *sf* wealth.
risa ['risa] *sf* laughter; laugh. **riseño** *adj* smiling; happy.
ristre ['ristre] *sm* **en ristre** at the ready.
ritmo ['ritmo] *sm* rhythm. **rítmico** *adj* rhythmic.
rito ['rito] *sm* rite. **ritual** *sm* ritual. **ritualismo** *sm* ritualism. **ritualista** *adj* ritualistic.
rival [ri'βal] *s(m+f)*, *adj* rival. **rivalidad** *sf* rivalry. **rivalizar** *v* vie. **rivalizar con** rival.
rizar [ri'θar] *v* (*pelo*) curl. **rizado** *sm* curling. **rizador** *sm* curling-iron. **rizo** *adj* curly.
robar [ro'βar] *v* rob, steal; kidnap. **robo** *sm* robbery.
roble ['roβle] *sm* oak.
*robustecer [roβuste'θer] *v* strengthen. **robustecerse** *v* gain strength. **robustecimiento** *sm* strengthening. **robustez** *sf* robustness. **robusto** *adj* robust.
roca ['roka] *sf* rock.
roce ['roθe] *sm* friction; rubbing; chafing.
rociar [ro'θjar] *v* sprinkle; spray; strew; moisten. **rociada** *sf* sprinkling; spraying; dew. **rociadera** *sf* watering can. **rociador** *sm* sprinkler.

rocín [ro'θin] *sm* nag; hack.

rodapié [roða'pje] *sm* skirting-board.

*rodar [ro'ðar] *v* roll; revolve; rotate. **rodado** *adj* (*auto*) run-in. **tránsito rodado** *sm* road traffic. **rodaja** *sf* small wheel. **rodaje** *sm* wheels *pl*.

rodear [roðe'ar] *v* encircle; enclose; go round. **rodearse** *v* surround oneself. **rodeo** *sm* detour; evasion; rodeo.

rodezno [ro'ðeθno] *sm* waterwheel; cogwheel.

rodilla [ro'ðiʎa] *sf* knee. **de rodillas** kneeling.

rodillo [ro'ðiʎo] *sm* rolling pin; roller; mangle.

*roer [ro'er] *v* gnaw; nibble. **roerse** *v* bite. **roedor** *adj* gnawing.

*rogar [ro'gar] *v* beg; pray. **rogación** *sf* petition. **rogativa** *sf* supplication.

rojo ['roxo] *adj* red. *sm* red; rouge. **rojear** *v* redden. **rojizo** *adj* reddish.

rollizo [ro'ʎiθo] *adj* chubby; plump.

rollo ['roʎo] *sm* roll; cylinder; (*foto*) film.

romance [ro'manθe] *sm*, *adj* romance. *sm* ballad. **romancero** *sm* ballad collection; ballad singer. **romántico** *adj* romantic.

romería [rome'ria] *sf* pilgrimage. **romero, -a** *sm*, *sf* pilgrim; *sm* rosemary.

romo ['romo] *adj* snub-nosed; blunt; dull.

rompecabezas [rompeka'βeθas] *sm invar* puzzle; jigsaw; riddle.

rompeolas [rompe'olas] *sm invar* breakwater.

romper [rom'per] *v* break; fracture; break out. **rompimiento** *sm* break; breach.

ron [ron] *sm* rum.

roncar [ron'kar] *v* snore; roar; boast. **ronca** *sf* bellow. **ronquido** *sm* snore.

ronco ['ronko] *adj* hoarse. **ronquedad** *sf* hoarseness.

rondar [ron'dar] *v* patrol; go round; pursue; haunt; serenade. **rondador** *sm* patrolman. **ronda** *sf* patrol; round of drinks.

ronronear [ronrone'ar] *v* purr.

ronzal [ron'θal] *sm* halter.

roña ['roɲa] *sf* filth; mange; rust; (*fam*) meanness. *adj* stingy. **roñoso** *adj* mangy; filthy; stingy.

ropa ['ropa] *sf* clothes *pl*, clothing. **ropa de cama** bed linen. **ropa interior** underclothes. **ropero** *sm* wardrobe.

roque ['roke] *sm* (*ajedrez*) rook.

rosa ['rosa] *sf* rose. **novela rosa** *sf* romantic novel. **rosado** *adj* rose-coloured. **rosal** *sm* rosebush.

rosario [ro'sarjo] *sm* rosary.

rosca ['roska] *sf* thread of a screw; doughnut; bread roll.

rostro ['rostro] *sm* countenance, face. **hacer rostro a** face.

rotación [rota'θjon] *sf* rotation. **rotativo** *adj* rotary.

roto ['roto] *adj* broken; torn. *sm* hole.

rotular [rotu'lar] *v* label. **rótula** *sf* label; placard.

rotundo [ro'tundo] *adj* round; (*fig*) emphatic. **rotundidad** *sf* roundness.

roturar [rotu'rar] *v* (*tierra*) break up. **rotura** *sf* breaking.

rozar [ro'θar] *v* graze; scrape. **rozarse** *v* be tongue-tied; trip over one's feet. **rozamiento** *sm* rubbing, friction.

rubí [ru'βi] *sm*, *pl* **rubíes** ruby.

rubio ['ruβjo] *sm*, *adj* blond. **rubia** *sf* blonde.

rubor [ru'βor] *sm* blush. **ruborizarse** *v* blush. **ruboroso** *adj* blushing.

rúbrica ['ruβrika] *sf* rubric; heading; flourish after a signature. **rubricar** *v* sign with a flourish.

rudeza [ru'ðeθa] *sf* roughness, rudeness. **rudo** *adj* rough; coarse; crude.

rudimento [ruði'mento] *sm* rudiment.

rueca [ru'eka] *sf* distaff.

rueda [ru'eða] *sf* wheel. **rueda de recambio** spare wheel.

ruedo [ru'eðo] *sm* edge; hem; round mat.

ruego [ru'ego] *sm* request; supplication.

rugir [ru'xir] *v* roar; bellow; howl. **rugido** *sm* roar; bellow; howl.

rugoso [ru'goso] *adj* wrinkled.

ruibarbo [rui'βarβo] *sm* rhubarb.

ruido [ru'iðo] *sm* noise; rumour. **meter ruido** make a noise. **ruidoso** *adj* noisy.

ruin [ru'in] *adj* mean; foul; puny. **ruindad** *sf* meanness; villainy.

ruina [ru'ina] *sf* ruin; ruins *pl*. **ruinoso** *adj* ruinous.

ruiseñor [ruise'ɲor] *sm* nightingale.

rumbo ['rumbo] *sm* course; direction; (*fam*) pomp. **hacer rumbo** set a course. **rumboso** *adj* splendid; lavish.

rumiar [ru'mjar] *v* ruminate; chew; grumble. **rumiante** *sm* ruminant.

rumor [ru'mor] *sm* rumour; noise; murmur. **rumorear** *v* rumour. **rumoroso** *adj* murmuring.

ruptura [rup'tura] *sf* rupture; break.
rural [ru'ral] *adj* rural.
Rusia ['rusja] *sf* Russia. **ruso. -a** *sm. sf* Russian.
rústico ['rustiko] *adj* rustic.
ruta ['ruta] *sf* route; road.
rutina [ru'tina] *sf* routine. **rutinario** *adj* routine; unimaginative.

S

sábado ['saβaðo] *sm* Saturday.
sabana [sa'βana] *sf* savannah.
sábana ['saβana] *sf* sheet.
sabanilla [saβa'niʎa] *sf* small cloth. napkin.
sabañón [saβa'ɲon] *sm* chilblain.
***saber** [sa'βer] *v* know; know how to; be aware, of. **a saber** namely. **sabedor** *adj* well-informed. **sabidillo, -a** *sm, sf* (*fam*) know-all. **sabido** *adj* known; learned. **sabiduría** *sf* knowledge; wisdom. **sabio** *adj* wise.
sabor [sa'βor] *sm* taste; flavour. **saborear** *v* taste; savour. **saborearse** *v* smack one's lips. **saboroso** *adj* tasty; savoury.
sabotear [saβote'ar] *v* sabotage. **saboteador, -a** *sm, sf* saboteur. **sabotaje** *sm* sabotage.
sabroso [sa'βroso] *adj* delicious; tasty; pleasant; racy.
sabueso [sa'βweso] *sm* bloodhound.
sacabocados [sakaβo'kaðos] *sm invar* (*tecn*) punch.
sacacorchos [saka'kortʃos] *sm invar* corkscrew.
sacamanchas [saka'mantʃas] *sm invar* stain-remover.
sacar [sa'kar] *v* get out; put out; draw; publish; take out; buy tickets; (*tenis*) serve. **saca** *sf* extraction; exportation.
sacarina [saka'rina] *sf* saccharine.
sacerdote [saker'ðote] *sm* priest. **sacerdocio** *sm* priesthood. **sacerdotal** *adj* priestly. **sacerdotisa** *sf* priestess.
saciar [sa'θjar] *v* satiate. **saciedad** *sf* satiety.
saco ['sako] *sm* sack; bag; plunder. **entrar a saco** plunder.
sacramento [sakra'mento] *sm* sacrament. **sacramental** *adj* sacramental.

sacrificar [sakrifi'kar] *v* sacrifice. **sacrificadero** *sm* slaughterhouse. **sacrificio** *sm* sacrifice; slaughter.
sacrilegio [sakri'lexjo] *sm* sacrilege. **sacrílego** *adj* sacrilegious.
sacro ['sakro] *adj* sacred. **sacrosanto** *adj* sacrosanct.
sacudir [saku'ðir] *v* shake, jolt. **sacudirse** *v* shake off; repel. **sacudida** *sf* shake, jolt.
sádico ['saðiko] *adj* sadistic. **sadismo** *sm* sadism. **sadista** *s(m + f)* sadist.
saeta [sa'eta] *sf* arrow; watch *or* clock hand. **saetada** *sf* arrow wound. **saetera** *sf* loophole. **saetero** *sm* bowman.
sagacidad [sagaθi'ðað] *sf* shrewdness. **sagaz** *adj* shrewd, wise.
sagrado [sa'graðo] *adj* sacred, holy. *sm* sanctuary.
sajón [sa'xon], **-ona** *s. adj* Saxon.
sal [sal] *sf* salt; wit; charm. **salero** *sm* salt cellar; wit; charm. **saleroso** *adj* (*fam*) witty; charming.
sala ['sala] *sf* hall; drawing-room; (*med*) ward; (*teatro*) house. **sala de conferencias** lecture hall. **sala de espera** waiting-room.
salacidad [salaθi'ðað] *sf* lechery.
salar [sa'lar] *v* salt. **salado** *adj* salty; witty.
salario [sa'larjo] *sm* salary, pay.
salchicha [sal'tʃitʃa] *sf* sausage. **salchichón** *sm* salami.
saldar [sal'ðar] *v* settle; liquidate; pay off. **saldo** *sm* payment; balance; bargain sale.
salida [sa'liða] *sf* departure; exit; start; outskirts *pl*; pretext; (*del sol*) rising; outcome; projection; witticism. **calle sin salida** *sf* cul-de-sac. **dar salida a** sell. **tener buenas salidas** be full of witty remarks. **saliente** *adj* projecting.
salina [sa'lina] *sm* salt mine. **salino** *adj* saline.
***salir** [sa'lir] *v* leave; emerge; (*astron*) rise; happen. **salir para** leave for. **salir por alguien** vouch for someone. **salirse** *v* leak; overflow; escape.
saliva [sa'liβa] *sf* saliva. **salivar** *v* salivate.
salmo ['salmo] *sm* psalm. **salmista** *s(m + f)* psalmist. **salmodia** *sf* psalmody.
salmón [sal'mon] *sm* salmon.
salmuera [sal'mwera] *sf* brine.
salón [sa'lon] *sm* large hall; drawing-room.
salpicar [salpi'kar] *v* splash; sprinkle. **salpicadura** *sf* splash; spatter.
salpimentar [salpimen'tar] *v* season with salt and pepper.

salpullido [salpuˈʎiðo] *sm* (*med*) rash.
salsa [ˈsalsa] *sf* sauce. gravy.
saltamontes [saltaˈmontes] *sm invar* grasshopper.
saltar [salˈtar] *v* jump; skip; break; explode. **salto** *sm* jump; hop; chasm. **salto de agua** waterfall. **salto de altura** high jump. **salto con garrocha** pole vault. **salto mortal** somersault.
saltear [salteˈar] *v* rob; assault. **salteador** *sm* highwayman. **salteamiento** *sm* highway robbery.
salubre [saˈluβre] *adj* salubrious, healthy. **salubridad** *sf* wholesomeness. **salud** *sf* health. ¡**salud!** cheers! **saludable** *adj* salutary. **saludador** *sm* quack doctor.
salvaguardar [salβagwarˈðar] *v* safeguard. **salvaguardia** *sf* safeguard.
saludar [saluˈðar] *v* salute; greet. **le saluda atentamente** yours faithfully. **saludo** *sm* greeting; salute. **saludos** *sm pl* regards *pl*, best wishes *pl*. **salutación** *sf* greeting.
salvaje [salˈβaxe] *adj* wild; uncultivated; savage. **salvajada** *sf* barbarity. **salvajería** *sf* savagery.
salvamanteles [salβamanˈteles] *sm invar* table mat.
salvar [salˈβar] *v* save, rescue; except; cross; overcome. **salvarse** *v* escape. **salvamento** *sm* salvation; salvage. **salvador** *adj* healing; saving.
salvavidas [salβaˈβiðas] *sm invar* lifebelt; life buoy; lifeboat.
salvedad [salβeˈðað] *sf* proviso; reservation; distinction.
salvia [ˈsalβja] *sf* sage.
salvo [ˈsalβo] *adv* except, saving. *adj* safe. **a salvo** safe. **poner a salvo** rescue. **salvo que** unless.
salvoconducto [salβokonˈdukto] *sm* safe-conduct.
san [san] *adj* saint; holy. *V* **santo**.
sanar [saˈnar] *v* heal; cure; get better. **sanable** *adj* curable. **sanatorio** *sm* sanatorium.
sanción [sanˈθjon] *sf* sanction. **sancionar** *v* sanction.
sandalia [sanˈdalja] *sf* sandal.
sandía [sanˈdia] *sf* watermelon.
sanear [saneˈar] *v* guarantee; drain; repair. **saneado** *adj* unencumbered; nett. **saneamiento** *sm* surety; drainage.
sangrar [sanˈgrar] *v* bleed; drain off. **sangradera** *sf* lancet. **sangre** *sf* blood. **a sangre fría** in cold blood. **sangriento** *adj* bloody. **sanguinario** *adj* bloodthirsty. **sanguinolento** *adj* bloody.
sangría [sanˈgria] *sf* bleeding; drink made of fruit and red wine.
sanguijuela [sangiˈxwela] *sf* leech.
sanidad [saniˈðað] *sf* health; sanitation. **sanitario** *adj* sanitary. **sano** *adj* healthy; wholesome; sound; good.
santiamén [santjaˈmen] *sm* instant. **en un santiamén** in a jiffy.
santificar [santifiˈkar] *v* sanctify, consecrate. **santificación** *sf* sanctification.
santiguar [santiˈgwar] *v* bless. **santiguarse** *v* cross oneself.
santo [ˈsanto], **-a** *sm, sf* saint. *adj* sacred; saintly; holy. **santo y bueno** all well and good.
santuario [sanˈtwarjo] *sm* sanctuary, shrine.
saña [ˈsaɲa] *sf* rage; cruelty. **sañoso** *adj* furious; cruel.
sapo [ˈsapo] *sm* toad.
saquear [sakeˈar] *v* plunder. **saqueo** *sm* plunder. **saqueador, -a** *sm, sf* looter.
sarampión [saramˈpjon] *sm* measles.
sarcasmo [sarˈkasmo] *sm* sarcasm. **sarcástico** *adj* sarcastic.
sarcófago [sarˈkofago] *sm* sarcophagus.
sardina [sarˈðina] *sf* sardine.
sardónico [sarˈðoniko] *adj* sardonic.
sargento [sarˈxento] *sm* sergeant.
sarna [ˈsarna] *sf* scabies; itch. **sarnoso** *adj* mangy.
sartén [sarˈten] *sf* frying pan.
sastre [ˈsastre] *sm* tailor. **sastrería** *sf* tailoring; tailor's shop.
satélite [saˈtelite] *sm* satellite.
sátira [ˈsatira] *sf* satire. **satírico** *adj* satirical. **satirizar** *v* satirize.
*****satisfacer** [satisfaˈθer] *v* satisfy; please. **satisfacerse** *v* satisfy oneself; take revenge. **satisfacción** *sf* satisfaction. **satisfactorio** *adj* satisfactory. **satisfecho** *adj* satisfied.
saturar [satuˈrar] *v* saturate. **saturación** *sf* saturation.
sauce [ˈsauθe] *sm* willow.
saúco [saˈuko] *sm* (*bot*) elder.
savia [ˈsaβja] *sf* sap.
saxófono [sakˈsofono] *sm* saxophone.
saya [ˈsaja] *sf* skirt, petticoat. **sayo** *sm* smock.
sazonar [saθoˈnar] *v* (*culin*) season; ripen.

sazón *sf* season; (*culin*) flavour; mellowness. **a la sazón** at the time. **sazonado** *adj* tasty; well seasoned.

se [se] *pron* himself; herself; yourself; oneself; itself; themselves; yourselves; one another; each other. **se dice** they say. **se habla inglés** English is spoken.

sebo ['seβo] *sm* grease. **seboso** *adj* greasy.

secar [se'kar] *v* dry. **secarse** *v* dry oneself; dry up. **seca** *sf* drought; sandbank. **secador** *sm* hair-dryer. **secadora** *sf* clothes-dryer. **secano** *sm* dry land. **secante** *sm* blotting paper. **seco** *adj* dry; lean; hoarse. **en seco** high and dry.

sección [sek'θjon] *sf* section.

secretario [sekre'tarjo], **-a** *sm, sf* secretary. **secretaría** *sf* secretariat.

secreto [se'kreto] *adj* secret; private; hidden. *sm* secrecy, secret knowledge. **secreto a voces** open secret. **secreteo** *sm* private conversation.

secta ['sekta] *sf* sect. **sectario, -a** *sm, sf* sectarian.

secuaz [se'kwaθ] *sm* follower, supporter.

secuestrar [sekwes'trar] *v* kidnap; hijack. **secuestrador, -a** *sm, sf* kidnapper; hijacker. **secuestro** *sm* kidnap; hijack.

secular [seku'lar] *adj* secular. **secularizar** *v* secularize.

secundar [sekun'dar] *v* second, support.

sed [seð] *sf* thirst. **tener sed** be thirsty. **sediento** *adj* thirsty.

seda ['seða] *sf* silk. **sedoso** *adj* silky.

sedante [se'ðante] *sm* sedative. *adj* calming.

sede ['seðe] *sf* (*rel*) see; (*de gobierno*) seat. **Santa Sede** Holy See.

sedentario [seðen'tarjo] *adj* sedentary.

sedería [seðe'ria] *sf* silk trade; drapery.

sedición [seði'θjon] *sf* sedition. **sedicioso** *adj* seditious.

sedimento [seði'mento] *sm* sediment. **sedimentar** *v* deposit.

*****seducir** [seðu'θir] *v* seduce; attract. **seducción** *sf* seduction. **seductivo** *adj* seductive. **seductor, -a** *sm, sf* seducer.

*****segar** [se'gar] *v* reap; mow. **segadora** *sf* mower; reaper.

seglar [se'glar] *sm* layman. *adj* secular.

segmento [seg'mento] *sm* segment.

segregar [segre'gar] *v* segregate. **segregación** *sf* segregation.

*****seguir** [se'gir] *v* follow; pursue; continue. **seguida** *sf* continuation. **en seguida** at once. **seguido** *adj* successive; straight.

cuatro días seguidos four days running. **seguimiento** *sm* pursuit; following.

según [se'gun] *prep* according to. *adv* it all depends. *conj* as.

segundo [se'gundo] *adj, sm* second.

segundón [segun'don] *sm* second son.

seguro [se'guro] *adj* sure; safe. *sm* safety catch; insurance. **seguridad** *sf* safety; certainty.

seis ['seis] *sm, adj* six.

selección [selek'θjon] *sf* selection. **seleccionar** *v* select. **selectivo** *adj* selective. **selecto** *adj* select.

selva ['selβa] *sf* forest; jungle. **selvoso** *adj* wooded, forested.

sello ['seʎo] *sm* stamp; seal. **selladura** *sf* sealing. **sellar** *v* stamp; seal.

semáforo [se'maforo] *sm* semaphore; traffic lights *pl.*

semana [se'mana] *sf* week. **semanal** *adj* weekly. **semanario** *sm* weekly publication.

semblante [sem'blante] *sm* face; appearance.

*****sembrar** [sem'brar] *v* sow; scatter. **sembradera** *sf* seed-drill. **sembrador, -a** *sm, sf* sower.

semejar [seme'xar] *v* resemble. **semejante** *adj* similar. **semejanza** *sf* similarity.

semen ['semen] *sm* semen. **semental** *sm* sire. **sementera** *sf* sowing; seed-time.

semestre [se'mestre] *sm* semester. **semestral** *adj* half-yearly.

semicírculo [semi'θirkulo] *sm* semicircle. **semicircular** *adj* semicircular.

semilla [se'miʎa] *sf* seed. **semillero** *sm* seedbed.

seminario [semi'narjo] *sm* seminary; seminar; seedbed.

senado [se'naðo] *sm* senate. **senador** *sm* senator.

sencillo [sen'θiʎo] *adj* simple; easy. **sencillez** *sf* simplicity.

senda ['senda] *sf* path. **sendero** *sm* path.

sendos ['sendos] *adj pl* each.

senectud [senek'tuð] *sf* old age.

senil [se'nil] *adj* senile. **senilidad** *sf* senility.

seno ['seno] *sm* bosom, breast; haven, refuge.

sensación [sensa'θjon] *sf* sensation. **sensacional** *adj* sensational.

sensatez [sensa'teθ] *sf* good sense. **sensato** *adj* sensible.

sensibilidad [sensiβili'ðað] *sf* sensibility; sensitivity. **sensible** *adj* sensitive; sensible; considerable.

sensiblería [sensiβle'ria] *sf* sentimentality. **sensiblero** *adj* sentimental.

sensitivo [sensi'tiβo] *adj* relating to the senses; sensitive.

sensual [sen'swal] *adj* sensual. **sensualidad** *sf* sensuality.

***sentar** [sen'tar] *v* seat; place; locate; establish; press; suit; fit. **sentarse** *v* sit down; settle. **sentada** *sf* sit-in. **sentado** *adj* seated; established.

sentencia [sen'tenθja] *sf* (*jur*) sentence. **sentenciar** *v* (*jur*) sentence. **sentencioso** *adj* sententious.

sentido [sen'tiðo] *sm* sense; meaning; direction; feeling. **sin sentido** meaningless. **tener sentido** make sense. *adj* heartfelt; moving; sincere.

sentimiento [senti'mjento] *sm* feeling; emotion; sentiment; grief. **sentimental** *adj* sentimental.

***sentir** [sen'tir] *v* feel; hear; regret. **lo siento mucho** I am very sorry. **sentirse** *v* feel; suffer from. **sentirse enfermo** feel ill. **sentirse obligado a** feel obliged to.

seña ['seɲa] *sf* mark; sign; signal; password. **señas** *sf pl* address *sing*.

señal [se'ɲal] *sf* signal; sign; mark. **en señal de** in proof of. **señaladamente** *adv* signally. **señalado** *adj* famous. **señalar** *v* mark; signal; point out; denote. **señalarse** *v* distinguish oneself.

señor [se'ɲor] *sm* mister; gentleman; lord; master. **El Señor** the Lord. **señora** *sf* lady; wife; mistress; madam. **la señora de García** Mrs García. **señorear** *v* domineer. **señorearse** *v* take possession. **señoría** *sf* lordship. **señorío** *sm* dominion; stateliness. **señorita** *sf* miss; young lady.

separar [sepa'rar] *v* separate; divide; discharge. **separable** *adj* separable. **separación** *sf* separation; dismissal. **separado** *adj* separate. **por separado** separately.

septentrional [septentrjo'nal] *adj* northern.

séptico ['septiko] *adj* septic.

septiembre [sep'tjembre] *sm* September.

séptimo ['septimo] *adj* seventh.

septuagésimo [septwa'xesimo] *adj* seventieth.

sepulcro [se'pulkro] *sm* tomb, grave.

sepultar [sepul'tar] *v* bury. **sepultura** *sf* grave; burial. **sepulturero** *sm* gravedigger.

sequedad [seke'ðað] *sf* dryness; curtness. **sequía** *sf* drought.

séquito ['sekito] *sm* entourage, followers *pl*.

***ser** [ser] *v* be; exist; occur. **a no ser por** but for. **sea lo que sea** come what may. **si no es que** unless.

seráfico [se'rafiko] *adj* seraphic. **serafín** *sm* seraph.

serenar [sere'nar] *v* calm; settle. **sereno** *adj* serene; calm. **serenidad** *sf* serenity; calmness.

serenata [sere'nata] *sf* serenade.

serie ['serje] *sf* series. **fabricación en serie** *sf* mass production.

serio ['serjo] *adj* serious. **tomar en serio** take seriously. **seriedad** *sf* seriousness; sincerity.

sermón [ser'mon] *sm* sermon.

serpiente [ser'pjente] *sf* serpent. **serpiente de cascabel** rattlesnake. **serpentear** *v* wriggle. **serpentino** *adj* serpentine.

serrano [ser'rano] *adj* of the mountains. *sm* highlander. **serranía** *sf* mountainous country.

***serrar** [ser'rar] *v* saw. **serrado** *adj* serrated. **serrín** *sm* sawdust.

servicio [ser'βiθjo] *sm* service; attendance. **estar de servicio** be on duty. **servicios** *sm pl* toilet *sing*. **servible** *adj* serviceable. **servidor, -a** *sm, sf* servant. **su seguro servidor** yours faithfully. **servidumbre** *sf* household staff; servitude. **servil** *adj* servile. **servilismo** *sm* servility.

servilleta [serβi'ʎeta] *sf* napkin.

***servir** [ser'βir] *v* serve. **para servir a usted** at your service. **servir de** act as. **servirse** *v* help oneself. **servirse de** make use of.

sesenta [se'senta] *sm, adj* sixty.

sesgar [ses'gar] *v* slant; twist. **sesgo** *sm* slant; twist.

sesión [se'sjon] *sf* session; conference.

seso ['seso] *sm* brain; sense, understanding, wisdom. **perder el seso** go mad.

seta ['seta] *sf* mushroom.

setenta [se'tenta] *sm, adj* seventy.

setiembre *V* septiembre.

seto ['seto] *sm* fence.

seudónimo [seu'ðonimo] *sm* pseudonym. **seudo** *adj* (*fam*) pseudo.

severo [se'βero] *adj* severe; harsh. **severidad** *sf* severity.
sexagésimo [seksa'xesimo] *adj* sixtieth. sexagenario. **-a** *sm, sf* sexagenarian.
sexo ['sekso] *sm* sex. **sexual** *adj* sexual. sexualidad *sf* sexuality.
sexto ['seksto] *adj* sixth. **sexteto** *sm* sexteto.
si [si] *conj* if; whether. **si bien** although.
si¹ [si] *adv* yes; indeed. **eso sí que es** yes, that's it. *sm* consent. **dar el sí** agree.
sí² *pron* himself; herself; itself; yourself; oneself; themselves; yourselves. **de por sí** in itself. **entre sí** among themselves. **metido en sí** pensive.
sibilante [siβi'lante] *adj* sibilant.
siderurgia [siðe'rurxja] *sf* iron and steel industry.
sidra ['siðra] *sf* cider.
siega ['sjega] *sf* reaping, harvesting.
siembra ['sjembra] *sf* sowing.
siempre ['sjempre] *adv* always. **siempre jamás** for ever and ever. **siempre que** whenever; provided that.
sien [sjen] *sf* (*anat*) temple.
sierra ['sjerra] *sf* saw; mountain range.
siervo ['sjerβo] *sm* slave; servant.
siesta ['sjesta] *sf* siesta.
siete ['sjete] *adj, sm* seven.
sífilis ['sifilis] *sm* syphilis. **sifilítico, -a** *s, adj* syphilitic.
sifón [si'fon] *sm* soda water; syphon.
sigilar [sixi'lar] *v* conceal. **sigilo** *sm* secrecy. **sigiloso** *adj* secretive.
siglo ['siglo] *sm* century. **siglo de oro** golden age.
signar [sig'nar] *v* sign, seal. **signarse** *v* cross oneself. **signatura** *sf* signature.
significar [signifi'kar] *v* signify; notify. **significado** *sm* meaning; significance. **significativo** *adj* significant.
signo ['signo] *sm* sign; symbol.
siguiente [si'gjente] *adj* following, next.
sílaba ['silaβa] *sf* syllable.
silbar [sil'βar] *v* whistle; hiss. **silbido** *sm* whistle, hiss.
silencio [si'lenθjo] *sm* silence. **silenciador** *sm* (*de arma*) silencer. **silenciar** *v* silence. **silencioso** *adj* silent.
silueta [si'lweta] *sf* silhouette, outline.
silvestre [sil'βestre] *adj* wild. **silvicultura** *sf* forestry.
silla ['siʎa] *sf* chair; seat; saddle. **silla de tijera** deck chair. **sillón** *sm* armchair.
sima ['sima] *sf* abyss.

símbolo ['simbolo] *sm* symbol. **simbólico** *adj* symbolic. **simbolismo** *sm* symbolism. **simbolizar** *v* symbolize.
simetría [sime'tria] *sf* symmetry. **simétrico** *adj* symmetrical.
simiente [si'mjente] *sf* seed.
símil ['simil] *adj* similar. *sm* comparison; simile. **similar** *adj* similar. **similitud** *sf* similarity.
simpatía [simpa'tia] *sf* affection; sympathy; friendliness; charm. **simpático** *adj* charming; friendly; nice. **simpatizar** *v* sympathize; get on.
simple ['simple] *adj* simple; pure; naïve. **simplemente** *adv* merely. **simpleza** *sf* simplicity; simpleness; silly thing. **simplicidad** *sf* simplicity. **simplificar** *v* simplify. **simplón, -ona** *sm, sf* simpleton.
simulacro [simu'lakro] *sm* image; semblance.
simular [simu'lar] *v* simulate. **simulación** *sf* pretence. **simulado** *adj* sham.
simultáneo [simul'taneo] *adj* simultaneous. **simultaneidad** *sf* simultaneousness.
sin [sin] *prep* without; but for; apart from. **sin embargo** nevertheless. **sin falta** without fail. **sin que** without.
sinagoga [sina'goga] *sf* synagogue.
sincero [sin'θero] *adj* sincere. **sinceridad** *sf* sincerity.
síncopa ['sinkopa] *sf* syncopation. **sincopar** *v* syncopate.
sindicato [sindi'kato] *sm* trade union; syndicate. **sindical** *adj* trade-union. **sindicalismo** *sm* trade-unionism. **síndico** *sm* trustee.
sinfín [sin'fin] *sm* endless number.
sinfonía [sinfo'nia] *sf* symphony. **sinfónico** *adj* symphonic.
singular [singu'lar] *adj* singular; exceptional; unique; excellent. **singularidad** *sf* singularity; excellence. **singularizar** *v* single out. **singularizarse** *v* distinguish oneself.
siniestro [si'njestro] *adj* (*dirección*) left; sinister. *sm* catastrophe. **siniestrado, -a** *sm, sf* victim of an accident.
sinnúmero [sin'numero] *sm* endless number.
sino¹ ['sino] *conj* but, except. **no sólo ... sino ...** not only ... but also ... .
sino² *sm* fate.
sinónimo [si'nonimo] *sm* synonym. *adj* synonymous.

sinopsis [si'nopsis] *sf* synopsis (*pl* -ses).

sinrazón [sinra'θon] *sf* injustice.

sinsabor [sinsa'βor] *sm* trouble.

sintaxis [sin'taksis] *sf* syntax. **sintáctico** *adj* syntactic.

síntesis ['sintesis] *sf* synthesis (*pl* -ses). **sintético** *adj* synthetic.

síntoma ['sintoma] *sm* symptom. **sintomático** *adj* symptomatic.

sintonizar [sintoni'θar] *v* (*radio*) tune in. **sintonía** *sf* signature tune.

sinvergüenza [sinβer'gwenθa] *adj* shameless. *s*(*m*+*f*) cad.

siquiera [si'kjera] *adv* at least; even; just. **ni siquiera** not at all. *conj* even if; even though. **siquiera … siquiera …** whether … or whether … .

sirena [si'rena] *sf* (*ninfa*) siren, mermaid; (*tecn*) siren, fog-horn.

sirviente [sir'βjente] *sm* servant.

sisar [si'sar] *v* pilfer; cheat. **sisa** *sf* theft, pilfering.

sísmico ['sismiko] *adj* seismic. **sismógrafo** *sm* seismograph.

sistema [sis'tema] *sm* system, method. **sistemático** *adj* systematic.

sitiar [si'tjar] *sm* besiege; surround.

sitio ['sitjo] *sm* place; room, space; siege. **no hay sitio** there is no room.

situar [si'twar] *v* situate; put. **situación** *sf* situation.

so [so] *prep* under. **so pena de** under penalty of.

sobaco [so'βako] *sm* armpit.

sobado [so'βaðo] *adj* kneaded; (*fam*) shabby, well-worn. **sobar** *v* knead; thrash; crumple; fondle.

soberanía [soβera'nia] *sf* sovereignty. **soberano, -a** *s, adj* sovereign.

soberbia [so'βerβja] *sf* pride; magnificence, pomp. **soberbio** *adj* proud; superb.

sobornar [soβor'nar] *v* bribe. **soborno** *sm* bribe; bribery.

sobrar [so'βrar] *sf* surplus. **de sobra** in excess. **sobras** *sf pl* remains *pl*. **sobradamente** *adv* excessively. **sobrado** *adj* abundant; superfluous. **sobrancero** *adj* unemployed. **sobrante** *adj* spare.

sobre[1] ['soβre] *prep* on; upon; over; above; about. **sobre las diez** about ten o'clock. **sobre todo** above all.

sobre[2] *sm* envelope.

sobrecama [soβre'kama] *sm* bedspread.

sobrecargar [soβrekar'gar] *v* overload. **sobrecarga** *sf* extra burden. **sobrecargo** *sm* purser.

sobrecejo [soβre'θexo] *sm* frown.

sobrecoger [soβreko'xer] *v* surprise, take aback. **sobrecogerse** *v* be startled.

sobredicho [soβre'ðitʃo] *adj* aforesaid.

sobrehumano [soβreu'mano] *adj* superhuman.

sobremanera [soβrema'nera] *adv* exceedingly.

sobremesa [soβre'mesa] *sf* dessert; table cover; after-dinner chat.

sobrenatural [soβrenatu'ral] *adj* supernatural.

sobrepasar [soβrepa'sar] *v* surpass.

*****sobreponer** [soβrepo'ner] *v* superimpose. **sobreponerse a** overcome. **sobrepuesto** *adj* superimposed.

sobreprecio [soβre'preθjo] *sm* surcharge.

*****sobresalir** [soβresa'lir] *v* excel. **sobresaliente** *adj* outstanding.

sobresaltar [soβresal'tar] *v* attack; frighten. **sobresalto** *sm* sudden attack; shock. **de sobresalto** suddenly.

sobrescrito [soβres'krito] *sm* (*en un sobre*) address.

sobretodo [soβre'toðo] *sm* overcoat.

*****sobrevenir** [soβreβe'nir] *v* happen suddenly.

sobrevivir [soβreβi'βir] *v* survive. **sobreviviente** *s*(*m*+*f*) survivor.

sobriedad [soβrie'ðað] *sf* sobriety. **sobrio** *adj* sober, moderate.

sobrino [so'βrino] *sm* nephew. **sobrina** *sf* niece.

socarrón [sokar'ron] *adj* sarcastic; sly. **socarronería** *sf* sarcasm; slyness.

socavar [soka'βar] *v* undermine. **socavón** *sm* excavation.

sociable [so'θjaβle] *adj* sociable. **sociabilidad** *sf* sociability.

social [so'θjal] *adj* social. **socializar** *v* socialize. **socialismo** *sm* socialism. **socialista** *s*(*m*+*f*) socialist.

sociedad [soθje'ðað] *sf* society. **socio, -a** *sm, sf* associate.

sociología [soθjolo'xia] *sf* sociology. **sociólogo, -a** *sm, sf* sociologist.

socorrer [sokor'rer] *v* help. **socorrido** *adj* helpful; handy. **socorro** *sm* succour; relief. **¡socorro!** help!

soda ['soða] *sf* soda-water.

soez [so'eθ] *adj* obscene; vulgar.

sofá [so'fa] *sf* sofa, settee.
sofocar [sofo'kar] *v* suffocate. **sofocación** *sf* suffocation. **sofocado** *adj* breathless. **sofoco** *sm* suffocation.
soga ['soga] *sf* rope, cord. **hacer soga** lag behind.
soja ['soxa] *sf* soya.
sojuzgar [soxuθ'gar] *v* subdue.
sol [sol] *sm* sun; sunlight. **hace sol** it's sunny. **tomar el sol** sunbathe.
solamente [sola'mente] *adv* only. **no solamente** not only.
solapa [so'lapa] *sf* flap; lapel; (*fig*) pretext. **solapado** *adj* sly. **solapar** *v* overlap; (*fig*) cover up, hide.
***solar** [so'lar] *adj* solar. *sm* lot; plot; building site.
solaz [so'laθ] *sm* recreation; solace. **a solaz** with pleasure. **solazar** *v* distract; amuse; solace.
soldado [sol'ðaðo] *sm* soldier.
***soldar** [sol'ðar] *v* solder; weld; (*huesos*) knit. **soldador** *sm* soldering iron. **soldadura** *sf* welding.
soledad [sole'ðað] *sf* loneliness, solitude.
solemne [so'lemne] *adj* solemn. **solemnidad** *sf* solemnity. **solemnizar** *v* solemnize.
***soler** [so'ler] *v* be in the habit of; usually be *or* do. **suele comer mucho** he usually eats a lot.
solera [so'lera] *sf* prop; stone pavement; tradition; strong old wine.
solicitar [soliθi'tar] *v* request; pursue; canvass. **solicitación** *sf* solicitation; application. **solicitador, -a** *sm, sf or* **solicitante** *sm* petitioner; applicant. **solícito** *adj* solicitous. **solicitud** *sf* solicitude.
solidaridad [soliðari'ðað] *sf* solidarity. **solidar** *v* consolidate. **solidario** *adj* mutual. **solidez** *sf* solidity. **solidificar** *v* solidify. **sólido** *adj* solid.
solitario [soli'tarjo], **-a** *sm, sf* hermit, recluse. *adj* lonely; solitary; alone; single.
solo ['solo] *adj* alone; single; unique; only; (*música*) solo. *sm* (*música*) solo.
sólo ['solo] *adv* only, merely.
***soltar** [sol'tar] *v* release; free; loosen; break; shed. **soltarse** *v* break loose; become unscrewed; lose one's inhibitions.
soltero [sol'tero] *sm* bachelor. *adj* single. **soltera** *sf* spinster. **soltería** *sf* celibacy. **solterona** *sf* old maid.

soltura [sol'tura] *sf* looseness; agility; fluency. **con soltura** fluently.
soluble [so'luβle] *adj* soluble. **solubilidad** *sf* solubility. **solución** *sf* solution. **solucionar** *v* solve.
solvencia [sol'βenθja] *sf* solvency; settlement. **solvente** *adj* solvent.
sollo ['soʎo] *sm* sturgeon.
sollozar [soʎo'θar] *v* sob. **sollozo** *sm* sob.
sombra ['sombra] *sf* shadow; shade. **dar sombra a** shade.
sombrero [som'brero] *sm* hat.
sombrilla [som'briʎa] *sf* parasol.
sombrío [som'brio] *sm* shady spot. *adj* shady; gloomy. **sombroso** *adj* shady.
somero [so'mero] *adj* superficial.
someter [some'ter] *v* submit; subdue. **sometimiento** *sm* submission.
somnífero [som'nifero] *sm* sleeping pill.
somnolencia [somno'lenθja] *sf* sleepiness. **somnámbulo, -a** *sm, sf* sleepwalker. **somnolente** *adj* sleepy.
son [son] *sm* sound; rumour; manner. **por este son** by this means.
***sonar** [so'nar] *v* sound; ring; chime. **sonarse** *v* blow one's nose. **sonante** *adj* sounding; ringing.
sondear [sonde'ar] *v* fathom; sound out.
soneto [so'neto] *sm* sonnet.
sonido [so'niðo] *sm* sound.
sonoro [so'noro] *adj* sonorous; resonant. **sonoridad** *sf* sonority.
***sonreír** [sonre'ir] *v* smile. **sonriente** *adj* smiling. **sonrisa** *sf* smile.
sonrojar [sonro'xar] *v* blush; flush. **sonrojo** *sm* blush.
***soñar** [so'nar] *v* dream. **soñador, -a** *sm, sf* dreamer. **soñera** *sf* drowsiness. **soñoliento** *adj* drowsy.
sopa ['sopa] *sf* soup. **como una sopa** soaked to the skin. **sopero** *sm* soup plate.
sopapo [so'papo] *sm* (*fam*) blow, punch. **sopapear** *v* chuck under the chin; punch.
soplar [so'plar] *v* blow; blow out; blow away; prompt. **sopladura** *sf* blowing. **soplillo** *sm* fan; blower. **soplo** *sm* blowing; puff of wind. **soplón, -ona** *sm, sf* informer.
sopor [so'por] *sm* drowsiness.
soportar [sopor'tar] *v* support; tolerate; endure. **soporte** *sm* support; stand.
sor [sor] *sf* (*rel*) sister.
sorber [sor'βer] *v* sip; suck; soak up. **sorbete** *sm* sherbet; water ice. **sorbetón**

sm large draught. **sorbo** *sm* sip; swallow; gulp.

sordera [sor'ðera] *sf* deafness. **sordo** *adj* deaf; muffled.

sórdido ['sorðiðo] *adj* squalid. **sordidez** *sf* squalor.

sordomudo [sorðo'muðo], **-a** *sm, sf* deaf-mute. *adj* deaf and dumb.

sorprender [sorpren'der] *v* surprise. **sorprendente** *adj* surprising. **sorpresa** *sf* surprise.

sortear [sorte'ar] *v* cast lots for; avoid, get round. **sorteable** *adj* avoidable. **sorteo** *sm* raffle; casting of lots; dodging. **sortija** [sor'tixa] *sf* ring; (*de pelo*) curl.

sortilegio [sorti'lexjo] *sm* sorcery; charm. **sortilega** *sf* sorceress. **sortilego** *sm* sorcerer.

*****sosegar** [sose'gar] *v* calm, quieten. **sosiego** *sm* calm, quiet.

soslayar [sosla'jar] *v* place obliquely; dodge; avoid. **soslayo** *adj* oblique.

soso ['soso] *adj* tasteless; dull.

sospechar [sospe'tʃar] *v* suspect. **sospecha** *sf* suspicion. **sospechoso** *adj* suspicious, suspect.

*****sostener** [soste'ner] *v* support; sustain. **sostén** *sm* support; brassière. **sostenedor, -a** *sm, sf* supporter. **sostenido** *adj* sustained; constant.

sota ['sota] *sf* (*deporte*) jack; (*fam*) hussy.

sotana [so'tana] *sf* cassock.

sótano ['sotano] *sm* basement, cellar.

soto ['soto] *sm* thicket, copse.

soviet [so'βjet] *sm* Soviet. **soviético** *adj* Soviet.

spaghettis [spa'getis] *sm pl* spaghetti *sing*.

su [su] *adj* his; her; its; your; their; one's.

suave ['swaβe] *adj* smooth; soft; mild. **suavidad** *sf* smoothness; softness. **suavizar** *v* soften; smooth; strop.

*****subarrendar** [suβarren'dar] *v* sublet, sublease. **subarriendo** *sm* subletting.

subasta [su'βasta] *sf* auction. **subastar** *v* auction.

subcampeón [subkam'pjon], **-ona** *sm, sf* runner-up.

subconsciencia [subkons'θjenθja] *sf* subconscious. **subconsciente** *adj* subconscious.

subdesarrollado [suβðesarro'ʎaðo] *adj* underdeveloped. **subdesarrollo** *sm* underdevelopment.

súbdito ['suβðito] *sm* subject, citizen.

subdividir [suβðiβi'ðir] *v* subdivide. **subdivisión** *sf* subdivision.

subir [su'βir] *v* climb; go up; rise; lift; promote. **subir al coche** get into the car. **subirse** *v* rise; become conceited. **subida** *sf* ascent. **subido** *adj* (*color*) bright.

súbito ['suβito] *adj* sudden. *adv* suddenly.

subjuntivo [subxun'tiβo] *sm* (*gram*) subjunctive.

sublevar [suβle'βar] *v* incite to rebellion. **sublevarse** *v* rebel. **sublevación** *sf* rebellion.

sublime [su'βlime] *adj* sublime, lofty. **sublimación** *sf* sublimation. **sublimidad** *sf* sublimity.

submarino [suβma'rino] *adj* underwater. *sm* submarine.

subordinado [suβorði'naðo] *adj* subordinate. **subordinar** *v* subordinate.

subproducto [suβpro'ðukto] *sm* by-product.

subrayar [suβra'jar] *v* underline, underscore; emphasize. **subrayado** *sm* underlining; emphasis.

subsanar [suβsa'nar] *v* excuse; redeem.

subscribir [suβskri'βir] *v* subscribe; sign. **subscripción** *sf* subscription.

*****subseguir** [suβse'gir] *v* follow. **subsiguiente** *adj* subsequent.

subsidiario [suβsi'ðjarjo] *adj* subsidiary.

subsidio [suβ'siðjo] *sm* subsidy, grant, allowance.

subsistir [suβsis'tir] *v* subsist; exist. **subsistencia** *sf* permanence; subsistence. **subsistente** *adj* subsisting.

substancia [suβ'staθja] *sf* substance. **en substancia** briefly. **substancial** *adj* substantial. **substanciar** *v* summarize; substantiate. **substancioso** *adj* substantial.

*****substituir** [suβstitu'ir] *v* substitute. **substitución** *sf* substitution. **substitutivo** *adj* substitute.

*****substraer** [suβstra'er] *v* subtract; remove; steal. **substraerse** *v* evade; withdraw. **substracción** *sf* subtraction; stealing.

subterfugio [suβter'fuxjo] *sm* subterfuge.

subterráneo [suβter'raneo] *adj* subterranean.

subtítulo [suβ'titulo] *sm* subtitle.

suburbio [suβ'urβjo] *sm* outskirts *pl*; slum. **suburbano** *adj* suburban.

subvención [suββen'θjon] *sf* subsidy. **subvencionar** *v* subsidize.

subvertir [suββer'tir] v subvert. subversión sf subversion. subversivo adj subversive.

subyugar [suβju'gar] v subjugate. subyugación sf subjugation.

suceder [suθe'ðer] v succeed; follow; happen. sucedido sm event. sucediente adj following. sucesión sf succession; offspring. sucesivamente adv successively. sucesivo adj successive. en lo sucesivo hereafter. suceso sm event; outcome.

suciedad [suθje'ðað] sf dirt, dirtiness. sucio adj dirty; vile, mean.

sucinto [su'θinto] adj succinct, brief.

sucumbir [sukum'bir] v succumb.

sucursal [sukur'sal] sm branch.

sud [suð] adj, sm south.

sudamericano [suðameri'kano], -a s, adj South American.

sudar [su'ðar] v sweat. sudar tinta (fam) sweat blood. sudor sm sweat. sudoroso adj sweaty.

sudeste [su'ðeste] adj, sm south-east.

sudoeste [suðo'este] sm, adj south-west.

Suecia ['sweθja] sf Sweden.

sueco ['sweko], -a sm, sf Swede. sm (idioma) Swedish. adj Swedish.

suegro ['swegro] sm father-in-law.

suela ['swela] sf (de zapato) sole. suelas sf pl sandals pl.

sueldo ['swelðo] sm salary; wage; pay. a sueldo paid.

suelo ['swelo] sm ground; soil; floor. echar al suelo demolish.

suelto ['swelto] adj free; loose; separate; agile.

sueño ['sweɲo] sm dream; sleep. tener sueño be sleepy.

suero ['swero] sm serum; whey.

suerte ['swerte] sf luck; fate; chance; kind; manner; quality. ¡buena suerte! good luck! de otra suerte otherwise. de tal suerte que in such a way that.

suéter ['sweter] sm sweater.

suficiencia [sufi'θjenθja] sf sufficiency; ability; self-importance. suficiente adj sufficient; capable.

sufragar [sufra'gar] v help; finance. sufragar por vote for. sufragio sm suffrage.

sufrir [suf'rir] v suffer; endure. sufrido adj long-suffering. sufrimiento sm suffering; patience.

*sugerir [suxe'rir] v suggest, hint. sugerencia sf suggestion. sugerente adj suggestive. sugestión sf suggestion. sugestionable adj suggestible. sugestionar v influence. sugestivo adj suggestive; stimulating.

suicidarse [swiθi'ðarse] v commit suicide. suicida s(m+f) (persona) suicide. suicidio sm suicide.

Suiza ['swiθa] sf Switzerland. swizo, -a s, adj Swiss.

sujetar [suxe'tar] v secure; hold; fasten; seize; tie; restrain; subordinate. sujetarse v hang on; hold up; subject oneself to; abide by. sujerción sf subjection; control. sujetapapeles sm invar paperclip. sujeto sm subject; individual.

sumar [su'mar] v add, add up. sumarse v join in. suma sf sum; summary; essence. en suma in short. sumadora sf adding machine. sumamente adv extremely. sumaria sf (jur) indictment. sumario sm summary.

sumergir [sumer'xir] v submerge, plunge. sumersión sf submersion.

suministrar [suminis'trar] v supply, provide. suministro sm supply. suministros sm pl supplies pl, provisions pl.

sumir [su'mir] v submerge; sink.

sumisión [sumi'sjon] sf submission. sumiso adj submissive.

sumo ['sumo] adj greatest; supreme. tribunal supremo sm supreme court.

suntuoso [sun'twoso] adj sumptuous. suntuosidad sf sumptuousness.

supeditar [supeði'tar] v subdue, subordinate. supeditación sf subjection.

superar [supe'rar] v surpass; overcome. superable adj surmountable. superación sf overcoming.

superávit [supe'raβit] sm surplus.

superchería [supertʃe'ria] sf fraud; swindle.

superficial [superfi'θjal] adj superficial. superficie sf surface; area.

superfluo [super'fluo] adj superfluous. superfluidad sf superfluity.

superior [supe'rjor] adj better; superior. sm superior.

superlativo [superla'tiβo] adj superlative.

supermercado [supermer'kaðo] sm supermarket.

supersecreto [superse'kreto] adj top secret.

superstición [supersti'θjon] *sf* superstition. **supersticioso** *adj* superstitious.
supervivencia [superβi'βenθja] *sf* survival. **superviviente** *s(m+f)* survivor.
supino [su'pino] *adj* supine.
suplantar [suplan'tar] *v* supplant; forge.
suplemento [suple'mento] *sm* supplement. **suplementario** *adj* supplementary; extra. **horas suplementarias** *sf pl* overtime *sing.*
suplente [su'plente] *s, adj* substitute.
súplica ['suplika] *sf* supplication; petition. **suplicación** *sf* supplication; wafer biscuit. **suplicante** *s(m+f)* supplicant. **suplicar** *v* implore; beseech.
suplicio [su'pliθjo] *sm* torture.
suplir [su'plir] *v* make up for; substitute.
***suponer** [supo'ner] *v* suppose; believe; mean; guess. **suposición** *sf* supposition; slander.
supremo [su'premo] *adj* supreme. **supremacía** *sf* supremacy.
suprimir [supri'mir] *v* suppress; delete; omit; eliminate. **supresión** *sf* suppression; deletion.
supuesto [su'pwesto] *adj* supposed; so-called; hypothetical; feigned. **¡por supuesto!** of course! **supuesto que** since; if. *sm* hypothesis (*pl* -ses).
sur [sur] *adj* southern. *sm* south.
surcar [sur'kar] *v* plough; cleave.
surgir [sur'xir] *v* rise; spring forth; appear; anchor. **surgidero** *sm* anchorage.
surrealista [surreal'ista] *s(m+f)* surrealist. **surrealismo** *sm* surrealism.
surtido [sur'tiðo] *adj* assorted. **bien surtido** well stocked. *sm* stock; range; assortment. **surtidor** *sm* jet; fountain; petrol pump. **surtir** *v* supply. **surtir un pedido** fill an order.
susceptibilidad [susθeptiβili'ðað] *sf* susceptibility. **susceptible** *adj* susceptible.
suscitar [susθi'tar] *v* agitate, stir up. **suscitar interés** arouse interest.
suscribir *V* **subscribir**.
susodicho [suso'ðitʃo] *adj* aforementioned.
suspender [suspen'der] *v* suspend; adjourn; hang; fail; interrupt. **suspensión** *sf* suspension. **suspenso** *sm* (*examen*) failure.
suspicacia [suspi'kaθja] *sf* suspicion; misgiving. **suspicaz** *adj* suspicious.
suspirar [suspi'rar] *v* sigh. **suspirado** *adj* longed for, wished for. **suspiro** *sm* sigh.

sustancia *V* **substancia**.
sustentar [susten'tar] *v* sustain; maintain. **sustentamiento** *sm* sustenance; maintenance. **sustento** *sm* sustenance.
***sustituir** *V* **substituir**.
susto ['susto] *sm* fright. **dar susto a** frighten.
susurrar [susur'rar] *v* whisper; murmur. **susurrarse** *v* be rumoured. **susurrante** *adj* whispering. **susurro** *sm* whisper; murmur.
sutil [su'til] *adj* subtle; sharp; slender; delicate. **sutileza** *sf* subtlety; thinness; sharpness. **sutilizar** *v* thin down; polish; sharpen.
sutura [su'tura] *sf* suture.
suyo ['sujo] *adj* of his; of hers; of yours; of theirs. *pron* his; hers; yours; its; theirs. **lo suyo** one's share. **muy suyo** typical of one.

T

tabaco [ta'βako] *sm* tobacco. **tabacalero, -a** *sm, sf* tobacconist.
tábano ['taβano] *sm* horsefly.
taberna [ta'βerna] *sf* tavern; public house.
tabique [ta'βike] *sm* partition; dividing wall. **tabicar** *v* wall up.
tabla ['taβla] *sf* board, plank; tablet; slab; index; vegetable plot. **tablas** *sf pl* (*teatro*) stage *sing.* **pisar las tablas** go on the stage. **tablado** *sm* wooden platform; bedstead; gallows. **tablaje** *sm* boards *pl.* **tablajería** *sf* gambling. **tablear** *vb* saw into planks. **tablero** *sm* planking; blackboard; gambling den. **tableta** *sf* tablet. **tablilla** *sf* notice-board. **tablón** *sm* beam.
tabú [ta'βu] *sm* taboo.
tabular [tabu'lar] *adj* tabular. *v* tabulate.
taburete [taβu'rete] *sm* stool.
tacaño [ta'kaɲo] *adj* mean, stingy. **tacañería** *sf* meanness.
tácito ['taθito] *adj* tacit. **taciturnidad** *sf* taciturnity. **taciturno** *adj* taciturn.
taco ['tako] *sm* wad; plug; billiard cue; draught; oath. **soltar un taco** utter an oath.

tacón [ta'kon] *sm* heel. **taconazo** *sm* blow *or* tap with the heel.
tacto ['takto] *sm* touch; sense of touch; tact.
tachar [ta'tʃar] *v* accuse; erase. **tacha** *sf* fault; tack, small nail. **poner tacha** find fault. **tachón** *sm* (*carpintería*) stud. **tachonado** *adj* studded. **tachonar** *v* stud. **tachoso** *adj* defective. **tachuela** *sf* small tack.
tahona [ta'ona] *sf* bakery.
taimado [tai'maðo] *adj* sly, crafty; sullen.
tajar [ta'xar] *v* cut; hew; cleave. **taja** *sf* incision. **tajada** *sf* slice. **sacar tajada** profit. **tajadero** *sm* chopping-block. **tajador** *sm* chopper.
tal [tal] *adj* such; such a. **el tal** that fellow. **tal como** such as. **tal vez** perhaps. *pron* someone; such a person *or* thing. **como tal** as such. *adv* so; as though.
taladrar [tala'ðrar] *v* bore, drill. **taladro** *sm* bore, drill.
talante [ta'lante] *sm* mood; look; grace. **de buen/mal talante** in a good/bad mood.
talar[1] [ta'lar] *v* cut down, fell.
talar[2] *adj* full-length.
talco ['talko] *sm* tinsel; talcum powder.
talega [ta'lega] *sf* money bag; nappy.
talento [ta'lento] *sm* talent. **talentoso** *adj* talented. **talentudo** *adj* over-talented.
talón [ta'lon] *sm* heel; counterfoil; voucher; coupon.
talud [ta'luð] *sm* slope.
tallar [ta'ʎar] *v* carve; appraise; deal cards.
tallarín [taʎa'rin] *sm* noodle.
talle ['taʎe] *sm* figure; waist.
taller [ta'ʎer] *sm* workshop; studio.
tallo ['taʎo] *sm* stem, stalk.
tamaño [ta'maɲo] *sm* size. **de tamaño natural** life-size.
tambalearse [tambale'arse] *v* stagger; wobble; sway.
también [tam'bjen] *adv* also, too.
tambor [tam'bor] *sm* drum. **tambor-mayor** drum major.
Támesis ['tamesis] *sm* Thames.
tamiz [ta'miθ] *sm* sieve. **pasar por tamiz** sift.
tampoco [tam'poko] *adv* neither.
tan [tan] *adv* so. **tan siquiera** even if only.
tanda ['tanda] *sf* turn; shift; relay; gang.
tangente [tan'xente] *sm, adj* tangent.

tangerina [tanxe'rina] *sf* tangerine.
tangible [tan'xiβle] *adj* tangible.
tanque ['tanke] *sm* tank.
tantear [tante'ar] *v* try; test; sound; keep score. **tantearse** *v* think carefully. **tanteo** *sm* calculation; score.
tanto ['tanto] *adj* as much; so much; as great; so great. *adv* so much; as much; so; thus. **tanto como** as much as. **por lo tanto** therefore. *sm* amount; sum. **otro tanto** as much again.
***tañer** [ta'ɲer] *v* (*música*) play. **tañido** *sm* tune; twanging.
tapacubo [tapa'kuβo] *sm* hub-cap.
tapar [ta'par] *v* cover up; plug; cap; cork. **tapa** *sf* lid; cover. **tapadero** *sm* stopper. **taparrabo** *sm* loincloth. **tapón** *sm* cork; stopper.
tapia ['tapja] *sf* garden wall. **tapiar** *v* wall up.
tapicería [tapiθe'ria] *sf* tapestry; upholstery. **tapicero, -a** *sm, sf* upholsterer. **tapiz** *sm* tapestry. **tapizar** *v* hang with tapestry; upholster.
taquigrafía [takigra'fia] *sf* shorthand. **taquígrafo, -a** *sm, sf* stenographer.
taquilla [ta'kiʎa] *sf* box office; till.
tararear [tarare'ar] *v* hum.
tardar [tar'ðar] *v* delay; take a long time. **tardanza** *sf* slowness.
tarde ['tarðe] *sf* afternoon; evening. *adv* late. **se hace tarde** it's getting late. **tardecer** *v* grow late.
tarea [ta'rea] *sf* task; homework.
tarifa [ta'rifa] *sf* tariff; price list; rate.
tarima [ta'rima] *sf* stand; platform.
tarjeta [tar'xeta] *sf* card. **tarjeta postal** postcard.
tarro ['tarro] *sm* jar.
tarta ['tarta] *sf* cake, tart.
tartamudear [tartamuðe'ar] *v* stammer, stutter. **tartamudeo** *sm* stammer, stutter. **tartamudo, -a** *sm, sf* stutterer.
tasar [ta'sar] *v* appraise; value. **tasa** *sf* rate; valuation. **sin tasa** without limit. **tasación** *sf* valuation.
tatarabuelo [tatara'βwelo] *sm* great-great-grandfather. **tatarabuela** *sf* great-great-grandmother.
tatuaje [ta'twaxe] *sm* tattoo. **tatuar** *v* tattoo.
tauromaquia [tauro'makja] *sf* bullfighting.
taxidermia [taksi'ðermja] *sf* taxidermy. **taxidermista** *s(m+f)* taxidermist.

taxi ['taksi] *sm* taxi. **taxímetro** *sm* taximeter. **taxista** *s(m+f)* taxi-driver.

taza ['taθa] *sf* cup.

te [te] *pron* you; to you; yourself; to yourself.

té [te] *sm* tea.

teatro [te'atro] *sm* theatre. **teátrico** *adj* theatrical. **teatrero. -a** *sm. sf* theatregoer.

tecla ['tekla] *sf* key. **teclado** *sm* keyboard. **teclear** *v* strum; try.

técnica ['teknika] *sf* technique. **técnico. -a** *sm. sf* technician. **tecnología** *sf* technology. **tecnólogo. -a** *sm. sf* technologist.

techado [te'tʃaðo] *sm* roof; ceiling. **bajo techado** under cover. **techar** *v* put a roof on. **techo** *sm* roof; ceiling.

tedio ['teðjo] *sm* tedium. **tedioso** *adj* tedious.

teja ['texa] *sf* tile. **tejado** *sm* tiled roof. **tejar** *v* tile. **tejaroz** *sm* eaves *pl*.

tejer [te'xer] *v* knit; weave. **tejedor. -a** *sm. sf* weaver. **tejedura** *sf* texture; weaving.

tejón [te'xon] *sm* (*zool*) badger.

tela ['tela] *sf* cloth; material. **tela de araña** spider's web. **telar** *sm* loom.

telaraña [tele'raɲa] *sf* cobweb.

telefonear [telefone'ar] *v* telephone. **teléfono** *sm* telephone.

telegrafiar [telegra'fjar] *v* telegraph. **telegrafia** *sf* telegraphy. **telégrafo** *sm* telegraph.

telegrama [tele'grama] *sm* telegram.

telemando [tele'mando] *sm* remote control.

telepatía [telepa'tia] *sf* telepathy. **telepático** *adj* telepathic.

telescopio [tele'skopjo] *sm* telescope. **telescópico** *adj* telescopic.

telestudio [tele'stuðjo] *sm* television studio.

televisión [teleβi'sjon] *sf* television. **televisar** *v* televise. **televisor** *sm* television set.

telina [te'lina] *sf* clam.

telón [te'lon] *sm* curtain. **telón de acero** Iron Curtain.

tema ['tema] *sm* theme. **temático** *adj* thematic.

*****temblar** [tem'blar] *v* tremble. shiver. shake. **temblor** *sm* shudder. **temblor de tierra** earthquake. **tembloroso** *adj* trembling. shuddering.

temer [te'mer] *v* fear. be afraid. **temeridad** *sf* temerity. **temeroso** *adj* fearful. **temor** *sm* fear.

temperamento [tempera'mento] *sm* temperament. nature. **temperancia** *sf* temperance. **temperar** *v* temper.

temperatura [tempera'tura] *sf* temperature.

tempestad [tempes'taθ] *sf* storm. **tempestuoso** *adj* stormy.

templar [tem'plar] *v* temper; moderate. **templado** *adj* temperate.

temple ['temple] *sm* temperature; mood; distemper. **pintura al temple** *sf* painting in distemper.

templo ['templo] *sm* temple.

temporada [tempo'raða] *sf* space of time. season. period.

temporal [tempo'ral] *adj also* **temporáneo** temporary; temporal, worldly, secular. *sm* bad weather.

temprano [tem'prano] *adj. adv* early.

tenaz [te'naθ] *adj* tenacious. **tenacidad** *sf* tenacity. **tenazas** *sf pl* pincers pl.

tendedero [tende'ðero] *sm* clothes line; place for drying clothes.

tendencia [ten'denθja] *sf* tendency.

*****tender** [ten'der] *v* spread out; extend; hang up; lay; set.

tendero [ten'dero]. **-a** *sm. sf* shopkeeper.

tendón [ten'don] *sm* (*anat*) tendon.

tenebroso [tene'βroso] *adj* dark, gloomy. **tenebrosidad** *sf* gloom.

tenedor [tene'ðor] *sm* fork; holder. **tenedor de libros** bookkeeper. **teneduría** *sf* bookkeeping.

tenencia [te'nenθja] *sf* tenancy. occupancy; tenure.

*****tener** [te'ner] *v* have; possess; hold; spend. **tener en mucho** esteem. **tener para sí** think. **tener puesto** wear.

tenería [tene'ria] *sf* tannery.

tenia ['tenja] *sf* tapeworm.

teniente [te'njente] *sm* lieutenant. **teniente coronel** *sm* lieutenant-colonel.

tenis ['tenis] *sm* tennis.

tenor[1] ['tenor] *sm* tenor.

tenor[2] *sm* meaning. purport.

tenso ['tenso] *adj* tense. taut. **tensión** *sf* tension. **tensión arterial** blood pressure.

*****tentar** [ten'tar] *v* tempt; feel; attempt; examine. **tentación** *sf* temptation. **tentador** *sm* tempter. **tentadora** *sf* temptress. **tentativa** *sf* attempt. **tentativo** *adj* tentative.

tentáculo [ten'takulo] *sm* tentacle.
tentempié [tentempi'e] *sm* (*fam*) snack.
tenue ['tenwe] *adj* tenuous: faint: subdued. **tenuidad** *sf* slightness.
*teñir [te'ɲir] *v* dye. stain. colour. **teñidura** *sf* dyeing.
teología [teolo'xia] *sf* theology. **teólogo** *sm* theologian.
teorema [teo'rema] *sf* theorem.
teoría [teo'ria] *sf* theory. **teórico** *adj* theoretical. **teorizar** *v* theorize.
teosofía [teoso'fia] *sf* theosophy.
tercero [ter'θero] *adj. sm* third.
terapéutico [tera'peutiko] *adj* therapeutic. **teurapéutica** *sf* therapeutics.
terciar [ter'θjar] *v* tilt sideways: divide into three: mediate. **tercio** *adj* third.
terciopelo [terθjo'pelo] *sm* velvet. **terciopelado** *adj* velvety.
terco ['terko] *adj* stubborn.
tergiversar [terxiβer'sar] *v* misrepresent: distort. **tergiversación** *sf* distortion.
terminar [termi'nar] *v* finish. end: complete. **terminación** *sf* end. **terminal** *adj* terminal. **terminante** *adj* decisive. **terminología** *sf* terminology.
término ['termino] *sm* end. **dar termino a** bring to an end. **termino medio** average.
termita [ter'mita] *sf also* **termite** *sm* termite.
termo ['termo] *sm* vacuum flask.
termodinámica [termoði'namika] *sf* thermodynamics.
termómetro [ter'mometro] *sm* thermometer.
termonuclear [termonukle'ar] *adj* thermonuclear.
termostato [termo'stato] *sm* thermostat.
ternero [ter'nero] *sm* calf: veal.
terneza [ter'neθa] *sf* tenderness: endearment.
ternilla [ter'niʎa] *sf* gristle.
terquedad [terke'ðað] *sf* stubbornness. obstinacy.
terraplén [terra'plen] *sm* terrace: embankment.
terraza [ter'raθa] *sf* terrace.
terremoto [terre'moto] *sm* earthquake.
terreno [ter'reno] *sm* terrain: land. **ceder terreno** give ground.
terrestre [ter'restre] *adj* terrestrial.
terrible [ter'riβle] *adj* terrible. **terrífico** *adj* terrifying.
territorial [territo'rjal] *adj* territorial. **territorio** *sm* territory.

terrón [ter'ron] *sm* lump of sugar: clod of earth.
terror [ter'ror] *sm* terror. **terrorismo** *sm* terrorism. **terrorista** *s(m+f)* terrorist.
terso ['terso] *adj* smooth: glossy: polished. **tersar** *v* smooth. **tersura** *sf* smoothness.
tertulia [ter'tulja] *sf* social gathering: company.
tesis ['tesis] *sf invar* thesis.
tesón [te'son] *sm* tenacity: persistence: inflexibility. **tesonería** *sf* doggedness.
tesoro [te'soro] *sm* treasure. **tesorería** *sf* treasury. **tesorero. -a** *sm. sf* treasurer.
testa ['testa] *sf* head.
testar [tes'tar] *v* make a will. **testamento** *sm* will. testament.
testarudo [testa'ruðo] *adj* stubborn. obstinate. **testarudez** *sf* obstinacy.
testificar [testifi'kar] *v* testify: witness. **testigo** *sm* witness. **testimonial** *adj* bearing witness. **testimoniar** *v* bear witness to. **testimonio** *sm* witness: testimony.
testículo [tes'tikulo] *sm* testicle.
teta ['teta] *sf* teat. nipple: mammary gland: udder.
tetera [te'tera] *sf* teapot.
tétrico ['tetriko] *adj* gloomy: grave: sullen.
textil [teks'til] *sm. adj* textile.
texto ['teksto] *sm* text: textbook.
textura [teks'tura] *sf* texture.
tez [teθ] *sf* complexion. skin.
ti [ti] *pron* (*fam*) you. **de ti para mi** between you and me.
tía ['tia] *sf* aunt: old mother: (*fam*) tart. **no hay tu tía** nothing doing.
tibio ['tiβjo] *adj* lukewarm. **tibieza** *sf* tepidity.
tiburón [tiβu'ron] *sm* shark.
tiempo ['tjempo] *sm* time: weather: (*gram*) tense. **al poco tiempo** soon after. **tiempo atrás** some time ago. **tiempo de perros** filthy weather.
tienda ['tjenda] *sf* shop. store: tent. **tienda de modas** boutique.
tienta ['tjenta] *sf* probe. **andar a tientas** feel one's way.
tiento ['tjento] *sm* feel. tough: tact. **a tiento** by touch.
tierno ['tjerno] *adj* tender: fresh. **pan tierno** fresh bread.
tierra ['tjerra] *sf* earth: land: country: ground. **echar por tierra** wreck. **tierra vegetal** topsoil.

tieso ['tjeso] *adj* stiff; firm. **adv** strongly. **tiesura** *sf* stiffness.

tiesto ['tjesto] *sm* flower pot.

tifo ['tifo] *sm* typhus.

tifoideo [tifoi'ðeo] *adj* typhoid. **fiebre tifoidea** *sf* typhoid fever.

tifón [ti'fon] *sm* typhoon.

tigre ['tigre] *sm* tiger.

tijeras [ti'xeras] *sf pl* scissors; shears.

tilín [ti'lin] *sm* ting-a-ling. **en un tilín** in a flash.

tilo ['tilo] *sm* lime, linden tree.

timar [ti'mar] *v* cheat. **timador** *sm* swindler.

timbrar [tim'brar] *v* stamp; seal. **timbre** *sm* bell; postage stamp.

tímido ['timiðo] *adj* timid. **timidez** *sf* timidity.

timo ['timo] *sm* cheat; swindle.

timón [ti'mon] *sm* helm; rudder. **timonear** *v* (*mar*) steer. **timonero** *sm* helmsman.

tímpano ['timpano] *sm* (*anat*) eardrum; (*música*) kettledrum.

tina ['tina] *sf* tub. **tinaja** *sf* large earthen jar.

tinglado [tin'glaðo] *sm* shed; platform.

tinieblas [ti'njeβlas] *sf pl* darkness *sing*; (*fig*) confusion *sing*.

tino ['tino] *sm* tact; moderation; skill. **sin tino** stupidly.

tinta ['tinta] *sf* ink; hue, colour. **tinte** *sm* dye; stain; shade. **tintero** *sm* inkstand, inkwell. **tintorería** *sf* dyeing; dry-cleaning. **tintorero, -a** *sm, sf* dyer; dry-cleaner. **tintura** dye; rouge.

tintín [tin'tin] *sm* tinkle. **tintinear** *v* tinkle.

tinto ['tinto] *adj* dyed. **vino tinto** *sm* red wine.

tiña ['tiɲa] *sf* ringworm.

tío ['tio] *sm* uncle.

tiovivo [tjo'βiβo] *sm* merry-go-round.

típico ['tipiko] *adj* typical; characteristic.

tiple ['tiple] *sm* (*música*) treble. *sf* soprano.

tipo ['tipo] *sm* type, pattern; model; standard; (*fam*) fellow. **tipo de cambio** rate of exchange.

tipografía [tipogra'fia] *sf* printing. **tipógrafo** *sm* printer.

tira ['tira] *sf* long strip, band.

tirada [ti'raða] *sf* throw; stretch; circulation. **tirador** *sm* marksman; handle.

tirado [ti'raðo] *adj* streamlined; (*fam*) dead easy; (*fam*) dirt cheap.

tiranía [tira'nia] *sf* tyranny. **tirano, -a** *sm, sf* tyrant. **tiranizar** *v* tyrannize.

tirante [ti'rante] *adj* taut. **tirantez** *sf* tautness.

tirar [ti'rar] *v* throw, fling; pull. **tirar por una calle** turn down a street.

tiritar [tiri'tar] *v* shiver. **tiritón** *sm* shiver.

tiro ['tiro] *sm* throw; shot; discharge; report; blow; practical joke. **tiro al blanco** target practice.

tiroides [ti'rojðes] *sm* thyroid.

tirón [ti'ron] *sm* haul, jerk; cramp; tyro, beginner. **de un tirón** straight off.

tiroteo [tiro'teo] *sm* firing, crossfire. **tirotear** *v* snipe at.

tisis ['tisis] *sf* tuberculosis.

títere ['titere] *sm* puppet; marionette.

titubear [tituβe'ar] *v* vacillate; totter, stagger; stammer. **titubeo** *sm* staggering; hesitation.

título ['titulo] *sm* title; license, diploma; degree. **titular** *adj* titular.

tiza ['tiθa] *sf* chalk.

tiznar [tiθ'nar] *v* stain, tarnish. **tiznado** *adj* stained, grimy. **tiznajo** *sm* smudge.

toalla [to'aʎa] *sf* towel. **toalla de baño** bathtowel. **toallero** *sm* towel-rail.

tobillo [to'βiʎo] *sm* ankle.

tobagán [toβa'gan] *sm* slide; chute.

tocadiscos [toka'ðiskos] *sm invar* record-player.

tocado [to'kaðo] *sm* coiffure.

tocador [toka'ðor] *sm* dressing-table.

tocar [to'kar] *v* touch; feel; (*música*) play; belong; concern; border on; be one's turn. **tocarse** *v* put on one's hat.

tocino [to'θino] *sm* bacon; salt pork.

todavía [toða'βia] *adv* yet, still; nevertheless. **todavía más** even more.

todo ['toðo] *adj* all; entire; every; each. **todo el mundo** everybody. **todo o nada** all or nothing.

toldo ['toldo] *sm* awning.

tolerar [tole'rar] *v* tolerate; bear. **tolerable** *adj* tolerable. **tolerancia** *sf* tolerance. **tolerante** *adj* tolerant.

tomar [to'mar] *v* take; hold; get; gather. **tomarse** *v* get rusty. **tomada** *sf* capture. **tomadura** *sf* taking.

tomate [to'mate] *sm* tomato. **tomatera** *sf* tomato plant.

tomillo [to'miʎo] *sm* thyme.

tomo ['tomo] *sm* tome, volume; bulk.

ton [ton] *sm* motive; occasion. **sin ton ni son** without rhyme or reason.

tonada [to'naða] *sf* song. **tonalidad** *sf* tonality.

tonel [to'nel] *sm* cask, barrel.

tonelada [tone'laða] *sf* ton. **tonelaje** *sm* tonnage.

tónico ['toniko] *sm, adj* (*música*) tonic. **tonificar** *v* (*med*) tone up.

tono ['tono] *sm* (*música*) pitch; tone; manner. **darse tono** put on airs.

tontería [tonte'ria] *sf* foolishness, nonsense. **tonto** *adj* foolish, silly; stupid; ignorant.

topacio [to'paθjo] *sm* topaz.

topar [to'par] *v* collide with; strike against; encounter; meet by chance.

tope ['tope] *sm* top, summit; end. **al tope** end to end.

tópico ['topiko] *sm* topic. *adj* topical.

topo ['topo] *sm* mole. **topera** *sf* molehill.

topografía [topogra'fia] *sf* topography. **topográfico** *adj* topographical.

toque ['toke] *sm* touch; peal of bells; test, trial.

tórax ['toraks] *sm* thorax.

torbellino [torβe'ʎino] *sm* whirlwind; whirlpool.

*torcer [tor'θer] *v* twist; turn; wrench; bend. **torcedura** *sf* twisting; sprain. **torcido** *adj* twisted; bent. **torcimiento** *sm* distortion.

tordo ['torðo] *sm* thrush.

torear [tore'ar] *v* fight the bull. **torero** *sm* bullfighter.

tormenta [tor'menta] *sf* storm. **tormentoso** *adj* stormy.

tormentar [tormen'tar] *v* torment. **tormento** *sm* torment; affliction; pain.

tornar [tor'nar] *v* turn; return; do again. **torna** *sf* return. **tornarse** *v* become.

tornasol [torna'sol] *sm* (*bot*) sunflower; litmus.

torneo [tor'neo] *sm* tournament.

tornillo [tor'niʎo] *sm* screw.

torniquete [torni'kete] *sm* tourniquet; turnstile.

toro ['toro] *sm* bull. **toros** *sm pl* bullfight.

toronja [to'ronxa] *sf* grapefruit.

torpe ['torpe] *adj* clumsy; indecent. **torpeza** *sf* clumsiness; indecency.

torpedo [tor'peðo] *sm* torpedo. **torpedero** *sm* torpedo-boat.

tórpido ['torpiðo] *adj* torpid. **torpor** *sm* torpor.

torre ['torre] *sf* tower.

torrente [tor'rente] *sm* torrent. **torrencial** *adj* torrential.

tórrido ['torriðo] *adj* torrid.

torta ['torta] *sf* cake; pie. **tortada** *sf* meat pie. **tortera** *sf* pie dish.

tortilla [tor'tiʎa] *sf* omelette.

tortuga [tor'tuga] *sf* tortoise; turtle.

tortura [tor'tura] *sf* torture. **tortuoso** *adj* tortuous.

tos [tos] *sf* cough. **tos ferina** whooping-cough. **toser** *v* cough.

tosco ['tosko] *adj* coarse; crude; clumsy. **tosquedad** *sf* roughness; crudeness.

*tostar [tos'tar] *v* toast; roast; tan. **tostada** *sf* piece of toast.

total [to'tal] *sm* total. **totalidad** *sf* totality. **totalitario** *adj* totalitarian. **totalizar** *v* total.

tóxico ['toksiko] *sm* poison. *adj* poisonous. **toxicar** *v* poison.

toxicómano [toksi'komano], **-a** *sm, sf* drug-addict. **toxicomanía** *sf* drug-addiction.

tozudo [to'θuðo] *adj* stubborn.

traba ['traβa] *sf* link; fetter; hindrance. **poner trabas** hinder. **trabadura** *sf* bond. **trabamiento** *sm* joining. **trabar** *v* join; fetter; strike up. **trabar amistad** become friends. **trabón** *sm* fetter.

trabajar [traβa'xar] *v* work; work on; elaborate; trouble; deal in. **trabajado** *adj* elaborate. **trabajador, -a** *sm, sf* worker. **trabajo** *sm* work; toil; exertion; hardship. **trabajoso** *adj* laborious.

trabalenguas [traβa'lengwas] *sm invar* tongue-twister.

tracción [trak'θjon] *sf* traction. **tractor** *sm* tractor.

tradición [traði'θjon] *sf* tradition. **tradicional** *adj* traditional.

*traducir [traðu'θir] *v* translate; interpret. **traducción** *sf* translation. **traductor, -a** *sm, sf* translator.

*traer [tra'er] *v* bring; carry; fetch; result in; wear. **traer a mal traer** treat roughly. **traer a cuento** mention. **traerse** *v* be dressed; behave.

traficar [trafi'kar] *v* trade; travel. **traficante** *s(m+f)* dealer. **tráfico** *sm* trade; traffic.

tragaluz [traga'luθ] *sf* skylight.

tragar [tra'gar] *v* swallow. **no puedo tragarle** I can't stand him. **tragadero** *sm* gullet. **trago** *sm* swallow; gulp.

tragedia [tra'xeðia] *sf* tragedy. **tragico** *adj* tragic.

traicionar [traiθjo'nar] *v* betray. **traición** *sf* treason; treachery. **traicionero** *adj* treacherous. **traidor, -a** *sm, sf* traitor.

traje ['traxe] *sm* dress; suit; costume. **traje de etiqueta** evening dress. **baile de trajes** *sm* fancy-dress ball.

trajín [tra'xin] *sm* haulage; coming and going. **trajinante** *sm* (*com*) carrier.

tramar [tra'mar] *v* weave; plan, plot. **trama** *sf* weft; plot.

tramitar [trami'tar] *v* negotiate, arrange. **tramitación** *sf* arrangements *pl*. **trámite** *sm* procedure; formality.

tramo ['tramo] *sm* (*puente*) span; (*escaleras*) flight; (*terreno*) strip.

trampa ['trampa] *sf* trap; trapdoor; fraud. **tramposo** *adj* deceitful.

trampear [trampe'ar] *v* defraud; scrape by. **trampeador, -a** *sm, sf* swindler.

trampolin [trampo'lin] *sm* ski jump; springboard.

trancar [tran'kar] *v* (*puerta*) bar; stride. **tranca** *sf* stick; club; (*fam*) drunkenness. **tranco** *sm* stride.

trance ['tranθe] *sm* trance; critical situation. **a todo trance** at all costs.

tranquilizar [trankili'θar] *v* tranquillize. **tranquilidad** *sf* tranquillity. **tranquilo** *adj* tranquil.

transacción [transak'θjon] *sf* transaction.

transatlántico [transat'lantiko] *adj* transatlantic. *sm* (*mar*) liner.

transbordar [transβor'ðar] *v* transfer. **transbordo** *sm* transfer.

transcribir [transkri'βir] *v* transcribe. **transcripción** *sf* transcription.

transcurrir [transkur'rir] *v* elapse. pass. **transcurso** *sm* course *or* lapse of time.

transeúnte [transe'unte] *adj* transitory, transient. *s*(*m+f*) transient, passer-by.

*****transferir** [transfe'rir] *v* transfer. **transferible** *adj* transferable.

transfigurar [transfigu'rar] *v* transfigure. **transfiguración** *sf* transfiguration.

transformar [transfor'mar] *v* transform. **transformación** *sf* transformation.

tránsfuga ['transfuga] *sm* deserter.

*****transgredir** [transgre'ðir] *v* transgress, violate. **transgresión** *sf* transgression. **transgresor, -a** *sm, sf* transgressor.

transición [transi'θjon] *sf* transition.

transido [tran'siðo] *adj* overwhelmed; stricken.

transigir [transi'xir] *v* compromise. **transigencia** *sf* tolerance. **transigente** *adj* tolerant.

transistor [transis'tor] *sm* transistor.

transitar [transi'tar] *v* travel; pass. **transitivo** *adj* (*gram*) transitive. **tránsito** *sm* transit; passage; transition. **transitorio** *adj* transitory.

transmitir [transmi'tir] *v* transmit. **transmisión** *sf* transmission. **transmisor** *sm* transmitter.

transparencia [transpa'renθja] *sf* transparency. **transparente** *adj* transparent.

transpirar [transpi'rar] *v* perspire; transpire. **transpiración** *sf* perspiration.

*****transponer** [transpo'ner] *v* transpose; transplant. **transponerse** *v* get down; get sleepy.

transportar [transpor'tar] *v* transport; (*música*) transpose. **transportarse** get carried away. **transporte** *sm* transport. **transposición** *sf* transposition.

tranvía [tran'βia] *sm* tramway; tram.

trapaza [tra'paθa] *sf* swindle, fraud; trick. **trapacear** *v* defraud. **trapacista** *s*(*m+f*) swindler.

trapecio [tra'peθjo] *sm* trapeze.

trapo ['trapo] *sm* rag. *pl* old clothes.

traquetear [trakete'ar] *v* shake up; rattle. **traqueteo** *sm* rattling; jolting.

tras [tras] *prep* after; behind; beyond. **tras de** in addition to.

*****trascender** [trasθen'der] *v* transcend; leak out; spread. **trascendencia** *sf* transcendence. **trascendental** *adj* momentous. **trascendente** *adj* transcendent.

*****trasegar** [trase'gar] *v* decant; upset.

trasero [tra'sero] *adj* rear. *sm* behind. **trasera** *sf* back; rear.

trasladar [trasla'ðar] *v* transfer; translate; postpone. **trasladarse** *v* go; move. **traslación** *sf* transfer; translation. **traslado** *sm* copy; transfer.

*****traslucirse** [traslu'θirse] *v* shine; show through. **traslúcido** *adj* translucent.

traslumbrar [traslum'brar] *v* dazzle.

trasmutar [trasmu'tar] *v* transmute. **trasmutación** *sf* transmutation.

trasnochar [trasno'tʃar] *v* be up all *or* most of the night.

traspasar [traspa'sar] *v* transfer; transfix; transgress. **traspasador, -a** *sm, sf* transgressor. **traspaso** *sm* transfer; transgression.

traspié [tras'pje] *sm* stumble.
trasplantar [trasplan'tar] *v* transplant.
trasplantarse *v* migrate. **trasplante** *sm*
transplant.
trasquilar [traski'lar] *v* shear, snip, clip.
trasquilado *adj* sheared; cropped.
traste ['traste] *sm* (*música*) fret. **ir al
traste** fall through, fail.
trasto ['trasto] *sm* tool; weapon; equipment; piece of furniture.
trastornar [trastor'nar] *v* upset; turn
upside down. **trastornado** *adj* unbalanced. **trastorno** *sm* upheaval; inconvenience.
trasunto [tra'sunto] *sm* copy, reproduction; likeness. **trasuntar** *v* copy.
tratar [tra'tar] *v* treat; deal with; handle.
tratable *adj* manageable. **tratamiento** *sm*
treatment. **trato** *sm* treatment; behaviour; bargain. **mal trato** ill-treatment.
través [tra'βes] *sm* slant; bias; reverse. **a
través de** across.
travesero [traβe'sero] *adj* transverse.
travesía *sf* crossroad.
travesura [traβe'sura] *sf* trick, prank.
traviesa [tra'βjesa] *sf* (*ferrocarril*) sleeper;
(*arq*) rafter; bet.
travieso [tra'βjeso] *adj* transverse, cross;
lively; mischievous. **a campo traviesa**
cross-country.
trayecto [tra'jekto] *sm* route; fare stage;
distance; way; itinerary. **trayectoria** *sf*
trajectory.
trazar [tra'θar] *v* draw; plot; trace;
design. **traza** *sf* sketch. **bien/mal trazado**
good/bad looking. **trazador, -a** *sm, sf*
designer.
trébol ['treβol] *sm* clover.
trece ['treθe] *adj, sm* thirteen.
trecho ['tretʃo] *sm* space; distance; lapse;
stretch.
tregua ['tregwa] *sf* truce; respite.
treinta ['treinta] *adj, sm* thirty.
tremendo [tre'mendo] *adj* tremendous.
trémulo ['tremulo] *adj* tremulous.
tren [tren] *sm* train. **tren botijo** excursion
train.
trenzar [tren'θar] *v* braid. **trenza** *sf* plait,
braid.
trementina [tremen'tina] *sf* turpentine.
trepar [tre'par] *v* climb. **trepa** *sf* climbing.
trepadoras *sf pl* climbing plants.
trepidar [trepi'ðar] *v* shake, tremble.
trepidación *sf* tremor.

tres [tres] *adj, sm* three.
triángulo [tri'angulo] *sm* triangle. **triangular** *adj* triangular.
tribu ['triβu] *sf* tribe.
tribuna [tri'βuna] *sf* tribune; gallery;
grandstand. **tribunal** *sm* tribunal.
tributar [triβu'tar] *v* pay. **tributable** *adj*
tributary. **tributación** *sf* tax. **tributante**
s(m + f) taxpayer. **tributo** *sm* tribute; tax.
triciclo [tri'θiklo] *sm* tricycle.
tricotar [triko'tar] *v* knit.
trigo ['trigo] *sm* wheat. **trigal** *sm*
wheatfield.
trigésimo [tri'xesimo] *adj* thirtieth.
trigonometría [trigonome'tria] *sf* trigonometry.
trillar [tri'ʎar] *v* thresh; beat. **trilla** *sf*
threshing. **trillador, -a** *sm, sf* threshing
machine.
trimestre [tri'mestre] *sm* three-month
term. **trimestral** *adj* quarterly.
trinar [tri'nar] *v* trill. **trinado** *sm* trill.
trincar [trin'kar] *v* break; bind; hold
down.
trinchar [trin'tʃar] *v* carve. **trinchante** *sm*
carving-knife. **trinchero** *adj* carving.
trinchera [trin'tʃera] *sf* trench.
trineo [tri'neo] *sm* sledge, sled, sleigh.
trinidad [trini'ðað] *sf* trinity.
trinitaria [trini'tarja] *sf* pansy.
tripa ['tripa] *sf* intestine. **tener malas
tripas** be cruel.
triple ['triple] *adj* triple.
trípode ['tripoðe] *sm* tripod.
tripulación [tripula'θjon] *sf* crew. **tripu-
lante** *sm* member of the crew.
triscar [tris'kar] *v* mingle; stamp; frisk.
trisca *sf* crunch.
triste ['triste] *adj* sad, mournful, gloomy.
tristeza *sf* sadness.
triturar [tritu'rar] *v* grind, crush. **tritura-
ción** *sf* grinding.
triunfar [triun'far] *v* triumph. **triunfador,
-a** *sm, sf* victor. **triunfal** *adj* triumphal.
triunfante *adj* triumphant. **triunfo** *sm* triumph.
trivial [tri'βjal] *adj* trivial. **trivialidad** *sf*
triviality.
triza ['triθa] *sf* shred; particle, fragment.
trocar [tro'kar] *v* exchange. **trocarse** *v*
change into. **trocamiento** *sm* exchange.
trochemoche [trotʃe'motʃe] *adv* higgledy-
piggledy.
trofeo [tro'feo] *sm* trophy.

trole ['trole] *sm* trolley.
tromba ['tromba] *sf* waterspout.
trombón [trom'bon] *sm* trombone.
trompa ['trompa] *sf* hunting horn; (*elefante*) trunk; proboscis.
trompada [trom'paða] *sf* bump; thump.
trompeta [trom'peta] *sf* trumpet. **trompetero** *sm* trumpeter.
*__tronar__ [tro'nar] *v* thunder. **tronada** *sf* thunderstorm. **tronante** *adj* thunderous. **tronido** *sm* thunderclap.
tronco ['tronko] *sm* tree trunk; stalk; stern.
tronchar [tron't∫ar] *v* bring down; break up.
trono ['trono] *sm* throne.
tropa ['tropa] *sf* troop.
tropel [tro'pel] *sm* crowd. **en tropel** in a rush. **tropelía** *sf* rush, hurry.
*__tropezar__ [trope'θar] *v* stumble; run into. **tropiezo** *sm* stumble.
trópico ['tropiko] *sm* tropic. **tropical** *adj* tropical.
trotar [tro'tar] *v* trot. **trote** *sm* trot.
trozo ['troθo] *sm* piece, fragment, bit.
truco ['truko] *sm* trick.
trucha ['trut∫a] *sf* trout; (*mec*) crane.
trueno [tru'eno] *sm* thunder.
trueque [tru'eke] *sm* exchange, barter.
trufa ['trufa] *sf* truffle.
truncar [trun'kar] *v* truncate, abridge. **truncado** *adj* truncated.
tu [tu] *adj* (*fam*) your.
tú [tu] *pron* (*fam*) you.
tubérculo [tu'βerkulo] *sm* tubercle; tuber. **tuberculosis** *sf* tuberculosis. **tuberculoso** *adj* tubercular.
tubo ['tuβo] *sm* tube, pipe. **tubería** *sf* tubing. **tubular** *adj* tubular.
tuerca ['twerka] *sf* (*mec*) nut. **tuerca a mariposa** wing nut.
tuerto ['twerto], -a *sm, sf* one-eyed person. *adj* one-eyed.
tuétano [tu'etano] *sm* (*anat*) marrow.
tufo ['tufo] *sm* vapour; fume; stench. **tufarada** *sf* whiff.
tul [tul] *sm* tulle.
tulipán [tuli'pan] *sm* tulip.
tullido [tu'λiðo] *adj* cripple. **tullirse** *v* be crippled.
tumba¹ ['tumba] *sf* tomb.
tumba² *sf* tumble. **tumbar** *v* knock down; tumble.
tumor [tu'mor] *sm* tumour.

tumulto [tu'multo] *sm* tumult. **tumultuoso** *adj* tumultuous.
tunante [tu'nante] *s(m+f)* rascal, crook. *adj* rascally. **tunantería** *sf* crookedness.
túnel ['tunel] *sm* tunnel.
túnica ['tunika] *sf* tunic.
tuno ['tuno] *sm* rogue.
tupé [tu'pe] *sm* toupee.
tupido [tu'piðo] *adj* thick; dense.
turba ['turβa] *sf* crowd; heap; peat. **turbal** *sm* peat bog.
turbante [tur'βante] *sm* turban.
turbar [tur'βar] *v* disturb. **turbarse** *v* be embarrassed.
turbina [tur'βina] *sf* turbine.
turbulento [turβu'lento] *adj* turbulent, disorderly. **turbulencia** *sf* turbulence.
turismo [tu'rismo] *sm* tourism. **turista** *s(m+f)* tourist.
turnar [tur'nar] *v* alternate, take turns. **turno** *sm* turn, shift. **por turno** in turn.
turón [tu'ron] *sm* polecat.
turquesa [tur'kesa] *sf* turquoise.
turrón [tur'ron] *sm* nougat.
tutear [tute'ar] *v* address as *tú*.
tutela [tu'tela] *sf* protection; tutelage. **tutelar** *adj* guardian.
tutor [tu'tor] *sm* tutor; guardian. **tutoría** *sf* guardianship.
tuyo ['tujo] *pron* (*fam*) yours; of yours.

U

u [u] *conj* or (before words beginning with *o* or *ho*).
ubicar [uβi'kar] *v* be situated; (*auto*) park. **ubicarse** *v* place oneself. **ubicuidad** *sf* ubiquity. **ubicuo** *adj* ubiquitous.
ubre ['uβre] *sf* udder.
ufanarse [ufa'narse] *v* boast. **ufano** *adj* proud, conceited. **ufanía** *sf* pride, arrogance.
ujier [u'xjer] *sm* usher.
úlcera ['ulθera] *sf* ulcer. **ulcerado** *adj* ulcerated.
ulterior [ulte'rjor] *adj* further, farther; ulterior. **ulteriormente** *adj* later.
ultimar [ulti'mar] *v* conclude, finish. **ultimación** *sf* conclusion. **últimamente**

adv finally; recently. **ultimátum** *sm* ultimatum. **último** *adj* last; latest. **por último** finally.
ultrajar [ultra'xar] *v* outrage; insult. **ultraje** *sm* outrage. **ultrajoso** *adj* outrageous.
ultramarino [ultrama'rino] *adj* overseas. **ultramar** *sm* overseas countries *pl.* **ir a ultramar** go abroad.
ultranza [ul'tranθa] *adv* **a ultranza** to the death; at all costs.
umbral [um'bral] *sm* threshold. **pisar los umbrales** cross the threshold.
umbrío [um'brio] *adj also* **umbroso** shady.
un [un] *art also* **una** a; one. *adj* one.
unánime [u'nanime] *adj* unanimous. **unanimidad** *sf* unanimity
unción [un'θjon] *sf* anointing, unction. **extremaunción** *sf* (*rel*) extreme unction.
uncir [un'θir] *v* yoke.
undécimo [un'deθimo], **-a** *s, adj* eleventh.
undoso [un'doso] *adj* wavy. **undulación** *sf* undulation. **undulante** *adj* undulating. **undular** *v* undulate.
ungir [un'xir] *v* anoint. **ungimiento** *sm* unction. **ungüento** *sm* ointment.
único ['uniko] *adj* only, sole, single; unique. **únicamente** *adv* only, solely.
unicornio [uni'kornjo] *sm* unicorn.
unidad [uni'ðað] *sf* unity; union; unit. **unido** *adj* united. **unificación** *sf* unification. **unificar** *v* unify.
uniformar [unifor'mar] *v* make uniform; standardize. **uniforme** *adj, sm* uniform. **uniformidad** *sf* uniformity.
unión [u'njon] *sf* union; unity; marriage. **unir** *v* join; mix. **unirse** *v* join; mingle.
Unión Soviética [u'njon so'βjetika] *sf* Soviet Union.
unísono [u'nisono] *adj* harmonious. **al unísono** in unison; unanimously.
universidad [uniβersi'ðað] *sf* university. **universitario** *adj* of a university.
universo [uni'βerso] *sm* universe. **universal** *adj* universal. **universalidad** *sf* universality.
uno ['uno] *adj* one; only. *pron* one; someone. **unos** *pron pl* some; a few. **unos y otros** all.
untar [un'tar] *v* grease; smear; stain; spread. **unto** *sm* grease; ointment.
uña ['uɲa] *sf* (*anat*) nail; talon, claw; hoof. **esconder las uñas** hide one's feelings. **uñero** *sm* ingrowing toenail.

uranio [u'ranjo] *sm* uranium.
urbano [ur'βano] *adj* urban; urbane. **urbanidad** *sf* urbanity. **urbanístico** *adj* urban. **urbanización** *sf* town planning. **urbe** *sf* large city.
urdir [ur'ðir] *v* warp; (*fig*) plot, scheme.
urgencia [ur'xenθja] *sf* urgency; emergency. **urgente** *adj* urgent. **urgir** *v* be urgent; urge. **me urge el tiempo** I am pressed for time.
urinario [uri'narjo] *sm* urinal.
urna ['urna] *sf* urn; ballot box.
urogallo [uro'gaʎo] *sm* (*zool*) grouse.
urraca [ur'raka] *sf* magpie.
usar [u'sar] *v* use; employ; be accustomed. **usado** *adj* used; worn. **usanza** *sf* custom; usage. **uso** *sm* use; wear; custom; enjoyment; fashion. **al uso de** in the style of.
usted [us'teð] *pron also* **Vd** you. **¡a usted!** thank you!
usual [u'swal] *adj* usual.
usufructo [u'sufrukto] *sm* use; enjoyment.
usura [u'sura] *sf* usury. **usurero, -a** *sm, sf* usurer.
usurpar [usur'par] *v* usurp. **usurpación** *sf* usurpation. **usurpador, -a** *sm, sf* usurper.
utensilio [uten'siljo] *sm* utensil; implement, tool.
útero ['utero] *sm* uterus. **uterino** *adj* uterine.
útil ['util] *sm* tool. *adj* useful; fit. **utilidad** *sf* utility, usefulness. **utilitario** *adj* utilitarian. **utilizar** *v* utilize, use.
uva ['uβa] *sf* grape. **uva pasa** raisin.

V

vaca ['βaka] *sf* cow; beef.
vacaciones [βaka'θjones] *sf pl* vacation *sing*; holidays *pl.* **irse de vacaciones** go on holiday.
vacante [βa'kante] *adj* vacant. *sf* vacancy. **vacar** *v* fall vacant.
vacilar [βaθi'lar] *v* hesitate. **vacilante** *adj* unstable, unsteady. **vacilación** *sf* vacillation.
vacío [βa'θio] *adj* empty. *sm* void; vacuum. **vaciar** *v* empty; pour out. **vacuo** *adj* empty; vacuous.

vacunar [βaku'nar] *v* vaccinate. **vacunación** *sf* vaccination.

vadear [βaðe'ar] *v* wade; surmount, overcome. **vadeable** *adj* fordable.

vagar [βa'gar] *v* wander, move about. *sm* leisure; ease. **vagabundo, -a** *sm, sf* vagabond. **vagante** *adj* vagrant.

vago ['βago] *adj* vague; indolent. *sm* tramp; loafer. **vaguedad** *sf* vagueness.

vagón [βa'gon] *sm* railway carriage; wagon. **vagón restaurante** dining-car. **vagoneta** *sf* small truck.

vahear [βae'ar] *v* steam. **vaho** *sm* vapour.

vahído [βa'iðo] *sm* vertigo, dizziness.

vaina ['βaina] *sf* sheath; scabbard; pod.

vainilla [βai'niʎa] *sf* vanilla.

vaivén [βai'βen] *sm* fluctuation; sway; swinging movement.

vajilla [βa'xiʎa] *sf* tableware, dishes *pl*.

vale ['βale] *sm* voucher; receipt; IOU.

valedero [βale'ðero] *adj* valid.

valentía [βalen'tia] *sf* valour, courage; brave *or* courageous act; bragging. **valentón, -ona** *sm, sf* braggart.

*****valer** [βa'ler] *v* be worth; cost; be equal to. **vale la pena** be worthwhile. **válgame la frase** if you don't mind my saying so. **valerse** *v* make use of. **valía** *sf* value, worth.

valeroso [βale'roso] *adj* brave; valuable.

validar [βali'ðar] *v* validate; make binding. **validación** *sf* validation; ratification. **válido** *adj* valid. **validez** *sf* validity.

valiente [βa'ljente] *adj* valiant, courageous; strong; first-rate.

valija [βa'lixa] *sf* valise; case; mail bag.

valimiento [βali'mjento] *sm* value; good will; protection; favour.

valor [βa'lor] *sm* value, worth; price; valour, courage. *adj* valuable. **valoración** *sf* valuation. **valorar** *v* value, appraise.

valsar [βal'sar] *v* waltz. **vals** *sm* waltz.

valuar [βalu'ar] *v* value, appraise, assess. **valuacción** *sf* valuation.

válvula ['βalβula] *sf* valve.

vallar [βa'ʎar] *v* fence in, enclose. **valla** *sf* fence. **vallado** *sm* enclosure.

valle ['βaʎe] *sm* valley.

vampiro [βam'piro] *sm* vampire.

vanagloriarse [βanaglo'rjarse] *v* boast. **vanagloria** *sf* boasting, vainglory.

vándalo ['βandalo] *sm, adj* vandal. **vandalismo** *sm* vandalism.

vanguardia [βan'gwarðja] *sf* vanguard; avant-garde.

vano ['βano] *adj* vain; idle. **en vano** in vain. **vanidad** *sf* vanity. **vanidoso** *adj* vain.

vapor [βa'por] *sm* vapour; steam; (*mar*) steamer. **vaporización** *sf* evaporation. **vaporizar** *v* evaporate.

vaquero [βa'kero] *sm* cowboy. **vaquería** *sf* herd of cows.

vaqueta [βa'keta] *sf* cowhide.

vara ['βara] *sf* rod, pole, staff; (*medida*) yard. **tener vara alta** have the upper hand.

varar [βa'rar] *v* launch; run aground.

variar [βa'rjar] *v* vary, change. **variable** *adj* variable. **variación** *sf* variation. **variado** *adj* varied. **variante** *sf* variant; version.

varice [βa'riθe], *sf* also **várice** varicose vein.

varilla [βa'riʎa] *sf* small stick; jawbone; curtain rail.

vario ['βarjo] *adj* varied, diverse. **varios** *adj* several.

varón [βa'ron] *sm, adj* male. **varonil** *adj* manly, virile.

vaselina ® [βase'lina] *sf* Vaseline ®.

vasija [βa'sixa] *sf* vessel; bowl; dish. **vaso** *sm* glass, tumbler.

vástago ['βastago] *sm* stem, shoot, sprout; scion, offspring.

vasto ['βasto] *adj* vast. **vastedad** *sf* vastness.

vaticinar [βatiθi'nar] *v* predict, foretell. **vaticinador, -a** *sm, sf* prophet, seer. **vaticinio** *sm* divination, prophecy.

vatio ['βatjo] *sm* (*elec*) watt.

vecino [βe'θino], **-a** *sm, sf* neighbour. **vecinal** *adj* local. **vecindad** *sf* neighbourhood.

vedar [βe'ðar] *v* veto; prohibit; hinder. **veda** *sf* prohibition. **vedado** *sm* game preserve.

vega ['βega] *sf* plain; tract of fertile ground.

vegetación [βexeta'θjon] *sf* vegetation. **vegetal** *adj* vegetable. **vegetar** *v* grow; (*fig*) vegetate. **vegetariano, -a** *sm, sf* vegetarian.

vehemencia [βee'menθja] *sf* vehemence. **vehemente** *adj* vehement.

vehículo [βe'ikulo] *sm* vehicle.

veinte ['βeinte] *sm, adj* twenty.

vejar [βe'xar] *v* vex, harass, annoy. **vejación** *sf* vexation. **vejatorio** *adj* vexatious.

vejez [βe'xeθ] *sf* old age.
vejiga [βe'xiga] *sf* blister; bladder.
vela ['βela] *sf* vigil, watch; candle; sail.
velar *v* keep watch; stay awake.
veleidad [βelei'ðað] *sf* whim; fickleness.
veleidoso *adj* fickle.
velero [βe'lero] *sm* sailing ship; glider.
velo ['βelo] *sm* veil.
velocidad [βeloθi'ðað] *sf* velocity.
velocímetro *sm* speedometer. **veloz** *adj*
fast, quick.
vello ['βeʎo] *sm* soft hair, down; fluff.
velloso *adj* dowry.
vena ['βena] *sf* vein; scan. **trabajar por
venas** work in fits and starts.
venablo [βe'naβlo] *sm* javelin.
venado [βe'naðo] *sm* deer; (*culin*) venison.
venal [βe'nal] *adj* venal.
vencer [βen'θer] *v* defeat; win; (*com*) fall
due. **vencerse** *v* control oneself. **vencible**
adj beatable. **los vencidos** the losers.
vencimiento *sm* victory; (*com*) expiration, falling due.
vendar [βen'dar] *v* bandage. **venda** *sf also*
vendaje *sm* bandage.
vendaval [βenda'βal] *sm* gale.
vender [βen'der] *v* sell. **vendedor** *sm* seller, vendor; salesperson. **vendible** *adj*
saleable.
vendimia [βen'ðimja] *sf* grape harvest;
vintage.
veneno [βe'neno] *sm* venom, poison.
venenoso *adj* poisonous.
venerar [βene'rar] *v* venerate. **venerable**
adj venerable. **veneración** *sf* veneration.
venéreo [βe'nereo] *adj* venereal.
venero [βe'nero] *sm* spring of water;
source, origin, root.
vengar [βen'gar] *v* avenge. **vengador, -a**
sm, sf avenger. **venganza** *sf* vengeance.
vengativo *adj* vindictive.
venia ['βenja] *sf* forgiveness, pardon; permission, leave.
*venir [βe'nir] *v* come. **venir bien** be suitable *or* convenient. **venirse** *v* come *or* go
back. **venida** *sf* arrival, coming; return.
venidero *adj* coming, future.
venta ['βenta] *sf* sale, market; inn. **venta
a plazos** hire purchase. **ventero, -a** *sm, sf*
innkeeper.
ventaja [βen'taxa] *sf* advantage. **ventajoso**
adj advantageous.
ventana [βen'tana] *sf* window.
ventilar [βenti'lar] *v* ventilate. **ventilación**

sf ventilation. **ventilador** *sm* ventilator;
fan.
ventosa [βen'tosa] *sf* vent.
ventoso [βen'toso] *sf* vent.
ventoso [βen'toso] *adj* windy. **ventosidad**
sf flatulence.
ventrílocuo [βen'trilokwo] *sm* ventriloquist. **ventriloquia** *sf* ventriloquism.
ventura [βen'tura] *sf* joy, happiness; good
luck. **mala ventura** ill luck. **venturado,
venturero** *or* **venturoso** *adj* lucky; happy.
*ver [βer] *v* see. *sm* view; aspect; opinion; looks *pl*, appearance. **echar de ver**
notice. **estar viendo** have a feeling. **vamos
a ver** let's see.
vera ['βera] *sf* border, edge.
verano [βe'rano] *sm* summer. **veranear** *v*
spend the summer. **veraneo** *sm* summer
holiday.
veras ['βeras] *sf pl* truth *sing*. **de veras**
indeed, really. **veracidad** *sf* veracity. **veraz** *adj* truthful.
verbo ['βerβo] *sm* verb. **verbosidad** *sf* ver-
bosity. **verboso** *adj* verbose.
verdad [βer'ðað] *sf* truth. **verdadero** *adj*
true; real, authentic; sincere; truthful.
verde ['βerðe] *adj* green; immature; fresh;
young; immodest, obscene. **darse un
verde** amuse oneself.
verdugo [βer'ðugo] *sm* executioner; hangman; scourge. **verdugón** *sm* weal (from
whiplash).
verdulero [βerðu'lero] *sm* greengrocer.
verdulería *sf* greengrocer's. **verdura** *sf*
greenness. **verduras** *sf pl* vegetables.
veredicto [βere'ðikto] *sm* verdict.
vergüenza [βer'gwenθa] *sf* shame;
affront; disgrace; shyness, timidity. **sin
vergüenza** shameless. **vergonzoso** *adj*
shy; shameful.
verídico [βe'riðiko] *adj* truthful.
verificar [βerifi'kar] *v* verify; examine,
inspect; check. **verificarse** *v* prove true;
be verified. **verificación** *sf* verification.
verificativo *adj* corroborative.
verosímil [βero'simil] *adj* likely, probable.
verosimilitud *sf* probability.
verruga [βer'ruga] *sf* wart.
versado [βer'saðo] *adj* versed, experienced; skilful.
versar [βer'sar] *v* go round; spin. **versar
sobre** to treat of, deal with.
versátil [βer'satil] *adj* versatile; variable;
inconstant. **versatilidad** *sf* versatility;
changeableness.

versículo [βer'sikulo] *sm* verse. **versificar** *v* versify. **verso** *sm* verse. **verso suelto** blank verse.

versión [βer'sjon] *sf* version.

vértebra ['βerteβra] *sf* vertebra. **vertebrado** *sm, adj* vertebrate.

***verter** [βer'ter] *v* spill, empty; pour; interpret, translate. **vertedero** *sm* drain. **vertedor** *sm* sewer.

vertical [βerti'kal] *adj* vertical.

vértice ['βertiθe] *sm* apex.

vértigo ['βertigo] *sm* vertigo. **vertiginoso** *adj* giddy.

vesícula [βe'sikula] *sf* (*anat*) vesicle; blister.

vestíbulo [βes'tiβulo] *sm* vestibule, entrance hall; lobby.

vestigio [βes'tixjo] *sm* vestige; footstep; trace.

***vestir** [βes'tir] *v* dress; clothe. **vestirse** get dressed. **vestido** *sm* dress.

veta ['βeta] *sf* vein of ore, etc.; grain in wood; streak.

veterano [βete'rano] *sm, adj* veteran.

veterinaria [βeteri'narja] *sf* veterinary science. **veterinario** *sm* vet.

veto ['βeto] *sm* veto.

vez [βeθ] *sf* turn; time; occasion. **a la vez** at once. **a veces** sometimes. **otra vez** once more. **tal vez** perhaps.

vía ['βia] *sf* road; way; track. **vía aérea** air mail. **en vías de** in the process of. **Vía Láctea** Milky Way.

viable ['βjaβle] *adj* viable.

viaducto [βja'ðukto] *sm* viaduct.

viajar [βja'xar] *v* travel. **viajante** *s(m+f)* traveller. **viaje** *sm* trip, journey. **viajero, -a** *sm, sf* traveller; passenger.

víbora ['βiβora] *sf* viper.

vibrar [βi'βrar] *v* vibrate, shake. **vibración** *sf* vibration. **vibrador** *sm* vibrator. **vibrante** *adj* vibrating; vibrant.

vicario [βi'karjo] *sm* vicar.

viciar [βi'θjar] *v* vitiate; corrupt. **vicio** *sm* vice; defect. **de vicio** for no reason at all. **vicioso** *adj* vicious.

vicisitud [βiθisi'tuð] *sf* vicissitude, mishap.

víctima ['βiktima] *sf* victim; sacrifice.

victoria [βik'torja] *sf* victory. **victorioso** *adj* victorious.

vid [βið] *sf* vine.

vida ['βiða] *sf* life. **en mi vida** never in my life. **nivel de vida** *sm* standard of living.

vidriar [βi'ðrjar] *v* glaze. **vidriera** *sf* stained glass. **vidrio** *sm* glass. **vidrioso** *adj* glassy.

viejo ['βjexo] *adj* old. *sm* old man. **vieja** *sf* old woman.

viento ['βjento] *sm* wind.

vientre ['βjentre] *sm* abdomen, belly; womb; bowels *pl*.

viernes ['βjernes] *sm* Friday. **Viernes Santo** Good Friday.

viga ['βiga] *sf* beam; timber.

vigente [βi'xente] *adj* (*jur*) in force, valid. **vigencia** *sf* validity. **en vigencia** in effect; in force.

vigésimo [βi'xesimo] *adj* twentieth.

vigilar [βixi'lar] *v* watch over. **vigilancia** *sf* vigilance. **vigilante** *adj* vigilant. **vigilia** *sf* watchfulness; vigil.

vigor [βi'gor] *sm* vigour. **vigoroso** *adj* vigorous.

vil [βil] *adj* vile. **vileza** *sf* vileness.

vilo ['βilo] *adv* **en vilo** aloft; suspended; (*fig*) on tenterhooks.

villa ['βiʎa] *sf* villa; town.

villancico [βiʎan'θiko] *sm* Christmas carol.

villanía [βiʎa'nia] *sf* villainy; coarse expression.

vinagre [βi'nagre] *sm* vinegar. **vinagroso** *adj* vinegary.

vínculo ['βinkulo] *sm* link; chain; tie.

vindicar [βindi'kar] *v* vindicate. **vindicación** *sf* vindication.

vino¹ ['βino] *sm* wine. **vino tinto** red wine. **vino de solera** vintage wine. **vinícola** *adj* relating to wine *or* wine production. **viña** *sf* vineyard.

viñeta [βi'ɲeta] *sf* vignette.

violar [βjo'lar] *v* violate; rape. **violación** *sf* violation; rape. **violador** *sm* rapist.

violencia [βjo'lenθja] *sf* violence. **violentar** *v* force, open by force; violate; do violence to.

violeta [βjo'leta] *adj, sf* violet.

violín [βjo'lin] *sm* violin. **violinista** *s(m+f)* violinist. **violón** *sm* double-bass.

virar [βi'rar] *v* veer; change direction; (*mar*) tack.

virgen [βir'xen] *adj, sf* virgin. **virginidad** *sf* virginity.

viril [βi'ril] *adj* virile. **virilidad** *sf* virility.

virtual [βir'twal] *adj* virtual; potential.

virtud [βir'tuð] *sf* virtue. **virtuoso** *adj* virtuous. **virtuosidad** *sf* virtuosity.

viruela [βi'rwela] *sf* smallpox.
virulencia [βiru'lenθja] *sf* virulence. **virulento** *adj* virulent.
visado [βi'saδo] *sm* visa.
visaje [βi'saxe] *sm* smirk, grimace. **visajero** *adj* grimacing.
vísceras ['βisθeras] *sf pl* viscera *pl.*
viscoso [βis'koso] *adj* viscous. **viscosidad** *sf* viscosity.
visera [βi'sera] *sf* visor.
visible [βi'siβle] *adj* visible. **visibilidad** *sf* visibility.
visión [βi'sjon] *sf* vision, eyesight; dream, fantasy; view. **visionario, -a** *sm, sf* visionary.
visitar [βisi'tar] *v* visit; inspect. **visita** *sf* visit; visitor. **hacer una visita** pay a visit.
vislumbrar [βislum'brar] *v* catch a glimpse of. **vislumbre** *sf* glimpse; glimmer.
viso ['βiso] *sm* aspect, appearance; gleam.
víspera ['βispera] *sf* eve; (*fig*) approach. **en vísperas de** on the eve of.
vista ['βista] *sf* view; eyesight; appearance, look; gaze. **a primera vista** at first sight. **con vistas de** with a view to. **¡hasta la vista!** good-bye!
visto ['βisto] *adj* seen; obvious. **bien visto** approved of. **visto bueno** authorized. **visto que** seeing that.
vistoso [βis'toso] *adj* showy; (*fam*) loud.
visual [βi'swal] *adj* visual.
vital [βi'tal] *adj* vital. **vitalidad** *sf* vitality.
vitamina [βita'mina] *sf* vitamin.
vitela [βi'tela] *sf* vellum.
vitorear [βitore'ar] *v* shout, cheer, acclaim. **¡vítor!** bravo!
vitreo [βi'treo] *adj* vitreous. **vitrina** *sf* showcase.
vitriólico [βi'trjoliko] *adv* vitriolic. **vitriolo** *sm* vitriol.
vituperar [βitupe'rar] *v* vituperate; abuse; insult. **vituperación** *sf* blame.
viuda ['βjuδa] *sf* widow. **viudo** *sm* widower. **viudez** *sf* widowhood.
vivaz [βi'βaθ] *adj* vivacious. **vivacidad** *sf* vivacity.
víveres ['βiβeres] *sm pl* provisions *pl.*
vivero [βi'βero] *sm* fishpond.
viveza [βi'βeθa] *sf* gaiety, liveliness.
vivienda [βi'βjenda] *sf* housing; dwelling, lodgings *pl.* **vividero** *adj* habitable.
vivificar [βiβifi'kar] *v* animate, bring to life.

vivir [βi'βir] *v* live. **¿quién vive?** who goes there? *sm* way of life.
vivisección [βiβisek'θjon] *sf* vivisection.
vivo ['βiβo] *adj* living, alive; vivid. **al vivo** to the life.
vizconde [βiθ'konde] *sm* viscount. **vizcondesa** *sf* viscountess.
vocablo [βo'kaβlo] *sm* word. **vocabulario** *sm* vocabulary.
vocación [βoka'θjon] *sf* vocation.
vocal [βo'kal] *adj* vocal. *sm* voter. *sf* vowel.
vocear [βoθe'ar] *v* bawl. **vocerío** *sm* bawling. **vocero** *sm* spokesman.
vociferar [βoθife'rar] *v* bawl; shout.
vocinglero [βoθin'glero] *adj* vociferous; loud-mouthed; talkative. **vocinglería** *sf* clamour, uproar.
volante [βo'lante] *adj* flying. *sm* steering-wheel; shuttlecock.
*volar [βo'lar] *v* fly; blow up, explode. **volarse** *v* become furious.
volátil [βo'latil] *adj* volatile.
volcán [βol'kan] *sm* volcano. **volcánico** *adj* volcanic.
*volcar [βol'kar] *v* upset; capsize. **volcarse** *v* fall over; bend over backwards.
volear [βole'ar] *v* volley. **voleo** *sm* volley.
volición [βoli'θjon] *sf* volition.
voltaje [βol'taxe] *sm* voltage. **voltio** *sm* volt.
voltear [βolte'ar] *v* overturn; revolve; tumble. **volteador, -a** *sm, sf* tumbler. **volteo** *sm* somersault.
voluble [βo'luβle] *adj* changeable. **volubilidad** *sf* changeable.
volumen [βolu'men] *sm* volume. **voluminoso** *adj* voluminous.
voluntad [βolun'taδ] *sf* volition; affection. **a voluntad** at will. **buena voluntad** goodwill.
voluntario [βolun'tarjo] *adj* voluntary. **voluntariedad** *sf* free will.
voluptuoso [βolup'twoso] *adj* voluptuous. **voluptuosidad** *sf* voluptuousness.
*volver [βol'βer] *v* return; turn; turn over. **volver sobre sí** pull oneself together. **volverse** *v* become; go back. **volverse loco** go mad.
vomitar [βomi'tar] *v* vomit. **vómito** *sm* vomit.
voraz [βo'raθ] *adj* voracious. **voracidad** *sf* voracity.
vórtice ['βortiθe] *sm* vortex.

vosotros [βo'sotros] *pron pl* (*fam*) you.
votar [βo'tar] *v* vote. **votante** *s*(*m+f*) voter. **voto** *sm* vote; vow.
voz [βoθ] *sf* voice; shout; report. **a media voz** in a whisper. **dar voces** call out.
vuelco ['βwelko] *sm* upset; overturning.
vuelo ['βwelo] *sm* flight; flying; wing. **al vuelo** in flight. **en un vuelo** in a jiffy.
vuelta ['βwelta] *sf* turn; return; bend; reverse; recompense. **dar una vuelta** take a stroll. **estar de vuelta** be back.
vuestro ['βwestro] *pron* yours. *adj* your.
vulcanizar [βulkani'θar] *v* vulcanize.
vulgar [βul'gar] *adj* common; ordinary; vulgar. **el hombre vulgar** the common man.
vulnerar [βulne'rar] *v* wound. **vulnerabilidad** *sf* vulnerability. **vulnerable** *adj* vulnerable.

X

xilófono [ksi'lofono] *sm* xylophone.

Y

y [i] *conj* and.
ya [ja] *adv* already; now; yet; later. **ya que** since. **ya voy** I'm just coming.
yacimiento [jaθi'mjento] *sm* (*minerales*) bed. **yacente** *adj* recumbent.
yanqui [jan'ki] *adj, sm* (*fam*) Yankee.
yarda ['jarða] *sf* yard.
yate ['jate] *sm* yacht.
yedra ['jeðra] *sf* ivy.
yegua ['jegwa] *sf* mare.
yelmo ['jelmo] *sm* helmet.
yema ['jema] *sf* yolk; bud; button. **yema del dedo** tip of the finger.
yerba ['jerβa] *sf* grass; herb.
yermo ['jermo] *sm* waste land. *adj* barren; desert.
yerno ['jerno] *sm* son-in-law.
yerro ['jerro] *sm* error; mistake.
yeso ['jeso] *sm* gypsum; plaster; plaster cast.
yo [jo] *pron* I; myself; me; ego.

yodo ['joðo] *sm* iodine.
yogur [jo'gur] *sm* yoghurt.
yugo ['jugo] *sm* yoke.
yugular [jugu'lar] *adj* jugular.
yunque ['junke] *sm* anvil.
yunta ['junta] *sf* couple, pair; (*de bueys*) yoke.
yute ['jute] *sm* jute.
*yuxtaponer [jukstapo'ner] *v* juxtapose. **yuxtaposición** *sf* juxtaposition. **yuxtapuesto** *adj* juxtaposed.

Z

zafar [θa'far] *v* loosen; free; clear; lighten. **zafarse** *v* run away.
zafio ['θafjo] *adj* uncouth.
zafiro [θa'firo] *sm* sapphire.
zaga ['θaga] *sf* rear; back.
zaguán [θa'gwan] *sm* entrance hall.
*zaherir [θae'rir] *v* censure; mock; reproach.
zahurda [θa'urða] *sf* pigsty.
zalamería [θalame'ria] *sf* flattery. **zalamero, -a** *sm, sf* flatterer.
zamarra [θa'marra] *sf* sheepskin jacket.
zambo ['θambo] *adj* knock-kneed. *sm* half-breed; monkey.
*zambullir [θambu'ʎir] *v* dive. **zambullida** *sf* dive.
zampar [θam'par] *v* polish off; shove in; devour. **zamparse** *v* rush.
zanahoria [θana'orja] *sf* carrot.
zancada [θan'kaða] *sf* long stride. **en dos zancadas** in a trice. **zancadilla** *sf* trip; trap. **echar la zancadilla** trip up.
zanco ['θanko] *sm* stilt.
zancudo [θan'kuðo] *adj* long-legged.
zángano ['θangano] *sm* (*insecto*) drone; (*fig*) loafer; fool.
zangolotear [θangolote'ar] *v* shake; fidget; rattle. **zangoloteo** *sm* shaking; rattling.
zanja ['θanxa] *sf* ditch; trench. **abrir las zanjas** lay the foundations.
zapa ['θapa] *sf* spade; trench. **zapapico** *sm* pickaxe. **zapar** *v* undermine.
zapatear [θapate'ar] *v* kick; ill-treat; tap-dance. **zapateado** *sm* Andalusian dance. **zapatería** *sf* shoe shop; shoe factory.

zapatero, -a *sm*, *sf* shoemaker. zapatilla *sf* slipper. zapato *sm* shoe.

zar [θar] *sm* tsar.

zarandear [θarande'ar] *v* sift; winnow; shake. zaranda *sf* sieve.

zaraza [θa'raθa] *sf* chintz.

zarcillo [θar'θiλo] *sm* hoe; barrel hoop; vine tendril; ear-ring.

zarco ['θarko] *adj* (*ojos*) light blue.

zarpa ['θarpa] *v* claw; paw. echar la zarpa grab hold. zarpar *v* weigh anchor. zarpazo *sm* whack.

zarza ['θarθa] *sf* bramble, blackberry bush. zarzamora *sf* (*fruto*) blackberry.

zarzo ['θarθo] *sm* hurdle.

zarzuela [θar'θwela] *sf* light *or* comic opera.

zeta ['θeta] *sf* letter *z*.

zigzaguear [θigθage'ar] *v* zigzag. zigzag *sm* zigzag.

zinc [θink] *sm* zinc.

zócalo ['θokalo] *sm* plinth; skirting board.

zodíaco [θo'δjako] *sm* zodiac.

zona ['θona] *sf* zone; area. zona edificada built-up area. zonas verdes green belt *sing.*

zoología [θoolo'xia] *sf* zoology. zoológico *adj* zoological. parque zoológico *sm* zoological gardens *pl*, zoo. zoólogo, -a *sm*, *sf* zoologist.

zoquete [θo'kete] *sm* chunk of wood; piece of stale bread; (*fam*) blockhead.

zorro ['θorro] *sm* fox. zorra *sf* vixen. zorrera *sf* foxhole.

zozobrar [θoθo'βrar] *v* wreck; capsize; founder; (*fig*) worry. zozobra *sf* foundering; worry.

zueco ['θweko] *sm* clog; galosh.

zumbar [θum'bar] *v* buzz; hum; strike; whack. zumbarse de make fun of. zumbido *sm* humming; buzzing.

zumbón [θum'bon], -a *sm*, *sf* jester; tease. *adj* waggish.

zumo ['θumo] *sm* juice. zumoso *adj* juicy.

zurcir [θur'θir] *v* darn. zurcido *sm* darn; stitch. zurcidura *sf* darning.

zurdo ['θurδo], -a *sm*, *sf* left-handed person. *adj* left-handed.

zurrar [θur'rar] *v* thrash; (*cuero*) dress; curry. zurra *sf* tanning; thrashing. zurrador *sm* tanner.

zurrón [θur'ron] *sm* leather bag; husk.

zutano [θu'tano], -a *sm*, *sf* so-and-so. fulano, zutano y mengano Tom, Dick, and Harry.